New 1996-1997 Edition

CALIFORNIA CAMPING

The Complete Guide

by Tom Stienstra

Foghorn
Press
BOOKS BUILDING COMMUNITY™

ISBN 0-935701-99-0

51995

9 780935 701999

Foghorn Press
555 DeHaro Street, Suite 220
San Francisco, CA 94107
(415) 241-9550

To order individual books, please call Foghorn Press:
1-800-FOGHORN (364-4676) or (415) 241-9550.

Foghorn Press titles are distributed to the book trade by Publishers Group West, Emeryville, California. To contact your local sales representative, call 1-800-788-3123.

Library of Congress ISSN Data:
February 1996
California Camping: The Complete Guide to More Than 50,000 Campsites for Tenters, RVers, and Car Campers
1996-1997 Edition
ISSN: 1078-957X

CREDITS

Research Editor	Janet Connaughton
Editorial/Production Manager	Ann-Marie Brown
Copyediting	Sherry McInroy
Publishing Manager	Rebecca Poole Forée
Production Manager	Michele Thomas
Production Assistant	Alexander Lyon
Acquisitions Editor	Judith Pynn
Cover Design	Stuart L. Silberman, Michele Thomas
Cover Photo	Frank Herholdt

Printed in the United States of America.

New 1996-1997 Edition

CALIFORNIA CAMPING

The Complete Guide

by Tom Stienstra

Foghorn
Press
BOOKS BUILDING COMMUNITY™

Dear Campers,

As part of a massive, two-year revision of *California Camping* by author Tom Stienstra, about 1,000 of this edition's campground reviews have been completely rewritten, including new, easier-to-follow directions and more detailed trip notes. And as with every edition of this comprehensive guidebook, all of the other information has been reviewed and updated by more than 50 recreation specialists who worked with research editor Janet Connaughton.

In response to suggestions from readers, we have added a Five Percent Club symbol to highlight the state's most primitive, difficult-to-reach and hidden camps (see page 9 for more details). We have also incorporated dozens of other changes inspired by readers' requests, including the addition of phone numbers for state park district offices.

While our information is as current as possible, changes to fees or facilities are sometimes made after we go to press. Please contact the campgrounds you plan to visit for updated information.

The improvements in this year's edition are part of our mission to make *California Camping* the most accurate, easy-to-use and comprehensive guidebook in America. We always welcome your comments and suggestions about the book. Please write to the Publishing Manager, Foghorn Press, 555 DeHaro Street, Suite 220, San Francisco, CA 94107.

Like you, we love the outdoors. Please enjoy and protect it.

—*The Editors*

The Color of Commitment

Foghorn Press has always been committed to printing on recycled paper, but up to now, we hadn't taken the final plunge to use 100% recycled paper because we were unconvinced of its quality. And until now, those concerns were valid. But the good news is that quality recycled paper is now available. We are thrilled to announce that Foghorn Press books are printed with Soya-based inks on 100% recycled paper, which has a 50% post-consumer waste content. The only way you'd know we made this change is by looking at the hue of the paper—a small price to pay for environmental integrity. You may even like the color better. We do. And we know the earth does, too.

PREFACE

If the great outdoors is so great, then why don't people enjoy it more? The answer is because of the time trap, and I will tell you exactly how to beat it.

For many, the biggest problem is finding the time to go, whether it is camping, hiking, fishing, boating, backpacking, biking or even just for a good drive in the country. The solution? Well, believe it or not, the answer is to treat your fun just like you treat your work, and I'll tell you just how.

Consider how you treat your job: Always on time? Go there every day you are scheduled? Do whatever it takes to get there and get it done? Right? No foolin' that's right. Now imagine if you took the same approach to the outdoors. Suddenly your life would be a heck of a lot better.

The secret is to schedule all of your outdoor activities. For instance, I go fishing every Thursday evening, hiking every Sunday morning and on an overnight trip every new moon (when stargazing is best). No matter what, I'm going. Just like going to work, I've scheduled it. The same approach works with longer adventures. The only reason I was able to hike from Yosemite to Tahoe last summer was because I scheduled two weeks to do it. The reason I spend 125 to 150 days a year in the field is because I schedule them.

If you get out your calendar and write in the exact dates you are going, then you'll go. If you don't, you won't. Suddenly, with only a minor change in your life plan, you can be living the life you were previously dreaming about.

See you out there….

—Tom Stienstra

TABLE OF CONTENTS

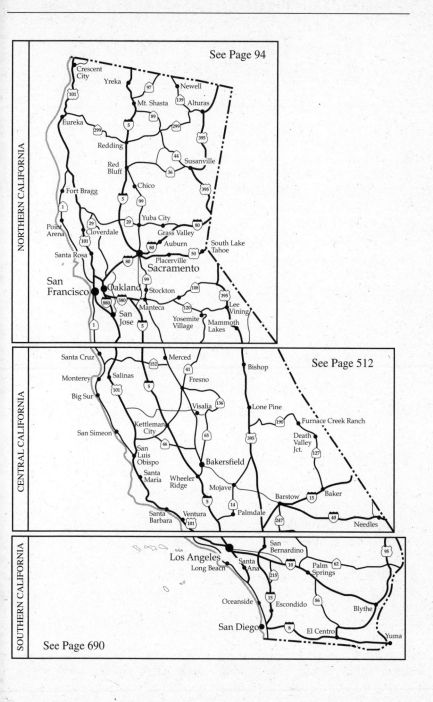

NORTHERN CALIFORNIA

See Page 94

Crescent City
Yreka
Newell
Mt. Shasta
Alturas
Eureka
Redding
Susanville
Red Bluff
Fort Bragg
Chico
Point Arena
Cloverdale
Yuba City
Grass Valley
Auburn
South Lake Tahoe
Santa Rosa
Placerville
Sacramento
San Francisco
Oakland
Stockton
Lee Vining
San Jose
Manteca
Yosemite Village
Mammoth Lakes

CENTRAL CALIFORNIA

See Page 512

Santa Cruz
Merced
Bishop
Monterey
Salinas
Fresno
Big Sur
Visalia
Lone Pine
San Simeon
Furnace Creek Ranch
Kettleman City
Death Valley Jct.
San Luis Obispo
Bakersfield
Santa Maria
Wheeler Ridge
Mojave
Barstow
Baker
Santa Barbara
Ventura
Palmdale
Needles

SOUTHERN CALIFORNIA

San Bernardino
Los Angeles
Santa Ana
Palm Springs
Long Beach
Oceanside
Escondido
Blythe
San Diego
El Centro
Yuma

See Page 690

HOW TO USE THIS BOOK

You can search for your ideal camping spot in two ways:
1) If you know the name of the campsite you'd like to visit, or the name of the corresponding geographical area (town name, national or state forest name, national or state park name, lake or river name, etc.), use the index beginning on page 806 to locate it, and turn to the corresponding page. If you are looking for a specific campsite name, you'll find that all campsites are listed in the index in capital letters.

2) If you'd like to camp in a particular part of the state, and want to find out what camps are available there, use the California state map on page 10 or in the back of this book. Find the zone you'd like to camp in (such as E1 for the San Francisco Bay Area or H3 for Santa Barbara), then turn to the corresponding pages in the book.

This book is conveniently divided into Northern, Central and Southern California. Within these sections, the book is further divided into map sections to allow for greater detail.

Northern California, Pages 93-510 (maps AØ-E5)

Central California, Pages 511-688 (maps F1-H9)

Southern California, Pages 689-805 (maps I2-J9)

• *See the bottom of every page for reference to corresponding maps.*

What the Ratings Mean

Every camping spot in this book is designated with a scenic beauty rating of 1 through 10. The ratings are based on the scenic beauty of the area only, and do not reflect quality issues such as the cleanliness of the camp or the temperament of the management, which can change from day to day.

SCENIC RATING

🔺1 🔺2 🔺3 🔺4 🔺5 🔺6 🔺7 🔺8 🔺9 🔺10

Poor.. Fair .... Great

What the Activity Symbols Mean

Each camp listing has one or more activity symbols next to its name. These symbols denote recreational activities and sidetrip possibilities located at or near the camp. They also indicate whether or not a camp has any wheelchair facilities or wheelchair-accessible areas. (Always phone ahead to be sure that the camp's definition of wheelchair facilities matches your particular needs.)

Key to the Symbols

Boating	Canoeing/ Rafting	Fishing	Golf	Hiking	Historical Site	Horseback Riding

Hot Springs	Swimming	Waterskiing	Wheelchair Access	Five Percent Club	RV

The Five Percent Club

Approximately 100 of the camps in *California Camping* are marked with the Five Percent Club symbol: . It has been documented that 95 percent of American vacationers use only five percent of the available recreation areas. Campgrounds marked with the Five Percent Club symbol are for the other five percent of the people—those who want to escape the crowds and camp in California's hard-to-reach, hidden sites.

Note to RVers

Those of you with recreational vehicles will find *California Camping* easy to use. Every camp listing that has RV sites also has an easy-to-spot RV symbol. Just flip the pages of the book and look for this symbol: . Occasionally you will find a campground listing that mentions RV sites but does not feature the RV symbol. This occurs in listings in which the camps have access routes that may not be safe for RVs.

Note to Tent Campers

Remember that an RV symbol featured next to a camp listing does not mean that the camp is an exclusive RV resort or unsuitable for tent campers. Many campgrounds offer quality campsites for both tenters and RVers.

CHAPTER REFERENCE MAP

CAMPING TIPS

INTRODUCTION

Going on a camping trip can be like trying to put hiking boots on an octopus. You've tried it too, eh? Instead of the relaxing, exciting sojourn that was intended, a camping trip can turn into a scenario called You Against The World. It can turn out to be about as easy as fighting an earthquake.

But it doesn't have to be that way and that's what this book is all about. If you give it a chance, it can put the mystery, excitement and fun back into your camping vacations—and remove the fear of snarls, confusion and occasional temper explosions of volcanic proportions that keep people at home, locked away from the action.

Mystery? There are hundreds of hidden, rarely used campgrounds listed and mapped in this book that you have never dreamed of. Excitement? At many of them you'll find the sizzle with the steak, the hike to a great lookout, the big fish at the end of the line. Fun? The how-to section of this book can help you take the futility out of your trips and put the fun back in. Add it up, put it in your cash register and you can turn a camping trip into the satisfying adventure it is meant to be, whether it's just an overnight quicky or a month-long expedition.

It has been documented that 95 percent of American vacationers use only five percent of the available recreation areas. With this book, you can leave the herd to wander and be free, and join the inner circle, the Five Percenters who know the great, hidden areas used by so few people. To join the Five Percent Club, you should take a hard look at the maps for the areas you wish to visit and the corresponding listings of campgrounds. As you study the camps, you will start to feel a sense of excitement building, a feeling that you are about to unlock a door and venture into a world that is rarely viewed. When you feel that excitement, act on it. Parlay that energy into a great trip.

The campground maps and listings can serve in two ways: 1) If you're on the road late in the day and you are stuck for a spot for the night, you can likely find one nearby; or 2) If you are planning in advance, you can tailor a vacation to fit exactly into your plans, rather than heading off, and hoping—maybe praying—it turns out all right.

For the latter, you may wish to obtain additional maps, particularly if you are venturing into areas governed by the U.S. Forest Service or Bureau of Land Management. Both are federal agencies and have low-cost maps available that detail all hiking trails, lakes, streams and backcountry camps reached via logging roads. How to obtain these and other maps is described in the Resource Guide on pages 86 to 90.

Backcountry camps listed in this book are often in primitive and rugged settings, but provide the sense of isolation that you may want for a trip. They also provide good jump-off points for backpacking trips, if that is your calling. These camps are also often free, and we have listed hundreds of them.

At the other end of the spectrum are the developed parks for motor homes, parks that offer a home away from home with everything from full hookups to a grocery store and laundromat. These spots are just as important as the remote camps with no facilities. Instead of isolation, an RV park provides a place to shower and get outfitted for food and clean clothes. For motor home cruisers, it is a place to stay in high style while touring the area. RV parks range in price from $8 to $20 per night, depending on location, and an advance deposit may be necessary in summer months.

Somewhere between the two extremes—the remote, unimproved camps and the lavish motor home parks—are hundreds and hundreds of campgrounds that provide a compromise: beautiful settings and some facilities, with a small overnight fee. Piped water, vault toilets and picnic tables tend to come with the territory, along with a fee that usually ranges from $7 to $15, with the higher-priced sites located near population centers. Because they offer a bit of both worlds, they are in high demand. Reservations are usually advised, and at state parks, particularly during the summer season, you can expect company. This does not mean you need to abandon them in hopes of a less confined environment. For one thing, most state parks have set up quotas so that you don't feel like you've been squeezed in with a shoehorn, and for another, the same parks are often uncrowded during the off-season or on weekdays.

Prior to your trip, you will want to get organized, and that's where you must start putting socks on that giant octopus. The key to organization for any task is breaking it down to its key components, then solving each element independent of the others. Remember the octopus. Grab a moving leg, jam on a boot and make sure it's on tight before reaching for another leg. Do one thing at a time, in order, and all will get done quick and right.

In the stories that follow, we have isolated the different elements of camping, and you should do the same when planning for your trip. There are separate stories on each of the primary ingredients for a successful trip: 1) Food and cooking gear; 2) Clothing and weather protection; 3) Hiking and foot care and how to choose the right boots and socks; 4) Sleeping gear; 5) Combatting bugs and some common sense first-aid; 6) Catching fish, avoiding bears and camp fun; 7) Outdoors with kids; 8) Weather prediction. We've also included sections on boat-in and desert camping and ethics in the outdoors, as well as a camping gear checklist.

Now you can become completely organized for your trip in just one week, spending just a little time each evening. Getting organized is an unnatural act for many. By splitting up the tasks, you take the pressure out of planning and put the fun back in.

As a full-time outdoors writer, the question I get asked more than any other is, "Where are you going this week?" All of the answers are in this book.

FOOD & COOKING GEAR

It was a warm, crystal clear day, the kind of day when if you had ever wanted to go skydiving, you would go skydiving. That was exactly the case for my old pal Foonsky, who had never before tried the sport. But a funny thing happened after he jumped out of the plane and pulled on the rip cord for the first time: His parachute didn't open.

In total free-fall, Foonsky watched the earth below getting closer and closer. Not one to panic, he calmly pulled the rip cord on the emergency parachute. But nothing happened then either. No parachute, no nothing.

The ground was getting closer and closer, and as he tried to search for a soft place to land, Foonsky detected a small object shooting up toward him, getting larger as it approached. It looked like a camper.

Foonsky figured this could be his last chance, so as they passed in mid-flight, he shouted, "Hey, do you know anything about parachutes?"

The other fellow just shouted back as he headed off into space, "Do you know anything about lighting camping stoves?"

Well, Foonsky got lucky and his parachute opened. As for the other fellow, well, he's probably in orbit like a NASA weather satellite. If you've ever had a mishap lighting a camping stove, you know exactly what I'm talking about.

When it comes to camping, all gear is not created equal. Nothing is more important than lighting your stove easily and having it reach full heat without feeling like you're playing with a short fuse to a miniature bomb. If your stove does not work right, your trip can turn into a disaster, regardless of how well you have planned the other elements. In addition, a bad stove will add an underlying sense of foreboding to your day. You will constantly have the inner suspicion that your darn stove is going to foul up again.

Camping Stoves

If you are buying a camping stove, remember this one critical rule: Do not leave the store with a new stove unless you have been shown exactly how to use it.

Know what you are getting. Many stores that specialize in

outdoor recreation equipment now provide experienced campers/ employees who will demonstrate the use of every stove they sell, and while they're at it, describe their respective strengths and weaknesses.

Never buy a stove that uses kerosene for fuel. Kerosene is smelly and messy, provides low heat, needs priming, and in America, is virtually obsolete as a camp fuel. As a test, I tried using a kerosene stove once. I could scarcely boil a pot of water. In addition, some kerosene leaked out when the stove was packed, and it ruined everything it touched. The smell of kerosene never did go away. Kerosene remains popular in Europe only because the campers haven't heard much of white gas yet, and when they do, they will demand it.

That leaves white gas or butane as the best fuels, and either one can be right for you, depending on your special preferences.

White gas is the most popular, because it can be purchased at most outdoor recreation stores, at many supermarkets, and is inexpensive and effective. It burns hot, has virtually no smell, and evaporates quickly if it should spill. If you get caught in wet, miserable weather and can't get a fire going, you can use it as an emergency fire starter, although its use as such should be sparing and never on an open flame.

White gas is a popular fuel both for car campers who use the large, two-burner stoves equipped with a fuel tank and a pump, and for hikers who use a lightweight backpacking stove. On the latter, lighting can require priming with a gel called priming paste, which some people dislike. Another problem with white gas is that it can be extremely explosive.

As an example, I once almost burned off my beard completely in a mini-explosion while lighting one of the larger stoves designed for car camping. I was in the middle of cooking dinner when the flame suddenly shut down. Sure enough, the fuel tank was empty, and after refilling it, I pumped the tank 50 or 60 times to regain pressure. When I lit a match, the sucker ignited from three feet away. The resulting explosion was like a stick of dynamite going off, and immediately the smell of burning beard was in the air. In the quick flash of an erred moment, my once thick, dark beard had been reduced to a mass of little, yellow, burned curly-Qs.

My error? After filling the tank, I forgot to shut the fuel cock off while pumping up the pressure in the tank. As a result, when I pumped the tank, the stove burners were slowly producing the gas/air mixture, filling the air space above the stove. The strike of a match even from a few feet away and ka-boom!

That problem can be solved by using stoves that use bottled

butane fuel. Butane requires no pouring, pumping or priming, and stoves that use butane are the easiest to light of all camping stoves. Just turn a knob and light—that's it. On the minus side, because it comes in bottles, you never know precisely how much fuel you have left, and when a bottle is empty, you have a potential piece of litter. Never litter. Ever.

The other problem with butane as a fuel is that it just plain does not work well in cold weather, or when there is little fuel left in the cartridge. Since you cannot predict mountain weather in spring or fall, you can use more fuel than originally projected. That can be frustrating, particularly if your stove starts wheezing with several days left in your trip. In addition, with most butane cartridges, if there is any chance of the temperature falling below freezing, you often have to sleep with the cartridge to keep it warm, or otherwise forget using it come morning.

Personally, I prefer using a small, lightweight stove that uses white gas so I can closely gauge fuel consumption. My pal Foonsky uses one with a butane bottle because it lights so easily. We have contests to see who can boil a pot of water faster and the difference is usually negligible. Thus, other factors are important when choosing a stove.

Of the other elements, ease of cleaning the burner is the most important. If you camp much, especially with the smaller stoves, the burner holes will eventually become clogged. Some stoves have a built-in cleaning needle; a quick twist of a knob and you're in business. On the other hand, others require disassembling and a protracted session using special cleaning tools. If a stove is difficult to clean, you will tend to put off doing it, and your stove will sputter and pant while you get humiliated watching the cold pot of water sitting on it.

Before making a purchase, have the salesman show you how to clean the burner head. Except in the case of the large, multi-burner family camping stoves, which rarely require cleaning, this test can do more to determine the long-term value of a stove than any other factor.

Building Fires

One summer expedition took me to the Canadian wilderness in British Columbia for a 75-mile canoe trip on the Bowron Lake Circuit, a chain of 13 lakes, six rivers and seven portages. It is one of the truly great canoe trips of the world, a loop trip that ends just a few hundred feet from its starting point. But at the first camp at Kibbee Lake, my camp stove developed a fuel leak at the base of the burner and the nuclear-like blast that followed just about turned Canada into a giant crater.

As a result, the final 70 miles of the trip had to be completed without a stove, cooking on open fires each night. The problem was compounded by the weather. It rained eight of the ten days. Rain? In Canada, raindrops the size of silver dollars fall so hard they actually bounce on the lake surface. We had to stop paddling a few times in order to empty the rainwater out of the canoe. At the end of the day, we'd make camp, and then came the test. Either make a fire or go to bed cold and hungry.

With an ax, at least we had a chance for success. As soaked as all the downed wood was, I was able to make my own fire-starting tinder from the chips of splitting logs; no matter how hard it rains, the inside of a log is always dry.

In miserable weather, matches don't stay lit long enough to get the tinder started. Instead, we used either a candle or the little, wax-like fire-starter cubes that stay lit for several minutes. From those, we could get the tinder going. Then we added small, slender strips of wood that had been axed from the interior of the logs. When the flame reached a foot high, we added the logs, with the dry interior of them facing in. By the time the inside of the logs had caught fire, the outside would be drying from the heat. It wasn't long before a royal blaze was brightening the rainy night.

That's a worst case scenario and hopefully you will never face anything like it. Nevertheless, being able to build a good fire and cook on it can be one of the more satisfying elements of a camping trip. At times, just looking into the flames can provide a special satisfaction at the end of a good day.

However, never expect to build a fire for every meal, or in some cases, even to build one at all. Many state and federal campgrounds have been picked clean of downed wood, or forest fire danger forces rangers to prohibit fires altogether during the fire season. In either case, you either use your camp stove or you go hungry.

But when you can build a fire, and the resources are available to do so, it will add to the quality of your camping trip. Of the campgrounds listed in this book, the sites that allow you to build fires will usually already have fire rings available. In primitive areas where you can make your own, you should dig a ring eight inches deep, line the edges with rock, and clear all the needles and twigs in a five-foot radius. The next day, when the fire is dead, you can discard the rocks, fill over the black charcoal with dirt, then scatter pine needles and twigs over it. Nobody will even know you camped there. That's the best way I know to keep a secret spot a real secret.

When you start to build a campfire, the first thing you will notice is that no matter how good your intentions, your fellow campers will not be able to resist moving the wood around. Watch. You'll just be getting ready to add a key piece of wood at just the right spot, and your companion will stick his mitts in, confidently believing he has a better idea. He'll shift the fire around and undermine your best thought-out plans.

So I make a rule on camping trips. One person makes the fire and everybody else stands clear, or is involved with other camp tasks, like gathering wood, getting water, putting up tents or planning dinner. Once the fire is going strong, then it's fair game; anyone adds logs at their discretion. But in the early, delicate stages of the campfire, it's best to leave it to one person.

Before a match is struck, a complete pile of firewood should be gathered. Then start small, with the tiniest twigs you can find, and slowly add in larger twigs as you go, criss-crossing them like a miniature tepee. Eventually, you will get to the big chunks that will produce high heat. The key is to get one piece of wood burning into another, which then burns into another, setting off what I call the "chain of flame." Conversely, single pieces of wood, set apart from each other, will not burn.

On a dry, summer evening, at a campsite where plenty of wood is available, about the only way you can blow the deal is to get impatient and try to add the big pieces too quickly. Do that and you'll just get smoke, not flames, and it won't be long before every one of your fellow campers is poking at your fire. It will drive you crazy, but they just won't be able to help it.

Cooking Gear

I like traveling light, and I've found all I need for cooking is a pot, small frying pan, metal pot grabber, fork, knife, cup and matches. If you want to keep the price of food low and also cook customized dinners each night, a small pressure cooker can be just the ticket. (See "Keeping the Price Down" on page 21.) I keep all my gear in one small bag, which fits into my pack. If I'm camping out of my four-wheel drive rig, the little bag of cooking gear is easy to keep track of. Going simple, not complicated, is the key to keeping a camping trip on the right track.

You can get more elaborate by purchasing complete cook kits with plates, a coffee pot, large pots and other cookware, but what really counts is having one single pot you're happy with. It needs to be just the right size, not too big or small, and stable enough so it won't tip over, even if it is at a slight angle on a fire, full of water at a full boil. Mine is just six inches wide and four-and-a-half inches deep. It holds better than a quart of water and has served well for several hundred camp dinners.

The rest of your cook kit is easy to complete. The frying pan should be small, light-gauge aluminum, teflon-coated, with a fold-in handle so it's no hassle to store. A pot grabber is a great addition. It's a little aluminum gadget that will clamp to the edge of pots and allow you to lift them and pour water with total control, without burning your fingers. For cleanup, take a small bottle filled with dish cleaner and a plastic scrubber, and you're in business.

A Sierra Cup, which is a wide aluminum cup with a wire handle, is an ideal cup to carry because you can eat out of it as well as use it for drinking. This means no plates to clean after dinner, so cleanup is quick and easy. In addition, if you go for a hike, you can clip it to your belt with its wire handle.

If you want a more formal setup, complete with plates, glasses, silverware and the like, you can end up spending more time preparing and cleaning up from meals than you do enjoying the country you are exploring. In addition, the more equipment you bring, the more loose ends you will have to deal with, and loose ends can cause plenty of frustration. If you have a choice, choose simple.

And remember what Thoreau said: "A man is rich in proportion to what he can do without."

Food and Cooking Tricks

On a trip to the Bob Marshall Wilderness in western Montana, I woke up one morning, yawned, and said, "What've we got for breakfast?"

The silence was ominous. "Well," finally came the response, "we don't have any food left."

"What!?"

"Well, I figured we'd catch trout for meals every other night."

On the return trip, we ended up eating wild berries, buds and yes, even roots (not too tasty). When we finally landed the next day at a suburban pizza parlor, we nearly ate the wooden tables.

Running out of food on a camping trip can do more to turn reasonable people into violent grumps than any other event. There's no excuse for it, not when a system for figuring meals can be outlined with precision and little effort. You should not go out and buy a bunch of food, throw it in your rig and head off for yonder. That leaves too much to chance. And if you've ever been in the woods and real hungry, you'll know to take a little effort to make sure a day or two of starvation will not occur. A three-step process offers a solution:

    1—Make a general meal-by-meal plan and make sure your companions like what is on it.

    2—Tell your companions to buy any specialty items (like a special brand of coffee) on their own and not to expect you to take care of everything.

    3—Put all the food on your living room floor and literally figure every day of your trip meal-by-meal, bagging the food in plastic bags as you go. You will know exact food quotas and will not go hungry.

Fish for meals? There's a guaranteed rule for that: If you expect to catch fish for meals, you will most certainly get skunked. If you don't expect to catch fish for meals, you will probably catch so many they'll be coming out of your ears. I've seen it a hundred times.

Keeping the Price Down

"There must be some mistake," I said with a laugh. "Who ever paid $750 for some camp food?"

But the amount was as clear as the digital numbers on the cash register: $753.27.

"How is this possible?" I asked the clerk at the register.

"Just add it up," she responded, irritated.

Then I started figuring. The freeze-dried backpack dinners cost $6 apiece. A small pack of beef jerky went for $2, the beef sticks for 75 cents, granola bars for 50 cents apiece. Then multiply it by four hungry men, including Foonsky, for 21 days. This food was for a major expedition—four guys hiking 250 miles over three weeks from Mount Whitney to Yosemite Valley.

The dinners alone cost close to $500. Add in the usual goodies—the jerky, granola bars, soups, dried fruit, oatmeal, Tang, candy and coffee—and I was handed a bill that felt like an earthquake.

A lot of campers have received similar shocks. In preparation for their trips, campers shop with enthusiasm. Then after hearing the price, they pay the bill in horror.

Well, there are solutions, lots of them. You can eat gourmet style in the outback without having your wallet cleaned out. But it means do-it-yourself cooking, more planning, and careful shopping. It also means transcending the push-button "I-want-it-now" attitude that so many people try to take with them to the mountains.

The secret is to bring along a small pressure cooker. A reader,

Mike Bettinger of San Francisco, passed this tip on to me. Little pressure cookers weigh about two pounds, and for backpackers and backcountry campers, that may sound like a lot. But when three or four people are on a trip, it actually saves weight.

The key is that it allows campers to bring items that are difficult to cook at high altitudes, such as brown and white rice, red, black, pinto and lima beans, and lentils. You pick one or more for a basic staple and then add a variety of freeze-dried ingredients to make a complete dish. Available are packets of meat, vegetables, onions, shallots and garlic. Sun-dried tomatoes, for instance, reconstitute wonderfully in a pressure cooker. Add herbs, spices and maybe a few rainbow trout and you will be eating better out of a backpack than most people eat in their homes.

"In the morning, I have used the pressure cooker to turn dried apricots into apricot sauce to put on the pancakes we made with sourdough starter," Bettinger said. "The pressure cooker is also big enough for washing out cups and utensils. The days when backpacking meant eating terrible freeze-dried food are over. It doesn't take a gourmet cook to prepare these meals, only some thought beforehand."

Now when Foonsky, Mr. Furnai, Rambob and me sit down to eat such a meal, we don't call it "eating." We call it "hodgepacking," or "time to pack your hodge." After a particularly long day on the trail, you can do some serious hodgepacking.

If your trip is a shorter one, like for a weekend, that means you can bring more fresh food to add some sizzle to the hodge. You can design a hot soup/stew mix that is good enough to make and eat at home.

You start by bringing a pot of water to a full boil, then adding pasta, ramen noodles or macaroni. While it simmers, cut in a potato, carrot, onion and garlic clove, and let it cook for about 10 minutes. When the vegetables have softened, add in a soup mix or two, maybe some cheese, and you are just about in business. But you can still ruin it and turn your hodge into sledge. Make sure you read the directions on the soup mix to determine cooking time. It can vary widely. In addition, make sure you stir the whole thing up, otherwise you will get these hidden dry clumps of soup mix that can taste like garlic sawdust.

How do I know? Well, it was up near Kearsage Pass in the Sierra Nevadas, where, feeling half-starved, I dug into our nightly hodge. I will never forget that first bite—I damn near gagged to death. Foonsky laughed at me, until he took his first bite (a nice big one), then turned green.

Another way to trim food costs is to make your own beef jerky, the trademark staple of campers for more than 200 years. But hey, a tiny, little packet of beef jerky costs $2. On that 250-mile expedition, I spent $150 on jerky alone. Never again. Now we make our own and get big strips of jerky that taste better than anything you can buy.

Foonsky settled on the following recipe, starting with a couple pieces of meat, lean top round, sirloin or tri-tip. At home, cut it in 3/16-inch strips across the grain, trimming out the membrane, gristle and fat. Marinate the strips for 24 hours, placing them in a glass dish. The fun begins in picking a marinade. Try two-thirds teriyaki sauce, one-third Worcestershire. You can customize the recipe by adding pepper, ground mustard, bay leaf, red wine vinegar, garlic and, for the brave, Tabasco sauce. After a day or so, squeeze out each strip of meat with a rolling pin, lay them in rows on a cooling rack over a cookie sheet, place them in an oven and dry them at 125 degrees for 12 hours. Thicker pieces can take as long as 18 to 24 hours.

That's it. The hardest part is cleaning the cookie sheet when you are done. The easiest part is eating your own homemade jerky while sitting at a lookout on a mountain ridge. The do-it-yourself method for jerky may take a day or so, but it is cheaper and can taste better than anything you can buy pre-made.

If all this still doesn't sound like your idea of a gourmet but low-cost camping meal, well, you are forgetting the main course: rainbow trout. Remember: If you don't plan on catching them for dinner, you'll probably snag more than you can finish in one night's hodgepacking.

Some campers go to great difficulties to cook their trout, bringing along frying pans, butter, grills, tin foil and more, but all you really need is some seasoned salt and a campfire.

Rinse the gutted trout off, and while it's still wet, sprinkle a good dose of seasoned salt on it, both inside and out. Clear any burning logs to the side of the campfire, then lay the trout right on the coals, turning it once so both sides are cooked. Sound ridiculous? Sound like you are throwing the fish away? Sound like the fish will burn up? Sound like you will have to eat the campfire ash? Wrong on all counts. The fish cooks perfectly, the ash doesn't stick, and after cooking trout this way, you may never fry a trout again.

But if you can't convince your buddies, who may insist the trout should be fried, then make sure you have butter to fry them in, not oil. And also make sure you cook them all the way through, so the meat strips off the backbone in two nice, clean fillets. The fish should end up looking like Sylvester the Cat just dipped it in his mouth, leaving only the head, tail and a perfect skeleton.

You can supplement your eats with sweets, nuts, freeze-dried fruits and drink mixes. In any case, make sure you keep the dinner menu varied. If you and your buddies look into your dinner cups and groan, "Ugh, not this again," you will soon start dreaming of cheeseburgers and french fries on your trip instead of hiking, fishing and finding beautiful campsites.

If you are car camping and have a big ice chest, you can bring virtually anything to eat and drink. If you are on the trail, and don't mind paying the price, the new era of pre-made freeze-dried dinners provide another option.

Some of the biggest advances in the outdoors industry have come in freeze-dried dinners now available for campers. Some of them are almost good enough to serve in restaurants. Sweet-and-sour pork over rice, tostadas, Burgundy chicken . . . it sure beats the poopy goop we used to eat, like the old, soupy chili mac dinners that tasted bad and looked so unlike "food" that consumption was near impossible, even for my dog, Rebel. Foonsky usually managed to get it down, however, but just barely.

To provide an idea of how to plan a menu, consider what my companions and I ate while hiking 250 miles on California's John Muir Trail:

• Breakfast—Instant soup, oatmeal (never get plain), one beef or jerky stick, coffee or hot chocolate.

• Lunch—One beef stick, two jerky sticks, one granola bar, dried fruit, half cup of pistachio nuts, Tang, one small bag of M&Ms.

• Dinner—Instant soup, one freeze-dried dinner, one milk bar, rainbow trout.

What was that last item? Rainbow trout? Right! Lest you plan on it, you can catch them every night.

CLOTHING & WEATHER PROTECTION

What started as an innocent pursuit of a perfect campground evolved into one heck of a predicament for Foonsky and me.

We had parked at the end of a logging road and then bushwhacked our way down a canyon to a pristine trout stream. On my first cast, a little flip into the plunge pool of a waterfall, I caught a 16-inch rainbow trout, a real beauty that jumped three times. Magic stuff.

Then just across stream, we saw it. The Perfect Camping Spot. On a sandbar on the edge of the forest, there lay a flat, high and dry spot above the river. Nearby was plenty of downed wood collected by past winter storms that we could use for firewood. And, of course, this beautiful trout stream was bubbling along just 40 yards from the site.

But nothing is perfect, right? To reach it, we had to wade across the river, although it didn't appear to be too difficult. The cold water tingled a bit, and the river came up surprisingly high, just above the belt. But it would be worth it to camp at The Perfect Spot.

Once across the river, we put on some dry clothes, set up camp, explored the woods, and fished the stream, catching several nice trout for dinner. But late that afternoon, it started raining. What? Rain in the summertime? Nature makes its own rules. By the next morning, it was still raining, pouring like a Yosemite waterfall from a solid gray sky.

That's when we noticed The Perfect Spot wasn't so perfect. The rain had raised the river level too high for us to wade back across. We were marooned, wet and hungry.

"Now we're in a heck of a predicament," said Foonsky, the water streaming off him.

Getting cold and wet on a camping trip with no way to get warm is not only unnecessary and uncomfortable, but it can be a fast ticket to hypothermia, the Number One killer of campers in the woods. By definition, hypothermia is a condition where body temperature is lowered to the point where it causes illness. It is particularly dangerous because the afflicted are usually unaware it is setting in. The first sign is a sense of apathy, then a state of confusion, which can lead eventually to collapse (or what appears to be sleep), then death.

You must always have a way to get warm and dry in short order, regardless of any conditions you may face. If you have no way of getting dry, then you must take emergency steps to prevent hypothermia. Those steps are detailed in the following pages on first-aid.

But you should never reach that point. For starters, always have different sets of clothes tucked away, so no matter how cold and wet you might get, you always have something dry. On hiking trips, I always carry a second set of clothes, sealed to stay dry, in a plastic garbage bag. I keep a third set waiting back at the truck.

If you are car camping, your vehicle can cause an illusory sense of security. But with an extra set of dry clothes stashed safely away, there is no illusion. The security is real. And remember, no matter how hot the weather is when you start on your trip, always be prepared for the worst. Foonsky and I learned the hard way.

So both of us were soaking wet on that sandbar, and with no other choice, we tried holing up in the tent for the night. A sleeping bag with Quallofil™, or another polyester fiber fill, can retain warmth even when wet, because the fill is hollow and retains its loft. So as miserable as it was, we made it through the night.

The rain finally stopped the next day, and the river dropped a bit, but it was still rolling big and angry. Using a stick as a wading staff, Foonsky crossed about 80 percent of the stream before he was dumped, but he made a jump for it and managed to scramble to the river bank. He waved for me to follow. "No problem," I thought.

It took me 20 minutes to reach nearly the same spot where Foonsky had been dumped. The heavy river current was above my belt and pushing hard. Then, in the flash of an instant, my wading staff slipped on a rock. I teetered in the river current, and was knocked over like a bowling pin. I became completely submerged. I went tumbling down the river, heading right toward the waterfall. While underwater, I looked up at the river surface and can remember how close it appeared, yet how out of control I was. Right then, this giant hand appeared, and I grabbed it. It was Foonsky. If it wasn't for that hand, I would have sailed right over the nearby waterfall.

My momentum drew Foonsky right into the river, and we scrambled in the current, but I suddenly sensed the river bottom under my knees. On all fours, the two of us clambered ashore. We were safe.

"Thanks ol' buddy," I said.

"Man, we're wet," he responded. "Let's get to the rig and get some dry clothes on."

Dressing in Layers

After falling in the river, Foonsky and I looked like a couple of cold swamp rats. When we eventually reached the truck and finally started getting into warm clothes, a strange phenomenon hit both of us. Now that we were warming up, we started shivering and shaking like old engines trying to start. Shivering is the body's built-in heater. That's how the body tries to warm itself, producing as much heat as if you were jogging.

To retain that heat, you should dress in "layers." The interior layer, what you wear closest to your skin, and the exterior layer, what you wear to repel the weather, are the most important.

In the good ol' days, campers wore long underwear made out of wool, which was scratchy, heavy and often sweaty. Well, times have changed. You can now wear long underwear made of polypropylene, a synthetic material that is warm, light, and wicks dampness away from your skin. It's ideal to wear in a sleeping bag on cold nights, during cool evenings after the sun goes down, or for winter snow sports. Poly shirts come in three weights: light, medium and heavy. The medium weight is ideal for campers. The light weight clings too much to your body. We call it Indian Underwear, because it keeps creeping up on you. And the heavy weight is too warm and bulky. For most folks, the medium is just right.

The next layer of clothes should be a light cotton shirt or a long-sleeve cotton/wool shirt, or both, depending on the coolness of the day. For pants, many just wear blue jeans when camping, but blue jeans can be hot, tight, and once wet, they tend to stay that way. Putting on wet blue jeans on a cold morning is a torturous way to start the day. I can tell you that from experience since I have suffered that fate a number of times. A better choice are pants made from a cotton/canvas mix, which are available at outdoors stores. They are light, have a lot of give, and dry quickly. If the weather is quite warm, shorts that have some room to them can be the best choice.

Vests and Parkas

In cold weather, you should take the layer system one step further with a warm vest and a parka jacket. Vests are especially useful because they provide warmth without the bulkiness of a parka. The warmest vests and parkas are either filled with down, Quallofil™, or are made with a cotton/wool mix. Each has its respective merits and problems. Down fill provides the most warmth for the amount of weight, but becomes useless when wet, taking on a close resemblance to a wet dish rag. Quallofil™ keeps much of its heat-retaining quality even when wet, but is expensive. Vests made of cotton/wool mixes are the most attractive and also are quite warm, but they can be as heavy as a ship's anchor when wet.

Sometimes the answer is combining the two. One of my best camping companions wears a good-looking, cotton/wool vest, and a parka filled with Quallofil™. The vest never gets wet, so weight is not a factor.

Rain Gear

One of the most miserable nights I ever spent in my life was on a camping trip where I didn't bring my rain gear or a tent. Hey, it was early August, the temperature had been in the 90s for weeks, and if anybody told me it was going to rain, I would have told them to consult a brain doctor. But rain it did. And as I got more and more wet, I kept saying to myself, "Hey, it's summer, it's not supposed to rain." Then I remembered one of the Ten Commandments of camping: forget your rain gear and you can guarantee it will rain.

To stay dry, you need some form of water-repellent shell. It can be as simple as a $5 poncho made out of plastic or as elaborate as a Gore-Tex™ rain jacket and pants set that costs $300. What counts is not how much you spend, but how dry you stay.

Some can do just fine with a cheap poncho, and note that ponchos can serve other uses in addition to a rain coat. Ponchos can be used as a ground tarp, as a rain cover for supplies or a backpack, or in a pinch, can be roped up to trees to provide a quick storm ceiling if you don't have a tent. The problem with ponchos is that in a hard rain, you just don't stay dry. First your legs get wet, then they get soaked. Then your arms follow the same pattern. If you're wearing cotton, you'll find that once part of the garment gets wet, the water will spread until, alas, you are dripping wet, poncho and all. Before long you start to feel like a walking refrigerator.

One high-cost option is buying a Gore-Tex™ rain jacket and pants. Gore-Tex™ is actually not a fabric, as is commonly believed, but a laminated film that coats a breathable fabric. The result is a lightweight, water repellent, breathable jacket and pants. They are perfect for campers, but they cost a fortune.

Some hiking buddies of mine have complained that the older Gore-Tex™ rain gear loses its water-repellent quality over time. However, manufacturers insist that this is the result of water seeping through seams, not leaks in the jacket. At each seam, tiny needles have pierced through the fabric, and as tiny as the holes are, water will find a way through. An application of Seam Lock™, especially at major seams around the shoulders of a jacket, can usually end the problem.

If you don't want to spend the big bucks for Gore-Tex™ rain gear, but want more rain protection than a poncho affords, a coated nylon jacket is the compromise that many choose. They are inexpensive, have the highest water-repellent quality of any rain gear, and are warm, providing a good outer shell for your layers of clothing. But they are not without fault. These jackets don't breathe at all, and if you zip them up tight, you can sweat like an Eskimo.

My brother, Rambob, gave me a $20 nylon jacket prior to a mountain climbing expedition. I wore that $20 special all the way to the top with no complaints; it's warm and 100% waterproof. The one problem with nylon is when the temperatures drop below freezing. It gets so stiff that it feels like you are wearing a straight jacket. But at $20, it seems like a treasure, especially compared to the $180 Gore-Tex™ jackets. And its value increases every time it rains.

Other Gear... And a Few Tips

What are the three items most commonly forgotten on a camping trip? A hat, sunglasses and chapstick. A hot day is unforgiving without them.

A hat is crucial, especially when you are visiting high elevations. Without one you are constantly exposed to everything nature can give you. The sun will dehydrate you, sap your energy, sunburn your head, and in worst cases, cause sunstroke. Start with a comfortable hat. Then finish with sunglasses, chapstick and sunscreen for additional protection. They will help protect you from extreme heat.

To guard against extreme cold, it's a good idea to keep a pair of thin ski gloves stashed away with your emergency clothes, along with a wool ski cap. The gloves should be thick enough to keep your fingers from stiffening up, but pliable enough to allow full movement, so you don't have to take them off to complete simple tasks, like lighting a stove. An alternative to gloves are glovelets, which look like gloves with no fingers. In any case, just because the weather turns cold doesn't mean that your hands have to.

And if you fall into a river like Foonsky and I did, well, I hope you have a set of dry clothes waiting back at your rig. Oh, and a hand reaching out to you.

HIKING & FOOT CARE

We had set up a nice little camp in the woods, and my buddy, Foonsky, was strapping on his hiking boots, sitting against a big Douglas fir.

"New boots," he said with a grin. "But they seem pretty stiff."

We decided to hoof it down the trail for a few hours, exploring the mountain wildlands that are said to hide Bigfoot and other strange creatures. After just a short while on the trail, a sense of peace and calm seemed to settle in. The forest provides you the chance to be purified with clean air and the smell of trees, freeing you from all troubles.

But it wasn't long before the look of trouble was on Foonsky's face. And no, it wasn't from seeing Bigfoot.

"Got a hot spot on a toe," he said.

Immediately we stopped. He pulled off his right boot, then socks, and inspected the left side of his big toe. Sure enough, a blister had bubbled up, filled with fluid, but hadn't popped. From his medical kit, Foonsky cut a small piece of moleskin to fit over the blister, then taped it to hold it in place. A few minutes later, we were back on the trail.

A half hour later, there was still no sign of Bigfoot. But Foonsky stopped again and pulled off his other boot. "Another hot spot." Another small blister had started on the little toe of his left foot, over which he taped a Band-Aid to keep it from further chafing against the inside of his new boot.

In just a few days, ol' Foonsky, a strong, 6-foot-5, 200-plus pound guy, was walking around like a sore-hoofed horse that had been loaded with a month of supplies and then ridden over sharp rocks. Well, it wasn't the distance that had done Foonsky in; it was those blisters. He had them on eight of his ten toes and was going through Band-Aids, moleskin and tape like he was a walking emergency ward. If he used any more tape, he would've looked like a mummy from an Egyptian tomb.

If you've ever been in a similar predicament, then you know the frustration of wanting to have a good time, wanting to hike and explore the area at which you have set up a secluded camp, only to be turned gimp-legged by several blisters. No one is immune—all are created equal before the blister god. You can be forced to bow to it unless you get your act together.

That means wearing the right style boots for what you have in mind and then protecting your feet with a careful selection of socks. And then, if you are still so unfortunate as to get a blister or two, it means knowing how to treat them fast so they don't turn your walk into a sore-footed endurance test.

What causes blisters? In almost all cases, it is the simple rubbing of your foot against the rugged interior of your boot. That can be worsened by several factors:

1—A very stiff boot, or one in which your foot moves inside the boot as you walk, instead of the boot flexing as if it was another layer of skin.

2—Thin, ragged or dirty socks. This is the fastest route to blisters. Thin socks will allow your feet to move inside of your boots, ragged socks will allow your skin to chafe directly against the boot's interior, and dirty socks will wrinkle and fold, also rubbing against your feet instead of cushioning them.

3—Soft feet. By themselves, soft feet will not cause blisters, but in combination with a stiff boot or thin socks, they can cause terrible problems. The best way to toughen up your feet is to go barefoot. In fact, some of the biggest, toughest-looking guys you'll ever see from Hells Angels to pro football players have feet that are as soft as a baby's butt. Why? Because they never go barefoot and don't hike much.

Selecting the Right Boots

One summer I hiked 400 miles, including 250 miles in three weeks, along the crest of California's Sierra Nevada, and another 150 miles over several months in an earlier general training program. In that span, I got just one blister, suffered on the fourth day of the 250-miler. I treated it immediately, and suffered no more. One key is wearing the right boot, and for me, that means a boot that acts as a thick layer of skin that is flexible and pliable to my foot. I want my feet to fit snugly in them, with no interior movement.

There are three kinds of boots: mountaineering boots, hiking boots and canvas walking shoes. Either select the right one for you or pay the consequences.

The stiffest of the lot is the mountaineering boot. These boots are often identified by mid-range tops, laces that extend almost as far as the toe area, and ankle areas that are as stiff as a board. The lack of "give" in them is what endears them to mountaineers. Their stiffness is preferred when rock climbing, walking off-trail on craggy surfaces, or hiking down the edge of stream beds where walking across small rocks can cause you to turn your ankle. Because these boots don't give on rugged, craggy terrain, they reduce ankle injuries and provide better traction.

The drawback to stiff boots is that if careful selection of socks is not made and your foot starts slipping around in them, you will get a set of blisters that would raise even Foonsky's eyebrows. But if you just want to go for a walk, or a good tromp with a backpack, then hiking shoes or backpacking boots will serve you better.

Canvas walking shoes are the lightest of all boots, designed for day walks or short backpacking trips. Some of the newer models are like rugged tennis shoes, designed with a canvas top for lightness and a lug sole for traction. These are perfect for people who like to walk but rarely carry a backpack. Because they are flexible, they are easy to break in, and with fresh socks, they rarely cause blister problems. And because they are light, general hiking fatigue is greatly reduced.

On the negative side, because canvas shoes have shallow lug soles, traction can be far from good on slippery surfaces. In addition, they provide less than ideal ankle support, which can be a problem in rocky areas, such as along a stream where you might want to go trout fishing. Turn your ankle and your trip can be ruined.

My preference is for a premium backpacking boot, the perfect medium between the stiff mountaineering boots and the soft canvas hiking shoes. The deep lug bottom provides traction, the high ankle coverage provides support, yet the soft, waterproof leather body gives each foot a snug fit. Add it up and that means no blisters. On the negative side, they can be quite hot, weigh a ton, and, if they get wet, take days to dry.

There are a zillion styles, brands and price ranges of boots to choose from. If you wander about, comparing all their many features, you will get as confused as a kid in a toy store. Instead, go into the store with your mind clear with what you want, then find it and buy it. If you want the best, expect to spend $60 to $80 for canvas walking shoes, from $100 to $140 and sometimes more for hiking or mountaineering boots. This is one area you don't want to scrimp on, so try not to yelp about the high cost. Instead, walk out of the store believing you deserve the best, and that's exactly what you just paid for.

If you plan on using the advice of a shoe salesman for your purchase, first look at what kind of boots he is wearing. If he isn't even wearing boots, then any advice he might tender may not be worth a plug nickel. Most people I know who own quality boots, including salesmen, will wear them almost daily if their job allows, since boots are the best footwear available. However, even these well-meaning folks can offer sketchy advice. Every hiker I've ever met will tell you he wears the world's greatest boot.

Instead, enter the store with a precise use and style in mind. Rather than fish for suggestions, tell the salesman exactly what you want, try two or three different brands of the same style, and always try on the matching pair of boots simultaneously so you know exactly how they'll feel. If possible, walk up and down stairs with them. Are they too stiff? Are your feet snug yet comfortable, or do they slip? Do they have that "right" kind of feel when you walk?

If you get the right answers to those questions, then you're on your way to blister-free, pleasure-filled days of walking.

Socks

The poor gent was scratching his feet like ants were crawling over them. I looked closer. Huge yellow calluses had covered the bottom of his feet, and at the ball and heel, the calluses were about a quarter of an inch thick, cracking and sore.

"I don't understand it," he said. "I'm on my feet a lot, so I bought a real good pair of hiking boots. But look what they've done to my feet. My feet itch so much I'm going crazy."

People can spend so much energy selecting the right kind of boot that they virtually overlook wearing the right kind of socks. One goes with the other.

Your socks should be thick enough to provide a cushion for your feet, as well as a good, snug fit. Without good socks, you might try to get the boot laces too tight and that's like putting a tourniquet on your feet. You should have plenty of clean socks on hand, or plan on washing what you have on your trip. As socks are worn, they become compressed, dirty and damp. Any one of those factors can cause problems.

My camping companions believe I go overboard when it comes to socks, that I bring too many and wear too many. But it works, so that's where the complaints stop. So how many do I wear? Well, would you believe three socks on each foot? It may sound like overkill, but each has its purpose, and like I said, it works.

The interior sock is thin, lightweight, and made out of polypropylene or silk synthetic materials designed to transport moisture away from your skin. With a poly interior sock, your foot stays dry when it sweats. Without a poly sock, your foot can get damp and mix with dirt, which can cause a "hot spot" to start on your foot. Eventually you get blisters, lots of them.

The second sock is for comfort, and can be cotton, but a thin wool-based composite is ideal. Some made of the latter can wick moisture away from the skin, much like polypropylene does. If wool itches your feet, a thick cotton sock can be suitable, though cotton collects moisture and compacts more quickly than other socks. If you're on a short hike though, cotton will do just fine.

The exterior sock should be made of high quality, thick wool—at least 80 percent wool. It will cushion your feet, provide that "just right" snug fit in your boot, and in cold weather, give you some additional warmth and insulation. It is critical to keep the wool sock clean. If you wear a dirty wool sock over and over again, it will compact and lose its cushion, start wrinkling while you hike, and your feet will catch on fire from the blisters that start popping up.

A Few More Tips

If you are like most folks, that is, the bottom of your feet are rarely exposed and quite soft, you can take additional steps in their care. The best tip is keeping a fresh foot pad in your boot made of sponge rubber. Another cure for soft feet is to get out and walk or jog on a regular basis prior to your camping trip.

If you plan to use a foot pad and wear three socks, you will need to use these items when sizing boots. It is an unforgiving error to wear thin cotton socks when buying boots, then later trying to squeeze all this stuff, plus your feet, into your boots. There just won't be enough room.

The key to treating blisters is fast work at the first sign of a hot spot. But before you remove your socks, first check to see if the sock has a wrinkle in it, a likely cause of the problem. If so, either change socks or pull them tight, removing the tiny folds, after taking care of the blister. Cut a piece of moleskin to cover the offending toe, securing the moleskin with white medical tape. If moleskin is not available, small Band-Aids can do the job, but these have to be replaced daily, and sometimes with even more frequency. At night, clean your feet and sleep without socks.

Two other items that can help your walking is an Ace bandage and a pair of gaiters.

For sprained ankles and twisted knees, an Ace bandage can be like an insurance policy to get you back on the trail and out of trouble. Over the years, I have had serious ankle problems and have relied on a good wrap with a four-inch bandage to get me home. The newer bandages come with the clips permanently attached, so you don't have to worry about losing them.

Gaiters are leggings made of plastic, nylon or Gore-Tex™ which fit from just below your knees, over your calves, and attach under your boots. They are of particular help when walking in damp areas, or in places where rain is common. As your legs brush against ferns or low-lying plants, gaiters will deflect the moisture. Without them, your pants will be soaking wet in short order.

Should your boots become wet, a good tip is never to try to force dry them. Some well-meaning folks will try to speed-dry them at the edge of a campfire or actually put the boots in an oven. While this may dry the boots, it can also loosen the glue that holds them together, ultimately weakening them until one day they fall apart in a heap.

A better bet is to treat the leather so the boots become water repellent. Silicone-based liquids are the easiest to use and least greasy of the treatments available.

A final tip is to have another pair of lightweight shoes or moccasins that you can wear around camp, and in the process, give your feet the rest they deserve.

SLEEPING GEAR

One mountain night in the pines on an eve long ago, my dad, brother and I had rolled out our sleeping bags and were bedded down for the night. After the pre-trip excitement, a long drive, an evening of trout fishing and a barbecue, we were like three tired doggies who had played too much.

But as I looked up at the stars, I was suddenly wide awake. The kid was still wired. A half hour later? No change—wide awake.

And as little kids can do, I had to wake up ol' dad to tell him about it. "Hey, Dad, I can't sleep."

"This is what you do," he said. "Watch the sky for a shooting star and tell yourself that you cannot go to sleep until you see at least one. As you wait and watch, you will start getting tired, and it will be difficult to keep your eyes open. But tell yourself you must keep watching. Then you'll start to really feel tired. When you finally see a shooting star, you'll go to sleep so fast you won't know what hit you."

Well, I tried it that night and I don't even remember seeing a shooting star, I went to sleep so fast.

It's a good trick, and along with having a good sleeping bag, ground insulation, maybe a tent or a few tricks for bedding down in a pickup truck or motor home, you can get a good sleep on every camping trip.

Some 20 years after that camping episode with my dad and brother, we made a trip to the Planetarium at the Academy of Sciences in San Francisco to see a show on Halley's Comet. The lights dimmed, and the ceiling turned into a night sky, filled with stars and a setting moon. A scientist began explaining phenomenons of the heavens.

After a few minutes, I began to feel drowsy. Just then, a shooting star zipped across the Planetarium ceiling. I went into a deep sleep so fast it was like I was in a coma. I didn't wake up until the show was over, the lights were turned back on, and the people were leaving.

Feeling drowsy, I turned to see if ol' Dad had liked the show. Oh yeah? Not only had he gone to sleep too, but he apparently had no intention of waking up, no matter what. Just like a camping trip.

Sleeping Bags

Question: What could be worse than trying to sleep in a cold, wet sleeping bag on a rainy night without a tent in the mountains?

Answer: Trying to sleep in a cold, wet sleeping bag on a rainy night without a tent in the mountains, when your sleeping bag is filled with down.

Water will turn a down-filled sleeping bag into a mushy heap. Many campers do not like a high-tech approach, but the state-of-the-art polyfiber sleeping bags can keep you warm even when wet. That factor, along with temperature rating and weight, is key when selecting a sleeping bag.

A sleeping bag is a shell filled with a heat-retaining insulation. By itself, it is not warm. Your body provides the heat, and the sleeping bag's ability to retain that heat is what makes it warm or cold.

The old-style canvas bags are heavy, bulky, cold and, when wet, useless. With other options available, their use is limited. Anybody who sleeps outdoors or backpacks should choose otherwise. Instead, buy and use a sleeping bag filled with down or one of the quality poly-fills. Down is light, warm and aesthetically pleasing to those who don't think camping and technology mix. If you choose a down bag, be sure to keep it double wrapped in plastic garbage bags on your trips in order to keep it dry. Once wet, you'll spend your nights howling at the moon.

The polyfiber-filled bags are not necessarily better than those filled with down, but they can be. Their one key advantage is that even when wet, some poly-fills can retain up to 80 to 85 percent of your body heat. This allows you to sleep and get valuable rest even in miserable conditions. And my camping experience is that no matter how lucky you may be, there comes a time when you will get caught in an unexpected, violent storm and everything you've got will get wet, including your sleeping bag. That's when a poly-fill bag becomes priceless. You either have one and can sleep, or you don't have one and suffer. It is that simple. Of the synthetic fills, Quallofil™ made by Dupont is the leader of the industry.

But as mentioned, just because a sleeping bag uses a high-tech poly-fill doesn't necessarily make it a better bag. There are other factors.

The most important are a bag's temperature rating and weight. The temperature rating of a sleeping bag refers to how cold it can get before you start actually feeling cold. Many campers make the mistake of thinking, "I only camp in the summer, so a bag rated at 30 or 40 degrees should be fine." Later, they find out it isn't so fine, and all it takes is one cold night to convince them of that. When selecting the right temperature rating, visualize the coldest weather you might ever confront, and then get a bag rated for even colder weather.

For instance, if you are a summer camper, you may rarely experience a night in the low 30s or high 20s. A sleeping bag rated at 20 degrees would be appropriate, keeping you snug, warm and asleep. For most campers, I advise bags rated at zero or ten degrees.

If you buy a polyfilled sleeping bag, never leave it squished in your stuff sack between camping trips. Instead, keep it on a hanger in a closet or use it as a blanket. One thing that can reduce a polyfilled bag's heat-retaining qualities is if you lose the loft out of the tiny hollow fibers that make up the fill. You can avoid this with proper storage.

The weight of a sleeping bag can also be a key factor, especially for backpackers. When you have to carry your gear on your back, every ounce becomes important. To keep your weight to a minimum, sleeping bags that weigh just three pounds are available, although expensive. But if you hike much, it's worth the price. For an overnighter, you can get away with a four or four-and-a-half-pound bag without much stress. However, bags weighing five pounds and up should be left back at the car.

I have two sleeping bags: a seven-pounder that feels like I'm in a giant sponge, and a little three-pounder. The heavy-duty model is for pickup truck camping in cold weather and doubles as a blanket at home. The lightweight bag is for hikes. Between the two, I'm set.

Insulation Pads

Even with the warmest sleeping bag in the world, if you just lay it down on the ground and try to sleep, you will likely get as cold as a winter cucumber. That is because the cold ground will suck the warmth right out of your body. The solution is to have a layer of insulation between you and the ground. For this, you can use a thin Insulite™ pad, a lightweight Therm-a-Rest™ inflatable pad, or an air mattress. Here is a capsule summary of them:

•**Insulite™ pads**—They are light, inexpensive, roll up quick for transport, and can double as a seat pad at your camp. The negative side is that in one night, they will compress, making you feel like you are sleeping on granite.

•**Therm-a-Rest™ pads**—They are a real luxury, because they do everything an Insulite pad does, but also provide a cushion. The negative side to them is that they are expensive by comparison, and if they get a hole in them, they become worthless without a patch kit.

•**Air mattress**—These are okay for car campers, but their bulk, weight and the amount of effort necessary to blow them up make them a nuisance.

A Few Tricks

When surveying a camp area, the most important consideration should be to select a good spot to sleep. Everything else is secondary. Ideally, you want a flat spot that is wind-sheltered, on ground soft enough to drive stakes into. Yeah, and I want to win the lottery, too.

Sometimes that ground will have a slight slope to it. In that case, always sleep with your head on the uphill side. If you sleep parallel to the slope, every time you roll over in your sleep, you'll find yourself rolling down the hill. If you sleep with your head on the downhill side, you'll get a headache that feels like an ax is embedded in your brain.

When you've found a good spot, clear it of all branches, twigs and rocks, of course. A good tip is to dig a slight indentation in the ground where your hip will fit. Since your body is not flat, but has curves and edges, it will not feel comfortable on flat ground. Some people even get severely bruised on the sides of their hips when sleeping on flat, hard ground. For that reason alone, they learn to hate camping. Instead, bring a spade, dig a little depression in the ground for your hip, and sleep well.

After the ground is prepared, throw a ground cloth over the spot, which will keep much of the morning dew off you. In some areas, particularly where fog is a problem, morning dew can be quite heavy and get the outside of your sleeping bag quite wet. In that case, you need overhead protection, such as a tent or some kind of roof, like that of a poncho or tarp, with its ends tied to trees.

Tents and Weather Protection

All it takes is to get caught in the rain once without a tent and you will never go anywhere without one again. A tent provides protection from rain, wind and mosquito attacks. In exchange, you can lose a starry night's view, though some tents now even provide moon roofs.

A tent can be as complex as a four-season, tubular-jointed dome with a rain fly, or as simple as two ponchos snapped together and roped up to a tree. They can be as cheap as a $10 tube tent, which is nothing more than a hollow piece of plastic, or as expensive as a $500 five-person deluxe expedition dome model. They vary greatly in size, price and put-up time. If you plan on getting a good one, then plan on doing plenty of shopping and asking lots of questions. The key ones are: Will it keep me dry? How hard is it to put up? Is it roomy enough? How much does it weigh?

With a little bit of homework, you can get the right answers to these questions.

• *Will it keep me dry?* On many one-person and two-person tents, the rain fly does not extend far enough to keep water off the bottom sidewalls of the tent. In a driving rain, water can also drip from the rain fly and to the bottom sidewalls of the tent. Eventually the water can leak through to the inside, particularly through the seams where the tent has been sewed together.

You must be able to stake out your rain fly so it completely covers all of the tent. If you are tent shopping and this does not appear possible, then don't buy the tent. To prevent potential leaks, use a seam water proofer like Seam Lock™, a glue-like substance, to close potential leak areas on tent seams. On the large umbrella tents, keep a patch kit handy.

Another way to keep water out of your tent is to store all wet garments outside the tent, under a poncho. Moisture from wet clothes stashed in the tent will condense on the interior tent walls. If you bring enough wet clothes in the tent, by the next morning you can feel like you're camping in a duck blind.

• *How hard is it to put up?* If a tent is difficult to erect in full sunlight, you can just about forget it at night. Some tents can go up in just a few minutes, without requiring help from another camper. This might be the kind of tent you want.

The way to compare put-up time of tents when shopping is to count the number of connecting points from the tent poles to the tent, and also the number of stakes required. The fewer, the better. Think simple. My tent has seven connecting points and, minus the rain fly, requires no stakes. It goes up in a few minutes. If you need a lot of stakes, it is a sure tip-off to a long put-up time. Try it at night or in the rain, and you'll be ready to cash your chips and go for broke.

Another factor is the tent poles themselves. Some small tents have poles that are broken into small sections that are connected by bungee cords. It takes only an instant to convert them to a complete pole.

Some outdoor shops have tents on display on their showroom floor. Before buying the tent, have the salesman take the tent down and put it back up. If it takes him more than five minutes, or he says he "doesn't have time," then keep looking.

• *Is it roomy enough?* Don't judge the size of a tent on floor space alone. Some tents small on floor space can give the illusion of roominess with a high ceiling. You can be quite comfortable in them and snug.

But remember that a one-person or two-person tent is just that. A two-person tent has room for two people plus gear. That's it. Don't buy a tent expecting it to hold more than it is intended to.

• *How much does it weigh?* If you're a hiker, this becomes the preeminent question. If it's much more than six or seven pounds, forget it. A 12-pound tent is bad enough, but get it wet and it's like carrying a piano on your back. On the other hand, weight is scarcely a factor if you camp only where you can take your car. My dad, for instance, used to have this giant canvas umbrella tent that folded down to this neat little pack that weighed about 500 pounds.

Bivouac Bags

If you like going solo and choose not to own a tent at all, a bivvy bag, short for bivouac bag, can provide the weather protection you require. A bivvy bag is a water-repellent shell in which your sleeping bag fits. They are light and tough, and for some, are a perfect alternative to a heavy tent. On the down side, however, there is a strange sensation when you try to ride out a rainy night in one. You can hear the rain hitting you, and sometimes even feel the pounding of the drops through the bivvy bag. It can be unsettling to try and sleep under such circumstances.

Pickup Truck Campers

If you own a pickup truck with a camper shell, you can turn it into a self-contained campground with a little work. This can be an ideal way to go: it's fast, portable, and you are guaranteed a dry environment.

But that does not necessarily mean it is a warm environment. In fact, without insulation from the metal truck bed, it can be like trying to sleep on an iceberg. That is because the metal truck bed will get as cold as the air temperature, which is often much colder than the ground temperature. Without insulation, it can be much colder in your camper shell than it would be on the open ground.

When I camp in my rig, I use a large piece of foam for a mattress and insulation. The foam measures four inches thick, is 48 inches wide and 76 inches long. It makes for a bed as comfortable as anything one might ask for. In fact, during the winter, if I don't go camping for a few weeks because of writing obligations, I sometimes will throw the foam on the floor, lay down the old sleeping bag, light a fire and camp right in my living room. It's in my blood, I tell you.

Motor Homes

The problems motor home owners encounter come from two primary sources: lack of privacy and light intrusion.

The lack of privacy stems from the natural restrictions of where a "land yacht" can go. Without careful use of the guide portion of this book, motor home owners can find themselves in parking lot settings, jammed in with plenty of neighbors. Because motor homes often have large picture windows, you lose your privacy, causing some late nights, and come daybreak, light intrusion forces an early wake-up. The result is you get shorted on your sleep.

The answer is always to carry inserts to fit over the inside of your windows. This closes off the outside and retains your privacy. And if you don't want to wake up with the sun at daybreak, you don't have to. It will still be dark.

FIRST AID & INSECT PROTECTION

The mountain night could not have been more perfect, I thought as I lay in my sleeping bag.

The sky looked like a mass of jewels and the air tasted sweet and smelled of pines. A shooting star fireballed across the sky, and I remember thinking, "It just doesn't get any better."

Just then, as I was drifting into sleep, this mysterious buzz appeared from nowhere and deposited itself inside my left ear. Suddenly awake, I whacked my ear with the palm of my hand, hard enough to cause a minor concussion. The buzz disappeared. I pulled out my flashlight and shined it on my palm, and there, lit in the blackness of night, lay the squished intruder. A mosquito, dead amid a stain of blood.

Satisfied, I turned off the light, closed my eyes, and thought of the fishing trip planned for the next day. Then I heard them. It was a squadron of mosquitos, flying landing patterns around my head. I tried to grab them with an open hand, but they dodged the assault and flew off. Just 30 seconds later another landed in my left ear. I promptly dispatched the invader with a rip of the palm.

Now I was completely awake, so I got out of my sleeping bag to retrieve some mosquito repellent. But while en route, several of the buggers swarmed and nailed me in the back and arms. Later, after applying the repellent and settling snugly again in my sleeping bag, the mosquitos would buzz a few inches from my ear. After getting a whiff of the poison, they would fly off. It was like sleeping in a sawmill.

The next day, drowsy from little sleep, I set out to fish. I'd walked but 15 minutes when I brushed against a bush and felt this stinging sensation on the inside of my arm, just above the wrist. I looked down: A tick had his clamps in me. I ripped it out before he could embed his head into my skin.

After catching a few fish, I sat down against a tree to eat lunch and just watch the water go by. My dog, Rebel, sat down next to me and stared at the beef jerky I was munching as if it was a T-bone steak. I finished eating, gave him a small piece, patted him on the head, and said, "Good dog." Right then, I noticed an itch on my arm where a mosquito had drilled me. I unconsciously scratched it. Two days later, in that exact spot, some nasty red splotches started popping up. Poison oak. By petting my dog and then scratching my arm, I had transferred the oil residue of the poison oak leaves from Rebel's fur to my arm.

On returning back home, Foonsky asked me about the trip.

"Great," I said. "Mosquitos, ticks, poison oak. Can hardly wait to go back."

"Sorry I missed out," he answered.

Mosquitos, No-See-Ums, Gnats and Horseflies

On a trip to Canada, Foonsky and I were fishing a small lake from the shore when suddenly a black horde of mosquitos could be seen moving across the lake toward us. It was like when the French Army looked across the Rhine and saw the Wehrmacht coming. There was a literal buzz in the air. We fought them off for a few minutes, then made a fast retreat to the truck and jumped in, content the buggers had been fooled. But somehow, still unknown to us, the mosquitos gained entry to the truck. In 10 minutes, we squished 15 of them while they attempted to plant their oil derricks in our skin. Just outside the truck, the black horde waited for us to make a tactical error, like roll down a window. It finally took a miraculous hailstorm to wipe out the attack.

When it comes to mosquitos, no-see-ums, gnats and horseflies, there are times when there is nothing you can do. However, in most situations you can muster a defense to repel the attack.

The first key with mosquitos is to wear clothing too heavy for them to drill through. Expose a minimum of skin, wear a hat and tie a bandanna around your neck, preferably one that has been sprayed with repellent. If you try to get by with just a cotton T-shirt, you will be declared a federal mosquito sanctuary.

So first your skin must be well covered, exposing only your hands and face. Second, you should have your companion spray your clothes with repellent. Third, you should dab liquid repellent directly on your skin.

Taking Vitamin B1 and eating garlic are reputed to act as natural insect repellents, but I've met a lot of mosquitos that are not convinced. A better bet is to examine the contents of the repellent in question. The key is the percentage of the ingredient called "non-diethyl-metatoluamide." That is the poison, and the percentage of it in the container must be listed and will indicate that brand's effectiveness. Inert ingredients are just excess fluids used to fill the bottles.

At night, the easiest way to get a good sleep without mosquitos buzzing in your ear is to sleep in a bug-proof tent. If the nights are warm and you want to see the stars, new tent models are available that have a skylight covered with mosquito netting. If you don't like tents on summer evenings, mosquito netting rigged with an air space at your head can solve the problem. Otherwise prepare to get bit, even with the use of mosquito repellent.

If your problems are with no-see-ums or biting horseflies, then you need a slightly different approach.

No-see-ums are tiny, black insects that look like nothing more than a sliver of dirt on your skin. Then you notice something stinging, and when you rub the area, you scratch up a little no-see-um. The results are similar to mosquito bites, making your skin itch, splotch and, when you get them bad, swell. In addition to using the techniques described to repel mosquitos, you should go one step further.

The problem is, no-see-ums are tricky little devils. Somehow they can actually get under your socks and around your ankles where they will bite to their heart's content all night long while you sleep, itch, sleep and itch some more. The best solution is to apply a liquid repellent to your ankles, then wear clean socks.

Horseflies are another story. They are rarely a problem, but when they get their dander up, they can cause trouble you'll never forget.

One such episode occurred when Foonsky and I were paddling a canoe along the shoreline of a large lake. This giant horsefly, about the size of a fingertip, started dive-bombing the canoe. After 20 minutes, it landed on his thigh. Foonsky immediately slammed it with an open hand, then let out a blood-curdling "yeeeee-ow" that practically sent ripples across the lake. When Foonsky whacked it, the horsefly had somehow turned around and bit him in the hand, leaving a huge, red welt.

In the next 10 minutes, that big fly strafed the canoe on more dive-bomb runs. I finally got my canoe paddle, swung it as if it was a baseball bat and nailed that horsefly like I'd hit a home run. It landed about 15 feet from the boat, still alive and buzzing in the water. While I was trying to figure what it would take to kill this bugger, a large rainbow trout surfaced and snatched it out of the water, finally avenging the assault.

If you have horsefly or yellowjacket problems, you'd best just leave the area. One, two or a few can be dealt with. More than that and your fun camping trip will be about as fun as being roped to a tree and stung by an electric shock rod.

On most trips, you will spend time doing everything possible to keep from getting bit by mosquitos or no-see-ums. When that fails, you must know what to do next, and fast, if you are among those ill-fated campers who get big, red lumps from a bite inflicted from even a microscopic-sized mosquito.

A fluid called After Bite™ or a dab of ammonia should be applied immediately to the bite. To start the healing process, apply a first-aid gel, not a liquid, such as Campho-Phenique™.

Ticks

Ticks are nasty little vermin that will wait in ambush, jump on unsuspecting prey, and then crawl to a prime location before filling their bodies with their victim's blood.

I call them Dracula Bugs, but by any name they can be a terrible camp pest. Ticks rest on grass and low plants and attach themselves to those who brush against the vegetation (dogs are particularly vulnerable). Typically, they are no more than 18 inches above ground, and if you stay on the trails, you can usually avoid them.

There are two common species of ticks. The common coastal tick is larger, brownish in color, and prefers to crawl around prior to putting its clamps on you. The latter habit can give you the creeps, but when you feel it crawling, you can just pick it off and dispatch it. The coastal tick's preferred destination is usually the back of your neck, just where the hairline starts. The other species, a wood tick, is small and black, and when he puts his clamps in, it's immediately painful. When a wood tick gets into a dog for a few days, it can cause a large, red welt. In either case, ticks should be removed as soon as possible.

If you have hiked in areas infested with ticks, it is advisable to shower as soon as possible, washing your clothes immediately. If you just leave your clothes in a heap, a tick can crawl from your clothes and invade your home. They like warmth, and one way or another, they can end up in your bed. Waking up in the middle of the night with a tick crawling across you chest can really give you the creeps.

Once a tick has its clampers on you, you must decide how long it has been there. If it has been a short time, the most painless and effective method for removal is to take a pair of sharp tweezers and grasp the little devil, making certain to isolate the mouth area, then pull him out. Reader Johvin Perry sent in the suggestion to coat the tick with Vaseline, which will cut off its oxygen supply, after which it may voluntarily give up the hunt.

If the tick has been in longer, you may wish to have a doctor extract it. Some people will burn a tick with a cigarette, or poison it with lighter fluid, but this is not advisable. No matter how you do it, you must take care to remove all of it, especially its claw-like mouth.

The wound, however small, should then be cleansed and dressed. This is done by applying liquid peroxide, which cleans and sterilizes, and then applying a dressing coated with a first-aid gel such as First-Aid Cream™, Campho-Phenique™, or Neosporin™.

Lyme disease, which can be transmitted by the bite of the deer tick, is rare but common enough to warrant some attention. To prevent tick bites, some people tuck their pant legs into their hiking socks and spray tick repellent, called Permamone™, on their pants.

The first symptom of Lyme disease is that the bite area will develop a bright red, splotchy rash. Other early symptoms sometimes include headache, nausaea, fever and/or a stiff neck. If this happens, or if you have any doubts, you should see your doctor immediately. If you do get Lyme disease, don't panic. Doctors say it is easily treated in the early stages with simple antibiotics. If you are nervous about getting Lyme disease, carry a small plastic bag with you when you hike. If a tick manages to get his clampers into you, put it in the plastic bag after you pull it out. Then give it to your doctor for analysis, to see if the tick is a carrier of the disease.

During the course of my hiking and camping career, I have removed ticks from my skin hundreds of times without any problems. However, if you are really worried about ticks, you can purchase a tick removal kit from any outdoors store. These kits allow you to remove ticks in such a way that their toxins are guaranteed not to enter your bloodstream.

Poison Oak

After a nice afternoon hike, about a five-miler, I was concerned about possible exposure to poison oak, so I immediately showered and put on clean clothes. Then I settled into a chair with my favorite foamy elixir to watch the end of a baseball game. The game went 18 innings and meanwhile, my dog, tired from the hike, went to sleep on my bare ankles.

A few days later I had a case of poison oak. My feet looked like they had been on fire and put out with an ice pick. The lesson? Don't always trust your dog, give him a bath as well, and beware of extra-inning ball games.

You can get poison oak only from direct contact with the oil residue from the leaves. It can be passed in a variety of ways, as direct as skin to leaf contact or as indirect as leaf to dog, dog to sofa, sofa to skin. Once you have it, there is little you can do but itch yourself to death. Applying Caladryl™ lotion or its equivalent can help because it contains antihistamines, which attack and dry the itch.

A tip that may sound crazy but seems to work is advised by my pal Furniss. You should expose the afflicted area to the hottest water you can stand, then suddenly immerse it in cold water. The hot water opens the skin pores and gets the "itch" out, and the cold water then quickly seals the pores.

In any case, you're a lot better off if you don't get poison oak to begin with. Remember the old Boy Scout saying: "Leaves of three, let them be." Also remember that poison oak can disguise itself. In the spring, it is green, then it gradually turns reddish in the summer. By fall, it becomes a bloody, ugly-looking red. In the winter, it loses its leaves altogether and appears to be nothing more than barren, brown sticks of small plant. However, at any time and in any form, skin contact can cause quick infection.

Some people are more easily afflicted than others, but if you are one of the lucky few who aren't, don't cheer too loudly. While some people can be exposed to the oil residue of poison oak with little or no effect, the body's resistance can gradually be worn down with repeated exposures. At one time, I could practically play in the stuff and the only symptom would be a few little bumps on the inside of my wrist. Now, some 15 years later, my resistance has broken down. If I merely rub against poison oak now, in a few days the exposed area can look like it was used for a track meet.

So regardless if you consider yourself vulnerable or not, you should take heed to reduce your exposure. That can be done by staying on trails when you hike and making sure your dog does the same. Remember, the worst stands of poison oak are usually brush-infested areas just off the trail. Protect yourself also by dressing so your skin is completely covered, wearing long-sleeve shirts, long pants and boots. If you suspect you've been exposed, immediately wash your clothes, then wash yourself with aloe vera, rinsing with a cool shower.

And don't forget to give your dog a bath as well.

Sunburn

The most common injury suffered on camping trips is sunburn, yet some people wear it as a badge of honor, believing that it somehow enhances their virility. Well, it doesn't. Neither do suntans. And too much sun can lead to serious burns or sunstroke.

It is easy enough to avoid. Use a high-level sunscreen on your skin, chapstick on your lips, and wear sunglasses and a hat. If any area gets burned, apply first-aid cream, which will soothe and provide moisture for your parched, burned skin.

The best advice is not to get even a suntan. Those who do are involved in a practice that can be eventually ruinous to their skins.

A Word About Giardia

You have just hiked in to your backwoods spot, you're thirsty and a bit tired, but you smile as you consider the prospects. Everything seems perfect—there's not a stranger in sight, and you have nothing to do but relax with your pals.

You toss down your gear, grab your cup and dip it into the stream, and take a long drink of that ice-cold mountain water. It seems crystal pure and sweeter than anything you've ever tasted. It's not till later that you find out that it can be just like drinking a cup of poison.

Whether you camp in the wilderness or not, if you hike, you're going to get thirsty. And if your canteen runs dry, you'll start eyeing any water source. Stop! Do not pass Go. Do not drink.

By drinking what appears to be pure mountain water without first treating it, you can ingest a microscopic protozoan called *Giardia lamblia.* The pain of the ensuing abdominal cramps can make you feel like your stomach and intestinal tract are in a knot, ready to explode. With that comes long-term diarrhea that is worse than even a bear could imagine.

Doctors call the disease giardiasis, or Giardia for short, but it is difficult to diagnose. One friend of mine who contracted Giardia was told he might have stomach cancer before the proper diagnosis was made.

Drinking directly from a stream or lake does not mean you will get Giardia, but you are taking a giant chance. There is no reason to take such a risk, potentially ruining your trip and enduring weeks of misery.

A lot of people are taking that risk. I made a personal survey of campers in the Yosemite National Park wilderness, and found that roughly only one in 20 were equipped with some kind of water-purification system. The result, according to the Public Health Service, is that an average of 4 percent of all backpackers and campers suffer giardiasis. According to the Parasitic Diseases Division of the Center for Infectious Diseases, the rates range from 1 percent to 20 percent across the country.

But if you get Giardia, you are not going to care about the statistics. "When I got Giardia, I just about wanted to die," said Henry McCarthy, a California camper. "For about 10 days, it was the most terrible thing I have ever experienced. And through the whole thing, I kept thinking, 'I shouldn't have drunk that water, but it seemed all right at the time.'"

That is the mistake most campers make. The stream might be running free, gurgling over boulders in the high country, tumbling into deep, oxygenated pools. It looks pure. Then the next day, the problems suddenly start. Drinking untreated water from mountain streams is a lot like playing Russian roulette. Sooner or later, the gun goes off.

Anyone venturing into the outdoors should be acquainted with the several solutions to the water-purification problem. I have tested them all. Here are my findings:

• **Katadyn Water Filter:** This is the best system for screening out Giardia, as well as other microscopic bacteria more commonly found in stream and lake water that can cause stomach problems.

To work the filter, place the nozzle in the water, then pump the water directly from a spout at the top of the pump into a canteen. This can require fairly rigorous pumping, especially as the filter becomes plugged. On the average, it takes a few minutes to fill a canteen.

The best advantages are that the device has a highly advanced screening system (a ceramic element), and it can be cleaned repeatedly with a small brush.

The drawbacks are that the filter is expensive, it can easily break when dropped because its body is made of porcelain, and if you pack very light, its weight (about two pounds) may be a factor. But those are good trade-offs when you can drink ice-cold stream water without risk.

• **First-Need or Sweetwater Water Purifiers:** These are the most cost-effective water-purification systems for a variety of reasons.

They are far less expensive than the Katadyn, yet provide much better protection than anything cheaper. They are small and light-weight, so they don't add much weight to your pack. And if you use some care to pump water from sediment-free sources, the purifiers will easily last a week, the length of most outdoor trips.

These devices consist of a plastic pump and a hose that connects to a separate filter canister. They pump faster and with less effort than the Katadyn, mainly because the filter is not as fine-screened.

The big drawback is that if you pump water from a mucky lake, the filter can clog in a few days. Therein lies the weakness. Once plugged up, it is useless and you have to replace it or take your chances.

One trick to extend the filter life is to fill your cook pot with water, let the sediment settle, then pump from there. As an added insurance policy, always have a spare filter canister on hand.

• **Boiling water:** Except for water filtration, this is the only treatment that you can use with complete confidence. According to the federal Parasitic Diseases Division, it takes a few minutes at a rolling boil to be certain you've killed *Giardia lamblia.* At high elevations, boil for three to five minutes. A side benefit is that you'll also kill other dangerous bacteria that live undetected in natural waters.

But to be honest, boiling water is a thorn for most people on backcountry trips. For one thing, if you boil water on an open fire, what should taste like crystal-pure mountain water tastes instead like a mouthful of warm ashes. If you don't have a campfire, it wastes stove fuel. And if you are thirsty *now,* forget it. The water takes hours to cool.

The only time boiling always makes sense, however, is when you are preparing dinner. The ash taste will disappear in whatever freeze-dried dinner, soup, or hot drink you make.

• **Water-purification pills:** Pills are the preference for most backcountry campers, and this can get them in trouble. At just $3 to $8 per bottle, which can figure up to just a few cents per canteen, they do come cheap. In addition, they kill most of the bacteria, regardless of whether you use iodine crystals or potable aqua iodine tablets.

The problem is they just don't always kill *Giardia lamblia,* and that is the one critter worth worrying about on your trip. That makes water-treatment pills unreliable and dangerous.

Another key element is the time factor. Depending on the water's temperature, organic content, and pH level, these pills can take a long time to do the job. A minimum wait of 20 minutes is advised. Most people don't like waiting that long, especially when they're hot and thirsty after a hike and thinking, "What the heck, the water looks fine."

And then there is the taste. On one trip, my water filter clogged and we had to use the iodine pills instead. It doesn't take long to get tired of the iodine-tinged taste of the water. Mountain water should be one of the greatest tasting beverages of the world, but the iodine kills that.

• **No treatment:** This is your last resort and, using extreme care, can be executed with success. One of my best hiking buddies, Michael Furniss, is a nationally-renowned hydrologist, and on wilderness trips he has showed me the difference between "safe" and "dangerous" water sources.

Long ago, people believed that just finding water running over a rock used to be a guarantee of its purity. Imagine that. What we've learned is that the safe water sources are almost always small creeks or springs located in high, craggy mountain areas. The key is making sure no one has been upstream from where you drink.

Furniss mentioned that another potential problem in bypassing water treatment is that even in settings free of Giardia, you can still ingest other bacteria that can cause stomach problems.

The only sure way to beat the problem is to filter or boil your water before drinking, eating, or brushing your teeth. And the best way to prevent the spread of Giardia is to bury your waste products at least eight inches deep and 100 feet away from natural waters.

Hypothermia

No matter how well planned your trip might be, a sudden change in weather can turn it into a puzzle for which there are few answers. Bad weather or an accident can set in motion a dangerous chain of events.

Such a chain of episodes occurred for my brother, Rambob, and me on a fishing trip one fall day just below the snow line. The weather had suddenly turned very cold and ice was forming along the shore of the lake. Suddenly, the canoe became terribly imbalanced and just that quick, it flipped. The little life vest seat cushions were useless, and using the canoe as a paddle board, we tried to kick our way back to shore where my dad was going crazy at the thought of his two sons drowning before his eyes.

It took 17 minutes in that 38-degree water, but we finally made it to the shore. When they pulled me out of the water, my legs were dead, not strong enough even to hold up my weight. In fact, I didn't feel so much cold as tired, and I just wanted to lay down and go to sleep.

I closed my eyes, and my brother-in-law, Lloyd Angal, slapped me in the face several times, then got me on my feet and pushed and pulled me about.

In the celebration over making it to shore, only Lloyd had realized that hypothermia was setting in. Hypothermia is the condition in which the temperature of the body is lowered to the point that it causes poor reasoning, apathy and collapse. It can look like the afflicted person is just tired and needs to sleep, but that sleep can be the first step to a coma.

Ultimately, my brother and I shared what little dry clothing remained. Then we began hiking around to get muscle movement, creating internal warmth. We ate whatever munchies were available because the body produces heat by digestion. But most important, we got our heads as dry as possible. More body heat is lost through wet hair than any other single factor.

A few hours later, we were in a pizza parlor replaying the incident, talking about how only a life vest can do the job of a life vest. We decided never again to rely on those little flotation seat cushions that disappear when the boat flips.

Almost by instinct we had done everything right to prevent hypothermia: Don't go to sleep, start a physical activity, induce shivering, put dry clothes on, dry your head and eat something. That's how you fight hypothermia. In a dangerous situation, whether you fall in a lake or a stream or get caught unprepared in a storm, that's how you can stay alive.

After being in that ice-bordered lake for almost 20 minutes and then finally pulling ourselves to the shoreline, we discovered a strange thing. My canoe was flipped right-side up, and almost all of its contents were lost: tackle box, floatation cushions and cooler. But remaining was one paddle and one fishing rod, the trout rod my grandfather had given me for my 12th birthday.

Lloyd gave me a smile. "This means that you are meant to paddle and fish again," he said with a laugh.

Getting Unlost

You could not have been more lost. But there I was, a guy who is supposed to know about these things, transfixed by confusion, snow and hoof prints from a big deer.

I discovered it is actually quite easy to get lost. If you don't get your bearings, getting found is the difficult part. This occurred on a wilderness trip where I'd hiked in to a remote lake and then set up a base camp for a deer hunt.

"There are some giant bucks up on that rim," confided Mr. Furnai, who lives near the area. "But it takes a mountain man to even get close to them."

That was a challenge I answered. After four-wheeling it to the trailhead, I tromped off with pack and rifle, gut-thumped it up 100 switchbacks over the rim, then followed a creek drainage up to a small but beautiful lake. The area was stark and nearly treeless, with bald granite broken only by large boulders. To keep from getting lost, I marked my route with piles of small rocks to act as directional signs for the return trip.

But at daybreak the next day, I stuck my head out of my tent and found eight inches of snow on the ground. I looked up into a gray sky filled by huge, cascading snowflakes. Visibility was about 50 yards, with fog on the mountain rim. "I better get out of here and get back to my truck," I said to myself. "If my truck gets buried at the trailhead, I'll never get out."

After packing quickly, I started down the mountain. But after 20 minutes, I began to get disoriented. You see, all the little piles of rocks I'd stacked to mark the way were now buried in snow, and I had only a smooth white blanket of snow to guide me. Everything looked the same, and it was snowing even harder now.

Five minutes later I started chewing on some jerky to keep warm, then suddenly stopped. Where was I? Where was the creek drainage? Isn't this where I was supposed to cross over a creek and start the switchbacks down the mountain?

Right then I looked down and saw the tracks of a huge deer, the kind Mr. Furnai had talked about. What a predicament: I was lost and snowed in, and seeing big hoof prints in the snow. Part of me wanted to abandon all safety and go after that deer, but a little voice in the back of my head won out. "Treat this as an emergency," it said.

The first step in any predicament is to secure your present situation, that is, to make sure it does not get any worse. I unloaded my rifle (too easy to slip, fall and have a misfire), took stock of my food (three days worth), camp fuel (plenty), and clothes (rain gear keeping me dry). Then I wondered, "Where the hell am I?"

I took out my map, compass and altimeter, then opened the map and laid it on the snow. It immediately began collecting snowflakes. I set the compass atop the map and oriented it to north. Because of the fog, there was no way to spot landmarks, such as prominent mountain tops, to verify my position. Then I checked the altimeter, which read 4,900 feet. Well, the elevation at my lake was 5,320 feet. That was critical information.

I scanned the elevation lines on the map and was able trace the approximate area of my position, somewhere downstream from the lake, yet close to a 4,900-foot elevation. "Right here," I said, point to a spot on the map with a finger. "I should pick up the switchback trail down the mountain somewhere off to the left, maybe just 40 or 50 yards away."

Slowly and deliberately, I pushed through the light, powdered snow. In five minutes, I suddenly stopped. To the left, across a 10-foot depression in the snow, appeared a flat spot that veered off to the right. "That's it! That's the crossing."

In minutes, I was working down the switchbacks, on my way, no longer lost. I thought of the hoof prints I had seen, and now that I knew my position, I wanted to head back and spend the day hunting.

Then I looked up at the sky, saw it filled with falling snowflakes, and envisioned my truck buried deep in snow. Alas, this time logic won out over dreams.

In a few hours, now trudging through more than a foot of snow, I was at my truck at a spot called Doe Flat, and next to it was a giant, all-terrain Forest Service vehicle and two rangers.

"Need any help?" I asked them.

They just laughed. "We're here to help you," one answered. "It's a good thing you filed a trip plan with our district office in Gasquet. We wouldn't have known you were out here."

"Winter has arrived," said the other. "If we don't get your truck out now, it will be stuck here until next spring. If we hadn't found you, you might have been here until the end of time."

They connected a chain from the rear axle of their giant rig to the front axle of my truck and started towing me out, back to civilization. On the way to pavement, I figured I had gotten some of the more important lessons of my life. Always file a trip plan, have plenty of food, fuel and a camp stove you can rely on. Make sure your clothes, weather gear, sleeping bag and tent will keep you dry and warm. Always carry a compass, altimeter and map with elevation lines, and know how to use them, practicing in good weather to get the feel of it.

And if you get lost and see the hoofprints of a giant deer, well, there are times when it is best to pass them by.

CATCHING FISH, AVOIDING BEARS & HAVING FUN

Feet tired and hot, stomachs hungry, we stopped our hike for lunch beside a beautiful little river pool that was catching the flows from a long but gentle waterfall. My brother, Rambob, passed me a piece of jerky. I took my boots off, then slowly dunked my feet into the cool, foaming water.

I was gazing at a towering peak across a canyon, when suddenly, Wham! There was a quick jolt at the heel of my right foot. I pulled my foot out of the water and incredibly, a trout had bitten it.

My brother looked at me like I had antlers growing out of my head. "Wow!" he exclaimed. "That trout almost caught himself an outdoors writer!"

It's true that in remote areas trout sometimes bite on almost anything, even feet. On one high-country trip, I have caught limits of trout using nothing but a bare hook. The only problem is that the fish will often hit the splitshot sinker instead of the hook. Of course, fishing isn't usually that easy. But it gives you an idea of what is possible.

America's wildlands are home for a remarkable abundance of fish and wildlife. Deer browse with little fear of man, bears keep an eye out for your food, and little critters like squirrels and chipmunks are daily companions. Add in the fishing and you've got yourself a camping trip.

Your camping adventures will evolve into premium outdoor experiences if you can work in a few good fishing trips, avoid bear problems, and occasionally add a little offbeat fun with some camp games.

Trout and Bass

He creeps up on the stream as quiet as an Indian scout, keeping his shadow off the water. With his little spinning rod, he'll zip his lure within an inch or two of its desired mark, probing along rocks, the edges of riffles, pocket water or wherever he can find a change in river habitat. It's my brother, Rambob, trout fishing, and he's a master at it.

In most cases, he'll catch a trout on his first or second cast. After that it's time to move up the river, giving no spot much more than five minutes due. Stick and move, stick and move, stalking the stream like a bobcat zeroing in on an unsuspecting rabbit. He might keep a few trout for dinner, but mostly he releases what he catches. Rambob doesn't necessarily fish for food. It's the feeling that comes with it.

Fishing can give you a sense of exhilaration, like taking a hot shower after being coated with dust. On your walk back to camp, the steps come easy. You suddenly understand what John Muir meant when he talked of developing a oneness with nature, because you have it. That's what fishing can provide.

You don't need a million dollars worth of fancy gear to catch fish. What you need is the right outlook, and that can be learned. That goes regardless of whether you are fishing for trout or bass, the two most popular fisheries in America. Your fishing tackle selection should be as simple and as clutter-free as possible.

At home, I've got every piece of fishing tackle you might imagine, more than 30 rods and many tackle boxes, racks and cabinets filled with all kinds of stuff. I've got one lure that looks like a chipmunk and another that resembles a miniature can of beer with hooks. If I hear of something new, I want to try it, and usually do. It's a result of my lifelong fascination with the sport.

But if you just want to catch fish, there's an easier way to go. And when I go fishing, I take that path. I don't try to bring everything. It would be impossible. Instead, I bring a relatively small amount of gear. At home I will scan my tackle boxes for equipment and lures, make my selections and bring just the essentials. Rod, reel and tackle will fit into a side pocket of my backpack or a small carrying bag.

So what kind of rod should be used on an outdoor trip? For most camper/anglers, I suggest the use of a light, multi-piece spinning rod that will break down to a small size. One of the best deals on the fishing market is the six-piece Daiwa 6.5-foot pack rod, No. 6752. It retails for as low as $30, yet is made of a graphite/glass composite that gives it the quality of a much more expensive model. And it comes in a hard plastic carrying tube for protection. Other major rod manufacturers, such as Fenwick, offer similar premium rods. It's tough to miss with any of them.

The use of graphite/glass composites in fishing rods has made them lighter and more sensitive, yet stronger. The only downside to graphite as a rod material is that it can be brittle. If you rap your rod against something, it can crack or cause a weak spot. That weak spot can eventually snap when under even light pressure, like setting a hook or casting. Of course, a bit of care will prevent that from ever occurring.

If you haven't bought a fishing reel in some time, you will be surprised at the quality and price of micro spinning reels on the market. The reels come tiny and strong, with rear-control drag systems. Sigma, Shimano, Cardinal, Abu and others all make premium reels. They're worth it. With your purchase, you've just bought a reel that will last for years and years.

The one downside to spinning reels is that after long-term use, the bail spring will weaken. The result is that after casting and beginning to reel, the bail will sometimes not flip over and allow the reel to retrieve the line. Then you have to do it by hand. This can be incredibly frustrating, particularly when stream fishing, where instant line pickup is essential. The solution is to have a new bail spring installed every few years. This is a cheap, quick operation for a tackle expert.

You might own a giant tackle box filled with lures, but on your fishing trip you are better off to fit just the essentials into a small container. One of the best ways to do that is to use the Plano Micro-Magnum 3414, a tiny two-sided tackle box for trout fishermen that fits into a shirt pocket. In mine, I can fit 20 lures in one side of the box and 20 flies, splitshot and snap swivels in the other. For bass lures, which are larger, you need a slightly larger box, but the same principle applies.

There are more fishing lures on the market than you can imagine, but a few special ones can do the job. I make sure these are in my box on every trip. For trout, I carry a small black Panther Martin spinner with yellow spots, a small gold Kastmaster, a yellow Roostertail, a gold Z-Ray with red spots, a Super Duper, and a Mepps Lightning spinner.

You can take it a step further using insider's wisdom. My old pal Ed the Dunk showed me his trick of taking a tiny Dardevle spoon, then spray painting it flat black and dabbing five tiny red dots on it. It's a real killer, particularly in tiny streams where the trout are spooky.

The best trout catcher I've ever used on rivers is a small metal lure called a Met-L Fly. On days when nothing else works, it can be like going to a shooting gallery. The problem is that the lure is near impossible to find. Rambob and I consider the few we have remaining so valuable that if the lure is snagged on a rock, a cold swim is deemed mandatory for its retrieval. These lures are as hard to find in tackle shops as trout can be to catch without one.

For bass, you can also fit all you need into a small plastic tackle box. I have fished with many bass pros and all of them actually use just a few lures: a white spinner bait, a small jig called a Gits-It, a surface plug called a Zara Spook, and plastic worms. At times, like when the bass move into shoreline areas during the spring, shad minnow imitations like those made by Rebel or Rapala can be dynamite. My favorite is the one-inch blue-silver Rapala. Every spring, as the lakes begin to warm and the fish snap out of their winter doldrums, I like to float and paddle around in my small raft. I'll cast that little Rapala along the shoreline and catch and release hundreds of bass, bluegill and sunfish. The fish are usually sitting close to the shoreline, awaiting my offering.

Fishing Tips

There's an old angler's joke about how you need to "think like a fish." But if you're the one getting zilched, you may not think it's so funny.

The irony is that it is your mental approach, what you see and what you miss, that often determines your fishing luck. Some people will spend a lot of money on tackle, lures and fishing clothes, and that done, just saunter up to a stream or lake, cast out and wonder why they are not catching fish. The answer is their mental outlook. They are not attuning themselves to their surroundings.

You must live on nature's level, not your own. Try this and you will become aware of things you never believed even existed. Soon you will see things that will allow you to catch fish. You can get a head start by reading about fishing, but to get your degree in fishing, you must attend the University of Nature.

On every fishing trip, regardless what you fish for, try to follow three hard-and-fast rules:

1—Always approach the fishing spot so you will be undetected.

2—Present your lure, fly or bait in a manner so it appears completely natural, as if no line was attached.

3—Stick and move, hitting one spot, working it the best you can, then move to the next.

Here's a more detailed explanation.

1—**Approach:** No one can just walk up to a stream or lake, cast out and start catching fish as if someone had waved a magic wand. Instead, give the fish credit for being smart. After all, they live there.

Your approach must be completely undetected by the fish. Fish can sense your presence through sight and sound, though this is misinterpreted by most people. By sight, this rarely means the fish actually see you, but more likely, they will see your shadow on the water, or the movement of your arm or rod while casting. By sound, it doesn't mean they hear you talking, but that they will detect the vibrations of your footsteps along the shore, kicking a rock, or the unnatural plunking sound of a heavy cast hitting the water. Any of these elements can spook them off the bite. In order to fish undetected, you must walk softly, keep your shadow off the water, and keep your casting motion low. All of these keys become easier at sunrise or sunset, when shadows are on the water. At midday, a high sun causes a high level of light penetration in the water, which can make the fish skittish to any foreign presence.

Like hunting, you must stalk the spots. When my brother Rambob sneaks up on a fishing spot, he is like a burglar sneaking through an unlocked window.

2—Presentation: Your lure, fly or bait must appear in the water as if no line was attached, so it appears as natural as possible. My pal Mo Furniss has skin-dived in rivers to watch what the fish see when somebody is fishing.

"You wouldn't believe it," he said. "When the lure hits the water, every trout within 40 feet, like 15, 20 trout, will do a little zigzag. They all see the lure and are aware something is going on. Meanwhile, onshore the guy casting doesn't get a bite and thinks there aren't any fish in the river."

If your offering is aimed at fooling a fish into striking, it must appear as part of its natural habitat, as if it is an insect just hatched or a small fish looking for a spot to hide. That's where you come in.

After you have snuck up on a fishing spot, you should zip your cast upstream, then start your retrieve as soon as it hits the water. If you let the lure sink to the bottom, then start the retrieve, you have no chance. A minnow, for instance, does not sink to the bottom then start swimming. On rivers, the retrieve should be more of a drift, as if the "minnow" was in trouble and the current was sweeping it downstream.

When fishing on trout streams, always hike and cast up river, then retrieve as the offering drifts downstream in the current. This is effective because trout will sit almost motionless, pointed upstream, finning against the current. This way they can see anything coming their direction, and if a potential food morsel arrives, all they need to do is move over a few inches, open their mouths, and they've got an easy lunch. Thus you must cast upstream.

Conversely, if you cast downstream, your retrieve will bring the lure from behind the fish, where he cannot see it approaching. And I've never seen a trout that had eyes in its tail. In addition, when retrieving a downstream lure, the river current will tend to sweep your lure inshore to the rocks.

3—Finding spots: A lot of fishermen don't catch fish and a lot of hikers never see any wildlife. The key is where they are looking.

The rule of the wild is that fish and wildlife will congregate wherever there is a distinct change in the habitat. This is where you should begin your search. To find deer, for instance, forget probing a thick forest, but look for when it breaks into a meadow, or a clear-cut has splayed a stand of trees. That's where the deer will be.

In a river, it can be where a riffle pours into a small pool, a rapid that plunges into a deep hole and flattens, a big boulder in the middle of a long riffle, a shoreline point, a rock pile, a submerged tree. Look for the changes. Conversely, long straight stretches of shoreline will not hold fish—the habitat is lousy.

On rivers, the most productive areas are often where short riffles tumble into small oxygenated pools. After sneaking up from the downstream side and staying low, you should zip your cast so the lure plops gently in the white water just above the pool. Starting your retrieve instantly, the lure will drift downstream and plunk into the pool. Bang! That's where the trout will hit. Take a few more casts, then head upstream to the next spot.

With a careful approach and lure presentation, and by fishing in the right spots, you have the ticket to many exciting days on the water.

Of Bears and Food

The first time you come nose-to-nose with a bear, it can make your skin quiver.

Even the sight of mild-mannered black bears, the most common bear in America, can send shock waves through your body. They range from 250 to 400 pounds and have large claws and teeth that are made to scare campers. When they bound, the muscles on their shoulders roll like ocean breakers.

Bears in camping areas are accustomed to sharing the mountains with hikers and campers. They have become specialists in the food-raiding business. As a result, you must be able to make a bear-proof food hang, or be able to scare the fellow off. Many campgrounds provide bear- and raccoon-proof food lockers. You can also stash your food in your vehicle, but that limits the range of your trip.

If you are staying at one of the easy backpack sites listed in this book, there will be no food lockers available. (The exceptions are the High Sierra camps in Yosemite National Park, where rangers have placed high wires for food hangs, the next best thing to food lockers.) Your car will not be there, either. The solution is to make a bear-proof food hang, suspending all of your food wrapped in a plastic garbage bag from a rope in midair, 10 feet from the trunk of a tree and 20 feet off the ground. (Counter-balancing two bags with a rope thrown over a tree limb is very effective, but finding an appropriate limb can be difficult.)

This is accomplished by tying a rock to a rope, then throwing it over a high but sturdy tree limb. Next, tie your food bag to the rope, and hoist it up in the air. When you are satisfied with the position of the food bag, tie off the end of the rope to another tree. In an area frequented by bears, a good food bag is a necessity—nothing else will do.

I've been there. On one trip, my pal Foonsky and my brother Rambob had left to fish, and I was stoking up an evening campfire when I felt the eyes of an intruder on my back. I turned around and this big bear was heading straight for our camp. In the next half hour, I scared the bear off twice, but then he got a whiff of something sweet in my brother's pack.

The bear rolled into camp like a semi truck, grabbed my brother's pack, ripped it open, and plucked out the Tang and the Swiss Miss. The 350-pounder then sat astride a nearby log and lapped at the goodies like a thirsty dog drinking water.

Once a bear gets his mitts on your gear, he considers it his. I took two steps toward the pack and that bear jumped off the log and galloped across the camp right at me. Scientists say a man can't outrun a bear, but they've never seen how fast I can go up a granite block with a bear on my tail.

Shortly thereafter, Foonsky returned to find me perched on top of the rock, and demanded to know how I could let a bear get our Tang. It took all three of us, Foonsky, Rambob, and myself, charging at once and shouting like madmen, to clear the bear out of the camp and send him off over the ridge. We learned never to let food sit unattended.

The Grizzly

When it comes to grizzlies, well, my friends, you need what we call an "attitude adjustment." Or that big ol' bear may just decide to adjust your attitude for you, making your stay at the park a short one.

Grizzlies are nothing like black bears. They are bigger, stronger, have little fear and take what they want. Some people believe there are many different species of this critter, like Alaskan brown, silvertip, cinnamon and Kodiak, but the truth is they are all grizzlies. Any difference in appearance has to do with diet, habitat and life habits, not speciation. By any name, they all come big.

The first thing you must do is determine if there are grizzlies in the area where you are camping. That can usually be done by asking local rangers. If you are heading into Yellowstone or Glacier National Park, or the Bob Marshall Wilderness of Montana, well, you don't have to ask. They're out there, and they're the biggest and potentially most dangerous critters you could run into.

One general way to figure the size of a bear is from his footprint. Take the width of the footprint in inches, add one to it—and you'll have an estimated length of the bear in feet. For instance, a nine-inch footprint equals a 10-foot bear. Any bear that big is a grizzly, my friends. In fact, most grizzly footprints average about nine to ten inches across, and black bears (though they may be brown in color) tend to have footprints only four-and-a-half to six inches across.

If you are hiking in a wilderness area that may have grizzlies, then it becomes a necessity to wear bells on your pack. That way, the bear will hear you coming and likely get out of your way. Keep talking, singing or maybe even debating the country's foreign policy, but whatever, do not fall into a silent hiking vigil. And if a breeze is blowing in your face, you must make even more noise (a good excuse to rant and rave about the government's domestic affairs). Noise is important, because your smell will not be carried in the direction you are hiking. As a result, the bear will not smell you coming.

If a bear can hear you and smell you, it will tend to get out of the way and let you pass without your knowing it was even close by. The exception is if you are carrying fish or lots of sweets in your pack, or if you are wearing heavy, sweet deodorants or makeup. All three are bear attractants.

Most encounters with grizzlies occur when hikers fall into a silent march in the wilderness with the wind in their faces, and they walk around a corner and right into a big, unsuspecting grizzly. If you do this, and see a big hump just behind its neck, well, don't think twice: It's a grizzly.

And then what should you do? Get up a tree, that's what. Grizzlies are so big that their claws cannot support their immense weight, and thus they cannot climb trees. And although their young can climb, they rarely want to get their mitts on you.

If you do get grabbed, every instinct in your body will tell you to fight back. Don't believe it. Play dead. Go limp. Let the bear throw you around a little, because after awhile you become unexciting play material, and the bear will get bored. My grandmother was grabbed by a grizzly in Glacier National Park and after a few tosses and hugs, was finally left alone to escape.

Some say it's a good idea to tuck your head under his chin, since that way, the bear will be unable to bite your head. I'll take a pass on that one. If you are taking action, any action, it's a signal that you are a force to be reckoned with, and he'll likely respond with more aggression. And bears don't lose many wrestling matches.

What grizzlies really like to do, believe it or not, is to pile a lot of sticks and leaves on you. Just let them, and keep perfectly still. Don't fight them; don't run. And when you have a 100-percent chance (not 98 or 99) to dash up a nearby tree, that's when you let fly. Once safely in a tree, then you can hurl down insults and let your aggression out.

In a wilderness camp, there are special precautions you should take. Always hang your food at least 100 yards downwind of your camp and get it high, 30 feet is reasonable. In addition, circle your camp with rope, and hang the bells from your pack on it. Thus, if a bear walks into your camp, he'll run into your rope, the bells will ring, and everybody will have a chance to get up a tree before ol' griz figures out what's going on. Often, the unexpected ringing of bells is enough to send him off in search of a quieter environment.

You see, more often than not, grizzlies tend to clear the way for campers and hikers. So, be smart, don't act like bear bait, and always have a plan if you are confronted by one.

My pal Foonsky had such a plan during a wilderness expedition in Montana's northern Rockies. On our second day of hiking, we started seeing scratch marks on the trees, 13 to 14 feet off the ground.

"Mr. Griz made those," Foonsky said. "With spring here, the grizzlies are coming out of hibernation and using the trees like a cat uses a scratch board to stretch the muscles."

The next day, I noticed Foonsky had a pair of track shoes tied to the back of his pack. I just laughed.

"You're not going to outrun a griz," I said. "In fact, there's hardly any animals out here in the wilderness that man can outrun."

Foonsky just smiled.

"I don't have to outrun a griz," he said. "I just have to outrun you!"

Fun and Games

"Now what are we supposed to do?" the young boy asked his dad.

"Yeah, Dad, think of something," said another son.

Well, Dad thought hard. This was one of the first camping trips he'd taken with his sons and one of the first lessons he received was that kids don't appreciate the philosophic release of mountain quiet. They want action, and lots of it. With a glint in his eye, Dad searched around the camp and picked up 15 twigs, breaking them so each was four inches long. He laid them in three separate rows, three twigs in one row, five twigs in another, and seven in the other.

"OK, this game is called 3-5-7," said dad. "You each take turns picking up sticks. You are allowed to remove all or as few as one twig from a row, but here's the catch: You can only pick from one row per turn. Whoever picks up the last stick left is the loser."

I remember this episode well because those two little boys were my brother Bobby, as in Rambobby, and me. And to this day, we still play 3-5-7 on campouts, with the winner getting to watch the loser clean the dishes. What I have learned in the span of time since that original episode is that it does not matter what your age is: Campers need options for camp fun.

Some evenings, after a long hike or ride, you are likely to feel too worn-out to take on a serious romp downstream to fish, or a climb up to a ridge for a view. That is especially true if you have been in the outback for a week or more. At that point a lot of campers will spend their time resting and gazing at a map of the area, dreaming of the next day's adventure, or just take a seat against a rock, watching the colors of the sky and mountain panorama change minute-by-minute. But kids in the push-button video era, and a lot of adults too, want more. After all, "I'm on vacation; I want some fun."

There are several options, like the 3-5-7 twig game, and they should be just as much a part of your pre-trip planning as arranging your gear.

For kids, plan on games, the more physically challenging the competition, the better. One of the best games is to throw a chunk of wood into a lake, then challenge the kids to hit it by throwing rocks. It wreaks havoc on the fishing, but it can keep kids totally absorbed for some time. Target practice with a wrist-rocket slingshot is also all-consuming for kids, firing rocks away at small targets like pine cones set on a log.

You can also set kids off on little missions near camp, like looking for the footprints of wildlife, searching out good places to have a "snipe hunt," picking up twigs to get the evening fire started, or having them take the water purifier to a stream to pump some drinking water into a canteen. The latter is an easy, fun, yet important task that will allow kids to feel a sense of equality they often don't get at home.

For adults, the appeal should be more to the intellect. A good example is star and planet identification, and while you are staring into space, you're bound to spot a few asteroids, or shooting stars. A star chart can make it easy to locate and identify many distinctive stars and constellations, such as Pleiades (the Seven Sisters), Orion and others from the zodiac, depending on the time of year. With a little research, this can add a unique perspective to your trip. You could point to Polaris, one of the most easily identified of all stars, and note that navigators in the 1400s used it to find their way. Polaris, of course, is the "North Star," and is at the end of the handle of the Little Dipper. Pinpointing Polaris is quite easy. First find the Big Dipper, then locate the outside stars of the ladle of the Big Dipper. They are called the "Pointer Stars" because they point right at Polaris.

A tree identification book can teach you a few things about your surroundings. It is also a good idea for one member of the party to research the history of the area you have chosen and another to research the geology. With shared knowledge, you end up with a deeper love of wild places.

Another way to add some recreation into your trip is to bring a board game, a number of which have been miniaturized for campers. The most popular are chess, checkers and cribbage. The latter comes with an equally miniature set of playing cards. And if you bring those little cards, that opens a vast set of other possibilities. With kids along, for instance, just take the Queen of Clubs out of the deck and you can instantly play Old Maid.

But there are more serious card games and they come with high stakes. Such occurred on one high country trip where Foonsky, Rambob and myself sat down for a late afternoon game of poker. In a game of seven-card stud, I caught a straight on the sixth card and felt like a dog licking on a T-bone. Already, I had bet several Skittles and peanut M&Ms on this promising hand.

Then I examined the cards Foonsky had face up. He was showing three sevens, and acting as happy as a grizzly with a pork chop, like he had a full house. He matched my bet of two peanut M&Ms, then raised me three SweetTarts, one Starburst and one sour apple Jolly Rancher. Rambob folded, but I matched Foonsky's bet and hoped for the best as the seventh and final card was dealt.

Just after Foonsky glanced at that last card, I saw him sneak a look at my grape stick and beef jerky stash.

"I raise you a grape stick," he said.

Rambob and I both gasped. It was the highest bet ever made, equivalent to a million dollars laid down in Las Vegas. Cannons were going off in my chest. I looked hard at my cards. They looked good, but were they good enough?

Even with a great hand like I had, a grape stick was too much to gamble, my last one with 10 days of trail ahead of us. I shook my head and folded my cards. Foonsky smiled at his victory.

But I still had my grape stick.

Old Tricks Don't Always Work

Most people are born honest, but after a few camping trips, they usually get over it.

I remember some advice I got from Rambob, normally an honest soul, on one camping trip. A giant mosquito had landed on my arm and he alerted me to some expert advice.

"Flex your arm muscles," he commanded, watching the mosquito fill with my blood. "He'll get stuck in your arm, then he'll explode."

For some unknown reason, I believed him. We both proceeded to watch the mosquito drill countless holes in my arm.

Alas, the unknowing face sabotage from their most trusted companions on camping trips. It can arise at any time, usually in the form of advice from a friendly, honest-looking face, as if to say, "What? How can you doubt me?" After that mosquito episode, I was a little more skeptical of my dear old brother. Then, the next day, when another mosquito was nailing me in the back of the neck, out came this gem:

"Hold your breath," he commanded. I instinctively obeyed. "That will freeze the mosquito," he said, "then you can squish him."

But in the time I wasted holding my breath, the little bugger was able to fly off without my having the satisfaction of squishing him. When he got home, he probably told his family, "What a dummy I got to drill today!"

Over the years, I have been duped numerous times with dubious advice:

On a grizzly bear attack: "If he grabs you, tuck your head under the grizzly's chin, then he won't be able to bite you in the head." This made sense to me until the first time I looked face-to-face with a nine-foot grizzly, 40 yards away. In seconds, I was at the top of a tree, which suddenly seemed to make the most sense.

On coping with animal bites: "If a bear bites you in the arm, don't try to jerk it away. That will just rip up your arm. Instead force your arm deeper into his mouth. He'll lose his grip and will have to open it to get a firmer hold, and right then you can get away." I was told this in the Boy Scouts, and when I was 14, I had a chance to try it out when a friend's dog bit me when I tried to pet it. What happened? When I shoved my arm deeper into his mouth, he bit me about three extra times.

On cooking breakfast: "The bacon will curl up every time in a camp frying pan. So make sure you have a bacon stretcher to keep it flat." As a 12-year-old Tenderfoot, I spent two hours looking for the bacon stretcher until I figured out the camp leader had forgotten it. It wasn't for several years until I learned that there is no such thing.

On preventing sore muscles: "If you haven't hiked for a long time and you are facing a rough climb, you can keep from getting sore muscles in your legs, back and shoulders by practicing the 'Dead Man's Walk.' Simply let your entire body go slack, and then take slow, wobbling steps. This will clear your muscles of lactic acid, which causes them to be so sore after a rough hike." Foonsky pulled this one on me. Rambob and I both bought it, then tried it while we were hiking up Mount Whitney, which requires a 6,000-foot elevation gain in six miles. In one 45-minute period, about 30 other hikers passed us and looked at us as if we were suffering from some rare form of mental aberration.

Fish won't bite? No problem: "If the fish are not feeding or will not bite, persistent anglers can still catch dinner with little problem. Keep casting across the current, and eventually, as they hover in the stream, the line will feed across their open mouths. Keep reeling and you will hook the fish right in the side of the mouth. This technique is called 'lining.' Never worry if the fish will not bite, because you can always line 'em." Of course, heh, heh, heh, that explains why so many fish get hooked in the side of the mouth.

How to keep bears away: "To keep bears away, urinate around the borders of your campground. If there are a lot of bears in the area, it is advisable to go right on your sleeping bag." Yeah, surrrrrre.

What to do with trash: "Don't worry about packing out trash. Just bury it. It will regenerate into the earth and add valuable minerals." Bears, raccoons, skunks and other critters will dig up your trash as soon as you depart, leaving one huge mess for the next camper. Always pack out everything.

Often the advice comes without warning. That was the case after a fishing trip with a female companion, when she outcaught me two-to-one, the third such trip in a row. I explained this to a shopkeeper, and he nodded, then explained why.

"The male fish are able to detect the female scent on the lure, and thus become aroused into striking."

Of course! That explains everything!

Getting Revenge

I was just a lad when Foonsky pulled the old snipe-hunt trick on me. It's taken 30 years to get revenge.

You probably know about snipe hunting. That is where the victim is led out at night in the woods by a group, then is left holding a bag.

"Stay perfectly still and quiet," Foonsky explained. "You don't want to scare the snipe. The rest of us will go back to camp and let the woods settle down. Then when the snipe are least expecting it, we'll form a line and charge through the forest with sticks, beating bushes and trees, and we'll flush the snipe out right to you. Be ready with the bag. When we flush the snipe out, bag it. But until we start our charge, make sure you don't move or make a sound or you will spook the snipe and ruin everything."

I sat out there in the woods with my bag for hours, waiting for the charge. I waited, waited and waited. Nothing happened. No charge, no snipe. It wasn't until well past midnight that I figured something was wrong. When I finally returned to camp, everybody was sleeping.

Well, I tell ya, don't get mad at your pals for the tricks they pull on you. Get revenge. Some 25 years later, on the last day of a camping trip, the time finally came.

"Let's break camp early," Foonsky suggested to Mr. Furnai and me. "Get up before dawn, eat breakfast, pack up, then be on the ridge to watch the sun come up. It will be a fantastic way to end the trip."

"Sounds great to me," I replied. But when Foonsky wasn't looking, I turned his alarm clock ahead three hours. So when the alarm sounded at the appointed 4:30 a.m. wakeup time, Mr. Furnai and I knew it was actually only 1:30 a.m.

Foonsky clambered out of his sleeping bag and whistled with a grin. "Time to break camp."

"You go ahead," I answered. "I'll skip breakfast so I can get a little more sleep. At the first sign of dawn, wake me up, and I'll break camp."

"Me too," said Mr. Furnai.

Foonsky then proceeded to make coffee, cook a breakfast and eat it, sitting on a log in the black darkness of the forest, waiting for the sun to come up. An hour later, with still no sign of dawn, he checked his clock. It now read 5:30 a.m. "Any minute now we should start seeing some light," he said.

He made another cup of coffee, packed his gear and sat there in the middle of the night, looking up at the stars, waiting for dawn. "Anytime now," he said. He ended up sitting there all night long.

Revenge is sweet. Prior to a fishing trip at a lake, I took Foonsky aside and explained that the third member of the party, Jimbobo, was hard of hearing and very sensitive about it. "Don't mention it to him," I advised. "Just talk real loud."

Meanwhile, I had already told Jimbobo the same thing. "Foonsky just can't hear very good.".

We had fished less than 20 minutes when Foonsky got a nibble.

"GET A BITE?" shouted Jimbobo.

"YEAH!" yelled back Foonsky, smiling. "BUT I DIDN'T HOOK HIM!"

"MAYBE NEXT TIME!" shouted Jimbobo with a friendly grin.

Well, they spent the entire day yelling at each other from the distance of a few feet. They never did figure it out. Heh, heh, heh.

That is, I thought so, until we made a trip salmon fishing. I got a strike that almost knocked my fishing rod out of the boat. When I grabbed the rod, it felt like Moby Dick was on the other end. "At least a 25-pounder," I said. "Maybe bigger."

The fish dove, ripped off line and then bulldogged. "It's acting like a 40-pounder," I announced, "Huge, just huge. It's going deep. That's how the big ones fight."

Some 15 minutes later, I finally got the "salmon" to the surface. It turned out to be a coffee can that Foonsky had clipped on the line with a snap swivel. By maneuvering the boat, he made the coffee can fight like a big fish.

This all started with a little old snipe hunt years ago. You never know what your pals will try next. Don't get mad. Get revenge!

CAMPING OPTIONS

Boat-in Seclusion

Most campers would never think of trading in their car, pickup truck or motor home for a boat, but people who go by boat on a camping trip have a virtual guarantee of seclusion and top-quality outdoor experiences.

Camping with a boat is a do-it-yourself venture in living in primitive circumstances. Yet at the same time you can bring along any luxury item you wish, from giant coolers, stoves and lanterns to portable gasoline generators. Weight is almost never an issue.

In California, many outstanding boat-in campgrounds are available in many beautiful areas. The best are on the shores of lakes accessible by canoe or skiff, and at offshore islands reached by saltwater cruisers. Several boat-in camps are detailed in this book.

If you want to take the adventure a step further and create your own boat-in camp, perhaps near a special fishing spot, this is a go-for-it deal that provides the best way possible to establish your own secret campsite. But most people who set out free-lance style forget three critical items for boat-in camping: a shovel, a sunshade and an ax. Here is why these three items can make a key difference in your trip:

1—A shovel: Many lakes and virtually all reservoirs have steep, sloping banks. At reservoirs subject to drawdowns, what was lake bottom in the spring can be a prospective campsite in late summer. If you want a flat area for a tent site, the only answer is to dig one out yourself. A shovel gives you that option.

2—A sunshade: The flattest spots to camp along lakes often have a tendency to support only sparse tree growth. As a result, a natural shield from sun and rain is rarely available. What? Rain in the summer? Oh yeah, don't get me started. A light tarp, set up with poles and staked ropes, solves the problem.

3—An ax: Unless you bring your own firewood, which is necessary at some sparsely wooded reservoirs, there is no substitute for a good, sharp ax. With an ax, you can almost always find dry firewood, since the interior of an otherwise wet log will be dry. When the weather turns bad is precisely when you will most want a fire. You may need an ax to get one going.

In the search to create your own personal boat-in campsite, you will find that the flattest areas are usually the tips of peninsulas and points, while the protected back ends of coves are often steeply sloped. At reservoirs, the flattest areas are usually near the mouths of the feeder streams, and the points are quite steep. On rivers, there are usually sand bars on the inside of tight bends that make for ideal campsites.

At boat-in campsites developed by government agencies, virtually all are free of charge, but you are on your own. Only in extremely rare cases is piped water available.

Any way you go, by canoe, skiff or power cruiser, you end up with a one-in-a-million campsite you can call your own.

Desert Outings

It was a cold, snowy day in Missouri when 10-year-old Rusty Ballinger started dreaming about the vast deserts of the West.

"My dad was reading aloud from a Zane Grey book called *Riders of the Purple Sage*," Ballinger said. "He would get animated when he got to the passages about the desert. It wasn't long before I started to have the same feelings."

That was in 1947. Ballinger, now in his 50s, has spent a good part of his life exploring the West, camping along the way. "The deserts are the best part. There's something about the uniqueness of each little area you see," Ballinger said. "You're constantly surprised. Just the time of day and the way the sun casts a different color. It's like the lady you care about. One time she smiles, the next time she's pensive. The desert is like that. If you love nature, you can love the desert. After awhile, you can't help but love it."

A desert adventure is not just an antidote for a case of cabin fever in the winter. Whether you go by motor home, pickup truck, car or on foot, it provides its own special qualities.

If you go camping in the desert, your approach has to be as unique as the setting. For starters, don't plan on any campfires, but bring a camp stove instead. And unlike in the mountains, do not camp near a water hole. The reason is an animal, like a badger, coyote or desert bighorn might be desperate for water, and if you set up camp in the animal's way, you may be forcing a confrontation.

In some areas, there is a danger of flash floods. An intense rain can fall in one area, collect in a pool, then suddenly burst through a narrow canyon. If you are in its path, you could be injured or drowned. The lesson? Never camp in a gully.

"Some people might wonder, 'What good is this place?'" Ballinger said. "The answer is that it is good for looking at. It is one of the world's unique places."

ETHICS & CAMP POLITICS

The perfect place to set up a base camp for a camping trip turned out to be not so perfect. In fact, according to Doug Williams of California, "it did not even exist."

Williams and his son, James, had driven deep into Angeles National Forest, prepared to set up camp and then explore the surrounding area on foot. But when they reached their destination, no campground existed.

"I wanted a primitive camp in a national forest where I could teach my son some basics," said the senior Williams. "But when we got there, there wasn't much left of the camp and it had been closed. It was obvious that the area had been vandalized."

It turned out not to be an isolated incident. A lack of outdoor ethics practiced by a few people using the non-supervised campgrounds available on national forest land has caused the U.S. Forest Service to close a few of them, and make extensive repairs to others.

"There have been sites closed, especially in Angeles and San Bernardino national forests in Southern California," said David Flohr, regional campground coordinator for the Forest Service. "It's an urban type of thing, affecting forests near urban areas, and not just Los Angeles. They get a lot of urban users and they bring with them a lot of the same ethics they have in the city. They get drinking and they're not afraid to do things. They vandalize and run. Of course, it is a public facility, so they think nobody is getting hurt."

But somebody is getting hurt, starting with the next person who wants to use the campground. And if the ranger district budget doesn't have enough money to pay for repairs, the campground is then closed for the next arrivals. Just ask Doug and James Williams.

In an era of considerable fiscal restraint for the Forest Service, vandalized campgrounds could face closures instead of repair in the next few years. The Williams had a taste of it, but Flohr, as camping coordinator, gets a steady diet.

"It starts with behavior," Flohr said. "General rowdiness, drinking, partying and then vandalism. It goes all the way from the felt tip pen things (graffiti) to total destruction, blowing up toilet buildings with dynamite. I have seen toilets destroyed totally with shotguns.

They burn up tables, burn barriers. They'll burn up signs for fire-wood, even the shingles right off the roofs of the bathrooms. They'll shoot anything, garbage cans, signs. It can get a little hairy. A favorite is to remove the stool out of a toilet building. We've had people fall in the open hole."

The National Park Service had a similar problem 10 years ago, especially with rampant littering. Park Director Bill Mott responded by creating an interpretive program that attempts to teach visitors the wise use of natural areas, and to have all park workers set examples by picking up litter and reminding others to do the same.

The Forest Service has responded with a similar program, with brochures available that detail the wise use of national forests. The four most popular brochures are titled: "Rules for Visitors to the National Forest," "Recreation on the National Forests," "Is the Water Safe?" and "Backcountry Safety Tips." These include details on campfires, drinking water from lakes or streams, hypothermia, safety and outdoor ethics. They are available for free by writing Public Affairs, U.S. Forest Service, 630 Sansome Street, San Francisco, CA 94111.

Flohr said even experienced campers sometimes cross over the ethics line unintentionally. The most common example, he said, is when campers toss garbage into the outhouse toilet, rather than packing it out in a plastic garbage bag.

"They throw it in the vault toilet bowls, and that just fills them up," Flohr said. "That creates an extremely high cost to pump it. You know why? Because that stuff has to be picked out piece-by-piece by some poor guy. It can't be pumped."

At most backcountry sites, the Forest Service has implemented a program called, "Pack it in, pack it out," even posting signs that remind all visitors to do so. But a lot of people don't do it, and others may even uproot the sign and burn it for firewood.

On a trip to a secluded lake near Carson Pass in the Sierra Nevada, I arrived at a small, little-known camp where the picnic table had been spray-painted and garbage had been strewn about. A pristine place, the true temple of God, had been defiled.

Then I remembered back 30 years, and a story my dad told me: "There are two dogs inside of you," he said, "a good one, and a bad one. The one you feed is the one that will grow. Always try to feed the good dog."

Getting Along with Fellow Campers

The most important thing about a camping, fishing or hunting trip is not where you go, how many fish you catch or how many shots you fire. It often has little to do with how beautiful the view is, how easy the campfire lights, or how sunny the days are.

Oh yeah? Then what is the most important factor? The answer: The people you are with. It is that simple.

Who would you rather camp with? Your enemy at work or your dream mate in a good mood? Heh, heh. You get the idea. A camping trip is a fairly close-knit experience, and you can make lifetime friends or lifelong enemies in the process. That is why your choice of companions is so important. Your own behavior is equally consequential.

Yet most people spend more time putting together their camping gear than considering why they enjoy or hate the company of their chosen companions. Here are rules of behavior for good camping mates:

1—No whining: Nothing is more irritating than being around a whiner. It goes right to the heart of adventure, since often the only difference between a hardship and an escapade is simply whether or not an individual has the spirit for it. The people who do can turn a rugged day in the outdoors into a cherished memory. Those who don't can ruin it with their incessant sniveling.

2—Activities must be agreed upon: Always have a meeting of the minds with your companions over the general game plan. Then everybody will possess an equal stake in the outcome of the trip. This is absolutely critical. Otherwise they will feel like merely an addendum to your trip, not an equal participant, and a whiner will be born (see No. 1).

3—Nobody's in charge: It is impossible to be genuine friends if one person is always telling another what to do, especially if the orders involve simple camp tasks. You need to share the space on the same emotional plane, and the only way to do that is to have a semblance of equality, regardless of differences in experience. Just try ordering your mate around at home for a few days. You'll quickly see the results, and they aren't nice.

4—Equal chances at the fun stuff: It's fun to build the fire, fun to get the first cast at the best fishing spot, and fun to hoist the bagged food for a bear-proof food hang. It is not fun to clean the dishes, collect firewood, or cook every night. So obviously, there must be an equal distribution of the fun stuff and the not-fun stuff, and everybody on the trip must get a shot at the good and the bad.

5—No heroes: No awards are bestowed for achievement in the outdoors, yet some guys treat mountain peaks, big fish and big game as if they are a trophy competition. Actually, nobody cares how wonderful you are, which is always a surprise to trophy chasers. What people care about is the heart of the adventure, the gut-level stuff.

6—Agree on a wakeup time: It is a good idea to agree on a general wakeup time before closing your eyes for the night, and that goes regardless of whether you want to sleep in late or get up at dawn. Then you can proceed on course regardless of what time you crawl out of your sleeping bag in the morning, without the risk of whining (see No. 1).

7—Think of the other guy: Be self-aware instead of self-absorbed. A good test is to count the number of times you say, "What do you think?" A lot of potential problems can be solved quickly by actually listening to the answer.

8—Solo responsibilities: There are a number of essential camp duties on all trips, and while they should be shared equally, most should be completed solo. That means that when it is time for you to cook, you don't have to worry about me changing the recipe on you. It means that when it is my turn to make the fire, you keep your mitts out of it.

9—Don't let money get in the way: Of course everybody should share equally in trip expenses, such as the cost of food, and it should be split up before you head out yonder. Don't let somebody pay extra, because that person will likely try to control the trip. Conversely, don't let somebody weasel out of paying a fair share.

10—Accordance on the food plan: Always have complete agreement on what you plan to eat each day. Don't figure that just because you like Steamboat's Sludge, everybody else will, too, especially youngsters. Always, always, always check for food allergies such as nuts, onions, or cheese, and make sure each person brings their own personal coffee brand. Some people drink only decaffeinated; others might gag on anything but Burma monkey beans.

Obviously, it is difficult to find companions who will agree on all of these elements. This is why many campers say that the best camping buddy they'll ever have is their mate, someone who knows all about them and likes them anyway.

OUTDOORS WITH KIDS

How do you get a boy or girl excited about the outdoors? How do you compete with the television and remote control? How do you prove to a kid that success comes from persistence, spirit and logic, which the outdoors teaches, and not from pushing buttons?

The answer is in the Ten Camping Commandments for Kids. These are lessons that will get youngsters excited about the outdoors, and will make sure adults help the process along, not kill it. Some are obvious, some are not, but all are important:

1—Trips with children should be to places where there is a guarantee of action. A good example is camping in a park where large numbers of wildlife can be viewed, such as squirrels, chipmunks, deer and even bear. Other good choices are fishing at a small pond loaded with bluegill, or hunting in a spot where a kid can shoot a .22 at pine cones all day. Boys and girls want action, not solitude.

2—Enthusiasm is contagious. If you aren't excited about an adventure, you can't expect a child to be. Show a genuine zest for life in the outdoors, and point out everything as if it is the first time you have ever seen it.

3—Always, always, always be seated when talking to someone small. This allows the adult and child to be on the same level. That is why fishing in a small boat is perfect for adults and kids. Nothing is worse for youngsters than having a big person look down at them and give them orders. What fun is that?

4—Always show how to do something, whether it is gathering sticks for a campfire, cleaning a trout or tying a knot. Never tell—always show. A button usually clicks to "off" when a kid is lectured. But they can learn behavior patterns and outdoor skills by watching adults, even when the adults are not aware they are being watched.

5—Let kids be kids. Let the adventure happen, rather than trying to force it within some preconceived plan. If they get sidetracked watching pollywogs, chasing butterflies or sneaking up on chipmunks, let them be. A youngster can have more fun turning over rocks and looking at different kinds of bugs that sitting in one spot, waiting for a fish to bite.

6—Expect young peoples' attention spans to be short. Instead of getting frustrated about it, use it to your advantage. How? By bringing along a bag of candy and snacks. Where there is a lull in the camp activity, out comes the bag. Don't let them know what goodies await, so each one becomes a surprise.

7—Make absolutely certain the child's sleeping bag is clean, dry and warm. Nothing is worse than discomfort when trying to sleep, but a refreshing sleep makes for a positive attitude the next day. In addition, kids can become quite scared of animals at night. The parent should not wait for any signs of this, but always play the part of the outdoor guardian, the one who will "take care of everything."

8—Kids quickly relate to outdoor ethics. They will enjoy eating everything they kill, building a safe campfire and picking up all their litter, and they will develop a sense of pride that goes with it. A good idea is to bring extra plastic garbage bags to pick up any trash you come across. Kids long remember when they do something right that somebody else has done wrong.

9—If you want youngsters hooked on the outdoors for life, take a close-up photograph of them holding up fish they have caught, blowing on the campfire or completing other camp tasks. Young children can forget how much fun they had, but they never forget if they have a picture of it.

10—The least important word you can ever say to a kid is "I." Keep track of how often you are saying "Thank you" and "What do you think?" If you don't say them very often, you'll lose out. Finally, the most important words of all are: "I am proud of you."

PREDICTING WEATHER

Foonsky climbed out of his sleeping bag, glanced at the nearby meadow and scowled hard.

"It doesn't look good," he said. "Doesn't look good at all."

I looked at my companion of 20 years of adventures, noted his discontent, and then I looked at the meadow and immediately understood why: *"When the grass is dry at morning light, look for rain before the night."*

"How bad you figure?" I asked him.

"We'll know soon enough, I reckon," Foonsky answered. "Short notice, soon to pass. Long notice, long it will last."

When you are out in the wild, spending your days fishing and your nights camping, you learn to rely on yourself for weather predictions. It can make or break you. If a storm hits the unprepared, it can quash the trip and possibly endanger the participants. If you are ready for it, what could be a hardship ends up as an added adventure.

You can't rely on TV weather forecasters either, people who don't even know that when all the cows on a hill are pointed north, it will rain that night for sure. God forbid if the cows are all sitting. But what do you expect from TV's talking heads?

Foonsky made a campfire, started boiling some water for coffee and soup, and we started to plan the day. In the process, I noticed the smoke of the campfire: It was sluggish, drifting and hovering.

"You notice the smoke?" I asked, chewing on a piece of home-made jerky.

"Not good," Foonsky said. "Not good." He knew that sluggish, hovering smoke indicates rain.

"You'd think we'd have been smart enough to know last night that this was coming," Foonsky said. "Did you take a look at the moon or the clouds?"

"I didn't look at either," I answered. "Too busy eating the trout we caught." You see, if the moon is clear and white, the weather will be good the next day. But if there is a ring around the moon, you can count the number of stars inside the ring, and that is how many days until the next rain. As for clouds, the high, thin clouds called cirrus indicate a change in the weather.

We were quiet for a while, planning our strategy, but while we did so, some terrible things happened: A chipmunk scattered past with his tail high, a small flock of geese flew by very low, and a little sparrow perched on a tree limb quite close to the trunk.

"We're in for trouble," I told Foonsky.

"I know, I know," he answered. "I saw 'em, too. And come to think of it, no crickets were chirping last night either."

"Damn, that's right!"

These are all signs of an approaching storm. Foonsky pointed at the smoke of the campfire and shook his head as if he had just been condemned. Sure enough, now the smoke was blowing towards the north, a sign of a south wind. *"When the wind is from the south, the rain is in its mouth."*

"We'd best stay hunkered down until it passes," Foonsky said.

I nodded. "Let's gather as much firewood now as we can, get our gear covered up, then plan our meals."

"Then we'll get a poker game going."

As we accomplished these camp tasks, the sky clouded up, then darkened. Within an hour, we had gathered enough firewood to make a large pile, enough wood to keep a fire going no matter how hard it rained. The day's meals had been separated out of the food bag, so it wouldn't have to be retrieved during the storm. We buttoned two ponchos together, staked two of the corners with ropes to the ground, and tied the other two with ropes to different tree limbs to create a slanted roof/shelter.

As the first raindrop fell with that magic sound on our poncho roof, Foonsky was just starting to shuffle the cards.

"Cut for deal," he said.

Just as I did so, it started to rain a bit harder. I pulled out another piece of beef jerky and started chewing on it. It was just another day in paradise...

Weather lore can be valuable. Small signs provided by nature and wildlife can be translated to provide a variety of weather information. Here is the list I have compiled over the years:

When the grass is dry at morning light,
Look for rain before the night.

Short notice, soon to pass.
Long notice, long it will last.

When the wind is from the east,
'Tis fit for neither man nor beast.
When the wind is from the south,
The rain is in its mouth.
When the wind is from the west,
Then it is the very best.

CAMPING TIPS

Red sky at night, sailors' delight.
Red sky in the morning, sailors take warning.

When all the cows are pointed north,
Within a day rain will come forth.

Onion skins very thin, mild winter coming in.
Onion skins very tough, winter's going to be very rough.

When your boots make the squeak of snow,
Then very cold temperatures will surely show.

If a goose flies high, fair weather ahead.
If a goose flies low, foul weather will come instead.

A thick coat on a woolly caterpillar means a big, early snow is
coming.

Chipmunks will run with their tails up before a rain.

Bees always stay near their hives before a rainstorm.

When the birds are perched on large limbs near tree trunks, an
intense but short storm will arrive.

On the coast, if groups of seabirds are flying a mile inland, look for
major winds.

If crickets are chirping very loud during the evening, the next day will
be clear and warm.

If the smoke of a campfire at night rises in a thin spiral, good weather
is assured for the next day.
If the smoke of a campfire at night is sluggish, drifting and hovering,
it will rain the next day.

If there is a ring around the moon, count the number of stars inside
the ring, and that is how many days until the next rain.
If the moon is clear and white, the weather will be good the next day.

The high, thin clouds called cirrus indicate a change in the weather.
The oval-shaped clouds called lenticular indicate high winds.

Two different levels of clouds moving in different directions indicate changing weather soon.

Huge, dark billowing clouds called cumulonimbus, suddenly forming on warm afternoons in the mountains, mean that a short but intense thunderstorm with lightning can be expected.

When squirrels are busy gathering food for extended periods, it means good weather is ahead in the short term, but a hard winter is ahead in the long term.

And God forbid if all the cows are sitting down…

LEAVE NO TRACE

"Enjoy America's country and leave no trace." That is the motto of the Leave No Trace organization, and we strongly support it. The following list was developed from the policies of Leave No Trace, with their input and support for its publication. For a free, pocket-sized, weatherproof card printed with these policies, as well as information that details how to minimize human impact on wild areas, phone (800) 332-4100.

Plan ahead and prepare
1. Learn about the regulations and issues that apply to the area you are visiting.
2. Avoid heavy-use areas.
3. Obtain all maps and permits.
4. Bring extra garbage bags to pack out any refuse you come across.

Keep the wilderness wild
1. Let nature's sound prevail. Avoid loud voices and noises.
2. Leave radios and tape players at home. At drive-in camping sites, never open car doors with music playing.
3. Careful guidance is necessary when choosing any games to bring for children. Most toys, especially any kind of gun toys with which children simulate shooting at each other, should not be allowed on a camping trip.
3. Control pets at all times, or leave them with a sitter at home.
4. Treat natural heritage with respect. Leave plants, rocks and historical artifacts where you find them.

Respect other users
1. Horseback riders have priority over hikers. Step to the downhill side of the trail and talk softly when encountering horseback riders.
2. Hikers and horseback riders have priority over mountain bikers. When mountain bikers encounter other users, even on wide trails, they should pass at an extremely slow speed. On very narrow trails, they should dismount and get off to the side, so the hiker or horseback rider can pass without having their trip disrupted.
3. Mountain bikes are not permitted on most single-track trails and are expressly prohibited on all portions of the Pacific Crest Trail, in

designated wilderness areas and on most state park trails. Mountain bikers breaking these rules should be confronted, told to dismount and walk their bikes until they reach a legal area.

4. It is illegal for horseback riders to break off branches that may lay in the path of wilderness trails.

5. Horseback riders on overnight trips are prohibited from camping in many areas, and are usually required to keep stock animals in specific areas where they can do no damage to the landscape.

Travel lightly
1. Visit the backcountry in small groups.
2. Below tree line, always stay on designated trails.
3. Do not cut across switchbacks.
4. When traveling cross-country where no trails are available, follow animal trails or spread out with your group so no new routes are created.
5. Read your map and orient yourself with landmarks, a compass and altimeter. Avoid marking trails with rock cairns, tree scars or ribbons.

Camp with care
1. Choose a pre-existing, legal site. Restrict activities to areas where vegetation is compacted or absent.
2. Camp at least 75 steps (200 feet) from lakes, streams and trails.
3. Always choose sites that will not be damaged by your stay.
4. Preserve the feeling of solitude by selecting camps that are out of view when possible.
5. Do not construct structures or furniture or dig trenches.

Campfires
1. Fire use can scar the backcountry. If a fire ring is not available, use a lightweight stove for cooking.
2. Where fires are permitted, use exisiting fire rings, away from large rocks or overhangs.
3. Do not char rocks by building new rings.
4. Gather sticks from the ground that are no larger than the diameter of your wrist.
5. Do not snap branches of live, dead or downed trees, which can cause personal injury and also scar the natural setting.
6. Put the fire "dead out" and make sure it is cold before departing. Remove all trash from the fire ring.
7. Remember that some forest fires can be started by a campfire that

appears to be out. Hot embers burning deep in the pit can cause tree roots to catch on fire and burn underground. If you ever see smoke rising from the ground, seemingly from nowhere, dig down and put the fire out.

Sanitation

If no refuse facility is available:

1. Deposit human waste in "cat holes" dug six to eight inches deep. Cover and disguise the cat hole when finished.
2. Deposit human waste at least 75 paces (200 feet) from any water source or camp.
3. Use toilet paper sparingly. When finished, carefully burn it in the cat hole, then bury it.
4. If no appropriate burial locations are available, such as in popular wilderness camps above tree line in hard granite settings—Devil's Punchbowl in the Siskiyou Wilderness is such an example—then all human refuse should be double-bagged and packed out.
5. At boat-in campsites, chemical toilets are required. Chemical toilets can also solve the problem of larger groups camping or long stays at one location where no facilities are available.
6. To wash dishes or your body, carry water away from the source and use small amounts of biodegradable soap. Scatter dishwater after all food particles have been removed.
7. Scour your campsites for even the tiniest piece of trash and any other evidence of your stay. Pack out all the trash you can, even if it's not yours. Finding cigarette butts, for instance, provides special irritation for most campers. Pick them up and discard them properly.
8. Never litter. Never. Or you become the enemy of all others.

RESOURCE GUIDE

Now you're ready to join the Five Percent Club, that is, the five percent of campers who know the secret spots where they can camp, fish and hike, and have the time of their lives doing it.

To aid in that pursuit, here are a number of contacts, map sources and reservation systems available for your use:

National Forests

The Forest Service provides many secluded camps and permits camping anywhere except where it is specifically prohibited. If you ever want to clear the cobwebs and get away from it all, this is the way to go.

Many Forest Service campgrounds are quite remote and have no developed water. You don't need to check in, you don't need reservations and there is no fee. At many Forest Service campgrounds that provide piped water, the camping fee is often only a few dollars, with payment made on the honor system. Because most of these camps are in mountain areas, they are subject to closure for snow or mud during the winter. More popular Forest Service camps cost from $6 to $10. Group sites are available on a reservation basis, and usually cost $50 to $100 per night, accomodating up to 100 people.

Dogs are permitted in national forests with no extra charge and no hassle. Conversely, in state and national parks, dogs are not allowed on trails and must be leashed. Always carry documentation of current shots.

Some of the more popular camps in national forests are on the Biospherics reservation system. The phone number to make a reservation at these camps is (800) 280-2267 (CAMP). The fee to make a reservation for a campground in national forests is usually $7.50 for single sites and $15 for group sites.

Maps for national forests are among the best you can get. They detail all backcountry streams, lakes, hiking trails and logging roads for access. They now cost $3, sometimes more for wilderness maps, and can be obtained by writing to the USDA-Forest Service, Office of Information, Pacific Southwest Region, 630 Sansome Street, San Francisco, CA 94111. For information, phone (415) 705-2874.

I've found the Forest Service personnel to be the most helpful of the government agencies for obtaining camping or hiking trail information. Unless you are buying a map, it is advisable to phone, not write, to get the best service. As long as you are phoning, you might also remind them that national forests are for campers as well as timber companies. For specific information on a national forest, write or phone the following addresses and phone numbers.

Angeles National Forest, located northeast of Los Angeles: write to 701 North Santa Anita Avenue, Arcadia, CA 91006, or phone (818) 574-5200.

Cleveland National Forest, located east of San Diego: write to 10845 Rancho Bernardo Road, Suite 200, San Diego, CA 92127, or phone (619) 557-5050.

Eldorado National Forest, located east of Placerville: write to 100 Forni Road, Placerville, CA 95667, or phone (916) 644-6048.

Inyo National Forest, located in the eastern Sierra Nevada: write to 873 North Main Street, Bishop, CA 93514, or phone (619) 873-5841.

Klamath National Forest, located northeast of Eureka: write to 1312 Fairlane Road, Yreka, CA 96097, or phone (916) 842-6131.

Lake Tahoe Basin, located west of Lake Tahoe: write to 870 Emerald Bay Road, Suite 1, South Lake Tahoe, CA 96150, or phone (916) 573-2600.

Lassen National Forest, located east of Redding: write to 55 South Sacramento Street, Susanville, CA 96130, or phone (916) 257-2151.

Los Padres National Forest, located south of Monterey: write to 6144 Calle Real, Goleta, CA 93117, or phone (805) 683-6711.

Mendocino National Forest, located northeast of Ukiah: write to 825 N. Humboldt Ave., Willows, CA 95988, or phone (916) 934-3316.

Modoc National Forest, located in the northeastern corner of the state: write to 800 West 12th Street, Alturas, CA 96101, or phone (916) 233-5811.

Plumas National Forest, located northwest of Lake Tahoe: write to P.O. Box 11500, Quincy, CA 95971, or phone (916) 283-2050.

San Bernardino National Forest, located east of San Bernardino: write to 1824 S. Commercenter Circle, San Bernardino, CA 92408-3430, or phone (714) 383-5588.

Sequoia National Forest, located south of Sequoia National Park: write to 900 West Grand Avenue, Porterville, CA 93257, or phone (209) 784-1500.

Shasta-Trinity National Forest, located northwest of Redding: write to 2400 Washington Avenue, Redding, CA 96001, or phone (916) 246-5222.

Sierra National Forest, located south of Yosemite: write to 1600 Tollhouse Road, Clovis, CA 93611, or phone (209) 487-5155.

Six Rivers National Forest, located between Eureka and Crescent City: write to 1330 Bayshore Way, Eureka, CA 95501, or phone (707) 442-1721.

Stanislaus National Forest, located east of Sonora: write to 19777 Greenley Road, Sonora, CA 95370, or phone (209) 532-3671.

Tahoe National Forest, located northwest of Lake Tahoe: write to 631 Coyote Street, Box 6003, Nevada City, CA 95959, or phone (916) 265-4531.

Toiyabe National Forest, located in eastern Sierra Nevada, near Bridgeport: write to P.O. Box 595, Bridgeport, CA 93517, or phone (916) 932-7070 or (702) 355-5300.

State Parks

The California State Parks system provides many popular camping spots. Reservations are often necessary during the summer months. The camps include drive-in numbered sites, tent spaces and picnic tables, with showers and bathrooms provided nearby. Although some parks are well known, there are still some little-known gems in the state parks system where campers can get seclusion, even in the summer months.

Reservations can be obtained through Destinet, which can be reached toll-free from anywhere in California by calling (800) 444-7275 (PARK). Destinet charges $6.75 for camp reservations, plus a separate charge for the campsite fee. Most state parks charge from $12 to $18 per night for a campsite, less for walk-in sites, often more for sites with beach frontage. In addition, there are also fees for peak season ($1), Friday and Saturday nights during peak season ($1), pets ($1), and, in some rare cases, premium sites. For campers 62 and older, discounts are available.

Reservations at state parks are available up to seven months in advance. For instance, in January, reservations are available for campgrounds in July. That means that campers who plan their vacations well in advance will have a significant advantage in obtaining quality campsites.

Because of a budget shortage, many state park telephones are no longer staffed. For this reason, the district office phone numbers have been added to state park listings in this book. District offices can usually provide any information visitors require about state parks.

For general information about California State Parks, write to California State Parks, Office of Information, P.O. Box 942896, Sacramento, CA 94296-0001; (916) 653-6995.

National Parks

The California National Parks are natural wonders, ranging from the spectacular yet crowded Yosemite Valley to the remote and rugged beauty of Lava Beds National Monument in northeastern California. At national parks, reservations, when taken, are usually made directly through the park at the following numbers. At many campgrounds at national parks, sites are first come, first served. Beginning January 15, 1996, Destinet will accept reservation requests for Yosemite National Park four months in advance for a one-month block. Call Destinet at (800) 365-2267 (CAMP) for more details.

The eight most popular parks are:

Yosemite National Park at (209) 372-0200 (for a touch-tone menu selection), (209) 372-0301 or (209) 372-0302.
Sequoia National Park at (209) 565-3341.
Kings Canyon National Park at (209) 565-3341.
Death Valley National Park at (619) 786-2331.
Devils Postpile National Monument at (619) 934-2289.
Point Reyes National Seashore at (415) 663-1092.
Joshua Tree National Park at (619) 367-7511.
Channel Islands National Park at (805) 658-5730.

The best of the rest are:

Lassen Volcanic National Park at (916) 595-4444.
Lava Beds National Monument at (916) 667-2282.
Whiskeytown National Recreation Area at (916) 241-6584.
Pinnacles National Monument at (408) 389-4462.
Redwoods National Park at (707) 464-6101.
Smith River National Recreation Area at (707) 457-3131.

RV Parks

The charge for hookups at RV parks varies from $10 to $20 per night. In populated areas, the charge often climbs to the $20 range. Many RV parks, particularly those in rural counties, must be contacted directly by phone. Many require a deposit with a reservation, which is usually just an advance payment for your first night's stay. No reservation service is available that links privately operated parks.

Other Useful Organizations

U.S. Geologic Survey, Western Distribution Branch, P.O. Box 25286, Federal Center, Denver, CO 80225; (303) 236-7477.

United States Bureau of Land Managment, California State Office, 2800 Cottage Way, E-2841, Sacramento, CA 95825; (916) 978-4474.

California Department of Boating and Waterways, 1629 "S" Street, Sacramento, CA 95814-7291; (916) 445-6281.

California Department of Fish and Game, 1416 Ninth Street, Sacramento, CA 95814; (916) 653-6420.

Catalina Camping Reservations, Doug Bombard Enterprises, P.O. Box 5044, Two Harbors, CA 90704; (310) 510-2800.

Lake County Visitor Information Center, 875 Lakeport Boulevard, Lakeport, CA 95453; (800) 525-3743 or (707) 263-9544.

Mammoth Lakes Visitors Bureau, P.O. Box 48, Mammoth Lakes, CA 93546; (800) 367-6572.

Mendocino Coast Chamber of Commerce, P.O. Box 1141, Fort Bragg, CA 95437; (707) 961-6300.

Plumas County Chamber of Commerce, P.O. Box 11018, Quincy, CA 95971; (800) 326-2247 or (916) 283-2045.

East Bay Regional Parks District, 2950 Peralta Oaks Court, P.O. Box 5381, Oakland, CA 94605-0381; (510) 635-0135, ext. 2200.

Shasta Cascade Wonderland Association, 14250 Holiday Road, Redding, CA 96003; (800) 474-2782.

Map Companies

Earthwalk Press, 2239 Union Street, Eureka, CA 95501; (800) 828-MAPS.

Map Link, 25 East Mason Street, Santa Barbara, CA 93101; (805) 965-4402.

Olmsted Brothers, P.O. Box 5351, Berkeley, CA 94705; (510) 658-6534.

Tom Harrison Cartography, 333 Bellam Boulevard, San Rafael, CA 94901; (415) 456-7940.

Maps are also available from the U.S. Forest Service (see page 86) and the U.S. Geologic Survey (see above).

CAMPING GEAR CHECKLIST

• Cooking Gear

Matches bagged in zip-lock bags
Fire-starter cubes or candle
Camp stove
Camp fuel
Pot, pan, cup
Pot grabber
Knife, fork
Dish soap and scrubber
Salt, pepper, spices
Itemized food
Plastic spade

Optional Cooking Gear:

Ax or hatchet
Wood or charcoal for barbecue
Ice chest
Spatula
Grill
Tin foil
Dust pan
Tablecloth
Whisk broom
Clothespins
Can opener

• Camping Clothes

Polypropylene underwear
Cotton shirt
Long sleeve cotton/wool shirt
Cotton/canvas pants
Vest
Parka
Rain jacket, pants or poncho
Hat
Sunglasses
Chapstick

Optional Clothing:

Seam Lock™
Shorts
Swimming suit
Gloves
Ski cap

• Hiking Gear

Quality hiking boots
Backup lightweight shoes
Polypropylene socks
Thick cotton socks
80% wool socks
Strong boot laces
Innersole or foot cushion
Moleskin and medical tape
Gaiters
Water-repellent boot treatment

• Sleeping Gear

Sleeping bag
Insulite™ or Therm-a-Rest™ pad
Ground tarp
Tent

Optional Sleeping Gear:

Air pillow
Mosquito netting
Foam pad for truck bed
Windshield light screen for RV
Catalytic heater

• First Aid

Band-Aids
Sterile gauze pads
Roller gauze
Athletic tape
Moleskin
Thermometer
Aspirin
Ace bandage
Mosquito repellent
After-Bite™ or ammonia
Campho-Phenique™ gel
First-Aid Cream™
Sunscreen
Neosporin™
Caladryl™
Biodegradable soap
Towelette
Tweezers

Optional First Aid:

Water purification system
Coins for emergency phoning
Extra set of matches
Mirror for signaling

• Fishing/Recreational Gear

Fishing rod
Fishing reel with fresh line
Small tackle box with lures,
    splitshot, snap swivels
Pliers
Knife

Optional Recreation Gear:

Stargazing chart
Tree identification handbook
Deck of cards
Backpacking cribbage board
Knapsack for each person

• Miscellaneous

Maps
Flashlight
Lantern and fuel
Nylon rope for food hang
Handkerchief
Camera and film
Plastic garbage bags
Toilet paper
Toothbrush and toothpaste
Compass
Watch
Feminine hygiene products

Optional Miscellaneous:

Binoculars
Notebook and pen
Towel

Nᴏʀᴛʜᴇʀɴ Aʀᴇᴀ Cᴀᴍᴘɢʀᴏᴜɴᴅs

Sᴄᴇɴɪᴄ Rᴀᴛɪɴɢ

△1 △2 △3 △4 △5 △6 △7 △8 △9 △10

Poor.. Fair .... Great

Kᴇʏ ᴛᴏ ᴛʜᴇ Sʏᴍʙᴏʟs

 Boating

 Canoeing/ Rafting

 Fishing

 Golf

 Hiking

 Historical Site

 Horseback Riding

 Hot Springs

 Swimming

 Waterskiing

 Wheelchair Access

 Five Percent Club

 RV

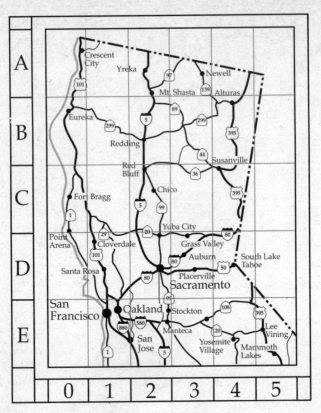

Map AØ .... (38 campgrounds)
Featuring: Smith River, Six Rivers National Forest, Redwood National Park, Klamath River, Del Norte Redwoods State Park, Prairie Creek Redwoods State Park, Humboldt Lagoons State Park; pages 96-113

Map A1 .... (23 campgrounds)
Featuring: Six Rivers National Forest, Klamath National Forest, Klamath River, Elk Creek, Scott River, North Fork Salmon River; pages 114-125

Map A2 .... (9 campgrounds)
Featuring: Klamath National Forest, Klamath River; pages 126-131

Map A3 .... (8 campgrounds)
Featuring: Klamath National Forest, Lava Beds National Monument, Modoc National Forest, Medicine Lake; pages 132-135

Map A4 .... (1 campground)
Featuring: Modoc National Forest; pages 136-137

Map BØ .... (29 campgrounds)
Featuring: Humboldt Bay, Six Rivers National Forest, Van Duzen River, Mattole River, Humboldt Redwoods State Park, Eel River, Kings Range; pages 138-151

Map B1 .... (61 campgrounds)
Featuring: Salmon River, Klamath National Forest, Trinity River, New River, Shasta-Trinity National Forest, Coffee Creek, Six Rivers National Forest, Canyon Creek, Stuarts Fork, Trinity Lake, Weaver Creek, Lewiston Lake, Ruth Lake; pages 152-179

Map B2 .... (63 campgrounds)
Featuring: Shasta-Trinity National Forest, Klamath National Forest, Mount Shasta, McCloud River, Sacramento River, Trinity Lake, Iron Canyon Reservoir, Shasta Lake, Whiskeytown Reservoir, Latour State Forest, Macumber Reservoir; pages 180-207

Map B3 .... (31 campgrounds)
Featuring: Shasta-Trinity National Forest, Modoc National Forest, Memorial State Park, Lake Britton, Hat Creek, Lassen National Forest, Lassen Volcanic National Park, Silver Lake, Eagle Lake; pages 208-221

Map B4 .... (21 campgrounds)
Featuring: Modoc National Forest, Cedar Pass, Eagle Lake; pages 222-231

Map CØ .... (35 campgrounds)
Featuring: Kings Range, Eel River, Richardson Grove State Park, Standish Hickey State Recreation Area, Navarro River, Lake Mendocino; pages 232-247

Map C1 .... (36 campgrounds)
Featuring: Shasta-Trinity National Forest, Mendocino National Forest, Lake Pillsbury, Letts Lake, Lower Blue Lake, Upper Blue Lake; pages 248-263

Map C2 .... (18 campgrounds)
Featuring: Sacramento River, Lassen National Forest, Black Butte Lake, Lake Oroville; pages 264-271

Map C3 .... (83 campgrounds)
Featuring: Lassen Volcanic National Park, Lassen National Forest, Lake Almanor, Feather River, Humbug Valley, Butt Valley Reservoir, Plumas National Forest, Bucks Lake, Little Grass Valley Reservoir, Sly Creek Reservoir, Tahoe National Forest, Packer Lake, Bullards Bar Reservoir, North Yuba River; pages 272-305

Map C4 .... (19 campgrounds)
Featuring: Antelope Lake, Plumas National Forest, Lake Davis, Frenchman Lake, Tahoe National Forest, Toiyabe National Forest; pages 306-315

Map DØ .... (20 campgrounds)
Featuring: Sonoma County Regional Park, Lake Sonoma, Russian River, Sonoma Coast State Beach, Bodega Bay; pages 316-325

Map D1 .... (45 campgrounds)
Featuring: Clear Lake, Russian River, Cache Creek, Lake Berryessa; pages 326-345

Map D2 .... (9 campgrounds)
Featuring: Colusa-Sacramento River State Recreation Area; pages 346-349

Map D3 .... (85 campgrounds)
Featuring: Bullards Bar Reservoir, Yuba River, Tahoe National Forest, Bowman Lake, Faucherie Lake, Jackson Meadow Reservoir, Sugar Pine Reservoir, Big Reservoir, American River, French Meadows Reservoir, Eldorado National Forest, Hell Hole Reservoir, Stumpy Meadows Lake, Gerle Creek Reservoir, Folsom Lake State Recreation Area, Ice House Reservoir, Union Valley Reservoir, Jenkinson Lake, Mokelumne River, Bear River Reservoir; pages 350-389

Map D4 .... (63 campgrounds)
Featuring: Tahoe National Forest, Stampede Reservoir, Prosser Reservoir, Boca Reservoir, Donner Lake, Truckee River, Lake Tahoe, Lake Tahoe Basin, Eldorado National Forest, Loon Lake, Carson River, Toiyabe National Forest, Carson Pass, Blue Lakes, Stanislaus National Forest; pages 390-417

Map E1 .... (26 campgrounds)
Featuring: Mount Tamalpais State Park, Point Reyes National Seashore, San Francisco Skyline Ridge; pages 418-431

Map E2 .... (23 campgrounds)
Featuring: Sacramento River Delta, Sacramento River, Mokelumne River, San Joaquin River Delta, San Joaquin River, Stanislaus River; pages 432-443

Map E3 .... (35 campgrounds)
Featuring: Pardee Reservoir, Camanche Reservoir, New Hogan Reservoir, Calaveras Big Trees State Park, Stanislaus National Forest, New Melones Lake, Tuolumne River, Don Pedro Reservoir, Lake McClure, Merced River; pages 444-459

Map E4 .... (89 campgrounds)
Featuring: Stanislaus National Forest, Stanislaus River, Lake Alpine, Donnells Reservoir, Middle Fork Stanislaus River, Walker River, Toiyabe National Forest, Pinecrest Lake, Twin Lakes, Cherry Lake, Tuolumne River, Inyo National Forest, Yosemite National Park, Tenaya Lake, Merced River, Sierra National Forest, San Joaquin River; pages 460-499

Map E5 .... (24 campgrounds)
Featuring: Mono Lake, Inyo National Forest, June Lake, Twin Lakes; pages 500-510

MAP A∅

NOR-CAL MAP .... see page 94
adjoining maps
NORTH .... no map
EAST (A1) .... see page 114
SOUTH (B∅) .... see page 138
WEST .... no map

38 LISTINGS
PAGES 96-113

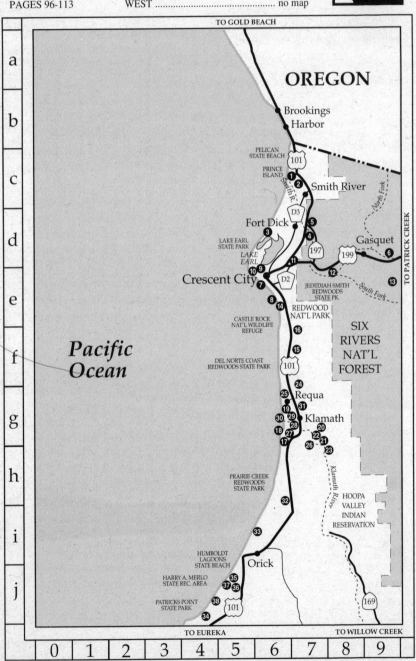

TO GOLD BEACH

OREGON

Brookings
Harbor

PELICAN
STATE BEACH

PRINCE
ISLAND

101

Smith River

Smith R.

Fort Dick

D3

Gasquet

LAKE EARL
STATE PARK

LAKE
EARL

197

U.S. 199

TO PATRICK CREEK

North Fork

Crescent City

D2

JEDEDIAH SMITH
REDWOODS
STATE PK.

South Fork

REDWOOD
NAT'L PARK

CASTLE ROCK
NAT'L WILDLIFE
REFUGE

SIX
RIVERS
NAT'L
FOREST

Pacific
Ocean

DEL NORTE COAST
REDWOODS STATE PARK

101

Requa

Klamath

Klamath River

HOOPA
VALLEY
INDIAN
RESERVATION

PRAIRIE CREEK
REDWOODS
STATE PARK

HUMBOLDT
LAGOONS
STATE BEACH

Orick

HARRY A. MERLO
STATE REC. AREA

PATRICKS POINT
STATE PARK

101

169

TO EUREKA

TO WILLOW CREEK

a
b
c
d
e
f
g
h
i
j

0 1 2 3 4 5 6 7 8 9

Map AØ featuring: Smith River, Six Rivers National Forest, Redwood National Park, Klamath River, Del Norte Redwoods State Park, Prairie Creek Redwoods State Park, Humboldt Lagoons State Park

1. SALMON HARBOR RESORT 🐟 ⚓   RV 6

Reference: **On Smith River; map AØ, grid c7.**

Campsites, facilities: There are 98 sites for tents or motor homes, 88 with full hookups and cable TV. Picnic tables, fire grills, flush toilets, showers, and a recreation room are provided. A laundromat, ice, gas, restaurant, bar and a bait and tackle shop are available nearby. Pets are allowed on leashes.

Reservations, fee: Reservations accepted; $14.50 fee per night.

Who to contact: Phone (707) 487-3341.

Location: From Crescent City, drive north on US 101 for 13 miles to the town of Smith River. Continue three miles north on US 101 to Salmon Harbor Road exit. Turn left on Salmon Harbor Road, drive two blocks and look for Salmon Harbor Resort on the left side of the road.

Trip note: If location is everything, then this privately-operated campground rates high for salmon fishermen in the fall months. It is set near the mouth of the Smith River, where salmon enter and school in the deep river holes in October. The fish are big, occasionally even surpassing 40 pounds. Year-round, this is a good layover spot for motor home cruisers looking for a spot near the Oregon border. It is actually a motor home parking area with hookups, set within a mobile home park. Located at the mouth of the Smith River, it overlooks the ocean, with good beachcombing and driftwood and agate hunting nearby.

2. SHIP ASHORE RV PARK 🐟 ⚓ ♿   RV 7

Reference: **On Smith River; map AØ, grid c7.**

Campsites, facilities: There are 200 motor home sites, most with full hookups, and a separate area for tents. Tables, flush toilets, showers, a whirlpool, a recreation room and a boat dock and ramp and some patios are provided. A laundromat, LP gas, groceries and boat rentals are available. Pets are allowed on leashes.

Reservations, fee: Reservations accepted; $15 fee per night.

Who to contact: Phone (707) 487-3141, extension 6.

Location: From Crescent City, drive north on US 101 for 19 miles (three miles past the town of Smith River) to the Ship Ashore sign at Chinook Street. At Chinook Street, turn left and drive a short distance (less than half a block) to the camp store at the campground entrance.

Trip note: This is a famous spot for Smith River fishermen, where the tales get taller as the evening gets late. The park is set on five acres of land adjacent to the lower Smith River. The salmon and steelhead seem to come in one size here—giant—but they can be as elusive as Bigfoot. If you want to hear how big, just check into the Ship Ashore Restaurant any fall or winter evening. In the summer, the resort has become quite popular with people cruising the coast on US 101.

3. LAKE EARL AND TALAWA STATE PARK

Reference: **Near Crescent City; map AØ, grid d6.**

Campsites, facilities: There are six primitive sites and a ride-in horse camp with 16 individual corrals. There is **no piped water**, but picnic tables, food lockers and composting toilets are provided. Fire rings are provided for the walk-in sites and fire pits for the horse camp. Pets are allowed on leashes.

Reservations, fee: Reservations are accepted; $7 fee per night for walk-in sites. In the horse camp, there is a $4 fee per night per horse and rider with a group rate of $50 per night for 13 or more riders. From June through August, registration is required and can be done at either Del Norte or Jedediah Smith State Parks.

Who to contact: Call (707) 464-9533, (707) 445-6547 or (707) 458-3310.

Location: In Crescent City, drive on US 101 to the lighted intersection at Northcrest Drive. Turn left (northwest) on Northcrest Drive and drive about five miles (Northcrest becomes Lake Earl Drive) to Lower Lake Road. Turn left on Lower Lake Road and drive 2.5 miles to Kellogg Road. Turn left on Kellogg Road and drive about a mile. A small metal gate and parking area large enough for a few cars is the access point on the right side of the road. Park, then walk a quarter-mile, with access trails for sites on the left side of the trail.

For the horse camp: In Crescent City, turn northwest on Northcrest Drive and drive five miles to Lower Lake Road. At Lower Lake Road, turn left and drive about seven miles to Palo Road. At Palo Road, turn left and drive to the parking area. The horse camp is about a half-mile southwest of the Palo Road parking lot.

For trail and walk-in beach access: In Crescent City, turn northwest on Northcrest Drive and continue 1.5 miles to Old Mill Road. Turn west (left) on Old Mill Road and drive three miles to Sand Hill Road. For the state park trailhead, turn left at Sand Hill Road and drive one-quarter mile to the trail entrance. For Fish and Game trail and walk-in beach access, continue on Old Mill Road to the locked gate at the road's end (about 100 yards past the Sand Hill Road turnoff).

For Lake Earl boat launch: In Crescent City, turn northwest on Northcrest Drive and drive about 3.5 miles to Lake View Road. At Lake View Road, turn left and drive one mile to the road's end at Lake Earl.

For drive-in beach access: From Crescent City, turn northwest on Northcrest Drive and drive north for about five miles to Lower Lake Road. At Lower Lake Road, turn left and drive 2.5 miles to Kellogg Road. At Kellogg Road turn left and drive 1.5 miles to the beach parking lot at the end of the road.

For picnicking and birdwatching: In Crescent City, turn northwest on Northcrest Drive and drive north for about five miles to Lower Lake Road. At Lower Lake Road, turn left and drive about seven miles to Palo Road on the left.

Trip note: This campground is one of the great discoveries available to people who love the outdoors. The walk-in sites are extremely secluded, quiet and sheltered. Smith River and Lake Earl are not only pretty and pleasant, but attract a wide variety of bird life thanks to their proximity to the ocean and surrounding marshes. Lake Earl is actually two—count 'em, two—lakes in one. Lake Earl proper is on the west side and is connected to Lake Talawa on the east. The campgrounds are not located right next to Lake Earl, but are only a short drive away. The access trail provides an outstanding bicycle trip.

Talawa borders coastal sand dunes and after heavy rainfall sometimes runs into the ocean. That is how sea-run cutthroat trout and flounder enter the brackish waters, caught rarely at the narrows between the lakes. Lakes Earl and Talawa offer 7.5 miles of ocean frontage, 15 miles of horseback riding and numerous hiking trails, an opportunity for canoeing and kayaking, and the bonus of the Smith River located nearby to the north. Guided walks are offered by state park volunteers in July and August.

4. RAMBLIN' ROSE RESORT

Reference: **Near Smith River; map AØ, grid d7.**

Campsites, facilities: There are 110 motor home sites, most with full hookups. Restrooms, showers, picnic tables and a recreation hall are provided. A gift store, groceries, ice, a laundromat, and a sanitary disposal station are also available. Pets are allowed on leashes.

Reservations, fee: Reservations accepted; $17 fee per night.

Who to contact: Call (707) 487-4831.

Location: From Crescent City, take US 101 north for five miles to the junction of US 199. Continue north on US 101 for another six miles to the campground. It is located at 6701 US 101 North, Crescent City.

Trip note: Ramblin' Rose is a motor home park set amid redwood trees, some of them giant. The big trees are the feature of the area, of course, with Redwood National Park and Jedediah Smith Redwoods State Park set to the nearby east on US 199. Nearby attractions include the beach to the immediate west and the Smith River to the nearby north.

5. CRESCENT CITY REDWOODS KOA

Reference: **On Smith River; map AØ, grid d7.**

Campsites, facilities: There are 44 tent sites and 50 sites for motor homes with full hookups. Cabins are also available. A sanitary disposal station, flush toilets, showers, picnic tables, a laundromat, fire grills and a playground are provided. LP gas, groceries, ice and wood are also available. Pets are allowed.

Reservations, fee: Reservations accepted; $18.50-$22.50 fee per night ($34.50-$39.50 for cabins).

Who to contact: Call (707) 464-5744.

Location: From Crescent City, take US 101 north for five miles to the junction of US 101 and US 199. Continue north on US 101 for one mile and look for the campground entrance on the right (east) side of the road.

Trip note: This KOA camp is located on the edge of a recreation wonderland, a perfect jumpoff spot for a vacation. The camp itself includes those little KOA Kamping Kabins, which are cute log cabins with electricity and heat; just make sure you bring your sleeping bag and pillows. With the camp's nearby location to US 199, it is only a 10-minute drive to Redwood National Park, Jedediah Smith Redwoods State Park, and the Smith River National Recreation Area. It is also only a 10-minute drive to the beach and Lake Earl to the east, and to Crescent City Harbor to the south.

6. PANTHER FLAT ⌂ 🐟 🏃🚶 ♿ 〰   RV 8

Reference: **On Smith River in Six Rivers National Forest; map AØ, grid d9.**

Campsites, facilities: There are 39 sites for tents, trailers up to 40 feet long and motor homes, some up to 22 feet long. Piped water, flush toilets, hot showers, fire grills and picnic tables are provided. Propane gas, groceries and a laundromat are available nearby. One campsite is **wheelchair accessible**. Pets are permitted on leashes or otherwise controlled.

Reservations, fee: Reservations recommended; phone (800) 280-CAMP; $7.85 reservation fee; $12 fee per night; $6 fee for extra vehicles.

Who to contact: Write to Smith River National Recreation Area, Six Rivers National Forest at P.O. Box 228, Gasquet, CA 95543 or call (707) 457-3131.

Location: From Crescent City, drive north on US 101 for five miles to the junction with Highway 199. At Highway 199, turn east and drive 17 miles to Gasquet. From Gasquet, continue for 2.5 miles east on US 199 and look for the entrance to the campground on the left side of the highway.

Trip note: This is an ideal alternative to the often crowded Jedediah Smith State Park. The park provides easy road access since it is set right along Highway 199, the two-laner that runs aside the Smith River. This is one of the feature campgrounds in the Smith River National Recreation Area, which is highlighted by excellent prospects for salmon and steelhead fishing in the fall and winter, respectively, and outstanding hiking and backpacking in the summer. A great nearby hike is the Stoney Creek Trail, an easy walk along the North Fork Smith River; the trailhead is in nearby Gasquet on Stoney Creek Road. Redwood National Park is a short drive to the west. The Siskiyou Wilderness is a short drive to the southeast via forest roads, detailed on Forest Service maps. The Wild and Scenic Smith River system provides swimming, sunbathing, kayaking for experts, and beautiful scenery. The camp is open year-round.

7. SUNSET HARBOR RV PARK ⌂ 🐟 ⚓ 🏃🚶 ♿   RV 4

Reference: **In Crescent City; map AØ, grid e6.**

Campsites, facilities: There are 70 motor home sites with full hookups. Picnic tables, flush toilets and showers are provided. A laundromat, grocery store and recreation room are available. Pets are allowed on leashes.

Reservations, fee: Reservations accepted; $17 fee per night.

Who to contact: Phone (707) 464-3423.

Location: In Crescent City on US 101, drive to King Street. At King Street, turn east and drive one block to the park entrance.

Trip note: People camp here with their motor homes in order to be close to the action in Crescent City and the nearby harbor and beach frontage. For starters, drive a few minutes to the northwest side of town, where the sea is sprinkled with gigantic rocks and boulders, for dramatic ocean views and spectacular sunsets. For finishers, go down to the west side of town for great walks along the ocean parkway, or south to the harbor and adjacent beach, which is long and expansive.

8. HARBOR RV ANCHORAGE ⌂ 🐟 ⚓ 🏃🚶 ♿   RV 7

Reference: **In Crescent City; map AØ, grid e6.**

Campsites, facilities: There are 123 motor home sites with full hookups. Picnic tables, flush toilets, showers and a sanitary disposal station are provided. A laundromat is available. Cable TV is also available. Pets are allowed on leashes.

Reservations, fee: Reservations accepted; $14 fee per night.

Who to contact: Phone (707) 464-1724.

Location: From US 101 at the southern end of Crescent City, turn west at Anchor Way and drive a short distance to Starfish Way. At Starfish Way, turn north and drive to the campground.

Trip note: The Crescent City Harbor, restaurants and a beach walk are all within close walking distance. The beach walk, located immediately to the south, is spectacular during low tides for beachcombing, especially for driftwood. Get the picture? Right—this park is right on the ocean, complete with salt air. If you don't mind the largely asphalt surroundings, more of a parking lot than anything else, you can get yourself a classic setup right on the edge of the sea.

---

9. BAYSIDE RV PARK 〜🐟⚓   RV 6

Reference: In Crescent City; map AØ, grid e6.

Campsites, facilities: There are 131 motor home sites with full hookups. Picnic tables, patios, flush toilets and showers are provided. A laundromat is available. Pets are allowed on leashes.

Reservations, fee: Reservations accepted; $15 fee per night.

Who to contact: Phone (707) 464-9482.

Location: From US 101 at the southern end of Crescent City, turn west at Citizen Dock Road and drive a very short distance to the campground.

Trip note: If you are towing a boat, you just found your own personal heaven. That is because this RV park is located directly adjacent to the boat docking area in Crescent City Harbor. There are several walks in the immediate area, including exploring the harbor and ocean frontage. For a quick change of scenery, it is only a 15-minute drive to Redwood National Park and Jedediah Smith Redwoods State Park along US 199 to the north.

---

10. VILLAGE CAMPER INN ♿🚶   RV 8

Reference: In Crescent City; map AØ, grid e6.

Campsites, facilities: There are 135 motor home sites, most with full hookups, and a separate area for tents. Picnic tables, a sanitary disposal station, flush toilets and showers are provided. A laundromat and cable TV hookups are available. Pets are allowed on leashes.

Reservations, fee: Reservations accepted; $14-$18 fee per night.

Who to contact: Call (707) 464-3544.

Location: From US 101 in Crescent City, turn east on Washington Boulevard and drive one block to Parkway Drive. At Parkway Drive, turn left and drive one block to 1543 Parkway Drive on the right side of the road.

Trip note: Woods and water, that's what attracts visitors to California's north coast. Village Camper Inn provides nearby access to big woods and big water. This motor home park is located on 20 acres of wooded land, with the giant redwoods along US 199 about a 10-minute drive away. In addition, there is also some premium beachcombing for driftwood and agates just a mile away on spectacular rocky beaches, just west of town.

11. HIOUCHI HAMLET RV RESORT

Reference: **Near Smith River; map AØ, grid e8.**

Campsites, facilities: There are 120 sites for tents or motor homes, most with full hookups. Flush toilets, showers and a sanitary disposal station are provided. A laundromat, LP gas, groceries and a golf course are available nearby. The facilities are **wheelchair accessible**. Pets are permitted.

Reservations, fee: Reservations accepted; $15-$20 fee per night.

Who to contact: Call (707) 458-3321.

Location: From Crescent City, drive five miles north on US 101 to Highway 199. Turn east on Highway 199 and drive about 10 miles (just past the entrance to Jedediah Smith State Park) to the town of Hiouchi. In Hiouchi, turn left at the well-signed campground entrance.

Trip note: The folks that run this outfit are among the nicest you'll ever find, and hey, the fried chicken at the Hamlet is always good for a quick hit. The park is out of the wind and fog you get on the coast, and set instead in the heart of the forest country. It makes a good base camp for a steelhead trip in winter. An excellent side trip is to drive just east of Hiouchi on US 199, then turn right and cross over two bridges, where you will reach a fork in the road; turn left for a great scenic drive along the South Fork Smith River or turn right to get back-door (and free) access to Jedediah Smith Redwoods State Park and three great trailheads for hiking in the redwoods. My favorite of the latter is the Boy Scout Tree Trail.

12. JEDEDIAH SMITH REDWOODS STATE PARK

Reference: **On Smith River; map AØ, grid e8.**

Campsites, facilities: There are 108 sites for tents or motor homes up to 30 feet long and several hike-in/bike-in sites. Piped water, flush toilets, showers, picnic tables, fire grills and a sanitary disposal station are provided. Propane gas, groceries and a laundromat are nearby. Pets are allowed on leashes.

Reservations, fee: Reserve by phoning Destinet at (800) 444-7275 ($6.75 Destinet fee); $15-$17 fee per night.

Who to contact: Phone (707) 458-3310, (707) 464-9533 or (707)445-6547.

Location: From Crescent City, drive north on US 101 for five miles to the junction with US 199. At US 199, turn north and drive nine miles. Turn right at the well-signed entrance station.

Trip note: This is a beautiful redwood park set along the Smith River, where the campsites are sprinkled amid a beautiful grove of redwoods. During the summer months, reservations are usually a necessity. The park has hiking trails that lead right out of the campground, one that is routed along the beautiful Smith River, another that heads through forest, across US 199 and hooks up with the Simpson-Reed Interpretive Trail. In the summer, guided walks are available. There is also a good put-in spot at the park for river access in a drift boat, canoe or raft. The fishing is best for steelhead from mid-January through March. An excellent side trip is available on the opposite bank of the Smith River; for access, see trip note for Hiouchi Hamlet RV Resort.

13. BIG FLAT

Reference: **On Hurdy-Gurdy Creek in Six Rivers National Forest; map AØ, grid e9.**

Campsites, facilities: There are 16 tent sites and 14 sites for tents or motor homes up to 22 feet long. Vault toilets, picnic tables and fire grills are provided but there is no garbage service. There is **no piped water**, so bring your own. Pets are permitted on leashes or otherwise controlled.

Reservations, fee: No reservations; $4 fee per night, $2 for each extra vehicle.

Who to contact: Write to Smith River National Recreation Area, Six Rivers National Forest at P.O. Box 228 Gasquet, CA 95543, or call (707) 457-3131.

Location: From Crescent City, drive north on US 101 for five miles to the junction with US 199. At US 199, turn north and drive 10 miles to Hiouchi. Continue just past Hiouchi and turn right at South Fork Road and cross two bridges. At the Y, turn left on South Fork Road and drive about 15 miles to Big Flat Road. At Big Flat Road, turn left and drive about a half-mile and look for the campground entrance on the left side of the road.

Trip note: This camp provides an ideal setting for those who know of it, and that is why it gets quite a bit of use for a relatively remote camp. It is set along Hurdy-Gurdy Creek, near where the creek enters the South Fork of the Smith River. It provides nearby access to old Kelsey Trail, an outstanding hiking route whether you are walking for a few hours or backpacking for days. From January through March, this is also an ideal base camp for a steelhead fishing trip (if you don't mind the inevitable rain), with a good stretch of water located within walking distance of the camp. In the summer, it is a good layover spot for rafters or kayakers paddling the South Fork of the Smith River. Open year-round, with limited services (like just about nothing) in the fall and winter.

14. NICKEL CREEK WALK-IN

Reference: **In Redwood National Park; map AØ, grid e6.**

Campsites, facilities: There are five hike-in tent sites. There is **no piped water**, but picnic tables, fire grills and composting toilets are provided. No pets are allowed.

Reservations, fee: No reservations; no fee.

Who to contact: Write to Redwood National Park Headquarters at 1111 Second Street, Crescent City, CA 95531, or call (707) 464-6101.

Location: From Crescent City, drive south on US 101 for two miles to Enderts Beach Road. At Enderts Beach Road, turn right (west) and drive about one mile to the trailhead at the end of the road. From the trailhead, hike in about one-half mile to the campground.

Trip note: This camp is set about 100 yards from the beach on a bluff, right near the mouth of Nickel Creek. It is one of the least-known national park campgrounds in the state. It provides a backpacking-like experience, yet with only a short walk. In return for the effort, you get seclusion and beach frontage, with seashore walks and tidepools available for your personal exploration. Open year-round.

15. DE MARTIN

Reference: **In Redwood National Park; map AØ, grid f7.**

Campsites, facilities: There are 10 tent sites. Piped water, composting toilets and caches for food storage are provided. No pets are allowed.

Reservations, fee: No reservations; no fee.

Who to contact: Write to 1111 Second Street, Crescent City, CA 95531, or call (707) 464-6101.

Location: From Crescent City, drive south for approximately 18 miles on US 101 to Wilson Creek Road. At Wilson Creek Road, turn left and drive about one-quarter mile to the trailhead at the end of the road. From the trailhead, hike in about 2.5 miles to the campground.

Trip note: This camp is primarily used by overnighters who are hiking the Pacific Coastal Trail. It is set in a grassy, prairie area on a bluff overlooking the ocean along the De Martin section of the Pacific Coastal Trail, right aside Wilson Creek. Sound good? You can chase the waves, hike the Coastal Trail, or just hunker down and let the joy of a peaceful spot renew your spirit. Open year-round.

---

16. DEL NORTE COAST REDWOODS STATE PARK

Reference: **Near Crescent City; map AØ, grid f7.**

Campsites, facilities: There are 38 tent sites and 107 sites for tents or motor homes up to 31 feet long. Hiker/biker sites are also available. Piped water, a sanitary disposal station, flush toilets, showers, fire grills and picnic tables are provided. Pets are allowed on leashes.

Reservations, fee: Reserve by phoning Destinet at (800) 444-7275 ($6.75 Destinet fee); $15-$17 fee per night; $5 fee for hiker/biker sites.

Who to contact: Call Del Norte Coast Redwoods State Park at (707) 464-9533 or (707) 445-6547.

Location: From Crescent City, drive nine miles south on US 101 to a signed access road for Del Norte Redwoods State Park. Turn left at the park entrance.

Trip note: The campsites are set in a series of loops in the forest, so while there are a lot of camps, you still feel a sense of privacy here. In addition to redwoods, there are also good stands of alders, along with a pretty stream fed by several creeks. It makes for a very pretty setting, with a good loop hike available right out of the camp. One reason for the lush growth is what rangers call the "nurturing" coastal climate. Nurturing, in this case, means rain like you wouldn't believe in the winter and lots of fog in the summer. Evening ranger programs are conducted here. Open April to October.

---

17. RIVERWOODS CAMPGROUND

Reference: **On Klamath River; map AØ, grid g7.**

Campsites, facilities: There are 74 motor home sites, many with full hookups, and a separate area for tents. Piped water, picnic tables, fire grills, flush toilets, showers and a sanitary disposal station are provided. Ice and wood are available. Satellite TV is available with full hookup sites. A few rental trailers are available. A convenience store and a fishing tackle store are located at the campground. Pets are allowed on leashes.

Reservations, fee: Reservations accepted; $10-$14 fee per night.

Who to contact: Phone (707) 482-5591.

Location: From the town of Klamath, drive one mile south on US 101 to Klamath

Beach Road. Turn west on Klamath Beach Road and drive two miles. Look for the campground entrance on the right side of the road.

Trip note: This motor home park provides direct access to the Klamath River, with pretty sites located in a grove of alder trees. Though the camp is set aside the Klamath, it is actually very close to the ocean as well, so the river is often more like a big lagoon. From mid-August through September, salmon will enter the Klamath and hold here, becoming acclimated to changes in salinity and water temperature. In the spring, usually late March and April, lampreys will enter this area and provide unusual shoreline fishing prospects. Nearby hiking is available on the Coastal Trail, with a trailhead located about a five-minute drive to the west on Klamath Beach Road, where you will arrive at a spectacular ocean bluff. Open year-round.

---

18. FLINT RIDGE WALK-IN

Reference: In Redwood National Park; map AØ, grid g6.

Campsites, facilities: There are 10 hike-in tent sites. Piped water and composting toilets are provided. No pets are allowed.

Reservations, fee: No reservations; no fee.

Who to contact: Write to Redwood National Park Headquarters at 1111 Second Street, Crescent City, CA 95531, or call (707) 464-6101.

Location: From Eureka, drive north on US 101 to the Klamath River. Just before reaching the bridge at the Klamath River, take the Coastal Drive exit and head west up the hill for 2.5 miles to a dirt parking area on the right side of the road. Park here. The trailhead for the campground is adjacent to the parking area, on the east side of the road. Hike five minutes to the camp.

Trip note: This little-known camp is located on a grassy bluff overlooking the ocean, along the Flint Ridge section of the Pacific Coastal Trail. From the parking area at the trailhead, it is only about a five-minute walk to reach a meadow surrounded by a thicket of wild blackberries, alders and redwoods, with the ocean looming huge to the west. The parking area, by the way, is an excellent perch to watch for the "puff-of-smoke" spouts from passing whales. A hike out of camp is routed into the forest, about a two-mile climb to reach a hill filled solid with redwoods; only problem is, there is no real destination, just in, then back.

---

19. DEL'S CAMP

Reference: On Klamath River; map AØ, grid g7.

Campsites, facilities: There are 53 motor home sites, many with full hookups, and a separate area for tents. Cable TV, picnic tables, fire grills, piped water, flush toilets and showers are provided. Boat rentals, a dock and a bait and tackle shop are available. Pets are allowed on leashes.

Reservations, fee: Reservations accepted; $11-$14 fee per night.

Who to contact: Phone (707) 482-4922.

Location: From Eureka, drive north on US 101 to Klamath. In Klamath, continue north on US 101 for another 2.5 miles to Requa Road. Turn west on Requa Road and drive a quarter mile to the campground.

Trip note: The campsites at Del's Camp are set near where Salt Creek, a feeder stream, pours into the adjacent Klamath River. It is a popular camp in the summer for its proximity to US 101 and the Klamath River, and also during the late summer and early fall when the salmon arrive on the Klamath. An outstanding hike, involving what can be a wheezing climb for many, is available nearby to the west on Requa Road—taking the trail up to Requa Ridge. Here is one of the most mind-blowing views available anywhere. On a clear day you can actually look out to sea and see the curvature of the earth. The camp is open from May 15 to October 30.

20. CRIVELLI'S TRAILER PARK

Reference: **Near Klamath River; map AØ, grid g7.**
Campsites, facilities: There are 31 motor home sites with full hookups. Flush toilets and showers are provided. A laundromat is available. No pets allowed.
Reservations, fee: Reservations accepted; $12-$15 fee per night.
Who to contact: Phone (707) 482-3713.
Location: From Eureka, drive north on US 101 to Klamath and the junction with Highway 169. Turn east on Highway 169 and drive 2.5 miles to the trailer park entrance.
Trip note: This motor home park is adjacent to a motel, surrounded by trees, with the Klamath River one mile away. It's a good base camp for a salmon fishing trip during the fall run. When the salmon arrive en masse, it can be difficult to get a reservation. Some regulars show up every year, same time, same place, staying for a week or more, fishing daily for salmon in the lower river. A café and lounge are available. Open year-round.

21. STEELHEAD LODGE

Reference: **On Klamath River; map AØ, grid g7.**
Campsites, facilities: There are 36 motor home sites (10 drive-through) with full hookups. Picnic tables, flush toilets and showers are provided. Ice is available. A bar, restaurant and motel are also available. Pets are allowed on leashes.
Reservations, fee: Reservations accepted; $15 fee per night.
Who to contact: Phone (707) 482-8145.
Location: From Eureka, drive north on US 101 to Klamath and the junction with Highway 169. Turn east on Highway 169 and drive 3.2 miles to Terwer Riffle Road. Turn south on Terwer Riffle Road and drive one block to Steelhead Lodge.
Trip note: Many anglers use this park as headquarters when the salmon and steelhead get going in August. The park has grassy sites near the Klamath River. The lodge usually provides good fishing reports by telephone. Open year-round.

22. REDWOOD REST

Reference: **On Klamath River; map AØ, grid g7.**
Campsites, facilities: There are 100 sites for tents or motor homes (30 drive-through) with full or partial hookups. Picnic tables, flush toilets and showers are provided. Wood is available. Pets are allowed on leashes.
Reservations, fee: Reservations accepted; $10-$14 fee per night.
Who to contact: Phone (707) 482-5033.
Location: From Eureka, drive north on US 101 to Klamath and the junction with Highway 169. Turn east on Highway 169 and drive 3.2 miles to the park.
Trip note: While there are quite a few privately operated parks on the lower Klamath River, this is the only park with redwood trees actually in the

campground. Reservations are advised during summer and are a necessity when salmon fishing picks up in mid-August. Open May through October.

23. TERWER PARK

Reference: **On Klamath River; map AØ, grid g7.**

Campsites, facilities: There are 98 motor home sites with full hookups. Picnic tables, flush toilets and hot showers are provided. LP gas, ice, a laundromat, cable TV and a dock are available. Pets are allowed on leashes.

Reservations, fee: Reservations accepted; $14 fee per night.

Who to contact: Phone (707) 482-3855.

Location: From Eureka, drive north on US 101 to Klamath and the junction with Highway 169. Turn east on Highway 169 and drive 3.2 miles to Terwer Riffle Road. Turn right on Terwer Riffle Road and drive 10 blocks (about a half-mile) to the park, located at 641 Terwer Riffle Road.

Trip note: This motorhome park is situated near the Terwer Riffle, one of the better shorefishing spots for steelhead and salmon on the lower Klamath River. You get grassy sites, river access and some fair trails along the Klamath. When the salmon arrive in late August and September, Terwer Riffle can at times be loaded with fish—as well as boaters and shore anglers, a wild scene. Open year-round.

24. CAMP MARIGOLD

Reference: **Near the Klamath River; map AØ, f6.**

Campsites, facilities: There are 40 sites for tents or motor homes with full hookups. Picnic tables, barbecues, cable TV, restrooms, hot showers and a coin-operated laundry are provided. Cabins (with fully equipped kitchenettes and bedding, for two to six persons) and a group lodge (with kitchen) for up to 15 people are also available.

Reservations: Reservations recommended; $10-$15 fee per night; cabins rent for $38.50-$60 per night; the lodge rents for $150 per night for the first 10 people, $5 for each additional person (maximum 15).

Who to contact: Phone (707) 482-3285 or (800) 621-8513.

Location: From Eureka, drive 60 miles north on US 101 to the campground at 16101 US Highway 101 (four miles north of the Klamath River Bridge, on the right side of US 101).

Trip note: Camp Marigold is surrounded by Redwood National Park, towering redwoods, Pacific Ocean beaches, driftwood, agates, fossilized rocks, black-berries, Fern Canyon, Lagoon Creek Park, and Trees of Mystery. It also has world-famous fishing nearby—for chinook and silver salmon, steelhead, sturgeon, trout, red tail perch, and candlefish. The camp has 3.5 acres of landscaped gardens with hiking trails...Get the idea? Well, there's more: It is only two miles to the Klamath River, if you can't find enough to do already.

25. MYSTIC FOREST RV PARK

Reference: **Near Klamath River; map AØ, grid g7.**

Campsites, facilities: There are 30 motor home sites, many with full hookups (15 drive-through) and a separate area for tents. Picnic tables, fire rings, piped water, flush toilets, showers, a playground and a solar-heated pool are provided. A laundromat and wood are available. Pets are allowed on leashes.

Reservations, fee: Reservations accepted; $10-$15 fee per night.

Who to contact: Phone (707) 482-4901.

Location: From Eureka, drive north on US 101 to Klamath. In Klamath, continue north for 3.2 miles. Look for the entrance sign on the left (west) side of the road. If you reach the Trees of Mystery, you have gone one mile too far north.

Trip note: Yes, Paul Bunyan exists. After all, how do you think the Mojave got turned into a desert? Babe, the giant blue ox, is still around too. This is true, you will discover at the Trees of Mystery north of Klamath, where a dinosaur-size Paul Bunyan guards the parking lot. Less than a mile away is the Mystic Forest RV Park. Though Mystic Forest and Trees of Mystery are not associated business-wise, the link is obvious as soon as you arrive.

---

26. BLACKBERRY PATCH

Reference: On Klamath River; map AØ, grid g7.

Campsites, facilities: There are 35 motor home sites with full hookups and one cabin for rent. Flush toilets, showers and picnic tables are provided. A laundromat is available. Pets are allowed on leashes.

Reservations, fee: Reservations accepted; $13 fee per night. Cabin rental is $40 per night.

Who to contact: Phone (707) 482-4782.

Location: From Eureka, drive north on US 101 to Klamath and the junction with Highway 169. Turn east on Highway 169 and drive 3.2 miles east to Terwer Riffle Road. At Terwer Riffle Road, turn west and drive one-quarter mile to the campground entrance on the right side of the road.

Trip note: It's no secret how this RV park got its name: There are tons of blackberry bushes in the park, and guests are allowed to pick to their heart's content during the berry season from mid- to late summer. The Klamath River is a few blocks away, with the Terwer Riffle, a great salmon spot in September, a highlight. Open year-round.

---

27. CAMPER CORRAL

Reference: On Klamath River; map AØ, grid g7.

Campsites, facilities: There are 140 sites for tents or motor homes, many with full hookups. Flush toilets, showers, picnic tables, fire grills, a recreation hall and a playground are provided. A sanitary disposal station, LP gas, a laundromat, cable TV, ice and a bait and tackle shop are available. Pets are allowed on leashes.

Reservations, fee: Reservations accepted; $12-$18 fee per night.

Who to contact: Phone (707) 482-5741.

Location: From Eureka, drive north on US 101 to Klamath. Just after crossing the Klamath River Bridge, take the Terwer Valley Road exit. Drive west for a short distance to the campground.

Trip note: This resort has 3,000 feet of Klamath River frontage, grassy tent sites, berry picking, the ocean and hiking trails nearby. And of course, in the fall it has salmon, the main attraction on the lower Klamath. Open April 1 to November 1.

---

28. KING SALMON RESORT

Reference: On Klamath River; map AØ, grid g7.

Campsites, facilities: There are 70 motor home sites, many with full hookups, and a separate area for tents. Piped water and flush toilets are provided. Showers, a laundromat, cable TV and a boat dock are available. Pets are allowed on leashes.

Reservations, fee: Reservations recommended; $10-$15 fee per night.

Who to contact: Phone (707) 482-4151.

Location: From Eureka, drive north to Klamath and the junction with Highway 169. Turn west on Highway 169 and drive a half-mile to the campground.

Trip note: King Salmon Resort has RV sites that are located adjacent to the Klamath River, and in addition, the resort property is wooded and private. It has become a very popular spot during the salmon run, making reservations a must when the fishing is best from mid-August through September. A bonus is that the property borders Redwood National Park.

---

29. KAMP KLAMATH 🐟 ⚓   RV 6

Reference: **On Klamath River; map AØ, grid g7.**

Campsites, facilities: There are 99 motor home sites with full hookups. Picnic tables, fire grills, flush toilets, showers and a recreation room are provided. Ice, a laundromat, cable TV, boat rentals, a tackle shop and a boat dock are available. Pets are allowed on leashes.

Reservations, fee: Reservations accepted; $11-$15 fee per night.

Who to contact: Write to Kamp Klamath at P.O. Box 128, Klamath, CA 95548, or call (707) 482-3405.

Location: From Eureka, drive north on US 101 to Klamath. In Klamath, continue north on US 101 for 1.5 miles to the campground.

Trip note: This camp is level and grassy with many sites along the lower Klamath River. Since it is located right along US 101, it is well-known to RV campers, and since it has a boat dock with direct access to the Klamath River, it is well known to fishermen. A bonus here is the hot tub. Open year-round (as is the camp). Redwood National Park is nearby.

---

30. CHINOOK RV RESORT 🐟 ⚓   RV 7

Reference: **On Klamath River; map AØ, grid g7.**

Campsites, facilities: There are 72 motor home sites with full hookups. Picnic tables, fire grills, flush toilets, showers, a playground, a laundromat and a recreation room are provided. LP gas, groceries, RV supplies, a boat ramp and a tackle shop are available. Pets are allowed.

Reservations, fee: Reservations accepted; $16 fee per night.

Who to contact: Phone (707) 482-3511.

Location: From Eureka, drive north on US 101 to Klamath. After crossing the bridge at the Klamath River, continue north on US 101 for one mile to the campground.

Trip note: Chinook RV Resort is another of the more well-known parks set on the lower Klamath. A boat ramp, fishing supplies and all the advice you can ask for are available. The camping area consists of grassy RV sites that overlook the river. Open year-round.

---

31. RIVERSIDE RV PARK 🐟 ⚓ 🚶 ♿   RV 7

Reference: **On Klamath River; map AØ, grid g7.**

Campsites, facilities: There are 93 motor home sites with full hookups (30 drive-through). Flush toilets, showers and a recreation room are provided. Boat rentals and a dock are available. Pets are allowed on leashes.

Reservations, fee: Reservations accepted; $12 fee per night.

Who to contact: Phone (707) 482-2523.

Location: From Eureka, drive north on US 101 to Klamath and the junction with Highway 169. Continue north on US 101 for 1.5 miles to the campground.

Trip note: This is one in a series of RV parks located near the town of Klamath along the lower Klamath River. It provides an option for motor home cruisers looking for a layover spot on a US 101 tour or a base of operations for a Klamath River fishing trip. There's good salmon fishing during the fall run on the Klamath River. Open April through October.

---

32. ELK PRAIRIE 👫 ♿ ⚓   RV 9

Reference: In Prairie Creek Redwoods State Park; map AØ, grid h6.

Campsites, facilities: There are 75 sites for tents or motor homes up to 27 feet long. Piped water, flush toilets, coin-operated showers, picnic tables and fire grills are provided. The facilities are **wheelchair accessible**. Pets are allowed on leashes.

Reservations, fee: Reserve by phoning Destinet at (800) 444-7275 ($6.75 Destinet fee); $15-$17 fee per night; $1 pet fee.

Who to contact: Call Prairie Creek Redwoods State Park at (707) 488-2171 or (707) 445-6547.

Location: From Eureka, drive north on US 101 for 41 miles to Orick. At Orick, continue north on US 101 for six miles to the Newton B. Drury Scenic Parkway. Take the exit for the Newton B. Drury Scenic Parkway, and drive north for two miles to the park. Turn left at the park entrance.

Trip note: In this remarkable park, herds of Roosevelt elk wander free. Great opportunities for photographs abound, often right beside the highway. Where there are meadows, there are elks, it's about that simple. An elky here, an elky there, making this one of the best places to see wildlife in California. The park also has excellent hiking and some mountain biking, including a trailhead for a great bike ride at the campground. There are many additional trailheads and a beautiful tour of giant redwoods along the Drury Scenic Parkway.

---

33. GOLD BLUFF BEACH 🐟 👫 ♿ ⚓   8

Reference: In Prairie Creek Redwoods State Park; map AØ, grid i6.

Campsites, facilities: There are 25 primitive sites for tents or motor homes up to 20 feet long (no trailers or vehicles wider than seven feet). Piped water, flush toilets, solar showers, fire grills and tables are provided. Pets are allowed on leashes.

Reservations, fee: No reservations; $15-$17 fee per night; $1 pet fee.

Who to contact: Call Prairie Creek Redwoods State Park at (707) 488-2171 or (707) 445-6547.

Location: From Eureka, drive north on US 101 for 41 miles to Orick. At Orick, continue north on US 101 for three miles to Davison Road. Turn left (west) on Davison Road and drive four miles to the campground. Note: No trailers are allowed on Davison Road, which is narrow and sometimes very bumpy.

Trip note: The campsites here are set in a sandy, exposed area with man-made windbreaks, at the head of a huge, expansive beach. You can walk for miles at this beach, often without seeing another soul. In addition, Fern Canyon Trail, one of the best 10-minute hikes in California, is located at the end of Davison Road. Hikers walk along a stream in a narrow canyon, its vertical walls covered with magnificent ferns. There are some herds of elk in the area, often right along the access road. Open year-round, but these camps are rarely used in the winter because of the region's heavy rain and winds.

34. PATRICK'S POINT STATE PARK

Reference: Near Trinidad; map AØ, grid j4.

Campsites, facilities: There are 124 sites for tents or motor homes up to 31 feet long. Piped water, flush toilets, coin-operated showers, fire grills and picnic tables are provided. The facilities are **wheelchair accessible**. Pets are permitted on leashes, but not on trails or beaches.

Reservations, fee: Reserve by phoning Destinet at (800) 444-7275 ($6.75 Destinet fee); $15-$17 fee per night; $1 pet fee.

Who to contact: Phone Patrick's Point State Park at (707) 677-3570 or (707) 445-6547.

Location: From Eureka, drive north on US 101 for 22 miles to Trinidad. At Trinidad, continue north on US 101 for 2.5 miles and take the well-signed exit. At the stop sign, turn left and drive a short distance to the park entrance.

Trip note: This pretty park is filled with Sitka spruce, dramatic coastal lookouts, and several beautiful beaches, including one with agates, one with tidepools and another with an expansive stretch of beachfront leading to a lagoon. You can best see all of it on the Rim Trail, which has many little cut-off routes to the lookouts and down to the beaches. The campground is sheltered in the forest, and while it is often foggy and damp in the summer, it is always beautiful. Count on making reservations.

35. STONE LAGOON BOAT-IN

Reference: In Humboldt Lagoons State Park; map AØ, grid j5.

Campsites, facilities: There are six primitive tent sites accessible by boat only. There is **no piped water**, but pit toilets, picnic tables and fire rings are provided. No pets are allowed.

Reservations, fee: No reservations; $10-$12 fee per night.

Who to contact: Call Prairie Creek Redwoods State Park at (707) 488-2171 or (707) 445-6547.

Location: From Eureka, drive north on US 101 for 43 miles (15 miles north of Trinidad) to Stone Lagoon. At Stone Lagoon, turn left at the visitor information center. The boat-in campground is located in a cove directly across the lagoon from the visitor center. The campsites are dispersed in an area covering about 300 yards in the landing area.

Trip note: This is an ideal spot for canoeists that virtually nobody knows about. While Stone Lagoon is located directly adjacent to US 101, the camp is set in a cove that is out of sight of the highway. That makes it a secret spot for many. It is a great place to explore by canoe or kayak, especially paddling upstream to the lagoon's inlet creek. After having set up camp, a hike is possible to a secluded sand spit and stretch of beachfront. Rarely, you may see elk in this area. The water is usually calm in the morning, but often gets choppy from afternoon winds. Translation: Get your paddling done early on Stone Lagoon. There is also good fishing for cutthroat trout here. Open year-round.

36. STONE LAGOON 🐟 ⚓ 👥

Reference: In Humboldt Lagoons State Park; map AØ, grid j5.

Campsites, facilities: There are 20 primitive, dispersed campsites. There is **no piped water**, but pit toilets, picnic tables, food lockers and fire rings are provided. A boat ramp is available. Pets are permitted on leashes.

Reservations, fee: No reservations; $10-$12 fee per night; $1 pet fee.

Who to contact: Call Prairie Creek Redwoods State Park at (707) 488-2171 or (707) 445-6547.

Location: From Eureka, drive north on US 101 for 43 miles to Orick (15 miles north of Trinidad) to Stone Lagoon (a good suggestion is to stop at the visitor center on the left side of the road). The campground entrance is located on the left side of US 101 at the north end of Stone Lagoon.

Trip note: Several campsites are available along the access route at the north end of Stone Lagoon. If the boat-in sites are filled (see previous listing), this drive-in site provides an alternative. Of the three lagoons on this stretch of coast, Stone Lagoon is the most unique. Every winter it rises from storm runoff and bursts open to the sea. This, in turn, allows sea-run cutthroat trout access to the lagoon's quiet waters. A very primitive boat ramp is available on the lagoon near the visitor center. It's often foggy in summer.

37. DRY LAGOON WALK-IN 👥 👥

Reference: In Humboldt Lagoons State Park; map AØ, grid j5.

Campsites, facilities: There are six primitive tent sites. There is **no piped water**, but pit toilets, fire rings and picnic tables are provided. No pets are allowed.

Reservations, fee: No reservations; $10-$12 fee per night.

Who to contact: Call Prairie Creek Redwoods State Park at (707) 488-2171 or (707) 445-6547.

Location: From Eureka, drive north on US 101 for 22 miles to Trinidad. At Trinidad, continue north on US 101 for 13 miles to the campground parking entrance at Milepost 114.5. After parking, walk 200 yards to the camp.

Trip note: This is a walk-in camp, that is, you need to walk about 200 yards from the parking area to reach the campsites. This makes it a dream for members of the Five Percent Club, because most tourists are unwilling to walk at all. It is beautiful here, set in the woods, with ocean views and beach access.

38. BIG LAGOON COUNTY PARK

🐟 ⚓ 🏊 🍴

Reference: Overlooking Pacific Ocean; map AØ, grid j5.

Campsites, facilities: There are 26 sites for tents or motor homes. Piped water, flush toilets, fire grills and picnic tables are provided. A boat ramp is available. Pets are permitted.

Reservations, fee: No reservations; $10 fee per night; $1 pet fee.

Who to contact: Phone Big Lagoon County Park at (707) 445-7651.

Location: From Eureka, drive north on US 101 for 22 miles to Trinidad. At Trinidad, continue north on US 101 for eight miles to Big Lagoon Park Road. Turn left (west) at Big Lagoon Park Road and drive two miles to the park.

Trip note: This is a remarkable, huge lagoon that borders the Pacific Ocean. It provides good boating, excellent exploring, fair fishing, and in winter, good duck hunting. It's a good spot to paddle a canoe around on a calm day. A lot of out-of-towners cruise by, note the lagoon's proximity to the ocean, and figure it must be saltwater. Wrong! It is not only freshwater, but it provides a long shot for fishermen trying for rainbow trout. One reason not many motor home drivers stop here is because most of them are drawn farther north (another eight miles) to Freshwater Lagoon, where there is a wide shoulder along the highway that allows them to line up their rigs, like a convoy parking parade, an unbelievable sight. Open year-round.

MAP A1

NOR-CAL MAP .... see page 94
adjoining maps
NORTH .... no map
EAST (A2) .... see page 126
SOUTH (B1) .... see page 152
WEST (AØ) .... see page 96

23 LISTINGS
PAGES 114-125

a

b

c

d

e

f

g

h

i

j

Kerby

Cave Junction

O'Brien

OREGON

Whiskey Peak
EL. 6,480

Patrick
Creek

199

Smith
River

South Fork

ROGUE RIVER
NATIONAL FOREST

TO CRESCENT CITY

① ②

③

④

Happy Camp

⑤

⑦

Seiad Valley

⑥

Horse
Creek

⑧

Hamburg

Scott Bar

TO I-5 NORTH OF YREKA

Clear Creek

River

Bear Peak
EL. 5,740

96

⑩

Buckhorn Mountain
EL. 6,917

MARBLE
MOUNTAIN
WILDERNESS

⑭

⑪

⑫

Scott River

Klamath

**SIX
RIVERS
NAT'L
FOREST**

⑨

⑬

**KLAMATH
NAT'L
FOREST**

Greenview

TO YREKA

Somes Bar

⑮

Salmon Mountains

Etna

3

Orleans

⑰ ⑳ ㉑ ⑱

⑲

⑯

Salmon River

Forks of
Salmon

㉒

Sawyers
Bar

㉓

Salmon Mountain
Summit
EL. 5,958

Weitchpec

TO WILLOW CREEK

North Fork

TO CECILVILLE

TO CALLAHAN

0 1 2 3 4 5 6 7 8 9

Map A1 featuring: Six Rivers National Forest, Klamath National Forest, Klamath River, Elk Creek, Scott River, North Fork Salmon River

1. GRASSY FLAT ⌇🐟 ♿ ✕   RV. **4**

Reference: **On Smith River in Six Rivers National Forest; map A1, grid d0.**

Campsites, facilities: There are eight tent sites and 11 sites for tents or motor homes up to 22 feet long. Piped water, vault toilets, fire grills and picnic tables are provided. Propane gas, groceries and a laundromat are available nearby. Some facilities are **wheelchair accessible**. Pets are permitted on leashes or otherwise controlled.

Reservations, fee: Reservations accepted; phone (800) 280-CAMP; $8 fee per night, $6 for each extra vehicle.

Who to contact: Write to Smith River National Recreation Area, Six Rivers National Forest at P.O. Box 228 Gasquet, CA 95543, or phone (707) 457-3131.

Location: From Crescent City, drive north on US 101 for five miles to the junction with US 199. At US 199, turn north and drive 17 miles to Gasquet. From Gasquet, continue east on US 199 for five miles and look for the campground entrance on the right side of the road.

Trip note: This is one in a series of three easy-to-reach Forest Service camps set near US 199 along the beautiful Smith River. It's a classic wild river, popular in the summer for kayakers, and the steelhead come huge in the winter for the crafty few. The camp itself is set directly across from a CalTrans waste area, and if you hit it wrong, when the crews are working, it can be noisy here. Most of the time, however, it is peaceful and quiet. Open May through mid-September. In the winter, when the camp is closed, fishermen will often park at the piped gate, then walk past the camp to access a good steelhead spot.

2. PATRICK CREEK ⌇🐟 🚶 ♿ ⚓   RV. **8**

Reference: **In Six Rivers National Forest; map A1, grid d1.**

Campsites, facilities: There are 13 sites for tents and motor homes. Piped water, flush toilets, picnic tables and fire grills are provided. Pets are permitted on leashes or otherwise controlled. Restrooms and water spigots are **wheelchair accessible**.

Reservations, fee: Reservations accepted; phone (800) 280-CAMP; $10 fee per night, $6 for each extra vehicle.

Who to contact: Write to Smith River National Recreation Area, Six Rivers National Forest at P.O. Box 228, Gasquet, CA 95543, or call (707) 457-3131.

Location: From Crescent City, drive north on US 101 for five miles to the junction with US 199. At US 199, turn north and drive 17 miles to Gasquet. From Gasquet, continue east on US 199 for eight miles and look for the campground entrance on the right side of the road.

Trip note: This is one of the prettiest spots along US 199, where Patrick Creek enters the upper Smith River. This section of the Smith looks something like a large trout stream, rolling green past a boulder-lined shore, complete with forest canopy. There are no trout, of course, but rather salmon and steelhead in the fall and winter, and only their little smolts pooling up in the summer months. A big plus for this camp is its nearby access to excellent hiking in the

Siskiyou Wilderness, especially the great day-hike to Buck Lake. It is essential
to have a map of Six Rivers National Forest, both for driving directions to the
trailhead and for the hiking route. Maps are available for $3 at the information
center for the Smith River National Recreation Area on the north side of US 199
in Gasquet. An option at this camp is Patrick Creek Lodge, located on the
opposite side of the highway from the campground, which has a fine restaurant
and bar available. The camp is open from May through mid-September.

---

3. WEST BRANCH

Reference: **In Klamath National Forest; map A1, grid d4.**

Campsites, facilities: There are 15 sites for tents or motor homes. Piped water,
vault toilets, picnic tables and fire grills provided. There are sanitary disposal
stations in Happy Camp at the Elk Creek Campground and the Happy Camp
Open Dump. Pack out your garbage. Pets are permitted on leashes or otherwise
controlled.

Reservations, fee: No reservations; no fee.

Who to contact: Phone the Klamath National Forest Happy Camp Ranger District
at (916) 493-2243.

Location: From Happy Camp on Highway 96, turn north on Indian Creek Road
(a gravel road) and drive 14.5 miles to the camp on the right side of the road.

Trip note: This is a virtually unknown, no-charge camp, set in a canyon near
Indian Creek, deep in Klamath National Forest. It is about a 20-minute drive
from the town of Happy Camp. The elevation is 2,200 feet. The best side trip
here is the winding four-mile drive on a bumpy dirt road to Kelly Lake, little
known and little used. A remote Forest Service station is located on the
opposite side of Indian Creek Road from the campground. Open May through
October.

---

4. FORT GOFF

Reference: **In Klamath National Forest; map A1, grid e6.**

Campsites, facilities: There are five tent sites. Vault toilets, picnic tables and fire
grills are provided, but there is **no piped water**, and you must pack out your
garbage. Pets are permitted on leashes or otherwise controlled. Supplies are
available in Seiad Valley.

Reservations, fee: No reservations; no fee.

Who to contact: Phone the Klamath National Forest Oak Knoll Ranger District
at (916) 465-2241.

Location: From Yreka, drive north on Interstate 5 to the junction with Highway
96. At Highway 96, turn west and drive to Seiad Valley. At Seiad Valley,
continue west on Highway 96 for five miles to the campground on the left
(south) side of the road.

Trip note: This small, primitive campground is set right along the Klamath River,
an ideal location for both fishing and rafting. Many of the most productive
shoreline fishing spots on the Klamath River are in this area, with fair trout
fishing in summer, good steelhead fishing in the fall and early winter, and a
wildcard for salmon in late September. There are pullouts along Highway 96
for parking, with short trails/scrambles down to the river. This is also a good
spot for rafting, especially for inflatable kayaks, and commercial rafting
operations have trips available on this stretch of river. On the opposite side of
Highway 96 (within walking distance to the west) is a trailhead for a hike that

is routed along Little Fort Goff Creek, an uphill tromp for five miles to Big Camp and the Boundary National Recreation Trail. The creek also runs nearby the camp.

5. ELK CREEK CAMPGROUND

Reference: **On Klamath River; map A1, grid f5.**

Campsites, facilities: There are 78 motor home sites, many with full or partial hookups, and a separate area for tents. Restrooms, hot showers, a recreation room, a beach, picnic tables and fire grills are provided. A laundromat, sanitary disposal station, ice, propane and wood are available. Pets are allowed on leashes.

Reservations, fee: Reservations accepted; $7 fee per person for tent campers, $18-$20 fee for motor homes.

Who to contact: Phone (916) 493-2208.

Location: From Highway 96 in the town of Happy Camp, turn south on Elk Creek Road and drive one mile to the campground.

Trip note: This is a year-round motor home park set where Elk Creek pours into the Klamath River. It is a beautiful RV park, with sites right on the water in a pretty wooded setting. The section of Klamath River nearby is perfect for inflatable kayaking and light rafting. While demure enough to keep it completely safe, it is still wild enough to make it exciting. In addition, the water is quite warm in the summer months and flows are maintained throughout the year, making it ideal for water sports.

6. O'NEIL CREEK

Reference: **In Klamath National Forest; map A1, grid f8.**

Campsites, facilities: There are 18 sites for tents or motor homes up to 22 feet. Vault toilets, piped water, picnic tables and fire grills are provided. Pack out your garbage. Pets are permitted on leashes or otherwise controlled. Supplies can be obtained in Seiad Valley.

Reservations, fee: No reservations; call for fees.

Who to contact: Phone the Klamath National Forest Oak Knoll Ranger District at (916) 465-2241.

Location: From Yreka, drive north on Interstate 5 to the junction with Highway 96. Turn west on Highway 96 and drive west to Hamburg. At Hamburg, continue west for three miles to the campground.

Trip note: This camp is set near O'Neil Creek, and though not far from the Klamath River, access to the river is not easy. To fish or raft, most people will use this as a base camp, then drive out for recreation during the day. That creates a predicament for owners of motor homes, who lose their campsites every time they drive off. In the fall hunting season, this is a good base camp for hunters branching out into the surrounding national forest. There are also historic mining sites nearby.

7. GRIDER CREEK

Reference: **In Klamath National Forest; map A1, grid f7.**

Campsites, facilities: There are 10 sites for tents or motor homes up to 16 feet long. Vault toilets, picnic tables and fire grills are provided, but there is **no piped water**, so bring your own and pack out your garbage. Pets are permitted on leashes or otherwise restrained.

Reservations, fee: No reservations; no fee.

Who to contact: Phone the Klamath National Forest Oak Knoll Ranger District at (916) 465-2241.

Location: From Yreka, drive north on Interstate 5 to the junction with Highway 96. At Highway 96, turn west and drive to Walker Creek Road (Forest Service Road 46N64, located one mile before reaching Seiad Valley). Turn left to enter Walker Creek Road, then stay to the right as it runs adjacent to the Klamath River to Grider Creek Road. At Grider Creek Road, turn left and drive south for three miles to the camp.

Trip note: This obscure little camp is used primarily by hikers, with a trailhead for the Pacific Crest Trail available, and by deer hunters in the fall. The camp is set at 1,700 feet along Grider Creek. From here, the Pacific Crest Trail is routed uphill along Grider Creek into the Marble Mountain Wilderness, about an 11-mile ripper to Huckleberry Mountain at 6,303 feet. There are no lakes along the route, only small streams and feeder creeks.

8. SARAH TOTTEN

Reference: **On Klamath River in Klamath National Forest; map A1, grid f8.**

Campsites, facilities: There are 12 tent sites, five sites for tents and motor homes up to 22 feet long, and one group site. Piped water, vault toilets, picnic tables and fire grills are provided. Pets are permitted on leashes or otherwise controlled. There's a small grocery store nearby.

Reservations, fee: No reservations; $6 fee per night.

Who to contact: Phone the Klamath National Forest Oak Knoll Ranger District at (916) 465-2241.

Location: From Yreka, drive north on Interstate 5 to the junction with Highway 96. At Highway 96, turn west and drive to Horse Creek. At Horse Creek, continue west for five miles to the campground on the right side of the road. (If you reach the town of Hamburg, you have gone a half-mile too far.)

Trip note: This is one of the more popular Forest Service camps on the Klamath River, and it's no mystery why. In the summer, its placement is perfect for rafters, who camp here and use it as a put-in spot. In fall and winter, fishermen arrive for the steelhead run. It's located in the "banana belt" or good weather area of the Klamath, in a pretty grove of oak trees. Fishing is often good here for salmon in early October and for steelhead from November through spring, providing there are fishable water flows.

9. DILLON CREEK

Reference: **On Klamath River in Klamath National Forest; map A1, grid g2.**

Campsites, facilities: There are 10 tent sites and 11 motor home sites. Piped water, vault toilets, picnic tables and fire grills are provided. There is a sanitary disposal station in Happy Camp (25 miles north of the campground) or at Aikens Campground (13 miles west of the town of Orleans). Pets are permitted on leashes or otherwise controlled.

Reservations, fee: No reservations; $6 fee per night.

Who to contact: Phone the Klamath National Forest at (916) 842-6131.

Location: From Yreka, drive north on Interstate 5 to the junction with Highway 96. Turn west on Highway 96 and drive to the town of Happy Camp. Continue west from Happy Camp for about 25 miles and look for the campground on the right side of the road. (Coming from the west, from Somes Bar, drive 15 miles north on Highway 96.)

Trip note: This is a prime base camp for a rafting or steelhead fishing trip. A put-in spot for rafting is located adjacent to the camp, with an excellent river run available from here on down past Presido Bar to the take-out at Ti-Bar. If you choose to go on, make absolutely certain to pull out at Somes Bar, or risk death at Ishi Pishi Falls. The water is warm here in the summer, and there are also many excellent swimming holes in the area. In addition, this is a great stretch of water for steelhead fishing in September and October, with 30-fish days (catch-and-release) possible in the same span of water from Dillon Beach to Ti-Bar. The elevation is 800 feet. Open year-round.

10. SULPHUR SPRINGS

Reference: **On Elk Creek in Klamath National Forest; map A1, grid g4.**
Campsites, facilities: There are several walk-in tent sites with vault toilets. Picnic tables and fire grills are provided. But there's **no piped water**, so bring your own, and pack out your garbage. Pets are permitted on leashes.
Reservations, fee: No reservations; no fee.
Who to contact: Phone the Klamath National Forest Happy Camp Ranger District at (916) 493-2243.
Location: From Yreka, drive north on Interstate 5 to the junction with Highway 96. At Highway 96, turn west and drive to Happy Camp. In Happy Camp, turn south on Elk Creek Road and drive 14 miles to the campground.
Trip note: This hidden spot is set along Elk Creek on the border of the Marble Mountain Wilderness. The camp is at a trailhead that provides access to miles and miles of trails that follow the streams into the backcountry of the Marble Mountain Wilderness. It is a 12-mile backpack trip one-way, and largely uphill, to Spirit Lake, one of the prettiest lakes in the entire wilderness. Sulphur Springs camp is set at 3,100 feet. The nearby hot springs (which are actually lukewarm) provide a side attraction. There are also some swimming holes nearby in Elk Creek, but expect the water to be cold.

11. BRIDGE FLAT

Reference: **In Klamath National Forest; map A1, grid g7.**
Campsites, facilities: There are eight sites for tents or motor homes up to 22 feet long. Piped water, vault toilets, fire grills and picnic tables are provided. Pets are permitted on leashes or otherwise restrained.
Reservations, fee: No reservations; $6 fee per night.
Who to contact: Phone Klamath National Forest Scott River Ranger District at (916) 468-5351.
Location: From Redding, drive north on Interstate 5 to Yreka. In Yreka, turn southwest on Highway 3 and drive 16.5 miles to Fort Jones. In Fort Jones, turn right (west) on Scott River Road and drive 21 miles to the campground on the right side of the road.
Trip note: This camp is set at 2,000 feet along the Scott River, adjacent to a remote Forest Service ranger station. Though commercial rafting trips are only rarely available here, the river is accessible during the early spring for skilled rafters and kayakers, with a good put-in spot located four miles downriver, and a take-out at Scott Bar at the mouth of the Klamath. For backpackers, a trailhead for the Kelsey Trail is nearby, leading into the Marble Mountain Wilderness.

12. LOVERS CAMP

Reference: **In Klamath National Forest; map A1, grid g7.**

Campsites, facilities: There are 10 walk-in sites. Vault toilets, fire grills and picnic tables are provided. There are also facilities for stock unloading and a corral. The only water available is for stock, so bring your own drinking water. Pets are permitted on leashes or otherwise restrained.

Reservations, fee: No reservations; no fee.

Who to contact: Phone the Klamath National Forest Scott River Ranger District at (916) 468-5351.

Location: From Redding, drive north on Interstate 5 to Yreka. In Yreka, turn southwest on Highway 3 and drive to Fort Jones. In Fort Jones, turn right and drive 18 miles on Scott River Road to Forest Service Road 43N45. Turn south on Forest Service Road 43N45 and drive nine miles to the campground at the end of the road.

Trip note: Lovers Camp isn't set up for lovers at all, but for horses and backpackers. This is a trailhead camp set at the edge of the Marble Mountain Wilderness, one of the best in the entire wilderness for packers with horses. It is set at 4,300 feet, and is open from June through October. The trail here is routed up along Canyon Creek to the beautiful Marble Valley at the foot of Black Marble Mountain. The most common destination is the Sky High Lakes, a good one-day huff-and-puff to get there. Now there's a place for lovers.

13. MARBLE MOUNTAIN RANCH

Reference: **Near Klamath River; map A1, grid h3.**

Campsites, facilities: There are 30 tent sites, 11 cabins, two houses and 30 motor home sites with full hookups. Restrooms, hot showers, a recreation room, picnic tables, fire grills, horseshoe pits, volleyball and basketball are provided. A laundromat, ice and wood are available. Pets are allowed on leashes.

Reservations, fee: Reservations accepted; $5-$14 fee per night; $27 per night for cabins; $40 per night for houses.

Who to contact: Phone (916) 469-3322 or (800) KLAMATH.

Location: From the junction of Highway 101 and Highway 299 near Arcata, turn east on Highway 299 and drive to Willow Creek. In Willow Creek, turn left (north) on Highway 96 and drive to Somes Bar. At Somes Bar, continue for 7.5 miles to Marble Mountain Ranch.

Trip note: The lodge is set just across the road from the Klamath River, an ideal location as headquarters for a rafting trip in the summer or a steelhead fishing trip in the fall. Commercial rafting trips are available here, as this piece of river is beautiful and fresh, with lots of wildlife and birds, yet not dangerous. However, be absolutely certain to take out at Somes Bar before reaching Ishi Pishi Falls, which cannot be run. If you like privacy and comfort, the cabin rentals available here are a nice bonus.

14. INDIAN SCOTTY

Reference: **On Scott River in Klamath National Forest; map A1, grid g7.**

Campsites, facilities: There are 32 sites, including several group sites, for tents or motor homes up to 22 feet long. Piped water, vault toilets, fire grills and picnic tables are provided. There is a playground in the group-use area. Pets are permitted on leashes or otherwise restrained.

Reservations, fee: Reservations accepted; $6 fee per night.

Who to contact: Phone the Klamath National Forest Scott River Ranger District at (916) 468-5351.

Location: From Redding, drive north on Interstate 5 to Yreka. In Yreka, turn southwest on Highway 3 for 16.5 miles to Fort Jones. In Fort Jones, turn right (west) on Scott River Road and drive 18 miles to a concrete bridge and the adjacent campground entrance (signed).

Trip note: This is a popular camp that provides direct access to the adjacent Scott River. Because it is easy to reach (no gravel roads) and it's shaded, it gets a lot of use. The camp is set at 2,400 feet. The levels, forces and temperatures on the Scott River fluctuate greatly from spring to fall. In the spring, it can be a raging cauldron, cold from snowmelt. Come summer, it quiets, with some deep pools providing swimming holes. By fall, it can be reduced to a trickle. Keep your expectations flexible according to the season.

---

15. OAK BOTTOM ON THE SALMON RIVER

Reference: In Klamath National Forest; map A1, grid i3.

Campsites, facilities: There are 35 sites for tents and motor homes and some group sites. Piped water, vault toilets, picnic tables and fire grills are provided. There is a sanitary disposal station at the Elk Creek Campground in Happy Camp or at Aikens Camp (13 miles west of the town of Orleans). Pets are permitted on leashes. Supplies are available in Somes Bar.

Reservations, fee: No reservations; $6 fee per night.

Who to contact: Phone the Klamath National Forest Ukonom Ranger District at (916) 627-3291.

Location: From the junction of US 101 and Highway 299 near Arcata, turn east on Highway 299 and drive to Willow Creek. At Willow Creek, turn left (north) on Highway 96 and drive to Somes Bar. At Somes Bar, turn east (right) on Somes Bar-Etna Road and drive three miles to the campground on the left side of the road.

Trip note: This camp is just far enough off Highway 96 that it gets missed by zillions of out-of-towners every year. It is set across the road from the lower Salmon River, a pretty, clean and cold stream that pours out of the surrounding wilderness high country. Swimming is decent in river holes, though the water is cold, especially when nearby Wooley Creek is full of snowmelt pouring out of the Marble Mountains to the north. In the fall, there is good shoreline fishing for steelhead, though the canyon bottom is shaded almost all day and gets very cold. Open year-round.

---

16. AIKENS CREEK

Reference: On Klamath River in Six Rivers National Forest; map A1, grid j1.

Campsites, facilities: There are 10 sites for tents only and 19 sites for motor homes up to 35 feet long. Piped water, flush toilets, picnic tables, fire grills and a sanitary disposal station are provided. Pets are permitted on leashes. Facilities are **wheelchair accessible**.

Reservations, fee: No reservations; $7 fee per night.

Who to contact: Phone Six Rivers National Forest, Orleans Ranger District at (916) 627-3291.

Location: From the junction of US 101 and Highway 299 near Arcata, turn east on Highway 299 and drive to Willow Creek. In Willow Creek, turn left (north) and drive to Weitchpec. In Weitchpec, continue on Highway 96 for five miles to the campground on the right side of the road.

Trip note: The Klamath River is warm and green here in summer, and this camp provides an ideal put-in spot for a day of easy rafting, especially for newcomers in inflatable kayaks. The camp is set at 340 feet in elevation, on Aikens Creek, a feeder stream a short distance from the Klamath. An easy paddle is from here to Weitchpec, with the take-out on the right side of the river just beyond Muddy Creek. The river is set in a beautiful canyon, with lots of birds, and enters the Hoopa Valley Indian Reservation. The steelhead fishing can be good in this area from August through mid-November, best downstream at Johnson's Bar from a boat, boondogging Glo Bugs. Highway 96 is a scenic but slow cruise.

---

17. FISH LAKE

Reference: **In Six Rivers National Forest; map A1, grid j1.**

Campsites, facilities: There are 10 sites for tents and 13 sites for tents or motor homes up to 35 feet long. Piped water, vault toilets, picnic tables and fire grills are provided. Pets are permitted on leashes.

Reservations, fee: No reservations; $6 fee per night, multiple family sites are $15 per night.

Who to contact: Phone Six Rivers National Forest, Orleans Ranger District at (916) 627-3291.

Location: *Note—The primary access road to this campground was closed by a landslide and will not be open in 1996. An alternate route is available but requires an additional 2.5 hours of driving time.* From the junction of US 101 and Highway 299 near Arcata, turn east on Highway 299 and drive to Willow Creek. At Willow Creek, turn north on Highway 96 and drive to Weitchpec. From Weitchpec, continue seven miles north on Highway 96 to Fish Lake Road. Turn left on Fish Lake Road and drive five miles (stay to the right at the Y) to Fish Lake.

Alternate directions: From Weitchpec, drive north on Highway 96 for 15 miles (past Fish Lake Road) to Forest Service Road 12N12. Turn left at Forest Service Road 12N12 (very twisty, dirt logging road) and drive about 25 miles to Forest Service Road 12N13. Turn left on Forest Service Road 12N13 and drive about nine miles (extremely twisty, with a hairpin right turn at the junction with road 12N10) to Forest Service Road 13N01. Turn left at 13N01 (largely paved) and drive about 20 miles to Forest Service Road 10N12 (Fish Lake Road). At Forest Service Road 10N12, turn left and drive three miles to the lake.

Trip note: This is a pretty little lake that provides good fishing for stocked rainbow trout from the season opener on Memorial Day weekend through July. The camp gets little pressure in other months. It's located in the heart of Bigfoot country, with numerous Bigfoot sightings occurring near Bluff Creek. No power boats are permitted on the lake, but it's too small for that anyway, being better suited for a float tube, raft or pram. The elevation is 1,800 feet. Open April to November.

Special note: With the short access road closed by a landslide, few people will take the time to drive the 2.5-hour alternate route. This means those who do will likely have the place entirely to themselves, rare for a pretty lake that you can reach without having to hike.

18. THE PINES TRAILER PARK

Reference: On Klamath River; map A1, grid j1.

Campsites, facilities: There are 25 motor home sites, all with full hookups, and a separate area for tents. Picnic tables, restrooms, showers and a sanitary disposal station are provided. A laundromat is available. Pets are allowed on leashes.

Reservations, fee: Reservations accepted; $12 fee per night.

Who to contact: Phone (916) 627-3425.

Location: From the junction of US 101 and Highway 299 near Arcata, drive east on Highway 299 to Willow Creek. At Willow Creek, turn north on Highway 96 and drive past Weitchpec and continue to Orleans. In Orleans, look for the park entrance on the left (north) side of the road.

Trip note: This is an option for motor home cruisers touring Highway 96, looking for a stopover in Orleans. The steelhead fishing is good in this area in the fall, with guide Roger Raynal of North Rivers Guide Service based out of this town. The campground is located in a wooded setting, across the highway from the Klamath River.

19. SIVSHANEEN

Reference: On Klamath River; map A1, grid j1.

Campsites, facilities: There are 25 motor home sites, all with full hookups. Restrooms, showers, a laundromat and a sanitary disposal station are available. Pets are allowed on leashes.

Reservations, fee: Reservations accepted; $12 fee per night.

Who to contact: Phone (916) 627-3354.

Location: From the junction of US 101 and Highway 299 near Arcata, drive east on Highway 299 to Willow Creek. At Willow Creek, turn north on Highway 96 and drive past Weitchpec and continue to Orleans. In Orleans, turn south on Red Cap Road and drive 1.5 miles to the campground.

Trip note: This makes a good base camp for a Klamath River fishing trip from August to December. That is when the steelhead and the "half-pounders," actually juvenile steelhead in the 12- to 16-inch class, arrive in huge numbers in this stretch of river. In the summer, the river is warm, with a good put-in spot for rafters available nearby. Open Memorial Day through October.

20. KLAMATH RIVERSIDE RV PARK & CAMP

Reference: On Klamath River; map A1, grid j2.

Campsites, facilities: There are 48 motor home sites with full hookups, and a separate area for tents. Picnic tables, restrooms, showers, a game room, a small store and a sanitary disposal station are provided. A laundromat is available. Horseback riding and river rafting services are also available nearby. Pets are allowed on leashes.

Reservations, fee: Reservations accepted; $8.50-$15 fee per night.

Who to contact: Phone (916) 627-3239, or (800) 627-9779.

Location: From the junction of US 101 and Highway 299 near Arcata, drive east on Highway 299 to Willow Creek. In Willow Creek, turn north on Highway 96

and drive past Weitchpec to Orleans. This campground is located at the west
end of the town of Orleans on Highway 96.

Trip note: This is one option for motor home cruisers touring Highway 96, looking
for a place in Orleans to tie up the horse for the night. The camp has large grassy
sites set amid pine trees, right on the river. There are spectacular views of Mt.
Orleans and the surrounding hills. Open year-round.

21. PEARCH CREEK

Reference: On Klamath River in Six Rivers National Forest; map A1, grid j2.

Campsites, facilities: There are nine sites for tents and two sites for tents or motor
homes up to 22 feet long. Piped water, vault toilets, picnic tables and fire grills
are provided. A grocery store, a laundromat and propane gas are available
nearby. Pets are allowed on leashes.

Reservations, fee: No reservations; $6 fee per night.

Who to contact: Phone Six Rivers National Forest at (916) 627-3291.

Location: From the junction of US 101 and Highway 299 near Arcata, drive east
on Highway 299 to Willow Creek. In Willow Creek, turn north on Highway 96
and drive past Weitchpec and continue to Orleans. In Orleans, continue for one
mile and look for the campground entrance on the right side of the road.

Trip note: This is one of the premium Forest Service camps on the Klamath River
because of its easy access from the highway and easy access to the river. The
camp is set on Pearch Creek, about a quarter-mile from the Klamath at a deep
bend in the river. It is open year-round and has fish smokers available, which
is either a sign of optimism or tells you how good the fishing can be. Indeed,
the fishing is excellent for one- to five-pound steelhead from August through
November. The elevation is 400 feet.

22. LITTLE NORTH FORK

Reference: In Klamath National Forest; map A1, grid j5.

Campsites, facilities: There are four tent sites with pit toilets, picnic tables and fire
grills. But there is **no piped water,** so bring your own and pack out your
garbage. Pets are permitted on leashes or otherwise restrained.

Reservations, fee: No reservations; no fee.

Who to contact: Phone Klamath National Forest Salmon River Ranger District at
(916) 467-5757.

Location: From Redding, drive north on Interstate 5 to Yreka. In Yreka, turn
southwest on Highway 3 and drive to Etna. In Etna, turn west on Etna-Somes
Bar Road (Main Street), and drive about 20 miles west to Sawyer's Bar. At
Sawyer's Bar, continue for 3.5 miles to the campground entrance on the right
side of the road.

Trip note: What the heck, ya can't beat the price, eh? And what you get is a tiny,
very primitive campground, at an elevation of 2,300 feet along the North Fork
Salmon River where it pours into the main stem Salmon. A trail is routed out
of camp that climbs up along the North Fork, where there are a few small pools
that can be used as spots for a summer dunking. In early summer, the water is
quite cold from snowmelt out of the nearby Marble Mountain Wilderness to the
north. In the fall, this campground can be used as a base camp for a steelhead
fishing trip on the nearby Salmon River.

23. IDLEWILD 🐟 🚶‍♀️   8

Reference: **On the North Fork of the Salmon River in Klamath National Forest; map A1, grid j7.**

Campsites, facilities: There are 23 sites, including two group sites, for tents or motor homes up to 22 feet long. Piped water, vault toilets, fire grills and picnic tables are provided. Pets are permitted on leashes or otherwise restrained.

Reservations, fee: No reservations; $4 fee per night.

Who to contact: Phone the Klamath National Forest Salmon River Ranger District at (916) 467-5757.

Location: From Redding, drive north on Interstate 5 to Yreka. In Yreka, turn southwest on Highway 3 and drive to Etna. In Etna, turn west on Etna-Somes Bar Road (Main Street in town) and drive about 16 miles to the campground on the right side of the road.

Trip note: This is one of the prettiest drive-to camps in the region, set near the confluence of the Salmon River and its South Fork. This is a beautiful, cold, clear stream and a major tributary to the Klamath River. Most campers are using this camp for its nearby trailhead (two miles north on a dirt Forest Service road out of camp). The hike here is routed to the north, climbing alongside the Salmon River for miles into the Marble Mountain Wilderness (wilderness permits are required). It's a rugged, 10-mile, all-day climb to Lake of the Island, with several other lakes (highlighted by Hancock Lake) to the nearby west, accessible on week-long trips. The camp is open from June through October.

MAP A2

NOR-CAL MAP .... see page 94
adjoining maps
NORTH .... no map
EAST (A3) .... see page 132
SOUTH (B2) .... see page 180
WEST (A1) .... see page 114

**9 LISTINGS
PAGES 126-131**

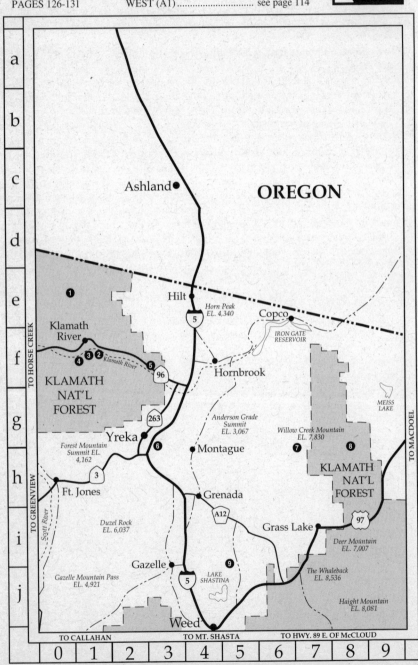

OREGON

Ashland

Hilt
Horn Peak
EL. 4,340
Copco
IRON GATE
RESERVOIR

Klamath
River
Klamath River
96

MEISS
LAKE

Hornbrook

KLAMATH
NAT'L
FOREST

263

Anderson Grade
Summit
EL. 3,067

Willow Creek Mountain
EL. 7,830

TO HORSE CREEK

Yreka

Forest Mountain
Summit EL.
4,162

Montague

KLAMATH
NAT'L
FOREST

TO MACDOEL

3

Ft. Jones

TO GREENVIEW

Scott River

Grenada

A12

Duzel Rock
EL. 6,037

Grass Lake

97

Deer Mountain
EL. 7,007

Gazelle

5

LAKE
SHASTINA

9

The Whaleback
EL. 8,536

Gazelle Mountain Pass
EL. 4,921

Haight Mountain
EL. 8,081

Weed

TO CALLAHAN

TO MT. SHASTA

TO HWY. 89 E. OF McCLOUD

a b c d e f g h i j

0 1 2 3 4 5 6 7 8 9

1. BEAVER CREEK ⌞⌐ ✕ ⚓ ⚓̇   RV 8

Reference: In Klamath National Forest; map A2, grid e1.

Campsites, facilities: There are eight sites for tents or small motor homes. Piped water, vault toilets, picnic tables and fire grills are provided. Pets are permitted on leashes or otherwise controlled.

Reservations, fee: No reservations; $4-$6 fee per night.

Who to contact: Phone the Klamath National Forest Oak Knoll Ranger District at (916) 465-2241.

Location: From Redding, drive north on Interstate 5 to Highway 96. Turn west on Highway 96 and drive approximately 15 miles (if you reach the town of Klamath River, you have gone a half-mile too far) to Beaver Creek Road. Turn right on Beaver Creek Road (Forest Service Road 11) and drive four miles to the campground.

Trip note: This camp is set along Beaver Creek, a feeder stream to the nearby Klamath River, with two small creeks entering Beaver Creek on the far side of the river near the campground. It is quiet and pretty. There are several historic mining sites in the area, with a map of Klamath National Forest (available for $3 at the district office) needed in order to find them. In the fall, this campsite is usually taken by deer hunters.

2. KLAMATH RIVER TRAILER PARK   RV 8
⌞⌐ ⚓ ≋ ✕ 🚶

Reference: On Klamath River; map A2, grid f1.

Campsites, facilities: There are 17 motor home sites with full hookups. Restrooms, hot showers and a laundromat are provided. Pets are allowed on leashes.

Reservations, fee: Reservations accepted; $10 fee per night.

Who to contact: Phone (916) 465-2324.

Location: From Redding, drive north on Interstate 5 to Highway 96. Turn west on Highway 96 and drive approximately 15 miles (if you reach the town of Klamath River, you have gone one mile too far) to the campground entrance.

Trip note: This privately-operated motor home park is located in one of the prettiest areas of the Klamath River. There's a good piece of river here for summer rafters or fall steelhead fishing. For rafting, the river is sprinkled with Class II and III rapids, ideal for inflatable kayaks. Several commercial rafting companies operate in this area. Every site has a view of the river and the beautiful Siskiyou Mountains. The camp is open year-round.

3. QUIGLEY'S GENERAL STORE   RV 7
& TRAILER PARK ⌞⌐ ≋ ≋ ✕

Reference: On Klamath River; map A2, grid f1.

Campsites, facilities: There are 20 motor home sites with full hookups. Tables, restrooms and hot showers are provided. A store and a laundromat are available. Pets are allowed on leashes.

Reservations, fee: Reservations accepted; $12 fee per night.

Who to contact: Phone (916) 465-2224.

Location: From Redding, drive north on Interstate 5 to Highway 96. Turn west on

Highway 96 and drive approximately 15 miles to the town of Klamath River and look for the campground entrance along the road.

Trip note: This year-round, privately operated park is set along the Klamath River. Many of the parking sites have clear views of the river, as well as good mountain views. Quigley's General Store is well stocked for such a remote little shop, and you can usually get reliable fishing information here, too.

4. THE OAKS RV PARK

Reference: **On Klamath River; map A2, grid f1.**

Campsites, facilities: There are 10 sites for tents and 12 sites for motor homes with full hookups. Picnic tables, fire grills, piped water, restrooms, hot showers, a snack bar and laundromat are available. Groceries are available in the town of Klamath River. Pets are allowed on leashes.

Reservations, fee: Reservations accepted; $10-$15 fee per night.

Who to contact: Phone (916) 465-2323.

Location: From Redding, drive north on Interstate 5 to Highway 96. Turn west on Highway 96 and drive approximately 15 miles to the town of Klamath River. Look for the park entrance across from the town post office.

Trip note: Fishing? Rafting? Canoeing? Hiking? This camp provides a good headquarters for all of these adventures. This stretch of the Klamath is ideal for boating, with summer flows warm and often set at perfect levels for rafting and canoeing. Fishing is best in the fall, when salmon, and later, steelhead, migrate through the area.

5. TREE OF HEAVEN

Reference: **In Klamath National Forest; map A2, grid f3.**

Campsites, facilities: There are 10 tent sites and 11 sites for moderate-sized motor homes. Piped water, vault toilets, picnic tables and fire grills are provided. Pets are permitted on leashes or otherwise controlled. A boat ramp is available.

Reservations, fee: No reservations; $6 fee per night.

Who to contact: Phone the Klamath National Forest Oak Knoll Ranger District at (916) 465-2241.

Location: From Redding, drive north on Interstate 5 to Highway 96. Turn west on Highway 96 and drive seven miles to the campground entrance on the left side of the road.

Trip note: This is an outstanding riverside campground that provides excellent access to the Klamath River for fishing, rafting and hiking. The best deal is to put in your raft, canoe or drift boat upstream at the ramp below Iron Gate Reservoir, then make the all-day run down to the take-out at Tree of Heaven. This section of river is an easy paddle, and also provides excellent steelhead fishing in the winter. There is also a trail out of the camp that is routed along the river and probes through vegetation, ending at a fair fishing spot (a better spot is nearby at the mouth of the Shasta River). On the drive in from the highway, you can watch the landscape turn from high chaparral to forest.

6. WALIAKA TRAILER HAVEN

Reference: **Map A2, grid g3.**

Campsites, facilities: There are 60 motor home sites with full or partial hookups. Restrooms, showers, a playground and a recreation room are provided. A laundromat and propane gas are available. Pets are allowed on leashes.

Reservations, fee: Reservations accepted; $19.50 fee per night.

Who to contact: Phone (916) 842-4500.

Location: From Redding, drive north on Interstate 5 to Yreka. In Yreka, take the Fort Jones exit and drive one block east to Fairlane Road. At Fairlane Road, turn north and drive to Sharps Road. At Sharps Road, turn east and drive one block to the motor home park.

Trip note: If it's late, you're tired and you're hunting for a spot to hunker down for the night, this is your only bet in the immediate Yreka vicinity. A string of fast-food restaurants are available nearby on the west side of the highway. It is not exactly paradise, but the views to the northwest of the Siskiyou Mountains are fair enough. The best side trip is heading north on Interstate 5 to the Klamath River; an exit with river access is available at the I-5 Bridge. Open year-round.

---

7. MARTIN'S DAIRY

Reference: On Little Shasta River in Klamath National Forest; map A2, grid g7.

Campsites, facilities: There are eight sites for tents or small motor homes. Piped water, vault toilets, picnic tables and fire grills provided. Pack out your garbage. Pets are permitted on leashes or otherwise controlled.

Reservations, fee: No reservations; no fee.

Who to contact: Phone the Klamath National Forest Goosenest Ranger District (916) 398-4391.

Location: From Redding, drive north on Interstate 5 to Weed. In Weed, turn north on Highway 97 and drive to Grass Lake. Continue about seven miles to Forest Service Road 70 (46N10) (note: if you reach Hebron Summit, you have driven about a mile too far). Turn left on Forest Service Road 70 (46N10) and drive about 10 miles to a Y. Take the left fork at the Y and drive three miles (including a very sharp right turn) to the campground on the right side of the road. A map of Klamath National Forest is advised.

Trip note: This camp is set at 6,000 feet, where the deer get big and the country seems wide open. A large meadow is nearby, located directly across the road from this remote camp, with fantastic wildflower displays in late spring. This is one of the prettiest camps around in the fall, with dramatic color from aspens and other hardwoods. It also makes a good base camp for hunters in the fall. Before heading into the surrounding back country, obtain a map of Klamath National Forest, available for $3 at the Goosenest Ranger Station on Highway 97, on your way in to camp.

---

8. JUANITA LAKE

Reference: In Klamath National Forest; map A2, grid g8.

Campsites, facilities: There are 12 tent sites and 11 sites for motor homes up to 32 feet. Piped water, vault toilets, picnic tables and fire grills provided. Boating is allowed, but no motorboats are permitted on the lake. This lake is **wheelchair accessible**. Pets are allowed on leashes.

Reservations, fee: No reservations; $6-$8 fee per night.

Who to contact: Phone the Klamath National Forest Goosenest Ranger District at (916) 398-4391.

Location: From Redding, drive north on Interstate 5 to Weed. In Weed, turn north on Highway 97 and drive approximately 40 miles to Macdoel. In Macdoel, turn west on Meiss Lake-Sam's Neck Road and drive 8.5 miles to Butte Valley

Road. At Butte Valley Road, turn south and drive to the campground.

Trip note: Small and relatively little-known, this camp is set along the shore of Juanita Lake at 5,100 feet. It is stocked with rainbow trout and brown trout, but a problem with golden shiners has cut into the lake's fishing productivity. It's a small lake and forested, set near the Butte Valley Wildlife Area in the plateau country just five miles to the northeast. The latter provides an opportunity to see waterfowl, and in the winter, bald eagles. Campers will discover a network of Forest Service roads in the area, providing an opportunity for mountain biking. There is also a paved trail around the lake that is **wheelchair accessible** and spans approximately 1.25 miles. Open May through October.

9. LAKE SHASTINA

Reference: **Near Klamath National Forest near Weed; map A2, grid j5.**

Campsites, facilities: There is a small primitive area designated for camping, but there is **no piped water** or other facilities. A boat launch is available. Supplies can be obtained in Weed. Pets are allowed on leashes.

Reservations, fee: No reservations; no fee.

Who to contact: Phone the Shasta Cascade Wonderland Association at (800) 474-2782.

Location: From Redding, drive north on Interstate 5 to Weed. In Weed, turn north on Highway 97 and drive about five miles to Big Springs Road. Turn left (west) on Big Springs Road and drive about one mile to Jackson Ranch Road. Turn left (west) on Jackson Ranch Road and drive a half-mile to an unpaved access road (watch for the signed turnoff). Turn left and drive to the campground.

Trip note: Lake Shastina is set at the northern foot of Mt. Shasta, offering spectacular views, good swimming on hot summer days, and a chance at crappie and trout fishing. One reason the views of Mt. Shasta are so good is because this is largely high sagebrush country, with few trees, and it can get very dusty, windy, and in the winter, nasty cold. When the lake is full and the weather is good, there are few complaints. This is one of the few lakes in Northern California that has property with lakeside housing, consisting of several small developments. Alas, the water slide, once offering great fun for kids, is now off-limits to the public.

MAP A3

NOR-CAL MAP .... see page 94
adjoining maps
NORTH .... no map
EAST (A4) .... see page 136
SOUTH (B3) .... see page 208
WEST (A2) .... see page 126

**8 LISTINGS
PAGES 132-135**

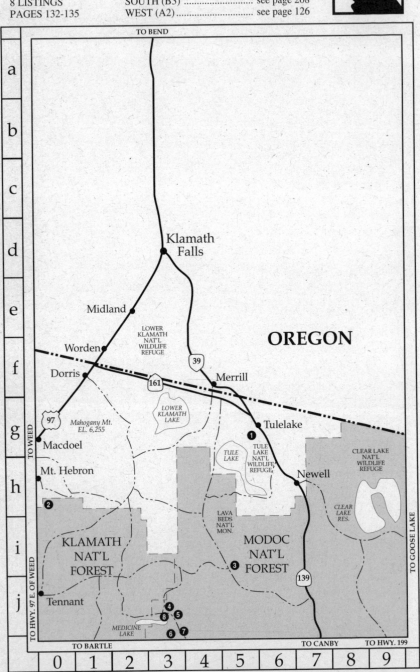

TO BEND

a

b

c

d

Klamath
Falls

e

Midland

Worden

LOWER
KLAMATH
NAT'L
WILDLIFE
REFUGE

OREGON

f

Dorris

39

Merrill

161

LOWER
KLAMATH
LAKE

97

*Mahogany Mt.
EL. 6,255*

Tulelake

1

g

Macdoel

TULE
LAKE

TULE
LAKE
NAT'L
WILDLIFE
REFUGE

CLEAR LAKE
NAT'L
WILDLIFE
REFUGE

TO WEED

Mt. Hebron

Newell

2

h

LAVA
BEDS
NAT'L
MON.

CLEAR
LAKE
RES.

i

**KLAMATH
NAT'L
FOREST**

**MODOC
NAT'L
FOREST**

TO HWY. 97 E. OF WEED

3

139

j

Tennant

4

8   5

*MEDICINE
LAKE*

6   7

TO GOOSE LAKE

TO BARTLE

TO CANBY

TO HWY. 199

0   1   2   3   4   5   6   7   8   9

Map A3 featuring: Klamath National Forest, Lava Beds National Monument, Modoc National Forest, Medicine Lake

1. SHADY LANE TRAILER PARK   RV. 3

Reference: **In Tulelake; map A3, grid g5.**

Campsites, facilities: There are 60 motor home sites with full hookups. Restrooms, showers and patios are provided, and a laundromat is available. Pets are allowed on leashes.

Reservations, fee: Reservations accepted; $15 fee per night.

Who to contact: Write to Shady Lane Trailer Park, 795 Modoc Avenue, P.O. Box 297, Tulelake, CA 96134, or call (916) 667-2617.

Location: From Redding, turn east on Highway 299 and drive to the junction with Highway 139. At Highway 139, turn north and drive 52 miles to Tulelake. At Tulelake, take the south exit on East West Road and drive to Modoc Avenue. At Modoc Avenue, turn left and drive to mid-block to the trailer park.

Trip note: There isn't much shade in Modoc County, but this private park manages to provide some. Good side trips include Tulelake Game Refuge, one of the best places in America (during the winter months) to see bald eagles, and a good bet year-round for birdwatching. Nearby is Lava Beds National Monument. Its northern edge is an excellent place to see deer in late fall and early winter.

2. SHAFTER   5% CLUB 4

Reference: **In Klamath National Forest; map A3, grid h0.**

Campsites, facilities: There are 14 sites for tents or small motor homes. Piped water, vault toilets, picnic tables and fire grills are provided. Pack out your own garbage. Pets are permitted on leashes or otherwise controlled.

Reservations, fee: No reservations; $6-$8 fee per night.

Who to contact: Phone the Klamath National Forest Goosenest Ranger District at (916) 398-4391.

Location: From Redding, drive north on Interstate 5 to Weed. In Weed, turn north on Highway 97 and drive 40 miles to Ball Mountain Road. At Ball Mountain Road, turn right and drive two miles to where the road dead-ends at an unnamed road. Turn right and drive seven miles (crossing railroad tracks after a quarter-mile) to the campground on the right side of the road.

Trip note: This is a little-used camp with trout fishing at nearby Butte Creek for small rainbow trout, primarily six to eight-inchers. Little Orr Lake, located about a 10-minute drive away on the southwest flank of Orr Mountain, provides fishing for larger rainbow trout, 10- to 12-inchers, as well as a sprinkling of smaller brook trout. This camp is primitive and not well known, set in a juniper- and sage-filled landscape. A great side trip is to the nearby Orr Mountain Lookout, where there are spectacular views of Mt. Shasta.

3. INDIAN WELL   9

Reference: **In Lava Beds National Monument; map A3, grid i5.**

Campsites, facilities: There are 40 sites for tents, pickup campers or small trailers. Picnic tables, fire rings and cooking grills are provided. From Memorial Day to Labor Day, water and flush toilets are available. During the winter, the water is turned off and only pit toilets are available. However, water and flush toilets are always available at the visitor center. The town of Tulelake (30 miles north) is the nearest supply station. Pets are allowed on leashes.

Reservations, fee: No reservations; $6 fee per night in winter, $10 in summer.

Who to contact: Call Lava Beds National Monument at (916) 667-2282.

Location: From Redding, drive east on Highway 299 to Canby and the junction with Highway 139. Turn left and drive about 30 miles to Forest Service Road 97 on the left (signed Lava Beds National Monument). Turn left and drive three miles to Forest Service Road 10. Bear right and drive 15 miles to the visitor center and the campground entrance road on the right. Turn right and drive one-quarter mile to the campground.

Trip note: This is a one-in-a-million spot with 20 lava tube caves, a cinder cone (climbable), Mammoth Crater, Native American pictographs and wildlife overlooks at Tule Lake. After winter's first snow, this is one of the best places in the West to photograph deer. Nearby Klamath National Wildlife Refuge is the largest bald eagle wintering area in the lower 48. If you are new to the outdoors, an interpretive center is available to explain it all to you.

---

4. MEDICINE LAKE

Reference: In Modoc National Forest; map A3, grid j3.

Campsites, facilities: There are 22 sites for tents or motor homes up to 22 feet long. Piped water, vault toilets, picnic tables and fire grills are provided. A boat ramp is available nearby. Pets are permitted on leashes. Supplies can be obtained in Bartle.

Reservations, fee: No reservations; $7 fee per vehicle per night.

Who to contact: Phone the Modoc National Forest District at (916) 667-2246.

Location: From Redding, drive north on Interstate 5 past Dunsmuir to Highway 89. Turn north on Highway 89 and drive 28 miles to Bartle. Just past Bartle, turn left on Forest Service Road 49 and drive 31 miles (it becomes Medicine Lake Road) to the lake. From Bartle, the route is signed.

Trip note: Lakeside campsites tucked away in conifers make this camp a winner. Medicine Lake was formed in a crater of an old volcano and is surrounded by sugar pine and fir trees. The lake is stocked with rainbow and brook trout in the summer, gets quite cold in the fall, and freezes over in winter. Many side trips are possible, including nearby Blanche Lake and Ice Caves (both signed, off the access road) and Lava Beds National Monument just 15 miles north. At 6,700 feet, temperatures can turn cold in summer and the season is short.

---

5. A.H. HOGUE

Reference: On Medicine Lake in Modoc National Forest; map A3, grid j3.

Campsites, facilities: There are 24 sites for tents or motor homes. Picnic tables, fire grills, piped water and vault toilets are provided. A boat ramp is available nearby. Pets are permitted on leashes. Supplies can be obtained in Bartle.

Reservations, fee: No reservations; $7 fee per vehicle per night.

Who to contact: Phone the Modoc National Forest District at (916) 667-2246.

Location: From Redding, drive north on Interstate 5 past Dunsmuir to Highway 89. Turn north on Highway 89 and drive 28 miles to Bartle. Just past Bartle, turn left on Forest Service Road 49 and drive 31 miles (it becomes Medicine Lake Road) to the lake. From Bartle, the route is signed.

Trip note: This camp was created in 1990 when the original Medicine Lake Campground was divided in half.

6. HEMLOCK

Reference: **On Medicine Lake in Modoc National Forest; map A3, grid j3.**

Campsites, facilities: There are 19 sites for tents or motor homes up to 22 feet long. Piped water, vault toilets, picnic tables and fire grills are provided. A boat ramp is available nearby. Pets are permitted on leashes. Supplies can be obtained in Bartle.

Reservations, fee: No reservations; $7 fee per vehicle per night.

Who to contact: Phone the Modoc National Forest District at (916) 667-2246.

Location: From Redding, drive north on Interstate 5 past Dunsmuir to Highway 89. Turn north on Highway 89 and drive 28 miles to Bartle. Just past Bartle, turn left on Forest Service Road 49 and drive 31 miles (it becomes Medicine Lake Road) to the lake. From Bartle, the route is signed.

Trip note: This is one of a series of campgrounds on Medicine Lake operated by the Forest Service. A special attraction at Hemlock Camp is the natural sand beach. For more information, see the trip note for Medicine Lake Campground.

7. HEADQUARTERS

Reference: **On Medicine Lake in Modoc National Forest; map A3, grid j3.**

Campsites, facilities: There are 10 sites for tents and motor homes. Piped water, vault toilets, picnic tables and fire grills are provided. A boat ramp is available nearby. Pets are permitted on leashes. Supplies can be obtained in Bartle.

Reservations, fee: No reservations; $7 fee per vehicle per night.

Who to contact: Phone Modoc National Forest District Office at (916) 667-2246.

Location: From Redding, drive north on Interstate 5 past Dunsmuir to Highway 89. Turn north on Highway 89 and drive 28 miles to Bartle. Just past Bartle, turn left on Forest Service Road 49 and drive 31 miles (it becomes Medicine Lake Road) to the lake. From Bartle, the route is signed.

Trip note: This is one of four campgrounds set beside Medicine Lake. For more information, see the trip note for Medicine Lake Campground.

8. BULLSEYE LAKE

Reference: **Near Medicine Lake in Modoc National Forest; map A3, grid j3.**

Campsites, facilities: There are a few primitive campsites, but **no piped water** or other facilities are available. Supplies are available in McCloud; limited supplies can be obtained at the Bartle Lodge. Pets are allowed on leashes.

Reservations, fee: No reservations; no fee.

Who to contact: Phone the Modoc National Forest District at (916) 667-2246.

Location: From Redding, drive north on Interstate 5 past Dunsmuir to Highway 89. Turn north on Highway 89 and drive 28 miles to Bartle. Just past Bartle, turn left on Forest Service Road 49 and drive 30 miles (if you reach Medicine Lake, you have gone about two miles too far). Turn right at the Bullseye Lake access road and drive a short distance to the lake.

Trip note: This tiny lake gets overlooked every year, mainly because of its proximity to nearby Medicine Lake. The lake is shallow, but because snow keeps it locked up until late May or early June, the water stays plenty cold for small trout through July. It is stocked with just 750 six- to eight-inch rainbow trout, not much to crow about. Nearby are some ice caves, created by ancient volcanic action, which are fun to poke around in and explore. The place is small, quiet and pretty, but most of all, small.

MAP A4

NOR-CAL MAP .... see page 94
adjoining maps
NORTH .... no map
EAST .... no map
SOUTH (B4) .... see page 222
WEST (A3) .... see page 132

1 LISTING
PAGES 136-37

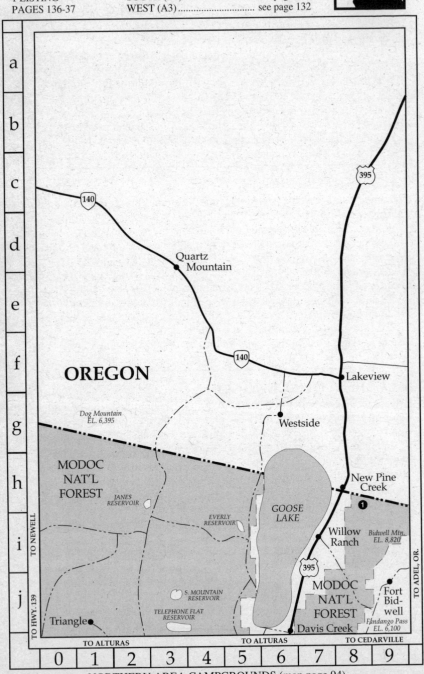

a
b
c
d
e
f
g
h
i
j

0 1 2 3 4 5 6 7 8 9

140

Quartz
Mountain

140

OREGON

Lakeview

Dog Mountain
EL. 6,395

Westside

MODOC
NAT'L
FOREST

JANES
RESERVOIR

EVERLY
RESERVOIR

GOOSE
LAKE

New Pine
Creek

1

Willow
Ranch

Bidwell Mtn.
EL. 8,820

395

S. MOUNTAIN
RESERVOIR

TELEPHONE FLAT
RESERVOIR

MODOC
NAT'L
FOREST

Fort
Bid-
well

Fandango Pass
EL. 6,100

Triangle

Davis Creek

395

TO NEWELL

TO HWY. 139

TO ADEL, OR.

TO ALTURAS

TO ALTURAS

TO CEDARVILLE

136   NORTHERN AREA CAMPGROUNDS (map page 94)

1. CAVE LAKE

Reference: **In Modoc National Forest; map A4, grid h8.**

Campsites, facilities: There are six sites for tents or motor homes up to 15 feet (trailers are not advised—steep access road). Piped water, vault toilets, fire grills and picnic tables are provided. A boat ramp is available for small boats (all motors are prohibited on the lake, including electric). Supplies are available in New Pine Creek, Fort Bidwell or Davis Creek. Pets are allowed on leashes.

Reservations, fee: No reservations; no fee.

Who to contact: Phone the Modoc National Forest District Office at (916) 279-6116, or write to P.O. Box 220, Cedarville, CA 96101.

Location: From Redding, turn east on Highway 299 and drive 146 miles to Alturas. In Alturas, turn north on US 395 and drive 40 miles to Forest Service Road 2 (if you reach the town of New Pine Creek on the Oregon/California border, you have driven one mile too far). Turn right (east) on Forest Service Road 2 (a steep, dirt road-trailers are not recommended) and drive six miles to the campground entrance on the left side of the road (just beyond the Lily Lake picnic area).

Trip note: A set of two lakes can be discovered out here in the middle of nowhere, with Cave Lake on one end and Lily Lake on the other. Together they make a very nice set, very quiet, extremely remote, with good fishing for rainbow trout and brook trout. Of the two lakes, it is nearby Lily Lake that is prettier and provides the better fishing. Cave Camp is set at 6,600 feet and is open from July through September. By camping here, you become a member of the Five Percent Club, that is, the five percent of campers who know of secret, isolated little spots such as this one.

MAP BØ

NOR-CAL MAP .... see page 94
adjoining maps
NORTH (AØ) .... see page 96
EAST (B1) .... see page 152
SOUTH (CØ) .... see page 232
WEST .... no map

29 LISTINGS
PAGES 138-151

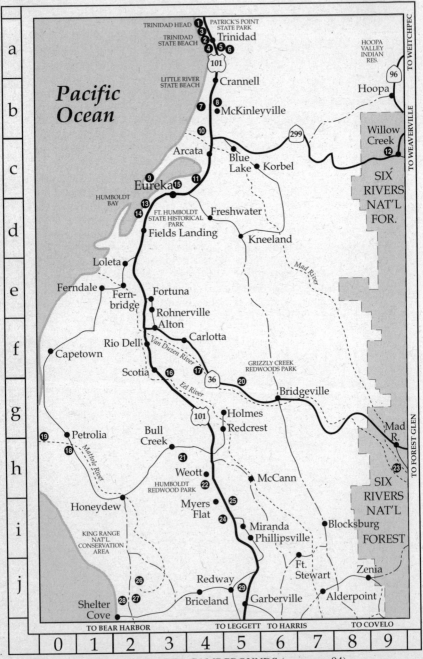

Pacific Ocean

TRINIDAD HEAD
PATRICK'S POINT STATE PARK
Trinidad
TRINIDAD STATE BEACH
101

LITTLE RIVER STATE BEACH
Crannell

McKinleyville

HOOPA VALLEY INDIAN RES.

96
Hoopa

299
Willow Creek

Arcata
Blue Lake
Korbel

SIX RIVERS NAT'L FOR.

Eureka
HUMBOLDT BAY
FT. HUMBOLDT STATE HISTORICAL PARK
Fields Landing
Freshwater
Kneeland

Loleta
Ferndale
Fern-bridge
Fortuna
Rohnerville
Alton
Carlotta
Rio Dell
Van Duzen River
GRIZZLY CREEK REDWOODS PARK
Mad River
Capetown
Scotia
36
Bridgeville
Eel River
101
Holmes
Redcrest
Mad R.

TO FOREST GLEN

Petrolia
Bull Creek
Mattole River
Weott
McCann
HUMBOLDT REDWOOD PARK

SIX RIVERS NAT'L FOREST

Honeydew
Myers Flat
Miranda
Phillipsville
Blocksburg
KING RANGE NAT'L CONSERVATION AREA
Ft. Stewart
Zenia

Redway
Briceland
Garberville
Alderpoint

Shelter Cove

TO BEAR HARBOR   TO LEGGETT   TO HARRIS   TO COVELO

a b c d e f g h i j

0   1   2   3   4   5   6   7   8   9

TO WEITCHPEC
TO WEAVERVILLE

Map BØ featuring: Humboldt Bay, Six Rivers National Forest, Van Duzen River, Mattole River, Humboldt Redwoods State Park, Eel River, King Range

1. SOUNDS OF THE SEA

Reference: In Trinidad; map BØ, grid a4.

Campsites, facilities: There are 52 motor home sites with full hookups. Picnic tables, fire rings, restrooms, showers and a sanitary disposal station are provided. RV storage, a laundromat, a grocery store, a gift shop, RV supplies, cable TV and ice are available. The facilities are **wheelchair accessible**. Pets are allowed on leashes.

Reservations, fee: Reservations accepted; $19 fee per night.

Who to contact: Phone (707) 677-3271.

Location: From Eureka, drive north on US 101 to Trinidad. In Trinidad, continue north on US 101 for 2.5 miles to the Patrick's Point exit. Take the Patrick's Point exit and turn left, and drive one-half mile to the campground.

Trip note: The Trinidad area, located about 20 miles north of Eureka, is one of the great places on this planet. Nearby Patrick's Point State Park is one the highlights, with a Sitka spruce forest, beautiful coastal lookouts, a great easy hike on the Rim Trail, and access to several secluded beaches. To the nearby south at Trinidad Head is a small harbor and dock, with deep sea and salmon fishing trips available. A pretty beach is located to the immediate north of the Seascape Restaurant. A bonus at this privately-operated motor home park is good berry picking.

2. SYLVAN HARBOR TRAILER PARK

Reference: In Trinidad; map BØ, grid a4.

Campsites, facilities: There are 73 motor home sites with full hookups. There are three cabins for rent. Restrooms, showers and a sanitary disposal station are provided. A laundromat and LP gas are available. Pets are allowed on leashes.

Reservations, fee: No reservations except for cabins; $12-$15 fee per night.

Who to contact: Phone (707) 677-9988.

Location: From Eureka, drive north on US 101 to Trinidad. Take the Trinidad exit, turn left at the stop sign and drive a short distance under the freeway to Patrick's Point Drive. Turn right and drive one mile to the campground.

Trip note: This is one of several privately-operated parks in the Trinidad area. It offers a choice of shaded or open sites near the ocean. Open year-round. For more information about recreation available nearby, see the trip note for Sounds of the Sea.

3. VIEW CREST CAMPGROUND

Reference: In Trinidad; map BØ, grid a4.

Campsites, facilities: There are 25 motor home sites (nine drive-through) with full hookups, and a separate area for tents. Picnic tables, fire rings, restrooms, showers, a playground and a sanitary disposal station are provided. Cable TV, RV storage, laundry facilities and wood are available. Pets are allowed on leashes.

Reservations, fee: Reservations accepted; $12-$17 fee per night.

Who to contact: Phone (707) 677-3393.

Location: From Eureka, drive north on US 101 to Trinidad. Take the Trinidad exit, turn left at the stop sign and drive a short distance under the freeway to Patrick's Point Drive. Turn right on Patrick's Point Drive and drive four miles to the campground.

Trip note: View Crest is one of the premium spots in Trinidad, with pretty cottages available as well as campsites for motor homes and tenters. It is one of the only camps in this area where glimpses of the ocean are available. A bonus here are the remarkable flights of swallows, many which have nests at the cottages. Recreation options include deep sea and salmon fishing at Trinidad Harbor to the nearby south, and outstanding easy hiking at Patrick's Point State Park to the nearby north.

---

4. MIDWAY RV PARK

Reference: **In Trinidad; map BØ, grid a4.**

Campsites, facilities: There are 65 motor home sites with full hookups. Picnic tables, restrooms, showers, cable TV, a club room and a playground are provided. RV storage is available. Pets are allowed on leashes.

Reservations, fee: Reservations recommended in summer; $18 fee per night.

Who to contact: Phone (707) 677-3934.

Location: From Eureka, drive north on US 101 to Trinidad. Take the Trinidad exit, turn left at the stop sign and drive a short distance under the freeway to Patrick's Point Drive. Turn right on Patrick's Point Drive and drive a half mile to the campground.

Trip note: This is one of several privately developed campgrounds in Trinidad. In summer, the salmon fishing can be excellent just off Trinidad Head. In the fall, rockfishing is the way to go, and in winter, crabbing is tops. Patrick's Point State Park provides a nearby side trip option to the north.

---

5. HIDDEN CREEK

Reference: **In Trinidad; map BØ, grid a5.**

Campsites, facilities: There are 56 motor home sites (six drive-through) with full or partial hookups, and four tent sites. Several group sites are also available. Picnic tables, patios, restrooms, showers, a sanitary disposal station and a recreation room are provided. LP gas is available. A laundromat and a grocery store are nearby. Pets are allowed on leashes.

Reservations, fee: Reservations recommended in summer; $12-$19 fee per night.

Who to contact: Phone (707) 677-3775.

Location: From Eureka, drive north on US 101 to Trinidad. Take the Trinidad exit, turn left at the stop sign, drive under the freeway and continue on Main Street to 199 North Westhaven.

Trip note: To tell you the truth, there really isn't much hidden about this RV park, and you might be hard-pressed to find the creek as well. Regardless, it is still in a very pretty location in Trinidad, with the Trinidad pier, adjacent harbor, restaurants and beach all within a drive of just a minute or two. Some of California's best deep sea fishing for salmon, lingcod and rockfish is available on boats out of Trinidad Harbor. There's also good beachcombing for agates and driftwood on the beach to the immediate north.

6. DEER LODGE

Reference: **In Trinidad; map BØ, grid a5.**

Campsites, facilities: There are 107 sites for tents or motor homes (two drive-through), some with full or partial hookups. Picnic tables, fire rings, restrooms, showers and a playground are provided. A grocery store, ice, wood, and LP gas are available. Pets are permitted on leashes.

Reservations, fee: Reservations recommended in summer; $12-$16 fee per night; $1 pet fee.

Who to contact: Phone (707) 677-3554.

Location: From Eureka, drive north on US 101 to Trinidad. Take the Trinidad exit, turn left at the stop sign and drive a short distance under the freeway to Patrick's Point Drive. Turn right on Patrick's Point Drive and about two miles north to the campground on the right side of the road.

Trip note: This campground is set on nine acres of redwoods, often dark and wet, with the ocean at Trinidad Head only about a five-minute drive away. There are also a series of cabins here, but some smell of mildew, others of cigarettes. It also appears that some people in beat-up trailers are "camping" here year-round, hardly a welcoming scene for carefree vacationers.

7. CLAM BEACH COUNTY PARK

Reference: **Near McKinleyville; map BØ, grid b4.**

Campsites, facilities: There are 50 sites for tents and motor homes. Piped water and vault toilets are provided. Propane gas, a grocery store and a laundromat are in McKinleyville. Pets are permitted.

Reservations, fee: No reservations; $8 fee per night; $1 pet fee.

Who to contact: Phone Clam Beach County Park at (707) 445-7652.

Location: From Eureka, drive north on US 101 to McKinleyville. Just past McKinleyville, turn west at the sign for Clam Beach and drive two blocks to the campground, which is adjacent to Little River State Beach.

Trip notes: Here awaits a beach that seems to stretch on forever, one of the great places to bring a lover, dog, children, or hey, all three. While the campsites are a bit exposed, making winds out of the north a problem in the spring, the direct beach access largely makes up for it. The park gets its name from the good clamming that is available, but you must come equipped with a clam gun or special clam shovel, and then be out when minus low tides arrive at daybreak. Most people just enjoy playing tag with the waves, long romantic walks, or throwing sticks for the dog.

8. WIDOW WHITE CREEK RV PARK

Reference: **In McKinleyville; map BØ, grid b4.**

Campsites, facilities: There are 40 motor home sites with full hookups and a separate area for tents. Picnic tables, restrooms, showers, a playground and a sanitary disposal station are provided. A laundromat is available. The facilities are **wheelchair accessible**. Pets are allowed on leashes.

Reservations, fee: Reservations accepted; $11-$15 fee per night.

Who to contact: Phone (707) 839-1137.

Location: From Eureka on US 101, drive north and continue for 4.5 miles past the junction with Highway 299 to the Murray Road exit. Take Murray Road exit, then turn east on Murray Road and drive one block to the campground.

Trip note: This privately-operated park provides extremely easy access from the highway. Nearby recreation options including the Mad River, where there is a good picnic site near the hatchery and steelhead fishing in the winter, a good perch fishing in the surf where the Mad River enters the ocean. The park offers horseshoes, volleyball, badminton, and get this, nearby are the "world's largest totem poles." They'll tell you all about it.

---

9. SAMOA BOAT LAUNCH COUNTY PARK

Reference: **On Humboldt Bay; map BØ, grid c3.**

Campsites, facilities: There are 10 tent sites and 40 motor home sites. Picnic tables, fire grills, piped water and flush toilets are provided. A boat ramp, a grocery store, LP gas and a laundromat are available in Eureka (about five miles away). Pets are permitted on leashes.

Reservations, fee: Reservations accepted; $8 fee per night; $1 pet fee.

Who to contact: Phone (707) 445-7652.

Location: From US 101 in Eureka, turn west on Highway 255 and drive two miles until it deadends at New Navy Base Road. At New Navy Base Road, turn left and drive five miles to the end of the Samoa Peninsula and the campground entrance.

Trip note: The nearby vicinity of the boat ramp, with access to Humboldt Bay and the Pacific Ocean, makes this a star attraction for campers towing their fishing boats. At the park, you get good beachcombing and clamming at low tides and a chance to see a huge variety of seabirds, highlighted by egrets and herons. There's a reason: Directly across the bay is the Humboldt Bay National Wildlife Refuge. This park is set near the famed all-you-can-eat, logger-style Samoa Cookhouse. Open year-round.

---

10. MAD RIVER RAPIDS RV PARK

Reference: **In Arcata; map BØ, grid b4.**

Campsites, facilities: There are 92 motor home sites (40 drive-through) with full hookups. Patios, picnic tables, fire grills, restrooms, showers, a sanitary disposal station, a recreation room, tennis courts, a fitness room, a playground, a swimming pool and a spa are provided. Cable TV, VCR rentals, a grocery store and a laundromat are available. Some facilities are **wheelchair accessible**. Pets are allowed on leashes.

Reservations, fee: Reservations accepted; $22-$28 fee per night.

Who to contact: Phone (707) 822-7275.

Location: From the junction of US 101 and Highway 299 in Arcata, drive a quarter-mile north on US 101 to the Guintoli Lane exit. Turn west on Janes Road and drive two blocks west to the campground.

Trip note: This camp is set near the farmlands on the outskirts of town, in a pretty, quiet setting. There is a great bike ride nearby on a trail routed along the Mad River, and it is also excellent for taking a dog for a walk. Nearby Arcata is a unique town, a bit of the old and a bit of the new, and the Arcata Marsh at the north end of Humboldt Bay provides a scenic and easy bicycle trip, as well as an excellent destination for hiking, sightseeing and birdwatching.

11. EUREKA KOA 🐟 ♿ 🚐 2

Reference: Map BØ, grid c4.

Campsites, facilities: There are 11 bike-in sites, 26 tent sites and 140 motor home sites (42 drive-through) with full or partial hookups. Group sites and four camping cabins are available. Piped water, flush toilets, showers, fire pits, picnic tables, a playground and a recreation room are provided. A grocery store, a laundromat, a sanitary disposal station, LP gas, ice and wood are available. Pets are permitted.

Reservations, fee: Reservations accepted; $14-$26 fee per night. Cabins are $32 per night for two people.

Who to contact: Phone Eureka KOA at (707) 822-4243.

Location: From Eureka, drive north on US 101 for four miles and look for the KOA sign on the right side of the highway at 4050 North US 101.

Trip note: This is a year-round KOA camp for US 101 cruisers looking for a layover spot in Eureka. A bonus here is a few of those little KOA Kamping Kabins, the little log-style jobs that win on cuteness alone. The closest significant recreation option is the Arcata Marsh on Humboldt Bay, a pretty spot with good trails for biking and hiking, or just parking and looking at the water. Another option is excellent salmon fishing in June, July and August, with party boats available just south of Eureka at King Salmon Charters.

12. BOISE CREEK 🐟 🥾 ♿ 🏊 🚐 7

Reference: In Six Rivers National Forest; map BØ, grid c4.

Campsites, facilities: There are three sites for bicyclists and hikers and 17 sites for tents or motor homes up to 40 feet long. Piped water, vault toilets, picnic tables and fire grills are provided. A grocery store, a laundromat and propane gas are available nearby. The facilities are **wheelchair accessible**. Pets are permitted on leashes.

Reservations, fee: No reservations; $4-$6 fee per night for first vehicle; $4 for each additional vehicle; $3 day-use fee (if not camping).

Who to contact: Phone the Lower Trinity Ranger District at (916) 629-2118.

Location: From the intersection of US 101 and Highway 299 near Arcata, turn east on Highway 299 and drive 39 miles and look for the campground entrance on the left side of the road. If you reach the town of Willow Creek, you have gone two miles too far.

Trip note: This camp features a quarter-mile long trail down to Boise Creek, and nearby access to the Trinity River. In addition, if you have ever wanted to see Bigfoot, you can do it while camping here, because there's a giant wooden Bigfoot on display in front of The Flame restaurant in nearby Willow Creek. After your Bigfoot experience, your best bet during summer is to head north on nearby Highway 96 (turn north in Willow Creek) to Tish Tang Campground, where there is excellent river access, swimming, and innertubing in the late summer's warm flows. The Trinity River also provides good salmon and steelhead fishing during fall and winter, respectively, with the best nearby access upriver along Highway 299 at Burnt Ranch. And hey, if you happen to see some giant footprints, tell 'em at The Flame. Open year-round.

13. E-Z LANDING 🐟 ⚓   RV 7

Reference: **On Humboldt Bay; map BØ, grid d3.**

Campsites, facilities: There are 55 motor home sites (20 drive-through) with full hookups. Patios, flush toilets and showers are provided. A sanitary disposal station, marine gas, ice, a laundromat, boat docks, a boat launch, bait and tackle are available. Party boat rentals are available nearby. Pets are permitted.

Reservations, fee: Reservations accepted; $14-$18 fee per night.

Who to contact: Phone E-Z Landing RV Park and Marina at (707) 442-1118.

Location: From Eureka, drive 2.5 miles south on US 101. Turn west on King Salmon Avenue and drive for a half-mile. Turn south on Buhne Drive and drive a half-mile to 1875 Buhne Drive.

Trip note: This is a good base camp for salmon trips in July and August when big schools of king and coho salmon often school just west of the entrance of Humboldt Bay. A boat ramp with access to Humboldt Bay and party boat fishing trips are both available out of E-Z Landing. It's not the prettiest camp in the world, with quite a bit of asphalt, but most people use this camp as a simple parking spot for sleeping while getting down to business during the day: fishing. This spot is ideal for ocean fishing, clamming, beachcombing and boating.

14. JOHNNY'S MARINA & RV PARK   RV 5

🐟 ⚓ 🏊

Reference: **On Humboldt Bay; map BØ, grid d2.**

Campsites, facilities: There are 53 motor home sites (four drive-through) with full hookups. Patios, restrooms, showers and a sanitary disposal station are provided. A laundromat and a boat dock are available. Pets are permitted.

Reservations, fee: Reservations accepted; $16-$17 fee per night.

Who to contact: Phone (707) 442-2284.

Location: From Eureka, drive 3.5 miles south on US 101. Turn west on King Salmon Avenue and drive a half-mile. Turn south on Buhne Drive and drive a half-mile to 1821 Buhne Drive.

Trip note: This is a good base camp for salmon fishing during the peak season in June, July and August. Boat rentals are available along with launching and mooring for private boats. Other recreation activities include beachcombing, clamming and perch fishing from shore. Charter fishing trips are available from King Salmon Charters. Open year-round.

15. EBB TIDE PARK   RV 2

Reference: **In Eureka; map BØ, grid c3.**

Campsites, facilities: There are 81 motor home sites (58 drive-through) with full or partial hookups. Restrooms, showers, picnic tables and patios are provided. A sanitary dump station, RV storage and a laundromat are available. Pets are permitted.

Reservations, fee: Reservations accepted; $11-$21 fee per night.

Who to contact: Phone Ebb Tide Park at (707) 445-2273.

Location: In Eureka, driving north on US 101, take the Mall 101 exit. Look for the park on the east side of the road. (Driving south on US 101, take the V Street exit and drive to the first stop light. Turn left and drive to Sixth Street. Turn left on Sixth Street and drive into Mall 101 and straight ahead to the park.)

Trip note: This year-round motor home park provides easy access off the highway and to stores and movie theatres. Not exactly a primitive spot in pristine wilderness. It is what it is: A place to park the rig for the night.

16. STAFFORD RV PARK

Reference: **Near Scotia; map BØ, grid f3.**

Campsites, facilities: There are 50 motor home sites (14 drive-through) with full or partial hookups, and 30 tent sites. Group sites are available. Piped water, flush toilets, showers, fire grills and picnic tables are provided. A laundromat, a playground, a sanitary disposal station, satellite TV and a store are available. Some facilities are **wheelchair accessible**. Pets are permitted.

Reservations, fee: Reservations accepted; $10-$20 fee per night; $1-$2 pet fee.

Who to contact: Phone Stafford RV Park at (707) 764-3416.

Location: From Eureka, drive south on US 101 to Scotia. At Scotia, continue south for three miles to Stafford Road. Turn right on Stafford Road and at the first stop sign, turn left under the overpass and drive a short distance to North Road. At North Road, turn right and drive one-quarter mile to 385 North Road.

Trip note: This is a privately-operated park for motor homes that provides several side trip options: a tour of the giant sawmill in Scotia, a tour of giant redwoods on the Avenue of the Giants, access to the nearby Eel River and best of all, the nearby Redwood National Park. One of the better park information centers in California is here, with maps and information about hikes, bike rides and driving tours.

17. VAN DUZEN COUNTY PARK

Reference: **On Van Duzen River; map BØ, grid f4.**

Campsites, facilities: There are 30 sites for tents or motor homes. Piped water, flush toilets, showers, fire grills and picnic tables are provided. A grocery store and laundromat are available nearby. Pets are permitted.

Reservations, fee: No reservations; $10 fee per night; $1 pet fee.

Who to contact: Phone (707) 445-7652.

Location: From Eureka, drive south on US 101 to the junction of Highway 36 at Alton. Turn east on Highway 36 and drive 12 miles to the campground.

Trip note: This campground is set at the headwaters of the Van Duzen River, one of the Eel River's major tributaries. The river is subject to tremendous fluctuations in flows and height, so low in the fall that it is often temporarily closed to fishing by the Department of Fish and Game, so high in the winter that only a fool would stick his toes in. For a short period in late spring, it provides a benign run for rafting and canoeing, putting in here and making the short run down to Grizzly Creek Redwoods State Park. In October, an excellent salmon fishing spot is where the Van Duzen enters the Eel. Open year-round.

18. A.W. WAY COUNTY PARK

Reference: **On Mattole River; map BØ, grid h1.**

Campsites, facilities: There are 30 sites for tents or motor homes. Piped water, flush toilets, showers, fire grills, picnic tables and a playground are provided. A grocery store, a laundromat and propane gas are available nearby. Pets are permitted.

Reservations, fee: Reservations accepted; $10 fee per night; $1 pet fee.

Who to contact: Phone (707) 445-7652.

Location: From Garberville, drive north on US 101 to the South Fork-Honeydew. Turn west on South Fork-Honeydew Road and drive 31 miles (the road alternates between pavement, gravel, dirt, then pavement again) to the park entrance on the left side of the road. The park is located 7.5 miles south of the town of Petrolia.

Trip note: This secluded camp provides home for visitors to the "Lost Coast," the beautiful coastal stretch of California located far from any semblance of urban life. The highlight here is the Mattole River, a great steelhead stream when flows are suitable between January and mid-March. Nearby is excellent hiking in the King Range National Conservation Area. For the great hike out to the abandoned Punta Gorda Lighthouse, drive to the trailhead on the left side of Lighthouse Road (see next listing). This area is typically bombarded with monsoon-level rains in winter.

---

19. MOUTH OF THE MATTOLE

Reference: On the Pacific Ocean; map BØ, grid g0.

Campsites, facilities: There are five sites for tents or motor homes up to 15 feet long. Vault toilets, fire grills and tables are provided. Pets are permitted. Piped water is available until September; after that, bring your own.

Reservations, fee: No reservations; no fee.

Who to contact: Phone Bureau of Land Management at (707) 825-2300.

Location: From US 101 north of Garberville, take the South Fork-Honeydew exit and drive west to Honeydew. At Honeydew, turn right on Mattole Road and drive toward Petrolia. At the second bridge over the Mattole River (one mile before Petrolia), turn west on Lighthouse Road and drive five miles to the campground at the end of the road.

Trip note: This is a little-known camp set at the mouth of the Mattole River, right where it pours into the Pacific Ocean. It is beautiful and isolated. An outstanding hike is available, with the trailhead (Prospect Ridge Road) located on the south side of Lighthouse Road (you'll see it while driving to camp). This trail is routed to the abandoned Punta Gorda Lighthouse, where it links up with the spectacular Lost Coast Trail. Perch fishing is good where the Mattole flows into the ocean, best during low tides. In the winter, the Mattole often provides excellent steelhead fishing. Check the Department of Fish and Game regulations for closed areas. Be sure to have a full tank on the way out—the nearest gas station is quite distant. Open year-round.

---

20. GRIZZLY CREEK REDWOODS ST. PARK

Reference: Map BØ, grid g5.

Campsites, facilities: There are nine tent sites and 21 sites for tents or motor homes up to 30 feet long. Piped water, flush toilets, showers, fire grills and picnic tables are provided. A laundromat and grocery store are available nearby. The facilities are **wheelchair accessible**. Pets are permitted on leashes.

Reservations, fee: Reserve by phoning Destinet at (800) 444-7275 ($6.75 Destinet fee); $15-$17 fee per night; $1 pet fee.

Who to contact: Phone (707) 946-2409, (707) 777-3683 or (707) 445-6547.

Location: From Eureka, drive south on US 101 to the junction of Highway 36 at Alton. Turn east on Highway 36 and drive about 10 miles to the campground.

Trip note: Most summer vacationers hit the campgrounds on the Redwood Highway, that is, US 101. Here is a camp just far enough off the beaten path to provide some semblance of seclusion. It is set in redwoods, quite beautiful, with fair hiking and good access to the adjacent Van Duzen River. In the winter, one of the better holes for steelhead fishing is accessible here. Open year-round.

---

21. ALBEE CREEK 🐟 🏃 🏊 ♱   RV. 8

Reference: **In Humboldt Redwoods State Park; map BØ, grid h3.**

Campsites, facilities: There are 14 sites for tents and 20 sites for tents or motor homes up to 33 feet long. Piped water, flush toilets, showers, fire grills and picnic tables are provided. Pets are permitted on leashes.

Reservations, fee: Reserve by phoning Destinet at (800) 444-7275 ($6.75 Destinet fee); $15-$17 fee per night; $1 pet fee.

Who to contact: Phone Humboldt Redwoods State Park at (707) 946-2409 or (707) 445-6547.

Location: From Eureka, drive south on US 101 south to Bull Creek Flats Road (if you reach Weott, you have gone two miles too far). At Bull Creek Flats Road, turn west and drive six miles to the campground.

Trip note: Humboldt Redwoods State Park is known for some unusual giant trees, including the Flat Iron Tree, the Dyerville Giant, as well as the Federation Grove and the Big Tree Area. A series of excellent hikes, both short and long, are available here. The camp is set in a redwood grove and the smell of these trees has a special magic. Nearby Albee Creek, a benign trickle most of the year, can flood in the winter after heavy rains. Open May through September.

---

22. BURLINGTON 🐟 🏃 🏊 ♱   RV. 7

Reference: **In Humboldt Redwoods State Park; map BØ, grid h4.**

Campsites, facilities: There are 58 sites for tents or motor homes up to 33 feet long. Piped water, a sanitary disposal station, flush toilets, showers, fire grills and picnic tables are provided. Pets are permitted on leashes.

Reservations, fee: Reserve by phoning Destinet at (800) 444-7275 ($6.75 Destinet fee); $15-$17 fee per night; $1 pet fee.

Who to contact: Phone Humboldt Redwoods State Park at (707) 946-2409 or (707) 445-6547.

Location: From Eureka, drive south on US 101 for 50 miles to the Weott/Newton Road exit. Turn right on Newton Road and continue to the T junction where Newton Road meets the Avenue of the Giants. Turn left on Avenue of the Giants and drive two miles to the campground entrance on the left.

Trip notes: This camp is often at capacity during the tourist months. You get shady campgrounds with big redwood stumps that kids can play on. There's good hiking on trails routed through the redwoods, and in winter, steelhead fishing is often good on the nearby Eel River. The park has 100 miles of trails, but it is the little half-mile Founders Grove Nature Trail that has the quickest payoff and the least effort, providing a route that passes the Dyerville Giant, the tallest tree in the park. Open year-round.

23. MAD RIVER

Reference: **In Six Rivers National Forest; map BØ, grid h9.**

Campsites, facilities: There are 40 sites, a few of which are for motor homes up to 22 feet long or trailers up to 30 feet long. Piped water is available from approximately mid-May to mid-October. Vault toilets, picnic tables and fire grills are provided.

Reservations, fee: No reservations; $4-$6 fee per night.

Who to contact: Phone the Six Rivers National Forest at (707) 442-1721.

Location: From Eureka, drive south on US 101 to the junction with Highway 36 at Alton. Turn east on Highway 36 and drive about 50 miles to the town of Mad River. Turn southeast on Lower Mad River Road and drive four miles to the campground on the right side of the road.

Trip note: This Forest Service campground is set in a hot, remote section of Six Rivers National Forest at an elevation of 2,600 feet. The headwaters of the Mad River pour right past the campground, about two miles downstream from the Ruth Lake Dam. People making weekend trips to Ruth Lake often end up at this camp. Ruth Lake is the only major recreation lake within decent driving range of Eureka, and offers a small marina with boat rentals, a good boat ramp for access to trout fishing, bass fishing and waterskiing. Open year-round.

24. GIANT REDWOODS RV CAMP

Reference: **On Eel River; map BØ, grid i4.**

Campsites, facilities: There are 25 tent sites and 57 motor home sites (25 drive-through), many with full or partial hookups. Picnic tables, fire rings, restrooms, showers and a sanitary disposal station are provided. A store, ice, LP gas, a laundromat, a playground and a recreation room are available. Pets are allowed.

Reservations, fee: Reservations recommended in summer; $16-$22 fee per night.

Who to contact: Phone Giant Redwoods RV Camp at (707) 943-3198.

Location: From Eureka, drive south 50 miles on US 101 to the Myers Flat/Avenue of the Giants exit. Turn right on Avenue of the Giants and make a quick left on Myers Avenue. Drive one-quarter mile on Myers Avenue into the campground entrance.

Trip note: The privately-operated park is set in a grove of redwoods and covers 23 acres, much of it fronting the Eel River. Trip options include the scenic drive on Avenue of the Giants. Open year-round.

25. HIDDEN SPRINGS

Reference: **In Humboldt Redwoods State Park; map BØ, grid i5.**

Campsites, facilities: There are 50 tent sites and 105 sites for tents or motor homes up to 33 feet long. Piped water, flush toilets, showers, fire grills and picnic tables are provided. A grocery store, a laundromat and LP gas are available in Myers Flat. Pets are permitted on leashes.

Reservations, fee: Reserve by phoning Destinet at (800) 444-7275 ($6.75 Destinet fee); $15-$17 fee per night; $1 pet fee.

Who to contact: Phone Humboldt Redwoods State Park at (707) 946-2409 or (707) 445-6547.

Location: From Garberville, drive north on US 101 to Myers Flat. At Myers Flat, take Avenue of the Giants and turn east and drive less than a mile to the campground entrance.

Trip note: This camp gets heavy use from May through September, but the campgrounds have been situated in a way that offers relative seclusion. Side trips include good hiking on trails routed through redwoods and a touring drive on Avenue of the Giants. The park has more than 100 miles of hiking trails, many of them spectacular in giant redwoods, including the Bull Creek Flats Trail and Founders Grove Nature Trail. In winter, nearby High Rock on the Eel River is one of the better shoreline fishing spots for steelhead.

26. HORSE MOUNTAIN 🚶 🐎   6

Reference: **In King Range; map BØ, grid j2.**

Campsites, facilities: There are nine sites for tents or motor homes up to 20 feet long. Piped water, vault toilets, fire grills and picnic tables are provided. Pets are permitted.

Reservations, fee: No reservations; $5 fee per night.

Who to contact: Phone the Bureau of Land Management at (707) 825-2300..

Location: From Eureka, drive 65 miles south on US 101 to the Redway exit. Take the Redway exit onto Redwood Drive in the town of Redway. Look on the right for the King Range Conservation Area sign. Turn right on Briceland-Thorne Road (which will become Shelter Cove Road) and drive 18 miles to Kings Peak Road. Turn right on Kings Peak Road and continue seven miles to the campground on the right.

Trip note: Few people know of this spot. The campground is set along the northwest flank of Horse Mountain. A primitive road (Saddle Mountain Road) leads west from the camp, then left at the Y, up to Horse Mountain (1,929 feet), which offers spectacular ocean and coastal views on clear days. If you turn right at the Y, the road leads to the trailhead for the King Crest Trail near Saddle Mountain (3,290 feet). This hike is an ambitious climb to Kings Peak (4,087 feet), rewarding hikers with a fantastic view in all directions, including picking out Mt. Lassen poking up above the Yolla Bolly Wilderness to the east. Open year-round.

27. SHELTER COVE 🐟 ⚓ 🚶   RV 9

Reference: **Overlooking Pacific Ocean; map BØ, grid j2.**

Campsites, facilities: There are 105 sites for tents or motor homes (15 drive-through), many with full hookups. Picnic tables, fire rings, restrooms, showers and sanitary disposal stations are provided. A laundromat, a grocery store, a deli, LP gas, ice, RV supplies, a boat ramp and boat rentals are available. Pets are allowed on leashes.

Reservations, fee: Reservations recommended; $14-$22 fee per night.

Who to contact: Phone (707) 986-7474.

Location: From Garberville on US 101, take the Shelter Cove-Redway-Redwood Drive exit. Drive 2.5 miles north on Redwood Road to Briceland-Shelter Cove Road. Turn west onto Briceland-Shelter Cove Road and drive 24 miles (following the truck/RV route signs) to Upper Pacific Drive. Turn south onto Upper Pacific Drive and go one-half mile.

Trip note: This is a prime oceanside spot to set up a base camp for deep sea fishing, whale watching, tide pooling, beachcombing and hiking. A relatively new six-lane boat ramp makes it perfect for campers with trailered boats who don't mind the long drive. Reservations are strongly advised here. The park's backdrop is the King Range National Conservation Area, offering spectacular views. The deli is world-famous for its fish and chips. The salmon fishing is quite good here in July and August, crabbing in December, clamming during winter's low tides, and hiking in the King Mountain Range during the summer. There is heavy rain in winter. Open year-round.

28. TOLKAN 🏃   6

Reference: **In King Range; map BØ, grid j2.**

Campsites, facilities: There are nine sites for tents or motor homes up to 20 feet long. Piped water, vault toilets, fire grills and picnic tables are provided. Pets are permitted on leashes. Facilities are **wheelchair accessible.**

Reservations, fee: No reservations; $8 fee per night.

Who to contact: Phone the Bureau of Land Management at (707) 825-2300.

Location: From Eureka, drive 65 miles south on US 101 to the Redway exit. Take the Redway exit onto Redwood Drive into the town of Redway. Look on the right for the King Range Conservation Area sign. Turn right on Briceland-Thorne Road (which will become Shelter Cove Road) and drive 18 miles to Kings Peak Road. Turn right on Kings Peak Road and continue eight miles to the campground on the right.

Trip note: This remote camp is set at 1,840 feet, a short drive south of the Horse Mountain Camp. For nearby side trip options, see the trip note for Horse Mountain Camp.

29. DEAN CREEK RESORT 🏃   RV 7

Reference: **On the South Fork of Eel River; map BØ, grid j5.**

Campsites, facilities: There are 64 motor home sites with full or partial hookups and 12 drive-through sites. Picnic tables, fire grills, restrooms, showers and a recreation room are provided. A laundromat, a store, RV supplies, wood, ice, a giant spa, a sauna, a pool, a sanitary dump station and a playground are available. In summer, inner tubes and tandem bikes are available. Pets are permitted.

Reservations, fee: Reservations recommended in summer; $14-$22 fee per night.

Who to contact: Phone Dean Creek Resort at (707) 923-2555.

Location: From Eureka, drive 60 miles south on US 101 to the Redway turnoff. Exit onto Redwood Drive and continue about one block to the campground entrance on the right.

Trip note: This year-round motor home park is set on the South Fork of the Eel River. In the summer, it makes a good base camp for a redwood park adventure, with the adjacent Humboldt Redwoods State Park providing 100 miles of hiking trails, many being routed through awesome stands of giant trees. In the winter, heavy rains feed the South Fork Eel, inspiring steelhead upstream on their annual winter journey. Fishing is good in this area, best by shore at nearby High Rock, though bank access is good at several other spots, particularly upstream near Benbow and in Cooks Valley. An excellent side trip is to drive on Avenue of the Giants, a tour through giant redwood trees, located three miles from the park. The campground also offers volleyball, shuffleboard, badminton and horseshoes. You get the idea.

NOR-CAL MAP .... see page 94
adjoining maps
NORTH (A1) .... see page 114
EAST (B2) .... see page 180
SOUTH (C1) .... see page 248
WEST (BØ) .... see page 138

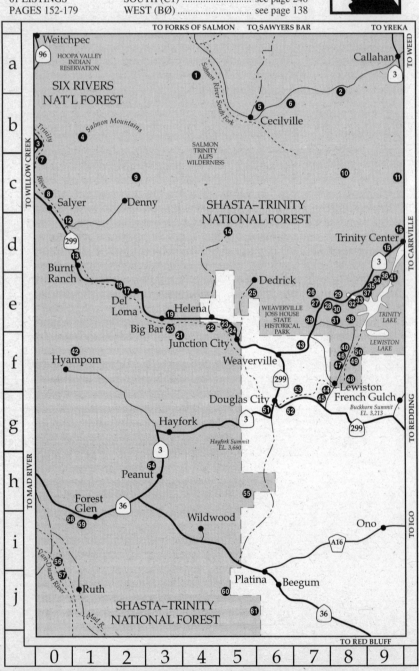

TO FORKS OF SALMON   TO SAWYERS BAR   TO YREKA

Weitchpec

96

HOOPA VALLEY
INDIAN
RESERVATION

Callahan

3

TO WEED

SIX RIVERS
NAT'L FOREST

1

Salmon River South Fork

2

5

6

Cecilville

Salmon Mountains

4

SALMON
TRINITY
ALPS
WILDERNESS

3

7

9

10

11

Trinity River

8

Salyer

Denny

SHASTA–TRINITY
NATIONAL FOREST

12

14

16

Trinity Center

15

299

13

Burnt
Ranch

Dedrick

34 35
37 36 41

26

29

32 33

31 38

Del
Loma

18 17

25

27 28 30

39

Helena

19

23

TRINITY
LAKE

Big Bar

20

22

24

43

LEWISTON
LAKE

21

Junction City

40

Hyampom

42

Weaverville

WEAVERVILLE
JOSS HOUSE
STATE
HISTORICAL
PARK

46 49
47 50
48

TO WILLOW CREEK

299

53

44

Lewiston

French Gulch

Douglas City

51

45

Buckhorn Summit
EL. 3,213

Hayfork

3

52

299

TO REDDING

Hayfork Summit
EL. 3,660

3

54

Peanut

Forest
Glen

36

55

58 59

Wildwood

Ono

TO MAD RIVER

A16

TO IGO

56

Van Duzen River

57

Ruth

Platina

Beegum

60

SHASTA–TRINITY
NATIONAL FOREST

61

Mad R.

36

TO RED BLUFF

0   1   2   3   4   5   6   7   8   9

Map B1 featuring: **Salmon River, Klamath National Forest, Trinity River, New River, Shasta-Trinity National Forest, Coffee Creek, Six Rivers National Forest, Canyon Creek, Stuarts Fork, Trinity Lake, Weaver Creek, Lewiston Lake, Ruth Lake**

1. MATTHEWS CREEK

Reference: **On Salmon River in Klamath National Forest; map B1, grid a5.**

Campsites, facilities: There are seven sites for tents or motor homes up to 16 feet long and seven sites for tents only. Piped water, vault toilets, fire grills and picnic tables are provided. Pets are permitted on leashes or otherwise restrained.

Reservations, fee: No reservations; $4 fee per night.

Who to contact: Phone the Klamath National Forest Salmon River Ranger District at (916) 467-5757.

Location: From the junction of US 101 and Highway 299 near Arcata, turn east on Highway 299 and drive to Willow Creek. In Willow Creek, turn north on Highway 96 and drive past Orleans to Somes Bar. At Somes Bar, turn east on Salmon River Road (Forest Service Road 2B01) and drive to the town of Forks of Salmon. Turn right on Cecilville Road (Forest Service Road 1002) and drive about nine miles to the campground. Cecilville Road is very narrow.

Trip note: This camp is set in a dramatic river canyon, with the beautiful South Fork of the Salmon River nearby. Rafters call it the "Cal Salmon," with good put-in and take-out spots located every few miles all the way to the confluence with the Klamath. In early summer, the water is quite cold from snowmelt, but by summer, it warms up significantly. The best fishing for steelhead on the Salmon is in December in the stretch of river downstream from Forks of Salmon (check regulations for closed areas). In winter, the mountain rims shield the canyon floor from sunlight and it gets so cold you'll feel like a human glacier. The elevation is 1,700 feet.

2. TRAIL CREEK

Reference: **In Klamath National Forest; map B1, grid a8.**

Campsites, facilities: There are seven sites for tents or motor homes up to 22 feet long and eight sites for tents only. Piped water, vault toilets, fire grills and picnic tables are provided. Pets are permitted on leashes or otherwise restrained.

Reservations, fee: No reservations; $4 fee per night.

Who to contact: Phone the Klamath National Forest Scott River Ranger District at (916) 468-5351.

Location: From Redding, drive north on Interstate 5 past Weed to the Edgewood exit. Take the Edgewood exit, turn left at the stop sign, and drive a short distance to another stop sign at Old Stage Road. Turn right at Old Stage Road and drive to Gazelle. In Gazelle, turn left on Gazelle-Callahan Road and drive to Callahan. In Callahan, turn southwest on Cecilville Road and drive 17 miles to the campground.

Trip note: This simple and quiet camp is set beside Trail Creek, a small tributary to the upper Salmon River, at an elevation of 4,700 feet. A trailhead is located about a mile to the south, accessible via a Forest Service road, providing access to a trail routed along Fish Creek for two miles, leading to little Fish Lake. From Fish Lake, the trail climbs steeply, switchbacking at times, for another two miles to larger Trail Gull Lake, a very pretty spot set below Deadman Peak (7,741 feet). Open May through October.

3. EAST FORK TRINITY

Reference: **On the Trinity River east of Willow Creek; map B1, grid b0.**

Campsites, facilities: There are eight sites for tents and motor homes. Picnic tables, fire rings and vault toilets with **wheelchair access** are provided. **No piped water** is available. Pets are permitted on leashes.

Reservations, fee: No reservations; $4 fee per night; $3 for each additional vehicle (Memorial Day through October 1, otherwise camping is free).

Who to contact: Phone the Lower Trinity Ranger District at (916) 629-2118; for a map, send $3 to Office of Information, U.S. Forest Service, 630 Sansome Street, San Francisco, CA 94111 and ask for Six Rivers National Forest.

Location: From the junction of US 101 and Highway 299 near Arcata, turn east on Highway 299 and drive to Willow Creek. From Willow Creek, continue six miles east on Highway 299, then look for the camp's signed turnoff on the south side of the road.

Trip note: This is a beautiful spot along the Trinity River. Set at a 2,000-foot elevation, it's one of the prettiest campgrounds in the area. In August and September, the river is often quite warm, ideal for swimming or innertubing. In the winter, it is one of the better camps for shoreline steelhead fishing. Way back in the 1950s and early 1960s, this was one of the better-known campgrounds in the area, but the flood of 1964 wiped it out. Only recently have rehabilitation efforts restored it to life.

4. MILL CREEK LAKE HIKE-IN

Reference: **On the edge of Trinity Alps Wilderness; map B1, grid b2**.

Campsites, facilities: There are three primitive tent sites at locations around the lake. Fire rings are provided. **No piped water** is available. No pets are allowed.

Reservations, fee: No reservations; no fee. A free wilderness permit is required from the U.S. Forest Service.

Who to contact: Phone the Lower Trinity Ranger District at (916) 629-2118; for a map, send $3 to Office of Information, U.S. Forest Service, 630 Sansome Street, San Francisco, CA 94111 and ask for Six Rivers National Forest.

Location: From the junction of US 101 and Highway 299 near Arcata, turn east on Highway 299 and drive to Willow Creek. In Willow Creek, turn north on Highway 96 and drive into the Hoopa Valley. At Hoopa on Highway 96, turn east on Big Hill Road and drive 12 miles to the national forest boundary. Turn right on Forest Road 10N02 and drive about 3.5 miles, where you will reach another junction. Turn right at the signed junction to Mill Creek Lake Trailhead and drive a short distance to the parking area. A one-hour walk is then required to reach the lake.

Trip note: Mill Creek Lake is a pretty and secret three-acre lake set at 5,000 feet on the edge of the Trinity Alps Wilderness. To reach it requires a two-mile hike from the wilderness boundary, with the little lake set just north of North Trinity Mountain (6,362 feet). This is a rare chance to reach a wilderness lake with such a short walk, backpacking without having to pay the penalty of days of demanding hiking. The lake features excellent swimming, with warmer water than in higher and more remote wilderness lakes, and decent fishing for rainbow trout. It is stocked with fingerlings yearly by airplane.

5. EAST FORK

Reference: **On Salmon River in Klamath National Forest; map B1, grid b6.**

Campsites, facilities: There are six tent sites and three sites for motor homes up to 16 feet long. Vault toilets, fire grills and picnic tables are provided. **No piped water** is provided, so bring your own. Pets are permitted on leashes or otherwise restrained.

Reservations, fee: No reservations; no fee.

Who to contact: Phone the Klamath National Forest Scott River Ranger District at (916) 467-5757.

Location: From Redding, drive north on Interstate 5 past Weed to the Edgewood exit. Take the Edgewood exit, turn left at the stop sign, and drive a short distance to another stop sign at Old Stage Road. Turn right at Old Stage Road and drive to Gazelle. In Gazelle, turn left on Gazelle-Callahan Road and drive to Callahan. In Callahan, turn southwest on Cecilville Road and drive about 30 miles to the campground on the right side of the road. If you reach the town of Cecilville, you have gone two miles too far.

Trip note: This is one of the more spectacular areas in the fall when the leaves turn different shades of gold. It's set at 2,400 feet along the Salmon River, just outside the town of Cecilville. Directly adjacent to the camp is Forest Service Road 37N02, which leads to a Forest Service station four miles away, and a trailhead for the Trinity Alps Wilderness three miles beyond that. Note to steelhead anglers: Check the Department of Fish and Game regulations for closed areas on the Salmon River.

6. SHADOW CREEK

Reference: **In Klamath National Forest; map B1, grid b6.**

Campsites, facilities: There are five tent sites and five sites for motor homes up to 16 feet long. Vault toilets, fire grills and picnic tables are provided. **No piped water** is available, so remember to bring your own. Pets are permitted on leashes or otherwise restrained.

Reservations, fee: No reservations; $4 fee per night.

Who to contact: Phone the Klamath National Forest Salmon River Ranger District at (916) 467-5757.

Location: From Redding, drive north on Interstate 5 past Weed to the Edgewood exit. Take the Edgewood exit, turn left at the stop sign, and drive a short distance to another stop sign at Old Stage Road. Turn right at Old Stage Road and drive to Gazelle. In Gazelle, turn left on Gazelle-Callahan Road and drive to Callahan. In Callahan, turn southwest on Cecilville Road and drive about 25 miles to the campground on the left side of the road.

Trip note: This tiny spot, secluded and quiet too, is along little Shadow Creek where it enters the East Fork Salmon River, adjacent to a deep bend in the road. An unusual side trip is to take the Forest Service road out of camp (turn north off Cecilville Road) and follow it as it winds back and forth, finally arriving at Grouse Point, 5,409 feet in elevation, for a view of the western slopes of nearby Russian and Trinity Alps Wilderness. Note that the river adjacent to the campground is a spawning area for steelhead and closed to fishing.

7. TISH TANG 🐟 ♒ 🍴   RV 🛡8

Reference: **In Six Rivers National Forest; map B1, grid c0.**

Campsites, facilities: There are 21 sites for tents and 19 sites for tents or motor homes up to 30 feet long and trailers up to 22 feet long. Piped water (available until approximately the end of October), vault toilets, picnic tables and fire grills are provided. Pets are permitted on leashes.

Reservations, fee: No reservations; $6 fee per night; $4 for each additional vehicle; $12 fee per night for multiple-family sites.

Who to contact: Phone the Lower Trinity Ranger District at (916) 629-2118.

Location: From the junction of US 101 and Highway 299 near Arcata, turn east on Highway 299 and drive to Willow Creek. In Willow Creek, turn north on Highway 96 and drive eight miles north to the campground entrance on the right side of the road.

Trip note: This camp is located adjacent to one of the best swimming holes in Northern California. By late July, the adjacent Trinity River is warm and slow, perfect for innertubing, falling in "by accident" and canoeing. There is a large gravel beach, and some people will bring shorty lawn chairs and just take a seat on the edge of the river in a few inches of water. Though Tish Tang is a good put-in spot for rafting in the late spring and early summer, taking the river north into the Hoopa Valley, it is too easy for most rafters to even ruffle a feather during the summer. The elevation is 400 feet. Open year-round, with limited service November through April.

---

8. LAZY DOUBLE "B" RV PARK 🐟 ♒ 🍴   RV 🛡7

Reference: **On Trinity River; map B1, grid c0.**

Campsites, facilities: There are 17 tent sites and 23 motor home sites with full or partial hookups. A grocery store, a laundromat, a sanitary dump station, a playground, hot showers, restrooms, picnic tables and fire grills are provided. Firewood is available. Pets are allowed on leashes.

Reservations, fee: Reservations accepted; $13-$17 fee per night.

Who to contact: Phone (916) 629-2156.

Location: From the junction of US 101 and Highway 299 near Arcata, turn east on Highway 299 and drive 46 miles to the park. From Redding, turn west on Highway 299 and drive 95 miles to the park.

Trip note: This is a privately-operated park set along the Trinity River, with easy and direct access to the river. There are sandy beaches nearby, a good area for rafting and innertubing, and a gold-panning area. Salmon fishing is best in the fall, and steelhead fishing in the winter, with good shorefishing access along Highway 299. There are on-site trailer rentals. Open year-round with limited winter facilities.

---

9. DENNY 🐟 ♒ 🚶

Reference: **On New River in Shasta-Trinity National Forest; map B1, grid c2.**

Campsites, facilities: There are 16 tent sites and six sites for tents or motor homes up to 25 feet long. Piped water, vault toilets, picnic tables and fire grills are provided. Pets are permitted on leashes. Supplies are available in Salyers Bar.

Reservations, fee: No reservations; no fee.

Who to contact: Phone the Shasta-Trinity National Forest, Big Bar Ranger District at (916) 623-6106.

Location: From the junction of US 101 and Highway 299 near Arcata, turn east on Highway 299 and drive to Willow Creek. In Willow Creek, continue east on Highway 299 and after reaching Salyer, continue for four miles to Denny Road (County Road 402). Turn north on Denny Road and drive about 14 miles on a paved but very windy road to the campground.

Trip note: This is a secluded and quiet campground located along the New River, a tributary to the Trinity River and a designated Wild and Scenic River. Trout fishing is decent, but the fish are small in the five miles of river near the campground. The stream here is OK for swimming, but too cold to even dip a toe in until late summer. If you drive north from the camp on Denny Road, you will find several trailheads for trips into the Trinity Alps Wilderness. The best of them is at the end of the road, where there is a good parking area, with a trail that is routed along the East Fork New River up toward Limestone Ridge. The campground is set at 1,400 feet.

10. GOLDFIELD 🚶‍♂️   6

Reference: **In Shasta-Trinity National Forest; map B1, grid c8.**

Campsites, facilities: There are six tent sites. Vault toilets, picnic tables, hitching posts for horses and fire grills are provided, but there is **no piped water**, so bring your own. Pets are permitted on leashes.

Reservations, fee: No reservations; no fee.

Who to contact: Phone the Shasta-Trinity National Forest District Office at (916) 623-2121.

Location: From Redding, turn east on Highway 299 and drive to Weaverville. In Weaverville, turn north on Highway 3 and drive just past the north end of Trinity Lake to Coffee Creek Road (104), adjacent to a Forest Service ranger station. Turn left (west) on Coffee Creek Road and drive 6.5 miles to the campground on the left side of the road.

Trip note: For hikers, this camp makes a perfect first stop after a long drive. You wake up, get your gear organized, then take the trailhead to the south. It is routed along Boulder Creek, and with a left turn at the junction (about four miles in), will take you to pretty Boulder Lake (another two miles), set inside the edge of the Trinity Alps Wilderness. It was 49er coach George Seifert who first told me about the beauty of this place, and how perfectly this campground is located for the hike. Campground elevation is 3,000 feet.

11. BIG FLAT 🐟 🚶‍♂️   RV 8

Reference: **On Coffee Creek in Klamath National Forest; map B1, grid c9.**

Campsites, facilities: There are nine sites for tents or motor homes up to 16 feet long. Vault toilets, fire grills and picnic tables are provided. But there is **no piped water**, so bring your own and pack out your garbage. Pets are permitted on leashes or otherwise restrained.

Reservations, fee: No reservations; no fee.

Who to contact: Phone the Klamath National Forest Salmon River Ranger District at (916) 467-5757.

Location: From Redding, turn east on Highway 299 and drive to Weaverville. In Weaverville, turn north on Highway 3 and drive just past the north end of Trinity Lake to Coffee Creek Road (104), adjacent to a Forest Service ranger station. Turn left (west) on Coffee Creek Road and drive 21 miles to the campground at the end of the road.

Trip note: This is a great jump-off spot for a wilderness backpacking trip into the adjacent Trinity Alps. An 11-mile hike will take you into the beautiful Caribou Lakes Basin for lakeside campsites, excellent swimming, dramatic sunsets, and fair trout fishing. The trail is routed out of camp, crosses the stream, then rises up a series of switchbacks to the ridge. From here it gets easier, rounding a mountain and depositing you in the basin. Bypass Little Caribou, Snowslide and Lower Caribou lakes, and instead head all the way to Caribou, the biggest and best of the lot. Big Flat Campground is set at 5,000 feet in elevation along Coffee Creek, and on the drive in, you'll see big piles of boulders along the stream, evidence of past goldmining activity.

12. GRAY'S FALLS 🐟 🏃 ♿ ✕   RV 8

Reference: **On Trinity River in Six Rivers National Forest; map B1, grid d0.**
Campsites, facilities: There are 17 tent sites and 16 sites for tents or motor homes up to 35 feet long and trailers up to 40 feet long. Piped water, flush toilets, picnic tables and fire grills are provided. One facility is **wheelchair accessible**. Pets are allowed on leashes.
Reservations, fee: No reservations; $6 fee per night; $4 each additional vehicle.
Who to contact: Phone the Lower Trinity Ranger District at (916) 629-2118.
Location: From the junction of US 101 and Highway 299 near Arcata, turn east on Highway 299 and drive to Willow Creek. In Willow Creek, continue east on Highway 299 for 12 miles to the campground.
Trip note: This is a prime summer spot to do absolutely nothing but enjoy the warm weather, cool water and watch the adjacent Trinity River flow past. It is a good put-in spot for a short trip on an innertube or inflatable kayak, with the water warm and benign by late summer. A nature trail is also nearby. Gray's Falls isn't actually much of a waterfall, but rather a short coursing piece of water over rocks that salmon have to leap over during their run upstream in mid-September. This is a good spot for fishing, not only for salmon, but for steelhead in late November and early December. The camp is open May to mid-September. The elevation is 1,000 feet.

13. BURNT RANCH 🐟 🏃   RV 7

Reference: **On Trinity River in Shasta-Trinity National Forest; map B1, grid d1.**
Campsites, facilities: There are 16 sites for tents or motor homes up to 25 feet long. Piped water, vault toilets, picnic tables and fire grills are provided. Pets are permitted on leashes. Supplies can be obtained in Hawkins Bar.
Reservations, fee: No reservations; no fee.
Who to contact: Phone the Shasta-Trinity National Forest, Big Bar Ranger District at (916) 623-6106.
Location: From Redding, take Highway 299 west and drive past Weaverville to Burnt Ranch. In Burnt Ranch, continue a half-mile and look for the campground entrance on the right (north) side of the road.
Trip note: This campground is set on a bluff above the Trinity River and is one of its most compelling spots. Burnt Ranch Falls isn't much of a waterfall, but provides a fantastic spot to watch salmon and steelhead leap like greyhounds to make it past the falls and into a calm pool above. The peak migration periods are in mid-September for salmon and in early winter and early spring for steelhead. On their migratory route, the fish will hold below the falls, gaining strength for their upriver surge, making it a natural fishing spot. This section

of river is very pretty, with deep dramatic canyons nearby. Open year-round. The elevation is 1,000 feet.

14. HOBO GULCH 🎣 🥾   RV 7

Reference: **On the North Fork of Trinity River in Shasta-Trinity National Forest; map B1, grid d4.**

Campsites, facilities: There are 10 sites for tents or motor homes. Vault toilets, picnic tables and fire grills are provided, but there is **no piped water**, so bring your own. Pets are permitted. Supplies can be obtained in Junction City.

Reservations, fee: No reservations; no fee.

Who to contact: Phone Shasta-Trinity National Forest, Big Bar Ranger District at (916) 623-6106.

Location: From Redding, turn west on Highway 299, drive past Weaverville and continue 13 miles to Helena. In Helena, turn north (right) and drive four miles on County East Fork Road to Hobo Gulch Road. At Hobo Gulch Road, turn north and drive 16 miles to the end of the road at the campground.

Trip note: Only the ambitious need apply. This is a trailhead camp set on the edge of the Trinity Alps Wilderness, and the reason only the ambitious show up is because it is a 20-mile uphill haul all the way to Grizzly Lake, set at the foot of the awesome Thompson Peak (8,663 feet), with no other lakes available en route. The camp is set at 2,900 feet elevation along the North Fork of the Trinity River. The adjacent slopes of the wilderness are known for little creeks, woods, and a few pristine meadows, and are largely devoid of lakes.

15. PREACHER MEADOW 🥾   RV 7

Reference: **In Shasta-Trinity National Forest; map B1, grid d9.**

Campsites, facilities: There are 45 sites for tents or motor homes up to 32 feet long. Piped water, vault toilets, picnic tables and fire grills are provided. Supplies, a laundromat and a small airport are available nearby. Pets are allowed on leashes.

Reservations, fee: No reservations; $5 fee per night.

Who to contact: Phone the Shasta-Trinity National Forest District Office at (916) 623-2121.

Location: From Redding, turn west on Highway 299 and drive to Weaverville at Highway 3. Turn north on Highway 3 and drive to Trinity Lake and continue towards Trinity Center and look for the campground entrance on the left side of the road (if you reach Trinity Center, you have gone two miles too far).

Trip note: The best thing about Preacher Meadow camp is its good view of the Trinity Alps, providing you seek out the right vantage point. Otherwise, compared to all the other camps in the area located so close to Trinity Lake, it has trouble matching up in the quality department. If the lakeside camps are full, this provides an overflow option.

16. WYNTOON RESORT 🎣 ⚓ 🥾 ♿ 🏊 🚶   RV 8

Reference: **On Trinity Lake; map B1, grid d9.**

Campsites, facilities: There are 78 tent sites and 136 full-hookup sites for trailers or motor homes. Piped water, picnic tables, fire rings, restrooms, showers and laundry facilities are provided. A playground, a pool, a sanitary dump station, gasoline, a hardware store, a grocery store, bicycle rentals, a fish cleaning area, boat rentals, slips and a boat launch are available. Trailers and cottages are also available for rent. Pets are permitted on leashes. The facilities are **wheelchair accessible**.

Reservations, fee: Reservations accepted; $17-$22 fee per night.

Who to contact: Phone the resort at (916) 266-3337.

Location: From Redding, turn west on Highway 299 and drive to Weaverville at Highway 3. Turn north on Highway 3 and drive to Trinity Lake. At Trinity Center, continue one-half mile north on Highway 3 to the resort.

Trip note: This huge resort is an ideal family vacation destination. It is set in a wooded area on the north shore of Trinity Lake and provides opportunities for fishing, boating, swimming and waterskiing, with access within walking distance. The lake is set at the base of the dramatic Trinity Alps, one of the most beautiful regions in the state.

---

17. DEL LOMA VILLAGE RV 7

Reference: **On Trinity River; map B1, grid e2.**

Campsites, facilities: There are 38 motor home sites with full or partial hookups. Picnic tables, fire grills, flush toilets, hot showers, and a sanitary dump station are provided. A grocery store, RV supplies, firewood, laundromat, propane gas, a recreation room, volleyball and horseshoe pits are available. Pets are allowed on leashes.

Reservations, fee: Reservations accepted; $17.50 fee per night.

Who to contact: Phone (916) 623-2834.

Location: From the junction of US 101 and Highway 299 in Arcata, turn east on Highway 299 and drive to Burnt Ranch. From Burnt Ranch, continue 10 miles east on Highway 299 to the town of Del Loma and look for the campground entrance along the road.

Trip note: Motor home cruisers looking for a layover spot near the Trinity River will find just that at Del Loma. Shady sites and sandy beaches are available here along the Trinity. Rafting and inner tube trips are popular in this area during summer months. Salmon fishing is best in the fall, steelhead fishing in the winter. Open year-round.

---

18. HAYDEN FLAT RV 7

Reference: **On Trinity River in Shasta-Trinity National Forest; map B1, grid e2.**

Campsites, facilities: There are 11 tent sites and 24 sites for tents or motor homes up to 25 feet long. Piped water, vault toilets, picnic tables and fire grills are provided. Pets are permitted on leashes.

Reservations, fee: No reservations; $5 fee per night.

Who to contact: Phone the Shasta-Trinity National Forest, Big Bar Ranger District at (916) 623-6106.

Location: From the junction of US 101 and Highway 299 in Arcata, turn east on Highway 299 and drive to Burnt Ranch. From Burnt Ranch, continue 10 miles east on Highway 299 and look for the campground entrance along the left (north) side of the road. If you reach the town of Del Loma, you have gone a half-mile too far.

Trip note: This campground is split into two pieces, with most of the sites grouped in a large, shaded area across the road from the river and a few on the river side. A beach is available along the river, which is a good spot for swimming as well as a popular put-in and take-out spot for rafters. The elevation is 1,200 feet. Open year-round.

19. BIG FLAT ◄🐟 🏃 🏊 RV 6

Reference: On Trinity River in Shasta-Trinity National Forest; map B1, grid e3.

Campsites, facilities: There are 10 sites for tents or motor homes up to 25 feet long. Piped water, vault toilets, picnic tables and fire grills are provided. Pets are permitted on leashes.

Reservations, fee: No reservations; $5 fee per night.

Who to contact: Phone the Shasta-Trinity National Forest, Big Bar Ranger District at (916) 623-6106.

Location: From Redding, turn west on Highway 299 and drive past Weaverville, Junction City and Helena, and continue for about seven miles. Look for the campground entrance on the right side of the road. If you reach the town of Big Bar, you have gone three miles too far.

Trip note: This level campground is set off Highway 299, just across the road from the Trinity River. The sites are close together, and it can be hot and dusty in midsummer. No problem. That is when you will be on the Trinity River, taking the lowest-priced rafting trip available anywhere in the West—as low as $25 to rent an inflatable kayak from Trinity River Rafting in nearby Big Bar. The price includes shuttle service. It's fun, exciting, easy (newcomers are welcome), and cheap.

20. BIG BAR ◄🐟 6

Reference: Near Trinity River in Shasta-Trinity National Forest; map B1, grid e3.

Campsites, facilities: There are three tent sites. Piped water, vault toilets, picnic tables and fire grills are provided. Supplies are available nearby. Pets are allowed on leashes.

Reservations, fee: No reservations; no fee.

Who to contact: Phone the Shasta-Trinity National Forest, Big Bar Ranger District at (916) 623-6106.

Location: From Redding, turn west on Highway 299 and drive past Weaverville, Junction City and Helena to the town of Big Bar. In Big Bar (just prior to reaching the ranger station), turn left on Forest Service Road 16 and drive one mile to the campground on the right side of the road.

Trip note: You name it, you got it—quiet, small campground, easy access, good fishing nearby (in the fall) and piped water. In addition, there is a good put-in spot for inflatable kayaks and rafts. It is an ideal piece of water for newcomers, with Trinity River Rafting offerings inflatable rentals for as low as $25, including shuttle charge. The elevation is 1,200 feet. If the shoe fits...

21. SKUNK POINT GROUP CAMP ◄🐟 🏊 ✕ 7

Reference: On the Trinity River in Shasta-Trinity National Forest; map B1, grid e3.

Campsites, facilities: There are two group sites that hold up to 30 people each. Vault toilets, picnic tables and fire grills are provided, but there is **no piped water**, so bring your own. Pets are permitted on leashes.

Reservations, fee: Reservations required; call for fee.

Who to contact: Phone the Shasta-Trinity National Forest, Big Bar Ranger District at (916) 623-6106.

Location: From Redding, turn west on Highway 299 and drive past Weaverville,

Junction City and Helena, and continue for about seven miles. Look for the campground entrance on the left side of the road. If you reach the town of Big Bar, you have gone two miles too far.

Trip note: This is an ideal site for groups on rafting trips. You get easy access to the nearby Trinity River with a streamside setting and privacy for the group. A beach on the river is nearby. In the spring, this section of river offers primarily Class II rapids (only more difficult during high water), but most of it is rated Class I. By late summer, the water is warm and benign, ideal for families. Guided rafting trips and inflatables are available for hire and rent in nearby Big Bar. The camp elevation is 1,200 feet. Open year-round.

22. PIGEON POINT 🛶 🐟 ♿ 🚤 ✕　　　RV 7

Reference: **On Trinity River in Shasta-Trinity National Forest; map B1, grid e4.**

Campsites, facilities: There are 10 sites for tents or motor homes up to 25 feet long. Vault toilets, picnic tables and fire grills are provided. There's **no piped water**, so bring your own. Supplies can be obtained in Big Bar or Junction City. Pets are permitted on leashes. The facilities are **wheelchair accessible**.

Reservations, fee: No reservations; $4 fee per night.

Who to contact: Phone the Shasta-Trinity National Forest, Big Bar Ranger District at (916) 623-6106.

Location: From Redding, turn west on Highway 299 and drive to Weaverville. Continue west on Highway 299 to Helena and continue two miles to the campground on the right (north) side of the road.

Trip note: In the good old days, huge flocks of bandtail pigeons flew the Trinity River Canyon, swooping and diving in dramatic shows. Nowadays, you don't see too many pigeons, but this camp still keeps its namesake. It is better known for its access to the Trinity River, with a large beach for swimming. The camp is not right on the Trinity, however—the highway is set between the camp and the river. The Forest Service road from the camp is routed north past several old mines on up to the Hobo Gulch Trailhead for the Trinity Alps. The elevation is 1,100 feet. Open May through October.

23. BIGFOOT CAMPGROUND AND RV PARK 　RV 8
🛶 🏃 ♿ 🚤 ✕

Reference: **On Trinity River; map B1, grid e5.**

Campsites, facilities: There are 45 motor home sites with full or partial hookups and a separate area for tent camping. From December 1 to May 1, only self-contained vehicles are allowed. Flush toilets, hot showers (for a fee), a laundromat, a grocery store, a sanitary dump station, television, propane gas, a swimming pool and horseshoe pits are available. Some facilities are **wheelchair accessible**. Pets are allowed on leashes.

Reservations, fee: Reservations recommended from July through October; $12-$16 fee per night.

Who to contact: Phone (916) 623-6088.

Location: From Redding, turn west on Highway 299 and drive to Junction City. At Junction City, continue west on Highway 299 for three miles to the camp.

Trip note: This private RV park has excellent access to the nearby Trinity River. It is a popular layover for Highway 299 cruisers, but provides the option for longer stays with rafting, goldpanning, and in the fall and winter, fishing for salmon and steelhead, respectively.

24. JUNCTION CITY CAMP 🐟 ⚓ 🏊 🍴 RV 7

Reference: On Trinity River in Shasta-Trinity National Forest; map B1, grid e5.

Campsites, facilities: There are 26 sites for motor homes up to 30 feet long. Piped water (available only from the pump house from November through April), vault toilets, picnic tables and fire grills are provided. Groceries and propane gas are available in Junction City. Pets are allowed on leashes.

Reservations, fee: No reservations; $7 fee per night from May through October.

Who to contact: Phone the Bureau of Land Management at (916) 224-2100.

Location: From Redding, turn west on Highway 299 and drive to Junction City. At Junction City, continue west on Highway 299 for 1.5 miles to the camp.

Trip note: Some of the Trinity River's best fall salmon fishing is in this area in September and early October, with steelhead following from mid-October into the winter. That makes it an ideal base camp for a fishing or camping trip.

---

25. RIPSTEIN 🐟 🚶 8

Reference: On Canyon Creek in Shasta-Trinity National Forest; map B1, grid e6.

Campsites, facilities: There are 10 tent sites. Vault toilets, picnic tables and fire grills are provided, but there's **no piped water**, so bring your own. Pets are permitted on leashes. Supplies can be obtained in Junction City.

Reservations, fee: No reservations; no fee.

Who to contact: Phone Shasta-Trinity National Forest, Big Bar Ranger District at (916) 623-6106.

Location: From Redding, turn west on Highway 299 and drive to Junction City. At Junction City, turn right (north) on Canyon Creek Road and drive 15 miles to the campground on the left side of the road.

Trip note: This is one of the great trailhead camps for the neighboring Trinity Alps. It is set at 2,600 feet in elevation on the southern edge of the wilderness and is a popular spot for a late-night arrival, followed by a backpacking trip the next morning. Waiting are the Canyon Creek Lakes, via a six-mile uphill hike along Canyon Creek. The destination is extremely beautiful—two alpine lakes set in high granite mountains. The route out passes Canyon Creek Falls, a set of two different waterfalls, about 3.5 miles out.

---

26. BRIDGE CAMP 🚶 🏇 8

Reference: On Stuarts Fork in Shasta-Trinity National Forest; map B1, grid e7.

Campsites, facilities: There are 10 sites for tents or trailers up to 12 feet long. Piped water (spring, summer and fall only), vault toilets, picnic tables and fire grills are provided. Horse corrals are available. Pets are permitted on leashes.

Reservations, fee: No reservations; $4 fee per night.

Who to contact: Phone the Shasta-Trinity National Forest District Office at (916) 623-2121.

Location: From Redding, turn west on Highway 299 and drive to Weaverville. In Weaverville, turn north on Highway 3 and drive 17 miles to Trinity Alps Road (at Stuarts Fork of Trinity Lake). At Trinity Alps Road, turn left and drive about 2.5 miles to the campground on the right side of the road.

Trip note: This remote spot is an ideal jump-off point for backpackers. It's located at the head of Stuarts Fork Trail, about two miles from the western shore of Trinity Lake. The trail leads into the Trinity Alps Wilderness, along Stuarts

Fork, past Oak Flat, Morris Meadows, and up to Emerald Lake and the Sawtooth Ridge. It is a long and grueling climb, but fishing is excellent at Emerald Lake, as well as at neighboring Sapphire Lake. There's a great view of the Alps from this camp. It is set at 2,700 feet and open year-round, but there's **no piped water** in the winter and it gets mighty cold up here.

---

27. PINEWOOD COVE CAMPGROUND

Reference: **On Trinity Lake; map B1, grid e7.**

Campsites, facilities: There are 42 motor home sites with full or partial hookups and 37 tent sites. Picnic tables and fire grills are provided. Restrooms, showers, a laundromat, a sanitary disposal station, RV supplies, free movies three nights a week, a recreation room, pinball and video machines, a grocery store, ice, fishing tackle, a library, a boat dock with 32 slips, a beach and boat rentals are available. Pets are permitted.

Reservations, fee: Reservations recommended in summer; $15-$20 fee per night.

Who to contact: Phone (916) 286-2201.

Location: From Redding, turn west on Highway 299 and drive to Weaverville. In Weaverville, turn north on Highway 3 and drive 14 miles to the campground entrance.

Trip note: This is a privately-operated camp with full boating facilities at Trinity Lake. If you don't have a boat, but want to get on Trinity Lake, this can be a good starting point. A reservation is advised during the peak summer season. The elevation is 2,300 feet. Open April 15 to October 31.

---

28. RIDGEVILLE ISLAND BOAT-IN CAMP

Reference: **On Trinity Lake in Shasta-Trinity National Forest; map B1, grid e8.**

Campsites, facilities: There are three tent sites. Vault toilets, picnic tables and fire grills are provided. There is **no piped water,** so bring your own. Boat ramps can be found near Clark Springs Campground, Alpine View Campground or further north at Trinity Center. Pets are allowed on leashes.

Reservations, fee: No reservations; no fee.

Who to contact: Phone the Shasta-Trinity National Forest District Office at (916) 623-2121.

Location: From Redding, turn west on Highway 299 and drive to Weaverville. In Weaverville, turn north on Highway 3 and drive seven miles to the Stuarts Fork arm of Trinity Lake. Boat launches are located at Stuarts Fork. After launching, drive your boat to the mouth of Stuarts Fork; the campground is set on a small island here.

Trip note: This is one of the 100 featured campgrounds in my book, *Easy Camping in Northern California.* Why? Well, how would you like to be on a deserted island for a week? You'll learn the answer from this tiny, little-known island with a great view of the Trinity Alps. It is one of several boat-in camps in this region of Trinity Lake. The elevation is 2,500 feet.

29. RIDGEVILLE BOAT-IN CAMP

Reference: **On Trinity Lake in Shasta-Trinity National Forest; map B1, grid e8.**

Campsites, facilities: There are 11 tent sites. Vault toilets, picnic tables and fire grills are provided. There is **no piped water,** so bring your own. Boat ramps can be found near Clark Springs Campground, Alpine View Campground or further north at Trinity Center. Pets are allowed on leashes.

Reservations, fee: No reservations; no fee.

Who to contact: Phone Shasta-Trinity National Forest District Office at (916) 623-2121.

Location: From Redding, turn west on Highway 299 and drive to Weaverville. In Weaverville, turn north on Highway 3 and drive seven miles to the Stuarts Fork arm of Trinity Lake. Boat launches are located at Stuarts Fork. After launching, drive your boat to the mouth of Stuarts Fork. The campground is set on the western shore at the end of a peninsula at the entrance to that part of the lake.

Trip note: This is one of the ways to get a camping spot to call your own—go by boat. The camp is exposed on a peninsula, providing beautiful views. Good prospects for waterskiing and fishing for trout or bass make for a highlight film. The early part of the season is the prime time here for boaters, prior to the furnace heat of full summer, with trout and bass both on the bite. A great view of the Trinity Alps is a bonus. The only downer is the typical lake drawdown at the end of summer and beginning of fall, when this boat-in camp is left a long traipse from water's edge.

---

30. HAYWARD FLAT

Reference: **On Trinity Lake in Shasta-Trinity National Forest; map B1, grid e8.**

Campsites, facilities: There are 94 sites for tents or motor homes up to 40 feet long and four multi-family sites. Piped water, flush toilets, picnic tables and fire grills are provided. Supplies and a boat ramp are available nearby. Pets are allowed on leashes.

Reservations, fee: Reserve by calling (800) 280-CAMP; $10-$17 fee per night; $7.50 reservation fee.

Who to contact: Phone the Shasta-Trinity National Forest District Office at (916) 623-2121.

Location: From Redding, turn west on Highway 299 and drive to Weaverville. In Weaverville, turn north on Highway 3 and drive about 20 miles (about three miles past the Mule Creek Ranger Station). Turn right at the signed access road for Hayward Flat and drive about three miles to the campground at the end of the road.

Trip note: When giant Trinity Lake is full of water, Hayward Flat is one of the prettiest places you could ask for. The camp has become one of the most popular Forest Service campgrounds on Trinity Lake, because it sits right along the shore and offers a "private" beach for Hayward Flat campers only. The elevation is 2,400 feet. Open mid-May through mid-September.

31. MINERSVILLE ⌐🐟 ⚓ 🏃 ⚓ 🎣   RV 7

Reference: On Trinity Lake in Shasta-Trinity National Forest; map B1, grid e8.
Campsites, facilities: There are 21 sites for tents or motor homes up to 18 feet long.
  Piped water (spring, summer and fall only), flush toilets, picnic tables, fire
  grills and a low-water boat ramp are provided. Pets are allowed on leashes.
Reservations, fee: No reservations; $9-$15 fee per night.
Who to contact: Phone the Shasta-Trinity National Forest District Office at (916)
  623-2121.
Location: From Redding, turn west on Highway 299 and drive to Weaverville. In
  Weaverville, turn north on Highway 3 and drive about 18 miles (if you reach
  the Mule Creek Ranger Station, you have gone a half-mile too far). Turn right
  at the signed campground access road and drive a half-mile to the campground.
Trip note: This is a good camp for boaters, with a boat ramp located in the cove
  a short distance to the north. The setting is near lakeside, quite beautiful when
  Trinity Lake is fullest in the spring and early summer. The elevation is 2,500
  feet. Open year-round, but there's **no piped water** in the winter.

32. STONEY POINT ⌐🐟 ⚓ 🏃 🏊 🎣   7

Reference: On Trinity Lake in Shasta-Trinity National Forest; map B1, grid e8.
Campsites, facilities: There are 22 tent sites. Piped water, flush toilets, picnic
  tables and fire grills are provided. Pets are permitted on leashes.
Reservations, fee: No reservations; $8 fee per night.
Who to contact: Phone the Shasta-Trinity National Forest District Office at (916)
  623-2121.
Location: From Redding, turn west on Highway 299 and drive to Weaverville. In
  Weaverville, turn north on Highway 3 and drive 14 miles (about a quarter-mile
  past the Stuarts Fork Bridge) to the campground.
Trip note: This is a popular spot at Trinity Lake, easily discovered and easily
  reached. It is set near the inlet of Stuarts Fork and often fills up. Two other
  campgrounds close by provide overflow options. The elevation is 2,400 feet.
  Open November to April.

33. TANNERY GULCH ⌐🐟 ⚓ 🏃 🏊 🎣   RV 8

Reference: On Trinity Lake in Shasta-Trinity National Forest; map B1, grid e8.
Campsites, facilities: There are 83 sites for tents or motor homes up to 40 feet long
  and four multi-family sites. Piped water, flush and vault toilets, picnic tables,
  a boat ramp and fire grills are provided. A grocery store is available nearby.
  Pets are permitted on leashes.
Reservations, fee: Reserve by calling (800) 280-CAMP ($7.50 reservation fee);
  $9-$15 fee per night.
Who to contact: Phone the Shasta-Trinity National Forest at (916) 623-2121.
Location: From Redding, turn west on Highway 299 and drive to Weaverville. In
  Weaverville, turn north on Highway 3 and drive 13.5 miles north to County
  Road 172. Turn right (east) on County Road 172 and drive 1.5 miles to the
  campground on the left side of the road.
Trip note: This is one of the more popular Forest Service camps set on the
  southwest shore of huge Trinity Lake. There's a nice beach near the campground, provided the infamous Bureau of Reclamation hasn't drawn the lake
  level down too far. It can be quite low in the fall. The elevation is 2,400 feet.

34. STONEY CREEK GROUP CAMP

Reference: On Trinity Lake in Shasta-Trinity National Forest; map B1, grid e8.

Campsites, facilities: This group campground can hold up to 50 people. Sites are for tents only. Piped water (spring, summer and fall only), flush toilets, picnic tables and fire grills are provided. Pets are permitted on leashes.

Reservations, fee: Reservations required; $30 fee per night.

Who to contact: Phone the Shasta-Trinity National Forest District Office at (916) 623-2121.

Location: From Redding, turn west on Highway 299 and drive to Weaverville. In Weaverville, turn north on Highway 3 and drive 14 .5 miles (about a half-mile past the Stuarts Fork Bridge) to the campground.

Trip note: A series of camps are located on the northern shore of the Stuarts Fork arm of Trinity Lake. This is one of two designed for groups (the other is Bushy Tail), and it is clearly the better. It is set along the Stoney Creek Arm, a cove with a feeder creek, with the camp large but relatively private. A swimming beach nearby is a bonus. The elevation is 2,400 feet. Open year-round, but there's **no piped water** in the winter.

35. BUSHY TAIL GROUP CAMP

Reference: On Trinity Lake in Shasta-Trinity National Forest; map B1, grid e8.

Campsites, facilities: This group campground can hold up to 200 people. Sites are for tents or motor homes up to 22 feet long. Piped water, flush toilets, picnic tables and fire grills are provided. Supplies and a boat ramp are available nearby. Pets are allowed on leashes.

Reservations, fee: Reservations required; $30 group fee per night.

Who to contact: Phone the Shasta-Trinity National Forest District Office at (916) 623-2121.

Location: From Redding, turn west on Highway 299 and drive to Weaverville. In Weaverville, turn north on Highway 3 and drive 17 miles (about three miles past the Stuarts Fork Bridge) to the campground entrance road on the right. Turn right and drive a short distance to the camp on the left side of the road.

Trip note: This is a huge group camp at Trinity Lake, the kind of place where you might want to have a political convention. Then you could tell some politician to go jump in a lake. (Haven't you always wanted to do that?) What the heck, it's pretty enough to want to jump in yourself, and with a boat launch nearby, you get a bonus. The elevation is 2,500 feet. Open May through September.

36. CLARK SPRINGS

Reference: On Trinity Lake in Shasta-Trinity National Forest; map B1, grid e8.

Campsites, facilities: There are 21 tent sites. Piped water (spring, summer and fall only), flush toilets, picnic tables and fire grills are provided. A grocery store and boat ramp are nearby. Pets are allowed on leashes.

Reservations, fee: No reservations; no fee.

Who to contact: Phone the Shasta-Trinity National Forest District Office at (916) 623-2121.

Location: From Redding, turn west on Highway 299 and drive to Weaverville. In Weaverville, turn north on Highway 3 and drive 18 miles (about five miles past the Stuarts Fork Bridge) to the campground entrance road on the right.

Trip note: This used to be a day-use-only picnic area, but by popular demand, the Forest Service has opened it for camping. That makes sense because people were bound to declare it a campground anyway, since it has a nearby boat ramp and a beach. The elevation is 2,400 feet. Open year-round, but there's **no piped water** in the winter.

37. MARINERS ROOST BOAT-IN CAMP

Reference: On Trinity Lake in Shasta-Trinity National Forest; map B1, grid e8.

Campsites, facilities: There are seven tent sites. Vault toilets, picnic tables and fire grills are provided. There is **no piped water,** so bring your own. Boat ramps can be found near Clark Springs Campground, Alpine View Campground or further north at Trinity Center. Pets are allowed on leashes.

Reservations, fee: No reservations; no fee.

Who to contact: Phone the Shasta-Trinity National Forest District-Office at (916) 623-2121.

Location: From Redding, turn west on Highway 299 and drive to Weaverville. In Weaverville, turn north on Highway 3 and drive seven miles to the Stuarts Fork arm of Trinity Lake. Boat launches are located at Stuarts Fork. After launching, drive your boat to the mouth of Stuarts Fork and look for the camp on the Peninsula just east of Ridgeville Island Boat-In Camp, on the opposite shore from Ridgeville Boat-In Camp.

Trip note: A perfect boat camp? This comes close at Trinity. It is positioned perfectly for boaters, with spectacular views of the Trinity Alps to the west, an ideal spot for waterskiers. That is because it is located on the western side of the lake's major peninsula, topped by Bowerman Ridge. This area is secluded and wooded, set at 2,400 feet elevation.

38. FAWN GROUP CAMP

Reference: On Trinity Lake in Shasta-Trinity National Forest; map B1, grid e8.

Campsites, facilities: This group campground can hold up to 300 people. Sites are for tents or motor homes up to 37 feet long. Piped water, flush toilets, picnic tables and fire grills are provided. Pets are permitted on leashes.

Reservations, fee: Reservations required; $40 fee per night.

Who to contact: Phone the Shasta-Trinity National Forest District Office at (916) 623-2121.

Location: From Redding, turn west on Highway 299 and drive to Weaverville. In Weaverville, turn north on Highway 3 and drive 15 miles to the campground.

Trip note: If you want Trinity Lake all to yourself, one way to do it is to get a group together and then reserve this camp near the shore of Trinity Lake. The elevation is 2,500 feet. Open May through September.

39. RUSH CREEK

Reference: In Shasta-Trinity National Forest, north of Weaverville; map B1, grid f6.

Campsites, facilities: There are 10 sites for tents only. Picnic tables and fire pits are provided. Vault toilets are available. **No piped water** is available. No trash facilities are provided, so bring a garbage bag to pack out all refuse.

Reservations, fee: No reservations; no fee.

Who to contact: Phone Shasta-Trinity National Forest at (916) 623-2121.

Location: From Redding, turn west on Highway 299 and drive to Weaverville. In Weaverville, turn north on Highway 3 and drive about eight miles to the signed turnoff on the left side of the road. Turn left and drive one-quarter mile on the short spur road to the campground on the left side of the road. If you get to Forest Road 113, you've gone too far.

Trip notes: This small, primitive camp provides overflow space during busy holiday weekends when the camps at Lewiston and Trinity lakes are near capacity. It may not be much, but hey, at least if you know about Rush Creek, you'll never get stuck for a spot. The camp is set along Rush Creek, and secluded, but again, it is nearly five miles to the nearest access point to Trinity Lake.

40. CAPTAIN'S POINT BOAT-IN CAMP

Reference: **On Trinity Lake in Shasta-Trinity National Forest; map B1, grid f8.**

Campsites, facilities: There are three tent sites. Vault toilets, picnic tables and fire grills are provided. There's **no piped water,** so bring your own. Boat ramps can be found near Clark Springs Campground, Alpine View Campground or further north at Trinity Center. Pets are allowed on leashes.

Reservations, fee: No reservations; no fee.

Who to contact: Phone the Shasta-Trinity National Forest District Office at (916) 623-2121.

Location: From Redding, turn west on Highway 299 and drive to Weaverville. In Weaverville, turn north on Highway 3 and drive about seven miles to the signed turnoff on the right side of the road for Trinity Alps Marina. Turn right and drive about 10 miles to the marina and boat ramp. Launch your boat and cruise north about four miles up the main Trinity River arm of the lake. Look for Captain's Point on the left side of the lake.

Trip note: The Trinity River arm of Trinity Lake is a massive piece of water, stretching north from the giant Trinity Dam for nearly 20 miles. This camp is the only boat-in camp along this entire stretch of shore, and it is situated at a prominent spot, where a peninsula juts well out into the main lake body. This is a perfect boat-in site for waterskiers or fishermen. The fishing is often excellent for smallmouth bass in the cove adjacent to Captain's Point, using grubs. The elevation is 2,400 feet.

41. ALPINE VIEW

Reference: **On Trinity Lake in Shasta-Trinity National Forest; map B1, grid e9.**

Campsites, facilities: There are 66 sites for tents or motor homes up to 32 feet long. Piped water, flush toilets, picnic tables and fire grills are provided. Pets are permitted on leashes. The Bowerman Boat Ramp is next to the camp.

Reservations, fee: No reservations; $9 fee per night.

Who to contact: Phone the Shasta-Trinity National Forest District Office at (916) 623-2121.

Location: From Redding, turn west on Highway 299 and drive to Weaverville. In Weaverville, turn north on Highway 3 and drive to Covington Mill (six miles south of Trinity Center). Turn right (south) on Guy Covington Road and drive three miles to the camp (one mile past Bowerman Boat Ramp) on the right side of the road.

Trip note: It is an attractive area, set on the shore of Trinity Lake at a creek inlet, and is again open after a temporary closure due to a major restoration project. The boat ramp nearby provides a bonus. It is a very pretty spot, with views to the west across the lake arm and to the Trinity Alps, featured by Granite Peak. The Forest Service also runs tours from the campground to historic Bowerman Barn, which was built in 1894. The elevation is 2,400 feet. Open mid-May through mid-September (rarely it is closed temporarily when lake levels are extremely low.)

42. BIG SLIDE

Reference: On the South Fork of Trinity River in Shasta-Trinity National Forest; map B1, grid f0.

Campsites, facilities: There are four tent sites and four sites for tents or motor homes. Piped water, vault toilets, picnic tables and fire grills are provided. Pets are permitted on leashes.

Reservations, fee: No reservations; no fee.

Who to contact: Phone the Shasta-Trinity National Forest District Office at (916) 628-5227.

Location: From Redding, turn west on Highway 299 and drive over the Buckhorn Summit and continue to the junction with Highway 3 near Douglas City. Turn left (south) on Highway 3 and drive to Hayfork. From Hayfork, turn right (west) on County Road 301 and drive about 20 miles to the town of Hyampom. In Hyampom, turn right on Lower South Fork Road (County Road 311) and drive five miles on County Road 311.

Trip note: This camp is literally out in the middle of nowhere. Free? Of course it's free. Otherwise, someone would actually have to show up now and then to collect. It's a tiny, secluded, little-visited spot set along the South Fork of the Trinity River. The elevation is 1,200 feet. Open April through November.

43. EAST WEAVER

Reference: On the east branch of Weaver Creek in Shasta-Trinity National Forest; map B1, grid f7.

Campsites, facilities: There are eight tent sites and seven sites for tents or motor homes up to 16 feet long. Piped water (spring, summer and fall only), vault toilets, picnic tables and fire grills are provided. Pets are permitted on leashes. Supplies and a laundromat are available in Weaverville.

Reservations, fee: No reservations; $5 fee per night.

Who to contact: Phone Shasta-Trinity National Forest District Office at (916) 623-2121.

Location: From Redding, turn west on Highway 299 and drive to Weaverville. In Weaverville, turn right (north) on Highway 3 and drive about two miles to East Weaver Road. Turn left (north) on East Weaver Road and drive 3.5 miles to the campground.

Trip note: This camp is set along East Weaver Creek. Another mile to the west on East Weaver Road, the road deadends at a trailhead, a good side trip. From here, the hiking trail is routed four miles, a significant climb, to tiny East Weaver Lake, set to the southwest of Monument Peak (7,771 feet elevation). The elevation at East Weaver Camp is 2,700 feet. Open year-round, but there's **no piped water** in the winter.

44. OLD LEWISTON BRIDGE RV RESORT

Reference: **On Trinity River; map B1, grid f7.**

Campsites, facilities: There are 52 motor home sites with full hookups and a separate area for tents. Restrooms, hot showers, a laundromat and picnic tables are provided. A grocery store and propane gas refills are available. A group picnic area is available by reservation. Supplies can be obtained in Lewiston. Pets are allowed on leashes.

Reservations, fee: Reservations required; $18 fee per night.

Who to contact: Phone (916) 778-3894.

Location: From Redding, turn west on Highway 299 and drive over Buckhorn Summit and continue for five miles to County Road 105. Turn right on County Road 105 and drive four miles to Lewiston and continue north to the junction of Rush Creek Road and Trinity Dam Road. Turn west on Rush Creek Road and drive three-quarters of a mile to the resort.

Trip note: Though much of the water from Trinity and Lewiston lakes is diverted via tunnel to Whiskeytown Lake (en route to the valley and points south), enough escapes downstream to provide a viable fishery on the stretch of river near the town of Lewiston. This upstream portion below Lewiston Lake is prime in the early summer for trout, particularly the chance for a huge brown trout (special regulations in effect). In the winter, the stretch near Steel Bridge is often good for steelhead. The campground is in a hilly area, but has level sites, with nearby Lewiston Lake a major attraction.

45. TRINITY RIVER LODGE RV RESORT

Reference: **On Trinity River, Map B1, grid f7.**

Campsites, facilities: There are 60 motor home sites, all with full hookups, and 18 tent sites. Restrooms, hot showers, laundromat, cable TV, a recreation room with movies, a playground, propane gas, a camp store, ice, wood, furnished trailer rentals, boat and trailer storage, volleyball, horseshoes, badminton and croquet are available. There is lake fishing nearby. Pets are allowed on leashes.

Reservations, fee: Reservations required; $12-$18 fee per night.

Who to contact: Phone (916) 778-3791.

Location: From Redding, turn west on Highway 299 and drive over Buckhorn Summit and continue for five miles to County Road 105. Turn right on County Road 105 and drive four miles to Lewiston and continue north to the junction of Rush Creek Road and Trinity Dam Road. Turn west on Rush Creek Road and drive two miles to the campground.

Trip note: For many, this privately-operated park is set in an ideal location. You get level, grassy sites along the Trinity River, yet it is just a short drive north to Lewiston Lake or a bit farther to giant Trinity Lake. Lake or river, take your pick. Open year-round.

46. ACKERMAN

Reference: **On Lewiston Lake in Shasta-Trinity National Forest; map B1, grid f8.**

Campsites, facilities: There are 66 sites for tents or motor homes up to 40 feet long. Piped water (spring, summer and fall only), flush toilets, picnic tables and fire grills are provided. A sanitary dump station is available. Pets are permitted on leashes.

Reservations, fee: No reservations; $9 fee per night.

Who to contact: Phone the Shasta-Trinity National Forest District Office at (916) 623-2121.

Location: From Redding, turn west on Highway 299 and drive over Buckhorn Summit and continue for five miles to County Road 105. Turn right on County Road 105 and drive four miles to Lewiston and continue north on County Road 105 (Buckeye Creek Road) for eight miles to the campground.

Trip note: Of the camps and parks at Lewiston Lake, Ackerman is located closest to the lake's headwaters. This stretch of water below Trinity Dam is the best area for trout fishing on Lewiston Lake. Nearby Pine Cove Fishing Access, located two miles south of the camp, offers the only boat ramp on Lewiston Lake with docks and a fish-cleaning station—a popular spot for fishermen. When the Trinity powerhouse is running, trout fishing is excellent in this area. The elevation is 2,000 feet. Open year-round, but there's **no piped water** in winter.

47. LAKEVIEW TERRACE RESORT

Reference: **On Lewiston Lake; map B1, grid f8.**

Campsites, facilities: There are 35 motor home sites with full hookups and cabins with one to five bedrooms. Restrooms, hot showers, a laundromat, a dump station, a heated pool, propane gas and boat rentals are available. A grocery store is nearby. Pets are allowed on leashes.

Reservations, fee: Reservations accepted; $17 fee per night. Cabins are $42-$80 per night.

Who to contact: Phone (916) 778-3803.

Location: From Redding, turn west on Highway 299 and drive over Buckhorn Summit and continue for five miles to County Road 105. Turn right on County Road 105 and drive four miles to Lewiston, then continue north on Trinity Dam Boulevard for five miles to the resort on the left side of the road.

Trip note: This might be your Golden Pond. It's a terraced motor home park—with cabin rentals and campsites also available—that overlooks Lewiston Lake, one of the prettiest drive-to lakes in the region. Fishing for trout is excellent from Lakeview Terrace on upstream toward the dam. Lewiston Lake is perfect for fishing, with a 10-mile-per-hour speed limit in effect (all the hot boats go to nearby Trinity), along with excellent prospects for rainbow and brown trout. The topper is that Lewiston Lake is always full to the brim, just the opposite of the up-and-down nightmare of its neighboring big brother, Trinity Lake.

48. MARY SMITH

Reference: **On Lewiston Lake in Shasta-Trinity National Forest; map B1, grid f8.**

Campsites, facilities: There are 18 tent sites. Piped water, flush and vault toilets, picnic tables and fire grills are provided. Pets are permitted on leashes. Supplies and a laundromat are available in Lewiston.

Reservations, fee: No reservations; $8 fee per night.

Who to contact: Phone the Shasta-Trinity National Forest Weaverville District

Office at (916) 623-2121.

Location: From Redding, turn west on Highway 299 and drive over Buckhorn Summit and continue for five miles to County Road 105. Turn right on County Road 105 and drive four miles to Lewiston, and continue 2.5 miles north on County Road 105 (Buckeye Creek Road) to the campground.

Trip note: This is one of the prettiest spots you'll ever see, set along the southwestern shore of Lewiston Lake. When you wake up, peek out of your sleeping bag and see this serene lake so nearby, the natural beauty can take your breath away. Hand-launch boats, such as canoes, are ideal here. Trolling for trout is only fair in this end of the lake; most of the fish are below the Trinity Dam. Birdwatching is good, however. The elevation is 2,000 feet. Open April through October.

---

49. COOPER GULCH 🐟 🏃 ♿

Reference: **On Lewiston Lake in Shasta-Trinity National Forest; map B1, grid f8.**

Campsites, facilities: There are five sites for tents or motor homes up to 16 feet long. Vault toilets, picnic tables and fire grills are provided, but there's **no piped water,** so bring your own. Pets are permitted on leashes. Supplies and a laundromat are available in Lewiston. Some facilities are **wheelchair accessible.**

Reservations, fee: No reservations; no fee.

Who to contact: Phone the Shasta-Trinity National Forest District Office at (916) 623-2121.

Location: From Redding, turn west on Highway 299 and drive over Buckhorn Summit and continue for five miles to County Road 105. Turn right on County Road 105 and drive four miles to Lewiston, then continue another four miles north on County Road 105 (Buckeye Creek Road) to the campground.

Trip note: Here is a nice spot along a beautiful lake, featuring a short trail to Baker Gulch, where a pretty creek enters Lewiston Lake. The trout fishing is good on the upper end of the lake (where the current starts) and upstream. The lake was recently designated as a wildlife viewing area, with large numbers of water-fowl and other birds often spotted near the tules offshore Lakeview Terrace. Bring all of your own supplies and plan on hunkering down here for a while. Open April through November.

---

50. TUNNEL ROCK 🐟 🏃 ⑦

Reference: **On Lewiston Lake in Shasta-Trinity National Forest; map B1, grid f8.**

Campsites, facilities: There are six tent sites. Vault toilets, picnic tables and fire grills are provided, but there is **no piped water,** so bring your own. Pets are allowed on leashes.

Reservations, fee: No reservations; no fee.

Who to contact: Phone the Shasta-Trinity National Forest District Office at (916) 623-2121.

Location: From Redding, turn west on Highway 299 and drive over Buckhorn Summit and continue for five miles to County Road 105. Turn right on County Road 105 and drive four miles to Lewiston, then continue another seven miles north on County Road 105 (Buckeye Creek Road) to the campground.

Trip note: This is a very small, primitive alternative to the Ackerman Camp, which is more developed and located another mile up the road to the north. The proximity to the Pine Cove boat ramp and fish-cleaning station, located less than two miles to the south, is a primary attraction. The elevation is 1,900 feet. Open year-round.

51. DOUGLAS CITY

Reference: On Trinity River; map B1, grid g6.

Campsites, facilities: There are 19 sites for tents or motor homes up to 30 feet long. Piped water, restrooms, picnic tables and fire grills are provided. Pets are permitted on leashes or otherwise controlled. Supplies are available in Douglas City.

Reservations, fee: No reservations; $8 fee per night.

Who to contact: Phone the Bureau of Land Management at (916) 224-2100.

Location: From Redding, turn west on Highway 299 and continue over the bridge at the Trinity River near Douglas City to Steiner Flat Road. Turn left on Steiner Flat Road and drive a half mile to the campground.

Trip note: If you want to camp along this stretch of the main Trinity River, this camp is your best bet. It is set off the main road, near the river, with good bank fishing access, the prime season being from mid-August through winter for salmon and steelhead. There's paved parking and a nice beach. This can be a good base camp for an off-season fishing trip on the Trinity River or a lounging spot during the summer. The elevation is 2,000 feet. Open May through October.

52. INDIAN CREEK RV & MOBILE HOME

Reference: On Trinity River; map B1, grid g6.

Campsites, facilities: There are 12 motor home sites with full hookups. Water, showers, flush toilets, picnic tables and a laundromat are provided. Supplies are available in Douglas City. Pets are allowed on leashes.

Reservations, fee: Reservations accepted; $17 fee per night.

Who to contact: Phone (916) 623-6332.

Location: From Redding, drive west on Highway 299 for 36 miles to the Indian Creek Park sign on the left. Turn left at the sign, drive a short distance, and look for the park entrance on the right.

Trip note: This privately-operated motor home park is set in the heart of Trinity River country across the road from the Trinity River. The elevation is 1,650 feet. Open year-round.

53. STEELBRIDGE

Reference: On Trinity River; map B1, grid g7.

Campsites, facilities: There are eight sites for tents or motor homes up to 30 feet long. There is **no piped water,** but pit toilets, picnic tables and fire grills are provided. Pets are permitted on leashes or otherwise controlled. Supplies are available in Douglas City.

Reservations, fee: No reservations; no fee.

Who to contact: Phone the Bureau of Land Management at (916) 224-2100.

Location: From Redding, turn west on Highway 299, drive over Buckhorn Summit and continue toward Douglas City to Steel Bridge Road (if you reach

Douglas City, you have gone 2.3 miles too far). At Steel Bridge Road, turn right and drive about four miles to the campground at the end of the road.

Trip note: Very few campers know of this spot, primarily because it is operated by the publicity-shy Bureau of Land Management, but it is a prime spot for angler/campers. It's one of the better stretches of water in the area for steelhead, with good shorefishing access. The prime time is from October through December. In the summer, the shade of conifers will keep you cool. Don't forget to bring your own water. The elevation is 2,000 feet. Open year-round.

54. PHILPOT

Reference: **On the North Fork of Salt Creek in Shasta-Trinity National Forest; map B1, grid h3.**

Campsites, facilities: There are six sites for tents or motor homes. Piped water, vault toilets, picnic tables and fire grills are provided. Pets are permitted on leashes.

Reservations, fee: No reservations; no fee.

Who to contact: Phone the Shasta-Trinity National Forest District Office at (916) 628-5227.

Location: From Redding, turn west on Highway 299 and drive over the Buckhorn Summit and continue to the junction with Highway 3 near Douglas City. Turn left (south) on Highway 3 and drive to Hayfork. From Hayfork, continue south on Highway 3 for about six miles to Plummer Lookout Road in Peanut. Turn right (west) on Plummer Lookout Road and drive one mile to the campground.

Trip note: It's time to join the Five Percent Club, that is, the five percent of the people who know the little-used, beautiful spots in California. This is one of those spots, set on the North Fork of Salt Creek on national forest land. The elevation is 2,600 feet. Open April through November. Remember: 95 percent of the people use five percent of the available areas. Why would anyone come here? To join the Five Percent Club, that's why.

55. DEERLICK SPRINGS

Reference: **On Browns Creek in Shasta-Trinity National Forest; map B1, grid h5.**

Campsites, facilities: There are 13 sites for tents or motor homes up to 20 feet long. Vault toilets, picnic tables and fire grills are provided. Pets are permitted on leashes or otherwise controlled.

Reservations, fees: No reservations; no fee.

Who to contact: Phone the Shasta-Trinity National Forest District Office at (916) 352-4211.

Location: From Red Bluff, turn west on Highway 36 (very twisty) and drive to the Forest Service ranger station in Platina. In Platina, turn north on Harrison Gulch Road and drive 10 miles to the campground.

Trip note: It's a long, twisty drive to this remote and primitive camp set on the edge of the Chanchelulla Wilderness, located in the transition zone where the valley's oak grasslands give way to conifers. This quiet little spot is set along Browns Creek. A trailhead just north of camp provides a streamside walk. The elevation is 3,100 feet. Open May through November.

56. BAILEY COVE

Reference: **On Ruth Lake in Six Rivers National Forest; map B1, grid i0.**

Campsites, facilities: There are 25 sites, a few of which are for motor homes up to 22 feet long. Piped water, vault toilets, picnic tables and fire grills are provided. A boat ramp and small marina is available nearby. Pets are allowed on leashes.

Reservations, fee: No reservations; $6 fee per night.

Who to contact: Phone the Six Rivers National Forest, Mad River Ranger District at (707) 574-6233.

Location: From Eureka, drive south on US 101 to Alton and the junction with Highway 36. Turn east on Highway 36 and drive about 50 miles to the town of Mad River. Turn right at the sign for Ruth Lake (Lower Mad River Road) and drive 13 miles to the campground on the right side of the road.

Trip note: Ruth Lake is the only major lake within a reasonable driving distance, although some people might argue with you over how reasonable this twisty drive is. Regardless, you end up at a camp along the east shore of Ruth Lake, where fishing for trout or bass and waterskiing are popular. What really wins out is that it is hot and sunny all summer, the exact opposite of the fogged-out Humboldt Coast. The elevation is 2,600 feet. Open May through October.

57. FIR COVE CAMPGROUND

Reference: **On Ruth Lake in Six Rivers National Forest; map B1, grid i0.**

Campsites, facilities: There are 19 single and three group sites. Several sites can accommodate motor homes up to 22 feet long. Piped water, vault toilets, picnic tables and fire grills are provided. Pets are allowed on leashes.

Reservations, fee: The campground is available for single family camping on summer weekends only, from Fridays after 2 p.m. to Mondays at 2 p.m. No reservations for single sites; $6 fee per night. This is a group camp the rest of the year; reserve group sites through the Mad River Ranger Station at (707) 574-6233; $15-$20 fee per night.

Who to contact: Phone the Six Rivers National Forest, Mad River Ranger Station, at (707) 574-6233.

Location: From Eureka, drive south on US 101 to Alton and the junction with Highway 36. Turn east on Highway 36 and drive about 50 miles to the town of Mad River. Turn right at the sign for Ruth Lake (Lower Mad River Road) and drive 12 miles to the campground on the right side of the road.

Trip note: This spot is situated along Ruth Lake adjacent to the Bailey Canyon Campground. It's a unique setup for groups only (and individual families on weekends). The elevation is 2,600 feet. Open May through October.

58. HELL GATE

Reference: **On the South Fork of Trinity River in Shasta-Trinity National Forest; map B1, grid i1.**

Campsites, facilities: There are 17 tent sites and seven sites for tents or motor homes up to 15 feet long. Piped water, vault toilets, picnic tables and fire grills are provided. The facilities are **wheelchair accessible**. Supplies are available in Forest Glen. Pets are permitted on leashes. There are 10 additional campsites that will take tents and motor homes up to 20 feet long, just a half-mile beyond this campground on the dirt road.

Reservations, fee: No reservations; $4 fee per night.

Who to contact: Phone the Shasta-Trinity National Forest District Office at (916) 628-5227.

Location: From Red Bluff, turn west on Highway 36 (very twisty) and drive past Platina to the junction with Highway 3. Continue west on Highway 36 for 10 miles to the campground entrance on the left side of the road. If you reach Forest Glen, you have gone one mile too far.

Trip note: This is a pretty spot set along the South Fork of the Trinity River that is visited by virtually no one. The prime feature is for hikers. The South Fork National Recreation Trail begins at the campground and follows the river for many miles. Additional trails branch off and up into the South Fork Mountains. The area is extremely hot in summer. The elevation is 2,300 feet. Open April through November.

59. FOREST GLEN

Reference: **On the South Fork of Trinity River in Shasta-Trinity National Forest; map B1, grid i1.**

Campsites, facilities: There are 15 sites for tents or motor homes up to 15 feet long. Piped water, vault toilets, picnic tables and fire grills are provided. Pets are permitted on leashes. Facilities are **wheelchair accessible**. Supplies are available in Forest Glen.

Reservations, fee: No reservations; $4 fee per night.

Who to contact: Phone the Shasta-Trinity National Forest District Office at (916) 628-5227.

Location: From Red Bluff, turn west on Highway 36 (very twisty) and drive past Platina to the junction with Highway 3. Continue west on Highway 36 for 11 miles to Forest Glen. The campground is set at the west end of town on the right side of the road.

Trip note: If you get stuck for a spot in this region, this camp almost always has sites open, even during three-day weekends. It is on the edge of a forest near the South Fork of the Trinity River. Open April through November.

60. BASIN GULCH

Reference: **In Shasta-Trinity National Forest; map B1, grid j5.**

Campsites, facilities: There are 13 sites for tents or motor homes up to 20 feet. Piped water, vault toilets, picnic tables and fire grills are provided. Pets are permitted on leashes or otherwise controlled.

Reservations, fees: No reservations; $6 fee per night.

Who to contact: Phone the Shasta-Trinity National Forest District Office at (916) 352-4211.

Location: From Red Bluff, drive about 45 miles west on Highway 36 to the Yolla Bolly District Ranger Station. From the ranger station, turn south on Stuart Gap Road and drive two miles to the campground.

Trip note: This is one of three little-known campgrounds set in the vicinity, which rarely get much use. A trail out of this camp climbs Noble Ridge, eventually rising to a good lookout at 3,933 feet elevation, providing sweeping views of the north valley. Of course, you could also just drive there, taking a dirt road out of Platina. There are many backcountry Forest Service roads in the area. Your best bet is to get a Shasta-Trinity National Forest map, which details them. The elevation is 2,600 feet. Open April through November.

61. BEEGUM GORGE 🚶🚶

Reference: **In Shasta-Trinity National Forest; map B1, grid j5.**

Campsites, facilities: There are two sites for tents or motor homes up to 20 feet. There is **no piped water**, but vault toilets, picnic tables and fire grills are provided. Pets are permitted on leashes or otherwise controlled.

Reservations, fees: No reservations; no fee.

Who to contact: Phone the Shasta-Trinity National Forest District Office at (916) 352-4211.

Location: From Red Bluff, turn west on Highway 36 and drive to Platina. In Platina, turn south on Forest Service Road 29N06 and drive 6.5 miles to the campground.

Trip note: If you want to get the heck away from anything and everything, this spot should be your calling. The camp is set along little Beegum Creek. The road to this camp dead-ends another mile down the road (west), at a trailhead for a hike that is routed along the creek for nearly five miles to North Fork Beegum Campground. Another route heads up nearby Little Red Mountain, but involves a 2,000-foot climb, often across dry, hot terrain. The payoffs include incredible views of the Yolla Bolly Middle Eel Wilderness and spectacular wildflower displays in the spring. The elevation at the camp is 2,200 feet. Open April through November.

MAP B2

NOR-CAL MAP .... see page 94
adjoining maps
NORTH (A2) .... see page 126
EAST (B3) .... see page 208
SOUTH (C2) .... see page 264
WEST (B1) .... see page 152

63 LISTINGS
PAGES 180-207

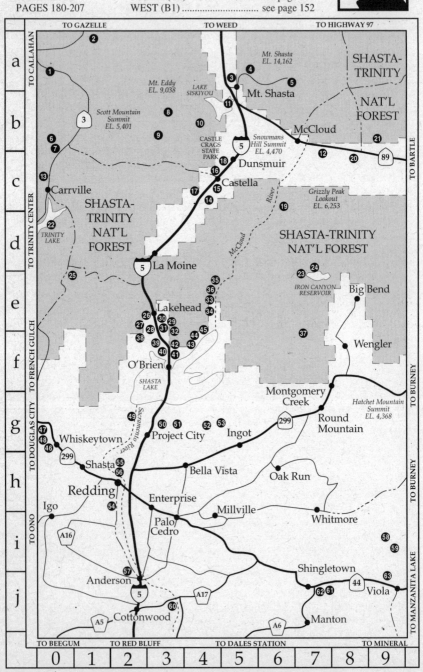

Map B2 featuring: Shasta-Trinity National Forest, Klamath National Forest, Mount Shasta, McCloud River, Sacramento River, Trinity Lake, Iron Canyon Reservoir, Shasta Lake, Whiskeytown Reservoir, Latour State Forest, Macumber Reservoir

1. SCOTT MOUNTAIN 👫

Reference: **In Shasta-Trinity National Forest; map B2, grid a0.**

Campsites, facilities: There are seven tent sites. Vault toilets, picnic tables and fire grills are provided, but there is **no piped water**, so bring your own. Pets are permitted on leashes.

Reservations, fee: No reservations; no fee.

Who to contact: Phone the Shasta-Trinity National Forest District Office at (916) 623-2121.

Location: From Redding, drive north on Interstate 5 just past Weed and take the Edgewood turnoff. At the stop sign, turn left and drive a short distance to a stop sign at Old Stage Road. Turn right on Old Stage Road and drive six miles to Gazelle. In Gazelle, turn left at Gazelle-Callahan Road and drive to Callahan. In Callahan, turn south on Highway 3 and drive to Scott Mountain Summit and look for the campground on the right side of the road.

Trip note: This camp is a jump-off point for hikers, with the Pacific Crest Trail passing right by the camp. If you hike southwest, it leads into the Scott Mountains and skirts the northern edge of the Trinity Alps Wilderness. Another option here is driving on Forest Service Road 40N08, which starts directly across Highway 3 from camp, and is only two miles to Big Carmen Lake, a small, largely unknown and pretty little spot. Campground elevation is 5,400 feet. Open year-round.

2. KANGAROO LAKE WALK-IN 🐟 👫 ♿ 🏊

Reference: **In Klamath National Forest; map B2, grid a1.**

Campsites, facilities: There are 15 walk-in sites for tents. Piped water, vault toilets, fire grills and picnic tables are provided. Pets are permitted on leashes or otherwise restrained. A fishing pier is available. Facilities are **wheelchair accessible**.

Reservations, fee: No reservations; $6-$8 fee per night.

Who to contact: Phone the Klamath National Forest Scott River Ranger District at (916) 468-5351.

Location: From Redding, drive north on Interstate 5 just past Weed and take the Edgewood turnoff. At the stop sign, turn left, drive a short distance to a stop sign at Old Stage Road. Turn right on Old Stage Road and drive six miles to Gazelle. In Gazelle, turn left at Gazelle-Callahan Road and drive over the summit. From the summit, continue about five miles to Rail Creek Road. Turn left at Rail Creek Road and drive about five miles to where the road dead-ends at Kangaroo Lake Campground.

Trip note: A remote paved road leads right to Kangaroo Lake, set at 6,050 feet, providing a genuine rarity: A beautiful and pristine mountain lake with a walk-in campground, good fishing for brook and rainbow trout, and an excellent trailhead for hikers. The walk to the campsites is very short, under five minutes tops, with many located within a minute's walk. Reaching the lake requires another five minutes, but a paved **wheelchair-accessible** trail is available. In addition, a switchbacked ramp for wheelchairs makes it one of the best wheelchair fishing experiences available anywhere in California. For hiking, a trail rises up steeply out of the campground and connects to the Pacific Crest Trail, from which you turn left to gain a dramatic lookout of Northern California peaks as well as the lake below.

3. KOA MT. SHASTA ♿ 🐟

Reference: **In Mt. Shasta; map B2, grid a5.**

Campsites, facilities: There are 41 motor home sites with full hookups, two camping cabins, and 89 additional sites for tents or motor homes (partial hookups). Restrooms, showers, fire grills, picnic tables, and a playground are provided. Propane gas, a grocery store and a laundromat are available. Pets are allowed on leashes.

Reservations, fee: Reservations accepted; $17.95-$24.95 fee per night. Cabins are $37 per night.

Who to contact: Phone (916) 926-4029.

Location: From Redding, drive north on Interstate 5 to the town of Mt. Shasta. Continue past the first Mt. Shasta exit and take the Central Mt. Shasta exit. Turn right at the stop sign and drive to the stoplight at Mt. Shasta Boulevard. Turn left and drive one-half mile to East Hinckley Boulevard. Turn right on East Hinckley, drive a very short distance, then turn left at the entrance to the extended driveway for Mt. Shasta KOA.

Trip note: Despite this KOA camp's relative proximity to the town of Mt. Shasta, the extended driveway, wooded grounds and view of Mt. Shasta offer a feeling of some seclusion. A bonus here is that those cute little KOA log cabins are available, providing additional privacy. There are many excellent side trips. The best is driving up Everitt Memorial Highway, which rises up the slopes of Mt. Shasta to tree line at Bunny Flat, where you can take outstanding, short day-hikes with great views to the south of the Sacramento River canyon and Castle Crags. In the winter, you can play in the snow.

4. McBRIDE SPRINGS 🚶 ⬛8

Reference: **In Shasta-Trinity National Forest; map B2, grid a5.**

Campsites, facilities: There are nine tent sites or motor home sites. Maximum length allowed for motor homes is 10 feet. Piped water, vault toilets, picnic tables and fire grills provided. Supplies and laundromat are available in the town of Mt. Shasta. Pets are permitted on leashes.

Reservations, fee: No reservations; $6 fee per night.

Who to contact: Phone the Shasta-Trinity National Forest District Office at (916) 926-4511.

Location: From Redding, drive north on Interstate 5 to the town of Mt. Shasta and take the Central Mt. Shasta exit. Turn right and continue on Lake Street through town; once out of town, it turns to the left and becomes Everitt Memorial Highway. Continue on Everitt Memorial Highway for four miles to the campground entrance on the left side of the road.

Trip note: This camp is set on the slopes of the awesome Mt. Shasta (14,162 feet), California's most majestic mountain. Stargazing is fantastic here, and during full moons, an eerie glow is cast on the adjoining high mountain slopes. A good side trip is to drive to the end of Everitt Memorial Highway, which tops out above 7,000 feet. You get great lookouts to the west and a jumpoff point for a Shasta expedition or day-hike to Panther Meadows. Open May through October.

5. PANTHER MEADOWS WALK-IN 🚶🚶

Reference: In Shasta-Trinity National Forest; map B2, grid a6.

Campsites, facilities: There are ten walk-in tent sites (trailers not recommended). Vault toilets, picnic tables and fire grills are provided, but there is **no piped water**. Supplies are available in the town of Mt. Shasta. Pets are permitted on leashes.

Reservations, fee: No reservations; no fee.

Who to contact: Phone the Shasta-Trinity National Forest District Office at (916) 926-4511.

Location: From Redding, drive north on Interstate 5 to the town of Mt. Shasta and take the Central Mt. Shasta exit. Turn right and continue on Lake Street through town; once out of town, it turns to the left and becomes Everitt Memorial Highway. Continue on Everitt Memorial Highway for about 10 miles to the Bunny Flat parking area (where the road is gated). Park, walk past the gate and continue for one mile to the campground entrance on the right side of the road.

Trip note: This quiet site, located on the slopes of Mt. Shasta at 7,400 feet, features access to the pristine Panther Meadows, a high mountain meadow set just below treeline. It's a sacred place, regardless of your religious orientation. The hiking is excellent here, with a short hike out to Gray Butte (8,108 feet) for a perfect look to the south of Castle Crags, Mt. Lassen and the Sacramento River Canyon.

6. HORSE FLAT 🚶🚶 🐎

Reference: On Eagle Creek in Shasta-Trinity National Forest; map B2, grid b0.

Campsites, facilities: There are five tent sites and 11 sites for tents or motor homes up to 16 feet long. Vault toilets, picnic tables and fire grills are provided, but there is **no piped water**, so bring your own. Pets are permitted on leashes. Horse corrals available.

Reservations, fee: No reservations; no fee.

Who to contact: Phone the Shasta-Trinity National Forest District Office at (916) 623-2121.

Location: From Redding, drive west on Highway 299 to Weaverville and Highway 3. Turn north on Highway 3 and drive to Trinity Center at the north end of Trinity Lake. From Trinity Center, continue north on Highway 3 for 16.5 miles to Eagle Creek Campground (on the right) and Forest Service Road 38N27 on the left. Turn left on Forest Service Road 38N27 and drive two miles to the campground.

Trip note: This camp gets used by commercial pack operations, as well as horse owners preparing for trips into the Trinity Alps. The camp even has a corral, though it was unused on our visit. A trail starts right out of camp and is routed deep into the Trinity Alps Wilderness. It starts at 3,200 feet in elevation, then climbs all the way along Eagle Creek to Eagle Peak, where it intersects with the Pacific Crest Trail, then drops over the ridge to little Telephone Lake, a nine-mile hike. Note: Horse owners should call for the condition of the corral prior to making your trip.

7. EAGLE CREEK

Reference: In Shasta-Trinity National Forest; map B2, grid b0.

Campsites, facilities: There are five tent sites and 12 sites for tents or motor homes up to 27 feet long. Piped water (spring, summer, and fall only), vault toilets, picnic tables and fire grills are provided. Pets are permitted on leashes.

Reservations, fee: No reservations, $5 fee per night.

Who to contact: Phone the Shasta-Trinity National Forest District Office at (916) 623-2121.

Location: From Redding, drive west on Highway 299 to Weaverville and Highway 3. Turn north on Highway 3 and drive to Trinity Center at the north end of Trinity Lake. From Trinity Center, continue north on Highway 3 for 16.5 miles to the campground on the right side of the road.

Trip note: This campground is set where little Eagle Creek enters the north Trinity River. Some campers use it as a base camp for a fishing trip, with the rainbow trout often abundant but predictably small in this stretch of water. The campground is open year-round, but there is **no piped water** in the winter. The elevation is 2,800 feet.

8. TOAD LAKE WALK-IN

Reference: In Shasta-Trinity National Forest; map B2, grid b3.

Campsites, facilities: There are six walk-in tent sites. Vault toilets are provided, but **no piped water**. Pets are permitted on leashes.

Reservations, fee: No reservations; no fee.

Who to contact: Phone the Shasta-Trinity National Forest District Office at (916) 926-4511.

Location: From the town of Mt. Shasta on Interstate 5, take the Central Mt. Shasta exit and drive to the stop sign. Turn left, cross the highway, and continue to another stop sign at W.A. Barr Road. Turn left and drive past Lake Siskiyou and continue up the mountain (the road becomes Forest Service Road 26). Just past a concrete bridge, turn right and drive a short distance, then turn left on Morgan Meadow Road and continue for 10 miles to the parking area. The road is extremely bumpy and twisty, and the final quarter-mile to the trailhead is rough. High-clearance, four-wheel-drive vehicles are recommended.

Trip note: If you want the remote beauty and splendor of an alpine lake on the Pacific Crest Trail, yet don't want to walk far to get there, this is the place. Little Toad Lake is no easy trick to get to, a bone-jarring ride for the last half hour, followed by a 15-minute walk, but it's worth the effort. It's a beautiful little lake in the Mt. Eddy Range, with lakeside sites, excellent swimming, fair fishing for small trout, and great hiking. The best of the latter is a 45-minute hike out of the Toad Lake Basin (follow the trail counterclockwise around the lake and up to the ridge) to Porcupine Lake, a pristine mountain lake. Open May (call first for snow conditions) through October.

9. GUMBOOT LAKE

Reference: In Shasta-Trinity National Forest; map B2, grid b3.

Campsites, facilities: There are four sites for tents or motor homes up to 10 feet long, and across the creek there are four tent sites. Vault toilets and picnic tables are provided, but there is **no piped water**. Pets are permitted on leashes.

Reservations, fee: No reservations; no fee.

Who to contact: Phone the Shasta-Trinity National Forest District Office at (916) 926-4511.

Location: From the town of Mt. Shasta on Interstate 5, take the Central Mt. Shasta exit and drive to the stop sign. Turn left, cross the highway, and continue to another stop sign at W.A. Barr Road. Turn left and drive past Lake Siskiyou and continue up the mountain (the road becomes Forest Service Road 26). Near the summit, look for the signed turn on the left side of the road for Gumboot Lake. Turn left and drive a half-mile to the lake.

Trip note: This pretty spot provides a few small camps set beside a small yet beautiful high mountain lake, the kind of place many think you can only reach with long hikes. Not so, not with Gumboot. In addition, the fishing is good here, with rainbow trout in the 12-inch class. The lake is small, almost too small for even a canoe, but better suited to a pram, raft or float tube. When the fishing gets good, it can get crowded, with both out-of-towners and locals making casts from the shoreline. An excellent hike is available here, tromping off-trail up the back slope of the lake to the Pacific Crest Trail, then turning left and scrambling to a great lookout of Mt. Shasta in the distance and Gumboot in the foreground. Open May through October.

---

10. CASTLE LAKE ⌇ ⬥ 🏃 ≋   🔺10

Reference: **In Shasta-Trinity National Forest; map B2, grid b4.**

Campsites, facilities: There are six sites for tents or motor homes up to 16 feet long. There is **no piped water,** but vault toilets, a picnic table and a fireplace are provided. Pets are permitted.

Reservations, fee: No reservations; no fee.

Who to contact: Phone the Shasta-Trinity National Forest District Office at (916) 926-4511.

Location: From the town of Mt. Shasta on Interstate 5, take the Central Mt. Shasta exit and drive to the stop sign. Turn left, cross the highway, and continue to another stop sign at W.A. Barr Road. Turn left and proceed over Box Canyon Dam at Lake Siskiyou, then one mile later, to Castle Lake Road. Turn left at Castle Lake Road and drive seven miles to the campground access road on the left. Turn left and drive a short distance to the campground. Note: Castle Lake is another quarter-mile up the road; there are no legal campsites along the lake's shoreline.

Trip note: Castle Lake is a beautiful spot, a deep blue lake set in a granite bowl with a spectacular wall on the far side. The views of Mt. Shasta are great, fishing is good (especially ice fishing in winter), canoeing or floating around on a raft is a lot of fun, and there is a terrific hike that loops around the left side of the lake, rising to the ridge overlooking the lake for dramatic views. The campground is not set right on the lake, to ensure the pristine clear waters remain untouched, but is rather just a short distance downstream along Castle Lake Creek. Open mid-May through October. The elevation is 5,450 feet.

---

11. LAKE SISKIYOU CAMP ⌇ ⬥ 🐟 ⚓ ≋ 🏃   🚐 🔺8

Reference: **Near Mt. Shasta; map B2, grid b5.**

Campsites, facilities: There are 124 motor home sites, (24 with partial and 75 with full hookups) and 225 additional sites for tents, four of which are group areas. There are also 11 RV rentals available. Piped water, flush toilets, fire grills, picnic tables, showers, a playground, propane, a grocery store, a gift shop, a deli, a laundromat and a sanitary disposal station are all available for campers' use. There are also boat rentals (canoes, kayaks, motorized boats), free boat launching, a wheelchair-accessible fishing dock, a fish-cleaning station, a beach, a recreation room, a banquet room, a restaurant and a snack bar. There is also a Geodesic dome housing complex and kitchen facilities. (Call for use fees). There is a free movie every night in the summer. Pets are allowed on leashes. Some facilities are **wheelchair-accessible.**

Reservations, fee: Reservations accepted; $13-$18 camping fee per night. RVs rent for $50-$70 per night. A $1 day-use fee is charged at the entrance station.

Who to contact: Phone (916) 926-2618.

Location: From the town of Mt. Shasta on Interstate 5, take the Central Mt. Shasta exit and drive to the stop sign. Turn left, cross the highway, and continue to another stop sign at W.A. Barr Road. Turn left and proceed over Box Canyon Dam at Lake Siskiyou. Two miles further, turn right at the entrance road for Lake Siskiyou Campground and Marina and drive a short distance to the entrance station.

Trip note: This is true gem of a lake, set virtually in the shadow of Mt. Shasta, always full or close to it, offering a variety of recreation. The campground complexes are huge, yet set in the forest so visitors don't get their style cramped. The lake is located within walking distance, but fishermen will want to drive, since a good boat ramp is available. The 10-mile-per-hour speed limit is strictly enforced. There is an excellent beach and swimming area, the latter protected by a buoy line. A restaurant and bar on the property add a bonus.

---

12. FOWLER'S CAMP

Reference: **On McCloud River in Shasta-Trinity National Forest; map B2, grid b7.**

Campsites, facilities: There are 39 sites for tents or motor homes up to 30 feet long. Piped water, vault toilets, picnic tables and fire grills are provided. Pets are permitted on leashes. The facilities are **wheelchair accessible**.

Reservations, fee: No reservations; $8 fee per night.

Who to contact: Phone the Shasta-Trinity National Forest District Office at (916) 964-2184.

Location: From Redding, drive north on Interstate 5 and continue just past Dunsmuir to the junction with Highway 89. Turn east on Highway 89 and drive to McCloud. From McCloud, drive five miles east on Highway 89 to the campground entrance road on the right. Turn right and drive a short distance to a Y, then turn left at the Y to the campground.

Trip note: This campground is set beside the beautiful McCloud River, providing the chance for an easy to hike to two waterfalls, including one of the most dramatic in Northern California. From the camp, the trail is routed upstream through forest, a near-level walk for only 15 minutes, then arriving at awesome Middle Falls, a wide-sweeping and powerful cascade, best viewed in April. By summer, the flows subside and warm to the point that some people will swim in the pool at the base of the falls. Another trail is routed from camp on downstream to Lower Falls, an outstanding swimming hole in midsummer. Fishing the McCloud River here is poor, with trout stocks suspended to protect native species of redband trout. If this camp is full, Cattle Camp and Algoma Camp offer overflow areas.

13. TRINITY RIVER

Reference: **In Shasta-Trinity National Forest; map B2, grid c0.**

Campsites, facilities: There are seven sites for tents or motor homes up to 32 feet long. Piped water (spring, summer, and fall only), vault toilets, picnic tables and fire grills are provided. Pets are permitted on leashes.

Reservations, fee: No reservations; $5 fee per night.

Who to contact: Phone the Shasta-Trinity National Forest District Office at (916) 623-2121.

Location: From Redding, drive west on Highway 299 to Weaverville and Highway 3. Turn north on Highway 3 and drive to Trinity Center at the north end of Trinity Lake. From Trinity Center, continue north on Highway 3 for 9.5 miles to the campground on the left side of the road.

Trip note: This camp provides easy access off Highway 3, yet is fairly secluded and provides streamside access to the upper Trinity River. It's a good base camp for a trout fishing trip when the upper Trinity is loaded with small trout. Open year-round, but there is **no piped water** in the winter. The elevation is 2,500 feet.

14. SIMS FLAT

Reference: **On Sacramento River; map B2, grid c4.**

Campsites, facilities: There are 19 sites for tents or motor homes up to 16 feet. Piped water, flush and vault toilets, picnic tables and fire grills are provided. Pets are permitted on leashes. A grocery store is nearby. The campground is **wheelchair accessible**.

Reservations, fee: No reservations; $8 fee per night.

Who to contact: Phone the Shasta-Trinity National Forest District Office at (916) 926-4511.

Location: From Redding, drive north on Interstate 5 for about 40 miles to the Sims Road exit. Take the Sims Road exit (on the east side of the highway) and drive south for one mile to the campground.

Trip note: The Upper Sacramento River is again becoming the No. 1 trout stream in America with direct access off an interstate highway. This camp is an example of the best of it. It sits beside the Upper Sacramento River, providing access to some of the better spots for trout fishing, particularly from mid-May through July. The trout population has largely recovered since the devastating spill from a train derailment that occurred in 1991. There is a **wheelchair-accessible** interpretive trail. If you want to literally get away from it all, there is a trailhead about three miles east on Sims Flat Road. This trail climbs along South Fork, including a terrible, steep, one-mile section near the top, eventually popping out at Tombstone Mountain. Open March through October.

15. CRAG VIEW VALLEY CAMP

Reference: **On Sacramento River; map B2, grid c4.**

Campsites, facilities: There are 10 sites (four drive-through), most with full hookups. There is a separate area for tents only. Picnic tables, fire grills, restrooms and hot showers are provided. A laundromat is available. Pets are allowed on leashes.

Reservations, fee: Reservations accepted; $10-$15 fee per night.

Who to contact: Phone (916) 235-0081.

Location: From Redding, drive north on Interstate 5 for 44 miles to the Castella exit. Turn right (south) on the frontage road on the east side of the highway and drive three-quarters of a mile to the campground.

Trip note: This camp is situated on the Sacramento River, below nearby Castle Crags State Park, and also near Castle Creek. There is access for trout fishing and good views of Castle Crags directly to the west and Mt. Shasta to the north. Open year-round.

---

16. CASTLE CRAGS STATE PARK   RV 9

Reference: **On Sacramento River; map B2, grid c4.**

Campsites, facilities: There are 64 sites for tents or motor homes up to 27 feet. Picnic tables, fire grills, piped water, hot showers and flush toilets are provided. Wood is available. Pets are permitted.

Reservations, fee: Reserve by phoning Destinet at (800) 444-7275 ($6.75 Destinet fee); $15-$17 fee per night.

Who to contact: Call (916) 235-2684.

Location: From Redding, drive north on Interstate 5 for 45 miles to the Castle Crags State Park exit. Turn west and drive (well-signed) to the park entrance on the right side of the road.

Trip note: Ancient granite spires tower 6,000 feet above the park, and beyond to the north, is the giant Mt. Shasta. Those prominent features make for a spectacular natural setting. The campsites are set in forest, shaded, very pretty, and sprinkled along a paved access road. At the end of the access road is a parking area for the two-minute walk to the Crags Lookout, a beautiful view. Nearby is the trailhead (at 2,500 feet elevation) for hikes up the Crags, featuring a six-mile round-trip that rises to Castle Dome at 4,966 feet, the leading spire on the crags ridge. Trout fishing is good in the nearby Sacramento River, but requires driving, walking and exploring to find the best spots. This is a popular state park, with reservations often required in summer months, yet with your choice of any campsite even in late spring. Open year-round.

---

17. BEST IN THE WEST RESORT   RV 3

Reference: **Near Dunsmuir; map B2, grid c4.**

Campsites, facilities: There are 16 motor home sites, most with full hookups. Five cabins are also available. Picnic tables are provided. Restrooms, hot showers, cable TV, ice, a laundromat, a playground, propane gas and horseshoes are available. Pets are allowed on leashes.

Reservations, fee: Reservations accepted; $15 fee per night. Cabins are $32-36 per night.

Who to contact: Phone at (916) 235-2603.

Location: From Redding, drive north on Interstate 5 for about 40 miles to the Sims Road exit. Take the Sims Road exit and drive one block west on Sims Road to the campground.

Trip note: This is a good layover spot for motor home cruisers looking to take a break. The proximity to Castle Crags State Park, the Sacramento River and Mt. Shasta make the location a winner.

18. RAILROAD PARK RESORT

Reference: **On Sacramento River; map B2, grid c5.**

Campsites, facilities: There are 60 sites, many with full hookups, and a separate area for tents only. Restrooms, hot showers, satellite TV hookups, grocery store, ice, laundromat, a restaurant, a recreation room, a playground and horseshoes are available. Pets are allowed.

Reservations, fee: Deposit required with reservation; $13-$18 fee per night.

Who to contact: Phone (916) 235-0420

Location: From Redding, drive north on Interstate 5 for 45 miles to Railroad Park Road. Turn west and drive a half-mile to the campground.

Trip note: This camp is set in the spirit of the railroad, when the steam trains ruled the rails. The property features old stage cars (which are available for overnight lodging) and a steam locomotive. Many good side trips are available in the area, including excellent hiking and sightseeing at Castle Crags State Park (where there are a series of awesome granite spires) and outstanding trout fishing on the upper Sacramento River.

19. AH-DI-NA

Reference: **On McCloud River in Shasta-Trinity National Forest; map B2, grid c6.**

Campsites, facilities: There are 16 tent sites. Piped water, flush toilets, picnic tables and fire grills are provided. Pets are permitted on leashes.

Reservations, fee: No reservations; $5 fee per night.

Who to contact: Phone the Shasta-Trinity National Forest District Office at (916) 964-2184.

Location: From Redding, drive north on Interstate 5 past Dunsmuir to the junction with Highway 89. Turn right and drive to McCloud. In McCloud, turn right on Squaw Valley Road and drive to Lake McCloud. Turn right at Lake McCloud and continue along the lake to a signed turnoff on the right side of the road (at a deep cove in the lake). Turn right (the road turns to dirt) and drive four miles to the campground entrance on the left side of the road. Turn left and drive a short distance to the campground.

Trip note: This is the perfect base camp for trout fishing on Lower McCloud River, with campsites set just a cast away from one of the prettiest streams in California. Downstream of the camp is a special two-mile stretch of river governed by The Nature Conservancy, where all fish must be released, no bait is permitted, single, barbless hooks are mandated, and only 10 rods are allowed on the river at any one time. Wildlife is abundant in the area, the Pacific Crest Trail passes adjacent to the camp, and an excellent nature trail is also available along the river in the McCloud Nature Conservancy.

20. CATTLE CAMP

Reference: **On McCloud River in Shasta-Trinity National Forest; map B2, grid c8.**

Campsites, facilities: There are 30 sites for tents or motor homes. **No piped water** is available, but vault toilets, picnic tables and fire grills are provided. Pets are permitted on leashes.

Reservations, fee: No reservations; no fee.

Who to contact: Phone the Shasta-Trinity National Forest District Office at (916)

964-2184.

Location: From Redding, drive north on Interstate 5 and continue just past Dunsmuir to the junction with Highway 89. Turn east on Highway 89 and drive to McCloud. From McCloud, drive 11 miles east on Highway 89 to the campground entrance road on the right. Turn right and drive a half mile to the campground on the left side of the road.

Trip note: This primitive campground is ideal for motor home campers that want a rustic setting, or as an overflow area if the more attractive Fowler's Camp is filled. One of the best swimming holes in the McCloud River is located near this camp, although the water is typically cold. There are several good side trips in the area, including fishing on the nearby McCloud River, visiting the three waterfalls near Fowler's Camp, or exploring the north slopes of Mt. Shasta (a map of Shasta-Trinity National Forest details the back roads).

21. ALGOMA

Reference: **On McCloud River in Shasta-Trinity National Forest; map B2, grid b9.**

Campsites, facilities: There are eight sites for tents or motor homes. There is **no piped water,** but vault toilets, picnic tables and fire grills are provided. Pets are permitted on leashes.

Reservations, fee: No reservations; no fee.

Who to contact: Phone the Shasta-Trinity National Forest District Office at (916) 964-2184.

Location: From Redding, drive north on Interstate 5 and continue just past Dunsmuir to the junction with Highway 89. Turn east on Highway 89 and drive to McCloud. From McCloud, drive 14 miles east on Highway 89 to the campground entrance road on the right. Turn right and drive one mile to the campground on the right side of the road.

Trip note: This little-known, undeveloped spot along the McCloud River is quite dusty in August. It is an alternative to Fowler's Camp and Cattle Camp. See the trip note for those camps for side-trip options. A dirt road out of camp (turn right at the junction) follows along the headwaters of the McCloud River, past Cattle Camp to Upper Falls, a parking area for a short walk to view Middle Falls, and on to Fowler's Camp and Lower Falls.

22. JACKASS SPRINGS

Reference: **On Trinity Lake in Shasta-Trinity National Forest; map B2, grid d0.**

Campsites, facilities: There are 21 sites for tents or motor homes up to 32 feet long. Piped water (spring, summer and fall only), vault toilets, picnic tables and fire grills are provided. Pets are permitted on leashes.

Reservations, fee: No reservations; no fee.

Who to contact: Phone the Shasta-Trinity National Forest District Office at (916) 623-2121.

Location: From Redding, turn west on Highway 299 and drive to Weaverville and the junction with Highway 3. Turn right on Highway 3 and drive 29 miles to Trinity Center. Continue five miles past Trinity Center, to County Road 106. Turn right on County Road 106 and drive 12 miles to the Jackass Springs turnoff (County Road 119). Turn right on County Road 119 and drive four miles to the campground at the end of the road.

Trip note: If you're poking around for a more secluded campsite on this end of the lake, halt your search and pick the best spot you can find at this campground, since it's the only one in this area of Trinity Lake. The camp is set on the remote east shore in a large, beautiful cove, complete with a little island just offshore. The only downer is that when the lake level is down, the water is a steep tromp from the campground. The elevation is 2,500 feet. Open year-round, but there's **no piped water** in winter.

23. HAWKINS LANDING 🐟 ⚓ 👫 🏊   RV 7

Reference: **On Iron Canyon Reservoir; map B2, grid d7.**

Campsites, facilities: There are 10 sites for tents or motor homes up to 16 feet long. Hand-pumped well water is available. Vault toilets, picnic tables and fire grills are provided. A boat ramp is available. Supplies can be obtained in Big Bend. Pets are allowed on leashes.

Reservations, fee: No reservations; $10 fee per night; $1 pet fee.

Who to contact: Phone PG&E at (916) 386-5164.

Location: From Redding, drive east on Highway 299 for 37 miles to Big Bend Road. At Big Bend Road, turn left (north) and drive 15.2 miles to the town of Big Bend. Continue for five miles to the lake, veering right at the T intersection, and continue for one mile to the boat launch/campground turnoff. Turn left and drive a quarter-mile to the campground.

Trip note: The adjacent boat ramp makes Hawkins Landing the better of the two camps at Iron Canyon Reservoir for campers with trailered boats (though Deadlun Camp is far more secluded). Iron Canyon provides good fishing for trout, has a resident bald eagle or two, and also has nearby hot springs available in the town of Big Bend. One problem with this lake is the annual drawdown in late fall, which causes the shoreline to be extremely muddy if visited in the spring; the lake usually rises high enough to make the boat ramp functional by mid-April.

24. DEADLUN 🐟 👫 🏊   RV 8

Reference: **On Iron Canyon Reservoir in Shasta-Trinity National Forest; map B2, grid d7.**

Campsites, facilities: There are 30 sites for tents or motor homes up to 24 feet long. There is **no piped water**, so bring your own. Vault toilets, picnic tables and fire grills are provided. A boat ramp is available one mile from the camp. Pets are permitted on leashes.

Reservations, fee: No reservations; no fee.

Who to contact: Phone the Shasta-Trinity National Forest District Office at (916) 275-1587.

Location: From Redding, drive east on Highway 299 for 37 miles to Big Bend Road. At Big Bend Road, turn left (north) and drive 15.2 miles to the town of Big Bend. Continue for five miles to the lake, veering right at the T intersection and continue for two miles (past the boat launch turnoff) to the campground turnoff on the left side of the road. Turn left and drive one mile to the campground.

Trip note: Deadlun is a pretty campground set in the forest, shaded and quiet, with a five-minute walk or one-minute drive to the Deadlun Creek arm of Iron Canyon Reservoir. Drive? If you have a canoe to launch or fishing equipment to carry, driving is the choice. Trout fishing is good here, both in April and May, then again in October and early November. One downer is that the shoreline is often very muddy here in March and early April. Because of an engineering error with the dam, the lake never fills completely, causing the lakeshore to be strewn with stumps and quite muddy after spring rains and snowmelt.

25. CLEAR CREEK

Reference: In Shasta-Trinity National Forest; map B2, grid e1.

Campsites, facilities: There are two tent sites and six sites for tents or motor homes up to 22 feet long. Vault toilets, picnic tables and fire grills are provided, but there is **no piped water**, so bring your own. Pets are allowed on leashes.

Reservations, fee: No reservations; no fee.

Who to contact: Phone the Shasta-Trinity National Forest District Office at (916) 623-2121.

Location: From Redding, turn west on Highway 299 and drive 17 miles to Trinity Lake Road (just west of Whiskeytown Lake). Turn north on Trinity Lake Road and continue past the town of French Gulch for about 12 miles to the Trinity Mountain ranger station. Turn right on County Road 106 (East Side Road, a gravel road) and drive north for about 11 miles to the campground access road (dirt) on right. Turn right on the access road and drive two miles to the campground.

Trip note: This is a primitive, little-known camp that gets extremely little use. It is set near Clear Creek at 3,500 feet elevation. In fall months, hunters will occasionally turn it into a deer camp, with the adjacent slopes of Blue Mountain and Damnation Peak in the Trinity Divide Country providing fair numbers of large bucks, three points or better. Trinity Lake is located only seven miles to the west, but seems like it's in a different world. That's because it is.

26. LAKESHORE VILLA RV PARK & CAMP

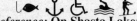

Reference: On Shasta Lake; map B2, grid e3.

Campsites, facilities: There are 92 sites with partial or full hookups. Picnic tables are provided. Restrooms, hot showers, a sanitary disposal station, satellite TV, a laundromat, a playground, a recreation room and a boat dock are available. Pets are permitted on leashes.

Reservations, fee: Deposit required with reservation; $20 fee per night.

Who to contact: Phone (916) 238-8688.

Location: From Redding, drive north on Interstate 5 for 24 miles to the Lakeshore-Antlers Road exit in Lakehead. Take that exit and, at the stop sign, turn left and drive under the freeway to Lakeshore Drive. Turn left on Lakeshore Drive and drive a half-mile to the campground on the right.

Trip note: This is a large campground with level, shaded sites for motor homes and tents, set near the northern Sacramento River arm of giant Shasta Lake. Prime time is from April through July, when lake levels are highest and the bass are on the bite.

27. LAKESHORE

Reference: On Shasta Lake; map B2, grid e3.

Campsites, facilities: There are 28 motor home sites with partial and full hookups. Picnic tables are provided. Restrooms, hot showers, a swimming pool, boat rentals, a boat dock and a small grocery store are available. Pets are allowed on leashes.

Reservations, fee: Reservations recommended; $12-$14 fee per night.
Who to contact: Phone (916) 238-2004.
Location: From Redding, drive north on Interstate 5 for 24 miles to the Lakeshore-Antlers Road exit in Lakehead. Take that exit and, at the stop sign, turn left and drive under the freeway to Lakeshore Drive. Turn left on Lakeshore Drive and drive one mile to the campground.
Trip note: Shasta Lake is a boater's paradise, and this camp is an ideal spot for campers with boats, with a boat ramp and private marina located available. It is located on the Sacramento River Arm of Shasta Lake.

28. SHASTA LAKE RV RESORT & CAMP

Reference: On Shasta Lake; map B2, grid e3.
Campsites, facilities: There are 21 tent sites and 53 motor home sites with full hookups. Picnic tables and fire grills are provided. Restrooms, hot showers, a grocery store, wood, a laundromat, a playground and a swimming pool are available. Pets are permitted. There is also a private dock with 36 boat slips.
Reservations, fee: Deposit required with reservation; $13-$20 fee per night.
Who to contact: Phone (916) 238-2370.
Location: From Redding, drive north on Interstate 5 for 24 miles to the Lakeshore-Antlers Road exit in Lakehead. Take that exit and, at the stop sign, turn left and drive under the freeway to Lakeshore Drive. Turn left on Lakeshore Drive and drive 1.5 miles to the campground.
Trip note: This camp is one of a series located on the upper end of Shasta Lake., with easy access off Interstate 5 by car, then easy access by boat to premium fishing for trout or bass as well as waterskiing.

29. GREGORY CREEK

Reference: On Shasta Lake in Shasta-Trinity National Forest; map B2, grid e3.
Campsites, facilities: There are five tent sites and 13 sites for tents or motor homes up to 24 feet long. Piped water, flush toilets, picnic tables and fire grills are provided. Pets are allowed on leashes.
Reservations, fee: Reservations accepted; $10 fee per night; $4 for each additional vehicle. For reservations call Shasta Recreation Company at (916) 238-2844.
Who to contact: Phone the Shasta-Trinity National Forest District Office at (916) 275-1587, or the Shasta Recreation Company at (916) 238-2844.
Location: From Redding, drive north on Interstate 5 for 21 miles to the Salt Creek exit. Take the Salt Creek exit and head east, driving four miles north on Gregory Creek Road to the campground at the end of the road.
Trip note: This is one of the more secluded Forest Service campgrounds on Shasta Lake. It is set just above lakeside, on the eastern shore of the northern Sacramento River arm of the lake. When the lake is fullest in the spring and early summer, this is a great spot. Open May to September.

30. ANTLERS RV RESORT & CAMPGROUND

Reference: On Shasta Lake; map B2, grid e3.
Campsites, facilities: There are 36 tent sites and 70 motor home sites, many with full hookups, and a separate area for tents. Restrooms, hot showers, a snack bar,

a grocery store, ice, a laundromat, a recreation room, a playground, shuffle-board, volleyball, swimming pool, propane gas, boats for rent, houseboats, moorage and a complete marina are available. Pets are permitted.

Reservations, fee: Deposit required with reservation; $12.50-$20 per night fee.

Who to contact: Phone (916) 238-2322.

Location: From Redding, drive north on Interstate 5 for 24 miles to the Lakeshore-Antlers Road exit in Lakehead. Take that exit and, at the stop sign, turn right and drive a short distance to Antlers Road. At Antlers Road, turn right and drive 1.5 miles south to the campground.

Trip note: Antlers Resort is set along the Sacramento River arm of Shasta Lake at 1,215 feet. The prime time to visit is from March through June when the lake levels are highest. This is a full-service spot for campers, boaters and anglers.

31. LAKEHEAD CAMP 🐟 ⚓ 🏊 🧍   RV 6

Reference: On Shasta Lake; map B2, grid e3.

Campsites, facilities: There are 20 tent sites and 30 motor home sites with full or partial hookups. Picnic tables, fire grills, restrooms, hot showers, a dump station, a store, wood, a laundromat, a heated swimming pool, bike rentals, horseshoes, volleyball and video games are available. An outdoor pavilion for groups is available. Pets are permitted on leashes. There's a boat ramp less than a mile from the campground.

Reservations, fee: Deposit required with reservation; $14-$18 fee per night from Memorial Day through Labor Day, with a 10% discount from October through April.

Who to contact: Call (916) 238-2671 or (800) 238-2627.

Location: From Redding, drive north on Interstate 5 for 24 miles to the Lakeshore-Antlers Road exit in Lakehead. Take that exit and, at the stop sign, turn right and drive a short distance to Antlers Road. At Antlers Road, turn left and drive a quarter-mile north to the campground on the right.

Trip note: This is one of the many campgrounds set around Shasta Lake. This one is particularly suited for motor home or pickup truck campers with trailer boats because there's a boat launch just a few minutes from the camp. The elevation is 1,200 feet. Open year-round, but best from March through June, when lake levels are highest.

32. ANTLERS 🐟 ⚓ 🏊 🧍   RV 7

Reference: On Shasta Lake in Shasta-Trinity National Forest; map B2, grid e3.

Campsites, facilities: There are 41 single sites and 18 double sites for tents or motor homes up to 30 feet long. Piped water, flush and vault toilets, picnic tables and fire grills are provided. A boat ramp, a grocery store and a laundromat are nearby. Pets are allowed on leashes.

Reservations, fee: Reservations accepted; phone the Shasta Recreation Company at (916) 238-2844; $12-$22 fee per night (reduced rates in winter).

Who to contact: Phone Shasta-Trinity National Forest District Office at (916) 275-1587.

Location: From Redding, drive north on Interstate 5 for 24 miles to the Lakeshore-Antlers Road exit in Lakehead. Take that exit and, at the stop sign, turn right and drive a short distance to Antlers Road. At Antlers Road, turn right and drive one mile south to the campground.

Trip note: This spot is set on the primary Sacramento River inlet of giant Shasta

Lake. Antlers is a well-known spot that gets returning campers and boaters year after year. It is the farthest upstream marina/camp on the lake. Because of that, lake levels can fluctuate greatly from spring through fall, and the operators will move their docks to compensate. Easy access off Interstate 5 is a big plus for boaters. Open year-round, with limited winter facilities.

33. ELLERY CREEK 🐟 ⚓ ♿ 🏊 🚣   RV 7

Reference: **On Shasta Lake in Shasta-Trinity National Forest; map B2, grid e4.**

Campsites, facilities: There are 19 sites for tents or motor homes up to 30 feet long. Piped water, vault toilets, picnic tables and fire grills are provided. Toilet facilities are **wheelchair accessible**. Pets are permitted on leashes.

Reservations, fee: Reservations accepted; phone the Shasta Recreation Company at (916) 238-2844; $10 fee per night.

Who to contact: Phone the Shasta-Trinity National Forest District Office at (916) 275-1587.

Location: From Redding, drive north on Interstate 5 for about 20 miles to the Gilman exit. Take Gilman Road (County Road 7H009) and drive northeast for 15 miles to the campground on the right side of the road.

Trip note: This camp is set at a pretty spot where Ellery Creek empties into the upper McCloud arm of Shasta Lake. This stretch of water is excellent for trout fishing in the summer, with bankfishing access available two miles upstream at the McCloud Bridge. In the spring, there are tons of small spotted bass along the shore from the camp on upstream to the inlet of the McCloud River. Open April to September.

34. MOORE CREEK 🐟 ⚓ 🏊 🚣   RV 7

Reference: **On Shasta Lake in Shasta-Trinity National Forest; map B2, grid e4.**

Campsites, facilities: There are 12 sites for tents or motor homes up to 16 feet long. Piped water, vault toilets, picnic tables and fire grills are provided. Pets are permitted on leashes.

Reservations, fee: Reservations accepted; phone the Shasta Recreation Company at (916) 238-2844; $10 fee per night.

Who to contact: Phone the Shasta-Trinity National Forest District Office at (916) 275-1587.

Location: From Redding, drive north on Interstate 5 for about 20 miles to the Gilman exit. Take Gilman Road (County Road 7H009) and drive northeast for 11 miles to the campground on the right side of the road.

Trip note: The McCloud arm of Shasta Lake is the most beautiful of the five arms at Shasta, with its emerald-green waters and limestone canyon towering overhead to the east. That beautiful setting is taken advantage of at this camp, with a good view of the lake and limestone, along with good trout fishing on the adjacent section of water. Open year-round.

35. McCLOUD BRIDGE 🐟 🥾   RV 7

Reference: **On Shasta Lake in Shasta-Trinity National Forest; map B2, grid e4.**

Campsites, facilities: There are 20 sites for tents or motor homes up to 16 feet long. Piped water, flush and vault toilets, picnic tables and fire grills are provided. Pets are permitted on leashes.

Reservations, fee: Reservations accepted; phone the Shasta Recreation Company at (916) 238-2844; $10 fee per night; $4 for each additional vehicle.

Who to contact: Phone the Shasta-Trinity National Forest District Office at (916) 275-1587.

Location: From Redding, drive north on Interstate 5 for about 20 miles to the Gilman exit. Take Gilman Road (County Road 7H009) and drive northeast for 19 miles to the campground.

Trip note: Even though reaching this camp requires a long drive, it remains popular. That is because the best shorefishing access at the lake is available at the nearby McCloud Bridge. It is common to see 15 or 20 people shorefishing here for trout on weekends. In the fall, big brown trout migrate through this section of lake en route to their upstream spawning grounds. Open April to September.

36. PINE POINT

Reference: **On Shasta Lake in Shasta-Trinity National Forest; map B2, grid e4.**

Campsites, facilities: There are 14 sites for tents or motor homes up to 24 feet. Vault toilets, picnic tables and fire rings are provided. There is piped water most of the year; it is turned off in the winter months. Pets are permitted on leashes.

Reservations, fee: Reservations accepted; phone the Shasta Recreation Company at (916) 238-2844; $10 fee per night.

Who to contact: Phone the Shasta-Trinity National Forest District Office at (916) 275-1587.

Location: From Redding, drive north on Interstate 5 for about 20 miles to the Gilman exit. Take Gilman Road (County Road 7H009) and drive northeast for 17 miles to the campground entrance road on the right. Turn right and drive a short distance to the campground.

Trip note: Pine Point is a pretty little camp, set on a ridge above the McCloud Arm of Shasta Lake amid oak trees and scattered Ponderosa pines. The view is best in spring, when lake levels are generally highest, with seeming miles of emerald-green water bordering the limestone mountains. Some people will launch elsewhere, then park their boat at shore below the camp, while the rest of their party arrives at the camp by car. That provides a chance not only for camping, but for boating, swimming, waterskiing and fishing as well. Open April to September.

37. MADRONE CAMP

Reference: **On Squaw Creek in Shasta-Trinity National Forest; map B2, grid e6.**

Campsites, facilities: There are 13 sites for tents or motor homes up to 16 feet long. There is **no piped water**, but vault toilets, picnic tables and fire grills are provided. Pets are permitted on leashes or otherwise controlled.

Reservations, fee: No reservations; no fee.

Who to contact: Phone the Shasta-Trinity National Forest District Office at (916) 275-1587.

Location: From Redding, drive 29 miles east on Highway 299 to the town of Montgomery Creek. Turn north (left) on Fenders Ferry Road (Forest Service Road 27) and drive 22 miles to the camp (the road starts as a gravel road and then becomes dirt).

Trip note: Tired of people? Then you came to the right place. This remote camp is set along Squaw Creek, a feeder stream of Shasta Lake to the southwest. It's way out there, far away from anybody. Even though Shasta Lake is relatively close, about 10 miles away, it is literally in another world. A network of four-wheel-drive roads provides a recreation option, detailed on a map of Shasta-Trinity National Forest.

38. LAKESHORE EAST 🌊 🎣 ⚓ 🏃 ♿ 🏊   RV 7

Reference: On Shasta Lake in Shasta-Trinity National Forest; map B2, grid f2.

Campsites, facilities: There are 36 sites for tents or motor homes up to 30 feet long. Piped water, flush toilets, picnic tables and fire grills are provided. Pets are permitted on leashes. A boat ramp, grocery store and laundromat are nearby. All facilities are **wheelchair accessible.**

Reservations, fee: Reservations accepted; phone the Shasta Recreation Company at (916) 238-2844; $12-$22 fee per night.

Who to contact: Phone the Shasta-Trinity National Forest District Office at (916) 275-1587.

Location: From Redding, drive north on Interstate 5 for 24 miles to the Antlers exit at Lakehead. Take the Antlers exit, and, at the stop sign, turn left and drive under the freeway to Lakeshore Drive. Turn left on Lakeshore Drive and drive three miles. Look for the campground entrance on the left side of the road.

Trip note: Two Forest Service campgrounds are nestled along the west shore of the Sacramento River of Shasta Lake, just upstream from Sugarloaf Marina and across from where Salt Creek enters this arm of the lake. They are called Lakeshore West and Lakeshore East, even though they are both on the western side of the Sacramento River arm. It's a nice spot, with a good boat ramp and marina nearby at Sugarloaf. Open May to September.

39. SALT CREEK RV PARK & CAMPGROUND   RV 5

🌊 🎣 ⚓ 🏊 🏃

Reference: Near Shasta Lake; map B2, grid f3.

Campsites, facilities: There are 56 sites, many with full hookups. Picnic tables and fire grills are provided. Restrooms, hot showers, a sanitary disposal station, a grocery store, wood, a laundromat, a playground, a heated pool, horseshoes and volleyball are available. Pets are permitted.

Reservations, fee: Reservations accepted; $14.50-$17.50 fee per night.

Who to contact: Phone (916) 238-8500.

Location: From Redding, drive north on Interstate 5 for about 20 miles to the Salt Creek Road exit. Take that exit, look for the signs, and drive a half-mile to the campground.

Trip note: This camp is located on a ridge across the highway from Shasta Lake. The sites are wooded and offer a view of the lake when the water level is high. There's boating, waterskiing, swimming and fishing on the upper end of Shasta Lake. Some private, shaded RV sites are available. Open year-round.

40. NELSON POINT 🌊 🎣 ⚓ 🏊 🏃   RV 7

Reference: On Shasta Lake in Shasta-Trinity National Forest; map B2, grid f3.

Campsites, facilities: There are eight sites for tents or motor homes up to 16 feet long. Vault toilets, picnic tables and fire grills are provided. **No piped water** is provided, so bring your own. Pets are permitted on leashes. A grocery store and a laundromat are nearby.

Reservations, fee: Reservations accepted; phone the Shasta Recreation Company at (916)238-2844; $5 fee per night; $4 for each additional vehicle.

Who to contact: Phone the Shasta-Trinity National Forest District Office at (916) 275-1587.

Location: From Redding, drive north on Interstate 5 for about 20 miles to the Salt Creek Road exit. Take that exit, turn left and drive one mile west to the campground.

Trip note: This is an easy-to-reach campground, only a few minutes from Interstate 5. It's set beside the Salt Creek inlet of Shasta Lake, deep in a cove. In low water years, or when the lake level is low in the fall and early winter, this camp can seem quite distant from water's edge. Open May through September.

41. HOLIDAY HARBOR

Reference: On Shasta Lake; map B2, grid f3.

Campsites, facilities: There 27 motor home sites with full hookups. Restrooms, hot showers, picnic tables and fire grills are provided. A grocery store, a laundromat, boat moorage, a playground, propane gas and boat rentals are available. Pets are allowed on leashes.

Reservations, fee: Reservations accepted; $13.50-$17.50 fee per night for two people.

Who to contact: Phone (916) 238-2383 or (800) 776-2628.

Location: From Redding, drive 18 miles north on Interstate 5 to the Shasta Caverns Road exit. Turn right at Shasta Caverns Road and drive about one mile to the campground entrance on the right.

Trip note: This camp is one of the more popular year-round, all-service resorts on Shasta Lake. It is set on the lower McCloud arm of the lake, which is extremely beautiful with a limestone mountain ridge off to the east. It is an ideal jumpoff for all water sports, especially houseboating and fishing. A good boat ramp, boat rentals and a store with all the goodies are bonuses. Another bonus is the side trip to Shasta Caverns, a privately guided adventure (fee charged) into limestone caves.

42. TRAIL IN RV CAMPGROUND

Reference: On Shasta Lake; map B2, grid f3.

Campsites, facilities: There are 39 sites, some pull-through, with full hookups. Picnic tables and fire grills are provided. Restrooms, hot showers, TVs, sanitary disposal station, a swimming pool, a grocery store, ice, wood and a laundromat are available. The facilities are **wheelchair accessible**. Pets are permitted.

Reservations, fee: Deposit required with reservation; $16.50 fee per night.

Who to contact: Phone (916) 238-8533.

Location: From Redding, drive 22 miles north on Interstate 5. Take the Gilman Road-Salt Creek Road exit and drive a short distance west on Gilman Road to Gregory Creek Road. Turn north on Gregory Creek Road and drive one mile to the campground.

Trip note: This is a privately-operated campground near the Salt Creek arm of giant Shasta Lake. Open, level sites are available. The lake is about three miles away and offers fishing, boating and swimming. Its proximity to Interstate 5 makes this a popular spot, fast and easy to reach, which is extremely attractive for drivers of RVs and trailers who want to avoid the many twisty roads surrounding Shasta Lake.

43. HIRZ BAY GROUP CAMP   RV 7

Reference: **On Shasta Lake in Shasta-Trinity National Forest; map B2, grid f4.**

Campsites, facilities: There are four group sites for tents and motor homes up to 24 feet long. Piped water, vault toilets, picnic tables and fire grills are provided. Pets are permitted on leashes.

Reservations, fee: Reservations required; phone the Shasta Recreation Company at (916) 238-2844; call for fees.

Who to contact: Phone the Shasta-Trinity National Forest District Office at (916) 275-1587.

Location: From Redding, drive north on Interstate 5 for about 20 miles to the Gilman exit. Take Gilman Road (County Road 7H009) and drive northeast for 10 miles to the campground/boat launch access road on the right. Turn right and drive a half-mile to the campground on the left side of the road.

Trip note: This is the spot for your own private party, providing you get a reservation, set on a point at the entrance of Hirz Bay on the McCloud River arm of Shasta Lake. A boat ramp is located only a half-mile away on the camp access road, providing access to the McCloud River arm. This is an excellent spot to make a base camp for a fishing trip, with great trolling for trout in this stretch of the lake. Open May through September.

44. HIRZ BAY   RV 7

Reference: **On Shasta Lake in Shasta-Trinity National Forest; map B2, grid f4.**

Campsites, facilities: There are 38 single sites and 10 double sites for tents or motor homes up to 30 feet long. Piped water, flush toilets, picnic tables and fire grills are provided. A boat ramp is nearby. The facilities are **wheelchair accessible**. Pets are permitted on leashes.

Reservations, fee: Reservations required; phone the Shasta Recreation Company at (916) 238-2844; $12-$22 fee per night for single sites. Reduced rates and services in the winter.

Who to contact: Phone the Shasta-Trinity National Forest District Office at (916) 275-1587.

Location: From Redding, drive north on Interstate 5 for about 20 miles to the Gilman exit. Take Gilman Road (County Road 7H009) and drive northeast for 10 miles to the campground/boat launch access road on the right. Turn right and drive a half-mile to the campground on the left side of the road.

Trip note: This is one of two camps in the immediate area (the other is Hirz Bay Group Camp) that provides nearby access to a boat ramp (a half-mile down the road) and the McCloud River arm of Shasta Lake. The camp is set on a point at the entrance of Hirz Bay. This is an excellent spot to make a base camp for a fishing trip, with great trolling for trout in this stretch of the lake. Open May through September.

45. DEKKAS ROCK GROUP CAMP   RV 8

Reference: **On Shasta Lake in Shasta-Trinity National Forest; map B2, grid f4.**

Campsites, facilities: There are four sites for tents or motor homes up to 16 feet long. Piped water, vault toilets, picnic tables and fire grills are provided. Pets are permitted on leashes. A grocery store is nearby.

Reservations, fee: Reservations required; phone the Shasta Recreation Company at (916) 238-2844; call for fees.

Who to contact: Phone the Shasta-Trinity National Forest District Office at (916) 275-1587.

Location: From Redding, drive north on Interstate 5 for about 20 miles to the Gilman exit. Take Gilman Road (County Road 7H009) and drive northeast for 11 miles to the campground on the right side of the road.

Trip note: The few people who know about this camp love this little spot. It is an ideal group camp, set on a flat above the McCloud arm of Shasta Lake, shaded primarily by bays and oaks, with a boat ramp located two miles to the south at Hirz Bay. The views are pretty here, looking across the lake at the limestone ridge that borders the McCloud arm. In late summer and fall, when the lake level drops, it can be a hike from the camp down to water's edge.

---

46. BRANDY CREEK

Reference: **On Whiskeytown Lake; map B2, grid g0.**

Campsites, facilities: There are 46 motor home sites for self-contained vehicles up to 25 feet long. A dump station and piped water are available. Pets are permitted on leashes.

Reservations, fee: No reservations; no fee.

Who to contact: Phone the Whiskeytown National Recreation Area at (916) 241-6584.

Location: From Redding, drive 10 miles west on Highway 299. Turn left at the Visitor Center (Kennedy Memorial Drive) and drive five miles to the campground entrance road on the right. Turn right and drive a short distance to the camp.

Trip note: For campers with boats, this is the best place to stay at Whiskeytown Lake, with a boat ramp located less than a quarter-mile away. Whiskeytown is popular for sailing and windsurfing, getting a lot more wind than other lakes in the region. Fishing for kokanee salmon is good in the early morning, prior to the wind coming up.

---

47. OAK BOTTOM

Reference: **On Whiskeytown Lake; map B2, grid g0.**

Campsites, facilities: There are 101 walk-in tent sites with picnic tables and fire grills. There are 50 motor home sites in the large parking area near the launch ramp and restrooms. Piped water, flush toilets, coin-operated showers, groceries, ice, wood, a sanitary dump station, a boat ramp and boat rentals are available. Some facilities are **wheelchair accessible**. Pets are permitted on leashes.

Reservations, fee: No reservations in off-season; reservations required in summer and available through Destinet, phone (800) 365-CAMP; $15-$17 fee per night in summer, $9-$11 fee the rest of the year.

Who to contact: Phone Whiskeytown National Recreation Area at (916) 241-6584.

Location: From Redding, drive 15 miles west on Highway 299 (past the visitor center) to the campground entrance road on the left. Turn left and drive a short distance to the campground.

Trip note: The prettiest hiking trails at Whiskeytown Lake are at the far western end of the reservoir, and this camp provides excellent access to them. One hiking and biking trail skirts the north shoreline of the lake and is routed to the lake's inlet at the Judge Carr Powerhouse. The other, with the trailhead just a short drive to the west, is routed along Mill Creek, a pristine, clear-running stream where the trail jumps over the stream many times, the kind of place you may never want to leave. The campground sites seem a little close, but the location is next to a beach area with a self-guided nature trail nearby. There are junior ranger programs for kids 6 to 12 years old, and evening ranger seminars at the Oak Bottom Amphitheater are available every night from mid-June through Labor Day.

48. DRY CREEK GROUP CAMP

Reference: **On Whiskeytown Lake; map B2, grid g0.**

Campsites, facilities: There are two group sites which can accommodate 80 people each. Piped water, pit toilets, picnic tables and fire grills are provided. Pets are permitted on leashes.

Reservations, fee: Reservations required and because the camp is very popular, should be made the first working day of the year to reserve any date through the summer months. Group fee is $30-$50 per night for single group sites and $100 for both; maximum stay is seven days.

Who to contact: Phone the Whiskeytown National Recreation Area at (916) 241-6584, extension 221.

Location: From Redding, drive 10 miles west on Highway 299. Turn left at the Visitor Center (Kennedy Memorial Drive) and drive six miles to the campground on the right side of the road.

Trip note: If you're in a group and take the time to reserve this spot, you'll be rewarded with some room and the quiet that goes along with it. This is the most remote drive-to camp at Whiskeytown Lake. A boat ramp is located about two miles away (to the east) at Brandy Creek. You'll pass it on the way in.

49. SHASTA

Reference: **On Sacramento River in Shasta-Trinity National Forest; map B2, grid g3.**

Campsites, facilities: There are 30 sites for tents or motor homes up to 24 feet long. Piped water, vault toilets, picnic tables and fire rings are provided. A boat ramp is nearby. Groceries and bait are available in Summit City. Pets are permitted on leashes.

Reservations, fee: Reservations accepted; phone the Shasta Recreation Company at (916) 238-2844; $10 fee per night; $4 for each additional vehicle.

Who to contact: Phone the Shasta-Trinity National Forest District Office at (916) 275-1587.

Location: From Interstate 5 just north of Redding, take the exit for the town of Shasta Lake City/Shasta Dam. Turn west on Shasta Dam Boulevard and drive three miles to Lake Boulevard. Turn right (north) on Lake Boulevard and drive two miles. Cross Shasta Dam and follow the signs to the campground.

Alternate directions due to road closure over Shasta Dam: When you reach Shasta Dam, turn left on a primitive dirt road which is routed down the canyon to the base of the dam. Cross the bridge to reach the western side of the river, then drive a short distance to the campground. Note: The Forest Service advises campers to stop at Shasta Dam, look for the guard shack, and get information from the guard on duty.

Trip note: This campground is located between Shasta Dam and the Sacramento River, and adjacent to an off-highway-vehicle staging area. Get the idea? Right, this place is for ATVs and dirt bikes, loud and wild, and hey, it's a perfect spot for them. It's barren and there isn't much to look at. Open year-round.

Special note: An engineering project at Shasta Dam has made reaching this campground difficult, with the road over Shasta Dam closed until 1997. Use alternate directions.

---

50. WONDERLAND RV PARK   RV 5

Reference: **Near Shasta Lake; map B2, grid g3.**

Campsites, facilities: There are 36 motor home sites, many with full hookups. Restrooms, showers, a laundromat, cable TV, a heated swimming pool and horseshoes are available. Pets are allowed on leashes.

Reservations, fee: Reservations required with deposit; $14.50 fee per night.

Who to contact: Phone (916) 275-1281.

Location: From Redding, drive north on Interstate 5 for 11 miles to the Fawndale exit. Exit south onto Wonderland Boulevard and drive a quarter mile to 15203 Wonderland Boulevard.

Trip note: This RV park is located within a mobile home park south of Shasta Lake. The tour of Shasta Cavern is a recreation option, via a short drive to Holiday Harbor. The city of Redding offers an extensive visitor center, the Carter House Natural History Museum in Caldwell Park, public golf courses and the Sacramento River trails, which are paved, making them accessible for **wheelchairs** and bikes. Open year-round.

---

51. BEAR MOUNTAIN RV RESORT   RV 3

Reference: **Near Shasta Lake; map B2, grid g4.**

Campsites, facilities: There are 17 tent sites and 97 motor home sites with full or partial hookups. Piped water, flush toilets, a laundromat, a grocery store, a dump station, picnic tables and fire rings are provided, as well as a swimming pool, recreation hall, arcade, and a horseshoe pit. Nearby is a free boat launch ramp. Pets are allowed on leashes.

Reservations, fee: Reservations accepted; $12-$16 fee per night.

Who to contact: Phone (916) 275-4728 or (800) 952-0551.

Location: From Redding, drive north on Interstate 5 for three miles to the Oasis Road exit. Turn east (right) on Oasis Road (Old Oregon Trail) and drive 3.5 miles. Turn right on Bear Mountain Road and drive 3.5 miles to the campground.

Trip note: This is a privately-operated park set up primarily for motor homes in the remote Jones Valley area along Shasta Lake.

---

52. JONES INLET   RV 7

Reference: **On Shasta Lake in Shasta-Trinity National Forest; map B2, grid g4.**

Campsites, facilities: There are an undesignated number of primitive sites for tents or motor homes up to 30 feet long. There is **no piped water**, but vault toilets are provided. A boat ramp is two miles from camp. Pets are permitted on leashes.

Reservations, fee: No reservations; $5 fee per night; $4 fee for each additional vehicle.

Who to contact: Phone the Shasta-Trinity National Forest District Office at (916) 275-1587.

Location: From Redding, turn east on Highway 299 and drive 7.5 miles just past the town of Bella Vista. At Dry Creek Road, turn left (north) and drive nine miles to a Y in the road. Veer right (left will take you to Silverthorn Resort) at the Y and drive a short distance to the campground entrance on the left side of the road.

Trip note: This is one of the few primitive camp areas on Shasta Lake, set on the distant Pit River arm of the lake. It is an ideal camp for hiking and biking, with the nearby Clickipudi Trail routed for miles along the lake's shore, in and out of coves, and then entering the surrounding foothills and oak/bay woodlands. The camp is pretty, if a bit exposed, with two nearby resorts, Jones Valley and Silverthorn, providing boat rentals and supplies.

53. UPPER & LOWER JONES VALLEY CAMPS

Reference: **On Shasta Lake in Shasta-Trinity National Forest; map B2, grid g5.**

Campsites, facilities: There are 27 sites for tents or motor homes up to 16 feet long in two adjacent campgrounds. Picnic tables, fire grills, piped water and vault toilets are provided. A boat ramp is two miles from camp. Pets are permitted on leashes.

Reservations, fee: Reservations accepted; phone the Shasta Recreation Company at (916) 238-2844; $10 fee per night; $4 for each additional vehicle.

Who to contact: Phone the Shasta-Trinity National Forest District Office at (916) 275-1587.

Location: From Redding, turn east on Highway 299 and drive 7.5 miles just past the town of Bella Vista. At Dry Creek Road, turn left (north) and drive nine miles to a Y in the road. Veer right (left will take you to Silverthorn Resort) at the Y and drive a short distance to the campground entrances, on the left side for Lower Jones and on the right side for Upper Jones.

Trip note: Lower Jones is a small, pretty camp sheltered by oaks and bays along a deep cove in the remote Pit River arm of Shasta Lake. There is a trailhead at camp that provides access to the Clickipudi Trail, a great hiking and biking trail that traces the lake's shore, routed through pretty woodlands. Two nearby resorts, Jones Valley and Silverthorn, provide boat rentals and supplies.

54. KOA OF REDDING

Reference: **In Redding; map B2, grid h2.**

Campsites, facilities: There are 124 sites, 54 with full hookups, and a separate area for tents. Piped water, flush toilets, showers, a playground, a swimming pool, a laundromat, a dump station, picnic tables and fire grills are provided. A grocery store and propane gas are also available. Pets are permitted.

Reservations, fee: Reservations accepted; $17.50-$20.50 fee per night.

Who to contact: Phone (916) 246-0101.

Location: In Redding, drive north on Interstate 5 to the Lake Boulevard (Alturas-Burney) exit. Turn west on Lake Boulevard and drive a quarter-mile to North Boulder Drive. Turn north on North Boulder Drive and drive one block to 280 North Boulder Drive.

Trip note: If you're stuck with no place to go, this large park could be your savior, but expect very hot weather in the summer. Nearby recreation options include the Sacramento River, which runs through town, Whiskeytown Lake to the west, and Shasta Lake to the north.

55. TWIN VIEW TERRACE RV PARK

Reference: **Near Redding; map B2, grid h2.**

Campsites, facilities: There are 48 drive-through motor home sites with full hookups. Restrooms, showers, laundromat, and a swimming pool are available. Pets are allowed on leashes.

Reservations, fee: No reservations; $17 fee per night.

Who to contact: Phone (916) 243-8114.

Location: In Redding, take the Twin View exit off Interstate 5. Turn south on Twin View and drive one mile on Twin View Boulevard to the RV park.

Trip note: This is one of several motor home parks open year-round in the Redding area. This park is located within a mobile home park.

56. MARINA RV PARK

Reference: **On Sacramento River; map B2, grid h2.**

Campsites, facilities: There are 86 motor home sites with full or partial hookups. Restrooms, hot showers, a laundromat, a grocery store, a swimming pool, a whirlpool, a boat ramp and a dump station are on park grounds. Pets are permitted.

Reservations, fee: Reservations accepted; $20 fee per night.

Who to contact: Phone (916) 241-4396.

Location: In Redding, turn west on Highway 299 and drive to Park Marina Drive. At Park Marina Drive, turn south and drive one mile to the park.

Trip note: The riverside setting is a highlight, with the Sacramento River providing relief from the dog days of summer. An easy, paved walking and bike trail is available nearby at the Sacramento River Parkway, providing river views and sometimes a needed breeze on hot summer evenings. A miniature golf course is located nearby. This park is open year-round.

57. SACRAMENTO RIVER RV PARK

Reference: **Map B2, grid i2.**

Campsites, facilities: There are 20 tent sites and 140 motor home sites with full hookups. Restrooms, hot showers, a grocery store, a laundromat, a dump station, cable TV, a bait and tackle shop, propane gas, a launch and thirty slips, two tennis courts and a large swimming pool are available. Pets are allowed on leashes.

Reservations, fee: Reservations accepted; $14-$21 fee per night. All discount coupons are honored for RVs.

Who to contact: Phone (916) 365-6402.

Location: From Redding, drive south on Interstate 5 for five miles to the Knighton Road exit. Turn west and drive a short distance to Riverland Drive. Turn left (south) on Riverland Drive and drive two miles to the end of the road.

Trip note: This makes a good headquarters for a fall fishing trip on the Sacramento River, where the salmon come big from August through October. In the summer, trout fishing is very good from this area as well, with a boat a must. No problem; there's a boat ramp at the park. In addition, fishing guides can be hired who launch from here daily. The park is open year-round, and if you want to stay close to home, a three-acre pond is available at the park. You also get great views of Mt. Shasta and Mt. Lassen.

58. OLD COW MEADOWS

Reference: **In Latour State Forest; map B2, grid i9.**

Campsites, facilities: There are three sites for tents or motor homes. There is **no piped water,** but picnic tables, fire grills and pit toilets are provided. Pets are permitted.

Reservations, fee: No reservations; no fee.

Who to contact: Phone the Latour State Forest at (916) 225-2505 or (916) 225-2438.

Location: In Redding, turn east on Highway 44 and drive about 9.5 miles to Millville Road. Turn left (north) on Millville Road and drive one-half mile to the intersection of Millville Road and Whitmore Road. Turn right (east) on Whitmore Road and drive 13 miles, through Whitmore, until Whitmore Road becomes Tamarac Road. Continue for one mile to a fork at Bateman Road. Take the right fork on Bateman Road and drive 3.5 miles (where the road turns to gravel), then continue 12 miles to the entrance to the campground.

Trip note: Nobody finds this campground without this book. You want quiet? You don't want to be bugged by anybody? You want piped water, too? Well, two out of three ain't bad. This tiny camp, virtually unknown, is set at 5,900 feet in a wooded area along Old Cow Creek. Recreation options include off-road-vehicle use, and walking the dirt roads that crisscross the area. Open June through October.

59. SOUTH COW CREEK MEADOWS

Reference: **In Latour State Forest; map B2, grid i9.**

Campsites, facilities: There are two sites for tents or motor homes. Non-piped water is available. Pit toilets, picnic tables and fire grills are provided. Pets are allowed.

Reservations, fee: No reservations; no fee.

Who to contact: Phone the Latour State Forest at (916) 225-2505 or (916) 225-2438.

Location: In Redding, turn east on Highway 44 and drive about 9.5 miles to Millville Road. Turn left (north) on Millville Road and drive one-half mile to the intersection of Millville Road and Whitmore Road. Turn right (east) on Whitmore Road and drive 13 miles, through Whitmore, until Whitmore Road becomes Tamarac Road. Continue for one mile to a fork at Bateman Road. Take the right fork on Bateman Road and drive 3.5 miles (where the road turns to gravel), then continue for 11 miles to the entrance to the campground.

Trip note: This camp is set in a pretty wooded area next to a small meadow along South Cow Creek. It's mostly used in the fall for hunting, with off-highway-vehicle use on the surrounding roads in the summer. The camp is set at 5,600 feet. If you want to get away from it all without leaving your vehicle, this is one way to do it. Open June through October.

60. READING ISLAND 🐟 ⚓ ♿   RV 7

Reference: On Sacramento River; map B2, grid j3.

Campsites, facilities: There are eight sites for tents or motor homes up to 30 feet long. Piped water, vault toilets, picnic tables and fire grills are provided. A boat ramp, groceries, propane gas and a laundromat are available nearby. The facilities are **wheelchair accessible**. Pets are allowed on leashes.

Reservations, fee: No reservations; $5 fee per night.

Who to contact: Phone the Bureau of Land Management at (916) 224-2100.

Location: From Redding, drive 15 miles south on Interstate 5 to Cottonwood. In Cottonwood, turn east on Balls Ferry Road and drive five miles to Adobe Road. Take Adobe Road to the campground entrance.

Trip note: This is a prime spot along the Sacramento River amid the best stretch of river for salmon. The state record 88-pounder was caught near here at the mouth of Old Battle Creek (the "Barge Hole"). The average salmon ranges from 12 to 25 pounds, best from mid-August through October. The river is usually too high and too cold for swimming, even when temperatures are in the 100s in the summer months. Innertubers without life jackets will be ticketed and taken off the water by the Shasta County sheriff's patrol boat. The Coleman Fish Hatchery offers a nearby side trip.

61. KOA LASSEN/SHINGLETOWN 🐟 🚶   RV 5

Reference: Near Lassen Volcanic National Park; map B2, grid j7.

Campsites, facilities: There are 50 sites for tents or motor homes; some are drive-through sites with full or partial hookups. Picnic tables, fire grills, piped water, flush toilets, hot showers, a playground, a heated pool and a dump station are provided. Groceries, ice, wood, a laundromat and propane gas are available. Pets are permitted.

Reservations, fee: Deposit required with reservation; $16-$21.50 fee per night.

Who to contact: Phone (916) 474-3133.

Location: From Redding, turn east on Highway 44 and drive to Shingletown. In Shingletown, continue east for four miles and look for the KOA sign on the side of the road.

Trip note: This is a popular KOA camp set 14 miles from the entrance of Lassen Volcanic National Park with pretty, wooded sites. Location is always the critical factor on vacations, and this park is set up perfectly for launching trips to the nearby east. Mill Creek provides trout fishing along Highway 44, and just inside the Highway 44 entrance station at Lassen Park is Manzanita Lake, providing good fishing and hiking. Open year-round.

62. MILL CREEK PARK 🐟 🚶   RV 7

Reference: Near Shingletown; map B2, grid j7.

Campsites, facilities: There are 34 sites for tents or motor homes; some are drive-through sites with full or partial hookups. Picnic tables, fire grills, piped water, flush toilets, a dump station and a laundromat are available. A fishing pond and creek are also available. Pets are permitted.

Reservations, fee: Deposit required with reservation; $12-$16 fee per night.

Who to contact: Phone (916) 474-5384.

Location: From Redding, drive east on Highway 44 to Shingletown. In Shingletown, continue east on Highway 44 for two miles to the campground.

Trip note: This year-round park is set up primarily for motor homes, but has sites for tenters. Its elevation is 4,000 feet and it's set amid conifers on the western slopes of Mt. Lassen. Its nearby location to Lassen Volcanic National Park is a key attraction here.

63. McCUMBER RESERVOIR

Reference: **On Macumber Reservoir; map B2, grid j9.**

Campsites, facilities: There are seven sites for tents or motor homes and five walk-in sites. Piped water, vault toilets, picnic tables and fire grills are provided. Pets are permitted on leashes.

Reservations, fee: No reservations; $11 fee per night; $1 pet fee.

Who to contact: Phone the PG&E District Office at (916) 386-5164.

Location: In Redding, turn east on Highway 44 and drive towards Viola to Lake McCumber Road (if you reach Viola, you have gone four miles too far). At Lake McCumber Road, turn left (north) and drive two miles to the reservoir and campground.

Trip note: Here's a little lake, easy to reach from Redding, that is little known and rarely visited. McCumber Reservoir is set at 3,500 feet in elevation and is stocked with 6,000 rainbow trout each year, providing fair fishing. No gas motors are permitted here. That's fine, and guarantees quiet, calm water, ideal for car-top boats—prams, canoes, rafts and small aluminum boats.

MAP B3

NOR-CAL MAP .... see page 94
adjoining maps
NORTH (A3) .... see page 132
EAST (B4) .... see page 222
SOUTH (C3) .... see page 272
WEST (B2) .... see page 180

31 LISTINGS
PAGES 208-221

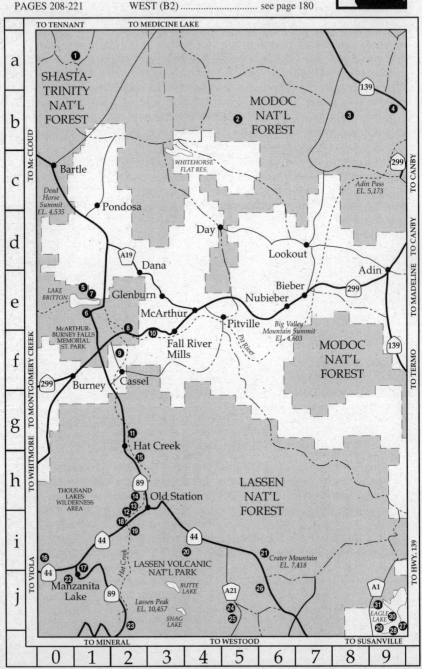

TO TENNANT   TO MEDICINE LAKE

a

SHASTA-
TRINITY
NAT'L
FOREST

MODOC
NAT'L
FOREST

b

139

③

④

②

c

Bartle

WHITEHORSE
FLAT RES.

299

Dead
Horse
Summit
EL. 4,535

Adin Pass
EL. 5,173

d

Pondosa

Day

Lookout

A19

Dana

Adin

e

LAKE
BRITTON

⑤ ⑦

Glenburn

Bieber
Nubieber

299

⑥

McArthur

Pitville

139

McARTHUR-
BURNEY FALLS
MEMORIAL
ST. PARK

⑧

⑩

Big Valley
Mountain Summit
EL. 4,603

MODOC
NAT'L
FOREST

f

Fall River
Mills

⑨

Pit River

299

Burney

Cassel

g

⑪

Hat Creek

⑮

h

89

LASSEN
NAT'L
FOREST

THOUSAND
LAKES
WILDERNESS
AREA

⑭

Old Station

⑬

⑫

⑱

⑲

44

44

i

⑯

⑰

⑳

㉑ Crater Mountain
EL. 7,418

44

Hat Creek

LASSEN VOLCANIC
NAT'L PARK

A1

j

44

㉒

Manzanita
Lake

89

BUTTE
LAKE

A21

㉖

㉛

EAGLE
LAKE

㉚

Lassen Peak
EL. 10,457

㉔

㉙ ㉘ ㉗

㉓

SNAG
LAKE

㉕

TO MINERAL   TO WESTOOD   TO SUSANVILLE

TO McCLOUD   TO MONTGOMERY CREEK   TO WHITMORE   TO VIOLA

TO CANBY   TO CANBY   TO MADELINE   TO TERMO   TO HWY. 139

0   1   2   3   4   5   6   7   8   9

Map B3 featuring: Shasta-Trinity National Forest, Modoc National Forest, Memorial State Park, Lake Britton, Hat Creek, Lassen National Forest, Lassen Volcanic National Park, Silver Lake, Eagle Lake

1. HARRIS SPRINGS 🏃🏃

Reference: **In Shasta-Trinity National Forest; map B3, grid a1.**

Campsites, facilities: There are 15 sites for tents or motor homes up to 32 feet long. Piped water, vault toilets, picnic tables and fire grills provided. Pets are permitted on leashes.

Reservations, fee: No reservations; no fee.

Who to contact: Phone the Shasta-Trinity National Forest District Office at (916) 964-2184.

Location: From Redding, drive north on Interstate 5 past Dunsmuir to the junction with Highway 89. Turn east on Highway 89 and drive to McCloud, then continue on Highway 89 for 17 miles just past the town of Bartle. Turn left (north) on Medicine Lake Road and drive about five miles to a Y. Turn left at the Y on Harris Springs Road (Forest Service Road 15) and drive 12 miles. Turn right at a Forest Service road signed for the Harris Springs ranger station, drive a short distance, and look for the campground entrance on the right side of the road.

Trip note: This camp is a hidden spot in remote Shasta-Trinity National Forest, nestled in the long, mountainous ridge that runs east from Mt. Shasta to the Lava Beds National Monument. The camp is set at 4,800 feet, with a ranger station located within a quarter-mile on the opposite side of the access road. The area is best explored by four-wheel-drive, venturing to a series of small buttes, mountaintops and lookouts in the immediate area. A map of Shasta-Trinity National Forest is a must.

2. LAVA CAMP 🏃🏃

Reference: **In Modoc National Forest; map B3, grid b5.**

Campsites, facilities: There are 12 sites for tents or motor homes up to 32 feet long. Vault toilets, tables and fire grills are provided. **No piped water** is available, so bring your own. Pets are allowed on leashes.

Reservations, fee: No reservations; no fee.

Who to contact: Phone the Modoc National Forest District Office at (916) 299-3215.

Location: From Redding, take Highway 299 east to Bieber (about 90 miles). Continue just past Bieber to County Road 91 and turn right (north), and drive seven miles to the town of Lookout. After crossing the Pit River, turn right on County Road 91 and drive about 13 miles to Forest Service Road 42N03. Turn left on Forest Service Road 42N03 and drive seven miles to the junction with Forest Service Road 42N23. Turn right and drive five miles to the campground on the right side of the road. A map of Modoc Forest is a must.

Trip note: Modoc country is "old country." It feels like it hasn't changed since the beginning of time. If that's what you are looking for, this camp is for you. It's virtually unknown, yet in a prime spot in the area, on the outskirts of Long Bell State Game Refuge. Glass Mountain and nearby lava flows offer good side trips. The elevation is 4,400 feet, set atop Sugar Pine Ridge. In the fall, it's a good base camp for a hunting trip. Open May through October.

3. COTTONWOOD FLAT 👣

Reference: **In Modoc National Forest; map B3, grid b8**

Campsites, facilities: There are 10 sites for tents or motor homes up to 22 feet long. Potable spring water, vault toilets, fire grills and picnic tables are provided. Pets are permitted on leashes or otherwise controlled. Supplies are available in Canby.

Reservations, fee: No reservations; no fee.

Who to contact: Phone the Modoc National Forest District Office at (916) 233-5811.

Location: From Redding, drive east on Highway 299 for about 100 miles to Adin. Continue on Highway 299 for about 20 miles to the Canby Bridge at the Pit River and the junction with Forest Service Road 84. Turn left on Forest Service Road 84 and drive eight miles to Forest Service Road 42N95. Turn right and drive a half-mile to the campground entrance on the left side of the road.

Trip note: The camp is wooded and shady, set at 4,700 feet in elevation in the rugged and remote Devils Garden area of Modoc National Forest. The region is known for large mule deer, and the camp is well situated as a base camp for a hunting trip in the fall. Temperatures get extremely cold early and late in the season. Open June to October.

4. HOWARD'S GULCH 🐟 👣 ♿ RV 6

Reference: **Near Duncan Reservoir in Modoc National Forest; map B3, grid b9.**

Campsites, facilities: There are 11 sites for tents or motor homes up to 22 feet long. Vault toilets, tables and fire grills are provided. One toilet is **wheelchair accessible**. There is **no piped water.** Pets are permitted on leashes. Supplies are available in Canby.

Reservations, fee: No reservations; no fee.

Who to contact: Phone the Modoc National Forest District Office at (916) 233-5811.

Location: From Redding, drive east on Highway 299 for about 100 miles to Adin. Continue on Highway 299 for about 25 miles to Canby. In Canby, turn left (northwest) on Highway 139 and drive six miles to the campground on the left side of the road.

Trip note: This is the nearest campground to Duncan Reservoir, located three miles to the north, which is stocked with trout each year by the Department of Fish and Game. The camp is set in the typically sparse woods of Modoc National Forest, but a beautiful grove of aspen is located three miles to the west on Highway 139, on the left side of the road. By the way, Highway 139 isn't much of a highway at all, but it is paved and will get you there. The elevation is 4,700 feet. Open May through October.

5. McARTHUR-BURNEY FALLS RV 9
🐟 ⚓ 👣 ♿ 🏊

Reference: **In McArthur-Burney Falls State Park; map B3, grid e1.**

Campsites, facilities: There are 128 sites for tents or motor homes up to 32 feet long. Piped water, flush toilets, hot showers, a sanitary dump station, picnic tables and fire grills are provided. The restrooms are **wheelchair accessible**.

Pets are permitted on leashes, but not on park trails or the beach. A grocery store and boat rentals are available in the summer.

Reservations, fee: Reserve through Destinet by phoning (800) 444-7275 ($6.75 Destinet fee); $15-$17 fee per night; $1 pet fee.

Who to contact: Phone (916) 335-2777 or (916) 538-2200.

Location: From Redding, drive east on Highway 299 to Burney, then continue for five miles to the junction with Highway 89. At Highway 89, turn left (north) and drive six miles to the campground entrance on the left side of the road.

Trip note: The 129-foot waterfall here, Burney Falls, is a beautiful cascade, split at the top by a little grove of trees, with little trickles oozing and falling out of the adjacent moss-lined wall. Since it is fed primarily by a spring, it runs strong and glorious most of the year. The Headwaters Trail provides an outstanding hike, both to see the waterfall and Burney Creek, as well as for an easy adventure and fishing access to the stream. There are other stellar recreation options at this state park. At the end of the campground access road is a boat ramp for Lake Britton, with rentals available for canoes and paddleboats. This is a beautiful lake, with awesome canyon walls on its upper end, and good trout and crappie fishing. There is also a good swimming beach. The Pacific Crest Trail is routed right through the park, and provides an additional opportunity for a day hike, best explored downstream from the dam. Reservations for sites are essential during the summer months.

---

6. NORTHSHORE

Reference: **On Lake Britton; map B3, grid e1.**

Campsites, facilities: There are 30 sites for tents or motor homes up to 16 feet long. Piped water, vault toilets, picnic tables and fire grills are provided. An unimproved boat ramp is available at the camp and an improved boat ramp is available in Burney Falls State Park (about four miles away). Supplies can be obtained in Fall River Mills or Burney. Pets are allowed on leashes.

Reservations, fee: No reservations; $11 fee per night; $1 pet fee; $3 launch fee.

Who to contact: Phone the PG&E District Office at (916) 386-5164.

Location: From Redding, drive east on Highway 299 to Burney, then continue for five miles to the junction with Highway 89. At Highway 89, turn left (north) and drive 9.7 miles (past the state park entrance and over the Lake Britton Bridge) to Clark Creek Road. Turn left (west) on Clark Creek Road and drive about a mile to the camp access road on the left. Turn left and drive to the camp.

Trip note: This peaceful campground is set among the woodlands near the shore of Lake Britton, directly across the lake from McArthur-Burney Falls Memorial State Park (see trip note for preceding campground). Boating and fishing are popular here, and once the water warms up in midsummer, swimming is also a winner. The best trout fishing in the area is on the Pit River near Powerhouse No. 3, but skilled and aggressive wading is required. A hot spring is available in Big Bend, about a 30-minute drive from camp.

---

7. DUSTY CAMPGROUND

Reference: **On Lake Britton; map B3, grid e1.**

Campsites, facilities: There are seven primitive sites for tents or motor homes up to 20 feet long and two primitive group sites which can accommodate up to 25 people each. There is **no piped water**, so bring your own. Vault toilets, picnic tables and fire rings are provided. Pets are allowed on leashes.

Reservations, fee: No reservations; $6 fee per night; $1 pet fee; group sites are $12 per night.

Who to contact: Phone the PG&E District Office at (916) 386-5164.

Location: From Redding, drive east on Highway 299 to Burney, then continue for five miles to the junction with Highway 89. At Highway 89, turn left (north) and drive 7 miles (past the state park entrance and over the Lake Britton Bridge) to Clark Creek Road. Turn left (west) on Clark Creek Road and drive about a 7.5 miles to the camp access road on the left. Turn right (east) and drive three-quarters of a mile to the campground directly ahead

Trip note: This is one of a series of campgrounds near the north shore of Lake Britton. See trip note for preceding camp.

8. BURNEY FALLS TRAILER RESORT

Reference: **Map B3, grid e2.**

Campsites, facilities: There are 28 motor home sites with full hookups. Restrooms, hot showers, a laundromat, horseshoes and a swimming pool are on the premises. Pets are allowed on leashes.

Reservations, fee: Reservations accepted; $16 fee per night.

Who to contact: Phone (916) 335-2781.

Location: From Redding, drive east on Highway 299 to Burney, then continue for five miles to the junction with Highway 89. At Highway 89, turn left (north) and drive 9.7 miles (past the state park entrance and over the Lake Britton Bridge) to Clark Creek Road. Turn left (west) on Clark Creek Road and drive a short distance to the campground entrance.

Trip note: This is a year-round motor home park located near Lake Britton, Burney Creek, and the Pit River. McArthur-Burney Falls Memorial State Park with its spectacular waterfall is within a five-minute drive. The region is loaded with adventure, with Lassen Volcanic National Park, Hat Creek and Fall River all within a 30-minute drive.

9. CASSEL

Reference: **On Hat Creek; map B3, grid f2.**

Campsites, facilities: There are 27 sites for tents or motor homes up to 20 feet long. Piped water, vault toilets, picnic tables and fire grills are provided. Pets are permitted on leashes.

Reservations, fee: No reservations; $11 fee per night; $1 pet fee.

Who to contact: Phone the PG&E District Office at (916) 386-5164.

Location: From Redding, drive east on Highway 299 to Burney, then continue for five miles to the junction with Highway 89. At the junction, continue straight on Highway 299 for two miles to Cassel Road. At Cassel Road, turn right (south) and drive 3.6 miles to the campground entrance on the left.

Trip note: This is an outstanding location for a base camp for a fishing trip, with nearby Crystal Lake, Baum Lake and Hat Creek, all set in the Hat Creek Valley, providing trout fishing. This section of Hat Creek is well known for its challenging flyfishing, with typically an excellent evening hatch and surface rise. Long leaders and very small flies are critical. A good source of fishing information is Vaughn's Sporting Goods in Burney. Baum Lake is ideal for car-top boats with electric motors.

10. PIT RIVER 🐟 🚶

Reference: **Map B3, grid f3.**

Campsites, facilities: There are 10 sites for tents or motor homes. There is **no piped water**, but vault toilets, picnic tables and fire grills are provided. Pets are permitted. There are supplies and a laundromat in Fall River Mills.

Reservations, fee: No reservations; no fee.

Who to contact: Phone the Bureau of Land Management at (916) 257-5381

Location: From Redding, drive east on Highway 299 to Burney, then continue for five miles to the junction with Highway 89. At the junction, continue straight on Highway 299, cross the Pit River Bridge, and drive about three miles to Pit River Powerhouse Road (a dirt road) on the right. Turn right (south) and drive along the river for about a mile to the campground.

Trip note: Very few out-of-towners know about this hidden and primitive campground set along the Pit River. It can provide a good base camp for a fishing trip adventure. The best stretch of trout water on the Pit is near Powerhouse No. 3. There are many other recreation options. A parking area and trail along Hat Creek are available where the Highway 299 Bridge crosses Hat Creek. Baum Lake, Crystal Lake and the Cassel section of Hat Creek are all within five miles of this camp.

11. HAT CREEK RANCH CAMPGROUND 🐟

Reference: **Map B3, grid g2.**

Campsites, facilities: There are 40 tent sites and 40 motor home sites with full or partial hookups. Restrooms, hot showers, a sanitary dump station, a laundromat, a playground and a grocery store are on the premises. No pets are allowed.

Reservations, fee: Reservations recommended; $13.75-$16.95 fee per night.

Who to contact: Phone (916) 335-7171.

Location: From Redding, drive east on Highway 299 to Burney, then continue for five miles to the junction with Highway 89. Turn right (south) on Highway 89 and drive 13 miles to the second Doty Road exit and the entrance to the campground.

Trip note: This privately-operated campground is set in a working cattle ranch, so if you go for a stroll, watch where you plant your Vibrams. Fishing is available in Hat Creek or in the nearby stocked trout pond. Sightseeing is excellent with Burney Falls, Lassen Volcanic National Park and Subway Caves all within 30 miles. Open April through October.

12. CAVE 🐟 🚶 ♿

Reference: **On Hat Creek in Lassen National Forest; map B3, grid h2.**

Campsites, facilities: There are 46 sites for tents or motor homes up to 22 feet long. Piped water, vault toilets, picnic tables and fire grills are provided. Supplies can be obtained in Old Station. Pets are allowed on leashes.

Reservations, fee: No reservations; $10 fee per night.

Who to contact: Phone the Lassen National Forest District Office at (916) 336-5521.

Location: From Redding, drive east on Highway 299 to Burney, then continue for five miles to the junction with Highway 89. Turn right (south) on Highway 89 and drive 23 miles to the campground entrance on the right side of the road. If you reach Old Station, you have gone one mile too far.

Trip note: Cave Camp is set right along Hat Creek, with both easy access off

Highway 89 and a fisherman's trail available along the stream. This stretch of Hat Creek is planted with rainbow trout twice per month by the Department of Fish and Game, and for campers, the prospects are all or nothing; all after a plant, nothing the rest of the time. Nearby side trips include Lassen Volcanic National Park, located about a 15-minute drive to the south on Highway 89, and Subway Cave Viewpoint, located three miles to the east on Highway 44 (turn left at the junction just across the road from the campground). A rare bonus at this camp is that **wheelchair-accessible** fishing is available. Open May to November.

13. BRIDGE

Reference: On Hat Creek in Lassen National Forest; map B3, grid h2.

Campsites, facilities: There are 25 sites for tents or motor homes up to 22 feet long. Piped water, vault toilets, picnic tables and fire grills are provided. A grocery store and propane gas are also available nearby. Pets are allowed on leashes.

Reservations, fee: No reservations; $9 fee per night.

Who to contact: Phone the Lassen National Forest District Office at (916) 336-5521.

Location: From Redding, drive east on Highway 299 to Burney, then continue for five miles to the junction with Highway 89. Turn right (south) on Highway 89 and drive 19 miles to the campground entrance on the right side of the road. If you reach Old Station, you have gone four miles too far.

Trip note: This camp is one of four along Highway 89 in the area set along Hat Creek. It is set at 3,800 feet elevation, with shaded sites and the stream within very short walking distance. Trout are stocked on this stretch of creek, with fishing access available out of camp, as well as at Rocky and Cave Camps to the south and Honn Camp to the north. In a weekend, you might hit all four. See trip note for Cave Camp.

14. ROCKY

Reference: On Hat Creek in Lassen National Forest; map B3, grid h2.

Campsites, facilities: There are eight tent sites. There is **no piped water**, but vault toilets, picnic tables and fire grills are provided. A grocery store and propane gas are also available nearby. Pets are allowed on leashes.

Reservations, fee: No reservations; $5 fee per night.

Who to contact: Phone the Lassen National Forest District Office at (916) 336-5521.

Location: From Redding, drive east on Highway 299 to Burney, then continue for five miles to the junction with Highway 89. Turn right (south) on Highway 89 and drive 20 miles to the campground entrance on the right side of the road. If you reach Old Station, you have gone three miles too far.

Trip note: This is a small, primitive camp located on Hat Creek on Highway 89, usually a second choice for campers if nearby Cave and Bridge camps have filled. Streamside fishing access is a plus here, with this section of stream stocked with rainbow trout. See trip note for Cave Camp.

15. HONN

Reference: On Hat Creek in Lassen National Forest; map B3, grid h2.

Campsites, facilities: There are six tent sites. There is **no piped water**, but vault toilets, picnic tables and fire grills are provided. A grocery store, a laundromat and propane gas are also available nearby. Pets are allowed on leashes.

Reservations, fee: No reservations; $5 fee per night.

Who to contact: Phone the Lassen National Forest District Office at (916) 336-5521.

Location: From Redding, drive east on Highway 299 to Burney, then continue for five miles to the junction with Highway 89. Turn right (south) on Highway 89 and drive 15 miles to the campground entrance on the left side of the road.

Trip note: This primitive, tiny camp is set near where Honn Creek enters Hat Creek, at 3,400 feet elevation. The river is extremely pretty here, shaded and flowing emerald-green. The camp provides streamside access for trout fishing, though this stretch of river is sometimes overlooked by the Department of Fish and Game in favor of stocking the river at the more popular Cave and Bridge campgrounds. See trip note for Cave Camp.

16. NORTH BATTLE CREEK RESERVOIR

Reference: Map B3, grid i0.

Campsites, facilities: There are 10 sites for tents or motor homes and five walk-in tent sites. Piped water, vault toilets, picnic tables and fire grills are provided. Pets are permitted on leashes. A car-top boat launch is available.

Reservations, fee: No reservations; $9 fee per night; $1 pet fee.

Who to contact: Phone the PG&E District Office at (916) 386-5164.

Location: From Redding, drive east on Highway 44 to Viola. From Viola, continue east for 3.5 miles to Forest Service Road 32N17. Turn left (north) on Forest Service Road 32N17 and drive five miles. Turn left (east) on Forest Service Road 32N31 and drive four miles. Turn right on Road 32N18 and drive a half-mile to the reservoir and the campground on the right side of the road.

Trip note: This little-known lake is set at 5,600 feet in elevation, largely surrounded by Lassen National Forest. No gas engines are permitted on the lake, making it ideal for canoes, rafts and car-top aluminum boats equipped with electric motors. When the lake level is up in early summer, it is a pretty setting with good trout fishing.

17. CRAGS CAMP

Reference: In Lassen Volcanic National Park; map B3, grid i1.

Campsites, facilities: There are 45 sites for tents or motor homes up to 35 feet long. Piped water, pit toilets, picnic tables and fire grills are provided. Pets are permitted on leashes.

Reservations, fee: No reservations; $6 fee per night.

Who to contact: Phone Lassen Volcanic National Park at (916) 595-4444.

Location: From Redding, drive east on Highway 44 for 42 miles to the junction with Highway 89. At Highway 89, turn right and drive one mile to the entrance station at Lassen Volcanic National Park. Continue on Highway 89 for about six miles to the campground on the left side of the road.

Trip note: Crags Camp is sometimes overlooked as a prime spot at Lassen Volcanic National Park because there is no lake nearby. No problem, because even though this camp is small compared to the giant complex at Manzanita Lake, the campsites are more spacious, a lot more private, and many are backed by forest. In addition, the Emigrant Trail runs out of camp, routed east and meeting up with pretty Lost Creek after a little over a mile, a great short hike. Directly across from Crags Camp are the towering Chaos Crags, topping out at 8,503 feet. The camp is set at 5,400 feet.

18. HAT CREEK 🐟 👫 ♿   RV. ⚠7

Reference: **In Lassen National Forest; map B3, grid i2.**

Campsites, facilities: There are 73 sites for tents or motor homes up to 22 feet long. Piped water, flush toilets, a sanitary dump station, picnic tables and fire grills are provided. A grocery store, a laundromat and propane gas are also available nearby. Pets are allowed on leashes.

Reservations, fee: No reservations; $10 fee per night.

Who to contact: Phone the Lassen National Forest District Office at (916) 336-5521.

Location: From Redding, drive east on Highway 44 to the junction with Highway 89 (near the entrance to Lassen Volcanic National Park). Turn north on Highway 89 and drive about 12 miles to the campground entrance on the left side of the road. (If you reach Old Station, you have gone one mile too far). Turn left and drive a short distance to the campground.

Trip note: This is one of a series of Forest Service camps set beside beautiful Hat Creek, a good trout stream stocked regularly by the Department of Fish and Game. The elevation is 4,400 feet. The proximity to Lassen Volcanic National Park to the south is a big plus, with supplies available in the little town of Old Station one mile to the north. Open May through October.

19. BIG PINE CAMP 🐟 👫   RV. ⚠7

Reference: **On Hat Creek in Lassen National Forest; map B3, grid i2.**

Campsites, facilities: There are 19 sites for tents or motor homes up to 22 feet long. Two hand pumps provide water. Vault toilets, picnic tables and fire grills are provided. A sanitary disposal station, a grocery store and propane gas are nearby. Pets are allowed on leashes.

Reservations, fee: No reservations; $7 fee per night.

Who to contact: Phone the Lassen National Forest District Office at (916) 336-5521.

Location: From Redding, drive east on Highway 44 to the junction with Highway 89 (near the entrance to Lassen Volcanic National Park). Turn north on Highway 89 and drive about eight miles (one mile past the vista point) to the campground entrance on the right side of the road. Turn right and drive a half-mile to the campground.

Trip note: This campground is set on the headwaters of Hat Creek, a pretty spot amid lodgepole pines. A dirt road out of camp parallels Hat Creek, providing access for trout fishing. A great vista point is set on the highway, a mile south of the campground entrance road. It is only a 10-minute drive to the south to the Highway 44 entrance station for Lassen Volcanic National Park.

20. BUTTE CREEK 🐟 👫   RV. ⚠6

Reference: **In Lassen National Forest; map B3, grid i4.**

Campsites, facilities: There are 10 unimproved sites for tents or motor homes up to 22 feet long. **No piped water** is available. Vault toilets, fire grills and tables are provided. Pets are permitted on leashes.

Reservations, fee: No reservations; no fee.

Who to contact: Call the Lassen National Forest at (916) 257-2151 or write to 55 South Sacramento Street, Susanville, CA 96130.

Location: From Redding, drive east on Highway 44 to the junction with Highway 89 (near the entrance to Lassen Volcanic National Park). Turn north on

Highway 89 and drive to Highway 44. Turn right (east) on Highway 44 and drive 11 miles to Forest Service Road 18. Turn right at Forest Service Road 18 and drive three miles to the campground on the left side of the road.

Trip note: This primitive, little-known spot is just three miles from the northern boundary of Lassen Volcanic National Park, set on little Butte Creek. It is a four-mile drive south out of camp on Forest Service Road 18 to Butte Lake in Lassen Park, as well as to the trailhead for a great hike up to the Cinder Cone (6,907 feet), with dramatic views of the Lassen wilderness. Open May through October.

21. CRATER LAKE

Reference: **In Lassen National Forest; map B3, grid i6.**

Campsites, facilities: There are 17 sites for tents or motor homes up to 16 feet long. Well water is available. Vault toilets, fire grills and picnic tables are provided. Pets are permitted on leashes.

Reservations, fee: No reservations; $10 fee per night.

Who to contact: Call Lassen National Forest at (916) 257-4188.

Location: From Redding, drive east on Highway 44 to the junction with Highway 89 (near the entrance to Lassen Volcanic National Park). Turn north on Highway 89 and drive to Highway 44. Turn right (east) on Highway 44 and drive to the Bogard Work Center and adjacent rest stop. Turn left at Forest Service Road 32N08 (signed Crater Lake) and drive one mile to a T. Bear right and continue on Forest Service Road 32N08 for six miles (including two hairpin left turns) to the campground on the left side of the road.

Trip note: This camp is set near Crater Lake at 6,800 feet in remote Lassen National Forest, just below Crater Mountain (that's it up there to the northeast at 7,420 feet). Crater Lake is less than a quarter-mile from the campground, with the access road continuing all the way to the lake. This primitive hideaway provides fishing, boating, and if you can stand the ice cold water, a quick dunk. Open June through October.

22. MANZANITA LAKE

Reference: **In Lassen Volcanic National Park; map B3, grid j0.**

Campsites, facilities: There are 179 sites for tents or motor homes up to 35 feet long. Piped water, flush toilets, showers, a sanitary dump station, picnic tables, and fire grills are provided. Pets are permitted. Propane gas, groceries and a laundromat are also available nearby.

Reservations, fee: No reservations; $10 fee per night.

Who to contact: Phone Lassen Volcanic National Park at (916) 595-4444.

Location: From Redding, drive east on Highway 44 to the junction with Highway 89. Turn right on Highway 89 and drive one mile to the entrance station to Lassen Volcanic National Park. Continue a short distance on Highway 89 and turn right at the campground entrance road and drive a half-mile to the campground.

Trip note: Manzanita Lake, set at 5,890 feet, is one of the prettiest lakes in Lassen Volcanic National Park and has good catch-and-release trout fishing for experienced fly fishers in prams and other non-powered boats. This is no place for a dad and a youngster to fish from shore with Power Bait. Because of the great natural beauty of the lake, the campground is often crowded, and the campsites are closer together than at other camps in the park. Evening walks around the lake are very beautiful. A major visitor center and small store are available nearby.

23. SUMMIT LAKE, NORTH AND SOUTH   RV. 9

Reference: In Lassen Volcanic National Park; map B3, grid j2.
Campsites, facilities: There are 94 sites for tents or motor homes up to 30 feet long. Piped water, flush and pit toilets (flush toilets on the north side, pit toilets on the south side), picnic tables, and fire grills are provided. Pets are permitted on leashes.
Reservations, fee: No reservations; $8-$10 fee per night.
Who to contact: Phone Lassen Volcanic National Park at (916) 595-4444.
Location: From Redding, drive east on Highway 44 to the junction with Highway 89. Turn right on Highway 89 and drive one mile to the entrance station to Lassen Volcanic National Park. Continue on Highway 89 for 12 miles to the campground entrance on the left (east) side of the road.
Trip note: Summit Lake is a beautiful spot where deer often visit each evening on the adjacent meadow just east of the campground. The lake is small, and since trout plants were suspended, it is about fished out. Evening walks around the lake are perfect for families. A more ambitious trail is routed out of camp and leads past lavish wildflower displays in early summer to a series of wilderness lakes.

24. SILVER BOWL   RV. 7

Reference: On Silver Lake in Lassen National Forest; map B3, grid j5.
Campsites, facilities: There are 18 sites for tents or motor homes. Piped water, vault toilets, fire grills and picnic tables are provided. Pets are permitted on leashes.
Reservations, fee: No reservations; $8 fee per night.
Who to contact: Phone the Lassen National Forest at (916) 258-2141
Location: From Red Bluff, drive east on Highway 36 to the junction with Highway 89. Continue east on Highway 89/36 past Lake Almanor to Westwood. In Westwood, turn north on County Road A21 and drive 12.5 miles to Silver Lake Road. Turn left (west) on Silver Lake Road (County Road 110) and drive 8.5 miles north to Silver Lake. At Silver Lake, turn right and drive a short distance to the campground.
Trip note: Silver Lake is a pretty lake set at 6,400 feet elevation at the edge of Caribou Wilderness. It is stocked with 9,000 Eagle Lake trout and 900 brown trout each year and provides a good summer fishery for campers. There is an unimproved boat ramp at the southern end of the lake. A trailhead from adjacent Caribou Lake is routed west into the wilderness, with routes available both to Emerald Lake to the northwest, and Betty, Trail and Shotoverin lakes nearby to the southeast. Open May to October.

25. BOGARD   RV. 6

Reference: In Lassen National Forest; map B3, grid j5.
Campsites, facilities: There are 21 sites for tents or motor homes up to 28 feet long. Water, vault toilets, tables and fire grills are provided. Pets are permitted on leashes.

Reservations, fee: No reservations; $8 fee per night.

Who to contact: Phone the Lassen National Forest at (916) 257-4188 or write to 55 South Sacramento Street, Susanville, CA 96130.

Location: From Redding, drive east on Highway 44 to the junction with Highway 89 (near the entrance to Lassen Volcanic National Park). Turn north on Highway 89 and drive to Highway 44. Turn right (east) on Highway 44 and drive to the Bogard Work Center (about seven miles past Poison Lake) and adjacent rest stop. Continue east on Highway 44 for two miles to a gravel road on the right side of the road (Forest Service Road 31N26). Turn right on Forest Service Road 31N26 and drive two miles. Turn right on Forest Service Road 31N21 and drive a half-mile to the campground at the end of the road.

Trip note: This little camp is set along Pine Creek, which flows through Pine Creek Valley at the foot of the Bogard Buttes. It is a relatively obscure camp that gets missed by many travelers. To the nearby west is a network of Forest Service Roads, and beyond is the Caribou Wilderness. Open May to October.

---

26. ROCKY KNOLL

Reference: **On Silver Lake in Lassen National Forest; map B3, grid j5.**

Campsites, facilities: There are seven tent sites and 11 sites for motor homes up to 27 feet long. Piped water, vault toilets, fire grills and picnic tables are provided. Pets are permitted on leashes.

Reservations, fee: No reservations; $8 fee per night.

Who to contact: Phone the Lassen National Forest at (916) 258-2141

Location: From Red Bluff, drive east on Highway 36 to the junction with Highway 89. Continue east on Highway 89/36 past Lake Almanor to Westwood. In Westwood, turn north on County Road A21 and drive 12.5 miles to Silver Lake Road. Turn left (west) on Silver Lake Road (County Road 110) and drive 8.5 miles north to Silver Lake. At Silver Lake, turn left and drive a short distance to the campground.

Trip note: This is one of two camps at pretty Silver Lake, set at 6,400 feet elevation at the edge of Caribou Wilderness. The other camp is Silver Bowl to the nearby north, which is larger and provides better access for hikers. This camp, however, is located closer to the boat ramp, which is set at the south end of the lake. Silver Lake provides a good summer fishery for campers. Open May to October.

---

27. ASPEN GROVE

Reference: **On Eagle Lake in Lassen National Forest; map B3, grid j9.**

Campsites, facilities: There are 26 tent sites. Picnic tables, fire grills, piped water, a phone and flush toilets are provided. Pets are permitted on leashes. A boat ramp is available.

Reservations, fee: No reservations; $10 fee per night.

Who to contact: Phone the Lassen National Forest at (916) 257-4188.

Location: From Red Bluff, drive east on Highway 36 to the junction with Highway 89. Drive east on Highway 89/36 to the junction with Highway 36 and continue for three miles to County Road A1. Turn left on County Road A1 and drive 15.5 miles to County Road 231. Turn right on County Road 231 and drive two miles to the campground on the left side of the road.

Trip note: Eagle Lake is one of the great trout lakes in California, producing the fast-growing and often huge Eagle Lake trout, which are common in the 18- to

22-inch class. This camp is one of three located at the south end of the lake, and is a popular one for anglers, with a boat ramp available adjacent to the campground. The one problem with Eagle Lake is the wind, which can whip the huge but shallow lake into a froth in the early summer. It is imperative that fishermen/boaters get on the water early, and then get back to camp early, with the fishing for the day often done by 10:30 a.m. A bonus here is a good chance to see bald eagles and osprey. Open May to October.

28. EAGLE

Reference: **On Eagle Lake in Lassen National Forest; map B3, grid j9.**

Campsites, facilities: There are 45 sites for tents or motor homes up to 32 feet long. Piped water, flush toilets, picnic tables and fire grills are provided. The facilities are **wheelchair accessible**. There is a boat launch nearby at Aspen Grove. Pets are permitted on leashes.

Reservations, fee: Reserve by phoning (800) 280-CAMP ($7.50 reservation fee); $12 fee per night.

Who to contact: Phone the Lassen National Forest at (916) 257-4188.

Location: From Red Bluff, drive east on Highway 36 to the junction with Highway 89. Drive east on Highway 89/36 to the junction with Highway 36 and continue for three miles to County Road A1. Turn left on County Road A1 and drive 15.5 miles to County Road 231. Turn right on County Road 231 and drive one mile to the campground on the left side of the road.

Trip note: Eagle Camp is set just up the road from Aspen Grove Camp; the latter is more popular because of the adjacent boat ramp. For information about Eagle Lake, see trip note for Aspen Grove Camp. Open May to October.

29. WEST EAGLE GROUP CAMPS

Reference: **On Eagle Lake in Lassen National Forest; map B3, grid j9.**

Campsites, facilities: There are two group camps for tents and motor homes up to 35 feet long. Piped water, flush toilets, tables and picnic areas are provided. The facilities are **wheelchair accessible**. Pets are permitted on leashes. A grocery store and a boat ramp are nearby. The campground capacity is limited to 100 people for camp one and 75 people for camp two.

Reservations, fee: Reservations required; $70-$110 fee per night for camp one; $60-$80 fee per night for camp two.

Who to contact: Reserve by calling (800) 280-CAMP ($15 reservation fee).

Location: From Red Bluff, drive east on Highway 36 to the junction with Highway 89. Drive east on Highway 89/36 to the junction with Highway 36 and continue for three miles to County Road A1. Turn left on County Road A1 and drive 15.5 miles to County Road 231. Turn right on County Road 231 and drive one mile to the campground (just beyond Eagle Group Camp) on the left side of the road.

Trip note: If you are coming in a big group to Eagle Lake, you better get on the horn first and reserve this camp. Then you can have your own private slice of solitude along the southern shore of Eagle Lake. Bring your boat. The Aspen Boat Ramp is only about a mile away.

30. MERRILL 🐟 ⚓ 🚶 ♿ 🏊 🚶 RV 9

Reference: **On Eagle Lake in Lassen National Forest; map B3, grid j9.**

Campsites, facilities: There are 181 sites for tents or motor homes up to 32 feet long. Piped water, flush toilets, picnic tables and fire grills are provided. A sanitary disposal station is available. The facilities are **wheelchair accessible**. A grocery store and boat ramp are nearby. Pets are allowed on leashes.

Reservations, fee: No reservations (except for lake sites); $12-$14 fee per night.

Who to contact: Phone Lassen National Forest at (916) 257-4188.

Location: From Red Bluff, drive east on Highway 36 to the junction with Highway 89. Drive east on Highway 89/36 to the junction with Highway 36 and continue for three miles to County Road A1. Turn left on County Road A1 and drive 15.5 miles to County Road 231. Bear left at that junction (staying on County Road 231) and drive one mile to the campground entrance on the right side of the road.

Trip note: This is one of the largest, most developed Forest Service campgrounds in the entire county. It is set along the southern shore of huge Eagle Lake at 5,100 feet. The nearest boat launch is adjacent to Aspen Grove Camp; see trip note for that camp. Open May to December.

---

31. CHRISTIE 🐟 ⚓ 🚶 ♿ 🏊 🚶 RV 9

Reference: **On Eagle Lake in Lassen National Forest; map B3, grid j9.**

Campsites, facilities: There are 69 sites for tents or motor homes up to 50 feet long. Piped water, flush toilets, fire grills and picnic tables are provided. The facilities are **wheelchair accessible**. A grocery store is nearby. Pets are permitted on leashes. A disposal station is two miles away at Merrill Camp.

Reservations, fee: No reservations (except for lake sites); $12-$18 fee per night.

Who to contact: Phone the Lassen National Forest at (916) 257-2151.

Location: From Red Bluff, drive east on Highway 36 to the junction with Highway 89. Drive east on Highway 89/36 to the junction with Highway 36 and continue for three miles to County Road A1. Turn left on County Road A1 and drive 15.5 miles to County Road 231. Bear left at that junction (staying on County Road 231) and drive four miles to the campground entrance on the right side of the road.

Trip note: This camp is set along the southern shore of Eagle Lake at 5,100 feet. Eagle Lake is well known for its big trout (yea) and big winds (boo). This camp offers some protection from the north winds. Its location is also good for seeing osprey, with the Osprey Management Area, which covers a six-mile stretch of shoreline, located just two miles to the north above Wildcat Point. A nearby resort is a bonus. The nearest boat ramp is at Aspen Grove Camp (see trip note). Open May to October.

NOTE: For more camps at Eagle Lake, see Chapter B4.

MAP B4

NOR-CAL MAP .... see page 94
adjoining maps
NORTH (A4) .... see page 136
EAST .... no map
SOUTH (C4) .... see page 306
WEST (B3) .... see page 208

21 LISTINGS
PAGES 222-231

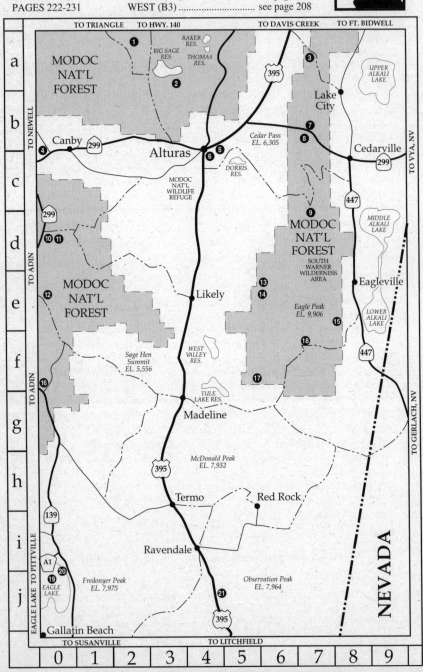

TO TRIANGLE   TO HWY. 140   TO DAVIS CREEK   TO FT. BIDWELL

MODOC NAT'L FOREST

RAKER RES.
BIG SAGE RES.
THOMAS RES.

UPPER ALKALI LAKE

395

Lake City

Cedar Pass EL. 6,305

Canby
299
Alturas

DORRIS RES.

Cedarville
299

TO NEWELL

MODOC NAT'L WILDLIFE REFUGE

447

299

MODOC NAT'L FOREST

MIDDLE ALKALI LAKE

TO ADIN

SOUTH WARNER WILDERNESS AREA

Eagleville

MODOC NAT'L FOREST

Likely

Eagle Peak EL. 9,906

LOWER ALKALI LAKE

447

TO ADIN

Sage Hen Summit EL. 5,556

WEST VALLEY RES.

TULE LAKE RES.

Madeline

TO GERLACH, NV

McDonald Peak EL. 7,932

395

Termo   Red Rock

139

Ravendale

NEVADA

A1

Fredonyer Peak EL. 7,975

Observation Peak EL. 7,964

EAGLE LAKE TO PITTVILLE

EAGLE LAKE

21

395

Gallatin Beach

TO SUSANVILLE   TO LITCHFIELD

0 1 2 3 4 5 6 7 8 9

a b c d e f g h i j

TO VYA, NV

Map B4 featuring: Modoc National Forest, Cedar Pass, Eagle Lake

1. RESERVOIR C 〜

Reference: **Near Alturas in Modoc National Forest; map B4, grid a2.**

Campsites, facilities: There are six primitive sites, but there is **no piped water**, so bring your own. A vault toilet and picnic tables are provided. Pets are allowed on leashes.

Reservations, fee: No reservations; no fee.

Who to contact: Phone the Modoc National Forest District Office at (916) 233-5811.

Location: From Alturas, drive west on Highway 299 for three miles to Crowder Flat Road (County Road 73). Turn right on Crowder Flat Road and drive 9.5 miles to Triangle Ranch Road (Forest Service Road 43N18). Turn left on Triangle Ranch Road and drive seven miles to Forest Service Road 44N32. Turn right on Forest Service Road 44N32, drive a half-mile, then turn right on the access road for the lake and campground and drive a half-mile to the camp at the end of the road.

Trip note: It is a hell of an adventure to explore the "alphabet lakes," located in the remote Devils Garden area of Modoc County. Reservoir C and Reservoir F provide the best of the lot, but the success can go up and down like a yo-yo, just like the water levels in the lakes. The lake is stocked with both Eagle Lake trout and brown trout. A sidelight to this area is the number of primitive roads that are routed through Modoc National Forest, perfect for four-wheel-drive cowboys. Open May to October.

2. BIG SAGE RESERVOIR 〜 ⚓

Reference: **In Modoc National Forest; map B4, grid a3.**

Campsites, facilities: There are primitive, dispersed sites for tents or motor homes of any length. Vault toilets and picnic tables are provided. **No piped water** is available, so bring your own. Pack out your garbage. A boat ramp is available. Pets are permitted on leashes. Supplies can be obtained in Alturas.

Reservations, fee: No reservations; no fee.

Who to contact: Phone the Modoc National Forest District Office at (916) 233-5811.

Location: From Alturas, drive west on Highway 299 for three miles to Crowder Flat Road (County Road 73). Turn right on Crowder Flat Road and drive about five miles to County Road 180. Turn right on County Road 180 and drive four miles. Turn left at the access road for the campground and boat ramp and drive a short distance to the camp on the left side of the road.

Trip note: This is a do-it-yourself camp, that is, pick your own spot, bring your own water, and don't expect to see any Forest Service rangers, or, for that matter, anybody else. This camp is set along Big Sage Reservoir—that's right, sagebrush country at 4,900 feet elevation. It is a big lake, covering 5,000 acres, and a boat ramp is located adjacent to the campground. This is one of the better bass lakes in Modoc County. Catfishing is also available here. Open May to October.

3. PLUM VALLEY

Reference: **Near the South Fork of Davis Creek in Modoc National Forest; map B4, grid a7.**

Campsites, facilities: There are 15 sites for tents or motor homes up to 15 feet long. Vault toilets, fire grills and picnic tables are provided. **No piped water** is available. Pets are permitted on leashes. Supplies are available in Davis Creek.

Reservations, fee: No reservations; no fee.

Who to contact: Phone the Modoc National Forest District Office at (916) 279-6116.

Location: From Alturas, drive north on US 395 for 18 miles to the town of Davis Creek. Turn east (right) on County Road 11 and drive two miles to a Y. Bear right on Forest Service Road 45N35 and drive one mile to the signed entrance to the campground on the left side of the road.

Trip note: This secluded and primitive camp is set near the South Fork of Davis Creek, at 5,600 feet elevation. Davis Creek provides fair trout fishing, with the trout short but chunky, and sometimes quite deeply colored. There are no other campgrounds within 15 miles. Open May to October.

4. BELLY ACRES CAMPGROUND

Reference: **Near Canby; map B4, grid b0.**

Campsites, facilities: There are 15 motor home sites with full hookups. Hot showers, flush toilets and a sanitary disposal station are available. Supplies are available in Canby. Pets are allowed on leashes.

Reservations, fee: Reservations accepted; $15 fee per night.

Who to contact: Phone (916) 233-4759.

Location: From Redding, drive east on Highway 299 past Adin and toward Canby. Just before reaching Canby, turn left (northwest) on County Road 214 and drive about a half-mile to the campground.

Trip note: This privately-developed motor home park has open, level sites and is located near Highway 299. It is set near the Devils Garden district of Modoc National Forest, known for large bucks with impressive antlers. The upper stretch of the Pit River runs right aside Highway 299 downstream of Canby. The elevation at the campground is 4,200 feet.

5. BRASS RAIL CAMPGROUND

Reference: **Near Alturas; map B4, grid b4.**

Campsites, facilities: There are 70 motor home sites, some with full hookups, and a separate tent area. Picnic tables are provided. Hot showers, flush toilets, a sanitary disposal station, a laundromat, ice, propane gas, a playground, a tennis court and a swimming pool are available. Pets are permitted on leashes. Supplies can be obtained in Alturas.

Reservations, fee: Reservations accepted; $8-$14 fee per night.

Who to contact: Phone (916) 233-2906.

Location: In Alturas at the junction of Highway 299 and US 395, turn east on US 395 and drive a half-mile to the signed campground entrance on the right.

Trip note: This private motor home park has easy access from the highway. The elevation is 4,400 feet. Open March through October. Alturas is the biggest "small town" in Modoc County and offers a nice city park with a playground, a museum, an old time saloon, and, just south of town, the Modoc National Wildlife Refuge. The Warner Mountains to the distant east provide a backdrop.

6. SULLY'S TRAILER LODGE ♿ ⚲   RV 4

Reference: **Near Alturas; map B4, grid b4.**

Campsites, facilities: There are 15 motor home sites, some with full hookups. Hot showers, flush toilets, a laundromat and horseshoe pits are available. Cable TV is available for an extra fee. Supplies can be obtained in Alturas. Pets are allowed on leashes.

Reservations, fee: Reservations accepted; $10.40-$14.40 fee per night.

Who to contact: Phone (916) 233-2253.

Location: In Alturas at the junction of Highway 299 and US 395, turn south on US 395 and drive a half-mile (look for the steam engine) to County Road 56. Turn east on County Road 56 and drive one block to the campground.

Trip note: This year-round, privately-operated park is located next to the playground, the city park and the Modoc County Museum, which details the history of the area. The surrounding Modoc National Wildlife Refuge requires only a short drive to reach, either a mile southwest of town along the Pit River, or three miles east of town at Dorris Reservoir. Big Sage Reservoir (see Big Sage Campground) provides another getaway option.

7. STOWE RESERVOIR CAMPGROUND 🚶🚶   RV 8

Reference: **In Modoc National Forest; map B4, grid b7.**

Campsites, facilities: There are eight sites for tents or motor homes up to 20 feet long. Piped water, vault toilets, picnic tables and fire grills are provided. Pets are permitted on leashes. Supplies can be obtained in Cedarville.

Reservations, fee: No reservations; no fee.

Who to contact: Phone the Modoc National Forest District Office at (916) 279-6116.

Location: From Redding, drive east on Highway 299 to Alturas. In Alturas, continue north on Highway 299/US 395 for five miles. Turn right on Highway 299 and drive about 12 miles (just pass Cedar Pass). Look for the signed entrance road on the left side of the road. Turn left and drive one mile to the campground on the right side of the road.

Trip note: Stowe Reservoir looks kind of like a large country pond where cattle would drink. You know why? Because it was. That is, it actually was a cattle pond on a family ranch, which has since been converted to Forest Service property. It is located in the north Warner Mountains (not to be confused with the South Warner Wilderness), which features many back roads and remote four-wheel-drive routes. Open May to October.

Special note: You may find this campground named "Stough Reservoir" on some maps and in previous editions of this book. The name is now officially spelled "Stowe Reservoir," after the family that originally owned the property.

8. CEDAR PASS   5

Reference: **On Cedar Pass in Modoc National Forest; map B4, grid b7.**

Campsites, facilities: There are 17 sites for tents or motor homes up to 22 feet long. Vault toilets, picnic tables and fire grills are provided. **No piped water** is available, so bring your own. Pack out your garbage. Pets are permitted on leashes. Supplies can be obtained in Cedarville or Alturas.

Reservations, fee: No reservations; no fee.

Who to contact: Phone the Modoc National Forest District Office at (916) 279-6116.

Location: From Redding, drive east on Highway 299 to Alturas. In Alturas, continue north on Highway 299/US 395 for five miles. Turn right on Highway 299 and drive about nine miles. Look for the signed entrance road on the right side of the road.

Trip note: Cedar Pass is at 5,900 feet in elevation, set on the ridge between Cedar Mountain (8,152 feet) to the north and Payne Peak (7,618) to the south, high in the north Warner Mountains. Bear Creek enters Thomas Creek adjacent to the camp, both small streams, but a pretty spot. Open May to October.

---

9. PEPPERDINE 🚶🏇   5%CLUB RV 5

Reference: **In Modoc National Forest; map B4, grid c7.**

Campsites, facilities: There are five sites for tents or motor homes up to 22 feet long. Piped water, vault toilets, picnic tables and fire grills are provided. Corrals are available with stock watering facilities. Pack out your garbage. Pets are permitted on leashes. Supplies are available in Cedarville or Alturas.

Reservations, fee: No reservations; no fee.

Who to contact: Phone the Modoc National Forest District Office at (916) 279-6116.

Location: In Alturas, drive south on Highway 395 to the southern end of town to County Road 56. Turn east (right) on County Road 56 and drive 13 miles to the Modoc Forest boundary and the junction with Parker Creek Road. Bear left on Parker Creek Road and continue for six miles to the signed campground access road on the right. Turn right and drive a half-mile to the campground on the right side of the road.

Trip note: This camp is outstanding for hikers planning a backpacking trip into the adjacent South Warner Wilderness. The camp is at 6,680 feet, set along the south side of tiny Porter Reservoir, with a horse corral located within walking distance. A trailhead out of camp provides direct access to the Summit Trail, the best hike in the South Warner Wilderness. Open July through October.

---

10. LOWER RUSH CREEK 🐟   RV 6

Reference: **In Modoc National Forest; map B4, grid d0.**

Campsites, facilities: There are five sites for tents and five sites for motor homes up to 22 feet long. Piped water, vault toilets, picnic tables and fire grills are provided. Pets are permitted on leashes. Supplies are available in Canby.

Reservations, fee: No reservations; $5 fee per night.

Who to contact: Phone the Modoc National Forest District Office at (916) 299-3215.

Location: From Redding, turn east on Highway 299 and drive to Adin. Continue east on Highway 299 for about seven miles to a signed campground turnoff on the right side of the road. Turn right and drive one mile to the campground.

Trip note: This is one of two obscure campgrounds set a short distance from Highway 299 off Rush Creek in southern Modoc County. Lower Rush Creek Camp is the first camp you will come to, with flat campsites, surrounded by an outer fence, and set along little Rush Creek. This camp is better suited for trailers than the camp at Upper Rush Creek. It is little-known and little-used. It's set at 4,400 feet in elevation. Open May to October.

11. UPPER RUSH CREEK

Reference: **In Modoc National Forest; map B4, grid d0.**

Campsites, facilities: There are 13 sites for tents or motor homes up to 22 feet long, but Lower Rush Creek Camp is better for trailers. Piped water, vault toilets, fire grills and tables are provided. Pets are permitted on leashes. Supplies can be obtained in Adin or Canby.

Reservations, fee: No reservations; $4 fee per night.

Who to contact: Phone the Modoc National Forest District Office at (916) 299-3215.

Location: From Redding, turn east on Highway 299 and drive to Adin. Continue east on Highway 299 for about seven miles to a signed campground turnoff on the right side of the road. Turn right and drive 2.5 miles to the campground at the end of the road.

Trip note: This is a pretty campground, set along little Rush Creek, a quiet, wooded spot that gets little use. It sits in the shadow of nearby Manzanita Mountain (7,036 feet elevation) to the east, where there is an old forest service lookout for a great view. To reach it from the camp, drive back toward Highway 299, and just before reaching the highway, turn left on Forest Service Road 22. A mile from the summit, turn left at a four-way junction and drive to the top. You get dramatic views of the Warm Springs Valley to the north and the Likely Flats to the east, looking across miles and miles of open country. Open May to October.

12. ASH CREEK

Reference: **In Modoc National Forest; map B4, grid e0.**

Campsites, facilities: There are seven sites for tents only. Vault toilets, tables and fire grills are provided. **No piped water** is available so bring your own. Pack out your garbage. Pets are permitted on leashes. Supplies can be obtained in Adin.

Reservations, fee: No reservations; no fee.

Who to contact: Phone the Modoc National Forest District Office at (916) 299-3215, or write to P.O. Box 885, Adin, CA 96006.

Location: From Redding, turn east on Highway 299 and drive to Adin. In Adin, turn right (southeast) on Ash Valley Road (County Road 88/527) and drive eight miles. Turn left at a signed entrance road and drive one mile to the campground on the right side of the road.

Trip note: This remote camp has stark beauty and is set along Ash Creek, a stream with small trout. This region of Modoc National Forest has an extensive network of backcountry roads, popular for deer hunters in the fall. Summer comes relatively late out here, and it can be cold and wet even in early June. Stash some extra clothes, just in case. That will probably guarantee nice weather. Open May to October.

13. SOUP SPRINGS

Reference: **In Modoc National Forest; map B4, grid e6.**

Campsites, facilities: There are eight tent sites and six sites for tents or motor homes up to 22 feet long. Piped water, vault toilets, picnic tables and fire grills are provided. Pets are permitted on leashes. Corrals are available. Supplies can be obtained in Likely.

Reservations, fee: No reservations; no fee.

Who to contact: Phone the Modoc National Forest District Office at (916) 279-6116.

Location: From Alturas, drive south on US 395 for 17 miles to the town of Likely. Turn left on Jess Valley Road (County Road 64) and drive nine miles to the fork. Bear left on West Warner Road (Forest Service Road 5) for 4.5 miles to Soup Loop Road. Turn right on Soup Loop Road (Forest Service Road 40N24), and continue on that gravel road for six miles to the campground entrance on the right.

Trip note: This is a beautiful, quiet, wooded campground at a trailhead into the South Warner Wilderness. Soup Creek originates at Soup Springs in the meadow adjacent to the campground. The trailhead here is routed two miles into the wilderness, where it junctions with the Mill Creek Trail. From here, turn left for a beautiful walk along Mill Creek and into Mill Creek Meadow, an easy yet pristine stroll that can provide a serene experience. The elevation at the campground is 6,800 feet. Open June to October.

---

14. MILL CREEK FALLS 🚶🏇   RV 9

Reference: **In Modoc National Forest; map B4, grid e6.**

Campsites, facilities: There are 11 sites for tents and eight sites for tents or motor homes up to 22 feet long. Piped water, vault toilets, tables and fire grills are provided. Pets are permitted on leashes. Supplies are available in Likely.

Reservations, fee: No reservations; $5 fee per night.

Who to contact: Phone the Modoc National Forest District Office at (916) 279-6116.

Location: From Alturas, drive 17 miles south on US 395 to the town of Likely. Turn left on Jess Valley Road (County Road 64) and drive nine miles to the fork. Bear left on Forest Service Road 5 for 2.5 miles, then turn right on Forest Service Road 40N46 and proceed two miles to the campground entrance at the end of the road.

Trip note: This nice, wooded campground is a good base camp for a wilderness backpacking trip into the South Warner Wilderness. The camp is set on Mill Creek, 5,700 feet in elevation. To see Mill Creek Falls, take the trail out of camp and bear left at the Y. To enter the interior of South Warner Wilderness, bear right at the Y, after which the trail passes Clear Lake, heads on to Poison Flat and Poison Creek, and then reaches a junction. Left will take you to the Mill Creek Trail, right will take you up to the Summit Trail. Take your pick. Here you can't go wrong. Open May through October.

---

15. EMERSON 🎣 🚶

Reference: **In Modoc National Forest; map B4, grid e8.**

Campsites, facilities: There are four sites for tents or motor homes up to 16 feet long. Vault toilets, picnic tables and fire grills are provided. **No piped water** is available, so bring your own. Pets are permitted on leashes. Supplies can be obtained in Eagleville.

Reservations, fee: No reservations; no fee.

Who to contact: Phone the Modoc National Forest District Office at (916) 279-6116.

Location: From Alturas, drive north on US 395/Highway 299 for about five miles to the junction with Highway 299. Turn right on Highway 299 and drive to Cedarville. From Cedarville, drive 15 miles south on County Road 1 to Eagleville. From Eagleville, continue one mile south on County Road 1 to County Road 40. Turn right on County Road 40 and drive three miles to the campground at the end of the road. The access road is steep and very slick in wet weather. Trailers are not recommended.

Trip note: This tiny camp is virtually unknown, nestled at 6,000 feet on the eastern boundary of the South Warner Wilderness. Big alkali lakes and miles of the Nevada flats can be seen on the other side of the highway as you drive along the entrance road to the campground. This primitive setting is used by backpackers hitting the trail, a steep, sometimes wrenching climb for 4.5 miles to North Emerson Lake (poor to fair fishing). For many, this is a true butt-kicker. Open July to October.

16. WILLOW CREEK   RV 7

Reference: **In Modoc National Forest; map B4, grid f0.**

Campsites, facilities: There are eight sites for tents or motor homes up to 32 feet long. Piped water, vault toilets, tables and fire grills are provided. Pets are permitted on leashes. A **wheelchair-accessible** toilet is located across from the picnic area.

Reservations, fee: No reservations; $5 fee per night.

Who to contact: Phone the Modoc National Forest at (916) 299-3215.

Location: From Redding, drive east on Highway 299 to Adin. From Adin, turn right on Highway 139 and drive to the campground on the left side of the road.

Trip note: This remote camp and picnic area is set along little Willow Creek amid pine, aspen and willows, with Lower McBride Springs set on the north side of the campground. To the southwest is a state game refuge, with access available by vehicle, and with several four-wheel-drive routes near its border. Open May through October.

17. BLUE LAKE   RV 6

Reference: **In Modoc National Forest; map B4, grid f6.**

Campsites, facilities: There are 48 sites for tents or motor homes up to 25 feet long. Piped water, vault toilets, tables and fire grills are provided. A paved boat launch is available on the lake. A **wheelchair-accessible** fishing pier is also available. Pets are permitted on leashes. Supplies are available in Likely.

Reservations, fee: No reservations; $6 fee per night.

Who to contact: Phone the Modoc National Forest District Office at (916) 279-6116.

Location: From Alturas, drive south on US 395 for 7 miles to the town of Likely. In Likely, turn left on Jess Valley Road (County Road 64) and drive nine miles to the fork. At the fork, bear right on Forest Service Road 64 and drive seven miles to Forest Service Road 38N60. Turn right on Forest Service Road 38N60 and drive two miles to the campground.

Trip note: This is a wooded campground with some level sites near the shore of Blue Lake. The lake, which covers 160 acres, provides fishing for brown trout and rainbow trout. A five-mile-per-hour speed limit assures quiet water for small boats and canoes. A trail circles the lake and takes less than an hour to hike. The elevation is 6,000 feet. Open June through October. Over the years, a highlight here has been occasional sightings of bald eagles. A clear decline in the eagle population here may cause this camp to be temporarily closed during the nesting season in the spring and early summer. Call before visiting.

18. PATTERSON 🚶🐃🏇 ▲7

Reference: In Modoc National Forest; map B4, grid f7.

Campsites, facilities: There are five sites for tents or motor homes up to 20 feet long. Piped water, vault toilets, tables and fire grills provided. Pack out your garbage. Supplies are available in Likely or Eagleville. Pets are allowed on leashes.

Reservations, fee: No reservations; no fee.

Who to contact: Phone the Modoc National Forest District Office at (916) 279-6116.

Location: From Alturas, drive 17 miles south on US 395 to the town of Likely. Turn left on Jess Valley Road (County Road 64) and drive nine miles to the fork. Bear right on Forest Service Road 64 and drive for 16 miles to the campground.

Trip note: This quiet, wooded campground is set across the road from Patterson Meadow at 7,200 feet in elevation. It's an ideal jumpoff spot for a backpacking trip into the South Warner Wilderness, with a trailhead at the camp providing access to the southern wilderness boundary. A great hike from here is the East Creek Loop, a 15-miler that can be completed in a weekend, and provides a capsule look at the amazing contrasts of the Warners, from small pristine streams to high, barren mountain rims. The camp is rarely open before July.

19. EAGLE LAKE RV PARK 🐟 ⚓ 🏊 RV 7

Reference: Map B4, grid i0.

Campsites, facilities: There are 30 tent sites and 69 motor home sites, most with full or partial hookups. There is a separate area for tents only. Picnic tables and fire grills are provided. Restrooms, showers, a laundromat, a sanitary disposal station, a grocery store, propane gas, RV supplies, wood, a recreation room and a boat ramp are available. Pets are allowed on leashes.

Reservations, fee: Reservations recommended; $13-$18.50 fee per night.

Who to contact: Phone (916) 825-3133.

Location: From Red Bluff, drive east on Highway 36 toward Susanville. Just before reaching Susanville, turn left on County Road A1 and drive to County Road 518 near Spalding Tract. Turn right on County Road 518 and drive through a small neighborhood to the lake frontage road (look for The Strand). Turn right on Palmetto Way and drive eight blocks to the store at the RV park entrance at 687-125 Palmetto Way.

Trip note: Eagle Lake RV Park has become something of a headquarters for anglers in pursuit of Eagle Lake trout, which typically range 18 to 22 inches. A nearby boat ramp provides access to Pelican Point and Eagle Point, where the fishing is often best in the summer. In the fall months, the north end of the lake provides better prospects (see North Eagle Lake camp). This motor home park has all amenities, including a small store. That means no special trips into town, just vacation time, lounging beside Eagle Lake, maybe catching a big trout now and then. One downer: The wind typically howls here most summer afternoons.

20. NORTH EAGLE LAKE 🐟 ⚓ 🏊 🎿 RV 8

Reference: Map B4, grid i0.

Campsites, facilities: There are 20 sites for tents or motor homes. Piped water, vault toilets, picnic tables and fire grills are provided. A private sanitary dump station and a boat ramp are nearby. Pets are permitted on leashes.

Reservations, fee: No reservations; $6 fee per night.

Who to contact: Phone the Bureau of Land Management at (916) 257-5381.

Location: From Red Bluff, drive east on Highway 36 to Susanville. In Susanville, turn left (north) on Highway 139 and drive 29 miles to County Road A1. Turn left at County Road A1 and drive a half-mile to the campground.

Trip note: This camp provides direct access in the fall months to the best fishing area of huge Eagle Lake. When the weather turns cold, the lake's population of big Eagle Lake trout migrate to their favorite haunts just outside the tules, often in water only five to eight feet deep. From shore, fish with inflated nightcrawlers near the lake bottom, just outside the tules. A boat ramp is located about two miles south. From there, troll a Needlefish along the tules, or anchor or tie up, and use a nightcrawler for bait. In the summer months, this area is quite exposed and can be hammered by north winds, which typically howl from midday to sunset. Open Memorial Day through December 31. The elevation is 5,100 feet.

21. RAMHORN SPRING 👫 🐎

Reference: **Map B4, grid j4.**

Campsites, facilities: There are 12 sites for tents or motor homes up to 28 feet long. Piped water, vault toilets, picnic tables and fire grills are provided. Pets are permitted on leashes.

Reservations, fee: No reservations; $0-$5 fee per night.

Who to contact: Phone the Bureau of Land Management at (916) 257-5381.

Location: From Red Bluff, drive east on Highway 36 to Susanville. In Susanville, turn north on US 395 and drive 50 miles to Post Camp Road. Turn right on Post Camp Road and drive two miles east to the campground.

Trip note: This very remote, little-known spot is set in an area with good numbers of antelope. Though being drawn for tags is nearly an impossibility, the lucky few hunters can use this camp for their base. It is located way out in Nowhere Land, near the flank of Shinn Peak (7,562 feet). This is the only camp in this book where the fee charged ranges from $0 to $5 per night. Why? Because in the summer, this camp is usually abandoned to the pine squirrels, and the BLM can't collect a camp fee from those furry little guys.

MAP CØ

NOR-CAL MAP .... see page 94
adjoining maps
NORTH (BØ) .... see page 138
EAST (C1) .... see page 248
SOUTH (DØ) .... see page 316
WEST .... no map

35 LISTINGS
PAGES 232-247

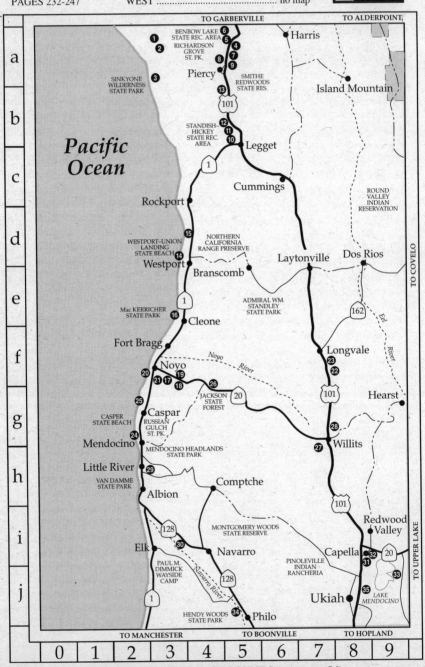

TO GARBERVILLE

TO ALDERPOINT

BENBOW LAKE
STATE REC. AREA

RICHARDSON
GROVE
ST. PK.

Harris

Piercy

SINKYONE
WILDERNESS
STATE PARK

SMITHE
REDWOODS
STATE RES.

Island Mountain

101

*Pacific
Ocean*

STANDISH-
HICKEY
STATE REC.
AREA

Legget

1

Cummings

ROUND
VALLEY
INDIAN
RESERVATION

Rockport

WESTPORT–UNION
LANDING
STATE BEACH

NORTHERN
CALIFORNIA
RANGE PRESERVE

Westport

Branscomb

Laytonville

Dos Rios

TO COVELO

1

ADMIRAL WM.
STANDLEY
STATE PARK

162

Eel River

Mac KERRICHER
STATE PARK

Cleone

Fort Bragg

Novo River

Longvale

Noyo

20

JACKSON
STATE
FOREST

Hearst

CASPER
STATE BEACH

Caspar

RUSSIAN
GULCH
ST. PK.

28

101

Willits

Mendocino

MENDOCINO HEADLANDS
STATE PARK

27

Little River

VAN DAMME
STATE PARK

Albion

Comptche

101

128

MONTGOMERY WOODS
STATE RESERVE

Redwood
Valley

TO UPPER LAKE

Elk

PAUL M.
DIMMICK WAYSIDE
CAMP

Navarro

PINOLEVILLE
INDIAN
RANCHERIA

Capella

20

128

Navarro River

LAKE
MENDOCINO

Ukiah

HENDY WOODS
STATE PARK

Philo

1

TO MANCHESTER

TO BOONVILLE

TO HOPLAND

| 0 | 1 | 2 | 3 | 4 | 5 | 6 | 7 | 8 | 9 |

Map CØ featuring: Kings Range, Eel River, Richardson Grove State Park, Standish Hickey State Recreation Area, Navarro River, Lake Mendocino

1. NADELOS
Reference: In King Range; map CØ, grid a3.
Campsites, facilities: There are eight single and one group tent sites. Piped water, vault toilets, picnic tables and fire grills are provided. Pets are permitted on leashes.
Reservations, fee: No reservations; $8 fee per night.
Who to contact: Call the Bureau of Land Management at (707) 825-2300.
Location: From US 101 north of Garberville, take the Redway exit, turn west on Shelter Cove Road and drive 17 miles to Chemise Mountain Road. Turn (left) south on Chemise Mountain Road and drive two miles to the campground on the right.
Trip note: Nadelos Campground is set at 1,840 feet near the South Fork Bear Creek, located at the southern end of the King Range National Conservation Area. This provides access to a rare geographic dynamic, where mountains and coast adjoin. Nearby Chemise Mountain, 2,598 feet, is one of the highest points in California within two miles of the sea. You can hike to the top of this mountain from a trailhead, which provides a dramatic lookout on clear days.

2. WAILAKI
Reference: In King Range; map CØ, grid a3.
Campsites, facilities: There are 13 sites for tents or motor homes up to 20 feet long. Piped water, vault toilets, picnic tables and fire grills are provided. Pets are permitted on leashes.
Reservations, fee: No reservations; $8 fee per night.
Who to contact: Phone the Bureau of Land Management at (707) 825-2300.
Location: From US 101 north of Garberville, take the Redway exit, turn west on Shelter Cove Road and drive 17 miles to Chemise Mountain Road. Turn (left) south on Chemise Mountain Road and drive 2.5 miles to the campground on the right.
Trip note: This is the most southerly-located camp in the King Range National Conservation Area, just a half-mile down the road from the preceding listed campground. A trailhead from this camp is routed via a short connector link to the Lost Coast Trail, and from there, hikers can venture south to the Sinkyone Wilderness and the coast, or make the day trip to Chemise Mountain (2,598 feet). The camp is set at 1,840 feet. Open year-round.

3. SINKYONE WILDERNESS
Reference: In Richardson Grove State Park; map CØ, grid a3.
Campsites, facilities: There are 15 tent sites, each with a fire ring and a picnic table, at Usal Beach. There is **no piped water**, but water is available, if you purify it. Pit toilets are provided. Between Bear Harbor and Jones Beach there are 25 primitive tent sites, some of which have tables, fire rings and pit toilets. (You can drive within three-quarters of a mile of Bear Harbor and park at

Orchard Creek, provided the weather is good and the gate is open at Needle Rock Ranch House.) Pets are allowed on leashes.

Reservations, fee: No reservations; $6 per night.

Who to contact: Phone Richardson Grove State Park (707) 247-3318 or (707) 445-6547.

Location: To reach the northern boundary of the Sinkyone Wilderness: From US 101 north of Garberville, take the Redway exit, turn west on Briceland Road and drive 17 miles to Whitethorn. From Whitethorn, continue six more miles to the four corners fork. Take the middle left fork and drive four miles on gravel road to the Needle Rock Ranger Station.

To reach the southern boundary of the Sinkyone Wilderness: From Leggett on US 101, turn southwest on Highway 1 (toward Fort Bragg) and drive 14.66 miles to milepost 90.88 at County Road 431. Turn right (north) on County Road 431 (a dirt road, often unsigned) and drive six miles to the Usal Beach campground. Note: the roads can be quite rough.

Trip note: This is a great jumpoff point for a backpacking trip in Sinkyone Wilderness on the Lost Coast, one of the few wilderness areas where a trip can be made any month of the year. The terrain is primitive and steep, often wet, but provides a rare coastal wilderness experience. Starting at the northern trailhead at Orchard Camp, or the southern trailhead at the Usal Beach Campground, it is a 17-mile trip, an ambitious weekend tromp.

---

4. MADRONE 🐟 🚶 ♿ 🛶   RV 8

Reference: **In Richardson Grove State Park; map CØ, grid a5.**

Campsites, facilities: There are 40 sites for tents or motor homes up to 30 feet long. Piped water, flush toilets, coin-operated showers, fire grills and picnic tables are provided. A grocery store and a sanitary disposal station are available. The facilities are **wheelchair accessible**. Pets are permitted.

Reservations, fee: Reserve by phoning Destinet at (800) 444-7275 ($6.75 Destinet fee); $15-$17 fee per night; $1 pet fee.

Who to contact: Call Richardson Grove State Park at (707) 247-3318 or (707) 445-6547.

Location: From the junction of US 101 and Highway 1 in Leggett, drive north on US 101 past Piercy to the park entrance along the west side of the road.

Trip note: The highway cuts a swath right through Richardson Grove State Park, and everyone slows to gawk at the giant trees, one of the most impressive groves of redwoods you can drive through in California. To explore further, there are several campgrounds available at the park, as well as a network of outstanding hiking trails. The best are the short Redwood Exhibit Trail, Settlers Loop and Toumey Trail.

---

5. BENBOW LAKE ST. RECREATION AREA   RV 7

🐟 ⚓ 🚶 🛶 🍴

Reference: **On Eel River; map CØ, grid a5.**

Campsites, facilities: There are 75 sites for tents or motor homes up to 27 feet long. Piped water, flush toilets, coin-operated showers, fire grills and picnic tables are provided. A boat ramp (no motors) and boat rentals are available. Supplies and a laundromat are available in Garberville. Pets are allowed on leashes.

Reservations, fee: Reservations recommended from May through September; reserve by phoning Destinet at (800) 444-7275 ($6.75 Destinet fee); $14-$16 fee per night; $1 pet fee.

Who to contact: Phone Benbow Lake State Recreation Area at (707) 923-3238 or (707) 247-3318.

Location: From the junction of US 101 and Highway 1 in Leggett, drive north on US 101 past Richardson Grove State Park to the park entrance (two miles south of Garberville).

Trip note: This camp is set along the South Fork of the Eel River, with easy access from US 101. It gets heavy use in summer. The river is dammed each summer, which temporarily creates Benbow Lake, an ideal spot for swimming and light boating. In winter, this stretch of river can be quite good for steelhead fishing. The campground is open from April through October.

6. BENBOW VALLEY RESORT

Reference: **On Eel River; map CØ, grid a5.**

Campsites, facilities: There are 112 motor home sites (60 drive-through) with full hookups and picnic tables. Cable TV, rest rooms, showers, a laundromat, a grocery store, LP gas, a restaurant, a playground, a recreation room, a heated swimming pool, a whirlpool, RV supplies and a nine-hole golf course are available. A boat dock and boat rentals (in summer) are available nearby at Benbow Lake. Pets are allowed on leashes.

Reservations, fee: Reservations accepted; $18-$27 fee per night.

Who to contact: Phone Benbow Valley RV Park at (707) 923-2777.

Location: From the junction of US 101 and Highway 1 in Leggett, drive north on US 101 past Richardson Grove State Park to Benbow Drive (two miles south of Garberville). Turn north on Benbow Drive and travel a short distance to the campground.

Trip note: This is an RV park set along US 101 and the South Fork Eel River, with both a small golf course and little Benbow Lake providing nearby recreation. It takes on a dramatically different character in the winter, when the highway is largely abandoned, the river comes up, and steelhead migrate upstream to the stretch of water here. Cooks Valley and Benbow provide good shorefishing access. Open year-round.

7. HUCKLEBERRY

Reference: **In Richardson Grove State Park; map CØ, grid a5.**

Campsites, facilities: There are 36 sites for tents or motor homes up to 30 feet. Piped water, flush toilets, coin-operated showers, fire grills and picnic tables are provided. A grocery store and a sanitary disposal station are available. The facilities are **wheelchair accessible**. Pets are permitted on leashes.

Reservations, fee: Reserve by phoning Destinet at (800) 444-7275 ($6.75 Destinet fee); $15-$17 fee per night; $1 pet fee.

Who to contact: Call Richardson Grove State Park at (707) 247-3318 or (707) 445-6547.

Location: From the junction of US 101 and Highway 1 in Leggett, drive north on US 101 past Piercy to the park entrance on the west side of the road.

Trip note: This camp is set in a giant grove of coastal redwoods, the tallest trees in the world. The park is one of the prettiest and most popular state parks, making reservations a necessity from Memorial Day through Labor Day. There is good hiking and sightseeing, but it is often crowded near the visitor center in the summer months. It's a good base camp in the winter for steelhead fishing in the South Fork of the Eel River.

8. RICHARDSON GROVE CAMPGROUND 🐟 🚐 7

Reference: **On Eel River; map CØ, grid a5.**

Campsites, facilities: There are 91 sites for tents or motor homes (28 drive-through), many with full or partial hookups, and two cabins. Picnic tables, fire rings, restrooms, showers, a sanitary disposal station, and a playground are provided. A laundromat, a grocery store, LP gas and ice are available. Pets are allowed on leashes.

Reservations, fee: Reservations recommended; $13.50-$18 fee per night; cabin rentals are $26 per night.

Who to contact: Phone (707) 247-3380.

Location: From the junction of US 101 and Highway 1 in Leggett, drive north on US 101 a half-mile past Richardson Grove State Park to the camp entrance on the west side of the road.

Trip note: This private camp provides a nearby alternative to Richardson Grove State Park, complete with cabin rentals. The state park with its grove of giant redwoods and excellent hiking is the primary attraction. The adjacent South Fork Eel River may look like a trickle in the summer, but it is an excellent steelhead stream with good shorefishing access in this area, as well as to the south in Cooks Valley. Open year-round.

9. OAK FLAT 🐟 🚶 ♿ 🏊 🚐 8

Reference: **In Richardson Grove State Park; map CØ, grid a5.**

Campsites, facilities: There are 94 sites for tents or motor homes up to 30 feet long. Piped water, flush toilets, coin-operated showers, fire grills and picnic tables are provided. A grocery store, a sanitary disposal station and propane gas are available nearby. Pets are allowed on leashes.

Reservations, fee: Reserve by phoning Destinet at (800) 444-7275 ($6.75 Destinet fee); $15-$17 fee per night; $1 pet fee.

Who to contact: Call Richardson Grove State Park at (707) 247-3318 or (707) 445-6547.

Location: From the junction of US 101 and Highway 1 in Leggett, drive north on US 101 past Piercy to the park entrance on the west side of the road.

Trip note: This camp is set on the east side of the Eel River in the shade of forest and provides easy access to the river. The camp is open only in summer. For side trip information, see trip note for Toumey and Huckleberry camps.

10. REDWOOD CAMPGROUND 🚐 8

🐟 🚶 ♿ 🏊

Reference: **On Eel River in Standish-Hickey State Recreation Area; map CØ, grid b5.**

Campsites, facilities: There are 63 sites for tents or motor homes up to 18 feet long. Piped water, coin-operated showers, flush toilets, picnic tables and fire rings are provided. Some facilities are **wheelchair accessible**. Pets are allowed on leashes.

Reservations, fee: Reserve by phoning Destinet at (800) 444-7275 ($6.75 Destinet fee); $14-$16 fee per night; $1 pet fee.

Who to contact: Phone Standish-Hickey State Recreation Area at (707) 925-6482 or (707) 445-6547.

Location: From the junction of US 101 and Highway 1 in Leggett, drive north on US 101 for one mile to the park entrance.

Trip note: This is one of three camps in Standish-Hickey State Recreation Area, and is by far the most unusual. To reach Redwood Campground requires driving over a temporary "summer bridge," providing access to a pretty spot along the South Fork Eel River. The camp is typically open from Memorial Day Weekend through Labor Day Weekend. In the winter, out comes the bridge and up comes the river. The elevation at the camp is 800 feet.

---

11. ROCK CREEK

Reference: On Eel River in Standish-Hickey State Recreation Area; map CØ, grid b5.

Campsites, facilities: There are 36 sites for tents or motor homes up to 27 feet long and trailers to 24 feet long. Piped water, coin-operated showers, flush toilets, picnic tables and fire rings are provided. Some facilities are **wheelchair accessible**. Pets are allowed on leashes.

Reservations, fee: Reserve by phoning Destinet at (800) 444-7275 ($6.75 Destinet fee); $14-$16 fee per night; $1 pet fee.

Who to contact: Phone Standish-Hickey State Recreation Area at (707) 925-6482 or (707) 445-6547.

Location: From the junction of US 101 and Highway 1 in Leggett, drive north on US 101 for one mile to the park entrance on the west side of the road.

Trip note: This is one of two main campgrounds set in a redwood grove at Standish-Hickey State Recreation Area (the other is Hickey). It is the classic state park camp, with numbered sites, flat tent spaces, picnic tables and food lockers. Hiking is only fair in this park, but most people enjoy the short tromp down to the nearby South Fork Eel River. In winter, steelhead migrate through the area.

---

12. HICKEY

Reference: On Eel River in Standish-Hickey State Recreation Area; map CØ, grid b5.

Campsites, facilities: There are 65 sites for tents or motor homes up to 27 feet long and trailers to 24 feet long. There are also several hike-in/bike-in sites. Piped water, showers, flush toilets, picnic tables and fire rings are provided. A grocery store and laundromat are nearby. Some facilities are **wheelchair accessible**. Pets are allowed on leashes.

Reservations, fee: Reserve by phoning Destinet at (800) 444-7275 ($6.75 Destinet fee); $14-$16 fee per night; $1 pet fee.

Who to contact: Phone Standish-Hickey State Recreation Area at (707) 946-2409 or (707) 445-6547.

Location: From the junction of US 101 and Highway 1 in Leggett, drive north on US 101 for one mile to the park entrance on the west side of the road.

Trip note: This is an ideal layover spot for US 101 cruisers yearning to spend a night in the redwoods. The park is best known for its camps set amid redwoods, as well as the nearby South Fork Eel River with its steelhead fishing in the winter. The camp is set at 800 feet.

13. REDWOODS RIVER RESORT

Reference: **On Eel River; map CØ, grid b5.**

Campsites, facilities: There are 14 tent sites and 27 motor home sites (nine drive-through) with full hookups, and two cabins with kitchenettes. Fire pits and picnic tables are provided. Restrooms, hot showers, a heated pool, a playground, a recreation room, a mini-mart, a laundromat, a group kitchen, a dump station and an evening campfire are among the amenities offered here. Pets are permitted.

Reservations, fee: Reservations recommended in the summer; $14-$20 fee per night; cabin rentals are $30 per night.

Who to contact: Phone (707) 925-6249.

Location: From the junction of US 101 and Highway 1 in Leggett, drive north on US 101 for seven miles to the campground entrance.

Trip note: This resort is situated in a 20-acre grove of redwoods on US 101. Many of the campsites are shaded. It is one in a series of both public and private campgrounds located along the highway between Leggett and Garberville. This spot is set at 700 feet. Open year-round.

14. WAGES CREEK BEACH CAMPGROUND

Reference: **Overlooking Pacific Ocean; map CØ, grid d3.**

Campsites, facilities: There are 175 sites for tents or motor homes. Piped water, fire grills, picnic tables and flush toilets are provided. Hot showers, a sanitary disposal station, wood and ice are available. Pets are allowed on leashes.

Reservations, fee: Reservations accepted; $10-$17 fee per night.

Who to contact: Phone (707) 964-2964.

Location: From Fort Bragg, drive north on Highway 1 to Westport. In Westport, continue north on Highway 1 for a half-mile to the campground entrance.

Trip note: This camp is set above the beach near the mouth of Wages Creek, with creekside sites available, some with glimpses of the ocean. You will notice that as you venture north from Fort Bragg, the number of vacationers in the area falls way off, providing a chance for quiet beaches and serene moments. The best nearby hiking is to the north out of the trailhead for the Sinkyone Wilderness (see directions and trip note for that camp). Open March through November.

15. WESTPORT UNION LANDING ST. BEACH

Reference: **Overlooking Pacific Ocean; map CØ, grid d4.**

Campsites, facilities: There are 100 primitive sites for tents or motor homes up to 35 feet long. Piped water, chemical toilets, fire grills and picnic tables are provided. Pets are permitted. A grocery store is nearby.

Reservations, fee: No reservations; $10-$12 fee per night; $1 pet fee.

Who to contact: Phone (707) 937-5804 or (707) 865-2391.

Location: From Fort Bragg, drive north on Highway 1 to Westport. In Westport, continue north on Highway 1 for three miles to the campground entrance.

Trip note: The northern Mendocino coast is remote, beautiful, and gets far less people pressure than the Fort Bragg area. That is the key to its appeal. The campsites are on an ocean bluff, relatively sheltered from coastal winds. Open year-round.

16. MACKERRICHER STATE PARK

Reference: **Overlooking Pacific Ocean; map CØ, grid e3.**
Campsites, facilities: There are 142 sites for tents or motor homes up to 35 feet long and 10 walk-in sites. Piped water, showers, flush toilets, a dump station, picnic tables and fire grills are provided. Pets are permitted. The facilities are **wheelchair accessible**.
Reservations, fee: Reserve by phoning Destinet at (800) 444-7275 ($6.75 Destinet fee); $15-$17 fee per night; $1 pet fee.
Who to contact: Phone (707) 937-5804 or (707) 865-2391.
Location: From Fort Bragg, drive north on Highway 1 for three miles to the campground entrance on the left side of the road.
Trip notes: MacKerricher is a beautiful park on the Mendocino Coast, a great destination for adventure and exploration. The camps are set in a coastal forest, with gorgeous walk-in sites. Nearby are a small beach, great tidepools, a rocky point where harbor seals lay in the sun, a small lake (Cleone) with trout fishing, a great bike trail and outstanding short hikes. The short jaunt around little Cleone Lake has many romantic spots, often tunneling through vegetation, then emerging for lake views. The coastal walk to the point to see seals and tidepools is equally captivating, and if you can't get a kiss here, you're in trouble. Open year-round.

17. WILDWOOD CAMPGROUND

Reference: **Near Fort Bragg; map CØ, grid f3.**
Campsites, facilities: There are 65 sites for tents or motor homes, many with full or partial hookups. Restrooms, picnic tables, fire rings, hot showers and a sanitary disposal station are provided. A laundromat and wood are available. No pets are permitted.
Reservations, fee: Reservations accepted; $15-$20 fee per night.
Who to contact: Phone (707) 964-8297.
Location: In Fort Bragg at the junction of Highway 1 and Highway 20, turn east on Highway 20 and drive 3.5 miles to the campground.
Trip note: The drive from Willits to Fort Bragg on Highway 20 is always a favorite, a curving two-laner through redwoods, not too slow, not too fast, best seen from the saddle of a Harley-Davidson. At the end of it is the coast, and just three miles out is this privately-operated campground. Within short drives are Noyo Harbor in Fort Bragg, Russian Gulch State Park and Mendocino to the south, and MacKerricher State Park to the north, enough to explore for days.

18. FORT BRAGG LEISURE TIME RV PARK

Reference: **In Fort Bragg; map CØ, grid f3.**
Campsites, facilities: There are 82 sites for tents or motor homes, many with full or partial hookups. Restrooms, picnic tables, cable TV, fire rings, hot showers (coin-operated) and a sanitary disposal station are provided. A laundromat is

available. The facilities are **wheelchair accessible**. Pets are allowed on leashes.

Reservations, fee: Reservations accepted; $12.50-$17.50 fee per night.

Who to contact: Phone (707) 964-5994.

Location: In Fort Bragg, at the junction of Highway 1 and Highway 20, turn east on Highway 20 and drive 2.2 miles to the campground entrance on the right (south) side of the road.

Trip note: This privately-operated park offers volleyball, horseshoes and badminton. You get the idea. See the trip note for the previous camp for side trip options.

19. POMO CAMPGROUND & MOTOR HOME PARK

Reference: **In Fort Bragg; map CØ, grid f3.**

Campsites, facilities: There are 30 sites for tents and 94 motor home sites with full or partial hookups. Restrooms, hot showers (coin-operated), cable TV hookups, a store, wood, ice, RV supplies, propane gas, a laundromat, a sanitary disposal station, a fish cleaning table, horseshoe pits and a large grass playing field are available. Picnic tables and fire rings are at each campsite. Pets are allowed on leashes.

Reservations, fee: Reservations recommended in summer; $16-$22 fee per night.

Who to contact: Phone (707) 964-3373.

Location: In Fort Bragg, at the junction of Highway 1 and Highway 20, drive south on Highway 1 for one mile to Tregoning Lane. Turn east and drive a short distance to 17999 Tregoning Lane.

Trip note: This park covers 17 acres near the ocean, one of several camps located on the Fort Bragg and Mendocino coast. Nearby Noyo Harbor offers busy restaurants, deep sea fishing, a boat ramp, harbor and walk out to the Noyo Harbor jetty.

20. WOODSIDE RV PARK & CAMPGROUND

Reference: **In Fort Bragg; map CØ, grid f3.**

Campsites, facilities: There are 18 sites for tents only and 86 sites for tents or motor homes with full or partial hookups. Group sites are available. Picnic tables, fire rings, restrooms, showers, a recreation room, a sauna and a sanitary disposal station are provided. Cable TV, RV supplies, ice, wood and a fish cleaning table are available. Boating and fishing access are nearby. Pets are allowed on leashes.

Reservations, fee: Reservations accepted; $14-$20 fee per night.

Who to contact: Phone (707) 964-3684.

Location: In Fort Bragg, at the junction of Highway 1 and Highway 20, drive south on Highway 1 for one mile to the campground.

Trip note: This privately-operated park is set up primarily for motor homes. It covers nine acres, is somewhat wooded, and provides access to nearby Fort Bragg and the ocean.

21. DOLPHIN ISLE MARINA 🐟 ⚓ ♿   RV 7

Reference: **On Noyo River in Fort Bragg; map CØ, grid f3.**

Campsites, facilities: There are 83 motor home sites with full or partial hookups. Restrooms, picnic tables, fire rings, hot showers (coin-operated), recreation room and a sanitary disposal station are provided. A laundromat, delicatessen, propane gas, a boat ramp and a dock are available. The facilities are **wheelchair accessible**. Pets are allowed on leashes.

Reservations, fee: Reservations accepted; $12-$20 fee per night.

Who to contact: Phone (707) 964-4113.

Location: In Fort Bragg, at the junction of Highway 1 and Highway 20, drive east on Highway 20 for a quarter mile to South Harbor Drive. Turn left (north) on South Harbor Drive and drive a quarter-mile to Basin Street. Turn right (east) on Basin Street and drive one mile to the campground.

Trip note: Noyo Harbor is headquarters at Fort Bragg, the place where everything starts from. For vacationers, that include wharfside restaurants, fishing trips, boat docks and a chance for a nice stroll out to the Noyo Harbor jetty. This motor home park is right at the marina, providing an ideal jumpoff point for all of those adventures. Beach access is available one mile away.

22. HIDDEN VALLEY CAMPGROUND ♿   RV 5

Reference: **North of Willits; map CØ, grid f7.**

Campsites, facilities: There are 50 sites for tents or motor homes, some with full or partial hookups. Picnic tables, fire grills, restrooms and showers are provided. Pets are allowed on leashes.

Reservations, fee: Reservations accepted; $15-$17 fee per night.

Who to contact: Phone (707) 459-2521 or (800) 458-8368 (California only).

Location: From Willits on US 101, drive north for 6.5 miles on US 101 to the campground on the east side of the road.

Trip note: The privately-operated park is located in a pretty valley, primarily oak/bay woodlands with a sprinkling of conifers. The most popular nearby recreation option is taking the Skunk Train in Willits for the ride out to the coast at Fort Bragg. Open year-round.

23. SLEEPYHOLLOW RV PARK 🐟 ⚓ 🚶   RV 5

Reference: **North of Willits; map CØ, grid f7.**

Campsites, facilities: There are six sites for tents and 24 motor home sites (seven drive-through) with full or partial hookups. Picnic tables, restrooms, showers, a playground, a pond, a recreation room and a sanitary dump station are provided. Pets are allowed on leashes.

Reservations, fee: Reservations accepted; $10-$13 fee per night.

Who to contact: Phone (707) 459-0613.

Location: From Willits on US 101, drive north for eight miles to the 55.5 mile marker (two-tenths of a mile beyond the Shimmins Ridge Road sign). At the beginning of the divided four-lane highway, turn right at the signed campground access road and drive to the entrance.

Trip note: This year-round, privately-operated park provides easy access off the highway. A nearby recreation option is riding the Skunk Train in Willits.

24. RUSSIAN GULCH STATE PARK   RV 9

Reference: **Near the Pacific Ocean; map CØ, grid g2.**

Campsites, facilities: There are 30 sites for tents or motor homes up to 27 feet long. Hiker/biker sites are also available. Piped water, showers, flush toilets, picnic tables and fire grills are provided. Pets are permitted. The facilities are **wheelchair accessible**.

Reservations, fee: Reserve by phoning Destinet at (800) 444-7275 ($6.75 Destinet fee); $15-$17 fee per night; $1 pet fee.

Who to contact: Phone (707) 937-5804 or (707) 865-2391.

Location: From Mendocino, drive two miles north on Highway 1 to the campground.

Trip note: This camp is set near some of California's most beautiful coastline, but the camp speaks to the woods, not the water, with the campsites set in a wooded canyon. They include some of the prettiest and secluded drive-in sites available on the Mendocino Coast. There is a great hike here, an easy hour-long walk to Russian Gulch Falls, a wispy 35-foot waterfall that falls into a rock basin, always pretty, awesome in late winter. Much of the route is accessible by bicycle, with a rack available where the trail narrows and turns to dirt. Open mid-March to mid-October.

25. CASPAR BEACH RV PARK   RV 8

Reference: **Near Mendocino; map CØ, grid g2.**

Campsites, facilities: There are 19 sites for tents only and 50 motor home sites with full or partial hookups. Picnic tables, fire grills, cable TV hookups, flush and pit toilets, showers (coin-operated) and a sanitary disposal station are provided. A store, wood, a playground and a laundromat are available. Pets are allowed on leashes.

Reservations, fee: Reservations accepted; $16-$23 fee per night.

Who to contact: Phone (707) 964-3306.

Location: From Mendocino on Highway 1, drive north for 3.5 miles to the Point Cabrillo exit. Turn west (left) on Point Cabrillo Road and drive three-quarters of a mile to the campground on the left.

Trip note: This privately-operated park has ocean frontage and good lookouts for whale watching. The park is somewhat wooded, with a small creek running behind it. Open year-round.

26. JACKSON STATE FOREST   6

Reference: **Near Fort Bragg; map CØ, grid g4.**

Campsites, facilities: There are 18 separate campgrounds throughout this state forest, with as few as two or as many as 24 campsites. **No piped water** is available, but pit toilets, picnic tables and fire grills are provided. Pets are permitted on leashes. Two horseback riding-equestrian campgrounds are also available.

Reservations, fee: Reservations recommended; no fee. A camping permit is required and a campground map is advised. Both can be obtained from the State Department of Forestry office at 802 North Main Street (Highway 1) in Fort Bragg.

Who to contact: Phone (707) 964-5674.

Location: From Willits on US 101, turn west on Highway 20 and drive 17 miles (the midway point between Willits and Fort Bragg). Turn right on Road 200 to gain access to Jackson State Forest, and only proceed for an overnight stay if you have a reserved camp and map from the Forestry Department.

Trip note: Primitive campsites set in a vast forest of redwoods and Douglas fir are the prime attraction here. Even though Highway 20 is a major connecting link to the coast in the summer months, these camps get bypassed because they are primitive and largely unknown. Why? Because reaching them requires driving on dirt roads sometimes frequented by logging trucks, and there are no campground signs along the highway. A highlight of the area is a 50-foot waterfall on Chamberlain Creek. Set in a steep canyon amid giant firs and redwoods, it can be reached with a 10-minute walk. The elevation is in the 2,000-foot range. What to do first? Get a map from the State Forestry Department. Open year-round, but the roads are extremely dusty in summer, muddy in winter.

---

27. WILLITS KOA

Reference: **Near Willits; map CØ, grid g7.**

Campsites, facilities: There are 21 sites for tents and 50 motor home sites (27 drive-through) with full or partial hookups. Group sites are available. Piped water, flush toilets, showers, picnic tables, a playground, a swimming pool, a fishing pond and a sanitary dump station are provided. A grocery store, RV supplies and a laundromat are available. Pets are allowed on leashes.

Reservations, fee: Reservations accepted; $17-$25.50 fee per night.

Who to contact: Phone (707) 459-6179.

Location: From Willits, at the junction of US 101 and Highway 20, turn west on Highway 20 and drive 1.5 miles to the campground.

Trip note: This is an ideal spot to park your motor home if you plan on taking the Skunk Train west to Fort Bragg. A depot for the train is within walking distance from the campground. The campground also offers nightly entertainment and weekend barbecues. The elevation is 1,377 feet. Open year-round.

---

28. QUAIL MEADOWS CAMPGROUND

Reference: **In Willits; map CØ, grid g7.**

Campsites, facilities: There are 49 motor home sites, most with full or partial hookups. There is a separate section for tents only. Patios, picnic tables, fire grills, restrooms, showers and a sanitary disposal station are provided. A grocery store, a laundromat, propane gas, ice and TV hookups are available. Pets are allowed on leashes.

Reservations, fee: Reservations accepted; $12-$20 fee per night.

Who to contact: Phone (707) 459-6006.

Location: In Willits, at the junction of US 101 and Highway 20, drive north on US 101 for one mile to the campground.

Trip note: This is one of several motor home parks in the Willits area. Nearby is Lake Emily, set near the Brook Trails development, which is stocked in the spring and early summer with trout by the Department of Fish and Game. It's like a backyard fishing hole for the folks around here. Another recreation option is the Skunk Train, which runs from Willits to Fort Bragg.

29. VAN DAMME STATE PARK

Reference: Near Mendocino; map CØ, grid h3.

Campsites, facilities: There are 74 sites for tents or motor homes up to 35 feet long, 10 primitive hike-in sites and one group campsite. Piped water, flush toilets, a sanitary disposal station, showers, picnic tables and fire grills are provided. A grocery store, a laundromat and propane gas are available nearby. Pets are permitted.

Reservations, fee: Reserve by phoning Destinet at (800) 444-7275 ($6.75 Destinet fee); $15-$17 fee per night; $1 pet fee.

Who to contact: Phone (707) 937-5804 or (707) 865-2391.

Location: From Mendocino on Highway 1, drive south for three miles to the town of Little River and the park entrance road on the east side of the road.

Trip note: The campsites at Van Damme are extremely popular, usually requiring reservations, but with a bit of planning your reward is a base of operations in a beautiful park with redwoods and a remarkable fern understory. A great option are the hike-in sites on the Fern Canyon Trail. The latter is one of the most popular hikes in the Mendocino area, crossing the Little River several times and weaving among old trees. The trail was wiped out temporarily by flooding in the winter of 1994-95. Just across from the entrance of the park is a small but beautiful coastal bay with a pretty beach, ideal for launching sea kayaks. Open year-round.

30. PAUL M. DIMMICK WAYSIDE STATE CAMP

Reference: On Navarro River in Navarro River Redwoods State Park; map CØ, grid i3.

Campsites, facilities: There are 28 sites for tents or motor homes up to 30 feet long. Piped water (summer only), vault toilets, fire grills and picnic tables are provided. Pets are permitted.

Reservations, fee: No reservations; $10-$12 fee per night; $1 pet fee.

Who to contact: Phone (707) 937-5804 or (707) 865-2391.

Location: From Cloverdale on US 101, turn north on Highway 128 and drive 49 miles. Look for the signed campground entrance on the left side of the road.

Trip note: A pretty grove of redwood trees and the nearby Navarro River are the highlights for this campground. It's a nice spot, but alas, lacks any significant hiking trails that could make this a spectacular spot; all the trailheads along Highway 128 turn out to be just little spur routes from the road to the river. Open year-round.

31. CHE-KAKA

Reference: At Lake Mendocino; map CØ, grid i8.

Campsites, facilities: There are 22 sites for tents or motor homes up to 35 feet long. Piped water, **vault toilets,** picnic tables and fire grills are provided. A boat ramp is nearby. Pets are allowed on leashes.

Reservations, fee: No reservations; $9 fee per night.

Who to contact: Phone the U.S. Corps of Engineers, Lake Mendocino at (707) 462-7581.

Location: From Ukiah, drive north on US 101 to the Highway 20 turnoff. Drive east on Highway 20 to Lake Mendocino Drive. Exit east (right) on Lake

Mendocino Drive and continue to the first stoplight. Turn left on North State Street and drive to the next stoplight. Turn right (which will put you back on Lake Mendocino Drive) and drive about one mile to the signed entrance to the campground at Coyote Dam.

Trip note: This campground sits beside the dam at the south end of Lake Mendocino, the lake with the leg-biting catfish. What? Right: the Department of Fish and Game installed "catfish condominiums" in the lake, that is, homes for catfish on the lake bottom. When swimmers started wading out and stepping on them, the catfish would come out and chomp them in the legs. Lake Mendocino is also known for good striped bass fishing, waterskiing and boating. Nearby, upstream of the lake, is Potter Valley and the East Fork Russian River, also called Cold Creek, which provides trout fishing in the summer. A boat ramp located at the corner of the dam is a bonus. The elevation is 750 feet. Open April through September.

32. KY-EN

Reference: **At Lake Mendocino; map CØ, grid i9.**

Campsites, facilities: There are 103 sites for tents or motor homes up to 35 feet long. Restrooms, showers, a playground (in the adjacent day-use area), a sanitary dump station, picnic tables and fire grills are provided. A boat ramp, boat rentals and limited supplies are available at the nearby marina. Some sites are **wheelchair accessible.** Pets are allowed on leashes.

Reservations, fee: Reserve group and handicapped sites only; $13-$15 fee per night in summer; no fee in winter.

Who to contact: Phone the U.S. Corps of Engineers, Lake Mendocino at (707) 462-7581.

Location: From Ukiah, drive north on US 101 to the Highway 20 turnoff. Drive east on Highway 20 to Marina Drive. Turn right and drive to the north end of the lake and the campground.

Trip note: This camp is located on north shore of Lake Mendocino. With the access road off Highway 20 instead of US 101 (as with Che-Kaka Camp), it can be overlooked by newcomers. A nearby boat ramp makes it especially attractive. During the winter months, this camp has 30 campsites and no fee is charged. For more information, see trip note for preceding camp.

33. BU-SHAY

Reference: **At Lake Mendocino; map CØ, grid i9.**

Campsites, facilities: There are 164 sites for tents or motor homes up to 35 feet long. There are three group sites for up to 120 people each. Restrooms, showers, a playground (in the adjacent day-use area), a sanitary dump station, picnic tables and fire grills are provided. The boat ramp is two miles from camp near Ky-en Campground. Some sites are **wheelchair accessible.** Pets are allowed on leashes.

Reservations, fee: Reserve group and handicapped sites only; $13 fee per night for individual sites; $80-$120 fee per night for groups.

Who to contact: Phone the U.S. Corps of Engineers, Lake Mendocino at (707) 462-7581.

Location: From Ukiah, drive north on US 101 to the Highway 20 turnoff. Drive east on Highway 20 to Marina Drive. Turn right and drive to the northeast side of the lake and the campground.

Trip note: Bu-Shay Camp, on the northeast end of Lake Mendocino, is set on a point that provides a pretty southern exposure when the lake is full. The lake is about three miles long and one mile wide. It offers fishing for striped bass and bluegill, as well as waterskiing and power boating. A nearby visitor center offers exhibits of local Native American history. The elevation is 750 feet. Open April through September. For more information about Lake Mendocino, see trip note for Che-Kaka Camp.

34. HENDY WOODS STATE PARK

Reference: **Near Booneville; map CØ, grid j5.**

Campsites, facilities: There are 92 sites for tents or motor homes up to 35 feet long. Piped water, flush toilets, showers, a sanitary disposal station, picnic tables and fire grills are provided. A grocery store and a propane gas station are available nearby. Pets are permitted. The facilities are **wheelchair accessible**.

Reservations, fee: Reserve by phoning Destinet at (800) 444-7275 ($6.75 Destinet fee); $15-$17 fee per night; $1 pet fee.

Who to contact: Phone (707) 937-5804 or (707) 865-2391.

Location: From Cloverdale on US 101, turn northwest on Highway 128 and drive about 35 miles to Philo Greenwood Road. Turn left (west) on Philo Greenwood Road and drive a short distance to the park entrance.

Trip note: This is a remarkable setting where the flora changes from open valley grasslands and oaks to a cloaked redwood forest with old-growth, as if you had waved a magic wand. The camps are set in forest, with a great trail routed amid the old redwoods and up to the Hermit Hut, where a hobo made his home for 18 years in a few giant tree stumps covered with branches. Open year-round. Note: It is illegal to fish in the park's river.

35. MANOR OAKS OVERNIGHTER PARK

Reference: **In Ukiah; map CØ, grid j8.**

Campsites, facilities: There are 53 motor home sites (15 drive-through) with full hookups. Picnic tables, fire grills, restrooms, showers and a swimming pool (in summer) are provided. A laundromat and ice are available. The camp is **wheelchair accessible**. Pets are allowed on leashes.

Reservations, fee: Reservations accepted; $18 fee per night.

Who to contact: Phone (707) 462-0529.

Location: From US 101 in Ukiah, take the Central Ukiah-Gobbi Street exit and drive east for a short distance to 700 East Gobbi Street on the left.

Trip note: This is a motor home park in an urban setting for Highway 101 motor-home cruisers. Nearby Lake Mendocino provides a side trip option, with access to boating, waterskiing and fishing. Open year-round.

MAP C1

NOR-CAL MAP .... see page 94
adjoining maps
NORTH (B1) .... see page 152
EAST (C2) .... see page 264
SOUTH (D1) .... see page 326
WEST (C0) .... see page 232

36 LISTINGS
PAGES 248-263

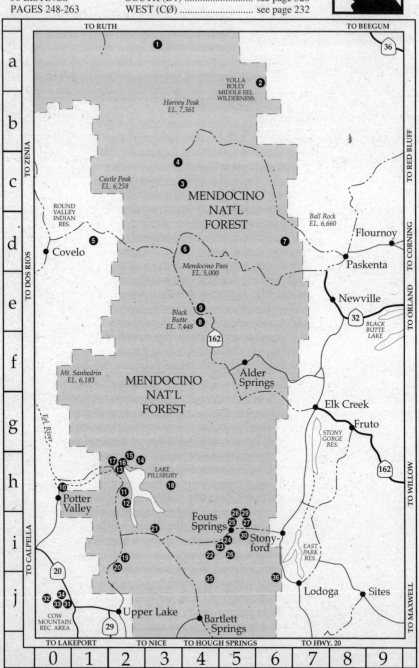

Map C1 featuring: Shasta-Trinity National Forest, Mendocino National Forest, Lake Pillsbury, Letts Lake, Lower Blue Lake, Upper Blue Lake

1. TOMHEAD SADDLE 👫 🐎

Reference: In Shasta-Trinity National Forest; map C1, grid a3.

Campsites, facilities: There are five sites for tents or motor homes. There is **no piped water**, so bring your own. Vault toilets, picnic tables and fire grills are provided. Pets are permitted. A horse corral is available.

Reservations, fee: No reservations; no fee.

Who to contact: Phone the Shasta-Trinity National Forest District Office at (916) 352-4211.

Location: From Interstate 5 in Red Bluff, turn west on Highway 36 and drive about 13 miles. Turn left on Cannon Road and drive about five miles to Pettyjohn Road. Turn west on Pettyjohn Road to and drive to Saddle Camp, then turn south on Forest Service Road 27N06 and drive three miles to the campground. A map of Shasta-Trinity National Forest is advised.

Trip note: This one is way out there in booger country. Little-known and rarely visited, it's primarily a jumpoff point for ambitious backpackers. It is located on the edge of the Yolla Bolly Middle Eel Wilderness Area. A trailhead here is routed to the South Fork of Cottonwood Creek, with eight miles of dry, hot hiking to get there. The elevation is 5,700 feet.

2. WHITE ROCK

Reference: In Shasta-Trinity National Forest; map C1, grid a6.

Campsites, facilities: There are three tent sites. Vault toilets, picnic tables and fire grills are provided. Pets are permitted on leashes.

Reservations, fee: No reservations; no fee.

Who to contact: Phone the Shasta-Trinity National Forest District Office at (916) 352-4211.

Location: From Red Bluff, drive about 45 miles west on Highway 36 to the Yolla Bolly Ranger Office. Continue west for about eight miles to Forest Service Road 30. Turn left on Forest Service Road 30 and drive nine miles to Forest Service Road 35. Turn left and drive (on a gravel road, very twisty) nine miles to the campground.

Trip note: There's a reason that there's no charge to camp here: Usually nobody's around. It's primitive, little-known, and likely to be empty. If you don't want to see anybody, you've found the right place. The big attraction here is watching the turtles swim at nearby White Rock Pond. A trailhead is available nearby out of Stuart Gap, which provides access to the North Yolla Bolly Mountains.

3. LITTLE DOE 🐟 👫

Reference: Near Howard Lake in Mendocino National Forest; map C1, grid c3.

Campsites, facilities: There are 13 tent sites. **No piped water** is available, so bring your own. Fire pits are provided. Supplies are available in Covelo. Pets are allowed on leashes.

Reservations, fee: No reservations; no fee. Open June through October.

Who to contact: Phone the Mendocino National Forest District Office at (707) 983-6118. For a map, send $3 to Office of Information, U.S. Forest Service, 630 Sansome Street, San Francisco, CA 94111.

Location: From Willits, drive north on US 101 for 13 miles to Longvale and the junction with Highway 162. Turn northeast on Highway 162 and drive to Covelo. Continue east on Highway 162 to the Eel River Bridge. Turn left at the bridge on Forest Service Road M1 and drive about 11 miles to campground at the north end of the lake.

Trip note: Little Howard Lake is tucked deep in the interior of Mendocino National Forest between Espee Ridge to the south and Little Doe Ridge to the north, elevation 3,600 feet. For a drive-to lake, it is surprisingly remote and provides fair trout fishing, primitive camping and an opportunity for car-top boating. Side trip opportunities include Hammerhorn Lake, about six miles away, and several four-wheel-drive roads in the area.

---

4. HAMMERHORN LAKE

Reference: Near Covelo in Mendocino National Forest; map C1, grid c3.

Campsites, facilities: There are eight sites for tents or motor homes up to 16 feet long. Piped water, picnic tables, fire grills and vault toilets are provided. Supplies are available in Covelo. There are two **wheelchair-accessible** piers and a trail. Pets are allowed on leashes.

Reservations, fee: No reservations; no fee. Open June through October.

Who to contact: Phone the Mendocino National Forest District Office at (707) 983-6118. For a map, send $3 to Office of Information, U.S. Forest Service, 630 Sansome Street, San Francisco, CA 94111.

Location: From Willits, drive north on US 101 for 13 miles to Longvale and the junction with Highway 162. Turn northeast on Highway 162 and drive to Covelo. Continue east on Highway 162 to the Eel River Bridge. Turn left at the bridge on Forest Service Road M1 and drive about 17 miles to campground at the north end of the lake.

Trip note: This is a veritable dot of a lake, just five acres, obscure and hidden, set at 3,500 feet in Mendocino National Forest. But it gets stocked with good-sized trout and can provide good fishing, camping and adventuring. The lake is set near the border of the Yolla Bolly Wilderness, with the trailhead located nearby to the northeast. A great side trip is the drive up to Hammerhorn Mountain Lookout.

---

5. EEL RIVER

Reference: In Mendocino National Forest; map C1, grid d2.

Campsites, facilities: There are 16 sites for tents or motor homes. Piped water, vault toilets, picnic tables and fire grills are provided. You must pack out your garbage. Pets are permitted on leashes or otherwise controlled.

Reservations, fee: No reservations; no fee.

Who to contact: Phone the Mendocino National Forest Covelo Ranger District at (707) 983-6118.

Location: From Willits, drive north on US 101 for 13 miles to Longvale and the junction with Highway 162. Turn northeast on Highway 162 and drive to Covelo. Continue east on Highway 162 for 13 miles to the campground.

Trip note: This is a little-known spot, set in the oak woodlands at the confluence of the Middle Fork of the Eel River and Black Butte River. The elevation is

1,500 feet, and it's often extremely hot in summer. At no cost, the camp's price is right. The camp is a major archeological site, an ancient Native American campsite. For this reason, restoration has been limited and at times, the camp is overgrown and weedy. Who cares, right? Right, after all, you're camping. Open May through October.

6. WELLS CABIN

Reference: **In Mendocino National Forest; map C1, grid d3.**

Campsites, facilities: There are 25 sites for tents or motor homes up to 22 feet long. Piped water, vault toilets, picnic tables and fire grills are provided. You must pack out your own garbage. Pets are permitted on leashes or otherwise controlled. There is **no piped water** in the winter.

Reservations, fee: No reservations; no fee.

Who to contact: Phone the Mendocino National Forest District at (916) 824-5196.

Location: From Corning on Interstate 5, turn west on County Road A9 and drive 20 miles to Paskenta. In Paskenta, turn left on County Road 55 and drive into Mendocino National Forest (where the road becomes Forest Service Road M4). Continue on Forest Service Road M4 all the way near the ridge at Government Flat at Forest Service Road 24N02. Turn left on Forest Service Road 24N02 and drive two miles to the campground.

Trip note: You'll join the Five Percent Club when you reach this spot. It is situated one mile from Anthony Peak Lookout (6,900 feet), where, on a clear day, you can get great views all the way to the Pacific Ocean, and sweeping views of the Sacramento Valley to the east. This campground is hardly used during the summer and often provides a cool escape from the heat of the valley. The elevation is 6,300 feet. Open July through October.

7. WHITLOCK

Reference: **In Mendocino National Forest; map C1, grid d6.**

Campsites, facilities: There are three sites for tents or motor homes up to 22 feet long. Piped water, vault toilets, picnic tables and fire grills are provided. You must pack out your own garbage. Pets are permitted on leashes or otherwise controlled.

Reservations, fee: No reservations; no fee.

Who to contact: Phone the Mendocino National Forest at (916) 824-5196.

Location: From Corning on Interstate 5, turn west onto County Road A9 (Corning Road) and drive 20 miles to Paskenta. Turn north on Toomes Camp Road (County Road 122) and drive 14 miles to the campground.

Trip note: This obscure Forest Service camp is often empty or close to empty. It is set at 4,300 feet, where conifers have taken over from the valley grasslands to the nearby east, amid good deer range, and makes a good hunting base camp in the fall, with a network of Forest Service roads in the area. It is advisable to obtain a Forest Service map. Open June through October.

8. PLASKETT MEADOWS

Reference: **In Mendocino National Forest; map C1, grid e4.**

Campsites, facilities: There are 32 sites for tents or motor homes up to 16 feet long. Piped water, vault toilets, fire grills and picnic tables are provided. Pets are allowed on leashes.

Reservations, fee: No reservations; $5 fee per night.

Who to contact: Phone the Mendocino National Forest at (916) 963-3128.

Location: In Willows on Interstate 5, turn west on Highway 162 and drive toward the town of Elk Creek. Just after crossing the Stony Creek Bridge, turn north on County Road 306 and drive four miles. Turn left (west) on Alder Springs Road (Forest Service Road 7) and drive 31 miles to the campground.

Trip note: This is a little-known camp in the mountains, near Plaskett Lakes, a pair of connected dot-size mountain lakes that form the headwaters of little Plaskett Creek. Trout fishing is best at the western-most of the two lakes. No motors are permitted. For a side trip option, there is a good hike that heads along Plaskett Creek and then south up to Chimney Rock (which can also be reached from the south via Bushy Mountain Road and a ton of backcountry driving). Open June through October.

9. MASTERSON GROUP CAMP

Reference: Near Plaskett Lakes in Mendocino National Forest; map C1, grid e4.

Campsites, facilities: This group camp can accommodate up to 100 people, with 20 tent sites, piped water, vault toilets, fire grills and picnic tables provided. Pets are allowed on leashes.

Reservations, fee: Reservations required; $20 group fee per night.

Who to contact: Phone the Mendocino National Forest at (916) 963-3128.

Location: In Willows on Interstate 5, turn west on Highway 162 and drive toward the town of Elk Creek. Just after crossing the Stony Creek Bridge, turn north on County Road 306 and drive four miles. Turn left (west) on Alder Springs Road (Forest Service Road 7) and drive 31 miles to the camp on the right.

Trip note: This is a group camp only. It is located just a mile away from the Plaskett Lakes, two small lakes set at 6,000 feet and surrounded by mixed conifer forest. No swimming and no motors are permitted at either lake. It is advisable to obtain a map of Mendocino National Forest, which details nearby streams, lakes and hiking trails. One notable trail is the Black Butte Trail. Open mid-May through mid-October. For more information, see trip note for Plaskett Meadows.

10. TROUT CREEK

Reference: Near East Van Arsdale Reservoir; map C1, grid h0.

Campsites, facilities: There are 15 sites for tents or motor homes. Piped water, picnic tables, fire grills and vault toilets are provided. Pets are permitted on leashes or otherwise controlled.

Reservations, fee: No reservations; $10 fee per night; $1 pet fee.

Who to contact: Phone the PG&E District Office at (916) 386-5164.

Location: From Ukiah on US 101, drive north to the junction with Highway 20. Turn east on Highway 20 and drive five miles. Turn northwest on County Road 240 (Potter Valley-Lake Pillsbury Road) toward Lake Pillsbury. From the Eel River Bridge, drive two miles to the campground entrance.

Trip note: This is a spot that relatively few campers know of. Most others looking over this area are setting up shop at nearby Lake Pillsbury to the east. But, if you like to watch the water roll by, this could be your port of call, since it is located at the confluence of Trout Creek and Eel River (not far from the East Van Arsdale Reservoir). Insider's note: Nearby in Potter Valley to the south, the East Fork Russian River (Cold Creek) is stocked with trout during the summer months. The elevation is 1,500 feet. Open May through October.

11. FULLER GROVE ⌐🐟⚓🏃🏊 🚐 7

Reference: **On Lake Pillsbury in Mendocino National Forest; map C1, grid h2.**

Campsites, facilities: There are 30 sites for tents or motor homes. Picnic tables and fire grills are provided. Piped water and vault toilets are available. A boat ramp is nearby. Pets are permitted on leashes or otherwise controlled.

Reservations, fee: No reservations; $6 fee per night, $3 per extra vehicle.

Who to contact: Phone the Mendocino National Forest Upper Lake Ranger Station at (707) 275-2361.

Location: From Ukiah on US 101, drive north to the junction with Highway 20. Turn east on Highway 20 and drive five miles. Turn northwest on County Road 240 (Potter Valley-Lake Pillsbury Road) and drive to the Eel River Information Kiosk at Lake Pillsbury. Continue for one mile, then turn right at the campground access road and drive a quarter-mile to the campground.

Trip note: This is one of several campgrounds bordering Lake Pillsbury, which at 2,000 acres is by far the largest lake in Mendocino National Forest. It has lakeside camping, good boat ramps, and in the spring, good fishing for trout. This camp is set along the northwest shore of the lake, with a boat ramp located only about a quarter-mile away to the north. There are numerous backcountry roads in the area, which provide access to a state game refuge to the north and the Snow Mountain Wilderness to the east.

12. LAKE PILLSBURY RESORT ⌐🐟⚓♿🏊 🚐 6

Reference: **Map C1, grid h2.**

Campsites, facilities: There are 40 sites for tents or motor homes, with no hookups. There are also eight cabins for rent. A snack bar, restrooms, showers, boat rentals, fuel, a dock, fishing supplies, and a pier are available. Pets are allowed on leashes.

Reservations, fee: Reservations recommended; $14 fee per night. Small cabins are $47 per night, large cabins are $59 per night.

Who to contact: Phone (707) 743-1581.

Location: From Ukiah on US 101, drive north to the junction with Highway 20. Turn east on Highway 20 and drive five miles. Turn northwest on County Road 240 (Potter Valley-Lake Pillsbury Road) and drive to Lake Pillsbury and Forest Service Road 301F. Turn right at Forest Service Road 301F and drive two miles to the resort.

Trip note: This is a pretty spot beside the shore of Lake Pillsbury in the heart of Mendocino National Forest. It can make a headquarters for a vacation involving boating, fishing, waterskiing or exploring the surrounding national forest. A boat ramp, small marina and full facilities make this place a prime attraction in a relatively remote location. This is the only resort on the lake that accepts reservations, and it has some lakefront sites. Open May through November.

13. POGIE POINT ⌐🐟⚓🏃🏊 🚐 7

Reference: **On Lake Pillsbury in Mendocino National Forest; map C1, grid h2.**

Campsites, facilities: There are 50 sites for tents or motor homes. Piped water is provided, except in winter. Picnic tables and fire grills are provided. Vault toilets are available. Pets are permitted on leashes or otherwise controlled.

Reservations, fee: No reservations; $6 fee per night, $3 per extra vehicle.

Who to contact: Phone the Mendocino National Forest Upper Lake Ranger

Station at (707) 275-2361.

Location: From Ukiah on US 101, drive north to the junction with Highway 20. Turn east on Highway 20 and drive five miles. Turn northwest on County Road 240 (Potter Valley-Lake Pillsbury Road) and drive 26 miles to the Eel River Information Kiosk at Lake Pillsbury. Continue for two miles, then turn right at the campground access road and drive a short distance to the campground.

Trip note: This camp is set beside Lake Pillsbury in Mendocino National Forest, located in the back of a cove at the lake's northwest corner. When the lake is full, this spot is quite pretty. When the lake level is way down, well, you can't win 'em all. A boat ramp is located about a quarter-mile to the south, a bonus. The elevation is 1,900 feet. Open year-round.

---

14. SUNSET CAMPGROUND 🎣 ⚓ 🚶 🏊   RV 7

Reference: On Lake Pillsbury in Mendocino National Forest; map C1, grid h2.

Campsites, facilities: There are 54 sites for tents or motor homes. Piped water (except in the winter), picnic tables, fire grills and vault toilets are provided. Pets are permitted on leashes or otherwise controlled. A boat ramp is nearby.

Reservations, fee: No reservations; $6 fee per night, $3 per extra vehicle.

Who to contact: Phone the Mendocino National Forest Upper Lake Ranger Station at (707) 275-2361.

Location: From Ukiah on US 101, drive north to the junction with Highway 20. Turn east on Highway 20 and drive five miles. Turn northwest on County Road 240 (Potter Valley-Lake Pillsbury Road) and drive 26 miles to the Eel River Information Kiosk at Lake Pillsbury. Continue for five miles around the north end of the lake and look for the camp entrance on the right side of the road.

Trip note: This camp is located on the northeast corner of Lake Pillsbury, with a boat ramp located at the mouth of Squaw Creek Cove less than a quarter-mile to the south. The adjacent, designated nature trail along the shore of the lake here is another attraction. The surrounding national forest offers side trip possibilities. Open year-round.

---

15. OAK FLAT 🎣 🚶   RV 6

Reference: On Lake Pillsbury in Mendocino National Forest; map C1, grid h2.

Campsites, facilities: There are 12 primitive sites for tents or motor homes. There is **no piped water**, but picnic tables, fire grills and vault toilets are provided. Pets are permitted on leashes or otherwise controlled.

Reservations, fee: No reservations; no fee.

Who to contact: Phone the Mendocino National Forest Upper Lake Ranger Station at (707) 275-2361.

Location: From Ukiah on US 101, drive north to the junction with Highway 20. Turn east on Highway 20 and drive five miles. Turn northwest on County Road 240 (Potter Valley-Lake Pillsbury Road) and drive 26 miles to the Eel River Information Kiosk at Lake Pillsbury. Continue for four miles around the north end of the lake and look for the camp entrance on the right side of the road.

Trip note: This primitive camp is used primarily by riders of off-road motorcycles and as an overflow area if Lake Pillsbury's other camps are full. It is set at 1,850 feet near the north shore of Lake Pillsbury in the heart of Mendocino National Forest. Trails leading into the backcountry are nearby, detailed on a Forest Service map. Open year-round.

16. NAVY

Reference: **On Lake Pillsbury in Mendocino National Forest; map C1, grid h2.**

Campsites, facilities: There are 20 sites for tents or motor homes. Picnic tables are provided. Piped water and vault toilets are available, and a boat ramp is nearby. Facilities are **wheelchair accessible.** Pets on leashes are permitted.

Reservations, fee: No reservations; $6 fee per night.

Who to contact: Phone the Mendocino National Forest Upper Lake Ranger Station at (707) 275-2361. For a map, send $3 to Office of Information, U.S. Forest Service, 630 Sansome Street, San Francisco, CA 94111, and ask for Mendocino National Forest.

Location: From Ukiah on US 101, drive north to the junction with Highway 20. Turn east on Highway 20 and drive five miles. Turn northwest on County Road 240 (Potter Valley-Lake Pillsbury Road) and drive 26 miles to the Eel River Information Kiosk at Lake Pillsbury. Continue for four miles around the north end of the lake and look for the campground entrance on the right side of the road. The campground is on the north shore, just west of Oak Flat Camp.

Trip note: When Pillsbury is full of water, this is one of the most attractive of the many camps at the lake. It is set in the lake's north cove, sheltered from north winds. Surrounded by forest, the camp is in quite a pretty setting. However, when the lake level is down, such as is common from late July through fall, it can seem that this camp is set on the edge of a dust bowl.

17. FULLER GROUP

Reference: **On Lake Pillsbury in Mendocino National Forest; map C1, grid h2.**

Campsites, facilities: This group campsite can accommodate up to 100 people in tents or motor homes. Group cooking and eating facilities are provided. Piped water and vault toilets are available, and a boat ramp is nearby. Facilities are **wheelchair accessible**. Pets on leashes are permitted.

Reservations, fee: Reservations required; call for fees.

Who to contact: Phone the Mendocino National Forest Upper Lake Ranger Station at (707) 275-2361. For a map, send $3 to Office of Information, U.S. Forest Service, 630 Sansome Street, San Francisco, CA 94111, and ask for Mendocino National Forest.

Location: From Ukiah on US 101, drive north to the junction with Highway 20. Turn east on Highway 20 and drive five miles. Turn northwest on County Road 240 (Potter Valley-Lake Pillsbury Road) and drive to the Eel River Information Kiosk at Lake Pillsbury. Continue for one mile, then turn right at the campground access road and drive a quarter-mile to the campground.

Trip note: With a giant group camp, you can have your own personal party headquarters. Every year there are groups that do exactly that at this camp set on the northwest shore of Lake Pillsbury. Unlike many other group camps, this one actually comes equipped with facilities designed for a large number of people, a giant grill being one of the main features. A boat ramp is available about a half-mile to the north.

18. LOWER NYE

Reference: **In Mendocino National Forest; map C1, grid h3.**

Campsites, facilities: There are six sites for tents or motor homes. There is **no piped water**, but picnic tables, fire grills and vault toilets are provided. Pets are permitted on leashes or otherwise controlled.

Reservations, fee: No reservations; no fee.

Who to contact: Phone the Mendocino National Forest Upper Lake Ranger Station at (707) 275-2361.

Location: From Ukiah on US 101, drive north to the junction of Highway 20. Turn east on Highway 20 and drive to the town of Upper Lake and to Elk Mountain Road. Turn left (north) on Elk Mountain Road (which becomes Forest Service Road 1N02) and drive 17 miles. Turn right (east) on Forest Service Road 18N01 (Bear Creek Road) and drive seven miles. Turn north on Forest Service Road 18N04 (Rice Creek Road) and drive 14 miles to the campground.

Trip note: This camp is on the northern border of the Snow Mountain Wilderness. It is a good jumpoff point for backpackers, or a spot for folks who don't want to be bugged by anybody to hunker down for a while. It is set at 3,300 feet on Skeleton Creek near the Eel River. A detailed USGS topographic map is strongly advised. Open May to mid-September.

19. DEER VALLEY CAMPGROUND 🚶🚶

Reference: **In Mendocino National Forest; map C1, grid i2.**

Campsites, facilities: There are 13 sites for tents or motor homes. There is **no piped water**, but picnic tables, fire grills and vault toilets are provided. Pets are permitted on leashes or otherwise controlled.

Reservations, fee: No reservations; no fee.

Who to contact: Phone the Mendocino National Forest Upper Lake Ranger Station at (707) 275-2361.

Location: From Ukiah on US 101, drive north to the junction of Highway 20. Turn east on Highway 20 and drive to the town of Upper Lake and to Elk Mountain Road. Turn left (north) on Elk Mountain Road (which becomes Forest Service Road 1N02) and drive 12 miles (the latter section is extremely twisty). Turn right on Forest Service Road 16N01 and drive four miles to the campground.

Trip note: This one is out there in booger country. It is used primarily in the fall by deer hunters. It is set at 3,700 feet in Deer Valley, about five miles from the East Fork of Middle Creek. Open April to November.

20. MIDDLE CREEK CAMPGROUND

Reference: **In Mendocino National Forest; map C1, grid i2.**

Campsites, facilities: There are 12 sites for tents or small motor homes. Piped water, picnic tables and fire grills are provided. Vault toilets are available. Pets are permitted on leashes or otherwise controlled.

Reservations, fee: No reservations; $4 fee per night.

Who to contact: Phone Mendocino National Forest, Upper Lake Ranger Station at (707) 275-2361.

Location: From Ukiah on US 101, drive north to the junction of Highway 20. Turn east on Highway 20 and drive to the town of Upper Lake and to Elk Mountain Road. Turn left (north) on Elk Mountain Road (which becomes Forest Service Road 1N02) and drive eight miles to the camp on the right side of the road.

Trip note: This camp is not widely known, but known well enough. Sometimes there's a problem with off-road motorcycles making a lot of noise in the area. That ruins an otherwise quiet spot, which is set at 2,000 feet at the confluence of the West and East Forks of Middle Creek. Open year-round.

21. BEAR CREEK CAMPGROUND

Reference: **In Mendocino National Forest; map C1, grid i3.**

Campsites, facilities: There are 16 sites for tents or small motor homes. There is **no piped water**, but picnic tables, fire grills and vault toilets are provided. Pets are permitted on leashes or otherwise controlled.

Reservations, fee: No reservations; no fee.

Who to contact: Phone the Mendocino National Forest Upper Lake Ranger Station at (707) 275-2361.

Location: From Ukiah on US 101, drive north to the junction of Highway 20. Turn east on Highway 20 and drive to the town of Upper Lake and to Elk Mountain Road. Turn left (north) on Elk Mountain Road (which becomes Forest Service Road 1N02) and drive 17 miles (the latter stretch is extremely twisty). Turn east on Forest Service Road 301C (Bear Creek Road) and drive eight miles to the campground on the right side of the road.

Trip note: Bet you didn't know about this one—a primitive spot out in the boondocks of Mendocino National Forest, set at 2,000 feet. It's a pretty spot too, set beside Bear Creek near its confluence with Blue Slides Creek. It's about a 10-minute drive to the Summit Springs Trailhead at the southern end of the Snow Mountain Wilderness. There are also numerous four-wheel-drive roads in this region, detailed on a map of Mendocino National Forest. Open May to mid-October.

---

22. LETTS LAKE COMPLEX

Reference: **In Mendocino National Forest; map C1, grid i4.**

Campsites, facilities: There are 40 sites for tents or motor homes up to 20 feet long. Piped water, vault toilets, picnic tables and fire grills are provided. Pets are permitted on leashes or otherwise controlled.

Reservations, fee: No reservations; $5 fee per night.

Who to contact: Phone the Mendocino National Forest Stonyford Ranger District at (916) 963-3128.

Location: From Interstate 5 at Maxwell, turn west on Maxwell-Sites Road and drive to Sites. Bear right on Peterson Road for one-half mile, turn left on Sites-Lodoga Road and continue to Lodoga. Turn right on Lodoga-Stonyford Road and loop around East Park Reservoir to reach Stonyford. From Stonyford, turn west on Fouts Springs Road (County Road M10) and drive about 17 miles into national forest (where the road becomes Forest Service 17N02) to the campground on the east side of Letts Lake.

Trip note: Letts Lake is a spot not too many folks know about, a 35-acre lake set in a mixed conifer forest at 4,500 feet just south of the Snow Mountain Wilderness. There are three camps set on the east side of the lake, so take your pick. No motors are allowed on the lake, making it ideal for canoes, rafts and float tubes. This lake is stocked with brook trout in the early summer. It's a designated historical landmark, the site where the homesteaders known as the Letts brothers were murdered. While that may not impress you, what will are the views to the north of the Snow Mountain Wilderness. In addition, there are several natural springs that can be fun to hunt up. By the way, after such a long drive to get here, don't let your eagerness cause you to stop at Lily Pond (on the left, one mile before reaching Letts Lake), because there's no trout in it. Open mid-April through October.

23. MILL VALLEY

Reference: **Near Letts Lake in Mendocino National Forest; map C1, grid i4.**

Campsites, facilities: There are 15 sites for tents or motor homes up to 18 feet long. Piped water, vault toilets, picnic tables and fire grills are provided. Pets are permitted on leashes or otherwise controlled.

Reservations, fee: No reservations; $3 fee per night.

Who to contact: Phone the Mendocino National Forest Stonyford Ranger District at (916) 963-3128.

Location: From Interstate 5 at Maxwell, turn west on Maxwell-Sites Road and drive to Sites. Bear right on Peterson Road for one-half mile, turn left on Sites-Lodoga Road and continue to Lodoga. Turn right on Lodoga-Stonyford Road and loop around East Park Reservoir to reach Stonyford. From Stonyford, turn west on Fouts Springs Road (County Road M10) and drive about 17 miles into national forest (where the road becomes Forest Service 17N02) to the camp access road on the left. Turn left and drive a half-mile to the camp.

Trip note: This camp is set beside Lily Pond, a little, teeny guy, with larger Letts Lake just a mile away. Since Lily Pond does not have trout, and Letts Lake does, this camp gets far less traffic than its counterpart. The area is crisscrossed with numerous creeks, four-wheel-drive routes and Forest Service roads, making it a great adventure for owners of four-wheel-drives. The elevation is 4,200 feet. Open mid-April through October.

24. DIXIE GLADE HORSE CAMP

Reference: **Near Snow Mountain Wilderness Area in Mendocino National Forest; map C1, grid i5.**

Campsites, facilities: This group campsite can accommodate up to 50 people in tents or motor homes. A horse corral, troughs, picnic tables and fire grills are provided. Piped water is available.

Reservations, fee: No reservations; no fee.

Who to contact: Phone Stonyford Ranger District at (916) 963-3128. For a map, send $3 to Office of Information, U.S. Forest Service, 630 Sansome Street, San Francisco, CA 94111, and ask for Mendocino National Forest.

Location: From Interstate 5 at Maxwell, turn west on Maxwell-Sites Road and drive to Sites. Bear right on Peterson Road for one-half mile, turn left on Sites-Lodoga Road and continue to Lodoga. Turn right on Lodoga-Stonyford Road and loop around East Park Reservoir to reach Stonyford. From Stonyford, turn west on Fouts Springs Road (County Road M10) and drive 10 miles to the camp on the left side of the road. The old Sanborn Cabin is adjacent to the camp.

Trip note: Got a horse who likes to tromp? No? Then take a pass on this one. Yes? Then sign right up, because this is a trailhead camp for people preparing to head north by horseback into the adjacent Snow Mountain Wilderness.

25. MILL CREEK

Reference: **In Mendocino National Forest; map C1, grid i5.**

Campsites, facilities: There are six tent sites. There is **no piped water**, but vault toilets, picnic tables and fire grills are provided. Pets are permitted on leashes or otherwise controlled.

Reservations, fee: No reservations; no fee.

Who to contact: Phone the Mendocino National Forest Stonyford Ranger District at (916) 963-3128.

Location: From Interstate 5 at Maxwell, turn west on Maxwell-Sites Road and drive to Sites. Bear right on Peterson Road for one-half mile, turn left on Sites-Lodoga Road and continue to Lodoga. Turn right on Lodoga-Stonyford Road and loop around East Park Reservoir to reach Stonyford. From Stonyford, turn west on Fouts Springs Road (County Road M10) and drive about eight miles. Turn right (north) on Forest Service Road 18N03 and you'll see the campground on your right.

Trip note: This tiny, pretty, secluded camp is set beside Mill Creek near Fouts Springs at the southeastern boundary of the Snow Mountain Wilderness. A nearby trailhead, a mile to the west, provides a hiking route into the wilderness that connects along Trout Creek, a great little romp. Mill Creek is quite pretty in the late spring, but by late summer, the flow drops way down. The elevation is 1,700 feet. Open year-round.

---

26. OLD MILL

Reference: **Near Mill Creek in Mendocino National Forest; map C1, grid i5.**

Campsites, facilities: There are eight sites for tents and two sites for tents or motor homes up to 16 feet long. (However, the access road to the campground is narrow.) There is **no piped water**, but toilets, picnic tables and fire grills are provided. Pets are permitted on leashes or otherwise controlled.

Reservations, fee: No reservations; no fee.

Who to contact: Phone the Mendocino National Forest Stonyford Ranger District at (916) 963-3128.

Location: From Interstate 5 at Maxwell, turn west on Maxwell-Sites Road and drive to Sites. Bear right on Peterson Road for one-half mile, turn left on Sites-Lodoga Road and continue to Lodoga. Turn right on Lodoga-Stonyford Road and loop around East Park Reservoir to reach Stonyford. From Stonyford, turn west on Fouts Springs Road (County Road M10) and drive about six miles. Turn left (south) on Forest Service Road M5 (Trough Springs Road) and drive 7.5 miles (on a narrow road) to the campground on your right.

Trip note: Little known and little used, this camp is set at 3,700 feet amid a mature stand of pine and fir on Trough Spring Ridge. It's just a short walk to Mill Creek. It's located at the site of—guess what? An old mill. Open May through October.

---

27. NORTH FORK

Reference: **On Stony Creek in Mendocino National Forest; map C1, grid i5.**

Campsites, facilities: There are four tent sites. There is **no piped water**, but vault toilets, picnic tables and fire grills are provided. Pets are permitted on leashes or otherwise controlled.

Reservations, fee: No reservations; no fee.

Who to contact: Phone the Mendocino National Forest Stonyford Ranger District at (916) 963-3128.

Location: From Interstate 5 at Maxwell, turn west on Maxwell-Sites Road and drive to Sites. Bear right on Peterson Road for one-half mile, turn left on Sites-Lodoga Road and continue to Lodoga. Turn right on Lodoga-Stonyford Road and loop around East Park Reservoir to reach Stonyford. From Stonyford, turn west on Fouts Springs Road (County Road M10) and drive about eight miles.

Turn right (north) on Forest Service Road 18N03 and drive two miles to the campground.

Trip note: This quiet, primitive camp is set in a grove of oak trees at the confluence of the north, south and middle forks of Stony Creek. There are many trailheads for hiking in the area, located with a few miles for the Snow Mountain Wilderness, but none at this camp. There are great views of St. John Mountain and Snow Mountain. See trip note for Mill Creek Camp for additional information. The elevation is 1,700 feet. Open year-round.

28. FOUTS CAMPGROUND 🏃 ♿   RV 6

Reference: **On Stony Creek in Mendocino National Forest; map C1, grid i5.**

Campsites, facilities: There are 11 sites for tents or motor homes up to 16 feet long. Piped water, vault toilets, picnic tables and fire grills are provided. Pets are permitted on leashes or otherwise controlled.

Reservations, fee: No reservations; no fee.

Who to contact: Phone the Mendocino National Forest Stonyford Ranger District at (916) 963-3128.

Location: From Interstate 5 at Maxwell, turn west on Maxwell-Sites Road and drive to Sites. Bear right on Peterson Road for one-half mile, turn left on Sites-Lodoga Road and continue to Lodoga. Turn right on Lodoga-Stonyford Road and loop around East Park Reservoir to reach Stonyford. From Stonyford, turn west on Fouts Springs Road (County Road M10) and drive about eight miles. Turn right (north) on Forest Service Road 18N03 and drive one mile to the campground on your right.

Trip note: This camp is located in a brushy area shaded by digger pines. It is set beside Stony Creek near Davis Flat and Fouts Springs. Several equally remote camps are nearby—North Fork, South Fork and Mill Creek. To the west is the Snow Mountain Wilderness and excellent hiking trails, to the south is an extensive Forest Service road network that provides access for four-wheel-drive vehicles and dirt bikes. The elevation is 1,700 feet.

29. SOUTH FORK 🏃 ♿   6

Reference: **On the South Fork of Stony Creek in Mendocino National Forest; map C1, grid i5**

Campsites, facilities: There are five tent sites. Vault toilets, picnic tables and fire rings are provided. There is **no piped water**. Pets are permitted on leashes.

Reservations, fee: No reservations; no fee.

Who to contact: Phone the Mendocino National Forest Stonyford District at (916) 963-3128.

Location: From Interstate 5 at Maxwell, turn west on Maxwell-Sites Road and drive to Sites. Bear right on Peterson Road for one-half mile, turn left on Sites-Lodoga Road and continue to Lodoga. Turn right on Lodoga-Stonyford Road and loop around East Park Reservoir to reach Stonyford. From Stonyford, turn west on Fouts Springs Road (County Road M10) and drive about eight miles. Turn right (north) on Forest Service Road 18N03 and drive one mile to the campground on your right.

Trip note: This camp is set on the South Fork of Stony Creek near Fouts and Davis Flat campgrounds. These camps are located in a designated off-highway-vehicle area and are used primarily by dirt bikers, so if you're looking for quiet, this probably isn't your camp. The elevation is 1,700 feet. Open year-round.

30. DAVIS FLAT 👫 ♿   🚐 4

Reference: **In Mendocino National Forest; map C1, grid i5**

Campsites, facilities: There are 70 dispersed sites for tents or motor homes of any length. Piped water, vault toilets, fire rings and picnic tables are provided. Pets are permitted on leashes.

Reservations, fee: No reservations; no fee.

Who to contact: Phone the Mendocino National Forest Stonyford District at (916) 963-3128.

Location: From Interstate 5 at Maxwell, turn west on Maxwell-Sites Road and drive to Sites. Bear right on Peterson Road for one-half mile, turn left on Sites-Lodoga Road and continue to Lodoga. Turn right on Lodoga-Stonyford Road and loop around East Park Reservoir to reach Stonyford. From Stonyford, turn west on Fouts Springs Road (County Road M10) and drive about eight miles. Turn right (north) on Forest Service Road 18N03 and drive one mile to the campground on your right.

Trip note: This camp is located across the road from Fouts and South Fork campgrounds. All three are located in a designated off-highway-vehicle area, so beware of motorcyclists, especially in the winter months. This isn't the quietest camp around, but there is some good hiking in the area to the immediate west in the Snow Mountain Wilderness. Elevation is 1,700 feet. Open year-round.

---

31. LE TRIANON RESORT 🎣 ⚓ 🏊   🚐 7

Reference: **On Lower Blue Lake; map C1, grid j0.**

Campsites, facilities: There are 200 sites for tents or motor homes with water and electric hookups, and 17 cabins for rent. Picnic tables are provided. Flush toilets, showers, a sanitary disposal station, a playground, a boat ramp, boat rentals, fishing supplies, a laundromat, a snack bar, propane gas and a grocery store are available. Pets are allowed on leashes.

Reservations, fee: No reservations; call for fees.

Who to contact: Phone the park at (707) 275-2262.

Location: From Ukiah, drive north on US 101 for five miles to the junction with Highway 20. Turn east on Highway 20 and drive 12 miles to 5845 West Highway 20.

Trip note: This is the biggest of the camps on the Blue Lakes, the overlooked lakes not far from giant Clear Lake. This one is an angler's special with good trout fishing in spring and no waterskiing permitted. The better fishing is in Upper Blue Lake, which is stocked with 28,000 trout per year, and where the water is much clearer than at the lower lake. The best fishing is in the spring, in April, May and June. A plus at this park is a few lakeside campsites. Open April through October.

---

32. MAYACMUS 👫 🐎

Reference: **Near Ukiah; map C1 grid j0.**

Campsites, facilities: There are nine tent sites. Piped water, vault toilets, picnic tables and fire grills are provided. Pets are permitted on leashes.

Reservations, fee: No reservations; no fee. Stay limit is 14 days.

Who to contact: Phone the Bureau of Land Management, Ukiah District at (707) 468-4000.

Location: From US 101 in Ukiah, turn east on Talmage Road and drive 1.5 miles to Eastside Road. Turn right and drive a third of a mile to Mill Creek Road. Turn left and drive three miles. Just beyond Mill Creek County Park, look for the North Cow Mountain sign on the left. Make a left there and drive seven miles to the campground.

Trip note: This campground is set within the Cow Mountain Recreation Area on the slopes of Cow Mountain, the oft overlooked wild region east of Ukiah. The primitive area is ideal for hiking and horseback riding. In the fall, it is a popular hunting area as well, for the few who know of it. This section of the Rec Area is quiet, with hiking on the Mayacmus Trail providing access to Willow Creek, Mill Creek and several overlooks of Clear Lake to the south. The flora is chaparral and oak/bay grasslands, with the weather extremely hot in the summer. By the way, off-road vehicles frequent the southern portion of the Rec Area, but not this immediate region.

33. PINE ACRES BLUE LAKE RESORT

Reference: **On Upper Blue Lake; map C1, grid j0.**

Campsites, facilities: There are 32 motor home sites, most with full or partial hookups. Picnic tables and fire grills are provided. Flush toilets, showers, a sanitary disposal station, boat rentals, boat launching, moorings, a boat ramp, a grocery store, fishing supplies and lake frontage sites are available. Pets are allowed on leashes.

Reservations, fee: Reservations accepted; $16-$19 fee per night.

Who to contact: Phone the park at (707) 275-2811.

Location: From Ukiah, drive north on US 101 for five miles to the junction with Highway 20. Turn east on Highway 20 and drive about 11 miles to Irvine Street. Turn right on Irvine Street and drive one block to Blue Lakes Road. Turn right and drive one block to the resort.

Trip note: Because of their proximity to Clear Lake, the Blue Lakes are often overlooked. But these lovely lakes offer good fishing for trout, especially in spring and early summer on Upper Blue Lake. With a speed limit in place, quiet boating is the rule. Swimming is good here. No waterskiing is permitted. Open year-round.

34. NARROWS LODGE RESORT

Reference: **On Upper Blue Lake; map C1, grid j0.**

Campsites, facilities: There are 28 sites for tents or motor homes, with full or partial hookups. Picnic tables are provided. Flush toilets, showers, a sanitary disposal station, a recreation room, boat rentals, pier, a boat ramp, boat rentals, fishing supplies and ice are available. A motel and cabins are also available. Pets are allowed on leashes, but not in motel rooms or cabins.

Reservations, fee: Reservations accepted; $19-$21 fee per night.

Who to contact: Phone the park at (707) 275-2718.

Location: From Ukiah, drive north on US 101 for five miles to the junction with Highway 20. Turn east on Highway 20 and drive about 11.5 miles to Blue Lakes Road. Turn left on Blue Lakes Road and drive to 5690 Blue Lakes Road.

Trip note: This is one of four campgrounds in the immediate vicinity. The Blue

Lakes are often overlooked because of their proximity to Clear Lake, but they are a quiet and pretty alternative, with good trout fishing in the spring and early summer. Open year-round.

35. CEDAR CAMP

Reference: **In Mendocino National Forest; map C1, grid j4.**

Campsites, facilities: There are five sites for tents or small motor homes (the access road is poor for trailers). There is **no piped water**, but vault toilets, picnic tables and fire grills are provided. Pets are permitted on leashes or otherwise controlled.

Reservations, fee: No reservations; no fee.

Who to contact: Phone the Mendocino National Forest Stonyford Ranger District at (916) 963-3128.

Location: From Interstate 5 at Maxwell, turn west on Maxwell-Sites Road and drive to Sites. Bear right on Peterson Road for one-half mile, turn left on Sites-Lodoga Road and continue to Lodoga. Turn right on Lodoga-Stonyford Road and loop around East Park Reservoir to reach Stonyford. From Stonyford, turn west on Fouts Springs Road (County Road M10) and drive about six miles. Turn left (south) on County Road M5 (Trough Springs Road) and drive 13 miles to the campground on your right.

Trip note: This camp is set at 4,300 feet elevation, just below Goat Mountain (6,121 feet), to the west about a mile away. Why did anybody decide to build a campground way out here? Because a small spring starts nearby, creating a trickle that runs into the nearby headwaters of Little Stony Creek. Open mid-June through mid-October.

36. DIGGER PINE FLAT

Reference: **On Little Stony Creek in Mendocino National Forest; map C1, grid j6.**

Campsites, facilities: There are seven sites for tents or small motor homes. There is **no piped water**, but vault toilets, picnic tables and fire grills are provided. Pets are permitted on leashes or otherwise controlled.

Reservations, fee: No reservations; no fee.

Who to contact: Phone the Mendocino National Forest Stonyford Ranger District at (916) 963-3128.

Location: From Interstate 5 at Maxwell, turn west on Maxwell-Sites Road and drive to Sites. Bear right on Peterson Road for one-half mile, turn left on Sites-Lodoga Road and continue to where the road crosses Stony Creek. Just after the bridge, turn left (southwest) on Goat Mountain Road and drive four miles (a rough, country road) to the campground on the left.

Trip note: This pretty spot is set in Little Stony Canyon, beside Little Stony Creek at 1,500 feet. Very few people know of this spot, and you will find it is appropriately named: It is little, it is stony, and the little trout amid the stones fit right in. The camp provides streamside access, and with Goat Mountain Road running along most of the stream, it is easy to fish much of this creek in an evening.

MAP C2

NOR-CAL MAP .... see page 94
adjoining maps
NORTH (B2) .... see page 180
EAST (C3) .... see page 272
SOUTH (D2) .... see page 346
WEST (C1) .... see page 248

18 LISTINGS
PAGES 264-271

TO COTTONWOOD   TO A-17   TO MANTON

TO BEEGUM

A5

5

36

A6

Paynes
Creek

Morgan Summit
EL. 5,750

Dales

36

2

TO MINERAL

a

1

36

36

3

Red Bluff

TO PASKENTA

b

4

99

TEHAMA
WILDLIFE
AREA

LASSEN

6
5

STATE
GAME
REFUGE

Dairyville

A8

Proberta

Dewitt Peak
EL. 2,064

NAT'L
FOREST

TO CHESTER

c

Gerber

Tehama

Los Molinos

ISHI
WILDERNESS

Henleyville

TO FLOURNOY

Rich
Field

Butte
Meadows

d

A9

Corning

WOODSON BRIDGE
STATE REC. AREA

7

Lomo

TO NEWVILLE

A9

10

Vina

Promontory Point
EL. 3,622

e

9

BLACK
BUTTE
LAKE

Kirkwood

Sacramento River

Forest
Ranch

Stirling
City

8

5

De Sabla

12

11

BIDWELL
MANSION
ST. HIST.
PARK

f

Orland

32

Nord

Chico

32

Magalia

TO FRUTO

Hamilton
City

Paradise

14

g

45

13

Artios

Ordbend

191

70

h

Willows

162

Durham

LAKE
OROVILLE

TO BERRY CREEK

Glenn

Nelson

i

Butte
City

99

70

SACRAMENTO
NAT'L
WILDLIFE
REFUGE

162

Richvale

15

162

Princeton

Afton

162

16

Oroville

17

TO BROWNVILLE

j

5

DELEVAN
NAT'L
WILDLIFE
REFUGE

Biggs

18

Palermo

TO SITES

45

Feather River

70

Maxwell

Gridley

Bangor

TO WILLIAMS   TO COLUSA   TO LIVE OAK   TO MARYSVILLE

0   1   2   3   4   5   6   7   8   9

Map C2 featuring: Sacramento River, Lassen National Forest, Black Butte Lake, Lake Oroville

1. BEND RV PARK AND FISHING RESORT

Reference: **On Sacramento River; map C2, grid a2.**

Campsites, facilities: There are 18 sites for motor homes, with full or partial hookups. There is a separate area for tents only. Piped water, showers, flush toilets and picnic tables are provided. A grocery store, bait and tackle shop, boat ramp, boat dock, laundromat and sanitary dump station are nearby. Pets are permitted.

Reservations, fee: Reservations accepted; $11-$17.50 fee per night.

Who to contact: Phone (916) 527-6289.

Location: From the junction of Interstate 5 and Highway 36 in Red Bluff, drive four miles north on Interstate 5 to the Jelly's Ferry Road exit. Turn northeast on Jelly's Ferry Road and drive 2.5 miles to the resort.

Trip note: For motor home cruisers, here's a spot to tie up your horse for a while. It's open year-round and is set beside the Sacramento River. Salmon average 15 to 25 pounds in this area, with the best results from mid-August through October. In recent years, the Bureau of Reclamation has been raising the gates of the Red Bluff Diversion Dam in early September. When that occurs, huge numbers of salmon charge upstream from Red Bluff to Anderson, holding in each deep river hole. Expect very hot weather in July and August.

2. BATTLE CREEK

Reference: **On Battle Creek in Lassen National Forest; map C2, grid a9.**

Campsites, facilities: There are 12 tent sites and 38 sites for tents or motor homes. Piped water, picnic tables and fire grills are provided. Flush toilets are available. Supplies can be obtained in the town of Mineral. Pets are permitted on leashes.

Reservations, fee: No reservations; $10 fee per night.

Who to contact: Phone the Lassen National Forest Almanor Ranger District Office at (916) 258-2141.

Location: From Red Bluff, turn east on Highway 36 and drive 41 miles to the campground (if you reach Mineral, you have gone two miles too far).

Trip note: This pretty spot offers easy access and streamside camping along Battle Creek. The trout fishing can be good in May, June and early July, when the creek is stocked by the Department of Fish and Game, which plants 23,000 rainbow trout and 2,000 smaller brook trout. Many people drive right by without knowing there is a stream here, and that the fishing can be good. The elevation is 4,800 feet. Open May through October.

3. O'NITE PARK

Reference: **Near Sacramento River; map C2, grid b2.**

Campsites, facilities: There are 74 motor home sites with full hookups. Picnic tables, restrooms, showers and a swimming pool are provided. A laundromat, propane gas and ice are available. Pets are permitted.

Reservations, fee: Reservations accepted; $19 fee per night.

Who to contact: Phone (916) 527-5868.

Location: From Interstate 5 and the junction of Highways 99 and 36 (in Red Bluff), drive west on Highway 36 (Antelope Boulevard) for one block to Gilmore Road. Turn south on Gilmore Road and drive one block to the camp.

Trip notes: Easy access from the highway, nearby supermarkets and restaurants, and many nearby side trips make this spot a winner. The park is only one block from the Sacramento River, which gets a big salmon run from mid-August through October. It's about a 45-minute drive east to Lassen Park. The elevation is approximately 300 feet and temperatures are typically in the 100s from mid-June through August.

---

4. LAKE RED BLUFF

Reference: **On Sacramento River near Red Bluff; map C2, grid b2.**

Campsites, facilities: There are 30 sites for tents or motor homes, with no hookups. Piped water, showers, vault and flush toilets, picnic areas, two boat ramps and a fish viewing plaza are available. Pets are permitted on a leash.

Reservations, fee: No reservations; $10 fee per night.

Who to contact: Phone the Mendocino National Forest, Corning Ranger District at (916) 824-5196.

Location: From Interstate 5 at Red Bluff, take the Highway 99-Lassen Park exit. Turn right at Sale Lane and travel about two miles south to the campground.

Trip note: Lake Red Bluff is created by the Red Bluff Diversion Dam on the Sacramento River, and waterskiing, birdwatching, hiking and fishing are the most popular activities. It has become a backyard swimming hole for local residents in the summer when the temperatures reach the high 90s and low 100s almost every day. In early September, the Bureau of Reclamation raises the gates at the Diversion Dam in order to allow migrating salmon an easier course on the upstream journey, and in the process Lake Red Bluff reverts to its former self as the Sacramento River.

---

5. BLACK ROCK

Reference: **On eastern edge of Ishi Wilderness Area; map C2, grid c9.**

Campsites, facilities: There are four tent sites. Picnic tables and fire pits are provided, and a vault toilet is available. There is **no piped water**. Mill Creek is adjacent to the camp and is a viable water source through early summer.

Reservations, fee: No reservations; $5 fee per night.

Who to contact: Phone Almanor Ranger District at (916) 258-2141 or (916) 258-3844. For a map, send $3 to Office of Information, U.S. Forest Service, 630 Sansome Street, San Francisco, CA 94111, and ask for Lassen National Forest.

Location: From Red Bluff, drive east on Highway 36 for about 35 miles to the town of Paynes Creek. In Paynes Creek, turn right on Little Giant Mill Road and continue for five miles to Plum Creek Road. Turn right on Plum Creek Road and drive two miles to Ponderosa Way. Turn right on Ponderosa Way and continue for about 20 miles to the campground on the right. Note: Only vehicles with high clearance are advised. No motor homes or trailers are allowed.

Trip note: This remote, primitive camp is set at the base of the huge, ancient Black Rock, one of the oldest geological points in Lassen National Forest. A bonus is that Mill Creek runs adjacent to the sites, providing a water source. This is the edge of the Ishi Wilderness, where remote hiking in solitude is possible without a wilderness permit and without venturing to high mountain elevations. A trailhead is available right out of the camp. The trail here is routed downstream along Mill Creek, extending five miles into the Ishi Wilderness, downhill all the way.

6. SOUTH ANTELOPE 👬 5% CLUB 6

Reference: **Near eastern edge of Ishi Wilderness Area; map C2, grid c9.**

Campsites, facilities: There are four tent sites. Picnic tables and fire pits are provided. A vault toilet is available. There is **no piped water.**

Reservations, fee: No reservations; no fee.

Who to contact: Phone Almanor Ranger District at (916) 258-2141 or (916) 258-3844. For a map, send $3 to Office of Information, U.S. Forest Service, 630 Sansome Street, San Francisco, CA 94111, and ask for Lassen National Forest.

Location: From Red Bluff, drive east on Highway 36 for about 35 miles to the town of Paynes Creek. In Paynes Creek, turn right on Little Giant Mill Road and continue for five miles to Plum Creek Road. Turn right on Plum Creek Road and drive two miles to Ponderosa Way. Turn right on Ponderosa Way and continue for about nine miles to the campground on the right. No motor homes or trailers are advised.

Trip note: This primitive campsite is for visitors who want to explore the Ishi Wilderness without an extensive drive (compared to other camps in the wilderness here). The South Fork of Antelope Creek runs west from the camp and provides an off-trail route for the ambitious. For easier hikes, trailheads along Ponderosa Way provide access into the eastern flank of the Ishi. The best nearby trail is the Lower Mill Creek Trail, with the trailhead located eight miles south at Black Rock Campground.

---

7. BUTTE MEADOWS 🐟 RV 6

Reference: **On Butte Creek in Lassen National Forest; map C2, grid d9.**

Campsites, facilities: There are 12 sites for tents or motor homes. Piped water, vault toilets, fire grills, picnic tables are provided. Pets are permitted on leashes. Supplies are available in Butte Meadows.

Reservations, fee: No reservations; $8 fee per night.

Who to contact: Phone the Lassen National Forest Almanor Ranger District at (916) 258-2141.

Location: From Chico, drive about 15 miles north on Highway 32 to the town of Forest Ranch. Continue on Highway 32 for another nine miles. Turn right onto Humboldt Road and drive five miles to Butte Meadows.

Trip note: On hot summer days, when a cold stream sounds better than a cold beer, Butte Meadows Campground provides a hide-out in national forest east of Chico. This is a summer camp situated along Butte Creek, which is stocked with 5,000 rainbow trout by the Department of Fish and Game. Nearby Doe Mill Ridge and the surrounding Lassen National Forest can provide a good side trip adventure. The elevation is 4,600 feet. Open May through October.

---

8. ORLAND BUTTES 🐟 ⚓ 👬 🏊 RV 7

Reference: **On Black Butte Lake; map C2, grid e0.**

Campsites, facilities: There are four tent sites and 31 sites for tents or motor homes up to 35 feet long. Piped water, restrooms, showers, fire grills, picnic tables, a boat-launch ramp and a sanitary disposal station are provided. Pets are allowed on leashes.

Reservations, fee: No reservations; $12 fee per night.

Who to contact: Phone the U.S. Army Corps of Engineers at (916) 865-4781.

Location: From Interstate 5 in Orland, take the Black Butte Lake exit. Drive west on Road 200 (Newville Road) for eight miles to the east shore of the lake.

Trip note: Black Butte Lake isn't far from Highway 5, but a lot of campers zoom right by it. The prime time to visit is in late spring and early summer, when the bass and crappie fishing can be quite good. There's a boat launch nearby. Expect very hot weather in the summer, when this part of the state turns into a hell-hole for campers. Open March through September.

9. BUCKHORN

Reference: On Black Butte Lake; map C2, grid e0.

Campsites, facilities: There are 85 sites for tents or motor homes up to 35 feet long. Piped water, picnic tables, fire grills, flush toilets, a sanitary dump station, showers and a playground are provided. A boat ramp, propane gas and a grocery store are nearby. Pets are permitted on leashes.

Reservations, fee: No reservations; $12 fee per night.

Who to contact: Phone the U.S. Corps of Engineers Black Butte Lake at (916) 865-4781.

Location: From Interstate 5 in Orland, take the Black Butte Lake exit. Drive about 12 miles west on Road 200 (Newville Road) to Buckhorn Road. Turn left and drive a short distance to the campground on the north shore of the lake.

Trip note: Black Butte Lake is set in the foothills of the north valley at 500 feet. It is one of the best 10 lakes in Northern California for crappie, best in spring. Recreation options include boating and hiking (an interpretive trail is available below the dam). For dirt bikers, an off-road motorcycle park is available at the Buckhorn Recreation Area. Open year-round.

10. WOODSON BRIDGE
STATE RECREATION AREA

Reference: On Sacramento River; map C2, grid e3.

Campsites, facilities: There are 46 sites for tents or motor homes up to 31 feet long. Group sites are available. Piped water, picnic tables, and fire grills are provided. Showers, flush toilets, a playground and a boat launch are available. Some facilities are **wheelchair accessible**, but the restrooms are not.

Reservations, fee: Reserve by phoning Destinet at (800) 444-7275 ($6.75 Destinet fee); $12-$14 fee per night; $1 pet fee.

Who to contact: Phone (916) 839-2112 or (916) 538-2200.

Location: From Interstate 5 in Corning, take the South Avenue exit and drive nine miles east to the campground.

Trip note: This campground features direct access to the Sacramento River, with a boat ramp making it an ideal spot for campers with trailered boats. In June, the nearby Tehama Riffle is one of the best spots on the entire river for shad. By mid-August, salmon start arriving, en route to their spawning grounds.

11. OLD ORCHARD RV PARK

Reference: Near Orland; map C2, grid f1.

Campsites, facilities: There are 52 motor home sites with partial or full hookups and a separate site for tents only. Showers, a sanitary disposal station, propane, a laundromat and a store are available. Pets are allowed on leashes.

Reservations, fee: Reservations accepted; $16-$19 fee per night.

Who to contact: Phone at (916) 865-5335 or write to Route 4, P.O. Box 4037, Orland, CA 95963.

Location: From Interstate 5 at Orland, take the Chico/Highway 32 exit, then head one block west and turn right. The park is one block down.

Trip note: Most folks use this as a layover spot while on long trips up or down Interstate 5 in the Central Valley. If you're staying longer than a night, there are two side trips that have appeal for anglers. Nearby Black Butte Lake to the west, with crappie in the early summer, and the Sacramento River to the east, with salmon in the late summer and early fall, can add some spice to your trip. The elevation is 250 feet.

12. KOA GREEN ACRES 🐟   RV 3

Reference: **Near Orland; map C2, grid f1.**

Campsites, facilities: There are 68 motor home sites with partial or full hookups and 24 tent sites. A store, a laundromat, a sanitary dump station, barbecues, a recreation room, a swimming pool and ice are available. Pets are allowed on leashes.

Reservations, fee: Reservations recommended; $16-$20 fee per night.

Who to contact: Phone KOA Green Acres at (916) 865-9188 or write to Route 4, P.O. Box 4048, Orland, CA 95963.

Location: From Orland on Interstate 5, take the Highway 32 exit and drive a half-mile west to the campground.

Trip note: This is a layover spot near Interstate 5 in the Central Valley, set in the heart of olive and almond country. It's a restful setting, but hot in summer, at times unbearable without air conditioning. Salmon fishing is available on the nearby Sacramento River, best from mid-August through October.

13. QUAIL TRAILS VILLAGE ⚓ ♿   RV 4

Reference: **Near Paradise; map C2, grid g8.**

Campsites, facilities: There are 20 motor home sites with full hookups (all are drive-through) and six tent sites. Picnic tables are provided. Restrooms, hot showers and a laundromat are available. Pets are allowed on leashes.

Reservations, fee: Reservations accepted; $10.60-$15.90 fee per night.

Who to contact: Phone (916) 877-6581.

Location: From Highway 99 in Chico, take the Paradise turnoff (Skyway). Turn right at the first signal in Paradise (Pearson Road). Go about 4.5 miles all the way to the end of the road and turn right on Pentz Magalia Highway. Drive 1.5 miles south to the park at 5110 Pentz Road.

Trip note: This is a rural motor home campground, set near the west branch of the Feather River, with nearby Lake Oroville the feature attraction. The Lime Saddle section of the Lake Oroville State Recreation Area is nearby, with a beach, boat launching facilities and concessions. Open year-round.

14. PINE RIDGE PARK   RV 5

Reference: **Near Paradise; map C2, grid g8.**

Campsites, facilities: There are 46 motor home sites with full hookups. Piped water, flush toilets, showers and a laundromat are available. Pets are permitted.

Reservations, fee: Reservations accepted; $16 fee per night.

Who to contact: Phone at (916) 877-0677.

Location: From Highway 191 in Paradise (at the south end of town), turn east on Pearson Road and drive two miles. Turn south on Pentz Road and drive one mile to 5084 Pentz Road.

Trip note: This privately-operated motor home park offers shaded sites in the pines and is set at 1,700 feet, in the transition zone where the foothill country with oak and bay grasslands starts to give way to pines and other conifers. A good side trip is to the northernmost part of the Lake Oroville State Recreation Area, the Lime Saddle Area. It offers a beach, a boat ramp, concessions and a picnic area. Open year-round.

15. BIDWELL CANYON

Reference: On Lake Oroville; map C2, grid i8.

Campsites, facilities: There are 70 sites for tents or motor homes up to 40 feet long and trailers up to 31 feet long (including boat trailers), all with full hookups. Piped water, flush toilets, showers, tables and fire grills are provided. A laundromat, a grocery store and propane gas are available nearby. Pets are permitted on leashes, but are not permitted on trails or beaches and must be enclosed at night.

Reservations, fee: Reserve by phoning Destinet at (800) 444-7275 ($6.75 Destinet fee); $14-$16 per night; $1 pet fee.

Who to contact: Call the Lake Oroville State Recreation Area at (916) 538-2200.

Location: From Oroville, drive eight miles east on Highway 162. Turn north on Kelly Ridge Road and drive 1.5 miles to the campground on the right.

Trip note: Bidwell Canyon is a major destination at giant Lake Oroville, as the campground is located near a major marina and boat ramp. It is set along the southern shore of the lake, on a point directly adjacent to the massive Oroville dam to the west. Many campers use this spot for boating headquarters. It is popular for waterskiing, as the water is warm enough in the summer for all water sports, and there is enough room for both fishermen and waterskiers. Recent habitat work has given the bass fishing a big help, with 30- and 40-fish days possible in the spring, casting plastic worms in the backs of coves where there is floating wood debris. What a lake—there are even floating outhouses here (imagine that!). It is very hot in mid-summer.

16. LOAFER CREEK

Reference: On Lake Oroville; map C2, grid i9.

Campsites, facilities: There are 137 sites for tents and motor homes up to 40 feet long and trailers to 31 feet long (including boat trailers). A sanitary disposal station, piped water, flush toilets, showers, fire grills and tables are provided. A boat ramp is available. The facilities are **wheelchair accessible**. Propane, groceries and a laundromat are available nearby. Pets are permitted on leashes, but are not permitted on trails or beaches.

Reservations, fee: Reserve by phoning Destinet at (800) 444-7275 ($6.75 Destinet fee); $10-$12 fee per night; $1 pet fee.

Who to contact: Phone Lake Oroville State Recreation Area at (916) 538-2200.

Location: From Oroville, drive east on Highway 162 about two miles past the Kelly Ridge Road turnoff to the signed campground entrance on the left.

Trip note: Loafer Creek Campground is set directly adjacent to a boat ramp on a deep cove at Lake Oroville, just across the water from Bidwell Canyon.

Campers come here to avoid the high number of people at Bidwell Marina, but hey, this spot is no secret, believe me. It's a primary option for campers with boats. The fishing is best for bass and trout in the spring and early summer. Open mid-March through October.

17. LOAFER CREEK GROUP CAMPS

Reference: On Lake Oroville; map C2, grid i9.

Campsites, facilities: There are six group camps that can accommodate up to 25 people each. The sites can be combined to accommodate up to 150 people. RV parking is limited and the maximum length is 20 feet; no trailers are permitted. Piped water, flush toilets, showers, fire grills and picnic tables are provided. A laundromat, a grocery store and propane gas are available nearby. Pets are permitted on leashes, but are not permitted on trails or beaches and must be enclosed at night. A large boat-in group camp is also available; call Lake Oroville Recreation Area at the number below for more information.

Reservations, fee: Reserve by phoning Destinet at (800) 444-7275 ($6.75 Destinet fee); $37.50 fee per night for groups; boat-in group camp is $60 per night; $1 pet fee.

Who to contact: Phone Lake Oroville State Recreation Area at (916) 538-2200.

Location: From Oroville, drive east on Highway 162 about two miles past the Kelly Ridge Road turnoff to the signed campground entrance on the left.

Trip note: This is an ideal base camp for Boy Scout troops or other large groups that need some privacy and a spot to call their own at Lake Oroville. It is located adjacent to the previous listing, Loafer Creek. A lakeside setting (pretty much), beach and nearby boat ramp are the primary attractions. Open April through October.

18. DINGERVILLE USA

Reference: Near Oroville; map C2, grid j6.

Campsites, facilities: There are 29 sites for motor homes with full hookups. Picnic tables are provided. Restrooms, showers, a swimming pool, a laundromat, a horseshoe pit and a nine-hole executive golf course are available. Facilities are **wheelchair accessible**.

Reservations, fee: Reservations recommended; $17.25 fee per night.

Who to contact: Call (916) 533-9343 or write to Route 6, P.O. Box 2225, Oroville, CA 95965.

Location: From Oroville and north, drive south on Highway 70. Turn right at the second Pacific Heights Road turnoff and continue on Pacific Heights Road to the campground. (From Highway 70 and south, turn left at Palermo-Welsh Road and continue north on Pacific Heights Road for a half-mile to camp.)

Trip note: You're right, they thought of this name all by themselves, needed no help. It is an RV park set in the Oroville foothill country—hot, dry and sticky in the summer, but with a variety of side trips available nearby. It is located adjacent to a wildlife area and the Feather River, within short range of Lake Oroville and the Thermolito Afterbay for boating, water sports and fishing. In the fall, the Duck Club in nearby Richvale is one of the few privately-owned properties that offers duck hunting on a single-day basis. The RV park is a clean, quiet campground with easy access from the highway. Open year-round.

MAP C3

NOR-CAL MAP .... see page 94
adjoining maps
NORTH (B3) .... see page 208
EAST (C4) .... see page 306
SOUTH (D3) .... see page 350
WEST (C2) .... see page 264

83 LISTINGS
PAGES 272-305

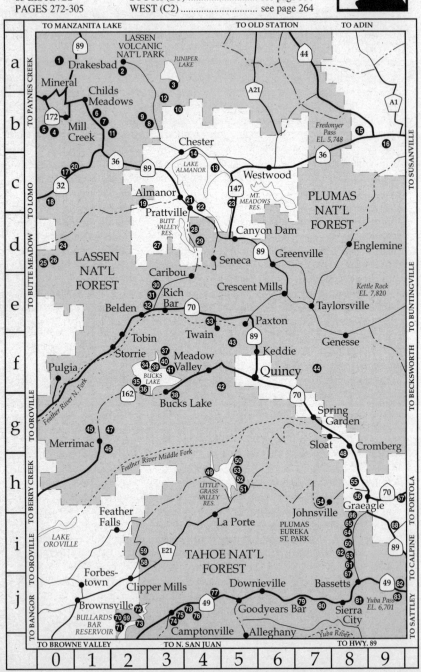

Map C3 featuring: Lassen Volcanic National Park, Lassen National Forest, Lake Almanor, Feather River, Humbug Valley, Butt Valley Reservoir, Plumas National Forest, Bucks Lake, Little Grass Valley Reservoir, Sly Creek Reservoir, Tahoe National Forest, Packer Lake, Bullards Bar Reservoir, North Yuba River

1. SOUTHWEST WALK-IN

Reference: In Lassen Volcanic National Park; map C3, grid a0.

Campsites, facilities: There are 21 walk-in tent sites. Picnic tables, fire pits, piped water and flush toilets are available. Pets are allowed on leashes.

Reservations, fee: No reservations; $8 fee per night.

Who to contact: Phone Lassen Volcanic National Park at (916) 595-4444.

Location: From Red Bluff, take Highway 36 east for 44 miles to the junction with Highway 89. Turn left on Highway 89 and drive to the park's entrance. Just after passing through the park entrance gate, look for the camp parking area on the east side of the road.

Trip note: Just taking the short walk required to reach this camp will launch you into an orbit beyond most of the highway cruisers visiting Lassen. In addition, the nearby trail for Bumpass Hell will put you into a different universe; it is located about five miles north on Highway 89 on the right side of the road. The route will take you past steam vents, boiling mud pots and hot springs, all set in prehistoric-looking volcanic rock.

2. WARNER VALLEY

Reference: On Hot Springs Creek in Lassen Volcanic National Park; map C3, grid a2.

Campsites, facilities: There are 18 tent or motor home sites. Piped water, pit toilets, fire grills and picnic tables are provided. Pets are permitted.

Reservations, fee: No reservations; $8 fee per night.

Who to contact: Phone the Lassen Volcanic National Park at (916) 595-4444.

Location: From Red Bluff, take Highway 36 east for 44 miles to the junction with Highway 89. Continue east on Highway 36/89 to Chester. In Chester, turn left (north) on Warner Valley Road (County Road 312, a dirt road, RVs not recommended) and drive 16 miles to the campground.

Trip note: Lassen is one of the great national parks of the West, yet it gets surprisingly little use compared to Yosemite, Sequoia and Kings Canyon National Parks. This camp gets overlooked because of its remote access out of Chester. The camp is set along Hot Springs Creek at 5,650 feet. A highlight here is a great 2.5-mile trail with an 800-foot climb to pretty Drake Lake. Another trail, about the same distance and flatter, is routed out to the unique Devil's Kitchen Geothermal Area, a great hike. It's also a good horseback riding area. The Drakesbad Resort is located near the campground, where reservations are about as difficult to get as finding Bigfoot. Open May through September.

3. JUNIPER LAKE 👥

Reference: **In Lassen Volcanic National Park; map C3, grid a4.**

Campsites, facilities: There are 18 sites for tents. Fire pits and pit toilets are provided. **No piped water** is available. Pets are allowed on leashes.

Reservations, fee: No reservations; $6 fee per night.

Who to contact: Phone Lassen Volcanic National Park at (916) 595-4444.

Location: From Red Bluff, take Highway 36 east for 44 miles to the junction with Highway 89. Continue east on Highway 36/89 to Chester. In Chester, turn left (north) on Warner Valley Road (County Road 312) and drive one mile to the Y and the junction for County Road 318. Bear right (marked for Juniper Lake) on County Road 318 and drive 11 miles to the campground on the east side of the lake. Note: This is a very rough dirt road; motor homes and trailers are not recommended.

Trip note: This pretty spot is on the eastern shore of Juniper Lake, at a elevation of 6,792 feet. It is far distant from the busy Highway 89 corridor that is routed through central Lassen Volcanic National Park. From the north end of the lake, a great side trip is to make the half-mile, 400-foot climb to Inspiration Point, which provides a panoramic view of the park's backcountry. A wilderness trailhead is located adjacent to the Juniper Lake Ranger Station. Since **no piped water is provided**, it is critical to bring a water purification pump or plenty of bottled water.

4. MILL CREEK RESORT 🐟 👥

Reference: **On Mill Creek in Lassen National Forest; map C3, grid b0.**

Campsites, facilities: There are 16 sites for tents or motor homes up to 22 feet long. Nine one- and two-bedroom cabins are also available. Picnic tables, fire grills, piped water and vault toilets are provided. Showers, a laundromat, a small grocery store and coffee shop are available. Pets are permitted.

Reservations, fee: Reservations accepted; $8 fee per night.

Who to contact: Phone at (916) 595-4449.

Location: From Red Bluff, drive east on Highway 36 to the town of Mineral and the junction with Highway 172. Turn right (south) and drive six miles to the town of Mill Creek. In Mill Creek, look for the sign for Mill Creek Resort on the right side of the road.

Trip note: This is a great spot, surrounded by Lassen National Forest and within close range of the southern Highway 89 entrance to Lassen Volcanic National Park. It is set at 4,800 feet along oft-bypassed Highway 172. A highlight here is Mill Creek (to reach it, turn south on the Forest Service road in town and drive to a parking area at the end of the road along the stream), where there is a great easy walk along the stream and fair trout fishing. Open May through October.

5. HOLE-IN-THE-GROUND 🐟 👥

Reference: **On Mill Creek in Lassen National Forest; map C3, grid b0.**

Campsites, facilities: There are four tent sites and nine sites for tents or motor homes. Piped water, vault toilets, picnic tables and fire grills are provided. Pets are permitted on leashes. Supplies are available in Mineral.

Reservations, fee: No reservations; $8 fee per night.

Who to contact: Phone the Lassen National Forest Almanor Ranger District Office at (916) 258-2141.

Location: From Red Bluff, drive 43 miles east on Highway 36 to the town of Mineral and the junction with Highway 172. Turn right (south) on Highway 172 and drive six miles to the town of Mill Creek. In Mill Creek, turn south onto a Forest Service road (signed), and drive five miles to the campground access road. Turn left and drive a quarter-mile to the camp.

Trip note: This is one of two campgrounds set along Mill Creek at 4,300 feet. Take your pick. The highlight here is a trail that follows along Mill Creek for many miles, which provides good fishing access. The stream is stocked with 2,000 rainbow trout each summer, joining residents and holdovers. Another option is to drive two more miles to the end of the Forest Service road, where there is a parking area for a trail that is routed downstream along Mill Creek and into a state game refuge. To keep things easy, obtain a map of Lassen National Forest that details the recreational opportunities. Open May to October.

---

6. GURNSEY CREEK GROUP CAMP

Reference: **In Lassen National Forest; map C3, grid b1.**

Campsites, facilities: This group campground can accommodate up to 100 people, with 20 sites for tents or motor homes. Piped water, vault toilets, picnic tables and fire grills are provided. A large community fireplace is centrally located for group use. Pets are permitted on leashes. Supplies are available in Mineral or Chester.

Reservations, fee: Reservations required; $75 fee per night with a deposit of 50%. The deposit is refundable if cancellation notice is given 10 days prior to the reservation date.

Who to contact: Phone the Lassen National Forest Almanor Ranger District Office at (916) 258-2141.

Location: From Red Bluff, drive east on Highway 36 for drive 55 miles (five miles east of Childs Meadow). Turn left at the campground entrance road and drive a short distance to the campground.

Trip note: This is a group camp. It's an ideal spot for a Boy Scout troop. For more information, see trip note for the adjacent Gurnsey Creek Campground. Open May to October.

---

7. GURNSEY CREEK

Reference: **In Lassen National Forest; map C3, grid b1.**

Campsites, facilities: There are 32 sites for tents or motor homes. Piped water, vault toilets, picnic tables and fire grills are provided. Pets are permitted on leashes. Supplies are available in Mineral.

Reservations, fee: No reservations; $9 fee per night.

Who to contact: Phone the Lassen National Forest Almanor Ranger District Office at (916) 258-2141.

Location: From Red Bluff, drive east on Highway 36 for drive 55 miles (five miles east of Childs Meadow). Turn left at the campground entrance road and drive a short distance to the campground.

Trip note: This camp is set at 5,000 feet in Lassen National Forest, with extremely easy access off Highway 36. The camp is set along the headwaters of little Gurnsey Creek, a highlight of the surrounding Lost Creek Plateau. Gurnsey Creek runs downstream and pours into Deer Creek, a good trout stream with access along narrow, winding Highway 32 to the nearby south. Open May through October.

8. HIGH BRIDGE

Reference: **On the North Fork of Feather River in Lassen National Forest; map C3, grid b2.**

Campsites, facilities: There are 12 sites for tents or motor homes. Non-piped water, vault toilets, picnic tables and fire grills are provided. Pets are permitted on leashes. Groceries and propane gas are available nearby.

Reservations, fee: No reservations; $9 fee per night.

Who to contact: Phone the Lassen National Forest Almanor Ranger District at (916) 258-2141.

Location: From Red Bluff, take Highway 36 east for 44 miles to the junction with Highway 89. Continue east on Highway 36/89 to Chester. In Chester, turn left (north) on Warner Valley Road (a dirt road, RVs not recommended) and drive five miles to the campground entrance road on the left.

Trip note: This camp is ideal for many people. It is just far enough off pavement that it is missed by thousands of campers wishing for such a spot. The payoff includes a pretty, adjacent trout stream, the headwaters of the North Fork Feather. Trout fishing is often good here, including some rare large brown trout, a surprise considering the relatively small size of the stream. Nearby access to the Warner Valley/Drakesbad entrance of Lassen Volcanic National Park provides a must-do side trip. The area is wooded and the road dusty. Open June through September.

9. DOMINGO SPRINGS

Reference: **In Lassen National Forest; map C3, grid b2.**

Campsites, facilities: There are nine sites for tents and nine sites for tents or motor homes. Piped water, vault toilets, picnic tables and fire grills are provided. Pets are permitted on leashes.

Reservations, fee: No reservations; $9 fee per night.

Who to contact: Phone the Lassen National Forest Almanor Ranger District at (916) 258-2141.

Location: From Red Bluff, take Highway 36 east for 44 miles to the junction with Highway 89. Continue east on Highway 36/89 to Chester. In Chester, turn left (north) on Warner Valley Road (a dirt road, RVs not recommended) and drive six miles to a Y with Red Bluff Road (Forest Service Road 311). Bear left on Forest Service Road 311 and drive two miles to the campground entrance road on the left.

Trip note: This camp is named after a small nearby spring located adjacent to the site. It is a small fountain that pours into the headwaters of the North Fork Feather River, a good trout stream. The Pacific Crest Trail is routed from this camp north for four miles to Little Willow Lake and the southern border of Lassen Volcanic National Park. The elevation is 5,200 feet. Open May through October.

10. BENNER CREEK

Reference: **On Benner Creek in Lassen National Forest; map C3, grid b4.**

Campsites, facilities: There are nine sites for tents or motor homes up to 20 feet long. Fire grills, picnic tables and vault toilets are provided. Pets are permitted on leashes.

Reservations, fees: No reservations; $6 fee per night.

Who to contact: Phone Almanor Ranger District at (916) 258-2141.

Locations: In Chester, on Highway 36, turn west on Juniper Lake Road and drive seven miles to Benner Creek Campground on the right.

Trip note: Benner Creek Camp is set outside the remote eastern border of Lassen Volcanic National Park and its stellar but primitive Juniper Lake Campground. If that national park camp is full, this provides a nearby option. For drivers of motor homes, this camp is preferable to navigating the rough road to Juniper Lake. In the fall, the camp gets occasional use by deer hunters.

11. WILLOW SPRINGS

Reference: **Near Lost Creek Spring in Lassen National Forest; map C3, grid b2.**

Campsites, facilities: There are 15 primitive sites for tents. Picnic tables and fire grills are provided. A vault toilet is available. **No piped water** is available.

Reservations, fee: No reservations; $5 fee per night.

Who to contact: Phone Almanor Ranger District at (916) 258-2141 or (916) 258-3844. For a map, send $3 to Office of Information, U.S. Forest Service, 630 Sansome Street, San Francisco, CA 94111, and ask for Lassen National Forest.

Location: From Red Bluff, drive east on Highway 36 for about 55 miles. About two miles past Childs Meadows Parking Area, turn left on Wilson Lake Road (Forest Road 29N19) and drive 1.5 miles to Forest Service Road 29N19. Turn right on Forest Service Road 29N19 and drive about 3.5 miles to the campground on the left side of the road.

Trip note: This is a primitive, undeveloped camp set on the southwest flank of North Stover Mountain (6,035 feet), used primarily by hunters during the fall deer season, and ignored the rest of the time. A network of Forest Service roads in the area provide vehicle access. Though there is **no piped water** available, Lost Creek Spring, to the east of camp, and Lost Creek, are viable water sources during wet years. The headwaters of Lost Creek run by the camp, flowing downstream into nearby Deer Creek to the south.

12. WARNER CREEK

Reference: **In Lassen National Forest; map C3, grid b3.**

Campsites, facilities: There are 13 sites for tents or motor homes up to 22 feet long. There is **no piped water**, but vault toilets, picnic tables and fire grills are provided. Pets are permitted on leashes.

Reservations, fee: No reservations; $6 fee per night.

Who to contact: Phone the Lassen National Forest Almanor Ranger District at (916) 258-2141.

Location: From Red Bluff, take Highway 36 east for 44 miles to the junction with Highway 89. Continue east on Highway 36/89 to Chester. In Chester, turn left (north) on Warner Valley Road (County Road 312 is dirt, RVs not recommended) and drive seven miles to the campground on the right side of the road.

Trip note: Some people find this camp by accident. They are driving to the Drakesbad/Warner Valley entrance of Lassen Volcanic National Park and discover this little, primitive camp on the way in, always an option during crowded weekends. It is set at 5,000 feet elevation along little Warner Creek, a tributary to the North Fork Feather River. Warner Valley is located two miles to the north, and the entrance to Lassen Park is another six miles. Open June through September.

13. LAST CHANCE CREEK 🐟 🚶 RV 7

Reference: **On Lake Almanor; map C3, grid b4.**

Campsites, facilities: There are 12 sites for tents or motor homes up to 30 feet long, and 13 group-camp units. Piped water, vault toilets, picnic tables and fire grills are provided. Pets are permitted on leashes.

Reservations, fee: Reservations required for the group camp, phone (916) 386-5164; $11 fee per night for individual sites; $15 for group sites; $1 pet fee.

Who to contact: Phone PG&E at (916) 386-5164.

Location: From Red Bluff, take Highway 36 east for 44 miles to the junction with Highway 89. Continue east on Highway 36/89 to Chester and continue for two miles over the causeway at the north end of Lake Almanor. About a quarter-mile after crossing the causeway, turn left and drive about four miles to the campground.

Trip note: This secluded camp is adjacent to where Last Chance Creek empties into the north end of Lake Almanor. It is an unpublicized PG&E Camp that is known primarily by locals and missed almost every time by out-of-towners. The adjacent lake area is a breeding area in the spring for white pelicans, and the beauty of these birds in large flocks can be extraordinary.

---

14. NORTHSHORE CAMPGROUND

🐟 ⚓ ♿ 🏊 🎣

Reference: **On Lake Almanor; map C3, grid b4.**

Campsites, facilities: There are 94 motor home sites, many with partial hookups, and 34 tent sites. Piped water, picnic tables, fire grills, flush toilets and showers are provided. A boat ramp and a dock are available. Pets are allowed on leashes.

Reservations, fee: Reservations accepted; $12.50-$16 fee per night.

Who to contact: Phone (916) 258-3376.

Location: From Red Bluff, take Highway 36 east for 44 miles to the junction with Highway 89. Continue east on Highway 36/89 to Chester and continue for six miles to the campground.

Trip note: This large, privately-developed park is primarily for motor homes on the northern shoreline of beautiful Lake Almanor. Open April through October.

---

15. GOUMAZ 🐟 🚶 🐎 RV 7

Reference: **On Susan River in Lassen National Forest; map C3, grid b8.**

Campsites, facilities: There are five sites for tents or motor homes up to 30 feet long. Vault toilets, picnic tables and fire rings are provided. There is **no piped water**. Pets are permitted.

Reservations, fee: No reservations; $5 fee per night.

Who to contact: Phone the Lassen National Forest Eagle Lake District at (916) 257-4188.

Location: From Red Bluff, drive east on Highway 36 past Lake Almanor to the junction with Highway 44. Turn left (west) on Highway 44 and drive six miles (one mile past the Worley Ranch) to Goumaz Road (Forest Service Road 30N08). Turn left (south) on Goumaz Road and drive about five miles to the campground entrance road on the right.

Trip note: This camp is set beside the Susan River, adjacent to the historic Bizz Johnson Trail, a former route for a rail line that has been converted to a 25-mile trail. The trail runs from Susanville to Westwood, but this section provides access to many of its prettiest and most remote stretches as it runs in a half circle around Pegleg Mountain (7,112 feet) to the east. It is an outstanding route for biking, hiking and horseback riding in the summer, and cross-country skiing in the winter. Open May to October.

16. ROXIE PECONOM

Reference: **In Lassen National Forest; map C3, grid b9.**

Campsites, facilities: There are 10 tent sites. Piped water, a vault toilet, picnic tables and fire rings are provided. Pets are allowed on leashes.

Reservations, fee: No reservations; no fee.

Who to contact: Phone the Lassen National Forest Eagle Lake District at (916) 257-4188.

Location: From Red Bluff, drive east on Highway 36 past Lake Almanor and continue past Fredonyer Pass for three miles to Forest Service Road 29N03 on the right. Turn right and drive two miles to the campground on the left.

Trip note: This small camp is set next to Willard Creek, a seasonal stream in eastern Lassen National Forest. It's shaded and quiet. The best nearby recreation is the Bizz Johnson Trail, with a trailhead located on Highway 44 (two miles east) at a parking area on the left side of the highway. This is an outstanding biking and hiking route. Open May to October.

17. ALDER

Reference: **On Deer Creek in Lassen National Forest; map C3, grid c0.**

Campsites, facilities: There are five tent sites. There is **no piped water.** Vault toilets, picnic tables and fire grills are provided. Pets are permitted on leashes.

Reservations, fee: No reservations; $5 fee per night.

Who to contact: Phone the Lassen National Forest Almanor Ranger District Office at (916) 258-2141.

Location: From Red Bluff, take Highway 36 east for 44 miles to the junction with Highway 89. Continue east on Highway 36/89 to the junction with Highway 32. Turn right (south) on Highway 32 and drive eight miles to the campground on the right side of the road. Trailers are not recommended.

Trip note: Deer Creek is a great little trout stream that runs along Highway 32. Alder is one of four camps set along Highway 32 with streamside access; this one is at 3,900 feet elevation, set near where both Alder Creek and Round Valley Creek pour into Deer Creek. The stream's best stretch of trout water is from here on upstream to Elam Creek Camp. Open April to November.

18. POTATO PATCH

Reference: **On Deer Creek in Lassen National Forest; map C3, grid c0.**

Campsites, facilities: There are 20 sites for tents and 12 sites for tents or motor homes. Piped water, vault toilets, picnic tables and fire grills are provided. Pets are permitted on leashes.

Reservations, fee: No reservations; $9 fee per night.

Who to contact: Phone the Lassen National Forest Almanor Ranger District Office at (916) 258-2141.

Location: From Red Bluff, take Highway 36 east for 44 miles to the junction with Highway 89. Continue east on Highway 36/89 to the junction with Highway 32. Turn right (south) on Highway 32 and drive 11 miles to the campground on the right side of the road. Trailers are not recommended.

Trip note: You get good hiking and fishing at this camp. It is set beside Deer Creek, 3,400 feet elevation, with good access for trout fishing, best in May and June. In early summer, a side trip adventure is heading two miles up Highway 32 to find Deer Creek Falls. Open May through October.

19. SOLDIER MEADOW

Reference: **On Soldier Creek in Lassen National Forest; map C3, grid c3**.

Campsites, facilities: There are 15 sites for tents or motor homes. Vault toilets, picnic tables and fire rings are provided. There is **no piped water,** so bring your own. Pets are permitted on leashes.

Reservations, fees: No reservations; $5 fee per night.

Who to contact: Phone Almanor Ranger District at (916) 258-2141.

Location: From Chester, drive south on Highway 89 to Humboldt Road. Turn right on Humboldt Road and drive one mile, bear right at the fork and continue five more miles to the intersection at Fanani Meadows. Turn right and drive one mile to the campground on the left.

Trip note: This camp is little-known and primitive, and is primarily used by fishermen and hunters in season. The campsites here are shaded, set in forest on the edge of meadows, and near a stream. The latter is Soldier Creek, which is stocked with trout by the Department of Fish and Game. In the fall, early storms can drive deer through this area on their annual migration to their wintering habitat in the valley, making this a decent base camp for hunters. However, no early storms often mean no deer.

20. ELAM

Reference: **On Deer Creek in Lassen National Forest; map C3, grid c1.**

Campsites, facilities: There are 15 sites for tents or motor homes. Piped water, vault toilets, picnic tables and fire grills are provided. Pets are permitted on leashes.

Reservations, fee: No reservations; $9 fee per night.

Who to contact: Phone the Lassen National Forest Almanor Ranger District Office at (916) 258-2141.

Location: From Red Bluff, take Highway 36 east for 44 miles to the junction with Highway 89. Continue east on Highway 36/89 to the junction with Highway 32. Turn right (south) on Highway 32 and drive three miles to the campground on the right side of the road. Trailers are not recommended.

Trip note: Of the campgrounds set on Deer Creek along Highway 32, Elam gets the most use. It is the first stopping point visitors arrive at, while heading west on narrow, curvy Highway 32, and it has an excellent day-use picnic area available. The stream here is stocked with rainbow trout in late spring and early summer, with good access for fishing. It is a pretty area, set where Elam Creek enters Deer Creek. A Forest Service Information Center is nearby. If the camp has too many people to suit your style, consider other more distant and primitive camps located downstream on Deer Creek. The elevation here is 4,600 feet. Open May to October.

21. LAKE ALMANOR CAMPGROUNDS

Reference: **On Lake Almanor; map C3, grid c4.**

Campsites, facilities: There are 130 sites for tents or motor homes up to 30 feet long. Piped water, vault toilets, picnic tables and fire grills are provided. A sanitary disposal station is available. Pets are permitted on leashes.

Reservations, fee: No reservations; $11 fee per night; $1 pet fee.

Who to contact: Phone PG&E at (916) 386-5164.

Location: From Red Bluff, take Highway 36 east for 44 miles to the junction with Highway 89. Continue east on Highway 36/89 to Lake Almanor and the junction with Highway 89 (two miles before reaching Chester). Turn right on Highway 89 and drive about 10 miles to the southeast end of Lake Almanor. Turn left at your choice of four campground entrances.

Trip note: What you get here are a series of four campgrounds along the southwest shore of Lake Almanor provided by PG&E as mitigation for their hydroelectric activities on the Feather River system. The camps are set upstream from the dam, with boat ramps available on each side of the dam. This is a pretty spot, with giant Almanor ringed by lodgepole pine and firs. The lake is usually full, or close to it, well into summer, with Mt. Lassen set in the distance to the north—bring your camera. Though it can take a day or two to locate the fish, once that effort is made, fishing is good for large trout and salmon in the spring and fall, and for smallmouth bass in the summer. In recent years, it has become extremely difficult for vacationers to get campground information from PG&E, a major breach in the public trust.

22. ALMANOR

Reference: **On Lake Almanor in Lassen National Forest; map C3, grid c4.**

Campsites, facilities: There are 15 sites for tents and 86 sites for tents or motor homes. Piped water, vault toilets, picnic tables and fire grills are provided. A boat ramp is available nearby. Pets are permitted on leashes.

Reservations, fee: No reservations; $11 fee per night.

Who to contact: Phone the Lassen National Forest Almanor Ranger District at (916) 258-2141.

Location: From Red Bluff, take Highway 36 east for 44 miles to the junction with Highway 89. Continue east on Highway 36/89 to Lake Almanor and the junction with Highway 89 (two miles before reaching Chester). Turn right on Highway 89 and drive six miles to County Road 310. Turn left (east) on County Road 310 and drive one mile to the campground.

Trip note: This is one of Lake Almanor's best-known and most popular Forest Service campgrounds. It is set along the western shore of beautiful Almanor, 4,519 feet elevation, directly across from the famous Almanor Peninsula. There is an excellent view of Mt. Lassen to the north, along with gorgeous sunrises. This section of lake provides good fishing for smallmouth bass in the summer, best using live crickets for bait. Open May through October.

23. LASSEN VIEW

Reference: **At Lake Almanor east of Red Bluff; map C3, grid c4.**

Campsites, facilities: There are 17 cabins, and 59 tent and motor home sites with full or partial hookups. Piped water, a restroom with showers, fire pits and picnic tables are provided. A small store, fishing equipment, boat rentals, a boat dock and fish-cleaning facility are also available. A fishing guide can be hired through the store.

Reservations, fee: Reservations recommended; call for fees.

Who to contact: Phone Lassen View Resort at (916) 596-3437.

Location: From Red Bluff, take Highway 36 east for 44 miles to the junction with Highway 89. Continue east on Highway 36/89 to Chester and drive through Chester to the junction with County Road A13. Turn right (south) and drive about four miles to the junction with Highway 147. Turn right on Highway 147 and drive one mile to the camp entrance (well signed) on the right .

Trip note: This is one of the few classic fishing camps in California, designed from start to finish with fishing in mind. Its location is near one of the best fishing spots on the entire lake, Big Springs, at the mouth of the Hamilton Branch. After launching a boat or renting one at Lassen View, Big Springs is just a five-minute ride, "right around the corner," as they say here. This is where salmon congregate in the spring and big brown and rainbow trout show up in the fall to feed on the lake's huge supply of pond smelt. The camp is rustic but friendly, and the folks here can help put you on to the fish. Lake Almanor, of course, is a big, beautiful lake set at 4,600 feet, ringed by conifers, and kept full most of the year. Open May 1 to November 1.

24. CHERRY HILL 🐟🥾   RV🚐 ▲7

Reference: **On Butte Creek in Lassen National Forest; map C3, grid d0.**

Campsites, facilities: There are 13 walk-in tent sites and 12 sites for tents or motor homes. Picnic tables, fire grills, piped water and vault toilets are provided. Pets are permitted on leashes. Supplies are available in the town of Butte Meadows.

Reservations, fee: No reservations; $9 fee per night.

Who to contact: Phone the Lassen National Forest Almanor Ranger District at (916) 258-2141.

Location: From Chico, drive about 15 miles north on Highway 32 to the town of Forest Ranch. Continue on Highway 32 for another nine miles to the junction with Humboldt Road. Turn right and drive five miles to Butte Meadows. Continue on Humboldt Road for three miles to the campground on the right side of the road.

Trip note: The camp is set along little Butte Creek at the foot of Cherry Hill, just downstream from the confluence of Colby Creek and Butte Creek. It is also on the western edge of the alpine zone in Lassen National Forest. A four-mile drive to the north, much of it along Colby Creek, will take visitors to the Colby Mountain Lookout, at 6,002 feet, for a dramatic view of the Ishi Wilderness to the west. Nearby to the south is Philbrook Lake (see next listing). Open May to October.

25. PHILBROOK RESERVOIR   RV🚐 ▲7

🐟 ⚓ ♿ 🏊

Reference: **Map C3, grid d0.**

Campsites, facilities: There are 20 sites for tents or motor homes up to 30 feet long. Picnic tables, fire grills, piped water and vault toilets are provided. Trailer and car-top boat launches are available. Pets are allowed on leashes.

Reservations, fee: No reservations; $11 fee per night; $1 pet fee.

Who to contact: Phone PG&E at (916) 386-5164.

Location: At Orland on Interstate 5, take the Highway 32/Chico exit and drive to Chico and the junction with Highway 99. Turn south on Highway 99 and drive to Skyway Road/Paradise (in south Chico). Turn east on Skyway Road and drive through Paradise and continue for 27 miles to Humbug Summit Road. Turn right and drive two miles to Philbrook Road. Turn right and drive four miles to the campground at the north end of the lake.

Trip note: Philbrook Reservoir is set at 5,500 feet elevation on the western mountain slopes above Chico, on the southwest edge of Lassen National Forest. It is a pretty lake, though subject to late-season drawdowns, with a scenic lookout located a short distance from camp. The lake is loaded with small trout—a dink here, a dink there, a dink everywhere. Open June through September.

26. WEST BRANCH

Reference: On Feather River in Lassen National Forest; map C3 grid d0.

Campsites, facilities: There are eight sites for tents and seven sites for tents or motor homes. Picnic tables, fire grills, piped water and vault toilets are provided. Pets are permitted on leashes.

Reservations, fee: No reservations; $8 fee per night.

Who to contact: Phone the Lassen National Forest Almanor Ranger District at (916) 258-2141.

Location: At Orland on Interstate 5, take the Highway 32/Chico exit and drive to Chico and the junction with Highway 99. Turn south on Highway 99 and drive to Skyway Road/Paradise (in south Chico). Turn east on Skyway Road and drive through Paradise and continue for 27 miles to Humbug Summit Road. Turn right and drive two miles to Philbrook Road and the campground access road on the right. Turn right and drive a half-mile to the campground.

Trip note: This is a small and remote campground set on the West Branch Feather River, 5,000 feet elevation, just upstream from where Philbrook Creek joins the Feather. It is set on the western edge of Lassen National Forest, with a network of backcountry roads in the area. Nearby destinations include Spring Valley Lake, Snag Lake and Snow Mountain, and several roads accessible only to four-wheel-drive vehicles. Because of its proximity to Philbrook Reservoir, located two miles to the east, this camp is often overlooked. Open June through September.

27. YELLOW CREEK

Reference: In Humbug Valley; map C3, grid d3.

Campsites, facilities: There are 10 sites for tents or motor homes. Piped water, vault toilets, picnic tables and fire grills are provided. Pets are permitted.

Reservations, fee: No reservations; $11 fee per night; $1 pet fee.

Who to contact: Phone PG&E at (916) 386-5164.

Location: From Oroville, drive north on Highway 70 to Belden. At Belden, turn left on Forest Service Road 26N26 and drive north about 11 miles to the campground entrance road on the left side of the road. (From Red Bluff, take Highway 36 east for 44 miles to the junction with Highway 89. Continue east on Highway 36/89 to Lake Almanor and the junction with Highway 89 (two miles before reaching Chester). Turn right on Highway 89 and drive about fives miles to Humbug Road (County Road 308/309). Turn right (west) and drive a mile to the junction of County Road 308 and 309. Bear left on County Road 309 and drive two miles to the junction with County Road 308. Bear right on County Road 307 and drive about five miles to a Y. Bear left at the Y and drive 1.2 miles to the campground entrance on the right side of the road.

Trip note: Yellow Creek is one of Cal Trout's pet projects. It's a beautiful stream for fly fishers, demanding the best from skilled anglers: approaching with complete stealth, making delicate casts with long leaders and small dry flies during the evening rise. This camp is set at 4,400 feet in Humbug Valley, and provides access to this stretch of water. An option is to fish Butt Creek, much easier fishing for small planted rainbow trout, with access available along the road on the way in. Some of the area was logged in the late 1980s by PG&E. Open May through October.

28. PONDEROSA FLAT

Reference: **On Butt Lake; map C3, grid d4.**

Campsites, facilities: There are 63 sites for tents or motor homes. Piped water, vault toilets, picnic tables and fire grills are provided. A boat ramp is available. Pets are permitted on leashes.

Reservations, fee: No reservations; $11 fee per night; $1 pet fee.

Who to contact: Phone PG&E at (916) 386-5164.

Location: From Red Bluff, take Highway 36 east for 44 miles to the junction with Highway 89. Continue east on Highway 36/89 to Lake Almanor and the junction with Highway 89 (two miles before reaching Chester). Turn right on Highway 89 and drive about seven miles to Butt Valley Road. Turn right (southwest) on Butt Valley Road and drive 3.2 miles to the campground on the right side of the road.

Trip note: This camp is set at the north end of Butt Lake, the little brother to nearby Lake Almanor. This camp is fairly popular, with the boat ramp a prime attraction, allowing camper/anglers on vacation a lakeside spot with easy access. Technically, Butt is the "afterbay" for Almanor, fed by a four-mile pipe with water from Almanor. What occurs is that pond smelt from Almanor get ground up in the Butt Lake powerhouse, providing a huge amount of feed for trout at the head of the lake; that's why the trout often get huge at Butt Lake. The one downer here is that lake drawdowns are common, so common that some locals call it "Stump Lake" from all the exposed tree stumps. Open May through October.

29. COOL SPRINGS

Reference: **On Butt Lake; map C3, grid d4.**

Campsites, facilities: There are 30 sites for tents or motor homes. Piped water, vault toilets, picnic tables and fire grills are provided. A boat ramp is available. Pets are permitted on leashes.

Reservations, fee: No reservations; $11 fee per night; $1 pet fee.

Who to contact: Phone PG&E at (916) 386-5164.

Location: From Red Bluff, take Highway 36 east for 44 miles to the junction with Highway 89. Continue east on Highway 36/89 to Lake Almanor and the junction with Highway 89 (two miles before reaching Chester). Turn right on Highway 89 and drive about seven miles to Butt Valley Road. Turn right (southwest) on Butt Valley Road and drive five miles to the campground on the right side of the road.

Trip note: This is one of two camps at Butt Lake, this one set about midway down the lake on its eastern shore, two miles south of Ponderosa Flat Campground. Cool Springs Creek enters the lake near the camp. For more information about Butt Lake, see trip note for preceding camp. Open May through October.

30. QUEEN LILY 🐟 🏃 🏊   RV 7

Reference: **On the North Fork of Feather River in Plumas National Forest; map C3, grid e3.**

Campsites, facilities: There are 12 sites for tents or motor homes up to 16 feet long. Piped water, flush toilets, fire grills and picnic tables are provided. Pets are permitted on leashes. A grocery store and a laundromat are nearby.

Reservations, fee: No reservations; $11 fee per night.

Who to contact: Phone Plumas National Forest at (916) 283-0555.

Location: From Oroville, drive north on Highway 70 to Caribou Road (two miles past Belden at Gasner Ranch Ranger Station). Turn left on Caribou Road and drive about three miles to the campground on the left side of the road.

Trip note: The North Fork Feather River is a prime destination for camping and trout fishing, especially for families. This is one of three camps along the river on Caribou Road. The stretch of river is well stocked. Insider's note: the first 150 yards of river below the dam at Caribou typically have large but elusive trout. Open May through September.

31. NORTH FORK 🐟 🏃 ♿ 🏊   RV 7

Reference: **On the North Fork of the Feather River, in Plumas National Forest; map C3, grid e3.**

Campsites, facilities: There are 20 sites for tents or motor homes up to 32 feet long. Piped water, flush toilets, showers, fire grills and picnic tables are provided. Pets are permitted on leashes. A grocery store and laundromat are nearby.

Reservations, fee: No reservations; $11 fee per night.

Who to contact: Phone Plumas National Forest at (916) 283-0555.

Location: From Oroville, drive north on Highway 70 to Caribou Road (two miles past Belden at Gasner Ranch Ranger Station). Turn left on Caribou Road and drive about two miles to the campground on the left side of the road.

Trip note: This camp is set between Queen Lily Camp to the nearby north and Gasner Bar to the nearby south, all three set on the North Fork Feather River. The elevation is 2,600 feet. Fishing access is good, trout plants are decent, making for a good fishing/camping trip. Note that all three camps are extremely popular on summer weekends. Open May through September.

32. GANSNER BAR 🐟 🏃 ♿ 🏊   RV 7

Reference: **On the North Fork of Feather River in Plumas National Forest; map C3, grid e3.**

Campsites, facilities: There are 14 sites for tents or motor homes up to 32 feet long. Piped water, flush toilets, fire grills and picnic tables are provided. Pets are permitted on leashes. A grocery store and laundromat are nearby. Facilities are **wheelchair accessible.**

Reservations, fee: No reservations; $11 fee per night.

Who to contact: Phone Plumas National Forest at (916) 283-0555.

Location: From Oroville, drive north on Highway 70 to Caribou Road (two miles past Belden at Gasner Ranch Ranger Station). Turn left on Caribou Road and drive a short distance to the campground on the left side of the road.

Trip note: This is the first of three camps along Caribou Road, which runs parallel to the North Fork Feather River. Of the three, this one receives the highest trout stocks, rainbow trout in the 10- to 12-inch class. Caribou Road runs upstream to Caribou Dam, with stream and fishing access along almost all of it. The camps often fill on summer weekends. Open April through October.

33. HALLSTED 🏊🐟   RV 7

Reference: **On the North Fork of Feather River in Plumas National Forest; map C3, grid e4.**

Campsites, facilities: There are 20 sites for tents or motor homes up to 22 feet long. Piped water, flush toilets, picnic tables and fire grills are provided. Pets are permitted on leashes. A grocery store is nearby.

Reservations, fee: Reserve by phoning (800) 280-CAMP ($7.50 reservation fee); $9 fee per night.

Who to contact: Phone Plumas National Forest at (916) 283-0555.

Location: From Oroville, drive northeast on Highway 70 to Belden. Continue past Belden for about 12 miles to the campground entrance on the right side of the road. Turn right and drive a quarter-mile to the campground.

Trip note: Easy highway access and a pretty trout stream right alongside have made this an extremely popular campground. It typically fills on summer weekends. Hallsted is set on the East Branch North Fork River, 2,800 feet elevation. The river is stocked with trout by the Department of Fish and Game. Open May through September.

34. LOWER BUCKS 🐟 ⚓ 🚶 🏊   RV 7

Reference: **On Lower Bucks Lake in Plumas National Forest; map C3, grid f2.**

Campsites, facilities: There are six sites for motor homes up to 26 feet long. **No piped water** or toilet facilities are provided. Picnic tables, a boat ramp and fire rings are available. Pets are allowed on leashes.

Reservations, fee: No reservations; $6 fee per night.

Who to contact: Phone the Plumas National Forest at (916) 283-0555.

Location: From Oroville, drive north on Highway 70 to the junction with Highway 89. Turn south on Highway 89/70 and drive 11 miles to Quincy. In Quincy, turn right at Bucks Lake Road and drive 17 miles to Bucks Lake and the junction with Bucks Lake Dam Road (Forest Service Road 33). Turn right and drive four miles around the lake, cross over the dam, drive a quarter-mile, then turn left on the campground entrance road.

Trip note: This camp is located on Lower Bucks Lake, which is actually the afterbay for Bucks Lake, set below the Bucks Lake Dam. It is a small, primitive and quiet spot that is often overlooked because it is not located on the main lake. Open May through October.

35. GRIZZLY CREEK 🐟 ⚓ 🏊 🎿   RV 4

Reference: **Near Bucks Lake in Plumas National Forest; map C3, grid f2.**

Campsites, facilities: There are eight sites for tents or motor homes up to 50 feet long. There is **no piped water**, but vault toilets, picnic tables and fire grills are provided. A boat ramp is available at Bucks Lake. Pets are permitted on leashes. A grocery store and laundromat are nearby.

Reservations, fee: No reservations; $9 fee per night.

Who to contact: Phone Plumas National Forest at (916) 283-0555.

Location: From Oroville, drive north on Highway 70 to the junction with Highway 89. Turn south on Highway 89/70 and drive 11 miles to Quincy. In

Quincy, turn right at Bucks Lake Road and drive 17 miles to Bucks Lake and the junction with Bucks Lake Dam Road (Forest Service Road 33). Turn right and drive one mile to the junction with Oroville-Quincy Road (Forest Service Road 36). Bear left and drive one mile to the campground on the right side of the road.

Trip note: This is an alternative to the more developed, more crowded camp-grounds at Bucks Lake. It is a small, primitive camp set near Grizzly Creek at 5,400 feet elevation. Nearby Bucks Lake provides good trout fishing, resorts and boat rentals. Open June through October.

---

36. HASKINS VALLEY

Reference: **On Bucks Lake; map C3, grid f3.**

Campsites, facilities: There are 65 sites for tents or motor homes. Piped water, vault toilets, picnic tables and fire grills are provided. A sanitary disposal station and a boat ramp are available. Pets are permitted on leashes.

Reservations, fee: No reservations; $11 fee per night; $1 pet fee.

Who to contact: Phone PG&E at (916) 386-5164.

Location: From Oroville, drive north on Highway 70 to the junction with Highway 89. Turn south on Highway 89/70 and drive 11 miles to Quincy. In Quincy, turn right at Bucks Lake Road and drive 16.5 miles to the campground entrance on the right side of the road.

Trip note: This is the biggest and most popular of the campgrounds at Bucks Lake, a pretty alpine lake with excellent trout fishing and clean campgrounds. A boat ramp is available to the nearby north, along with Bucks Lodge. This camp is set deep in a cove at the extreme south end of the lake, where the water is quiet and sheltered from north winds. Bucks Lake, 5,200 feet elevation, is well documented for excellent fishing for rainbow and mackinaw trout, with high catch rates of rainbow trout and lake records in the 16-pound class. Open May through October.

---

37. SILVER LAKE

Reference: **In Plumas National Forest; map C3, grid f3.**

Campsites, facilities: There are eight tent sites. There is **no piped water**, but vault toilets, picnic tables and fire grills are provided. Pets are permitted on leashes.

Reservations, fee: No reservations; no fee.

Who to contact: Phone Plumas National Forest at (916) 283-0555.

Location: From Oroville, drive north on Highway 70 to the junction with Highway 89. Turn south on Highway 89/70 and drive 11 miles to Quincy. In Quincy, turn right at Bucks Lake Road and drive west for nine miles west to Silver Lake Road. Turn right (north) and drive seven miles to the campground at the north end of the lake.

Trip note: While tons of people go to Bucks Lake for the great trout fishing and lakeside camps, nearby Silver Lake gets little attention despite great natural beauty, good hiking and decent trout fishing. The camp is located at the north end of the lake, 5,800 feet elevation, a primitive and secluded spot. No power boats (or swimming) are allowed on Silver Lake, which makes it ideal for canoes and rafts. The lake has lots of small brook trout. The Pacific Crest Trail is routed on the ridge above the lake, skirting past Mt. Pleasant (6,924 feet) to the nearby west. Open May through October.

38. WHITEHORSE 🐟 ⚓ 🚶🚶 🏊   RV 7

Reference: **Near Bucks Lake in Plumas National Forest; map C3, grid f3.**

Campsites, facilities: There are 20 sites for tents or motor homes up to 43 feet long. Piped water, vault toilets, fire grills and picnic tables are provided. A grocery store and laundromat are nearby. Pets are allowed on leashes.

Reservations, fee: No reservations; $12 fee per night.

Who to contact: Phone Plumas National Forest at (916) 283-0555.

Location: From Oroville, drive north on Highway 70 to the junction with Highway 89. Turn south on Highway 89/70 and drive 11 miles to Quincy. In Quincy, turn right at Bucks Lake Road and drive 14.5 miles to the campground entrance on the right side of the road.

Trip note: This campground is set along Bucks Creek, about two miles from the boat ramps and south shore concessions at Bucks Lake. The trout fishing can be quite good at Bucks Lake, particularly on early summer evenings. The elevation is 5,200 feet. For more information, see trip note for Haskins Camp. Open June through September.

39. SUNDEW 🐟 ⚓ 🚶🚶 🏊   RV 7

Reference: **On Bucks Lake in Plumas National Forest; map C3, grid f3.**

Campsites, facilities: There are 19 sites for tents or motor homes up to 22 feet long. Piped water, vault toilets, fire grills and picnic tables are provided. Pets are permitted on leashes. There is a boat ramp two miles north of the camp.

Reservations, fee: No reservations; $12 fee per night.

Who to contact: Phone Plumas National Forest at (916) 283-0555.

Location: From Oroville, drive north on Highway 70 to the junction with Highway 89. Turn south on Highway 89/70 and drive 11 miles to Quincy. In Quincy, turn right at Bucks Lake Road and drive 17 miles to Bucks Lake and the junction with Bucks Lake Dam Road (Forest Service Road 33). Turn right and drive around the lake, cross over the dam, continue for a half-mile and turn right at the campground access road.

Trip note: Sundew Camp is set on the northern shore of Bucks Lake, just north of Bucks Lake Dam. A boat ramp is located about two miles north in the Mill Creek Cove, providing access to one of the better trout spots on the lake. You want fish? At Bucks Lake, you can get fish—it's one of state's top mountain trout lakes. Sunrises are often spectacular from this camp, with the light glowing on the lake's surface.

40. MILL CREEK 🐟 ⚓ 🚶🚶 🏊   RV 7

Reference: **At Bucks Lake in Plumas National Forest; map C3, grid f3.**

Campsites, facilities: There are eight sites for tents or motor homes up to 58 feet long and two walk-in tent sites. Piped water, flush toilets, fire grills and picnic tables are provided. Groceries are available within five miles. Pets are permitted on leashes.

Reservations, fee: No reservations; $12 fee per night.

Who to contact: Phone Plumas National Forest at (916) 283-0555.

Location: From Oroville, drive north on Highway 70 to the junction with Highway 89. Turn south on Highway 89/70 and drive 11 miles to Quincy. In Quincy, turn right at Bucks Lake Road and drive 17 miles to Bucks Lake and the junction with Bucks Lake Dam Road (Forest Service Road 33). Turn right, drive around the lake, cross over the dam, and continue for about three miles to the campground.

Trip note: When Bucks Lake is full, this is one of the prettiest spots on the lake. The camp is set deep in Mill Creek Cove, adjacent to where Mill Creek enters the northernmost point of Bucks Lake. A boat ramp is located a half-mile away to the south, providing boat access to one of the better trout fishing spots at the lake. Unfortunately, when the lake level falls, this camp is left high and dry, some distance from the water. The elevation is 5,200 feet.

41. HUTCHINS GROUP CAMP

Reference: Near Bucks Lake in Plumas National Forest; map C3, grid f3.

Campsites, facilities: There are three group sites for tents or motor homes. Piped water, vault toilets, picnic tables and fire grills are provided. A sanitary disposal station and a boat ramp are available. Pets are permitted on leashes.

Reservations, fee: Reservations required; $43.60 group fee per night.

Who to contact: Phone the Plumas National Forest at (916) 283-0555.

Location: From Oroville, drive north on Highway 70 to the junction with Highway 89. Turn south on Highway 89/70 and drive 11 miles to Quincy. In Quincy, turn right at Bucks Lake Road and drive 17 miles to Bucks Lake and the junction with Bucks Lake Dam Road (Forest Service Road 33). Turn right, drive around the lake, cross over the dam, continue for a short distance and turn right. Drive a half-mile, cross the stream (passing an intersection) and continue straight for a half-mile to the campground.

Trip note: This is a prime spot for a Boy Scout outing or any other trip that has a large group and would like a pretty spot. An amphitheater is available. It is set at 5,200 feet near Bucks and Lower Bucks Lakes. For more information, see trip note for Lower Bucks, Sundew and Haskins camps. Open May through October.

42. DEANES VALLEY

Reference: On Rock Creek in Plumas National Forest; map C3, grid f4.

Campsites, facilities: There are seven sites for tents or motor homes. There is **no piped water**, but vault toilets, picnic tables and fire grills are provided. Pets are allowed on leashes.

Reservations, fee: No reservations; no fee.

Who to contact: Phone Plumas National Forest at (916) 283-0555.

Location: From Oroville, drive north on Highway 70 to the junction with Highway 89. Turn south on Highway 89/70 and drive 11 miles to Quincy. In Quincy, turn right at Bucks Lake Road and drive 3.5 miles to Forest Service Road 24N28. Turn left and drive seven miles to the campground.

Trip note: This secret spot is set on South Fork Rock Creek, deep in a valley in Plumas National Forest. The trout here are very small natives. If you want a pure, quiet spot, great. If you want great fishing, not great. The surrounding region has a network of backcountry roads, including routes passable only for four-wheel-drives; to drive them, get a map of Plumas National Forest. Open April through October.

43. SNAKE LAKE

Reference: In Plumas National Forest; map C3, grid f5.

Campsites, facilities: There are seven tent sites. There is **no piped water**, but vault toilets, picnic tables and fire grills are provided. Pets are permitted on leashes.

Reservations, fee: No reservations; no fee.

Who to contact: Phone Plumas National Forest at (916) 283-0555.

Location: From Oroville, drive north on Highway 70 to the junction with Highway 89. Turn south on Highway 89/70 and drive 11 miles to Quincy. In Quincy, turn right at Bucks Lake Road and drive five miles to County Road 422. Turn right and drive two miles to the Snake Lake access road. Turn right and drive one mile to the campground.

Trip note: Snake Lake is a rarity in the northern Sierra, a mountain lake that has bass, catfish and bluegill. That is because it is a shallow lake, set at 4,200 feet in Plumas National Forest. The camp is located on the west side of the lake. A road circles the lake that provides a good bicycle route for youngsters. A side trip to the nearby north is Smith Lake, about a five-minute drive, with the Butterfly Valley Botanical Area bordering it. Open May through October.

44. BRADY'S CAMP

Reference: On Pine Creek in Plumas National Forest; map C3, grid f7.

Campsites, facilities: There are four tent sites. There is **no piped water,** but vault toilets, picnic tables and fire grills are provided. Pets are allowed on leashes.

Reservations, fee: No reservations; no fee.

Who to contact: Phone Plumas National Forest at (916) 283-0555.

Location: From Oroville, drive north on Highway 70 to the junction with Highway 89. Turn south on Highway 89/70 and drive 11 miles to Quincy. In Quincy, continue on Highway 89/70 for six miles to Squirrel Creek Road. Turn left and drive seven miles (after two miles bear right at the Y) to Forest Service Road 25N29. Turn left and drive one mile to the campground on the right side of the road.

Trip note: Don't expect any company here. This is a tiny, little-known, primitive camp near Pine Creek, roughly 7,000 feet elevation. A side trip is to make the half-mile drive up to Argentine Rock, at 7,209 feet, for a lookout onto this remote forest country. To the east is many miles of national forest, accessible by vehicle, although there is significant logging activity in portions of it. Open May through October.

45. ROGERS COW CAMP

Reference: In Plumas National Forest; map C3, grid g1.

Campsites, facilities: There are five sites for tents or motor homes. Tables, fire grills and vault toilets are provided, but **no piped water** is available. Pets are permitted on leashes.

Reservations, fee: No reservations; no fee.

Who to contact: Phone Plumas National Forest at (916) 534-6500.

Location: In Oroville, drive east on Highway 162 (Oroville-Quincy Highway) for 26.5 miles to the Brush Creek Ranger Station. Continue on Oroville-Quincy Highway for eight miles to the campground entrance road on the left side of the road. Turn left and drive a short distance to the camp.

Trip note: First note that the Oroville-Quincy "Highway" is actually a bumpy, twisty dirt Forest Service Road, a backcountry route that connects Oroville to Quincy and passes Lake Oroville and Bucks Lake in the process. That puts this camp way out there in No Man's Land, set in Plumas National Forest at 4,000 feet. You want quiet, you get it. You want water, you bring it yourself. The camp is set near the headwaters of Coon Creek. There are no other natural destinations in the area, and I'm not saying Coon Creek is anything to see. It's advisable to obtain a map of Plumas National Forest, which details all backcountry roads. There has been logging activity in the area. Open May to October.

46. MILSAP BAR

Reference: **On the Middle Fork of Feather River in Plumas National Forest; map C3, grid g1.**

Campsites, facilities: There are 20 sites for tents or motor homes up to 16 feet long. There is **no piped water,** but tables, fire grills and vault toilets are provided. Pets are permitted on leashes.

Reservations, fee: No reservations; no fee.

Who to contact: Phone the Plumas National Forest at (916) 534-6500.

Location: In Oroville, drive east on Highway 162 (Oroville-Quincy Highway) for 26.5 miles to the Brush Creek Ranger Station. Turn right (south) on Bald Rock Road and drive for about one-half mile to Forest Service Road 22N62 (Milsap Bar Road). Turn left and drive eight miles to the campground (a narrow, steep, mountainous dirt road).

Trip note: Among whitewater river rafters, Milsap Bar is a well-known access point to the Middle Fork Feather River. This river country features a deep canyon, beautiful surroundings, and is formally recognized as the Feather Falls Scenic Area (named after the 640-foot waterfall), with trips offered by several rafting companies. The elevation is 1,600 feet. Open May to October.

47. LITTLE NORTH FORK

Reference: **On the Middle Fork of Feather River in Plumas National Forest; map C3, grid g1.**

Campsites, facilities: There are eight sites for tents or motor homes up to 16 feet long. There is **no piped water**, but vault toilets, tables and fire grills are provided. Pets are permitted on leashes.

Reservations, fee: No reservations; no fee.

Who to contact: Phone Plumas National Forest at (916) 534-6500.

Location: From Oroville, turn east on Highway 162 (Oroville-Quincy Highway) and drive 26 miles to the Brush Creek Ranger Station. Continue northeast on Oroville-Quincy Highway for about six miles to Forest Service Road 60. Turn right and drive about eight miles to the campground entrance road on the left side of the road. Turn left and drive a quarter-mile to the campground. Note: This route is long, twisty, bumpy, and narrow for most of the way.

Trip note: Guaranteed quiet? You got it. This is a primitive camp in the outback that few know of. It is set along the Little North Fork of the Middle Fork of the Feather River at 2,700 feet. The surrounding backcountry of Plumas National Forest features an incredible number of roads, giving four-wheel-drive owners a chance to get so lost they'll need this camp. Instead, get a map of Plumas National Forest before venturing out. Open May through October.

48. GOLDEN COACH TRAILER RESORT

Reference: Near Feather River; map C3, grid g8.

Campsites, facilities: There are 50 motor home sites with full hookups. Restrooms, showers, picnic tables and fire grills are provided. A laundromat, wood and LP gas are also available. A store and a cafe are within walking distance. Pets are allowed on leashes.

Reservations, fee: Reservations recommended in July and August; $15-$20 fee per night.

Who to contact: Phone (916) 836-2426.

Location: In Truckee, at the junction of Highway 80 and Highway 89, take Highway 89 north to the junction with Highway 70. Drive north on Highway 89/Highway 70 for 6.5 miles to Cromberg and look for the signed entrance to the campground at 59704 Highway 70.

Trip note: This is a good layover spot for RV cruisers looking to hole up for the night. The park is wooded, and set near the Feather River. You'll find mostly older adults here. Open May through mid-September.

49. BLACK ROCK

Reference: On Little Grass Valley Reservoir in Plumas National Forest; map C3, grid h4.

Campsites, facilities: There are 10 walk-in tent sites and 20 sites for tents or motor homes up to 22 feet long. Piped water, vault toilets, picnic tables and fire grills are provided. A sanitary dump station, boat ramp and grocery store are nearby. Pets are permitted on leashes.

Reservations, fee: No reservations; $9 fee per night.

Who to contact: Phone Plumas National Forest (916) 534-6500.

Location: From Oroville, drive east on Highway 162 for about eight miles to the junction signed Challenge/LaPorte. Bear right and drive east past Challenge and Strawberry Valley to LaPorte. Continue two miles past LaPorte to the junction with County Road 514 (Little Grass Valley Road). Turn left and drive about five miles to the campground access road on the west side of the lake. Turn right on the access road and drive a quarter-mile to the campground.

Trip note: This is the only campground on the west shore of Little Grass Valley Reservoir, with an adjacent boat ramp making it an attractive choice for fishermen. The lake is set at 5,000 feet in Plumas National Forest and provides lakeside camping and decent fishing for rainbow trout and kokanee salmon. If you don't like the company, there are four other camps to choose from at the lake, all set on the opposite eastern shore. The elevation is 5,000 feet. Open June through October.

50. RUNNING DEER

Reference: On Little Grass Valley Reservoir in Plumas National Forest; map C3, grid h5.

Campsites, facilities: There are 40 sites for tents or motor homes. Piped water, flush toilets, picnic tables and fire grills are provided. A boat ramp, grocery store, and sanitary dump station are nearby. Pets are permitted on leashes.

Reservations, fee: No reservations; $11 fee per night.

Who to contact: Phone Plumas National Forest at (916) 534-6500.

Location: From Oroville, drive east on Highway 162 for about eight miles to the junction signed Challenge/LaPorte. Bear right and drive east past Challenge and Strawberry Valley to LaPorte. Continue two miles past LaPorte to the junction with County Road 514 (Little Grass Valley Road). Turn left and drive one mile to a junction. Turn right and drive three miles to the campground on the left side of the road.

Trip note: Little Grass Valley Reservoir is a pretty mountain lake set at 5,000 feet in Plumas National Forest, providing lakeside camping, boating, and fishing for rainbow trout and kokanee salmon. This is one of four campgrounds set on the eastern shore, this one on the far northeastern end of the lake. Looking straight north from the camps is a pretty view, gazing across the water and up at Bald Mountain, 6,255 feet in elevation. A trailhead for the Pacific Crest Trail is available nearby, located at little Fowler Lake about four miles north of Little Grass Valley Reservoir. Open June through September.

51. WYANDOTTE 🐟 ⚓ 🚶 🚤 🎣   RV 7

Reference: **On Little Grass Valley Reservoir in Plumas National Forest; map C3, grid h5.**

Campsites, facilities: There are 28 sites for tents or motor homes up to 22 feet long. Piped water, flush toilets, picnic tables and fire grills are provided. A sanitary dump station, boat ramp and grocery store are nearby. Pets are permitted on leashes.

Reservations, fee: No reservations; $11-$15 fee per night.

Who to contact: Phone Plumas National Forest at (916) 534-6500.

Location: From Oroville, drive east on Highway 162 for about eight miles to the junction signed Challenge/LaPorte. Bear right and drive east past Challenge and Strawberry Valley to LaPorte. Continue two miles past LaPorte to the junction with County Road 514 (Little Grass Valley Road). Turn left and drive one mile to a junction. Turn left and drive one mile to the campground entrance road on the right.

Trip note: Of the five camps on Little Grass Valley Reservoir, this is the favorite. It is set on a small peninsula that extends well into the lake, with a boat ramp set nearby. For more information, see the trip note for Running Deer Camp. Open May to October.

52. LITTLE BEAVER 🐟 ⚓ 🚶 🚤 🎣   RV 7

Reference: **On Little Grass Valley Reservoir in Plumas National Forest; map C3, grid h5.**

Campsites, facilities: There are 120 sites for tents or motor homes. Piped water, flush toilets, picnic tables and fire grills are provided. A grocery store, sanitary dump station and boat ramp are nearby. Pets are permitted on leashes.

Reservations, fee: No reservations; $11-$12 fee per night.

Who to contact: Phone Plumas National Forest at (916) 534-6500.

Location: From Oroville, drive east on Highway 162 for about eight miles to the junction signed Challenge/LaPorte. Bear right and drive east past Challenge and Strawberry Valley to LaPorte. Continue two miles past LaPorte to the junction with County Road 514 (Little Grass Valley Road). Turn left and drive one mile to a junction. Turn right and drive two miles to the campground entrance road on the left.

Trip note: This is one of five campgrounds on Little Grass Valley Reservoir, set at 5,000 feet. Take your pick. For more information, see the trip note for Running Deer Camp. Open June through October.

53. RED FEATHER CAMP

Reference: On Little Grass Valley Reservoir in Plumas National Forest; map C3, grid h5.

Campsites, facilities: There are 60 sites for tents or motor homes up to 22 feet long. Piped water, flush toilets, picnic tables and fire grills are provided. A sanitary dump station, boat ramp and grocery store are nearby. Pets are permitted on leashes.

Reservations, fee: Reserve sites by phoning (800) 280-CAMP ($7.50 reservation fee); $12 fee per night.

Who to contact: Phone Plumas National Forest at (916) 534-6500.

Location: From Oroville, drive east on Highway 162 for about eight miles to the junction signed Challenge/LaPorte. Bear right and drive east past Challenge and Strawberry Valley to LaPorte. Continue two miles past LaPorte to the junction with County Road 514 (Little Grass Valley Road). Turn left and drive one mile to a junction. Turn right and drive three miles to the campground entrance road on the left.

Trip note: This camp is well developed and popular, set on the eastern shore of Little Grass Valley Reservoir, just south of Running Deer Camp and just north of Little Beaver Camp. For more information, see the trip note for Running Deer Camp. Open June through October.

54. PLUMAS-EUREKA STATE PARK

Reference: Near Graeagle; map C3, grid h7.

Campsites, facilities: There are 67 sites for tents, trailers or motor homes up to 30 feet long. Piped water, showers, flush toilets, a sanitary dump station, picnic tables and fire grills are provided. A grocery store, laundromat and propane gas are available in Graeagle. Pets are allowed on leashes.

Reservations, fee: No reservations; $15-17 fee per night; $1 pet fee.

Who to contact: Phone (916) 836-2380 or (916) 525-7232.

Location: In Truckee, drive north on Highway 89 and drive to Graeagle. Just after passing Graeagle (one mile from the junction of Highway 70), turn left (west) on County Road A14 (Graeagle-Johnsville Road) and drive west for about five miles to the park entrance.

Trip note: Plumas-Eureka State Park is a beautiful chunk of parkland, featuring great hiking, a pretty lake, and this well-maintained campground. For newcomers to the area, Jamison Camp at the southern end of the park makes for an excellent first stop. So does the nearby hike to Grass Lake, a first-class tromp that takes about two hours and features a streamside walk along Jamison Creek, with the chance to take a five-minute cutoff to see 40-foot Jamison Falls. Other must-see destinations in the park include Eureka Lake, and from there, the 1,100-foot climb up to Eureka Peak, 7,447 feet, for a dramatic view of all the famous peaks in this region. Camp elevation is 5,200 feet. Open May through September.

55. LITTLE BEAR RV PARK 🐟 ♿ ⊒ ✕   🚐 ⚠7

Reference: **On Feather River; map C3, grid h8.**

Campsites, facilities: There are 95 motor home sites, 80 with full hookups. Restrooms, showers, picnic tables and fire grills are provided. A laundromat, a grocery store, and ice are also available. Pets are allowed on leashes.

Reservations, fee: Reservations accepted; $17-$20 fee per night.

Who to contact: Phone (916) 836-2774.

Location: In Truckee, drive north on Highway 89 and drive to Blairsden and the junction with Highway 70. Turn north and drive one mile to Little Bear Road. Turn left (south) on Little Bear Road and drive a short distance to the campground.

Trip note: This is a privately operated motor home park set near the Feather River, open April through October. Nearby destinations include Plumas-Eureka State Park and the Lakes Basin Recreation Area. The elevation is 4,300 feet.

56. MOVIN' WEST TRAILER RANCH 🐟 🏃   🚐 ⚠4

Reference: **Near Graeagle; map C3, grid h8.**

Campsites, facilities: There are 32 motor home sites with full or partial hookups. Piped water, picnic tables, fire grills, flush toilets, showers and a laundromat are provided. Propane gas is available nearby. Pets are allowed on leashes.

Reservations, fee: Reservations accepted; $20 fee per night.

Who to contact: Phone (916) 836-2614.

Location: From Truckee, drive northwest on Highway 89 about 50 miles to Graeagle. Continue just past Graeagle to County Road A14. Turn left and drive a quarter-mile northwest to the campground.

Trip note: This RV area is set within a mobile home park. If that's what you want, you've found it. The elevation is 4,300 feet. Open May through October.

57. SIERRA SPRINGS TRAILER RESORT   🚐 ⚠5

Reference: **Map C3, grid h9.**

Campsites, facilities: There are 40 motor home sites, 30 with full hookups. Piped water, showers, flush toilets, picnic tables and fire grills are provided. A sanitary dump station, a laundromat, cable TV, a playground, a recreation room and a volleyball court are available. Pets are allowed on leashes.

Reservations, fee: Reservations accepted; $18 fee per night.

Who to contact: Phone (916) 836-2747.

Location: From Truckee, drive northwest on Highway 89 about 50 miles to Blairsden and the junction with Highway 70. Turn right and drive 3.5 miles east to Sierra Springs Drive. Turn left on Sierra Springs Drive and drive one-quarter mile to 70099 Sierra Springs Road on the left.

Trip note: This privately operated park provides all amenities. Possible side trips include the Feather River Park, located four miles away in the town of Blairsden. The elevation is 5,000 feet. Open April through October 31.

58. STRAWBERRY 🐟 ⚓ ♿ ⊒   🚐 ⚠7

Reference: **On Sly Creek Reservoir in Plumas National Forest; map C3, grid i2.**

Campsites, facilities: There are 17 sites for tents, trailers or motor homes. Piped water, vault toilets, picnic tables and fire grills are provided. A car-top boat launch is available on Sly Creek Reservoir. Pets are allowed on leashes.

Reservations, fee: No reservations; $8 fee per night.

Who to contact: Phone the Plumas National Forest at (916) 534-6500.

Location: From Oroville, drive east on Highway 162 for about eight miles to the junction signed Challenge/LaPorte. Bear right and drive east on LaPorte Road past Challenge and continue for about 14 miles to a signed turnoff on the left for Sly Creek Reservoir. Turn left and drive one mile to the campground on the eastern end of the lake.

Trip note: Sly Creek Reservoir is a long narrow lake set in western Plumas National Forest. There are two campgrounds on opposite ends of the lake, with different directions to each. This camp is set in the back of a cove on the lake's eastern arm, with a nearby boat ramp available. This is a popular lake for trout fishing in the summer.

---

59. SLY CREEK

Reference: On Sly Creek Reservoir in Plumas National Forest; map C3, grid i2.

Campsites, facilities: There are 21 sites for tents, trailers or motor homes. Five walk-in tent cabins are also available. Piped water, vault toilets, picnic tables and fire grills are provided. A car-top boat launch is available on Sly Creek Reservoir. Pets are allowed on leashes.

Reservations, fee: No reservations; $10 fee per night.

Who to contact: Phone the Plumas National Forest at (916) 675-2462.

Location: From Oroville, drive east on Highway 162 for about eight miles to the junction signed Challenge/LaPorte. Bear right and drive east on LaPorte Road past Challenge and continue for 10 miles to Forest Service Road 16 (a signed turnoff on the left). Turn left and drive 4.5 miles to the campground.

Trip note: Sly Creek Camp is set on Sly Creek Reservoir's southwestern shore near Lewis Flat, with a boat ramp located about a mile to the north. Both camps are well set for campers/fishermen. This camp provides direct access to the lake's main body, with good trout fishing well upstream on the main lake arm. You get quiet water and decent fishing.

---

60. DIABLO

Reference: On Packer Creek in Tahoe National Forest; map C3, grid i8.

Campsites, facilities: This is an undeveloped, designated camping area for tents and motor homes. There is **no piped water**, but vault toilets are provided. Pets are permitted on leashes or otherwise controlled. Supplies are available in Bassetts and Sierra City.

Reservations, fee: No reservations; no fee.

Who to contact: Phone Tahoe National Forest at (916) 288-3231.

Location: From Truckee, turn north on Highway 89 and drive 20 miles to Sierraville. At Sierraville, turn left on Highway 49 and drive about 10 miles to the Bassetts Store. Turn right (north) on Gold Lake Road and drive 1.5 miles to Packer Lake Road. Turn left, drive a short distance, and at the fork, bear right and drive one mile to the campground on the right side of the road.

Trip note: This is a primitive camping area set on Packer Creek, about two miles from Packer Lake. This area is extremely beautiful with several lakes nearby, including the Sardine Lakes and Packer Lake, and this camp provides an overflow area when the more developed campgrounds have filled.

61. SALMON CREEK 🚶🚶

RV **9**

Reference: **In Tahoe National Forest; map C3, grid i8.**

Campsites, facilities: There are 31 sites for tents or motor homes up to 22 feet long. Piped water, vault toilets, picnic tables and fire grills are provided. Pets are permitted on leashes or otherwise controlled. Supplies and a laundromat are available in Sierra City.

Reservations, fee: No reservations; $8 fee per night.

Who to contact: Phone Tahoe National Forest at (916) 288-3231.

Location: From Truckee, turn north on Highway 89 and drive 20 miles to Sierraville. At Sierraville, turn left on Highway 49 and drive about 10 miles to the Bassetts Store. Turn right (north) on Gold Lake Road and drive two miles to the campground on the left side of the road.

Trip note: This campground is set at the confluence of Packer and Salmon Creeks, 5,800 feet in elevation, with easy access off the Gold Lakes Highway. It is on the edge of the Lakes Basin Recreation Area, with literally dozens of lakes located within 15 miles, plus great hiking, fishing and low-speed boating. Open June through October.

---

62. PACKSADDLE 🚶🚶 🏇

6

Reference: **Near Packer Lake in Tahoe National Forest; map C3, grid i8.**

Campsites, facilities: There are 12 sites for tents or motor homes. There is **no piped water**, but vault toilets are provided. Pack and saddle stock are permitted. Hitching rails are available. Pets are permitted on leashes or otherwise controlled. Supplies are available in Bassetts and Sierra City.

Reservations, fee: No reservations; $10 fee per night

Who to contact: Phone Tahoe National Forest at (916) 288-3231.

Location: From Truckee, turn north on Highway 89 and drive 20 miles to Sierraville. At Sierraville, turn left on Highway 49 and drive about 10 miles to the Bassetts Store. Turn right (north) on Gold Lake Road and drive 1.5 miles to Packer Lake Road. Turn left, drive a short distance, and at the fork, bear right and drive 2.5 miles to the campground.

Trip note: Packsaddle Camp is a primitive spot, located about a half-mile from Packer Lake, with an additional 15 lakes within a five-mile radius, and one of America's truly great hiking trails available nearby. Packer Lake, 6,218 feet, is located at the foot of the dramatic Sierra Buttes, and has lakefront log cabins, good trout fishing and low-speed boating. The trail nearby to the Sierra Buttes features a climb of 2,369 feet over the course of five miles. It is highlighted by a stairway with 176 steps that literally juts out into open space, and crowned by an astounding view for hundreds of miles in all directions.

---

63. BERGER CREEK 🐟 🚶🚶

RV **6**

Reference: **In Tahoe National Forest; map C3, grid i8.**

Campsites, facilities: There are 10 sites for tents or motor homes up to 16 feet long. There is **no piped water**, but vault toilets, picnic tables and fire grills are provided. Pets are permitted on leashes or otherwise controlled. Supplies are available in Bassetts and Sierra City.

Reservations, fee: No reservations; no fee.

Who to contact: Phone Tahoe National Forest at (916) 288-3231.

Location: From Truckee, turn north on Highway 89 and drive 20 miles to

Sierraville. At Sierraville, turn left on Highway 49 and drive about 10 miles to the Bassetts Store. Turn right (north) on Gold Lake Road and drive 1.5 miles to Packer Lake Road. Turn left, drive a short distance, and at the fork, bear right and drive two miles to the campground.

Trip note: Berger Creek Camp, primitive and undeveloped, provides an overflow alternative to the nearby Diablo Camp (also extremely primitive). On busy summer weekends, when an open campsite can be difficult to find at a premium location in the Lakes Basin Recreation Area, these two camps provide a safety valve to keep you from being stuck for the night. Nearby is Packer Lake, the trail to the Sierra Buttes, Sardine Lakes and Sand Pond, all excellent destinations. The elevation is 5,900 feet. Open June through October.

---

64. SNAG LAKE

Reference: In Tahoe National Forest; map C3, grid i8.

Campsites, facilities: There are 16 sites for tents or motor homes up to 16 feet long. There is **no piped water**, but vault toilets, picnic tables and fire grills are provided. Only hand boat launching is allowed. Pets are permitted on leashes or otherwise controlled. Supplies are available in Bassetts and Sierra City.

Reservations, fee: No reservations; no fee.

Who to contact: Phone Tahoe National Forest at (916) 288-3231.

Location: From Truckee, turn north on Highway 89 and drive 20 miles to Sierraville. At Sierraville, turn left on Highway 49 and drive about 10 miles to the Bassetts Store. Turn right (north) on Gold Lake Road and drive five miles to the campground.

Trip note: Snag Lake is an ideal little lake for camping anglers with canoes. There are no boat ramps and you can have the place virtually to yourself. It is set at 6,600 feet elevation, an easy-to-reach lake in the Lakes Basin Recreation Area. Trout fishing is only fair, as in fair numbers and fair size, mainly rainbow trout in the 10 to 12-inch class. This is a primitive camp, so bring everything you will need, including water. Open June through October.

---

65. LAKES BASIN GROUP CAMP

Reference: In Plumas National Forest; map C3, grid i8.

Campsites, facilities: This group camp can accommodate up to 25 people in tents or small motor homes. Piped water, vault toilets, picnic tables and fire grills are provided. Pets are permitted on leashes or otherwise controlled. Supplies are available in Graeagle.

Reservations, fee: Reserve by phoning (800) 280-CAMP ($15 reservation fee); $40 group fee per night.

Who to contact: Phone the Plumas National Forest Beckwourth Ranger District at (916) 836-2575.

Location: From Truckee, drive north on Highway 89 toward Graeagle to the Gold Lake Highway (one mile before reaching Graeagle). Turn left on the Gold Lake Highway and drive about seven miles to the campground.

Trip note: This is a Forest Service group camp that is ideal for the Boy or Girl Scouts. It is set at 6,400 feet in elevation, just a short drive from the trailhead to beautiful Frazier Falls, and also near Gold Lake, Little Bear Lake and some 15 lakes set below nearby Mt. Elwell.

Special note: The camp was closed for renovation and is schedule to reopen during the summer of 1996. Call for status.

66. LAKES BASIN 🐟 🚶 🏊

RV **8**

Reference: **In Plumas National Forest; map C3, grid i8.**

Campsites, facilities: There are 24 sites for tents or small motor homes. Piped water, vault toilets, picnic tables and fire grills are provided. Pets are permitted on leashes. Supplies are available in Graeagle.

Reservations, fee: No reservations; $10 fee per night.

Who to contact: Phone the Plumas National Forest Beckwourth Ranger District at (916) 836-2575.

Location: From Truckee, drive north on Highway 89 toward Graeagle to the Gold Lake Highway (one mile before reaching Graeagle). Turn left on the Gold Lake Highway and drive about seven miles to the campground.

Trip note: The renovation of this camp for 1996 makes it far more accessible to small motor homes and trailers. That done, it is a great location for a base camp to explore the surrounding Lakes Basin Recreation Area. From nearby Gold Lake or Elwell Lodge, there are many short hikes available to small pristine lakes. A must-do trip is the easy hike to Frazier Falls, only a mile round-trip to see the spectacular 176-foot waterfall, though the trail is crowded during the middle of the day. The camp elevation is 6,400 feet. Open June through October.

Special note: The camp was closed for renovation and is schedule to reopen during the summer of 1996. Call for status.

---

67. SARDINE LAKE 🐟 ⚓ 🚶 🏊

8

Reference: **In Tahoe National Forest; map C3, grid i8 .**

Campsites, facilities: There are 29 sites for tents or motor homes up to 22 feet long. Piped water, vault toilets, picnic tables and fire grills are provided. Pets are permitted on leashes or otherwise controlled. Limited supplies are available at Sardine Lake Lodge.

Reservations, fee: No reservations; $8 fee per night.

Who to contact: Phone Tahoe National Forest at (916) 288-3231.

Location: From Truckee, turn north on Highway 89 and drive 20 miles to Sierraville. At Sierraville, turn left on Highway 49 and drive about 10 miles to the Bassetts Store. Turn right (north) on Gold Lake Road and drive 1.5 miles to Packer Lake Road. Turn left, drive a short distance, and at the fork, bear left and drive a half-mile to the campground.

Trip note: Lower Sardine Lake is a jewel set below the Sierra Buttes, one of the prettiest settings in California. The campground is actually about a mile east of the lake. Nearby is the beautiful Sand Pond Interpretive Trail. A great hike is routed along the shore of Lower Sardine Lake to a hidden waterfall (in spring) that feeds the lake, and ambitious hikers can explore beyond and discover Upper Sardine Lake. Trout fishing is excellent in Lower Sardine Lake, with a primitive boat ramp available for small boats. The speed limit and small size of the lake keeps boaters slow and quiet. A small marina and boat rentals are available. Open June through October.

---

68. CLIO'S RIVER'S EDGE 🐟 ♿ 🚣 🍴

RV **7**

Reference: **On Feather River; map C3, grid i9.**

Campsites, facilities: There are 220 motor home sites with full hookups. Piped water, showers (coin operated), picnic tables, flush toilets, a laundromat and cable TV are provided. A grocery store is nearby. Pets are allowed on leashes.

Reservations, fee: Reservations accepted; $20 fee per night.

Who to contact: Phone (916) 836-2375.

Location: From Truckee, drive north on Highway 89 toward Graeagle and Blairsden. Near Clio (4.5 miles south of Highway 70 at Blairsden), look for the campground entrance.

Trip note: This is a giant motor home park set adjacent to a pretty and easily accessible stretch of the Feather River. There are many possible side trip destinations, including Plumas-Eureka State Park, Lakes Basin Recreation Area, and several nearby golf courses. Open May through mid-October. The elevation is about 4,500 feet.

69. GARDEN POINT BOAT-IN

Reference: On Bullards Bar Reservoir; map C3, grid j2.

Campsites, facilities: There are 16 sites, accessible by boat only. There is **no piped water**, but picnic tables, fire grills and vault toilets are provided. You must burn or pack out your garbage. Pets are permitted on leashes or otherwise controlled. Supplies are available in Emerald Cove Marina.

Reservations, fee: Reservations required; $10 fee per night.

Who to contact: Managed by the Emerald Cove Resort and Marina for the Yuba County Water Agency; phone (916) 692-3200 or (916) 741-6278.

Location: From Marysville, drive northeast on Highway 20 to Marysville Road. Turn north at Marysville Road (signed Bullards Bar Reservoir) and drive about 10 miles to Old Marysville Road. Turn right and drive 14 miles to reach the Cottage Creek Launch Ramp and the marina (turn right just before the dam). To reach the ramp at the Dark Day Campground, continue over the dam and drive four miles, then turn left on Garden Valley Road and continue to the ramp. From the boat launch, continue to the campground on the northwest side.

Trip note: Bullards Bar Reservoir is one of the few lakes in the Sierra Nevada to offer boat-in camping not only at developed boat-in sites, but to allow boaters to create their own primitive sites anywhere along the lake's shoreline. A chemical toilet is required gear. Garden Point Boat-In Camp is located on the western shore of the northern Yuba River arm. This lake provides good fishing for kokanee salmon, waterskiing, and many coves for playing in the water.

70. DARK DAY WALK-IN

Reference: On Bullards Bar Reservoir; map C3, grid j2.

Campsites, facilities: There are 16 walk-in tent sites. Picnic tables and fire pits are provided. Piped water and flush and vault toilets are available. A boat ramp is available nearby, and supplies are available at Emerald Cove Marina. Pets are permitted on leashes or otherwise controlled.

Reservations, fee: Reservations required; $10 fee per night.

Who to contact: Phone Emerald Cove Resort at (916) 692-3200, or the Yuba County Water Agency at (916) 741-6278.

Location: From Marysville, drive northeast on Highway 20 to Marysville Road. Turn north at Marysville Road (signed Bullards Bar Reservoir) and drive about 10 miles to Old Marysville Road. Turn right and drive 14 miles and continue over the dam to Garden Valley Road. Turn left and drive past the boat launch to the campground on the northwest side of the lake.

Trip note: This is the only car-accessible campground at Bullards Bar Reservoir with direct shoreline access. You park in a central area, and then walk a short distance to the campground. The lake is a very short walk farther. Bullards Bar is a great camping lake, pretty and large with several lake arms and good fishing for kokanee salmon (as long as you have a boat). It is set at 2,000 feet in the foothills, like a silver dollar in a field of pennies. A bonus at Bullards Bar is that there is never a charge for day use, parking or boat launching. Open year-round.

71. SHORELINE CAMP BOAT-IN

Reference: On Bullards Bar Reservoir; map C3, grid j2.

Campsites, facilities: Boaters may choose their own primitive campsite anywhere on the shore of Bullards Bar Reservoir. You must burn or pack out your garbage. Supplies are available at Emerald Cove Marina. Pets are permitted.

Reservations, fee: Reservations and a shoreline camping permit are required; phone for fees. Note: A portable chemical toilet is required for boat-in campers.

Who to contact: Phone Emerald Cove Resort at (916) 692-3200.

Location: From Marysville, turn east on Highway 20 and drive 12 miles. Turn left on Marysville Road (look for the sign for Bullards Bar Reservoir) and drive 10 miles. Turn right on Old Marysville Road and drive 14 miles to the Cottage Creek Launch Ramp (turn right just before the dam). To reach the boat launch, continue to the campgrounds on the west side.

Trip note: There are two boat-in campgrounds on Bullards Bar Reservoir, but another option is to throw all caution to the wind and just head out on your own, camping wherever you want. It is critical to bring a shovel to dig a flat site for sleeping, a large tarp for sun protection, and of course, plenty of water or a water purification pump. This is a big, beautiful lake, with good trolling for kokanee salmon. Note: A portable chemical toilet is required.

72. MADRONE COVE BOAT-IN

Reference: On Bullards Bar Reservoir; map C3, grid j2.

Campsites, facilities: There are 10 sites, accessible by boat only. There is **no piped water**, but picnic tables, fire grills and vault toilets are provided. You must burn or pack out your garbage. Pets are permitted on leashes or otherwise controlled. Supplies are available at the marina.

Reservations, fee: Reservations required; phone for fees.

Who to contact: Managed by Emerald Cove Resort and Marina for the Yuba County Water Agency; call (916) 692-3200.

Location: From Marysville, drive 12 miles east on Highway 20. Turn left at the sign for Bullards Bar Reservoir (Marysville Road). Drive 10 miles north, then turn right on Old Marysville Road and drive 14 miles to reach the Cottage Creek Launch Ramp and the marina (turn right just before the dam). To reach the ramp, continue over the dam and drive four miles, then turn left on Garden Valley Road and continue to the ramp. From the boat launch, continue to the campground on the west side.

Trip note: This is one of several boat-in campgrounds at Bullards Bar Reservoir. It is set on the main Yuba River arm of the lake, along the western shore. This is a premium boat-in site. The elevation is 2,000 feet.

73. SCHOOLHOUSE

Reference: On Bullards Bar Reservoir; map C3, grid j2.

Campsites, facilities: There are 67 sites for tents or motor homes. Picnic tables, fire grills, piped water and flush and vault toilets are provided. A boat ramp is nearby. Pets are permitted on leashes or otherwise controlled. Supplies are available in North San Juan, Camptonville, Dobbins and at the marina.

Reservations, fee: Reservations required; phone for fees.

Who to contact: Managed by Emerald Cove Resort and Marina for the Yuba County Water Agency; phone (916) 692-3200.

Location: From Marysville, turn east on Highway 20 and drive 12 miles. Turn left on Marysville Road (look for the sign for Bullards Bar Reservoir) and drive 10 miles. Turn right on Old Marysville Road and drive 14 miles to the dam, then continue for another three miles to the campground entrance road on the left.

Trip note: Bullards Bar Reservoir is one of the better lakes in the Sierra Nevada for camping, primarily because the lake levels tend to be higher here than at many other lakes. The camp is set on the southeast shore, with a trail available out of the camp to a beautiful lookout of the lake. Bullards Bar is known for good fishing for trout and kokanee salmon, waterskiing and all water sports. A three-line concrete boat ramp is located to the south at Cottage Creek. Boaters should consider the special boat-in camps at the lake. The elevation is 2,200 feet. Open year-round with limited winter facilities.

---

74. FIDDLE CREEK

Reference: On North Yuba River in Tahoe National Forest; map C3, grid j3.

Campsites, facilities: There are 13 tent sites. There is **no piped water**, but vault toilets, picnic tables and fire pits are provided. Pets are permitted on leashes or otherwise controlled. Limited supplies are available nearby at the Indian Valley Outpost. Facilities are **wheelchair accessible,** including a paved trail to the Yuba River.

Reservations, fee: No reservations; $10 fee per night.

Who to contact: Phone Tahoe National Forest at (916) 288-3231.

Location: From Auburn, take Highway 49 north to Nevada City and continue (the road jogs left, then narrows) to Camptonville. Continue 9.5 miles to the campground entrance.

Trip note: This camp is situated on the North Yuba River in a quiet, forested area. This is a beautiful stream, one of the prettiest to flow westward out of the Sierra Nevada, with deep pools and miniature waterfalls. It is popular for rafting out of Goodyear's Bar, and if you can stand the cold water, there are many good swimming holes along Highway 49. Fiddle Bow Trail leads out from the camp to Halls Ranch Station or Indian Rock. Bring your own drinking water or a water purifier. It's set at 2,200 feet. There are a series of campgrounds located on this stretch of the Yuba River. Open year-round.

---

75. CAL-IDA/CARLTON FLAT

Reference: On North Yuba River in Tahoe National Forest; map C3, grid j3.

Campsites, facilities: There are two undeveloped camping areas. There is **no piped water**, but vault toilets are provided (one is **wheelchair accessible**). Pets are permitted on leashes or otherwise controlled. Some supplies are available at the Indian Valley Outpost nearby.

Reservations, fee: No reservations; $10 fee per night.

Who to contact: Phone Tahoe National Forest at (916) 288-3231.

Location: From Auburn, take Highway 49 north to Nevada City and continue (the road jogs left, then narrows) to Camptonville. Continue nine miles to the campground entrance. The camping area at Lower Carlton Flat is located one mile northeast of the Highway 49 bridge at Indian Valley. The camping area at Upper Carlton Flat is located behind the Indian Valley Outpost on the Cal Ida Road.

Trip note: Lower Carlton Flat is on the North Yuba River, and Upper Carlton Flat is across the road. Both are right next door to Fiddle Creek Camp. For more information, see the trip note for the preceding camp.

76. ROCKY REST ⌐◣ 🎣 🚶 🏊   7

Reference: **On North Yuba River in Tahoe National Forest; map C3, grid j4.**

Campsites, facilities: This is an undeveloped camping area. There is **no piped water**, but vault toilets are provided. Pets are permitted on leashes or otherwise controlled. Limited supplies are available at the Indian Valley Outpost nearby.

Reservations, fee: No reservations; $10 fee per night.

Who to contact: Phone Tahoe National Forest at (916) 288-3231.

Location: From Auburn, take Highway 49 north to Nevada City and continue (the road jogs left, then narrows) to Camptonville. Continue 10 miles north to the campground entrance.

Trip note: This is one in a series of campgrounds set at streamside on the North Yuba River. Primitive and undeveloped, it is used primarily as an overflow camp if the other campgrounds in the area (that have piped water) are filled. The elevation is 2,200 feet. A newly constructed footbridge is now available that crosses the North Yuba and provides an outstanding seven-mile hike.

77. RAMSHORN ⌐◣ 🎣 🚶 🏊   RV 7

Reference: **On North Yuba River in Tahoe National Forest; map C3, grid j4.**

Campsites, facilities: There are 16 sites for tents or motor homes up to 22 feet long. Piped water, vault toilets, picnic tables and fire pits are provided. Pets are permitted on leashes or otherwise controlled. Supplies are available in Downieville.

Reservations, fee: No reservations; $10 fee per night.

Who to contact: Phone Tahoe National Forest at (916) 288-3231.

Location: From Auburn, take Highway 49 north to Nevada City and continue (the road jogs left, then narrows) to Camptonville. Continue 15 miles north to the campground entrance.

Trip note: This camp is set on Ramshorn Creek, just across the road from the North Yuba River. It's one in a series of camps on this stretch of the beautiful North Yuba River. A short distance downstream is a picnic area with a trailhead for a great hike that follows the Yuba downstream. Goodyear's Bar, located one mile east, is a famous access point for whitewater rafting trips on the Yuba. The camp's elevation is 2,600 feet. Open year-round.

78. INDIAN VALLEY ⌐◣ 🎣 🚶 🏊   RV 7

Reference: **On North Yuba River in Tahoe National Forest; map C3, grid j4.**

Campsites, facilities: There are 17 sites for tents or motor homes up to 22 feet long. Piped water, vault toilets, picnic tables and fire pits are provided. Pets are permitted on leashes or otherwise controlled. Limited supplies are available nearby at the Indian Valley Outpost.

Reservations, fee: No reservations; $8 fee per night.

Who to contact: Phone Tahoe National Forest at (916) 288-3231.

Location: From Auburn, take Highway 49 north to Nevada City and continue (the road jogs left, then narrows) to Camptonville. Continue 10 miles to the camp entrance.

Trip note: This is an easy-to-reach spot set at 2,200 feet beside the North Yuba River. Highway 49 runs adjacent to the Yuba for miles eastward, providing easy access to the river in many areas. There are several other camps in the immediate area; see trip notes for Fiddle Creek and Upper and Lower Carlton, all located within a mile. Open year-round.

---

79. UNION FLAT

Reference: **On North Yuba River in Tahoe National Forest; map C3, grid j6.**

Campsites, facilities: There are 14 sites for tents or motor homes up to 22 feet long. Piped water, vault toilets, picnic tables and fire pits are provided. Facilities are **wheelchair accessible**. Pets are permitted on leashes or otherwise controlled. Supplies are available in Downieville.

Reservations, fee: No reservations; $8 fee per night.

Who to contact: Phone Tahoe National Forest at (916) 288-3231.

Location: From Auburn, take Highway 49 north to Nevada City and continue (the road jogs left, then narrows) to Downieville. Continue six miles east to the campground entrance.

Trip note: Of all the campgrounds on the North Yuba River along Highway 49, this one has the best swimming. The camp is set near Quartz Point and Granite Mountain and has a nice swimming hole next to it if you can stand the cold. Recreational mining is also an attraction here. The elevation is 3,400 feet. Open May through October.

---

80. LOGANVILLE

Reference: **On North Yuba River in Tahoe National Forest; map C3, grid j7.**

Campsites, facilities: There are 20 sites for tents or motor homes up to 22 feet long. Piped water, vault toilets and picnic tables are provided. Pets are permitted on leashes or otherwise controlled. Supplies and a laundromat are available in Sierra City.

Reservations, fee: No reservations; $8 fee per night.

Who to contact: Phone Tahoe National Forest at (916) 288-3231.

Location: From Auburn, take Highway 49 north to Nevada City and continue (the road jogs left, then narrows) to Downieville. Continue 12 miles east to the campground entrance on the right (two miles west of Sierra City).

Trip note: Nearby Sierra City is only two miles away, meaning you can make a quick getaway for a prepared meal or any food or drink you may need to add to your camp. Loganville is set on the North Yuba River, elevation 4,200 feet, It offers a good stretch of water in this region for trout fishing, with many pools set below miniature waterfalls. Open May through October.

---

81. WILD PLUM

Reference: **On Haypress Creek in Tahoe National Forest; map C3, grid j8.**

Campsites, facilities: There are 47 sites for tents or motor homes up to 22 feet long. Piped water, vault toilets, picnic tables and fire pits are provided. Pets are permitted on leashes or otherwise controlled. Supplies and a laundromat are available in Sierra City.

Reservations, fee: No reservations; $8 fee per night.

Who to contact: Phone Tahoe National Forest at (916) 288-3231.

Location: From Auburn, take Highway 49 north to Nevada City and continue (the road jogs left, then narrows) past Downieville to Sierra City at Wild Plum Road. Turn right (south) on Wild Plum Road and drive two miles to the campground entrance road on the right.

Trip note: This popular Forest Service camp is set on Haypress Creek at 4,400 feet. There are several hidden waterfalls in the area, which makes this a well-loved camp for the people who know of them. There's a scenic hike up the Haypress Trail. It goes past a waterfall, to Haypress Valley. Two other nearby waterfalls are Loves Falls (on the North Yuba on Highway 49 two miles east of Sierra City) and Hackmans Falls (remote, set in a ravine one mile south of Sierra City, no road access). Open May through October.

82. CHAPMAN CREEK 🐟 👫 🏊   RV 8

Reference: On North Yuba River in Tahoe National Forest; map C3, grid j9.

Campsites, facilities: There are 29 sites for tents or motor homes up to 22 feet long. Piped water, showers, vault toilets, picnic tables and fire pits are provided. Pets are permitted on leashes or otherwise controlled. Supplies are available in Bassetts.

Reservations, fee: No reservations; $10 fee per night.

Who to contact: Phone Tahoe National Forest at (916) 288-3231.

Location: From Truckee, turn north on Highway 89 and drive 20 miles to Sierraville. At Sierraville, turn left on Highway 49 and drive over Yuba Pass and continue for four miles to the campground on the right .

Trip note: This camp is set along Chapman Creek at 6,000 feet, just across the highway from where it enters the North Yuba River. A good side trip is to hike the Chapman Creek Trail, which leads out of camp to Beartrap Meadow or to Haskell Peak (8,107 feet). Open June through October.

83. SIERRA 🐟 👫 🏊   7

Reference: On North Yuba River in Tahoe National Forest; map C3, grid j9.

Campsites, facilities: There are nine sites for tents and seven sites for tents or motor homes up to 22 feet long. There is **no piped water**, but vault toilets, picnic tables and fire pits are provided. Pets are permitted on leashes or otherwise controlled. Supplies are available in Bassetts.

Reservations, fee: No reservations; $6 fee per night.

Who to contact: Phone Tahoe National Forest at (916) 288-3231.

Location: From Truckee, turn north on Highway 89 and drive 20 miles to Sierraville. At Sierraville, turn left on Highway 49 and drive over Yuba Pass. Continue for five miles to the campground on the left (south) side of the road.

Trip note: This is a primitive and easy-to-reach spot set along the North Yuba River, used primarily as an overflow area from the nearby Chapman Creek Camp (located one mile upstream). Nearby recreation options include the Chapman Creek Trail (see trip note for Chapman Creek Camp), several waterfalls (see Wild Plum Camp) and the nearby Lakes Basin Recreation Area to the north off the Gold Lake Highway. The elevation is 5,600 feet. Open June through October.

NOR-CAL MAP .... see page 94
adjoining maps
NORTH (B4) .... see page 222
EAST .... no map
SOUTH (D4) .... see page 390
WEST (C3) .... see page 272

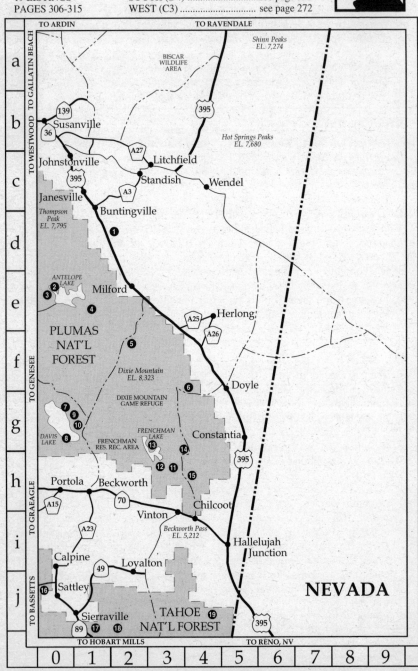

Map C4 featuring: Antelope Lake, Plumas National Forest, Lake Davis, Frenchman Lake, Tahoe National Forest, Toiyabe National Forest

1. HONEY LAKE CAMPGROUND   RV. 4

Reference: **Near Milford; map C4, grid d2.**

Campsites, facilities: There are 44 sites for tents or motor homes, some with full or partial hookups. Picnic tables are provided. Restrooms, showers, a laundromat, a sanitary disposal station, propane gas, a grocery store, ice, wood and a game room are available. Pets are allowed on leashes.

Reservations, fee: Reservations accepted; $12.50-$16.50 fee per night.

Who to contact: Phone (916) 253-2508.

Location: From Susanville on US 395, drive 22 miles south (if you reach Milford, you have gone two miles too far) to the campground.

Trip note: For newcomers, Honey Lake is a strange looking place; it's a vast, flat alkali lake with not much around it. It sits in a huge basin that, from a distance, looks almost moon-like. The campground is set at 4,300 feet and covers 27 acres, most of it overlooking the lake. There are a lot of junipers and scraggly-looking aspens in the area, with a waterfowl management area located along the north shore of the lake.

2. BOULDER CREEK   RV. 7

Reference: **At Antelope Lake in Plumas National Forest; map C4, grid e0.**

Campsites, facilities: There are 70 sites for tents or motor homes. Piped water, vault toilets, picnic tables and fire grills are provided. A sanitary dump station, boat ramp and grocery store are nearby. Pets are permitted on leashes.

Reservations, fee: Reserve by phoning (800) 280-CAMP ($7.50 reservation fee); $10-$12 fee per night.

Who to contact: Phone Plumas National Forest at (916) 283-0555.

Location: From Red Bluff, drive east on Highway 36 to Susanville and US 395. Turn south on US 395 and drive about 10 miles (one mile past Janesville) to County Road 208. Turn right on County Road 208 (signed Antelope Lake) and drive about 15 miles to a Y (one mile before Antelope Lake). Turn left at the Y and drive four miles to the campground entrance on the right side of the road (on the northwest end of the lake).

Trip note: Antelope Lake is a pretty mountain lake circled by conifers with nice campsites and good trout fishing. It is set at 5,000 feet in remote eastern Plumas National Forest, far enough away so the marginally-inclined never make the trip. Campgrounds are located at each end of the lake (this one is just north of Lone Rock at the north end), with a boat ramp at Lost Cove on the east side of the lake. The lake isn't huge, but it is big enough, with 15 miles of shoreline and little islands, coves and peninsulas to give it an intimate feel. Open May through October.

3. LONE ROCK   RV. 9

Reference: **At Antelope Lake in Plumas National Forest; map C4, grid e0.**

Campsites, facilities: There are 86 sites for tents or motor homes up to 45 feet long. Piped water, vault toilets, picnic tables and fire grills are provided. A sanitary dump station, boat ramp and grocery store are nearby. Pets are permitted on leashes.

Reservations, fee: Reserve by phoning (800) 280-CAMP ($7.50 reservation fee); $12-$14 fee per night.

Who to contact: Phone Plumas National Forest at (916) 283-0555.

Location: From Red Bluff, drive east on Highway 36 to Susanville and US 395. Turn south on US 395 and drive about 10 miles (one mile past Janesville) to County Road 208. Turn right on County Road 208 (signed Antelope Lake) and drive about 15 miles to a Y (one mile before Antelope Lake). Turn left at the Y and drive three miles to the campground entrance on the right side of the road (on the northwest end of the lake).

Trip note: This camp provides an option to nearby Boulder Creek Camp, located to the immediate north at the northwest shore of Antelope Lake. See trip note for preceding camp. The elevation is 5,000 feet. Campfire programs are offered in the summer at the camp's amphitheater. Open May through October.

---

4. LONG POINT

Reference: **At Antelope Lake in Plumas National Forest; map C4, grid e1.**

Campsites, facilities: There are 38 single sites and four group sites for tents or motor homes up to 50 feet long. Piped water, vault toilets, picnic tables and fire grills are provided. A grocery store, boat ramp and sanitary dump station are nearby. Pets are permitted on leashes.

Reservations, fee: Reserve by phoning (800) 280-CAMP ($7.50 reservation fee); $12-$14 fee per night; group sites are $20-$33 per night.

Who to contact: Phone Plumas National Forest at (916) 284-7126.

Location: From Red Bluff, drive east on Highway 36 to Susanville and US 395. Turn south on US 395 and drive about 10 miles (one mile past Janesville) to County Road 208. Turn right on County Road 208 (signed Antelope Lake) and drive about 15 miles to a Y (one mile before Antelope Lake). Turn right at the Y and drive one mile to the campground entrance on the left side of the road.

Trip note: Long Point is a pretty camp set on a peninsula that extends well into Antelope Lake, facing Lost Cove. There are actually two camps here, with a bonus group camp set on the east side of the main campground. The lake's boat ramp is at Lost Cove, a three mile drive around the lake's northeast shore. Trout fishing is often good here, with a wide variety of sizes, from the little stocked Slim Jim rainbow trout on up to some large brown trout. A **wheelchair-accessible** nature trail and fishing pier are available. Open May through October.

---

5. CONKLIN PARK

Reference: **On Willow Creek in Plumas National Forest; map C4, grid f2.**

Campsites, facilities: There are nine sites for tents or motor homes up to 22 feet long. There is **no piped water**, but vault toilets, picnic tables and fire grills are provided. Pets are permitted on leashes.

Reservations, fee: No reservations; no fee.

Who to contact: Phone Plumas National Forest at (916) 836-2575.

Location: From Susanville on US 395, drive south for 24 miles to Milford. In Milford, turn right (east) on County Road 336 and drive about four miles to a Y. Bear to the left on Forest Service Road 70/26N70 and drive three miles. Turn right at the bridge at Willow Creek, then turn left on Forest Service Road 70 (now paved) and drive three miles to the camp entrance road on the left side.

Trip note: This camp is located along little Willow Creek on the northeastern border of the Dixie Mountain State Game Refuge. Much of the area is recovering from a fire that burned during the summer of 1989. Although the area has greened up, there remains significant evidence of the fire. The campground is little-known, primitive, and rarely-used, and not likely to change any time soon. The elevation is 5,900 feet. Open May through October.

6. MEADOW VIEW   RV 6

Reference: **Near Last Chance Creek in Plumas National Forest; map C4, grid f4.**

Campsites, facilities: There are six sites for tents or motor homes. There is **no piped water**, but vault toilets, picnic tables and fire grills are provided. Pets are permitted on leashes.

Reservations, fee: No reservations; no fee.

Who to contact: Phone Plumas National Forest at (916) 836-2575.

Location: From Reno, drive north on US 395 for 43 miles to Doyle. At Doyle, turn west on Doyle Grade Road (County Road 331, a dirt road most of the way) and drive 7.5 miles to the campground.

Trip note: This little-known, primitive camp is set along the headwaters of Little Last Chance Creek, along the eastern border of the Dixie Mountain State Game Refuge. The access road continues along the creek, and connects with primitive roads that enter the interior of the game refuge. Side trip options include Frenchman Lake to the south, and the drive up to Dixie Mountain, 8,323 feet in elevation. Campground elevation is 6,100 feet. Open May through October.

7. LIGHTNING TREE   RV 7

Reference: **On Lake Davis in Plumas National Forest; map C4, grid g0.**

Campsites, facilities: There are 38 sites for motor homes. There is **no piped water** or toilets. A sanitary dump station and a car-top boat launch are nearby. Pets are permitted on leashes.

Reservations, fee: No reservations; no fee.

Who to contact: Phone Plumas National Forest at (916) 836-2575.

Location: From Truckee, turn north on Highway 89 and drive to Sattley and County Road A23. Turn right on County Road A23 and drive 13 miles to Highway 70. Turn left on Highway 70 and drive one mile to Grizzly Road. Turn right on Grizzly Road and drive about six miles to Davis Lake. Continue north on Davis Lake Road along the lake's east shore and drive about five miles to the campground entrance on the left side of the road.

Trip note: Davis Lake is one of the top mountain lakes for fishing in California, with large rainbow trout in the early summer and fall, and an improving bass fishery in the summer. This camp is set perfectly for a fishing trip. It is located at Lightning Tree Point on the lake's remote northeast shore, directly across the lake from Freeman Creek, one of the better spots for big trout. A boat launch is available on the north side of the camp, a great bonus. Davis is a good-sized lake, with 30 miles of shoreline. It is set high in the northern Sierra at 5,775 feet, so it gets lots of snow and freezes over in winter.

8. GRIZZLY 🐟 ⚓ 🏊 🎣   RV 7

Reference: **On Lake Davis in Plumas National Forest; map C4, grid g0.**

Campsites, facilities: There are 55 sites for tents or motor homes up to 32 feet long. Piped water, flush toilets, picnic tables and fire grills are provided. A boat ramp, a grocery store and a sanitary dump station are nearby. Pets are permitted on leashes.

Reservations, fee: No reservations; $12 fee per night.

Who to contact: Phone Plumas National Forest at (916) 836-2575.

Location: From Truckee, turn north on Highway 89 and drive to Sattley and County Road A23. Turn right on County Road A23 and drive 13 miles to Highway 70. Turn left on Highway 70 and drive one mile to Grizzly Road. Turn right on Grizzly Road and drive about six miles to Davis Lake. Continue north on Davis Lake Road for less than a mile to the campground entrance on the left side of the road.

Trip note: This is one of the better developed campgrounds at Lake Davis and is a popular spot for camping anglers. Its proximity to the Grizzly Store, located just over the dam to the south, makes getting last-minute supplies a snap. In addition, a boat ramp is located to the north in Honker Cove, providing access to the southern reaches of the lake, including the island area, where trout trolling is good in early summer and fall. Open May through October.

---

9. GRASSHOPPER FLAT 🐟 ⚓ 🏊 🎣   RV 7

Reference: **On Lake Davis in Plumas National Forest; map C4, grid g0.**

Campsites, facilities: There are 70 sites for tents or motor homes up to 32 feet long. Piped water, flush toilets, picnic tables and fire grills are provided. A boat ramp, grocery store and sanitary dump station are nearby. Pets are permitted on leashes.

Reservations, fee: No reservations; $12 fee per night.

Who to contact: Phone Plumas National Forest at (916) 836-2575.

Location: From Truckee, turn north on Highway 89 and drive to Sattley and County Road A23. Turn right on County Road A23 and drive 13 miles to Highway 70. Turn left on Highway 70 and drive one mile to Grizzly Road. Turn right on Grizzly Road and drive about six miles to Davis Lake. Continue north on Davis Lake Road for a mile (just past Grizzly Camp) to the campground entrance on the left side of the road.

Trip note: Grasshopper Flat provides a nearby alternative to Grizzly Camp at Davis, with the nearby boat ramp at adjacent Honker Cove a primary attraction for campers with trailered boats for fishing. The camp is set at the southeast end of the lake, 5,800 feet elevation. Davis Lake is known for its large rainbow trout that bite best in early summer and fall. Open May through October.

---

10. CROCKER 🐟   RV 5

Reference: **In Plumas National Forest; map C4, grid g1.**

Campsites, facilities: There are 10 sites for tents or motor homes up to 32 feet long. There is **no piped water**, but vault toilets, picnic tables and fire grills are provided. Pets are permitted on leashes.

Reservations, fee: No reservations; no fee.

Who to contact: Phone Plumas National Forest at (916) 836-2575.

Location: From Reno, drive north on US 395 to the junction with Highway 70.

Turn west on Highway 70 and drive to Beckwourth and County Road 111 (Beckwourth-Genessee Road). Turn right (north) on County Road 111 and drive six miles to the campground on the left side of the road.

Trip note: Even though this camp is located just four miles east of Davis Lake, it is little-known and little-used, with three lakeside camps available close by at Davis. This camp is set in Plumas National Forest at 5,800 feet elevation, and it is about a 15-minute drive north to the border of the Dixie Mountain State Game Refuge. Open May through October.

---

11. FRENCHMAN 🐟 ⚓ 🏊 🎣   RV 7

Reference: On Frenchman Lake in Plumas National Forest; map C4, grid g3.

Campsites, facilities: There are 38 sites for tents or motor homes. Piped water, vault toilets, picnic tables and fire grills are provided. A sanitary dump station and a boat ramp are nearby. Pets are permitted on leashes.

Reservations, fee: Reserve by phoning (800) 280-CAMP ($7.50 reservation fee); $12 fee per night.

Who to contact: Phone Plumas National Forest at (916) 836-2575.

Location: From Reno, drive north on US 395 to the junction with Highway 70. Turn west on Highway 70 and drive to Chilcoot and the junction with Frenchman Lake Road. Turn right on Frenchman Lake Road and drive nine miles to the lake and to a Y. At the Y, turn right and drive 1.5 miles to the campground on the left side of the road.

Trip note: Frenchman Lake is set at 5,500 feet elevation, on the edge of high desert to the east and forest to the west. This camp is set at the southeast end of the lake, where there are four other campgrounds, including a group camp and a boat ramp. The lake provides good fishing for stocked rainbow trout. The best fishing is in the cove near the campgrounds and the two inlets, one along the west shore and one at the head of the lake. The proximity to Reno, only 35 miles away, keeps gambling in the back of the minds of many anglers. Because of water demands downstream, the lake often drops significantly by the end of summer. Open May through October.

---

12. COTTONWOOD SPRINGS   RV 7
🐟 ⚓ 🏊 ♿

Reference: Near Frenchman Lake in Plumas National Forest; map C4, grid g3.

Campsites, facilities: There are 20 sites for tents or motor homes up to 50 feet long and two group camping areas. Piped water, flush toilets, picnic tables and fire grills are provided. A boat ramp and sanitary dump station are nearby. Pets are permitted on leashes.

Reservations, fee: Reserve by phoning (800) 280-CAMP ($7.50 reservation fee); $12 fee per night; $44-$87 fee per night for groups.

Who to contact: Phone Plumas National Forest at (916) 836-2575.

Location: From Reno, drive north on US 395 to the junction with Highway 70. Turn west on Highway 70 and drive to Chilcoot and the junction with Frenchman Lake Road. Turn right on Frenchman Lake Road and drive nine miles to the lake and to a Y. At the Y, turn left and drive 1.5 miles to the campground on the left side of the road.

Trip note: Cottonwood Springs, elevation 5,700 feet, is largely an overflow camp at Frenchman Lake. The more popular Big Cove, Spring Creek and Frenchman camps are located along the southeast shore of the lake near a boat ramp. Cottonwood Springs, on the other hand, is set on a creek about two miles from the dam. However, there is a great side trip here, taking Forest Service Road 24N52 out of camp to the southwest and driving through the Little Last Chance Canyon Scenic Area; the road deadends about seven miles in. Open May through October.

13. BIG COVE 🐟 ⚓ ♿ 🏊 🎣   🚐 ⛺

Reference: **At Frenchman Lake in Plumas National Forest; map C4, grid g3.**
Campsites, facilities: There are 38 sites for tents or motor homes up to 50 feet long (19 sites are multiple-family units; 11 sites are **wheelchair-accessible**). Piped water, flush toilets, picnic tables and fire grills are provided. A boat ramp, sanitary dump station, grocery store and propane gas are available nearby. Pets are permitted.
Reservations, fee: Reserve by phoning (800) 280-CAMP ($7.50 reservation fee); $12-$24 fee per night.
Who to contact: Phone Plumas National Forest at (916) 836-2575.
Location: From Reno, drive north on US 395 to the junction with Highway 70. Turn west on Highway 70 and drive to Chilcoot and the junction with Frenchman Lake Road. Turn right on Frenchman Lake Road and drive nine miles to the lake and to a Y. At the Y, turn right and drive two miles to Forest Service Road 24N01. Turn left and drive a short distance to the campground entrance on the left side of the road.
Trip note: Big Cove is one of four camps set in the southeastern end of Frenchman Lake, with a boat ramp available about a mile away, located near the Frenchman and Spring Creek Camps. See trip note for Frenchman Camp. Open May through September.

14. SPRING CREEK 🐟 ⚓ 🎣 ♿   🚐 ⛺

Reference: **On Frenchman Lake in Plumas National Forest; map C4, grid g4.**
Campsites, facilities: There are 35 sites for tents or motor homes up to 55 feet long. Piped water, vault toilets, picnic tables and fire grills are provided. A boat ramp and sanitary dump station are nearby. Pets are permitted on leashes.
Reservations, fee: Reserve by phoning (800) 280-CAMP ($7.50 reservation fee); $12 fee per night.
Who to contact: Phone Plumas National Forest at (916) 836-2575.
Location: From Reno, drive north on US 395 to the junction with Highway 70. Turn west on Highway 70 and drive to Chilcoot and the junction with Frenchman Lake Road. Turn right on Frenchman Lake Road and drive nine miles to the lake and to a Y. At the Y, turn right and drive two miles to the campground on the left side of the road.
Trip note: Frenchman Lake is set at 5,500 feet elevation, on the edge of high desert to the east and forest to the west. This camp is set at the southeast end of the lake, where there are four other campgrounds, including a group camp and a boat ramp. The lake provides good fishing for stocked rainbow trout, best in the cove near the campgrounds.

15. CHILCOOT 🐟 🚶 🏊 RV. 7

Reference: On Last Chance Creek in Plumas National Forest; map C4, grid h4.

Campsites, facilities: There are five sites for tents and 35 sites for tents or motor homes up to 45 feet long. Piped water, flush toilets, picnic tables and fire grills are provided. A boat ramp, grocery store and sanitary dump station are nearby. Pets are permitted on leashes.

Reservations, fee: Reserve by phoning (800) 280-CAMP ($7.50 reservation fee); $12 fee per night.

Who to contact: Phone Plumas National Forest at (916) 836-2575.

Location: From Reno, drive north on US 395 to the junction with Highway 70. Turn west on Highway 70 and drive to Chilcoot and the junction with Frenchman Lake Road. Turn right on Frenchman Lake Road and drive six miles to the campground on the left side of the road.

Trip note: This little camp is set along Little Last Chance Creek, 5,400 feet in elevation, about three miles downstream from Frenchman Lake. This stream once provided excellent trout fishing, but it is now largely overgrown with brush, making fishing access very difficult. Open May through October.

16. YUBA PASS 🚶 RV. 6

Reference: In Tahoe National Forest; map C4, grid j0.

Campsites, facilities: There are 20 sites for tents or motor homes up to 22 feet long. Piped water, vault toilets, picnic tables and fire grills are provided. Pets are permitted on leashes or otherwise controlled. Supplies are available in Bassetts.

Reservations, fee: No reservations; $9 fee per night.

Who to contact: Phone Tahoe National Forest at (916) 288-3231.

Location: From Truckee, drive north on Highway 89 past Sattley to the junction with Highway 49. Turn west on Highway 49 and drive about six miles to the campground on the left side of the road.

Trip note: This camp is set right at Yuba Pass at an elevation of 6,700 feet. In the winter, the surrounding area is a ski park, which gives it an unusual look in summer months. From Yuba Pass, a Forest Service road provides access to nearby Berry Creek to the south. Open June through November.

17. COTTONWOOD CREEK 🐟 🚶 ♨ RV. 7

Reference: In Tahoe National Forest; map C4, grid j1.

Campsites, facilities: There are 21 sites for tents and 28 sites for tents or motor homes up to 22 feet long. There is also a group camp that can accommodate up to 125 people. Piped water, vault toilets, picnic tables and fire grills are provided. Pets are permitted on leashes or otherwise controlled. Supplies are available in Sierraville.

Reservations, fee: Reserve by phoning (800) 280-CAMP ($7.50 reservation fee); $9 fee per night; $5 for each additional vehicle; group camp is $167.50 per night.

Who to contact: Phone Tahoe National Forest at (916) 288-3231, or California Land Management at (916) 582-0120.

Location: From Truckee, drive north on Highway 89 for about 20 miles to the campground entrance road (a half-mile past Cold Creek Camp). Turn right and drive a quarter-mile to the campground.

Trip note: This camp is set along the Cottonwood Creek at 5,800 feet. An interpretive trail starts at the camp and makes a short loop, and there are several nearby side trip options, including trout fishing on the Little Truckee River to the nearby south, visiting the Campbell Hot Springs out of Sierraville to the nearby north, or venturing into the surrounding Tahoe National Forest. Open May through October.

18. BEAR VALLEY 🎣 🚶

Reference: **On Bear Valley Creek in Tahoe National Forest; map C4, grid j2.**

Campsites, facilities: There are 10 tent sites. Piped water, vault toilets, picnic tables and fire grills are provided. Pets are permitted on leashes or otherwise controlled. Supplies are available in Sierraville.

Reservations, fee: No reservations; no fee.

Who to contact: Phone Tahoe National Forest at (916) 288-3231.

Location: From Truckee, drive north on Highway 89 to Sierraville and the junction with Highway 49. Turn right at that junction (the road becomes Lemon Canyon Road) and drive east for eight miles to the campground at a five-way Forest Service road junction. This road is not recommended for trailers.

Trip note: The surrounding national forest area was largely burned by the historic Cottonwood Fire of 1994, but the camp itself was saved. It is set on the headwaters of Bear Valley Creek, 6,700 feet in elevation, with a spring adjacent to the campground. The road leading southeast out of camp is routed to Sardine Peak (8,134 feet), where there is a dramatic view of the surrounding burned region. Open June through October.

19. LOOKOUT 🚶

Reference: **In Toiyabe National Forest; map C4, grid j4.**

Campsites, facilities: There are 15 sites for tents and four sites for tents or motor homes up to 22 feet long, plus a group camp which can accommodate up to 16 people. Pit toilets, picnic tables and fire grills are provided. **No piped water** is available. Pets are permitted on leashes or otherwise controlled.

Reservations, fee: No reservations; $3 fee per night; group fee is $7.50 per night.

Who to contact: Phone Toiyabe National Forest Headquarters, Carson Ranger District at (702) 882-2766.

Location: From Truckee on Interstate 80, drive east across the state line into Nevada to Verdi. Take the Verdi exit and drive north on Old Dog Valley Road for 11 miles to the campground entrance.

Trip note: This primitive camp is set in remote country near the California/Nevada border at 6,700 feet. It is a former mining site, and the highlight here is a quartz crystal mine a short distance from the camp. Stampede Reservoir provides a side trip option, about 10 miles to the southwest. Open June through September.

MAP DØ

NOR-CAL MAP .... see page 94
adjoining maps
NORTH (CØ) .... see page 232
EAST (D1) .... see page 326
SOUTH .... no map
WEST .... no map

20 LISTINGS
PAGES 316-325

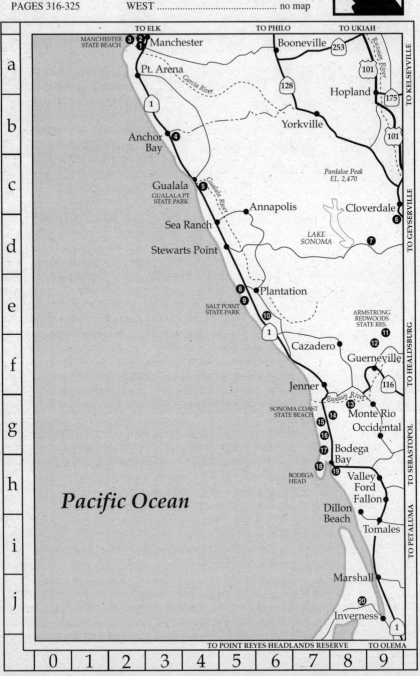

Pacific Ocean

Map DØ featuring: Sonoma County Regional Park, Lake Sonoma, Russian River, Sonoma Coast State Beach, Bodega Bay

1. MANCHESTER STATE BEACH

Reference: **Near Point Arena; map DØ, grid a2.**

Campsites, facilities: There are 48 sites for tents or motor homes up to 30 feet long. Piped water, chemical toilets, picnic tables and fire grills are provided. A sanitary dump station is available. No pets are allowed.

Reservations, fee: Reserve by phoning Destinet at (800) 444-7275 ($6.75 Destinet fee); $10-$12 fee per night; $1 pet fee.

Who to contact: Phone (707) 937-5804 or (707) 865-2391.

Location: From Santa Rosa on US 101, turn west on Highway 12 (it becomes Highway 116 at Forestville) and drive to Highway 1 at Jenner. Turn north on Highway 1 and drive 55 miles to Point Arena. From Point Arena, continue about two miles north to the park on the left side of the road.

Trip note: Manchester State Beach is a beautiful park on the Sonoma coast, set near the Garcia River with the town of Point Arena to the nearby north providing a supply point. If you hit it during one of the rare times when the skies are clear and the wind is down, the entire area will seem aglow in magical sunbeams. The Alder Creek Trail is a great hike here, routed north along beachfront to the mouth of Alder Creek and its beautiful coastal lagoon. This is where the San Andreas Fault heads off from land and into the sea. Open year-round.

2. MANCHESTER BEACH KOA

Reference: **North of Point Arena at Manchester State Beach; map DØ, grid a2.**

Campsites, facilities: There are 63 sites for motor homes, some with full or partial hookups. There are also 18 cabins and 44 tent sites. Restrooms, showers, a heated pool (seasonal), a hot tub and spa, a recreation room, a playground, a dump station, picnic tables and fire grills are provided. A grocery store, ice, wood, laundromat and propane gas are available. Pets are permitted.

Reservations, fee: Reservations accepted; $26-$32 fee per night for two people; each additional person is $5. Cabins are $36 per night.

Who to contact: Manchester Beach KOA, P.O. Box 266, Manchester, CA 95459; (707) 882-2375.

Location: From Santa Rosa on US 101, turn west on Highway 12 (it becomes Highway 116 at Forestville) and drive to Highway 1 at Jenner. Turn north on Highway 1 and drive 55 miles to Point Arena. From Point Arena continue north for about two miles to the park on the left side of the road.

Trip note: This is a privately-operated KOA park set beside Highway 1 and near the beautiful Manchester State Beach. A great plus here is the cute little log cabins, with electric heat provided. They can provide a great sense of privacy, and after a good sleep, campers are ready to explore the adjacent state park. Open year-round.

3. ROLLERVILLE JUNCTION ♿

Reference: **Near Point Arena; map DØ, grid a2.**

Campsites, facilities: There are 51 sites for tents or motor homes (12 are drive-through), 41 with full hookups. Restrooms, hot showers, a hot tub, a clubhouse with full kitchen, a playground, cable TV hookups, a sanitary dump station, picnic tables and fire grills are provided. A laundromat, a small store and propane gas are available. Pets are allowed on leashes. Facilities are **wheelchair accessible.**

Reservations, fee: Reservations accepted; $20-$24 fee per night.

Who to contact: Phone (707) 882-2440.

Location: From Santa Rosa on US 101, turn west on Highway 12 (it becomes Highway 116 at Forestville) and drive to Highway 1 at Jenner. Turn north on Highway 1 and drive 55 miles to Point Arena. From Point Arena, continue north for two miles to the campground.

Trip note: This privately-operated campground has gone through recent renovation, with more future improvements anticipated. Its location makes it an attractive spot, with the beautiful Manchester State Beach, Alder Creek and Garcia River all located nearby on one of California's most attractive stretches of coastline. Set at 220 feet elevation, and open year-round.

---

4. ANCHOR BAY CAMPGROUND 🌊 🚶

Reference: **Near Gualala; map DØ, grid b3.**

Campsites, facilities: There are 66 sites for tents or motor homes, many with water and electrical hookups. Restrooms, hot showers, a sanitary dump station, picnic tables and fire grills are provided. Pets are allowed on leashes.

Reservations, fee: Reservations accepted; $21-$25 fee per night.

Who to contact: Phone (707) 884-4222.

Location: From Santa Rosa on US 101, turn west on Highway 12 (it becomes Highway 116 at Forestville) and drive to Highway 1 at Jenner. Turn north on Highway 1 and drive 38 miles to Gualala. From Gualala, continue four miles north on Highway 1 to the campground on the left side of the road.

Trip note: This is a quiet and beautiful stretch of California coast. The campground is located on the oceanside of Highway 1 north of Gualala, with sites set on an ocean bluff as well as amid trees—take your pick. Nearby Gualala Regional Park provides an excellent easy hike, the headlands-to-beach loop with coastal views, a lookout of the Gualala River, and many giant cypress trees. In winter, the nearby Gualala River attracts large but elusive steelhead. Open year-round.

---

5. GUALALA POINT 🌊 🚶 ♿

Reference: **Sonoma County Regional Park; map DØ, grid c4.**

Campsites, facilities: There are 19 sites for tents and motor homes up to 28 feet long, six walk-in tent sites. Restrooms, a sanitary dump station, picnic tables and fire grills are provided. Wood is available. The facilities are **wheelchair accessible**. Pets are allowed on leashes.

Reservations, fee: No reservations; $3 fee per person for walk-in sites, $14 fee per night for other sites; $4 fee per extra vehicle; $1 pet fee.

Who to contact: Phone (707) 785-2377.

Location: From Santa Rosa on US 101, turn west on Highway 12 (it becomes

Highway 116 at Forestville) and drive to Highway 1 at Jenner. Turn north on Highway 1 and drive 38 miles to Gualala. Turn right at the park entrance (a day-use area is located on the west side of the highway).

Trip note: This is a dramatic spot right on the ocean, adjacent to the mouth of the Gualala River. A trail along the bluff provides an easy hiking adventure, and on the west side of the highway, other trails are available to the beach. Open year-round.

6. DUTCHER CREEK RV PARK & CAMP ✕

Reference: **Near Lake Sonoma; map DØ, grid d9.**

Campsites, facilities: There are 10 tent sites and 38 motor home sites (two are drive-through) with full or partial hookups. Picnic tables are provided. Flush toilets, showers, a sanitary disposal station and a laundromat are available. Pets are allowed on leashes.

Reservations, fee: Reservations accepted; $12-$18 fee per night.

Who to contact: Phone the park at (707) 894-4829.

Location: From Santa Rosa, drive north on US 101 beyond Healdsburg to the Dutcher Creek exit (just south of Cloverdale). Take the Dutcher Creek exit and drive west on Theresa Drive, under the freeway, continue a half-mile to the end of Theresa Drive and follow signs to the park office at 230 Theresa Drive.

Trip note: This privately-operated camp provides a layover for Highway 101 cruisers. It has both native and seasonal plant displays, and the nearby Asti Vineyard provides a side trip. Lake Sonoma is located to the west, with the best access provided to the south out of Dry Creek Road (see listing for Lake Sonoma). Elevation is 385 feet. Open year-round.

7. LAKE SONOMA RECREATION AREA 🐟 ⚓ 🚶 🏊 🎣

Reference: **Near Healdsburg; map DØ, grid d9.**

Campsites, facilities: There are 15 primitive boat-in sites around the lake, and 113 tent sites and two group sites at Liberty Glen Campground located 2.5 miles from the lake. Picnic tables, fire grills, and portable toilets are provided at the primitive sites, but **no piped water** is available. Piped water, flush toilets, solar-heated showers and a sanitary disposal station are available in Liberty Glen. A boat ramp and boat rentals are available. Saturday night campfire talks are held at the two amphitheaters during the summer. Campsites have limited facilities in winter. Pets are allowed on leashes.

Reservations, fee: Reservations accepted. No fee for primitive sites, but a permit is required from the visitor center. Liberty Glen fees are $12 per night; call for group fees and reservations.

Who to contact: Phone the U.S. Army Corps of Engineers, Lake Sonoma at (707) 433-9483.

Location: From Santa Rosa, drive north on US 101 to Healdsburg. In Healdsburg, take the Dry Creek Road exit, turn left and drive northwest for 11 miles. After crossing a small bridge, the visitor center will be on your right side.

Trip note: Lake Sonoma is rapidly becoming one of the best weekend vacation sites for Bay Area campers. The developed campground (Liberty Glen) is fine for car campers, but the boat-in sites are ideal for folks who desire a quiet and pretty lakeside setting. This is a big lake, extending nine miles north on the Dry Creek arm and four miles west on the Warm Springs Creek arm. There is an adjacent 8,000-acre wildlife area with 40 miles of hiking trails. The waterskiers vs. fishermen conflict has been resolved by limiting high-speed boats to specified areas. Laws are strictly enforced, making this lake excellent for either sport. The best fishing is in the protective coves of the Warm Springs and Dry Creek arms of the lake; use live minnows for bass, which are available at the Dry Creek Store located on the access road south of the lake. The visitor center is adjacent to a public fish hatchery. Salmon and steelhead come to spawn from the Russian River between October and March. Open year-round.

8. SALT POINT STATE PARK

Reference: **Map DØ, grid e5.**

Campsites, facilities: There are 109 sites for tents or motor homes up to 31 feet long, 20 walk-in tent sites, 10 hiker/biker sites, and one group camp. Picnic tables, fire grills and piped water are provided. Flush and pit toilets and a sanitary disposal station are available. The picnic areas and some hiking trails are **wheelchair accessible**. Pets are allowed on leashes, except on trails.

Reservations, fee: Reserve by phoning Destinet at (800) 444-7275 ($6.75 Destinet fee); $6-$17 fee per night.

Who to contact: Phone the park at (707) 847-3221 or (707) 865-2391.

Location: From Santa Rosa on US 101, turn west on Highway 12 (it becomes Highway 116 at Forestville) and drive to Highway 1 at Jenner. Turn north on Highway 1 and drive about 20 miles to the park entrance at Gerstle Cove.

Trip note: This is a gorgeous piece of Sonoma Coast, highlighted by Fisk Mill Cove, inshore kelp beds, outstanding short hikes and abalone diving. Great hikes include the Bluff Trail and Stump Beach Trail (great views, but crowded). During abalone season, this is one of the best and most popular spots on the Northern California coast. Camp reservations are advised. Open year-round.

9. OCEAN COVE CAMPGROUND

Reference: **Near Fort Ross; map DØ, grid e5.**

Campsites, facilities: There are 115 sites for tents or motor homes. Piped water, picnic tables, fire grills, cold showers and chemical toilets are provided. A boat launch, a grocery store, fishing supplies and diving gear rentals are available. Pets are permitted.

Reservations, fee: No reservations; $11 fee per night; $1 pet fee.

Who to contact: Phone the campground store at (707) 847-3422.

Location: From Santa Rosa on US 101, turn west on Highway 12 (it becomes Highway 116 at Forestville) and drive to Highway 1 at Jenner. Turn north on Highway 1 and drive 17 miles north on Highway 1 (five miles north of Fort Ross) to the campground entrance.

Trip note: The highlights here are the campsites on a bluff overlooking the ocean. Alas, it can be foggy during the summer. A good side trip is to Fort Ross, with a stellar easy hike available on the Fort Ross Trail, which features a walk through an old colonial fort as well as great coastal views. There is also excellent hiking at Stillwater Cove Regional Park, located just a mile to the south off Highway 1. Open April through November.

10. STILLWATER COVE REGIONAL PARK   RV 8

Reference: **Near Fort Ross; map DØ, grid e6.**

Campsites, facilities: There are 23 sites for tents or motor homes up to 35 feet long. Picnic tables, fire grills and piped water are provided. Flush toilets, showers, and a sanitary disposal station are available. Pets are permitted. Supplies can be obtained in Ocean Cove (one mile north) and Fort Ross. The facilities are **wheelchair accessible**.

Reservations, fee: No reservations; $14 fee per night, $4 for each additional vehicle; $1 pet fee.

Who to contact: Phone the park at (707) 847-3245.

Location: From Santa Rosa on US 101, turn west on Highway 12 (it becomes Highway 116 at Forestville) and drive to Highway 1 at Jenner. Turn north on Highway 1 and drive 16 miles north on Highway 1 (four miles north of Fort Ross) to the park entrance.

Trip note: Stillwater Cove has a dramatic rock-strewn cove and sits on a classic chunk of Sonoma coast. The campground is sometimes overlooked, since it is a county-operated park and not on the state's Destinet reservation system. One of the region's great hikes is available here, the Stockoff Creek Loop, with the trailhead located at the day-use parking lot. In little over a mile, the trail is routed through forest with both firs and redwoods, and then along a pretty stream. To get beach access, you will need to cross Highway 1, then drop down to the cove. Open year-round.

11. AUSTIN CREEK STATE   RV 7
   RECREATION AREA

Reference: **Near Russian River; map DØ, grid e9.**

Campsites, facilities: There are 24 sites for tents or motor homes up to 20 feet long. No trailers are allowed. (The access road is very narrow.) Picnic tables, fire grills, piped water and flush toilets are provided. Pets are permitted on leashes in the main campground. There are also four primitive, hike-in, backcountry campsites with tables, fire rings and pit toilets, but **no piped water** is available and no pets are permitted. The camps are 2.5 to four miles from the main campground. Obtain a backcountry camping permit from the office.

Reservations, fee: No reservations; $10-$12 fee per night; $1 pet fee.

Who to contact: Phone the park at (707) 869-2015 or (707) 865-2391.

Location: From Santa Rosa on US 101, turn west on Highway 12 (it becomes Highway 116 at Forestville) to Guerneville. At Armstrong Woods Road, turn right and drive 2.5 miles to the entrance of Armstrong Redwoods State Park. Continue 3.5 miles through Armstrong Redwoods to Austin Creek State Recreation Area to the campground.

Trip note: Austin Creek State Recreation Area and Armstrong Redwoods State Park are actually coupled, forming 5,000 acres of continuous parkland. Most visitors prefer the redwood park. The highlight at the Recreation Area is hiking trails that lead to a series of small creeks: Stonehouse Creek, Gilliam Creek and Austin Creek. They involve pretty steep climbs, and in the summer, it's hot here. There are many attractive side-trip possibilities, including the adjacent Armstrong Redwoods, of course, but also canoeing on the Russian River, fishing (smallmouth bass in summer, steelhead in winter), and wine tasting.

12. FAERIE RING CAMPGROUND

Reference: **Near Russian River; map DØ, grid e9.**

Campsites, facilities: There are 41 sites for tents or motor homes up to 31 feet long, four with full hookups. Picnic tables and fire grills are provided. Piped water, flush toilets, showers and a sanitary disposal station are available. Pets are allowed on leashes.

Reservations, fee: Reservations accepted; $10 fee per night (adults); $4 fee for kids.

Who to contact: Phone the park at (707) 869-2746.

Location: From Santa Rosa on US 101, turn west on Highway 12 (it becomes Highway 116 at Forestville) to Guerneville. At Armstrong Woods Road, turn right and drive 1.8 miles to the campground.

Trip note: If location is everything, then this privately operated campground is set right in the middle of the best of it in the Russian River region. It is one mile north of the Russian River and less than a mile south of Armstrong Redwoods State Park.

---

13. CASINI RANCH FAMILY CAMPGROUND

Reference: **On Russian River; map DØ, grid f8.**

Campsites, facilities: There are 225 sites for tents and motor homes (28 drive-through), many with full or partial hookups. Picnic tables and fire grills are provided. Flush toilets, showers, a playground, a sanitary disposal station, a laundromat, cable TV, a video arcade, a game arcade, boat and canoe rentals, propane gas and a grocery store are available. Some facilities are **wheelchair accessible**. Pets are allowed on leashes.

Reservations, fee: Reservations recommended; $17-$24 fee per night.

Who to contact: Phone (707) 865-2255, or (800) 451-8400 for reservations.

Location: From Santa Rosa on US 101, turn west on Highway 12 (it becomes Highway 116 at Forestville) to Duncan Mills. In Duncan Mills, turn southeast on Moscow Road and drive a half-mile to the campground.

Trip note: Woods and water, this campground has both, with campsites set near the Russian River in both sun-filled or shaded sites. Its location on the lower river makes a side trip to the coast easy, with the Sonoma Coast State Beach about a 15-minute drive to the nearby west. Open year-round.

---

14. POMO CANYON WALK-IN

Reference: **In Sonoma Coast State Beach; map DØ, grid g7.**

Campsites, facilities: There are 20 walk-in tent sites. Picnic tables and fire grills are provided. Piped water and pit toilets are available. No pets are permitted.

Reservations, fees: No reservations; $9 fee per night, $2 fee per night each additional vehicle.

Who to contact: Phone Sonoma Coast State Beach at (707) 875-3483 or write to 3095 Highway 1, Bodega Bay, CA 94923.

Location: From San Francisco, drive north of US 101 to Petaluma. In Petaluma, take the East Washington exit. Turn west on Bodega Avenue (it merges) and drive through Petaluma for 26 miles to Bodega Bay, where the road merges with Highway 1. Continue north on Highway 1 past Bodega Bay for about 10 miles. Turn east (right) on Willow Creek Road and drive about three miles to the campground. Reaching the campsites requires a one- to five-minute walk.

Trip note: This is a gorgeous camp, well-hidden, and offers a great trailhead and nearby beach access. The camp is actually not on the coast at all, but on the east-facing slope of Pomo Canyon (just over the ridge from the coast), where the campsites are set within a beautiful second-growth redwood forest. A trail is routed through the redwoods (with many cathedral trees) and up to the ridge, where there are divine views of the mouth of the Russian River, Goat Rock, and the beautiful Sonoma coast. The trail continues all the way to Shell Beach, where you can spend hours poking around and beachcombing. The camp's seclusion and proximity to the Bay Area make it a rare winner.

15. BODEGA DUNES CAMPGROUND   RV 8

Reference: **In Sonoma Coast State Beach; map DØ, grid g7.**

Campsites, facilities: There are 98 sites for tents or motor homes up to 31 feet long. Picnic tables, fire grills and piped water are provided. Flush toilets, showers and a sanitary disposal station are available. Pets are permitted on leashes except on trails. A laundromat, supplies and horse rentals are available nearby.

Reservations, fee: Reserve by phoning Destinet at (800) 444-7275 ($6.75 Destinet fee); $14-$16 fee per night; $1 pet fee.

Who to contact: Phone the Sonoma Coast State Beach at (707) 875-3483 or (707) 865-2391.

Location: From Petaluma on US 101, take the Washington Boulevard exit and drive west through Petaluma (it becomes Bodega Avenue) and continue to Highway 1. Turn north on Highway 1 and drive to Bodega Bay. In Bodega Bay, drive one mile north to the campground entrance.

Trip note: Sonoma Coast State Beach features several great campgrounds, and if you like the beach, this one rates high. It is set at the end of a beach that stretches for miles, providing stellar beach walks and excellent beachcombing during low tides. To the nearby south is Bodega Bay, including a major deep sea sportfishing operation with excellent salmon fishing in June and July, and outstanding prospects for rockfish and lingcod from August through November. The town of Bodega Bay offers a full marina and restaurants.

16. WRIGHTS BEACH CAMPGROUND   RV 8

Reference: **In Sonoma Coast State Beach; map DØ, grid g7.**

Campsites, facilities: There are 30 sites for tents or motor homes up to 27 feet long. Picnic tables, fire grills, piped water and flush toilets are provided. Pets are permitted.

Reservations, fee: Reserve by phoning Destinet at (800) 444-7275 ($6.75 Destinet fee); $20-$22 fee per night; $1 pet fee.

Who to contact: Phone the Sonoma Coast State Beach at (707) 875-3483 or (707) 865-2391.

Location: From Petaluma on US 101, take the Washington Boulevard exit and drive west through Petaluma (it becomes Bodega Avenue) and continue to Highway 1. Turn north on Highway 1 and drive to Bodega Bay. In Bodega Bay, drive six miles north to the campground entrance.

Trip note: This state park campground is at the north end of a beach that stretches south for several miles, yet to the north, it is steep and rocky. There are many excellent side trips. The best is to the north, where you can explore dramatic Shell Beach (the turnoff is on the west side of Highway 1), or take the Pomo-Ohlone (trailhead on the east side of the highway, across from Shell Beach) up the adjacent foothills for sweeping views of the coast.

17. BODEGA BAY RV PARK

Reference: **In Bodega Bay, map DØ, grid h7.**

Campsites, facilities: There are 64 sites for motor homes, 37 with full hookups. Picnic tables, fire grills, piped water, flush toilets and showers are provided. A laundromat, volleyball court and horseshoes are available. Pets are permitted.

Reservations, fee: Reservations recommended; $22 fee per night for two people; $2 for each additional person.

Who to contact: Bodega Bay RV Park, 2000 Highway One, P.O. Box 96, Bodega Bay, CA 94923; (707) 875-3701 or fax to (707) 875-9811.

Location: From Petaluma on US 101, take the Washington Boulevard exit and drive west through Petaluma (it becomes Bodega Avenue) and continue to Highway 1. Turn north on Highway 1 and drive to Bodega Bay. In Bodega Bay, continue north for 1.2 miles past the Union 76 station to the RV park.

Trip note: This is one of the oldest RV parks in the state, and there are few coastal destinations better than Bodega Bay. Excellent seafood restaurants are available within five minutes, some of the best deep sea fishing is available out of Bodega Bay Sportfishing, and there is a great view of the ocean at nearby Bodega Head to the west. What more could you want?

18. WESTSIDE REGIONAL PARK

Reference: **On Bodega Bay; map DØ, grid h7.**

Campsites, facilities: There are 47 sites for tents or motor homes. Piped water, picnic tables and fire grills are provided. Flush toilets, showers, a sanitary disposal station, a fish-cleaning station and a boat ramp are available. Pets are permitted on leashes. Supplies can be obtained in Bodega Bay.

Reservations, fee: No reservations; $14 fee per night; $1 pet fee.

Who to contact: Phone Sonoma County Parks Department at (707) 875-3540.

Location: From Petaluma on US 101, take the Washington Boulevard exit and drive west through Petaluma (it becomes Bodega Avenue) and continue to Highway 1. Turn north on Highway 1 and drive to Bodega Bay. In Bodega Bay, continue north to Bay Flat Road. Turn left on Bay Flat Road and drive two miles (looping around the bay) to the campground on the right.

Trip note: This campground is located on the west shore of Bodega Bay. One of the great boat launches on the coast is nearby to the south, providing access to prime fishing waters. Salmon fishing is excellent from mid-June through August. A small, protected beach (for kids to dig in the sand and wade) is available at the end of the road beyond the campground.

19. DORAN REGIONAL PARK

Reference: **On Bodega Bay; map DØ, grid h8.**

Campsites, facilities: There are 10 sites for tents and 124 sites for tents or motor homes. Picnic tables, fire grills and piped water are provided. Flush toilets, showers, sanitary disposal stations, a fish-cleaning station and a boat ramp are available. Pets are permitted on leashes. Supplies can be obtained in Bodega Bay.

Reservations, fee: No reservations; $14 fee per night; $1 pet fee.

Who to contact: Phone Sonoma County Parks Department at (707) 875-3540.

Location: From Petaluma on US 101, take the Washington Boulevard exit and drive west through Petaluma (it becomes Bodega Avenue) and continue to Highway 1. Turn north on Highway 1 and drive toward Bodega Bay and look for the campground entrance on the right. (If you reach the town of Bodega Bay, you have gone one mile too far).

Trip note: This campground is set beside Doran Beach on Bodega Bay, which offers complete fishing and marina facilities. In season, it's also a popular clamming and crabbing spot. Salmon fishing is often excellent during the summer months at the Whistle Buoy offshore from Bodega Head and rockfishing is good year-round at Cordell Bank. Fishing is also available off the rock jetty in the park. Open year-round.

---

20. TOMALES BAY STATE PARK WALK-IN

Reference: Map DØ, grid j8.

Campsites, facilities: There are 10 tent sites for hikers and bicyclists only. Piped water is provided. No pets are allowed.

Reservations, fee: No reservations; $15-$17 fee per night.

Who to contact: Phone (415) 669-1140 or (415) 456-1286.

Location: From Marin on US 101, take the Sir Francis Drake Boulevard exit. Turn west and drive about 20 miles to the town of Olema. Turn right on Highway 1 and drive a short distance, then turn left at Bear Valley Road and drive north for 8.2 miles to Pierce Ranch Road (Bear Valley Road rejoins with Sir Francis Drake). Turn right and drive 1.2 miles to the access road for Tomales Bay State Park. Turn right and drive 1.5 miles to the park entrance.

Trip note: Few know of this tiny campground, not even the many bicyclists touring Highway 1 who are looking for exactly such a spot. This camp is for hikers and bikers only. The park is on the secluded western shore of Tomales Bay, pretty, quiet and protected from the coastal winds. The park offers good hiking, picnicking and, during low tides, clamming (make sure you have a fishing license). There are several excellent hikes in this park, including the Johnstone Trail that ranges from Heart's Desire Beach to Shell Beach and beyond, and the Indian Nature Trail.

MAP D1

NOR-CAL MAP .... see page 94
adjoining maps
NORTH (C1) .... see page 248
EAST (D2) .... see page 346
SOUTH (E1) .... see page 418
WEST (DØ) .... see page 316

45 LISTINGS
PAGES 326-345

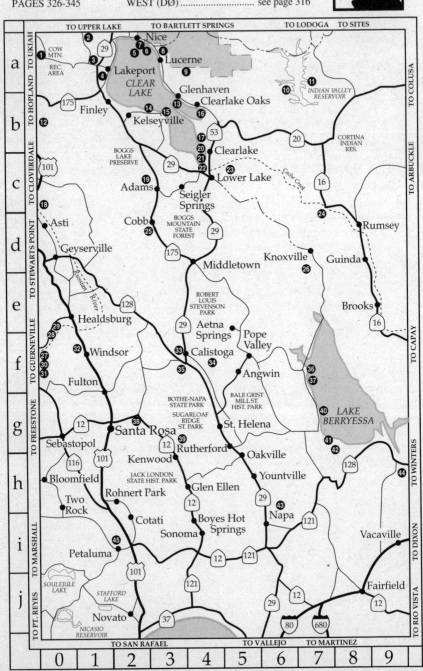

Map D1 featuring: Clear Lake, Russian River, Cache Creek, Lake Berryessa

1. RED MOUNTAIN 🏃🏇   🔺3

Reference: **Near Ukiah; map D1, grid a0.**

Campsites, facilities: There are 10 tent sites. Piped water, vault toilets, picnic tables and fire grills are provided. Pets are permitted on leashes or otherwise controlled.

Reservations, fee: No reservations; no fee.

Who to contact: Phone the Bureau of Land Management, Ukiah District at (707) 468-4000.

Location: From Ukiah on US 101, drive to Talmage Road. Turn east and drive 1.5 miles to Eastside Road. Turn right and drive a short distance to Mill Creek Road. Turn left and drive nine miles to the campground.

Trip note: Like Mayacmus Campground in Chapter C1, this camp is also set in the Cow Mountain Area east of Ukiah, but be forewarned: This is a popular spot for off-road motorcycles. If you don't like bikes, go to the other camp. Besides motorcycle trails, there are opportunities for hiking, horseback riding and hunting.

2. KELLY'S KAMP 🐟 🏊   RV 🔺6

Reference: **On Scotts Creek near Clear Lake; map D1, grid a1.**

Campsites, facilities: There are 75 sites for tents or motor homes, many with full or partial hookups. Picnic tables and fire grills are provided. Flush toilets, showers, a sanitary disposal station, a laundromat, ice and a small camp store are available. Pets are allowed on leashes.

Reservations, fee: Reservations accepted; $15-$17 fee per night.

Who to contact: Phone the park at (707) 263-5754.

Location: From Ukiah on US 101, drive north to the junction with Highway 20. Turn east and drive 14 miles (five miles from Upper Lake) to Scotts Valley Road. Turn south and drive to the park at 8220 Scotts Valley Road.

Trip note: This privately-operated park is set beside Scotts Creek, within short driving range of Blue Lakes to the north on Highway 20 and the north end of Clear Lake to the south. Closed November through March.

3. U-WANNA CAMP 🐟♿   RV 🔺3

Reference: **Near Clear Lake; map D1, grid a1.**

Campsites, facilities: There are 30 sites for tents or motor homes (four drive-through), with full or partial hookups. Picnic tables, fire grills, restrooms, showers, a sanitary disposal station, a laundromat, a playground and a recreation room are provided. Pets are allowed on leashes.

Reservations, fee: Reservations accepted; $14.50 fee per night; $1 pet fee.

Who to contact: Phone the park at (707) 263-6745.

Location: From Highway 29 in Lakeport, drive to 11th Street. Turn west and drive a half-mile to Riggs Road. Turn left on Riggs Road and drive three-quarters of a mile to Scotts Creek Road. Turn right and drive three-quarters of a mile to the campground at 2699 Scotts Creek Road.

Trip note: Whether U-Wanna or not, this could be where you end up if you're hunting for a site on a good-weather summer weekend. The camp is set about two miles from Clear Lake, with a boat ramp at nearby Lakeport. A small fishing pond for kids here is a plus. Open year-round.

4. WILL-O-POINT RESORT

Reference: On Clear Lake; map D1, grid a1.

Campsites, facilities: There are 124 sites for tents or motor homes, 10 motor home sites with full hookups and 10 cabins. Restrooms, showers, a boat ramp, a laundromat, a game room, jet ski rentals, fishing supplies, propane gas, a restaurant and a small grocery store are available. Pets are allowed on leashes.

Reservations, fee: Reservations required; $17-$20 fee per night; cabins are $60-$71 per night; $3 pet fee.

Who to contact: Phone the park at (707) 263-5407.

Location: In Lakeport on Highway 29 (which becomes Main Street in town), drive to First Street. The camp is on the corner of Main Street and First Street.

Trip note: Will-o-Point Resort is an attractive spot on Clear Lake, with a public park nearby that offers picnic facilities and a children's playground. There are two beaches within walking distance of the campsites. Tent cabins are available. Possible side trips include visiting the nearby Chateau du Lac/Kendall-Jackson Winery. The nearby shore is a good area for bass fishing, and the resort occasionally hosts fishing tournaments. Open year-round.

5. SANDPIPER SHORES

Reference: On Clear Lake; map D1, grid a2.

Campsites, facilities: There are 30 motor home sites with full or partial hookups. Picnic tables, restrooms, showers and a boat ramp are provided. Moorings, a pier, a laundromat and propane gas are available. Pets are allowed on leashes.

Reservations, fee: Reservations accepted; $16 fee per night.

Who to contact: Phone the park at (707) 274-4448.

Location: From Ukiah on US 101, drive north to the junction with Highway 20. Turn east on Highway 20 and drive to the town of Nice and Hammond Avenue. Turn south and drive a half-mile to Lakeshore Boulevard. Turn left (east) and drive to 2630 Lakeshore Boulevard.

Trip note: Sandpiper Shores provides boating access to the northern end of Clear Lake. Fishing for catfish is good near here, both in Rodman Slough and just outside the mouth of Rodman Slough. This is where the legendary Catfish George Powers caught 4,000 to 5,000 catfish per year, using dead minnows for bait. In addition, the old submerged pilings in this area provide good bass fishing for boaters casting spinner baits. Several beaches are also available at the north end of the lake.

6. NORTH SHORE RESORT AND MARINA

Reference: On Clear Lake; map D1, grid a2.

Campsites, facilities: There are 10 sites for tents or motor homes, with full or partial hookups. Picnic tables and fire grills are provided. Restrooms, showers, a laundromat, a boat ramp, a pier and a bookstore are available. Pets are allowed on leashes.

Reservations, fee: Reservations accepted; $18 fee per night.

Who to contact: Phone the park at (707) 274-7771.

Location: From Ukiah on US 101, drive north to the junction with Highway 20. Turn east on Highway 20 and drive to the town of Nice and Hammond Avenue. Turn south on Hammond Avenue and drive a half-mile to Lakeshore Boulevard. Turn right (west) and drive to 2345 Lakeshore Boulevard.

Trip note: This is one of a half-dozen privately-run parks in the immediate vicinity.

---

7. HOLIDAY HARBOR RV PARK

Reference: On Clear Lake; map D1, grid a2.

Campsites, facilities: There are 30 motor home sites with full or partial hookups. An enclosed marina with 150 boat slips, a boat ramp and an adjacent beach are available. Picnic tables, restrooms, showers, a recreation room and a sanitary disposal station are provided. A laundromat and ice are available. Pets are allowed on leashes.

Reservations, fee: Reservations accepted; $16 fee per night.

Who to contact: Phone the park at (707) 274-1136.

Location: From north of Ukiah on US 101, drive north to the junction with Highway 20. Turn east on Highway 20 and drive to the town of Nice and Hammond Avenue. Turn south on Hammond Avenue and drive a half-mile to Lakeshore Boulevard. Turn left (east) and drive to 3605 Lakeshore Boulevard.

Trip note: This is one of the most popular resorts at the north end of Clear Lake. It is ideal for boaters, with a full-service marina and a major docking complex. Fishing for bass is good in this area, along old docks and submerged pilings. Waterskiing just offshore is also good, with the north end of the lake often more calm than the water to points south. The elevation is about 2,000 feet.

---

8. ARROW TRAILER PARK

Reference: On Clear Lake; map D1, grid a3.

Campsites, facilities: There are 24 sites for motor homes, many with full or partial hookups. Restrooms, showers, a laundromat, boat rentals, moorings, fishing supplies, a boat ramp, a grocery store, beer, wine and ice are available. Pets are allowed on leashes.

Reservations, fee: Reservations accepted; $18 fee per night.

Who to contact: Phone the park at (707) 274-7715 or write to PO Box 1735, Lucerne, CA 95458.

Location: From north of Ukiah on US 101 or from Williams on Interstate 5, turn on Highway 20 and drive to Clear Lake and the town of Lucerne. Look for the campground at 6720 East Highway 20.

Trip note: Lucerne is known for its harbor and its long stretch of well-kept, public beaches along the shore of Clear Lake. The town offers a shopping district, restaurants and cafes. In summer months, crappie fishing is good at night from the boat docks, as long as there are bright lights to attracts gnats, which in turn attract minnows, the prime food for crappie.

9. LAKEVIEW CAMPGROUND 👭

Reference: **Near Clear Lake in Mendocino National Forest; map D1, grid a4.**

Campsites, facilities: There are nine sites for tents or motor homes. There is **no piped water**, but picnic tables, fire grills and vault toilets are provided. Pets are permitted on leashes or otherwise controlled.

Reservations, fee: No reservations; no fee.

Who to contact: Phone the Mendocino National Forest Upper Lake Ranger Station at (707) 275-2361.

Location: From north of Ukiah on US 101 or from Williams on Interstate 5, turn west on Highway 20 and drive to Clear Lake. Drive two miles north of the town of Lucerne to Bartlett Springs Road (Forest Service Road 8). Turn east on Bartlett Springs Road and drive five miles to High Valley Road (Forest Service Road 15N09). Turn southwest and drive three miles to the camp.

Trip note: When Clear Lake is packed to the rafters with campers, this spot offers a perfect alternative, if you don't mind roughing it a bit. It is set at 3,400 feet (above the town of Lucerne) overlooking the lake. A trail from camp leads down to the town; it's a two-mile hike, but most folks wouldn't want to make the uphill, return trip, especially on a hot summer day. Options include fishing and boating at Clear Lake, of course, but also venturing east on Bartlett Springs Road to the north end of remote Indian Valley Reservoir, where there is excellent fishing for bass. Open May to mid-October.

---

10. BLUE OAK 🎣 ⚓ 👭 🏊

Reference: **At Indian Valley Reservoir; map D1, grid a6.**

Campsites, facilities: There are five sites for tents or motor homes. Picnic tables and fire rings are provided. Piped water and pit toilets are available.

Reservations, fee: No reservations; no fee; 14-day stay limit.

Who to contact: Phone the Clear Lake Resource Area at (707) 468-4000, or write Bureau of Land Management, 2550 North State Street, Ukiah, CA 95482. A detailed map is available from the BLM.

Location: From Williams on Interstate 5, turn west on Highway 20 and drive 25 miles into the foothills to Walker Ridge Road. Turn north on Walker Ridge Road (a dirt road) and drive north for about four miles to a "major" intersection of two dirt roads. Turn left and drive about 2.5 miles toward the Indian Valley Dam. The Blue Oak Campground is located just off the road to your right, about 1.5 miles from Indian Valley Reservoir.

Trip note: Indian Valley Reservoir is kind of like an ugly dog that you love more than anything because inside it beats a heart that will never betray you. The camp is out in the middle of nowhere in oak woodlands, about a mile from the dam. It is primitive and little-known. For many, that kind of isolation is perfect. While there are good trails nearby, it is the outstanding fishing for bass and bluegill at the lake every spring and early summer that is the key reason to make the trip.

---

11. WINTUN 👭

Reference: **Near Indian Valley Reservoir; map D1, grid a6.**

Campsites, facilities: There is one primitive tent site with a picnic table and a fire ring. Piped water and pit toilets are available.

Reservations, fee: No reservations; no fee.

Who to contact: Phone Clear Lake Resource Area at (707) 468-4000, or write Bureau of Land Management, 2550 North State Street, Ukiah, CA 95482. A detailed map is available from the BLM.

Location: From Williams on Interstate 5, turn west on Highway 20 and drive 25 miles into the foothills to Walker Ridge Road. Turn north on Walker Ridge Road (a dirt road) and drive north for about four miles to a "major" intersection of two dirt roads. Continue straight on Walker Ridge Road for another five miles. At the sign for Wintun Camp, turn left and drive about one mile on a spur road that deadends at the campground. Note: To reach Indian Valley Reservoir from Wintun Camp, you must backtrack one mile, then turn left on Walker Ridge Road and drive eight or nine miles to the north end of the lake.

Trip note: If you want to feel like you are out in the middle of nowhere without being out in the middle of nowhere, then this camp answers your call. Wintun Camp is the smallest and most obscure camp anywhere, yet it has excellent trails nearby for hiking and biking and is about a 20-minute drive away from the north end of Indian Valley Reservoir (which has outstanding bass fishing). Note: Summer temperatures can burn you into a crispy enchilada, so bring a tarp that you can rig for shade cover.

---

12. SHELDON CREEK

Reference: Near Hopland; map D1, grid b0.

Campsites, facilities: There are six sites for tents. Piped water, vault toilets, picnic tables and fire grills are provided. Pets are permitted on leashes or otherwise controlled.

Reservations, fee: No reservations; no fee.

Who to contact: Phone the Bureau of Land Management, Ukiah District at (707) 462-3873.

Location: From Santa Rosa on US 101, drive north to Hopland and the junction with Highway 175. Turn east on Highway 175 and drive three miles to Old Toll Road. Turn right (south) on Old Toll Road and drive eight miles to the camp.

Trip note: Only the locals know about this spot, and hey, there aren't a lot of locals around. The camp is set amid rolling hills, grasslands and oaks, along little Sheldon Creek. It is pretty and quiet in the spring when the hills have greened up, but hot in the summer. Recreational possibilities include hiking, horseback riding (bring your own horse, pardner), and in the fall, hunting.

---

13. GLENHAVEN BEACH CAMP & MARINA

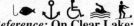

Reference: On Clear Lake; map D1, grid b3.

Campsites, facilities: There are 21 sites for motor homes up to 26 feet long, with full or partial hookups. Picnic tables, fire grills, restrooms, showers and a recreation room are provided. A boat ramp and boat rentals are available. Pets are allowed on leashes.

Reservations, fee: Reservations accepted; $16-$18 fee per night.

Who to contact: Phone the park at (707) 998-3406.

Location: From north of Ukiah on US 101 or Interstate 5 at Williams, turn on Highway 20 and drive to Clear Lake and the town of Glenhaven (four miles northwest of Clearlake Oaks). In Glenhaven, drive to the camp at 9625 East Highway 20.

Trip note: This makes a good base camp for all boaters, waterskiers and fishermen. It is set on a peninsula on the eastern shore of Clear Lake, with nearby Indian Beach providing a good recreation and waterplay spot. In addition, it is a short boat ride out to Anderson Island, Weekend Island and Buckingham Point, where bass fishing can be excellent along shaded tules. Open February through November.

14. CLEAR LAKE STATE PARK

Reference: **Map D1, grid b3.**

Campsites, facilities: There are 147 sites for tents or motor homes, located in four campgrounds, and several primitive hike-in or bike-in sites. Picnic tables, fire grills, restrooms, showers, a sanitary disposal station and a boat ramp are available. A grocery store, a laundromat, and propane gas are nearby. Pets are permitted. The boat ramp, picnic area and some campsites are **wheelchair accessible**.

Reservations, fee: Reserve by phoning Destinet at (800) 444-7275 ($6.75 Destinet fee); $22 fee per night for "lakeside premium" sites; $17 fee per night for other sites; $6 fee per night for hiker/biker sites; $1 pet fee.

Who to contact: Phone the park at (707) 279-4293 or (707) 938-1519.

Location: From Vallejo, drive north on Highway 29 to Lower Lake. Turn left on Highway 29 and drive eight miles to Soda Bay Road. Turn right on Soda Bay Road and drive about 10 miles to the park entrance on the right side of the road.

Or from Kelseyville on Highway 29, take the Kelseyville exit and turn north on Main Street. Drive a short distance to State Street. Turn north and drive to Gaddy Lane. Continue north on Gaddy Lane for about two miles to Soda Bay Road. Turn right and drive a half-mile to the park entrance on the left.

Trip note: If you have fallen in love with Clear Lake and its surrounding oak woodlands, it is difficult to find a better spot than at Clear Lake State Park. It is set on the western shore of Clear Lake, and though the oak woodlands flora means you can seem quite close to your camping neighbors, the proximity to quality boating, watersports and fishing makes the lack of privacy worth it. Reservations are a necessity in summer months. That stands to reason, with excellent bass fishing from boats beside a tule-lined shoreline near the park and good catfishing in the sloughs that run through the park. Some campsites have water frontage. A few short hiking trails are also available. Rangers here are friendly, helpful, and provide reliable fishing information. The elevation is 2,000 feet.

15. EDGEWATER RESORT AND RV PARK

Reference: **On Clear Lake; map D1, grid b3.**

Campsites, facilities: There are 59 motor home sites with full hookups. Picnic tables, fire grills, restrooms, showers and a boat ramp are provided. Wood is available. No pets are allowed

Reservations, fee: Reservations accepted; $25 fee per night.

Who to contact: Phone the park at (707) 279-0208.

Location: In Kelseyville on Highway 29, take the Merritt Road exit and drive on Merritt for two miles (it becomes Gaddy Lane) to Soda Bay Road. Turn right on Soda Bay Road and drive three miles to the campground entrance on the left.

Trip note: Soda Bay is one of Clear Lake's prettiest and most intimate spots, and this camp provides excellent access. Both waterskiing and fishing for bass and bluegill are excellent in this part of the lake, sheltered from north winds for quiet water, with a tule-lined shore from Henderson Point all the way around to Dorn Bay, nearly three miles of prime fishing territory.

16. M & M CAMPGROUNDS

Reference: **On Clear Lake; map D1, grid b4.**

Campsites, facilities: There are 37 motor home sites. Flush toilets, showers and a boat ramp are provided. Boat rentals and a grocery store are nearby. Pets are allowed.

Reservations, fee: Reservations required; $12.50 fee per night; $5 launch fee.

Who to contact: Phone the park at (707) 998-9943.

Location: From north of Ukiah on US 101 or at Williams on Interstate 5, turn on Highway 20 and drive to Clearlake Oaks and Island Drive. Turn south (the only way you can turn) on Island Drive and drive two blocks to 13050 Island Drive.

Trip note: This park has a unique setting, located on an island in the shaded lagoons and waterways that lead from Clear Lake into the town of Clearlake Oaks. That means the boat ramp is extremely sheltered from wakes. Fishing for bass and catfish is good in the immediate area, with an excellent catfish hole located off nearby Rattlesnake Island. Open year-round.

17. AUSTIN'S CAMPGROUND AND MARINA

Reference: **On Clear Lake; map D1, grid b4.**

Campsites, facilities: There are 26 motor home sites with water and electrical hookups. Flush toilets, showers, a sanitary disposal station, a pier, a boat ramp, a laundromat, propane gas and a small grocery store are available. Pets are allowed on leashes.

Reservations, fee: Reservations recommended; $13-$15 fee per night; $3 boat-launch fee and $4 fee per night for a boat slip.

Who to contact: Phone the park at (707) 994-7623.

Location: From Lower Lake at the junction of Highway 29 and Highway 53, drive north on Highway 53 to Olympic Drive. Turn west (toward the lake), and drive past Lakeshore Drive to the campground entrance (signed).

Trip note: This privately-operated park has lake frontage sites available on the southeast shore of Clear Lake. The view from here can be divine—miles of lake with Mt. Konocti in the background. This part of the lake has good fishing for catfish at the mouth of Cache Creek. Open year-round.

18. CLOVERDALE KOA

Reference: **Near Russian River; map D1, grid c0.**

Campsites, facilities: There are 58 sites for tents, 104 motor home sites (six drive-through), most with full hookups, and eight cabins. Picnic tables and fire grills are provided. Flush toilets, showers, a swimming pool, a playground, a sanitary disposal station, a laundromat, a recreation room, mini-golf, nature trails, a catch-and-release fish pond, nightly entertainment in the summer, propane gas, and a grocery and gift store are available. Pets are permitted.

Reservations, fee: Reservations accepted; $19.50-$24 fee per night; cabins $34.

Who to contact: Phone the park at (707) 894-3337, or for reservations phone (800) 368-4558.

Location: From Cloverdale on US 101, take the Central Cloverdale exit, which puts you on Asti Road. Drive straight on Asti Road to First Street. Turn east and drive a short distance to River Road. Turn south and drive four miles to KOA Road. Turn left and drive to the campground entrance.

In summer/fall: South of Cloverdale on US 101, take the Asti exit and drive east one block to Asti Road. Turn south and drive a short distance to Washington School Road. Turn east and drive 1.5 miles to KOA Road. Turn right and drive to the campground entrance. (Note: this route is open May 15 to December 15, when a seasonal bridge is in place). Both routes are well-signed.

Trip note: This KOA campground is set just above the Russian River in the Alexander Valley wine country, just south of Cloverdale. Since new owners took over in 1994, the place has undergone considerable renovation, and is now both rustic and tidy, with adorable little camping cabins a great bonus. In addition, a fishing pond is stocked with largemouth bass, bluegill, catfish, and when water temperatures are cool enough, trout. The nearby Russian River is an excellent beginner's route in an inflatable kayak or canoe. The nearby winery in Asti makes for a popular side trip. Open year-round.

---

19. LOCH LOMOND PARK ≥   RV 4

Reference: **Near Middletown; map D1, grid c3.**

Campsites, facilities: There are 37 motor home sites, 10 with full or partial hookups. Picnic tables, fire grills, restrooms and showers are provided. There is a swimming pool and grocery store across the street. No pets are allowed.

Reservations, fee: Reservations accepted; $8-$10 fee per night.

Who to contact: Phone the park at (707) 928-5044.

Location: From Vallejo, drive north on Highway 29 past Calistoga to Middletown and the junction with Highway 175. Turn north on Highway 175 and drive 12 miles to the park entrance on the left side of the road.

Trip note: This park is located midway between Clear Lake and the Napa Valley and is favored primarily by seniors with motor homes. Though the Highway 29 corridor gets tons of vacation traffic, you can escape most of it here on little Highway 175. The valley setting is pretty in the spring when everything is still green, with Cobb Mountain nearby. Open year-round.

---

20. SHAW'S SHADY ACRES ⌐ ♆ ⚓ ≥   RV 7

Reference: **On Cache Creek; map D1, grid c4.**

Campsites, facilities: There are 16 sites for tents or motor homes, many with partial or full hookups. Picnic tables and fire grills are provided. Restrooms, showers, a sanitary disposal station, a pier, boat rentals, a boat ramp, a laundromat, a swimming pool, a recreation patio, a beer and wine bar, fishing supplies and a grocery store are available. Pets must be on leashes and may not be left unattended in camp.

Reservations, fee: Reservations recommended; $16 fee per night; $0.50 pet fee.

Who to contact: Phone the park at (707) 994-2236.

Location: From the town of Lower Lake, drive north on Highway 53 for 1.3 miles to Old Highway 53. Turn left (a frontage road) and drive a quarter-mile to the park entrance road.

Trip note: This is one of several privately-operated campgrounds set beside Cache Creek, just south of Clear Lake. The fishing for catfish is often quite good on summer nights in Cache Creek, a deep green, slow-moving water that looks more like a slough in a Mississippi bayou than a creek. Waterfront campsites with scattered walnut, ash and oak trees are available. Clear Lake is a short drive to the north.

21. END O' THE RAINBOW

Reference: On Cache Creek; map D1, grid c4.
Campsites, facilities: There are 10 motor home sites with full hookups and a grassy area for tents or motor homes. Picnic tables, fire grills and shade umbrellas are provided. Restrooms, showers, a laundromat, a playground, a game room, fishing supplies and a small store are available. Pets are permitted on leashes or otherwise controlled.
Reservations, fee: Reservations recommended; $15 fee per night.
Who to contact: Phone the park at (707) 994-3282.
Location: From the town of Lower Lake, drive north on Highway 53 for 1.3 miles to Old Highway 53. Turn left (a frontage road) and drive a short distance to the campground entrance road at 7425 Old Highway 53.
Trip note: This is one of several resorts on Cache Creek, the outlet stream that pours south from Clear Lake. Fishing for catfish can be quite good at night from the dock at this resort, and on our visit, crawdads for bait were available for sale. The nearby town of Lower Lake is one of the oldest towns in Lake County and offers numerous historic sites. Clear Lake is a short drive to the north.

22. GARNERS' RESORT

Reference: On Cache Creek; map D1, grid c4.
Campsites, facilities: There are 25 sites for tents and 40 motor home sites with full hookups. Flush toilets, showers, a sanitary disposal station, boat rentals, a pier, a boat ramp, a recreation room, a swimming pool, a wading pool, fishing supplies, a laundromat and a grocery store are available. Pets are allowed on leashes.
Reservations, fee: Reservations accepted; $14-$16 fee per night.
Who to contact: Phone the park at (707) 994-6267.
Location: From the town of Lower Lake, drive north on Highway 53 for 1.3 miles to Old Highway 53. Turn left (a frontage road) and drive 1.5 miles to the resort entrance on the left.
Trip note: This is one of several privately-operated parks in the immediate area along Cache Creek just south of Clear Lake. This park offers site for tents as well as RVs, many near Cache Creek, which actually looks more like a slough—deep, wide, green and slow-moving. Open year-round.

23. AZTEC RV PARK

Reference: On Cache Creek; map D1, grid c5.
Campsites, facilities: There are 30 motor home sites with full or partial hookups and six tent sites. This is as an "adult park" (no children or pets allowed). Restrooms, showers, a pier, a ramp, a laundromat and river frontage sites are available. Propane gas is available nearby.
Reservations, fee: Reservations recommended; $15 fee per night.
Who to contact: Phone the park at (707) 994-4377.

Location: From the town of Lower Lake, drive north on Highway 29 for one mile to Dam Road. Turn right and drive to Tish-a-Tang Road and continue to the campground at 16150 Tish-a-Tang Road.

Trip note: This is an adults-only RV park set near Cache Creek, just south of Clear Lake.

---

24. CACHE CREEK CANYON REGIONAL PARK

Reference: **Near Rumsey; map D1, grid c7.**

Campsites, facilities: There are 45 sites for tents or motor homes and three group camps which can accommodate 20-50 people. Picnic tables, fire grills and piped water are provided. Flush toilets and a sanitary disposal station are available. Pets are permitted.

Reservations, fee: No reservations; $10-$15 fee per night; $1 fee for pets.

Who to contact: Phone the park at (916) 666-8115.

Location: From Vacaville on Interstate 80, turn north on Interstate 505 and drive 21 miles to Madison and the junction with Highway 16. Turn north on Highway 16 and drive northwest for about 45 miles to the town of Rumsey. From Rumsey, continue west on Highway 16 for five miles to the park entrance.

Trip note: This is the best campground in Yolo County, yet it's known by few out-of-towners. It is set at 1,300 feet, beside Cache Creek, which is the closest river to the Bay Area that provides whitewater rafting opportunities. This section of river features primarily Class I and II water, ideal for inflatable kayaks and overnight trips. Occasionally, huge catfish are caught in this area. Open year-round.

---

25. BEAVER CREEK RV PARK & CAMP

Reference: **Near Cobb Mountain; map D1, grid d3.**

Campsites, facilities: There are 10 tent sites and 97 sites for motor homes up to 40 feet long. Most are pull-through and all have full hookups. Piped water is provided. Picnic tables, fire rings, restrooms, showers, a group area, a pool, kayaks and paddle boats, a boating pond, a playground, horseshoes, a recreation hall, a convenience store and laundromat are available. Some facilities are **wheelchair accessible.** Pets are allowed on leash.

Reservations, fee: Reservations recommended; $17-$20 fee per night.

Who to contact: Beaver Creek RV Park, 14417 Bottle Rock Road, P.O. Box 49, Cobb Mountain, CA 95426; (707) 928-4322 or (800) 307-CAMP.

Location: From Vallejo, drive north on Highway 29 past Calistoga to Middletown and the junction with Highway 175. Turn north on Highway 175 and drive 8.5 miles to Bottle Rock Road. Turn left and drive three miles to the campground entrance on the left side of the road.

Trip note: This camp has a trout creek, a pond with canoes and kayaks in summer, plus plenty of hiking and birding opportunities. In addition, horseback riding and hot air balloon rides are available nearby. This camp is set near Highway 175 between Middletown and Clear Lake, and while there is a parade of vacation traffic on Highway 29, relatively few people take the longer route on Highway 175. Cobb Mountain looms nearby.

26. LOWER HUNTING CREEK

Reference: **Near Lake Berryessa; map D1, grid d7.**

Campsites, facilities: There are five sites for tents or motor homes. Piped water, picnic tables, fire grills, shade shelters and vault toilets are provided. Pets are permitted on leashes or otherwise controlled.

Reservations, fee: No reservations; no fee.

Who to contact: Phone the Bureau of Land Management at (707) 468-4000.

Location: In Lower Lake on Highway 29, turn southeast on Morgan Valley Road (Berryessa-Knoxville Road) and drive 15 miles to Devilhead Road. Turn south and drive two miles to the campground.

Trip note: This little-known camp might seem like it's out in the middle of nowhere for the folks who wind up here accidentally (we did), and it turns out that it is. If you plan on a few days here, it's advisable to get information or a map of the surrounding area from the Bureau of Land Management prior to your trip. There are 25 miles of trails for off-highway-vehicle use. In the fall, the area provides access for deer hunting with poor to fair success. Open year-round.

27. MIRABEL TRAILER PARK AND CAMP

Reference: **On Russian River; map D1, grid f0.**

Campsites, facilities: There are 125 sites for tents or motor homes, many with full or partial hookups. Picnic tables and fire grills are provided. Flush toilets, showers, a playground, a laundromat, a sanitary disposal station and canoe rentals are available. Pets, except pit bulls, are allowed on leashes.

Reservations, fee: Reservations recommended; $15-$20 fee per night.

Who to contact: Phone the park at (707) 887-2383.

Location: North of Santa Rosa on US 101, take the River Road exit and head west. Drive eight miles to the campground at 7600 River Road.

Trip note: The big attraction here during the summer is swimming and paddling around in canoes. This privately-operated park is set near the Russian River, but in the summer, the "river" is actually a series of small lakes, with temporary dams stopping most of the water flow. In winter, out come the dams, up comes the water, and in come the steelhead, migrating upstream past this area. Armstrong Redwoods State Park just north of Guerneville provides a nearby trip option. Open March through October.

28. SCHOOLHOUSE CANYON CAMPGROUND

Reference: **Near Russian River; map D1, grid f0.**

Campsites, facilities: There are 45 sites for tents or motor homes. Picnic tables and fire grills are provided. Piped water, flush toilets, showers and wood are available. Pets are allowed on leashes.

Reservations, fee: Reservations accepted; $20 fee per night for two people; $5 for each additional person.

Who to contact: Phone the park at (707) 869-2311.

Location: From Santa Rosa, drive north on US 101 about 2.5 miles and take the River Road/Guerneville exit. Drive to the stop sign, turn left on River Road and drive 12.5 miles to the campground entrance.

Trip note: This campground feature a half-mile of sandy beach along the Russian River, campsites in a grove of large redwoods, and a parklike setting on 210 acres of land originally homesteaded in the 1850s. A one-mile scenic hiking trail is available, routed up to a ridge for some nice views of the countryside. Open May through October.

29. BURKE'S RESORT & CANOE TRIPS

Reference: On Russian River; map D1, grid f0.

Campsites, facilities: There are 60 sites for tents or motor homes. Picnic tables and fire grills are provided. Flush toilets, showers, wood and canoe rentals are available. Pets are not allowed.

Reservations, fee: Reservations recommended; $12-$15 fee per night.

Who to contact: Phone the park at (707) 887-1222.

Location: In Marin, drive north on US 101 to Rohnert Park and the junction with Highway 116. Turn north on Highway 116 and drive 14 miles to Forestville and Mirabel Road. Turn right and drive one mile until it deadends at the Russian River and the campground.

Trip note: Burke's is the long-established canoe rental service and campground on the Russian River. The favorite trip is the 10-miler from Burke's in Forestville to Guerneville, which is routed right through the heart of the area's redwoods, about a 3.5-hour trip with plenty of time for sunbathing, swimming or anything else you can think of. The cost is $30, including a return by shuttle. Many other trips are available. Open April through October.

30. RIVER BEND CAMPGROUND

Reference: On Russian River; map D1, grid f0.

Campsites, facilities: There are 108 sites for tents or motor homes, many with full hookups (including cable TV). Picnic tables and fire rings are provided. Piped water, flush toilets, showers, a laundromat, a recreation room, a dog walking area, canoe and tube rentals, a volleyball court and a grocery store are available. Pets are permitted.

Reservations, fee: Reservations accepted; $15-$20 fee per night; $3 pet fee.

Who to contact: Phone the park at (707) 887-7662.

Location: From US 101 north of Santa Rosa, take the River Road-Guerneville exit. Drive west for 11 miles (just after the bridge) to the campground on the left side of the road at 11820 River Road.

Trip note: This privately-owned campground offers grassy sites beside the Russian River. There is a wide variety of recreation in the area, including canoe rentals, fishing on the Russian River, hiking Armstrong Redwoods State Park north of Guerneville, or heading west on 116 to the coast and the Sonoma Coast State Beach.

31. HILTON PARK

Reference: On Russian River; map D1 grid f0.

Campsites, facilities: There are 35 tent sites and five motor home sites with no hookups. Picnic tables, fire rings, showers, restrooms, a beach, laundry facilities, a playground, firewood and ice are available. Canoe rentals are available nearby. Pets are permitted on leashes.

Reservations, fee: Reservations recommended; $20-$25 fee per night.

Who to contact: Phone the park at (707) 887-9206.

Location: From US 101 north of Santa Rosa, take the River Road-Guerneville exit. Drive west for 11.5 miles (shortly after the bridge) to the campground on the left side of the road, just behind the Russian River Pub.

Trip note: This lush, wooded park is set on the banks of the Russian River, with a choice of open or secluded sites. The highlight of the campground is a large, beautiful beach, which offers access for swimming, fishing and canoeing. The folks here are very friendly and you get a choice of many recreation options in the area. Open year-round.

---

32. WINDSORLAND RV PARK ≈

RV. 3

Reference: **Near Santa Rosa; map D1, grid f1.**

Campsites, facilities: There are 55 motor home sites with full hookups. Patios are provided. Flush toilets, showers, a swimming pool, a sanitary disposal station, a laundromat, a recreation room and a playground are available. Pets are permitted.

Reservations, fee: Reservations accepted; $20-$25 fee per night. No credit cards.

Who to contact: Phone the park at (707) 838-4882.

Location: From Santa Rosa on US 101, drive north for nine miles to Windsor. Take the Windsor exit and turn north on Old Redwood Highway and drive a half-mile to 9290 Old Redwood Highway.

Trip note: This developed park is located close to the Russian River, wine country to the east, redwoods to the west, and Lake Sonoma to the northwest. But with a swimming pool, playground and recreation room, many visitors are content to stay right here, spend the night, then head out on their vacation. Open year-round.

---

33. NAPA COUNTY FAIRGROUNDS

RV. 2

Reference: **In Calistoga; map D1, grid f3.**

Campsites, facilities: There are 50 motor home sites (all drive-through and with hookups) and a lawn area for tents. Group sites are available by reservation only. Restrooms, showers and a sanitary disposal station are available. No fires are permitted. A nine-hole golf course is adjacent to the campground area. Pets are allowed on leashes.

Reservations, fee: No reservations (except for groups); $10-15 fee per night.

Who to contact: Phone the campground at (707) 942-5111.

Location: From Napa on Highway 29, drive north to Calistoga and Lincoln Avenue and drive four blocks to Fairway. Turn left and drive to the end of the road to the campground.

Trip note: What this really is, folks, is just the county fairgrounds, converted to a motor home park for 11 months each year. It is closed to camping from mid-June through mid-July, but what the heck, you can stick around and try to win a stuffed animal. What is more likely, of course, is that you have come here for the health spas, with great natural hot springs, mud baths and assorted goodies at the health resorts in Calistoga. Nearby parks for hiking include Bothe-Napa Valley and Robert Louis Stevenson state parks.

34. CALISTOGA RANCH CAMPGROUND

Reference: **Near Calistoga; map D1, grid f4.**

Campsites, facilities: There are 60 sites for tents, 84 motor home sites with full or partial hookups, four cabins and two trailers. Picnic tables and barbecue grills are provided. Flush toilets, showers, a sanitary disposal station, a laundromat, a lake, a swimming pool and a snack bar are available. Pets are permitted.

Reservations, fee: Reservations accepted; $19-$25 fee per night; $45 fee per night for cabins and $79 fee per night for trailers; $2 pet fee.

Who to contact: Phone the park at (707) 942-6565.

Location: From Napa on Highway 29, drive north through St. Helena and continue for about five miles to Larkmead Lane. Turn east and drive a short distance to the Silverado Trail. Turn left (north) and drive about 200 yards to Lommel Road. Turn right and drive a quarter-mile to the campground.

Trip note: This is a large, privately-run camp set in the heart of the wine country, about a 15-minute drive from the famous Calistoga spas and mud baths. Elevation is 600 feet. Open year-round.

35. BOTHE-NAPA VALLEY STATE PARK

Reference: **Near Calistoga; map D1, grid f4.**

Campsites, facilities: There are nine sites for tents and 49 sites for tents or motor homes up to 31 feet long. Picnic tables, fire grills and piped water are provided. Flush toilets, showers, a sanitary disposal station and a swimming pool (in the summer) are available. The facilities are **wheelchair accessible**. Pets are permitted. Supplies can be obtained in Calistoga or St. Helena.

Reservations, fee: Reserve by phoning Destinet at (800) 444-7275 ($6.75 Destinet fee); $15-$17 fee per night; $1 pet fee.

Who to contact: Phone the park at (707) 942-4575 or (707) 938-1519.

Location: From Napa on Highway 29, drive north to St. Helena and continue north for five miles (one mile past the entrance to Bale Grist Mill State Park) to the park entrance road on the left.

Trip note: It's always a stunner for newcomers to discover this beautiful park with redwoods and a pretty stream so close to the Napa Valley wine-and-spa country. Though the campsites are relatively exposed, they are set beneath a pretty oak/bay/madrone forest, with trailheads for hiking nearby. One trail is routed south for 1.2 miles to the restored Bale Grist Mill, a giant mill wheel on a pretty creek. Another more scenic route heads up Ritchey Canyon, amid redwoods and along Ritchey Creek, beautiful and intimate. Open year-round.

36. RANCHO MONTICELLO RESORT

Reference: **On Lake Berryessa; map D1, grid f7.**

Campsites, facilities: There are 59 sites for tents and 45 motor home sites with full hookups. Picnic tables, fire grills and piped water are provided. Restrooms, showers, a snack bar, complete marina facilities, ice, propane gas and groceries are available. Pets are allowed on leashes.

Reservations, fee: Reservations recommended; $14-$24 fee per night.

Who to contact: Phone (707) 966-2188.

Location: From Vallejo, drive north on Interstate 80 to the Suisun Valley Road exit. Take Suisun Valley Road north to Highway 121. Turn north on Highway 121 and drive five miles to Highway 128. Turn north (left) on Highway 128 and drive five miles to Berryessa-Knoxville Road and drive ten miles to 6590 Knoxville Road.

Trip note: This is a fully-developed, privately-operated park set on the shore of Lake Berryessa. Berryessa is the third largest man-made lake in Northern California, smaller than only Shasta and Oroville. It is a popular spot for waterskiing and fishing for trout and bass. Elevation is 475 feet. Open year-round.

37. PUTAH CREEK PARK

Reference: On Lake Berryessa; map D1, grid f7.

Campsites, facilities: There are 130 sites for tents or motor homes, many with full or partial hookups. Restrooms, showers, a sanitary disposal station, a laundromat, a boat ramp, rowboat rentals, a snack bar, a restaurant, propane gas, ice and groceries are available. Pets are permitted on leashes.

Reservations, fee: Reservations recommended; $17-$23 fee per night.

Who to contact: Phone the park at (707) 966-2116.

Location: From Vallejo, drive north on Interstate 80 to the Suisun Valley Road exit. Take Suisun Valley Road and drive north to Highway 121. Turn north on Highway 121 and drive five miles to Highway 128. Turn north (left) on Highway 128 and drive five miles to Berryessa-Knoxville Road and drive 13 miles to 7600 Knoxville Road.

Trip note: This campground is set at 400 feet elevation on the northern end of Lake Berryessa. The Putah Creek arm provides very good bass fishing in the spring and trout trolling in the summer. The north end of the lake has a buoy line that keeps powerboats out, but it can still be explored by paddling a canoe, which allows you to fish in relatively untouched waters and see deer during the evening on the eastern shore. In the fall, usually by mid-October, the trout come to the surface and provide excellent fishing at the mouth of Pope Creek or Putah Creek for anglers drifting live minnows. The resort also has apartment-style rentals. Open year-round.

38. SPRING LAKE REGIONAL PARK

Reference: In Santa Rosa; map D1, grid g2.

Campsites, facilities: There are four sites for tents and 30 sites for tents or motor homes of any length. Picnic tables, fire grills, and piped water are provided. Flush toilets, showers, a sanitary disposal station, a boat ramp (no motorboats), boat rentals and bike paths are available (summer). Pets are permitted with proof of rabies vaccination. A grocery store, a laundromat, wood and propane gas are available nearby.

Reservations, fee: Reservations accepted; phone (707) 539-8092; $14 fee per night; $1 pet fee, with proof of rabies vaccination. Note: The limit is eight people and two vehicles per campsite.

Who to contact: Phone the park at (707) 539-8082.

Location: From Santa Rosa on US 101, turn east on Highway 12 (it will become

Hoen Avenue) and continue to Newanga Avenue. Turn left and drive to the park at the end of the road.

Trip note: Spring Lake is one of the few lakes in the greater Bay Area that provides lakeside camping. Not only that, Spring Lake is stocked twice each month in late winter and spring with rainbow trout by the Department of Fish and Game. It is a small, pretty lake. Only non-powered boats are permitted, which keeps things fun and quiet for everybody. An easy trail along the west shore of the lake to the dam, then into adjoining Howarth Park, provides a pleasant evening stroll. Open daily from mid-May through mid-September, and on weekends and holidays only during the off-season.

---

39. SUGARLOAF RIDGE STATE PARK

Reference: **Near Santa Rosa; map D1, grid g4.**

Campsites, facilities: There are 50 sites for tents or motor homes up to 27 feet long. Picnic tables, fire grills, piped water and flush toilets are provided. Pets are permitted.

Reservations, fee: Reserve by phoning Destinet at (800) 444-PARK ($6.75 Destinet fee); $15-$17 fee per night; $1 pet fee.

Who to contact: Phone the park at (707) 833-5712 or (707) 938-1519.

Location: From Santa Rosa on US 101, turn east on Highway 12 and drive seven miles to Adobe Canyon Road. Turn north and drive three miles to the park entrance.

Trip note: Sugarloaf Ridge State Park is a perfect example of a place that you can't make a final judgement about from your first glance. Your first glance will lead you to believe that this is just hot foothill country, with old ranch roads set in oak woodlands for horseback riding and sweaty hiking or biking. A little discovery here, however, is that the Canyon Trail (trailhead located on the south side of the park access road) will deliver you to a rock-studded 25-foot waterfall, beautifully set in a canyon, complete with a redwood canopy. It will launch your perspective and your camping trip into a new dimension. Open year-round.

---

40. LAKE BERRYESSA MARINA RESORT

Reference: **Map D1, grid g7.**

Campsites, facilities: There are 70 sites for tents and 53 motor home sites with water and electrical hookups. Flush toilets, showers, a sanitary disposal station, a laundromat, a snack bar, complete marina facilities (including boat repair), RV supplies and groceries are available. Pets are permitted on leashes.

Reservations, fee: Reservations recommended; $12-$24 fee per night; $1 pet fee.

Who to contact: Phone (707) 966-2161.

Location: From Vallejo, drive north on Interstate 80 to the Suisun Valley Road exit. Take Suisun Valley Road and drive north to Highway 121. Turn north on Highway 121 and drive five miles to Highway 128. Turn north (left) on Highway 128 and drive five miles to Berryessa-Knoxville Road and then nine miles to 7600 Knoxville Road.

Trip note: Lake Berryessa is the Bay Area's backyard water recreation headquarters, the No. 1 lake (in the greater Bay Area) to waterski, loaf and fish. This resort is set on the west shore of the main lake, one of several resorts at the lake. Open year-round.

41. SPANISH FLAT RESORT

RV 🔺**7**

Reference: On Lake Berryessa; map D1, grid g7.

Campsites, facilities: There are 120 sites for tents or motor homes, a few with partial hookups. Picnic tables, fire grills and piped water are provided. Flush toilets, showers, a boat launch, complete marina facilities, boat rentals and groceries are available. A laundromat, restaurant, post office and RV supplies are nearby. The facilities are **wheelchair accessible**. Pets are permitted on leashes.

Reservations, fee: Reservations accepted; $17-$20 fee per night.

Who to contact: Phone (707) 966-7700.

Location: From Vallejo, drive north on Interstate 80 to the Suisun Valley Road exit. Take Suisun Valley Road and drive north to Highway 121. Turn north on Highway 121 and drive five miles to Highway 128. Turn north (left) on Highway 128 and drive five miles to Berryessa-Knoxville Road and drive four miles to 4290 Knoxville Road.

Trip note: This is one of several lakeside camps at Lake Berryessa. Berryessa, considered the Bay Area's backyard fishing hole, is the third largest man-made lake in Northern California (Shasta and Oroville lakes are bigger). It is a popular lake for power boating, waterskiing and fishing. Trout fishing is good, trolling deep in the summer or drifting with minnows in fall and winter. The elevation is approximately 500 feet. Open year-round.

42. PLEASURE COVE RESORT

RV 🔺**7**

Reference: On Lake Berryessa; map D1, grid g8.

Campsites, facilities: There are 105 sites for tents or motor homes (20 have water and electrical hookups). Picnic tables and fire grills are provided. Restrooms, showers, ice, a restaurant, a bar, a boat ramp, propane gas and groceries are available. Pets are permitted.

Reservations, fee: Reservations accepted; $16-$18 fee per night; $2 pet fee.

Who to contact: Phone (707) 966-2172.

Location: From Vallejo, drive north on Interstate 80 about 10 miles to the Suisun Valley Road exit. Take Suisun Valley Road and drive north another 10 miles to Highway 121. Turn north (right) on Highway 121 and drive about eight miles to the end of Highway 121 and the junction with Highway 128. Bear right (southeast) on Highway 128 and proceed four miles to Wragg Canyon Road. Turn north (left) and continue three miles to the resort entrance.

Trip note: Pleasure Cove is set on the south end of Lake Berryessa, an excellent area for trout and bass fishing. Top spots that are nearby include the Monticello Dam, the narrows and Skier's Cove for trout, and the back of the coves of the Markley Cove arm for bass. This park is family-oriented.

43. NAPA TOWN & COUNTRY FAIRGROUNDS ♿

RV 🔺**2**

Reference: In Napa; map D1, grid h6.

Campsites, facilities: There are 100 motor home sites, many with electrical and water hookups, and an open area with space for 400 self-contained units.

Restrooms, showers, laundry facilities and a sanitary disposal station are provided. A grocery store and restaurant are within walking distance. Pets are permitted on leashes.

Reservations, fee: No reservations except for groups of 15 or more; $15 fee per night.

Who to contact: Phone (707) 253-4900.

Location: From Napa on Highway 29, drive to the Napa/Lake Berryessa exit. Turn east and drive to Third Street. Turn right and drive to Burnell Street and the campground entrance.

Trip note: This campground is actually the parking area for the Napa Fairgrounds. When the fair is in operation in early August, it is closed temporarily. The rest of the year, it is simply a large parking lot near Napa.

44. LAKE SOLANO COUNTY PARK

RV 6

Reference: Near Lake Berryessa; map D1, grid h9.

Campsites, facilities: There are 67 sites for tents or motor homes up to 35 feet long, 17 with full hookups. Piped water, fire grills and tables are provided. A sanitary disposal station, flush toilets, showers, a boat ramp and boat rentals are available. A grocery store is nearby. Some facilities are **wheelchair accessible**. Pets are accepted with proof of vaccination.

Reservations, fee: No reservations; $8-$18 fee per night; $1 pet fee.

Who to contact: Phone Lake Solano County Park at (916) 795-2990.

Location: In Vacaville, turn north on Interstate 505 and drive 11 miles to the junction of Highway 128. Turn west on Highway 128 and drive about five miles (past Winters) to Pleasant Valley Road. Turn left on Pleasant Valley Road and drive to the park at 8685 Pleasant Valley Road.

Trip note: Lake Solano provides a low-pressure option to nearby Lake Berryessa. It is a long, narrow lake set below the outlet at Monticello Dam at Lake Berryessa, technically called the afterbay. Compared to Berryessa, life moves at a much slower pace and some people prefer it. The lake has fair trout fishing in the spring. The camp can also be used as an overflow area if the camps at Berryessa fill on popular weekends. Open year-round.

45. SAN FRANCISCO NORTH/ PETALUMA KOA

RV 3

Reference: Near Petaluma; map D1, grid i2.

Campsites, facilities: There are 312 sites for tents or motor homes (161 drive-through), many with full or partial hookups, and 34 cabins. Picnic tables and fire grills are provided. Flush toilets, showers, cable TV hookups, a sanitary disposal station, a playground, recreation rooms, a swimming pool, a jacuzzi, a petting zoo, shuffleboard, a laundromat, propane gas and a grocery store are available. Some facilities are **wheelchair accessible**. Pets are permitted.

Reservations, fee: Reservations recommended; $26-$31 fee per night; cabins are $36 per night.

Who to contact: Phone the park at (707) 763-1492.

Location: From Petaluma on US 101, take the Penngrove exit and drive west for a quarter-mile on Petaluma Boulevard to Stony Point Road. Turn north on Stony Point Road and drive to Rainsville Road. Turn west on Rainsville Road and drive to 20 Rainsville Road.

Trip note: This campground is less than a mile from US 101, yet it has a rural feel. It's a good base camp for folks who require some quiet mental preparation before heading south to the Bay Area or to the nearby wineries, redwoods and the Russian River. The big plus here is that this KOA has the cute log cabins called "Kamping Kabins," providing privacy for those who want it. Open year-round.

NOR-CAL MAP .... see page 94
adjoining maps
NORTH (C2) .... see page 264
EAST (D3) .... see page 350
SOUTH (E2) .... see page 432
WEST (D1) .... see page 326

9 LISTINGS
PAGES 346-349

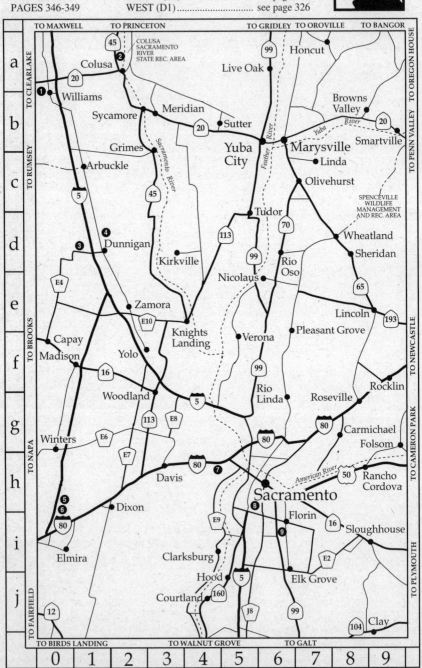

TO MAXWELL TO PRINCETON TO GRIDLEY TO OROVILLE TO BANGOR

TO CLEARLAKE

a

45

2

COLUSA
SACRAMENTO
RIVER
STATE REC. AREA

Colusa

99

Honcut

Live Oak

20

1

Williams

Browns
Valley

20

b

Sycamore

Meridian

20

Sutter

Yuba

River

Smartville

TO RUMSEY

Grimes

Yuba
City

Marysville

Linda

c

Arbuckle

45

Olivehurst

Sacramento River

Feather River

SPENCEVILLE
WILDLIFE
MANAGEMENT
AND REC. AREA

TO PENN VALLEY

TO OREGON HOUSE

5

Tudor

70

Wheatland

d

3

4

Dunnigan

113

Sheridan

Kirkville

99

Rio
Oso

E4

Nicolaus

65

e

Zamora

E10

Lincoln

193

TO BROOKS

Knights
Landing

Verona

Pleasant Grove

TO NEWCASTLE

Capay

99

f

Madison

Yolo

16

Rio
Linda

Rocklin

Woodland

5

Roseville

g

113

E8

80

80

Carmichael

TO NAPA

Winters

E6

Folsom

E7

80

American River

TO CAMERON PARK

h

Davis

7

80

Sacramento

50

Rancho
Cordova

5

8

Florin

16

i

6

Dixon

9

Sloughhouse

80

Clarksburg

E9

E2

TO PLYMOUTH

Elmira

Hood

5

Elk Grove

j

Courtland

160

TO FAIRFIELD

12

J8

99

104

Clay

TO BIRDS LANDING TO WALNUT GROVE TO GALT

| 0 | 1 | 2 | 3 | 4 | 5 | 6 | 7 | 8 | 9 |

1. ALMOND GROVE MOBILE HOME PARK RV4 A1

Reference: **In Williams; map D2, grid a0.**

Campsites, facilities: There are several motor home sites with full hookups. Picnic tables, restrooms and showers are provided. A laundromat is available. Pets are permitted. A store is nearby.

Reservations, fee: Reservations accepted; $10-$12 fee per night.

Who to contact: Phone (916) 473-5620.

Location: From the Central Valley on Interstate 5, drive to Williams and the Central Williams exit. Take that exit and drive west on E Street for eight blocks to 12th Street. Turn left on 12th Street and drive three blocks to the park entrance on the right side at 880 12th Street.

Trip note: The town of Williams is set in the middle of the Sacramento Valley, a popular spot to stop and grab a bite at its outstanding delicatessen (Granzella's), where there is a gigantic stuffed polar bear. Open year-round.

2. COLUSA-SACRAMENTO RIVER STATE RECREATION AREA RV4 A5

Reference: **Near Colusa; map D2, grid a2.**

Campsites, facilities: There are 14 sites for tents or motor homes up to 30 feet long. Restrooms, hot showers, a sanitary dump station, picnic tables and fire grills are provided. A grocery store and laundromat are nearby. A boat ramp is available. Pets are allowed on leashes.

Reservations, fee: Reserve by phoning Destinet at (800) 444-PARK ($6.75 Destinet fee); $12-$14 fee per night; $5 boat fee; $5 fee per extra vehicle.

Who to contact: Phone (916) 458-4927 or (916) 538-2200.

Location: In Williams at the junction of Interstate 5 and Highway 20, drive east on Highway 20 for 10 miles to the town of Colusa. Turn north on 10th Street and drive a short distance to the park.

Trip note: This region of the Sacramento Valley is well known as a high-quality habitat for birds. Nearby Delevan National Wildlife Refuge is an outstanding destination for wildlife viewing, and provides good duck hunting in December. In summer months, the nearby Sacramento River is a bonus with shad fishing in June and July, salmon fishing from August through October, sturgeon fishing in the winter, and striped bass fishing in the spring. Open year-round.

3. CAMPERS INN RV4 A1

Reference: **Near Dunnigan; map D2, grid d1.**

Campsites, facilities: There are 13 tent sites and 72 motor home sites (44 drive-through) with full or partial hookups. Flush toilets, picnic tables, showers, a heated pool, a clubhouse, horseshoes, a nine-hole golf course, a laundromat, propane gas, ice and groceries are available. The facilities are **wheelchair accessible**. Pets are allowed on leashes.

Reservations, fee: Reservations accepted; $15-$19 fee per night.

Who to contact: Phone the park at (916) 724-3350.

Location: From Interstate 5, take the Dunnigan exit (just north of the Interstate 505 cutoff). Drive west on County Road E-4 for one mile to County Road 88.

Turn north and drive for 1.5 miles to the park.

Trip note: This private park has a rural valley atmosphere, and it provides a layover for drivers cruising Interstate 5. The Sacramento River, located to the east, is the closest body of water, but this section of river is hardly a premium side trip destination. There are no nearby lakes. Open year-round.

4. HAPPY TIME RV PARK

Reference: **Near Dunnigan; map D2, grid d1.**

Campsites, facilities: There are eight tent sites and 30 motor home sites (18 drive-through) with full hookups. Flush toilets, showers, picnic tables, a playground, a laundromat and a swimming pool are available. Pets are allowed on leashes.

Reservations, fee: Reservations accepted; $20 fee per night.

Who to contact: Phone (916) 724-3336.

Location: From Interstate 5 near the Interstate 505 intersection, take the County Road 8 exit. Drive east on County Road 8 for a short distance to Road 99W. Turn left (north) on Road 99W and drive one block to the campground.

Trip note: If you are cruising Interstate 5 and are exhausted, or need to take a deep breath before hitting the Bay Area or Sacramento, this private park can provide a respite, and to be honest, not a whole lot more. Restaurants are available in nearby Dunnigan. Open year-round.

5. NEIL'S VINEYARD RV PARK

Reference: **Near Vacaville; map D2, grid h0.**

Campsites, facilities: There are 10 tent sites and 110 motor home sites (20 drive-through), many with full or partial hookups. Flush toilets, showers, picnic tables, a swimming pool, a laundromat, a sanitary disposal station, a recreation room and ice are available. Pets are permitted.

Reservations, fee: Reservations recommended; $18-$22.50 fee per night.

Who to contact: Phone (707) 447-8797 or write to 4985 Midway Road, Vacaville, CA 95688.

Location: From Vacaville on Interstate 80, turn north on Interstate 505 and drive three miles to Midway Road. Turn east on Midway Road and travel a half-mile to the campground on the left.

Trip note: This is one of two privately-operated parks set up primarily for motor homes. This one is set in a eucalyptus grove, with clean, well-kept sites. If you are heading to the Bay Area, it is late in the day and you don't have your destination set, this spot offers a chance to hole up for the night and formulate your travel plans. The Nut Tree offers a nearby side trip. Open year-round.

6. GANDY DANCER

Reference: **Near Vacaville; map D2, grid h0.**

Campsites, facilities: There are 51 motor home sites, all are drive-through with full hookups. Flush toilets, showers, picnic tables, a swimming pool, a children's pool, a laundromat, a sanitary disposal station and ice are available. Pets are permitted.

Reservations, fee: Reservations recommended; $18 fee per night.

Who to contact: Phone (707) 446-7679.

Location: From Vacaville on Interstate 80, turn north on Interstate 505 and drive three miles to Midway Road. Turn east on Midway Road and travel a quarter-mile to the campground.

Trip note: This layover spot for motor home cruisers is set near the Nut Tree, a famous restaurant for travelers. Marine World U.S.A. in Vallejo is located within a half-hour drive. Open year-round.

7. SACRAMENTO-METRO KOA ♿ 🏊 🚰　　🚐 ▲1

Reference: **Map D2, grid h4.**
Campsites, facilities: There are 49 tent sites and 95 motor home sites with full hookups. Flush toilets, showers, a playground, a swimming pool, a laundromat, propane gas and groceries are available. Pets are permitted.
Reservations, fee: Reservations recommended; $22-$28 fee per night.
Who to contact: Phone the park at (916) 371-6771 or (800) 545-KAMP.
Location: From Sacramento, drive west on Interstate 80 about four miles to the West Capitol Avenue exit. Exit and turn left onto West Capitol Avenue, going under the freeway to the first stop light and the intersection with Lake Road. Turn left onto Lake Road and continue about one-half block to the camp on the left at 3951 Lake Road.
Trip note: This is the choice of car and motor home campers touring California's capital, looking for a layover spot. It is located in downtown Sacramento near the Capitol building and the railroad museum. Open year-round.

8. STILLMAN TRAILER PARK ♿ 🏊 🚰　　🚐 ▲1

Reference: **In Sacramento; map D2, grid h5.**
Campsites, facilities: There are 65 motor home sites with full hookups. Flush toilets, showers, laundromat, a clubhouse and a swimming pool are available. Adults only. Small pets are permitted.
Reservations, fee: Reservations accepted; $24 fee per night.
Who to contact: Phone the park at (916) 392-2820.
Location: In Sacramento on Highway 99, take the 47th Avenue West exit and go to the first light at Stillman Park Circle. Turn right and the park will be just ahead at 3880 Stillman Park Circle.
Trip note: This is an adults-only motor home park located in downtown Sacramento near the Capitol and the railroad museum. It's a popular layover spot in summer months. Open year-round.

9. 99 TRAILER PARK　　🚐 ▲2

Reference: **Near Sacramento; map D2, grid i6.**
Campsites, facilities: There are 26 motor home sites with full hookups, including phone. There are no restroom facilities. Weekly residents preferred. A grocery store, a laundromat and propane gas are nearby. Pets are allowed on leashes.
Reservations, fee: Reservations accepted; $15 fee per night.
Who to contact: Phone the park at (916) 423-4078.
Location: From Sacramento, drive south on Highway 99 to the Sheldon Road exit. Turn west and drive to Stockton Boulevard (frontage road). Make a hard right on Stockton Boulevard and drive a short distance to the park.
Trip note: This is a popular motor home park for folks touring Sacramento because it's about a five-minute drive from the city. Most of the sites are tree-shaded, and it's a good thing, because Sacramento does a good job of imitating a furnace in the summer. Maybe it's all the hot air emanating from the mouths of politicians. Side trips include all the sights of California's capital city, of course, and the nearby Consumnes River.

MAP D3

NOR-CAL MAP .... see page 94
adjoining maps
NORTH (C3) .... see page 272
EAST (D4) .... see page 390
SOUTH (E3) .... see page 444
WEST (D2) .... see page 346

85 LISTINGS
PAGES 350-389

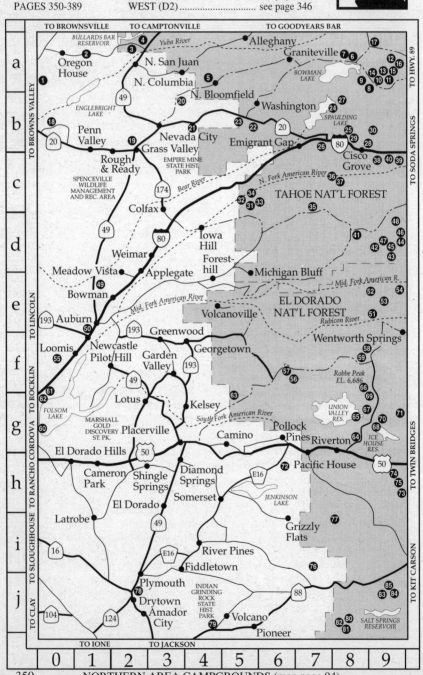

Map D3 featuring: Bullards Bar Reservoir, Yuba River, Tahoe National Forest, Bowman Lake, Faucherie Lake, Jackson Meadow Reservoir, Sugar Pine Reservoir, Big Reservoir, American River, French Meadows Reservoir, Eldorado National Forest, Hell Hole Reservoir, Stumpy Meadows Lake, Gerle Creek Reservoir, Folsom Lake State Recreation Area, Ice House Reservoir, Union Valley Reservoir, Jenkinson Lake, Mokelumne River, Bear River Reservoir

1. COLLINS LAKE RECREATION AREA

Reference: Near Marysville; map D3, grid a0.

Campsites, facilities: There are 159 sites for tents or motor homes (29 drive-through), many with full or partial hookups (52 are located along the lakefront). Picnic tables, fire grills and piped water are provided. There is also a large open camping area nearby, which requires no reservations and has piped water and chemical toilets. Flush toilets, a sanitary disposal station, showers (fee charged), a boat ramp, boat rentals, a sandy swimming beach, a marina, a grocery store, a laundromat, wood, ice and propane gas are available. Many facilities are **wheelchair accessible.** Pets are allowed on leashes.

Reservations, fee: Reservations recommended; $13.75-$18.75 fee per night.

Who to contact: Phone the campground at (916) 692-1600.

Location: From Marysville, drive east on Highway 20 for 12 miles to Marysville Road. Turn north and drive eight miles to the recreation area entrance road on the right. Turn right and drive one mile to the entrance station, then continue to the campground on the left side of the road.

Trip note: Collins Lake is set in the foothill country east of Marysville, 1,200 feet in elevation, ideal in spring and early summer for the camper, boater and angler. The lake has 12 miles of shoreline, and is quite pretty in the spring. Fishing is good for trout until late June, and after that, the warm water makes the lake exceptional for waterskiing. There is a marina adjacent to the campground, and further south is a swimming beach and boat ramp. Open year-round.

2. LAKE FRANCIS RESORT

Reference: On Lake Francis; map D3, grid a1.

Campsites, facilities: There are 86 sites for tents or motor homes up to 50 feet long, 56 with full and 26 with partial hookups. There are also eight cabins. Fire rings, restrooms, showers, RV storage, a dump station, laundry facilities, a pool, playgrounds, horseshoe pits, a softball field, a volleyball court, a croquet area, pool tables, and a video game room are provided. A spa/sauna, boat ramp, mooring, boat and waterski rentals, fishing facilities, a three-hole golf course, a snackbar, a grocery store, gasoline and propane gas are available. The resort allows group camping and has a meeting/club room with fireplace available. Some sites are **wheelchair accessible.** Pets are permitted on leashes, except in cabin rentals.

Reservations, fee: Reservations requested; call for fees.

Who to contact: Phone the resort at (916) 692-2046, or write to Lake Francis Resort, P.O. Box 45, Dobbins, CA 95935-0045.

Location: From Marysville, drive east on Highway 20 for12 miles to Marysville Road. Turn north (left) on Marysville Road and drive seven miles to Lake Francis Road. Turn south (right) and drive one-quarter mile to the resort entrance on the right.

Trip note: This resort was originally a public recreation area. It was bought a few years ago by a membership organization and closed to the public. Now it is open to the public again. A special feature is an "Old Western Town" consisting of a large,6,094-foot building that has its own saloon, restaurant and fireplace. There is "gate-guarded" access. Camp elevation is 2,000 feet. The summary— quiet, peaceful and wooded, with all the amenities.

---

3. MOONSHINE CAMPGROUND

Reference: Near Yuba River near Bullards Bar Reservoir; map D3, grid a2.

Campsites, facilities: There are 25 sites for tents or motor homes, all with partial hookups. Picnic tables, fire rings, and piped water are provided. Vault toilets, ice and firewood are available. A grocery store and propane gas are available in North San Juan. Pets are allowed on leashes.

Reservations, fee: Reservations required; $17-$20 fee per night.

Who to contact: Phone the campground at (916) 288-3585.

Location: From Auburn, drive north on Highway 49 to Nevada City, then continue for 17 miles through the town of North San Juan. Continue on Highway 49, cross a bridge over the Middle Fork Yuba to Moonshine Road. Turn left on Moonshine Road and drive three-quarters of a mile to the campground.

Trip note: This campground features shaded sites and a swimming hole on the nearby Middle Fork Yuba River. Both are needed, with the weather hot here in the summer, at roughly 2,400 feet in the Sierra foothills. It's a seven-mile drive to a three-lane boat ramp at Dark Day Picnic Area at Bullards Bar Reservoir, the feature side trip. Open May through October 5.

---

4. HORNSWOGGLE GROUP CAMP

Reference: On Bullards Bar Reservoir in Tahoe National Forest; map D3, grid a2.

Campsites, facilities: There are four 25-person group sites and one 50-person group site. Picnic tables, fire grills, piped water and flush and vault toilets are provided. A boat ramp is nearby. Pets are permitted on leashes or otherwise controlled. Supplies are available at the marina.

Reservations, fee: Reservations required; $25-$50 fee per night.

Who to contact: Phone the Tahoe National Forest at (916) 288-3231.

Location: From Auburn, drive north on Highway 49 to Nevada City, then continue for 17 miles through the town of North San Juan. Continue on Highway 49, cross a bridge over the Middle Fork Yuba to Moonshine Road. Turn left on Moonshine Road and drive five miles to Marysville Road. Turn north and drive about a mile to the campground on the right.

Trip note: This camp is designed for group use. A three-lane concrete boat ramp is located two miles north at the Dark Day Picnic Area. For information about family campgrounds and boat-in sites, see the listings for Bullards Bar Reservoir in Chapter C3. Open year-round.

5. MALAKOFF DIGGINS STATE HISTORIC PARK 🚶 ♿ 🏇 🛉

Reference: **Map D3, grid a4.**

Campsites, facilities: There are 30 sites for tents or motor homes up to 24 feet long. Piped water, flush toilets (except Mid-November through February), picnic tables and fire grills are provided. A small grocery store is nearby. Pets are permitted.

Reservations, fee: Reserve by phoning Destinet at (800) 444-7275 ($6.75 Destinet fee); $12 camping fee per night; $1 pet fee.

Who to contact: Phone (916) 265-2740 or (916) 445-7373.

Location: From Auburn, drive north on Highway 49 to Nevada City, then continue for 11 miles to the junction of Tyler Foote Crossing Road. Turn right and drive for 16 miles to the park entrance. The last two miles are over a steep gravel road to the park entrance.

Trip note: This camp is set near a small lake in the park, but the main attraction of the area is the gold mining history. The area was formerly a gold mining center, and there are tours available during summer months to the numerous historic sites. The elevation is 3,400 feet. Open year-round.

6. JACKSON CREEK 🎣 🚶

Reference: **Near Bowman Lake in Tahoe National Forest; map D3, grid a8.**

Campsites, facilities: There are 14 tent sites. There is **no piped water**, but vault toilets, picnic tables, and fire grills are provided. Pack out your garbage. Pets are permitted on leashes or otherwise controlled.

Reservations, fee: No reservations; no fee.

Who to contact: Phone the Tahoe National Forest at (916) 265-4538.

Location: From Sacramento, drive east on Interstate 80 past Emigrant Gap to Highway 20. Turn west on Highway 20 and drive to Bowman Road (County Road 18). Turn right and drive about 12 miles to Bowman Lake (much of the road is quite rough), then continue for one mile east of the lake to the campground on the left.

Trip note: This primitive campground is located at 5,600 feet, adjacent to Jackson Creek, a primary feeder stream to Bowman Lake to the nearby west. There are several lakes within a five-mile radius, including Bowman Lake, Jackson Meadow Reservoir, Sawmill Lake and Faucherie Lake, all within a five-minute drive from this camp. A trailhead is available one mile south (right side of the road) at the north end of Sawmill Lake. The trail is routed to a series of pretty Sierra lakes to the west of Haystack Mountain (7,391 feet). Open June through October.

7. BOWMAN LAKE 🎣 ⚓ 🚶 🏊

Reference: **In Tahoe National Forest; map D3, grid a8.**

Campsites, facilities: There are seven tent sites. There is **no piped water**, but vault toilets are provided. Pack out your garbage. Pets are permitted on leashes or otherwise controlled.

Reservations, fee: No reservations; no fee.

Who to contact: Phone the Tahoe National Forest at (916) 265-4538.

Location: From Sacramento, drive east on Interstate 80 past Emigrant Gap to Highway 20. Turn west on Highway 20 and drive to Bowman Road (County Road 18). Turn right and drive about 12 miles (much of the road is quite rough) to Bowman Lake and the campground on the right side of the road at the head of the lake.

Trip note: Bowman is a sapphire jewel set in Sierra granite at 5,568 feet, extremely pretty, and ideal for campers with car-top boats. There is no boat ramp (you wouldn't want to trailer a boat on the access road anyway), but there are lots of small rainbow trout, and they are eager to please during the evening bite. The camp is set on the eastern end of the lake, just below where Jackson Creek pours in. The lake is flanked by Bowman Mountain (7,392 feet) and Red Hill (7,075 feet) to the south and Quartz Hill (7,025) to the north.

8. FAUCHERIE LAKE GROUP CAMP

Reference: **Near Bowman Lake in Tahoe National Forest; map D3, grid a8.**

Campsites, facilities: There is one large group camp for tents or motor homes up to 22 feet long. There is **no piped water**, but vault toilets, picnic tables and fire grills are provided. Pack out your garbage. Pets are permitted on leashes or otherwise controlled.

Reservations, fee: Reserve by phoning (800) 280-CAMP ($15 reservation fee); $30 fee per night.

Who to contact: Phone the Tahoe National Forest at (916) 265-4538.

Location: From Sacramento, drive east on Interstate 80 past Emigrant Gap to Highway 20. Turn west on Highway 20 and drive to Bowman Road (County Road 18). Turn right and drive about 12 miles (much of the road is quite rough) to Bowman Lake and continue one mile to a Y. Bear right at the Y and drive about three miles to the campground at the end of the road.

Trip note: Faucherie Lake is the kind of place that most people believe can only be reached by long, difficult hikes with a backpack. Guess again: Here it is, set in Sierra granite, 6,100 feet in elevation, quiet and pristine, a classic alpine lake. It is ideal for car-top boating and has decent fishing for both rainbow and brown trout. This is a group camp set on the lake's northern shore, a prime spot, with the lake's outlet creek nearby. Open June through October.

9. CANYON CREEK

Reference: **Near Faucherie Lake in Tahoe National Forest; map D3, grid a8.**

Campsites, facilities: There are nine sites for tents and 11 sites for motor homes up to 22 feet long. There is **no piped water**, but vault toilets, picnic tables, and fire grills are provided. Pack out your garbage. Pets are permitted on leashes or otherwise controlled.

Reservations, fee: No reservations; no fee.

Who to contact: Phone the Tahoe National Forest at (916) 265-4538.

Location: From Sacramento, drive east on Interstate 80 to Emigrant Gap. Take the off-ramp, then head north on the short connector road to Highway 20. Turn west on Highway 20 and drive a half-mile to Bowman Road (County Road 18). Turn right and drive about 12 miles (much of the road is quite rough) to Bowman Lake and continue one mile to a Y. Bear right at the Y and drive about two miles to the campground on the right side of the road.

Trip note: This pretty spot is at 6,000 feet in Tahoe National Forest, one mile from Sawmill Lake (which you pass on the way in), and one mile from pretty Faucherie Lake. It is set along Canyon Creek, the stream that connects those two lakes. Of the two, Faucherie provides better fishing, and because of that, there are fewer people at Sawmill. Take your pick. A trailhead is available at the north end of Sawmill Lake with a hike to several small, alpine lakes, a great day or overnight backpacking trip. Open June through October.

10. SILVER TIP GROUP CAMP 🐟 ⚓ 🚶 🏊 RV 7

Reference: At Jackson Meadow Reservoir in Tahoe National Forest; map D3, grid a9.

Campsites, facilities: There are two 25-person group sites for tents or motor homes up to 22 feet long. Piped water, vault toilets, picnic tables and fire grills are provided. Pets are permitted on leashes. Supplies are available in Truckee or Sierraville. A boat ramp is nearby.

Reservations, fee: Reserve by phoning (800) 280-CAMP ($15 reservation fee); $37.50 group fee per night.

Who to contact: Phone California Land Management at (916) 582-0120, or Tahoe National Forest District Office at (916) 994-3401; or write to P.O. Box 95, Sierraville, CA 96126.

Location: From Truckee, drive north on Highway 89 for 17.5 miles to Forest Service Road 7. Turn west on Forest Service Road 7 and drive 16 miles to Jackson Meadow Reservoir. At the lake, continue around the west shoreline, then turn left at the campground access road.

Trip note: This group camp is set on the southwest edge of Jackson Meadow Reservoir at 6,200 feet, in a pretty area with pine forest, high meadows and the trademark granite look of the Sierra Nevada. A boat ramp and swimming beach are located nearby at Woodcamp. For more information, see the trip note for Woodcamp. Open June through November.

11. WOODCAMP 🐟 ⚓ 🚶 🏊 RV 7

Reference: At Jackson Meadow Reservoir in Tahoe National Forest; map D3, grid a9.

Campsites, facilities: There are 10 sites for tents and 10 sites for tents or motor homes up to 22 feet long. Piped water, flush toilets, picnic tables and fire grills are provided. Pets are permitted on leashes or otherwise controlled. Supplies are available in Truckee or Sierraville. A boat ramp is adjacent to the camp.

Reservations, fee: Reservations accepted; $10 fee per night; $4 for each additional vehicle.

Who to contact: Phone Tahoe National Forest at (916) 994-3401, or California Land Management at (916) 582-0120.

Location: From Truckee, drive north on Highway 89 for 17.5 miles to Forest Service Road 7. Turn west on Forest Service Road 7 and drive 16 miles to Jackson Meadow Reservoir. At the lake, continue around the west shoreline, then turn left at the campground access road.

Trip note: Woodcamp and Pass Creek Camp (see next listing), are the best two camps for boaters at Jackson Meadow Reservoir because each have boat ramps directly adjacent to the camp. That is critical because fishing is far better by boat here than from shore, with a good mix of both rainbow and brown trout. The camp is set at 6,100 feet along the lake's southwest shore, in a pretty spot, with a swimming beach and short interpretive hiking trail nearby. This is a beautiful lake in the Sierra Nevada, complete with pine forest and a classic granite backdrop. Open June through November.

12. PASS CREEK ↪ 🐟 ⚓ 👫 🏊   RV 7

Reference: At Jackson Meadow Reservoir in Tahoe National Forest; map D3, grid a9.

Campsites, facilities: There are 15 sites for tents and 15 sites for motor homes up to 22 feet long. Piped water, a sanitary dump station, vault toilets, picnic tables and fire grills are provided. A boat ramp is nearby. Pets are permitted on leashes or otherwise controlled. Supplies are available in Truckee or Sierraville.

Reservations, fee: Reserve by phoning (800) 280-CAMP ($7.50 reservation fee); $11 fee per night.

Who to contact: Phone Tahoe National Forest at (916) 994-3401, or California Land Management at (916) 582-0120.

Location: From Truckee, drive north on Highway 89 for 17.5 miles to Forest Service Road 7. Turn west on Forest Service Road 7 and drive 16 miles to Jackson Meadow Reservoir and the campground on the left at the north end of the lake.

Trip note: This is the premium campground at Jackson Meadow Reservoir, a developed site with water, a concrete boat ramp, a swimming beach nearby at Aspen Creek Picnic Area, and a trailhead for the Pacific Crest Trail a half-mile to the east (you'll pass it on the way in). This lake has the trademark look of the high Sierra, and the bonus here is that lake levels are often kept higher than at other reservoirs on the western slopes of the Sierra Nevada. Trout stocks are excellent, with 85,000 rainbow and brown trout planted each summer after ice-out. The elevation is 6,100 feet. Open June through October.

13. FIR TOP ↪ 🐟 ⚓ 👫 ♿ 🏊   RV 7

Reference: At Jackson Meadow Reservoir in Tahoe National Forest; map D3, grid a9.

Campsites, facilities: There are 12 sites for tents or motor homes up to 22 feet long. Piped water, a sanitary dump station, flush toilets, picnic tables and fire grills are provided. Pets are permitted on leashes or otherwise controlled. Supplies are available in Truckee or Sierraville. A boat ramp is nearby. Some facilities are **wheelchair accessible**.

Reservations, fee: Reserve by phoning (800) 280-CAMP ($7.50 reservation fee); $11 fee per night.

Who to contact: Phone Tahoe National Forest at (916) 994-3401, or California Land Management at (916) 582-0120.

Location: From Truckee, drive north on Highway 89 for 17.5 miles to Forest Service Road 7. Turn left (west) on Forest Service Road 7 and drive 16 miles to Jackson Meadow Reservoir. Continue around the lake to the west side and the campground on the left side of the road.

Trip note: Jackson Meadow is a great destination for a short vacation, and that's why there are so many campgrounds available; it's not exactly a secret. This camp is set on a cove on the lake's southwest shore, less than a mile from a boat ramp near Woodcamp. See the trip notes for Woodcamp and Pass Creek Camp. The elevation is 6,200 feet. Open June through November.

14. FINDLEY 🐟 ⚓ 🏃 ♿ 🏊   RV 7

Reference: At Jackson Meadow Reservoir in Tahoe National Forest; map D3, grid a9.

Campsites, facilities: There are 15 sites for tents or motor homes up to 22 feet long. Piped water, flush toilets, picnic tables and fire grills are provided. Pets are permitted on leashes or otherwise controlled. Supplies are available in Truckee or Sierraville. A boat ramp is nearby. The facilities are **wheelchair accessible**.

Reservations, fee: Reserve by phoning (800) 280-CAMP ($7.50 reservation fee); $11 fee per night.

Who to contact: Phone Tahoe National Forest at (916) 994-3401, or California Land Management at (916) 582-0120.

Location: From Truckee, drive north on Highway 89 for 17.5 miles to Forest Service Road 7. Turn left (west) on Forest Service Road 7 and drive 16 miles to Jackson Meadow Reservoir. Continue around the lake to the west side, just past the entrance to Fir Top Camp, to the campground entrance on the left side of the road.

Trip note: Findley Camp is set near Woodcamp Creek, a quarter-mile from where it pours into Jackson Meadow Reservoir. Though it is not a lakeside camp, it is quite pretty just the same, and within a half-mile of the boat ramp near Woodcamp. It is set at 6,200 feet. This is one of several camps at the lake. Open June through November.

15. JACKSON POINT BOAT-IN 🐟 ⚓ 🏊   5% CLUB 9

Reference: Jackson Meadow Reservoir in Tahoe National Forest; map D3, grid a9.

Campsites, facilities: There are 10 tent sites. There is **no piped water**, but vault toilets, picnic tables and fire grills are provided. Supplies are available in Truckee or Sierraville. Pets are allowed on leashes.

Reservations, fee: Reservations accepted; no fee.

Who to contact: Phone Tahoe National Forest at (916) 994-3401, or California Land Management at (916) 582-0120.

Location: From Truckee, drive north on Highway 89 for 17.5 miles to Forest Service Road 7. Turn left (west) on Forest Service Road 7 and drive 16 miles to Jackson Meadow Reservoir. Drive to Pass Creek Campground and boat launch (on the left at the north end of the lake). Launch your boat and cruise a half-mile south to Jackson Point and the boat-in campsites.

Trip note: This is one of the few boat-in camps available anywhere in the high Sierra. This gorgeous spot is situated on the end of a peninsula that extends from the east shore of Jackson Meadow Reservoir. Small and primitive, it's the one spot at the lake where you can gain entry into the Five Percent Club. Because the lake levels are kept near full all summer, this boat-in camp is doubly appealing. There are several lakeside sites, where from your tent, you can see the trout rising during the evening bite. The elevation is 6,100 feet. Open June through October.

16. EAST MEADOW 🐟 ⚓ 🏃 ♿ 🏊   RV 7

Reference: At Jackson Meadow Reservoir in Tahoe National Forest; map D3, grid a9.

Campsites, facilities: There are 20 tent sites and 26 sites for tents or motor homes up to 22 feet long. Piped water, flush toilets, a sanitary dump station, picnic tables and fire grills are provided. There is a boat ramp nearby. Pets are permitted on leashes or otherwise controlled. Supplies are available in Truckee or Sierraville. The facilities are **wheelchair accessible**.

Reservations, fee: Reserve by phoning (800) 280-CAMP ($7.50 reservation fee); $11 fee per night.

Who to contact: Phone Tahoe National Forest at (916) 994-3401, or California Land Management at (916) 582-0120.

Location: From Truckee, drive north on Highway 89 for 17.5 miles to Forest Service Road 7. Turn left (west) on Forest Service Road 7 and drive 15 miles to the campground entrance road on the left (if you reach Pass Creek Camp, you have gone one mile too far). Turn left and drive one mile to the campground on the right.

Trip note: This camp is in a beautiful setting on the east side of Jackson Meadow Reservoir, on the edge of a sheltered cove. The Pacific Crest Trail passes right by camp, providing access for a historic day-trip, though no stellar destinations are nearby on this stretch of the PCT. The nearest boat ramp is at Pass Creek Camp, two miles away. The elevation is 6,100 feet. Open June through November.

17. ASPEN GROUP CAMP

Reference: At Jackson Meadow Reservoir in Tahoe National Forest; map D3, grid a9.

Campsites, facilities: There are two 25-person group sites and one 50-person group site for tents or motor homes up to 22 feet long. Piped water, vault toilets, a sanitary dump station, picnic tables, fire grills and a campfire circle are provided. There is a boat ramp nearby on Jackson Meadow Reservoir. Pets are permitted on leashes or otherwise controlled. Supplies are available in Truckee or Sierraville.

Reservations, fee: Reserve by phoning (800) 280-CAMP ($15 reservation fee); $40-$75 group fee per night.

Who to contact: Phone the Tahoe National Forest District Office at (916) 994-3401, or California Land Management at (916) 582-0120.

Location: From Truckee, drive north on Highway 89 for 17.5 miles to Forest Service Road 7. Turn left (west) on Forest Service Road 7 and drive 16 miles (one mile past Pass Creek Camp) to the campground entrance on the right.

Trip note: A swimming beach, boat ramp and easy access to adjacent Jackson Meadow Reservoir make this a premium group camp. The elevation is 6,100 feet. Open June through October.

18. ENGLEBRIGHT LAKE BOAT-IN

Reference: Near Marysville; map D3, grid b0.

Campsites, facilities: There are 100 boat-in sites along the shores of Englebright Lake and a group camping area which accommodates 40 people (by reservation only). Picnic tables, fire grills and pit toilets are provided. Two boat ramps are available on either side of Skippers Cove (and more boat-in campsites). Boat rentals (including houseboats), mooring, a fuel dock and groceries are available. Pets are allowed on leashes.

Reservations, fee: No reservations (except group-use area); $2 boat-launch fee from May to October.

Who to contact: Phone the U.S. Corps of Engineers, Englebright Lake at (916) 639-2342, or call the concessionaire at Skippers Cove at (916) 639-2272.

Location: From Auburn, drive north on Highway 49 to Grass Valley and the junction with Highway 20. Turn west on Highway 20 and drive to Mooney Flat Road (if you reach Smartville, you have gone one mile too far). Turn north on Mooney Flat and drive three miles to a fork. Turn left at the fork and drive one mile to park headquarters and the boat ramp just east of the dam.

Trip note: Englebright Lake is the perfect destination for boat-in camping, fishing and waterskiing. Remember this place. It always seem to have plenty of water, and there are more developed boat-in campsites than at any other lake in California. The lake looks like a huge water snake, long and narrow, set in the Yuba River canyon at 520 feet in elevation. Trout fishing is good in the spring, when waterskiing is prohibited on the upper end of the lake. In summer, it is a waterskiing mecca, with the water warm and calm. Open year-round.

---

19. NEVADA COUNTY FAIRGROUNDS

Reference: **At the fairgrounds near Grass Valley; map D3, grid b2.**

Campsites, facilities: There are 143 sites for motor homes, all with hookups. Two sanitary dump stations, showers and flush toilets are available. Pets are permitted on leashes.

Reservations, fee: Reservations accepted; $13 fee per night. A 14-day stay limit is enforced.

Who to contact: Phone (916) 273-6217 or write to Nevada County Fairgrounds, P.O. Box 2687, Grass Valley, CA 95945.

Location: From Auburn, drive north on Highway 49 to Grass Valley and the McKnight Way or Empire Street exits. Take either and follow the signs to the Nevada County Fairgrounds.

Trip note: The motto here is "California's Most Beautiful Fairgrounds," and they're right. The area is set at 2,300 feet in the Sierra foothills, with a good number of pines sprinkled about. The park is located adjacent to the fairgrounds, and even though the fair runs for a few weeks every summer, the park is open year-round. A caretaker at the park is available to answer any questions. Kids can fish at a small lake nearby.

---

20. SOUTH YUBA

Reference: **Near Yuba River; map D3, grid b3.**

Campsites, facilities: There are 17 sites for tents or motor homes up to 27 feet long. Piped water, pit toilets, picnic tables and fire grills are provided. Pets are permitted on leashes.

Reservations, fee: No reservations; $3 fee per night.

Who to contact: Phone the Bureau of Land Management at (916) 985-4474.

Location: From Auburn, turn north on Highway 49 and drive to Nevada City, then continue a short distance to North Bloomfield Road. Turn right (east) and drive 10 miles to the campground on the right side of the road (the road becomes quite rough). *RVs or vehicles with trailers should take this route:* From Auburn, turn north on Highway 49 to Nevada City, then continue to Tyler Foote Crossing Road. Turn right and drive to Grizzly Hills Road (just past North Columbia). Turn right and drive three miles to North Bloomfield Road. Turn left and drive a short distance to the campground on the right.

Trip note: This little-known BLM camp is set next to where little Kenebee Creek enters the Yuba River. The Yuba is about a mile away, with some great swimming holes to explore. A good side trip is to nearby Malakoff Diggins State Park and the town of North Bloomfield (about a 10-minute drive to the northeast on North Bloomfield Road), which is being completely restored to its 1850s character. Hopefully, that does not include the food. The elevation is 2,600 feet. Open March through October.

21. SCOTTS FLAT LAKE RECREATION AREA

Reference: **Map D3, grid b4.**

Campsites, facilities: There are 182 sites for tents or motor homes up to 35 feet long. Restrooms, showers, and a sanitary dump station are provided. A general store, a bait and tackle shop, boat rentals, a boat ramp and a playground are also available. Pets are permitted on leashes. Most facilities are **wheelchair accessible**.

Reservations, fee: Reservations recommended in summer; $14-$19 fee per night; $2 pet fee.

Who to contact: Phone (916) 265-5302.

Location: From Auburn, drive north on Highway 49 to Nevada City and the junction with Highway 20. Turn right (east) and drive five miles to Scotts Flat Road. Turn right (south) and drive four miles (three miles paved, one mile gravel) to the camp entrance road on the right (on the north shore of the lake).

Trip note: Scotts Flat Reservoir at 3,100 feet in elevation is shaped like a large teardrop, one of the prettier lakes in the Sierra foothills, with 7.5 miles of shoreline circled by forest. The camp is set on the lake's north shore, largely protected from spring winds, and within short range of the marina and one of the lake's two boat launches. Trout fishing is good here in the spring and early summer, and then when the lake heats up, waterskiing and power boating become more popular. Open year-round, weather permitting.

22. SKILLMAN GROUP CAMP

Reference: **In Tahoe National Forest; map D3, grid b5.**

Campsites, facilities: This group campsite can accommodate up to 80 people. Piped water, vault toilets, picnic tables and fire grills are provided. Pets are permitted on leashes. A horse corral is available.

Reservations, fee: Reserve by phoning (800) 280-CAMP; $15-$50 fee per night.

Who to contact: Phone Tahoe National Forest at (916) 265-4538.

Location: From Sacramento, drive east on Interstate 80 past Emigrant Gap to Highway 20. Turn west on Highway 20 and drive 18 miles to the campground entrance on the left.

Trip note: Skillman Group Camp is set at 4,400 feet, on a loop access road just off of Highway 20, with the historic Pioneer Trail running right through the camp. See the trip note for White Cloud Camp. Open May through November, depending on the weather.

23. WHITE CLOUD

Reference: **In Tahoe National Forest; map D3, grid b5.**

Campsites, facilities: There are 46 sites for tents or motor homes up to 22 feet long. Piped water, vault and flush toilets, picnic tables and fire grills are provided. Pets are permitted on leashes or otherwise controlled.

Reservations, fee: No reservations; $9 fee per night.

Who to contact: Phone the Tahoe National Forest at (916) 265-4538.

Location: From Sacramento, drive east on Interstate 80 to Emigrant Gap. Take the offramp, then head north on the short connector road to Highway 20. Turn west on Highway 20 and drive about 15 miles to the campground entrance on the left.

Trip note: This camp is set along the historic Pioneer Trail, which has turned into one of the top mountain bike routes in the Sierra Nevada, easy and fast. This trail traces the route of the first wagon road opened by emigrants and gold seekers in 1850. It is best suited for mountain biking, with a lot of bikers learning of the one-way downhill ride (with an extra car for a shuttle ride) from Bear Valley to Lone Grave. The Omega Overlook is the highlight, with dramatic views of granite cliffs and the Yuba River. The camp is set at 4,200 feet in Tahoe National Forest. Open May through October.

---

24. FULLER LAKE

Reference: **In Tahoe National Forest; map D3, grid b7.**

Campsites, facilities: There are nine tent sites, with **no piped water**, but vault toilets, picnic tables and fire grills are provided. Pack out your garbage. Pets are permitted on leashes or otherwise controlled.

Reservations, fee: No reservations; no fee.

Who to contact: Phone the Tahoe National Forest at (916) 265-4538.

Location: From Sacramento, drive east on Interstate 80 past Emigrant Gap to Highway 20. Turn west on Highway 20 and drive to Bowman Road (County Road 18). Turn right (north) and drive four miles to the campground on the right side of the road.

Trip note: Fuller Lake is the gateway to a region off Bowman Road filled with more than a dozen lakes. It is the first you will come to, at 5,600 feet in elevation. The camp is primitive but pretty, set on the west side of Fuller Lake. A small unimproved boat ramp is available. It is not only easy for campers to reach, but also easy for the Department of Fish and Game, and they stock this lake with both rainbow and brown trout starting in early summer. The access road is usually free of snow by mid-May, but late-season snowstorms are not unusual. Open May through October.

---

25. LAKE SPAULDING

Reference: **Near Emigrant Gap; map D3, grid b7.**

Campsites, facilities: There are 25 sites for tents or motor homes up to 20 feet long. Piped water, picnic tables, fire grills and restrooms are provided. A boat ramp is available. Supplies are available in Nevada City. Pets are allowed on leashes.

Reservations, fee: No reservations; $10 fee per night; $1 pet fee.

Who to contact: Phone PG&E at (916) 386-5164.

Location: From Sacramento, drive east on Highway 80 past Emigrant Gap to Highway 20. Drive west on Highway 20 to Lake Spaulding Road. Turn right on Lake Spaulding Road and travel a half-mile to the lake.

Trip note: Lake Spaulding is set at 5,000 feet in the Sierra Nevada, complete with huge boulders and a sprinkling of conifers. Its clear, pure, very cold water has startling effects on swimmers. The lake is extremely pretty, with the Sierra granite backdrop looking as if it has been cut, chiseled and smoothed. The drive here is nearly a straight shot up Interstate 80, the boat ramp is fine for small aluminum boats, and if there is any problem here, it is that there will be plenty of company at the campground. Fishing for kokanee salmon and rainbow trout is often good, as well as fishing for trout at the nearby South Fork Yuba River. There are many other lakes set in the mountain country to the immediate north that can make for excellent side trips, including Bowman, Weaver and Faucherie lakes.

26. LODGEPOLE 🐟 ⚓ 🏊   RV 8

Reference: **On Lake Valley Reservoir in Tahoe National Forest; map D3, grid b7.**

Campsites, facilities: There are 18 sites for tents or motor homes up to 20 feet long. Piped water, picnic tables, fire grills and restrooms are provided. A boat ramp is available. Supplies can be obtained off Interstate 80. Pets are allowed on leashes.

Reservations, fee: No reservations; $10 fee per night; $1 pet fee.

Who to contact: Phone PG&E at (916) 386-5164.

Location: From Interstate 80, take the Yuba Gap exit and drive south for a quarter-mile to Lake Valley Road. Turn right on Lake Valley Road and drive for one mile until the road forks. Bear right and continue for 1.5 miles to the campground entrance road to the right on another fork.

Trip note: Lake Valley Reservoir is set at 5,786 feet and covers 300 acres. It is gorgeous when full, its shoreline sprinkled with conifers and boulders. The lake provides decent results for fishermen, with the best luck while trolling. A speed limit prohibits waterskiing and jet-skiing, and that keeps the place quiet and peaceful. The campground is set about a quarter-mile from the lake's southwest shore, about two miles from the boat ramp located on the north shore. A trailhead from camp is routed south up Monumental Ridge and to Monumental Creek (three miles, one-way) set on the northwestern flank of Quartz Mountain (6,931 feet).

27. GROUSE RIDGE 🐟 🚶 🏊   RV 6

Reference: **Near Bowman Lake in Tahoe National Forest; map D3, grid b7.**

Campsites, facilities: There are nine sites for tents or motor homes up to 16 feet long. Piped water, vault toilets, picnic tables and fire grills are provided. Pack out your garbage. Pets are permitted on leashes or otherwise controlled.

Reservations, fee: No reservations; no fee.

Who to contact: Phone the Tahoe National Forest at (916) 265-4538.

Location: From Sacramento, drive east on Interstate 80 past Emigrant Gap to Highway 20. Turn west on Highway 20 and drive to Bowman Road (County Road 18). Turn north on Bowman Road and drive five miles to Grouse Ridge Road. Turn right on Grouse Ridge Road and drive six miles on rough gravel to the campground.

Trip note: This camp is set at 7,400 feet at the gateway to some beautiful hiking country filled with small high-Sierra lakes. The camp is primarily used as a trailhead and jumpoff point, not as a destination itself. The closest hike is the half-mile tromp up to the Grouse Ridge Lookout, 7,707 feet, which provides a spectacular view to the north of this area and its many small lakes. Hiking north, the trail passes Round Lake (to the left) in the first mile and Middle Lake (on the right) two miles later, with opportunities to take cutoff trails on either side of the ridge to visit numerous other lakes. Open June through October.

28. WOODCHUCK

Reference: **On Rattlesnake Creek in Tahoe National Forest; map D3, grid b8.**

Campsites, facilities: There are eight sites for tents or motor homes up to 16 feet long. There is **no piped water**, but vault toilets, picnic tables and fire grills are provided. Pets are permitted on leashes or otherwise controlled. A grocery store and propane gas are also available nearby.

Reservations, fee: No reservations; no fee.

Who to contact: Phone the Tahoe National Forest at (916) 265-4538.

Location: From Sacramento, drive east on Interstate 80 to Yuba Pass and continue for about four miles to Cisco Grove exit north. Take that exit, then turn left on the frontage road and drive a short distance to Rattlesnake Road (just prior to reaching Thousand Trails). Turn right on Rattlesnake Road (gravel, steep and curvy, trailers not recommended) and drive three miles to the campground on the right.

Trip note: This little camp is only a few miles from Interstate 80, but it is quite obscure and little-known to most travelers. It is set on Rattlesnake Creek at 6,300 feet in Tahoe National Forest, at the threshold of some great backcountry and four-wheel-drive roads that access many beautiful lakes. To explore, a map of Tahoe National Forest is a must. Open June through October.

29. INDIAN SPRINGS

Reference: **Near Yuba River in Tahoe National Forest; map D3, grid b8.**

Campsites, facilities: There are 35 sites for tents or motor homes up to 25 feet long. Piped water, vault toilets, picnic tables and fire grills are provided. Pets are permitted on leashes or otherwise controlled. A grocery store and propane gas are also available nearby.

Reservations, fee: Reserve by phoning (800) 280-CAMP ($7.50 reservation fee); $10 fee per night.

Who to contact: Phone the Tahoe National Forest at (916) 265-4538.

Location: From Sacramento, drive east on Interstate 80 to Yuba Pass and continue for about three miles to the Eagle Lakes exit. Take that exit, then head north on Eagle Lakes Road for one mile to the campground on the left side of the road.

Trip note: The camp is easy to reach from Interstate 80, yet is in a beautiful setting at 5,600 feet along the South Fork Yuba River. This is a gorgeous stream, running deep blue-green and pure through a granite setting, complete with giant boulders and beautiful pools. Trout fishing is fair. There is a small beach nearby where you can go swimming, though the water is cold. There are also several lakes in the vicinity. Open May through October.

30. LAKE STERLING

Reference: **In Tahoe National Forest; map D3, grid b9.**

Campsites, facilities: There are six tent sites. There is **no piped water**, but vault toilets, picnic tables and fire grills are provided. Pack out your garbage. Pets are permitted on leashes or otherwise controlled.

Reservations, fee: No reservations; no fee.

Who to contact: Phone the Tahoe National Forest at (916) 265-4538.

Location: From Sacramento, drive east on Interstate 80 to Yuba Pass and continue for about four miles to Cisco Grove exit north. Take that exit, then turn left on the frontage road and drive a short distance to Rattlesnake Road (just prior to reaching Thousand Trails). Turn right on Rattlesnake Road and drive four miles to Sterling Lake Road on the left. Turn left and drive 2.5 miles (steep, curvy, sometimes rough) to the campground on the right side of the road.

Trip note: This remote and primitive camp was renovated in 1995. It is set along Lake Sterling at 7,000 feet, an excellent camp for hikers or boaters with car-top boats. It is a very pretty, small lake, perched in a granite pocket, with the campground set along the western shore. A trailhead from the campground is routed north past a series of little mountain ponds, a great loop that takes only a few hours to complete. Fishing at Lake Sterling is fair, with the trout often very small. Note: Boy Scout Troops often have outings based out of the southeast side of the lake.

31. FORBES CREEK GROUP CAMP

Reference: **On Sugar Pine Reservoir in Tahoe National Forest; map D3, grid c5.**

Campsites, facilities: This group campsite can accommodate up to 50 people in tents or motor homes up to 30 feet long. Piped water, vault toilets, picnic tables and fire grills are provided. All facilities are **wheelchair accessible**. A campfire circle, central parking area, sanitary dump station and boat ramp are available nearby. Pets are permitted on leashes or otherwise controlled. Supplies can be obtained in Foresthill.

Reservations, fee: Reserve by phoning (800) 280-CAMP; ($15 reservation fee); $40 fee per night.

Who to contact: Phone the concessionaire at (801) 226-3564 or write to L&L Inc., 899 South Orem Boulevard, Orem, UT 84058. Or phone the Tahoe National Forest District Office at (916) 367-2224.

Location: From Sacramento, drive east on Interstate 80 to the north end of Auburn and the Foresthill Road exit. Take that exit and drive east for eight miles to Sugar Pine Road. Turn left and drive seven miles to a fork (just before reaching the lake). Turn right and drive for two miles around the south end of the lake to the campground on the left.

Trip note: This is a special group camp, ideal for Boy Scout troops. The boat launch is nearby, but note: a 10-mile-per-hour speed limit is the law. That makes for quiet water, perfect for anglers and canoeists and other small boats. A paved trail circles the lake. For more information, see Giant Gap Campground.

32. GIANT GAP CAMPGROUND

Reference: **On Sugar Pine Reservoir in Tahoe National Forest; map D3, grid c5.**

Campsites, facilities: There are 30 sites for tents or motor homes up to 30 feet long. Piped water, vault toilets, picnic tables and fire grills are provided. All facilities are **wheelchair accessible**. A sanitary dump station and a boat ramp are available on the south shore. Pets are permitted on leashes or otherwise controlled. Supplies can be obtained in Foresthill.

Reservations, fee: Reserve by phoning (800) 280-CAMP ($7.50 reservation fee); $8-$24 fee per night.

Who to contact: Phone the concessionaire at (801) 226-3564 or write to L&L Inc., 899 South Orem Boulevard, Orem, UT 84058. Or phone the Tahoe National Forest District Office at (916) 367-2224.

Location: From Sacramento, drive east on Interstate 80 to the north end of Auburn and the Foresthill Road exit. Take that exit and drive east to Foresthill and continue for eight miles to Sugar Pine Road. Turn left and drive seven miles to a fork (just before reaching the lake). Turn left and drive for about a mile to the campground on the right.

Trip note: This is a lakeside spot along the western shore of Sugar Pine Reservoir, at 3,500 feet in elevation in Tahoe National Forest. For boaters, there is a ramp on the south shore. Note that a 10-mile-per-hour speed limit is the law, making this lake ideal for anglers in search of quiet water. Other recreation notes: There's a paved trail around the lake, a beach nearby at Manzanita Picnic Area on the north shore, and several streams nearby in the surrounding national forest. Big Reservoir, located two miles to the east, is the only other lake in the region, and also has a campground. The trout fishing at Sugar Pine is fair, but much better than that at Big Reservoir.

---

33. BIG RESERVOIR 🐟 ⛵ ✕ 　 RV 🔺

Reference: On Big Reservoir in Tahoe National Forest; map D3, grid c5.

Campsites, facilities: There are 100 sites for tents or motor homes up to 25 feet long. Piped water, vault toilets, picnic tables and fire grills are provided. Firewood is limited. Pets are permitted on leashes or otherwise controlled. Supplies are available in Foresthill.

Reservations, fee: Reservations accepted; $15 fee per night.

Who to contact: Call DeAnza Placer Gold Mining Company at (916) 367-2129, or phone Tahoe National Forest at (916) 367-2224.

Location: From Sacramento, drive east on Interstate 80 to the north end of Auburn and the Foresthill Road exit. Take that exit and drive east to Foresthill. then continue for eight miles to Sugar Pine Road. Turn left and drive about three miles to Forest Service Road 24 (signed Big Reservoir). Bear right on Forest Service Road 24 and drive about five miles to the campground entrance road on the right.

Trip note: Here's a quiet lake where no boat motors are allowed. That makes it ideal for canoeists, row-boaters and tube floaters who don't like the idea of having to dodge waterskiers, or fishermen for that matter, because the fishing is zilch here. The lake is quite pretty, a 70-acre pocket of snowmelt surrounded by forest. A nice beach is available, not far from the resort. The elevation is 4,000 feet. Open May through October.

---

34. SHIRTTAIL CREEK 🐟 ⚓ 🏃 ♿ ⛵ 　 RV 🔺

Reference: On Sugar Pine Reservoir in Tahoe National Forest; map D3, grid c5.

Campsites, facilities: There are 30 sites for tents or motor homes up to 30 feet long (double and triple sites are available). Piped water, vault toilets, picnic tables and fire grills are provided. All facilities are **wheelchair accessible**. A sanitary dump station and a boat ramp are available on the south shore. Pets are permitted on leashes or otherwise controlled. Supplies can be obtained in Foresthill.

Reservations, fee: Reserve by phoning (800) 280-CAMP ($7.50 reservation fee); $8 fee per night.

Who to contact: Phone the concessionaire at (801)226-3564 or write to L&L Inc., 899 South Orem Boulevard, Orem, UT 84058. Or phone the Tahoe National Forest District Office at (916) 367-2224.

Location: From Sacramento, drive east on Interstate 80 to the north end of Auburn and the Foresthill Road exit. Take that exit and drive east to Foresthill, then continue for eight miles to Sugar Pine Road. Turn left and drive seven miles to a fork (just before reaching the lake). Turn left and drive for about three miles to the campground on the right.

Trip note: This camp is set near the little creek that feeds into the north end of Sugar Pine Reservoir. The boat ramp is located all the way around the other side of the lake in Sugar Pine Cove near Forbes Creek Group Camp. For recreation notes, see the trip note for Giant Gap Campground.

---

35. SECRET HOUSE

Reference: **In Tahoe National Forest; map D3, grid c7.**

Campsites, facilities: There are two tent sites. There is **no piped water**, but vault toilets, picnic tables and fire grills are provided. Pack out your garbage. Pets are permitted on leashes or otherwise controlled. Supplies are available in Foresthill.

Reservations, fee: No reservations; no fee.

Who to contact: Phone the Tahoe National Forest at (916) 367-2224.

Location: From Sacramento, drive east on Interstate 80 to the north end of Auburn and the Foresthill Road exit. Take that exit and drive east to Foresthill and Foresthill Divide Road. Continue northeast (the road eventually turns to gravel, and is narrow and curvy) and drive 19 miles to the campground on the right side of the road.

Trip note: Foresthill Divide Road is set on a mountain ridge with a series of trailheads on the left side of the road. They provide access to old mining trails that lead down to the North Fork American River. These are some of the steepest hiking trails in California, with 2,000-foot drops over the course of two miles typical for all the routes, but the payoff is a series of secluded and pristine streamside hikes and fishing spots. The camp itself is perched in forest on the flank of Whiskey Hill. The nearest trailhead is less than two miles up the road on the left. The elevation is 5,400 feet. Open May through October.

---

36. NORTH FORK

Reference: **On the North Fork of American River in Tahoe National Forest; map D3, grid c7.**

Campsites, facilities: There are 17 sites for tents or motor homes up to 16 feet long. Piped water, vault toilets, picnic tables and fire grills are provided. Pets are permitted on leashes or otherwise controlled. Supplies are available at Emigrant Gap, Cisco Grove and Soda Springs.

Reservations, fee: Reserve by phoning (800) 280-CAMP ($7.50 reservation fee); $9 fee per night.

Who to contact: Phone the Tahoe National Forest at (916) 265-4538.

Location: From Sacramento, drive east on Interstate 80 to the Emigrant Gap exit. Take that exit and drive south for a quarter-mile to Texas Hill Road (County Road 19). Turn right and drive about five miles to the camp on the right.

Trip note: This is gold mining country, and this camp is set along the Little North Fork of the North Fork American River, at 4,400 feet in elevation, where you might still find a few magic gold flecks. Unfortunately, they are probably fool's gold, not the real stuff. This feeder stream is small and pretty, and the camp is fairly remote and overlooked by most. It is set on the edge of a network of backcountry Forest Service Roads. To explore them, a map of Tahoe National Forest is a must. Open May through October.

37. TUNNEL MILL

Reference: **On the North Fork of American River in Tahoe National Forest; map D3, grid c7.**

Campsites, facilities: There are two group sites for tents or motor homes up to 16 feet long. There is **no piped water**, but vault toilets, picnic tables and fire grills are provided. Pets are permitted on leashes or otherwise controlled. Supplies are available at the Nyack exit of Emigrant Gap.

Reservations, fee: Reservations required; phone (800) 280-CAMP ($15 reservation fee); $40 fee for groups.

Who to contact: Phone the Tahoe National Forest at (916) 265-4538.

Location: From Sacramento, drive east on Interstate 80 to the Emigrant Gap exit. Take that exit and drive south for a quarter-mile to Texas Hill Road (County Road 19). Turn right and drive about seven miles to the campground on the right side of the road.

Trip note: This is a good spot for a Boy Scout campout. It's a rustic, quiet, group camp set all by itself along the (take a deep breath) East Fork of the North Fork of the North Fork of the American River (whew). See preceding camp (North Fork) for more recreation information. The elevation is 4,400 feet. Open June through October.

38. BIG BEND

Reference: **On Yuba River in Tahoe National Forest; map D3, grid c8.**

Campsites, facilities: There are 15 sites for tents or motor homes up to 16 feet long. Piped water, vault toilets, picnic tables and fire grills are provided. Pets are permitted on leashes or otherwise controlled. A grocery store, a restaurant and propane gas are available nearby.

Reservations, fee: Reserve by phoning (800) 280-CAMP ($7.50 reservation fee); $10 fee per night.

Who to contact: Phone the Tahoe National Forest at (916) 265-4538.

Location: From Sacramento, drive east on Interstate 80 to Cisco Grove and continue for one mile to the Big Bend exit. Take that exit (remaining just south of the highway), then turn left on the frontage road and drive east for a quarter-mile to the campground. (Traveling westbound on Interstate 80, take the Rainbow Road exit—if you reach Cisco Grove you have gone two miles too far—and continue west for 1.5 miles to the campground.)

Trip note: Big Bend is named after the big curve in the South Fork Yuba River. This camp is set next to that curve, at 5,900 feet in elevation, a pretty spot high in the Sierra Nevada, in Tahoe National Forest. Nearby access for Interstate 80 and an adjacent ranger station make this an easy camp to reach and use as a base. There are numerous nearby lakes to the north (Sterling and Fordyce, both drive-to) and south (Loch Leven, hike-in only) for great side trips. Open May through October.

39. KIDD LAKE GROUP CAMP

Reference: **West of Truckee; map D3, grid c9.**

Campsites, facilities: This group site will accommodate up to 100 people in tents only. Piped water, picnic tables, fire grills and restrooms are provided. An unimproved boat ramp is available. Supplies are available in Truckee. Pets are permitted on leashes.

Reservations, fee: Reservations required; $15 fee per night; $2 pet fee.

Who to contact: For reservations, write to Land Supervisor, PG&E, P.O. Box 1148, Auburn, CA 95603, or phone (916) 386-5164.

Location: From Sacramento, drive east on Interstate 80 toward Truckee and the Norden exit. Take that exit, drive a short distance, and turn south on Soda Springs Road and drive one mile to Pahatsi Road. Turn right (west) and drive two miles. When the road forks, bear right and drive one mile to the campground entrance road on the left.

Trip note: Kidd Lake is one of four lakes bunched in a series along the access road just south of Interstate 80. It is set in the northern Sierra's high country, at 6,500 feet, and gets loaded with snow every winter. In late spring and early summer, always call ahead for conditions on the access road. The fishing is frustrating, consisting of a lot of tiny brook trout. Only car-top boats are permitted on Kidd Lake. The camp is set just northeast of the lake, within walking distance of the shore.

40. HAMPSHIRE ROCKS

Reference: **On Yuba River in Tahoe National Forest; map D3, grid c9.**

Campsites, facilities: There are 31 sites for tents or motor homes up to 22 feet long. Piped water, vault toilets, picnic tables and fire grills are provided. Pets are permitted on leashes or otherwise controlled. A grocery store, restaurant and propane gas are available nearby.

Reservations, fee: Reserve by phoning (800) 280-CAMP ($7.50 reservation fee); $10 fee per night.

Who to contact: Phone the Tahoe National Forest at (916) 265-4538.

Location: From Sacramento, drive east on Interstate 80 to Cisco Grove and continue for one mile to the Big Bend exit. Take that exit (remaining just south of the highway), then turn left on the frontage road and drive east for 1.5 miles to the campground.

Trip note: This camp sits along the South Fork of the Yuba River, 5,900 feet in elevation, with easy access off Interstate 80 and a nearby Forest Service visitor information center. Fishing for trout is fair. There are some swimming holes, but the water is often very cold. Nearby lakes that can provide side trips include Sterling and Fordyce lakes (drive-to) to the north, and the Loch Leven Lakes (hike-to) to the south. Open May through October.

41. ROBINSON FLAT

Reference: **Near French Meadows Reservoir in Tahoe National Forest; map D3, grid d8.**

Campsites, facilities: There are five tent sites. There is **no piped water**, but vault toilets, picnic tables and fire grills are provided. Pack out your garbage. Pets are permitted on leashes or otherwise controlled. Supplies are available in Foresthill.

Reservations, fee: No reservations; no fee.

Who to contact: Phone the Tahoe National Forest at (916) 367-2224.

Location: From Sacramento, drive east on Interstate 80 to the north end of Auburn and the Foresthill Road exit. Take that exit and drive east to Foresthill and Foresthill Divide Road. Continue northeast (the road eventually turns to gravel, and is narrow and curvy) and drive 27 miles to the junction with County Road 43. Turn left and drive a short distance to the campground on the right side of the road.

Trip note: This camp is set at 6,800 feet in remote Tahoe National Forest, on the eastern flank of Duncan Peak (7,116 feet), with a two-mile drive to the south to Duncan Peak Lookout (7,182 feet). A trail out of camp follows along a small stream, a fork to Duncan Creek, in Little Robinsons Valley. French Meadows Reservoir is located to the nearby southeast. Open May through October.

---

42. POPPY HIKE-IN, BOAT-IN 🐟 ⚓ 🚶 🏊 **5% CLUB** **9**

Reference: **On French Meadows Reservoir in Tahoe National Forest; map D3, grid d9.**

Campsites, facilities: There are 12 tent sites, accessible by boat or by a one-mile-long foot trail from McGuire Picnic Site. There is **no piped water**, but vault toilets, picnic tables and fire grills are provided. Pets are permitted on leashes or otherwise controlled. Supplies are available in Foresthill.

Reservations, fee: No reservations; no fee.

Who to contact: Phone the Tahoe National Forest District Office at (916) 367-2224, or L&L Inc. at (801) 226-3564, or write 899 South Orem Boulevard, Orem, UT 84058.

Location: From Sacramento, drive east on Interstate 80 to the north end of Auburn and the Foresthill Road exit. Take that exit and drive east to Foresthill and Mosquito Ridge Road. Turn east and drive 36 miles (curvy) to a dirt road on the left (one mile before reaching Anderson Dam). Turn left and drive three miles to the end of the road. Park and hike one mile to the camp. Note: The trailhead access road is sometimes blocked by a locked gate, making it a three-mile hike to the campground. An option if the gate is locked is to drive around the lake and hike in one mile from the McGuire Picnic Area.

Trip note: Poppy Camp is located on the north side of French Meadows Reservoir, about midway along the lake's shore. This camp can be reached only by boat or on foot, supplying a great degree of privacy compared to the other camps on this lake. A trail that is routed along the north shore of this reservoir runs right through the camp, providing two different trailhead access points, as well as a good side trip hike. The lake is quite big, covering nearly 2,000 acres when full, at 5,300 feet in elevation on a dammed-up section of the Middle Fork American River. It is stocked with rainbow trout, but also has prime habitat for brown trout, including some big ones.

---

43. FRENCH MEADOWS 🐟 ⚓ 🚶 🏊 **RV** **7**

Reference: **On French Meadows Reservoir in Tahoe National Forest; map D3, grid d9.**

Campsites, facilities: There are 75 sites for tents or motor homes up to 22 feet long. Piped water, flush toilets, picnic tables and fire grills are provided. A concrete boat ramp is nearby. Pets are permitted on leashes or otherwise controlled. Supplies are available in Foresthill.

Reservations, fee: Reserve by phoning (800) 280-CAMP ($7.50 reservation fee); $8 fee per night.

Who to contact: Phone the Tahoe National Forest District Office at (916) 367-2224, or L&L Inc. at (801) 226-3564, or write 899 South Orem Boulevard, Orem, UT 84058.

Location: From Sacramento, drive east on Interstate 80 to the north end of Auburn and the Foresthill Road exit. Take that exit and drive east to Foresthill and Mosquito Ridge Road. Turn east and drive 36 miles (curvy) to Anderson Dam, then continue along the southern shoreline of French Meadows Reservoir for four miles to the campground.

Trip note: The nearby boat launch makes this the choice for boating campers. The camp is on French Meadows Reservoir at 5,300 feet. It is set on the lake's southern shore, with the boat ramp located about a mile to the south (you'll see the entrance road on the way in). This is a big lake set in remote Tahoe National Forest in the North Fork American River Canyon, with good trout fishing. The lake level often drops in late summer, then a lot of stumps and boulders start poking through the lake surface. This creates navigational hazards for boaters, but also makes it easier for fishermen to know where to fish. If the fish don't bite here, boaters should make the nearby side trip to awesome, steep-sided Hell Hole Reservoir to the south. Open June through October.

---

44. GATES GROUP CAMP 🎣 🏃 🏊   RV 7

Reference: **On North Fork of the American River in Tahoe National Forest; map D3, grid d9.**

Campsites, facilities: There are two 25-person group sites and one 75-person group site for tents or motor homes up to 22 feet long. Piped water, vault toilets, picnic tables, fire grills, central parking and a campfire circle are provided. Pets are permitted on leashes or otherwise controlled. Supplies are available in Foresthill.

Reservations, fee: Reserve by phoning (800) 280-CAMP ($15 reservation fee); $25-$50 fee per night.

Who to contact: Phone the concessionaire at (209) 294-4512, or write to Sierra Recreation, P.O. Box 478, Pioneer, CA 95666. Or phone the Tahoe National Forest at (916) 367-2224.

Location: From Sacramento, drive east on Interstate 80 to the north end of Auburn and the Foresthill Road exit. Take that exit and drive east to Foresthill and Mosquito Ridge Road. Turn east and drive 36 miles (curvy) to Anderson Dam, then continue for five miles along the southern shoreline to French Meadows Reservoir and a fork at the head of the lake. Bear right at the fork and drive one mile to the camp at the end of the road.

Trip note: This group camp is well secluded along the North Fork American River, just upstream from where it pours into French Meadows Reservoir. For recreation options, see trip notes for French Meadows Camp and Poppy Camp. Open June through October.

---

45. COYOTE GROUP CAMP 🎣 ⚓ 🏃 🏊   RV 6

Reference: **On French Meadows Reservoir, in Tahoe National Forest; map D3, grid d9.**

Campsites, facilities: There are three 25-person group sites and one 50-person group site for tents or motor homes up to 22 feet long. Piped water, vault toilets, picnic tables and fire grills are provided. A campfire circle and central parking area are also provided. Pets are permitted on leashes or otherwise controlled. Supplies are available in Foresthill.

Reservations, fee: Reserve by phoning (800) 280-CAMP ($15 reservation fee); $25-$50 fee per night or $1 per person.

Who to contact: Phone the concessionaire at (209) 294-4512 or write to Sierra Recreation, P.O. Box 478, Pioneer, CA 95666. Or phone the Tahoe National Forest District Office at (916) 367-2224.

Location: From Sacramento, drive east on Interstate 80 to the north end of Auburn and the Foresthill Road exit. Take that exit and drive east to Foresthill and Mosquito Ridge Road. Turn east and drive 36 miles (curvy) to Anderson Dam, then continue for five miles along the southern shoreline to French Meadows Reservoir and a fork at the head of the lake. Bear left at the fork and drive a half-mile to the camp on the left side of the road.

Trip note: This group camp is set right at the head of French Meadows Reservoir, at 5,300 feet in elevation. A boat ramp is located two miles to the south, just past Lewis Campground, on the lake's north shore. For recreation options, see the trip notes for French Meadows Camp and Poppy Camp. Open June through October.

---

46. AHART

Reference: **Near French Meadows Reservoir in Tahoe National Forest; map D3, grid d9.**

Campsites, facilities: There are 12 sites for tents or motor homes up to 22 feet long. There is **no piped water**, but vault toilets, picnic tables and fire grills are provided. Pets are permitted on leashes or otherwise controlled. Supplies are available in Foresthill.

Reservations, fee: No reservations; $8 fee per night.

Who to contact: Phone the Tahoe National Forest District Office at (916) 367-2224, or L&L Inc. at (801) 226-3564, or write to 899 South Orem Boulevard, Orem, UT 84058.

Location: From Sacramento, drive east on Interstate 80 to the north end of Auburn and the Foresthill Road exit. Take that exit and drive east to Foresthill and Mosquito Ridge Road. Turn east and drive 36 miles (curvy) to Anderson Dam, then continue for five miles along the southern shoreline to French Meadows Reservoir and a fork at the head of the lake. Bear left at the fork and drive 1.5 miles to the campground.

Trip note: This camp is located one mile north of French Meadows Reservoir and set near where the Middle Fork of the American River enters the lake. It is primarily used as an overflow camp if lakeside camps are filled. This is bear country in the summer. Open June through October.

---

47. LEWIS

Reference: **On French Meadows Reservoir in Tahoe National Forest; map D3, grid d9.**

Campsites, facilities: There are 40 sites for tents or motor homes up to 22 feet long. Piped water, vault toilets, picnic tables and fire grills are provided. A concrete boat ramp is nearby. Pets are permitted on leashes or otherwise controlled. Supplies are available in Foresthill.

Reservations, fee: Reserve by phoning (800) 280-CAMP ($7.50 reservation fee);

$8 fee per night.

Who to contact: Phone the Tahoe National Forest District Office at (916) 367-2224, or L&L Inc. at (801) 226-3564, or write 899 South Orem Boulevard, Orem, UT 84058.

Location: From Sacramento, drive east on Interstate 80 to the north end of Auburn and the Foresthill Road exit. Take that exit and drive east to Foresthill and Mosquito Ridge Road. Turn east and drive 36 miles (curvy) to Anderson Dam, then continue for five miles along the southern shoreline to French Meadows Reservoir and a fork at the head of the lake. Bear left at the fork and drive a half-mile to the campground entrance road on the left. Turn left and drive one mile to the camp on the right.

Trip note: This camp is not set at lakeside, but is just across the road from French Meadows Reservoir. It is still quite pretty, set along a feeder creek near the lake's northeast shore. A boat ramp is available only a half-mile to the south, and the adjacent McGuire Picnic Area has a trailhead that is routed along the lake's northern shoreline. This lake is big (2,000 acres) and pretty, created by a dam on the Middle Fork American River, with good fishing for rainbow trout. Open May through October.

---

48. TALBOT

Reference: On Middle Fork of American River in Tahoe National Forest; map D3, grid d9.

Campsites, facilities: There are five tent sites. There is **no piped water**, but vault toilets, picnic tables and fire grills are provided. Pets are permitted on leashes or otherwise controlled. Supplies are available in Foresthill. The camp is within a state game refuge, so no firearms are permitted.

Reservations, fee: No reservations; no fee.

Who to contact: Phone the Tahoe National Forest District Office at (916) 367-2224.

Location: From Sacramento, drive east on Interstate 80 to the north end of Auburn and the Foresthill Road exit. Take that exit and drive east to Foresthill and Mosquito Ridge Road. Turn east and drive 36 miles (curvy) to French Meadows Reservoir and continue to the head of the lake to a fork. Bear left at the fork and continue for six miles to the campground.

Trip note: Talbot Camp is set at 5,600 feet along the Middle Fork of the American River, primarily used as a trailhead camp for backpackers heading into the Granite Chief Wilderness. The trail is routed along the Middle Fork American River, turning south into Picayune Valley, flanked by Needle Peak (8,971 feet), Granite Chief (9,886 feet) and Squaw Peak to the east, then beyond to connect with the Pacific Crest Trail. The camp has 10 stalls for trailer parking for horses and pack stock. Hitching rails are available at the trailhead. Open June through October.

---

49. AUBURN KOA

Reference: Map D3, grid e1.

Campsites, facilities: There are 10 tent sites and 66 motor home sites, some with hookups. Picnic tables, fire grills, flush toilets, showers and a sanitary dump station are provided. A playground, a swimming pool, a recreation room, a fishing pond, badminton, horseshoes, volleyball, a grocery store, a laundromat and propane gas are available. Pets are allowed on leashes.

Reservations, fee: Reservations accepted; $20-$27 fee per night.

Who to contact: Phone (916) 885-0990.

Location: From Auburn, drive north on Highway 49 for 3.5 miles to Rock Creek Road (one block past Bell Road). Turn right on Rock Creek Road and follow the signs to 3550 KOA Way.

Trip note: This year-round KOA park is set at 1,250 feet and has all the amenities. What the heck, it even has a swimming pool.

50. AUBURN STATE RECREATION AREA

Reference: Near Auburn; map D3, grid e1

Campsites, facilities: There are 53 tent sites and 22 boat-in sites. Pit toilets, picnic tables and fire rings are provided. There is **no piped water**. Pets are permitted on leashes or otherwise controlled.

Reservations, fee: Reserve boat-in sites only by phoning Destinet at (800) 444-7275 ($6.75 Destinet fee); $9-$11 fee per night.

Who to contact: Phone the park at (916) 885-4527 or (916) 988-0205 or write to P.O. Box 3266, Auburn, CA 95604.

Location: From Auburn, turn south on Highway 49 and drive one mile to the park entrance. The campsites are dispersed throughout the park. For directions to a specific campsite, contact the park office.

Trip note: This 42,000-acre state park is a jewel in the valley foothill country, at 500 feet in elevation. It is located in the scenic American River Canyon and just far enough out of Sacramento to make visitors feel like they're escaping the city treadmill. The American River runs through the park, offering visitors opportunities to fish, boat and raft. In addition, there are over 50 miles of hiking and horseback riding trails. Open year-round.

51. MIDDLE MEADOWS GROUP CAMP

Reference: On Long Canyon Creek in Eldorado National Forest; map D3, grid e8.

Campsites, facilities: There are two group sites for tents or small motor homes. Piped water, vault toilets, and picnic tables are provided. Supplies can be obtained in Foresthill. Pets are permitted on leashes or otherwise controlled.

Reservations, fee: Reserve by phoning (800) 280-CAMP ($15.85 reservation fee); $50 fee per night.

Who to contact: Phone the Eldorado National Forest Information Center at (916) 644-6048.

Location: From Sacramento, drive east on Interstate 80 to the north end of Auburn and the Foresthill Road exit. Take that exit and drive east to Foresthill and Mosquito Ridge Road. Turn east and drive 36 miles (curvy) to Anderson Dam at French Meadows Reservoir and the junction with Forest Service Road 22 (also called Forest Service Road 48). Bear right and drive about nine miles to the campground on the right side of the road.

Trip note: This group camp is set within range of several adventures. To the nearby east is Hell Hole Reservoir (you'll need a boat here to do it right), and to the nearby north is French Meadows Reservoir (you'll drive past the dam on the way in). Unfortunately, there isn't a hell of a lot to do at this spot other than watch the water flow by on adjacent Long Canyon Creek. Open June through September.

52. BIG MEADOWS

Reference: **Near Hell Hole Reservoir in Eldorado National Forest; map D3, grid e8.**

Campsites, facilities: There are 35 sites for tents or motor homes up to 22 feet long. Piped water, vault toilets, picnic tables and fire grills are provided. Pets are permitted on leashes or otherwise controlled. Supplies are available in Foresthill.

Reservations, fee: No reservations; no fee.

Who to contact: Phone the Eldorado National Forest Information Center at (916) 644-6048.

Location: From Sacramento, drive east on Interstate 80 to the north end of Auburn and the Foresthill Road exit. Take that exit and drive east to Foresthill and Mosquito Ridge Road. Turn east and drive 36 miles (curvy) to Anderson Dam at French Meadows Reservoir and the junction with Forest Service Road 22 (also called Forest Service Road 48). Bear right and drive about 11 miles to the campground entrance road on the left (about a mile from Hell Hole Reservoir). Turn left and drive a half-mile to the campground.

Trip note: This camp sits on a meadow near the ridge above Hell Hole Reservoir (which is about two miles away). See the trip note for Hell Hole. Open May through November.

53. HELL HOLE

Reference: **Near Hell Hole Reservoir in Eldorado National Forest; map D3, grid e9.**

Campsites, facilities: There are 10 sites for tents or motor homes. Piped water, vault toilets, picnic tables and fire grills are provided. Supplies can be obtained in Foresthill. Pets are permitted on leashes or otherwise controlled. A boat launch is available nearby at the reservoir.

Reservations, fee: No reservations; no fee.

Who to contact: Phone the Eldorado National Forest Information Center at (916) 644-6048.

Location: From Sacramento, drive east on Interstate 80 to the north end of Auburn and the Foresthill Road exit. Take that exit and drive east to Foresthill and Mosquito Ridge Road. Turn east and drive 36 miles (curvy) to Anderson Dam at French Meadows Reservoir and the junction with Forest Service Road 22 (also called Forest Service Road 48). Bear right and drive about 11 miles to Hell Hole Reservoir and a fork. Bear right and drive one mile to the campground entrance road on the left.

Trip note: Hell Hole sits at the bottom of a massive granite gorge, a mountain temple with water the color of sapphire blue bordered by high canyon walls. For the most part, there is no shore, and that's why there are no lakeside campsites or shoreline fishing prospects. This is the closest drive-to camp at Hell Hole Reservoir, about a mile away with a boat launch nearby. Bring a boat, then enjoy the awesome scenery while you troll for kokanee salmon, brown trout, mackinaw trout and a sprinkling of rainbow trout. This is a unique fishery compared to the put-and-take rainbow trout at so many other lakes. The lake elevation is 4,700 feet; the camp elevation is 5,200 feet.

54. UPPER HELL HOLE WALK-IN

Reference: **On Hell Hole Reservoir in Eldorado National Forest; map D3, grid e9.**

Campsites, facilities: There are 15 tent sites, accessible by trail or boat only. There is **no piped water**, but pit toilets, picnic tables and fire grills are provided. Pets are permitted on leashes or otherwise controlled. A boat launch is available at the reservoir. Supplies can be obtained in Foresthill.

Reservations, fee: No reservations; no fee.

Who to contact: Phone the Eldorado National Forest Information Center at (916) 644-6048.

Location: From Sacramento, drive east on Interstate 80 to the north end of Auburn and the Foresthill Road exit. Take that exit and drive east to Foresthill and to Mosquito Ridge Road. Turn east and drive 36 miles (curvy) to Anderson Dam at French Meadows Reservoir and the junction with Forest Service Road 22 (also called Forest Service Road 48). Bear right and drive about 11 miles to Hell Hole Reservoir and a fork. Bear right and drive three miles to the trailhead at the end of the road at the southeast corner of the lake.

Trip note: This is an awesome spot, set on the southern shore at the upper end of Hell Hole Reservoir, where there is Yosemite-like beauty in remote national forest, seen by relatively few people. To get here requires a 3.5-mile walk on a trail routed along the southern rim of the canyon overlooking Hell Hole. It is one of the prettiest hikes on planet earth. You arrive at this little trail camp, ready to explore onward the next day into the Granite Chief Wilderness, or just do nothing except enjoy adjacent Buck Meadow and the paradise you have discovered. Open May through October.

55. LOOMIS KOA

Reference: **In Loomis; map D3, grid f0.**

Campsites, facilities: There are 74 motor home sites (many with hookups), a separate tent area, and two cabins. Picnic tables, fire grills, flush toilets, showers and a sanitary dump station are provided. A playground, a swimming pool, a recreation room, volleyball, horseshoes, a grocery store, a laundromat and propane gas are available. Pets are allowed on leashes.

Reservations, fee: Reservations accepted; $20-$26 fee per night; $33 cabin fee per night.

Who to contact: Phone (916) 652-6737.

Location: From Sacramento, drive east on Interstate 80 to Loomis and the junction of Sierra College Boulevard. Drive north on Sierra College Boulevard for a half-mile to Taylor Road. Turn east and drive a half-block to the camp.

Trip note: This KOA park is set in the Sierra foothills, which are known for hot summer weather. The sites are on level gravel and some are shaded. In late summer, the 49ers hold their annual training camp at the college in this town. The elevation is 1,200 feet.

56. BLACK OAK GROUP CAMP

Reference: **Near Stumpy Meadows Lake in Eldorado National Forest; map D3, grid f6.**

Campsites, facilities: There are four group sites for tents or motor homes up to 16 feet long. Piped water, vault toilets, picnic tables and fire grills are provided.

Pets are permitted on leashes or otherwise controlled. A boat ramp is nearby.

Reservations, fee: Reserve by phoning (800) 280-CAMP ($15.85 reservation fee); $50 group-use fee.

Who to contact: Phone the Eldorado National Forest Information Center at (916) 644-6048.

Location: From Sacramento, drive east on Interstate 50 to Placerville and the junction with Highway 193. Turn north and drive 12 miles to Georgetown and Main Street (Georgetown-Wentworth Springs Road). Turn right and drive 20 miles to Stumpy Meadows Lake, then continue for two miles to the north shore of the lake and campground entrance road on the right side of the road.

Trip note: This group camp is set directly adjacent to Stumpy Meadows Campground. For trip note information, see the listing for Stumpy Meadows. The boat ramp for the lake is located just south of the Mark Edson Dam, near the picnic area. Elevation is 4,400 feet. Open April through November.

---

57. STUMPY MEADOWS

Reference: **On Stumpy Meadows Lake in Eldorado National Forest; map D3, grid f6.**

Campsites, facilities: There are 40 sites for tents or motor homes up to 16 feet long. Piped water, vault toilets, picnic tables and fire grills are provided. Pets are permitted on leashes or otherwise controlled. A boat ramp is nearby.

Reservations, fee: Reserve by phoning (800) 280-CAMP ($7.85 reservation fee); $8 fee per night; $15 for two-family site.

Who to contact: Phone the Eldorado National Forest Information Center at (916) 644-6048.

Location: From Sacramento, drive east on Interstate 50 to Placerville and the junction with Highway 193. Turn north and drive 12 miles to Georgetown and Main Street (Georgetown-Wentworth Springs Road). Turn right and drive 20 miles to Stumpy Meadows Lake, then continue for two miles to the north shore of the lake and campground entrance road on the right side of the road.

Trip note: This is the camp of choice for visitors to Stumpy Meadows Lake. The first thing visitors notice is the huge ponderosa pine trees, noted for their distinctive mosaic-like bark. The lake is set at 4,400 feet in Eldorado National Forest, and covers 320 acres with water that is cold and clear. The lake has both rainbow and brown trout, and in the fall, provides good fishing for big browns (they move up into the head of the lake, near where Pilot Creek enters). Open April through November.

---

58. GERLE CREEK

Reference: **on Gerle Creek Reservoir in Eldorado National Forest; map D3, grid f8.**

Campsites, facilities: There are 50 sites for tents or motor homes up to 22 feet long. Piped water, vault toilets, picnic tables, **wheelchair-accessible** trails, fire grills and a fishing pier are provided. Pets are permitted on leashes or otherwise controlled.

Reservations, fee: Reserve by phoning (800) 280-CAMP ($7.85 reservation fee); $8 fee per night.

Who to contact: Phone the Eldorado National Forest Information Center at (916) 644-6048.

Location: From Sacramento, drive east on US 50 to Riverton and the junction with

Ice House Road (Soda Springs-Riverton Road). Turn north and drive about 30 miles (past Union Valley Reservoir) to a fork with Forest Service Road 30. Turn left and drive two miles, then bear left on the campground entrance road and drive one mile to the campground.

Trip note: This is a small, pretty, but limited spot set along the northern shore of little Gerle Creek Reservoir, at 5,231 feet in elevation. The lake is ideal for canoes or other small boats because no motors are permitted and no boat ramp is available. That makes for quiet water. It is set in the Gerle Creek Canyon, which feeds into the South Fork Rubicon River. No trout plants are made at this lake, and fishing is correspondingly poor. A network of Forest Service roads to the north can provide great exploring. A map of Eldorado National Forest is a must. Open June through October.

59. SOUTH FORK 🐟 🥾   RV 8

Reference: On the South Fork of Rubicon River in Eldorado National Forest; map D3, grid f8.

Campsites, facilities: There are 17 sites for tents or motor homes up to 22 feet long. There is **no piped water**, but vault toilets, picnic tables and fire grills are provided. Pets are permitted on leashes or otherwise controlled.

Reservations, fee: No reservations; no fee.

Who to contact: Phone the Eldorado National Forest Information Center at (916) 644-6048.

Location: From Sacramento, drive east on US 50 Riverton and the junction with Ice House Road (Soda Springs-Riverton Road). Turn north and drive about 25 miles to the junction with Forest Service Road 13N28 (3.5 miles past Union Valley Reservoir). Bear left on Forest Service Road 13N28 and drive two miles to the campground entrance on the right.

Trip note: This primitive national forest camp is set alongside the South Fork Rubicon River, just over a mile downstream from the outlet at Gerle Creek Reservoir. Trout fishing is fair, the water tastes extremely sweet (always pump-filter with a water purifier), and there are several side trips available. These include Loon Lake (eight miles to the northeast), Gerle Creek Reservoir (to the nearby north) and Union Valley Reservoir (to the nearby south). Open June through October.

60. PENINSULA 🐟 ⚓ 🥾 ♿ 🏊 🏇 🚻 🚶   RV 6

Reference: In Folsom Lake State Recreation Area; map D3, grid g0.

Campsites, facilities: There are 100 sites for tents or motor homes. Picnic tables, fire grills and piped water are provided. Flush toilets, showers and a bike path are available. There are boat rentals, moorings, a snack bar, ice, and bait and tackle available at the Folsom Lake Marina. Pets are permitted.

Reservations, fee: Reserve by phoning Destinet at (800) 444-7275 ($6.75 Destinet fee); $14-$16 fee per night; $1 pet fee.

Who to contact: Phone Folsom Lake State Recreation Area at (916) 988-0205.

Location: From Placerville, drive east on US 50 to the Spring Street/Highway 49 exit. Turn left (north) on Highway 49 (toward the town of Coloma), and continue 8.3 miles into the town of Pilot Hill and Rattlesnake Bar Road. Turn left on Rattlesnake Bar Road and drive nine miles to the end of the road and the park entrance.

Trip note: This is one of the big camps at Folsom Lake, but it is also more remote than the other camps, requiring a circuitous drive to reach. It is set on the peninsula on the northeast shore, right where the North Fork American River arm of the lake enters the main lake area. A nearby boat ramp, marina, and boat rentals make this a great weekend spot. Fishing for bass and trout is often quite good in spring and early summer, and waterskiing is popular in the hot summer months.

61. NEGRO BAR 🛶 🐟 ⚓ 👫 ♿ 🏊 🐴 🧍   RV 6

Reference: **In Folsom Lake State Recreation Area; map D3, grid g0.**

Campsites, facilities: There are 20 sites for tents. Picnic tables, fire grills, and piped water are provided. Flush toilets, shower and a bike path are available. A grocery store and a laundromat are nearby. There are boat rentals, moorings, a snack bar, ice, and bait and tackle available at the Folsom Lake Marina.

Reservations, fee: Reserve by phoning Destinet at (800) 444-7275 ($6.75 Destinet fee); $14-$16 fee per night.

Who to contact: Phone Folsom Lake State Recreation Area at (916) 988-0205.

Location: From Interstate 80 north of Sacramento, take the Douglas Boulevard exit and head east for five miles to Auburn-Folsom Road. Turn right on Auburn-Folsom Road and drive south for six miles until the road dead-ends into Greenback Lane. Turn right on Greenback Lane and merge immediately into the left lane. The park entrance is approximately two-tenths of a mile on the left.

Trip note: Lake Natoma is the afterbay for Folsom Lake, but is nothing like Folsom Lake. Natoma is comparatively small (500 acres), very narrow instead of wide, with cold water instead of warm. This camp is set at the head of the lake on the northern shore, with an adjacent boat ramp available. Two nearby group camps are a bonus.

62. BEAL'S POINT 🛶 🐟 ⚓ 👫 ♿ 🏊 🐴 🧍🧍   RV 6

Reference: **In Folsom Lake State Recreation Area; map D3, grid g0.**

Campsites, facilities: There are 49 sites for tents or motor homes up to 31 feet long. Picnic tables, fire grills and piped water are provided. Flush toilets, showers, a dump station, a bike path and horseback riding facilities are available. Camping, picnicking and fishing areas are **wheelchair accessible**. There are boat rentals, moorings, a snack bar, ice, and bait and tackle available at the Folsom Lake Marina. Pets are permitted.

Reservations, fee: Reserve by phoning Destinet at (800) 444-7275 ($6.75 Destinet fee); $14-$16 fee per night; $1 pet fee.

Who to contact: Phone Folsom Lake State Recreation Area at (916) 988-0205.

Location: From Sacramento, drive east on US 50 to the Folsom Boulevard exit. Turn left at the stop sign and continue on Folsom Boulevard for 3.5 miles, following the road as it curves onto Leidesdorff Street. Head east on Leidesdorff Street for one-half mile, dead-ending into Riley Street. Turn left onto Riley Street and proceed over the bridge, turning right on Folsom-Auburn Road. Head north on Folsom-Auburn Road for 3.5 miles to the park entrance on the right.

Trip note: Folsom Lake is Sacramento's backyard vacation spot, a huge lake covering some 12,000 acres with 75 miles of shoreline, which means plenty of room for boating, waterskiing, fishing and suntanning. This camp is set on its southwest side, just north of the dam, with a boat ramp nearby at Granite Bay.

The lake has a productive trout fishery in the spring, a fast-growing population of kokanee salmon, and good prospects for bass in late spring and early summer. By summer, waterskiers usually take over the lake each day by at about 10 a.m. One problem with this lake is that a minor lake drawdown can cause major amounts of shoreline to become exposed on its upper arms. Open year-round.

63. FINNON LAKE RESORT

Reference: **Map D3, grid g5.**

Campsites, facilities: There are 35 sites for tents or motor homes. Piped water, chemical toilets, picnic tables and fire grills are provided. Pets are permitted.

Reservations, fee: No reservations; $8 fee per night.

Who to contact: Phone the county park at (916) 622-9314.

Location: From Placerville, turn east on US 50 and drive to Placerville and the junction with Highway 193. Turn north and drive four miles north on Highway 193 to Rock Creek Road. Turn right (east) and drive nine miles to the lake.

Trip note: Not many out-of-towners head to Finnon Lake, a little county recreation lake set up for small boats that are hand-launched and paddle-powered. But it does provide lakeside camping and fair fishing for a light mix of bass, sunfish and bluegill, with warm water for swimming. It is set at 2,200 feet in the foothills, a few miles north of the South Fork American River. Open year-round.

64. SILVER CREEK

Reference: **Near Ice House Reservoir in Eldorado National Forest; map D3, grid g8.**

Campsites, facilities: There are 11 tent sites. There is **no piped water**, but vault toilets, picnic tables and fire grills are provided. Pets are permitted on leashes or otherwise controlled.

Reservations, fee: No reservations; no fee.

Who to contact: Phone the Eldorado National Forest Information Center at (916) 644-6048.

Location: From Sacramento, drive east on US 50 to Riverton and the junction with Ice House Road (Soda Springs-Riverton Road). Turn left (north) and drive about seven miles to the campground entrance road on the left (if you reach the junction with Forest Service Road 3, you have gone a quarter-mile too far). Turn left and drive a quarter-mile to the campground.

Trip note: Silver Creek might be a pretty spot at 5,200 feet in elevation, but it is rarely the destination of campers. Rather, it is primarily used as an overflow spot if the camps at nearby Ice House Reservoir are full. Ice House is only two miles north, and Union Valley Reservoir is four miles north. Open June through October.

65. JONES FORK

Reference: **On Union Valley Reservoir in Eldorado National Forest; map D3, grid g8.**

Campsites, facilities: There are 10 sites for tents or motor homes up to 25 feet long. Vault toilets, picnic tables, fire rings and grills are provided. There is **no piped water**. Pets are allowed on leashes.

Reservations, fee: No reservations; no fee.

Who to contact: Phone the Eldorado National Forest Information Center at (916) 644-6048.

Location: From Sacramento, drive east on US 50 to Riverton and the junction with Ice House Road (Soda Springs-Riverton Road). Turn left (north) and drive 14 miles to the campground entrance road on the left (at the south end of Union Valley Reservoir). Turn left and drive a half-mile to the campground.

Trip note: The Crystal Basin Recreation Area is the most popular backcountry region for campers from the Sacramento area, and Union Valley Reservoir is the centerpiece. The area gets its name from the prominent granite Sierra ridge, which looks like crystal when it is covered with frozen snow. This is a big lake, set at 4,900 feet elevation, with four lakeside campgrounds and three boat ramps providing access. This is the first camp you will arrive at, set at the mouth of the Jones Fork Cove, and is the only camp that is free and without a developed water source. Open June through October.

66. YELLOWJACKET 🐟 ⚓ 🚣   RV 8

Reference: On Union Valley Reservoir in Eldorado National Forest; map D3, grid g8.

Campsites, facilities: There are 40 sites for tents or motor homes up to 22 feet long. Piped water, vault and flush toilets, picnic tables and fire grills are provided. Pets are permitted on leashes or otherwise controlled. A boat ramp is nearby.

Reservations, fee: Reserve by phoning (800) 280-CAMP ($7.85 reservation fee); $8 fee per night.

Who to contact: Phone the Eldorado National Forest Information Center at (916) 644-6048.

Location: From Sacramento, drive east on US 50 to Riverton and the junction with Ice House Road (Soda Springs-Riverton Road). Turn left (north) and drive 21 miles to Wolf Creek Road (at the head of Union Valley Reservoir). Turn left and drive one mile to the campground entrance road. Turn left and drive one mile to the campground.

Trip note: The camp, set at 4,900 feet, is located on the north shore of the reservoir. A boat launch adjacent to the camp makes this an ideal destination for trout-angling campers with boats. Union Valley Reservoir, a popular weekend destination for campers from the Central Valley, is stocked with brook trout and rainbow trout by the Department of Fish and Game. Open June through October.

67. SUNSET 🐟 ⚓ ♿ 🚣   RV 8

Reference: On Union Valley Reservoir in Eldorado National Forest; map D3, grid g8.

Campsites, facilities: There are 131 sites for tents or motor homes up to 22 feet long and 30 walk-in tent sites. Piped water, vault toilets, picnic tables and fire grills are provided. A boat ramp and sanitary disposal station are available. Pets are permitted on leashes or otherwise controlled. One site is **wheelchair accessible**.

Reservations, fee: Reserve by phoning (800) 280-CAMP ($7.85 reservation fee); $10 fee per night; $15 fee for two-family sites.

Who to contact: Phone the Eldorado National Forest Information Center at (916) 644-6048.

Location: From Sacramento, drive east on US 50 to Riverton and the junction with

Ice House Road (Soda Springs-Riverton Road). Turn left (north) and drive 15 miles to the campground entrance road (one mile past the turnoff for Jones Fork Camp). Turn left and drive 1.5 miles to the campground at the end of the road.

Trip note: This is the prettiest of all the camps at Union Valley Reservoir, set at the eastern tip of the peninsula that juts out into the lake at the mouth of Jones Fork. A nearby boat ramp (you'll see it on the left on the way in) is a big plus, along with a picnic area and beach. The lake has decent trout fishing, with both brook trout and rainbow trout. The place is gorgeous, set at 4,900 feet in the Sierra Nevada range. Open June through October.

68. ICE HOUSE 🐟 ⚓ 🚶 ♿ 🏊 RV 8

Reference: **On Ice House Reservoir in Eldorado National Forest; map D3, grid g9.**

Campsites, facilities: There are 17 sites for tents and 66 sites for tents or motor homes up to 22 feet long. Three sites are **wheelchair-accessible.** Piped water, vault toilets, picnic tables and fire grills are provided. A boat ramp and sanitary disposal station are available. Pets are permitted on leashes or otherwise controlled.

Reservations, fee: Reservations accepted; reserve by phoning (800) 280-CAMP; $10-$15 fee per night.

Who to contact: Phone the Eldorado National Forest Information Center at (916) 644-6048.

Location: From Sacramento, drive east on US 50 to Riverton and the junction with Ice House Road (Soda Springs-Riverton Road). Turn left (north) and drive about 11 miles to the junction with Forest Service Road 3 and Ice House Road. Turn right on Ice House Road and drive two miles to the campground access road on the right.

Trip note: Along with Loon Lake and Union Valley Reservoir, Ice House Reservoir is a feature destination in the Crystal Basin Recreation Area. Ice House gets most of the fishermen and Union Valley gets most of the campers. The camp here is set on the lake's northwestern shore, 5,500 feet in elevation, just up from the dam and adjacent to the lake's boat ramp. The lake was created by a dam on South Fork Silver Creek and covers 650 acres, with the deepest spot about 130 feet deep. It is stocked with rainbow trout, brook trout, and brown trout. Open June though October.

69. WENCH CREEK 🐟 ⚓ 🚶 🏊 RV 7

Reference: **On Union Valley Reservoir in Eldorado National Forest; map D3, grid g9.**

Campsites, facilities: There are 100 sites for tents or motor homes up to 22 feet long. There are also two group sites. Piped water, flush toilets, vault toilets, picnic tables and fire grills are provided. Pets are permitted on leashes or otherwise controlled. A boat ramp is three miles away at the Yellowjacket Campground.

Reservations, fee: No reservations for family sites; $8 fee per night; reserve group sites by phoning (800) 280-CAMP ($15.85 reservation fee); $50 group fee.

Who to contact: Phone the Eldorado National Forest Information Center at (916) 644-6048.

Location: From Sacramento, drive east on US 50 to Riverton and the junction with Ice House Road (Soda Springs-Riverton Road). Turn left (north) and drive 19 miles to the campground entrance road (three miles past the turnoff for Sunset Camp). Turn left and drive one mile to the campground at the end of the road.

Trip note: Wench Camp is set on the northeast shore of Union Valley Reservoir, one of four camps at the lake. See trip notes for Jones Fork and Sunset camps. The elevation is 4,900 feet. Open June through October.

70. NORTHWIND

Reference: **On Ice House Reservoir in Eldorado National Forest; map D3, grid g9.**

Campsites, facilities: There are 10 sites for tents or motor homes up to 25 feet. Vault toilets, picnic tables, fire rings and grills are provided. There is **no piped water**. Pets are allowed on leashes.

Reservations, fee: No reservations; no fee.

Who to contact: Phone the Eldorado National Forest Information Center at (916) 644-6048.

Location: From Sacramento, drive east on US 50 to Riverton and the junction with Ice House Road (Soda Springs-Riverton Road). Turn left (north) and drive about 11 miles to the junction with Forest Service Road 3 and Ice House Road. Turn right on Ice House Road and drive about three miles (two miles past the boat ramp) to the campground access road on the right.

Trip note: This camp is set on the north shore of Ice House Reservoir, one of two rare free campgrounds on the shore of the lake (the other is Strawberry Point). It is located slightly above the reservoir, offering prime views. See the trip note for Ice House Camp. Open June through October.

71. STRAWBERRY POINT

Reference: **On Ice House Reservoir in Eldorado National Forest; map D3, grid g9.**

Campsites, facilities: There are 10 sites for tents or motor homes up to 25 feet. Vault toilets, picnic tables, fire rings and grills are provided. There is **no piped water**. Pets are allowed on leashes.

Reservations, fee: No reservations; no fee.

Who to contact: Phone the Eldorado National Forest Information Center at (916) 644-6048.

Location: From Sacramento, drive east on US 50 to Riverton and the junction with Ice House Road (Soda Springs-Riverton Road). Turn left (north) and drive about 11 miles to the junction with Forest Service Road 3 and Ice House Road. Turn right on Ice House Road and drive about four miles (three miles past the boat ramp) to the campground access road on the right.

Trip note: This camp is one of two free camps set on the north shore of Ice House Reservoir, 5,400 feet in elevation. See the trip note for Ice House. Open March through December, weather permitting.

72. SLY PARK RECREATION AREA

Reference: **On Jenkinson Lake; map D3, grid h6.**

Campsites, facilities: There are 186 sites for tents or motor homes up to 32 feet long, with no hookups. Picnic tables, fire grills, piped water, pit toilets and two boat ramps are provided. Pets are permitted on leashes. Some facilities are **wheelchair accessible**. There are five group sites that can accommodate 50 to 100 people and an equestrian camp called Black Oak, which has 15 sites and two youth-group sites. A grocery store, snack bar, bait and propane gas are available nearby.

Reservations, fee: Reservations recommended; $13 fee per night; $110 minimum group fee for first 50 people, $1.50 for each additional camper; $1.50 pet fee; $5 boat-launch fee.

Who to contact: Phone (916) 644-2545.

Location: From Sacramento, drive east on US 50 to Pollock Pines and take the exit for Sly Park Road. Drive south for five miles to Jenkinson Lake and the campground access road. Turn left and drive a half-mile to the campground on the left.

Trip note: Jenkinson Lake is set at 3,500 feet in elevation in the lower reaches of Eldorado National Forest, with a climate that is perfect for waterskiing and fishing. The two sports get along, with most waterskiers motoring around the lake's main body, while fishermen head upstream into the Hazel Creek arm of the lake for trout (in the spring) and bass (in the summer). This is one of the better lakes in the Sierra for brown trout. The boat ramp is located in a cove on the southwest end of the lake, about two miles from the campground. The area also has several hiking trails, and the lake is good for swimming. A group camp is available for visitors with horses, complete with riding trails, hitching posts and corrals. One horse trail circles the lake. Open year-round.

---

73. SILVER FORK 🎣 🚶 ♿ 🏊 RV 7

Reference: **On the Silver Fork of the American River in Eldorado National Forest; map D3, grid h9.**

Campsites, facilities: There are 35 sites for tents or RVs up to 22 feet long and five double-family sites. One of the sites is **wheelchair-accessible**. Piped water, vault toilets, picnic tables and fire grills are provided. Pets are permitted on leashes or otherwise controlled.

Reservations, fee: No reservations; $9 fee per night; $14 for double-family sites.

Who to contact: Phone the Eldorado National Forest Information Center at (916) 644-6048.

Location: From Sacramento, drive east on US 50 to Kyburz and Silver Fork Road. Turn right (south) and drive eight miles to the campground on the right side of the road.

Trip note: The tons of vacationers driving US 50 along the South Fork American River always get frustrated when they try to fish or camp, because there are precious few opportunities for either, with about zero trout and camps alike. But, just 10 minutes off the beaten path, you can find both at Silver Fork Camp. The access road provides many fishing opportunities, and is stocked with rainbow trout by the state. The camp is set right along the river, at 5,500 feet in elevation, in Eldorado National Forest. Open May through October.

---

74. SAND FLAT 🎣 🏊 RV 7

Reference: **On the South Fork of American River in Eldorado National Forest; map D3, grid h9.**

Campsites, facilities: There are 29 sites for tents or motor homes up to 22 feet long. Piped water, vault toilets, picnic tables and fire grills are provided. Pets are permitted on leashes or otherwise controlled. Groceries, a restaurant and gas are available nearby.

Reservations, fee: No reservations; $9 fee per night.

Who to contact: Phone the Eldorado National Forest Information Center at (916) 644-6048.

Location: From Sacramento, drive east on US 50 to Placerville, then continue for 28 miles to the campground on right.

Trip note: This first-come, first-served campground often gets filled up by US 50 traffic. And why not? You get easy access, a well-signed exit, and a nice setting on the South Fork of the American River. The elevation is 3,900 feet. The river is very pretty here, but fishing is often poor. In winter, the snow level usually starts just a few miles uphill. Open year-round.

---

75. CHINA FLAT

Reference: **On the Silver Fork of American River in Eldorado National Forest; map D3, grid h9.**

Campsites, facilities: There are 23 sites for tents or motor homes up to 22 feet long. Piped water, vault toilets, picnic tables and fire grills are provided. Pets are permitted on leashes or otherwise controlled.

Reservations, fee: No reservations; $9 fee per night.

Who to contact: Phone the Eldorado National Forest Information Center at (916) 644-6048.

Location: From Sacramento, drive east on US 50 to Kyburz and Silver Fork Road. Turn right (south) and drive three miles to the campground on the left side of the road.

Trip note: China Flat Camp is set on the opposite side of the road of the Silver Fork American River, with a nearby access road that is routed along the river for a mile. This provides access for fishing, swimming, gold panning and exploring. It feels far off the beaten path, even though it is only five minutes from that parade of traffic on US 50. What a deal. Open May through October.

---

76. PI PI

Reference: **On the Middle Fork of Consumnes River in Eldorado National Forest; map D3, grid i7.**

Campsites, facilities: There are 51 sites for tents or motor homes up to 22 feet long (three double-family sites). Piped water, vault toilets, picnic tables and fire grills are provided. Pets are permitted on leashes. There is **wheelchair access** to some camping areas, restrooms and pathways.

Reservations, fee: Reserve by phoning 280-CAMP ($7.85 reservation fee); $9-$18 fee per night.

Who to contact: Phone the Eldorado National Forest Information Center at (916) 644-6048.

Location: From Jackson, drive east on Highway 88 to Pioneer, and continue for nine miles to Omo Ranch Road. Turn left (north) and drive one mile to North-South Road (Forest Service Road 6). Turn right and drive 5.5 miles to the campground on the left side of the road.

Trip note: This is far enough out of the way to get missed by most campers. It is set along the Middle Fork of the Consumnes River, at 4,100 feet. There are some good swimming holes in the area, but the water is cold in early summer (after all, it's snowmelt). There is a nature trail/boardwalk that is **wheelchair**

accessible along the river. Several sites border a pretty meadow in the back of the camp. This is also the gateway to a vast network of Forest Service roads to the north in Eldorado National Forest. Open May through November.

77. CAPPS CROSSING

Reference: **On the North Fork of Consumnes River in Eldorado National Forest; map D3, grid i8.**

Campsites, facilities: There are 11 tent sites. Piped water, vault toilets, picnic tables and fire grills are provided. Pets are permitted on leashes or otherwise controlled.

Reservations, fee: No reservations; $9 fee per night.

Who to contact: Phone the Eldorado National Forest Information Center at (916) 644-6048.

Location: From Sacramento, drive east on US 50 to Placerville, and continue for 12 miles to the Sly Park Road exit. Turn right and drive about six miles to the Mormon Emigrant Trail (Forest Service Road 5). Turn left (east) on Mormon Emigrant Trail and drive about 13 miles to North-South Road (Forest Service Road 6). Turn right (south) on North-South Road and drive about six miles to the campground on the left side of the road.

Trip note: Here's a candidate for the Five Percent Club. It's set out in the middle of nowhere along the North Fork of the Consumnes River. It's a primitive spot that doesn't get much use. This camp is in the western reaches of a vast number of backcountry Forest Service roads. A map of Eldorado National Forest is a must to explore them. The elevation is 5,200 feet. Open June through October.

---

78. FAR HORIZONS 49er TRAILER VILLAGE

Reference: **In Plumas; map D3, grid j2.**

Campsites, facilities: There are 329 motor home sites with full hookups. Flush toilets, a sanitary disposal station, showers, a playground, two swimming pools, a jacuzzi, a recreation room, a pool room, a TV lounge, a laundromat, a deli, propane gas and a general store are available. Pets are permitted.

Reservations, fee: Reservations recommended; $25-$30 fee per night.

Who to contact: Phone the park at (209) 245-6981 or (800) 339-6981.

Location: From Sacramento, drive east on US 50 for a short distance to the junction with Highway 16. Turn east on Highway 16 and drive to Highway 49. Turn north on Highway 49 and drive one mile to the campground on the left side of the road at 18265 Highway 49. Note: This is one mile south of Main Street in Plumas.

Trip note: This is the granddaddy of RV parks, set in the heart of the gold country 40 miles east of Stockton and Sacramento. It is rarely crowded, and offers warm pools, a huge spa and a friendly staff. Open year-round.

---

79. INDIAN GRINDING ROCK STATE HISTORICAL PARK

Reference: **Near Jackson; map D3, grid j4.**

Campsites, facilities: There are 23 sites for tents or motor homes up to 27 feet long. Picnic tables, fire grills and piped water are provided. Flush toilets and hot showers are available. Pets are permitted. Facilities are **wheelchair accesssible.**

Reservations, fee: No reservations; $15-$17 fee per night; $1 pet fee.

Who to contact: Phone the park at (209) 296-7488 or (209) 532-0150.

Location: From Jackson, drive east on Highway 88 for 11 miles to Pine Grove-Volcano Road. Turn left (north) Pine Grove-Volcano Road and drive 1.5 miles to the park.

Trip note: Visiting this park, about three miles from Sutter Creek, is like entering a time machine. It offers a reconstructed Miwok village with petroglyphs, bedrock mortars, a cultural center, and interpretive talks for groups, by reservation. Set at 2,500 feet in the Sierra foothills. Open year-round.

---

80. WHITE AZALEA

Reference: **On Mokelumne River in Eldorado National Forest; map D3, grid j8.**

Campsites, facilities: There are six tent sites. Vault toilets are provided. There is **no piped water**, so bring your own. Pets are permitted on leashes.

Reservations, fee: No reservations; no fee.

Who to contact: Phone the Eldorado National Forest Information Center at (916) 644-6048.

Location: From Jackson, drive east on Highway 88 to Pioneer, then continue for about 20 miles to Ellis Road (Forest Service Road 92), at a signed turnoff for Lumberyard Campground. Turn right on Forest Service Road 92 and drive and about eight miles. Cross the Bear River, and drive a short distance to a Forest Service Road turnoff (Forest Service Road 9). Turn right and drive three miles (past Mokelumne Camp) to the campground. The road is steep, narrow and winding in spots—not good for RVs or trailers.

Trip note: Out here in the remote Mokelumne River canyon are three primitive camps set on the Mokelumne's North Fork. White Azalea Camp, 3,500 feet in elevation, is the closest of the three to Salt Springs Reservoir, the prime recreation destination. It's about a three-mile drive to the dam and an adjacent parking area for a wilderness trailhead for the Mokelumne Wilderness. This trail makes a great day hike, routed for four miles along the north shore of Salt Springs Reservoir to Blue Hole at the head of the lake. Open May to November.

---

81. MOORE CREEK

Reference: **On Mokelumne River in Eldorado National Forest; map D3, grid j8.**

Campsites, facilities: There are eight tent sites. Vault toilets are provided. There is **no piped water**, so bring your own. Pets are permitted on leashes.

Reservations, fee: No reservations; no fee.

Who to contact: Phone the Eldorado National Forest Information Center at (916) 644-4048.

Location: From Jackson, drive east on Highway 88 to Pioneer, then continue for about 20 miles to Ellis Road (Forest Service Road 92), at a signed turnoff for Lumberyard Campground. Turn right on Forest Service Road 92 and drive and about eight miles. Cross the Bear River, and drive a short distance to a Forest Service Road turnoff (Forest Service Road 9). Turn right and drive two miles (past Mokelumne Camp) to the campground access road on the right. Turn right and drive a quarter-mile to the campground on the right. The road is steep, narrow and winding in spots—not good for RVs or trailers.

Trip note: This camp is set at 3,200 feet elevation on little Moore Creek, a feeder stream to the nearby North Fork Mokelumne River. It's one of three primitive camps within two miles. See the trip note for White Azalea Camp. Open May to November.

82. MOKELUMNE 🐟 〰️   △7

Reference: **On Mokelumne River in Eldorado National Forest; map D3, grid j8.**

Campsites, facilities: There are eight tent sites. Vault toilets are provided. There is **no piped water**, so bring your own. Pets are permitted on leashes.

Reservations, fee: No reservations; no fee.

Who to contact: Phone the Eldorado National Forest Information Center at (916) 644-6048.

Location: From Jackson, drive east on Highway 88 to Pioneer, then continue for about 20 miles to Ellis Road (Forest Service Road 92), at a signed turnoff for Lumberyard Campground. Turn right on Forest Service Road 92 and drive and about eight miles. Cross the Bear River and drive a short distance to a Forest Service Road turnoff (Forest Service Road 9). Turn right and drive two miles to the campground on the left side of the road.

Trip note: This primitive spot is set beside the Mokelumne River, 3,200 feet in elevation, one of three primitive camps in the immediate area. See the trip note for Azalea Camp. There are some good swimming holes nearby. Fishing is fair, with the trout on the small side. Open May to November.

83. SOUTH SHORE 🐟 ⚓ 🏃 〰️   RV △7

Reference: **On Bear River Reservoir in Eldorado National Forest; map D3, grid j9.**

Campsites, facilities: There are 13 sites for tents and nine sites for tents or motor homes. There are four two-family sites. Picnic tables, fire grills, piped water and vault toilets are provided. A boat ramp, a grocery store, boat rentals and propane gas are available at nearby Bear River Lake Resort. Pets are allowed on leashes.

Reservations, fee: No reservations; $9 fee per night; $18 fee per night for two-family sites.

Who to contact: Phone the Eldorado National Forest Information Center at (916) 644-6048.

Location: From Stockton, drive east on Highway 88 for about 80 miles to the lake entrance on the right side of the road. Turn right and drive four miles (past the dam) to the campground entrance on the right side of the road.

Trip note: Bear River Reservoir is set at 5,900 feet, which means it becomes ice-free earlier in the season each spring than its uphill neighbors to the east, Silver Lake and Caples Lake. It is a good-size lake—725 acres—and cold and deep, too. It gets double-barreled trout stocks, receiving fish from the state and the operator of the lake's marina and lodge. This campground is set on the lake's southern shore, just east of the dam. Explorers can drive south for five miles to Salt Springs Reservoir, which has a trailhead and parking area on the north side of the dam for a great day hike along the lake. Open June to November.

84. BEAR RIVER GROUP CAMP

RV **6**

Reference: On Bear River Reservoir in Eldorado National Forest; map D3, grid j9.

Campsites, facilities: There are three group sites for tents. Picnic tables, fire grills, piped water and vault toilets are provided. A grocery store, a boat ramp, boat rentals and propane gas are available nearby. Pets are allowed on leashes.

Reservations, fee: Reservations required; $35-$70 fee per night.

Who to contact: Contact the Eldorado National Forest Information Center at (916) 644-6048. For reservations, call Sierra Recreation Managers: (209) 295-4512.

Location: From Stockton, drive east on Highway 88 for about 80 miles to the lake entrance on the right side of the road. Turn right and drive five miles (past the dam) to the campground entrance on the left side of the road.

Trip note: This is a group camp set near Bear River Reservoir, a pretty lake that provides power boating and trout fishing. See the trip note for South Shore, which is located just a mile from this camp. Open June to November.

85. BEAR RIVER LAKE RESORT

RV **8**

Reference: On Bear River Reservoir; map D3 grid j9.

Campsites, facilities: There are 127 sites for tents or motor homes, all with partial hookups. Picnic tables, fire grills, and piped water are provided. Restrooms, showers, a sanitary disposal station, a boat ramp, boat rentals, firewood, ice, propane gas, a laundromat, a post office, a telephone, a restaurant and cocktail lounge, and a grocery store are available. Pets are permitted.

Reservations, fee: Reservations recommended; $18.50 fee per night.

Who to contact: Phone the resort at (209) 295-4868.

Location: From Stockton, drive east on Highway 88 for about 80 miles to the lake entrance on the right side of the road. Turn right and drive four miles to a junction (if you pass the dam, you have gone a quarter-mile too far). Turn left and drive a half-mile the campground entrance on the right side of the road.

Trip note: Bear River Lake Resort is a complete vacation service lodge, with everything you could ask for. A lot of people have been asking in recent years, making this a popular spot that often requires a reservation. The resort also sponsors fishing derbies in the summer, and sweetens the pot considerably by stocking exceptionally large rainbow trout. The resort is set at 6,000 feet. For more information about Bear River Reservoir, see the trip note for South Shore Camp. Open year-round.

MAP D4

NOR-CAL MAP .... see page 94
adjoining maps
NORTH (C4) .... see page 306
EAST .... no map
SOUTH (E4) .... see page 460
WEST (D3) .... see page 350

63 LISTINGS
PAGES 390-417

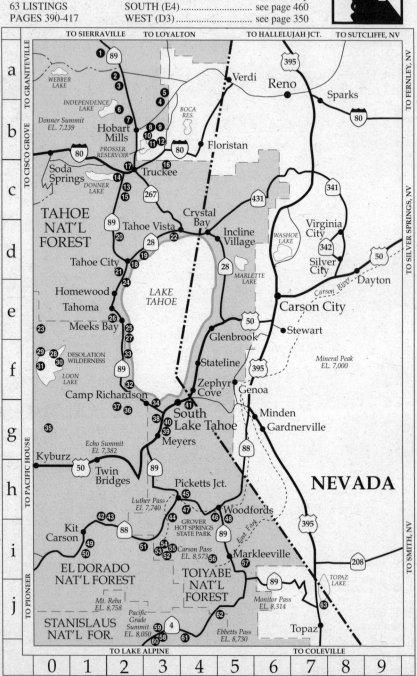

TO SIERRAVILLE TO LOYALTON TO HALLELUJAH JCT. TO SUTCLIFFE, NV

TO GRANITEVILLE

89

WEBBER LAKE

395

Verdi

Reno

Sparks

INDEPENDENCE LAKE

BOCA RES.

80

Donner Summit EL. 7,239

Hobart Mills

PROSSER RESERVOIR

80

Floristan

TO CISCO GROVE

80

Soda Springs

DONNER LAKE

Truckee

267

431

341

TO FERNLEY, NV

Crystal Bay

Incline Village

Washoe Lake

Virginia City

342

Silver City

50

Dayton

TAHOE NAT'L FOREST

89

Tahoe Vista

28

28

MARLETTE LAKE

Carson River

TO SILVER SPRINGS, NV

Tahoe City

LAKE TAHOE

Homewood

Tahoma

Carson City

Stewart

DESOLATION WILDERNESS

Meeks Bay

Glenbrook

50

89

Stateline

Mineral Peak EL. 7,000

LOON LAKE

Camp Richardson

Zephyr Cove

Genoa

395

South Lake Tahoe

Minden

Gardnerville

TO PACIFIC HOUSE

Echo Summit EL. 7,382

Meyers

88

NEVADA

Kyburz

50

Twin Bridges

89

Picketts Jct.

45

Luther Pass EL. 7,740

47

Woodfords

48

395

TO SMITH, NV

44

GROVER HOT SPRINGS STATE PARK

46

89

East Fork

Kit Carson

88

51

54

55

53

52

56

Carson Pass EL. 8,573

Markleeville

57

208

TO PIONEER

EL DORADO NAT'L FOREST

TOIYABE NAT'L FOREST

89

Monitor Pass EL. 8,314

TOPAZ LAKE

63

Mt. Reba EL. 8,758

Pacific Grade Summit EL. 8,050

STANISLAUS NAT'L FOR.

59

4

58

60

61

Ebbetts Pass EL. 8,730

62

Topaz

TO LAKE ALPINE TO COLEVILLE

0 1 2 3 4 5 6 7 8 9

Map D4 featuring: Tahoe National Forest, Stampede Reservoir, Prosser Reservoir, Boca Reservoir, Donner Lake, Truckee River, Lake Tahoe, Lake Tahoe Basin, Eldorado National Forest, Loon Lake, Carson River, Toiyabe National Forest, Carson Pass, Blue Lakes, Stanislaus National Forest

1. COLD CREEK 🐟 🚶 ♨ ︎ RV 8

Reference: **In Tahoe National Forest; map D4, grid a1.**

Campsites, facilities: There are 13 sites for tents or motor homes up to 22 feet long. Piped water, vault toilets, picnic tables and fire grills are provided. Pets are permitted on leashes or otherwise controlled. Supplies are available in Sierraville.

Reservations, fee: Reserve by phoning (800) 280-CAMP ($7.50 reservation fee); $9 fee per night.

Who to contact: Phone Tahoe National Forest at (916) 587-3558, or California Land Management at (916) 582-0120.

Location: From Truckee, drive north on Highway 89 for about 16 miles to the campground on the left (west side of the road). If you reach Sierraville, you have gone five miles too far north.

Trip note: There are four small campgrounds along Highway 89 between Sierraville and Truckee, all within close range of side trips to Webber Lake, Independence Lake, and Campbell Hot Springs in Sierraville. Cold Creek Camp is set just downstream of the confluence of Cottonwood Creek and Cold Creek, at 5,800 feet in elevation. Open May through October.

2. UPPER LITTLE TRUCKEE 🐟 🚶 RV 7

Reference: **On Little Truckee River in Tahoe National Forest; map D4, grid a2.**

Campsites, facilities: There are 26 sites for tents or motor homes up to 22 feet long. Piped water, vault toilets, picnic tables and fire grills are provided. Pets are permitted on leashes or otherwise controlled. Supplies are available in Sierraville.

Reservations, fee: Reserve by phoning (800) 280-CAMP ($7.50 reservation fee); $9 fee per night.

Who to contact: Phone Tahoe National Forest at (916) 587-3558, or California Land Management at (916) 582-0120.

Location: From Truckee, drive north on Highway 89 for about 11 miles to the campground on the left, a short distance beyond Lower Little Truckee Camp.

Trip note: This camp is set along the Little Truckee River at 6,100 feet, two miles from Stampede Reservoir. The Little Truckee is a pretty trout stream, with easy access not only from this campground, but for another three miles northward along Highway 89, then for another seven miles to the west along Forest Service Road 7, the route to Webber Lake. It only takes about 10 minutes of driving from this camp to reach Stampede Reservoir to the east or Independence Lake to the west. Open May through October.

3. LOWER LITTLE TRUCKEE 🐟 RV 7

Reference: **Near Stampede Reservoir in Tahoe National Forest; map D4, grid a2.**

Campsites, facilities: There are 15 sites for tents or motor homes up to 22 feet long. Piped water, vault toilets, picnic tables and fire grills are provided. Pets are permitted on leashes or otherwise controlled. Supplies are available in Sierraville.

Reservations, fee: Reserve by phoning (800) 280-CAMP ($7.50 reservation fee); $9 fee per night; $4 for each additional vehicle.

Who to contact: Phone Tahoe National Forest at (916) 587-3558, or California Land Management at (916) 582-0120.

Location: From Truckee, drive north on Highway 89 for about 11 miles to the campground on the left. If you reach Upper Little Truckee Camp, you have gone a quarter-mile too far.

Trip note: This pretty camp is set along the Little Truckee River at 6,000 feet, about two miles from Stampede Reservoir, and about a quarter-mile from Lower Little Truckee Camp. See the trip note for the preceding camp. Open May through October.

---

4. LOGGER 🐟 ⚓ 🚶 ♿ 🏊 RV 7

Reference: **At Stampede Reservoir in Tahoe National Forest; map D4, grid a3.**

Campsites, facilities: There are 252 sites for tents or motor homes up to 32 feet long. Piped water, a sanitary dump station, flush toilets, picnic tables and fire grills are provided. A concrete boat ramp is available one mile from camp. A grocery store is nearby. The facilities are **wheelchair accessible**. Pets are allowed on leashes.

Reservations, fee: Reserve by phoning (800) 280-CAMP ($7.50 reservation fee); $11 fee per night; $4 for each additional vehicle.

Who to contact: Phone California Land Management at (916) 582-0120.

Location: From Truckee, drive east on Interstate 80 for seven miles to the Boca-Hirschdale (County Road 270) exit. Take that exit and drive north on County Road 270 for about seven miles (past Boca Reservoir) to the junction with County Road S261 on the left. Turn left and drive 1.5 miles to the campground on the right.

Trip note: Stampede is a huge lake by Sierra standards, covering 3,400 acres, the largest lake in the region besides Lake Tahoe. It is set at 6,000 feet, surrounded by classic Sierra granite and pines, and is big and beautiful. The campground is also huge, set about a half-mile from the lake near its southern shore, a few minutes drive from the Captain Roberts Boat Ramp. This camp is ideal for campers, boaters and anglers. The lake is becoming one of the top fishing lakes in California for kokanee salmon (catchable only by trolling), and also has some large mackinaw trout and a sprinkling of planter-sized rainbow trout. One problem at Stampede is receding water levels from midsummer through fall, a real pain, which puts the campsites some distance from the lake. However, the boat ramp has been extended to assist boaters during drawdowns. Open May through October.

---

5. EMIGRANT GROUP CAMP 🐟 ⚓ 🚶 ♿ 🏊 RV 7

Reference: **At Stampede Reservoir in Tahoe National Forest; map D4, grid a3.**

Campsites, facilities: There are two 25-person group sites and two 50-person group sites for tents or motor homes up to 32 feet long. Piped water, a sanitary dump station, vault toilets, picnic tables and fire grills are provided. Bring your own firewood. A three-lane concrete boat ramp is available. The facilities are **wheelchair accessible**. Pets are allowed on leashes.

Reservations, fee: Reserve by phoning (800) 280-CAMP ($15 reservation fee); $38.50-$77 group fee per night.

Who to contact: Phone California Land Management at (916) 582-0120.

Location: From Truckee, drive east on Interstate 80 for seven miles to the Boca-Hirschdale (County Road 270) exit. Take that exit and drive north on County Road 270 for about seven miles (past Boca Reservoir) to the junction with County Road S261 on the left. Turn left and drive 1.5 miles to the campground access road on the right. Turn right and drive one mile to the camp on the left.

Trip note: Emigrant Group Camp is set at a beautiful spot on Stampede Reservoir, near a point along a cove on the southeastern corner of the lake. There is a beautiful view of the lake from the point, and a boat ramp is located two miles to the east. Elevation is 6,000 feet. See the trip note for the previous camp. Open May through September.

6. INDEPENDENCE LAKE

Reference: **North of Truckee; map D4, grid b1.**

Campsites, facilities: There are 20 sites for tents. **No piped water** or sewage facilities are available. A primitive boat ramp is available. Supplies can be obtained in Truckee. Pets are allowed on leashes.

Reservations, fee: No reservations. All campers must register at the caretaker's house before entering. No fee for walk-in sites; camping with a vehicle is $6-$9 per night.

Who to contact: Phone Sierra Pacific Power at (702) 689-3156.

Location: From Truckee, drive 12.5 miles north on Highway 89 to Forest Service Road 7 (Jackson Meadow Road). Turn west and travel 1.5 miles to Independence Lake Road. Turn south and drive 6.5 miles to the campground and boat ramp at the northeast end of the lake.

Trip note: When you turn left off Highway 89 and start heading west into the interior of Tahoe National Forest, this is the first of three lakes you come to, set at 5,600 feet. The others are Webber Lake (another seven miles) and Jackson Meadow Reservoir (another 14 miles). Independence has a fair fishery for Lahontan cutthroat trout, and provides a primitive drive-to setting. The lake is large and stark, with no facilities of any kind available other than this primitive boat ramp.

7. SAGE HEN CREEK

Reference: **In Tahoe National Forest; map D4, grid b2.**

Campsites, facilities: There are 10 sites for tents or motor homes up to 16 feet long. There is **no piped water**, but vault toilets are provided. Pack out your garbage. Pets are permitted on leashes or otherwise controlled.

Reservations, fee: No reservations; $6 fee per night.

Who to contact: Phone the Tahoe National Forest at (916) 587-3558.

Location: From Truckee, drive nine miles north on Highway 89 to Sagehen Summit Road on the left. Turn left and drive two miles to the campground. A gate on the road a short distance from the camp is sometimes locked early and late in the season.

Trip note: This is a small, primitive camp set at 6,500 feet beside little Sage Hen Creek, just north of a miniature mountain range called the Sagehen Hills, which top out at 7,707 feet. This camp is only five miles from the undeveloped southwestern shore of Stampede Reservoir. It is primarily used as an overflow site on popular weekends when the camps along Highway 89 and at Stampede, Boca, and Prosser Creek have filled. Open June through October.

8. LAKESIDE 🛶 🐟 ⚓ 🏊

Reference: **On Prosser Reservoir in Tahoe National Forest; map D4, grid b2.**

Campsites, facilities: There are 30 sites for tents or motor homes up to 33 feet long and one group site. There is **no piped water**, but vault toilets are provided. Pets are permitted on leashes or otherwise controlled. A boat ramp is available nearby.

Reservations, fee: No reservations; no fee.

Who to contact: Phone the Tahoe National Forest at (916) 587-3558.

Location: From Truckee, drive north on Highway 89 for three miles to the campground entrance road on the right. Turn right and drive less than a mile to the campground.

Trip note: This is a primitive campsite set in a deep cove in the northwestern end of Prosser Reservoir, near the lake's headwaters. This is a gorgeous lake, set at 5,741 feet, and a 10-mile-per-hour speed limit keeps the fast boats out. The adjacent shore is decent for hand-launch car-top boats, providing the lake level is up, and a concrete boat ramp is located a mile down the road. Lots of trout are stocked here every year, including 100,000 rainbow trout fingerlings added in an experiment by the Department of Fish and Game to see how fast they will grow. The trout fishing is often quite good after the ice breaks up in late spring. Open June through October.

9. ANNIE McCLOUD 🛶 🐟 ⚓ 🥾 🏊 🛶

Reference: **On Prosser Reservoir in Tahoe National Forest; map D4, grid b3.**

Campsites, facilities: There are 10 sites for tents or motor homes up to 16 feet long. There is **no piped water.** Chemical toilets are provided at the campground, and vault toilets are provided across the road from the campground entrance. Pets are allowed on leashes.

Reservations, fee: No reservations; no fee.

Who to contact: Phone the Tahoe National Forest at (916) 587-3558.

Location: From Interstate 80, drive north on Highway 89 for a half-mile to Prosser Dam Road. Turn right on Prosser Dam Road and drive 4.5 miles, over the dam and to the campground on the left side of the road.

Trip note: Annie McCloud Camp is set on the remote eastern shore of Prosser Reservoir, just north of the dam, just west of Boca Hill (6,669 feet). It's a primitive camp, with no boat ramp nearby; ramps are located all the way around the west side of the lake. See trip note for Lakeside Camp. Open June through October.

10. BOYINGTON MILL 🛶 🥾

Reference: **On Little Truckee River in Tahoe National Forest; map D4, grid b3.**

Campsites, facilities: There are 10 sites for tents or motor homes up to 32 feet long. There is **no piped water**, but vault toilets and picnic tables are provided. Pets are permitted on leashes or otherwise controlled.

Reservations, fee: No reservations; $8 fee per night.

Who to contact: Phone the Tahoe National Forest at (916) 587-3558.

Location: From Truckee, travel east on Interstate 80 for seven miles to the Boca-Hirschdale exit. Take that exit and drive north on County Road 270 for about four miles (past Boca Reservoir) to the campground on the right .

Trip note: Boyington Mill is a little Forest Service camp set between Boca Reservoir to the nearby south and Stampede Reservoir to the nearby north, along a little inlet creek to the adjacent Little Truckee River. This camp comes in use as an overflow camp when lakeside campsites at Boca, Stampede, and Prosser have already filled. The elevation is 5,700 feet. Open May through October.

11. BOCA REST CAMPGROUND

Reference: **On Boca Reservoir in Tahoe National Forest; map D4, grid b3.**

Campsites, facilities: There are 25 sites for tents or motor homes up to 22 feet long. Piped water, vault toilets, picnic tables, and fire grills are provided. Pets are permitted on leashes or otherwise controlled. A hand-launch boat ramp is available. A concrete boat ramp is three miles away on the southwest shore of Boca Reservoir. Truckee is the nearest place for telephones and supplies.

Reservations, fee: No reservations; $8 fee per night.

Who to contact: Phone the Tahoe National Forest at (916) 587-3558.

Location: From Truckee, travel east on Interstate 80 for seven miles to the Boca-Hirschdale exit. Take that exit and drive north on County Road 270 for about 2.5 miles to the campground on the right side of the road.

Trip note: The Boca Dam faces Interstate 80, so the lake is out of sight of the zillions of highway travelers who would otherwise certainly stop here. For those who do, they find the lake is very pretty, set at 5,700 feet, covering 1,000 acres with deep, blue water. This camp is set on its northeastern shore, not far from the inlet to the Little Truckee River. The boat ramp is some distance away (see listing for next camp). The elevation is 5,700 feet. Open May through October.

12. BOCA SPRINGS CAMPGROUND

Reference: **On Boca Reservoir in Tahoe National Forest; map D4, grid b3.**

Campsites, facilities: There are 20 sites for tents or motor homes up to 16 feet long. There is **no piped water**, but portable toilets and fire grills are provided. Pets are permitted on leashes or otherwise controlled. A concrete boat ramp is north of the campground on Boca Reservoir. Truckee is the nearest place for telephones and supplies.

Reservations, fee: No reservations; $8 fee per night.

Who to contact: Phone the Tahoe National Forest at (916) 587-3558.

Location: From Truckee, travel east on Interstate 80 for seven miles to the Boca-Hirschdale exit. Take that exit and drive north for a short distance to County Road 73 and continue for one mile to the campground on the right side of the road.

Trip note: Boca Reservoir is known for being a "big fish factory," with some huge but rare brown trout and rainbow trout sprinkled among a growing fishery for kokanee salmon. The lake is set at 5,700 feet, a Sierra gem within a few miles of Interstate 80. The camp is the best choice for fishermen/boaters, with a launch ramp set just down from the campground. Open May through October.

13. GRANITE FLAT 🐟 🚶 ♿   RV 6

Reference: **On Truckee River in Tahoe National Forest; map D4, grid c2.**

Campsites, facilities: There are 65 sites for tents or motor homes, and 10 walk-in tent sites. Piped water, vault toilets, fire grills and picnic tables are provided. Pets are permitted on leashes or otherwise controlled. The facilities are **wheelchair accessible**.

Reservations, fee: Reserve by phoning (800) 280-CAMP ($7.50 reservation fee); $12 fee per night.

Who to contact: Phone the Tahoe National Forest District Office at (916) 587-3558.

Location: From Truckee, drive south on Highway 89 for 1.5 miles to the campground entrance on the right.

Trip note: This camp is set along the Truckee River at 5,800 feet, in an area known for a ton of traffic on adjacent Highway 89, as well as decent trout fishing, and in the spring and early summer, rafting. It is about a 15-minute drive to Squaw Valley or Lake Tahoe. A bike route is also available along the Truckee River out of Tahoe City. Open May through October.

14. DONNER MEMORIAL STATE PARK   RV 10
🐟 ⚓ 🚶 ♿ 🏊 ⛪

Reference: **On Donner Lake; map D4, grid c2.**

Campsites, facilities: There are 154 sites for tents or motor homes up to 28 feet long. Piped water, flush toilets, showers, picnic tables and fire grills are provided. Pets are permitted on leashes. Supplies are available in Truckee. Facilities are **wheelchair accessible**.

Reservations, fee: Reserve by phoning Destinet at (800) 444-7275 ($6.75 Destinet fee); $15-$17 fee per night; $1 pet fee.

Who to contact: Phone (916) 582-7892 or (916) 525-7232.

Location: From Auburn, drive east on Interstate 80 just past Donner Lake to Donner Pass Road. Take that exit and drive south for one mile to the park entrance and the southeast end of the lake.

Trip note: The remarkable beauty of Donner Lake often evokes a deep, heartfelt response. The lake is big, three miles long and three-quarters of a mile wide, gem-like blue and set near the Sierra crest at 5,900 feet. The area is well developed, with a number of cabins and access roads, and this state park is the feature destination. It is located along the southeastern end of the lake, and is extremely pretty. Fishing is good here (typically only in the early morning), trolling for kokanee salmon or rainbow trout, with big mackinaw and brown trout providing wild cards. In summer, a wind often comes up in the early afternoon here. In winter, a good cross-country ski trail is available. One last note: Please bring plenty of food. You know why.

15. GOOSE MEADOWS 🐟 ✕   RV 6

Reference: **On Truckee River in Tahoe National Forest; map D4, grid c2.**

Campsites, facilities: There are 25 sites for tents or motor homes up to 30 feet long. Hand-pumped water is available. Vault toilets, fire grills and picnic tables are provided. Pets are permitted on leashes or otherwise controlled. Supplies are available in Truckee and Tahoe City.

Reservations, fee: Reserve by phoning (800) 280-CAMP ($7.50 reservation fee); $8 fee per night; $4 for each additional vehicle.

Who to contact: Phone the Tahoe National Forest District Office at (916) 587-3558, or California Land Management at (916) 582-0120.

Location: From Truckee, drive south on Highway 89 for four miles to the campground entrance on the left (river side) of the highway.

Trip note: There are three campgrounds set along the Truckee River off Highway 89, between Truckee and Tahoe City. Goose Meadows provides good fishing access with decent prospects, despite the high number of vehicles roaring past on the adjacent highway. This stretch of river is also popular for rafting. The elevation is 5,800 feet. Open May through October.

16. MARTIS CREEK LAKE 🐟 ⚓ ✗   RV 7

Reference: **Near Truckee; map D4, grid c3.**

Campsites, facilities: There are 25 sites for tents or motor homes up to 30 feet long. Piped water, vault toilets, picnic tables and fire grills are provided. Supplies are available in Truckee. Pets are allowed on leashes.

Reservations, fee: No reservations; $10 fee per night.

Who to contact: Phone the U.S. Corps of Engineers, Martis Creek Lake, at (916) 639-2342.

Location: From Truckee, drive south on Highway 267 for about three miles (past the airport) to the entrance road to the lake on the left. Turn left and drive another 2.5 miles to the campground at the end of the road.

Trip note: If only this lake wasn't so often windy in the afternoon, it would be heaven to flyfishers in float tubes, casting out with sinking lines and leech patterns, using a strip retrieve. To some, it's heaven anyway, with Lahontan cutthroat trout ranging to 25 inches here. This is a special catch-and-release fishery where anglers are permitted to use only artificial lures with single barbless hooks. The setting is somewhat sparse and open, a small lake on the eastern edge of the Martis Valley. No motors are permitted at the lake, making it ideal (when the wind is down) for float tubes or prams. The elevation is 5,800 feet. Open May through October.

17. COACHLAND RV PARK 🐟 🚶 ♿   RV 6

Reference: **In Truckee; map D4, grid c3.**

Campsites, facilities: There are 131 sites for trailers or motor homes up to 40 feet long. Picnic tables, restrooms, showers, laundry facilities, cable TV and propane are available. Pets are permitted on leashes. The facilities are **wheelchair accessible**.

Reservations, fee: Reservations recommended; $22 fee per night.

Who to contact: Phone the park at (916) 587-3071 or write to 10500 Highway 89 North, Unit 35, Truckee, CA 96161.

Location: From Truckee, drive north on Highway 89 for a short distance to the park at 10500 Highway 89 on the left side of the road.

Trip note: Truckee is the gateway to recreation at North Tahoe. Within minutes are Donner Lake, Prosser Creek Reservoir, Boca Reservoir, Stampede Reservoir and the Truckee River. Squaw Valley is a short distance to the south off Highway 89 and Northstar is the same off Highway 267. The park is set in a wooded area near the junction of Interstate 80 and Highway 89, providing easy access. The downtown Truckee area (with restaurants) is nearby. This is one of the only parks in the area that is open year-round. The elevation is 6,000 feet.

---

18. WILLIAM KENT

Reference: **Near Lake Tahoe in Lake Tahoe Basin; map D4, grid d2.**

Campsites, facilities: There are 55 tent sites and 40 sites for motor homes up to 24 feet long. Piped water, flush toilets, a sanitary dump station, picnic tables and fire grills are provided. Pets are permitted. A grocery store, a laundromat and propane gas are available nearby.

Reservations, fee: Reserve by phoning (800) 280-CAMP ($7.50 reservation fee); $12 fee per night.

Who to contact: Phone U.S. Forest Service at (916) 573-2600, or phone the campground at (916) 544-5994.

Location: From Truckee, drive south on Highway 89 to Tahoe City. Turn south on Highway 89 and drive three miles to the campground entrance on the right side of the road.

Trip note: William Kent Camp is a little pocket of peace set near the busy traffic of Highway 89 on the western shore corridor. It is set on the west side of the highway, meaning visitors have to cross the highway in order to get lakeside access. It is set at 6,300 feet and is wooded, with primarily lodgepole pines. The drive here is awesome or ominous, depending on how you look at it, with the view of incredible Lake Tahoe to the east, the deepest blue in the world. But you often have a lot of time to look at it, with traffic rarely moving quickly. Open June through September.

---

19. LAKE FOREST CAMPGROUND

Reference: **On Lake Tahoe; map D4, grid d2.**

Campsites, facilities: There are 21 sites for tents or motor homes up to 20 feet long. Piped water, flush toilets and picnic tables are provided. A boat ramp is available. A grocery store, a laundromat, and propane gas are available nearby.

Reservations, fee: No reservations; $10 fee per night.

Who to contact: Phone (916) 583-5544, ext. 2.

Location: From Truckee, drive south on Highway 89 to Tahoe City. Turn north on Highway 89 and drive two miles to the campground entrance on the right side of the road.

Trip note: The northwest shore of Lake Tahoe provides beautiful lookouts and excellent boating access. The latter is a highlight of this camp, with a boat ramp nearby. From here, it is a short cruise to Dollar Point and around the corner north to Carnelian Bay, one of the better stretches of water for trout fishing. The elevation is 6,200 feet. Open April through October.

---

20. SILVER CREEK

Reference: **On Truckee River in Tahoe National Forest; map D4, grid d2.**

Campsites, facilities: There are 20 sites for tents or motor homes up to 40 feet long and eight walk-in sites. Piped water, vault toilets, picnic tables and fire grills are provided. Pets are permitted on leashes or otherwise controlled. Supplies are available in Truckee and Tahoe City.

Reservations, fee: Reserve by phoning (800) 280-CAMP ($7.50 reservation fee);

$8 fee per night; $4 for each additional vehicle.

Who to contact: Phone the Tahoe National Forest District Office at (916) 587-3558.

Location: From Truckee, drive south on Highway 89 for six miles to the campground entrance on the river side of the highway.

Trip note: This pretty campground is set near where Deer Creek enters the Truckee River. The trout fishing is often good in this area and side trips include a good hike up the trail that runs along Deer Creek, with the trailhead right at the camp. This is one of three campgrounds along Highway 89 and the Truckee River, between Truckee and Tahoe City. The elevation is 5,800 feet. Open June through September.

21. TAHOE STATE RECREATION AREA   RV 9

Reference: On Lake Tahoe; map D4, grid d2.

Campsites, facilities: There are 39 sites for tents or motor homes up to 21 feet long. Piped water, coin-operated showers, flush toilets, picnic tables, fire grills, a playground and a pier are provided. Pets are permitted. Firewood, other supplies and a laundromat are available nearby.

Reservations, fee: Reserve by phoning Destinet at (800) 444-7275 ($6.75 Destinet fee); $14-$16 fee per night; $1 pet fee.

Who to contact: Phone (916) 583-3074 or (916) 525 7232.

Location: From Truckee, drive south on Highway 89 to Tahoe City. Turn north on Highway 89 and drive a quarter-mile to the campground entrance on the left side of the road.

Trip note: This is a popular summer-only campground at the northwest side of Lake Tahoe. The Recreation Area covers a large area just west of Highway 24 near Tahoe City, with the opportunity for hiking and horseback riding. A boat ramp is located two miles to the northwest at nearby Lake Forest, and bike rentals are available in Tahoe City for a route along Highway 89 near the shore of the lake.

22. SANDY BEACH CAMPGROUND   RV 8

Reference: On Lake Tahoe; map D4, grid d3.

Campsites, facilities: There are 50 sites with full or partial hookups for tents or motor homes up to 35 feet long. Piped water, showers, flush toilets, picnic tables and fire grills are provided. A boat ramp is available and pets are permitted. A grocery store, a laundromat and propane gas are available nearby.

Reservations, fee: Reservations accepted; $15-$20 fee per night.

Who to contact: Phone (916) 546-7682, or write Sandy Beach Campground, P.O. Box 6868, Tahoe City, CA 96145.

Location: From Truckee, drive south on Highway 89 to Tahoe City. Turn north on Highway 89 and drive eight miles to the campground (signed) on the left side of the road.

Trip note: Sandy Beach Camp is set at 6,200 feet near the northwest shore of Lake Tahoe. A nearby boat ramp provides access to one of the better fishing areas of the lake for mackinaw trout. The water in Tahoe is always cold, and though a lot of people will get suntans on beaches next to the lake, swimmers need to be members of the Polar Bear Club. A short drive to the east will take you past the town of Kings Beach and into Nevada, where there are some small casinos near the shore of Crystal Bay. Open May through October.

23. WENTWORTH SPRINGS 🐟 🚶

Reference: **Near Loon Lake in Eldorado National Forest; map D4, grid e0.**

Campsites, facilities: There are eight tent sites. There is **no piped water**, but vault toilets, picnic tables and fire grills are provided. Access is recommended for motorcycles or four-wheel-drive vehicles only. Pets are permitted on leashes or otherwise controlled.

Reservations, fee: No reservations; no fee.

Who to contact: Phone the Eldorado National Forest Information Center at (916) 644-6048.

Location: From Sacramento, drive east on US 50 to Riverton and the junction with Ice House Road (Soda Springs-Riverton Road) on the left. Turn left and drive 30 miles to the junction with Forest Service Road 30. Bear left and drive 3.5 miles to Forest Service Road 33. Turn right and drive seven miles to the campground on the left side of the road. (The access road is suitable for four-wheel-drive vehicles or off-road motorcycles).

Trip note: There is one reason people come here, to set up a base camp for an OHV adventure, whether they are the owners of four-wheel-drives, all-terrain vehicles or dirt bikes. A network of roads lead from this camp, passable only by these vehicles, roads that would flat destroy your average car. The camp is set deep in Eldorado National Forest, at 6,200 feet in elevation. While the north end of Loon Lake is located a mile to the east, the road to get there is extremely rough (perfect, right?). The road is gated along the lake, preventing access to this camp for those who drive directly to Loon Lake. Open June through October.

24. SUGAR PINE POINT STATE PARK 🐟 🚶 ♿ 🚤 ⛪

Reference: **On Lake Tahoe; map D4, grid e2.**

Campsites, facilities: There are 175 sites for tents or motor homes up to 30 feet long. There are also 10 group sites available. Piped water, coin-operated showers (except in winter), flush toilets, a sanitary dump station, picnic tables and fire grills are provided. A grocery store, laundry facilities, and propane gas are available nearby. There is **wheelchair access** to picnic areas. Pets are permitted on leashes.

Reservations, fee: Reserve by phoning Destinet at (800) 444-7275 ($6.75 Destinet fee); $15-$17 fee per night; $1 pet fee.

Who to contact: Call (916) 525-7982 or (916) 525-7232.

Location: From Truckee, drive south on Highway 89 to Tahoe City. Turn south on Highway 89 and drive 10 miles to the campground (signed) on the west side of the road.

Trip note: This is one of three beautiful and popular state parks set on the west shore of Lake Tahoe. This one is located just north of Meeks Bay on General Creek, with almost two miles of lake frontage available, though the camp-ground is located on the opposite side of Highway 89. A pretty trail is available routed four miles along the creek up to Lost Lake, set just outside the northern boundary of Desolation Wilderness. The elevation is 6,200 feet. Open year-round, but no showers are available during winter.

25. MEEKS BAY

Reference: **On Lake Tahoe in Lake Tahoe Basin; map D4, grid e2.**

Campsites, facilities: There are 40 sites for tents or motor homes up to 20 feet long. Piped water, flush toilets, picnic tables and fire grills are provided. Laundry facilities and groceries are available nearby. Pets are permitted.

Reservations, fee: Reserve by phoning (800) 280-CAMP ($7.50 reservation fee); $14 fee per night.

Who to contact: Phone Lake Tahoe Basin Management Unit at (916) 544-5994.

Location: In South Lake Tahoe at the junction of Highway 89 and US 50, turn north on Highway 89 and drive 17 miles to the campground.

Trip note: Meeks Bay is a beautiful spot along the western shore of Lake Tahoe. A bicycle trail is available nearby that is routed along the lake's shore, but requires occasionally crossing busy Highway 89. Open May through October.

26. KASPIAN

Reference: **On Lake Tahoe in Lake Tahoe Basin; map D4, grid e2.**

Campsites, facilities: There are 10 sites for tents or motor homes up to 20 feet long. Piped water, flush toilets, picnic tables and fire grills are provided. Pets are permitted if they are on leashes. A grocery store, a laundromat, and propane gas are available nearby.

Reservations, fee: No reservations; $10 fee per night.

Who to contact: Phone Lake Tahoe Basin Management Unit at (916) 573-2600.

Location: From Truckee, drive south on Highway 89 to Tahoe City. Turn south on Highway 89 and drive four miles to the campground (signed) on the east side of the road.

Trip note: As gorgeous and as huge as Lake Tahoe is, there are relatively few camps or even restaurants with lakeside settings. This is one of the few. Kaspian is set along the west shore of the lake, at 6,235 feet in elevation, between the little towns of Sunnyside and Tahoe Pines. A Forest Service Road (03) is available adjacent to the camp on the west side of Highway 89, routed west into national forest (becoming quite rough) to a trailhead. From here, you can hike up to Barker Peak (8,166 feet) for incredible views of Lake Tahoe, as well as access to the Pacific Crest Trail. Open May through September.

27. MEEKS BAY RESORT

Reference: **Map D4, grid e2.**

Campsites, facilities: There are 28 sites for motor homes, 10 with hookups. Showers, flush toilets, picnic tables and fire grills are provided. Laundry facilities, a snack bar, a gift shop and groceries are available nearby. A boat ramp and boat slips are available. No pets are allowed.

Reservations, fee: Reservations accepted; $15-$25 fee per night; $3-$5 day-use fee; $15 fee per night for boat slips.

Who to contact: Phone (916) 525-7242.

Location: In South Lake Tahoe at the junction of Highway 89 and US 50, turn north on Highway 89 and drive 17 miles to the campground.

Trip note: Prime access for boating makes this a camp of choice for the boater/camper at Lake Tahoe. A boat launch is not only nearby, but access to Rubicon

Bay and beyond to breathtaking Emerald Bay is possible, a six-mile trip, one-way, for boats large enough and fast enough to make it. Open June through September.

28. RED FIR GROUP CAMP

Reference: On Loon Lake in Eldorado National Forest; map D4, grid f0.

Campsites, facilities: This group site will accommodate up to six vehicles and 25 people. Piped water, vault toilets, fire rings and grills are provided. Pets are allowed on leashes.

Reservations, fee: Reserve by phoning (800) 280-CAMP ($15 reservation fee); $35 fee per night.

Who to contact: Phone the Eldorado National Forest Information Center at (916) 644-6048.

Location: From Sacramento, drive east on US 50 to Riverton and the junction with Ice House Road (Soda Springs-Riverton Road) on the left. Turn left and drive 34 miles to a fork at the foot of Loon Lake. Turn left and drive three miles to the campground (just beyond Northshore Camp).

Trip note: This is a pretty, wooded camp, ideal for medium-sized groups. The camp is set across the road from the water, offering a secluded, quiet spot. Lake access is a short hike away. See the trip note for Northshore Camp. The elevation is 6,500 feet. Open June through September.

29. LOON LAKE NORTHSHORE

Reference: On Loon Lake in Eldorado National Forest; map D4, grid f0.

Campsites, facilities: There are 15 sites for tents or self-contained motor homes. **No piped water** is available. Vault toilets, picnic tables, fire rings and grills are provided. Pets are allowed on leashes.

Reservations, fee: No reservations; no fee.

Who to contact: Phone the Eldorado National Forest Information Center at (916) 644-6048.

Location: From Sacramento, drive east on US 50 to Riverton and the junction with Ice House Road (Soda Springs-Riverton Road) on the left. Turn left and drive 34 miles to a fork at the foot of Loon Lake. Turn left and drive three miles to the campground.

Trip note: This camp is set on the northwestern shore of Loon Lake, where its water's edge sites make for an extremely pretty setting, even though few facilities and no boat ramp are available. (The boat ramp is located near the Loon Lake Campground and Picnic Area at the south end of the lake.) For more information about Loon Lake, see the trip notes for Pleasant Camp and Loon Lake Camp. Open June through September.

30. PLEASANT HIKE-IN, BOAT-IN

Reference: On Loon Lake in Eldorado National Forest; map D4, grid f0.

Campsites, facilities: There are 10 boat-in or hike-in tent sites. There is **no piped water**, but pit toilets, picnic tables and fire grills are provided. The camp is accessible by boat or trail only. Pets are permitted on leashes or otherwise controlled.

Reservations, fee: No reservations; no fee.

Who to contact: Phone the Eldorado National Forest Information Center at (916) 644-6048.

Location: From Sacramento, drive east on US 50 to Riverton and the junction with Ice House Road (Soda Springs-Riverton Road) on the left. Turn left and drive 34 miles to a fork at the foot of Loon Lake. Turn right and drive one mile to the Loon Lake Picnic Area or boat ramp. Either hike or boat 2.5 miles to the campground on the northeast shore of the lake.

Trip note: This a premium Sierra camp, hike-in or boat-in only, set on the remote northeast shore of Loon Lake, 6,378 feet in elevation. In many ways, this makes for a perfect short vacation. After reaching the camp, a trail is available routed east for four miles past Buck Island Lake (6,436 feet) and Rockbound Lake (6,529 feet), set just inside the northern border of Desolation Wilderness. When the trail is clear of snow, this makes for a fantastic day hike; a wilderness permit is required if staying overnight inside the wilderness boundary. Open June through October.

---

31. LOON LAKE 🐟 ⚓ 👫 ♿ 🏊   RV 9

Reference: In Eldorado National Forest; map D4, grid f0.

Campsites, facilities: There are 53 sites for tents or motor homes up to 22 feet long. Piped water, vault toilets, picnic tables and fire grills are provided. Pets are permitted on leashes or otherwise controlled. A boat ramp and swimming beach are nearby.

Reservations, fee: Reserve by phoning (800) 280-CAMP ($7.85 reservation fee); $9 fee per night.

Who to contact: Phone the Eldorado National Forest Information Center at (916) 644-6048.

Location: From Sacramento, drive east on US 50 to Riverton and the junction with Ice House Road (Soda Springs-Riverton Road) on the left. Turn left and drive 34 miles to a fork at the foot of Loon Lake. Turn right and drive one mile to the Loon Lake Picnic Area or boat ramp. Either hike or boat 2.5 miles to the campground on the northeast shore of the lake.

Trip note: Loon Lake is set near the Sierra Crest at 6,400 feet, covering 600 acres with depths up to 130 feet. This is the lake's primary campground, and it is easy to see why, with a picnic area, beach (includes a small unit to change your clothes in), and boat ramp located adjacent to the camp. The lake provides good trout fishing, and with the access road often not clear of snow until mid-June, the lake can be stocked every week of summer. Afternoon winds drive anglers off the lake, but are cheered by sailboarders. An excellent trail is also available here, with the hike routed along the lake's eastern shore to Pleasant Camp (a trailhead for the Desolation Wilderness is available at Pleasant Camp; see previous listing). Open June through September.

---

32. EMERALD BAY STATE PARK   RV 10

🐟 ⚓ 👫 🏊 ⚓

Reference: On Lake Tahoe; map D4, grid f2.

Campsites, facilities: There are 100 sites for tents or motor homes up to 21 feet long and trailers up to 18 feet long. Piped water, coin-operated showers, flush toilets, picnic tables and fire grills are provided. Pets are permitted. There are also 20 boat-in sites available on the north side of the bay with water and toilets provided.

Reservations, fee: Reserve by phoning Destinet at (800) 444-7275 ($6.75 Destinet fee); $12-$14 fee per night; $1 pet fee. No reservations for boat-in sites; $10-$12 fee per night.

Who to contact: Call (916) 541-3030 or (916) 525-7277 or (916) 525-7232.

Location: In South Lake Tahoe at the junction of Highway 89 and US 50, turn north on Highway 89 and drive eight miles to the state park turnoff on the east side of the road. Turn east and drive one mile to the park entrance.

Trip note: This is one of the most beautiful and popular state parks on the planet earth. It is set at Eagle Point, near the mouth of Emerald Bay on Lake Tahoe, a place of rare, divine beauty. Although the high number of people at Lake Tahoe, and at this park in particular, present an inevitable problem, the 20 boat-in sites provide a remarkable solution. There may be no more beautiful place anywhere to run a boat than in Emerald Bay, with its deep cobalt-blue waters, awesome surrounding ridgelines, glimpses out the mouth of the Bay of Lake Tahoe, and even a little island. The park also has several short hiking trails. Open June through September.

33. D.L. BLISS STATE PARK

Reference: On Lake Tahoe; map D4, grid f2.

Campsites, facilities: There are 168 sites for tents or motor homes up to 18 feet long and trailers up to 15 feet long. Piped water, showers, flush toilets, picnic tables and fire grills are provided. Pets are permitted on leashes.

Reservations, fee: Reserve through Destinet at (800) 444-7275 ($6.75 Destinet fee); $15-$17 fee per night; $1 pet fee.

Who to contact: Call (916) 525-7277 or (916) 525-7232.

Location: In South Lake Tahoe at the junction of Highway 89 and US 50, turn north on Highway 89 and drive 13 miles to the state park turnoff on the east side of the road. Turn east and drive to the park entrance.

Trip note: D.L. Bliss State Park is set on one of Lake Tahoe's most beautiful stretches of shoreline, from Emerald Point at the mouth of Emerald Bay on northward to Rubicon Point, spanning some three miles. The camp is set at the north end of the park, the sites nestled amid pines, with the lake about a quarter-mile away. A trail from the camp is routed south to Emerald Point (6,232 feet), where there is a beautiful view of the lake and beyond to the surrounding mountain rim, awesome in early summer when it is still covered with snow. Open June through mid-October.

34. CAMP RICHARDSON RESORT

Reference: On Lake Tahoe; map D4, grid f3.

Campsites, facilities: There are 223 sites for tents and 112 sites for motor homes, some with full or partial hookups. Piped water, showers, flush toilets, a sanitary dump station, a playground, a recreation hall, picnic tables and fire pits are provided. A boat ramp, boat rentals, groceries and propane gas are also available. No pets allowed.

Reservations, fee: Reservations recommended; $17-$22 fee per night.

Who to contact: Phone (916) 541-1801, or (800) 544-1801.

Location: In South Lake Tahoe at the junction of Highway 89 and US 50, turn north on Highway 89 and drive 2.5 miles to the resort on the right side of the road.

Trip note: Richardson's Resort is within minutes of boating, biking and gambling, and in the winter, skiing. It's a take-your-pick deal. With cabins and a hopping restaurant and night club also on the property, this is a place that offers one big package. The campsites are set in the woods, not on the lake itself. From here, you can gain access to an excellent bike route that runs for three miles, then loops around by the lake for another three miles, most of it flat and easy, all of it beautiful. Expect company. The elevation is 6,300 feet. Open June through October.

35. WRIGHTS LAKE

Reference: **In Eldorado National Forest; map D4, grid g0.**

Campsites, facilities: There are 35 sites for tents and 36 sites for tents or motor homes up to 22 feet long. Piped water, vault toilets, picnic tables and fire grills are provided. Pets are permitted on leashes or otherwise controlled.

Reservations, fee: Reserve by phoning (800) 280-CAMP ($7.85 reservation fee); $10 fee per night.

Who to contact: Phone the Eldorado National Forest Information Center at (916) 644-6048.

Location: From Sacramento, drive east on US 50 to Placerville, then continue for 34 miles (five miles past Kyburz) to Wrights Lake Road. Turn north on Wrights Lake Road and drive eight miles to the campground on the right side of the road.

Trip note: This high-mountain lake (7,000 feet) has shoreline camping, good fishing and hiking, yet is remote enough to be overlooked by many. There is no boat ramp, plus rules permit no motors, so it is ideal for canoes, rafts and prams, and people who like quiet. Fishing is fair for both rainbow trout and brown trout. It is a classic alpine lake, though small (65 acres), with a trailhead for the Desolation Wilderness located at its north end. From here, it is only a three-mile hike to the beautiful Twin Lakes and Island Lake, set on the western flank of Mt. Price (9,975 feet). Open June through October.

36. FALLEN LEAF CAMPGROUND

Reference: **In Lake Tahoe Basin; map D4, grid g2.**

Campsites, facilities: There are 75 sites for tents and 130 sites for tents or motor homes up to 40 feet long. Piped water, flush toilets, picnic tables and fire grills are provided. A boat ramp, laundromat and supplies are available nearby. Pets are allowed on leashes.

Reservations, fee: Reserve by phoning (800) 280-CAMP ($7.50 reservation fee); $14 fee per night.

Who to contact: Phone the U.S. Forest Service Tahoe Basin Management Unit at (916) 573-2600.

Location: In South Lake Tahoe at the junction of US 50 and Highway 89, turn north on Highway 89 and drive two miles to the Fallen Leaf Lake turnoff. Turn left and drive 1.5 miles to the campground.

Trip note: This is a large "tent city" near the north shore of Fallen Leaf Lake, set at 6,337 feet in elevation. This lake is almost as deep blue as nearby Tahoe. It's a big lake, three miles long, and also quite deep, 430 feet at its deepest point. The campground is operated by the concessionaire, which provides a variety of recreational opportunities, including a boat ramp and horseback riding rentals. Fishing is best in the fall for kokanee salmon. Because the lake is circled by forest and much of it private property, you need a boat to fish or explore the lake. A visitor center is available north of the Fallen Leaf Lake turnoff on Highway 89. Open May through October.

37. CAMP SHELLEY

Reference: **Near Lake Tahoe in Lake Tahoe Basin; map D4, grid g2.**

Campsites, facilities: There are 26 sites for tents or motor homes up to 22 feet long. Piped water, flush toilets, showers, picnic tables and fire grills are provided. A boat ramp, groceries and propane gas are available nearby at Camp Richardson. Pets are permitted on leashes and or otherwise controlled.

Reservations, fee: Reserve by writing the Livermore Recreation and Park District at 71 Trevarno Road, Livermore, CA 94550; $12 fee per night.

Who to contact: Phone the Livermore Area Recreation and Park District at (916) 541-6985.

Location: In South Lake Tahoe at the junction of US 50 and Highway 89, turn north on Highway 89 and drive 2.5 miles to Camp Richardson, then continue for 1.3 miles to the sign for Mt. Tallac. Turn left and drive to the campground (signed).

Trip note: This privately-owned campground is set near South Lake Tahoe, within close range of an outstanding bicycle trail. Nearby to the west is the drive to Inspiration Point and the incredible lookout of Emerald Bay, as well as the parking area for the short hike to Eagle Falls. Nearby to the east is Fallen Leaf Lake and south shore of Lake Tahoe. Open mid-June through Labor Day.

38. CHRIS HAVEN MOBILE HOME AND RV PARK

Reference: **Near South Lake Tahoe; map D4, grid g3.**

Campsites, facilities: There are 57 motor home sites with full hookups. Patios, restrooms, showers and laundry facilities are provided. Pets are allowed on leashes.

Reservations, fee: Reservations recommended; $23 fee per night.

Who to contact: Phone (916) 541-1895.

Location: Entering South Lake Tahoe on US 50, drive east to E Street (a half-mile south of the junction of US 50 and Highway 89). Turn east on E Street and drive one block to the park on the left.

Trip note: This is an RV-only park that is set within the boundaries of a mobile home park, within close range of the casinos to the east. Open year-round.

39. KOA SOUTH LAKE TAHOE

Reference: **Map D4, grid g3.**

Campsites, facilities: There are 16 sites for tents and 52 sites with full hookups for motor homes up to 30 feet long. Picnic tables, fire grills, restrooms, showers, a sanitary dump station, a recreation room, a swimming pool and a playground are on the premises. (Restrooms and showers are not available in very cold weather.) Laundry facilities, groceries, RV supplies and propane gas are also available. Pets are permitted.

Reservations, fee: Reservations recommended; $22-$28 fee per night; $1.50 pet fee.

Who to contact: Phone (916) 577-3693.

Location: Entering South Lake Tahoe on US 50, look for the KOA sign along the road (located five miles south of the junction of US 50 and Highway 89).

Trip note: Like so many KOA camps, this one is located on the outskirts of a major destination area, in this case, South Lake Tahoe. It is within close range of gambling, fishing, hiking, bike rentals, and, in winter, good skiing. The camp is set at 6,300 feet. Open April through December.

---

40. TAHOE VALLEY CAMPGROUND

Reference: **Near Lake Tahoe; map D4, grid g3.**

Campsites, facilities: There are 110 sites for tents and 305 sites for motor homes with full hookups. Restrooms, a sanitary dump station, picnic tables, fire grills, laundry facilities, a heated swimming pool, a playground, a grocery store, RV supplies, propane gas, ice, firewood, cable TV and a recreation room are all provided. Pets are permitted on leashes (limit of two pets).

Reservations, fee: Reservations recommended; $20-$27 fee per night, $2 pet fee.

Who to contact: Phone (916) 541-2222.

Location: Entering South Lake Tahoe on US 50, drive east on US 50 to Meyers (a quarter-mile south of the junction of US 50 and Highway 89) to the signed entrance on the right.

Trip note: This is a massive privately-operated park near South Lake Tahoe. The nearby attractions include five golf courses, horseback riding, casinos, and, of course, "The Lake." Open mid-April through mid-October.

---

41. EL DORADO RECREATION AREA

Reference: **Near Lake Tahoe; map D4, grid g4.**

Campsites, facilities: There are 170 sites for tents or motor homes up to 32 feet long. Piped water, flush toilets, showers, a sanitary dump station, a playground, picnic tables and fire grills are provided. A boat ramp is also available. Supplies and laundry facilities are nearby. Pets are permitted with proof of vaccinations.

Reservations, fee: Reservations accepted; $17-$20 fee per night; two-night minimum on weekends and holidays; $1 pet fee.

Who to contact: Call (916) 542-6096 or (916) 542-6055.

Location: Entering South Lake Tahoe on US 50, drive east on US 50 to Rufus Allen Boulevard. Turn right (south) and drive a quarter-mile to the campground on the right side of the road.

Trip note: This city-operated campground at South Lake Tahoe is primarily designed for RV drivers on tour. Open April through September and set at 6,200 feet.

---

42. KIRKWOOD LAKE

Reference: **In Eldorado National Forest; map D4, grid h1.**

Campsites, facilities: There are 12 tent sites. Piped water, vault toilets, picnic tables and fire rings are provided. Pets are permitted on leashes.

Reservations, fee: No reservations; $8 fee per night.

Who to contact: Phone the Eldorado National Forest Information Center at (916) 644-6048.

Location: From Jackson, drive east on Highway 88 for 60 miles (four miles past Silver Lake) to the campground entrance road on the left (if you reach the sign for Kirkwood Ski Resort, you have gone a half-mile too far). Turn left and drive a quarter-mile (road not suitable for trailers or RVs) to the campground.

Trip note: Little Kirkwood Lake is in a beautiful Sierra setting, with good shoreline access, fishing for small rainbow trout and quiet water. Despite that, it is often overlooked in favor of nearby Silver Lake and Caples Lake along Highway 88. Nearby Kirkwood Ski Resort stays open all summer and offers excellent opportunities for horseback riding, hiking and meals. The elevation is 7,600 feet. Open June through October.

---

43. CAPLES LAKE RV 8

Reference: In Eldorado National Forest; map D4, grid h2.

Campsites, facilities: There are 20 sites for tents and 15 sites for tents or motor homes up to 22 feet long. Piped water, vault toilets, picnic tables and fire rings are provided. Groceries, propane gas, a boat ramp and boat rentals are nearby. Pets are permitted on leashes.

Reservations, fee: No reservations; $9 fee per night.

Who to contact: Phone the Eldorado National Forest Information Center at (916) 644-6048.

Location: From Jackson, drive east on Highway 88 for 63 miles (one mile past the entrance road to Kirkwood Ski Area) to the camp entrance road on the left.

Trip note: Caples Lake, set in the high country at 7,800 feet, is a pretty lake right along Highway 88. It covers 600 acres, has a 10 mile-per-hour speed limit, and provides good trout fishing and excellent hiking. The camp is set across the highway (a little two-laner) from the lake, with the Caples Lake Resort and boat rental nearby. There is a parking area at the west end of the lake, and from here there is a great 3.5-mile hike to Emigrant Lake, set in the Mokelumne Wilderness on the western flank of Mt. Round Top (10,310 feet). Open June through October.

---

44. HOPE VALLEY RV 7

Reference: Near Carson River in Toiyabe National Forest; map D4, grid h3.

Campsites, facilities: There are 20 sites for tents or motor homes up to 22 feet long and one group area for up to 16 people. Piped water, vault toilets, picnic tables and fire grills are provided. Pets are permitted on leashes.

Reservations, fee: Reserve by phoning (800) 280-CAMP ($7.50 reservation fee); $7-$14 fee per night.

Who to contact: Phone the Toiyabe National Forest, Carson Ranger District at (702) 882-2766.

Location: From Sacramento, drive east on US 50 to the junction with Highway 89. Turn south on Highway 89 and drive over Luther Pass to the junction with Highway 88. Turn right (west) and drive two miles to Blue Lakes Road. Turn left (south) and drive 1.5 miles to the campground on the right side of the road. (From Jackson, drive east on Highway 88 over Carson Pass and continue east for five miles to Blue Lakes Road. Turn right (south) and drive 1.5 miles to the campground on the right side of the road.)

Trip note: The West Fork Carson River runs right through Hope Valley, a pretty trout stream with a choice of four streamside campgrounds. Trout stocks are made near the camps during summer. This is a very pretty area, with this camp just east of Carson Pass, at 7,300 feet in elevation. A trailhead for the Pacific Crest Trail is located three miles south of camp. The primary nearby destination is Blue Lakes, about a 10-minute drive. An insider's note is that little

Tamarack Lake, set just beyond the turnoff for Lower Blue Lake, is excellent for swimming. Open June through October.

45. KIT CARSON 🐟 🚶 RV 8

Reference: **On the West Fork of Carson River in Toiyabe National Forest; map D4, grid h4.**

Campsites, facilities: There are 12 sites for tents or motor homes up to 22 feet long. Piped water, vault toilets, picnic tables and fire grills are provided. Pets are permitted on leashes.

Reservations, fee: No reservations; $7 fee per night.

Who to contact: Phone the Toiyabe National Forest, Carson Ranger District at (702) 882-2766.

Location: From Sacramento, drive east on US 50 to the junction with Highway 89. Turn south on Highway 89 and drive over Luther Pass to the junction with Highway 88. Turn left (east) and drive one mile to the campground on the left side of the road. (From Jackson, drive east on Highway 88 over Carson Pass and to the junction with Highway 89, then continue for one mile to the campground on the left side of the road.)

Trip note: This is one in a series of pristine, high Sierra camps set along the West Fork of the Carson River. There's good trout fishing, thanks to regular stocks from the Department of Fish and Game. This is no secret, however, and the area from the Highway 89 bridge on downstream gets a lot of fishing pressure. The elevation is 6,600 feet. Open mid-May through mid-September.

46. CRYSTAL SPRINGS 🐟 🚶 RV 8

Reference: **On the West Fork of Carson River in Toiyabe National Forest; map D4, grid h4.**

Campsites, facilities: There are 20 sites for tents or motor homes up to 22 feet long. Piped water, vault toilets, picnic tables and fire grills are provided. Pets are permitted on leashes.

Reservations, fee: No reservations; $7 fee per night.

Who to contact: Phone the Toiyabe National Forest, Carson Ranger District at (702) 882-2766.

Location: From Sacramento, drive east on US 50 to the junction with Highway 89. Turn south on Highway 89 and drive over Luther Pass to the junction with Highway 88. Turn left (east) and drive 4.5 miles to the campground on the right side of the road. (From Jackson, drive east on Highway 88 over Carson Pass to the junction with Highway 89 and continue for 4.5 miles to the campground on the right side of the road.)

Trip note: For many, this camp is ideal. It is set at 6,000 feet, right alongside the West Fork of the Carson River. This stretch is stocked with trout by the Department of Fish and Game. It is easy to reach, just off Highway 88, and supplies can be obtained in nearby Woodfords. The hot springs in Markleeville provide a side trip. Open late April through September.

47. SNOWSHOE SPRINGS 🐟 🚶 8

Reference: **On the West Fork of Carson River in Toiyabe National Forest; map D4, grid h4.**

Campsites, facilities: There are 13 tent sites. Piped water, vault toilets, picnic tables and fire grills are provided. Pets are permitted on leashes.

Reservations, fee: No reservations; $7 fee per night.

Who to contact: Phone the Toiyabe National Forest, Carson Ranger District at (702) 882-2766.

Location: From Sacramento, drive east on US 50 to the junction with Highway 89. Turn south on Highway 89 and drive over Luther Pass to the junction with Highway 88. Turn left (east) and drive two miles to the campground on the right side of the road. (From Jackson, drive east on Highway 88 over Carson Pass to the junction with Highway 89 and continue for two miles to the campground on the right side of the road.)

Trip note: Take your pick of this or the other three camps set at the streamside of the West Fork of the Carson River. This one is at 6,600 feet. Trout are plentiful, but rarely large. Open June through September.

---

48. TURTLE ROCK PARK

Reference: **Near Woodfords; map D4, grid h5.**

Campsites, facilities: There are 25 sites for tents or motor homes up to 30 feet long. Piped water, pit toilets, picnic tables and fire grills are provided. Laundry facilities, groceries and propane gas are available nearby. Pets are allowed on leashes.

Reservations, fee: No reservations; $8 fee per night.

Who to contact: The camp is administered by Alpine County Parks. For information call (916) 694-2255.

Location: From Sacramento, drive east on US 50 to the junction with Highway 89. Turn south on Highway 89 and drive over Luther Pass to the junction with Highway 88. Turn left (east) and drive to Woodfords and the junction with Highway 89. Turn south and drive 4.5 miles to the park entrance on the right side of the road.

Trip note: This pretty, wooded campground, set at 6,000 feet, gets missed by a lot of folks. That's because it is administered at the county level and also because most vacationers want the more pristine beauty of the nearby camps along the Carson River. Open May through September or October. (Closure is determined by weather. If it snows, they close, so call ahead if you're planning an autumn visit.) Nearby side trips include Grover Hot Springs, and the hot springs in Markleeville.

---

49. SILVER LAKE WEST

Reference: **On Silver Lake; map D4, grid i1.**

Campsites, facilities: There are 17 sites for tents or motor homes. Picnic tables and fire pits are provided. Piped water and vault toilets are available. Pets are permitted (on leashes and under strict control).

Reservations, fee: No reservations; $10 fee per night.

Who to contact: Phone PG&E at (916) 386-5164.

Location: From Jackson, drive east on Highway 88 for 50 miles (to the north end of Silver Lake) to the campground entrance road on the left.

Trip note: The Highway 88 corridor provides access to three excellent lakes: Lower Bear River Reservoir, Silver Lake and Caples Lake. Silver is difficult to pass by, with cabin rentals, pretty campsites, decent trout fishing and excellent hiking. The lake is set at 7,200 feet in a classic granite cirque just below the Sierra Ridge. This camp is set on the west side of Highway 88, across the road from the lake. A great hike is available starting at the trailhead on the east side of the lake, a two-mile tromp to little Hidden Lake, one of several trails in the area. The camp is open May through October.

50. EAST SILVER LAKE 7

Reference: **In Eldorado National Forest; map D4, grid i1.**

Campsites, facilities: There are 28 sites for tents and 34 sites for tents or motor homes. Picnic tables, fire grills, vault toilets and piped water are provided. A grocery store, boat rentals, boat ramp and propane gas are nearby. Pets are permitted on leashes.

Reservations, fee: Reserve by phoning (800) 280-CAMP ($7.85 reservation fee); $9 fee per night.

Who to contact: Phone the Eldorado National Forest Information Center at (916) 644-6048.

Location: From Jackson, drive east on Highway 88 for 50 miles (to the north end of Silver Lake) to the campground entrance road on the right.

Trip note: Silver Lake is an easy-to-reach alpine lake set at 7,200 feet, which provides a beautiful setting, good trout fishing and hiking. This camp is set on the northeast side of the lake, with a boat ramp located nearby. See the trip note for Silver Lake West. Open June to November.

51. WOODS LAKE 9

Reference: **In Eldorado National Forest; map D4, grid i2.**

Campsites, facilities: There are 25 tent sites and one multiple-family unit. Hand-pumped water, vault toilets, picnic tables and fire rings are provided. Groceries and propane gas are available within five miles. No pets are allowed.

Reservations, fee: No reservations; $9-$18 fee per night.

Who to contact: Phone the Eldorado National Forest Information Center at (916) 644-6048.

Location: From Jackson, drive east on Highway 88 to Caples Lake and continue for one mile to the Woods Lake turnoff on the right (two miles west of Carson Pass). Turn south and drive one mile to the campground on the right (trailers and RVs are not recommended).

Trip note: Woods Lake is only two miles from Highway 88, yet can provide campers the feeling of visiting a far-off land. It is a small but beautiful lake in the granite backdrop of the high Sierra, set at 8,200 feet near Carson Pass. No boats with motors are permitted, making it ideal for canoes and row boats. Trout fishing is fair. A great trailhead is available here, a three-mile loop hike to little Round Top Lake and Winnemucca Lake (twice the size of Woods Lake) and back. They are set on the northern flank of Mt. Round Top (10,310 feet). The camp is open July through October.

52. LOWER BLUE LAKE 7

Reference: **Near Carson Pass; map D4, grid i3.**

Campsites, facilities: There are 16 sites for tents. Piped water, vault toilets, picnic tables and fire grills are provided. Pets are permitted on leashes.

Reservations, fee: No reservations; $10 fee per night; $1 pet fee.

Who to contact: The camp is managed by PG&E. For information call (916) 386-5164.

Location: From Sacramento, drive east on US 50 to the junction with Highway 89. Turn south on Highway 89 and drive over Luther Pass to the junction with

Highway 88. Turn right (west) and drive two miles to Blue Lakes Road. Turn left (south) and drive 11 miles to a junction at the south end of Lower Blue Lake. Turn right and drive a short distance to the campground on the left side of the road. (From Jackson, drive east on Highway 88 over Carson Pass and continue east for five miles to Blue Lakes Road. Turn right (south) and drive 11 miles (seven paved, four gravel) to a junction at the south end of Lower Blue Lake. Turn right and drive a short distance to the campground on the left.)

Trip note: This is the high country, 8,200 feet, where the terrain is stark and steep and edged by volcanic ridgelines, and where the deep blue-green hue of lake water brightens the landscape. Lower Blue Lake provides a popular trout fishery, with rainbow trout, brook trout and cutthroat trout all stocked regularly. The boat ramp is located adjacent to the campground. The access road crosses the Pacific Crest Trail, providing access to a series of small, pretty hike-to lakes just outside the edge of the Mokelumne Wilderness. Open June through September.

53. MIDDLE CREEK

Reference: Near Carson Pass and Blue Lakes; map D4, grid i3.

Campsites, facilities: There are five sites for tents or motor homes. Piped water, vault toilets, picnic tables and fire grills are provided. Pets are permitted on leashes.

Reservations, fee: No reservations; $10 fee per night; $1 pet fee.

Who to contact: The camp is managed by PG&E. For information call (916) 386-5164.

Location: From Sacramento, drive east on US 50 to the junction with Highway 89. Turn south on Highway 89 and drive over Luther Pass to the junction with Highway 88. Turn right (west) and drive two miles to Blue Lakes Road. Turn left (south) and drive 11 miles to a junction at the south end of Lower Blue Lake. Turn right and drive 1.5 miles to the campground on the left side of the road. (From Jackson, drive east on Highway 88 over Carson Pass and continue east for five miles to Blue Lakes Road. Turn right (south) and drive 11 miles (seven paved, four gravel) to a junction at the south end of Lower Blue Lake. Turn right and drive 1.5 miles to the campground on the left side of the road.)

Trip note: This is a tiny, captivating spot set along the creek that connects Upper and Lower Blue Lakes, providing a take-your-pick deal for anglers. See the trip note for Lower Blue Lake. The elevation is 8,200 feet. Open June through September.

54. UPPER BLUE LAKE

Reference: Near Carson Pass; map D4, grid i3.

Campsites, facilities: There are 32 sites for tents. Piped water, vault toilets, picnic tables and fire grills are provided. Pets are permitted on leashes.

Reservations, fee: No reservations; $10 fee per night; $1 pet fee.

Who to contact: The camp is managed by PG&E. For information call (916) 386-5164.

Location: From Sacramento, drive east on US 50 to the junction with Highway 89. Turn south on Highway 89 and drive over Luther Pass to the junction with Highway 88. Turn right (west) and drive two miles to Blue Lakes Road. Turn left (south) and drive 11 miles to a junction at the south end of Lower Blue Lake. Turn right and drive three miles to the campground on the left side of the road.

(From Jackson, drive east on Highway 88 over Carson Pass and continue east for five miles to Blue Lakes Road. Turn right (south) and drive 11 miles (seven paved, four gravel) to a junction at the south end of Lower Blue Lake. Turn right and drive three miles to the campground on the left side of the road.)

Trip note: This is one of two camps set along Upper Blue Lake and one of four camps in the immediate area. The trout fishing is usually quite good here in early summer. See the trip note for Lower Blue Lake Camp. The elevation is 8,200 feet. Open June through September.

55. UPPER BLUE LAKE DAM

Reference: **Near Carson Pass; map D4, grid i3.**

Campsites, facilities: There are 25 tent sites. Piped water, vault toilets, picnic tables and fire grills are provided. Pets are permitted on leashes.

Reservations, fee: No reservations; $10 fee per night; $1 pet fee.

Who to contact: For information, call PG&E at (916) 364-5164.

Location: From Sacramento, drive east on US 50 to the junction with Highway 89. Turn south on Highway 89 and drive over Luther Pass to the junction with Highway 88. Turn right (west) and drive two miles to Blue Lakes Road. Turn left (south) and drive 11 miles to a junction at the south end of Lower Blue Lake. Turn right and drive three miles to the campground next to the dam. (From Jackson, drive east on Highway 88 over Carson Pass and continue east for five miles to Blue Lakes Road. Turn right (south) and drive 11 miles (seven paved, four gravel) to a junction at the south end of Lower Blue Lake. Turn right and drive three miles to the campground next to the dam.)

Trip note: This is one of four camps set at the Blue Lakes, 8,200 feet in elevation, south of Carson Pass. A boat ramp is located near this camp. For recreation options, see the trip note for Lower Blue Lake Camp. Most years, the camp opens in June and stays open through September (depending on snowfall).

56. GROVER HOT SPRINGS STATE PARK

Reference: **Near Markleeville; map D4, grid i4.**

Campsites, facilities: There are 26 sites for tents, 13 sites for motor homes, and 37 sites for tents or motor homes up to 27 feet long. Piped water, flush toilets, coin-operated showers (except in the winter), a hot springs pool with **wheelchair access**, a swimming pool, picnic tables and fire grills are provided. A grocery store and a laundromat are nearby. Pets are permitted.

Reservations, fee: Reserve by phoning Destinet at (800) 444-PARK ($6.75 Destinet fee); $15-$17 fee per night; $1 pet fee; pool fees are $4 per adult, $2 per child seven or under.

Who to contact: Call (916) 694-2248 or (916) 525-7232.

Location: From Sacramento, drive east on US 50 to the junction with Highway 89. Turn south on Highway 89 and drive over Luther Pass to the junction with Highway 88. Turn left (east) and drive to Woodfords and the junction with Highway 89. Turn south and drive six miles to Markleeville and the junction with Hot Springs Road. Turn west and drive four miles to the park entrance.

Trip note: This is a famous spot for folks who like the rejuvenating powers of a hot spring. Some say they feel a glow about them for weeks. When touring the South Tahoe/Carson Pass area, many vacationers take part of a day to make the trip to the hot springs. Side trip options include a nature trail in the park, or driving to the Carson River (where the water is a mite cooler) and fishing for trout. The elevation is 5,800 feet. Open year-round.

57. MARKLEEVILLE RV 7

Reference: On Markleeville Creek in Toiyabe National Forest; map D4, grid i5.

Campsites, facilities: There are 10 sites for tents or motor homes up to 20 feet long. Piped water, vault toilets, picnic tables and fire grills are provided. A grocery store is nearby. Pets are allowed on leashes.

Reservations, fee: No reservations; $7 fee per night.

Who to contact: Phone the Toiyabe National Forest, Carson Ranger District at (702) 882-2766.

Location: From Sacramento, drive east on US 50 to the junction with Highway 89. Turn south on Highway 89 and drive over Luther Pass to the junction with Highway 88. Turn left (east) and drive to Woodfords and the junction with Highway 89. Turn south and drive six miles to Markleeville and continue for a half-mile to the campground.

Trip note: This is a pretty, streamside camp set at 5,500 feet along Markleeville Creek, one mile from the East Fork of the Carson River. The trout here are willing, but alas, are dinkers. This area is the transition zone where high mountains to the west give way to the high desert to the east. The hot springs in Markleeville provide a good side trip. Open late April through September.

58. PACIFIC VALLEY 7

Reference: Overlooking Pacific Creek in Stanislaus National Forest; map D4, grid j3.

Campsites, facilities: There are nine sites for tents. There is **no piped water**, but picnic tables and vault toilets are provided. Pets are permitted on leashes.

Reservations, fee: No reservations; no fee. A free campfire permit is required; get one from the district office.

Who to contact: Phone the Stanislaus National Forest Calaveras Ranger District at (209) 795-1381. For a map, send $3 to Office of Information, U.S. Forest Service, 630 Sansome Street, San Francisco, CA 94111, and ask for Stanislaus National Forest.

Location: From Angels Camp, drive east on Highway 4 to Lake Alpine and continue for about seven miles to the campground on the right side of the road.

Trip note: This is a do-it-yourself special, that is, more of a general area for camping than a campground, set up for backpackers heading out on expeditions into the Carson-Iceberg Wilderness to the south. It is set at 7,600 feet along Pacific Creek, a tributary to the Mokelumne River. The trail from camp is routed south and reaches three forks within two miles. The best is routed deep into the wilderness, flanking Hiram Peak (9,760 feet), Airola Peak (9,938 feet) and Iceberg Peak (9,720 feet). Open June through September.

59. HERMIT VALLEY 8

Reference: In Stanislaus National Forest; map D4, grid j3.

Campsites, facilities: There are three sites for tents. There is **no piped water**, but vault toilets are provided. Pets are permitted on leashes.

Reservations, fee: No reservations; no fee. A free campfire permit is required; get one from the district office.

Who to contact: Phone the Stanislaus National Forest Calaveras Ranger District at (209) 795-1381. For a map, send $3 to Office of Information, U.S. Forest Service, 630 Sansome Street, San Francisco, CA 94111, and ask for Stanislaus National Forest.

Location: From Angels Camp, drive east on Highway 4 to Lake Alpine and continue for about nine miles to the campground on the left side of the road.

Trip note: This tiny, remote, little-known spot is set near the border of the Mokelumne Wilderness near where Grouse Creek enters the Mokelumne River, at 7,500 feet in elevation. Looking north, there is a good view into Deer Valley. A primitive road is available, located a half-mile west of camp, that is routed through Deer Valley north for six miles to the Blue Lakes. On the opposite (south) side of the road from the camp, there is a little-traveled hiking trail that is routed up Grouse Creek to Milk Ranch Meadow at the border of the Carson-Iceberg Wilderness. Open June through September.

---

60. MOSQUITO LAKE

Reference: At Mosquito Lake in Stanislaus National Forest; map D4, grid j3.

Campsites, facilities: There are a small number of primitive, undesignated sites for tents. Picnic tables are provided and a vault toilet is available. **No piped water** is available.

Reservations, fee: No reservations; no fee. A free campfire permit is required; get one from the district office.

Who to contact: Phone the Stanislaus National Forest Calaveras Ranger District at (209) 795-1381. For a map, send $3 to Office of Information, U.S. Forest Service, 630 Sansome Street, San Francisco, CA 94111, and ask for Stanislaus National Forest.

Location: From Angels Camp, drive east on Highway 4 to Lake Alpine and continue for about six miles to the campground on the left side of the road.

Trip note: Mosquito Lake is a pristine Sierra setting at 8,260 feet, presenting remarkable beauty for a place that can be reached by car. Most people believe that Mosquito Lake is for day-use only, and that's why they get crowded into nearby Alpine Lake Camp (see chapter E4). But it's not for day-use only, and this camp is often overlooked because it is about a mile west of the little lake, and on the opposite side of the road. The lake is small, a pretty emerald green, and even has a few small trout in it.

---

61. BLOOMFIELD

Reference: In Stanislaus National Forest; map D4, grid j4.

Campsites, facilities: There are five sites for tents or motor homes. There is **no piped water**, but vault toilets, picnic tables and fire grills are provided. A grocery store, propane gas and a laundromat are available nearby. Pets are allowed on leashes.

Reservations, fee: No reservations; no fee. A free campfire permit is required; get one from the district office.

Who to contact: Phone the Stanislaus National Forest Calaveras Ranger District at (209) 795-1381. For a map, send $3 to Office of Information, U.S. Forest Service, 630 Sansome Street, San Francisco, CA 94111, and ask for Stanislaus National Forest.

Location: From Angels Camp, drive east on Highway 4 to Lake Alpine and continue for about 15 miles to Forest Service Road 8N01 on the right side of the road (1.5 miles west of Ebbetts Pass). Turn right and drive two miles to the campground on the right side of the road.

Trip note: This is a primitive and little-known camp set at 7,800 feet near Ebbetts Pass. The North Fork Mokelumne River runs right by the camp, with good stream access for about a mile on each side of the camp. The access road continues south to Highland Lakes, a destination that provides car-top boating, fair fishing, and trailheads for hiking into the Carson-Iceberg Wilderness. Open June through October.

62. SILVER CREEK

Reference: **In Toiyabe National Forest; map D4, grid j5.**

Campsites, facilities: There are 22 sites for tents or motor homes up to 22 feet long. Piped water, vault toilets, picnic tables and fire grills are provided. Pets are allowed on leashes.

Reservations, fee: Reserve by phoning (800) 280-CAMP ($7.50 reservation fee); $7 fee per night.

Who to contact: Phone the Toiyabe National Forest, Carson Ranger District at (702) 882-2766.

Location: From Angels Camp, drive east on Highway 4 all the way over Ebbetts Pass and continue for about six miles to the campground.

From Markleeville, drive south on Highway 89 to the junction with Highway 4. Turn west on Highway 4 and drive about five miles to the campground.

Trip note: This pretty spot, set near Silver Creek, has easy access from Highway 4 and good fishing in early summer for small trout. It is in the remote high Sierra, east of Ebbetts Pass. A side trip to Ebbetts Pass features Kinney Reservoir and a trailhead at the north end of the lake (on the west side of Highway 4) for a one-mile hike to Lower Kinney Lake. The elevation is 6,800 feet. Open June through October.

63. TOPAZ LAKE RV PARK

Reference: **Near Markleeville; map D4, grid j7.**

Campsites, facilities: There are 54 motor home sites with full hookups, cable TV and picnic tables. Restrooms, showers, a laundromat, propane gas and a boat ramp are available. Pets are permitted.

Reservations, fee: Reservations accepted; $15-$20 fee per night.

Who to contact: Phone the park at (916) 495-2357.

Location: From Carson City, drive south on US 395 for 33 miles to Topaz Lake and the campground on the left side of the road. (From Bridgeport, drive north on US 395 for 45 miles to the campground on the right side of the road.)

Trip note: Topaz Lake, set at 5,000 feet, is one of the hidden surprises for California anglers. The surprise is the size of the rainbow trout, with one of the highest rates of 15- to 18-inch trout of any lake in the mountain country. The setting is hardly pretty, a good-sized lake on the edge of the barren high desert country, with the Nevada border running right through the center of the lake. Wind is a problem for small boats, especially in the early summer. The RV park is set adjacent to Topaz Lake Marina, which offers boat rentals, as well as a tackle shop and a snack bar. Open year-round (weather permitting), with the owners requesting a phone call prior to visits in the offseason.

MAP E1

NOR-CAL MAP .... see page 94
adjoining maps
NORTH (D1) .... see page 326
EAST (E2) .... see page 432
SOUTH (F1) .... see page 514
WEST .... no map

26 LISTINGS
PAGES 418-431

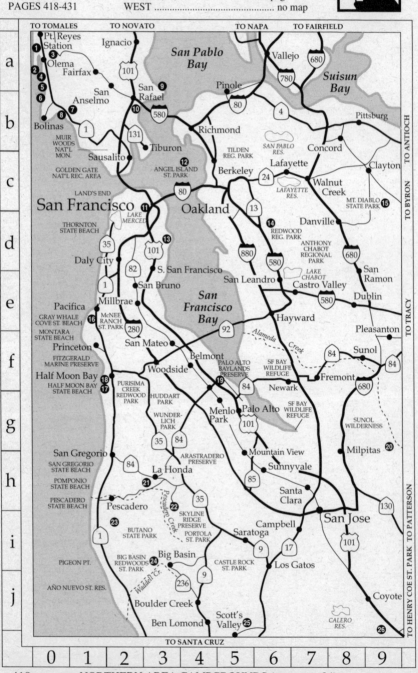

Map E1 featuring: Point Reyes National Seashore, Mount Tamalpais State Park, San Francisco, Skyline Ridge

1. OLEMA RANCH CAMPGROUND 👫 🐎　　RV. 5

Reference: **Map E1, grid a0.**

Campsites, facilities: There are 200 sites for tents or motor homes, some with full or partial hookups. Picnic tables are provided. Piped water, restrooms, showers, a sanitary disposal station, a laundromat and a recreation hall (for groups of 25 or more only) are available. Pets are allowed on leashes.

Reservations, fee: Reservations accepted; $16-$24 fee per night.

Who to contact: Phone (415) 663-8001.

Location: From US 101 in Marin, take the Sir Francis Drake Boulevard exit and drive west for about 20 miles to Highway 1 at Olema. Turn right on Highway 1 and drive a half-mile to the campground.

Trip note: This large, private park is in a perfect location for a Point Reyes adventure. Olema is a beautiful country town set in a valley amid Marin's coastal foothills. It borders the Point Reyes National Seashore to the west and the Golden Gate National Recreation Area to the east, with Tomales Bay to the nearby north. There are several excellent trailheads available within a 10-minute drive along Highway 1 to the south. While the wildfire on nearby Inverness Ridge and adjacent western slopes in the fall of 1995 ravaged an old-growth forest of Bishop pine, the land's regeneration has become a beautiful spectacle. Open year-round.

2. SKY CAMP HIKE-IN 👫　　7

Reference: **In Point Reyes National Seashore; map E1, grid a0.**

Campsites, facilities: There are 11 individual sites and one group site (walk-in only) with piped water and pit toilets provided. Fire grills are provided for use with charcoal, but no wood fires are permitted in the park. No vehicles or pets are permitted.

Reservations, fee: Reservations required; no fee; four-day maximum stay.

Who to contact: Call the park headquarters at (415) 663-1092.

Location: From US 101 in Marin, take the Sir Francis Drake Boulevard exit and drive west for about 20 miles to Highway 1 at Olema. Turn right on Highway 1 and drive a very short distance. Then turn left on Bear Valley Road and drive north for seven-tenths of a mile. Turn left at the "Seashore Information" sign and drive to the parking lot for park headquarters and the Bear Valley Trailhead.

Trip note: Sky Camp is set on the western flank of Mt. Wittenberg on Inverness Ridge, right at the edge of the area in Point Reyes National Seashore that burned in the 1995 fall wildfire. In fact, this hike-in camp was right at the edge of the fire break, and was partially burned. After a renovation it will reopen on April 1, 1996. To reach the camp, take the Bear Valley Trail from park headquarters and walk a mile to the Meadow Trail. Turn right (north) on the Meadow Trail and hike 1.5 miles to the Sky Trail, cross it, and continue one-half mile to the campground. From here, you get a dramatic view of the burned area and the adjacent Marin coast. No open fires and no pets are permitted. You must have a backcountry permit from the Bear Valley Visitor Center to camp here.

3. SAMUEL P. TAYLOR STATE PARK

🚶 ♿ 🐎 ⛺

Reference: **Near San Rafael; map E1, grid a0.**

Campsites, facilities: There are 25 sites for tents and 35 sites for tents or motor homes up to 27 feet long. Piped water, fire grills, tables, flush toilets, showers (coin-operated) and food lockers are provided. There is a small store two miles away in Lagunitas. Two campsites are **wheelchair accessible**. Pets are permitted on leashes in the campground only; they are not permitted on trails.

Reservations, fee: Reserve by phoning Destinet at (800) 444-7275 ($6.75 Destinet fee); $13-$17 fee per night; $1 pet fee.

Who to contact: Phone (415) 488-9897 or (415) 456-1286.

Location: From US 101 in Marin, take the Sir Francis Drake Boulevard exit and drive west for about 15 miles to the park entrance on the left side of the road.

Trip note: This is a beautiful park, with campsites set amid redwoods, complete with a babbling brook running nearby. Hikers will find 20 miles of hiking trails, a hidden waterfall, and some good mountain biking routes on service roads. The paved bike path that runs through the park and parallels Sir Francis Drake Boulevard is a terrific easy ride. Open year-round.

4. COAST CAMP HIKE-IN 🚶🚶

Reference: **Point Reyes National Seashore; map E1, grid a0.**

Campsites, facilities: There are 12 individual and two group hike-in sites, with piped water and pit toilets. Backpacking stoves are required for cooking. No vehicles or pets are permitted.

Reservations, fee: Reservations required; no fee; four-day maximum stay.

Who to contact: Call park headquarters at (415) 663-1092.

Location: From US 101 in Main, take the Sir Francis Drake Boulevard exit and drive about 20 miles to Highway 1 at Olema. Turn right on Highway 1 and drive a very short distance. Then turn left at Bear Valley Road and drive north for two miles to Limantour Road. Turn left at Limantour Road and drive six miles to the access road for the Point Reyes Hostel. Turn left and drive two-tenths of a mile to the trailhead on the right side of the road.

Trip note: This is a classic ocean-bluff setting, a hike-in camp set just above Santa Maria Beach on the Point Reyes National Seashore, providing an extended tour into a land of charm. It is a 2.8-mile hike to get here, the most northerly-located camp on the Coast Trail. (The complete Coast Trail is a 15-mile trip that is one of the best hikes in the Bay Area.) From Coast Camp, the trail contours south along the bluffs above the beach, routed south for 1.4 miles to Sculptured Beach, where there are a series of odd geologic formations, including caves, tunnels and sea stacks. Reservations and a backcountry permit are required. Note: This camp is set on the edge of the area that burned in the fall 1995 fire, and the camp will be closed until April 1, 1996 for renovation.

5. WILDCAT CAMP HIKE-IN 🚶🚶

Reference: **In Point Reyes National Seashore; map E1, grid a0.**

Campsites, facilities: There are seven individual and four group hike-in sites, with piped water and pit toilets. (The four group sites can hold 25 people each.) Fire grills are provided for use with charcoal, but no wood fires are permitted in the park. No vehicles or pets are permitted.

Reservations, fee: Reservations required; no fee; four-day maximum stay.

Who to contact: Phone park headquarters at (415)663-1092.

Location: From US 101 in Marin, take the Sir Francis Drake Boulevard exit and drive west for about 20 miles to Highway 1 at Olema. Turn left on Highway 1 and drive about 10 miles south to Olema-Bolinas Road (often unsigned). Turn right and drive 2.1 miles to Mesa Road. Turn right and drive 5.8 miles to the Palomarin Trailhead. It is a 5.6-mile hike to the campground on the Coast Trail.

Trip note: This backpack camp sits in a grassy meadow near a small stream that flows to the ocean, just above remote Wildcat Beach. Getting there takes you on a fantastic hike that crosses some of the Bay Area's most beautiful wildlands. The trail is routed along the ocean for about a mile, then heads up in the coastal hills, then turns left and skirts past Bass Lake, Crystal Lake, Pelican Lake and ultimately to Alamere Creek with its dramatic 40-foot waterfall, one of the rare ocean bluff waterfalls anywhere.

---

6. GLEN CAMP HIKE-IN

Reference: In Point Reyes National Seashore; map E1, grid b0.

Campsites, facilities: There are 12 hike-in sites with piped water and pit toilets. Backpacking stoves are required for cooking. No pets are permitted.

Reservations, fee: Reservations required; no fee; four-day maximum stay.

Who to contact: Phone park headquarters at (415) 663-1092.

Location: From US 101 in Marin, take the Sir Francis Drake Boulevard exit and drive about 20 miles to Highway 1 at Olema. Turn right on Highway 1 and drive a very short distance. Then turn left on Bear Valley Road and drive north for seven-tenths of a mile. Turn left at the "Seashore Information" sign and drive to the parking lot for park headquarters and the Bear Valley Trailhead. It is a 4.6-mile hike to the camp.

Trip note: Glen Camp is set in the coastal foothills of Point Reyes National Seashore, right at the edge of where forest gives way to grasslands. The hike to it starts at the Bear Valley Visitor Center, where you can obtain your backcountry permits and hiking information, and is routed on the popular Bear Valley Trail, a wide road made out of compressed rock. It is 1.6 miles to Divide Meadow, with a modest 215-foot climb, then another 1.6 miles through Bear Valley to the Glen Camp Trail. Turn left and hike 1.4 miles, with the trail lateralling in and out of two canyons to reach the camp. It is secluded and quiet. Get a map, a reservation, and bring everything you need.

---

7. PANTOLL CAMPGROUND

Reference: In Mount Tamalpais State Park; map E1, grid b1.

Campsites, facilities: There are 16 walk-in sites tent sites. Piped water, flush toilets, fire grills, food lockers, fire wood and tables are provided. Pets are permitted on leashes.

Reservations, fee: No reservations; $15-$17 fee per night; $1 pet fee.

Who to contact: Phone (415) 388-2070 or District Headquarters at (415) 456-1286.

Location: From US 101 in Marin, take the Stinson Beach/Highway 1 exit. Drive west to the stoplight at the T intersection (Highway 1). Turn left and drive about four miles uphill to the Panoramic Highway. Bear to the right on Panoramic Highway and continue for 5.5 miles (past the turnoff to Muir Woods). Turn left at the Pantoll parking area and ranger station. A 100-foot walk is required to reach the campground.

Trip note: When camping at Pantoll, you are within close range of the divine, including some of the best hiking, best lookouts and just plain best places to be anywhere in the Bay Area. The camp is set in the woods on the western slopes of Mt. Tamalpais, which some say is a place of special power. The Steep Ravine Trail is routed out of camp to the west into a wondrous gorge filled with redwoods and a stream with miniature waterfalls. After a good rain when everything is oozing with moisture, this can be one of the most romantic places on the planet earth. Another hike, on the Matt Davis/Coastal Trail, provides breathtaking views of the coast. Another must is the nearby drive to the East Peak Lookout, where the entire world seems within reach.

8. STEEP RAVINE ENVIRONMENTAL CAMPSITES 9

Reference: **Mount Tamalpais State Park; map E1, grid b1.**

Campsites, facilities: There are six walk-in sites for tents, and 10 primitive cabins, each with a wood stove, picnic table and flat wood surface for sleeping. Pit toilets, fire grills and tables are provided. Piped water is nearby and wood is available. No pets are permitted.

Reservations, fee: Reserve by phoning Destinet at (800) 444-7275 ($6.75 Destinet fee); $7-$9 fee per night.

Who to contact: Phone (415) 388-2070 or (415) 456-1286.

Location: From US 101 in Marin, take the Stinson Beach/Highway 1 exit and drive to the coast at Muir Beach overlook. Turn north on Highway 1 and drive about four miles to the Rocky Point access road (gated) on the left side of the highway.

Trip note: This is one of the most remarkable spots on the California coast, with primitive cabin/wood shacks set on a bluff on Rocky Point overlooking the ocean. It is primitive but dramatic, with passing ships, fishing boats, lots of marine birds, occasionally even whales, and a chance for heart-stopping sunsets. There is an easy walk to the north down to Redrock Beach, which is very secluded, and just across the road (with a short jog to the right) is a trailhead for the Steep Ravine Trail on the slopes of Mt. Tamalpais. After a while, you'll feel like you're a million miles from civilization.

9. CHINA CAMP STATE PARK WALK-IN 10

Reference: **On San Pablo Bay near San Rafael; map E1, grid a3.**

Campsites, facilities: There are 30 walk-in tent sites. Picnic tables and fire grills are provided. Piped water and a restroom are available. No pets are permitted.

Reservations, fees: No reservations; $9 fee per night; $2 fee per night for each additional vehicle.

Who to contact: Phone (415) 456-0766 or (415) 456-1286.

Location: From San Francisco, drive north on US 101 to San Rafael and take the North San Pedro Road exit. Drive west on North San Pedro Road for five miles to the park entrance station. Shortly after passing through the entrance station, bear right and drive a short distance to the campground parking lot. Reaching the sites requires a one-minute walk.

Trip note: This is one of the Bay Area's prettiest campgrounds. It is set in woodlands with a pretty creek running past. The camps are shaded and sheltered. Directly adjacent to the camp is a meadow, marshland, and then San

Pablo Bay. Deer can seem as tame as chipmunks. Hiking is outstanding here, either taking the Shoreline Trail for a pretty walk to the edge of San Pablo Bay, or the Bay View Trail for the climb up the ridge that borders the park, in the process gaining spectacular views of the bay and miles of charm.

10. MARIN PARK, INC. 🚶🏃 ♿ 🦦 🐟

Reference: **Near San Rafael; map E1, grid b2.**

Campsites, facilities: There are 89 motor home sites with full hookups. Showers, a laundromat, a swimming pool and RV supplies are available. Pets are permitted.

Reservations, fee: Reservations accepted with deposit; $28 fee per night.

Who to contact: Phone at (415) 461-5199.

Location: From US 101 in Marin, take the Lucky Drive exit (just south of San Rafael). Make an immediate left under the freeway and drive to the stop light. Turn left on the frontage road (Redwood Highway) and drive four blocks to the park at 2140 Redwood Highway.

Trip notes: For out-of-towners with motor homes, this can make an ideal base camp for Marin County adventures. To the west is Mt. Tamalpais State Park, Muir Woods National Monument, Samuel P. Taylor State Park and Point Reyes National Seashore. To the nearby east is the Loch Lomond Marina on San Pablo Bay, where fishing trips can be arranged for striped bass and sturgeon; phone (415) 456-0321. The park offers complete sightseeing information, and easy access to buses and ferry service to San Francisco.

11. SAN FRANCISCO RV PARK ♿

Reference: **In San Francisco; map E1, grid c3.**

Campsites, facilities: There are 200 sites with full hookups for motor homes. Water, barbecues, and tables are provided. A dump station, showers, a laundromat and a game room are available. Pets are permitted.

Reservations, fee: Reservations required; $32-$34 fee per night.

Who to contact: Phone (415) 986-8730 or write to 250 King Street, San Francisco, CA 94107.

Location: In San Francisco on Interstate 80, drive to the Fourth Street exit. Take the Fourth Street exit, turn right on Fourth Street and drive four blocks to King Street. Turn left on King Street and drive a half block to the RV parking area.

Trip note: San Francisco's only "campground" is strictly for motor homes. It consists of a long parking area set beneath a freeway structure. City buses leave from the park regularly. Traffic is often jammed up in this area. It is advisable to call prior to arrival to get a traffic report, and plan your arrival during non-peak traffic periods. Open year-round.

12. ANGEL ISLAND STATE PARK WALK-IN 🐟 ⚓ 🚶🏃 ♿ ⛪

Reference: **Map E1, grid c3.**

Campsites, facilities: There are nine walk-in sites with piped water, toilets, fire grills and tables provided. No pets are permitted. A cafe is available on the island. The facilities are **wheelchair accessible**.

Reservations, fee: Reserve by phoning Destinet at (800) 444-PARK ($6.75 Destinet fee); $12 fee per night (limit eight people per site).

Who to contact: Phone Angel Island State Park at (415) 435-1915 or district headquarters at (415) 456-1286.

Location: Angel Island is in northern San Francisco Bay and reachable by ferry from Pier 43 in San Francisco (for schedule information call (415) 546-2896); Tiburon (for schedule information call (415) 435-2131); and Vallejo (for schedule information call (707) 64-FERRY).

Trip note: Camping at Angel Island is one of the most unique adventures in the Bay Area, with the only catch being that the campsites require a walk of up to two miles to reach. The payoff comes at 4:30, when all the park's day visitors and most of the staff depart for the mainland., leaving the entire island to you. From start to finish, it's a great trip, featuring a ferry boat ride, a great hike in, and a private campsite, often with spectacular views of the Bay. The tromp up to 781-foot Mt. Livermore includes a short, very steep stretch but in return furnishes one of the most spectacular urban lookouts in America.

13. CANDLESTICK RV PARK

Reference: **In San Francisco; map E1, grid d3.**

Campsites, facilities: There are 118 sites for trailers or motor homes, all with full hookups. Restrooms and showers are provided. A laundromat, grocery store, game room and propane are available. Shuttles and bus tours are available. Small pets are permitted on leashes. The facilities are **wheelchair accessible**.

Reservations, fee: Reservations recommended; phone (800) 888-CAMP. Call for current fees.

Who to contact: Phone the park at (415) 822-2299.

Location: From San Francisco on US 101, take the Candlestick Park (3COM) exit. Turn east on the stadium entrance road and drive around the parking lot to the far end of the stadium. During baseball games, campers are advised to take the 3rd Street exit in order to avoid traffic.

Trip note: If you are arriving from out of town to see the Giants play baseball or 49ers play football, this park is your calling, set adjacent to the Candlestick Park, I mean 3COM Park (that will always sound ridiculous), parking lot. The location is four miles from downtown San Francisco. It is an ideal destination for out-of-towners who want to explore the city without having to drive, because the park offers tours and inexpensive shuttles to the downtown area.

14. ANTHONY CHABOT REGIONAL PARK

Reference: **Near Castro Valley; map E1, grid d6.**

Campsites, facilities: There are 10 walk-in tent sites, 12 motor home sites with partial hookups, and 43 sites for tents or motor homes. Fire grills and picnic tables are provided. Piped water, flush toilets, hot showers and a sanitary disposal station are available. Pets are permitted on leashes.

Reservations, fee: Reservations required; phone (510) 562-2267 ($5 reservation fee); $13-$19 fee per night; $5 per night for each additional vehicle; $1 pet fee.

Who to contact: For a brochure, call the East Bay Regional Parks District at (510) 635-0135, extension 2200.

Location: From Interstate 580 in the Oakland hills, take the 35th Avenue exit. Turn east on 35th Avenue and drive up the hill and straight across Skyline, where 35th Avenue becomes Redwood Road. Continue on Redwood Road for six miles to the park entrance on the right.

Trip note: The campground at Chabot Regional Park is set on a hilltop sheltered by eucalyptus, with good views and trails available. The best campsites are the walk-in units, requiring a walk of only a minute or so. Several provide views of Lake Chabot to the south a half-mile away. The lake provides good trout fishing in the winter and spring, and a chance for huge but elusive largemouth bass. The Huck Trail is routed down from the campground (near walk-in Site 20) to the lake at Honker Bay, a good fishing area. There is also a good 12-mile bike ride around the lake. Boat rentals at a small marina are available.

15. MOUNT DIABLO STATE PARK 🚶 ♿ 🐎　　RV 6

Reference: **Map E1, grid c9.**

Campsites, facilities: There are 60 sites for tents or motor homes up to 24 feet long (in three campgrounds). Piped water, vault or flush toilets, fire grills and tables are provided. Pets are allowed on leashes.

Reservations, fee: Reserve by phoning Destinet at (800) 444-7275 ($6.75 Destinet fee); $15-$17 fee per night; $1 pet fee.

Who to contact: Phone Mount Diablo State Park at (510) 837-2525 or (415) 330-6300.

Location: From Danville on Highway 680, take the Diablo Road exit. Follow Diablo Road for 1.5 miles to Mount Diablo Scenic Boulevard. Turn left (it eventually becomes Blackhawk Road) and drive to South Gate Road. Turn left and drive four miles to the park entrance.

Trip note: Mount Diablo, elevation 3,849 feet, provides one of the most all-encompassing lookouts anywhere in America. On crystal-clear days, you can see the Sierra Nevada and its white, snowbound crest. With binoculars, some claim to have seen Half Dome in Yosemite. The drive to the summit is a must-do trip, and the interpretive center right on top of the mountain is one of the best in the Bay Area. The camps at Mount Diablo are set in foothill/oak grassland country, with some shaded sites. Winter and spring are good times to visit, when the weather is still cool enough for good hiking trips. Most of the trails require long hikes, often including significant elevation losses and gains. In late summer, the park is sometimes closed to campers due to fire danger. No alcohol is permitted in the park.

16. PACIFIC PARK 🐟 🚶 ♿ 🏊 ⛳　　RV 8

Reference: **In Pacifica; map E1, grid e1.**

Campsites, facilities: There are 260 motor home sites with full hookups. Restrooms, showers, a heated swimming pool, a spa and a recreation room are provided. Cable TV, a grocery store, a laundromat and propane gas are available. Pets are allowed on leashes.

Reservations, fee: Reservations recommended; $27-$33 fee per night; $1 pet fee.

Who to contact: Phone (415) 355-2112 or (800) 992-0554 (California only).

Location: From San Francisco and north, drive south on Highway 1 into Pacifica. Take the Manor Drive exit and drive to the stop sign (you will be on the west side of the highway). Continue straight ahead (the road becomes Palmetto Avenue) for about one mile and look for the entrance to the park on the right side of the road at 700 Palmetto. (From the south, drive north on Highway 1 into Pacifica. Take the Manor Drive exit. At the stop sign, turn left on the frontage road (you will be on the east side of the highway) and drive one block to another stop sign. Turn left, drive a short distance over the highway to a stop sign at Manor/Palmetto, and turn left. Drive about one mile to the park on the right.)

Trip note: This has become the best motor home park in the Bay Area. It is set on the bluffs just above the Pacific Ocean, complete with beach access, a nearby fishing pier and sometimes excellent surf fishing. There is also a nearby golf course and the chance for dramatic ocean sunsets. The park is relatively new, kept clean and in good shape, and though there is too much asphalt, the proximity to the beach overcomes it. It is only 20 miles from San Francisco.

17. HALF MOON BAY STATE BEACH

Reference: **Map E1, grid f2.**

Campsites, facilities: There are 55 sites for tents or motor homes up to 36 feet long. Piped water, fire grills and picnic tables are provided. A sanitary disposal station and toilets are available. Pets are allowed on leashes.

Reservations, fee: No reservations; $15-$17 fee per night.

Who to contact: Phone (415) 726-8820 or (415) 330-6300.

Location: In Half Moon Bay at the junction of Highway 1 and Highway 92, turn south on Highway 1 and drive about a mile to Kelly Avenue. Turn right (west) on Kelly Avenue and drive two miles to the park entrance.

Trip note: During summer months, this park often fills to capacity with campers touring Highway 1. The campground has level, grassy sites for tents, a clean parking area for motor homes, and a state beach available just a short walk away. Side trips include Princeton and Pillar Point Marina, seven miles north on Highway 1, where fishing and whale watching trips are possible.

18. PELICAN POINT RV PARK

Reference: **In Half Moon Bay; map E1, grid f2.**

Campsites, facilities: There are 75 sites for motor homes, with full hookups and patios. Picnic tables, restrooms, showers, a laundromat, propane gas, a small store, a clubhouse and a sanitary disposal station are provided. Pets are allowed on leashes.

Reservations, fee: Reservations recommended; $27-$30 fee per night.

Who to contact: Phone (415) 726-9100.

Location: In Half Moon Bay at the junction of Highway 1 and Highway 92, turn south on Highway 1 and drive 2.5 miles to Miramontes Point Road. Turn right (west) and drive a short distance to the park entrance.

Trip note: This park is in a rural setting on the southern outskirts of the town of Half Moon Bay, set on an extended bluff near the ocean. All facilities are available nearby, with restaurants available in Half Moon Bay and 10 miles north in Princeton at Pillar Point Harbor. The harbor has an excellent boat launch, fish-cleaning station, party boat trips for salmon and rockfish, and in the winter, whale watching trips. Open year-round.

19. TRAILER VILLA

Reference: **In Redwood City; map E1, grid f5.**

Campsites, facilities: There are 50 motor home sites with full hookups. Restrooms, showers, a laundromat and a sanitary disposal station are available. Pets are allowed on leashes or otherwise controlled.

Reservations, fee: Reservations recommended; $20 fee per night.

Who to contact: Phone (415) 366-7880.

Location: In Redwood City on US 101, take the Seaport Boulevard exit east. Drive a short distance to East Bayshore Road. Turn right and drive one mile to 3401 East Bayshore Road.

Trip note: The Peninsula can seem like zoo on parade when driving the "Bayshore Freeway," but a short drive to Trailer Villa provides a quick return to some semblance of sanity. It is located near the Redwood City Harbor, a pretty spot adjacent to the unusual Leslie Salt site on the shore of the Bay, where there is often an unbelievably high pile of salt. A boat launch is available at the harbor, providing access to South San Francisco Bay. Open year-round.

---

20. SUNOL REGIONAL WILDERNESS

Reference: **Map E1, grid g9.**

Campsites, facilities: There are four tent sites. Piped water, tables, fire grills and vault toilets are provided. Pets are allowed on leashes.

Reservations, fee: Reservations required; phone (510) 562-2267 ($5 reservation fee); $10 fee per night; $1 pet fee.

Who to contact: Phone the East Bay Regional Parks District at (510) 635-0135, extension 2200, or Sunol Regional Wilderness at (510) 862-2244.

Location: In the East Bay on Interstate 680, drive to Sunol and take the Calaveras Road exit. Turn south on Calaveras and drive four miles to Geary Road. Turn left on Geary Road and drive two miles to the park entrance.

Trip note: Sunol Regional Wilderness is an outstanding park for offseason hiking and camping. In the spring and early summer, it is one of the best of the 250 parks in the Bay Area to see wildflowers, and in addition, that is when Alameda Creek in Little Yosemite forms several miniature pool-and-drop waterfalls. The park is set in rolling oak/bay grasslands. In addition to the drive-in sites, there are also a few trail camps available, the closest requiring a 3.4-mile hike from park headquarters. It is extremely quiet and secluded, with a nearby spring developed to provide drinking water. No alcohol is permitted in the park, and it is subject to temporary closures in late summer due to fire danger.

---

21. MEMORIAL COUNTY PARK

Reference: **Near La Honda; map E1, grid h3.**

Campsites, facilities: There are 136 sites for tents or motor homes. A horse camp, fire grills, picnic tables, piped water, showers and flush toilets are provided. A sanitary disposal station is available from May through October. No pets are allowed.

Reservations, fee: No reservations; $14 fee per night; $4 each additional vehicle.

Who to contact: Phone Memorial Park at (415) 879-0212, or (415) 363-4021.

Location: In Half Moon Bay at the junction of Highway 1 and Highway 92, drive south on Highway 1 for 15 miles to the Pescadero Road exit. Turn left (east) on Pescadero Road and drive about 10 miles to the park entrance.

Trip note: This beautiful redwood park is set on the western slopes of the Santa Cruz Mountains, tucked in a pocket between the tiny towns of La Honda and Loma Mar. The campground features access to a nearby network of 50 miles of trails, with the best hike along the headwaters of Pescadero Creek. In late winter, it is sometimes possible to see steelhead spawn (no fishing permitted, of course). The trails link up with others in nearby Portola State Park and Sam McDonald County Park, providing access to a vast recreation land. The camp is often filled on summer weekends, but the camps are spaced so it won't cramp your style. Open year-round.

22. PORTOLA STATE PARK 🚶🚶

Reference: **Near Skyline Ridge; map E1, grid h3.**

Campsites, facilities: There are 52 sites for tents or motor homes up to 24 feet long. Piped water, fire grills and tables are provided. Toilets and coin-operated showers are available. Pets are permitted.

Reservations, fee: Reserve by phoning Destinet at (800) 444-7275 ($6.75 Destinet fee); $17 fee per night; $1 pet fee. No reservations October through mid-May.

Who to contact: Phone (415) 948-9098 or (408) 429-2850/2851.

Location: From Palo Alto on Interstate 280, take the Page Mill exit. Turn east on Page Mill Road and drive (slow and twisty) to Skyline Boulevard (Highway 35). Cross Skyline and continue west on Alpine Road (very twisty) for about five miles to Portola State Park Road. Turn left on Portola State Park Road and drive about three miles to the campground.

Trip note: Portola State Park is very secluded, the result of visitors being required to travel on an extremely slow and winding series of roads to reach it. The park features redwoods and foothill grasslands on the western slopes of the Santa Cruz Mountains, the headwaters of Pescadero Creek, and 14 miles of hiking trails. A four-mile hike links up to nearby Memorial Park. At times in the summer, a low fog will move in along the San Mateo Coast, and from lookouts near Skyline, visitors can peer to the west at what seems like a pearlescent sea with little islands (hilltops) poking through.

23. BUTANO STATE PARK 🚶🚶

Reference: **Near Pescadero; map E1, grid i2.**

Campsites, facilities: There are 21 sites for tents or motor homes and 18 walk-in sites. Piped water, fire grills and picnic tables are provided. A restroom is available. Pets are permitted.

Reservations, fee: Reserve by phoning Destinet at (800) 444-7275 ($6.75 Destinet fee); $17 fee per night; $1 pet fee.

Who to contact: Phone (415) 879-2040 or (415) 330-6300.

Location: In Half Moon Bay at the junction of Highway 1 and Highway 92, drive south on Highway 1 for 15 miles to the Pescadero Road exit. Turn left (east) on Pescadero Road and drive past the town of Pescadero to Cloverdale Road. Turn right and drive about five miles to the park entrance on the left.

Trip note: The campground at Butano is set in a redwood forest, so pretty and with such good hiking that it has become popular enough to make reservations a must. It is the favorite campground for State Parks Director Don Murphy. The reason is because there are a series of exceptional hikes, including the one to the Ano Nuevo Lookout (pick a clear day), the Mill Ox Loop, and for the ambitious, the 11-mile Butano Rim Loop. The latter has a backpack camp set in the park's most remote area, but no water is available.

24. BIG BASIN REDWOODS STATE PARK

Reference: **Near Santa Cruz; map E1, grid i3.**

Campsites, facilities: There are 107 sites for tents or motor homes up to 27 feet long, 38 walk-in sites, 35 tent cabins (reservations required), and 10 backpack campsites. Piped water, picnic tables and fire grills are provided. Restrooms, coin-operated showers, a sanitary disposal station and groceries are available. Some campsites and facilities are **wheelchair accessible**. Pets are allowed on leashes in campsites only.

Reservations, fee: Reserve by phoning Destinet at (800) 444-7275 ($6.75 Destinet fee); $17-$19 fee per night. For tent cabin fees and reservations, phone (800) 874-8368.

Who to contact: Phone Big Basin State Park at (408) 338-6132 or (408) 429-2850.

Location: From Santa Cruz, turn north on Highway 9 and drive 12 miles to Boulder Creek. Turn west on Highway 236 and drive nine miles to the park headquarters.

Trip note: Big Basin is one of the best state parks in California, featuring giant redwoods near the park headquarters, secluded campsites set in forest, and rare opportunities to stay in a tent cabin or a backpacking trail site. It is a great park for hikers, with two waterfalls, one close and one far, making for stellar destinations. The close one is Sempervirens Falls, a long, narrow, silvery stream, an easy 1.5-hour roundtrip on the Sequoia Trail. The far one is the famous Berry Creek Falls, a spectacular 70-foot cascade set in a beautiful canyon, framed by redwoods. For hikers in good condition, figure two hours (4.7 miles) to reach Berry Creek Falls, five hours for the round trip in-and-out, and six hours for the complete loop (12 miles) that extends into the park's most remote areas. There is also an easy loop nature trail near the park headquarters in the valley floor that is routed past several mammoth redwoods.

25. CARBONERO CREEK TRAILER PARK

Reference: **Near Scotts Valley; map E1, grid j5.**

Campsites, facilities: There are 10 sites for tents and 104 motor home sites with full or partial hookups and picnic tables. Restrooms, showers, cable TV, a laundromat, a recreation room, a hot tub, whirlpool and a swimming pool are available. Pets are permitted on leashes by the RV sites only.

Reservations, fee: Reservations recommended; $22-$24 fee per night.

Who to contact: Phone (408) 438-1288, or (800) 546-1288.

Location: From Santa Cruz at the junction of Highways 1 and 17, turn east on Highway 17 and drive four miles to the Mount Hermon/Big Basin exit. Take that exit north onto Mount Hermon Road and drive to Scotts Valley Drive. Turn right and drive to Disc Drive. Turn right on Disc Drive and continue to 917 Disc Drive.

Trip note: This camp is just a short hop from Santa Cruz and the shore of Monterey Bay. There are many side trip options, making this a prime location for vacationers cruising the California coast. In Santa Cruz, there are several quality restaurants, plus fishing trips and boat rentals at Santa Cruz Wharf, as well as the famous Santa Cruz Boardwalk and amusement park. Open year-round.

26. PARKWAY LAKES RV PARK

Reference: **Near Morgan Hill; map E1, grid j9.**

Campsites, facilities: There are 113 motor home sites with electricity and piped water. Restrooms, showers, a sanitary disposal station, a laundromat and a recreation room are available. Pets are allowed on leashes.

Reservations, fee: Reservations required; $22-$25 fee per night.

Who to contact: Phone (408) 779-0244.

Location: From San Jose, drive south about 12 miles on US 101 to the Cochrane-Monterey Road exit. Turn right (west) on Cochrane Road and continue about 1.5 miles to the Monterey Highway turnoff. Drive south (right) on Monterey Highway about 3.5 miles to Ogier Road. Turn right on Ogier Road and drive to 100 Ogier Road on the right.

Trip note: This RV park provides a spot to park on the southern outskirts of the San Francisco Bay Area. It gets its name from nearby Parkway Lake, a pay-to-fish-lake where for $10 you get a chance to catch rainbow trout up to 10 pounds in the winter and spring, and catfish and sturgeon in the summer. There are several other reservoirs in the nearby foothills, including Coyote, Anderson, Chesbro, Uvas and Calero. The best nearby source for fishing and recreation is Coyote Discount Bait and Tackle at (408) 463-0711.

NOTE: **For Del Valle Regional Park, Joseph Grant County Park, and Henry Coe State Park, see Chapter E2.**

MAP E2

NOR-CAL MAP .... see page 94
adjoining maps
NORTH (D2) .... see page 346
EAST (E3) .... see page 444
SOUTH (F2) .... see page 528
WEST (E1) .... see page 418

23 LISTINGS
PAGES 432-443

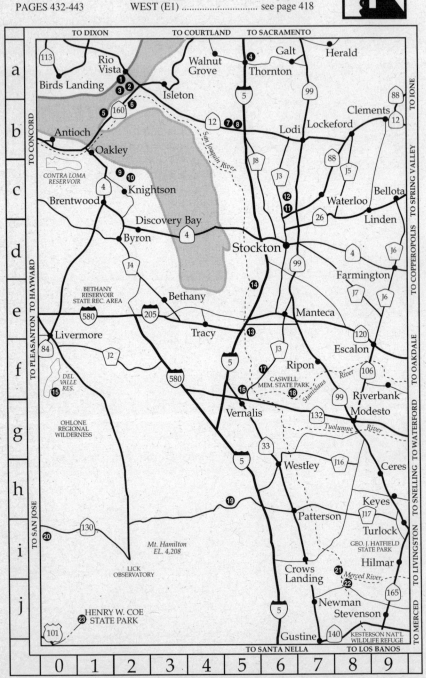

Map E2 featuring: Sacramento River Delta, Sacramento River, Mokelumne River, San Joaquin River Delta, San Joaquin River, Stanislaus River

1. SANDY BEACH COUNTY PARK 🐟 ⚓ ♿ 🚐 ⛺

Reference: **On Sacramento River; map E2, grid a2.**

Campsites, facilities: There are 42 sites for tents or motor homes. Electricity, picnic tables, fire grills and piped water are provided. Flush toilets, showers, a playground and a sanitary disposal station and a boat ramp are available. The facilities are **wheelchair accessible**. Supplies can be obtained nearby. Pets are permitted with proof of rabies vaccination.

Reservations, fee: Reservations accepted; $10-$15 fee per night; $1 pet fee.

Who to contact: Phone the park (707) 374-2097.

Location: From Fairfield on Interstate 80, take the Highway 12 exit and drive southeast for 14 miles to Rio Vista and the intersection with Main Street. Turn southeast on Main Street and drive a short distance to Second Street. Turn right and drive a half-mile to Beach Drive. Continue on Beach Drive to the park.

Trip note: This is a surprisingly little-known park, especially considering it provides beachside access to the Sacramento River. It is a popular spot for sunbathers in hot summer months, but in winter, it is one of the few viable spots where you can fish from the shore for sturgeon. It also provides outstanding boating access to the Sacramento River, including one of the best fishing spots for striped bass in the fall, the Rio Vista Bridge. Open year-round.

2. DUCK ISLAND RV PARK 🐟 ♿ 🚐 ⛺

Reference: **On Sacramento River; map E2, grid a2.**

Campsites, facilities: There are 51 motor home sites with full hookups. Picnic tables are provided. A recreation room with a kitchen is available. A boat ramp is available at Brannan Island State Recreation Area, a short drive away. Supplies and a laundromat are located in Rio Vista. The facilities are **wheelchair accessible**. Adults only. Pets are allowed on leashes.

Reservations, fee: Reservations accepted; reservation and deposit required for groups; $17 fee per night.

Who to contact: Phone (916) 777-6663.

Location: In Fairfield on Interstate 5, take the Highway 12 exit and drive 14 miles southeast to Rio Vista and continue to Highway 160 (at the signal before the bridge). Turn left on Highway 160 and drive just under a mile to the RV park.

Trip note: This pleasant rural park, set up for adults only, has riverside access that provides an opportunity for bank fishing on the Sacramento River. A boat ramp is available at the end of Main Street in Rio Vista. Both Hap's and The Trap provide reliable fishing information as well as all gear needed for fishing.

3. DELTA MARINA RV RESORT 🚐 ⛺ 🐟 ⚓ ♿ 🏃

Reference: **On Sacramento River Delta; map E2, grid a2.**

Campsites, facilities: There are 25 motor home sites with full hookups. Picnic tables and fire grills are provided. Restrooms, showers, a sanitary disposal station, a laundromat, a playground, a boat ramp, ice and propane gas are available. Pets are allowed on leashes (one pet per vehicle).

Reservations, fee: Reservations accepted; $17-$25 fee per night; $2 pet fee.

Who to contact: Phone (707) 374-2315.

Location: From Fairfield on Interstate 80, take the Highway 12 exit and drive southeast for 14 miles to Rio Vista and the intersection with Main Street. Turn right (southeast) on Main Street and drive a short distance to Second Street. Turn right and drive to the harbor.

Trip note: This is a prime spot for boat campers. Summers are hot and breezy, and waterskiing is popular on the nearby Sacramento River. From November to March, the striped bass fishing is quite good, often as close as just a half-mile upriver at the Rio Vista Bridge. The boat launch at the harbor is a bonus. Open year-round.

---

4. NEW HOPE LANDING

Reference: On Mokelumne River north of Stockton; map E2, grid a5.

Campsites, facilities: There are 25 sites for tents or motor homes, some with hookups. Piped water is provided. Restrooms, showers, a grocery store, propane gas and a full service marina are available. Pets are allowed on leashes.

Reservations, fee: Reservations accepted; $15 fee per night for two people; $3 fee each additional person.

Who to contact: Phone the camp at (209) 794-2627.

Location: From Stockton on Interstate 5, drive north for 25 miles to the Thornton exit. Take that exit and turn west on Walnut Grove Road and drive 3.3 miles to the campground entrance on the left.

Trip note: New Hope Landing is a privately-operated resort set along the Mokelumne River in the upper San Joaquin Delta. There's a marina available, which gives you access to 1,000 miles of Delta waterways via the Mokelumne River. The Lower Mokelumne is often an excellent area to troll for striped bass in April, and to waterski in summer. In late summer, water hyacinth is sometimes a problem farther upstream.

---

5. EDDO'S HARBOR AND RV PARK

Reference: On San Joaquin River Delta; map E2, grid b2.

Campsites, facilities: There are 33 sites for motor homes, with full hookups. Picnic tables and piped water are provided. Flush toilets, hot showers, a launch ramp, boat storage, fuel dock, a laundromat and a small grocery store are available. Pets are allowed on leashes.

Reservations, fee: Reservations recommended; $20 fee per night.

Who to contact: Phone the campground at (510) 757-5314,.

Location: In Fairfield on Interstate 5, take the Highway 12 exit and drive 14 miles southeast to Rio Vista and continue to Highway 160 (at the signal before the bridge). Turn right on Highway 160 and drive south to Sherman Island Levee Road. Turn left and drive to the campground along the San Joaquin River. Note: If arriving by boat, the camp is located adjacent to Light 21.

Trip note: This is an ideal spot for campers with boats. Eddo's is set on the San Joaquin River, upstream of the Antioch Bridge, in an outstanding region for fishing, powerboating and waterskiing. In summer months, boaters have access to 1,000 miles of Delta waterways, with the best of them in a nearby spider web of rivers and sloughs off the San Joaquin to False River, Frank's

Tract and Old River. Hot weather and sheltered sloughs make this ideal for
waterskiing. In the winter, a nearby fishing spot called Eddo's Bar as well as
the mouth of the False River attract striped bass.

6. BRANNAN ISLAND STATE RECREATION AREA 🐟 ⚓ ♿ 🏊 🎣
Reference: On Sacramento River; map E2, grid b2.

Campsites, facilities: There are 102 sites for tents or motor homes up to 36 feet
long. Picnic tables and fire grills are provided. Restrooms, showers (at the boat
launch site), a sanitary disposal station and a boat launch are available. Several
sites have boat berths. Facilities are **wheelchair accessible**. Supplies can be
obtained in Rio Vista. Pets are permitted.

Reservations, fee: Reserve by phoning Destinet at (800) 444-7275 ($6.75 Destinet
fee); $15-$17 fee per night; $1 pet fee.

Who to contact: Phone (916) 777-6671 or (916) 445-7373.

Location: In Fairfield on Interstate 5, take the Highway 12 exit and drive 14 miles
southeast to Rio Vista and continue to Highway 160 (at the signal before the
bridge). Turn right on Highway 160 and drive three miles to the park entrance.

Trip note: This state park is designed perfectly for boaters, set in the heart of the
Delta's vast waterways. You get year-round adventure: waterskiing and
fishing for catfish are popular in the summer, and in the winter, the immediate
area is often good for striped bass fishing. The proximity of the campgrounds
to the boat launch deserves a medal. What many people do is tow a boat here,
launch it and keep it docked, return to their site and set up, then come and go
as they please, boating, fishing and exploring in the Delta.

7. TOWER PARK MARINA AND RESORT 🐟 ⚓ ♿ 🎣
Reference: Near Stockton; map E2, grid b5.

Campsites, facilities: There are 500 sites for tents or motor homes, most with full
hookups (tent sites are closed in winter months). Picnic tables and barbecues
are provided. Restrooms, showers, a sanitary disposal station, a recreation
room, boat rentals, overnight boat slips, an elevator boat launch, a playground,
a restaurant, a laundromat, a gift shop, a grocery store and propane gas are
available. Pets are allowed on leashes.

Reservations, fee: Reservations recommended; $15-$27 fee per night.

Who to contact: Phone the park at (209) 369-1041.

Location: In Stockton at the junction of Interstate 5 and Highway 4, head north
on Interstate 5 for 14 miles to Highway 12. Turn west on Highway 12 and drive
about five miles to 14900 Highway 12.

Trip note: This huge resort is ideal for boat-in campers who desire a full-facility
marina. The camp is set on Little Potato Slough near the Mokelumne River. In
the summer, this is a popular waterskiing area. Some hot weekends are like a
continuous party. Open all year.

8. WESTGATE LANDING COUNTY PARK 🐟 ⚓ ♿ 🏊 🎣
Reference: In San Joaquin River Delta near Stockton; map E2, grid b5.

Campsites, facilities: There are 14 sites for tents or motor homes. Piped water, barbecues and picnic tables are provided. Flush toilets are available. Groceries and propane gas are nearby. Pets are permitted on leashes. There are 22 boat slips available.

Reservations, fee: No reservations; $9 fee per night; boat slips $10; $1 pet fee.
Who to contact: Phone the County Parks Department at (209) 953-8800.
Location: In Stockton at the junction of Interstate 5 and Highway 4, head north on Interstate 5 for 14 miles to Highway 12. Turn west on Highway 12 and drive about five miles to Glasscock Road. Turn right (north) and drive about a mile to the park.
Trip note: Summer temperatures typically reach the high 90s and low 100s here, and this county park provides a little shade and boating access to the South Fork Mokelumne River. On hot summer nights, some campers will stay up late and night-fish for catfish. In winter months between storms, the area typically gets smothered in dense fog. Open all year.

9. ISLAND PARK

Reference: On San Joaquin River Delta; map E2, grid c3.
Campsites, facilities: There are 66 motor home sites with full hookups. Restrooms, showers, a laundromat, a recreation room, cable TV and a swimming pool are available. Small pets are permitted.
Reservations, fee: Reservations accepted; $18 fee per night.
Who to contact: Phone (510) 684-2144.
Location: From Antioch, turn east on Highway 4 and drive to Oakley and Cypress Road. Turn east on Cypress Road, drive over the Bethel Island Bridge and continue a half-mile to Gateway Road. Turn right and drive a half-mile to Island Park.
Trip note: This privately-operated motor home park is set on the edge of the San Joaquin Delta's boating paradise, with more than 1,000 miles of waterways available. Nearby Frank's Tract, Old River, False River and the lower Mokelumne River are all spots that provide good waterskiing in the summer.

10. DELTA RESORT

Reference: On San Joaquin River Delta; map E2, grid c3.
Campsites, facilities: There are 80 motor home sites with full hookups. Restrooms, a sanitary disposal station, propane gas, a playground, a boat ramp and a full restaurant and bar are available. Pets are allowed on leashes.
Reservations, fee: Reservations required (with deposit); $18 fee per night.
Who to contact: Phone (510) 684-9351 or write to P.O. Box 455, Bethel Island, CA 94511.
Location: From Antioch, turn east on Highway 4 and drive to Oakley and Cypress Road. Turn east on Cypress Road, drive over the Bethel Island Bridge and continue a half mile to Gateway Road. Turn right and drive to River View Road. Turn left and drive to the park at 6777 River View Road.
Trip note: This park is set on Bethel Island in the heart of the San Joaquin Delta. The boat ramp here provides immediate access to an excellent area for waterskiing, and it turns into a playland on hot summer days. In the fall and winter, the area often provides good striper fishing at nearby Frank's Tract, False River and San Joaquin River. Catfishing in surrounding slough areas is good year-round. The Delta Sportsman Shop at Bethel Island has reliable fishing information.

11. SAHARA MOBILE PARK ♿ 〜

Reference: **In Stockton; map E2, grid c6.**

Campsites, facilities: There are 28 motor home sites with electric hookups. Restrooms, showers, a recreation room, a heated swimming pool (seasonal) and a laundromat are available. A playground, a grocery store and a donut shop are nearby. Small pets are permitted.

Reservations, fee: Reservations accepted; $20 fee per night.

Who to contact: Phone the park at (209) 464-9392.

Location: In Stockton on Highway 99, take the Cherokee exit, and drive west for about three miles to Sanguinetti Lane. Turn right and drive one mile to 2340 Sanguinetti Lane.

Trip note: They play Bingo every Tuesday night here, and that should tell you everything you need to know about this spot. Open year-round.

12. STOCKTON-LODI KOA 〜 🅁🅅 🅰

Reference: **In Stockton; map E2, grid c6.**

Campsites, facilities: There are 102 sites for tents or motor homes, many with full hookups. Picnic tables are provided. Restrooms, showers, a sanitary disposal station, a grocery store, propane gas, a laundromat, a recreation room, a swimming pool and a playground are available. Pets are permitted on leashes.

Reservations, fee: No reservations; $19-$23 fee per night.

Who to contact: Phone the park at (209) 941-2573 or 334-0309.

Location: From Stockton on Interstate 5, drive five miles north to Eight Mile Road. Turn east and drive five miles to the campground at 2851 East Eight Mile Road.

Trip note: This KOA camp is in the heart of the San Joaquin Valley. The proximity to Interstate 5 and Highway 99 make it work for long-distance vacationers looking for a spot to park the rig for the night. The San Joaquin Delta is located 15 miles to the west, with best access provided off Highway 12 to Isleton and Rio Vista; it's also a pretty drive. Open year-round.

13. DOS REIS COUNTY PARK 🐟 ⚓ ♿

Reference: **On San Joaquin River near Stockton; map E2, grid e5.**

Campsites, facilities: There are 26 motor home sites with full hookups and a separate section for tents only. Picnic tables and fire grills are provided. Restrooms, showers and a boat ramp are available. A grocery store, a laundromat and propane gas can be found nearby. Pets are permitted on leashes.

Reservations, fee: Reservations accepted; $13 fee per night; $1 pet fee.

Who to contact: Phone the County Parks at (209) 953-8800.

Location: From Stockton on Interstate 5, drive a short distance to the Lathrop exit. Turn northwest on Lathrop and drive one mile to Dos Reis Road. Turn toward the San Joaquin River and drive to the park on the east side of the river.

Trip note: This is a 90-acre county park that has a quarter-mile of San Joaquin River frontage, a boat ramp, and nearby access to the eastern Delta near Stockton. The sun gets scalding hot here in the summer, branding everything in sight. That's why boaters make quick work of getting in the water, then cooling off with water sports. In the winter, this area often has zero visibility from tule fog. Open all year.

14. OAKWOOD LAKE RESORT

Reference: **Near Stockton; map E2, grid e5.**

Campsites, facilities: There are 87 sites for tents, 116 sites for tents or motor homes, and 194 motor home sites. Picnic tables are provided. Piped water, electrical connections, and sewer hookups are provided at most sites. Restrooms, showers, a dump station, a grocery store, a laundromat, propane gas, a swimming lagoon, water slides, paddle boats, organized activities and a stocked 75-acre lake are available. The facilities are **wheelchair accessible**. Pets are allowed on leashes.

Reservations, fee: Reservations accepted; $18-$24 fee per night; $2 pet fee.

Who to contact: Phone the park at (209) 239-9566.

Location: In Manteca, turn east on Highway 120 and drive two miles to Airport Way. Turn south and drive a half-mile to Woodward Way. Turn right and drive two miles to the park entrance.

Trip note: This is huge, privately-operated "water theme" park that covers 375 acres and offers a wide array of water-related recreation activities. It is a great place for families to cool off and have fun on hot summer days, with youngsters lining up for trips down the water slides. Open all year.

15. DEL VALLE PARK

Reference: **Near Livermore; map E2, grid f0.**

Campsites, facilities: There are 129 sites for tents or motor homes, 21 with full hookups. Piped water, fire grills and picnic tables are provided. A sanitary disposal station, flush toilets, hot showers, a full marina and a boat launch are available. Pets are permitted.

Reservations, fee: Reservations required; phone (510) 562-2267 ($4 reservation fee); $13-$16 fee per night; $1 pet fee.

Who to contact: Phone the East Bay Regional Park District at (510) 635-0135, extension. 2200 or Del Valle Park at (510) 373-0332.

Location: On Interstate 580, drive to Livermore and the North Livermore Avenue exit. Turn south and drive on North/South Livermore Road (this will turn into Tesla Road) to Mines Road. Turn right and drive south for three miles to Del Valle Road. Turn right and drive for three miles to the entrance to the park.

Trip note: Of the 50 parks in the East Bay Regional Park District, it is Del Valle that provides the highest variety of recreation at the highest quality levels. Del Valle Reservoir is the centerpiece, a long narrow lake that fills a canyon, providing a good boat launch for powerboating, and fishing for trout, striped bass and catfish. The sites are somewhat exposed due to the grassland habitat, but they fill anyway on most weekends and three-day holidays. A trailhead south of the lake provides access to the Ohlone Wilderness Trail, and for the well conditioned, there is the 5.5-mile buttkicker of a climb to Murietta Falls, gaining 1,600 feet in 1.5 miles. Murietta Falls is the Bay Area's highest waterfall, 100 feet tall, though its thin, silvery cascade rarely evokes much emotional response after such an intense climb.

16. ORCHARD RV PARK

Reference: **Near Stockton; map E2, grid f5.**

Campsites, facilities: There are 20 tent sites and 88 drive-through motor home sites with full hookups. Picnic tables and fire grills are provided. Restrooms, showers, a laundromat, a sanitary disposal station, a swimming pool, a restaurant and horseshoe pits are available. The facilities are **wheelchair accessible**. Groceries, propane gas, and a weekend flea market can be found nearby. Pets are allowed on leashes.

Reservations, fee: Reservations accepted; $20 fee per night.

Who to contact: Phone the park at (209) 836-2090.

Location: From Interstate 5 near Vernalis, turn east on Highway 132 and drive three miles to the signed campground entrance at 2701 East Highway 132.

Trip note: The huge swimming pool and water slides here make this a popular campground for families. Temperatures in the 100-degree range in the summer months keep both in constant use. This privately-operated park is set up primarily for owners of motor homes. Its location near Interstate 5 makes it a winner for many of them.

17. DURHAM FERRY RECREATION AREA

Reference: **Near Stockton; map E2 grid f6.**

Campsites, facilities: There are 75 sites for tents or motor homes, some with full hookups. Picnic tables and fire grills are provided. Restrooms, showers and a sanitary dump station are available. Groceries and propane gas can be obtained nearby. Pets are permitted on leashes.

Reservations, fee: No reservations; $11 fee per night; $1 pet fee.

Who to contact: Phone the County Parks Department at (209) 953-8800.

Location: From Interstate 5 near Vernalis, turn east on Highway 132 and drive to County Road J3 (Airport Way). Turn right (south) on Airport Way and drive six miles (the road jogs left) to the park entrance.

Trip note: This is a county park that features nearly two miles of frontage along the San Joaquin River, along with an adjoining 176 acres. This section of the San Joaquin is not exactly a pristine babbling brook, but rather a slow-moving, greenish ick that can turn almost plasma-like in late summer from algae and weed growth. Regardless, out here, water is water, and shoreline fishing for catfish on summer nights and walking along the river to see birds still makes for a pleasant setting.

18. CASWELL MEMORIAL STATE PARK

Reference: **On Stanislaus River near Stockton; map E2, grid f6.**

Campsites, facilities: There are 65 sites for tents or motor homes up to 24 feet long. Piped water, fire grills and picnic tables are provided. Flush toilets, showers, wood and a nature trail and exhibits are available. The exhibits are **wheelchair accessible**. Pets are allowed on leashes.

Reservations, fee: Reserve by phoning Destinet at (800) 444-7275 ($6.75 Destinet fee); $15-$17 fee per night; $1 pet fee.

Who to contact: Phone the park at (209) 599-3810 or (209) 826-1196.

Location: From Manteca, drive south on Highway 99 for 1.5 miles to the Austin Road exit. Turn south and drive four miles to the park entrance.

Trip note: Caswell Memorial State Park features shoreline frontage along the Stanislaus River, along with an additional 250 acres of parkland. The Stanislaus provides shoreline fishing for catfish on summer nights. Other recreation options here include a fine visitor center and an interpretive nature trail. Open year-round.

19. FRANK RAINES REGIONAL PARK 🚶🚶

Reference: **Near Modesto; map E2, grid h5.**

Campsites, facilities: There are 34 tent or motor home sites. Fire grills, picnic tables, piped water, electrical connections and sewer hookups are provided. Restrooms, showers and a playground are available. Pets are permitted.

Reservations, fee: No reservations; $12-$16 fee per night; $2 pet fee; $2 fee for rough terrain vehicles.

Who to contact: Phone the park at (408) 897-3127.

Location: On Interstate 5 (south of the junction of Interstate 5 and Interstate 580), drive to the Patterson exit. Turn east and drive to Del Puerto Canyon Road. Turn west and drive 16 miles to the park.

Trip note: This park is primarily a riding area for dirt bikes and three- and four-wheel OHVs, who take advantage of the rough-terrain riding course available here. A side trip option is to visit Minniear Park, located directly to the east, which is a day-use wilderness park with hiking trails and a creek. This area is very pretty in the spring when the foothills are still green and many wildflowers are blooming. Open year-round.

20. JOSEPH GRANT COUNTY PARK 🚶🚶 ♿

Reference: **Near San Jose; map E2, grid i0.**

Campsites, facilities: There are 20 sites for tents or motor homes up to 28 feet long. Fire grills and tables are provided. Piped water, hot showers, a sanitary dump station and toilets are available. Pets are permitted.

Reservations, fee: No reservations; $8 fee per night; $1 pet fee.

Who to contact: Phone Grant County Park at (408) 274-6121.

Location: In San Jose at the junction of Interstate 680 and US 101, take Interstate 680 south to the Alum Rock Avenue exit. Turn east and drive four miles to Mt. Hamilton Road. Turn right and drive eight miles to the park headquarters entrance on the right side of the road.

Trip note: Grant Ranch is a great wild playland covering 9,000 acres in the foothills of nearby Mt. Hamilton to the east. It features 40 miles of hiking trails (horses permitted), 20 miles of old ranch roads that are perfect for mountain biking, a pretty lake (Grant Lake) and miles of foothills, canyons and grasslands. The campground is set amid oak grasslands, is shaded, and can be used as a base camp for planning the day's recreation. The best hikes are to Halls Valley, especially in the winter and spring when there are many secret little creeks and miniature waterfalls in hidden canyons, and the Hotel Trail and Canada de Pala Trail, which drops down to San Felipe Creek, the prettiest stream in the park. A great side trip is the slow, curvy drive east to Lick Observatory for great views of the Santa Clara Valley. Closed December through February. Open on weekends only in March.

21. FISHERMAN'S BEND RIVER CAMP

🐟 ⚓ ♿

Reference: **On San Joaquin River; map E2, grid i8.**

Campsites, facilities: There are 20 sites for tents only and 38 motor home sites with full hookups. Picnic tables and fire grills are provided. Piped water, restrooms, showers, a sanitary disposal station, a laundromat, a boat ramp, a fish cleaning station, a swimming pool, a playground and horseshoe pits are available. Pets are allowed on leashes.

Reservations, fee: Reservations accepted; $16-$21 fee per night.

Who to contact: Phone the park at (209) 862-3731.

Location: South of the junction of Interstate 5 and Interstate 580, drive on Interstate 5 to the Newman/Stuhr Road exit. Turn east on County Road J18 (Stuhr Road) and drive 6.5 miles to Hills Ferry Road. Turn left and drive one mile to River Road. Turn left on River Road and drive to 26836 River Road.

Trip note: This small, privately operated campground is set along the San Joaquin River on the southern outskirts of the San Joaquin Delta country. The park offers shaded sites and direct river access for boaters. This section of river provides fishing for catfish on hot summer nights. Open all year.

22. GEORGE J. HATFIELD STATE RECREATION AREA

Reference: **Near Newman; map E2, grid i8.**

Campsites, facilities: There are 21 family sites and one large group site for tents or motor homes up to 32 feet long. Picnic tables, fire grills and piped water are provided. Flush toilets are available. Supplies can be obtained in Newman. Pets are allowed on leashes.

Reservations, fee: Call ahead for group reservations and fees; $12-$14 fee for family sites; $1 pet fee.

Who to contact: Phone the Four Rivers District Office at (209) 826-1196.

Location: South of the junction of Interstate 5 and Interstate 580, drive on Interstate 5 to the Newman/Stuhr Road exit. Turn east on County Road J18 (Stuhr Road) and drive to Newman and the junction with Highway 33. Turn right (south) and drive a short distance to Hills Ferry Road. Turn left (east) and drive five miles to the park entrance.

Trip note: This is a small state park set in the heart of the San Joaquin Valley, near the confluence of the Merced River and San Joaquin River, well known for very hot summer days and very foggy winter nights. Some folks say if you eat enough catfish from this spot, you'll glow in the dark after a few years. It's advisable to throw them back. Open year-round.

23. HENRY W. COE STATE PARK

Reference: **Near Gilroy; map E2, grid j1.**

Campsites, facilities: There are seven sites for tents and 13 sites for tents or motor homes. Piped water, pit toilets, fire grills and tables are provided. Pets are permitted on leashes.

Reservations, fee: Reserve by phoning Destinet at (800) 444-7275 ($6.75 Destinet fee); $10-$12 fee per night; $1 pet fee.

Who to contact: Phone (408) 779-2728 or (209) 826-1196.

Location: From Morgan Hill on US 101, take the East Dunne Avenue exit and drive through Morgan Hill, over the bridge at Anderson Lake, and continue for 13 miles (very twisty) to the park entrance.

Trip note: This is the Bay Area's backyard wilderness, with 80,000 acres of wildlands, 100 lakes and ponds, and 150 miles of trails for hiking, biking and wilderness-style camping. The drive-in campground is set on a hilltop, and though exposed, it provides dramatic views and a good spot for stargazing. Before setting out for the outback, always consult with the rangers here—the ambitious plans of many hikers cause them to suffer dehydration and heat stroke. The park has excellent pond-style fishing, but requires extremely long hikes to reach the best lakes, including Mustang Pond, Coit Lake, Mississippi Lake, Kelly Lake and Hoover Lake. Expect hot weather in summer; spring and early summer are the prime times. Even though the park may appear to be 120 square miles of oak foothills, the terrain is sometimes steep, and there are many great secrets to be discovered here, including Rooster Comb and Coyote Creek. Bring a water purifier for hikes, because there is **no piped water** in the outback.

NOR-CAL MAP .... see page 94
adjoining maps
NORTH (D3) .... see page 350
EAST (E4) .... see page 460
SOUTH (F3) .... see page 534
WEST (E2) .... see page 432

35 LISTINGS
PAGES 444-459

STANISLAUS NAT'L FOREST

TO DRYTOWN
TO PIONEER
TO CLEMENTS

Ione
① 104
Jackson
Pine Grove

a

88
LAKE AMADOR
② PARDEE RES.
26
③

Buena Vista
CAMANCHE RESERVOIR
Valley Springs
Mokelumne Hill

CALAVERAS BIG TREES STATE PARK
④
⑫

b

TO BELLOTA
⑤
④
Wallace
⑧
San Andreas
Arnold
⑩
⑨
⑪

N. Fork Stanislaus River
Middle Fork

12
Burson
⑥ ⑦
28
NEW HOGAN RESERVOIR
Sheep Ranch

c

Jenny Lind
49
Murphys
S. Fork Stanislaus River

TO FARMINGTON
Milton
Angels Camp
Vallecito
⑯
Mi-Wuk Village

TO LONG BARN

d

J14
Copperopolis
NEW MELONES LAKE
⑭
Melones
⑮
Columbia
⑱
Twain Harte

4
4
⑬
Tuttletown
108
⑰

e

J14
Eugene
Sonora
Soulsbyville
Tuolumne

TO ESCALON
⑲
WOODWARD RESERVOIR
⑳
Jamestown

TULLOCH RESERVOIR

f

Knights Ferry
㉑
Chinese Camp

TO MODESTO
120
Stanislaus River
Tuolumne River
Bucks Meadow

108
Oakdale
J59
49
Groveland
⑳
⑳

g

⑳
㉖
㉕
Big Oak Flat
120

Waterford
23
132
DON PEDRO RESERVOIR
⑳
⑳

MODESTO RESERVOIR
㉔
La Grange
Coulterville

h

Hickman
Tuolumne River
㉗

TO TURLOCK
TURLOCK LAKE
㉜
Merced River

㉛
LAKE McCLURE

i

J17
J16
J59
Snelling
㉝
Bear Valley

99
Merced River
㉞
J16
Mt. Bullion

Delhi
Merced Falls
49

j

35
Hornitos
Catheys Valley

TO STEVENSON
Livingston
J17
Winton
140
140
Mariposa
Mormon Bar

TO NIPINNAWASSE

Atwater
TO MERCED
TO MERCED
TO RAYMOND

0 1 2 3 4 5 6 7 8 9

Map E3 featuring: Pardee Reservoir, Camanche Reservoir, New Hogan Reservoir, Calaveras Big Trees State Park, Stanislaus National Forest, New Melones Lake, Tuolumne River, Don Pedro Reservoir, Lake McClure, Merced River

1. LAKE AMADOR RECREATION AREA

Reference: Near Stockton; map E3, grid a1.

Campsites, facilities: There are 150 sites for tents or motor homes, 72 with full hookups, and 12 group sites. Picnic tables and fire grills are provided. Piped water, rest rooms, showers, a sanitary disposal station, a boat ramp, boat rentals, fishing supplies (including bait and tackle), a restaurant, a grocery store, propane gas, a swimming pond and a playground are available. Pets are permitted on leashes.

Reservations, fee: Reservations accepted; $12-$18 fee per night.

Who to contact: Phone the resort at (209) 274-4739.

Location: From Stockton, turn east on Highway 88 and drive 24 miles to Clements. Just east of Clements, continue straight on Highway 12 and drive 11 miles to Jackson Valley Road. Turn right (well signed) and drive four miles to Lake Amador Drive. Turn right and drive over the dam to the campground office.

Trip note: Lake Amador is set in the foothill country east of Stockton at an elevation of 485 feet, covering 425 acres with 13 miles of shoreline. Everything here is set up for fishing, with waterskiing and jet-skiing prohibited, large trout stocks from winter through late spring, and the chance for huge bass. The largest two-man bass limit in California was caught here, 80 pounds, and the lake record weighed 15 pounds, 13 ounces. The Carson Creek Arm and Jackson Creek Arm are the top spots. Open year-round.

2. PARDEE RECREATION AREA

Reference: On Pardee Reservoir; map E3, grid a2.

Campsites, facilities: There are 99 sites for tents or motor homes and 112 motor home sites with full hookups. Picnic tables, fire grills and piped water are provided. Restrooms, showers (in the motor home section), a sanitary disposal station, a boat ramp, boat rentals, a laundromat, a grocery store, propane gas, RV and boat storage and a swimming pool are available. Pets are permitted on leashes.

Reservations, fee: Reservations accepted for motor home sites only; $13-$18 fee per night; $1 pet fee.

Who to contact: Phone the resort at (209) 772-1472.

Location: From Stockton, drive east on Highway 88 for 24 miles to the town of Clements. Just east of Clements, turn left on Highway 88 and drive 11 miles to Jackson Valley Road. Turn right and drive to a four-way stop sign at Buena Vista. Turn right and drive for three miles to Stony Creek Road on the left. Turn left and drive a mile to the campground.

Trip note: Many people feel that Pardee is the prettiest lake in the Mother Lode Country, a big lake covering 2,257 acres with 37 miles of shoreline. It is a beautiful sight in the spring when the lake is full and the surrounding hills are green and glowing. Waterskiing, jet-skiing and swimming are prohibited at the lake. It is set up expressly for fishing, with high catch rates for rainbow trout and kokanee salmon, best while trolling in the north arm of the lake. Open mid-February through November.

3. GOLDEN TORCH RV RESORT & CAMP

Reference: **Near Arnold; map E3, grid a9.**

Campsites, facilities: There are 49 tent sites and 63 motor home sites with full hookups. Fire grills and picnic tables are provided. Piped water, restrooms, showers, a sanitary disposal station, a recreation room, a swimming pool and a playground are available. A grocery store, a laundromat and propane gas are nearby. Pets are permitted.

Reservations, fee: Reservations recommended; $13-$19 fee per night.

Who to contact: Phone the campground at (209) 795-2820.

Location: From Angels Camp, turn northeast on Highway 4 and drive 22 miles to Arnold. Continue for seven miles to the campground entrance.

Trip note: This is a privately-operated park set at 5,800 feet on the slopes of the Sierra Nevada, near Stanislaus National Forest, the North Stanislaus River and Calaveras Big Trees State Park (three miles away). The latter features 150 Giant Sequoias, along with the biggest stump you can imagine, and two easy hikes, one routed through the North Grove, another through the South Grove. Open year-round.

4. SOUTH CAMANCHE SHORE

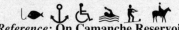

Reference: **On Camanche Reservoir; map E3, grid b1.**

Campsites, facilities: There are 330 sites for tents or motor homes, 125 with full hookups. Picnic tables, fire grills, and piped water are provided. Restrooms, showers, a sanitary disposal station, a trout pond, a boat ramp, boat rentals, a laundromat, a snackbar and a grocery store are available. Pets are permitted on leashes.

Reservations, fee: Reservations accepted for motor home sites only; $14-$18 fee per night.

Who to contact: Phone the resort at (209) 763-5178.

Location: From Stockton, drive east on Highway 88 for 24 miles to Clements. Just east of Clements, continue east on Highway 12 and drive six miles to South Camanche Parkway. Turn left and drive six miles to the entrance gate.

Trip note: Camanche Lake is a huge multi-faceted facility, covering 7,700 acres with 53 miles of shoreline, set in the foothills east of Lodi, at 325 feet in elevation. It is the No. 1 recreation lake for waterskiing and jet-skiing (in specified areas) as well as swimming. In the spring and summer, it provides outstanding fishing for bass, trout, crappie, bluegill and catfish. There are two campgrounds at the lake, and both have boat ramps nearby and all facilities. This one at South Shore has a large but exposed overflow area for campers, a way to keep from getting stuck for a spot on popular weekends. Open year-round.

5. CAMANCHE NORTHSHORE RESORT

Reference: On Camanche Reservoir; map E3, grid b1.

Campsites, facilities: There are 229 sites for tents or motor homes. There are no hookups. Picnic tables, fire grills and piped water are provided. Restrooms, showers, a sanitary disposal station, a boat ramp, boat rentals, a laundromat, a grocery store, a coffee shop/restaurant and a playground are available. Pets are permitted on leashes.

Reservations, fee: Reservations recommended (required for groups); $14-$18 fee per night; $5.50 boat launch fee.

Who to contact: Phone the resort at (209) 763-5121.

Location: From Stockton, drive east on Highway 88 for 24 miles to Clements. Just east of Clements, bear left on Highway 88 and drive six miles to Camanche Parkway. Turn right and drive seven miles to Camanche Northshore entrance gate.

Trip note: The sites at North Shore feature grassy spots with picnic tables, set above the lake, and though there are few trees and the sites seem largely exposed, the lake view is quite pretty. The lake will beckon you for water sports, excellent for boat owners. The warm, clean waters make for good waterskiing (in specified areas), and fishing for trout in spring, bass in early summer, and crappie, bluegill and catfish in summer. Open year-round.

6. ACORN WEST

Reference: At New Hogan Reservoir; map E3, grid b2.

Campsites, facilities: There are 59 sites for tents or motor homes. Fire pits and picnic tables are provided. Piped water, flush toilets, showers and a sanitary dump station are available. A four-lane paved boat ramp is located in adjacent Acorn East Campground. Groceries and propane gas are available nearby. Pets are permitted on leashes.

Reservations, fee: No reservations; $12 fee per night; $6 for each additional vehicle.

Who to contact: Phone New Hogan Marina at (209) 772-1462 or the U.S. Army Corps of Engineers at (209) 772-1343.

Location: From Stockton, drive east on Highway 26 for about 35 miles to Valley Springs and Hogan Dam Road. Turn right and drive about four miles to the campground.

Trip note: New Hogan is a big lake in the foothill country east of Stockton, covering 4,000 acres with 50 miles of shoreline. Acorn West is one of three campgrounds on the lake operated by the Army Corps of Engineers; the others are Acorn East and Oak Knoll. Boaters might also consider boat-in sites located near Deer Flat on the eastern shore. Boating and waterskiing are popular here. Fishing for largemouth bass is off-and-on, best in the spring up the Bear Creek and Whiskey Creek arms, and again in the fall when the striped bass come to life, chasing baitfish on the surface. An interpretive trail below the dam provides a side-trip option.

7. ACORN EAST

Reference: **At New Hogan Reservoir; map E3, grid b2.**

Campsites, facilities: There are 69 sites for tents or motor homes. Fire pits and picnic tables are provided. Piped water, flush toilets, showers and a sanitary dump station are available. A four-lane paved boat ramp is located near the campground. Groceries and propane gas are available nearby. Pets are permitted on leashes.

Reservations, fee: No reservations; $12 fee per night; $6 for each additional vehicle.

Who to contact: Phone U.S. Army Corps of Engineers at (209) 772-1343.

Location: From Stockton, drive east on Highway 26 for about 35 miles to Valley Springs and Hogan Dam Road. Turn right and drive about four miles to the campground (just beyond Acorn West Campground).

Trip note: This is the campground of choice for boaters who prefer drive-to camps instead of the boat-in sites located on the east side of the lake near Deer Flat. A four-lane concrete boat ramp near this camp makes access easy. New Hogan is a big lake, and waterskiing and high-speed boating are popular here, along with largemouth bass fishing in the spring and striped bass fishing in the fall. See the trip note for Acorn West.

8. OAK KNOLL

Reference: **At New Hogan Reservoir; map E3, grid b2.**

Campsites, facilities: There are 50 sites for tents or motor homes. Fire grills and picnic tables are provided. Piped water and vault toilets are available. Groceries, propane gas, a sanitary dump station and a four-lane boat ramp are available nearby. Pets are allowed on leashes.

Reservations, fee: No reservations; $8 fee per night; $4 for each additional vehicle.

Who to contact: Phone U. S. Army Corps of Engineers at New Hogan Reservoir at (209) 772-1343.

Location: From Stockton, drive east on Highway 26 for about 35 miles to Valley Springs and Hogan Dam Road. Turn right and drive about four miles to the campground (adjacent to Acorn camps).

Trip note: This is one of three camps at New Hogan Reservoir and is basically only used as overflow camping during busy years. The reservoir was created by an Army Corps of Engineers dam project on the Calaveras River. This camp is open as needed from April to October. See the trip note for Acorn West.

9. NORTH GROVE

Reference: **In Calaveras Big Trees State Park; map E3, grid b8.**

Campsites, facilities: There are 36 sites for tents, 14 sites for motor homes up to 18 feet long, 24 sites for motor homes up to 30 feet long and one site designed for **wheelchair use**. A group campground is also available. Fire grills and picnic tables are provided. Piped water, flush toilets, firewood, coin-operated showers and a sanitary disposal station are available. A nature trail and exhibits are **wheelchair accessible**. No bicycles are allowed on the paths, but they are permitted on fire roads. Pets are permitted on leashes, but not on trails.

Reservations, fee: Reserve by phoning Destinet at (800) 444-7275 ($6.75 Destinet fee); $15-$17 fee per night; $150 group fee; $1 pet fee.

Who to contact: Phone the Calaveras Big Trees State Park at (209) 795-2334 or (209) 532-0150.

Location: From Angels Camp, drive east on Highway 4 for 22 miles to Arnold, then continue another four miles to the park entrance.

Trip note: This is one of the two campgrounds at Calaveras Big Trees State Park, the state park known for its two groves of mountain redwoods, the Giant Sequoia. The trailhead for a hike on the North Grove Loop is available here, an easy one-mile walk that is routed among 150 Sequoias, where the sweet fragrance of the massive trees fills the air. These trees are known for their massive diameters, not for their heights, as is the case with coastal redwoods. Another hike, a five-miler, is available in the South Grove, where the park's two largest Sequoias (Agassiz Tree and Palace Hotel Tree) can be seen on a spur trail there. A visitor center is available during peak periods, offering exhibits on giant Sequoia and natural history. The North Fork Stanislaus River runs near Highway 4, providing trout fishing access. In the winter, this is a popular spot for cross-country skiing and snowshoeing. The elevation is 4,800 feet. Open year-round.

10. OAK HOLLOW

Reference: **In Calaveras Big Trees State Park; map E3, grid b8.**

Campsites, facilities: There are 31 sites for tents only, 19 sites for motor homes up to 18 feet long, and five sites for motor homes up to 30 feet long. Fire rings and picnic tables are provided. Piped water, flush toilets, a sanitary disposal station and coin-operated showers are available. Supplies can be purchased in Dorrington. A nature trail and exhibits are **wheelchair accessible**. Pets are permitted on leashes, but not on trails.

Reservations, fee: Reserve by phoning Destinet at (800) 444-7275 ($6.75 Destinet fee); $15-$17 fee per night; $1 pet fee.

Who to contact: Phone the Calaveras Big Trees State Park at (209) 795-2334 or (209) 532-0150.

Location: From Angels Camp, drive east on Highway 4 for 22 miles to Arnold, then continue another four miles to the park entrance.

Trip note: This is one of two campgrounds at Calaveras Big Trees State Park. See the trip note for North Grove for recreation information. Open May through September.

11. BOARDS CROSSING

Reference: **On the North Fork of Stanislaus River in Stanislaus National Forest; map E3, grid b9.**

Campsites, facilities: There are five tent sites. Piped water, picnic tables and vault toilets are available. Groceries and propane gas can be purchased nearby. Pets are permitted on leashes.

Reservations, fee: No reservations; no fee; campfire permits required (free).

Who to contact: Phone the Stanislaus National Forest Calaveras Ranger District at (209) 795-1381.

Location: From Angels Camp, turn east on Highway 4 and drive past Arnold to Dorrington and Boards Crossing Road on the right. Turn right and drive about two miles to the campground entrance road on the right. Turn right and drive about a mile to the campground on the right.

Trip note: This is one of the oldest campgrounds in the Western U.S., with a historic one-way bridge located nearby that crosses the North Fork Stanislaus River. It is a small, primitive camp set along the North Fork Stanislaus River, at 3,800 feet, with Beaver Creek located three miles to the east (continue on the access road after crossing the bridge). This camp is just far enough off Highway 4 to be overlooked by most campers. Open June to October.

12. SOURGRASS

Reference: **On the North Fork of Stanislaus River in Stanislaus National Forest; map E3, grid b9.**

Campsites, facilities: There are 15 sites for tents or motor homes up to 16 feet long. Piped water, fire grills and picnic tables are provided. Vault toilets are available. Supplies can be obtained in Dorrington. Pets are permitted on leashes.

Reservations, fee: No reservations; $5 fee per night.

Who to contact: Phone the Stanislaus National Forest Calaveras Ranger District at (209) 795-1381.

Location: From Angels Camp, turn east on Highway 4 and drive past Arnold to Dorrington and Boards Crossing Road on the right. Turn right and drive four miles (driving past the Board Crossing turnoff on the right) to the campground on the left side of the road, set adjacent to a hairpin turn.

Trip note: This is a wooded site set along the North Fork of the Stanislaus River, at 3,900 feet. The access road continues over Little Beaver Creek and enters a state game refuge, set directly to the east. Open April through October.

13. TUTTLETOWN RECREATION AREA

Reference: **At New Melones Lake; map E3, grid d5.**

Campsites, facilities: There are 95 sites for tents or motor homes. Picnic tables and fire grills are provided. Piped water, flush toilets, a sanitary dump station, showers, a playground and a boat ramp are available. Pets are allowed on leashes.

Reservations, fee: No reservations; $10 fee per night.

Who to contact: Phone the U.S. Department of Reclamation at (209) 536-9094.

Location: From Sonora, drive north on Highway 49 to Tuttletown to Reynolds Ferry Road. Turn left and drive about two miles to the campground on the left side of the road.

Trip note: This is one of two camps on Lake New Melones in the Sierra Nevada foothills. This is a huge reservoir that covers 12,250 acres and offers 100 miles of shoreline and good fishing. Waterskiing is permitted in specified areas. A boat ramp is located near camp. Although the lake's main body is huge, the better fishing is well up the lake's Stanislaus River arm (for trout) and in its coves (for bass and bluegill), where there are submerged trees providing perfect aquatic habitat. The lake level often drops dramatically in the fall. Open year-round.

14. GLORY HOLE

Reference: **At New Melones Lake; map E3, grid d5.**

Campsites, facilities: There are 144 sites for tents or motor homes. Picnic tables and fire grills are provided. Piped water, flush toilets, a sanitary dump station, showers, a marina, boat rentals, a volleyball court, a baseball diamond and a playground are available. Pets are allowed on leashes.

Reservations, fee: No reservations; $10 fee per night.

Who to contact: Phone the U.S. Department of Reclamation at (209) 536-9094.

Location: From Sonora, drive north on Highway 49 for about 15 miles (Glory Hole Market on the left side of the road) to Glory Hole Road. Turn left and drive five miles to the campground, with sites on both sides of the road.

Trip note: This is one of two camps on New Melones Lake in the Sierra Nevada foothills, a popular spot with a boat ramp nearby for access to outstanding waterskiing and fishing. See the trip note for the preceding camp. Open year-round.

15. MARBLE QUARRY RV PARK

Reference: **Near Columbia; map E3, grid d6.**

Campsites, facilities: There is a small area for tents and 85 sites for motor homes (26 have full hookups, 59 have partial hookups). Piped water and picnic tables are provided. Restrooms, showers, a swimming pool, a laundromat, a store, a sanitary dump station, a playground, two clubhouses, a lounge, two full kitchens, satellite TV and propane gas are available. Some facilities are **wheelchair accessible**. Pets are allowed on leashes.

Reservations, fee: Reservations accepted; $17-$25 fee per night.

Who to contact: Phone (209) 532-9539.

Location: From Sonora, turn north on Highway 49 and drive east for 2.5 miles to Parrotts Ferry Road. Bear right and drive two miles to Yankee Hill Road. Turn right and drive a half-mile to the campground at 11551 Yankee Hill Road.

Trip note: This RV park is set at 2,100 feet in the Mother Lode country, within nearby range of several adventures. Columbia State Historic Park is located within walking distance, and the Stanislaus River Arm of New Melones Lake is only a five-mile drive distant. Open year-round.

16. 49er RV RANCH

Reference: **Near Columbia; map E3, grid d6.**

Campsites, facilities: There are 45 sites for trailers and motor homes, all with full hookups. Piped water, picnic tables and barbecues are provided. Restrooms, hot showers, a laundromat, a store, a sanitary dump station, cable TV, propane gas and a large barn for group or club activities are available. Pets are allowed on leashes.

Reservations, fee: Reservations accepted; $21.50 fee per night. Group rates are available.

Who to contact: Phone (209) 532-4978.

Location: From Sonora, turn north on Highway 49 and drive east for 2.5 miles to Parrots Ferry Road. Turn right and drive 1.7 miles to Columbia Street. Turn right and drive 0.4 miles to Pacific. Turn left and drive one block to Italian Bar Road. Turn right and drive a half-mile to the campground on the right.

Trip note: This historic ranch/campground was originally built in 1852 as a dairy farm. Several original barns are still standing. The place has been brought up to date, of course, with a small store on the property providing last-minute supplies. Location is a plus, with the Columbia State Historic Park only a half-mile away, and the Stanislaus River arm of New Melones Reservoir within a five-minute drive. The elevation is 2,100 feet. Open year-round.

17. RIVER RANCH CAMPGROUND

Reference: **On Tuolumne River; map E3, grid d9.**

Campsites, facilities: There are 55 sites for tents or motor homes. Piped water, fire grills and picnic tables are provided. Restrooms and showers are available. A grocery store, a laundromat and propane gas are nearby. Pets are allowed on leashes.

Reservations, fee: Reservations accepted; $14 fee per night.

Who to contact: Phone (209) 928-3708.

Location: From Sonora, drive east on Highway 108 for three miles to Tuolumne Road. Bear right and drive a quarter-mile to another fork (Buchanan Mine Road). Bear left on Buchanan Mine Road and drive eight miles (the road becomes Cottonwood Creek Road) to the campground on the right side of the road.

Trip note: This is a pretty spot set at 2,700 feet, right where conifers begin to take over from the valley foothill grasslands. The campground is set near where Basin Creek enters the Tuolumne River, adding a peaceful element for campers, as well as a chance for trout fishing. Open March through November.

18. SUGARPINE RV PARK

Reference: **In Twain Harte; map E3, grid d9.**

Campsites, facilities: There are 17 tent sites and 65 sites with full hookups for motor homes. Piped water and picnic tables are provided. Restrooms, showers, a playground, a swimming pool, miniature golf, a laundromat and a store are available. Pets are allowed on leashes.

Reservations, fee: Reservations accepted; $12-$22 fee per night.

Who to contact: Phone (209) 586-4631.

Location: From Sonora, drive east on Highway 108 for 14 miles to the park on the right side of the road.

Trip note: Twain Harte is a beautiful little town, located right at the edge of the snow line in winter, and right where pines take over the alpine landscape. This park is set at the threshold of the mountain country, with Pinecrest, Dodge Ridge, and Beardsley Reservoir nearby. Note: Heading east out of Twain Harte, beware of the unannounced horseshoe turn at the town of Confidence. Some drivers are surprised by the turn and cross over into oncoming traffic.

19. WOODWARD RESERVOIR COUNTY PARK

Reference: **Map E3, grid e0.**

Campsites, facilities: There are 155 sites for tents or motor homes. Piped water, fire grills and picnic tables are provided. Flush toilets, showers, a sanitary disposal station, groceries, propane gas, boat ramps, mooring, boat rentals, dry boat storage, bait and fishing licenses are available. Pets are allowed on leashes.

Reservations, fee: No reservations; $12-$16 fee per night; $2 pet fee.

Who to contact: Phone the park at (209) 847-3304 or (209) 525-4107.

Location: From Manteca, drive east on Highway 120 for 20 miles to Oakdale and the junction with County Road J14 (26 Mile Road). Turn left (north) and drive five miles to 14528 26 Mile Road at Woodward Reservoir.

Trip note: Woodward Reservoir is a large lake covering 2,900 acres with 23 miles of shoreline, set in the rolling foothills just north of Oakdale. It is a good lake for both waterskiing and bass fishing, with minimal conflict between the two sports. That is because two large coves on the south and east ends of the lake, as well as the area behind Whale Island, are for low-speed boats only. That makes for good fishing, while the speedboats have the main lake body to let 'er rip. Open year-round.

20. LAKE TULLOCH RV CAMP & MARINA

Reference: On south shore of Lake Tulloch, map E3, grid e4.

Campsites, facilities: There are 130 sites for tents or motor homes. Piped water, fire rings and picnic tables are provided. Many sites have full hookups. An additional large area is available for lakefront tent camping and self-contained unit camping. Flush toilets, hot showers, a laundromat, a store, propane gas, a boat launch and boat ramp are provided. Many facilities are **wheelchair accessible.** Group sites and rates are available. Pets are allowed on leashes.

Reservations, fee: Reservations accepted; $15-$25 fee per night.

Who to contact: Lake Tulloch RV Camp and Marina, 14448 Tulloch Dam Road, Jamestown, CA 95327; (209) 881-0107.

Location: From Manteca, drive east on Highway 120 and drive about 35 miles to Tulloch Road on the left. Turn left and drive 4.6 miles to the campground entrance at the south shore of Lake Tulloch.

Trip note: Unlike so many reservoirs in the foothill country, this one is nearly always full of water. In addition, it is one of the rare places where fishermen and waterskiers live in harmony. That is due to the many coves and a six-mile-long arm with an enforced five-mile-per-hour speed limit. It's a big lake, shaped like a giant "X" with extended lake arms adding up to 55 miles of shoreline. The campground features mature oak trees which provide shade to most of the developed sites. A secret at Tulloch is that fishing is also good for crawdads. Open year-round.

21. KNIGHTS FERRY RESORT

Reference: On Stanislaus River; map E3, grid f2.

Campsites, facilities: There are 21 sites for tents or motor homes. A community fire grill, restrooms, showers and a restaurant are available. Pets are permitted on leashes.

Reservations, fee: Reservations accepted with deposit; $20-$23 fee per night; $3 pet fee. There is a two-night minimum on weekends and holidays.

Who to contact: Phone the park at (209) 881-3349.

Location: From Manteca, drive east on Highway 120 for about 35 miles to Knights Ferry and Kennedy Road. Turn left (north) and drive to a bridge; cross the bridge and continue a short distance to Sonora Road/Main Street. Turn left and drive to the Knights Ferry Restaurant, set at the entrance to the campground.

Trip note: This is a privately-run resort located in the small historic town of Knights Ferry. Side trips include tours of the covered bridge, "the longest west of the Mississippi," and several historic buildings and homes, all within walking distance of the park. River access and hiking trails are available at the east end of town. Raft and canoe rentals are also nearby.

22. MOCCASIN POINT

Reference: **At Don Pedro Reservoir; map E3, grid f6.**

Campsites, facilities: There are 65 sites for tents and 15 sites for motor homes with full hookups. Picnic tables and barbecue units are provided at all sites. Piped water, restrooms, showers, a store, a sanitary dump station, propane gas, ice, a snack bar, a boat ramp, motorboat and houseboat rentals, fuel, moorings, and bait and tackle are available. No pets are permitted.

Reservations, fee: Reservations accepted; $14-$18 fee per night.

Who to contact: Phone (209) 852-2396.

Location: From Manteca, drive east on Highway 120 for 30 miles to the Highway 120/Yosemite exit. Bear right on Highway 120 and drive five miles to Chinese Camp and the junction with Highway 49. Turn right on Highway 49/120 and drive six miles (just beyond the Quartz Mountain/Jamestown turnoff on the left) to the campground on the left side of the road.

Trip note: This camp is at the north end of Don Pedro Reservoir, with a boat ramp set adjacent to the campground. Moccasin Point juts out well into the lake, directly across from where the major Tuolumne River arm enters the lake. Don Pedro is a giant lake, nearly 13,000 surface acres and 160 miles of shoreline, but is subject to drawdowns from midsummer through early fall. At different times, fishing is excellent for salmon, trout or bass. Houseboating and boat-in camping (bring a sun screen) provide options. Open year-round.

---

23. BIG BEAR PARK

Reference: **On Tuolumne River near Modesto; map E3, grid g1.**

Campsites, facilities: There are 96 sites for tents and 116 motor home sites, most with full hookups. Piped water, restrooms, showers, a sanitary disposal station, a laundromat, propane, ice, a small store, three clubhouses and a playground are available. A miniature train ride and a water slide are available from May to September. Pets are allowed on leashes (RV section only).

Reservations, fee: Reservations accepted; $17-$21 fee per night.

Who to contact: Phone the park at (209) 874-1984.

Location: From Modesto, drive east on Highway 132 for 12 miles to the town of Waterford (where the road becomes Yosemite Boulevard) and drive to the park at 13400 Yosemite Boulevard.

Trip note: Big Bear Park is set at 2,500 feet in the foothill country east of Modesto. The park welcomes families with young children. The Tuolumne River runs right alongside the campground. Nearby side trips include Modesto Reservoir, Turlock Lake and Don Pedro Reservoir. Open year-round.

---

24. MODESTO RESERVOIR REGIONAL PARK

Reference: **Map E3, grid g2.**

Campsites, facilities: There are 100 sites for tents or motor homes, with partial hookups. Piped water, fire grills and picnic tables are provided. Flush toilets, a dump station, showers, two boat ramps, waterskiing, fishing, a marina and a store are available. Propane gas is available nearby. No pets allowed.

Reservations, fee: No reservations; $12-$16 fee per night.
Who to contact: Phone the park at (209) 874-9540.
Location: From Modesto, drive east on Highway 132 for 16 miles past Waterford to Reservoir Road. Turn left (north) and drive to the campground at 18139 Reservoir Road at Modesto Reservoir.
Trip note: Modesto Reservoir is not well known, but it is a surprisingly big lake, at 2,700 acres with 31 miles shoreline, set in the hot foothill country. Waterskiing is excellent here in the main lake body. Fishermen head to the southern shore of the lake, which is loaded with submerged trees and coves, and is also protected by a five-mile-per-hour speed limit. Fishing for bass is good, though the fish are often small. Open year-round.

25. FLEMING MEADOWS

Reference: **On Don Pedro Reservoir; map E3, grid g4.**
Campsites, facilities: There are 152 sites for tents or motor homes and 89 motor home sites with full hookups. Picnic tables are provided. Restrooms, showers, and a sanitary dump station are available. A laundromat, a store, ice, a snack bar, a restaurant, tackle and bait, motorboat and houseboat rentals, a boat ramp, berths, engine repairs and propane gas are nearby. No pets are permitted.
Reservations, fee: Reservations accepted; $14-$18 fee per night.
Who to contact: Phone (209) 852-2396.
Location: From Modesto, drive east on Highway 132 to La Grange and County Road J59 (La Grange Road). Turn left (north) and drive five miles to Bonds Flat Road. Turn right and drive two miles to the campground.
Trip note: Fleming Meadows is set near the shore of Don Pedro Lake at its extreme south end, just east of the dam. A boat ramp is available nearby, on the southeast side of the dam. This is a big camp, at the foot of a giant lake, where hot weather, warm water, waterskiing and bass fishing make for weekend vacations. Don Pedro has many extended lake arms, providing 160 miles of shoreline and nearly 13,000 surface acres when full. Open year-round.

26. BLUE OAKS

Reference: **At Don Pedro Reservoir; map E3, grid g4.**
Campsites, facilities: There are 197 sites for tents and motor homes. Piped water, picnic tables and barbecue units are provided. Flush toilets, showers and a sanitary disposal station are available. A grocery store, a laundromat, a boat ramp and propane gas are located nearby. No pets are permitted.
Reservations, fee: Reservations accepted; $14 fee per night.
Who to contact: Phone (209) 852-2396.
Location: From Modesto, drive east on Highway 132 to La Grange and County Road J59 (La Grange Road). Turn left (north) and drive five miles to Bonds Flat Road. Turn right and drive one mile to the campground.
Trip note: Blue Oaks Camp is located between the dam at Don Pedro Reservoir and Fleming Meadows Camp. The nearby boat ramp to the east is a big plus here. See the trip note for Fleming Meadows and Moccasin Point.

27. HORSESHOE BEND RECREATION AREA

Reference: **On Lake McClure; map E3, grid g7.**
Campsites, facilities: There are 110 sites for tents or motor homes, 35 with partial

hookups. Picnic tables are provided. Restrooms, showers, a sanitary disposal station and a boat ramp are available. Nearby are a grocery store and a laundromat. Pets are permitted on leashes.

Reservations, fee: Reservations required; $12-$16 fee per night; $2 pet fee.

Who to contact: Phone (800) 468-8889 (209) 378-2521.

Location: From Modesto, drive east on Highway 132 for 31 miles to La Grange, then continue for about 17 miles (toward Coulterville) to the north end of Lake McClure to the campground entrance road on the right side of the road. Turn right and drive a half-mile to the campground.

Trip note: Lake McClure is a unique, horseshoe-shaped lake in the foothill country west of Yosemite. It adjoins smaller Lake McSwain, connected by the Merced River. McClure is shaped like a giant "H," with its lake arms providing 81 miles of shoreline, warm water for waterskiing, and fishing for bass (on the left half of the "H" near Cotton Creek) and for trout (on the right half of the "H"). There is a boat launch adjacent to the campground. It's one of four lakes in the immediate area; the others are Don Pedro Reservoir to the north and Modesto Reservoir and Turlock Lake to the west. The elevation is 900 feet. The camp and marina are open year-round.

---

28. THE PINES

RV 4

Reference: **In Stanislaus National Forest; map E3, grid g9.**

Campsites, facilities: There are 12 sites for tents or motor homes up to 22 feet long. Piped water (May through October only), picnic tables and fire grills are provided. Vault toilets are available. A grocery store is nearby. Pets are allowed on leashes.

Reservations, fee: No reservations; $9 fee per night; $35 group fee.

Who to contact: Phone the Stanislaus National Forest Groveland Ranger District at (209) 962-7825.

Location: From Groveland, drive east on Highway 120 for eight miles (about a mile past the County Road J20 turnoff) to the signed campground entrance road on the right. Turn right (south) onto the campground entrance road and drive a short distance to the camp.

Trip note: The Pines Camp is set at 3,200 feet in elevation on the western edge of Stanislaus National Forest, only a half-mile from the Buck Meadows ranger station, about five miles from the Tuolumne River (see Lumsden Campground, Chapter E4). A Forest Service road is routed south of camp for two miles, climbing to Smith Peak Lookout (3,877 feet), providing sweeping views to the west of the San Joaquin Valley foothills. Open year-round.

---

29. MOORE CREEK GROUP CAMP

Reference: **In Stanislaus National Forest; map E3, grid g9.**

Campsites, facilities: There is one group campsite. Vault toilets and fire grills are provided. There is **no piped water,** so bring your own.

Reservations, fees: Reservations required; call for fees.

Who to contact: Phone Groveland Ranger District at (209) 962-7825.

Location: From Groveland, drive east on Highway 120 about 12 miles to Forest Road 2S95. Turn right (south) and drive 1.5 miles to the campground on the right.

Trip note: This group camp is set at 2,800 feet, just past where the Sierra alpine zone takes over from foothill oak woodlands. It is set near the access route (Highway 120) to the Crane Flat entrance station to Yosemite National Park.

30. TURLOCK LAKE ST. RECREATION AREA

Reference: **Map E3, grid h3.**

Campsites, facilities: There are 62 sites for tents or motor homes up to 27 feet long. Piped water, fire grills and picnic tables are provided. Flush toilets, showers, a boat ramp, moorings, ice, a grocery store, a bait shop and a snack bar are available. The boat facilities, grocery store, and snack bar are **wheelchair accessible**. Pets are allowed on leashes.

Reservations, fee: Reserve by phoning Destinet at (800) 444-7275 ($6.75 Destinet fee); $14-$16 fee per night.

Who to contact: Phone the park at (209) 874-2008, (209) 874-2056, or (209) 826-1195.

Location: From Modesto, drive east on Highway 132 for 11 miles to Waterford. Continue east on Highway 132 for eight miles to Roberts Ferry Road. Turn right (south) on Roberts Ferry Road and drive one mile to Lake Road. Turn left (east) on Lake Road and drive three miles to the park.

Trip note: Turlock Lake heats up like a big bathtub in the summer, making it ideal for boating and all water sports. It covers 3,500 acres with 26 miles of shoreline. A boat ramp and small marina are available near the camp, making it ideal for boaters/campers. Bass fishing is fair in the summer. In the late winter and spring, the surprise here is that the water is quite cold, being fed by snowmelt from the Tuolumne River, providing a once-a-year chance for trout fishing. By early summer, forget trout and think bass. If they don't bite, just give up and literally jump in the lake.

31. BARRETT COVE RECREATION AREA

Reference: **On Lake McClure; map E3, grid h6.**

Campsites, facilities: There are 275 sites for tents or motor homes. Piped water, electrical connections and sewer hookups are provided at some sites. Picnic tables are provided. Restrooms, showers, boat ramps, a dump station, a swimming lagoon and a playground are available. Nearby are a grocery store, a laundromat, boat and houseboat rentals and propane gas. Pets are permitted on leashes.

Reservations, fee: Reservations required; $12-$16 fee per night; $2 pet fee.

Who to contact: Phone (800) 468-8889 or (209) 378-2521.

Location: From Modesto, drive east on Highway 132 for 31 miles to La Grange, then continue for about 11 miles (toward Coulterville) to Merced Falls Road. Turn right and drive three miles to the campground entrance on the left. Turn left and drive one mile to the campground on the left side of the road.

Trip note: Lake McClure is shaped like a giant "H," with its lake arms providing 81 miles of shoreline. This camp is set on the left side of the "H," that is, on the western shore, within a park that provides a good boat ramp. This is the largest in a series of camps on Lake McClure. See Horseshoe Bend and McClure Point. Open year-round.

32. McCLURE POINT RECREATION AREA

Reference: On Lake McClure; map E3, grid h6.

Campsites, facilities: There are 100 sites for tents or motor homes up to 40 feet long. Piped water and electrical connections are provided at many sites. Picnic tables are provided. Restrooms, showers, a boat ramp, and a laundromat are available. A grocery store is nearby. Pets are permitted on leashes.

Reservations, fee: Reservations required; $12-$16 fee per night; $2 pet fee.

Who to contact: Phone (800) 468-8889 or (209) 378-2521.

Location: From Turlock, drive east on County Road J17 for 19 miles to the junction with Highway 59. Continue east on Highway 59/County Road J17 for 4.5 miles to Snelling, and bear right at Lake McClure Road. Drive seven miles to Lake McSwain Dam, and continue for seven miles to the campground at the end of the road.

Trip note: McClure Point Camp is the choice location for campers/boaters coming from the Turlock or Merced areas. It is a well-developed campground with an excellent boat ramp that provides access to the main lake area of Lake McClure. This is the best spot on the lake for waterskiing. The camp and marina are open year-round.

33. BAGBY RECREATION AREA

Reference: On upper Lake McClure; map E3, grid h8.

Campsites, facilities: There are 25 tent sites. Piped water, flush toilets, a small store and a boat ramp are available. Pets are permitted on leashes.

Reservations, fee: Reservations required; $12 fee per night; $2 pet fee.

Who to contact: Phone (800) 468-8889 or (209) 378-2521.

Location: From Modesto, drive east on Highway 132 for 31 miles to La Grange, then continue for 20 miles to Coulterville and the junction with Highway 49. Turn right (south) on Highway 49 and drive about 12 miles, cross the bridge and look for the campground entrance on the left side of the road. Turn left and drive a quarter-mile to the campground.

Trip note: This is the most distant and secluded camp on Lake McClure. It is set near where the Merced River enters the lake, way up adjacent to the Highway 49 Bridge, nearly an hour's drive from the dam. Trout fishing is good in the area, and it makes sense; when the lake heats up in summer, the trout naturally congregate near the cool incoming flows of the Merced River. Open year-round.

34. LAKE McSWAIN RECREATION AREA

Reference: Near McSwain Dam on Merced River; map E3, grid i6.

Campsites, facilities: There are 112 sites for tents or motor homes up to 40 feet long. Piped water, electrical connections and sewage disposal are provided. Picnic tables are provided. Restrooms, showers, a boat ramp, boat rentals, a laundromat, a playground and a dump station are available. A grocery store, boat rentals and propane gas are nearby. Pets are permitted on leashes.

Reservations, fee: Reservations required; $12-$16 fee per night; $2 pet fee.

Who to contact: Phone (800) 468-8889 or (209) 378-2521.

Location: From Turlock, drive east on County Road J17 for 19 miles to the junction with Highway 59. Continue east on Highway 59/County Road J17 for 4.5 miles to Snelling, and bear right at Lake McClure Road. Drive seven miles to the campground turnoff on the right.

Trip note: Lake McSwain is actually the afterbay for adjacent Lake McClure, with this camp located near the McSwain Dam on the Merced River. If you have a canoe or car-top boat, this lake is preferable to Lake McClure because waterskiing is not allowed. In terms of size, McSwain is like a puddle compared to the giant McClure, but unlike McClure, the water levels are kept up almost year-round at McSwain. The water is cold here and trout stocks are good in the spring. Open March to mid-October.

---

35. McCONNELL STATE RECREATION AREA 🚐 ⑥

Reference: **On Merced River; map E3, grid j1.**

Campsites, facilities: There are 17 sites for tents or motor homes up to 24 feet long and one group site for tents only. Piped water, fire grills, and picnic tables are provided. Flush toilets and hot showers are available. Supplies can be obtained in Delhi. Pets are allowed on leashes.

Reservations, fee: Phone for group reservations and fees; $12-$16 fee per night for family sites; $1 pet fee.

Who to contact: Phone the Four Rivers District Office at (209) 826-1196.

Location: From Modesto or Merced, drive on Highway 99 to Delhi and the El Capitan Way exit (well signed). Turn east on El Capitan Way and drive five miles to Pepper Street. Turn right and drive to the park.

Trip note: The weather gets scorching hot around these parts in the summer months, and a lot of out-of-towners would pay a bunch for a little shade and a river to sit next to. That's what this park provides, with the Merced River flowing past, along with occasional mermaids on the beach. In high-water years, the Merced River attracts salmon (in the fall). Open March through September.

MAP E4

NOR-CAL MAP .... see page 94
adjoining maps
NORTH (D4) .... see page 390
EAST (E5) .... see page 500
SOUTH (F4) .... see page 538
WEST (E3) .... see page 444

89 LISTINGS
PAGES 460-499

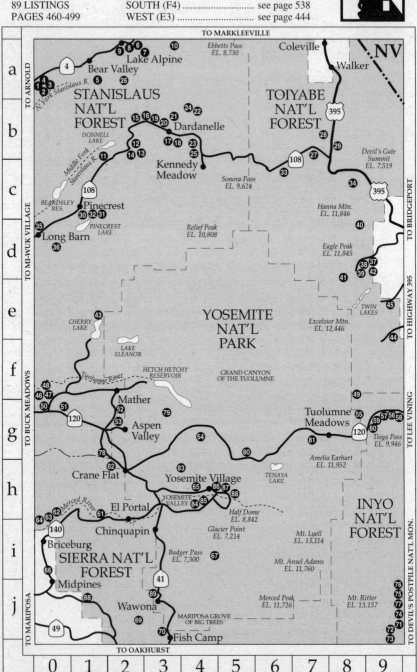

TO MARKLEEVILLE

NV

Coleville

Walker

TO ARNOLD

4

Bear Valley

Lake Alpine

Ebbetts Pass
EL. 8,730

STANISLAUS
NAT'L
FOREST

N. Fork Stanislaus R.

TOIYABE
NAT'L
FOREST

395

Dardanelle

DONNELL
LAKE

Middle Fork
Stanislaus R.

Kennedy
Meadow

28

29

Devil's Gate
Summit
EL. 7,519

108

27

TO BRIDGEPORT

108

Pinecrest

Sonora Pass
EL. 9,624

33

34

395

TO MI-WUK VILLAGE

BEARDSLEY
RES.

PINECREST
LAKE

Long Barn

Relief Peak
EL. 10,808

Hanna Mtn.
EL. 11,846

40

Eagle Peak
EL. 11,845

TWIN
LAKES

45

CHERRY
LAKE

YOSEMITE
NAT'L
PARK

Excelsior Mtn.
EL. 12,446

TO HIGHWAY 395

LAKE
ELEANOR

HETCH HETCHY
RESERVOIR

GRAND CANYON
OF THE TUOLUMNE

TO BUCK MEADOWS

Tuolumne River

Mather

120

Aspen
Valley

Tuolumne
Meadows

120

Tioga Pass
EL. 9,946

TO LEE VINING

Amelia Earhart
EL. 11,952

Crane Flat

Yosemite Village

YOSEMITE
VALLEY

TENAYA
LAKE

INYO
NAT'L
FOREST

El Portal

Merced R. iver

Half Dome
EL. 8,842

Glacier Point
EL. 7,214

Mt. Lyell
EL. 13,114

Chinquapin

140

Briceburg

Badger Pass
EL. 7,300

Mt. Ansel Adams
EL. 11,760

TO DEVIL'S POSTPILE NAT'L MON.

SIERRA NAT'L
FOREST

Midpines

TO MARIPOSA

41

Wawona

MARIPOSA GROVE
OF BIG TREES

Merced Peak
EL. 11,726

Mt. Ritter
EL. 13,157

Fish Camp

TO OAKHURST

Map E4 featuring: Stanislaus National Forest, Stanislaus River, Lake Alpine, Donnells Reservoir, Middle Fork Stanislaus River, Walker River, Toiyabe National Forest, Pinecrest Lake, Twin Lakes, Cherry Lake, Tuolumne River, Inyo National Forest, Yosemite National Park, Tenaya Lake, Merced River, Sierra National Forest, San Joaquin River

1. BIG MEADOWS GROUP CAMP

Reference: **In Stanislaus National Forest; map E4, grid a0.**

Campsites, facilities: There is one group campsite for tents or motor homes. Piped water, picnic tables and fire grills are provided. Vault toilets are available. Groceries, a laundromat and propane gas are nearby. Pets are permitted on leashes.

Reservations, fee: Reserve by phoning (800) 280-CAMP ($15 reservation fee); $25 fee per group per night or $1 per person.

Who to contact: Phone the Stanislaus National Forest Calaveras Ranger District at (209) 795-1381.

Location: From Angels Camp on Highway 49, turn east on Highway 4 and drive about 30 miles (three miles past Ganns Meadows) to the campground on the right.

Trip note: Big Meadows Group Camp is set at 6,500 feet on the western slopes of the Sierra Nevada. There are a number of recreation attractions nearby, the most prominent being the North Fork Stanislaus River two miles to the south in national forest (see Sand Flat Campground), with access available from a four-wheel-drive road just east of camp, or on Spicer Reservoir Road (see Stanislaus River Campground). Lake Alpine, a pretty, popular lake with trout fishing, is located nine miles east on Highway 4. Open May to October.

2. SAND FLAT

Reference: **On Stanislaus River in Stanislaus National Forest; map E4, grid a0.**

Campsites, facilities: There are four tent sites. Fire grills, picnic tables and vault toilets are available. There is **no piped water**, so bring your own. Pets are permitted on leashes.

Reservations, fee: No reservations; no fee; campfire permits are required (free).

Who to contact: Phone the Stanislaus National Forest Calaveras Ranger District at (209) 795-1381.

Location: From Angels Camp on Highway 49, turn east on Highway 4 and drive about 30 miles (3.5 miles past Ganns Meadows) and continue a half-mile past Big Meadows Group Camp to a dirt/gravel road on the right. Turn right and drive two miles on a steep, unimproved road (four-wheel drive required).

Trip note: This one is for four-wheel-drive cowboys who want to carve out a piece of the Sierra Nevada wildlands for themselves. It is set on the North Fork Stanislaus River, 5,900 feet, where there is decent fishing for small trout, with the fish often holding right where white water runs into pools. This is a tiny, primitive camp where you won't get bugged by anyone, and is named for the extensive sandy flat on the south side of the river. Open June to September.

3. STANISLAUS RIVER 🐟

Reference: **In Stanislaus National Forest; map E4, grid a0.**

Campsites, facilities: There are 25 sites for tents or motor homes up to 16 feet long. Fire grills and picnic tables are provided. Piped water and vault toilets are available. Pets are permitted on leashes. Tamarack has supplies.

Reservations, fee: No reservations; $5 fee per night.

Who to contact: Phone the Stanislaus National Forest Calaveras Ranger District at (209) 795-1381.

Location: From Angels Camp on Highway 49, turn east on Highway 4 and drive about 32 miles (five miles past Ganns Meadows) to Spicer Reservoir Road on the right. Turn right (south) and drive four miles to the campground on the right side of the road.

Trip note: As you might figure from its name, this camp provides excellent access to the adjacent North Fork Stanislaus River, but it is also the closest drive-in campground to Utica Reservoir, Union Reservoir and Spicer Meadow Reservoir, all located within seven miles to the east. Of the three, Spicer Meadow has the best trout fishing. The elevation is 6,200 feet, with timbered sites and the river just south of camp. Open June to October.

4. BIG MEADOW 🚶

Reference: **Near Stanislaus River in Stanislaus National Forest; map E4, grid a0.**

Campsites, facilities: There are 65 sites for tents or motor homes. Piped water, fire grills and picnic tables are provided and vault toilets are available. Groceries, a laundromat and propane gas are nearby. Pets are permitted.

Reservations, fee: Reserve by phoning (800) 280-CAMP ($7.50 reservation fee); $8 fee per night.

Who to contact: Phone the Stanislaus National Forest Calaveras Ranger District at (209) 795-1381.

Location: From Angels Camp on Highway 49, turn east on Highway 4 and drive about 30 miles (three miles past Ganns Meadows) to the campground on the right.

Trip note: Big Meadows Camp is set at 6,500 feet and features a number of nearby recreation options. The most prominent is North Fork Stanislaus River, with access available at Sand Flat and Stanislaus River campgrounds. In addition, Lake Alpine is located nine miles to the east, and three mountain reservoirs, Spicer Meadow, Utica and Union, are all within a 15-minute drive. Open June through October.

5. UNION RESERVOIR WALK-IN 🐟 ⚓ 🚶

Reference: **Northeast of Arnold in Stanislaus National Forest; map E4, grid a1.**

Campsites, facilities: There are 15 primitive walk-in tent sites. A restroom is available, along with a signboard explaining lake rules and camp policies. A boat ramp is available nearby.

Reservations, fee: No reservations; no fee.

Who to contact: Phone Calaveras Ranger District at (209) 795-1381. For a map, send $3 to Office of Information, U.S. Forest Service, 630 Sansome Street, San Francisco, CA 94111, and ask for Stanislaus National Forest.

Location: From Angels Camp, drive east on Highway 4 for about 32 miles to

Spicer Reservoir Road. Turn right and travel east for about seven miles to Forest Service Road 7N75. Turn left and drive three miles to Union Reservoir. There are four designated parking areas for the walk-in camps along the road here.

Trip note: Union Reservoir is set in Sierra granite at 6,850 feet, a beautiful and quiet lake that is kept that way with rules that mandate a five-mile-per-hour speed limit and walk-in camping only, with most of the sites providing lakeside views. Fishing is often good, but you need a boat, trolling for kokanee salmon. The setting is great, especially for canoes or other small boats. This camp is not well known, and those who visit usually keep quiet so everybody can enjoy a pristine experience.

6. PINE MARTEN

Reference: Near Lake Alpine in Stanislaus National Forest; map E4, grid a2.

Campsites, facilities: There are 33 sites for tents or motor homes up to 22 feet long. Piped water, flush toilets, picnic tables and fire grills are provided. A boat ramp is available. A grocery store, propane gas and a laundromat are nearby. Pets are permitted on leashes.

Reservations, fee: No reservations; $11.50 fee per night.

Who to contact: Phone the Stanislaus National Forest Calaveras Ranger District at (209) 795-1381.

Location: From Angels Camp, drive east on Highway 4 to Arnold and continue for 29 miles to Lake Alpine. Drive to the northeast end of the lake to the campground entrance on the right side of the road.

Trip note: Lake Alpine is a beautiful Sierra lake set at 7,320 feet, surrounded by granite and pines, located just above where the snowplows stop in winter. This camp is set on the northeast side, about a quarter-mile away from the lake's shore. Fishing for rainbow trout is good in May and early June, prior to the summer crush; despite the long drive to get here, this lake is getting well known for its beauty, camping and hiking. A trailhead is available out of nearby Silver Valley Camp that provides a two-mile hike to pretty Duck Lake and beyond into the Carson-Iceberg Wilderness. Open June to mid-October.

7. SILVER VALLEY

Reference: On Lake Alpine in Stanislaus National Forest; map E4, grid a2.

Campsites, facilities: There are 25 sites for tents or motor homes up to 22 feet long. Piped water, flush toilets, picnic tables and fire grills are provided. A boat launch is available. Facilities are **wheelchair accessible**. A grocery store, propane gas and a laundromat are nearby. Pets are permitted on leashes.

Reservations, fee: No reservations; $11.50 fee per night.

Who to contact: Phone the Stanislaus National Forest Calaveras Ranger District at (209) 795-1381.

Location: From Angels Camp, drive east on Highway 4 to Arnold and continue for 29 miles to Lake Alpine. Drive to the northeast end of the lake to the campground entrance on the right side of the road. Turn right and drive a half-mile to the campground.

Trip note: This is one of four camps at Lake Alpine. Silver Valley is set at the northeast end of the lake, 7,400 feet in elevation, with a trailhead nearby that provides access to the Carson-Iceberg Wilderness. For recreation information, see trip note for Pine Marten Camp. Open June through mid-October.

8. ALPINE CAMPGROUND

RV

Reference: **On Lake Alpine in Stanislaus National Forest; map E4, grid a2.**

Campsites, facilities: There are five tent sites and 22 sites for motor homes up to 22 feet long. Piped water, flush and vault toilets, showers, picnic tables, fire grills and a boat launch are provided. A grocery store, propane gas and a laundromat are nearby. Pets are permitted on leashes. The facilities are **wheelchair accessible**.

Reservations, fee: No reservations; $11.50 fee per night.

Who to contact: Phone the Stanislaus National Forest Calaveras Ranger District at (209) 795-1381.

Location: From Angels Camp, drive east on Highway 4 to Arnold and continue for 29 miles to Lake Alpine. Just before reaching the lake, turn right and drive a quarter-mile to the campground on the left.

Trip note: This is the campground that is in the greatest demand at Lake Alpine, and it is easy to see why. It is very small, the boat ramp is located adjacent to the camp, you can get supplies at a small grocery store within walking distance, and during the evening rise, you can often see the jumping trout from your campsite. Lake Alpine is one of the prettiest lakes you can drive to, set at 7,320 feet amid pines and Sierra granite. A trailhead is available out of nearby Silver Valley Camp that provides a two-mile hike to pretty Duck Lake and beyond into the Carson-Iceberg Wilderness. Open June through October.

9. SILVER TIP

RV

Reference: **Near Lake Alpine in Stanislaus National Forest; map E4, grid a2.**

Campsites, facilities: There are 24 sites for tents or motor homes up to 22 feet long. Piped water, flush toilets, picnic tables and fire grills are provided. A boat launch is about a mile away. A grocery store, propane gas and a laundromat are nearby. Pets are permitted on leashes.

Reservations, fee: No reservations; $11.50 fee per night.

Who to contact: Phone the Stanislaus National Forest Calaveras Ranger District at (209) 795-1381.

Location: From Angels Camp, drive east on Highway 4 to Arnold and continue for 29 miles to Lake Alpine. One mile before reaching the lake (adjacent to the Bear Valley/Mt. Reba turnoff), turn right at the campground entrance on the right side of the road.

Trip note: This camp is set about two miles from the shore of Lake Alpine. Why then would anyone camp here when there are campgrounds right at the lake? Two reasons. One, those lakeside camps often fill on summer weekends. Two, Highway 4 is snowplowed to this campground entrance, but not beyond. So in big snow years when the road is still closed in late spring and early summer, you can park your rig here to camp, then hike in to the lake. See the trip note for Alpine Campground.

10. UPPER & LOWER HIGHLAND LAKES

Reference: **In Stanislaus National Forest; map E4, grid a3.**

Campsites, facilities: There are a total of 35 sites for tents or motor homes. Piped water, vault toilets, picnic tables and fire rings are provided.

Reservations, fee: No reservations; $5 fee per night. Pets are allowed on leashes.

Who to contact: Phone the Stanislaus National Forest Calaveras Ranger District at (209) 795-1381.

Location: From Angels Camp, drive east on Highway 4 to Arnold, past Lake Alpine and continue for 14.5 miles to Forest Service Road 8N01 (one mile west of Ebbetts Pass). Turn right (south) and drive 7.5 miles to the campground on the right side of the road. Trailers are not recommended.

Trip note: This camp is set between Upper and Lower Highland Lakes, two beautiful alpine ponds that offer good fishing for small brook trout as well as spectacular panoramic views. Hiram Peak (9,760 feet), looms to the nearby south. A trail that starts at the north end of Highlands Lakes (a parking area is available) is routed east for two miles to Wolf Creek Pass, where it connects with the Pacific Crest Trail; from there, turn left or right, you can't lose.

11. CASCADE CREEK

Reference: **In Stanislaus National Forest; map E4, grid b1.**

Campsites, facilities: There are seven sites for tents or motor homes up to 22 feet long. Picnic tables and vault toilets are provided. There is **no piped water.** Pets are permitted on leashes. Dardanelle has supplies.

Reservations, fee: No reservations; no fee.

Who to contact: Phone the Stanislaus National Forest Summit Ranger District at (209) 965-3434.

Location: From Sonora, drive east on Highway 108 to Strawberry, and continue for eight miles to the campground on the left side of the road.

Trip note: This tiny, rarely-used spot along Cascade Creek is located at 6,000 feet. A Forest Service road, located about a quarter-mile west of camp on the south side of the highway, provides a side-trip drive three miles up to Pikes Peak, at 7,236 feet. Open May through October.

12. NIAGARA CREEK OFF-HIGHWAY-VEHICLE CAMP

Reference: **In Stanislaus National Forest; map E4, grid b2.**

Campsites, facilities: There are 10 sites for tents or motor homes up to 22 feet long. Stoves and picnic tables are provided. Vault toilets are available. There is **no piped water**, so bring your own. (A spring is nearby). Pets are permitted on leashes. Supplies can be purchased in Dardanelle.

Reservations, fee: No reservations; no fee.

Who to contact: Phone the Stanislaus National Forest Summit Ranger District at (209) 965-3434.

Location: From Sonora, drive east on Highway 108 to Strawberry, and continue for about 12 miles to Eagle Meadows Road (Forest Service Road 6N24) on the right. Turn right and drive one mile to the campground on the left.

Trip note: This camp is set beside Niagara Creek at 6,600 feet, high in Stanislaus National Forest on the western slopes of the Sierra. This camp provides direct access to a network of backcountry roads in national forest, including routes to Double Dome Rock and another to Eagle Meadows. So if you have a four-wheel-drive or dirt bike, this is the place to come. Open May through October.

13. NIAGARA CREEK 🐟 🚶   RV 6

Reference: **Near Donnells Reservoir in Stanislaus National Forest; map E4, grid b2.**

Campsites, facilities: There are seven sites for tents or motor homes up to 22 feet long. Stoves and picnic tables are provided. Vault toilets are available. There is **no piped water**, so bring your own. Pets are permitted on leashes. Supplies can be purchased in Dardanelle.

Reservations, fee: No reservations; no fee.

Who to contact: Phone the Stanislaus National Forest Summit Ranger District at (209) 965-3434.

Location: From Sonora, drive east on Highway 108 to Strawberry, and continue for about 12 miles to Eagle Meadows Road (Forest Service Road 6N24) on the right. Turn right and drive one mile to the campground on the left.

Trip note: This small, primitive camp is locted adjacent to the preceding camp, set up primarily for off-road vehicles. Open May through October.

14. MILL CREEK CAMP 🐟 🚶   7

Reference: **In Stanislaus National Forest; map E4, grid c2.**

Campsites, facilities: There are 12 sites for tents or motor homes. Vault toilets and fire grills are provided. There is **no piped water**, so bring your own.

Reservations, fees: No reservations; no fee.

Who to contact: Phone Summit Ranger District at (209) 965-3434.

Location: From Sonora, drive east on Highway 108 to Strawberry. From Strawberry, continue east on Highway 108 about 11.5 miles to the campground on the right.

Trip note: This pretty little camp is set at 6,200 feet in elevation, high in Stanislaus National Forest, near a variety of outdoor recreation. The camp is near the Middle Fork Stanislaus River, which is stocked with trout near Donnells. For hiking, there is an outstanding trailhead at Kennedy Meadows (east of Donnells). For fishing, both Beardsley Reservoir (boat necessary) and Pinecrest Lake (shoreline prospects okay) provide two nearby alternatives.

15. SPICER RESERVOIR 🐟 ⚓ ♿ 🏊   RV 8

Reference: **Near Spicer Reservoir in Stanislaus National Forest; map E4, grid b2.**

Campsites, facilities: There are 60 family sites, two double-family sites, and one triple-family site, all suitable for tents or motor homes. Piped water, vault toilets, a phone, picnic tables and fire grills are provided. Two sites are **wheelchair accessible**. A boat ramp is available nearby. Pets are allowed on leashes.

Reservations; fee: No reservations; $9-$11 fee per night.

Who to contact: Phone the Stanislaus National Forest, Calaveras District Office at (209) 795-1381. For a map, send $3 to Office of Information, U.S. Forest Service, 630 Sansome Street, San Francisco, CA 94111.

Location: From Angels Camp, drive east on Highway 4 for about 32 miles to Spicer Reservoir Road (Forest Service Road 7N01). Turn right and drive seven miles, bear right at a fork with a sharp right turn, and drive one mile to the campground at the west end of the lake.

Trip note: Spicer Meadow Reservoir, set at 6,418 feet, isn't a big lake by reservoir standards, covering 227 acres, but it is quite pretty from a boat, and is surrounded by canyon walls. The beauty is compounded by good trout fishing, sometimes even excellent trout fishing. A boat ramp is available near the campground. A trail has recently been completed that leads around the reservoir. Note that this area can really get hammered with snow in big winters, so in the spring and early summer, always check for access conditions before planning a trip.

16. FENCE CREEK 🛶

RV 4

Reference: **Near the Middle Fork of Stanislaus River in Stanislaus National Forest; map E4, grid b2.**

Campsites, facilities: There are 30 sites for tents or motor homes up to 22 feet long. Fire grills and picnic tables are provided. Pit toilets are available. There is **no piped water**, so bring your own. Pets are permitted on leashes. Supplies can be purchased in Dardanelle.

Reservations, fee: No reservations; no fee.

Who to contact: Phone the Stanislaus National Forest Summit Ranger District at (209) 965-3434.

Location: From Sonora, drive east on Highway 108 past Strawberry and at Donnells Vista, continue three miles to Clark Fork Road. Turn left (north) and drive one mile to the campground entrance on the left side of the road.

Trip note: Fence Creek is a feeder stream to Clark Fork, which runs a mile downstream and joins with the Middle Fork Stanislaus River en route to Donnells Reservoir. The camp sits along little Fence Creek, 6,100 feet elevation. Fence Creek Road continues east for another nine miles to an outstanding trailhead at Iceberg Meadow on the edge of the Carson-Iceberg Wilderness. Open May through October.

17. PIDGEON FLAT 🛶 🥾

7

Reference: **On the Middle Fork Stanislaus River in Stanislaus National Forest; map E4, grid b3.**

Campsites, facilities: There are seven walk-in tent sites. Fire grills and picnic tables are provided and vault toilets are available. There is **no piped water**, so bring your own. Pets are permitted. Supplies can be purchased in Dardanelle.

Reservations, fee: No reservations; $5 fee per night.

Who to contact: Phone the Stanislaus National Forest Summit Ranger District at (209) 65-3434.

Location: From Sonora, drive east on Highway 108 past Strawberry to Dardanelle. At Dardanelle, continue two miles east to the campground on the left side of the road.

Trip note: The prime attraction at Pidgeon Flat is the short trail to Columns of the Giants, a rare example of columnar hexagonal rock, similar to the phenomenon at Devils Postpile near Mammoth Lakes. In addition, the camp is set adjacent to the Middle Fork Stanislaus River; trout are small here and get fished hard. Supplies are available within walking distance in Dardanelle. Elevation is 6,000 feet. Open May through October.

18. EUREKA VALLEY

Reference: **On the Middle Fork of Stanislaus River in Stanislaus National Forest; map E4, grid b3.**

Campsites, facilities: There are 27 sites for tents or motor homes up to 22 feet long. Piped water, stoves and picnic tables are provided. Vault toilets are available. Pets are permitted. Supplies can be purchased in Dardanelle.

Reservations, fee: No reservations; $8 fee per night.

Who to contact: Phone the Stanislaus National Forest Summit Ranger District at (209) 965-3434.

Location: From Sonora, drive east on Highway 108 past Strawberry to Dardanelle. At Dardanelle, continue three miles east to the campground.

Trip note: There are some half-dozen campgrounds on this stretch of the Middle Fork Stanislaus River near Dardanelle, 6,100 feet in elevation. This stretch of river is planted with trout by the Department of Fish and Game, but is hit pretty hard despite its relatively isolated location. A good short and easy hike is to Columns of the Giants, accessible on a quarter-mile long trail out of the Pidgeon Flat Campground one mile to the west. Open May through October.

---

19. BOULDER FLAT

Reference: **Near the Middle Fork of Stanislaus River in Stanislaus National Forest; map E4, grid b3.**

Campsites, facilities: There are 23 sites for tents or motor homes up to 22 feet long. Stoves and picnic tables are provided. Piped water and vault toilets are available. Pets are permitted on leashes. Supplies can be purchased in Dardanelle.

Reservations, fee: No reservations; $8 fee per night.

Who to contact: Phone the Stanislaus National Forest Summit Ranger District at (209) 965-3434.

Location: From Sonora, drive east on Highway 108 past Strawberry to Clark Fork Road. At Clark Fork Road, continue east on Highway 108 for one mile to the campground on the left side of the road.

Trip note: You want camping on the Stanislaus River? Driving east on Highway 108, this is the first in a series of campgrounds along the Middle Fork Stanislaus. Boulder Flat is set at 5,600 feet, with easy access off the highway a bonus, supplies available in nearby Dardanelle, and this stretch of river stocked with trout. Open May through September.

---

20. BRIGHTMAN FLAT

Reference: **On the Middle Fork of Stanislaus River in Stanislaus National Forest; map E4, grid b3.**

Campsites, facilities: There are 30 sites for tents or motor homes up to 22 feet long. Fire grills and picnic tables are provided. Vault toilets are available. There is **no piped water**, so bring your own. Pets are permitted on leashes. Supplies can be purchased in Dardanelle.

Reservations, fee: No reservations; $5 fee per night.

Who to contact: Phone the Stanislaus National Forest Summit Ranger District at (209) 965-3434.

Location: From Sonora, drive east on Highway 108 past Strawberry to Clark Fork Road. At Clark Fork Road, continue east on Highway 108 for two miles to the campground on the left side of the road.

Trip note: This camp is located on the Middle Fork of the Stanislaus River and set at 5,600 feet, one mile east of Boulder Flat Campground and two miles west of Dardanelle. For recreation options, see trip note for Pidgeon Flat. Open May through October.

21. DARDANELLE ↳🐟 📺 7

Reference: **On the Middle Fork of Stanislaus River in Stanislaus National Forest; map E4, grid b3.**

Campsites, facilities: There are 28 sites for tents or motor homes up to 22 feet long. Piped water, fire grills and picnic tables are provided. Vault toilets are available. Pets are permitted on leashes. Supplies can be purchased in Dardanelle.

Reservations, fee: Reserve by phoning (800) 280-CAMP; ($7.50 reservation fee); $10 fee per night for single sites; $15 fee per night for double sites.

Who to contact: Phone the Stanislaus National Forest Summit Ranger District at (209) 965-3434.

Location: From Sonora, drive east on Highway 108 past Strawberry to Dardanelle and the campground on the left side of the road.

Trip note: This Forest Service camp is set within walking distance of supplies in Dardanelle, and is also located right alongside the Middle Fork Stanislaus River. This section of river is stocked with trout by the Department of Fish and Game. The trail to see Columns of the Giants is located 1.5 miles to the east out of Pidgeon Flat Campground. Open May through October.

22. SAND FLAT ↳🐟 🥾 🏊 📺 7

Reference: **On the Clark Fork of Stanislaus River in Stanislaus National Forest; map E4, grid b4.**

Campsites, facilities: There are 53 sites for tents or motor homes. Stoves and picnic tables are provided. Piped water and vault toilets are available. Pets are permitted on leashes. Supplies can be purchased in Dardanelle.

Reservations, fee: No reservations; $5 fee per night.

Who to contact: Phone the Stanislaus National Forest Summit Ranger District at (209) 965-3434.

Location: From Sonora, drive east on Highway 108 past Strawberry and at Donnells Vista, continue three miles to Clark Fork Road. Turn left (north) and drive seven miles to the campground entrance on the right side of the road.

Trip note: Sand Flat campground, at 6,200 feet, is set three miles (by vehicle on Clark Fork Road) from an outstanding trailhead for the Carson-Iceberg Wilderness. This camp is used primarily by late-arriving backpackers, who camp for the night, get their gear in order, then head off on the trail. The trail is routed out of Iceberg Meadow, with a choice of heading north to Paradise Valley (unbelievably green and loaded with corn lilies along a creek) and onward to the Pacific Crest Trail, or east to Clark Fork and upstream to Clark Fork Meadow below Sonora Peak. Two choices, both winners. Open May through September.

23. BAKER ↳🐟 📺 7

Reference: **On the Middle Fork of Stanislaus River in Stanislaus National Forest; map E4, grid b4.**

Campsites, facilities: There are 44 sites for tents or motor homes up to 22 feet long. Piped water, stoves and picnic tables are provided. Vault toilets are available.

Pets are permitted. Supplies can be purchased in Dardanelle.

Reservations, fee: No reservations; $7.50 fee per night.

Who to contact: Phone the Stanislaus National Forest Summit Ranger District at (209) 965-3434.

Location: From Sonora, drive east on Highway 108 past Strawberry to Dardanelle. From Dardanelle, continue five miles east to the campground on the right side of the road at the turnoff for Kennedy Meadows.

Trip note: Baker Camp is set at the turnoff for the well-known and popular Kennedy Meadows trailhead for the Emigrant Wilderness. The camp is set along the Middle Fork Stanislaus River, 6,200 feet elevation, downstream a short ways from the confluence with Deadman Creek. The trailhead, with a nearby horse corral, is located another two miles further on the Kennedy Meadow access road. From here, it is a 1.5-mile hike to a fork in the trail; to the right will take you two miles to Relief Reservoir, 7,226 feet, and to the left will route you up Kennedy Creek for five miles to pretty Kennedy Lake, set just north of Kennedy Peak (10,716 feet). Open May through October.

24. CLARK FORK

Reference: **On the Clark Fork of Stanislaus River in Stanislaus National Forest; map E4, grid b4.**

Campsites, facilities: There are 88 sites for tents or motor homes up to 22 feet long. 12 free sites with facilities for horses are available nearby. Stoves and picnic tables are provided. Piped water, flush or vault toilets and a sanitary disposal station are available. **Wheelchair accessible** sites are available. Pets are permitted on leashes. Supplies can be purchased in Dardanelle.

Reservations, fee: No reservations; $7-$8 fee per night.

Who to contact: Phone the Stanislaus National Forest Summit Ranger District at (209) 965-3434.

Location: From Sonora, drive east on Highway 108 past Strawberry and at Donnells Vista, continue three miles to Clark Fork Road. Turn left (north) and drive six miles to the campground entrance on the right side of the road.

Trip note: Clark Fork Camp is set on Clark Fork of the Stanislaus River, and is used both by drive-in vacationers and backpackers. A trailhead for hikers is located a quarter-mile away on the north side of Clark Fork Road (a parking area is available here). From here, the trail is routed up along Arnot Creek, skirting between Iceberg Peak on the left and Lightning Mountain on the right, for eight miles to Wolf Creek Pass and the junction with the Pacific Crest Trail. For another nearby trailhead, see trip note for nearby Sand Flat Campground. Open May through October.

25. DEADMAN

Reference: **On the Middle Fork of Stanislaus River in Stanislaus National Forest; map E4, grid b4.**

Campsites, facilities: There are 17 sites for tents or motor homes up to 22 feet long. Piped water, stoves and picnic tables are provided. Flush and vault toilets are available. Pets are permitted. Supplies can be purchased in Dardanelle.

Reservations, fee: No reservations; $7.50 fee per night.

Who to contact: Phone the Stanislaus National Forest Summit Ranger District at (209) 965-3434.

Location: From Sonora, drive east on Highway 108 past Strawberry to Dardanelle. From Dardanelle, continue five miles east to the campground on the right side of the road at the turnoff for Kennedy Meadows.

Trip note: This is a popular trailhead camp and an ideal jumpoff point for backpackers heading into the adjacent Emigrant Wilderness. The camp is located a short distance from Baker Camp; see trip note for hiking destinations.

26. SPICER RESERVOIR GROUP CAMP

Reference: Near Spicer Reservoir in Stanislaus National Forest; map E4, grid a2.

Campsites, facilities: There is one group site that can accommodate up to 50 people. Piped water, vault toilets, picnic tables, fire grills, a food preparation area, a primitive amphitheater and a group parking area are provided. A boat ramp is available approximately one mile away. Pets are allowed on leashes.

Reservations, fee: Reservations required; $30-$50 fee per night.

Who to contact: Phone the Stanislaus National Forest, Calaveras District Office at (209) 795-1381. For a map, send $3 to Office of Information, U.S. Forest Service, 630 Sansome Street, San Francisco, CA 94111.

Location: From Angels Camp, drive east on Highway 4 for about 32 miles to Spicer Reservoir Road (Forest Service Road 7N01). Turn right and drive seven miles, bear right at a fork with a sharp right turn, and drive one mile to the campground at the west end of the lake.

Trip note: Spicer Meadow Reservoir, set at 6,418 feet, isn't a big lake by reservoir standards, covering 227 acres, but it is quite pretty from a boat, and is surrounded by canyon walls. The beauty is compounded by good trout fishing. A boat ramp is available near the campground. A trail has recently been completed that leads around the reservoir. Note that this area can really get hammered with snow in big winters, so in the spring and early summer, always check for access conditions before planning a trip.

27. SONORA BRIDGE

Reference: Near Walker River in Toiyabe National Forest; map E4, grid b7.

Campsites, facilities: There are 23 sites for tents or motor homes up to 30 feet long. Piped water, fire grills and picnic tables are provided. Vault toilets are available. Pets are permitted on leashes.

Reservations, fee: Reserve by phoning (800) 280-CAMP; ($7.50 reservation fee); $7 fee per night.

Who to contact: Phone the Toiyabe National Forest, Bridgeport Ranger Station at (619) 932-7070.

Location: From north of Bridgeport, at the junction of US 395 and Highway 108, turn west on Highway 108 and drive two miles to the campground.

Trip note: The West Walker River is a pretty stream, flowing over boulders and into pools, with this stretch of river well-stocked by the Department of Fish and Game. This is one of several campgrounds located near the West Walker, this one set at 6,600 feet elevation, about a half-mile from the river. The setting is in the transition zone from high mountains to high desert on the eastern edge of the Sierra Nevada. Open May to October.

28. CHRIS FLAT 🐟 🚶 RV 7

Reference: **On Walker River in Toiyabe National Forest; map E4, grid b7.**
Campsites, facilities: There are 15 sites for tents or motor homes up to 22 feet long. Piped water, fire grills and picnic tables are provided. Vault toilets are available. Pets are permitted on leashes.
Reservations, fee: No reservations; $7 fee per night.
Who to contact: Phone the Toiyabe National Forest, Bridgeport Ranger Station at (619) 932-7070.
Location: From Carson City, drive south on US 395 to Coleville, then continue south for 15 miles to the campground on the east side of the road (located four miles north of the junction of US 395 and Highway 108).
Trip note: This is one of two campgrounds set along Highway 395 next to the West Walker River, a pretty trout stream with easy access and good stocks of rainbow trout. The plants are usually made at two campgrounds, making for good prospects here at Chris Flat, or west on Highway 108 at Sonora Bridge Campground. The elevation is 6,600 feet. Open May through November.

29. BOOTLEG 🐟 RV 6

Reference: **On Walker River in Toiyabe National Forest; map E4, grid b8.**
Campsites, facilities: There are 63 paved sites for tents or motor homes up to 45 feet long. Piped water, fire grills and picnic tables are provided. Flush toilets are available. Pets are permitted on leashes.
Reservations, fee: Reserve by phoning (800) 280-CAMP; ($7.50 reservation fee); $7 fee per night.
Who to contact: Phone the Toiyabe National Forest, Bridgeport Ranger Station at (619) 932-7070.
Location: From Carson City, drive south on US 395 to Coleville, then continue south for 13 miles to the campground on the west side of the highway (located six miles north of the junction of US 395 and Highway 108).
Trip note: Location is always a key, and easy access off US 395, the adjacent West Walker River, and good trout stocks in summer make this a popular spot. See trip note for Chris Flat and Sonora Bridge Campground. Note that this camp is on the west side of the highway, and that anglers will have to cross the road in order to gain fishing access (which makes Chris Flat Camp a better choice). The elevation is 6,600 feet. Open May to mid-September.

30. MEADOWVIEW 🐟 ⚓ 🚶 🏊 🏇 RV 7

Reference: **Near Pinecrest Lake in Stanislaus National Forest; map E4, grid c1.**
Campsites, facilities: There are 100 sites for tents or motor homes up to 22 feet long. Piped water, stoves and picnic tables are provided. Flush toilets and equestrian facilities are available. A grocery store, a laundromat, a boat ramp, pay showers (in summer months only) and propane gas are nearby. Pets are allowed on leashes.
Reservations, fee: No reservations; $9.50 fee per night.
Who to contact: Phone the Stanislaus National Forest Summit Ranger District at (209) 965-3434.
Location: From Sonora, drive east on Highway 108 for about 25 miles to Strawberry and the signed road for Pinecrest Lake. Turn right at the sign and drive a very short distance to the signed road for Pinecrest/Dodge Ridge. Turn

right and drive about 100 yards to the campground entrance on the left side of the road.

Trip note: No secret here, folks. This camp is located one mile from Pinecrest Lake, a popular weekend vacation area. Pinecrest Lake is set at 5,621 feet, covers 300 acres, is stocked with rainbow trout, and has a 20-mile-per-hour speed limit for boaters. This is a family-oriented vacation center, and a popular walk is the easy hike around the lake. If you want something more ambitious, there is a cutoff on the north side of the lake that is routed one mile up to little Catfish Lake. The Dodge Ridge Ski Area is nearby, with many privately owned cabins in the area. Open May to October.

31. PIONEER TRAIL GROUP CAMP ⚓ 🚶

Reference: **Near Pinecrest Lake in Stanislaus National Forest; map E4, grid c1.**

Campsites, facilities: There are three group sites here. Piped water, picnic tables and stoves are provided. Vault toilets are available. A grocery store, a laundromat, a boat ramp, pay showers (in summer months only), and propane gas are nearby. Pets are allowed on leashes.

Reservations, fee: Reserve by phoning (800) 280-CAMP; $15 reservation fee; $40-$55 group fee per night.

Who to contact: Phone the Stanislaus National Forest Summit Ranger District at (209) 965-3434.

Location: From Sonora, drive east on Highway 108 for about 25 miles to Strawberry and the signed road for Pinecrest Lake. Turn right at the sign and drive a very short distance to the signed road for Pinecrest/Dodge Ridge. Turn right and drive about one mile to the campground entrance on the right side of the road.

Trip note: If you're going to Pinecrest Lake with a Boy Scout troop, this is the spot, since it is set up specifically for groups. You get beautiful creek and canyon views. For recreation information, see trip note for nearby Meadowview Camp. Open May to September.

32. PINECREST 🐟 ⚓ 🚶 🏊 🐎

Reference: **Near Pinecrest Lake in Stanislaus National Forest; map E4, grid c1.**

Campsites, facilities: There are 200 sites for tents or motor homes up to 22 feet long. Piped water, picnic tables and stoves are provided. Vault toilets are available. Pets are permitted on leashes. A grocery store, a laundromat, pay showers (in summer months only), equestrian facilities, a boat ramp and propane gas are nearby.

Reservations, fee: Reserve by phoning (800) 280-CAMP; $7.50 reservation fee; $12 fee per night.

Who to contact: Phone the Stanislaus National Forest Summit Ranger District at (209) 965-3434.

Location: From Sonora, drive east on Highway 108 for about 25 miles. Turn right at the sign for Pinecrest Lake. Go about 100 yards past the turnoff for Pinecrest/Dodge Ridge and turn right onto the access road for Pinecrest Camp.

Trip note: This monster-sized Forest Service camp is set near Pinecrest Lake. In early summer, there is good fishing for stocked rainbow trout. A launch ramp is available, and a 20-mile-per-hour speed limit is enforced on the lake. A trail circles the lake and also branches off to nearby Catfish Lake. The elevation is 5,800 feet. Open May to October. Winter camping is allowed here.

33. LEAVITT MEADOWS 🐟 🥾   RV 9

Reference: **On Walker River in Toiyabe National Forest; map E4, grid c6.**

Campsites, facilities: There are 16 sites for tents or motor homes up to 22 feet long. Piped water, fire grills and picnic tables are provided. Vault toilets are available. Pets are permitted on leashes.

Reservations, fee: No reservations; $7 fee per night.

Who to contact: Phone the Toiyabe National Forest, Bridgeport Ranger Station at (619) 932-7070.

Location: From the junction of US 395 and Highway 108 north of Bridgeport, turn west on Highway 108 and drive seven miles to the campground on the south side of the road.

Trip note: While Leavitt Meadows is set right aside Highway 108, a little winding two-laner, there are several nearby off-pavement destinations that make this camp a winner. The camp is set in the high eastern Sierra, east of Sonora Pass, 7,000 feet elevation, where Leavitt Creek and Brownie Creek enter the West Walker River. There is a pack station for horseback riding nearby. The most popular side trip is driving four miles west on Highway 108, then turning south and driving four miles to Leavitt Lake, where the trout fishing is sometimes spectacular, trolling a gold Cripplure. The camp is set at 7,000 feet. Open May to October.

---

34. OBSIDIAN 🐟 🥾   RV 6

Reference: **On Molybdenite Creek in Toiyabe National Forest; map E4, grid c8.**

Campsites, facilities: There are 14 sites for tents or motor homes up to 30 feet long. Fire grills and picnic tables are provided. Vault toilets are available. There is **no piped water**, so bring your own. Pets are permitted on leashes.

Reservations, fee: No reservations; $4 fee per night.

Who to contact: Phone the Toiyabe National Forest, Bridgeport Ranger Station at (619) 932-7070.

Location: At the junction of US 395 and Highway 108 (12 miles north of Bridgeport), drive south a short distance on US 935 to an improved dirt road and a sign that says "Forest Service Campground." Turn west and drive four miles to the campground.

Trip note: This primitive, little-known camp, 7,800 feet elevation, is set up for backpackers, with an adjacent trailhead providing a jumpoff point into the wilderness. The trail here is routed up the Molybdenite Creek drainage and into the Hoover Wilderness. Open May to November.

---

35. FRASER FLAT 🐟 ♿   RV 7

Reference: **On South Fork of the Stanislaus River in Stanislaus National Forest; map E4, grid d0.**

Campsites, facilities: There are 16 sites for tents or motor homes up to 22 feet. Piped water, picnic tables and stoves are provided. Vault toilets are available. A grocery store and propane gas are nearby. A camping and fishing site for **wheelchair** use are provided. Pets are allowed on leashes.

Reservations, fee: No reservations; $5 fee per night.

Who to contact: Phone the Stanislaus National Forest Mi-Wok Ranger District at (209) 586-3234.

Location: From Sonora, drive east on Highway 108 to Long Barn. Continue east for six miles to the campground entrance road on the left. Turn left and drive two miles to the campground on the left side of the road.

Trip note: This camp is set along the South Fork of the Stanislaus River. If the fish aren't biting, a seven-mile side trip via Forest Service roads will route you north into the main canyon of the Middle Fork Stanislaus. A map of Stanislaus National Forest is required for this adventure. This camp also provides an overflow area if the camps at nearby Pinecrest Lake near Strawberry are filled. Open May through October.

36. HULL CREEK 🐟   RV 7

Reference: **In Stanislaus National Forest; map E4, grid d0.**

Campsites, facilities: There are 16 sites for tents or motor homes up to 22 feet long. Picnic tables and stoves are provided. Piped water and vault toilets are available. Pets are allowed on leashes.

Reservations, fee: No reservations; $5 fee per night.

Who to contact: Phone the Stanislaus National Forest Mi-Wok Ranger District at (209) 586-3234.

Location: From Sonora, drive east on Highway 108 to Long Barn and Hull Meadow Road. Turn right (south) and drive nine miles east on Hull Meadow Road to the campground on the left side of the road.

Trip note: This obscure camp is set on little Hull Creek (too small for trout fishing), at 5,600 feet elevation in Stanislaus National Forest. This a good spot for people testing out four-wheel-drive vehicles, with an intricate set of Forest Service roads set to the east. To explore that area, a map of Stanislaus National Forest is essential. Open May through October, with camping permitted in winter when accessible.

37. HONEYMOON FLAT 🐟 🚶   RV 8

Reference: **On Robinson Creek in Toiyabe National Forest; map E4, grid d9.**

Campsites, facilities: There are 47 sites for tents or motor homes up to 35 feet long. Piped water, fire grills and picnic tables are provided. Vault toilets are available. Pets are permitted on leashes.

Reservations, fee: Reserve by phoning (800) 280-CAMP; $7.50 reservation fee; $7 fee per night.

Who to contact: Phone the Toiyabe National Forest, Bridgeport Ranger Station at (619) 932-7070.

Location: On US 395, drive to Bridgeport and the junction with Twin Lakes Road. Turn west and drive eight miles to the campground.

Trip note: The camp is set aside Robinson Creek at 7,000 feet elevation, in the transition zone between the Sierra Nevada range to the west and the high desert to the east. It is easy to reach, located on the access road to Twin Lakes, only three miles further. The lake is famous for occasional huge brown trout. However, the fishing at Robinson Creek is often quite good, thanks to more than 50,000 trout planted each year by the Department of Fish and Game. Open May through November.

38. PAHA 🐟 ⚓ 🚶 🏊   RV 8

Reference: **Near Twin Lakes in Toiyabe National Forest; map E4, grid d8.**

Campsites, facilities: There are 22 paved sites for tents or motor homes up to 35 feet long. Piped water, fire grills and picnic tables are provided. Flush toilets are available. A boat launch, a store, showers and a laundromat are available nearby. Pets are permitted on leashes.

Reservations, fee: Reserve by phoning (800) 280-CAMP; $7.50 reservation fee; $8 fee per night.

Who to contact: Phone the Toiyabe National Forest, Bridgeport Ranger Station at (619) 932-7070.

Location: On US 395, drive to Bridgeport and the junction with Twin Lakes Road. Turn west and drive 10 miles to the campground.

Trip note: This is one in a series of camps near Robinson Creek and within close range of Twin Lakes. The elevation is 7,000 feet. Open May to October. See trip notes for Honeymoon Flat and Lower Twin Lake camps.

39. ROBINSON CREEK RV 9

Reference: **Near Twin Lakes in Toiyabe National Forest; map E4, grid d8.**

Campsites, facilities: There are 54 paved sites for tents or motor homes up to 45 feet long. Piped water, fire grills and picnic tables are provided. There is also an amphitheater. Flush toilets are available. Pets are permitted on leashes.

Reservations, fee: Reserve by phoning (800) 280-CAMP; $7.50 reservation fee; $8 fee per night.

Who to contact: Phone the Toiyabe National Forest, Bridgeport Ranger Station at (619) 32-7070.

Location: On US 395, drive to Bridgeport and the junction with Twin Lakes Road. Turn west and drive 10 miles to the campground.

Trip note: This campground, one of a series in the area, is set at 7,000 feet on Robinson Creek, not far from Twin Lakes. For recreation options, see the trip note for Lower Twin Lake and Honeymoon camps.

40. BUCKEYE RV 8

Reference: **Near Buckeye Creek in Toiyabe National Forest; map E4, grid d8.**

Campsites, facilities: There are 65 paved sites for tents or motor homes up to 30 feet long. There is one group site available. Piped water, fire grills and picnic tables are provided. Flush toilets are available. Pets are permitted on leashes.

Reservations, fee: Group site reservations are available by calling (800) 280-CAMP; $15 reservation fee; $30 fee per night. No reservations for individual sites; $7 fee per night.

Who to contact: Phone the Toiyabe National Forest, Bridgeport Ranger Station at (619) 932-7070.

Location: On US 395, drive to Bridgeport and the junction with Twin Lakes Road. Turn west and drive seven miles to Buckeye Road. Turn north on Buckeye Road (dirt, often impassable when wet) and drive 3.5 miles to the campground.

Trip note: Here's a little secret: A two-mile hike out of camp is Buckeye Hot Springs, an undeveloped hot springs. That is what inspires campers to bypass the fishing at nearby Robinson Creek (three miles away) and Twin Lakes (six miles away). The camp feels remote and primitive, set at 7,000 feet on the eastern slope of the Sierra near Buckeye Creek. Another secret is that brook trout are planted at the little bridge that crosses Buckeye Creek near the campground. A trail that starts near camp is routed through Buckeye Canyon and into the Hoover Wilderness. Open late May to October.

41. LOWER TWIN LAKE 🛶 🐟 ⚓ 🏃 🏊   RV 9

Reference: **In Toiyabe National Forest; map E4, grid d8.**

Campsites, facilities: There are 15 paved sites for tents or motor homes up to 35 feet long. Piped water, fire grills and picnic tables are provided. Flush toilets are available. A boat launch, a store, showers and a laundromat are available nearby. Pets are permitted on leashes.

Reservations, fee: Reserve by phoning (800) 280-CAMP; ($7.50 reservation fee); $8 fee per night.

Who to contact: Phone the Toiyabe National Forest, Bridgeport Ranger Station at (619) 932-7070.

Location: On US 395, drive to Bridgeport and the junction with Twin Lakes Road. Turn west and drive 11 miles to the campground.

Trip note: The Twin Lakes are actually two lakes, of course, set high in the eastern Sierra at 7,000 feet. The best of the two is Lower Twin, where a full resort, marina, boat ramp and some of the biggest brown trout in the West can be found. The state record brown was caught here, 26.5 pounds, and in 1991, 11-year-old Micah Beirle of Bakersfield caught one that weighed 20.5 pounds, one of the great fish catches by a youngster anywhere in America. Of course, most of the trout are your typical 10- to 12-inch planted rainbow trout, but nobody seems to mind, with the chance of a true monster-sized fish always in the back of the minds of anglers. An option for campers is an excellent trailhead for hiking near Mono Village at the head of Upper Twin Lake. Here you will find the Barney Lake Trail, which is routed up the headwaters of Robinson Creek, steeply at times, to little Barney Lake, an excellent day hike. Open May through October.

42. CRAGS CAMPGROUND 🛶 🐟 ⚓ 🏃 ♿   RV 8

Reference: **On Robinson Creek in Toiyabe National Forest; map E4, grid d8.**

Campsites, facilities: There are 27 sites for tents or motor homes up to 40 feet long. Picnic tables and fire grills are provided. Piped water, flush toilets and lighted bathrooms are available. The campground is **wheelchair accessible**. A boat launch (at Lower Twin Lake), store, laundromat and showers are located within a half mile. Pets are permitted on leashes.

Reservations, fee: No reservations; $8 fee per night.

Who to contact: Phone the Bridgeport Ranger District at (619)932-7070.

Location: On US 395, drive to Bridgeport and the junction with Twin Lakes Road. Turn west and drive 11 miles to a road on the left (just before reaching Lower Twin Lake. Turn left and drive over the bridge at Robinson Creek to another road on the left. Turn left and drive a short distance to the campground.

Trip note: Crags Camp is set at 7,000 feet in the Sierra, one of a series of campgrounds along Robinson Creek near Lower Twin Lake. While this camp does not offer direct access to Lower Twin, home of giant brown trout, it is very close. See the trip note for Lower Twin Lake Campground and Honeymoon Flat.

43. CHERRY VALLEY 🛶 🐟 ⚓ 🏃 🏊   RV 7

Reference: **On Cherry Lake in Stanislaus National Forest; map E4, grid e1.**

Campsites, facilities: There are 46 sites for tents or motor homes of any length. Piped water (only in summer months), picnic tables and stoves are provided.

Vault toilets are available. A boat ramp is nearby. Pets are allowed on leashes.

Reservations, fee: No reservations; $9 fee per night; $16 fee for double sites.

Who to contact: Phone the Stanislaus National Forest Groveland Ranger District at (209) 962-7825.

Location: From Groveland, drive east on Highway 120 for about 15 miles to Forest Service Road 1N07 (Cherry Valley Road) on the left side of the road. Turn left and drive 18 miles to the south end of Cherry Lake and the campground access road on the right. Turn right and drive one mile to the campground.

Trip note: Cherry Lake is a mountain lake surrounded by national forest, at 4,700 feet in elevation, set just outside the western boundary of Yosemite National Park. It is much larger than most people anticipate, and provides much better trout fishing than anything in Yosemite. The camp is set along the southwest shore of the lake, a very pretty spot, about a one-mile ride to the boat launch located on the west side of the Cherry Valley Dam. The lake is bordered to the east by Kibbie Ridge; just on the other side is Yosemite Park and Lake Eleanor. Open April through October.

---

44. TRUMBULL LAKE

Reference: **In Toiyabe National Forest; map E4, grid e9.**

Campsites, facilities: There are 45 sites for tents or motor homes up to 35 feet long. Piped water, fire grills and picnic tables are provided. Vault toilets are available. Pets are permitted on leashes. A store is nearby at the resort.

Reservations, fee: Reserve by phoning (800) 280-CAMP; ($7.50 reservation fee); $7 fee per night.

Who to contact: Phone the Toiyabe National Forest, Bridgeport Ranger Station at (619) 932-7070.

Location: From Bridgeport, drive south on US 395 for 13.5 miles to Virginia Lakes Road. Turn west on Virginia Lakes Road and drive 6.5 miles to the campground entrance road.

Trip note: This is a high-mountain camp at 9,500 feet, set at the gateway to a beautiful Sierra basin. Little Trumbull Lake is the first lake on the north side of Virginia Lakes Road, with Virginia Lakes set nearby, along with the Hoover Wilderness and access to many other small lakes by trail. A trail is available that is routed just north of Blue Lake, then leads west to Frog Lake, Summit Lake and beyond into a remote area of Yosemite National Park. If you don't want to rough it, cabins, boat rentals and a restaurant are available at Virginia Lakes Resort. Open June to October.

---

45. GREEN CREEK

Reference: **In Toiyabe National Forest; map E4, grid e9.**

Campsites, facilities: There are 11 sites for tents or motor homes up to 22 feet long. Piped water, fire grills and picnic tables are provided. Vault toilets are available. Pets are permitted.

Reservations, fee: No reservations; $7 fee per night.

Who to contact: Phone the Toiyabe National Forest, Bridgeport Ranger Station at (619) 932-7070.

Location: From Bridgeport, drive south on US 395 for six miles to Green Lakes Road (dirt). Turn west and drive seven miles to the campground.

Trip note: This camp is ideal for backpackers or campers who like to fish for trout in streams. That is because the camp is set at 7,500 feet, with a trailhead for a route that heads into the Hoover Wilderness and several high mountain lakes, including Green Lake, West Lake and East Lake; the ambitious can hike beyond in remote northeastern Yosemite National Park. The camp is set along Green Creek, a fair trout stream with small rainbow trout. Open May through October.

46. LUMSDEN

Reference: **On Tuolumne River in Stanislaus National Forest; map E4, grid f0.**

Campsites, facilities: There are 11 tent sites. Picnic tables and fire grills are provided. Vault toilets are available. There is **no piped water**. Pets are allowed on leashes.

Reservations, fee: No reservations; no fee.

Who to contact: Phone the Stanislaus National Forest Groveland Ranger District at (209) 962-7825.

Location: From Groveland, drive east on Highway 120 for about eight miles (just under a mile beyond County Road J20) to a dirt road on the left side of the highway. Turn left and drive to a Forest Service road intersection. Jog left, then right, and continue for four miles to the camp on the right side of the road.

Trip note: This is one of the great access points for whitewater rafting on the Wild and Scenic Tuolumne river and its premium stretch between Hetch Hetchy Reservoir in Yosemite and Don Pedro Reservoir in the Central Valley foothills. Unless you are an expert rafter, you are advised to attempt running this stretch of river only with a professional rafting company. The camp is set at 1,500 feet, just across the road from the river. The road in down the canyon is steep and bumpy. There are two other camps within a mile, South Fork and Lumsden Bridge. Open April through October.

47. LUMSDEN BRIDGE

Reference: **On Tuolumne River in Stanislaus National Forest; map E4, grid f0.**

Campsites, facilities: There are nine tent sites. Picnic tables and stoves are provided. Vault toilets are available. There is **no piped water**. Pets are allowed on leashes.

Reservations, fee: No reservations; no fee.

Who to contact: Phone the Stanislaus National Forest Groveland Ranger District at (209) 962-7825.

Location: From Groveland, drive east on Highway 120 for about eight miles (just under a mile beyond County Road J20) to a dirt road on the left side of the highway. Turn left and drive to a Forest Service road intersection. Jog left, then right, and continue for 5.5 miles to the campground on the left side of the road.

Trip note: This is one of three camps set in this immediate stretch along the Tuolumne River, one of the best whitewater rafting rivers in California. This camp is set at 1,500 feet on the north side of the river, accessible just after crossing the Lumsden Bridge, hence the name. See the trip note for Lumsden Camp.

48. SOUTH FORK 🐟 ✕

Reference: Near Tuolumne River in Stanislaus National Forest; map E4, grid f0.

Campsites, facilities: There are eight tent sites. Picnic tables and stoves are provided. Vault toilets are available. There is **no piped water**. Pets are allowed on leashes.

Reservations, fee: No reservations; no fee.

Who to contact: Phone the Stanislaus National Forest Groveland Ranger District at (209) 962-7825.

Location: From Groveland, drive east on Highway 120 for about eight miles (just under a mile beyond County Road J20) to a dirt road on the left side of the highway. Turn left and drive to a Forest Service road intersection. Jog left, then right, and continue for five miles to the camp on the right side of the road.

Trip note: South Fork Camp is located a half-mile upstream from Lumsden Campground and about a mile downstream from Lumsden Bridge Camp. Why do we say "upstream" and "downstream" instead of east and west? Because this is a camp for whitewater rafters, featuring the spectacular Tuolumne River and access to its most exciting stretches. You should only attempt to run this river with a professional rafting company. The elevation is 1,500 feet. Open April through October.

49. SADDLEBAG LAKE 🐟 ⚓ 🚶

Reference: In Inyo National Forest; map E4, grid f8.

Campsites, facilities: There are 22 sites for tents or motor homes up to 22 feet long. One group site can accommodate up to 40 people. Piped water, fire grills and picnic tables are provided. Vault toilets, boat rentals and a boat launch are available. A grocery store is nearby. Pets are allowed on leashes.

Reservations, fee: Reservations for group site only, phone (800) 280-CAMP; $8 fee per night for single sites; group site fee is $20 per night

Who to contact: Phone the Inyo National Forest District Office at (619) 647-3000.

Location: On US 395, drive to just south of Lee Vining and the junction with Highway 120. Turn west and drive about 11 miles to Saddlebag Lake Road. Turn right and drive three miles to the campground. (From Merced, turn east on Highway 140 and drive into Yosemite National Park and continue toward Yosemite Valley to the junction with Highway 120. Turn north and drive about 65 miles through the Tioga Pass entrance station. Continue three miles to Saddlebag Lake Road. Turn left and drive three miles to the campground.)

Trip note: This camp is set in spectacular high country above treeline, the highest drive-to camp and lake in California, with Saddlebag Lake at 10,087 feet. The camp is set about a quarter-mile from the lake, within walking range of the little store, boat ramp, rentals, and a one-minute drive with a boat for launching at the ramp. The scenery is stark, everything is granite, ice or water, with only a few slow-growing Jeffrey pines managing precarious toeholds, sprinkled across the landscape on the access road. An excellent trailhead is available for hiking, with the best hike routed out past little Hummingbird Lake to Lundy Pass. Open June to mid-October.

50. LOST CLAIM 🐟

Reference: **Near Tuolumne River in Stanislaus National Forest; map E4, grid g0.**

Campsites, facilities: There are 10 tent sites or small motor homes. Picnic tables and stoves are provided. Vault toilets and hand-pumped well water are available. A grocery store is nearby. Pets are allowed on leashes.

Reservations, fee: No reservations; $8 fee per night.

Who to contact: Phone the Stanislaus National Forest Groveland Ranger District at (209) 962-7825.

Location: From Groveland, drive east on Highway 120 for 14 miles (1.5 miles past the Buck Meadows ranger station) to the campground on left side of the road.

Trip note: This is one in a series of easy-access camps off Highway 120 that provide overflow areas when all the sites are taken in Yosemite National Park to the east. A feeder stream to the Tuolumne River runs by the camp. The elevation is 3,100 feet. Open May until Labor Day.

51. SWEETWATER 🐟

Reference: **Near South Fork of Tuolumne River in Stanislaus National Forest; map E4, grid g0.**

Campsites, facilities: There are 13 sites for tents or motor homes up to 22 feet long. Piped water, picnic tables and stoves are provided. Vault toilets are available. A grocery store is nearby. Pets are allowed on leashes.

Reservations, fee: No reservations; $9 fee per night.

Who to contact: Phone the Stanislaus National Forest Groveland Ranger District at (209) 962-7825.

Location: From Groveland, drive east on Highway 120 for about 18 miles (four miles past the Buck Meadows ranger station) to the campground on left side of the road.

Trip note: This camp is set at 3,000 feet, near the South Fork Tuolumne River, one of several camps along Highway 120 that can provide a safety valve for campers who can't find space in Yosemite National Park to the east. Open April through October.

52. MIDDLE FORK 🐟

Reference: **On the Middle Fork of Tuolumne River in Stanislaus National Forest; map E4, grid g2.**

Campsites, facilities: There are 24 sites for tents or motor homes up to 16 feet long. Stoves are provided. Vault toilets are available. There is **no piped water**, so bring your own. A grocery store is nearby. Pets are allowed on leashes.

Reservations, fee: No reservations; no fee.

Who to contact: Phone the Stanislaus National Forest Groveland Ranger District at (209) 962-7825.

Location: From Groveland, drive east on Highway 120 for 28 miles (six miles past Harden Flat) to Evergreen Road. Turn north (left) and drive five miles to the campground.

Trip note: Middle Fork Camp is named after the nearby Middle Fork Tuolumne River, which runs right by the camp, crossing under the bridge, then heading downstream into remote forest country. The camp is pretty, primitive, and is often overlooked by vacationers searching for a spot up and down Highway

120 after being shut out of Yosemite. To the nearby north is Camp Mather and a remote entrance to Yosemite National Park, with access to Hetch Hetchy Reservoir and a great side trip to Tueculala and Wapama Falls on the northwest side of the reservoir. The elevation is 4,400 feet. Open April through October.

53. CARLON ⌊⊶   RV 7

Reference: **On Crane Creek in Stanislaus National Forest; map E4, grid g2.**
Campsites, facilities: There are 16 sites for tents or motor homes up to 16 feet long. Picnic tables and stoves are provided. Vault toilets and hand-pumped well water are available. A grocery store is nearby. Pets are allowed on leashes.
Reservations, fee: No reservations; no fee.
Who to contact: Phone the Stanislaus National Forest Groveland Ranger District at (209) 962-7825.
Location: From Groveland, drive east on Highway 120 for 28 miles (six miles past Harden Flat) to Evergreen Road. Turn north (left) and drive a half-mile to the campground on the right side of the road.
Trip note: Carlon Camp is set at a deep bend in the road at a gulch, right where Crane Creek flows past. It is a pretty spot, 4,300 feet in elevation, surrounded by Stanislaus National Forest with both the Mather and Crane Flat entrance stations to Yosemite located within 10-minute drives. Open April (snowmelt permitting) through October.

54. YOSEMITE CREEK ⌊⊶ 🚶🚶   9

Reference: **On Yosemite Creek in Yosemite National Park; map E4, grid g4.**
Campsites, facilities: There are 75 tent sites. Picnic tables and fire pits are provided. Pit toilets are available. **No piped water** is available. Pets are permitted on leashes. A 14-day stay limit is enforced.
Reservations, fee: No reservations; $6-$8 fee per night.
Who to contact: Phone Yosemite National Park at (209) 372-0200 for a touch-tone menu, or (209) 372-0265.
Location: From Merced, drive east on Highway 140 to the Yosemite Park entrance and continue toward Yosemite Valley to the junction with Highway 120/Tioga Road. Turn north and drive about 30 miles (just beyond White Wolf turnoff on the left) to Yosemite Creek Campground Road on the right. Turn right (RVs and trailers not recommended) and drive five miles to the campground at the end of the road.
Trip note: This is the most remote drive-to camp in Yosemite National Park, a great alternative to camping in the valley or at Tuolumne Meadows, and the rough, curvy access road keeps many out-of-state tourists away. It is set along Yosemite Creek at 7,659 feet, with poor trout fishing but a trailhead for a spectacular hike. If you arrange a shuttle ride, you can make a great one-way trip down to the north side of the Yosemite canyon rim, skirting past the top of Yosemite Falls (a side trip to Yosemite Point is a must!), then tackling the unbelievable descent down to the valley, emerging at Sunnyside Campground.

55. JUNCTION ⌊⊶ 🚶🚶   RV 7

Reference: **Near Ellery and Tioga Lakes in Inyo National Forest; map E4, grid g8.**
Campsites, facilities: There are 14 sites for tents or motor homes up to 22 feet long. Fire grills and picnic tables are provided. Vault toilets are available. There is

no piped water, so bring your own. Pets are allowed on leashes.

Reservations, fee: No reservations; no fee.

Who to contact: Phone the Inyo National Forest District Office at (619) 647-3000.

Location: On US 395, drive to just south of Lee Vining and the junction with Highway 120. Turn west and drive about 10 miles to Saddlebag Road and the campground on the right side of the road. (From Merced: Turn east on Highway 140, drive into Yosemite National Park and continue toward Yosemite Valley to the junction with Highway 120/Tioga Road. Turn north and drive about 65 miles through the Tioga Pass entrance station. Continue four miles to Saddlebag Road and the campground on the left side of the road.)

Trip note: Which way do you go? From Junction Campground, any way you choose, you can't miss. Two miles to the north is Saddlebag Lake, the highest drive-to lake (10,087 feet) in California. Directly across the road is Ellery Lake, and a mile to south is Tioga Lake, two beautiful pristine waters with trout fishing. To the east is Mono Lake, and to the west is Yosemite National Park. Take your pick. Camp elevation is 9,600 feet. Open June to October.

56. LEE VINING CREEK CAMPS 🎣   RV 7

Reference: **Near Lee Vining; map E4, grid g9.**

Campsites, facilities: There are 131 sites for tents or motor homes up to 24 feet long in four separate campgrounds located next to each other. Pit toilets are available. There is no piped water, so bring your own. Pets are permitted on leashes. Supplies can be purchased in Lee Vining.

Reservations, fee: No reservations; $5 fee per night.

Who to contact: Phone the Mono County Building and Parks Department at (619) 932-5231.

Location: On US 395, drive to just south of Lee Vining and the junction with Highway 120. Turn west and drive about 3.5 miles to a county road on the left. Turn left and drive one to two miles and look for the campground entrances on the left side of the road.

Trip note: These camps can be a godsend for vacationers who show up at Yosemite National Park and make the discovery that there are no sites left— a terrible experience for some late-night arrivals. But these county campgrounds provide a great safety valve, even if they are extremely primitive, with the sites a bit bunched together in a largely open, edge-of-desert environment. Lee Vining Creek is the highlight, flowing right past the campgrounds, along Highway 120 bound for Mono Lake to the nearby east. A must-do side trip is venturing to the south shore of Mono Lake to walk amid the bizarre yet beautiful tufa spires. Open May through October.

57. BIG BEND 🎣   RV 8

Reference: **On Lee Vining Creek in Inyo National Forest; map E4, grid g9.**

Campsites, facilities: There are 17 sites for tents or motor homes up to 22 feet long. Piped water, fire grills and picnic tables are provided. Vault toilets are available. A grocery store is nearby. Pets are allowed on leashes.

Reservations, fee: No reservations; $8 fee per night.

Who to contact: Phone the Inyo National Forest District Office at (619) 647-3000.

Location: On US 395, drive to just south of Lee Vining and the junction with Highway 120. Turn west and drive about 3.5 miles to a county road on the left. Turn left and drive three miles west to the campground access road on the left.

Turn left and drive a short distance to the camp.

Trip note: This camp is set in sparse but beautiful country along Lee Vining Creek at 7,800 feet elevation. It is an excellent bet for an overflow camp if Tuolumne Meadows Camp in nearby Yosemite is packed. The view from the camp to the north features Mono Dome (10,614 feet) and Lee Vining Peak (11,691 feet). Open May to mid-October.

---

58. ASPEN GROVE

Reference: **On Lee Vining Creek; map E4, grid g9.**

Campsites, facilities: There are 56 sites for tents or motor homes up to 20 feet long. There is no piped water, so bring your own. Pit toilets are available. Pets are permitted on leashes. Supplies can be purchased in Lee Vining.

Reservations, fee: No reservations; $5 fee per night.

Who to contact: Phone the Mono County Building and Parks Department at (619) 932-5231.

Location: On US 395, drive to just south of Lee Vining and the junction with Highway 120. Turn west and drive about 3.5 miles to a county road on the left. Turn left and drive about four miles west to the campground on the left.

Trip note: This high-country, primitive camp is set along Lee Vining Creek at 8,000 feet, located on the eastern slopes of the Sierra just east of Yosemite National Park. Take the side trip to moon-like Mono Lake, best seen at the south shore tufa preserve. Open May through October.

---

59. TIOGA LAKE

Reference: **In Inyo National Forest; map E4, grid g9.**

Campsites, facilities: There are 12 tent sites. Piped water, picnic tables and fire grills are provided. Vault toilets are available. Pets are allowed on leashes.

Reservations, fee: No reservations; $8 fee per night.

Who to contact: Phone the Inyo National Forest District Office at (619) 647-3000.

Location: On US 395, drive to just south of Lee Vining and the junction with Highway 120. Turn west and drive about 11 miles (just past Ellery Lake) to the campground on the left side of the road. (From Merced, turn east on Highway 140 and drive into Yosemite National Park and continue toward Yosemite Valley to the junction with Highway 120/Tioga Road. Turn north and drive about 65 miles through the Tioga Pass entrance station. Continue three miles to the campground on the right side of the road.)

Trip note: Tioga Lake is a dramatic site, with gem-like blue waters circled by Sierra granite at 9,700 feet elevation. Together with adjacent Ellery Lake, they make up two gorgeous waters with near-lake camping, trout fishing (stocked with rainbow trout) and access to Yosemite National Park and Saddlebag Lake. See trip note for Ellery Lake. Open June to October.

---

60. ELLERY LAKE

Reference: **In Inyo National Forest; map E4 grid g9.**

Campsites, facilities: There are three tent sites and 14 sites for tents or motor homes up to 22 feet long. Piped water, fire grills and picnic tables are provided. Flush toilets are available. A grocery store is nearby. Pets are allowed on leashes.

Reservations, fee: No reservations; $8 fee per night.

Who to contact: Phone the Inyo National Forest District Office at (619) 647-3000.

Location: On US 395, drive to just south of Lee Vining and the junction with Highway 120. Turn west and drive about 10 miles to the campground on the left side of the road. (From Merced, turn east on Highway 140 and drive into Yosemite National Park and continue toward Yosemite Valley to the junction with Highway 120/Tioga Road. Turn north and drive about 65 miles through the Tioga Pass entrance station. Continue four miles to the campground on the right side of the road.)

Trip note: Ellery Lake offers all the spectacular beauty of Yosemite, but is two miles outside park borders. That means it is stocked with trout by the Department of Fish and Game (no lakes in Yosemite are planted, hence the lousy fishing). Just like at neighboring Tioga Lake, here are deep-blue waters set in rock in the 9,500-foot elevation range, one of the most pristine highway-access lake settings anywhere. Nearby Saddlebag Lake is a common side trip, the highest drive-to lake in California. Whenever Tuolumne Meadows Campground fills in Yosemite, this camp fills shortly thereafter. Camp elevation is 9,600 feet. Open June to October.

---

61. INDIAN FLAT 🐟 🏊

Reference: **On Merced River in Sierra National Forest; map E4, grid h1.**

Campsites, facilities: There are 18 sites for tents or motor homes up to 22 feet long. Piped water, fire grills and picnic tables are provided and vault toilets are available. A grocery store is nearby.

Reservations, fee: No reservations, but this camp usually fills by noon on Fridays; $12 fee per night.

Who to contact: Phone the Inyo National Forest District Office at (209) 683-4665.

Location: From Merced, turn east on Highway 140 and drive to Mariposa. Continue east for 24 miles to the campground (four miles from El Portal) on the right (south) side of the road.

Trip note: The beautiful Merced River runs along Highway 140, a great river in the spring and early summer for rafting, in the summer for trout fishing, and in the late summer for swimming. Deep holes, slicks and boulder-spiked rapids highlight the river all along the highway. This camp is set just across the road from the river, only four miles from El Portal and the Arch Rock entrance to Yosemite National Park. Elevation is 1,500 feet. Open year-round.

---

62. McCABE FLAT 🐟 🚶 🏊 ✕ 🐎

Reference: **On the Merced River east of Briceburg; map E4, grid h0.**

Campsites, facilities: There are seven tent sites. Picnic tables and fire rings are provided. Vault toilets are available. Pets are permitted on leashes.

Reservations, fee: No reservations; $2 fee per person per night.

Who to contact: Phone Folsom Resource Area at (916) 985-4474, or write to Bureau of Land Management, 63 Natoma Street, Folsom, CA 95630.

Location: From Merced, drive south on Highway 99 for just a few miles to its junction with Highway 140. Turn east on Highway 140 and drive through Mariposa and on to Briceburg. At the Briceburg Visitors Center, turn left at a dirt road that is signed "BLM Camping Areas" (the road remains paved for about 150 yards). Drive over the suspension bridge and turn left, traveling downstream on the road, parallel to the river. Drive for two miles to McCabe Flat.

Trip note: What a spot: McCabe Flat is secluded on one of the prettiest sections of the Merced River, where you can enjoy great hiking, swimming and fishing, all on the same day. The access road out of camp leads downstream to the Yosemite Railroad Grade, which has been converted into a great trail. If you don't mind cold water, the Merced River's pools can provide relief from summer heat. Evening flyfishing is good in many of the same spots through July.

63. WILLOW PLACER 🐟 🏃 🏊 ✕ 🐴   ⑧

Reference: **On the Merced River east of Briceburg; map E4, grid h0.**

Campsites, facilities: There are five tent sites. Picnic tables and fire rings are provided. Vault toilets are available. Pets are permitted on leashes. A 14-day stay limit is enforced.

Reservations, fee: No reservations; $2 fee per person per night.

Who to contact: Phone Folsom Resource Area at (916) 985-4474, or write to Bureau of Land Management, 63 Natoma Street, Folsom, CA 95630.

Location: From Merced, drive south on Highway 99 for just a few miles to its junction with Highway 140. Turn east on Highway 140 and drive through Mariposa and on to Briceburg. At the Briceburg Visitors Center, turn left at a dirt road that is signed "BLM Camping Areas" (the road remains paved for about 150 yards). Drive over the suspension bridge and turn left, traveling downstream on the road, parallel to the river. Drive for four miles (two miles past McCabe Flat) to Willow Placer Campground.

Trip note: Willow Placer is a small, beautiful campground that gets overlooked by many travelers streaming to Yosemite. Evening trout fishing is decent, and rafting and swimming can be outstanding in this stretch of the Merced. Just a quarter-mile away, down the road leading out of camp, is the trailhead for the old Yosemite Railroad Grade, now a trail for hikers, bikers and horseback riders.

64. RAILROAD FLAT 🐟 🏃 🏊 ✕ 🐴   ⑧

Reference: **On the Merced River east of Briceburg; map E4, grid h0.**

Campsites, facilities: There are eight tent sites. Picnic tables and fire rings are provided. Vault toilets are available. Pets are permitted on leashes.

Reservations, fee: No reservations; $2 fee per person per night.

Who to contact: Phone Folsom Resource Area at (916) 985-4474, or write to Bureau of Land Management, 63 Natoma Street, Folsom, CA 95630.

Location: From Merced, drive south on Highway 99 for just a few miles to its junction with Highway 140. Turn east on Highway 140 and drive through Mariposa and on to Briceburg. At the Briceburg Visitors Center, turn left at a dirt road that is signed "BLM Camping Areas" (the road remains paved for about 150 yards). Drive over the suspension bridge and turn left, traveling downstream on the road, parallel to the river. Drive for 4.5 miles to where the road deadends at Railroad Flat Campground, about one-quarter mile past Willow Placer Camp.

Trip note: The access road that leads to the three BLM camps on the Merced River—McCabe Flat, Willow Placer and Railroad Flat—is actually part of the old Yosemite Railroad Grade. And the gate that blocks cars at Railroad Flat doesn't keep anybody else out—the old railroad is a great hiking, biking or horseback riding route that runs all the way to Bagby. Access to the adjacent

Merced River is good. It's a stretch of water that can be excellent for rafting and trout fishing. Insider's note: The spring wildflower display, which usually happens in April, is probably better at Red Hills (located just outside Chinese Camp) than anywhere in the Sierra foothills.

65. SUNNYSIDE WALK-IN

Reference: **In Yosemite Valley in Yosemite National Park; map E4, grid h4.**
Campsites, facilities: There are 35 walk-in tent sites. Each site must be shared with as many as six other campers. Picnic tables and fire pits are provided. Piped water and flush toilets are available. A parking area, showers, groceries and a laundromat are nearby. No pets allowed. A seven-day stay limit is enforced.
Reservations, fee: No reservations; $3 fee per night; $5 park entrance fee.
Who to contact: Phone Yosemite National Park at (209) 372-0200 for a touch-tone menu, or (209) 372-0265.
Location: After entering Yosemite Valley, drive past the chapel and turn left at the first stop sign. Cross Sentinel Bridge and drive about a quarter-mile, then turn left (at the sign for Yosemite Lodge) at the next stop sign. Drive a half-mile past the base of Yosemite Falls and look for the large sign marking the parking area for Sunnyside Walk-in Camp on the right.
Trip note: The concept at Sunnyside was to provide a walk-in camp alternative to drive-in camps that sometimes resemble combat camping. Unfortunately, it doesn't really work, with the sites here jammed together. Regardless, the camp is in a great location, within walking distance of Yosemite Falls. It has a view of Leidig Meadow and the southern valley rim, and with Sentinel Rock directly across the valley. A trail is routed from camp to Lower Yosemite Falls. In addition, the trailhead for the Yosemite Falls Trail is a short distance away, a terrible buttkicking climb up Columbia Rock to the rim adjacent to the top of the falls, providing one of most incredible views in all the world.

66. YOSEMITE-MARIPOSA KOA CAMP

Reference: **Near Mariposa; map E4, grid i0.**
Campsites, facilities: There are 40 tent sites, 30 motor home sites with full hookups, and six cabins. Picnic tables and barbecues are provided. Restrooms, showers, a sanitary disposal station, a laundromat, a store, propane gas, a recreation room, a swimming pool and a playground are available. Pets are allowed on leashes.
Reservations, fee: Reservations accepted; $20-$30 fee per night; $38 fee per night for cabins.
Who to contact: Phone the park at (209) 966-2201.
Location: From Merced, drive east on Highway 140 to Mariposa. Continue on Highway 140 for six miles to Midpines and 6323 Highway 140 and turn left at the campground entrance.
Trip note: A little duck pond, cute log cabins, a swimming pool, and the KOA's proximity to Yosemite National Park make this one a winner. The RV sites are lined up along the entrance road, edged by grass. A 10 p.m. "quiet time" helps ensure a good night's sleep. It's a one-hour drive to Yosemite Valley, and your best bet is to get there early to enjoy the spectacular beauty before the park is packed with people.

67. BRIDALVEIL CREEK

Reference: **Near Glacier Point in Yosemite National Park, map E4, grid i4.**

Campsites, facilities: There are 110 tent sites and motor homes. Picnic tables and fire grills are provided. Piped water and flush toilets are available. Pets are permitted on leashes. A 14-day stay limit is enforced.

Reservations, fee: No reservations; $10 fee per night.

Who to contact: Phone Yosemite National Park at (209) 372-0200 for a touch-tone menu, or (209) 372-0265.

Location: In Yosemite, drive toward Yosemite Valley and the junction of Highway 140 and Highway 41. Turn right on Highway 41 (Wawona Road) and drive about 10 miles to Glacier Point Road. Turn left on Glacier Point Road and drive about 25 miles (a few miles past Badger Pass Ski Area) to Peregoy Meadow and the campground access road on the right. Turn right and drive a short distance to the campground.

Trip note: There may be no better view in the world than the one provided from Glacier Point, looking down into Yosemite Valley, where Half Dome looks like nature's perfect sculpture work. Then there's the perfect views of Yosemite Falls, Nevada Falls, Vernal Falls and several hundred square miles of Yosemite's wilderness backcountry. This is the closest camp to Glacier Point's drive-to view, but it is also the closest camp to the best day hikes in the entire park. Along Glacier Point Road are trailheads to Sentinel Dome (incredible view of Yosemite Falls) and Taft Point (breathtaking drop, incredible view of El Capitan), and McGurk Meadow (one of the most pristine and romantic spots on planet earth). At 7,200 feet, the camp is more than 3,000 feet higher than Yosemite Valley. A good day hike out of camp leads you to Ostrander Lake, set just below Horse Ridge. Open June through September, though the camp may open later after winters with large snow accumulations.

68. JERSEYDALE

Reference: **In Sierra National Forest; map E4, grid j1.**

Campsites, facilities: There are 10 tent sites and two sites for tents or motor homes up to 22 feet long. Piped water, fire grills and picnic tables are provided. Vault toilets are available. A grocery store is nearby. Pets are allowed on leashes.

Reservations, fee: No reservations; $10 fee per night.

Who to contact: Phone the Sierra National Forest Mariposa Ranger District at (209) 683-4665.

Location: From Mariposa, drive northeast on Highway 140 for about five miles to Triangle Road (if you reach Midpines, you have gone 1.5 miles too far). Turn right (east) on Triangle Road and drive about six miles to Darrah and Jerseydale Road. Turn left (north) and drive three miles to the campground on the left side of the road (adjacent to the Jerseydale Ranger Station).

Trip note: This little camp gets overlooked by many visitors shut out of nearby Yosemite National Park simply because they don't realize it exists. It is set southwest of the national park in Sierra National Forest, with two good side trips nearby. If you continue north on Jerseydale Road to its end (about six miles) you will come to a gated Forest Service road/trailhead that provides access east for miles along the South Fork of the Merced River, where there is often good fishing, swimming and rafting. In addition, a dirt road from the camp is routed east for many miles into the Chowchilla Mountains. Open May through November.

69. SUMMIT CAMP

Reference: **In Sierra National Forest; map E4, grid j2.**

Campsites, facilities: There are two tent sites. Piped water, fire grills and picnic tables are provided. Vault toilets are available. Pets are allowed on leashes.

Reservations, fee: No reservations; no fee.

Who to contact: Phone the Sierra National Forest Mariposa Ranger District at (209) 683-4665.

Location: From Oakhurst, drive north on Highway 41 toward the town of Fish Camp and a gravel Forest Service Road (Road 5S09X, one mile before Fish Camp) on the left. Turn left and drive six miles (twisty) to the campground on the left side of the road.

Trip note: The prime attraction of tiny Summit Camp is its proximity to the Wawona entrance to Yosemite National Park. It is located along a twisty Forest Service road, perched in the Chowchilla Mountains at 5,800 feet, about three miles from Big Creek. It's an extremely little-known alternative when the park campgrounds at Wawona are packed. Open June to November.

---

70. SUMMERDALE

Reference: **On the South Fork of Merced River in Sierra National Forest; map E4, grid j3.**

Campsites, facilities: There are 21 tent sites and nine sites for tents or motor homes up to 22 feet long. Piped water, fire grills and picnic tables are provided. Vault toilets are available. A grocery store is nearby. Pets are allowed on leashes.

Reservations, fee: No reservations, but this camp usually fills by noon on Fridays; $12 fee per night.

Who to contact: Phone the Sierra National Forest Mariposa Ranger District at (209) 683-4665.

Location: From Oakhurst, drive north on Highway 41 to Fish Camp and continue for one mile to the campground entrance on the left side of the road.

Trip note: You can't get much closer to Yosemite National Park. This camp is set within a mile of the Wawona entrance to Yosemite, about a five-minute drive to the Mariposa Grove. If you don't mind its proximity to the highway, this is a pretty spot in its own right, set along Big Creek, a feeder stream to the South Fork Merced River. Some good swimming holes are in this area. The elevation is 5,000 feet. Open May to October.

---

71. MINARET FALLS

Reference: **On San Joaquin River in Inyo National Forest; map E4, grid j9.**

Campsites, facilities: There are 28 sites for tents or motor homes up to 55 feet long. Piped water, fire grills and picnic tables are provided. Chemical toilets and horseback riding facilities are available. Supplies can be purchased in Mammoth Lakes. Pets are permitted on leashes.

Reservations, fee: No reservations; $8 fee per night.

Who to contact: Phone the Inyo National Forest District Office at (619) 924-5500.

Location: On US 935, drive to Mammoth Junction (Highway 203). Turn west on Highway 203 and drive for four miles, through the town of Mammoth Lakes to Minaret Road (still Highway 203). Turn right and drive 4.5 miles to the Devils Postpile entrance kiosk (adjacent to the Mammoth Lakes Ski Area). Continue ahead for six miles to the campground entrance road on the right.

Turn right and drive a quarter-mile to the campground.

Trip note: This camp has one of the prettiest settings of the series of camps along the upper San Joaquin River and near Devils Postpile National Monument. It is set at 7,600 feet near Minaret Creek, across from where beautiful Minaret Falls pours into the San Joaquin River. Devils Postpile National Monument, one of the best examples in the world of hexagonal columnar rock, is less than a mile from camp, where there is also a trail to awesome Rainbow Falls. The Pacific Crest Trail runs right through this area as well, and if you hike to the south, there is excellent streamside fishing access.

Special note: Non-campers arriving between 7:30 a.m. and 5:30 p.m. are required to take a shuttle bus ($7 per person) from the entrance kiosk for access to this area.

---

72. DEVILS POSTPILE NATIONAL MONUMENT 🚶🏇 ♿   🚐 ⑨

Reference: **Near San Joaquin River; map E4, grid j9.**

Campsites, facilities: There are 21 sites for tents or motor homes. Piped water, fire grills and picnic tables are provided. Flush toilets are available. Pets are allowed on leashes.

Reservations, fee: No reservations; $6-$8 fee per night.

Who to contact: Phone the National Park Service at (619) 934-2289.

Location: On US 935, drive to Mammoth Junction (Highway 203). Turn west on Highway 203 and drive for four miles, through the town of Mammoth Lakes to Minaret Road (still Highway 203). Turn right and drive 4.5 miles to the Devils Postpile entrance kiosk (adjacent to the Mammoth Lakes Ski Area). Continue ahead for 7.8 miles to the campground entrance road on the right.

Trip note: Devils Postpile is a spectacular and rare example of hexagonal, columnar rock that look like posts, hence the name. The camp is set at 7,600 feet in elevation and provides nearby access for the easy hike to the Postpile. If you keep walking, it is a 2.5-mile walk to Rainbow Falls, a breathtaking cascade which produces rainbows in its floating mist, seen only from the trail alongside the waterfall looking downstream. The camp is also adjacent to the Upper San Joaquin River and the Pacific Crest Trail. Open mid-June to mid-October.

Special note: Non-campers arriving between 7:30 a.m. and 5:30 p.m. are required to take a shuttle bus ($7 per person) from the entrance kiosk for access to this area.

---

73. RED'S MEADOW 🚶🏇   🚐 ⑥

Reference: **In Inyo National Forest; map E4, grid j9.**

Campsites, facilities: There are 54 sites for tents or motor homes up to 55 feet long. Piped water, fire grills and picnic tables are provided and flush toilets, a natural hot springs, shower house and horseback riding facilities are available. Supplies can be purchased in Mammoth Lakes. Pets are permitted on leashes.

Reservations, fee: No reservations; $10 fee per night.

Who to contact: Phone the Inyo National Forest District Office at (619) 924-5500.

Location: On US 935, drive to Mammoth Junction (Highway 203). Turn west on Highway 203 and drive for four miles, through the town of Mammoth Lakes to Minaret Road (still Highway 203). Turn right and drive 4.5 miles to the Devils Postpile entrance kiosk (adjacent to the Mammoth Lakes Ski Area).

Continue ahead for 7.8 miles to the entrance to Devils Postpile National Monument. Bear left and drive two miles to the campground entrance road.

Trip note: Red's Meadows has long been established as one of the best outfitters for horseback riding trips. To get the feel of it, five-mile round-trips are available to Rainbow Falls. Multi-day trips into the Ansel Adams Wilderness on the Pacific Crest Trail are also available. A small restaurant is a bonus here, always a must-stop for long-distance hikers getting a shot to chomp their first hamburger in weeks, something like a bear finding a candy bar, quite a sight for the drive-in campers. The nearby Devils Postpile National Monument, Minaret Falls and San Joaquin River provide recreation options. Open June to October.

Special note: Non-campers arriving between 7:30 a.m. and 5:30 p.m. are required to take a shuttle bus ($7 per person) from the entrance kiosk for access to this area.

---

74. PUMICE FLAT

Reference: **On San Joaquin River in Inyo National Forest; map E4, grid j9.**

Campsites, facilities: There are 17 sites for tents or motor homes up to 22 feet long. Piped water, fire grills and picnic tables are provided. Flush toilets and horseback riding facilities are available. Supplies in Mammoth Lakes. Pets are permitted on leashes.

Reservations, fee: No reservations; $10 fee per night.

Who to contact: Phone the Inyo National Forest District Office at (619) 924-5500.

Location: On US 935, drive to Mammoth Junction (Highway 203). Turn west on Highway 203 and drive for four miles, through the town of Mammoth Lakes to Minaret Road (still Highway 203). Turn right and drive 4.5 miles to the Devils Postpile entrance kiosk (adjacent to the Mammoth Lakes Ski Area). Continue ahead for five miles to the campground on the right side of the road.

Trip note: Pumice Flat, 7,700 feet in elevation, provides roadside camping within short range of several adventures. A trail out of camp links with the Pacific Crest Trail, where you can hike along the upper San Joaquin River for miles, providing excellent access for flyfishing, heading north into the Ansel Adams Wilderness. Devils Postpile National Monument is just two miles south, along with the trailhead for Rainbow Falls. Open June to mid-September.

Special note: Non-campers arriving between 7:30 a.m. and 5:30 p.m. are required to take a shuttle bus ($7 per person) from the entrance kiosk for access to this area.

---

75. UPPER SODA SPRINGS

Reference: **On San Joaquin River in Inyo National Forest; map E4, grid j9.**

Campsites, facilities: There are 29 sites for tents or motor homes up to 55 feet long. Piped water, fire grills and picnic tables are provided. Flush toilets and horseback riding facilities are available. Supplies can be purchased in Mammoth Lakes. Pets are permitted on leashes.

Reservations, fee: No reservations; $8 fee per night.

Who to contact: Phone the Inyo National Forest District Office at (619) 924-5500.

Location: On US 935, drive to Mammoth Junction (Highway 203). Turn west on Highway 203 and drive for four miles, through the town of Mammoth Lakes to Minaret Road (still Highway 203). Turn right and drive 4.5 miles to the Devils Postpile entrance kiosk (adjacent to the Mammoth Lakes Ski Area).

Continue ahead for five miles to the campground entrance road on the right. Turn right and drive a quarter-mile to the campground.

Trip note: This is a premium location, within earshot of the upper San Joaquin River and within minutes of many first-class recreation options. The river is stocked with trout at this camp, with several good pools within short walking distance. Farther upstream, accessible by an excellent trail, are smaller wild trout that provide good flyfishing. Devils Postpile National Monument, a massive formation of ancient columnar rock, is only three miles to the south. The Pacific Crest Trail passes right by the camp, providing a trailhead for access to numerous lakes in the Ansel Adams Wilderness. The elevation is 7,700 feet. Open June to October.

Special note: Non-campers arriving between 7:30 a.m. and 5:30 p.m. are required to take a shuttle bus ($7 per person) from the entrance kiosk for access to this area.

76. AGNEW MEADOWS ⌊🐟 🏃 🐎   RV 9

Reference: **In Inyo National Forest; map E4, grid j9.**

Campsites, facilities: There are 22 sites for tents or motor homes up to 22 feet long. A group camp is also available (reservations required for group camp). Piped water, fire grills and picnic tables are provided. Chemical toilets and horseback riding facilities are available. Supplies can be obtained in Mammoth Lakes. Pets are permitted on leashes.

Reservations, fee: No reservations; $8 fee per night. Reservations required for group camp, reserve by calling (800) 280-CAMP; $15 reservation fee; $20-$40 fee per night.

Who to contact: Phone the Inyo National Forest District Office at (619) 924-5500.

Location: On US 935, drive to Mammoth Junction (Highway 203). Turn west on Highway 203 and drive for four miles, through the town of Mammoth Lakes to Minaret Road (still Highway 203). Turn right and drive 4.5 miles to the Devils Postpile entrance kiosk (adjacent to the Mammoth Lakes Ski Area). Continue ahead for four miles to the campground entrance road on the right. Turn right and drive just under a mile to the campground.

Trip note: This is a perfect camp to use as a launching pad for a backpacking trip or day of flyfishing for trout. It is set along the upper San Joaquin River at 8,400 feet, with a trailhead for the Pacific Crest Trail available right at the camp. From here, you can hike six miles to the gorgeous Thousand Island Lake, a beautiful lake sprinkled with islands set below Banner and Ritter Peaks in the spectacular Minarets. For day hikes, another choice is walking the River Trail, which is routed from Agnew Meadows along the San Joaquin, providing excellent fishing, though the trout are small. Open late June to October.

Special note: Non-campers arriving between 7:30 a.m. and 5:30 p.m. are required to take a shuttle bus ($7 per person) from the entrance kiosk for access to this area. If you take the shuttle and wish to visit this camp for the excellent hiking and fishing access, be certain to tell the driver. Scheduled stops are not usually planned here.

77. PUMICE FLAT GROUP CAMP ⌊🐟 🏃 🐎   RV 6

Reference: **On San Joaquin River in Inyo National Forest; map E4, grid j9.**

Campsites, facilities: There are four group sites for tents or motor homes up to 22 feet long. Piped water, fire grills and picnic tables are provided. Flush toilets and horseback riding facilities are available. Supplies can be purchased in Mammoth Lakes. Pets are permitted on leashes.

Reservations, fee: Reserve by phoning (800) 280-CAMP; $15 reservation fee; $20-$55 fee per night per group.

Who to contact: Phone the Inyo National Forest District Office at (619) 924-5500.

Location: On US 935, drive to Mammoth Junction (Highway 203). Turn west on Highway 203 and drive for four miles, through the town of Mammoth Lakes to Minaret Road (still Highway 203). Turn right and drive 4.5 miles to the Devils Postpile entrance kiosk (adjacent to the Mammoth Lakes Ski Area). Continue ahead for five miles to the campground on the right side of the road.

Trip note: This camp is set at 7,700 feet in elevation near the Upper San Joaquin River, adjacent to Pumice Camp. For recreation information, see trip note for Pumice Camp. Open June to October.

---

78. HODGDON MEADOW   RV 7

Reference: **In Yosemite National Park; map E4, grid g1.**

Campsites, facilities: There are 105 family sites for tents or motor homes up to 35 feet long. There are also four group sites for up to 30 people and a few walk-in camps for tents only. Piped water, fire rings and picnic tables are provided. Flush toilets are available. A grocery store and propane gas are nearby. Pets are permitted on leashes in campgrounds, but not on trails.

Reservations, fee: Reserve by phoning Destinet at (800) 365-2267; $10-$12 fee per night; group campsite fee is $35 per night.

Who to contact: Phone Yosemite National Park at (209) 372-0200 for a touch-tone menu, or (209) 372-0265.

Location: From Groveland, drive east on Highway 120 to the Big Oak Flat entrance station for Yosemite National Park. Just after passing the entrance station, turn left and drive a short distance to the campground.

Trip note: Hodgdon Meadow is set on the outskirts of Yosemite, just inside the park's borders at the Highway 120 entrance station, at 4,900 feet in elevation. It is located near a small feeder creek to South Fork Tuolumne River. It is about a 20-minute drive on Highway 120 to a major junction, where a left turn takes you on Tioga Road and to Yosemite's high country, including Tuolumne Meadows, and a right routes you toward Yosemite Valley (25 miles from the camp). Open year-round.

---

79. WHITE WOLF   RV 8

Reference: **In Yosemite National Park; map E4, grid g4.**

Campsites, facilities: There are 87 sites for tents or motor homes up to 35 feet long. Piped water, fire rings and picnic tables are provided. Flush toilets and evening ranger programs are available. A grocery store is nearby. Pets are permitted on leashes in campground, but not on trails.

Reservations, fee: No reservations; $10 fee per night.

Who to contact: Phone Yosemite National Park at (209) 372-0200 for a touch-tone menu, or (209) 372-0265.

Location: From Merced, drive east on Highway 140 to the El Portal entrance station at Yosemite National Park. Continue east on Highway 140 to the junction with Highway 120/Tioga Road (just before entering the valley). Turn left and drive to the junction with Highway 120. Turn right and drive 15 miles to White Wolf Road on the left. Turn left and drive one mile to the campground entrance road on the right.

Trip note: This is one of Yosemite National Park's prime mountain camps for people who like to hike, either for great day hikes in the immediate area and beyond, or for overnight backpacking trips. The day hike to Lukens Lake is an easy two-mile trip, the payoff being this pretty little alpine lake set amid a meadow, pines and granite. Just about everybody who camps at White Wolf makes the trip. Backpackers can make the overnight trip into the Ten Lakes Basin, set below Grand Mountain and Colby Mountain. Bears are common at this camp, so be certain to secure your food in the bear-proof lockers. The elevation is 8,000 feet. Open June through mid-September.

80. PORCUPINE FLAT 🏃🏃   RV 6

Reference: **Near Yosemite Creek in Yosemite National Park; map E4, grid g5.**
Campsites, facilities: There are 52 sites for tents or motor homes up to 35 feet long. There is limited RV space. Fire rings and picnic tables are provided. Pit toilets are available. There is **no piped water**, so bring your own. No pets are permitted.
Reservations, fee: No reservations; $6 fee per night.
Who to contact: Phone Yosemite National Park at (209) 372-0200 for a touch-tone menu, or (209) 372-0265.
Location: From Merced, drive east on Highway 140 to the El Portal entrance station at Yosemite National Park. Continue east on Highway 140 to the junction with Highway 120/Tioga Road (just before entering the valley). Turn left and drive to the junction with Highway 120. Turn right and drive about 25 miles to the campground on the left side of the road (16 miles west from Tuolumne Meadows).
Trip note: Porcupine Flat, set at 8,100 feet, is southwest of Mt. Hoffman, one of the prominent nearby peaks along Tioga Road in Yosemite National Park. The trailhead to hike to May Lake, set just below Mt. Hoffman, is located about five miles away, on a signed turnoff on the north side of the road. There are several little peaks above the lake where hikers can gain great views, including one of the back side of Half Dome. Open June to October.

81. TUOLUMNE MEADOWS 🐟 🏃🏃 🐎   RV 8

Reference: **In Yosemite National Park; map E4, grid g7.**
Campsites, facilities: There are 314 sites for tents or motor homes up to 35 feet long. Piped water, flush toilets, picnic tables, fire grills and a dump station are provided, but no hookups. Pets are permitted on leashes. Showers and groceries are available nearby. There are also an additional 25 hike-in sites available for backpackers (usually those hiking the Pacific Crest Trail), and eight group sites that can accommodate 30 people each.
Reservations, fee: Reserve by phoning Destinet at (800) 365-2267. Only half of the sites are available through reservations; the other half are first come, first served. There is a $12 fee per night for family sites, $3 fee per night for walk-in sites, $35 fee per night for group sites. The 25 hike-in sites are free.
Who to contact: Phone Yosemite National Park at (209) 372-0200 for a touch-tone menu, or (209) 372-0265.
Location: From Merced, drive east on Highway 140 to the El Portal entrance station at Yosemite National Park. Continue east on Highway 140 to the junction with Highway 120/Tioga Road (just before entering the valley). Turn

left and drive to the junction with Highway 120. Turn right and drive 46 miles to the campground on the right side of the road. (From just south of Lee Vining at the junction of US 395 and Highway 120, turn west and drive to the Tioga Pass entrance station for Yosemite National Park. Continue for about 10 miles to the campground entrance on the left.)

Trip note: This is Yosemite's biggest camp, and for the variety of nearby adventures, it might also be the best. It is set in the high country, at 8,600 feet, and can be used as a base camp for fishing, hiking and horseback riding, or as a jumpoff point for a backpacking trip (wilderness permits required). There are two outstanding and easy day hikes from here, one heading north on the Pacific Crest Trail for the near-level walk to Tuolumne Falls, the other heading south up Lyell Fork, with good fishing for small brook trout. With a backpack, either route can be extended for as long as desired into remote and beautiful country. The campground is huge, and neighbors are guaranteed, but it is well wooded, feels somewhat secluded, even with all the RVs and tents. There are lots of food-raiding bears in the area, and using the food lockers is required. Open June through mid-October.

82. CRANE FLAT   RV 6

Reference: **Near Tuolumne Grove of Big Trees in Yosemite National Park; map E4, grid h2.**

Campsites, facilities: There are 166 sites for tents or motor homes up to 35 feet long. Piped water, fire rings and picnic tables are provided. Flush toilets, groceries, propane gas and evening ranger programs are available. A gas station is nearby.

Reservations, fee: Reserve by phoning Destinet at (800) 365-2267; $12 fee per night from May through October.

Who to contact: Phone Yosemite National Park at (209) 372-0200 for a touch-tone menu, or (209) 372-0265.

Location: From Groveland, drive east on Highway 120 to the Big Oak Flat entrance station for Yosemite National Park. After passing through the entrance station, drive about 10 miles to the campground entrance road on the right. Turn right and drive a half-mile to the campground.

Trip note: Crane Flat is located within a five-minute drive of the Tuolumne Grove of Big Trees, as well as the Merced Grove to the nearby west. This is the feature attraction in this part of Yosemite National Park, set near the western border near the Highway 120 entrance station. The camp is set at 6,200 feet. Reaching Yosemite Valley is about a 25-minute drive. Open May through October.

83. TAMARACK FLAT   RV 7

Reference: **On Tamarack Creek in Yosemite National Park; map E4, grid h3.**

Campsites, facilities: There are 52 tent sites or very small motor homes up to 24 feet long. Fire rings and picnic tables are provided. Pit toilets are available. No piped water is available, so bring your own. No pets are permitted.

Reservations, fee: No reservations; $6 fee per night.

Who to contact: Phone Yosemite National Park at (209) 372-0200 for a touch-tone menu, or (209) 372-0265.

Location: From Merced, drive east on Highway 140 to the El Portal entrance station at Yosemite National Park. Continue east on Highway 140 to the junction with Highway 120/Tioga Road (just before entering the valley). Turn left and drive to the junction with Highway 120. Turn right on Tioga Road and drive three miles to the campground entrance on the right side of the road. Turn right and drive 2.5 miles to the campground. Trailers and RVs are not advised.

Trip note: The road in to this campground looks something like the surface of the moon. Then you arrive and find one of the few primitive drive-to camps in Yosemite National Park, 6,300 feet in elevation. From the trailhead at camp, you can link up with the El Capitan Trail, then hike across Ribbon Meadow on up to the north valley rim at El Capitan, 7,569 feet. This is the largest single piece of granite in the world, and standing atop it for both the sensation and the divine view is a breathtaking experience. From camp, Yosemite Valley is 23 miles away. Open June through mid-October.

---

84. LOWER PINES 🛶 🐟 🚶 🏊 🍴 🐎   RV 9

Reference: In Yosemite Valley in Yosemite National Park; map E4, grid h4.

Campsites, facilities: There are 172 sites for tents or motor homes up to 35 feet long. Fire rings and picnic tables are provided. Piped water and flush toilets are available. A grocery store, a laundromat, propane gas, a recycling center and horse, bike and cross-country ski rentals are available nearby. Pets are allowed from November through March only.

Reservations, fee: Reserve by phoning Destinet at (800) 365-2267; $15 fee per night.

Who to contact: Phone Yosemite National Park at (209) 372-0200 for a touch-tone menu, or (209) 372-0265.

Location: After entering Yosemite Valley, drive past Curry Village (on the right) and Stoneman Meadow (on the left) to the campground entrance on the left side of the road (just before Clarks Bridge and the horse stables).

Trip note: For combat-style camping, this is a pretty good place. Lower Pines is set right along the Merced River, quite pretty, in the center of Yosemite Valley. Of course, the tents and RVs are jammed in quite close together. Within walking distance is the trail to Mirror Lake (a zoo on parade), as well as the trailhead at Happy Isles for the hike up to Vernal Falls and Nevada Falls. The park's shuttle bus picks up riders near the camp entrance. Open year-round.

---

85. UPPER RIVER 🛶 🐟 🚶 🏊 🍴 🐎   9

Reference: In Yosemite Valley in Yosemite National Park; map E4, grid h4.

Campsites, facilities: There are 124 tent sites. Fire rings and picnic tables are provided. Piped water and flush toilets are available. A grocery store, a laundromat, propane gas, a recycling center, and horse and bike rentals are available nearby. Pets are not allowed.

Reservations, fee: Reserve by phoning Destinet at (800) 365-2267; $15 fee per night.

Who to contact: Phone Yosemite National Park at (209) 372-0200 for a touch-tone menu, or (209) 372-0265.

Location: After entering Yosemite Valley, drive LeConte Memorial to an intersection (Curry Village is on the right). Turn left and drive over Stoneman Bridge and continue a short distance to the campground entrance on the right.

Trip note: Upper River Camp is set along the Merced River in Yosemite Valley, within walking distance of the Ahwahnee Hotel, located about a half-mile north. Bicycle rentals are available at nearby Curry Village, and from there, you can ride a circle around the valley floor for perfect views of Yosemite Falls,

Bridalveil Falls, Half Dome, El Capitan and the glacial-sculpted Yosemite Valley rim. A shuttle bus makes stops at the campground's entrance. Open May to mid-October.

86. LOWER RIVER 〽️🏕️🏊✕🐎   RV 9

Reference: **In Yosemite Valley in Yosemite National Park; map E4, grid h4.**

Campsites, facilities: There are 126 sites for tents or motor homes up to 40 feet long. Fire grills and picnic tables are provided. Piped water, flush toilets and a sanitary disposal station are available. A grocery store, a laundromat, propane gas, a recycling center, a visitor center and horse and bike rentals are available nearby. Pets are not allowed.

Reservations, fee: Reserve by phoning Destinet at (800) 365-2267; $15 fee per night.

Who to contact: Phone Yosemite National Park at (209) 372-0200 for a touch-tone menu, or (209) 372-0265.

Location: After entering Yosemite Valley, drive LeConte Memorial to an intersection (Curry Village is on the right). Turn left and drive over Stoneman Bridge and continue a short distance to the campground entrance on the left.

Trip note: It looks something like Tent City in summer months, and that's because it is. It can be a strange scene, all these campers jammed together in the center of Yosemite Valley, the world's greatest natural showpiece. This camp is located directly across the road from Upper River. See that trip note for recreation options. Open May to October.

87. UPPER PINES 〽️🏕️🏊✕🐎   RV 9

Reference: **In Yosemite Valley in Yosemite National Park; map E4, grid h5.**

Campsites, facilities: There are 238 sites for tents or motor homes up to 35 feet long. Fire rings and picnic tables are provided. Piped water, flush toilets and a sanitary disposal station are available. A grocery store, laundromat, propane gas, recycling center, and horse and bike rentals are available nearby. Pets are permitted on leashes in the campground, but not on trails.

Reservations, fee: Reserve by phoning Destinet at (800) 365-2267; $15 fee per night.

Who to contact: Phone Yosemite National Park at (209) 372-0200 for a touch-tone menu, or (209) 372-0265.

Location: After entering Yosemite Valley, drive past Curry Village (on the right) and Stoneman Meadow (on the left) to the campground entrance on the right side of the road (just before Clarks Bridge and the horse stables).

Trip note: Of the campgrounds in Yosemite Valley, Upper Pines is located closest to the jumpoff to paradise, providing you can get a campsite to the far south end of the camp. From here it is a short walk to the Happy Isles Trailhead, and with it, the chance to hike to Vernal Falls on the Mist Trail (steep), or beyond to Nevada Falls (very steep) at the foot of Liberty Cap. But crowded this camp is, and you'd best expect it. People come from all over the world to camp here. Sometimes it appears they are from other worlds as well. The elevation is 4,000 feet. Open April to November.

88. NORTH PINES 〽️🏕️🏊✕🐎   RV 9

Reference: **In Yosemite Valley in Yosemite National Park; map E4, grid h5.**

Campsites, facilities: There are 86 sites for tents or motor homes up to 30 feet long.

Piped water, fire grills and picnic tables are provided. Flush toilets are available. A grocery store, laundromat, recycling center, propane gas and horse and bike rentals are available nearby. No pets are allowed.

Reservations, fee: Reserve by phoning Destinet at (800) 365-2267; $15 fee per night.

Who to contact: Phone Yosemite National Park at (209) 372-0200 for a touch-tone menu, or (209) 372-0265.

Location: After entering Yosemite Valley, drive past Curry Village (on the right) and Stoneman Meadow (on the left). Continue past Upper and Lower Pines campgrounds, drive over Clarks Bridge, turn left (at the horse stables) and drive a short distance to the campground on the right.

Trip note: North Pines Camp is set along the Merced River, within a very short distance of the stables for horseback riding rentals. A trail out of camp heads east and links up the paved road/trail to Mirror Lake, a virtual parade of people. If you continue hiking past Mirror Lake you will get astounding views of Half Dome, and in addition, leave the masses behind as you enter Tenaya Canyon. The elevation is 4,000 feet. Open May to October.

---

89. WAWONA

Reference: **On the South Fork of the Merced River in Yosemite National Park; map E4, grid j3.**

Campsites, facilities: There are 100 sites for tents or motor homes up to 35 feet long and one group campsite. Piped water, fire rings and picnic tables are provided. Flush toilets are available. A grocery store, propane gas and horseback riding facilities are available nearby. Pets are permitted on leashes in the campground, but not on trails. There are also some stock handling facilities for camping with pack animals; call for further information.

Reservations, fee: No reservations for family camping; $10 fee per night. For a group campsite, write to Wawona Group Reservations, Wawona District Office, P.O. Box 2027, Yosemite National Park, CA 95389; $34 fee per night.

Who to contact: Phone Yosemite National Park at (209) 372-0200 for a touch-tone menu, or (209) 372-0265.

Location: From Oakhurst, drive north on Highway 41 to the Wawona entrance to Yosemite National Park. Continue north on Highway 41 past Wawona (golf course on the left) and drive one mile to the campground entrance on the left.

Trip note: Wawona Camp is an attractive alternative to the packed camps in Yosemite Valley, providing you don't mind the relatively long drives to the best destinations. The camp is pretty, set along the South Fork Merced River, with the sites more spaciously situated that at most other drive-to camps in the park. The nearest attraction is the Mariposa Grove of Giant Sequoias, but get your visit in early and be out by 9 a.m., because after that it turns into a zoo, complete with shuttle train. The best nearby hike is a strenuous eight-mile roundtrip to Chilnualna Falls, the prettiest sight in the southern region of the park, with its trailhead located at the east end of The Redwoods in North Wawona. It's a 45-minute drive to either Glacier Point or Yosemite Valley. Open year-round.

NOR-CAL MAP .... see page 94
adjoining maps
NORTH .... no map
EAST .... no map
SOUTH (F5) .... see page 564
WEST (E4) .... see page 460

24 LISTINGS
PAGES 500-510

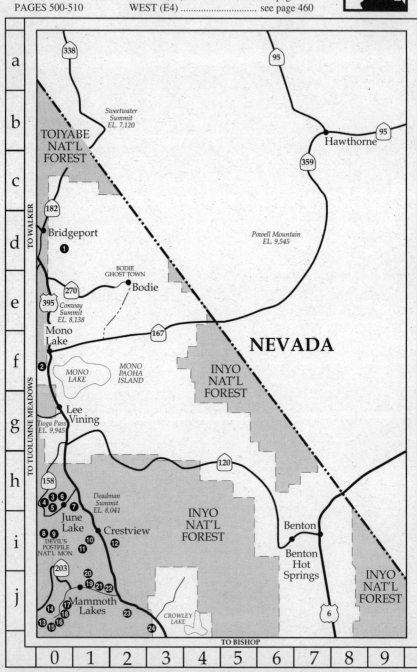

Map E5 featuring: Mono Lake, Inyo National Forest, June Lake, Twin Lakes

1. WILLOW SPRINGS TRAILER PARK   RV. 6

Reference: **Near Bridgeport; map E5, grid d0.**

Campsites, facilities: There are 25 motor home sites with picnic tables and full hookups. Restrooms, showers, a trout pond and a laundromat are available. Pets are allowed on leashes.

Reservations, fee: Reservations accepted; $18 fee per night.

Who to contact: Phone the park at (619) 932-7725.

Location: From Bridgeport on US 395, drive five miles south to the park.

Trip note: Willow Springs Trailer Park is set at 6,800 feet along US 395, which runs along the eastern Sierra from Carson City south to Bishop and Independence. The country is stark here, on the edge of the high Nevada desert, but there are many side trips that give the area life. The most popular destinations are to the nearby south, Mono Lake with its tufa towers and incredible populations of breeding gulls and waterfowl, and the ghost town of Bodie. For trout fishing, there's Bridgeport Reservoir to the north (good trolling) and downstream to the East Walker River (flyfishing), both excellent destinations, as well as Twin Lakes to the west (huge brown trout). Ken's Sporting Goods in Bridgeport provides excellent information. Open May to October.

2. LUNDY CREEK   RV. 7

Reference: **Near Lundy Lake; map E5, grid f0.**

Campsites, facilities: There are 50 sites for tents or motor homes up to 24 feet long. Pit toilets are available. There is **no piped water**, so bring your own. Pets are permitted on leashes. Supplies can be purchased in Lee Vining.

Reservations, fee: No reservations; $5 fee per night.

Who to contact: Phone the Mono County Building and Parks Department at (619) 932-5231.

Location: From Lee Vining, drive north on US 395 for seven miles to Lundy Lake Road. Turn left and drive a short distance to the campground.

Trip note: This camp is set high in the eastern Sierra at 7,800 feet elevation along pretty Lundy Creek, the mountain stream that feeds Lundy Lake and then runs downhill, eventually joining other creeks on its trip to nearby Mono Lake. Nearby Lundy Lake is a long narrow lake with good fishing for rainbow trout and brown trout. There is a trailhead just west of the lake that is routed steeply up into the Hoover Wilderness to several small pretty lakes, passing two waterfalls about two miles in. A must-do side trip is visiting Mono Lake and its spectacular tufa towers, best done at the Mono Lake Tufa State Reserve along the southern shore of the lake. Open May through October.

3. PINE CLIFF RESORT   RV. 7

Reference: **At June Lake; map E5, grid h0.**

Campsites, facilities: There are 55 sites for tents only, 17 partial-hookup sites for tents or motor homes, and 154 motor home sites with full or partial hookups. Fire rings, picnic tables, piped water, electrical connections and sewer hookups are provided at most sites. Restrooms, showers, a laundromat, a store and propane gas are available. A boat ramp, boat and tackle rentals, fish cleaning facilities and fuel are available nearby. Pets are permitted on leashes

Reservations, fee: Reservations recommended; $8-$15 fee per night.

Who to contact: Phone the park at (619) 648-7558.

Location: From Lee Vining, drive south on US 395 (past the first Highway 158/ June Lake Loop turnoff) to June Lake Junction (a gas station/store is on the west side of the road) and Highway 158. Turn west on Highway 158 and drive two miles to Oh! Ridge Road. Turn right (north) and drive one mile to the park entrance road on the left.

Trip note: This camp is in a pretty setting along the north shore of June Lake, 7,600 feet in elevation, the feature lake among four in the June Lake Loop. This is a 160-acre high-mountain lake set below snow-capped peaks, and gets large numbers of trout plants each summer, making it extremely popular for fishermen. Of the lakes in the June Lake Loop, this is the one that has the most everything—the most beauty, the most fish, the most developed accommodations, and alas, the most people. Open mid-April through October.

---

4. SILVER LAKE RV 9

Reference: In Inyo National Forest; map E5, grid h0.

Campsites, facilities: There are 65 sites for tents or motor homes up to 22 feet long. Piped water, fire grills, and picnic tables are provided. Flush toilets and horseback riding facilities are available. A grocery store, a laundromat, motorboat rentals, a boat ramp, bait, a snack bar, boat fuel and propane gas are available nearby. Pets are allowed on leashes.

Reservations, fee: No reservations; $10 fee per night.

Who to contact: Phone the Inyo National Forest District Office at (619) 647-3000.

Location: From Lee Vining on US 395, drive south to the first Highway 158/June Lake Loop turnoff. Turn west and drive nine miles (past Grant Lake) to Silver Lake. Just as you arrive at Silver Lake (a small store is on the right), turn left at the campground entrance.

Trip note: Silver Lake is set at 7,600 feet, an 80-acre lake in the June Lake Loop with Carson Peak looming in the background. Boat rentals, fishing for trout at the lake, a beautiful trout stream (Rush Creek) next to the camp, and a nearby trailhead for wilderness hiking and horseback riding (rentals available) are the highlights. The camp is largely exposed and vulnerable to winds, the only downer. Within walking distance to the south is Silver Lake, always a pretty sight, especially when afternoon winds cause the lake surface to sparkle in crackling silvers. Just across the road from the camp is a great trailhead for the Ansel Adams Wilderness, with a two-hour hike available that climbs up to pretty Agnew Lake overlooking the June Lake basin. Open May to October.

---

5. JUNE LAKE RV 9

Reference: In Inyo National Forest; map E5, grid h0.

Campsites, facilities: There are 22 sites for tents or motor homes up to 22 feet long. Piped water, fire grills and picnic tables are provided. Flush toilets and a boat ramp are available. A grocery store, a laundromat, boat and tackle rentals, moorings, and propane gas are available nearby. Pets are allowed on leashes.

Reservations, fee: No reservations; $10 fee per night.

Who to contact: Phone the Inyo National Forest District Office at (619) 647-3000.

Location: From Lee Vining, drive south on US 395 (past the first Highway 158/

June Lake Loop turnoff) to June Lake Junction (a gas station/store is on the west side of the road) and Highway 158. Turn west on Highway 158 and drive two miles to June Lake. Turn right (north) and drive a short distance to campground.

Trip note: There are three campgrounds at pretty June Lake; this is one of the two operated by the Forest Service (the other is Oh! Ridge). This one is located on the northeast shore of the lake, at 7,600 feet in elevation, a pretty spot with all supplies available just two miles to the south in the town of June Lake. The nearest boat launch is north of town. This is a good lake for trout fishing, receiving nearly 100,000 stocked trout per year. Open mid-April to November.

---

6. OH! RIDGE 🐟 ⚓ 🏊   RV 7

Reference: **On June Lake in Inyo National Forest; map E5, grid h0.**

Campsites, facilities: There are 148 sites for tents or motor homes up to 32 feet long. Piped water, fire grills and picnic tables are provided. Flush toilets and a playground are available. A grocery store, a laundromat, a boat ramp, boat and tackle rentals, a swimming beach, moorings, and propane gas are available nearby. Pets are allowed on leashes.

Reservations, fee: Reserve by calling (800) 280-CAMP ($7.50 reservation fee); $10 camping fee per night.

Who to contact: Phone the Inyo National Forest District Office at (619) 647-3000.

Location: From Lee Vining, drive south on US 395 (past the first Highway 158/June Lake Loop turnoff) to June Lake Junction (a gas station/store is on the west side of the road) and Highway 158. Turn west on Highway 158 and drive two miles to Oh! Ridge Road. Turn right (north) and drive one mile to the campground.

Trip note: This is the biggest of the campgrounds on June Lake, but it is not the most popular since it is not set at lakeshore, but back about a quarter-mile or so from the north end of the lake. Regardless, it is a beautiful setting, with the ridge of the high Sierra providing a backdrop, along with good trout fishing. The elevation is 7,600 feet. Open mid-April to November.

---

7. HARTLEY SPRINGS 🚶   RV 5

Reference: **In Inyo National Forest; map E5, grid h1.**

Campsites, facilities: There are 21 sites for tents or motor homes up to 40 feet long. Fire grills and picnic tables are provided. Vault toilets are available. There is **no piped water**, so bring your own. Pets are allowed on leashes.

Reservations, fee: No reservations; no fee.

Who to contact: Phone the Inyo National Forest District Office at (619) 647-3000.

Location: From Lee Vining, drive south on US 395 for 11 miles to June Lake Junction. Continue south for two miles to a dirt Forest Service road on the right. Turn right and drive two miles to the campground entrance road on the left.

Trip note: Even though this camp is only a five-minute drive from US 395, those five minutes will take you into another orbit. It has the feel of a remote, primitive camp, set in a dusty, spartan high mountain environment at 8,400 feet in elevation. About two miles to the immediate north is Obsidian Dome "Glass Flow," at 8,611 feet, which a craggy geologic formation that some people enjoy scrambling around and exploring; pick your access point carefully. Open June to mid-September.

8. REVERSED CREEK

Reference: **In Inyo National Forest; map E5, grid i0.**

Campsites, facilities: There are 17 sites for tents or motor homes up to 22 feet long. Piped water, fire grills and picnic tables are provided. Flush toilets are available. A grocery store, a laundromat and propane gas are nearby. Boating is available at nearby Silver Lake, two miles away. Pets are allowed on leashes.

Reservations, fee: No reservations; $10 fee per night.

Who to contact: Phone the Inyo National Forest District Office at (619) 647-3000.

Location: From Lee Vining, drive south on US 395 (past the first Highway 158/ June Lake Loop turnoff) to June Lake Junction (a gas station/store is on the west side of the road) and Highway 158. Turn west on Highway 158 and drive three miles to the campground on the left side of the road (across from Gull Lake).

Trip note: This camp is set at 7,600 feet near pretty Reversed Creek, the only stream in the region that flows towards the mountains, not away from them. It is a small, tree-lined stream that provides decent trout fishing. There are also cabins available for rent near here. Directly opposite the camp, on the other side of the road, is Gull Lake and the boat ramp. Two miles to the west, on the west side of the road, is the trailhead for the hike to Fern Lake on the edge of the Ansel Adams Wilderness, a little buttkicker of a climb. Open May to October.

9. GULL LAKE

Reference: **In Inyo National Forest; map E5, grid i0.**

Campsites, facilities: There are 10 sites for tents or motor homes up to 22 feet long. Piped water, fire grills and picnic tables are provided, and flush toilets are available. A grocery store, a laundromat, a boat ramp and propane gas are available nearby. Pets are allowed on leashes.

Reservations, fee: No reservations; $10 fee per night.

Who to contact: Phone the Inyo National Forest District Office at (619) 647-3000.

Location: From Lee Vining, drive south on US 395 (past the first Highway 158/ June Lake Loop turnoff) to June Lake Junction (a gas station/store is on the west side of the road) and Highway 158. Turn west on Highway 158 and drive three miles to the campground entrance on the right side of the road .

Trip note: Little Gull Lake, just 64 acres, is the smallest of the lakes on the June Lake Loop, but to many it is the prettiest. It is set at 7,600 feet, just west of June Lake, and with Carson Peak looming on the Sierra crest to the west, it is a dramatic and intimate setting. The lake is stocked with nearly 50,000 trout each summer, providing good fishing. A boat ramp is located on the lake's southwest corner. Open May to November.

10. GLASS CREEK

Reference: **In Inyo National Forest; map E5, grid i1.**

Campsites, facilities: There are 50 sites for tents or motor homes up to 22 feet long. Fire grills and picnic tables are provided. Vault toilets are available. There is **no piped water**, so bring your own. Pets are allowed on leashes.

Reservations, fee: No reservations; no fee.

Who to contact: Phone the Inyo National Forest District Office at (619) 647-3000.

Location: From Lee Vining, drive south on US 395 for 11 miles to June Lake Junction. Continue south for six miles to a Forest Service road (Glass Creek

Road) on the right side of the road. Turn right and drive a quarter-mile to the camp access road on the right. Turn right and drive a half-mile to the camp at the end of the road. (Note: If arriving from the south on US 395, you will pass the CalTrans Crestview Maintenance Station on the right. Continue north, make a U-turn when possible and follow the above directions.)

Trip note: This primitive camp is set along Glass Creek at 7,600 feet, about a mile from Obsidian Dome to the nearby west. A trail follows Glass Creek past the southern edge of the dome, a craggy, volcanic formation that tops out at 8,611 feet in elevation. That trail continues along Glass Creek, climbing to the foot of San Joaquin Mountain for a great view of the high desert to the east. An insider's note is that the Department of Fish and Game stocks Glass Creek with trout just once each June, right at the camp. Open mid-May to November.

11. DEADMAN 🐟 🏃 ██ 5

Reference: **On Deadman Creek in Inyo National Forest; map E5, grid i1.**

Campsites, facilities: There are 30 sites for tents or motor homes up to 22 feet long. A group camp is also available (reservations required). Fire grills and picnic tables are provided. Vault toilets are available. There is **no piped water**. Pets are allowed on leashes.

Reservations, fee: No reservations; no fee. Reservations required for group camps; $20 fee per day. Reserve by calling (800) 280-CAMP ($15 reservation fee).

Who to contact: Phone the Inyo National Forest District Office at (619) 647-3000.

Location: From Lee Vining, drive south on US 395 for 11 miles to June Lake Junction. Continue south for six miles to a Forest Service Road (Deadman Creek Road) on the right side of the road. Turn right and drive two miles to the camp access road on the right. Turn right and drive a half-mile to the camp. (Note: If arriving from the south on US 395, if you reach the CalTrans Crestview Maintenance Station on the right, you have gone one mile too far.)

Trip note: This little-known camp is set at 7,800 feet along little Deadman Creek. It is primitive and dusty in the summer, cold in the early summer and fall. From camp, hikers can drive west for three miles to the headwaters of Deadman Creek and to a trailhead for a route that runs past San Joaquin Mountain and beyond to little Yost Lake, a one-way hike of four miles. Open June to mid-October.

12. BIG SPRINGS 🐟 🏃 ██ 5

Reference: **On Deadman Creek in Inyo National Forest; map E5, grid i2.**

Campsites, facilities: There are 24 sites for tents or motor homes up to 22 feet long. Fire grills and picnic tables are provided. Vault toilets are available. There is **no piped water**, so bring your own. Pets are allowed on leashes.

Reservations, fee: No reservations; no fee.

Who to contact: Phone the Inyo National Forest District Office at (619) 647-3000.

Location: From Lee Vining, drive south on US 395 for 11 miles to June Lake Junction. Continue south for about seven miles to Owens River Road. Turn left (east) and drive two miles to a fork. Bear left at the fork and drive a quarter mile to the camp on the left side of the road.

Trip note: Big Springs Camp, at 7,300 feet, is set on the edge of the high desert, on the east side of US 395. The main attractions are Deadman Creek, which runs right by the camp, and Big Springs, which is set just on the opposite side of the river. There are several hot springs in the area, best reached by driving south on US 395 to the Mammoth Lakes Airport, and turning left on Hot Creek Road. Open June to October.

13. HORSESHOE LAKE GROUP CAMP

Reference: In Inyo National Forest; map E5, grid j0.

Campsites, facilities: There are four sites for tents or motor homes up to 45 feet long. Piped water, fire grills and picnic tables are provided. Flush toilets and a swimming beach are available. Supplies can be purchased in Mammoth Lakes. Pets are permitted on leashes.

Reservations, fee: Reserve by calling (800) 280-CAMP ($15 reservation fee); $22-$55 group fee per night.

Who to contact: Phone the Inyo National Forest District Office at (619) 924-5500.

Location: From Lee Vining on US 395, drive south for 25 miles to Mammoth Junction and Highway 203 (Minaret Summit Road). Turn west on Highway 203 and drive four miles to Lake Mary Road. Turn left and drive seven miles (past Twin Lakes, Lake Mary and Lake Mamie) to Horseshoe Lake and the campground on the left side of the road.

Trip note: Horseshoe Lake is a beautiful little lake, set at 8,900 feet, as pristine as any drive-to lake in the eastern Sierra. Unlike the other lakes in the Mammoth area, there is no resort, no boat rentals, no boat ramp, and fishing is only fair. But it is beautiful, and a trailhead is available on the northern side of the lake that heads west up to Mammoth Pass and connects with the Pacific Crest Trail. There are numerous wilderness lakes in the region. Open mid-June to mid-September.

14. TWIN LAKES

Reference: In Inyo National Forest; map E5, grid j0.

Campsites, facilities: There are 95 sites for tents and motor homes up to 55 feet long. Picnic tables, fire grills and piped water are provided. Flush toilets, a boat launch and horseback riding facilities are available. A grocery store, a laundromat and propane gas are nearby. Pets are permitted on leashes.

Reservations, fee: No reservations; $11 fee per night.

Who to contact: Phone the Inyo National Forest District Office at (619) 924-5500.

Location: From Lee Vining on US 395, drive south for 25 miles to Mammoth Junction and Highway 203 (Minaret Summit Road). Turn west on Highway 203 and drive four miles to Lake Mary Road. Turn left and drive 2.5 miles to Twin Lakes Road. Turn right and drive a half-mile to the campground.

Trip note: From Twin Lakes, you can look west and see pretty Twin Falls, a wide cascade that runs into the head of upper Twin Lake. There are actually two camps here, one on each side of the access road, at 8,700 feet. Lower Twin Lake is a favorite for flyfishers in float tubes. Open May to mid-October.

15. LAKE GEORGE

Reference: In Inyo National Forest; map E5, grid j0.

Campsites, facilities: There are 16 sites for tents or motor homes up to 16 feet long. Piped water, fire grills and picnic tables are provided. Flush toilets, a boat launch and horseback riding facilities are available. A grocery store, a laundromat and propane gas are available nearby. Pets are permitted on leashes.

Reservations, fee: No reservations; $11 fee per night.

Who to contact: Phone the Inyo National Forest District Office at (619) 924-5500.

Location: From Lee Vining on US 395, drive south for 25 miles to Mammoth Junction and Highway 203 (Minaret Summit Road). Turn west on Highway 203 and drive four miles to Lake Mary Road. Turn left and drive four miles to Lake Mary Loop Drive. Turn left and drive a short distance to Lake George Road. Turn right and drive a half-mile to the campground.

Trip note: The sites here have views of Lake George, a beautiful lake in a rock basin set below the spectacular Crystal Crag. Lake George is at 9,000 feet in elevation, a small lake fed by creeks coming from both Crystal Lake and TJ Lake. Both of the latter make excellent short hiking trips; TJ Lake is only about a 20-minute walk from the campground. Trout fishing at Lake George is decent—not great, not bad, but decent. Open mid-June to mid-September.

---

16. LAKE MARY ⌞🐟 👫🏃 🐎   RV 9

Reference: **In Inyo National Forest; map E5, grid j0.**

Campsites, facilities: There are 48 sites for tents or motor homes up to 30 feet long. Piped water, fire grills and picnic tables are provided. Flush toilets and horseback riding facilities are available. A grocery store, a laundromat and propane gas are nearby. Pets are permitted on leashes.

Reservations, fee: No reservations; $11 fee per night.

Who to contact: Phone the Inyo National Forest District Office at (619) 924-5500.

Location: From Lee Vining on US 395, drive south for 25 miles to Mammoth Junction and Highway 203 (Minaret Summit Road). Turn west on Highway 203 and drive four miles to Lake Mary Road. Turn left and drive four miles to Lake Mary Loop Drive. Turn left and drive a quarter-mile to the campground entrance.

Trip note: Lake Mary is the star of the Mammoth Lakes region. Of the 11 lakes in the region, this is the largest. It provides a resort, a boat ramp, and boat rentals and it receives the highest number of trout stocks. It is set at 8,900 feet, in a place of incredible natural beauty, one of the few places that literally has it all. Of course, that often includes quite a few other people. If there are too many for you, an excellent trailhead is available at nearby Coldwater Camp. Open mid-June to mid-September.

---

17. PINE CITY 👫🏃 🐎   RV 7

Reference: **Near Twin Lakes in Inyo National Forest; map E5, grid j0.**

Campsites, facilities: There are 10 sites for tents or motor homes up to 55 feet long. Piped water, fire grills and picnic tables are provided. Flush toilets and horseback riding facilities are available. A grocery store, a laundromat and propane gas are available nearby. Pets are permitted on leashes.

Reservations, fee: No reservations; $11 fee per night.

Who to contact: Phone the Inyo National Forest District Office at (619) 924-5500.

Location: From Lee Vining on US 395, drive south for 25 miles to Mammoth Junction and Highway 203 (Minaret Summit Road). Turn west on Highway 203 and drive four miles to Lake Mary Road. Turn left and drive four miles to Lake Mary Loop Drive. Turn left and drive a quarter-mile to the campground.

Trip note: This is one of two camps set amid the Twin Lakes. Of the 11 lakes in the region, Twin Lakes is the preferred favorite of flyfishers in float tubes. From the water, it is a dramatic scene, looking west at pretty Twin Falls cascading into the head of upper Twin Lake. The elevation is 8,700 feet. Open mid-June to mid-September.

18. COLDWATER 🐟 🚶 🐎   RV 7

Reference: **On Coldwater Creek in Inyo National Forest; map E5, grid j0.**

Campsites, facilities: There are 77 sites for tents or motor homes up to 22 feet long. Piped water, fire grills and picnic tables are provided. Flush toilets and horseback riding facilities are available. Supplies can be purchased in Mammoth Lakes. Pets are permitted on leashes.

Reservations, fee: No reservations; $11 fee per night.

Who to contact: Phone the Inyo National Forest District Office at (619) 924-5500.

Location: From Lee Vining on US 395, drive south for 25 miles to Mammoth Junction and Highway 203 (Minaret Summit Road). Turn west on Highway 203 and drive four miles to Lake Mary Road. Turn left and drive four miles to Lake Mary Loop Drive. Turn left and drive 3.5 miles to the camp entrance road.

Trip note: While this camp is not the first choice of many simply because there is no lake view, it has a special attraction all its own. First, it is a two-minute drive from the campground to Lake Mary, where there is a boat ramp, rentals and good trout fishing. Second, at the end of the campground access road is a trailhead for two outstanding hikes. From the Y at the trailhead, if you head right, you will be routed up Coldwater Creek and to Emerald Lake, a great short little hike. If you head to the left, you will have a more ambitious trip to Arrowhead, Skelton, and Red Lake, all within three miles. The elevation is 8,900 feet. Open mid-June to late September.

19. MAMMOTH MOUNTAIN RV PARK ♿ ⚓ RV 6

Reference: **Near Mammoth Lakes; map E5, grid j1.**

Campsites, facilities: There are 130 sites for tents and motor homes, some with full hookups. Piped water, electricity, picnic tables and fire grills provided. Restrooms, hot showers, cable TV hookups, a sanitary disposal station, a laundromat, a swimming pool and a jacuzzi are available. The facilities are **wheelchair accessible.** Supplies can be obtained in Mammoth Lakes. Pets are allowed on leashes.

Reservations, fee: Reservations accepted; $20-$25 fee per night.

Who to contact: Phone the park at (619) 934-3822, or write to P.O. Box 288, Mammoth Lakes, CA 93546.

Location: From Lee Vining on US 395, drive south for 25 miles to Mammoth Junction and Highway 203 (Minaret Summit Road). Turn west on Highway 203 and drive about three miles to the park.

Trip note: This motor home park is located just across the street from the Forest Service Visitors Center. Got a question? They've got an answer. This camp is open year-round, making it a great place to stay for a ski trip.

20. PINE GLEN 🚶 🐎   RV 6

Reference: **In Inyo National Forest; map E5, grid j1.**

Campsites, facilities: There are 11 family sites and six group sites for tents or motor homes up to 50 feet long. Piped water, fire grills and picnic tables are provided. Flush toilets and a sanitary disposal station are available. A grocery store, a laundromat, propane gas, and horseback riding facilities are nearby in Mammoth Lakes. Pets are permitted on leashes.

Reservations, fee: Reservations required for group sites only; reserve sites by calling (800) 280-CAMP ($7.50 reservation fee, $15 reservation fee for group sites); $10 fee per night for family sites; $20-$40 fee for group sites.

Who to contact: Phone the Inyo National Forest District Office at (619) 924-5500.

Location: From Lee Vining on US 395, drive south for 25 miles to Mammoth Junction and Highway 203 (Minaret Summit Road). Turn west on Highway 203 and drive about three miles to the Forest Service Visitor Center. Just past the visitor's center, turn right and drive a short distance to the campground.

Trip note: This is a well-located base camp for several side trips. The most popular is the trip to Devils Postpile National Monument, with a shuttle ride from the Mammoth Ski Area. Other nearby trips include exploring Inyo Craters, Mammoth Lakes and the hot springs near Mammoth Lakes Airport. The elevation is 7,800 feet. Open June to September.

---

21. NEW SHADY REST 🚶🏇   RV 6

Reference: **In Inyo National Forest; map E5, grid j1.**

Campsites, facilities: There are 97 sites for tents or motor homes up to 22 feet long. Piped water, fire grills and picnic tables are provided. Flush toilets, a dump station, a playground and horseback riding facilities are available. A grocery store, a laundromat and propane gas are nearby. Supplies can be obtained in Mammoth Lakes. Pets are permitted on leashes.

Reservations, fee: No reservations; $9 fee per night.

Who to contact: Phone the Inyo National Forest District Office at (619) 924-5500.

Location: From Lee Vining on US 395, drive south for 25 miles to Mammoth Junction and Highway 203 (Minaret Summit Road). Turn west on Highway 203 and drive about three miles to the Forest Service Visitor Center. Just past the visitor's center, turn right and drive a short distance to the campground.

Trip note: This easy-to-reach camp is set at 7,800 feet, not far from the Mammoth Visitor Center. The surrounding Inyo National Forest provides many side trip opportunities, including Devils Postpile National Monument (shuttles available from Mammoth), Upper San Joaquin River, and the Inyo National Forest backcountry trails, streams and lakes. Open May to October.

---

22. OLD SHADY REST 🚶🏇   RV 6

Reference: **In Inyo National Forest; map E5, grid j1.**

Campsites, facilities: There are 51 sites for tents or motor homes up to 55 feet long. Piped water, fire grills and picnic tables are provided. Flush toilets, a dump station, a playground and horseback riding facilities are available. A grocery store, a laundromat and propane gas are nearby. Supplies can be obtained in Mammoth Lakes. Pets are permitted on leashes.

Reservations, fee: No reservations; $10 fee per night.

Who to contact: Phone the Inyo National Forest District Office at (619) 924-5500.

Location: From Lee Vining on US 395, drive south for 25 miles to Mammoth Junction and Highway 203 (Minaret Summit Road). Turn west on Highway 203 and drive about three miles to the Forest Service Visitor Center. Just past the visitor's center, turn right and drive a short distance to the campground.

Trip note: Names like "Old Shady Rest" are usually reserved for mom-and-pop motor home parks, but the Forest Service has proved it is capable of all sorts of shenanigans. Like "New Shady Rest," this camp is located near the Mammoth Visitor Center, with the same side trips available. It is one of three camps in the immediate vicinity. The elevation is 7,800 feet. Open June through early September.

23. SHERWIN CREEK

Reference: **In Inyo National Forest; map E5, grid j2.**

Campsites, facilities: There are 87 sites for tents or motor homes up to 55 feet long. Piped water, fire grills and picnic tables are provided. Flush toilets are available. Horseback riding facilities are nearby. Supplies are available in Mammoth Lakes. Pets are permitted on leashes.

Reservations, fee: No reservations; $10 fee per night.

Who to contact: Phone the Inyo National Forest District Office at (619) 924-5500.

Location: From Lee Vining on US 395, drive south for 25 miles to Mammoth Junction and Highway 203 (Minaret Summit Road). Turn west on Highway 203 and drive about three miles to the Forest Service Visitor Center and continue a short distance to Old Mammoth Road. Turn left and drive about a mile to Sherwin Creek. Turn south and drive two miles to the campground on the left side of the road.

Trip note: This is a stark-looking camp set along little Sherwin Creek, at 7,600 feet in elevation, a short distance from the town of Mammoth Lakes. If you drive a mile east on Sherwin Creek Road, then turn right at the short spur road, you will find a trailhead for a hike that is routed up four miles to Valentine Lake in the John Muir Wilderness, set on the northwest flank of Bloody Mountain. Open mid-May through mid-September.

24. CONVICT LAKE

Reference: **In Inyo National Forest; map E5, grid j3.**

Campsites, facilities: There are 88 sites for tents or motor homes up to 55 feet long. Rental cabins are also available. Piped water, fire grills and picnic tables are provided. Flush toilets, a dump station, a boat ramp and horseback riding facilities are available. Pets are permitted on leashes.

Reservations, fee: No reservations; $10 fee per night.

Who to contact: Phone the Inyo National Forest District Office at (619) 924-5500.

Location: From Lee Vining on US 395, drive south for 31 miles (five miles past Mammoth Junction) to Convict Lake Road (adjacent to Mammoth Lakes Airport). Turn west on Convict Lake Road and drive three miles to Convict Lake. Cross the dam and drive a short distance to the campground entrance road on the left. Turn left and drive a quarter-mile to the campground.

Trip note: After driving in the stark desert on US 395 to get here, it is always astonishing to clear the rise and see Convict Lake (7,583 feet) and its gem-like waters set in a mountain bowl beneath a back wall of high, jagged wilderness peaks. The camp is set about a half-mile from the lake, but is right beside Convict Creek, which provides surprisingly good trout fishing, including some rare monster-size brown trout in the fall below the Convict Lake outlet. Fishing is also good in Convict Lake, with a chance of hooking a 10- or 15-pound trout. A bonus is an outstanding resort with a boat launch, boat rentals, cabin rentals, small store, restaurant and bar. Horseback rides and hiking are also available, with a trail routed along the north side of the lake, then along upper Convict Creek (a stream crossing is required about three miles in) and into the John Muir Wilderness. Open late April through October.

CENTRAL AREA CAMPGROUNDS

SCENIC RATING

▲1 ▲2 ▲3 ▲4 ▲5 ▲6 ▲7 ▲8 ▲9 ▲10

Poor.. Fair .... Great

KEY TO THE SYMBOLS

Boating

Canoeing/
Rafting

Fishing

Golf

Hiking

Historical
Site

Horseback
Riding

Hot Springs

Swimming

Waterskiing

Wheelchair
Access

Five Percent
Club

RV

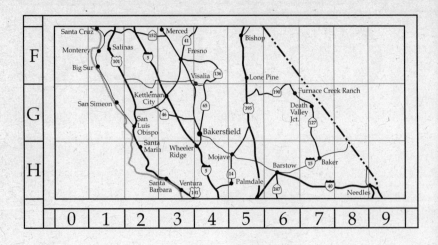

Map F1 .... (33 campgrounds)
Featuring: Anderson Lake, Mount Madonna, Monterey Bay, Los Padres National Forest, Big Sur; pages 514-527

Map F2 .... (12 campgrounds)
Featuring: San Luis Reservoir, Pinnacles National Monument; pages 528-533

Map F3 .... (5 campgrounds)
Featuring: Eastman Lake, Hensley Lake; pages 534-537

Map F4 .... (66 campgrounds)
Featuring: Sierra National Forest, Big Creek, Willow Creek, Bass Lake, Mammoth Pool Reservoir, Forebay Lake, Kerckhoff Reservoir, Huntington Lake, San Joaquin River, Shaver Lake, Courtright Reservoir, Pine Flat Lake, Kings River, Black Rock Reservoir, Wishon Reservoir, Sequoia National Forest, Kings Canyon National Park; pages 538-563

Map F5 .... (71 campgrounds)
Featuring: Inyo National Forest, Lake Crowley, Lake Edison, Sierra National Forest, San Joaquin River, Florence Lake, Pleasant Valley Reservoir, Lake Sabrina, South Lake, Sequoia National Forest, Kings Canyon National Park, Middle Fork Kaweah River, Mount Whitney; pages 564-589

Map F6 .... (5 campgrounds)
Featuring: Inyo National Forest; pages 590-593

Map G1 .... (6 campgrounds)
Featuring: Los Padres National Forest; pages 594-597

Map G2 .... (19 campgrounds)
Featuring: Lake San Antonio, San Simeon State Beach, Los Padres National Forest, Morro Bay, Santa Margarita Lake, San Luis Obispo Bay, Pismo State Beach; pages 598-605

Map G3 .... (4 campgrounds)
Featuring: Kern National Wildlife Refuge, Los Padres National Forest; pages 606-609

Map G4 .... (9 campgrounds)
Featuring: Lake Kaweah, Success Lake, Lake Ming; pages 610-613

Map G5 .... (58 campgrounds)
Featuring: Sequoia National Forest, Tule River, Mountain Home State Forest, John Muir Wilderness, Inyo National Forest, Kern River, Isabella Lake; pages 614-635

Map G6 .... (5 campgrounds)
Featuring: Death Valley National Monument; pages 636-639

Map G7 .... (4 campgrounds)
Featuring: Death Valley National Monument; pages 640-643

Map H2 .... (7 campgrounds)
Featuring: Pismo State Beach; Solvang; Santa Barbara; pages 644-647

CEN-CAL MAP .... see page 512
adjoining maps
NORTH (E1) .... see page 418
EAST (F2) .... see page 528
SOUTH (G1) .... see page 594
WEST .... no map

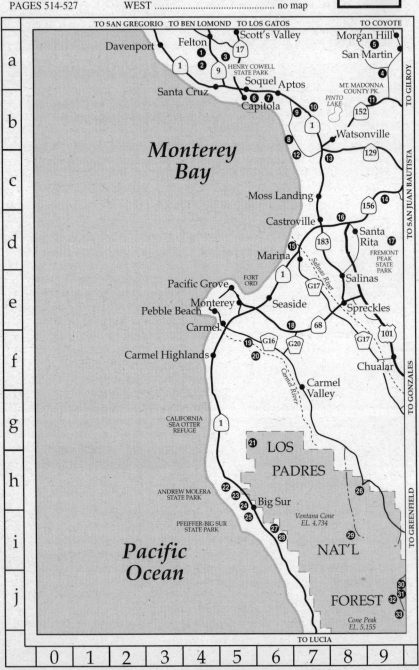

TO SAN GREGORIO   TO BEN LOMOND   TO LOS GATOS   TO COYOTE

Davenport
Felton
Scott's Valley
Morgan Hill
San Martin
HENRY COWELL STATE PARK
Soquel   Aptos
Santa Cruz
MT. MADONNA COUNTY PK.
Capitola
PINTO LAKE
152
Watsonville
Monterey Bay
129
TO SAN JUAN BAUTISTA
TO GILROY
Moss Landing
156
Castroville
Santa Rita
183
FREMONT PEAK STATE PARK
Marina
Salinas
Pacific Grove
FORT ORD
Spreckles
Monterey
Seaside
Pebble Beach
68
Carmel
Chualar
101
Carmel Highlands
TO GONZALES
Carmel River
Carmel Valley
CALIFORNIA SEA OTTER REFUGE
LOS PADRES
Salinas River
G17
G16
G20
G17
Andrew Molera State Park
Big Sur
Ventana Cone EL. 4,734
TO GREENFIELD
Pfeiffer-Big Sur State Park
NAT'L
Pacific Ocean
FOREST
Cone Peak EL. 5,155

TO LUCIA

a b c d e f g h i j

0 1 2 3 4 5 6 7 8 9

1. COTILLION GARDENS RV PARK

Reference: **Near Santa Cruz; map F1, grid a4.**

Campsites, facilities: There are two sites for tents and 80 for motor homes, many with full hookups. Picnic tables and fire grills are provided. Restrooms, showers, cable TV hookups, a recreation room, a swimming pool and a small store are available. Pets are allowed on leashes.

Reservations, fee: Reservations recommended; $20-$27 fee per night.

Who to contact: Phone (408) 335-7669, or write to 300 Old Big Trees, Felton, CA 95018.

Location: From Highway 17 five miles north of Santa Cruz, take the Felton-Scotts Valley exit. Drive 3.5 miles to Felton. Turn left (south) on Highway 9 and drive 1.5 miles to the campground.

Trip note: This is a pretty place with several possible sidetrips. It is set on the edge of the Santa Cruz Mountain redwoods, near Henry Cowell Redwoods State Park and the San Lorenzo River. Monterey Bay is only about a 10-minute drive from the park.

2. SMITHWOODS RESORT

Reference: **Near Santa Cruz; map F1, grid a4.**

Campsites, facilities: There are 142 motor home sites with full hookups. No tent camping is allowed. Picnic tables and fire grills are provided. Restrooms, showers, a recreation room, a swimming pool, a playground and a small store are available. Pets are allowed on leashes.

Reservations, fee: Reservations recommended; $25 fee per night.

Who to contact: Phone (408) 335-4321.

Location: From Highway 17 five miles north of Santa Cruz, take the Felton-Scotts Valley exit onto Mt. Hermon Road and at the bottom of the hill make a right into the town of Felton. Turn left (south) on Highway 9 and drive about 1.5 miles to the campground.

Trip note: You get a pretty redwood setting at this privately-operated park with its many sidetrip possibilities. Henry Cowell Redwoods State Park (good) and Big Basin Redwoods State Park (better) are two nearby parks that provide hiking opportunities. The narrow-gauge train ride through the area is fun too.

3. HENRY COWELL REDWOODS STATE PARK

Reference: **Near Santa Cruz; map F1, grid a5.**

Campsites, facilities: There are 112 sites for tents or motor homes up to 35 feet long. Piped water, fire grills and tables are provided. Coin-operated showers and toilets are available. Pets are permitted. Some facilities are **wheelchair accessible**.

Reservations, fee: Reservation service is closed from November through March, but reservations are advisable the rest of the year. Phone Destinet at (800) 444-7275 ($6.75 Destinet fee); $17-$19 per night fee; $1 pet fee.

Who to contact: Phone (408) 335-4598 or (408) 438-2396 or (408) 429-2850/ 2851.

Location: From Highway 1 in Santa Cruz, take the Ocean Street-Central Santa Cruz exit. Turn inland on Graham Hill Road towards Felton. Drive about three miles uphill to the park. The entrance is on the left.

Trip note: This is a quality redwood state park near Santa Cruz with good hiking, including one trail to a great lookout over Santa Cruz and the Pacific Ocean. The San Lorenzo River runs near the park and provides steelhead fishing in winter months on Wednesdays and weekends. The fishing prospects are much improved due to the private stocking program of a local sportsmen's club. This campground is open year-round.

---

4. UVAS CANYON COUNTY PARK ⌂🐟⚓ 🚐 6

Reference: **Near Morgan Hill; map F1, grid a9.**

Campsites, facilities: There are 15 sites for tents only and 15 sites for tents or motor homes up to 28 feet long. Fire grills and tables are provided. Piped water, a boat ramp and toilets are available. Pets are permitted.

Reservations fee: No reservations; $10 fee per night; $1 pet fee.

Who to contact: Call Uvas Canyon County Park at (408) 779-9232.

Location: From US 101 in San Jose, drive west on Bernal Avenue, then south on Santa Teresa Boulevard to Bailey Ave. Drive west on Bailey Avenue to McKean Road. Go south on McKean Road, which becomes Uvas Road. Continue on Uvas Road to Croy Road. Turn right on Croy Road and drive 4.5 miles to the park.

Trip note: Over the years, Uvas Reservoir has provided some of the better black bass and crappie fishing in the Bay Area among the 40 public access lakes. Best by far during the spring, when it is also stocked with rainbow trout. Call Coyote Discount Bait and Tackle at (408) 463-0711 for the latest fishing tips. Low water is sometimes a problem. Call first for lake levels.

---

5. OAK DELL 🚐 2

Reference: **Near Anderson Lake; map F1, grid a9.**

Campsites, facilities: There are 42 motor home sites, most with full hookups. Picnic tables, restrooms, showers and a sanitary disposal station are provided. Pets are permitted on leashes.

Reservations, fee: Reservations accepted; $19 fee per night for two people; $2 fee per night each additional person.

Who to contact: Phone (408) 779-7779 or write to 12790 Watsonville Road, Morgan Hill, CA 95037.

Location: From US 101 in Morgan Hill, take the Tennant Road exit and drive west for one mile to Monterey Road. Turn left (south) onto Monterey Road and drive a short distance to Watsonville Road. Turn right (west) on Watsonville Road and drive 3.5 miles to the RV park.

Trip note: The highlight of this park is nearby Anderson Lake, located about 10 miles away. The first thing you should ask is, "How much water is in Lake Anderson?" The answer may be the key to the success of your trip. When Anderson has plenty of water, it has the capacity to be a large, beautiful lake providing waterskiing, fishing for bass, bluegill, crappie and catfish, swimming and general relief on the hot summer days here. Open year-round.

6. NEW BRIGHTON STATE BEACH

Reference: **Near Santa Cruz; map F1, grid b5.**

Campsites, facilities: There are 112 sites for tents or motor homes up to 31 feet long. Piped water, fire grills, and picnic tables are provided. A sanitary disposal station, toilets, coin-operated showers, propane gas, groceries and a laundromat are available. Pets are permitted.

Reservations, fee: Reservations recommended from mid-March through October; reserve by phoning Destinet at (800) 444-7275 ($6.75 Destinet fee); $17-$19 fee per night; $1 pet fee.

Who to contact: Call the state park at (408) 475-4850 or (408) 429-2850/2851.

Location: From Santa Cruz, drive south on Highway 1 for about five miles to the Capitola-New Brighton Beach exit. The park is just off the highway.

Trip note: This is one in a series of camps set on the bluffs overlooking Monterey Bay. They are among the most popular and in-demand state campgrounds in California. Reservations are a necessity. Alas, the summer months are often foggy, especially in the morning. Beachcombing and surf fishing for perch provide recreation options along with skiff rentals at the nearby Capitola Wharf. The San Lorenzo River enters the ocean nearby.

7. SEACLIFF STATE BEACH

Reference: **Near Santa Cruz; map F1, grid b6.**

Campsites, facilities: There are 26 sites with hookups for motor homes up to 40 feet. Fire grills and tables are provided. Restrooms and coin-operated showers are available. Propane gas, groceries and a laundromat are available nearby. Some facilities are **wheelchair accessible**. Pets are allowed on leashes in the camping area, but not on the beach.

Reservations, fee: Reservations recommended; reserve by phoning Destinet at (800) 444-7275 ($6.75 Destinet fee); $26-$28 fee per night; $1 pet fee.

Who to contact: Call the state park rangers at (408) 429-2850, or Seacliff State Beach at (408) 688-3222 (phone sometimes unattended) or call the district office at (408) 429-2850/2851.

Location: From Santa Cruz, drive about six miles to the Seacliff Beach exit. Turn west and drive to the park entrance.

Trip note: This is a popular layover in summer months, but the best weather is from mid-August to early October. The spot is pretty and set on bluffs overlooking Monterey Bay. The "old cement ship" nearby provides some of the best shorefishing in the bay. An interpretive center is available in the summer months.

8. MANRESA BEACH STATE PARK

Reference: **On Pacific Ocean; map F1, grid b6**

Campsites, facilities: There are 64 tent sites. Piped water, picnic tables, restrooms, coin-operated showers, food lockers and fire rings are provided. Pets are permitted on leashes. The facilities are **wheelchair accessible**.

Reservations, fee: Reservations recommended from mid-March through October; reserve through Destinet at (800) 444-7275 (a reservation fee is charged); $17-$19 fee per night.

Who to contact: Phone the park at (408) 761-1795 or (408) 429-2850 or (408) 429-2850/2851.

Location: From Santa Cruz, drive south on Highway 17 to Highway 1. Turn south and proceed to the San Andreas Road exit. Drive eight miles south on San Andreas Road to Sand Dollar Drive and follow the signs to the park entrance. The parking area is about 1,000 yards from the camping area.

Trip note: This beautiful, extremely popular state park is set on a bluff overlooking the Pacific Ocean. Many sites have ocean views; others are set back in a secluded grove of pine trees. There is beach access for fishing, swimming or beachcombing. Santa Cruz and Monterey are each a short drive away and offer endless recreation possibilities.

9. SANTA CRUZ KOA   RV 8

Reference: **Near Watsonville; map F1, grid b7.**

Campsites, facilities: There are 12 sites for tents only and 213 motor home sites with full or partial hookups. There are also 50 camping cabins. Picnic tables and fire grills are provided. Restrooms, showers, a sanitary disposal station, a swimming pool, a jacuzzi, a wading pool, a playground, a recreation room, bicycle rentals, a store and propane gas are available. Pets are allowed on leashes.

Reservations, fee: Reservations accepted; $31.95-$35.95 fee per night; $42.95-$52.95 for cabins.

Who to contact: Phone (408) 722-0551.

Location: From Santa Cruz, drive 12 miles southeast on Highway 1. Take the San Andreas Road exit. Head southwest and drive 3.5 miles to 1186 San Andreas Road.

Trip note: This popular layover spot for motor home cruisers is not far from Manresa and Sunset State Beaches. Pinto Lake provides nearby trout fishing from winter to early summer. Open year-round.

10. PINTO LAKE PARK   RV 7

Reference: **Near Watsonville; map F1, grid b8.**

Campsites, facilities: There are motor home sites with full hookups at Pinto Lake Park. Picnic tables, piped water, sewer hookups, and electricity are provided. A boat ramp and boat rentals are available in the summer. Pets are allowed on leashes.

Reservations, fee: Reservations accepted; $16 fee per night; $1 pet fee.

Who to contact: Phone the park at (408) 722-8129.

Location: From Santa Cruz, drive 17 miles south on Highway 1 to the Watsonville-Highway 152 exit. At the first intersection, turn left on Green Valley Road and drive three miles to the lake. From Monterey, drive north on Highway 1, take a right at the Green Valley Road exit and drive three miles to the Lake.

Trip note: Pinto Lake is the only one of the seven lakes in the nine Bay Area counties that offers camping near the lake. For the few who know about it, it's an offer that can't be refused. From winter to early summer, the Department of Fish and Game stocks the lake twice a month with rainbow trout. The lake also has a crappie population that cycles up and down over the years, with some summers providing outstanding fishing.

11. MOUNT MADONNA COUNTY PARK

Reference: **Near Gilroy; map F1, grid b9.**

Campsites, facilities: There are 118 sites for tents or motor homes. Piped water, fire grills and tables are provided. Toilets are available. Pets are permitted on leashes.

Reservations, fee: No reservations; $8 fee per night; $1 pet fee.

Who to contact: Call Mount Madonna County Park at (408) 842-2341.

Location: From US 101 in Gilroy, take the Hecker Pass Highway (Highway 152) exit west. Drive about seven miles west to the park entrance. From Highway 1 in Watsonville, turn east onto Highway 152 and drive about 12 miles to the park entrance.

Trip note: It's a twisty son-of-a-gun road to reach the top of Mount Madonna, but the views are worth it. On clear days, visitors get great vistas of Monterey Bay to the west and Santa Clara Valley to the east. Recreation opportunities include horseback rentals and hiking trails. Elevation in the park reaches 1,896 feet.

---

12. SUNSET STATE BEACH

Reference: **Near Watsonville; map F1, grid c6.**

Campsites, facilities: There are 90 sites for tents or motor homes up to 31 feet long. Restrooms, showers, fire grills and picnic tables are provided. Pets are allowed on leashes.

Reservations, fee: Reservations recommended from mid-March through November; reserve by phoning Destinet at (800) 444-7275 ($6.75 Destinet fee); $17-$19 fee per night; $1 pet fee.

Who to contact: Phone the park rangers at (408) 724-1266 or (408) 429-2850/2851.

Location: From Highway 1 near Watsonville, take the Riverside Drive exit toward the ocean to Beach Road. Drive 3.5 miles on Beach Road to the San Andreas Road exit, turn right on San Andreas Road and follow signs to the beach.

Trip note: On clear evenings, the sunsets look like they are imported from Hawaii. The camp is set on a bluff overlooking Monterey Bay, a good spot for Pismo clams during minus low tides. The best weather is in late summer and fall. Spring can be windy here, early summer is often foggy.

---

13. LOMA LINDA TRAVEL PARK

Reference: **Near Salinas; map F1, grid c7.**

Campsites, facilities: There are 50 motor home sites with full hookups. A sanitary disposal station, picnic tables, restrooms and showers are provided. Propane gas and a golf course are available nearby. The facilities are **wheelchair accessible**. A golf course is nearby. Pets are allowed on leashes, except in the tent area.

Reservations, fee: Reservations required; $18 fee per night.

Who to contact: Phone the park at (408) 722-9311.

Location: Drive two miles south of Watsonville on Highway 1 to Salinas Road. Turn east and drive one mile to 890 Salinas Road.

Trip note: Location is everything, they say, and this motor home park's proximity to Monterey and Carmel gives RV cruisers what they're looking for. A possible sidetrip for trout anglers is too often overlooked at Pinto Lake near Watsonville. Open all year. Panoramic views of the surrounding mountains and ocean are available from most sites at this park.

14. MONTEREY VACATION RV PARK

Reference: **Near San Juan Bautista; map F1, grid c9.**

Campsites, facilities: There are 88 sites for motor homes with full hookups. Flush toilets, showers, a jacuzzi, a swimming pool, a laundromat and propane gas are available. Pets are permitted on leashes.

Reservations, fee: Reservations recommended for three-day holiday weekends; $18 fee per night.

Who to contact: Phone the park at (408) 757-8098.

Location: The park is located between Gilroy and Salinas at 1400 Highway 101 (two miles south of the Highway 156-San Juan Bautista exit).

Trip note: This motor home park is conveniently located. It's a 10-minute drive to San Juan Bautista, 30 minutes to the Monterey Bay Aquarium, and 40 minutes to Monterey's Fisherman's Wharf. It's a pretty, wooded location.

15. MARINA DUNES RV PARK

Reference: **Near Monterey Bay; map F1, grid d6.**

Campsites, facilities: There are 65 motor home sites, many with full or partial hookups. Piped water and picnic tables are provided. Restrooms, showers, a laundromat, cable TV, a recreation room and groceries are available. Pets are permitted.

Reservations, fee: Reservations recommended; $21-$36 fee per night; $1 pet fee.

Who to contact: Phone the park at (408) 384-6914.

Location: From Highway 1 in Marina, take the Reservation Road exit and drive one block west. Turn north onto Dunes Drive and drive to 3330 Dunes Drive.

Trip note: This is a popular motor home park for RV cruisers who are touring Highway 1 and want a layover spot near Monterey. This spot fills the bill, being open all year and located in Marina, a short drive from the sights in Monterey and Carmel. It is set in the sand dunes, about 200 yards from the ocean.

16. CABANA HOLIDAY

Reference: **Near Salinas; map F1, grid d8.**

Campsites, facilities: There are 96 motor home sites with full or partial hookups and some tent sites. Picnic tables and fire grills are provided. Restrooms, showers, a recreation room, a swimming pool, a playground, a laundromat and a store are available. Pets are permitted.

Reservations, fee: Reservations recommended; $25.56 fee per night; discounted to $23 per night for CSAA or Good Sam members.

Who to contact: Phone the park at (408) 663-2886.

Location: From Salinas, drive north on US 101 for seven miles to the junction with Highway 156. This park is at that intersection at 8710 Prunedale North Road.

Trip note: If Big Sur, Monterey and Carmel are packed, this spot provides some overflow space. It's about a half-hour drive from the Monterey area. Limited facilities available in the winter.

17. FREMONT PEAK STATE PARK 🚶🚶

Reference: **Near San Juan Bautista; map F1, grid d9.**

Campsites, facilities: There are 25 primitive sites for tents or motor homes up to 26 feet long; trailers to 18 feet long. Picnic tables, fire rings and piped water are provided. Pit toilets are available. Pets are permitted on leashes.

Reservations, fee: No reservations; $10-$12 fee per night; $1 pet fee.

Who to contact: Phone the park at (408) 623-4255 or (408) 649-2836.

Location: From Highway 156 in San Juan Bautista, turn south on San Juan Canyon Road and drive 11 miles to the park.

Trip note: Fremont Peak State Park is just far enough "out there" to get missed by a lot of folks. It is located on a ridge (2,900 feet) with great views of Monterey Bay available on the trail going up Fremont Peak. An observatory at the park is open to the public on specified Saturdays. There is no access from this park to the adjacent Hollister State Vehicular Recreation Area.

18. LAGUNA SECA RECREATION AREA
🐟 🚶🚶 ♿

Reference: **Near Monterey; map F1, grid e6.**

Campsites, facilities: There are 170 sites for tents or motor homes, many with partial hookups. Picnic tables and fire grills are provided. Restrooms, showers, a sanitary disposal station, a pond, a rifle and pistol range, and group camping facilities are available. Pets are allowed on leashes.

Reservations, fee: Reservations accepted; $15-$20 fee per night; $1 pet fee.

Who to contact: Phone the park at (408) 422-6138 or (408) 758-3185 or (408) 755-4899.

Location: From Monterey, drive nine miles east on Highway 68 to the entrance.

Trip note: This campground is just minutes away from the sights in Monterey and Carmel. It is situated in oak woodlands overlooking the world famous Laguna Seca Raceway. Open year-round.

19. RIVERSIDE RV PARK 🐟 🏊

Reference: **On the Carmel River; map F1, grid f5.**

Campsites, facilities: There are 35 motor home sites with full hookups and cable TV. Restrooms, showers, a recreational cabana, a game room with pool tables, a barbecue area, horseshoes, basketball courts and a river beach are available. A grocery store, a laundromat, and propane gas are nearby. Pets are permitted.

Reservations, fee: Reservations accepted; $30-$33 fee per night; $1 pet fee.

Who to contact: Phone the park at (408) 624-9329.

Location: From Carmel, drive 4.5 miles southeast on Carmel Valley Road to Schulte Road. Turn right and drive to 27680 Schulte Road.

Trip note: Location, location, location. That's what vacationers want to know. Well, this park is set on the Carmel River, minutes away from Carmel, Cannery Row, the Monterey Aquarium, golf courses and the beach. Each site is divided by hedges and flowers. Open year-round.

20. SADDLE MOUNTAIN RECREATION PARK 🚐 🔼 6

Reference: Near Carmel River; map F1, grid f5.

Campsites, facilities: There are 25 tent sites and 25 full-hookup sites for trailers or motor homes. Piped water, picnic tables, barbecues, restrooms and showers are provided. A swimming pool, playground, horseshoe pits, volleyball net, basketball court and a game room are available. Pets are permitted on leashes. The facilities are **wheelchair accessible**.

Reservations, fee: Reservations accepted; $20-$32 fee per night.

Who to contact: Phone the park at (408) 624-1617.

Location: From Carmel, drive 4.5 miles east on Carmel Valley Road to Schulte Road. Turn right and continue to the park at the end of the road.

Trip note: This pretty park is set about 100 yards from the Carmel River amid a grove of oak trees. The river is dry most of the year, and when there is water, it is usually closed to protect the migrating steelhead. So don't count on fishing here. But the park does offer several miles of good hiking trails, and it's only five miles from Carmel, so you won't be stuck with nothing to do.

21. BOTTCHER'S GAP 🚶 🚐 🔼 6

Reference: In Los Padres National Forest; map F1, grid g5.

Campsites, facilities: There are nine sites for tents only and 11 sites for tents or motor homes. Piped water, picnic tables and fire grills are provided. Vault toilets are available. Pets are permitted on leashes.

Reservations, fee: No reservations; no fee.

Who to contact: Phone Los Padres National Forest, Monterey Ranger District at (408) 385-5434.

Location: From Carmel, drive south on Highway 1 for about 10 miles to Palo Colorado Road. Turn left (east) and drive nine miles to the campground.

Trip note: Here is a surprise for all the Highway 1 cruisers who never leave the highway. Just inland is this little-known camp, set in beautiful Palo Colorado (redwood) Canyon. It's a good jumpoff spot for a hiking trip—the trail leading out of camp is routed all the way into the Ventana Wilderness. The elevation is 2,100 feet. Open all year.

22. ANDREW MOLERA STATE PARK WALK-IN 10

Reference: In Big Sur; map F1, grid h4.

Campsites, facilities: There are several primitive, walk-in sites with fire rings and picnic tables. Piped water and chemical toilets are available. Bring your own wood. Pets are allowed on leashes.

Reservations, fee: No reservations; $6 per night per person; $1 pet fee.

Who to contact: Phone the park at (408) 667-2315 or (408) 649-2836.

Location: From Carmel, drive 21 miles south on Highway 1 to the park.

Trip note: Considering the grandeur of Big Sur, some campers might find it hard to believe that any primitive campgrounds are available. Believe it. This park offers walk-in sites amid some beautiful country. A trail from the parking area leads one mile to a beautiful beach, complete with sea otters playing on the edge of kelp beds. Note: There is a three-day limit on stays here.

23. FERNWOOD PARK

Reference: On Big Sur River; map F1, grid h5.

Campsites, facilities: There are 16 sites for tents only and 49 motor home sites, some with water and electrical hookups. Fire grills and picnic tables are provided. Restrooms and showers are available. A grocery store is nearby. Pets are permitted on leashes.

Reservations, fee: Reservations accepted; $21-$23 fee per night; $3 pet fee.

Who to contact: Phone the park at (408) 667-2422.

Location: From Carmel, drive 28 miles south on Highway 1 to the campground.

Trip note: This motor home park is set on the banks of Big Sur River in the redwoods of the beautiful Big Sur coast. You can crown your trip with a first-class dinner at Nepenthe or the Ventana Inn (bring your bank with you).

24. BIG SUR CAMPGROUND

Reference: On Big Sur River; map F1, grid h5.

Campsites, facilities: There are 40 motor home sites with water and electrical hookups, and 4 sites for tents or motor homes. Piped water, fire grills and picnic tables are provided. Restrooms, showers, a dump station, a playground, a small store and a laundromat are available. Pets are allowed on leashes.

Reservations, fee: Reservations recommended; $22-$25 fee per night; $3 pet fee.

Who to contact: Phone the park at (408) 667-2322.

Location: From Carmel, drive 27 miles south on Highway 1 to the campground.

Trip note: This camp is located in the redwoods along the Big Sur River. Big Sur is a nationally famous area that offers the best of all worlds. Campers can stay near redwoods, use great trails through the forest, or explore nearby Pfeiffer Beach.

25. RIVERSIDE CAMPGROUND

Reference: On Big Sur River; map F1, grid h5.

Campsites, facilities: There are 46 sites for tents or motor homes, some of which have water and electrical hookups. Picnic tables and fire grills are provided. Restrooms, showers and a playground are available. Pets are permitted.

Reservations, fee: Reservations recommended; $22-$25 fee per night; $3 pet fee.

Who to contact: Phone the campground at (408) 667-2414.

Location: From Carmel, drive 25 miles south on Highway 1 to the campground.

Trip note: This is one in a series of privately-operated camps set up for Highway 1 cruisers touring the Big Sur area. This camp is set amid redwoods. Sidetrips include expansive beaches with sea otters playing on the edge of kelp beds (Andrew Molera State Park), redwood forests and waterfalls (Julia Pfeiffer-Burns State Park), and several quality restaurants (Nepenthe, Ventana Inn). Open year-round (weather permitting).

26. WHITE OAKS

Reference: Near Anastasia Creek in Los Padres National Forest; map F1, grid h8.

Campsites, facilities: There are eight tent sites. Piped water, picnic tables and fire grills are provided. Vault toilets are available. Pets are permitted on leashes.

Reservations, fee: No reservations; no fee.

Who to contact: Phone Los Padres National Forest, Monterey Ranger District at (408) 385-5434.

Location: From Highway 1 in Carmel, turn east on Carmel Valley Road and drive about 22 miles. Turn right (south) on Tassajara Road and drive eight miles to the campground.

Trip note: You can get some unexpected adventures in this area. I kept asking these bald guys about the hiking possibilities, and they just shook their heads. Turns out they were from a religious cult and on a one week vigil of silence. Either that, or they wanted to keep their favorite hikes secret. There's a good one that starts about a mile from the camp which is routed into the Ventana Wilderness. Several backcountry sites are available on the way. The camp is set at 4,200 feet, near Anastasia Creek.

---

27. VENTANA CAMPGROUNDS

Reference: In Big Sur; map F1, grid i6.

Campsites, facilities: There are 70 sites for tents or RVs up to 22 feet. Piped water, fire grills and tables are provided. A restroom and showers are available. A small grocery store is nearby. Pets must be on leashes.

Reservations, fee: Reservations accepted; $22 fee per night; $3 pet fee.

Who to contact: Phone the campground at (408) 667-2688 or write to P.O. Box 206, Big Sur, CA 93920.

Location: From Carmel, drive 28 miles south on Highway 1 to the campground in Big Sur.

Trip note: This rustic camp for tenters has wooded sites and an ideal location. Many premium sidetrips are available, from the beautiful beach at Andrew Molera State Park (a one-mile hike is necessary) to the redwoods and waterfalls in Julia Pfeiffer-Burns State Park. Open all year.

---

28. PFEIFFER BIG SUR STATE PARK

Reference: In Big Sur; map F1, grid i6.

Campsites, facilities: There are 218 sites for tents or motor homes up to 32 feet long and some primitive bike-in sites. Piped water, picnic tables and fire grills are provided. Restrooms, showers, a laundromat, groceries and propane gas are available. Campgrounds, restrooms, the grocery store, and food services are **wheelchair accessible**. Pets are permitted.

Reservations, fee: Reserve by phoning Destinet at (800) 444-7275 ($6.75 Destinet fee); $17-$19 fee per night; $1 pet fee; $6 fee per night for bike-in sites.

Who to contact: Phone the park headquarters at (408) 667-2315 or (408) 649-2836.

Location: From Carmel, drive 26 miles south on Highway 1.

Trip note: This is one of the most popular state parks in California, and it's easy to see why. You can have it all: fantastic coastal vistas (Highway 1), redwood forests and waterfalls (Julia Pfeiffer-Burns State Park), expansive beaches with sea otters playing on the edge of kelp beds (Andrew Molera State Beach), great restaurants (Nepenthe, Ventana Inn), and private, patrolled sites. Reservations are a necessity. Open year-round.

29. CHINA CAMP 🏃   **RV** 6

Reference: **In Los Padres National Forest; map F1, grid i8.**

Campsites, facilities: There are eight sites for tents only and five sites for tents or motor homes. Picnic tables and fire grills are provided. Vault toilets are available. Pets are permitted on leashes.

Reservations, fee: No reservations; no fee.

Who to contact: Phone Los Padres National Forest, Monterey Ranger District at (408) 385-5434.

Location: From Highway 1 in Carmel, turn east onto Carmel Valley Road and drive about 22 miles. Turn right (south) on Tassajara Road and drive 10 miles to the campground.

Trip note: A lot of folks might find it difficult to believe that a spot that feels so remote can be so close to the over-manicured Carmel Valley. But here it is, one of two camps on Tassajara Road. This one has a trail out of camp that is routed into the Ventana Wilderness. Tassajara Hot Springs is seven miles away at the end of Tassajara Road, and keep a lookout for the gents with shaved heads. The elevation is 4,300 feet. Open from April to December.

---

30. ARROYO SECO 🐟 🏃 ≈   **RV** 8

Reference: **In Los Padres National Forest; map F1, grid j9.**

Campsites, facilities: There are 51 sites for tents or motor homes. Piped water, picnic tables and fire grills are provided. Vault toilets are available. Supplies can be obtained in the town of Arroyo Seco. Pets are permitted on leashes.

Reservations, fee: No reservations; $10 fee per night; $15 fee per night for multi-family sites.

Who to contact: Phone Los Padres National Forest, Monterey Ranger District at (408) 385-5434.

Location: From US 101 in the town of Greenfield, turn west on Greenfield-Arroyo Seco Road (County Roads G16 and 3050) and drive 19 miles to the camp.

Trip note: This pretty spot near Arroyo Seco Creek, (900-foot elevation) is just outside the northern border of Ventana Wilderness. Open all year.

---

31. ARROYO SECO GROUP CAMP   **RV** 8

Reference: **In Los Padres National Forest; map F1, grid j9.**

Campsites, facilities: There is one group campsite for tents or motor homes. Piped water, picnic tables and fire grills are provided. Vault toilets are available. Supplies can be obtained in the nearby town of Arroyo Seco. Pets are permitted on leashes.

Reservations, fee: Reservations required; phone (800) 280-CAMP; $35 group fee per night.

Who to contact: Phone Los Padres National Forest, Monterey Ranger District at (408) 385-5434.

Location: From US 101 at the town of Greenfield, turn west on Greenfield-Arroyo Seco Road (County Roads G-16 and 3050) and drive 19 miles to the camp.

Trip note: If you have a larger group, give the folks at Arroyo Seco a break and use this adjoining spot instead. That way you'll get the privacy you all desire.

This camp is in a pretty spot, set near Arroyo Seco Creek near the northern border of the Ventana Wilderness. Open year-round.

32. MEMORIAL PARK

Reference: **In Los Padres National Forest; map F1, grid j9.**
Campsites, facilities: There are eight tent sites. Picnic tables and fire grills are provided. Vault toilets are available. Pets are permitted on leashes.
Reservations, fee: No reservations; $5 fee per night.
Who to contact: Phone Los Padres National Forest, Monterey Ranger District at (408) 385-5434.
Location: From US 101 in King City, turn south on County Route G14 and drive 18 miles to the town of Jolon. From there, turn north on Mission Road and drive six miles. Turn left on Del Venturi-Milpitas Road (Indian Road) and drive 16 miles to the campground.
Trip note: This is one of two backcountry camps in the area. The camp has a trailhead that provides access to the Ventana Wilderness trail network. The elevation is 2,000 feet, which gives hikers a nice head start on the climb. Open year-round.

33. ESCONDIDO

Reference: **In Los Padres National Forest; map F1, grid j9.**
Campsites, facilities: There are nine tent sites. Picnic tables and fire grills are provided. Vault toilets are available. Pets are permitted on leashes.
Reservations, fee: No reservations; no fee.
Who to contact: Phone Los Padres National Forest, Monterey Ranger District at (408) 385-5434.
Location: From US 101 in the town of Greenfield, turn west on Greenfield-Arroyo Seco Road and drive 19 miles to Indians Road. Turn south and drive seven miles on Indians Road (a narrow, winding, dirt road) to the campground.
Trip note: This is prime jumpoff spot for backpackers heading into the Ventana Wilderness. The camp is set at 900 feet at a trailhead that connects to a network of other trails. The only catch is you have to plan on walking up. Open from April to December.

MAP F2

CEN-CAL MAP .... see page 512
adjoining maps
NORTH (E2) .... see page 432
EAST (F3) .... see page 534
SOUTH (G2) .... see page 598
WEST (F1) .... see page 514

12 LISTINGS
PAGES 528-533

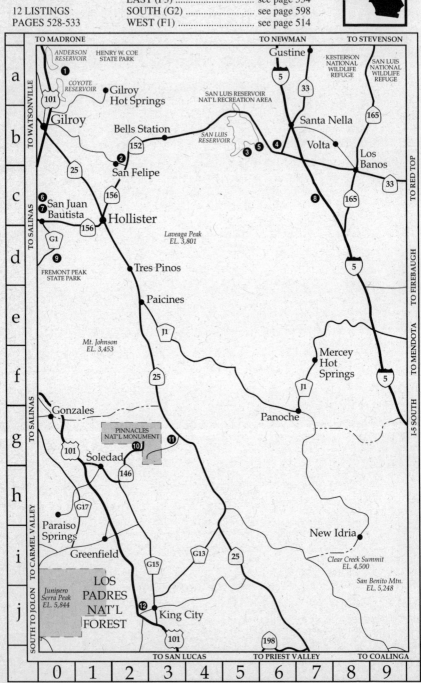

Map F2 featuring: San Luis Reservoir, Pinnacles National Monument

1. COYOTE LAKE COUNTY PARK 🐟 ⚓ 🚐 **7**

Reference: **Near Gilroy; map F2, grid a0.**

Campsites, facilities: There are 74 sites for tents or motor homes up to 24 feet long. Tables and fire grills are provided. Piped water, flush toilets and a boat ramp are available. Pets are allowed on leashes.

Reservations, fee: No reservations; $8 fee per night, $4 per second vehicle.

Who to contact: Phone for available space at (408) 842-7800.

Location: From US 101 in Gilroy, drive east via Leavesley Road (to New Avenue, to Roop Road, then to Coyote Lake Road) for a total of 5.5 miles to the park.

Trip note: All you need is a lake full of water for this to be a pretty spot, but because of severe draw downs that occur in some years, campers are advised to call ahead for lake levels. When the lake is full, trout stocks are made in spring months and bass fishing can be good. In summer, it can be hot and dry. Call Coyote Discount Bait and Tackle at (408) 463-0711 for a free map of the lakes in Santa Clara Valley.

2. CASA DE FRUTA ORCHARD RESORT 🚐 **1**
♿ 🏊

Reference: **Near Pacheco Pass; map F2, grid b2.**

Campsites, facilities: There are 300 motor home sites, all with water and electric hookups (some have sewer). Picnic tables and fire grills are provided. Also available are flush toilets, showers, a sanitary disposal station, cable TV, satellite TV, a laundromat, a playground, a swimming pool, a wading pool, an outdoor dance floor, horseshoes, volleyball courts, baseball diamonds, a wine and cheese tasting room, a candy factory, a bakery, a fruit stand, a petting zoo, a 24-hour restaurant, a gift shop and a grocery store. Pets are permitted.

Reservations, fee: Reservations accepted; $22-$24 fee per night.

Who to contact: Phone the park at (408) 842-9316.

Location: From Gilroy, drive 13 miles east, or from Los Banos, drive 28 miles west on Highway 152 to 10031 Pacheco Pass Highway.

Trip note: This 80-acre park has a festival-like feel to it with country music and dancing on summer weekends and barbecues on Sundays. It's a good thing, because there isn't a whole lot else to do around these parts. Huge but sparse San Luis Reservoir, 20 miles to the east, provides a possible side trip.

3. BASALT 🐟 ⚓ 🥾 ♿ 🏊 🚐 **5**

Reference: **On San Luis Reservoir; map F2, grid b5.**

Campsites, facilities: There are 79 sites for tents or motor homes. Piped water, fire grills and picnic tables are provided. Flush toilets, showers, a dump station and boat ramp are available. A grocery store, a laundromat and propane gas are nearby. The facilities are **wheelchair accessible**. Pets are allowed on leashes.

Reservations, fee: Phone Destinet at (800) 444-PARK ($6.75 Destinet fee); $14-$16 fee per night; $1 pet fee.

Who to contact: Phone the San Luis Reservoir State Recreation Area at (209) 826-1196.

Location: From Los Banos, drive 12 miles west on Highway 152 to the entrance road on left.

Trip note: San Luis Reservoir is a huge, man-made lake that is a storage facility along the California Aqueduct. When the Delta water pumps take the water, they also take the fish, filling this lake up with both. Striped bass fishing is best in the fall when the stripers chase schools of baitfish on the lake surface (indicated by the diving birds—birds never lie). Spring and early summer can be quite windy, but that makes for good sailboarding. The elevation is 575 feet. Open year-round.

4. MADEIROS

Reference: On San Luis Reservoir; map F2, grid b6.

Campsites, facilities: There are 350 primitive sites for tents or motor homes. Some shaded ramadas with fire grills and picnic tables are available. Tanked water and chemical toilets are available. A boat ramp is nearby. Pets are permitted on leashes.

Reservations, fee: No reservations; $9-$11 fee per night; $1 pet fee.

Who to contact: Phone the San Luis Reservoir State Recreation Area at (209) 826-1196.

Location: From Los Banos, drive 12 miles west on Highway 152 to the intersection of Highway 33. Turn north on Highway 33 and drive a short distance to the campground entrance.

Trip note: This campground, one of two on the vast, sparse expanse of San Luis Reservoir, gets windy in the spring, hot in the summer, and low on water in the fall. Striped bass fishing is best in the fall when the wind is down and stripers will corral schools of baitfish near the lake surface. The elevation is 225 feet. Open year-round.

5. MEADOWS CAMPGROUND

Reference: On San Luis Reservoir; map F2, grid b5.

Campsites, facilities: There are 53 sites for tents or motor homes with electrical and water hookups. Fire pits, picnic tables and pit toilets are provided. No dump station and no showers are provided. Pets are permitted on leashes.

Reservations, fee: No reservations; $14-$16 fee per night; $1 pet fee.

Who to contact: Phone the San Luis Reservoir State Recreation Area at (209) 826-1196.

Location: From Los Banos, drive 12 miles west on Highway 152 to the signed entrance on the right.

Trip note: Meadows Campground is located on Los Banos Creek near San Luis Reservoir. It is one in a series of camps operated by the state in the San Luis Recreation Area, adjacent to San Luis Reservoir and O'Neill Forebay, home of the biggest striped bass in California—and the world-record for landlocked stripers.

6. MISSION FARM RV PARK

Reference: Near San Juan Bautista; map F2, grid c0.

Campsites, facilities: There are four sites for tents and 165 motor home sites with full hookups and picnic tables. Flush toilets, showers, a barbecue area, a sanitary disposal station, a laundromat, propane gas and groceries are available. Pets are permitted on leashes; a dog run is available.

Reservations, fee: Reservations recommended; $15-20 fee per night.

Who to contact: Phone the park at (408) 623-4456.

Location: From US 101, drive three miles east on Highway 156. Turn right at the stop light and then left at the big sign for the park and drive a quarter mile down the road to 400 San Juan-Hollister Road.

Trip note: The close proximity to San Juan Bautista—it's within easy walking distance—is the main attraction of this privately-operated park. The park is set beside a walnut orchard, and in the fall, you can pick walnuts for free and keep them.

---

7. SAN JUAN BAUTISTA KOA

Reference: **Near San Juan Bautista; map F2, grid c0.**

Campsites, facilities: There are 17 sites for tents only, 27 sites with partial hookups for tents or motor homes, and 14 motor home sites with full hookups. Two cabins are also available. Picnic tables and fire grills are provided. Flush toilets, showers, a sanitary disposal station, a recreation room, a swimming pool, a laundromat, propane gas and groceries are available. Some facilities are **wheelchair accessible**. Pets are permitted on leashes.

Reservations, fee: Reservations accepted; $18-$24 fee per night; $28-$30 cabin rental fee per night.

Who to contact: Phone the park at (408) 623-4263.

Location: From US 101, take the Highway 129 exit west and drive 100 feet. Turn left onto Searle Road (frontage road) and drive to the stop sign. Turn left again on Anzar and drive under the freeway to 900 Anzar Road.

Trip note: Well, at least they have some spots for tenters; they are the only privately-operated park in the immediate area that does. Its proximity to Mission San Juan Bautista is a highlight, and it is also a short drive to the Monterey-Carmel area.

---

8. LOS BANOS CREEK RESERVOIR

Reference: **Near Los Banos; map F2, grid c7.**

Campsites, facilities: There are 25 sites for tents or motor homes up to 30 feet long. Fire grills and picnic tables are provided. Pit toilets and a boat ramp are available. There is **no piped water**, so bring your own. Pets are allowed on leashes.

Reservations, fee: No reservations; $7-$9 fee per night; $1 pet fee.

Who to contact: Phone the San Luis Reservoir State Recreation Area at (209) 826-1196.

Location: From Los Banos, drive five miles west on Highway 152. Turn south on Volta Road and drive about one mile. Turn left (east) on Pioneer Road and drive one mile. Turn south (right) onto Canyon Road and drive about five miles to the park.

Trip note: Los Banos Creek Reservoir is a small lake set amid surrounding pasture land and is relatively little-known compared to the nearby San Luis Reservoir. In summer and fall, it's a good spot for canoes or car-top boats (there's an enforced five-m.p.h. speed limit). In spring, it can be quite windy and is a popular spot for sailboarding. The elevation is 400 feet. Open year-round.

9. HOLLISTER HILLS STATE VEHICULAR RECREATION AREA

Reference: **Near Hollister; map F2, grid d0.**

Campsites, facilities: There are 125 sites for tents or motor homes. Some group sites are available. Picnic tables, fire grills and piped water are provided. Flush toilets, showers and a grocery store are available. Dogs are permitted on leashes.

Reservations, fee: No reservations; $8 fee per night; pets are free.

Who to contact: Phone the park at (408) 637-3874 or (408) 637-8186.

Location: From Highway 25 in Hollister, turn south on Cienega Road and drive eight miles to the park.

Trip note: This unique park was designed for off-road-vehicle enthusiasts. It provides 80 miles of trails for motorcycles and 40 miles of trails for four-wheel-drive vehicles. All trails close at sunset. There is no direct access to the Fremont Peak State Park, bordering directly to the west. The elevation is about 1,500 feet. Open year-round.

10. PINNACLES NATIONAL MONUMENT

Reference: **Map F2, grid g2.**

Campsites, facilities: There are 18 walk-in tent sites. There are two **wheelchair accessible** sites near **wheelchair accessible** restrooms. Picnic tables, fire grills and piped water are provided. Pets are permitted on leashes, except on trails.

Reservations, fee: No reservations; $10 fee per night.

Who to contact: Phone the park at (408) 389-4526.

Location: From US 101 in Soledad, drive 11 miles northeast on Highway 146 to the campground.

Trip note: The Pinnacles National Monument is like a different planet. It's a 16,000-acre park with volcanic clusters and strange caves, all great for exploring. This is one of two campgrounds at the Pinnacles, and don't get the two mixed up. This is the more primitive of the two, and far less visited. Does the shoe fit? If so, come prepared for hot weather, the chance of meeting up with a rattlesnake, and with plenty of ice in a cooler to keep your drinks cold. Closed on weekends from mid-February to June 1st.

11. PINNACLES CAMPGROUND

Reference: **Near Pinnacles National Monument; map F2, grid g3.**

Campsites, facilities: There are 125 sites for tents or motor homes. Picnic tables and fire grills are provided. Piped water, electricity, flush toilets, sanitary disposal station, showers, a store and a swimming pool are available. Bring your own firewood or purchase it at the campground. Pets are permitted on leashes, except on trails.

Reservations, fee: Reservations accepted for group sites, all others on a first-come first-served basis; $6 fee per night per person for a family site; $5 fee per night per person for a group site with a $50 minimum.

Who to contact: Phone the campground at (408) 389-4462.

Location: From Hollister, drive 32 miles south on Highway 25. Turn at the sign for the Pinnacles (Highway 146) and drive about 2.5 miles to the campground.

Trip note: This is one of two camps at the Pinnacles National Monument. This private one gets a lot more traffic—it has more facilities, the road in is in better shape, and the campground is closer to Bear Gulch Caves, a prime destination. The jagged pinnacles, for which the park was named, were formed by the erosion of an ancient volcanic eruption. If you are planning to stay over the weekend in the spring, arrive early on Friday evening to be sure you get a campsite. Beware of temperatures in the 90s and 100s in the summer.

12. SAN LORENZO REGIONAL PARK

Reference: **In King City; map F2, grid j2.**

Campsites, facilities: There are 119 sites for tents or motor homes with partial hookups. Tables and fire grills are provided. A dump station, restrooms and showers are available. Pets are allowed on leashes.

Reservations, fee: Reservations accepted; $12-$18 fee per night.

Who to contact: Phone the park at (408) 385-5964.

Location: Drive on US 101 to King City. The park is at 1160 Broadway.

Trip note: A lot of folks cruising Highway 101, underestimating the time it takes to travel the state, can get caught out near King City, and it can feel like No Man's Land to a visitor. Well, don't sweat it because this park offers a spot to overnight. It's set near the Salinas River, which isn't exactly the Mississippi, but it'll do. Open year-round.

CEN-CAL MAP .... see page 512
adjoining maps
NORTH (E3) .... see page 444
EAST (F4) .... see page 538
SOUTH (G3) .... see page 606
WEST (F2) .... see page 528

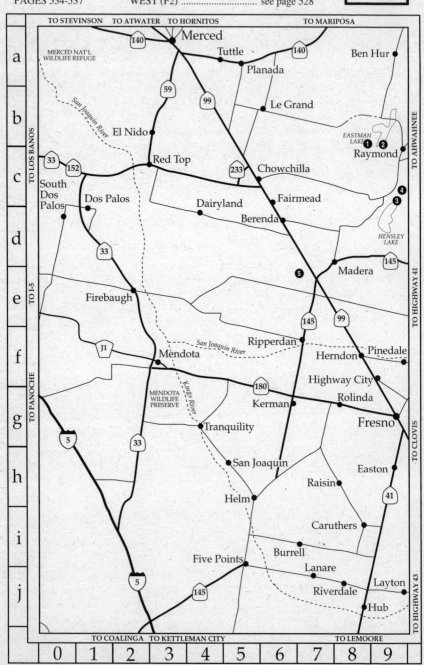

Map F3 featuring: Eastman Lake, Hensley Lake

1. CORDORNIZ RECREATION AREA RV 5

Reference: On Eastman Lake; map F3, grid b9.

Campsites, facilities: There are 62 sites for tents or motor homes. Group sites are also available. Piped water, fire grills and picnic tables are provided. Flush toilets, showers, a dump station and a boat ramp are available. Pets are allowed on leashes.

Reservations, fee: No reservations; $12 fee per night.

Who to contact: Phone the U.S. Army Corps of Engineers, Eastman Lake at (209) 689-3255.

Location: From Chowchilla on Highway 99, take the Avenue 26 exit. Drive 17 miles east on Avenue 26. Turn north on County Road 29 and drive eight miles to the lake.

Trip note: Eastman Lake, a typical federal reservoir, was created for agricultural use by damming the Chowchilla River. But on a 105-degree summer day, it can seem like a nice tub to cool off in. Ideal for waterskiing, swimming or just getting a quick dunk. Bass fishing is best in the spring, before the summer sun starts branding everything in sight. The elevation is 650 feet. Open year-round. Note: Eastman Lake was closed to water recreation in 1989 due to hydrilla infestation and overgrowth, but is now re-opened for boating year-round during daylight hours. The upper end of the lake is still closed to boats, with the area marked by a keep-out buoy line.

2. WILDCAT RECREATION AREA RV 5

Reference: On Eastman Lake; map F3, grid b9.

Campsites, facilities: There are 19 sites for tents or motor homes. Piped water, fire grills and picnic tables are provided. Vault toilets and a dump station are available. A boat ramp is nearby. Pets are allowed on leashes.

Reservations, fee: No reservations; $6 fee per night.

Who to contact: Phone the U.S. Army Corps of Engineers, Eastman Lake at (209) 689-3255.

Location: From Chowchilla on Highway 99, take the Avenue 26 exit. Drive 17 miles east on Avenue 26. Turn north on County Road 29 and drive eight miles to the lake.

Trip note: Eastman Lake was created by Buchanan Dam on the Chowchilla Reservoir. This is the smaller of the camps on the lake. Not exactly a pristine setting, but water is water, and during the 100-degree days of summer in the valley, that means plenty. It's ideal for waterskiing. Open March through September. Note: Eastman Lake was closed to water recreation in 1989 due to hydrilla infestation and overgrowth, but is now re-opened for boating year-round during daylight hours. The upper end of the lake is still closed to boats, with the area marked by a keep-out buoy line.

3. HENSLEY GROUP SITE 🎣 ⚓ 🏊 🎿   RV 5

Reference: On Hensley Lake; map F3, grid c9.

Campsites, facilities: There is one group site. Piped water, fire grills and picnic tables are provided. Flush toilets, showers, a dump station, a playground and a boat ramp are available. Pets are allowed on leashes.

Reservations, fee: Reservations recommended; $50 group fee per night (includes a $3 boat-launch fee).

Who to contact: Phone the U.S. Army Corps of Engineers, Hensley Lake at (209) 673-5151.

Location: From Madera, drive northeast on Highway 145 for about six miles. Bear left on County Road 400 and drive 11 miles to the campground at the reservoir.

Trip note: Hensley Lake is one of the two lakes that is a short drive east of Madera. (The other is Millerton Reservoir). Hensley is the smaller of the two and has a smaller access road as well and fewer people to compete with for boating space. The reservoir was created by a dam on the Fresno River. The elevation is 500 feet. Open year-round.

---

4. HIDDEN VIEW CAMPGROUND   RV 5

🎣 ⚓ 🏊 🎿

Reference: On Hensley Lake; map F3, grid c9.

Campsites, facilities: There are 52 sites for tents or motor homes. Piped water, fire grills and picnic tables are provided. Flush toilets, showers, a dump station and a boat ramp are available. Pets are permitted on leashes.

Reservations, fee: No reservations; $12 fee per night; $3 boat launch fee.

Who to contact: Phone the U.S. Army Corps of Engineers, Hensley Lake at (209) 673-5151.

Location: From Madera, drive northeast on Highway 145 for about six miles. Bear left on County Road 400 and drive 12 miles to the campground at the reservoir.

Trip note: This is the other camp at Hensley Lake, set in the foothills northeast of Madera. It is most popular with waterskiers in the summer. Because Millerton Lake is closer and easier to reach for Fresno boaters, this lake often gets overlooked. Open all year.

---

5. COUNTRY LIVING RV PARK ♿ 🏊   RV 1

Reference: In Madera; map F3, grid d6.

Campsites, facilities: There are 49 motor home sites. Picnic tables, piped water, electrical connections and sewer hookups are provided. Restrooms, showers and a laundromat are available. A swimming pool and jacuzzi are available in the summer only. A store is nearby. Pets are permitted.

Reservations, fee: Reservations accepted; $15 fee per night.

Who to contact: Phone the park at (209) 674-5343.

Location: In Madera, take the Avenue 16 exit from Highway 99 and drive one-quarter mile to the camp entrance on the right, at 24833 Avenue 16.

Trip note: It can be a dry piece of life driving this country on a hot summer afternoon, ready to stop, but knowing of nowhere to go. This RV park gives you an option. Open year-round.

MAP F4

CEN-CAL MAP .... see page 512
adjoining maps
NORTH (E4) .... see page 460
EAST (F5) .... see page 564
SOUTH (G4) .... see page 610
WEST (F3) .... see page 534

66 LISTINGS
PAGES 538-563

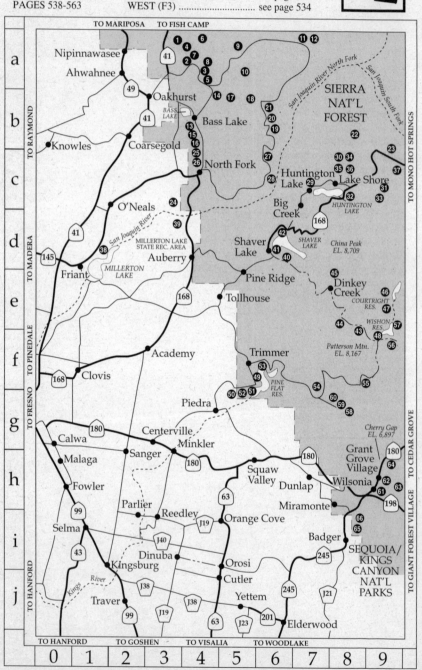

Map F4 featuring: **Sierra National Forest, Big Creek, Willow Creek, Bass Lake, Mammoth Pool Reservoir, Forebay Lake, Kerckhoff Reservoir, Huntington Lake, San Joaquin River, Shaver Lake, Courtright Reservoir, Pine Flat Lake, Kings River, Black Rock Reservoir, Wishon Reservoir, Sequoia National Forest, Kings Canyon National Park**

1. BIG SANDY

Reference: **On Big Creek in Sierra National Forest; map F4, grid a3.**

Campsites, facilities: There are 10 sites for tents only and four sites for tents or motor homes up to 16 feet long. Picnic tables and fire grills are provided. Vault toilets are available. There is **no piped water**, so bring your own. Pets are permitted on leashes.

Reservations, fee: No reservations; $9 fee per night.

Who to contact: Phone the Sierra National Forest Mariposa Ranger District at (209) 683-4665.

Location: From Oakhurst on Highway 41, drive about five miles north to Sky Ranch Road. Go northeast for approximately 14 miles to the campground.

Trip note: It's only six miles from the highway, but this camp gets overlooked by hundreds of thousands of campers heading to the nearby southern entrance of Yosemite National Park. If you want quiet, this is a better choice. It's a pretty camp set on Big Creek in the Sierra National Forest and just eight miles from the southern entrance to Yosemite National Park. It is one of two camps in the immediate area. The elevation is 5,800 feet. Open from June to November.

2. GREYS MOUNTAIN

Reference: **On Willow Creek in Sierra National Forest; map F4, grid a4.**

Campsites, facilities: There are 12 sites for tents and motor homes up to 22 feet long. Picnic tables and fire grills are provided. Pit toilets are available. Pets are permitted on leashes. **No piped water** is available, so bring your own.

Reservations, fee: No reservations; $9 fee per night.

Who to contact: Phone the Sierra National Forest Mariposa Ranger District at (209) 683-4665.

Location: From Fresno, drive 46 miles north on Highway 41 to Oakhurst. From there continue north on Highway 41 to Sky Ranch Road (about five miles). Turn right (east) and follow this road for about 10 miles to the campground.

Trip note: This is a small, little-known, primitive campground where you can just about guarantee solitude. Yet it is located on Willow Creek, only a 15-minute drive from Bass Lake. The series of campgrounds along Willow Creek don't get much traffic. The elevation is 5,200 feet. Open from June to November.

3. SOQUEL

Reference: **On the North Fork of Willow Creek in Sierra National Forest; map F4, grid a4.**

Campsites, facilities: There are 14 sites for tents and motor homes up to 22 feet long. Fire grills and picnic tables are provided. Vault toilets are available. There is **no piped water**, so bring your own. Pets are permitted on leashes.

Reservations, fee: No reservations; $9 fee per night.

Who to contact: Phone the Sierra National Forest Mariposa Ranger District at (209) 683-4665.

Location: From Fresno, drive about 52 miles north on Highway 41 to Sky Ranch Road (before Fish Camp, and five miles north of Oakhurst). Turn east and follow for about eight miles to campground.

Trip note: Located at 5,400 feet on the North Fork of Willow Creek, this is one of the several primitive, relatively isolated campgrounds in the area. It would be handy to have a map of the Sierra National Forest that details the back roads, trails and streams in the area. Open from June to November.

4. LITTLE SANDY

Reference: **On Big Creek in Sierra National Forest; map F4, grid a4.**

Campsites, facilities: There are eight tent sites and two sites for trailers or motor homes. Picnic tables and fire grills are provided. Vault toilets are available. There is **no piped water**, so bring your own. Pets are permitted on leashes.

Reservations, fee: No reservations; no fee.

Who to contact: Phone the Sierra National Forest Mariposa Ranger District at (209) 683-4665.

Location: From Oakhurst, drive about five miles north to Sky Ranch Road. Go northeast for approximately 15 miles to the campground.

Trip note: This quiet little spot is only nine miles from the southern entrance to Yosemite National Park. Like the camp, Big Sandy, it is set along Big Creek in the Sierra National Forest. If Yosemite is packed, this can be an ideal option. The elevation is 6,100 feet. Open from June to November.

5. NELDER GROVE

Reference: **In Sierra National Forest; map F4, grid a4.**

Campsites, facilities: There are seven sites for tents or motor homes up to 22 feet long. Fire grills and picnic tables are provided. Vault toilets are available. There is **no piped water**, so bring your own. Pets are permitted on leashes.

Reservations, fee: No reservations; no fee.

Who to contact: Phone the Sierra National Forest Mariposa Ranger District at (209) 683-4665.

Location: From Fresno, drive 46 miles north on Highway 41 to the town of Oakhurst. From there continue north on Highway 41 for five miles to Sky Ranch Road. Follow this road for about eight miles northeast to the campground.

Trip note: A fantastic spot, set amid the Nelder Grove of Giant Sequoias, the majestic mountain redwoods. It's surprising more people don't know about it. But since the southern entrance to Yosemite National Park is just 10 miles away, folks get sidetracked. The elevation is 5,300 feet. Open from May to October.

6. TEXAS FLAT GROUP CAMP

Reference: **On the North Fork of Willow Creek in Sierra National Forest; map F4, grid a4.**

Campsites, facilities: There are four sites for tents or motor homes up to 22 feet long. Fire grills and picnic tables are provided. Vault toilets and stock handling facilities are available. There is **no piped water**, so bring your own. Pets are allowed on leashes.

Reservations, fee: Reservations accepted; no fee. There is a fee for horses.

Who to contact: Phone the Sierra National Forest Mariposa Ranger District at (209) 683-4665.

Location: From Fresno, drive about 47 miles north on Highway 41 to Oakhurst. Go approximately five miles further north (on Highway 41) to Sky Ranch Road. Turn right (east) and follow for about 12 miles to campground.

Trip note: If you are on your honeymoon, this definitely ain't the place. Unless you like the smell of horses, that is. It's a pretty enough spot, set along the North Fork of Willow Creek, but it is primarily designed for groups with horses. Sidetrip options: This camp is 15 miles from the south entrance of Yosemite National Park and 15 miles north of Bass Lake. The elevation is 5,500 feet. Open from June through November.

---

7. FRESNO DOME

Reference: **On Big Creek in Sierra National Forest; map F4, grid a4.**

Campsites, facilities: There are 12 sites for tents or motor homes up to 22 feet long. Picnic tables and fire grills are provided. Pit toilets are available. There is **no piped water**, so bring your own. Pets are permitted on leashes.

Reservations, fee: No reservations; $9 fee per night.

Who to contact: Phone the Sierra National Forest Mariposa Ranger District at (209) 683-4665.

Location: From Oakhurst on Highway 41 drive north for five miles to Sky Ranch Road. Follow this road northeast for about 12 miles to campground.

Trip note: This is one in a series of primitive, backcountry Forest Service camps in the area, and hey, the price is right. Free. This one is set along Big Creek at 6,400 feet. A map of Sierra National Forest details backcountry roads, hiking trails and streams. Because Yosemite National Park is close and borders the National Forest, this little camp gets overlooked plenty.

---

8. KELTY MEADOW

Reference: **On Willow Creek in Sierra National Forest; map F4, grid a4.**

Campsites, facilities: There are 12 sites for tents and motor homes up to 22 feet long. Fire grills and picnic tables are provided. Vault toilets and stock handling facilities are available. There is **no piped water**, so bring your own. Pets are allowed on leashes.

Reservations, fee: Reservations required for equestrians; $9 fee per night.

Who to contact: Phone the Sierra National Forest Mariposa Ranger District at (209) 683-4665.

Location: From Oakhurst on Highway 41, drive five miles north to Sky Ranch Road (before Fish Camp). Follow Sky Ranch Road for about 10 miles northeast to the campground.

Trip note: This primitive campground located by Willow Creek has sites available for campers with horses. Nearby Fresno Dome and the Nelder Grove of Giant Sequoias provide possible sidetrips. The elevation is 5,800 feet. Open from June to November.

9. UPPER CHIQUITO 👫

Reference: **On Chiquito Creek in Sierra National Forest; map F4, grid a5.**

Campsites, facilities: There are 10 sites for tents only and 10 sites for tents or motor homes up to 22 feet long. Picnic tables and fire grills are provided. Vault toilets are available. There is **no piped water**, so bring your own. Pets are permitted on leashes.

Reservations, fee: No reservations; no fee.

Who to contact: Phone the Sierra National Forest Minarets Ranger District at (209) 877-2218.

Location: From Fresno, drive 50 miles north on Highway 41 to Yosemite Forks. Turn right (east) onto County Road 222 and drive six miles to the town of Bass Lake. Turn left (north) onto Beasore Road and drive 16 miles to the campground.

Trip note: This is one in a series of primitive, Forest Service camps set along Chiquito Creek. This one, set at 6,800 feet, is quite a bit easier to reach than the others. A map of the Sierra National Forest details the surrounding backcountry, roads, trails and streams. Open from June to October.

10. LOWER CHIQUITO

Reference: **On Chiquito Creek in Sierra National Forest; map F4, grid a6.**

Campsites, facilities: There are seven sites for tents or motor homes up to 22 feet long. Fire grills and picnic tables are provided. Vault toilets are available. There is **no piped water,** so bring your own. Pets are permitted on leashes.

Reservations, fee: No reservations; $9 fee per night.

Who to contact: Phone the Sierra National Forest Minarets Ranger District at (209) 877-2218.

Location: From the town of North Fork (south of Bass Lake), drive east and south on Mammoth Pool Road (County Road 225) to Minarets Road. Turn left (north) on Minarets Road (Road 4S81). The drive is a total distance of about 38 miles from North Fork. Turn left onto Forest Service Road 6S71 and drive three miles to the campground.

Trip note: This is a BOW-BOW camp: that is, "Bring your Own Water," said twice just for good measure. It gets hot up in this country and there's **no piped water** at the camp. It is small, little-known, and about eight miles from Mammoth Pool Reservoir. The elevation is 4,900 feet. Open from May to October.

11. CLOVER MEADOW 👫

Reference: **On Granite Creek in Sierra National Forest; map F4, grid a7.**

Campsites, facilities: There are seven sites for tents or motor homes up to 16 feet long. Picnic tables and fire grills are provided. Piped water and vault toilets are available. Pets are permitted on leashes.

Reservations, fee: No reservations; no fee.

Who to contact: Phone the Sierra National Forest Minarets Ranger District at (209) 877-2218.

Location: From the town of North Fork (south of Bass Lake), drive east and south on Mammoth Pool Road (County Road 225) to Minarets Road. Turn left (north) on Minarets Road (Road 4S81) and drive to the campground entrance road. The camp is adjacent to the Clover Meadow Ranger Station. The total distance from North Fork to the entrance road is about 43 miles—20 miles north of Mammoth Pool Reservoir on Minarets Road.

Trip note: This one of the better jumpoff camps in the area for backpackers. A trail from the camp leads into the Ansel Adams Wilderness where there are many beautiful high Sierra lakes. The camp is set at 7,000 feet, adjacent to the Clover Meadow Ranger Station. Open from June to October.

12. GRANITE CREEK 🐟 🥾 🏊

Reference: **In Sierra National Forest; map F4, grid a7.**

Campsites, facilities: There are 20 tent sites. Picnic tables and fire grills are provided. Pit toilets are available. There is **no piped water**, so bring your own. Pets are permitted on leashes.

Reservations, fee: No reservations; no fee.

Who to contact: Phone the Sierra National Forest Minarets Ranger District at (209) 877-2218.

Location: From the town of North Fork (south of Bass Lake), drive east and south on Mammoth Pool Road (County Road 225) to Minarets Road. Turn left (north) on Minarets Road (Road 4S81) and drive to the campground entrance road, which goes to the Clover Meadow Ranger Station (total distance from North Fork to the entrance road is about 41 miles—18 miles north of Mammoth Pool Reservoir on Minarets Road). Drive 3.5 miles to the campground.

Trip note: This camp can be a jumpoff point for backpackers, with a trail from camp leading north to numerous lakes in the Ansel Adams Wilderness. Clover Meadow camp may be more desirable because it has both piped water to tank up your canteens and a ranger station to obtain the latest trail information. The elevation is 6,900 feet. Open from June to October.

13. FORKS 🐟 ⚓ 🥾 🏊 🎣   RV 8

Reference: **On Bass Lake in Sierra National Forest; map F4, grid b3.**

Campsites, facilities: There are 25 sites for tents only and six sites for tents or motor homes up to 22 feet long. Fire grills and picnic tables are provided. Piped water and flush toilets are available. Pets are permitted on leashes. A laundromat and a grocery store are nearby.

Reservations, fee: From Memorial Day through Labor Day, reserve by calling (800) 280-CAMP ($7.50 reservation fee); $15 fee per night.

Who to contact: Phone the Sierra National Forest Mariposa Ranger District at (209) 683-4665.

Location: From Fresno, drive 50 miles north on Highway 41 to Yosemite Forks. Turn right (east) onto County Road 222 and drive six miles to the campground on Bass Lake.

Trip note: Bass Lake is set in a canyon. It's a long, narrow, deep lake that is popular for fishing in the spring and waterskiing in the summer. It's a pretty spot, set at 3,400 feet in the Sierra National Forest. It's one of several camps at the lake. Boats must be registered at the Bass Lake observation tower after launching. The only camp on Bass Lake that is open year around is the Lupine-Cedar Camp. Open from May through September.

14. CHILKOOT 🥾   RV 7

Reference: **Near Bass Lake in Sierra National Forest; map F4, grid b4.**

Campsites, facilities: There are seven sites for tents and RVs up to 22 feet long. Picnic tables and fire grills are provided. Vault toilets are available, but there is **no piped water**, so bring your own. Pets are permitted on leashes. Groceries and a laundromat are available at Bass Lake.

Reservations, fee: No reservations; $9 fee per night.

Who to contact: Phone the Sierra National Forest Mariposa Ranger District at (209) 683-4665.

Location: From Fresno, drive 50 miles north on Highway 41 to Yosemite Forks. Turn right (east) onto County Road 222 and drive six miles to the town of Bass Lake. Turn left (north) onto Beasore Road and drive 4.5 miles to the campground.

Trip note: A lot of people have heard of Bass Lake, but only a handful know about Chilcoot Creek. That's where this camp is located, but it's just two miles from Bass Lake. It provides a primitive option to use either as an overflow area for Bass Lake or for folks who don't want to get jammed into one of the Bass Lake campgrounds on a popular weekend. Open from May to September.

15. CRANE VALLEY GROUP & YOUTH CAMP

Reference: **On Bass Lake in Sierra National Forest; map F4, grid b4.**

Campsites, facilities: There are four sites that hold 30 to 50 people each at Youth Group Camp and seven sites that hold 30 to 50 people each at Crane Valley Camp. Fire grills and picnic tables are provided. Piped water and flush toilets are available; (there is no water at Crane Valley Camp). Pets are permitted on leashes. A grocery store is nearby.

Reservations, fee: Reserve by calling (800) 280-CAMP ($15 reservation fee); $20-$50 fee per night.

Who to contact: Phone the Sierra National Forest Mariposa Ranger District at (209) 683-4665.

Location: From Fresno, drive 50 miles north on Highway 41 to Yosemite Forks. Turn right (east) onto County Road 222 and drive six miles to Bass Lake.

Trip note: Bass Lake is a long, narrow, mountain lake set in the Sierra foothills at 3,400 feet. It's especially popular in the summer for waterskiers.

16. LUPINE-CEDAR

Reference: **On Bass Lake in Sierra National Forest; map F4, grid b4.**

Campsites, facilities: There are 113 sites for tents or motor homes up to 40 feet long, and several double-family sites. Picnic tables and fire grills are provided. Piped water and flush toilets are available. Some facilities are **wheelchair accessible**. Pets are permitted on leashes. Groceries and a boat ramp are available nearby.

Reservations, fee: Reserve by calling (800) 280-CAMP ($7.50 reservation fee); $15 fee per night; $30 per night for double-family sites.

Who to contact: Phone the Sierra National Forest Mariposa Ranger District at (209) 683-4665.

Location: From Fresno, drive 50 miles north on Highway 41 to Yosemite Forks. Turn right (east) onto County Road 222 and drive six miles to the campground on Bass Lake.

Trip note: This is *the* camping headquarters at Bass Lake and the only camp open year-round. Bass Lake is a popular vacation spot, especially for weekends or three-day holidays. Fishing is best in the spring for rainbow trout and large-mouth bass, and by mid-June, waterskiers have usually taken over. Boats must be registered at the Bass Lake observation tower after launching.

17. GAGGS CAMP 🚶‍♂️

Reference: **In Sierra National Forest; map F4, grid b5.**

Campsites, facilities: There are nine sites for tents or motor homes up to 16 feet long. Picnic tables and fire grills are provided. Pit toilets are available. There is **no piped water**, so bring your own. Pets are permitted on leashes.

Reservations, fee: No reservations; no fee.

Who to contact: Phone the Sierra National Forest Minarets Ranger District at (209) 877-2218.

Location: From North Fork (south of Bass Lake), drive 4.5 miles north on Mallum Ridge Road (Road 274). Turn right onto Central Camp Road (a narrow, winding road) and drive 11.5 miles to the campground

Trip note: The masses are not exactly beating a hot trail to this camp. It's a little spot, set along a little creek for campers who will have no trouble taking their pick of the sites here. It is set at 5,800 feet in the Sierra National Forest, with Bass Lake about 15 miles away. Open from June to November.

18. SODA SPRINGS 🎣 🚶‍♂️ 🏊

Reference: **On Chiquito Creek in Sierra National Forest; map F4, grid b5.**

Campsites, facilities: There are 16 sites for tents or motor homes up to 22 feet long. Fire grills and picnic tables are provided. Vault toilets are available. There is **no piped water**, so bring your own. Pets are permitted on leashes. A grocery store and a boat ramp are nearby.

Reservations, fee: No reservations; no fee.

Who to contact: Phone the Sierra National Forest Minarets Ranger District at (209) 877-2218.

Location: From the town of North Fork (south of Bass Lake), drive east and south on Mammoth Pool Road (County Road 225) to Minarets Road. Turn left (north) on Minarets Road (Road 4S81) and drive to the campground. The total distance from North Fork is about 37 miles on narrow, winding roads.

Trip note: This camp, one in a series on Chiquito Creek, is on the West Fork, about five miles from Mammoth Pool Reservoir and is used primarily as an overflow area if the more developed camps with piped water have filled up. The elevation is 4,400 feet. Open from April to November.

19. MAMMOTH POOL 🎣 ⚓ 🏊

Reference: **On Mammoth Pool Reservoir in Sierra National Forest; map F4, grid b6.**

Campsites, facilities: There are 18 sites for tents only, 29 sites for tents or motor homes up to 22 feet long, and five multi-family sites. Picnic tables and fire grills are provided. Piped water and vault toilets are available. A grocery store and a boat ramp are nearby. Pets are allowed on leashes.

Reservations, fee: No reservations; $12 fee per night.

Who to contact: Phone the Sierra National Forest Minarets Ranger District at (209) 877-2218.

Location: From the town of North Fork (south of Bass Lake), drive east and south on Mammoth Pool Road (County Road 225) to Minarets Road. Turn left (north) on Minarets Road (Road 4S81) and drive to the campground. The total distance from North Fork is about 42 miles on narrow, winding roads.

Trip note: You can plan on company here. Even though Mammoth Pool Reservoir is not widely known, those that know of it, like it. They'll be your neighbors, since the camp fills quickly on the weekends. Trout fishing can be good in the spring and early summer, with waterskiing dominant during warm weather. Get this: Lake use is restricted from May 1 to June 15 due to deer migrating across it—that's right, swimming—but the campgrounds here are still open. Open May to November.

20. PLACER

Reference: **Near Mammoth Pool Reservoir in Sierra National Forest; map F4, grid b6.**

Campsites, facilities: There are seven tent sites. Picnic tables and fire grills are provided. Vault toilets are available. There is **no piped water**. Pets are permitted on leashes.

Reservations, fee: No reservations; $10 fee per night.

Who to contact: Phone the Sierra National Forest Minarets Ranger District at (209) 877-2218.

Location: From the town of North Fork (south of Bass Lake), drive east and south on Mammoth Pool Road (County Road 225) to Minarets Road. Turn left (north) on Minarets Road (Road 4S81) and drive to the campground. The total distance from North Fork is about 39 miles on narrow, winding roads.

Trip note: This little camp is located just three miles from Mammoth Pool Reservoir. With piped water and a pretty setting along Chiquito Creek, it is one of the better campgrounds that is used as an overflow area for Mammoth Pool visitors. The elevation is 4,100 feet. Open from April to November.

21. SWEET WATER

Reference: **Near Mammoth Pool Reservoir in Sierra National Forest; map F4, grid b6.**

Campsites, facilities: There are five sites for tents only and five sites for motor homes up to 16 feet long. Picnic tables and fire grills are provided. Vault toilets are available. There is **no piped water**, so bring your own. Pets are permitted on leashes. A grocery store and a boat ramp are nearby.

Reservations, fee: No reservations; $10 fee per night.

Who to contact: Phone the Sierra National Forest Minarets Ranger District at (209) 877-2218.

Location: From the town of North Fork (south of Bass Lake), drive east and south on Mammoth Pool Road (County Road 225) to Minarets Road. Turn left (north) on Minarets Road (Road 4S81) and drive to the campground. The total distance from North Fork is about 41 miles on narrow, winding roads.

Trip note: It's small and primitive, but if the camp at Mammoth Pool Reservoir is filled up, this spot provides an alternative. It is set on Chiquito Creek, just a mile from the lake. The elevation is 3,800 feet. Open from May to November.

22. SAMPLE MEADOW

Reference: **On Kaiser Creek in Sierra National Forest; map F4, grid b8.**

Campsites, facilities: There are 16 sites for tents or small motor homes up to 16 feet long. Fire grills and picnic tables are provided. Vault toilets are available. There is **no piped water**, so bring your own. Pets are permitted on leashes.

Reservations, fee: No reservations; no fee.

Who to contact: Phone the Sierra National Forest Pineridge Ranger District at (209) 855-5360.

Location: From the town of Shaver Lake, drive 21 miles north on Highway 168 to the town of Lakeshore. From Lakeshore, turn northeast on Kaiser Pass Road (Forest Service Road 4S01) and drive for nine miles. Turn north onto the entrance road (dirt) and drive five miles to the campground.

Trip note: This is a pretty, secluded spot set at 7,800 feet along Kaiser Creek, with nearby trailheads available for backpackers. One trail accesses several lakes in the Kaiser Wilderness and another heads north and follows Kaiser Creek all the way to Mammoth Pool Reservoir (about 13 miles). There is another camp just off that trail called West Kaiser Campground. Open from June to October.

23. PORTAL FOREBAY 🎣 ⚓ 🚶 🏊 RV 8

Reference: On Forebay Lake in Sierra National Forest; map F4, grid b9.

Campsites, facilities: There are 11 sites for tents or small motor homes up to 16 feet long. Picnic tables and fire grills are provided. Vault toilets are available. There is **no piped water** is available. Pets are permitted on leashes. Groceries are available nearby at Mono Hot Springs.

Reservations, fee: No reservations; $10 fee per night.

Who to contact: Phone the Sierra National Forest Pineridge Ranger District at (209) 841-3311.

Location: From the town of Shaver Lake, drive 21 miles north on Highway 168 to the town of Lakeshore. From Lakeshore, drive northeast on Kaiser Pass Road (Forest Service Road 4S01) for about 13.5 miles to the campground entrance.

Trip note: This small, primitive camp set along the shore of Forebay Lake at 7,200 feet is a good jumpoff spot for hikers. Trails lead into the surrounding backcountry, including Lake Edison. Open from June to October.

24. SMALLEY COVE 🎣 🚶 ♿ 🏊 RV 7

Reference: On Kerckhoff Reservoir near Madera; map F4, grid c3.

Campsites, facilities: There are five sites for tents or motor homes. Piped water, fire grills, picnic tables and vault toilets are provided. Pets are permitted. There is a fee for pets. Supplies can be purchased in Auberry.

Reservations, fee: No reservations; $10 fee per night; $1 pet fee.

Who to contact: Phone PG&E at (916) 386-5164.

Location: From Highway 99 in Madera, drive 19 miles east on Highway 145. Turn right (south) on Road 206 to the town of Friant. From Friant, drive 19 miles northeast on Millerton Road and Auberry Road to Auberry. From Auberry, drive 8.5 miles north on Powerhouse Road to the campground.

Trip note: If you really want to get away from it all, this campground is a bit further than Squaw Leap Camp. Yet it is not quite as primitive since it does have piped water. There's access to the San Joaquin River for fishing. Open year-round.

25. SPRING COVE 🎣 ⚓ 🚶 🏊 🎣 RV 8

Reference: On Bass Lake in Sierra National Forest; map F4, grid c4.

Campsites, facilities: There are 54 sites for tents only and 11 sites for motor homes up to 30 feet long. Picnic tables and fire grills are provided. Piped water and flush toilets are available. Pets are permitted on leashes. Groceries and a boat ramp are available nearby.

Reservations, fee: From Memorial Day through Labor Day, reserve by calling (800) 280-CAMP ($7.50 reservation fee); $15 fee per night.

Who to contact: Phone the Sierra National Forest Mariposa Ranger District at (209) 683-4665.

Location: From Fresno, drive 50 miles north on Highway 41 to Yosemite Forks. Turn right (east) onto County Road 222 and drive six miles to the campground on Bass Lake.

Trip note: This is one of the several camps set beside Bass Lake, a long, narrow reservoir set in the Sierra foothill country. Expect hot weather in the summer. Boats must be registered at the Bass Lake observation tower after launching. The elevation is 3,400 feet. Open from May to September.

26. WISHON POINT   RV. 9

Reference: **On Bass Lake in Sierra National Forest; map F4, grid c4.**

Campsites, facilities: There are 47 sites for tents or motor homes up to 30 feet long and several double-family sites. Picnic tables, fire grills and piped water are provided. Flush toilets are available. Pets are permitted on leashes. Groceries and a boat ramp are nearby.

Reservations, fee: From Memorial Day through Labor Day, reserve by calling (800) 280-CAMP ($7.50 reservation fee); $15 fee per night; $30 per night for double-family sites.

Who to contact: Phone the Sierra National Forest Mariposa Ranger District at (209) 683-4665.

Location: From Fresno, drive 50 miles north on Highway 41 to Yosemite Forks. Turn right (east) onto County Road 222 and drive six miles to the campground on Bass Lake.

Trip note: This is the smallest, and many say the prettiest as well, of the camps at Bass Lake. It's located on Wishon Point. The elevation is 3,400 feet. Open from June to October.

27. ROCK CREEK   RV. 6

Reference: **In Sierra National Forest; map F4, grid c6.**

Campsites, facilities: There are 19 sites for tents or motor homes up to 32 feet long. Fire grills and picnic tables are provided. Piped water and vault toilets are available. Pets are permitted on leashes.

Reservations, fee: No reservations; $12 fee per night.

Who to contact: Phone the Sierra National Forest Minarets Ranger District at (209) 877-2218.

Location: From the town of North Fork (south of Bass Lake), drive east and south on Mammoth Pool Road (County Road 225) to Minarets Road. Turn left (north) on Minarets Road (Road 4S81) and drive to the campground (total distance from North Fork is about 27 miles).

Trip note: Piped water is the big bonus here. It's a heck of a lot easier to live with than the no-water situation at the Fish Creek Camp. It is also why this camp tends to fill up on weekends. A trail out of camp leads southeast for one mile and then connects with a trail that goes to Mammoth Pool Reservoir, five miles north. There is another campground at Mammoth Pool (but you can drive there). The elevation is 4,300 feet. Open from April to November.

28. FISH CREEK

Reference: **In Sierra National Forest; map F4, grid c6.**

Campsites, facilities: There are seven sites for tents or motor homes up to 16 feet long. Picnic tables, fire grills and vault toilets are available. There is **no piped water.** Pets are permitted on leashes.

Reservations, fee: No reservations; $10 fee per night.

Who to contact: Phone the Sierra National Forest Minarets Ranger District at (209) 877-2218.

Location: From the town of North Fork (south of Bass Lake), drive east and south on Mammoth Pool Road (County Road 225) to Minarets Road. Turn left (north) on Minarets Road (Road 4S81) and drive to the campground (total distance from North Fork is about 23 miles).

Trip note: This small, primitive camp isn't difficult to reach, yet is overlooked by many folks heading to Mammoth Pool Reservoir. It is set along Fish Creek at 4,600 feet in the Sierra National Forest. A trail near the camp leads to Mammoth Pool, six miles north, where there are two popular campgrounds. Of course, you could also drive there. Open from April to November.

29. BILLY CREEK

Reference: **On Huntington Lake in Sierra National Forest; map F4, grid c7.**

Campsites, facilities: There are 57 sites for tents only and 20 sites for tents or motor homes up to 25 feet long. Picnic tables, fire grills and piped water are provided. Vault and flush toilets are available. Pets are permitted on leashes. A small grocery store is nearby.

Reservations, fee: Reserve by calling (800) 280-CAMP ($7.50 reservation fee); $12 fee per night.

Who to contact: Phone the Sierra National Forest Pineridge Ranger District at (209) 841-3311.

Location: From the town of Shaver Lake, drive 21 miles north on Highway 168 to the town of Lakeshore. Turn left on County Road M2710 and drive about five miles west to the campground.

Trip note: With a half dozen camps available at Huntington Lake, vacationers can usually find a campsite to their liking. And if you don't like the company, just keep looking. The elevation is 7,000 feet. Open from June to October.

30. CATAVEE

Reference: **On Huntington Lake in Sierra National Forest; map F4, grid c8.**

Campsites, facilities: There are 31 sites for tents or motor homes up to 22 feet long. Picnic tables, fire grills and piped water are provided. Vault toilets are available. Pets are permitted on leashes. Horseback riding facilities and a small grocery store are nearby.

Reservations, fee: Reserve by calling (800) 280-CAMP ($7.50 reservation fee); $12 fee per night.

Who to contact: Phone the Sierra National Forest Pineridge Ranger District at (209) 841-3311.

Location: From the town of Shaver Lake, drive 21 miles north on Highway 168 to the town of Lakeshore. Turn left (west) on County Road M2710 and drive a half mile to the campground.

Trip note: This is one of the several camps set on the shore of Huntington Lake, a scenic, high country lake at 7,200 feet, where you can enjoy fishing, hiking and sailing. Sailboat regattas take place regularly during the summer. Nearby resorts offer boat rentals and guest docks. Tackle rentals and bait are also available. A trailhead near camp accesses the Kaiser Wilderness. Open from June through October.

31. BADGER FLAT GROUP CAMP 🚶 🐎   RV 7

Reference: On Rancheria Creek in Sierra National Forest; map F4, grid c8.

Campsites, facilities: This campground will accommodate groups of up to 100 people in tents or motor homes up to 22 feet long. Fire grills and picnic tables are provided. Vault toilets and horseback riding facilities are available. **No piped water** is available so bring your own. Pets are permitted on leashes. A grocery store is nearby.

Reservations, fee: Reserve by calling (800) 280-CAMP ($15 reservation fee); $100 fee per night per group.

Who to contact: Phone the Sierra National Forest Pineridge Ranger District at (209) 841-3311.

Location: From the town of Shaver Lake, drive 21 miles north on Highway 168 to the town of Lakeshore. From Lakeshore, turn northeast on Kaiser Pass Road (Forest Service Road 4S01) and drive for six miles to the campground.

Trip note: Badger Flat is a nearby option to other camps in the area. It's a primitive site along Rancheria Creek at 8,200 feet. A trail that passes through camp serves the Kaiser Wilderness to the north and Dinkey Lakes Wilderness to the south. Open from June through September.

32. RANCHERIA 🐟 🚶 🏊   RV 8

Reference: Near Huntington Lake in Sierra National Forest; map F4, grid c8.

Campsites, facilities: There are 150 sites for tents or motor homes up to 22 feet long. Picnic tables, fire grills and piped water are provided. Flush toilets are available. Pets are permitted on leashes. A grocery store and propane gas are available nearby.

Reservations, fee: Reserve by calling (800) 280-CAMP ($7.50 reservation fee); $12 fee per night.

Who to contact: Phone the Sierra National Forest Pineridge Ranger District at (209) 841-3311.

Location: From the town of Shaver Lake, drive 20 miles north on Highway 168 toward the town of Lakeshore.

Trip note: This is the granddaddy of the camps at Huntington Lake, and some say the best in the area. One reason is the nearby Rancheria Falls National Recreation Trail, which provides access to beautiful Rancheria Falls. The elevation is 7,000 feet. Open year-round.

33. BADGER FLAT 🚶 🐎   RV 7

Reference: On Rancheria Creek in Sierra National Forest; map F4, grid c8.

Campsites, facilities: There are 15 sites for tents or motor homes up to 22 feet long. Fire grills and picnic tables are provided. Vault toilets and horseback riding facilities are available. **No piped water** is available, so bring your own. Pets are permitted on leashes.

Reservations, fee: No reservations; $8 fee per night.

Who to contact: Phone the Sierra National Forest Pineridge Ranger District at (209) 841-3311.

Location: From the town of Shaver Lake, drive 21 miles north on Highway 168 to the town of Lakeshore. From Lakeshore, turn northeast on Kaiser Pass Road (Forest Service Road 4S01) and drive for seven miles to the campground.

Trip note: This camp is a good launching pad for backpackers. It is set at 8,200 feet along Rancheria Creek. The trail leading out of the camp is routed into the Kaiser Wilderness to the north and Dinkey Lakes Wilderness to the south. Open from June to October.

34. KINNIKINNICK

Reference: On Huntington Lake in Sierra National Forest; map F4, grid c8.

Campsites, facilities: There are 35 sites for tents or motor homes up to 22 feet long. Picnic tables, fire grills and piped water are provided. Flush toilets and horseback riding facilities are available. Pets are permitted on leashes. A grocery store is available nearby.

Reservations, fee: Reserve by calling (800) 280-CAMP ($7.50 reservation fee); $12 fee per night.

Who to contact: Phone the Sierra National Forest Pineridge Ranger District at (209) 841-3311.

Location: From the town of Shaver Lake, drive 21 miles north on Highway 168 to the town of Lakeshore. Turn left (west) on County Road M2710 and drive a half mile to the campground.

Trip note: Flip a coin; there are a half-dozen camps at Huntington Lake. The elevation is 7,000. Open from June to September.

35. DEER CREEK

Reference: On Huntington Lake in Sierra National Forest; map F4, grid c8.

Campsites, facilities: There are 28 sites for tents or motor homes up to 22 feet long. Picnic tables, fire grills and piped water are provided. Flush toilets and horseback riding facilities are available. Pets are permitted on leashes. A grocery store, and propane gas are nearby.

Reservations, fee: Reserve by calling (800) 280-CAMP ($7.50 reservation fee); $12 fee per night.

Who to contact: Phone the Sierra National Forest Pineridge Ranger District at (209) 841-3311.

Location: From the town of Shaver Lake, drive 21 miles north on Highway 168 to the town of Lakeshore. Turn left (west) on County Road M2710 and drive a half mile to the campground.

Trip note: This is another in the series of camps at Huntington Lake, a pretty mountain lake set at 7,000 feet. It's a popular vacation destination for hunkering down for a while or strapping on a backpack and taking off on the nearby trail routed into the Kaiser Wilderness. Open from June to October.

36. COLLEGE

Reference: On Huntington Lake in Sierra National Forest; map F4, grid c8.

Campsites, facilities: There are 11 sites for tents or motor homes up to 22 feet long. Piped water, fire grills and picnic tables are provided. Vault toilets are available. Pets are permitted on leashes. Horseback riding facilities, grocery store and propane gas are available nearby.

Reservations, fee: Reserve by calling (800) 280-CAMP ($7.50 reservation fee); $12 fee per night.

Who to contact: Phone the Sierra National Forest Pineridge Ranger District at (209) 841-3311.

Location: From the town of Shaver Lake, drive 21 miles north on Highway 168 to the town of Lakeshore. Turn left (west) on County Road M2710 and drive a half mile to the campground.

Trip note: This is a take-your-pick deal, one of six camps along the north shore of Huntington Lake. The elevation is 7,000. Open from June to October.

---

37. BOLSILLO

Reference: On Bolsillo Creek in Sierra National Forest; map F4, grid c9.

Campsites, facilities: There are three tent sites. Piped water, picnic tables and fire grills are provided. Vault toilets are available. Pets are permitted on leashes. Supplies can be purchased in Mono Hot Springs.

Reservations, fee: No reservations; no fee.

Who to contact: Phone the Sierra National Forest Pineridge Ranger District at (209) 841-3311.

Location: From the town of Shaver Lake, drive 21 miles north on Highway 168 to the town of Lakeshore. From Lakeshore, turn northeast on Kaiser Pass Road (Forest Service Road 4S01) and drive for 15 miles to the campground entrance on the right.

Trip note: This is a tiny, virtually unknown camp, yet there are several bonuses, including piped water. It is set at 7,400 feet along Bolsillo Creek. Sidetrip options include a hike on a trail that passes through the camp and goes north for two miles to Mono Hot Springs and south for 2.5 miles to Corbett Lake. Open from June to October.

---

38. MILLERTON LAKE STATE RECREATION AREA

Reference: Near Madera; map F4, grid d1.

Campsites, facilities: There are 138 sites for tents or motor homes up to 31 feet long and two group sites available. Fire grills and picnic tables are provided. Piped water, showers, flush toilets, sanitary disposal station and boat ramps are available. Some facilities are **wheelchair accessible**. Pets are permitted on leashes. Supplies can be purchased in Friant.

Reservations, fee: From March 10 through September 10, reserve through Destinet at (800) 444-PARK ($6.75 Destinet fee); $14-$16 fee per night; pets $1.

Who to contact: Phone (209) 822-2332 or (209) 822-2630.

Location: From Highway 99 in Madera, drive 22 miles east on Highway 145 (six miles past intersection with Highway 41) to the campground.

Trip note: As the temperature gauge goes up in the summer, the value of Millerton Lake increases at the same rate. A beach area is available at the day-use park across the lake from the campground. By midsummer, waterskiers take over the lake. Fishing can be good in spring, but by fall, the water level has usually dropped quite a bit in the attempt to quench the insatiable thirst of valley farms. A good side trip is to take the trail from camp to a lookout over the lake. Open year-round.

39. SQUAW LEAP

Reference: **On San Joaquin River near Madera; map F4, grid d3.**

Campsites, facilities: There are five family sites and two group sites for tents. All are walk-in sites. Fire grills and picnic tables are provided. Vault toilets and a hitching post are available. There is **no piped water**, so bring your own. Pets are permitted. Supplies can be purchased in Auberry.

Reservations, fee: No reservations; no fee.

Who to contact: Phone the Bureau of Land Management, Folsom Resource Area at (916) 985-4474.

Location: From State Highway 99 in Madera, drive 19 miles east on Highway 145. Turn right (south) on Road 206 to the town of Friant. From Friant, drive 19 miles northeast on Millerton/Auberry Road to Auberry. From Auberry, drive two miles north on Powerhouse Road. Turn left at the Squaw Leap Management Area sign at Smalley Road. Drive four miles to the campground.

Trip note: Not many folks know about this spot. It's a primitive setting, but it has some bonuses. For one thing, there's access to the San Joaquin River if you drive to the fishing access trailhead at the end of the road. From there, you get spectacular views of the San Joaquin River Gorge. The camp is a trailhead for two excellent hiking and equestrian trails. Beautiful wildflower displays are available in the spring. Open year-round.

40. SWANSON MEADOW

Reference: **Near Shaver Lake in Sierra National Forest; map F4, grid d6.**

Campsites, facilities: There are 12 sites for tents or motor homes up to 22 feet long. Fire grills and picnic tables are provided. Vault toilets are available. There is **no piped water** at this site, so bring your own. Pets are permitted on leashes. A grocery store is nearby.

Reservations, fee: No reservations; $8 fee per night.

Who to contact: Phone the Sierra National Forest Pineridge Ranger District at (209) 841-3311.

Location: From Highway 168 just south of the town of Shaver Lake, drive three miles east on Dinkey Creek Road.

Trip note: This smallest and most primitive of the camps near Shaver Lake is used primarily as an overflow area if lakeside camps are full. It is located about two miles from the Shaver Lake. The elevation is 5,600 feet. Open from May to November.

41. DORABELLE

Reference: **On Shaver Lake in Sierra National Forest; map F4, grid d6.**

Campsites, facilities: There are 68 sites for tents or motor homes up to 22 feet long. Picnic tables, fire grills and piped water are provided. Vault toilets are available. Pets are permitted on leashes. A grocery store is nearby.

Reservations, fee: Reserve by calling (800) 280-CAMP ($7.50 reservation fee); $12 fee per night.

Who to contact: Phone the Sierra National Forest Pineridge Ranger District at (209) 841-3311.

Location: From Highway 168 south of the town of Shaver Lake, turn east onto County Road N257 (Dorabelle Road) and drive a half mile to the campground.

Trip note: This is one of the few Forest Service camps in the state that is set up more for motor homes than for tenters. It's a popular lake for vacationers and well stocked with trout during summer months. Boat rentals and bait and tackle are available at the nearby marina. This is also a popular snow-play area in the winter. The elevation is 5,400 feet. Open from May to October.

42. CAMP EDISON

Reference: **On Shaver Lake; map F4, grid d6.**

Campsites, facilities: There are 252 sites for tents or motor homes up to 22 feet long. Forty-three of these sites are for full hookups. Piped water, sewer, electrical connections, fire grills, and picnic tables are provided. Flush toilets, showers, a sanitary disposal station, cable TV, a laundromat and a boat ramp are available. Pets are permitted on leashes. Some facilities are **wheelchair accessible**.

Reservations, fee: Reservations accepted; $18-$22 fee for two people per night; senior citizens get a discounted fee ($12.50 per night); $2 pet fee.

Who to contact: Phone the park at (209) 841-3444.

Location: From the town of Shaver Lake, drive one mile north on Highway 168 to the campground entrance road.

Trip note: Here is a series of camps along popular Shaver Lake. Boat rentals and bait and tackle are available at the nearby marina. You can expect company. The elevation is 5,400 feet. Open year-round with limited winter facilities.

43. BUCK MEADOW

Reference: **On Deer Creek in Sierra National Forest; map F4, grid e8.**

Campsites, facilities: There are 10 sites for tents only and five sites for tents or motor homes up to 22 feet long. Picnic tables, fire grills and vault toilets are available. There is **no piped water**, so bring your own. Pets are permitted on leashes.

Reservations, fee: No reservations; no fee.

Who to contact: Phone the Sierra National Forest Kings River Ranger District at (209) 855-8321.

Location: From Highway 168 just south of Shaver Lake, turn east on Dinkey Creek Road and drive about 12 miles. Turn right on McKinley Grove Road and drive eight miles to the campground.

Trip note: This is one of the three little-known, primitive camps in the area. This one is set at 6,800 feet along Deer Creek. It's about seven miles from Wishon Reservoir, a more popular destination. Open from June to October.

44. GIGANTEA

Reference: **On Dinkey Creek in Sierra National Forest; map F4, grid e8.**

Campsites, facilities: There are seven sites for tents or motor homes up to 16 feet long. Picnic tables are provided. Vault toilets and fire grills are available. There is **no piped water** at this site. Pets are permitted on leashes. Supplies can be purchased in Dinkey Creek.

Reservations, fee: No reservations; no fee.

Who to contact: Phone the Sierra National Forest Kings River Ranger District at (209) 855-8321.

Location: From Highway 168 just south of Shaver Lake, turn east on Dinkey Creek Road and drive about 12 miles. Turn right on McKinley Grove Road and drive six miles to the campground.

Trip note: Backpackers use this primitive camp along Dinkey Creek as a mountain access point. A trail passes through camp that follows the creek south for many miles and going north, follows Dinkey Creek up to the town of Dinkey Creek, where convenience and horseback riding facilities can be found. The elevation is 6,500 feet. Open from June to October.

45. DINKEY CREEK

Reference: **In Sierra National Forest; map F4, grid e8.**

Campsites, facilities: There are 128 sites for tents or motor homes up to 22 feet long. Piped water, fire grills and picnic tables are provided. Flush toilets and horseback riding facilities are available. Pets are permitted on leashes. Supplies can be purchased in Dinkey Creek.

Reservations, fee: From Memorial Day through Labor Day, reserve by calling (800) 280-CAMP ($7.50 reservation fee); $10 fee per night.

Who to contact: Phone the Sierra National Forest Kings River Ranger District at (209) 855-8321.

Location: From Highway 168 just south of the town of Shaver Lake, turn east on Dinkey Creek Road and drive 14 miles to the campground.

Trip note: This is a huge Forest Service camp set along Dinkey Creek at 5,700 feet. It serves both backpackers and folks who want to call it home for awhile. A trail passes through the camp that follows Dinkey Creek south for many miles. Taken north, the trail follows Dinkey Creek past Dinkey Dome up to Swamp Meadow, then along a dirt road for about 2.5 miles to a trailhead that leads to numerous lakes in the Dinkey Lakes Wilderness. Open from May to October.

46. TRAPPER SPRINGS

Reference: **On Courtright Reservoir in Sierra National Forest; map F4, grid e9.**

Campsites, facilities: There are 45 sites for tents or motor homes up to 22 feet long. Piped water, fire grills, and picnic tables are provided. Vault toilets are available. Pets are permitted on leashes. A boat ramp is nearby. This campground is **wheelchair accessible**.

Reservations, fee: No reservations; $10 fee per night.

Who to contact: Phone the Sierra National Forest Kings River Ranger District at (209) 855-8321.

Location: From Highway 168 just south of the town of Shaver Lake, turn east onto Dinkey Creek Road and drive 12 miles. Turn right (east) on McKinley Grove Road and drive 14 miles. Turn north onto Courtright Reservoir Road and drive 12 miles to the campground.

Trip note: This is one of the two camps on Courtright Reservoir, a pretty high mountain lake at 8,200 feet. Open June to October.

47. MARMOT ROCK WALK-IN

Reference: **On Courtright Reservoir in Sierra National Forest; map F4, grid e9.**

Campsites, facilities: There are 14 walk-in sites for tents only. Piped water, fire grills and picnic tables are provided. Vault toilets and a boat ramp are available. Pets are permitted on leashes.

Reservations, fee: No reservations; $10 fee per night; $1 pet fee.

Who to contact: Phone PG&E at (916) 386-5164 or the Sierra National Forest Kings River Ranger District at (209) 855-8321.

Location: From Highway 168 just south of the town of Shaver Lake, turn east onto Dinkey Creek Road and drive 12 miles. Turn right (east) on McKinley Grove Road and drive 14 miles. Turn north on Courtright Reservoir Road and drive 10 miles to the campground on the south shore.

Trip note: Courtright Reservoir is in the high country at 8,200 feet. It is a pretty Sierra lake that provides options for boaters and hikers. Trout fishing can be good here. Boaters must observe a 15-m.p.h. speed limit, which makes for quiet water. Hikers should consider the trail on the western side of the lake, which is routed into the Dinkey Lakes Wilderness or the trail on the eastern side of the lake that heads into the John Muir Wilderness. Open from June to October.

48. UPPER KINGS RIVER GROUP CAMP 8

Reference: On Lake Wishon; map F4, grid e9.

Campsites, facilities: There is one group site that will accommodate up to 50 people. Picnic tables and fire pits are provided. Piped water and vault toilets are available. Pets on leashes and kept under strict control are permitted.

Reservations, fee: Reservations are required; $100 fee per night with a two-night limit.

Who to contact: Phone PG&E at (916) 386-5164.

Location: On Highway 168 just south of the town of Shaver Lake, turn east on Dinkey Creek Road and drive 12 miles. Turn right on McKinley Grove Road and continue to the Wishon Dam. The campground is located near the base of the dam.

Trip note: Lake Wishon is a great place for a multi-day camping trip. When the lake is full, which is not often enough, the place has great natural beauty, set at 6,500 feet and surrounded by national forest. The fishing is fair enough on summer evenings, and a 15-m.p.h. speed limit keeps the lake quiet. A side trip option is hiking from the trailhead at Woodchuck Creek, which within the span of a one-day hike takes you into the John Muir Wilderness and past three lakes—Woodchuck, Chimney and Marsh. Open May through October.

49. DEER CREEK POINT GROUP SITE RV 7

Reference: On Pine Flat Lake; map F4, grid f5.

Campsites, facilities: There are two group sites (for 50 people) that will accommodate tents or motor homes. Piped water, fire grills, and picnic tables and vault toilets are provided. Pets are permitted on leashes. Boat rentals are available within five miles of camp.

Reservations, fee: Reservations required; $50-$75 per night per group.

Who to contact: Phone the U.S. Corps of Engineers at (209) 787-2589.

Location: From Fresno, take Belmont Avenue east. Belmont Avenue will merge into Trimmer Springs Road. Continue on Belmont/Trimmer Springs approximately eight miles past the community of Piedra. Look for the Island Park Campground sign on the right. Turn right there and continue past the Island Park camp about one-half mile to Deer Park Group Site campground entrance.

Trip note: This is one of the better camps at Pine Flat Lake. The relative smallness, and the good location, are pluses. The best time to visit is in the spring when the lake levels are the highest and the fishing for trout and bass is at its peak. When full, Pine Flat is 21 miles long and has 67 miles of shoreline, but it is subject to drawdowns in late summer when the water gets diverted for irrigation. The elevation is 1,000 feet. Open April through September.

50. PINE FLAT RECREATION AREA

Reference: On Kings River; map F4, grid f5.

Campsites, facilities: There are 52 sites for tents or motor homes. Piped water, fire grills and picnic tables are provided. Flush toilets, a dump station, a playground and a **wheelchair accessible** fishing area are available. A grocery store, a laundromat and propane gas are nearby. Pets are allowed on leashes.

Reservations, fee: No reservations; $11 fee per night.

Who to contact: Phone the park at (209) 488-3004.

Location: From Fresno, drive east on Belmont Road. Belmont Road will merge with Trimmer Springs Road. Continue on Belmont/Trimmer Springs to Pine Flat Road. Turn right on Pine Flat Road and drive three miles to the signed campground entrance.

Trip note: This is a county park that is open all year, set along the Kings River just above Pine Flat Lake. The lake can be subject to drawdowns due to irrigation demands, which makes spring the best time to visit. Hey, the fishing is best in the spring anyway, and by summer, waterskiers often monopolize the lake. There are several resorts on the lake that offer boat and ski rentals, bait and tackle.

51. ISLAND PARK

Reference: On Pine Flat Lake; map F4, grid f5.

Campsites, facilities: There are 52 designated sites for tents or motor homes and 60 overflow sites with picnic tables available. Piped water, fire grills and picnic tables are provided at designated sites. Flush toilets, showers, a boat ramp, fish cleaning stations and a dump station are available. Some facilities are **wheelchair accessible**. Pets are permitted on leashes. There is a seasonal store at the campground entrance. Boat rentals are available within five miles.

Reservations, fee: No reservations; $12 fee per night; $6 fee for each additional vehicle.

Who to contact: Phone the U.S. Corps of Engineers at (209) 787-2589.

Location: From Fresno, take Belmont Avenue east. Belmont Avenue will merge into Trimmer Springs Road. Continue on Belmont/Trimmer Springs approximately eight miles past the community of Piedra. Look for the Island Park Campground sign on the right. Turn right there and continue about one-quarter mile to the signed park entrance.

Trip note: This is one of the several campgrounds available at Pine Flat Lake, a popular lake set in the foothill country. The elevation is 1,000 feet.

52. SUNNYSLOPE CAMPGROUNDS

Reference: Near Pine Flat Lake; map F4, grid f5.

Campsites, facilities: There are 97 sites for tents or motor homes. Piped water, electrical connections and picnic tables are provided. Restrooms, hot showers, a laundromat, a playground, a grocery store, ice and propane gas are available. Boat rentals and marinas are available at Pine Flat Reservoir. Pets are permitted.

Reservations, fee: Reservations accepted; $12-$16 fee per night.

Who to contact: Phone the park at (209) 787-2730.

Location: From Piedra, drive three miles northeast on Trimmer Springs Road. Turn right onto Sunnyslope Road and drive 100 yards to the campground.

Trip note: This campground overlooks Pine Flat Lake, a pretty lake (when full of water) set in the foothill country. There are several resorts on the lake that offer boat and waterski rentals, bait and tackle.

53. SYCAMORE CREEK

Reference: **On Pine Flat Lake; map F4, grid f6.**

Campsites, facilities: There are 20 sites for tents or motor homes up to 22 feet long. Fire grills and picnic tables are provided. Vault toilets are available. There is **no piped water**, so bring your own. Pets are permitted on leashes.

Reservations, fee: No reservations; $6 fee per night.

Who to contact: Phone the U.S. Corps of Engineers at (209) 787-2589.

Location: From Fresno, drive east on Belmont Avenue which will merge with Trimmer Springs Road. Continue on Belmont/Trimmer Springs for about five miles past the community of Trimmer to the signed campground entrance on the right.

Trip note: This is the other of the two large, primitive group camps on the northeast shore of Pine Flat Lake. Several other camps at Pine Flat Lake are available.

54. KIRCH FLAT

Reference: **On Kings River in Sierra National Forest; map F4, grid f7.**

Campsites, facilities: There are 17 sites for tents or motor homes up to 22 feet long and one group camp that will accommodate up to 50 people. Fire grills and picnic tables are provided. Vault toilets are available. There is **no piped water**, so bring your own. Pets are permitted on leashes.

Reservations, fee: No reservations, no fee for family camping; to reserve group site call Trimmer Ranger Station at (209) 855-8321; group camp fee is $1 per person per night, 25 person minimum.

Who to contact: Phone the Sierra National Forest Kings River Ranger District at (209) 855-8321.

Location: From Trimmer, drive 18 miles east on Trimmer Springs Road.

Trip note: In the summer, it can feel like you're camping on a branding iron. It is set in the foothill country and is adjacent to Kings River. Pine Flat Lake, six miles away, provides another option. The elevation is 1,100 feet. Open year-round.

55. BLACK ROCK

Reference: **On Black Rock Reservoir in Sierra National Forest; map F4, grid f8.**

Campsites, facilities: There are seven sites for tents only and one trailer site. Piped water, fire grills and picnic tables are provided. Vault toilets are available. Pets are permitted on leashes.

Reservations, fee: No reservations; $8 fee per night.

Who to contact: Phone the Sierra National Forest Kings River Ranger District at (209) 855-8321.

Location: From Trimmer, drive east on Trimmer Springs Road for about 20 miles. Turn northwest onto Black Road and drive 10 miles to the campground.

Trip note: This relatively little-known spot is set at Black Rock Reservoir on the

North Fork of the Kings River. Exploring the Kings River Geological Area could be a possible side trip. The elevation is 4,200 feet. Open May to October.

56. LILY PAD

Reference: **On Wishon Reservoir in Sierra National Forest; map F4, grid f9.**

Campsites, facilities: There are six sites for tents only and 10 sites for tents or motor homes up to 16 feet long. Piped water, picnic tables and fire grills are provided. Vault toilets are available. Pets are permitted on leashes. Groceries, boat rentals, a boat ramp and propane gas are available nearby. This campground is **wheelchair accessible**. There is also a group campsite available nearby called Upper Kings River; it will accommodate up to 50 people.

Reservations, fee: No reservations for single sites; $10 fee per night; $75 group fee per night.

Who to contact: Phone the Sierra National Forest Kings River Ranger District at (209) 855-8321.

Location: From Highway 168 south of the town of Shaver Lake, turn east onto Dinkey Creek Road and drive 12 miles. Turn right (east) on McKinley Grove Road and drive 16 miles to the campground.

Trip note: This is the smaller of the two camps at Wishon Reservoir. It is set along the southwest shore at 6,500 feet.

57. WISHON VILLAGE

Reference: **On Wishon Reservoir; map F4, grid f9.**

Campsites, facilities: There are 26 sites for tents only and 96 RV sites with full hookups. Picnic tables, piped water, electrical connections and sewer hookups are provided. Restrooms, hot showers, flush toilets, a laundromat, a country store, ice, a boat ramp, motorboat rentals, bait, tackle and propane gas are available. Pets are allowed on leashes.

Reservations, fee: Reservations recommended; $12-$22 fee per night.

Who to contact: Phone the park at (209) 865-5361.

Location: From Highway 168 just south of the town of Shaver Lake, turn east onto Dinkey Creek Road and drive 12 miles. Turn right on McKinley Grove Road and drive 15 miles to 66500 McKinley Grove Road.

Trip note: This privately-operated mountain park is set on the North Fork of the Kings River near the shore of Wishon Reservoir. Trout stocks often make for good fishing in early summer, but anglers with boats should heed the 15-m.p.h. speed limit. Backpackers should head to nearby Coolidge Meadow, where a trailhead awaits that is routed to the Woodchuck Creek drainage and numerous lakes in the John Muir Wilderness. The elevation is 6,500 feet. Open May to November.

58. MILL FLAT

Reference: **On Kings River in Sequoia National Forest; map F4, grid g8.**

Campsites, facilities: There are five sites for tents only. Picnic tables and fire grills are provided. Vault toilets are available. **No piped water** is available, so bring your own. Pets are permitted on leashes.

Reservations, fee: No reservations; no fee.

Who to contact: Phone the Sequoia National Forest Hume Lake Ranger District at (209) 338-2251.

Location: From Trimmer, drive about 17 miles east on Trimmer Springs Road (Forest Service Road 11S12). Cross the river and drive one mile along the south side of the Kings River on Forest Service Road 11S12, parallel to the Keller Ranch. At the junction with the second bridge, turn right onto a dirt road (Forest Service Road 12S01) and drive about 2.5 miles to the campground on the south side of the river. Trailers not recommended.

Trip note: This spot is on the Kings River at the confluence of Mill Flat Creek. It's a very small, primitive spot and very hot in the summer. It's set upstream from Pine Flat Lake. Open year-round.

59. CAMP 4

Reference: **On Kings River in Sequoia National Forest; map F4, grid g8.**

Campsites, facilities: There are five sites for tents only. Picnic tables and fire grills are provided. Vault toilets are available. There is **no piped water**, so bring your own. Pets are permitted on leashes.

Reservations, fee: No reservations; no fee.

Who to contact: Phone the Sequoia National Forest Hume Lake Ranger District at (209) 338-2251.

Location: From Trimmer, drive about 17 miles east on Trimmer Springs Road (Forest Service Road 11S12). Cross the river and drive one mile along the south side of the Kings River on Forest Service Road 12S01. At the junction with the second bridge, turn right onto a dirt road (Forest Service Road 12S01 and drive about 1.5 miles to the campground on the south side of the river. Trailers not recommended.

Trip note: This is one in the series of camps set on the Kings River, upstream from Pine Flat Lake. The weather gets hot, so bring a cooler. A map of the Sequoia National Forest details the backcountry roads. Open year-round.

60. CAMP 4 & 1/2

Reference: **On Kings River in Sequoia National Forest; map F4, grid g8.**

Campsites, facilities: There are five sites for tents only. Picnic tables and fire grills are provided. Vault toilets are available. There is **no piped water**, so bring your own. Pets are permitted on leashes.

Reservations, fee: No reservations; no fee.

Who to contact: Phone the Sequoia National Forest Hume Lake Ranger District at (209) 338-2251.

Location: From Trimmer, drive about 17 miles east on Trimmer Springs Road (Forest Service Road 11S12). Cross the river and drive one mile along the south side of the Kings River on Forest Service Road 12S01. At the junction with the second bridge, turn right onto a dirt road (Forest Service Road 12S01) and drive about three-quarters of a mile to the campground. Trailers not recommended.

Trip note: We found five sites here, not "four and a half," though it's not easy to tell. It is one in the series of camps located just east of Pine Flat Lake along the Kings River. It's small, primitive and usually hot. Open year-round.

61. SUNSET

Reference: **In Kings Canyon National Park; map F4, grid h9.**

Campsites, facilities: There are 119 sites for tents or motor homes up to 30 feet long. Piped water, fire grills and picnic tables are provided. Flush toilets, evening ranger programs and horseback riding facilities are available (in the summer). A grocery store and a laundromat are nearby. Showers are available in Grant Grove. Pets are permitted on leashes, except on trails.

Reservations, fee: No reservations; $10 fee per night.

Who to contact: Phone the Kings Canyon National Park at (209) 565-3341.

Location: From Wilsonia in Kings Canyon National Park, drive a half mile north on Highway 180.

Trip note: This is the biggest of the camps that are located just inside the Kings Canyon National Park boundaries at Wilsonia. The Grant Grove of Giant Sequoias is the main attraction and close by. The elevation is 6,600 feet. Open May to October.

62. AZALEA 🏃 ♿ 🐎   RV 5

Reference: **In Kings Canyon National Park; map F4, grid h9.**

Campsites, facilities: There are 113 sites for tents or motor homes up to 30 feet long. Piped water, fire grills and picnic tables are provided. Flush toilets, a dump station, evening ranger programs and horseback riding facilities are available. The campgrounds and restroom facilities are **wheelchair accessible**. A grocery store is nearby. Showers are available in Grant Grove. Pets are permitted on leashes, except on trails.

Reservations, fee: No reservations; $10 fee per night.

Who to contact: Phone the Kings Canyon National Park at (209) 565-3341.

Location: From Wilsonia in Kings Canyon National Park, drive three-quarters of a mile north on Highway 180.

Trip note: This camp is tucked just inside the western border of Kings Canyon National Park. It is set at 6,600 feet near the Grant Grove of Giant Sequoias. Privately-owned Sequoia Lake is nearby for sight-seeing (no fishing or swimming for the public), just west of the camp. There's a side trip to the north on Highway 180: reenter the park at Cedar Grove, set near the spectacular canyon of Kings River, one of the deepest gorges in North America. Open year-round.

63. CRYSTAL SPRINGS 🏃 🐎   RV 5

Reference: **In Kings Canyon National Park; map F4, grid h9.**

Campsites, facilities: There are 63 sites for tents. Piped water, fire grills and picnic tables are provided. Flush toilets, a dump station, horseback riding facilities and evening ranger programs are available. Showers are available in Grant Grove. Groceries and propane gas are nearby. Pets are permitted on leashes, except on trails.

Reservations, fee: No reservations; $10 fee per night.

Who to contact: Phone the Kings Canyon National Park at (209) 565-3341.

Location: From Wilsonia in Kings Canyon National Park, drive three-quarters of a mile north on Highway 180.

Trip note: Kings Canyon National Park has protected one of the deepest gorges in North America. This camp offers a pretty spot, which is set at 6,600 feet. The giant Sequoias in the area are inspiring. As winter approaches, beware of bad road and snow conditions. Open from May to October.

64. PRINCESS 🐟   RV 7

Reference: **On Indian Creek in Sequoia National Forest; map F4, grid h9.**

Campsites, facilities: There are 50 tent sites and 40 sites for tents or motor homes up to 22 feet long. Picnic tables, fire grills and piped water are provided. Vault toilets and a dump station are available. Pets are permitted on leashes. A grocery store is nearby.

Reservations, fee: Reserve by calling (800) 280-CAMP ($7.50 reservation fee); $12 fee per night.

Who to contact: Phone the Sequoia National Forest, Hume Lake Ranger District at (209) 338-2251.

Location: From Grant Grove in Kings Canyon National Park, drive six miles north on Highway 180 to the campground entrance road.

Trip note: This mountain camp is at 5,900 feet. It is popular because of its close proximity to both Hume Lake and Kings Canyon National Park. Lake Hume is just four miles from the camp and the Grant Grove entrance to Kings Canyon National Park is only six miles away. Open from May to September.

---

65. ESHOM CREEK

Reference: On Eshom Creek in Sequoia National Forest; map F4, grid i8.

Campsites, facilities: There are 17 sites for tents or motor homes up to 22 feet long and seven multi-family units. Piped water, picnic tables and fire grills are provided. Vault toilets are available. Pets are permitted on leashes.

Reservations, fee: No reservations; $10-$12 fee per night.

Who to contact: Phone the Sequoia National Forest, Hume Lake Ranger District at (209) 338-2251.

Location: From Highway 99, drive east on Highway 198 through Visalia to Highway 245. Turn left (north) on Highway 245 and drive to Badger. From Badger, drive eight miles northeast on County Road 465.

Trip note: With everybody heading to nearby Sequoia National Park, this is the kind of spot that is often overlooked. Or you can use it if that park is too crowded. It is set just two miles from park boundaries along Eshom Creek at 4,800 feet. Open from May to October.

---

66. SIERRA LAKE CAMPGROUND

Reference: Near Visalia; map F4, grid i8.

Campsites, facilities: There are 10 sites for tents only and 25 motor home sites. Picnic tables, fire grills, piped water, electrical connections and sewer hookups are provided. Restrooms, showers, a laundromat, a store, a dump station and propane gas and a full service restaurant are available. Pets are allowed on leashes.

Reservations, fee: Reservations recommended; $12-$18 per night; $1 pet fee.

Who to contact: Phone the park at (209) 337-2520.

Location: From Highway 99, drive east on Highway 198 through Visalia to Lemon Cove. Turn left on Highway 216 and go a half mile. Turn right (north) on Dry Creek Road and drive 16 miles to Mountain Road 453 (Stagecoach Road). Turn right and drive 1.5 miles to the campground.

Trip note: This secluded, privately-managed, 106-acre park offers a 10-acre lake stocked with trout. The park is about a 30-minute drive from Kings Canyon and Sequoia National Parks and has three restaurants within three miles of the camp. Open year-round.

MAP F5

CEN-CAL MAP .... see page 512
adjoining maps
NORTH (E5) .... see page 500
EAST (F6) .... see page 590
SOUTH (G5) .... see page 614
WEST (F4) .... see page 538

71 LISTINGS
PAGES 564-589

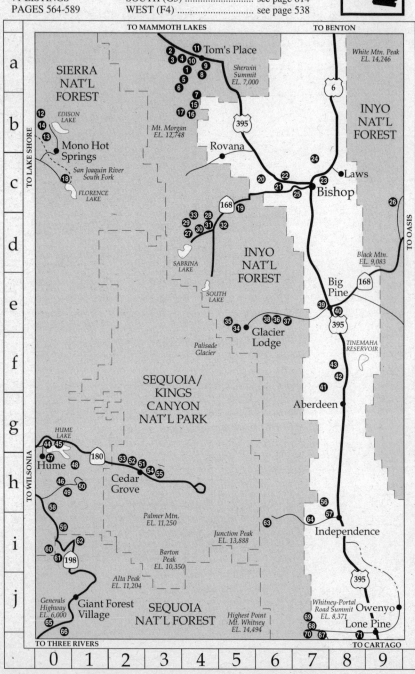

Map F5 featuring: Inyo National Forest, Lake Crowley, Lake Edison, Sierra National Forest, San Joaquin River, Florence Lake, Pleasant Valley Reservoir, Lake Sabrina, South Lake, Sequoia National Forest, Kings Canyon National Park, Middle Fork Kaweah River, Mount Whitney

1. IRIS MEADOW ↳🐟   RV 5

Reference: **Near Lake Crowley in Inyo National Forest; map F5, grid a3.**

Campsites, facilities: There are 15 sites for tents or motor homes up to 22 feet long. Piped water, fire grills, and picnic tables are provided. Flush toilets are available. Supplies can be purchased in Tom's Place. Pets are permitted on leashes.

Reservations, fee: No reservations; $10 fee per night.

Who to contact: Phone Inyo National Forest at (619) 873-2500.

Location: From the junction of US 395 and Highway 203 (the Mammoth Lakes turnoff), drive 15 miles south on US 395 to Tom's Place. Turn south on Rock Creek Road and drive three miles to the campground.

Trip note: This Forest Service camp, at the base of Reds Mountain, is another in the series of camps on Rock Creek. It is a popular layover area for campers visiting Lake Crowley. The elevation is 8,100 feet. Open from June to September.

2. McGEE CREEK RV PARK ↳🐟 👫   RV 4

Reference: **Near Lake Crowley in Inyo National Forest; map F5, grid a3.**

Campsites, facilities: There are 35 sites for tents or motor homes, many with partial or full hookups. Piped water, fire grills and picnic tables are provided. Flush toilets and hot showers are available. Pets are allowed on leashes.

Reservations, fee: Reservations accepted; $12-$15 fee per night.

Who to contact: Phone the park at (619) 935-4233.

Location: From the junction of US 395 and Highway 203 (the Mammoth Lakes turnoff), drive south on US 395 for 6.5 miles to a turnoff to the frontage road that runs along the west side of US 395 and parallel to it. Continue south on that road for about 1.5 miles to McGee Creek Road. Turn onto McGee Creek Road and you'll see the park entrance.

Trip note: This is a popular layover spot for folks visiting giant Lake Crowley. Lake Crowley once offered outstanding trout fishing, but in the 1990s, it's been closer to "fair to good." That means there are days where you need a Jaws of Life to get a trout to open its mouth. Convict Lake provides a nearby side trip option. The elevation is 7,000 feet. Open April to October.

3. McGEE CREEK 👫   RV 7

Reference: **In Inyo National Forest; map F5, grid a3.**

Campsites, facilities: There are 28 sites for tents or motor homes up to 22 feet long. Piped water, fire grills and picnic tables are provided. Flush toilets are available. Pets are permitted on leashes.

Reservations, fee: Reserve by phoning (800) 280-CAMP ($7.50 reservation fee); $8 fee per night.

Who to contact: Phone the Inyo National Forest District Office at (619) 873-2500.

Location: From the junction of US 395 and Highway 203 (the Mammoth Lakes turn off), drive south on US 395 for 6.5 miles to a turn off for the frontage road that runs along the west side of US 395 and parallel to it. Continue south for about two miles to McGee Creek Road. Turn right (southwest) and drive 1.5 miles to the campground.

Trip note: This Forest Service camp, set along little McGee Creek, is often used as a base camp for backpackers. A trailhead is available up the road that provides access along McGee Creek and is routed to the John Muir Wilderness. The elevation is 7,600 feet. Open from May through October.

4. CROWLEY LAKE

Reference: Map F5, grid a3.

Campsites, facilities: There are 47 sites for tents or motor homes. Fire grills and picnic tables are provided. Pit toilets and a dumpster are available. No piped water, so bring your own. A grocery store and a boat ramp are nearby on Lake Crowley. Pets are allowed on leashes.

Reservations, fee: No reservations; no fee.

Who to contact: Phone the Bureau of Land Management Bishop Resource Area at (619) 872-4881.

Location: From Bishop, drive north 30 miles on Highway 395 to the Hilton Creek/ Crowley Lake Road exit. Turn left on Crowley Lake Road and continue through the town of Hilton Creek to Old Highway 395. Turn right (north) on Old Highway 395 and drive five miles to the signed campground entrance on the left.

Trip note: This large BLM-managed camp is across US 395 from the south shore of Lake Crowley. Crowley, once the capital of trout fishing in the eastern Sierra, has lost some of its luster in recent years, and many anglers are fishing smaller mountain lakes instead. The elevation is 7,000 feet. Open from May to October.

5. BIG MEADOW

Reference: Near Lake Crowley in Inyo National Forest; map F5, grid a3.

Campsites, facilities: There are five sites for tents only and six sites for tents or motor homes up to 22 feet long. Picnic tables, fire grills, and piped water are provided. Flush toilets are available. Supplies can be purchased in Tom's Place. Pets are permitted on leashes.

Reservations, fee: No reservations; $11 fee per night.

Who to contact: Phone Inyo National Forest at (619) 873-2500.

Location: From the junction of US 395 and Highway 203 (the Mammoth Lakes turnoff), drive 15 miles south on US 395 to Tom's Place. Turn south on Rock Creek Road and drive four miles to the campground.

Trip note: This is a smaller, quieter camp in the series of camps that are set along Rock Creek. Nearby giant Lake Crowley and tiny Rock Creek Lake provide sidetrips. The elevation is 8,600 feet. Open from June to September.

6. PALISADE

Reference: Near Lake Crowley in Inyo National Forest; map F5, grid a3.

Campsites, facilities: There are two sites for tents only and three sites for tents or motor homes up to 22 feet long. Picnic tables, fire grills and piped water are provided. Flush toilets and horseback riding facilities are available. Supplies can be purchased in Tom's Place. Pets are permitted on leashes.

Reservations, fee: No reservations; $10 fee per night.

Who to contact: Phone the Inyo National Forest at (619) 873-2500.

Location: From the junction of US 395 and Highway 203 (the Mammoth Lakes turnoff), drive 15 miles south on US 395 to Tom's Place. Turn south on Rock Creek Road and drive five miles to the campground.

Trip note: This shoe might just fit. Considering how popular the Lake Crowley area has become, a tiny little spot like this one on Rock Creek could be just what the doctor ordered. The elevation is 8,600 feet. Open from May to October.

7. EAST FORK 🚶🏇   RV 8

Reference: **Near Lake Crowley in Inyo National Forest; map F5, grid a3.**

Campsites, facilities: There are 133 sites for tents or motor homes up to 22 feet long. Picnic tables, fire grills and piped water are provided. Flush toilets and horseback riding facilities are available. Supplies can be purchased in Tom's Place and Rock Creek Lake Resort. Pets are permitted on leashes.

Reservations, fee: Reservations accepted; $8 fee per night.

Who to contact: Phone Inyo National Forest at (619) 873-2500.

Location: From the junction of US 395 and Highway 203 (the Mammoth Lakes turnoff), drive 15 miles south on US 395 to Tom's Place. Turn south on Rock Creek Road and drive five miles to the campground.

Trip note: If you like plenty of company, this big Forest Service camp will provide it. This is a popular campground near Lake Crowley. It is set at 9,000 feet along Rock Creek. For more solitude, you might consider a side trip to little Rock Creek Lake. Open from June to October.

8. ASPEN GROUP CAMP 🐟 🚶   RV 5

Reference: **Near Lake Crowley in Inyo National Forest; map F5, grid a4.**

Campsites, facilities: There are five sites for tents or motor homes up to 16 feet long. Piped water, fire grills and picnic tables are provided. Flush toilets are available. Supplies can be purchased in Tom's Place. Pets are permitted on leashes.

Reservations, fee: Reserve by phoning (800) 280-CAMP ($15 reservation fee); $40 per night group fee.

Who to contact: Phone Inyo National Forest at (619) 873-2500.

Location: From the junction of US 395 and Highway 203 (the Mammoth Lakes turnoff), drive 15 miles south on US 395 to Tom's Place. Turn south on Rock Creek Road and drive three miles to the campground.

Trip note: This small, group campsite set on Rock Creek, is used primarily as a base camp for fishermen and campers heading to Lake Crowley. The elevation is 8,100 feet. Open from May to October.

9. F M D HOLIDAY 🐟 🚶   RV 5

Reference: **Near Lake Crowley in Inyo National Forest; map F5, grid a4.**

Campsites, facilities: There are 35 sites for tents or motor homes up to 22 feet long. Piped water, fire grills and picnic tables are provided. Vault toilets are available. Groceries are available nearby. Pets are permitted on leashes.

Reservations, fee: No reservations; $10 fee per night.

Who to contact: Phone Inyo National Forest at (619) 873-2500.

Location: From the junction of US 395 and Highway 203 (the Mammoth Lakes turnoff), drive 15 miles south on US 395 to Tom's Place. Turn south on Rock

Creek Road and drive a half mile to the campground on the left.

Trip note: During peak weekends, this campground is used as an overflow area, as needed. It is set near Rock Creek, not far from Lake Crowley. The elevation is 7,500 feet.

10. FRENCH CAMP ⟨🐟⟩   RV 5

Reference: **On Rock Creek near Lake Crowley in Inyo National Forest; map F5, grid a4.**

Campsites, facilities: There are six sites for tents only and 80 sites for tents or motor homes up to 22 feet long. Picnic tables, fire grills and piped water are provided. Flush toilets are available. Groceries are available nearby. Pets are permitted on leashes.

Reservations, fee: No reservations; $10 fee per night.

Who to contact: Phone Inyo National Forest at (619) 873-2500.

Location: From the junction of US 395 and Highway 203 (the Mammoth Lakes turnoff), drive 15 miles south on US 395 to Tom's Place. Turn south on Rock Creek Road and drive a quarter mile to the campground, on the right.

Trip note: This is a good alternative to nearby Lake Crowley. It's a pretty spot along Rock Creek, with side trip opportunities that include boating and fishing on giant Crowley and a westward drive on Rock Creek Road to little Rock Creek Lake 10 miles away. The elevation is 7,500 feet. Open from April to October.

11. TUFF ⟨🐟⟩   RV 5

Reference: **Near Lake Crowley in Inyo National Forest; map F5, grid a4.**

Campsites, facilities: There are 15 sites for tents only and 19 sites for tents or motor homes up to 22 feet long. Picnic tables, fire grills and piped water are provided. Flush toilets are available. Pets are permitted on leashes.

Reservations, fee: Reserve by phoning (800) 280-CAMP ($7.50 reservation fee); $8 fee per night.

Who to contact: Phone Inyo National Forest at (619) 873-2500.

Location: From the junction of US 395 and Highway 203 (the Mammoth Lakes turnoff), drive 15.5 miles south on US 395 just beyond Tom's Place.

Trip note: If the Owens Valley is packed with campers, knowing every available spot can come in handy. This is one of the several camps on Rock Creek, not far from Lake Crowley. The elevation is 7,000 feet. Open April to October.

12. VERMILLION ⟨🐟 ⚓ 🏃 🏊 🏇⟩   RV 8

Reference: **On Lake Edison in Sierra National Forest; map F5, grid b0.**

Campsites, facilities: There are 11 tent sites and 20 sites for tents or RVs up to 16 feet. Piped water, picnic tables and fire grills are provided. Vault toilets are available. Pets are permitted on leashes. A boat ramp and horseback riding facilities are nearby. Supplies can be purchased in Mono Hot Springs.

Reservations, fee: Reserve by phoning (800) 280-CAMP ($7.50 reservation fee); $10 fee per night.

Who to contact: Phone the Sierra National Forest Pineridge Ranger District at (209) 841-3311.

Location: From the town of Shaver Lake, drive 21 miles north on Highway 168 to the town of Lakeshore. From Lakeshore, drive northeast on Kaiser Pass Road (Forest Service Road 4S01). Kaiser Pass Road becomes Edison Lake

Road at Mono Hot Springs. Continue north for five miles past the town to the campground on the west shore of Lake Edison.

Trip note: Lake Edison is a premium vacation destination. The 15-m.p.h. speed limit on the lake guarantees quiet water. Trout fishing is often quite good in early summer. A side trip option is to hike the trail from the camp, which travels along the north shore of Lake Edison for five miles to Quail Meadows, where it intersects with the Pacific Crest Trail in the John Muir Wilderness. The elevation is 7,700 feet. Open from June through October.

13. MONO HOT SPRINGS

Reference: On San Joaquin River in Sierra National Forest; map F5, grid b0.

Campsites, facilities: There are four tent sites and 26 sites for trailers, tents or RVs, with horse pastures across from the campground. Picnic tables, fire grills are provided. Piped water and vault toilets are available. Pets are permitted on leashes. Supplies can be purchased in Mono Hot Springs. There is also a no fee campground at the Mono Creek Trailhead for overnight horse camping for people heading into the wilderness.

Reservations, fee: Reserve by phoning (800) 280-CAMP ($7.50 reservation fee); $10 fee per night.

Who to contact: Phone the Sierra National Forest Pineridge Ranger District at (209) 841-3311.

Location: From the town of Shaver Lake, drive 21 miles north on Highway 168 to the town of Lakeshore. From Lakeshore, turn northeast on Kaiser Pass Road (Forest Service Road 4S01). Kaiser Pass Road becomes Edison Lake Road at Mono Hot Springs. Continue north about three miles until you see the campground entrance sign on the left.

Trip note: This is a popular spot for the few folks that know of it. It is set in the Sierra at 6,500 feet along the San Joaquin River, directly adjacent to Mono Hot Springs Resort. Don't be surprised if you meet Mr. Ed at this camp. It's used primarily by horses, not people, to carry vacationers into the adjacent backcountry. There is a trail from the camp that forks to Lake Edison or into the backcountry of Ansel Adams Wilderness. It's a good idea to bring an apple along with you. Horsies like that. Open May through October.

14. MONO CREEK

Reference: Near Lake Edison in Sierra National Forest; map F5, grid b0.

Campsites, facilities: There are 14 sites for tents or motor homes up to 16 feet. Picnic tables, fire grills and piped water are provided. Vault toilets are available. Pets are permitted on leashes. Horseback riding facilities and a boat ramp are nearby. Supplies can be purchased in Mono Hot Springs.

Reservations, fee: Reserve by phoning (800) 280-CAMP ($7.50 reservation fee); $10 fee per night.

Who to contact: Phone the Sierra National Forest Pineridge Ranger District at (209) 841-3311.

Location: From the town of Shaver Lake, drive 21 miles north on Highway 168 to the town of Lakeshore. Then drive northeast on Kaiser Pass Road (Forest Service Road 4S01). Kaiser Pass Road becomes Edison Lake Road at Mono Hot Springs. Continue north for three miles past the town to the campground.

Trip note: Here's a beautiful spot along Mono Creek that offers a good alternative to nearby Lake Edison. The camp, set at 7,400 feet, is about a mile upstream from the dam at Lake Edison and has good evening trout fishing upstream from the camp. The Mono Hot Springs Resort is three miles away and there are numerous trails nearby that access the backcountry. Open from June to September.

15. PINE GROVE 🐟 🚶 🐎　　　RV 7

Reference: **Near Lake Crowley in Inyo National Forest; map F5, grid b3.**

Campsites, facilities: There are five sites for tents only and six sites for tents or motor homes up to 22 feet long. Picnic tables, fire grills and piped water are provided. Flush toilets and horseback riding facilities are available. Supplies can be purchased in Tom's Place and Rock Creek Lake Resort. Pets are permitted on leashes.

Reservations, fee: No reservations; $10 fee per night.

Who to contact: Phone Inyo National Forest at (619) 873-2500.

Location: From the junction of US 395 and Highway 203 (the Mammoth Lakes turnoff), drive 15 miles south on US 395 to Tom's Place. Turn south on Rock Creek Road and drive seven miles to the campground.

Trip note: This is one of the smaller camps in a series of spots along Rock Creek. The elevation is 9,300 feet. Open from May to October.

16. ROCK CREEK LAKE 🐟 🚶　　　RV 8

Reference: **In Inyo National Forest; map F5, grid b3.**

Campsites, facilities: There are 28 sites for tents or motor homes up to 22 feet long. Picnic tables, fire grills, flush toilets and piped water are provided. Supplies can be purchased in Tom's Place and Rock Creek Lake Resort. Pets are permitted on leashes.

Reservations, fee: No reservations; $10 fee per night.

Who to contact: Phone Inyo National Forest at (619) 873-2500.

Location: From the junction of US 395 and Highway 203 (the Mammoth Lakes turnoff), drive 15 miles south on US 395 to Tom's Place. Turn south on Rock Creek Road and drive seven miles to the campground.

Trip note: Considering how many people flock to Lake Crowley, this nearby alternative might end up being more what you're looking for. The elevation is 9,600 feet. Open from June through October.

17. ROCK CREEK LAKE GROUP CAMP 🐟 🚶　　　

Reference: **In Inyo National Forest; map F5, grid b3.**

Campsites, facilities: There is one group site for tent camping that can accommodate 20 to 50 people. Picnic tables, fire grills, flush toilets and piped water are provided. Supplies can be purchased in Tom's Place and Rock Creek Lake Resort. Pets are permitted on leashes.

Reservations, fee: Reserve by phoning (800) 280-CAMP ($15 reservation fee); $40 fee per night.

Who to contact: Phone Inyo National Forest at (619) 873-2500.

Location: From the junction of US 395 and Highway 203 (the Mammoth Lakes turnoff), drive 15 miles south on US 395 to Tom's Place. Turn south on Rock Creek Road and drive seven miles to the campground.

Trip note: This is a group camp and an option to Rock Creek Lake. It is also set on Rock Creek Lake at 9,700 feet. Open from mid-June through October.

18. JACKASS MEADOW

RV **7**

Reference: **On Florence Lake in Sierra National Forest; map F5, grid c0.**

Campsites, facilities: There are 44 sites for tents or motor homes up to 16 feet. Picnic tables, fire grills and a **wheelchair-accessible** fishing pier are provided. Vault toilets and piped water are available. Pets are permitted on leashes.

Reservations, fee: Reserve by phoning (800) 280-CAMP ($7.50 reservation fee); $10 fee per night.

Who to contact: Phone the Sierra National Forest Pineridge Ranger District at (209) 841-3311.

Location: From the town of Shaver Lake, drive 21 miles north on Highway 168 to the town of Lakeshore. From Lakeshore, turn northeast on Kaiser Pass Road (Forest Service Road 4S01) and drive to Florence Lake Road (two miles south of the town of Mono Hot Springs). Turn south on Florence Lake Road and drive five miles to the campground.

Trip note: Jackass Meadow is a pretty spot set adjacent to Florence Lake, near the Upper San Joaquin River. There are good canoeing, rafting and float-tubing possibilities—high Sierra style. The elevation is 7,200 feet. Open June to October.

---

19. BIG TREES

RV **7**

Reference: **On Bishop Creek in Inyo National Forest; map F5, grid c5.**

Campsites, facilities: There are nine sites for tents or motor homes. Piped water, flush toilets, fire grills and picnic tables are provided. Horseback riding facilities are available. Supplies can be purchased in Bishop. Pets are permitted on leashes.

Reservations, fee: No reservations; $11 fee per night.

Who to contact: Call the Inyo National Forest White Mountain Ranger District at (619) 873-2500.

Location: From Bishop on US 395, drive 11 miles south on Highway 168 to the campground entrance. Continue southwest on a dirt road to the campground.

Trip note: This is a small Forest Service camp set on Bishop Creek at 7,500 feet. Both South Lake and Lake Sabrina are about 10 miles away. Open from Memorial Day to Labor Day.

---

20. HORTON CREEK

RV **7**

Reference: **Near Bishop; map F5, grid c6.**

Campsites, facilities: There are 54 sites for tents or motor homes. Fire grills and picnic tables are provided. Pit toilets and a dumpster are available. There is **no potable water**, so bring your own. Pets are permitted on leashes.

Reservations, fee: No reservations; no fee.

Who to contact: Phone the Bureau of Land Management at (619) 872-4881.

Location: From Bishop, drive 8.5 miles north on US 395. Turn west on Round Valley Road and drive five miles to the campground on the left.

Trip note: This is a little-known, primitive BLM camp set along Horton Creek, northwest of Bishop. It is a popular base camp for hunters in the fall, with wild, rugged country to the west. The Inyo Mono Ecology Center is nearby. The elevation is 5,000 feet. Open from May to October.

21. MILLPOND CAMPGROUND

Reference: **Near Bishop; map F5, grid c6.**

Campsites, facilities: There are 60 sites for tents or motor homes, many with water and electrical hookups. Piped water, fire grills and picnic tables are provided. Flush toilets, showers and a laundromat are available. Pets are permitted on leashes.

Reservations, fee: Reservations accepted; $10-$13 fee per night.

Who to contact: Phone the campground at (619) 873-5342.

Location: From Bishop, drive six miles north on US 395. Turn west at the Millpond Recreation Area sign and drive one mile to the campground on the left.

Trip note: This privately-operated camp is adjacent to the Millpond Recreation Area which offers ball fields, playgrounds and a swimming lake. Open from March through November.

22. PLEASANT VALLEY COUNTY PARK

Reference: **Near Pleasant Valley Reservoir; map F5, grid c6.**

Campsites, facilities: There are 200 sites for tents or motor homes. Fire grills and picnic tables are provided. Piped water and pit toilets are available. Pets are permitted on leashes.

Reservations, fee: No reservations; $6 fee per night.

Who to contact: Phone the Inyo County Parks Department at (619) 878-0272 or (800) 447-4696.

Location: From Bishop, drive 5.5 miles north on US 395. Turn right (northeast) on the campground entrance road; or seven miles northwest of Bishop (on US 395) turn north on Pleasant Valley Road and drive one mile to the campground.

Trip note: This county park is set near long, narrow Pleasant Valley Reservoir, created by the Owens River. The elevation is 4,200 feet. Open year-round.

23. SHADY REST TRAILER PARK

Reference: **In Bishop; map F5, grid c7.**

Campsites, facilities: There are 25 sites for tents or motor homes. Piped water and full hookups are provided. Flush toilets, showers and a laundromat are available. Pets are permitted on leashes.

Reservations, fee: Reservations recommended; $16-$18 fee per night.

Who to contact: Phone the park at (619) 873-3430.

Location: In Bishop, drive to 399 East Yaney Street.

Trip note: This is an option for folks who want to find a layover in the Bishop area without going to much trouble to find it. Possible sidetrips include visiting the Indian Cultural Center in Bishop and the Pleasant Valley Reservoir. The latter takes about a 15-minute drive to reach. Open year-round.

24. HIGHLANDS RV PARK

Reference: **Near Bishop; map F5, grid c7.**

Campsites, facilities: There are 103 motor home sites with full hookups. Piped water and picnic tables are provided. Flush toilets, showers, a dump station, cable TV, propane gas and a laundromat are available. Groceries are nearby. Pets are allowed on leashes.

Reservations, fee: Reservations recommended; $20-$21 fee per night.

Who to contact: Phone the park at (619) 873-7616.

Location: From Bishop, drive two miles north on Highway 395/North Sierra Highway to 2275 North Sierra Highway.

Trip note: This is a privately-operated motor home park near Bishop that is set up for Highway 395 cruisers. Possible sidetrips include visiting the Indian Cultural Center in Bishop or Pleasant Valley Reservoir, about 10 miles northwest. The elevation is 4,300 feet. Open year-round.

25. BROWN'S TOWN SCHOBER LANE CAMP   RV. 5

Reference: **Near Bishop; map F5, grid c7.**

Campsites, facilities: There are 150 sites for tents or motor homes, many with water and electrical hookups. Piped water, fire grills and picnic tables are provided. Flush toilets, showers, cable TV, a museum, a store and a snack bar are available. Pets are permitted on leashes.

Reservations, fee: Reservations accepted; $10-$15 fee per night.

Who to contact: Phone the campground at (619) 873-8522.

Location: From Bishop, drive one mile south on US 395 to Schober Lane and exit left to the campground entrance.

Trip note: This privately-operated campground, one of several in the vicinity of Bishop, is the only one in the area that accepts tents. It's all shade and grass and next to the golf course. Open from March through November.

26. GRANDVIEW   RV. 6

Reference: **Near Big Pine in Inyo National Forest; map F5, grid c9.**

Campsites, facilities: There are 26 sites for tents or motor homes up to 22 feet long. Fire grills and picnic tables are provided. Vault toilets are available. There is **no piped water**, so bring your own. Pets are permitted on leashes.

Reservations, fee: No reservations; no fee.

Who to contact: Call the Inyo National Forest White Mountain Ranger District at (619) 873-2500.

Location: From Big Pine on US 395, turn east on Highway 168 and drive 13 miles. Turn north on Road 4S01 (White Mountain Road) and drive 5.5 miles to the campground.

Trip note: This is a primitive and little-known camp, and the folks who visit this area earn it. It is located in the high country in the White Mountains east of Bishop at 8,600 feet, along White Mountain Road. The road borders the Ancient Bristle Cone Pine Forest to the east and leads north to jumpoff spots for hikers heading up Mt. Barcroft (13,023 feet) or White Mountain (14,246 feet). A trail leads out of the camp up to an old mining site. Open from May through October.

27. SABRINA   RV. 7

Reference: **Near Lake Sabrina in Inyo National Forest; map F5, grid d4.**

Campsites, facilities: There are 18 sites for tents or motor homes. Piped water, vault toilets, fire grills and picnic tables are provided. A boat ramp and boat rentals are available. Supplies can be purchased in Bishop. Pets are permitted on leashes.

Reservations, fee: No reservations; $8 fee per night.

Who to contact: Call the Inyo National Forest White Mountain Ranger District at

(619) 873-2500.

Location: From Bishop on US 395, drive 17 miles south on Highway 168 to the campground.

Trip note: You get the best of both worlds at this camp. Set at 9,000 feet on Bishop Creek, the trails that are available here are routed into the high country of the John Muir Wilderness, and you're also just a half mile from Lake Sabrina. Take your pick. Whatever your choice, it's a good one. Open from June to September.

28. FORKS 🐎   RV 5

Reference: **Near South Lake in Inyo National Forest; map F5, grid d4.**

Campsites, facilities: There are eight sites for tents or motor homes. Piped water, flush toilets, fire grills and picnic tables are provided. Horseback riding facilities are available at North Lake. Supplies can be purchased in Bishop. Pets are permitted on leashes.

Reservations, fee: No reservations; $8 fee per night.

Who to contact: Call the Inyo National Forest White Mountain Ranger District at (619) 873-2500.

Location: From Bishop on US 395, drive 13 miles south on Highway 168 to the campground.

Trip note: This camp is located at the fork in the road, which gives you two options. You can turn south on South Lake Road and hunker down there for a spell, or keep driving on Highway 168 to Lake Sabrina, where hikers will find a trailhead that accesses the John Muir Wilderness. The elevation is 7,800 feet. Open from May to October.

29. CREEKSIDE RESORT 🐟   RV 3

Reference: **On the South Fork of Bishop Creek; map F5, grid d4.**

Campsites, facilities: There are four sites for tents only and 44 sites for motor homes with full or partial hookups. Piped water, flush toilets, hot showers, a laundromat, grocery store, fish cleaning facilities and propane gas are available. Pets are permitted.

Reservations, fee: Deposit required with reservation; $15-$25 fee per night; $1 pet fee.

Who to contact: Phone the park at (619) 873-4483.

Location: From Bishop on US 395, drive 15 miles south on Highway 168. Turn south on South Lake Road and drive two miles to the campground.

Trip note: This privately-operated park in the high country is set up primarily for motor homes. A lot of folks are surprised to find it here. North, Sabrina and South Lakes are in the area. The elevation is 8,400 feet. Open from May to October.

30. BISHOP PARK CAMP 🐟 🚶 🐎   RV 7

Reference: **Near Lake Sabrina in Inyo National Forest; map F5, grid d4.**

Campsites, facilities: There are 20 family sites and one group campsite for tents or motor homes up to 22 feet long. Piped water, flush toilets, fire grills and picnic tables are provided. Horseback riding facilities are available at North Lake. Supplies can be purchased in Bishop. Pets are permitted on leashes.

Reservations, fee: No reservations; $8 fee per night; $25 fee per night for a group campsite.

Who to contact: Call the Inyo National Forest White Mountain Ranger District at (619) 873-2500.

Location: From Bishop on US 395, drive 15 miles south on Highway 168 to the campground.

Trip note: This camp is one in a series of camps in the immediate area that are located along Bishop Creek. This one is about two miles from Lake Sabrina, and an ideal area for starting a backpacking expedition into the John Muir Wilderness. The elevation is 7,500 feet. Open from May through October.

---

31. INTAKE ⊾ ⚓ 🏃   RV 7

Reference: **On Sabrina Creek in Inyo National Forest; map F5, grid d4.**

Campsites, facilities: There are eight walk-in sites for tents only and nine sites for tents or motor homes. Piped water, flush toilets, fire grills and picnic tables are provided. Supplies can be purchased in Bishop. Pets are permitted on leashes.

Reservations, fee: No reservations; $8 fee per night.

Who to contact: Call the Inyo National Forest White Mountain Ranger District at (619) 873-2500.

Location: From Bishop on US 395, drive 14 miles south on Highway 168 to the campground entrance.

Trip note: This small camp, set at 7,500 feet, on an equally small reservoir on Bishop Creek, is about three miles from Lake Sabrina. The trailhead at Lake Sabrina leads into the John Muir Wilderness. Nearby North Lake and South Lake provide side trip options. Open April through October.

---

32. FOUR JEFFREY ⊾ 🏃 🐎   RV 7

Reference: **Near South Lake in Inyo National Forest; map F5, grid d4.**

Campsites, facilities: There are 106 sites for tents or motor homes up to 22 feet long. Piped water, flush toilets, fire grills and picnic tables are provided. Supplies can be purchased in Bishop. Pets are permitted on leashes.

Reservations, fee: No reservations; $11 fee per night.

Who to contact: Call the Inyo National Forest White Mountain Ranger District at (619) 873-2500.

Location: From Bishop on US 395, drive 13 miles south on Highway 168 to the campground entrance. Turn south on South Lake Road and drive a half mile to the campground.

Trip note: This is by far the largest of the Forest Service camps in the vicinity. There are three lakes in the area: North Lake, Lake Sabrina and South Lake. The camp is set on the South Fork of Bishop Creek at 8,100 feet, about four miles from South Lake. Open from mid-April through October.

---

33. NORTH LAKE ⊾ 🏃 🐎   8

Reference: **On Bishop Creek near North Lake in Inyo National Forest; map F5, grid d4.**

Campsites, facilities: There are 11 tent sites. Piped water, vault toilets, fire grills and picnic tables are provided. Horseback riding facilities are available. Supplies can be purchased in Bishop. Pets are permitted on leashes.

Reservations, fee: No reservations; $11 fee per night.

Who to contact: Call the Inyo National Forest White Mountain Ranger District at (619) 873-2500.

Location: From Bishop on US 395, drive 17 miles south on Highway 168. Turn north on Road 8S02 and drive for two miles to the campground.

Trip note: This prime trailhead camp set in the high country (9,500 feet) takes care of a lot of the "up" hikers have to contend with when entering the nearby John Muir Wilderness. The camp is set on the North Fork of Bishop Creek near North Lake and close to a trailhead that accesses numerous lakes in the John Muir Wilderness and eventually connects with the Pacific Crest Trail. Open from July through September.

34. BIG PINE CREEK

Reference: **In Inyo National Forest; map F5, grid e5.**

Campsites, facilities: There are five sites for tents only and 25 sites for tents or motor homes. Piped water, fire grills and picnic tables are provided. Vault toilets are available. Pets are permitted on leashes.

Reservations, fee: Reserve by phoning (800) 280-CAMP ($7.50 reservation fee); $8 fee per night.

Who to contact: Call the Inyo National Forest White Mountain Ranger District at (619) 873-2500.

Location: From US 395 in Big Pine, turn west onto Glacier Lodge Road and drive nine miles to the campground.

Trip note: This is another good spot for backpackers to launch a multi-day trip. The camp is set along Big Pine Creek at 7,700 feet, with trails near the camp that are routed to the numerous lakes in the high country of the John Muir Wilderness. A Forest Service map is essential. Open May to mid-October.

35. FIRST FALLS HIKE-IN CAMP

Reference: **In Inyo National Forest; map F5, grid e5.**

Campsites, facilities: There are five tent sites. Fire grills and picnic tables are provided. Pit toilets are available. There is **no piped water**. Pets are allowed on leashes.

Reservations, fee: No reservations; no fee.

Who to contact: Call the Inyo National Forest White Mountain Ranger District at (619) 873-2500.

Location: From US 395 in Big Pine, turn west onto Glacier Lodge Road and drive 8.5 miles. Park and hike two miles to the campground.

Trip note: This high country, hike-in camp is the first step for backpackers heading into the John Muir Wilderness. It is set at 8,300 feet on the South Fork of Big Pine Creek. Open from May to mid-October.

36. PALISADE GROUP CAMP

Reference: **On Big Pine Creek in Inyo National Forest; map F5, grid e6.**

Campsites, facilities: There are two group sites for tents or motor homes. Piped water, fire grills and picnic tables are provided. Vault toilets are available. Pets are permitted on leashes.

Reservations, fee: Reserve by phoning (800) 280-CAMP ($15 reservation fee); $25 fee per night.

Who to contact: Call the Inyo National Forest White Mountain Ranger District at (619) 873-2500.

Location: From US 395 in Big Pine, turn west onto Glacier Lodge Road and drive 8.5 miles to the campground.

Trip note: This trailhead camp, set at 7,600 feet, is popular for groups planning to rock climb the Palisades. The latter is for experienced mountaineers only; it's a dangerous expedition where risk of life is included in the bargain. Safer options include exploring the surrounding John Muir Wilderness. Open from May to mid-October.

37. SAGE FLAT 🐟 🚶   RV 8

Reference: **On Big Pine Creek near Big Pine in Inyo National Forest; map F5, grid e6.**

Campsites, facilities: There are 28 sites for tents or motor homes. Piped water, fire grills and picnic tables are provided. Vault toilets are available. Pets are permitted on leashes.

Reservations, fee: Reserve by phoning (800) 280-CAMP ($7.50 reservation fee); $8 fee per night.

Who to contact: Call the Inyo National Forest White Mountain Ranger District at (619) 873-2500.

Location: From US 395 in Big Pine, turn west onto Glacier Lodge Road and drive 8.5 miles to the campground.

Trip note: It just depends what route you want to take. This camp, like the others in the immediate vicinity, is set up for backpackers to start multi-day expeditions into the nearby John Muir Wilderness. It's a steep climb that starts at 7,400 feet. The camp is set along Big Pine Creek. Open from mid-April to mid-November.

38. UPPER SAGE FLAT 🐟 🚶   RV 8

Reference: **On Big Pine Creek in Inyo National Forest; map F5, grid e6.**

Campsites, facilities: There are 21 sites for tents or motor homes. Piped water, fire grills and picnic tables are provided. Vault toilets are available. Pets are permitted on leashes.

Reservations, fee: Reserve by phoning (800) 280-CAMP ($7.50 reservation fee); $8 fee per night.

Who to contact: Call the Inyo National Forest White Mountain Ranger District at (619) 873-2500.

Location: From US 395 in Big Pine, turn west onto Glacier Lodge Road and drive 8.5 miles to the campground.

Trip note: This is one in a series of Forest Service camps in the area set up primarily for backpackers to start wilderness expeditions. Several trails are available near the camp that head into the John Muir Wilderness. Even starting at 7,600 feet, expect a steep climb. Open from May to mid-October.

39. BAKER CREEK COUNTY PARK   RV 4

Reference: **Near Big Pine; map F5, grid e7.**

Campsites, facilities: There are 70 sites for tents or motor homes. Fire grills and picnic tables are provided. Pumped water and pit toilets are available. Pets are permitted on leashes. Supplies can be purchased in Big Pine.

Reservations, fee: No reservations; $5 fee per night.

Who to contact: Phone the Inyo County Parks Department at (619) 878-0272 or (800) 447-4696.

Location: From Big Pine, drive a half mile north on US 395. Turn west on Baker Creek Road and drive one mile to the campground on the left.

Trip note: A lot of cruisers touring the eastern Sierra on US 395 probably wish they knew of this spot. It's ideal for a quick overnighter, with easy access from Big Pine. It's set along Baker Creek at 4,000 feet.

40. BIG PINE TRIANGLE COUNTY PARK   RV 4

Reference: **Near Big Pine; map F5, grid e8.**

Campsites, facilities: There are 40 sites for tents or motor homes. Piped water, fire grills and picnic tables are provided. Flush toilets are available. Pets are permitted on leashes. Supplies can be purchased in Big Pine.

Reservations, fee: No reservations; $5 fee per night.

Who to contact: Phone the Inyo County Parks Department at (619) 878-0272 (800) 447-4696.

Location: From Big Pine, drive a half mile north on US 395 to the campground.

Trip note: This is one of two county camps near the town of Big Pine, providing US 395 cruisers with two options. The camp is set along the Big Pine Canal at 3,900 feet. Open from April to November.

41. GOODALE CREEK   RV 6

Reference: **Near Independence; map F5, grid f7.**

Campsites, facilities: There are 62 sites for tents or motor homes. Fire grills and picnic tables are provided. Pit toilets and a dumpster are available. There is **no potable water**, so bring your own. Pets are permitted on leashes.

Reservations, fee: No reservations; no fee.

Who to contact: Call the Bureau of Land Management at (619) 872-4881.

Location: From Independence, drive 12 miles north on US 395. Turn west on Aberdeen Road and drive two miles to the campground on the left.

Trip note: This obscure BLM camp is set along little Goodale Creek at 4,100 feet. It's good layover spot for US 395 cruisers. Open May to October.

42. TINNEMAHA CREEK   RV 6

Reference: **Near Big Pine; map F5, grid f8.**

Campsites, facilities: There are 55 sites for tents or motor homes. Fire grills and picnic tables are provided. Pit toilets are available. There is **no piped water**, so bring your own. Pets are permitted on leashes.

Reservations, fee: No reservations; $5 fee per night.

Who to contact: Phone the Inyo County Parks Department at (619) 878-0272 (800) 447-4696.

Location: From Independence, drive 19.5 miles north on US 395. Turn west (left) onto Fish Springs Road and drive a half mile. Turn right onto Tinnemaha Road and drive two miles to the campground on the left.

Trip note: This primitive, little-known (to out-of-towners) county park is located on Tinnemaha Creek at 4,400 feet. Sidetrip possibilities include Tinnemaha Reservoir, about five miles away. Open year-round.

43. TABOOSE CREEK   RV 4

Reference: **Near Big Pine; map F5, grid f8.**

Campsites, facilities: There are 55 sites for tents or motor homes. Fire grills and picnic tables are provided. Pumped water and pit toilets are available. Supplies can be purchased in Big Pine or Independence. Pets are permitted on leashes.

Reservations, fee: No reservations; $5 fee per night.

Who to contact: Phone the Inyo County Parks Department at (619) 878-0272 (800) 447-4696.

Location: From Big Pine, drive 11 miles south on US 395. Turn west at Taboose Creek and drive for one mile to the campground.

Trip note: The eastern Sierra is stark country, but this little spot provides a stream (Taboose Creek) and some trees in the vicinity of the campground. The easy access is a bonus. The elevation is 3,900 feet. Open year-round.

---

44. HUME LAKE

Reference: **In Sequoia National Forest; map F5, grid g0.**

Campsites, facilities: There are 60 tent sites and 14 sites for tents or motor homes up to 22 feet long. Picnic tables, fire grills and piped water are provided. Flush toilets are available. Pets are permitted on leashes. A grocery store is nearby.

Reservations, fee: Reservations accepted; phone (800) 280-CAMP; $14 fee per night.

Who to contact: Phone the Sequoia National Forest Hume Lake Ranger District (209) 338-2251.

Location: From Grant Grove in Kings Canyon National Park, drive six miles north on Highway 180 to the Hume Lake Road junction. Turn south and drive three miles to Hume Lake.

Trip note: This is the best of the camps in the area because it is near Hume Lake. The lake offers good trout fishing, especially in the spring and early summer. Entrances to Kings Canyon National Park are nearby. The elevation is 5,200 feet. Open from May to September.

---

45. ASPEN HOLLOW

Reference: **Near Hume Lake in Sequoia National Forest; map F5, grid g0.**

Campsites, facilities: There is a group campsite for up to 75 people with picnic tables, fire grills and piped water provided. Vault toilets are available. Pets are permitted on leashes. A grocery store is nearby.

Reservations, fee: Reserve by phoning (800) 280-CAMP; $112.50 fee per night.

Who to contact: Phone the Sequoia National Forest Hume Lake Ranger District at (209) 338-2251.

Location: From Grant Grove in Kings Canyon National Park, drive six miles north on Highway 180 to the Hume Lake Road junction. Turn south and drive three miles to Hume Lake.

Trip note: This large group camp is set at 5,200 feet, near Hume Lake. Entrances to Kings Canyon National Park are nearby. Open from May to September.

---

46. TEN MILE

Reference: **On Ten Mile Creek in Sequoia National Forest; map F5, grid h0.**

Campsites, facilities: There are 10 sites for tents or motor homes up to 22 feet long. Picnic tables and fire grills are provided. Vault toilets are available. There is **no piped water**, but a grocery store is nearby. Pets are permitted on leashes.

Reservations, fee: No reservations; no fee.

Who to contact: Phone the Sequoia National Forest, Hume Lake Ranger District at (209) 338-2251.

Location: From Grant Grove in Kings Canyon National Park, drive six miles north on Highway 180 to the Hume Lake Road junction. Turn south and drive eight miles around Hume Lake and up Ten Mile Road to the campground.

Trip note: This is one of the three small, primitive campgrounds set along Ten Mile Creek above Hume Lake. This one is about four miles from the lake. The elevation is 5,800 feet. Open from May to October.

---

47. LOGGER FLAT GROUP CAMP 🐟   7

Reference: **On Ten Mile Creek in Sequoia National Forest; map F5, grid h0.**

Campsites, facilities: This is a group campsite for up to 50 people with picnic tables and fire grills provided. Piped water and vault toilets are available. Pets are permitted on leashes. A grocery store is nearby.

Reservations, fee: Reserve by phoning (800) 280-CAMP; $75 fee per night.

Who to contact: Phone the Sequoia National Forest, Hume Lake Ranger District at (209) 338-2251.

Location: From Grant Grove in Kings Canyon National Park, drive six miles north on Highway 180 to the Hume Lake Road junction. Turn south and drive 6.5 miles around Hume Lake and up Ten Mile Road to the campground.

Trip note: This is the group site alternative to the Landslide Camp. See the trip note for the following camp for details.

---

48. LANDSLIDE 🐟   7

Reference: **On Ten Mile Creek in Sequoia National Forest; map F5, grid h0.**

Campsites, facilities: There are six sites for tents only and three sites for tents or motor homes up to 16 feet long. Picnic tables and fire grills are provided. Vault toilets are available. There is one outlet for **piped water**. Pets are permitted on leashes. A grocery store is nearby.

Reservations, fee: No reservations; no fee.

Who to contact: Phone the Sequoia National Forest Hume Lake Ranger District at (209) 338-2251.

Location: From Grant Grove in Kings Canyon National Park, drive six miles north on Highway 180 to the Hume Lake Road junction. Turn south and drive seven miles around Hume Lake and up Ten Mile Road to the campground.

Trip note: If you want quiet, you got it. Few folks know about this camp. If you want a stream nearby, you got it. Landslide Creek runs right beside the camp. If you want a lake nearby, you got it. Hume Lake is about two miles away. If you want a national park nearby, you got it. It's not far from the entrances to Kings Canyon National Park. Add it up: You got it. Set at 5,800 feet. Open from May to October.

---

49. BUCK ROCK   RV 4

Reference: **Near Big Meadows Creek in Sequoia National Forest; map F5, grid h0.**

Campsites, facilities: There are five primitive sites for tents or motor homes up to 16 feet long. Picnic tables and fire grills are provided. Vault toilets are available. There is **no piped water**, so bring your own. Pets are permitted on leashes.

Reservations, fee: No reservations; no fee.

Who to contact: Phone the Sequoia National Forest Hume Lake Ranger District at (209) 338-2251.

Location: From Grant Grove in Kings Canyon National Park, drive seven miles southeast on Generals Highway. Turn left on Big Meadows Road and drive four miles to the camp.

Trip note: The elevation is 7,500 feet. Open from June to October. Sequoia and Kings Canyon National Parks are nearby.

50. BIG MEADOWS 🐟 🚶   RV 7

Reference: On Big Meadows Creek in Sequoia National Forest; map F5, grid h1.

Campsites, facilities: There are numerous sites along Big Meadows creek and the Big Meadows Road for tents or motor homes up to 22 feet long. Picnic tables and fire grills are provided. Vault toilets are available. There is **no piped water**, so bring your own. Pets are permitted on leashes.

Reservations, fee: No reservations; no fee.

Who to contact: Phone the Sequoia National Forest Hume Lake Ranger District at (209) 338-2251.

Location: From Grant Grove, drive seven miles southeast on Generals Highway. Turn left on Big Meadows Road (Forest Service Road 14S11) and drive five miles to the camp.

Trip note: This primitive, high mountain camp (7,600 feet) is set beside little Big Meadows Creek. Backpackers can use this as a launching pad, with the nearby trail leading to the Jennie Lake Wilderness. Kings Canyon National Park is a nearby side trip, only a 12-mile drive to the entrance. Open from June to October.

51. SENTINEL 🚶 ♿ 🐎   RV 8

Reference: **In Kings Canyon National Park; map F5, grid h2.**

Campsites, facilities: There are 83 sites for tents or motor homes. Piped water, fire grills and picnic tables are provided. Flush toilets, an evening ranger program, showers and a dump station are available. Some facilities are **wheelchair accessible**. A grocery store, laundromat, showers and horseback riding facilities are nearby. Pets are permitted on leashes.

Reservations, fee: No reservations; $10 fee per night.

Who to contact: Phone the Kings Canyon National Park at (209) 565-3341.

Location: From Cedar Grove in Kings Canyon National Park, drive west on Highway 180 to the campground.

Trip note: This camp provides a nearby alternative to Sheep Creek Camp. They both tend to fill up quickly in the summer. It's a short walk to Cedar Grove, the center of activity in the park. The elevation is 4,600 feet. Open from April through October (depending on road and snow conditions).

52. SHEEP CREEK 🚶 🐎   RV 8

Reference: **In Kings Canyon National Park; map F5, grid h2.**

Campsites, facilities: There are 111 sites for tents or motor homes. Piped water, fire grills and picnic tables are provided. Flush toilets, showers and a dump station are available. A grocery store, a laundromat, showers and horseback riding facilities are available nearby. Pets are permitted on leashes.

Reservations, fee: No reservations; $10 fee per night.

Who to contact: Phone the Kings Canyon National Park at (209) 565-3341.

Location: From Cedar Grove in Kings Canyon National Park, drive a half mile west on Highway 180.

Trip note: This is one of the camps that always fills up fast on summer weekends. It's a pretty spot and just a short walk from Cedar Grove. The camp is set along Sheep Creek at 4,600 feet. Open from June to October.

53. CANYON VIEW GROUP CAMP 🚶 🐎   RV 8

Reference: **In Kings Canyon National Park; map F5, grid h2.**

Campsites, facilities: There are four sites for tents accommodating a minimum of 20 people and a maximum of 40 people per site. Piped water, fire grills and picnic tables are provided. Flush toilets and a dump station are available. A grocery store, a laundromat, showers and horseback riding facilities are nearby. Pets are permitted on leashes.

Reservations, fee: Reservations must be made by mail: Canyon View Group Sites, P.O. Box 948, Kings Canyon National Park, CA 93633. Phone (209) 335-2853 for information.

Who to contact: Phone the Kings Canyon National Park at (209) 565-3341.

Location: From Cedar Grove in Kings Canyon National Park, drive east on Highway 180 to the campground, a half mile past the ranger station.

Trip note: If you are in a large group, just plain forget trying to find a campground in Kings Canyon National Park where you can all be together—except for this spot. Reservations are required. The elevation is 4,600 feet. Open from June to September (depending on road and snow conditions).

54. CANYON VIEW 🚶 🐎   RV 8

Reference: **In Kings Canyon National Park; map F5, grid h3.**

Campsites, facilities: There are 37 sites for tents. Piped water, fire grills, flush toilets and picnic tables are provided. Showers, horseback riding facilities, a grocery store and a laundromat are nearby. Pets are permitted on leashes.

Reservations, fee: No reservations; $10 fee per night.

Who to contact: Phone the Kings Canyon National Park at (209) 565-3341.

Location: From Cedar Grove in Kings Canyon National Park, drive east on Highway 180 to the campground, a half mile past the ranger station.

Trip note: This is another of the several camps in the Cedar Grove area of the park. The road leads into the river canyon, where dramatic views of the deep Kings River Canyon are available. Kings River Canyon is one of the deepest gorges in North America. The elevation is 4,600 feet. Open from June to September (depending on road and snow conditions).

55. MORAINE 🚶 🐎   RV 8

Reference: **In Kings Canyon National Park; map F5, grid h3.**

Campsites, facilities: There are 120 sites for tents or motor homes. Piped water, fire grills, picnic tables and flush toilets are provided. Showers, horseback riding facilities, a grocery store and a laundromat are nearby. Pets are permitted on leashes.

Reservations, fee: No reservations; $10 fee per night.

Who to contact: Phone the Kings Canyon National Park at (209) 565-3341.

Location: From Cedar Grove in Kings Canyon National Park, drive east on Highway 180 to the campground, one mile past the ranger station.

Trip note: This is the last in the series of camps in the Cedar Grove area of Kings Canyon National Park. This camp is used only for overflow. Hikers should drive past the Cedar Grove Ranger Station to the end of the road at Copper

Creek—this is a prime jumpoff point for a hike with spectacular lookouts. The elevation is 4,600 feet. Open from June to October (depending on road and snow conditions).

56. OAK CREEK 🏃

Reference: **In Inyo National Forest; map F5, grid h7.**

Campsites, facilities: There are 24 sites for tents or motor homes. Piped water, fire grills and picnic tables are provided. Flush toilets are available. Supplies and a laundromat are available in Independence. Pets are permitted on leashes.

Reservations, fee: Reservations accepted; phone (800) 280-CAMP (2267); $7 fee per night.

Who to contact: Call Inyo National Forest Mt. Whitney Ranger District at (619) 876-6200.

Location: From Independence, drive two miles north on US 395. Turn left (west) onto North Oak Creek Drive and drive three miles to the campground.

Trip note: This is one in a series of little-known camps located west of Independence that provide jumpoff spots for backpackers. Caution: Plan on a steep climb up to the Sierra crest. This camp is set at 5,000 feet, with a trail from camp that is routed west (and up) into the California Bighorn Sheep Zoological Area, a rugged, stark country well above the tree line. Camp is open May to October.

57. INDEPENDENCE CREEK 🐟 ♿

Reference: **In Independence; map F5, grid h8.**

Campsites, facilities: There are 25 sites for tents or motor homes. Piped water and picnic tables are provided. Pit toilets are available. Some facilities are **wheelchair accessible**. Supplies and a laundromat are available in Independence. Pets are permitted on leashes.

Reservations, fee: No reservations; $5 fee per night.

Who to contact: Phone the Inyo County Parks Department at (619) 878-0272 or (800) 447-4696.

Location: From US 395 in Independence, drive a half mile west on Market Street to the campground.

Trip note: This is an oft-overlooked camp for US 395 cruisers because it is an unpublicized county park. It is set at 3,900 feet along Independence Creek. Open year-round.

58. DORST 🏃

Reference: **On Dorst Creek in Sequoia National Park; map F5, grid i0.**

Campsites, facilities: There are 218 family sites for tents or motor homes and five group sites. Piped water, fire grills and picnic tables are provided. Flush toilets, a dump station, and evening ranger programs are available. A grocery store and a laundromat are nearby. Pets are permitted on leashes.

Reservations, fee: No reservations for family sites; $10 fee per night. For group sites, reservations must be made by mail. Write Dorst Group Site, Box C, Lodgepole, Sequoia National Park, CA 93262.

Who to contact: Phone the Sequoia National Park at (209) 565-3341. For road and weather information, call (209) 565-3351.

Location: From Giant Forest Village in Sequoia National Park, drive 14 miles northwest on Generals Highway. There is a vehicle length advisory on

Generals Highway due to steep curves. Vehicles over 22 feet are not advised to drive here. Alternate route is to take Highway 180 into the park, then turn right on Generals Highway just after entering the park.

Trip note: This is one in a series of big, popular camps in Sequoia National Park. The camp is set on Dorst Creek at 6,700 feet, near a trail that is routed into the backcountry and through Muir Grove. Open from June to September.

---

59. STONY CREEK

Reference: **In Sequoia National Forest; map F5, grid i0.**

Campsites, facilities: There are 29 sites for tents, and 20 sites for motor homes up to 22 feet long. Piped water, fire grills and picnic tables are provided. Flush toilets are available. A grocery store and a laundromat are nearby. Pets are permitted on leashes.

Reservations, fee: Reserve by phoning (800) 280-CAMP; $8 fee per night.

Who to contact: Phone the Sequoia National Forest Hume Lake Ranger District at (209) 338-2251.

Location: From Grant Grove in Kings Canyon National Park, drive 13 miles southeast on Generals Highway.

Trip note: The elevation is 6,400 feet. Open from June to September. Sequoia and Kings Canyon National Parks are nearby.

---

60. FIR GROUP CAMPGROUND

Reference: **Near Stony Creek in Sequoia National Forest; map F5, grid i0.**

Campsites, facilities: There is a group campsite for up to 100 people with piped water, picnic tables and fire grills provided. Vault toilets are available. A grocery store and a laundromat are nearby. Pets are permitted on leashes.

Reservations, fee: Reserve by phoning (800) 280-CAMP ($15 reservation fee); $1 per person with $25 minimum.

Who to contact: For general information phone Sequoia National Forest, Hume Lake District at (209) 338-2251.

Location: From Grant Grove in Kings Canyon National Park, drive 14 miles southeast on Generals Highway.

Trip note: This is the second of the two large group camps in the immediate vicinity set along Stony Creek. Open from June to September.

---

61. COVE GROUP CAMP

Reference: **Near Stony Creek in Sequoia National Forest; map F5, grid i0.**

Campsites, facilities: There is a group campsite for up to 50 people. Piped water, picnic tables and fire grills are provided. Vault toilets are available. A grocery store and laundromat are available nearby. Pets are permitted on leashes.

Reservations, fee: Reserve by phoning (800) 280-CAMP ($15 reservation fee); $1 per person with $25 minimum.

Who to contact: For general information phone Sequoia National Forest, Hume Lake Ranger District at (209) 338-2251.

Location: From Grant Grove in Kings Canyon National Park, drive 14 miles southeast on Generals Highway.

Trip note: This large group camp is located beside Stony Creek. The elevation is 6,500 feet. Open from June to September.

62. LODGEPOLE 🚶🏇

Reference: **On the Marble Fork of Kaweah River in Sequoia National Park; map F5, grid i1.**

Campsites, facilities: There are 250 sites for tents or motor homes. Piped water, fire grills and picnic tables are provided. Flush toilets, showers, a dump station, horseback riding facilities, a gift shop and evening ranger programs are available. A grocery store, market, deli, pay showers, propane gas, and a laundromat are nearby. Pets are permitted on leashes.

Reservations, fee: Reserve by phoning Destinet at (800) 365-CAMP; ($6 Destinet fee); $12 fee per night.

Who to contact: Phone the Sequoia National Park at (209) 565-3341.

Location: From Giant Forest Village in Sequoia National Park, drive five miles northeast on Generals Highway. There is a vehicle length advisory on Generals Highway due to steep curves. Vehicles over 22 feet are not advised to drive here. An alternate route is to take Highway 180 into the park, then turn south on Generals Highway just after entering the park.

Trip note: This is a giant but pretty camp set on the Marble Fork of the Kaweah River. Plan on plenty of company. To escape, one option is to strap on your hiking boots and hoof it on the trails near the camp leading into the backcountry of Sequoia National Park. The elevation is 6,700 feet. Open year-round.

63. ONION VALLEY 🚶🚶

Reference: **In Inyo National Forest; map F5, grid i6.**

Campsites, facilities: There are 29 sites for tents only. Piped water, flush toilets, fire grills and picnic tables are provided. Pets are permitted on leashes.

Reservations, fee: Reservations accepted; phone (800) 280-CAMP; $7 fee per night.

Who to contact: Call the Inyo National Forest Mt. Whitney Ranger District at (619) 876-6200.

Location: From US 395 in Independence, drive 14 miles west on Onion Valley Road to the campground.

Trip note: A $2 Forest Service map and a free wilderness permit are your passports to the high country from this camp. Several trails leading out from the camp are routed deep into the John Muir Wilderness and Sequoia National Park and connect to the Pacific Crest Trail. It is set at 9,200 feet, which means there's a lot of the "up" that's behind you. Open from mid-June through September.

64. GRAY'S MEADOW 🐟

Reference: **On Independence Creek in Inyo National Forest; map F5, grid i7.**

Campsites, facilities: There are 52 sites for tents or motor homes. Piped water, fire grills and picnic tables are provided. Flush toilets are available. Supplies and a laundromat in Independence. Pets are permitted on leashes.

Reservations, fee: Reservations accepted; phone(800) 280-CAMP; $7 fee per night.

Who to contact: Call Inyo National Forest Mt. Whitney Ranger District at (619) 876-6200.

Location: From US 395 in Independence, turn west on Onion Valley Road and drive five miles to the campground.

Trip note: This stark but pretty spot, set in the eastern Sierra along Independence

Creek, is just far enough off US 395 to get missed by a lot of folks. Open from April to September.

65. POTWISHA 🏃🚶 ♿   RV 7

Reference: **On the Marble Fork of Kaweah River in Sequoia National Park; map F5, grid j0.**

Campsites, facilities: There are 44 sites for tents or motor homes up to 30 feet long. Piped water, picnic tables and fire grills are provided. Flush toilets, a dump station and evening ranger programs are available. The campgrounds and restroom facilities are **wheelchair accessible**. Pets are permitted on leashes.

Reservations, fee: No reservations; $10 fee per night.

Who to contact: Phone the Sequoia National Park at (209) 565-3341. For road weather information call (209) 565-3351.

Location: From Visalia, drive east on Highway 198 to the Ash Mountain Center. From the Ash Mountain Center, drive four miles northeast on Generals Highway. There is a vehicle length advisory in effect on Generals Highway, just past Potwisha. Vehicles of 22 feet or longer are advised not to drive on this road.

Trip note: This pretty spot on the Marble Fork of the Kaweah River is one of Sequoia National Park's smaller drive-to campgrounds. From Buckeye Flat, located east of the camp a few miles, there is a trail that runs along Paradise Creek. It can be very hot and dry in summer. Open year-round.

66. BUCKEYE FLAT 🏃🚶   8

Reference: **On the Middle Fork of Kaweah River in Sequoia National Park; map F5, grid j1.**

Campsites, facilities: There are 28 tent sites. Picnic tables, fire grills and piped water are provided. Flush toilets are available. Pets are permitted on leashes.

Reservations, fee: No reservations; $10 fee per night.

Who to contact: Phone the Sequoia National Park at (209) 565-3341.

Location: From Visalia, drive east on Highway 198 to the Ash Mountain Center. From the Ash Mountain Center, drive six miles northeast on Generals Highway. There is a vehicle length advisory in effect on Generals Highway, just past Potwisha. Vehicles of 22 feet or longer are advised not to drive on this road.

Trip note: In any big, popular national park like Sequoia, the smaller the campground, the better. Well, this is one of the smaller ones here. It is set on the Middle Fork of the Kaweah River. Just south of camp is a trail that runs beside pretty Paradise Creek. Open from April to October (depending on road and weather conditions).

67. LONE PINE 🐟 🏃🚶   RV 8

Reference: **Near Mt. Whitney in Inyo National Forest; map F5, grid j7.**

Campsites, facilities: There are 43 sites for tents or motor homes. Piped water, vault toilets, fire grills and picnic tables are provided. Supplies are available in Lone Pine. Pets are permitted on leashes.

Reservations, fee: Reservations are accepted for half of the sites; phone (800) 280-CAMP; $7 fee per night.

Who to contact: Call the Inyo National Forest Mt. Whitney Ranger District at (619) 876-6200.

Location: From Lone Pine, drive seven miles west on Whitney Portal Road.

Trip note: This is an alternative for campers preparing to hike Mt. Whitney or start the John Muir Trail. It is set at 6,000 feet, 2,000 feet below Whitney Portal (the jumpoff spot for hikers), providing a lower elevation spot for hikers to acclimate themselves to the altitude for a day. The camp is set on Lone Pine Creek and has a limited stay policy (14 days). You get decent fishing and spectacular views of Mt. Whitney. Open year-round.

68. WHITNEY PORTAL GROUP CAMP

Reference: **In Inyo National Forest; map F5, grid j7.**
Campsites, facilities: There are three group sites for tents or motor homes up to 16 feet long. Piped water, flush toilets, fire grills and picnic tables are provided. Supplies are available in Lone Pine. Pets are allowed on leashes.
Reservations, fee: Reserve by phoning (800) 280-CAMP; ($15 reservation fee); $25 fee per group per night.
Who to contact: Call the Inyo National Forest Mt. Whitney Ranger District at (619) 876-6200.
Location: From Lone Pine, drive 13 miles west on Whitney Portal Road.
Trip note: This is the spot for groups planning to hike to the top of Mt. Whitney. Permits and reservations are required to camp and climb. The elevation is 8,100 feet. Open from mid-May to mid-October.

---

69. WHITNEY TRAILHEAD

Reference: **In Inyo National Forest; map F5, grid j7.**
Campsites, facilities: There are 10 tent sites at this walk-in campground. Piped water, pit toilets, fire grills and picnic tables are provided. Supplies are available in Lone Pine. Stays are limited to one night only. Pets are allowed on leashes.
Reservations, fee: No reservations; $5 fee per night.
Who to contact: Call the Inyo National Forest Mt. Whitney Ranger District at (619) 876-6200.
Location: From Lone Pine, drive 13 miles west on Whitney Portal Road, then hike.
Trip note: If Whitney Portal is packed to the rafters, this camp provides a hike-in option (elevation 8,000 feet). The trailhead to the Mt. Whitney summit (14,495 feet) is nearby. Mt. Whitney is the beginning of the 211-mile John Muir Trail, which ends in Yosemite Valley. Open from mid-May to mid-October.

---

70. WHITNEY PORTAL

Reference: **Near Mt. Whitney in Inyo National Forest; map F5, grid j7.**
Campsites, facilities: There are 43 sites for tents or motor homes up to 16 feet long. Piped water, flush toilets, fire grills and picnic tables are provided. Supplies are available in Lone Pine. Pets are allowed on leashes.
Reservations, fee: Reservations accepted for half of the sites—call (800) 280-CAMP; $10 fee per night.
Who to contact: Call the Inyo National Forest Mt. Whitney Ranger District at (619) 876-6200.
Location: From Lone Pine, drive 13 miles west on Whitney Portal Road.
Trip note: The trailhead at this camp is one of the most popular jumpoff spots for backpackers in America. The trail is routed up to the top of Mt. Whitney (14,495 feet) and forks off at Trail Crest to the Pacific Crest Trail-John Muir

Trail. A maximum seven-day stay is enforced. Hikers must have a wilderness permit, available at the Forest Service office in Lone Pine, to climb Whitney. The camp is set at 8,000 feet. Open from mid-May to mid-October.

71. PORTAGEE JOE

Reference: **Near Lone Pine; map F5, grid j8.**

Campsites, facilities: There are 15 sites for tents or motor homes. Piped water, pit toilets, fire grills and picnic tables are provided. Supplies and a laundromat are available in Lone Pine. Pets are permitted on leashes.

Reservations, fee: No reservations; $6 fee per night.

Who to contact: Phone the County Parks Department at (619) 878-0272.

Location: In Lone Pine, drive one-half mile west on Whitney Portal Road to Tuttle Creek Road. At Tuttle Creek Road, turn south and drive a one-tenth of a mile to the campground.

Trip note: This small, little-known camp provides an option for both Mt. Whitney hikers or US 395 cruisers. It is located about five miles from Diaz Lake Camp and set on a small creek at 3,750 feet. Open year-round.

MAP F6

CEN-CAL MAP .... see page 512
adjoining maps
NORTH .... no map
EAST .... no map
5 LISTINGS   SOUTH (G6) .... see page 636
PAGES 590-593   WEST (F5) .... see page 564

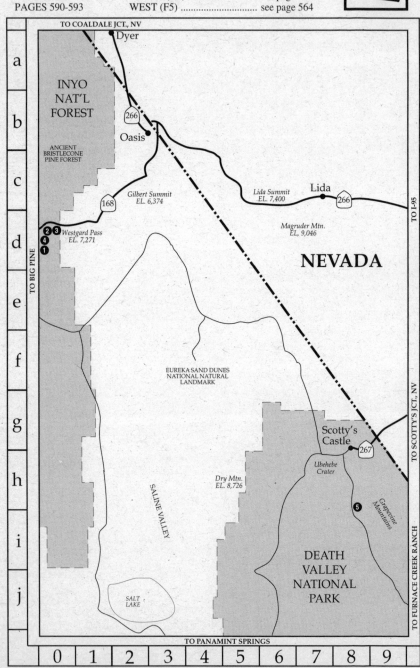

TO COALDALE JCT., NV

Dyer

a

INYO NAT'L FOREST

ANCIENT BRISTLECONE PINE FOREST

b

266

Oasis

c

168   Gilbert Summit EL. 6,374

Lida Summit EL. 7,400   Lida   266

TO I-95

Magruder Mtn. EL. 9,046

d

② ③ Westgard Pass EL. 7,271
④
①

TO BIG PINE

NEVADA

e

f

EUREKA SAND DUNES NATIONAL NATURAL LANDMARK

g

Scotty's Castle
267

TO SCOTTY'S JCT., NV

Ubehebe Crater

h

SALINE VALLEY

Dry Mtn. EL. 8,726

Grapevine Mountains

⑤

i

DEATH VALLEY NATIONAL PARK

TO FURNACE CREEK RANCH

j

SALT LAKE

TO PANAMINT SPRINGS

| 0 | 1 | 2 | 3 | 4 | 5 | 6 | 7 | 8 | 9 |

Map F6 featuring: Inyo National Forest

1. PINYON GROUP CAMP 👫

Reference: **Near Big Pine in Inyo National Forest; map F6, grid d0.**
Campsites, facilities: There are eight sites for tents or motor homes. Picnic tables and vault toilets are provided. There is **no piped water**, so bring your own. Pets are permitted on leashes.
Reservations, fee: Reserve by phoning (800) 280-CAMP ($15 reservation fee); $20 group fee per night.
Who to contact: Phone the Inyo National Forest White Mountain Ranger District at (619) 873-2500.
Location: From Big Pine on US 395, turn east on Highway 168 and drive 13 miles to the campground.
Trip note: This is one in a series of camps in the immediate area. For side-trip details, see the trip note for Fossil Group Camp.

2. POLETA GROUP CAMP 👫

Reference: **Near Big Pine in Inyo National Forest; map F6, grid d0.**
Campsites, facilities: There are eight sites for tents or motor homes. Picnic tables and vault toilets are provided. There is **no piped water**, so bring your own. Pets are permitted on leashes.
Reservations, fee: Reserve by phoning (800) 280-CAMP ($15 reservation fee); $20 group fee per night.
Who to contact: Phone the Inyo National Forest White Mountain Ranger District at (619) 873-2500.
Location: From Big Pine on US 395, turn east on Highway 168 and drive 13 miles to the campground.
Trip note: This is one of the four camps in the immediate area, so take your pick. For side-trip possibilities, see the trip note for Fossil Group Camp.

3. JUNIPER GROUP CAMP 👫

Reference: **Near Big Pine in Inyo National Forest; map F6, grid d0.**
Campsites, facilities: There are five sites for tents or motor homes. Picnic tables and vault toilets are provided. There is **no piped water**, so bring your own. Pets are permitted on leashes.
Reservations, fee: Reserve by phoning (800) 280-CAMP ($15 reservation fee); $20 fee per group per night.
Who to contact: Phone the Inyo National Forest White Mountain Ranger District at (619) 873-2500.
Location: From Big Pine on US 395, turn east on Highway 168 and drive 13 miles to the campground.
Trip note: Juniper Camp is a nearby option to Poleta Camp for group campers. See the trip note for Fossil Group Camp for sidetrip details.

4. FOSSIL GROUP CAMP 👫

Reference: **Near Big Pine in Inyo National Forest; map F6, grid d0.**
Campsites, facilities: There are 11 sites for tents or motor homes. Picnic tables and vault toilets are provided. There is **no piped water**, so bring your own. Pets are

permitted on leashes.

Reservations, fee: Reserve by phoning (800) 280-CAMP ($15 reservation fee);
$20 group fee per night.

Who to contact: Phone the Inyo National Forest White Mountain Ranger District
at (619) 873-2500.

Location: From Big Pine on US 395, turn east on Highway 168 and drive 13 miles
to the campground.

Trip note: This is a primitive and little-known Forest Service camp set at 7,220
feet elevation. Ambitious visitors have several side-trip options. From nearby
Cedar Flat, a trail leads west to Black Mountain (9,083 feet). Deep Spring Lake
is 10 miles from camp via Highway 168 and primitive roads; a Forest Service
map is a necessity. Another option is to drive north on White Mountain Road,
which is routed through the Ancient Bristle Cone Pine Forest.

---

5. MESQUITE SPRING 👫 ♿   🚐 7

Reference: **In Death Valley National Park; map F6, grid i8.**

Campsites, facilities: There are 30 sites for tents or motor homes. Picnic tables are
provided. Piped water, flush toilets and a sanitary dump station is available.
Facilities are **wheelchair accessible**. Pets are allowed on leashes.

Reservations, fee: No reservations; $6 fee per night.

Who to contact: Phone Death Valley National Park at (619)786-2331.

Location: Enter the park's southwest entrance gate on Highway 190, obtain a park
brochure, then continue on Highway 190 past Stovepipe Wells to the north end
of the park. The camp is located three miles south of Scotty's Castle.

Trip note: Mesquite Spring is the most remote and prettiest campground in Death
Valley. There are a number of sidetrips possible from here that make for little
adventures. A favorite is poking around Scotty's Castle. If you are a lover of
subzero desert beauty, then you must make this trip in late winter, when all
kinds of very tiny wildflowers bring the stark valley floor to life.

MAP G1

CEN-CAL MAP .... see page 512
adjoining maps
NORTH (F1) .... see page 514
EAST (G2) .... see page 598
SOUTH .... no map
WEST .... no map

6 LISTINGS
PAGES 594-597

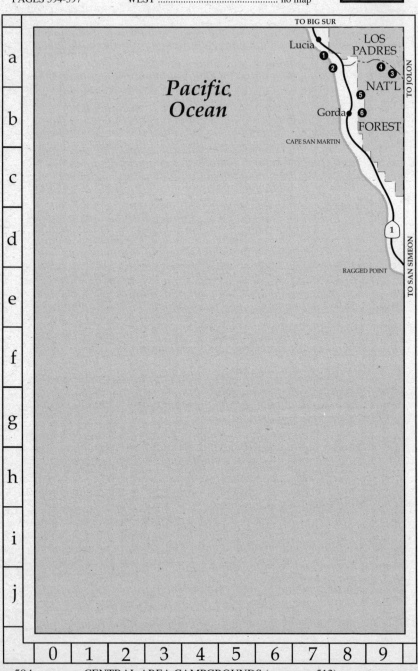

Map G1 featuring Los Padres National Forest

1. LIMEKILN STATE PARK

RV 9

Reference: **On Pacific Ocean; map G1, grid a7.**

Campsites, facilities: There are 43 sites for tents or motor homes up to 21 feet long; trailers to 15 feet long. There is a limit of one vehicle per campsite; extra passenger vehicles are allowed in parking areas only if space permits. Piped water, restrooms, showers, a dump station, a grocery store, bait and firewood are available. Pets are allowed on leashes, except on trails.

Reservations, fee: No reservations; $20-$24 fee per night; $6 fee each extra vehicle.

Who to contact: Phone the park at (408) 667-2403 or (408) 649-2836.

Location: From Big Sur, drive 26 miles south on Highway 1.

Trip note: This is a Highway 1 layover spot, set up primarily for motor homes. Drive-in campsites are set up both near the beach and the redwoods, take your pick. Several hiking trails are available, including one that is routed past some historic lime kilns. This camp was originally called Limekiln Beach Redwoods, and was privately operated. No more.

2. KIRK CREEK

RV 8

Reference: **Near Pacific Ocean in Los Padres National Forest; map G1, grid a8.**

Campsites, facilities: There are 33 sites for tents or motor homes. Piped water, picnic tables and fire grills are provided. Flush toilets are available. Pets are permitted on leashes.

Reservations, fee: No reservations; $10-$15 fee per night, $2-$3 fee per night for bicyclists.

Who to contact: Phone Los Padres National Forest, Monterey Ranger District at (408) 385-5434.

Location: From the little town of Lucia on Highway 1, drive four miles south on Highway 1 to the campground.

Trip note: This pretty camp is set along Kirk Creek near where it empties into the Pacific Ocean. A trail from camp branches north through the Ventana Wilderness, which is dotted with backcountry campsites. Open year-round.

3. PONDEROSA

RV 4

Reference: **In Los Padres National Forest; map G1, grid a9.**

Campsites, facilities: There are 23 sites for tents or motor homes up to 32 feet long. Piped water, picnic tables and fire grills are provided. Vault toilets are available. Pets are permitted on leashes.

Reservations, fee: No reservations; $5 fee per night.

Who to contact: Phone Los Padres National Forest, Monterey Ranger District at (408) 385-5434.

Location: From US 101 in King City, drive 18 miles south on County Route G14 to the town of Jolon. From Jolon, turn north on Mission Road and drive four miles. Turn left on Nacimiento-Fergusson Road and drive 12 miles to the campground.

Trip note: Not many folks know about this spot that's just far enough off the main track to get missed. It's set at 1,500 feet elevation in Los Padres National Forest, not far from the Ventana Wilderness (good hiking) and Hunter Liggett Military Reservation (wild pig hunting with permit). Open year-round.

4. NACIMIENTO

Reference: **In Los Padres National Forest; map G1, grid a9.**

Campsites, facilities: There are nine sites for tents and eight sites for tents or motor homes. Picnic tables and fire grills are provided. Vault toilets are available. Pets are permitted on leashes.

Reservations, fee: No reservations; no fee.

Who to contact: Phone Los Padres National Forest, Monterey Ranger District at (408) 385-5434.

Location: From the little town of Lucia on Highway 1, drive four miles south on Highway 1 to Nacimiento Road. Turn east and drive about eight winding miles to the campground. Or from the town of Jolon, drive 15 miles northwest on Nacimiento-Fergusson Road.

Trip note: This little-known spot near the Nacimiento River at 1,600 feet elevation makes for a good jumpoff spot for a backpack or hunting trip. The camp is set in Los Padres National Forest near the Ventana Wilderness and Hunter Liggett Military Reservation.

5. PLASKETT CREEK

Reference: **Overlooking Pacific Ocean in Los Padres National Forest; map G1, grid b8.**

Campsites, facilities: There are 43 sites for tents or motor homes. Piped water, picnic tables and fire grills are provided. Flush toilets are available. Pets are permitted on leashes.

Reservations, fee: No reservations; $10 fee per night; $15 for multi-family sites; $2-$3 for bicyclists.

Who to contact: Phone Los Padres National Forest, Monterey Ranger District at (408) 385-5434.

Location: From the town of Lucia, drive 9.5 miles south on Highway 1 to the campground.

Trip note: This is a premium coastal camp for Highway 1 cruisers, set at 200 feet elevation along little Plaskett Creek above the Pacific Ocean. A little cafe in Lucia provides open-air dining with a dramatic lookout down the coast. Open all year.

6. PLASKETT CREEK GROUP CAMP

Reference: **Overlooking Pacific Ocean in Los Padres National Forest; map G1, grid b8.**

Campsites, facilities: There are three group sites for tents or motor homes. Piped water, picnic tables and fire grills are provided. Vault toilets are available. Pets are permitted on leashes.

Reservations, fee: Reserve by phoning (800) 280-CAMP ($15 reservation fee); $50 group fee per night.

Who to contact: Phone Los Padres National Forest, Monterey Ranger District at (408) 385-5434.

Location: From the little town of Lucia, drive 9.5 miles south on Highway 1 to the campground.

Trip note: This is one of two prime, coastal camps in this immediate area along Highway 1, which is one of the prettiest drives in the West. This camp is for small groups and is set beside little Plaskett Creek. A great little cafe that overlooks the coast is available in Lucia. Open year-round.

MAP G2

CEN-CAL MAP .... see page 512
adjoining maps
NORTH (F2) .... see page 528
EAST (G3) .... see page 606
SOUTH (H2) .... see page 644
WEST (G1) .... see page 594

19 LISTINGS
PAGES 598-605

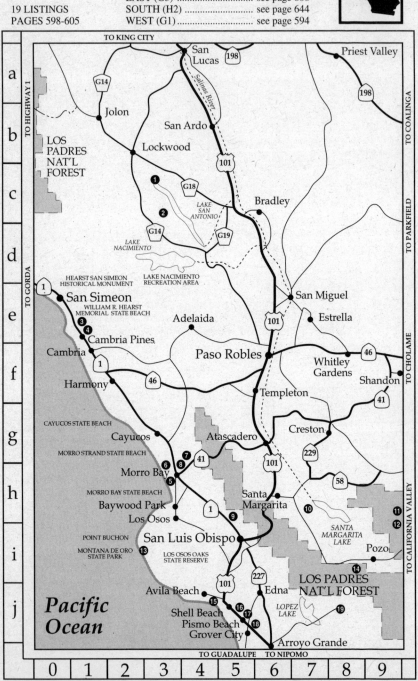

Map G2 featuring: Lake San Antonio, San Simeon State Beach, Los Padres National Forest, Morro Bay, Santa Margarita Lake, San Luis Obispo Bay, Pismo State Beach

1. NORTH SHORE

Reference: On Lake San Antonio; map G2, grid c3.

Campsites, facilities: There are 236 sites for tents or motor homes, some with full or partial hookups. Piped water, fire grills and tables are provided. A dump station, restrooms, showers, a boat ramp, boat rentals, stables, a playground, a recreation room, a laundromat and a grocery store are available. Pets are permitted on leashes.

Reservations, fee: Reservations accepted; $11-$21 fee per night; $1 pet fee.

Who to contact: Phone the resort at (805) 472-2311.

Location: From King City on US 101, turn south onto County Road G18 and drive 24 miles to the Lockwood intersection. Continue straight on County Road G18 (Jolon Road) and drive about 10 miles to the camp entrance road on the right.

Trip note: Lake San Antonio is a year-round spot for adventure. It is a narrow, 16-mile long reservoir that provides fishing for bass in the spring and waterskiing in the summer. In the winter you can take unique bald eagle tours that run from the south shore. It's a good spot for boaters and campers. Open year-round.

2. SOUTH SHORE

Reference: On Lake San Antonio; map G2, grid c3.

Campsites, facilities: There are three campgrounds with 458 campsites for tents or motor homes, many with full or partial hookups. Piped water, fire grills and tables are provided. A dump station, restrooms, showers, a boat ramp, boat rentals, a playground, a recreation room, a laundromat, a grocery store and a visitor information center are available. Pets are permitted on leashes.

Reservations, fee: Reservations accepted; $11-$21 fee per night; $1 pet fee.

Who to contact: Phone the resort at (805) 472-2311.

Location: From King City, drive 29 miles south on US 101. Take the County Road G19 (Nacimiento Lake Road) exit and drive 12 miles to County Road G14 (Interlake Road). Turn right and drive nine miles to the campground entrance road (San Antonio Road).

Trip note: Harris Creek, Redondo Vista and Lynch are the three campgrounds set near each other along the south shore of Lake San Antonio, a 16-mile reservoir that provides good bass fishing in the spring and waterskiing in the summer. In the winter months, the Monterey County Department of Parks offers a unique eagle watch program, which includes boat tours. Open all year.

3. WASHBURN

Reference: In San Simeon State Park; map G2, grid e1.

Campsites, facilities: There are 70 sites for tents or motor homes up to 31 feet long. Fire grills and picnic tables are provided. Piped water and chemical toilets are available. A grocery store, a laundromat, and propane gas can be found nearby in Cambria. Pets are permitted.

Reservations, fee: Reserve by phoning Destinet at (800) 444-7275 ($6.75 Destinet fee); $10-$12 fee per night; $1 pet fee.

Who to contact: Phone the state park at (805) 927-2035 or (805) 927-2020.

Location: From Cambria, drive three miles north on Highway 1 to the park entrance. This campground is just beyond San Simeon Creek Campground on the park entrance road.

Trip note: This camp is primarily used as an overflow area if the San Simeon Creek Campground is jammed to the rafters. It sits on the hill above the other camp and offers an ocean view, but it is less developed. That's good or bad depending on your viewpoint. Open year-round.

---

4. SAN SIMEON CREEK

Reference: In San Simeon State Park; map G2, grid e1.

Campsites, facilities: There are 132 sites for tents or motor homes up to 35 feet long. Fire grills and picnic tables are provided. Piped water, flush toilets, showers and a dump station are available. A grocery store, a laundromat, and propane gas can be found nearby in Cambria. Pets are permitted.

Reservations, fee: Reserve by phoning Destinet at (800) 444-7275 ($6.75 Destinet fee); $17-$19 fee per night; $1 pet fee.

Who to contact: Phone the state park at (805) 927-2035 or (805) 927-2020.

Location: From Cambria, drive three miles north on Highway 1 to the park entrance.

Trip note: Hearst Castle is only five miles northeast, so this spot is a natural for visitors planning to take the tour. For a tour reservation phone Destinet. The camp is set across the highway from the ocean, with easy access under the highway to the beach. San Simeon Creek, while not exactly the Mississippi, runs through the campground and adds a nice touch. Open year-round.

---

5. MORRO BAY STATE PARK

Reference: Map G2, grid h3.

Campsites, facilities: There are 20 motor home sites with water and electrical connections and 115 sites for tents or motor homes up to 31 feet long. Some sites are **wheelchair accessible**. Fire grills and picnic tables are provided. Piped water, flush toilets, coin-operated showers, a dump station, museum exhibits, nature walks and programs are available. A laundromat, a grocery store, propane gas, a boat ramp, mooring, rentals and food service are available in Morro Bay. The picnicking, museum and food service areas are **wheelchair accessible**. Pets are permitted.

Reservations, fee: Reserve by phoning Destinet at (800) 444-7275 ($6.75 Destinet fee); $17-$19 fee per night; $1 pet fee.

Who to contact: Phone the park at (805) 772-2560 or (805) 549-3312.

Location: On Highway 1, drive to the south end of Morro Bay and follow the signs to the park entrance.

Trip note: Reservations are strongly advised. This is one of the premium stopover spots for folks cruising north on Highway 1 out of the L.A. area. The park offers a wide range of activities and exhibits covering the natural and cultural history of the area. Sidetrips include fishing in Morro Bay, touring Hearst Castle, or visiting the Morro Bay Wildlife Refuge.

6. MORRO STRAND STATE BEACH

Reference: **Near Morro Bay; map G2, grid h3.**

Campsites, facilities: There are 23 sites for tents and 81 sites for motor homes up to 24 feet long. Piped water, fire grills, and picnic tables are provided. Flush toilets and cold, outdoor showers are available. Supplies and a laundromat are available in Morro Bay. Pets are permitted.

Reservations, fee: Reserve by phoning Destinet at (800) 444-7275 ($6.75 Destinet fee) from Memorial Day to Labor Day; $17-$19 fee per night; $1 pet fee.

Who to contact: Phone the state beach at (805) 772-2560 or (805) 549-3312.

Location: This campground is within the Morro Bay city limits, just off Highway 1. The exit to the campground is signed.

Trip note: A ton of Highway 1 cruisers plan to stay overnight at this state park. And why not? It is set along the ocean near Morro Bay, a pretty spot year-round. Sidetrip options include the Morro Bay Wildlife Refuge, Museum of Natural History, or an ocean fishing trip out of Morro Bay.

---

7. RANCHO COLINA RV PARK

Reference: **In Morro Bay; map G2, grid h4.**

Campsites, facilities: There are 57 motor home sites with full hookups. Picnic tables are provided. Restrooms, showers, a laundromat and a recreation room are available. Supplies can be found nearby. Pets are allowed on leashes.

Reservations, fee: Reservations accepted; $19 fee per night.

Who to contact: Phone the park at (805) 772-8420.

Location: From Morro Bay on Highway 1, drive one mile east on Atascadero Road (Highway 41) to 1045 Atascadero Road.

Trip note: This is a privately-operated motor home park, one of several camping options in the Morro Bay area. Open year-round.

---

8. MORRO DUNES TRAILER PARK & CAMP

Reference: **In Morro Bay; map G2, grid h4.**

Campsites, facilities: There are 43 sites for tents and 139 motor home sites. Picnic tables, fire grills, piped water, electrical connections, cable TV and, in most cases, sewer hookups are provided. Restrooms, showers, a laundromat, a store, wood, ice and a dump station are available. Propane gas can be obtained nearby. Pets are allowed on leashes.

Reservations, fee: Reservations accepted; $15-$25 fee per night.

Who to contact: Phone the park at (805) 772-2722.

Location: From Highway 1 in Morro Bay, drive west on Atascadero (Highway 41) for a half mile to 1700 Embarcadero/Atascadero Road.

Trip note: The many sidetrip possibilities make this an attractive destination. Available trips include deep sea fishing and clamming out of Morro Bay, the Hearst Castle tour, Montana de Oro State Park, the Museum of Natural History and the Morro Bay Wildlife Refuge. Open year-round.

---

9. EL CHORRO REGIONAL PARK

Reference: **Near San Luis Obispo; map G2, grid h5.**

Campsites, facilities: There are 75 undesignated sites for tents or motor homes.

Fire grills and picnic tables are provided. Piped water, flush toilets and a playground are available. Supplies and a laundromat are nearby in San Luis Obispo. Pets are permitted on leashes.

Reservations, fee: No reservations; $13-$20 fee per night; $1.50 pet fee.

Who to contact: Phone the park at (805) 781-5219.

Location: From San Luis Obispo, drive seven miles north on Highway 1 to the park entrance on the east side of the highway.

Trip note: Despite easy access just off Highway 1, this park is often overlooked for one reason: It isn't in the state park or Destinet reservation systems. That means there are times when coastal state parks can be jammed full and this regional park may still have space. Morro Bay, located six miles away, provides many possible sidetrips. Note that a men's prison is located about one mile away. For some people, this can be a real turnoff.

---

10. SANTA MARGARITA KOA

Reference: Near Santa Margarita Lake; map G2, grid h7.

Campsites, facilities: There are 54 sites for tents or motor homes. Picnic tables, fire grills, piped water and, in some cases, electrical connections and sewer hookups are provided. Restrooms, showers, a swimming pool, a playground, a laundromat, a store, a dump station and propane gas are available. Pets are permitted on leashes.

Reservations, fee: Reservations accepted; $19-$25 per night.

Who to contact: Phone the camp at (805) 438-5618.

Location: From San Luis Obispo, drive eight miles north on US 101 to the Highway 58/Santa Margarita exit. Drive through the town of Santa Margarita and turn right on Entrada. Within one mile, Entrada turns into Pozo Road. Continue six miles on Pozo Road to Santa Margarita Lake Road. Turn left and the campground is one-half mile on the right.

Trip note: This camp is set on the access road to Santa Margarita Lake, about one-quarter mile from the lake entrance. Santa Margarita Lake is set in the coastal oak woodlands east of San Luis Obispo, just below the Santa Lucia Mountains. It is a long narrow lake that has good fishing for bass in the spring but slows in late summer. Open year-round.

---

11. SELBY

Reference: At Carrizo Plain, northeast of San Luis Obispo; map G2, grid h9.

Campsites, facilities: This is a primitive camping area with no designated sites. A portable toilet is available. **No piped water** is provided. No trash facilities are available, so bring a garbage bag with you to collect all refuse.

Reservations, fee: No reservations; no fee.

Who to contact: Phone Caliente Resource Area at (805) 391-6000, or write to Bureau of Land Management, 3801 Pegasus Drive, Bakersfield, CA 93308.

Location: From Bakersfield, take Highway 58 west for about 30 miles to McKittrick (where Highway 33 merges with 58). Stay on Highway 58/33 for another two miles, then turn west on Highway 58 (signed for California Valley) and drive for about 30 miles. Turn left on Soda Lake Road and drive seven miles to the entrance of the Carrizo Plains Natural Area. Continue about six miles to the Selby Camping area, located on your right.

Trip note: Selby is a primitive camping area at the base of the Caliente Mountain Range, used primarily by hunters in the fall, early winter and spring, looking for deer, wild pigs and some upland game birds. Otherwise, there's not much out here, with hot temperatures scorching the hills during the summer months. In the winter, a great side trip is to Soda Lake, a nesting area for the endangered sandhill crane.

---

12. KCL

Reference: **At Carrizo Plain, northeast of San Luis Obispo; map G2, grid h9.**
Campsites, facilities: This is a primitive camping area with no designated sites. A portable toilet is available. **No piped water** is provided. No trash facilities are available, so bring a garbage bag with you to collect all refuse.
Reservations, fee: No reservations; no fee.
Who to contact: Phone Caliente Resource Area at (805) 391-6000 or write Bureau of Land Management, 3801 Pegasus Drive, Bakersfield, CA 93308.
Location: From Bakersfield, take Highway 58 west for about 30 miles to McKittrick (where Highway 33 merges with 58). Stay on Highway 58/33 for another two miles, then turn west on Highway 58 (signed for California Valley) and drive for about 30 miles. Turn left on Soda Lake Road and drive seven miles to the entrance of the Carrizo Plains Natural Area. Continue about 15 miles (pass Selby Camping area) to KCL Camp on the right.
Trip note: KCL is the name for the old ranch headquarters in the Carrizo, and what is left is an old broken-down barn and a water wagon—and not much else. At least there are some trees here (in comparison, there are almost none at nearby Selby Camp). Like Selby Camp, this camp is used primarily in the fall as a base for hunters. But the Carrizo Plain is best known for providing a habitat for many rare species of plants, in addition to furnishing the winter nesting sites at Soda Lake for the awesome migration of giant sandhill cranes. Occasionally these huge birds will fly down the valley and be visible here.

---

13. MONTANA DE ORO STATE PARK

Reference: **Near Morro Bay; map G2, grid i2.**
Campsites, facilities: There are 50 sites for tents or motor homes up to 24 feet long, four walk-in environmental sites and two group sites which will accommodate 25 campers per site. Fire grills and picnic tables are provided. Pit toilets, horse camping facilities and a nature trail are available. There is **no piped water**, but potable trucked water is available. Supplies and a laundromat are nearby. Pets are allowed on leashes.
Reservations, fee: Reserve by phoning Destinet at (800) 444-7275 ($6.75 Destinet fee); $7-$9 fee per night; $17-$19 group camp fee per night; $1 pet fee.
Who to contact: Phone the park at (805) 528-0513 or (805) 549-3312.
Location: From Morro Bay, drive two miles south on Highway 1. Turn on South Bay Boulevard and drive four miles to Los Osos. Turn right (west) on Pecho Valley Road and drive five miles to the park.
Trip note: This primitive, sprawling chunk of land includes coastline, 7,300 acres of foothills and Valencia Peak, elevation 1,345 feet. There's no water—that stops a lot of people. The camp is set on a bluff with stunning views of the ocean and cliffs.

14. HI MOUNTAIN 🏃

Reference: In Los Padres National Forest; map G2, grid i8.

Campsites, facilities: There are 11 sites for tents or motor homes up to 16 feet long (trailers not recommended). There is **no piped water**. Fire grills and picnic tables are provided. Vault toilets are available. Pets are permitted on leashes.

Reservations, fee: No reservations; no fee.

Who to contact: Phone the Los Padres National Forest Santa Lucia District at (805) 925-9538.

Location: From San Luis Obispo, drive eight miles north on US 101. Turn east on Highway 58 and drive four miles (two miles past Santa Margarita). Turn southeast on Pozo Road and drive for 16 miles to the town of Pozo. Turn on Hi Mountain Road and drive two miles to the campground.

Trip note: At an elevation of 2,800 feet, this is the highest point in the Santa Lucia Wilderness. It's near a trailhead camp with two trails starting here leading into the Garcia Mountain area to two other camps. In fall, it makes a good base camp for hunters. Open year-round (road may be closed during heavy rains).

---

15. AVILA HOT SPRINGS SPA AND RV PARK

Reference: On San Luis Obispo Bay; map G2, grid j5.

Campsites, facilities: There are 25 sites for tents and 50 motor home spaces, many with full or partial hookups. Picnic tables and some fire grills are provided. Restrooms, showers, a swimming pool, a hot mineral pool, a spa, cable TV, a dump station, a recreation room, an arcade and group barbecue pits are available. A grocery store, a laundromat, propane gas, a golf course and riding stables are nearby. Pets are allowed on leashes.

Reservations, fee: Reservations accepted; phone (800) 332-2359; $18-$28 fee per night. There is an extra charge for pool and spa facilities.

Who to contact: Phone the park at (805) 595-2359.

Location: From San Luis Obispo, drive nine miles south on US 101 to the Avila Beach Drive exit. Drive to 250 Avila Beach Drive.

Trip note: The hot mineral pool here is a featured attraction. Nearby recreation options include Avila State Beach and Pismo State Beach. Open year-round.

---

16. PISMO COAST VILLAGE

Reference: In Pismo Beach; map G2, grid j5.

Campsites, facilities: There are 400 motor home sites with full hookups, satellite TV, picnic tables, and fire grills. Restrooms, showers, playgrounds, swimming pools, a laundromat, a store, firewood, ice, a recreation room, propane gas, recreation programs, a restaurant and a miniature golf course are available. Pets are allowed on leashes.

Reservations, fee: Reservations accepted, phone (800) 458-1881; $22-$36 fee per night.

Who to contact: Phone the park at (805) 773-1811.

Location: In Pismo Beach drive to 165 South Dolliver Street (Highway 1).

Trip note: This big time motor home park gets a lot of use by Highway 1 cruisers. Its location is a plus, being set near the ocean. Open year-round.

17. NORTH BEACH 🐟 👫 🏇   RV 7

Reference: **In Pismo State Beach; map G2, grid j5.**

Campsites, facilities: There are 103 sites for tents or motor homes up to 31 feet long. Fire grills and picnic tables are provided. Piped water, flush toilets and a dump station are available. Horseback riding facilities, a grocery store, a laundromat and propane gas are nearby. Pets are permitted on leashes.

Reservations, fee: Reserve by phoning Destinet at (800) 444-7275 ($6.75 Destinet fee); $17-$19 fee per night; $1 pet fee.

Who to contact: Phone the park at (805) 489-2684 or (805) 549-3312.

Location: This campground is within Pismo Beach city limits, just off Highway 1. The exit is signed.

Trip note: Plan on a reservation and plenty of company. This is an exceptionally popular state beach, as an ultimate destination as well as for folks just wanting a stopover while cruising Highway 1. The adjacent dune area makes for great walks, or, for kids, great rolls.

18. LE SAGE RIVIERA 🐟 👫 🚩   RV 4

Reference: **Near Pismo State Beach; map G2, grid j5.**

Campsites, facilities: There are 60 motor home sites. Picnic tables, piped water, electrical connections and sewer hookups are provided. Restrooms, showers, and a laundromat are available. Stores, restaurants and golf courses are nearby. Pets are permitted on leashes.

Reservations, fee: Reservations accepted; $18-$22 fee per night.

Who to contact: Phone the park at (805) 489-2103.

Location: From Pismo Beach, drive two miles south on Grand Avenue or Dolliver Street to 319 North Highway 1.

Trip note: This is a year-round motor home park that can provide headquarters for visits to several nearby attractions. They include nearby Pismo State Beach and Lopez Lake, 10 miles to the east. Open year-round.

19. LOPEZ LAKE RECREATION AREA   RV 7

🐟 ⚓ 👫 ♿ 🏊 🚶 🏇

Reference: **Near Arroyo Grande; map G2, grid j8.**

Campsites, facilities: There are 356 sites for tents or motor homes of any length, many with full or partial hookups. Picnic tables and fire rings are provided. Restrooms, showers, a playground, a laundromat, a store, ice, a snack bar, a boat ramp, mooring, boat fuel, tackle, boat rentals and a water slide are available. Pets are permitted on leashes and with proof of rabies vaccination.

Reservations, fee: Reservations accepted; call (805) 489-8019; $12-$20 fee per night; $1.50 pet fee; $4 boat launch fee.

Who to contact: Phone the park at (805) 489-1122.

Location: From Arroyo Grande on US 101, take the Grand Avenue exit. Turn east and drive through Arroyo Grande. Turn northeast on Lopez Drive and drive 10 miles to the park.

Trip note: Lopez Lake is set amid oak woodlands southeast of San Luis Obispo. The lake is shaped something like a horseshoe, and in the spring, maybe it brings good luck to fishermen. By summer, waterskiers take over. Sidetrips include hiking or horseback riding, with a number of trails looping through the area. Open year-round.

CEN-CAL MAP .... see page 512
adjoining maps
NORTH (F3) .... see page 534
EAST (G4) .... see page 610
SOUTH (H3) .... see page 648
WEST (G2) .... see page 598

4 LISTINGS
PAGES 606-609

TO LOS BANOS   TO FIVE POINTS   TO HUB

TO LOS BANOS
TO FIVE POINTS
TO HANFORD

a
TO PRIEST VALLEY
198
5
Huron
198
Lemoore

269
Coalinga
41
Stratford

b
198
TO GUERNSEY
Summit
EL. 3,498

c
TO SAN MIGUEL
Avenal
33
1 Kettleman City
Parkfield

d
41
KETTLEMAN STATE REC. AREA
TO CONCORAN

e
Cholame
46
5
Devils Den

f
TO PASO ROBLES
Shandon
KERN NAT'L WILDLIFE REFUGE

g
46
Blackwells Corner
Lost Hills
2

h
TO SANTA MARGARITA
33
5
TO WASCO
TO SHAFFER

i
TO POZO
3
LOS PADRES NAT'L FOREST
Summit EL. 3,258
58
Buttonwillow

j
4
California Valley
58
McKittrick
TO WHEELER RIDGE

TO DERBY

0   1   2   3   4   5   6   7   8   9

Map G3 featuring: Kern National Wildlife Refuge, Los Padres National Forest

1. KETTLEMAN CITY RV PARK 🚶🏇   RV 2

Reference: **Near Kettleman City; map G3, grid c5.**
Campsites, facilities: There are 65 motor home sites, and unlimited tent sites. Picnic tables, piped water and full or partial hookups are provided. There are eight sites with telephone hookups, available on request. Restrooms, showers, playgrounds, video game room, a pool, a meeting room, a laundromat, a store, a dump station, a dog run, a restaurant, a snack bar, horseshoeing services, horseback riding facilities and propane gas are available. There is also a two-acre RV sales lot at the park. Pets are allowed on leashes. (Note: There is a 10% discount at the camp restaurant for overnight campers.)
Reservations, fee: Reservations accepted; $6-$17 fee per night.
Who to contact: Phone the park at (209) 386-4000.
Location: From Interstate 5 near Kettleman City, take the Highway 41 exit. Drive a half mile north on Highway 41. Turn left (west) on Hubert Way, then right on Cyril Place to 452 Cyril Place.
Trip note: Being stuck in Kings County looking for a place to park a motor home is no picnic. Unless, that is, you are lucky enough to have this book and know about Kettleman City RV Park. It's literally the "only game in town;" in fact, it's the only camp in the entire county. Visitors will find access to miles of open paths and roads for hiking or running. Open year-round.

2. LOST HILLS KOA ♿ 🏊   RV 4

Reference: **Near Kern National Wildlife Refuge; map G3, grid g8.**
Campsites, facilities: There are 10 sites for tents only and 80 motor home sites. Picnic tables, piped water, satellite TV, and full hookups are provided. Restrooms, showers, a swimming pool, a laundromat, a store, a video room and propane gas are available. Some facilities are **wheelchair accessible**. Restaurants are nearby. Pets are allowed on leashes.
Reservations, fee: Reservations accepted; $18-$22 fee per night; (800) 562-2793.
Who to contact: Phone the park at (805) 797-2719.
Location: Drive to the junction of Interstate 5 and Highway 46. If you are coming from the south, make a left hand turn on Highway 46 into the park entrance. Coming from the north, make a right hand turn on Highway 46 into the park entrance.
Trip note: The pickings can get slim around these parts if you're cruising north on Interstate 5, so if it's late, you'll likely be happy to find this KOA camp. The nearby Kern National Wildlife Refuge, about a 15-minute drive away, offers a sidetrip possibility. It's a waterfowl reserve that attracts a lot of ducks and geese in the fall and winter months. Open year-round.

3. LA PANZA 🚶🚶   RV 3

Reference: **In Los Padres National Forest; map G3, grid i0.**
Campsites, facilities: There are 16 sites for tents or motor homes up to 16 feet long. Fire grills and picnic tables are provided. Vault toilets are available. There is **no piped water**. Pets are allowed on leashes.

Reservations, fee: No reservations; $3 fee per night during deer season.

Who to contact: Phone the Los Padres National Forest Santa Lucia District at (805) 925-9538.

Location: From San Luis Obispo, drive eight miles north on US 101. Turn east on Highway 58 and drive four miles (two miles past Santa Margarita). Turn southeast on Pozo Road and drive for 16 miles to the town of Pozo. Continue 11.5 miles east past Pozo on County Road M3093 to the campground.

Trip note: This primitive spot is located at 2,400 feet in the La Panza Range, an oak woodland area which is crisscrossed by numerous trails and streams. This is a nearby option to the Hi Mountain Campground. Open year-round.

---

4. STONY CREEK

Reference: **In Los Padres National Forest; map G3, grid j0.**

Campsites, facilities: There are six sites for tents. Fire grills and picnic tables are provided. Vault toilets are available. There is **no piped water**, so bring your own. Pets are permitted on leashes.

Reservations, fee: No reservations; no fee.

Who to contact: Phone the Los Padres National Forest Santa Lucia District at (805) 925-9538.

Location: From Arroyo Grande on US 101, take the Grand Avenue exit. Turn east and drive through Arroyo Grande. Turn northeast on Lopez Drive and drive 1.5 miles. Turn right on Huasna Road and drive 11 miles east. Continue east on County Road M2023 (Huasna Road) for ten miles. Turn north (left) on Forest Service Road 30S02 and drive 2.5 miles to the trailhead. Hike in 2.5 miles past the locked gate to the campground.

Trip note: Just about nobody goes out here. It is a small, primitive spot set along little Stony Creek at 1,800 feet elevation, deep in the Los Padres National Forest. It's located on the outskirts of the Garcia Wilderness. You're not going to see Bigfoot around here, but you won't likely see any other folks either. Open year-round.

MAP G4

CEN-CAL MAP .... see page 512
adjoining maps
NORTH (F4) .... see page 538
EAST (G5) .... see page 614
SOUTH (H4) .... see page 662
WEST (G3) .... see page 606

9 LISTINGS
PAGES 610-613

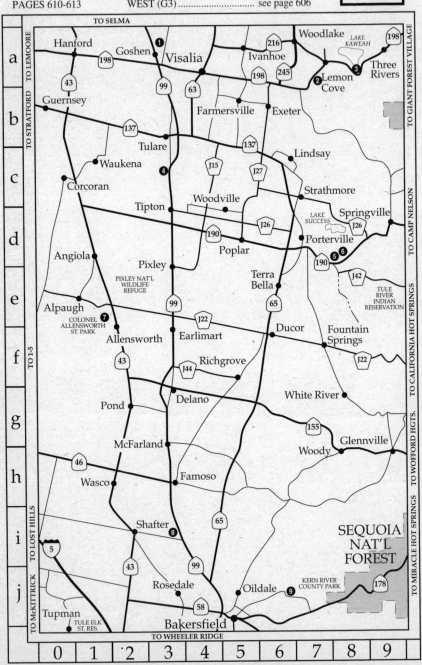

TO SELMA

TO LEMOORE
TO STRATFORD
TO I-5
TO McKITTRICK
TO LOST HILLS

Hanford
Goshen
198
Visalia
99
63
43
Guernsey
137
Tulare
Waukena
Corcoran
Tipton
190
Angiola
Pixley
Alpaugh
PIXLEY NAT'L
WILDLIFE
REFUGE
COLONEL
ALLENSWORTH
ST. PARK
Allensworth
43
99
J22
Earlimart
Richgrove
J44
Delano
Pond
McFarland
46
Wasco
Famoso
5
Shafter
43
99
Rosedale
Tupman
TULE ELK
ST. RES.
58
Bakersfield

Woodlake
216
Ivanhoe
198
245
Lemon
Cove
Three
Rivers
LAKE
KAWEAH
198
Farmersville
Exeter
137
Lindsay
J15
J27
Woodville
Strathmore
J26
LAKE
SUCCESS
Springville
J26
Poplar
Porterville
190
Terra
Bella
65
J42
TULE
RIVER
INDIAN
RESERVATION
Ducor
Fountain
Springs
J22
White River
155
Glennville
Woody
65
SEQUOIA
NAT'L
FOREST
Oildale
KERN RIVER
COUNTY PARK
178

TO GIANT FOREST VILLAGE
TO CAMP NELSON
TO CALIFORNIA HOT SPRINGS
TO WOFFORD HGTS.
TO MIRACLE HOT SPRINGS

TO WHEELER RIDGE

a b c d e f g h i j

0 1 2 3 4 5 6 7 8 9

1. GOSHEN-VISALIA KOA ⌇   RV 1

Reference: Map G4, grid a3.

Campsites, facilities: There are 30 sites for tents only, 48 motor home sites, and 38 sites for tents or motor homes. Piped water and full or partial hookups are provided. Restrooms, showers, a swimming pool, a laundromat, a playground, a recreation room, a store, a dump station and propane gas are available. Pets are allowed on leashes.

Reservations, fee: Reservations accepted; $17-$23.50 fee per night.

Who to contact: Phone the park at (209) 651-0544 or (800) 322-2336 in California.

Location: From Visalia, drive five miles west to 7480 Avenue 308; or drive one mile east of Highway 99; or drive one mile north of Highway 198.

Trip note: This is a layover spot for Highway 99 cruisers. If you're looking for a spot to park your rig for the night, don't get too picky around these parts.

2. LEMON COVE-SEQUOIA ⌇   RV 5

Reference: Near Lake Kaweah; map G4, grid a7.

Campsites, facilities: There are 55 sites for tents or motor homes as well as group camping facilities. Picnic tables, piped water and full or partial hookups are provided. Restrooms, showers, a playground, a swimming pool, a laundromat, a recreation room, cable TV, a store, a dump station and propane gas are available. Pets are allowed on leashes.

Reservations, fee: Reservations accepted; $15-$19 fee per night.

Who to contact: Phone the park at (209) 597-2346.

Location: From Visalia, drive east on Highway 198 to its intersection with Highway 65. Continue for eight miles on Highway 198 to the camp on the left.

Trip note: This year-round campground provides an option for campers who want a spot near Lake Kaweah.

3. HORSE CREEK RECREATION AREA   RV 6

Reference: On Lake Kaweah; map G4, grid a8.

Campsites, facilities: There are 80 sites for tents or motor homes. Piped water, fire grills and picnic tables are provided. Flush toilets, showers, a paved boat ramp, and a dump station are available. Some facilities are **wheelchair accessible**. Nearby are a grocery store, laundromat, boat and waterski rentals, ice, a snack bar and propane gas. Pets are allowed on leashes.

Reservations, fee: No reservations; $8-$12 fee per night.

Who to contact: Phone the U.S. Corps of Engineers at (209) 597-2301.

Location: From Visalia, drive 25 miles east on Highway 198 to Lake Kaweah's south shore.

Trip note: The sun brands everything in sight around this part of the valley. Lake Kaweah is the spot folks go for a quick dunk. The camp is set on the southern shore of the lake. Waterskiers tend to monopolize the lake, but in spring, before it gets too hot, trout and bass fishing are decent. The water level drops a great deal during late summer, as thirsty farms suck up every drop they can get. The elevation is 300 feet.

4. SUN AND FUN RV PARK ♿ 🏊 ⚑ RV 1

Reference: **Near Tulare; map G4, grid c3.**

Campsites, facilities: There are 60 motor home sites. Picnic tables, fire grills, piped water and full hookups are provided. Restrooms, showers, a dump station, a playground, a swimming pool, a spa, a laundromat, and a recreation room are available. Some facilities are **wheelchair accessible**. A golf course, a restaurant and a store are nearby. Pets are allowed on leashes.

Reservations, fee: Reservations accepted; $20 fee per night.

Who to contact: Phone the park at (209) 686-5779.

Location: From Tulare, drive three miles south on Highway 99 to the Avenue 200 exit west. Drive a short distance to 1000 Avenue 200. From Tipton, drive 10 miles north on Highway 99. Exit on Avenue 200, bearing right over the freeway to the campground entrance.

Trip note: We figured somebody should give the swimming pool a lifesaver award, so what the heck, we did. This motor home park is just off Highway 99, exactly halfway between San Francisco and Los Angeles. Are you having fun yet?

---

5. THE LAST RESORT 🐟 🏊 RV 4

Reference: **Near Success Lake; map G4, grid d8.**

Campsites, facilities: There are 250 sites for tents or motor homes, 50 with full or partial hookups. Picnic tables and, in some cases, fire grills are provided. Restrooms, showers, a recreation room, a playground, a swimming pool, fishing facilities, a laundromat, a store, a dump station, firewood, a dog-walking area and propane gas are available. Pets are permitted on leashes, but noisy or dangerous pets are not permitted at all.

Reservations, fee: Reservations accepted; $16-$25 fee per night.

Who to contact: Phone the park at (209) 784-3948.

Location: From Porterville on Highway 65, turn east on Highway 190 and drive five miles to 27798 Highway 190.

Trip note: This campground is in a parklike setting with trees and flowers. It is two miles from Success Lake. A small, stocked fishing pond is available, and pet geese and ducks are often wandering around. Open all year.

---

6. TULE RECREATION AREA 🐟 ⚓ 🚶 🏊 🎿 RV 7

Reference: **On Success Lake; map G4, grid d8.**

Campsites, facilities: There are 104 sites for tents or motor homes up to 30 feet long. Piped water, fire grills and picnic tables are provided. Flush toilets, a dump station, and a playground are available. Nearby are a grocery store, a boat ramp, boat and waterski rentals, bait, tackle and propane gas. Pets are permitted on leashes.

Reservations, fee: No reservations; $8-$12 fee per night for regular camping; several primitive, free sites are available; $2 launch fee.

Who to contact: Phone the U.S. Corps of Engineers at (209) 784-0215.

Location: From Porterville, drive eight miles east on Highway 190 to Success Lake and look for the campground entrance on the left.

Trip note: Success Lake is a popular spot for San Joaquin Valley waterskiers. The lake is set in the foothill country, where 100-degree weather is common in the summer. Fishing is best in the spring. The wildlife area along the west side of the lake is worth exploring. You can also hike the nature trail below the dam.

7. COLONEL ALLENSWORTH STATE HISTORIC PARK ⚓

Reference: **Near Earlimart; map G4, grid e1.**

Campsites, facilities: There are 15 sites for tents or motor homes up to 30 feet long. There is also a 51-site overflow area. Piped water, fire grills and picnic tables are provided. Restrooms with hot showers and visitor center are available. A grocery store is 12 miles away in Delano. Pets are permitted on leashes.

Reservations, fee: No reservations; $10 fee per night; $1 pet fee.

Who to contact: Phone the park at (805) 849-3433 or (209) 822-2630.

Location: From Fresno, drive south on Highway 99 about 60 miles to Earlimart. Turn right (west) on Avenue 56 and drive eight miles to the Highway 43 turnoff. Turn left on Highway 43 and travel south two miles to the park exit on the right. Drive 100 yards into the park directly ahead.

Trip note: What you have here is the old town (Allensworth) that has been restored as an historical park dedicated to the African American pioneers who founded it with Colonel Allen Allensworth, the highest ranking army chaplain of his time. One museum is available at the school here and another at the Colonel's house with a 30-minute movie on the history of Allensworth. Open year-round.

8. KOA BAKERSFIELD ♿ ≈

Reference: **Map G4, grid i3.**

Campsites, facilities: There are 12 tent sites and 62 motor home sites. Picnic tables, piped water and full or partial hookups are provided. Restrooms, showers, a swimming pool (in summer), a laundromat, a store, a dump station and propane gas are available. Pets are allowed on leashes.

Reservations, fee: Call for space available; $20-$25 fee per night.

Who to contact: Phone the park at (805) 399-3107.

Location: From Bakersfield, drive 12 miles north on Highway 99 to the Shafter-Lerdo Highway exit. Drive one mile west on Lerdo Way to 5801 Lerdo Highway.

Trip note: If you're stuck in the southern valley and the temperature feels like you're sitting in a cauldron, well, this spot provides a layover for the night, near the town of Shafter. It's not exactly a hotbed of excitement. Open year-round.

9. KERN RIVER COUNTY PARK

Reference: **At Lake Ming; map G4, grid j6.**

Campsites, facilities: There are 50 sites for tents or motor homes. Picnic tables, fire grills and piped water are provided. Flush toilets, showers, a dump station, a playground and a boat ramp are available. Pets are permitted on leashes. A grocery store is nearby.

Reservations, fee: No reservations; $12 fee per night; $2 pet fee.

Who to contact: Phone the County Parks Department at (805) 861-2345 or (805) 872-3179.

Location: From Bakersfield, drive east on Highway 178. Turn left (north) on Alfred Harrell Highway and follow the signs to Lake Ming. Turn left on Lake Ming Road and follow the signs to the campground on the right.

Trip note: This is a popular spot for southern valley residents, since it is only a 15-minute drive from Bakersfield. Waterskiing is permitted on Lake Ming, and dominates summer activity. Recreation options include Hart Park and the Foss-Kern River County Golf Course. The elevation is 450 feet. Open all year.

MAP G5

58 LISTINGS
PAGES 614-635

CEN-CAL MAP .... see page 512
adjoining maps
NORTH (F5) .... see page 564
EAST (G6) .... see page 636
SOUTH (H5) .... see page 674
WEST (G4) .... see page 610

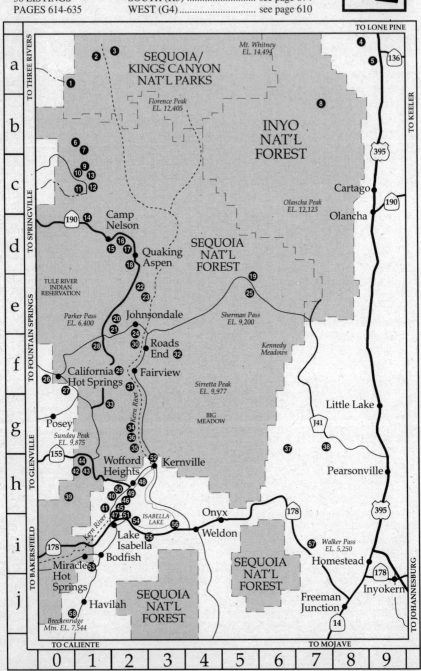

Map G5 featuring: Sequoia National Forest, Tule River, Mountain Home State Forest, John Muir Wilderness, Inyo National Forest, Kern River, Isabella Lake

1. SOUTH FORK 🥾🥾   7

Reference: On the South Fork of Kaweah River in Sequoia National Park; map G5, grid a0.

Campsites, facilities: There are 13 sites for tents only. Picnic tables and fire grills are provided. Pit toilets are available. There is **no piped water**. Pets are permitted on leashes.

Reservations, fee: No reservations; $5 fee per night from mid-May through October; no fee in other months.

Who to contact: Phone the Sequoia National Park at (209) 565-3341.

Location: From Visalia, drive to Three Rivers on Highway 198. In Three Rivers, turn east on South Fork Road and drive 13 miles to the campground.

Trip note: The smallest developed camp in Sequoia National Park might just be what you're looking for. It is set at 3,650 feet on the South Fork of the Kaweah River, just inside the southwestern border of Sequoia National Park. The ranger station here has maps and information. A trail heads east from the camp and traverses Dennison Ridge, eventually leading to Hocket Lakes and connecting to other backcountry trails.

2. ATWELL MILL 🥾🥾   8

Reference: On Atwell Creek in Sequoia National Park; map G5, grid a1.

Campsites, facilities: There are 21 tent sites. Picnic tables, fire grills and piped water are provided. Pit toilets are available. A grocery store is nearby. Pets are permitted on leashes.

Reservations, fee: No reservations; $5 fee per night.

Who to contact: Phone the Sequoia National Park at (209) 565-3341.

Location: From Visalia, take Highway 198 to Three Rivers. Continue north for three miles on Highway 198. Turn right (east) on Mineral King Road and drive 20 miles to the campground. Mineral King Road is quite rough—no RVs or trailers.

Trip note: This small, pretty camp in Sequoia National Park is located on Atwell Creek near the East Fork of the Kaweah River. Trails near camp provide access to the backcountry. The elevation is 6,650 feet. Open from May to September (depending on road and weather conditions).

3. COLD SPRINGS 🥾🥾   9

Reference: On the East Fork of Kaweah River in Sequoia National Park; map G5, grid a2.

Campsites, facilities: There are 40 tent sites. Picnic tables, fire grills and piped water are provided. Pit toilets are available. A grocery store is nearby. Pets are permitted on leashes.

Reservations, fee: No reservations; $5 fee per night.

Who to contact: Phone the Sequoia National Park at (209) 565-3341.

Location: From Visalia, take Highway 198 to Three Rivers. Continue to drive three miles north on Highway 198. Turn right (east) on Mineral King Road and drive 25 miles to the campground.

Trip note: This high country camp at Sequoia National Park is set at 7,500 feet on the East Fork of the Kaweah River. A trail is routed south of camp to a network of backcountry trails, including those to Mosquito Lakes (that sounds like fun, eh?), Eagle Lake, and, for the ambitious, White Chief Lake. Open from May to September.

---

4. TUTTLE CREEK 🏃 RV 4

Reference: **Near Mt. Whitney; map G5, grid a8.**

Campsites, facilities: There are 84 sites for tents or motor homes. There is **no piped water**, but pit toilets, fire grills, a dumpster and picnic tables are provided. Supplies are available in Lone Pine. Pets are permitted on leashes.

Reservations, fee: No reservations; no fee.

Who to contact: Phone the Bureau of Land Management at (619) 872-4881.

Location: From Lone Pine, drive 3.5 miles west on Whitney Portal Road. Turn south on Horseshoe Meadow Road and drive 1.5 miles. Turn west on Tuttle Creek Road (a winding, dirt road) and drive directly into the campground.

Trip note: This primitive, BLM camp is set at the base of Mt. Whitney along Tuttle Creek at 5,100 feet. It is often used as an overflow area if the camps farther up Whitney Portal Road are full. Open from May through October.

---

5. DIAZ LAKE 🐟 ⚓ 🏊 🚣 RV 6

Reference: **Near Lone Pine; map G5, grid a9.**

Campsites, facilities: There are 200 sites for tents or motor homes. Piped water, fire grills and picnic tables are provided. Flush toilets, a solar shower and a boat ramp are available. Supplies and a laundromat are available in Lone Pine. Pets are permitted on leashes.

Reservations, fee: No reservations; $8 fee per night.

Who to contact: Phone the County Parks Department at (619) 878-0272.

Location: From Lone Pine, drive two miles south on US 395 to the entrance on the right.

Trip note: A lot of people don't even know this place exists. It's a small lake near Lone Pine, 3,800 feet, providing an opportunity for boating, waterskiing and trout fishing. A 20-foot limit is enforced for boats. Open year-round.

---

6. HIDDEN FALLS 🐟 🏃 7

Reference: **On Tule River in Mountain Home State Forest; map G5, grid b1.**

Campsites, facilities: There are eight, walk-in sites for tents only. Picnic tables, fire grills and piped water are provided. Pit toilets are available. Pets are permitted on leashes.

Reservations, fee: No reservations; no fee.

Who to contact: Phone the Mountain Home State Forest at (209) 539-2855 or (209) 539-2329.

Location: From Porterville, drive 19 miles east on Highway 190 (one mile past the town of Springville). Turn left (north) onto Balch Park Road and drive about 23 miles to the Mountain Home State Forest sign on the right. Continue on Balch Road, following the signs to the State Forest Headquarters where a box of free forest maps is available. In addition, campgrounds are well-signed from this point. The total trip from the Highway 190/Balch Road turnoff to the campground is about 30 miles. Alternate route: After driving three miles on

Balch Park Road, turn right (east) on Bear Creek Road and drive 25 miles to the campground. This is not a good road for trailers and motor homes.

Trip note: One of the prettier camps in Mountain Home State Forest, this small, quiet camp is set along the Tule River, near Hidden Falls, at 6,000 feet. Open from June to October.

---

7. MOSES GULCH

Reference: **On Tule River in Mountain Home State Forest; map G5, grid b1.**

Campsites, facilities: There are ten sites for tents. Piped water, fire grills and picnic tables are provided. Vault toilets are available. Pets are permitted on leashes.

Reservations, fee: No reservations; no fee.

Who to contact: Phone the Mountain Home State Forest at (209) 539-2855 or (209) 539-2329.

Location: From Porterville, drive 19 miles east on Highway 190 (one mile past the town of Springville). Turn left (north) onto Balch Park Road and drive about 23 miles to the Mountain Home State Forest sign on the right. Continue on Balch Road, following the signs to the State Forest Headquarters where a box of free forest maps is available. In addition, campgrounds are well-signed from this point. The total trip from the Highway 190/Balch Road turnoff to the campground is about 31 miles. Alternate route: After driving three miles on Balch Park Road, turn right (east) on Bear Creek Road and drive 26 miles to the campground. This is not a good road for trailers and motor homes.

Trip note: This is another in the series of camps in the remote Mountain Home State Forest, so take your pick. And you can't beat the price.

---

8. HORSESHOE MEADOW

Reference: **Near John Muir Wilderness in Inyo National Forest; map G5, grid b7.**

Campsites, facilities: There are several walk-in sites and a few drive-in equestrian sites. Vault toilets, piped water, picnic tables, fire grills, a pack station and horseback riding facilities are available. Pets are permitted on leashes.

Reservations, fee: No reservations, $5 fee per night for walk-in sites; $10 for equestrians.

Who to contact: Call the Inyo National Forest Mt. Whitney Ranger District at (619) 876-6200.

Location: From Lone Pine, drive 3.5 miles west on Whitney Portal Road. Turn left on Horseshoe Meadows Road and drive 19 miles to the end of the road.

Trip note: This is an alternative for backpackers who want to avoid the mob climbing Mt. Whitney. The camp is set at 10,000 feet on the border of the John Muir Wilderness and Golden Trout Wilderness. Open from mid-May through mid-October.

---

9. FRAZIER MILL

Reference: **In Mountain Home State Forest; map G5, grid c1.**

Campsites, facilities: There are 46 sites for tents and a few motor homes. Piped water, fire grills and picnic tables are provided. Vault toilets are available. Pets are permitted on leashes.

Reservations, fee: No reservations; no fee.

Who to contact: Phone the Mountain Home State Forest at (209) 539-2855 or

(209) 539-2329.

Location: From Porterville, drive 19 miles east on Highway 190 (one mile past the town of Springville). Turn left (north) onto Balch Park Road and drive about 23 miles to the Mountain Home State Forest sign on the right. Continue on Balch Road, following the signs to the State Forest Headquarters where a box of free forest maps is available. In addition, campgrounds are well-signed from this point. The total trip from the Highway 190/Balch Road turnoff to the campground is about 35 miles. Alternate route: After driving three miles on Balch Park Road, turn right (east) on Bear Creek Road and drive 17 miles to the campground. However, this is not a good road for trailers and motor homes.

Trip note: The prime attraction here is the many old-growth giant Sequoias. A Forest Information Trail and the trailhead leading into the Golden Trout Wilderness are nearby. The Wishon Fork of the Tule River is the largest of the several streams that pass through this forest. And hey, you can't beat the price. Open from June to October.

---

10. SHAKE CAMP 🚶🏇   6

Reference: **In Mountain Home State Forest; map G5, grid c1.**

Campsites, facilities: There are 11 sites for tents or motor homes. Piped water, fire grills and picnic tables are provided. Vault toilets are available, and a public pack station with corrals is available nearby. Pets are permitted on leashes.

Reservations, fee: No reservations; no fee.

Who to contact: Phone the Mountain Home State Forest at (209) 539-2855 or (209) 539-2329.

Location: From Porterville, drive 19 miles east on Highway 190 (one mile past the town of Springville). Turn left (north) onto Balch Park Road and drive about 23 miles to the Mountain Home State Forest sign on the right. Continue on Balch Road, following the signs to the State Forest Headquarters where a box of free forest maps is available. In addition, campgrounds are well-signed from this point. The total trip from the Highway 190/Balch Road turnoff to the campground is about 36 miles. Alternate route: After driving three miles on Balch Park Road, turn right (east) on Bear Creek Road and drive 21 miles to the campground. This is not a good road for trailers and motor homes.

Trip note: This is a rare spot for horseback riding. Horses can be rented for the day, hour or night. This is a popular spot for backpackers. It is set at 6,500 feet and there's a trailhead here for a hiking trip into the Golden Trout Wilderness. The Balch Park Pack Station, a commercial outfitter, is located nearby, so you can expect horse traffic on the trail. Open from June to October.

---

11. BALCH COUNTY PARK 🚶♿   RV 6

Reference: **In Mountain Home State Forest; map G5, grid c1.**

Campsites, facilities: There are 71 sites for tents or motor homes up to 30 feet long. Piped water, fire grills and picnic tables are provided. Flush toilets are available. Pets are permitted on leashes.

Reservations, fee: No reservations; $8 fee per night; $1 pet fee.

Who to contact: Phone the park at (209) 733-6612.

Location: From Porterville, drive 19 miles east on Highway 190 (one mile past the town of Springville). Turn left (north) onto Balch Park Road and drive three miles to Bear Creek Road. Turn east (right) and drive 15 miles to the campground (trailers not recommended). Alternate route: After turning north onto Balch Park Road, drive 40 miles to the park.

Trip note: Secluded, hard-to-reach? Yes, and that's just what folks want here. Mountain Home State Forest has eight campgrounds, all surrounded by state land and Sequoia National Forest. Nearby there's a grove of giant Sequoias that's an attraction. The elevation is 6,500 feet. Open from May to October.

---

12. METHUSELAH GROUP CAMP 🥾   RV 6

Reference: **In Mountain Home State Forest; map G5, grid c1.**

Campsites, facilities: This group site can accommodate 20 to 100 people in tents or motor homes. Fire grills and some picnic tables are provided. Vault toilets are available. Pets are permitted on leashes. There is **no piped water**, so bring your own.

Reservations, fee: Reservations required; no fee.

Who to contact: Phone the Mountain Home State Forest at (209) 539-2855 or (209) 539-2329.

Location: From Porterville, drive 19 miles east on Highway 190 (one mile past the town of Springville). Turn left (north) onto Balch Park Road and drive about 23 miles to the Mountain Home State Forest sign on the right. Continue on Balch Road, following the signs to the State Forest Headquarters where a box of free forest maps is available. In addition, campgrounds are well-signed from this point. The total trip from the Highway 190/Balch Road turnoff to the campground is about 40 miles. Alternate route: After turning north onto Balch Park Road, drive 40 miles to the campground.

Trip note: This is one of the few free group camps available anywhere in California. Remember to bring water. The elevation is 5,900 feet. Open from June to October.

---

13. HEDRICK POND 🐟 🥾   RV 6

Reference: **In Mountain Home State Forest; map G5, grid c1.**

Campsites, facilities: There are 14 sites for tents or motor homes. Piped water, fire grills and picnic tables are provided. Vault toilets are available. Pets are permitted on leashes.

Reservations, fee: No reservations; no fee.

Who to contact: Phone the Mountain Home State Forest at (209) 539-2855 or (209) 539-2329.

Location: From Porterville, drive 19 miles east on Highway 190 (one mile past the town of Springville). Turn left (north) onto Balch Park Road and drive about 23 miles to the Mountain Home State Forest sign on the right. Continue on Balch Road, following the signs to the State Forest Headquarters where a box of free forest maps is available. In addition, campgrounds are well-signed from this point. The total trip from the Highway 190/Balch Road turnoff to the campground is about 35 miles. Alternate route: After driving three miles on Balch Park Road, turn right (east) on Bear Creek Road and drive 16 miles to the campground. However, this is not a good road for trailers and motor homes.

Trip note: Take your pick of the eight camps at Mountain Home State Forest at about 6,300 feet. The beautiful country is highlighted by the giant Sequoias, and Hedrick Pond provides a fishing opportunity, being stocked occasionally with rainbow trout. Open from June through October.

14. WISHON 🐟 🥾　　　　　　　RV 8

Reference: **On Tule River in Sequoia National Forest; map G5, grid d1.**

Campsites, facilities: There are nine sites for tents only and 26 sites for tents or motor homes up to 22 feet long. Picnic tables, fire grills and piped water are provided. Vault toilets are available. Pets are permitted on leashes.

Reservations, fee: For reservations, phone (800) 280-CAMP; $12 fee per night.

Who to contact: Phone the Sequoia National Forest Tule River Ranger District at (209) 539-2607.

Location: From Porterville, drive 25 miles east on Highway 190. Turn north (left) on County Road 208 (Wishon Drive) and drive 3.5 miles. This camp is located at the bottom of a canyon.

Trip note: There are two trails routed northeast right out of camp, including one that is routed northeast out of the camp along the Middle Fork that heads to Mountain Home State Forest. The elevation is 4,000 feet. Open from April to October.

---

15. COY FLAT 🐟 🥾　　　　　　　RV 4

Reference: **In Sequoia National Forest; map G5, grid d2.**

Campsites, facilities: There are 20 sites for tents or motor homes up to 22 feet long. Piped water, fire grills and picnic tables are provided. Vault toilets are available. Pets are permitted on leashes.

Reservations, fee: For reservations, phone (800) 280-CAMP; $10 fee per night.

Who to contact: Phone the Sequoia National Forest Tule River Ranger District at (209) 539-2607.

Location: From Porterville, drive 34 miles east on Highway 190 to Camp Nelson. Turn right (south) on Forest Service Road 21S94 and drive one mile.

Trip note: This is just far enough off the beaten path to get missed by most vacationers. It is set on Coy Creek at 5,000 feet. For hikers, there is a trail that is routed through Belknap Camp Grove and then south along Slate Mountain. Open from May to November 15.

---

16. BELKNAP 🐟 🥾　　　　　　　RV 7

Reference: **On the South Middle Fork of Tule Creek in Sequoia National Forest; map G5, grid d2.**

Campsites, facilities: There are 15 sites for tents or motor homes up to 22 feet long. Trailers are prohibited in this area. Piped water, fire grills, picnic tables and vault toilets are available. A grocery store is nearby. Pets are permitted on leashes.

Reservations, fee: For reservations, phone (800) 280-CAMP; $10 fee per night.

Who to contact: Phone the Sequoia National Forest Tule River Ranger District at (209) 539-2607.

Location: From Porterville, drive 34 miles east on Highway 190 to Camp Nelson. Turn right (east) on Nelson Drive and drive one mile to the campground.

Trip note: This quiet spot is set on the South Middle Fork of Tule Creek near McIntyre Grove and Belknap Camp Grove. A trail leads out of camp past Wheel Meadow Grove and winds through the backcountry. The elevation is 5,000 feet. Open from April to October.

17. QUAKING ASPEN GROUP CAMP

Reference: **Near Freeman Creek in Sequoia National Forest; map G5, grid d2.**

Campsites, facilities: There are three group sites for 12 people, two group sites for 25 people and two group sites for 50 people, suitable for tents. Piped water, fire grills, picnic tables and vault toilets are available. A grocery store is nearby. Pets are permitted.

Reservations, fee: For reservations, phone (800) 280-CAMP; $18-$75 group fee per night, depending on group size.

Who to contact: Phone the Sequoia National Forest Tule River Ranger District at (209) 539-2607.

Location: From Porterville, drive 34 miles east on Highway 190 to Camp Nelson. Continue about 11 miles east on Highway 190 to the campground.

Trip note: This is a group camp option to Peppermint Camp. See that trip note for sidetrips. The elevation is 7,000 feet. Open from May to October.

18. QUAKING ASPEN

Reference: **In Sequoia National Forest; map G5, grid d2.**

Campsites, facilities: There are 32 sites for tents or motor homes up to 22 feet long. Piped water, fire grills picnic tables and vault toilets are available. A grocery store is nearby. Pets are permitted on leashes.

Reservations, fee: For reservations, phone (800) 280-CAMP; $12 fee per night.

Who to contact: Phone the Sequoia National Forest Tule River Ranger District at (209) 539-2607.

Location: From Porterville, drive 34 miles east on Highway 190 to Camp Nelson. Continue 11 miles east of Camp Nelson on Highway 190.

Trip note: A pretty spot, especially in the fall, set at 7,000 feet near the head of Freeman Creek. A trail passes through camp that accesses other trails leading into the backcountry. Open from May to November 15.

19. TROY MEADOW

Reference: **On Fish Creek in Sequoia National Forest; map G5, grid d5.**

Campsites, facilities: There are 10 sites for tents only and 63 sites for tents or motor homes up to 22 feet long. Piped water, fire grills and picnic tables are provided. Vault toilets are available. Pets are permitted on leashes.

Reservations, fee: No reservations; no fee.

Who to contact: Phone the Sequoia National Forest Cannell Meadow Ranger District at (619) 376-3781.

Location: From the town of Brown on Highway 14, drive four miles north. Turn left (west) on Nine Mile Canyon Road and drive 31 miles northwest (road becomes Sherman Pass Road) to the campground.

Trip note: Obscure? Yes, but what the heck, it gives you an idea of what is possible out in the boondocks. The camp is set at 7,800 feet right along Fish Creek. An information station is available two miles northwest. You are advised to stop there prior to any backcountry trips. Off-highway-vehicle trails are available. Open from May to November.

20. LONG MEADOW 🐟 🚶   RV 6

Reference: In Sequoia National Forest; map G5, grid e1.

Campsites, facilities: There are four sites for tents or motor homes up to 16 feet long. Fire grills and picnic tables are provided. Vault toilets are available. There is **no piped water**, so bring your own. Pets are permitted on leashes.

Reservations, fee: For reservations, phone (800) 280-CAMP; $10 fee per night.

Who to contact: Phone the Sequoia National Forest Hot Springs Ranger District at (805) 548-6503.

Location: From Highway 99 in Earlimart, take the County Road J22 (Avenue 56) exit and drive east for 39 miles to the town of California Hot Springs. Turn north (left) on County Road M50 (Parker Pass Road) and drive 12 miles. Turn left on M107 (Western Divide Highway) and drive four miles to the entrance.

Trip note: This is a nearby option to the Redwood Meadow Camp, where the Trail of the Hundred Giants is an attraction. The elevation is 6,500 feet. Open from June to September.

21. REDWOOD MEADOW 🚶🚶 ♿   RV 7

Reference: Near Parker Meadow Creek in Sequoia National Forest; map G5, grid e1.

Campsites, facilities: There are 14 sites for tents or motor homes up to 40 feet long. Piped water, fire grills and picnic tables are provided. Vault toilets are available. Pets are permitted on leashes.

Reservations, fee: For reservations, phone (800) 280-CAMP; $12 fee per night.

Who to contact: Phone the Sequoia National Forest Hot Springs Ranger District at (805) 548-6503.

Location: From Highway 99 in Earlimart, take the County Road J22 (Avenue 56) exit and drive east for 39 miles to the town of California Hot Springs. Turn north (left) on County Road M50 (Parker Pass Road) and drive 12 miles. Turn left on M107 (Western Divide Highway) and drive three miles to the entrance.

Trip note: The highlight here is the half-mile Trail of the Hundred Giants, which is routed through a grove of giant Sequoias. It is usable by **wheelchair** hikers. The camp is set near Parker Meadow Creek. The elevation is 6,500 feet. If this camp is full, the Long Meadow Camp provides a nearby option. This is a popular camp, so get here early. Open from June to September.

22. PEPPERMINT 🐟 🚶   RV 7

Reference: On Peppermint Creek in Sequoia National Forest; map G5, grid e2.

Campsites, facilities: There are 19 sites for tents or motor homes up to 22 feet long. Fire rings and picnic tables are provided. Vault toilets are available. There is **no piped water**, so bring your own. A grocery store is nearby. Pets are permitted on leashes. A fire permit is required.

Reservations, fee: No reservations; no fee.

Who to contact: Phone the Sequoia National Forest Tule River Ranger District at (209) 539-2607.

Location: From Porterville, drive 34 miles east on Highway 190 to Camp Nelson. Continue about 15 miles southeast on Highway 190 to the entrance road.

Trip note: This is one of the two primitive camps at Peppermint Creek, but the two are not directly connected by a road. Several backcountry roads are in the area, detailed on a Forest Service map, and can make for some self-styled fortune hunts. For the ambitious, hiking the trail at the end of Forest Service Road 21S05 can lead to a fantastic lookout at The Needles (8,245 feet). The camp elevation is 7,100 feet. Open from May to October.

23. LOWER PEPPERMINT
Reference: **In Sequoia National Forest; map G5, grid e2.**
Campsites, facilities: There are 17 sites for tents or motor homes up to 40 feet long. Piped water, fire grills and picnic tables are provided. Vault toilets are available. Pets are permitted on leashes.
Reservations, fee: No reservations; $10 fee per night.
Who to contact: Phone the Sequoia National Forest Hot Springs Ranger District at (805) 548-6503.
Location: From the town of Lake Isabella, drive 35 miles north on Burlando Road and Sierra Way to the town of Johnsondale. Turn right (north) on Forest Service Road 22S82 (Lloyd Meadow Road) and drive about 14 miles on a paved road to the campground.
Trip note: This is a little-known camp in the Sequoia National Forest, set along Peppermint Creek at 5,300 feet. Many backcountry roads are available in the area, which are detailed on a Forest Service map. Open from June to October.

24. LIMESTONE
Reference: **On Kern River in Sequoia National Forest; map G5, grid e2.**
Campsites, facilities: There are 12 sites for tents only and 10 sites for tents or motor homes up to 22 feet long. Fire grills and picnic tables are provided. Vault toilets are available. There is **no piped water**, so bring your own. Pets are permitted on leashes. Supplies and a laundromat are available in Kernville.
Reservations, fee: For reservations, phone (800) 280-CAMP; $8 fee per night.
Who to contact: Phone the Sequoia National Forest Cannell Meadow Ranger District at (619) 376-3781.
Location: From Kernville, drive 19 miles north on Kern River Highway-Sierra Way Road.
Trip note: This is a small camp along the Kern River, set deep in the Sequoia National Forest at 3,800 feet. It is advisable to obtain a Forest Service map, which details the back roads. A mile to the west, South Creek Falls provides a possible sidetrip. Open from April through November.

25. FISH CREEK
Reference: **In Sequoia National Forest; map G5, grid e5.**
Campsites, facilities: There are 40 sites for tents or motor homes up to 22 feet long. Piped water, fire grills and picnic tables are provided. Vault toilets are available. A grocery store is nearby. Pets are allowed on leashes.
Reservations, fee: No reservations; no fee.
Who to contact: Phone the Sequoia National Forest Cannell Meadow Ranger District at (619) 376-3781.
Location: From Highway 395, 15 miles north of China Lake, turn left (west) on Nine Mile Canyon Road and drive 28 miles northwest (the road becomes Sherman Pass Road) to the campground.
Trip note: This is a pretty spot set at the confluence of Fish Creek and Jackass

Creek. They provide piped water, yet don't charge campers for its use. The elevation is 7,400 feet. Open from May to November. The nearby off-highway-vehicle trails can make this a noisy campground in the daytime.

26. LEAVIS FLAT

Reference: On Deer Creek in Sequoia National Forest; map G5, grid f0.

Campsites, facilities: There are five sites for tents only and four sites for motor homes up to 16 feet long. Piped water, fire grills and picnic tables are provided. Vault toilets are available. A grocery store, a laundromat and propane gas can be found nearby. Pets are permitted on leashes.

Reservations, fee: For reservations, phone (800) 280-CAMP; $10 fee per night.

Who to contact: Phone the Sequoia National Forest Hot Springs Ranger District at (805) 548-6503.

Location: From Highway 99 in Earlimart, take the County Road J22 (Avenue 56) exit and drive east for 39 miles to the campground. Or from Highway 65 follow the California Hot Springs Resort signs from Ducor.

Trip note: This is an easy-to-reach camp set on the western border of Sequoia National Forest along Deer Creek. The elevation is 3,100 feet. Open year-round.

27. WHITE RIVER

Reference: In Sequoia National Forest; map G5, grid f0.

Campsites, facilities: There are eight sites for tents and four sites for motor homes up to 16 feet long. Piped water, fire grills and picnic tables are provided. Vault toilets are available. Pets are permitted on leashes.

Reservations, fee: For reservations, phone (800) 280-CAMP; $10 fee per night.

Who to contact: Phone the Sequoia National Forest Hot Springs Ranger District at (805) 548-6503.

Location: From Highway 155 just west of Glennville, turn north on Linns Valley Road and drive about 2.5 miles. Turn left on County Road M10 and drive through Idlewild. Continue northeast on Forest Service Road 24S05 (dirt road) for six more miles.

Trip note: This relatively obscure spot gets missed by plenty of folks who wished they knew about it. The camp is set at 4,000 feet along the White River. It is advisable to obtain a Forest Service map. Open from May to October.

28. HOLEY MEADOW

Reference: On Double Bunk Creek in Sequoia National Forest; map G5, grid f1.

Campsites, facilities: There are 10 sites for tents or motor homes up to 16 feet long. Piped water, fire grills and picnic tables are provided. Vault toilets are available. Pets are permitted on leashes.

Reservations, fee: For reservations, phone (800) 280-CAMP; $10 fee per night.

Who to contact: Phone the Sequoia National Forest Hot Springs Ranger District at (805) 548-6503.

Location: From Highway 99 in Earlimart, take the County Road J22 (Avenue 56) exit and drive east for 39 miles to the town of California Hot Springs. Turn north (left) on County Road M50 (Parker Pass Road) and drive 12 miles. Turn left on M107 (Western Divide Highway) and drive a half mile to the entrance.

Trip note: This is a shaded, quiet spot to hunker down for awhile, maybe to lean against a tree and not be bugged by anything. The elevation is 6,400 feet. Open from June to October.

29. FROG MEADOW

Reference: **In Sequoia National Forest; map G5, grid f1.**

Campsites, facilities: There are 10 sites for tents or motor homes up to 16 feet long. Fire grills and picnic tables are provided. Vault toilets are available. Pets are permitted on leashes. There is **no piped water.**

Reservations, fee: No reservations; no fee.

Who to contact: Phone the Sequoia National Forest Hot Springs Ranger District at (805) 548-6503.

Location: From Highway 155 just west of Glennville, turn north on Linns Valley Road (County Road M3 and drive about four miles. Turn left onto the County Road (M-9) and drive 4.5 miles to Guernsey Mill (Sugarloaf Lodge) and this continues on Sugarloaf Road (Forest Service Road 23S16) for about seven miles. Turn left on Forest Service Road 24S50 (dirt road) to Frog Meadow and the campground.

Trip note: This small, primitive camp, set near Tobias Creek at 7,500 feet, is used primarily by hunters in the fall. Several trails, sometimes used by motorcyclists, lead out from the camp. Open from June to October.

30. FAIRVIEW

Reference: **On Kern River in Sequoia National Forest; map G5, grid f2.**

Campsites, facilities: There are 55 sites for tents or motor homes up to 27 feet long. Piped water, fire grills and picnic tables are provided. Vault toilets are available. Some sites are **wheelchair accessible**. Pets are permitted on leashes. Supplies and a laundromat are available in Kernville.

Reservations, fee: For reservations, phone (800) 280-CAMP; $12 fee per night.

Who to contact: Phone the Sequoia National Forest Kernville Office at (619) 376-3781.

Location: From Kernville, drive 16 miles north on Kern River Highway-Sierra Road to the town of Fairview. The campground is at north end of town.

Trip note: Easy-to-reach, easy-to-like, this Forest Service camp is set on the Kern River. The elevation is 3,500 feet. Open from May to October.

31. GOLD LEDGE

Reference: **On Kern River in Sequoia National Forest; map G5, grid f2.**

Campsites, facilities: There are 37 sites for tents or motor homes up to 22 feet long. Piped water, fire grills and picnic tables are provided. Vault toilets are available. Pets are permitted on leashes. Supplies and a laundromat are available in Kernville.

Reservations, fee: For reservations, phone (800) 280-CAMP ; $12 fee per night.

Who to contact: Phone the Sequoia National Forest Kernville Office at (619) 376-3781.

Location: From Kernville, drive 10 miles north on Kern River Highway-Sierra Way Road to the campground.

Trip note: This is another in the series of camps on the Kern River, north of Lake Isabella. This one is set at 3,200 feet. Open from May to September.

32. HORSE MEADOW 🐟 🚶‍♀️   RV 8

Reference: **On Salmon Creek in Sequoia National Forest; map G5, grid f3.**

Campsites, facilities: There are 18 sites for tents only and 15 sites for tents or motor homes up to 23 feet long. Piped water, fire grills and picnic tables are provided. Vault toilets are available. Pets are permitted on leashes. Pack out your garbage.

Reservations, fee: No reservations; $5 fee per night.

Who to contact: Phone the Sequoia National Forest Kernville Office at (619) 376-3781.

Location: From Kernville, drive north on Sierra Way for about 20 miles to the sign that says "Highway 395-Black Rock Ranger Station." Make a sharp right on Sherman Pass Road and drive about 6.5 miles to Cherry Hill Road (Forest Service Road 22512). There is a green gate with a sign that says "Horse Meadow-Big Meadow." Turn right and drive for about four miles. The road becomes dirt, and continues for about another three miles (follow the signs) to the campground entrance road.

Trip note: This is a virtually unknown spot set along Salmon Creek at 7,600 feet. It is a very pretty area of big meadows, forests and backcountry roads. A trail starts at the camp and follows along Salmon Creek to Salmon Creek Falls, a good sidetrip. Open from June to November.

33. PANORAMA 🚶‍♀️   5

Reference: **In Sequoia National Forest; map G5, grid g1.**

Campsites, facilities: There are 10 sites for tents or motor homes up to 40 feet long. Fire grills and picnic tables are provided. Vault toilets are available. There is **no piped water**, so bring your own. Pets are permitted on leashes.

Reservations, fee: No reservations; no fee.

Who to contact: Phone the Sequoia National Forest Hot Springs Ranger District at (805) 548-6503.

Location: From Highway 155 just west of Glennville, turn north on Linns Valley Road (County Road M3 and drive about four miles. Turn left onto County Road M-9 and drive about 4.5 miles to Guernsey Mill (Sugarloaf Lodge), and then continue on via Sugarloaf Road 23S16 for about six miles to the campground (paved all the way).

Trip note: This pretty spot, set near the end of an old logging spur, is the kind of place not many folks have a clue exists. Nearby Portuguese Pass provides a lookout and Portuguese Meadow a spot for lunch. The elevation is 6,800 feet. Open from June to September.

34. HOSPITAL FLAT 🐟 🏊 🍴   RV 8

Reference: **On the North Fork of Kern River in Sequoia National Forest; map G5, grid g2.**

Campsites, facilities: There are 40 sites for tents or motor homes up to 22 feet long. Piped water, fire grills and picnic tables are provided. Vault toilets are available. Pets are permitted on leashes. Supplies and a laundromat are available in Kernville.

Reservations, fee: For reservations, phone (800) 280-CAMP; $12 fee per night.

Who to contact: Phone the Sequoia National Forest Kernville Office at (619) 376-3781.

Location: From Kernville, drive seven miles north on Kern River Highway-Sierra Way Road to the campground.

Trip note: It's kind of like the old shell game, trying to pick the best of the camps set along the North Fork of the Kern River. This one is set seven miles north of Lake Isabella. The elevation is 2,800 feet. Open from May to September.

35. HEADQUARTERS ⌐🐟🏊🍴   RV 8

Reference: **On the North Fork of Kern River in Sequoia National Forest; map G5, grid g2.**

Campsites, facilities: There are 44 sites for tents or motor homes up to 22 feet long. Piped water, fire grills and picnic tables are provided. Vault toilets are available. Some facilities are **wheelchair accessible.** Supplies and a laundromat are available in Kernville. Pets are allowed on leashes.

Reservations, fee: For reservations, phone (800) 280-CAMP; $12 fee per night.

Who to contact: Phone the Sequoia National Forest Kernville Office at (619) 376-3781.

Location: From Kernville, drive three miles north on Sierra Way to the campground.

Trip note: As you head north from Lake Isabella on Sierra Way, this is the first in a series of Forest Service campgrounds that you have your pick of, all of them set along the North Fork of the Kern River. The North Fork is known for offering prime kayaking water. The elevation is 2,700 feet. Open year-round.

36. CAMP 3 ⌐🐟🏊🍴   RV 9

Reference: **On the North Fork of the Kern River in Sequoia National Forest; map G5, grid g2.**

Campsites, facilities: There are 52 sites for tents or motor homes up to 22 feet long. Piped water, fire grills and picnic tables are provided. Vault toilets are available. Pets are permitted on leashes. Supplies and a laundromat are available in Kernville.

Reservations, fee: For reservations, phone (800) 280-CAMP; $12 fee per night.

Who to contact: Phone the Sequoia National Forest Kernville Office at (619) 376-3781.

Location: From Kernville, drive five miles northwest on Kern River Highway-Sierra Way Road to the campground.

Trip note: This is one in a series of camps located along the Kern River, north of Lake Isabella (this camp is five miles north). These camps provide excellent put-in and take-out spots for kayakers. If you don't like this spot, the next camp is just two miles upriver. The elevation is 2,800 feet. Open from May to September.

37. LONG VALLEY ⌐🐟🥾🏊🍴   5% CLUB 5

Reference: **Near Dome Land Wilderness Area; map G5, grid g6.**

Campsites, facilities: There are 13 tent sites. Non-potable piped water, fire grills and picnic tables are provided. Pit toilets are available. Pack out your garbage. Pets are allowed on leashes.

Reservations, fee: No reservations; no fee.

Who to contact: Phone the Bureau of Land Management at (805) 391-6000.

Location: From north of San Bernardino, drive north on US 395 to the junction of US 395 and Highway 14. Continue north for 11 miles to Pearsonville. At

Pearsonville, continue two miles north to Nine Mile Canyon Road (at the Kennedy Meadows sign). Turn left (west) and drive 11 miles to the BLM Work Station. Turn left on the dirt road opposite the station and drive 14 miles.

Trip note: This one is way out there in booger country. It's set in Long Valley, a good spot for backpackers to take a leap into the surrounding wildlands. A trail from camp leads 2.5 miles west to the South Fork of the Kern River and the Dome Land Wilderness Area. The elevation is 5,200 feet. Open year-round.

38. CHIMNEY CREEK 🚶🚶

Reference: **On Pacific Crest Trail; map G5, grid g7.**

Campsites, facilities: There are 36 sites for tents or motor homes up to 25 feet long. Non-potable piped water, fire grills and picnic tables are provided. Pit toilets are available. Please pack out your own garbage. Pets are allowed on leashes.

Reservations, fee: No reservations, no fee.

Who to contact: Phone the Bureau of Land Management at (805) 391-6000.

Location: From north of San Bernardino, drive north on US 395 to the junction of US 395 and Highway 14. Continue north for 11 miles to Pearsonville. At Pearsonville, continue two miles north to Nine Mile Canyon Road (at the Kennedy Meadows sign). Turn left (west) and drive 11 miles to the BLM Work Station. Turn left on the dirt road opposite the station and drive three miles.

Trip note: This is one of the premium launching pads for a first-class backpacking trip. The Pacific Crest Trail runs right through camp, providing the ideal trailhead. Set at 5,900 feet on Chimney Creek. Open year-round.

39. EVANS FLAT 🚶🚶🐎

Reference: **In Sequoia National Forest; map G5, grid h0.**

Campsites, facilities: There are 20 sites for tents or motor homes up to 16 feet long. Fire grills and picnic tables are provided. Portable restroom is available. There is **no piped water** at this site, so bring your own. Four corrals with water troughs (though water for the troughs is not always available) and a pasture area are provided for horses. Pets are allowed on leashes.

Reservations, fee: No reservations; no fee.

Who to contact: Phone the Sequoia National Forest Greenhorn District at (805) 871-2223.

Location: From Greenhorn Summit on Highway 155, turn south on Rancheria Road (paved, then dirt) and drive 8.3 miles to the campground.

Trip note: You have to earn this one, but if you want solitude, Evans Flat can provide it. It is set at 6,200 feet, with Woodward Peak located a half mile to the east (an obvious sidetrip). Open from May to October.

40. HUNGRY GULCH 🚶🐟⚓🏊🏄

Reference: **On Lake Isabella; map G5, grid h1.**

Campsites, facilities: There are 78 sites for tents, motor homes or trailers. Piped water, fire grills and picnic tables are provided. Flush toilets, showers and a playground are available. Pets are permitted on leashes. Supplies and a laundromat are available in the town of Lake Isabella.

Reservations, fee: For reservations, phone (800) 280-CAMP; $14 fee per night.

Who to contact: Phone the Sequoia National Forest Lake Isabella Office at (619) 379-5646.

Location: From the town of Lake Isabella, drive four miles north on Highway 155 to the campground.

Trip note: This camp is located just across from Boulder Gulch Camp, near Lake Isabella. For details, see that trip note. Open from April through September.

41. PIONEER POINT

Reference: **On Lake Isabella; map G5, grid h1.**

Campsites, facilities: There are 78 sites for tents, motor homes or trailers up to 30 feet long. Piped water, fire grills and picnic tables are provided. Flush toilets, showers, a playground and a fish cleaning station are available. A boat ramp is three miles from camp. Pets are permitted on leashes. Supplies and a laundromat are available in the town of Lake Isabella.

Reservations, fee: For reservations, phone (800) 280-CAMP; $14 fee per night.

Who to contact: Phone the Sequoia National Forest Lake Isabella Office at (619) 379-5646.

Location: From the town of Lake Isabella, drive 2.5 miles on Highway 155 to the campground.

Trip note: Pioneer Point is one of the two camps in the immediate area near the main dam at Lake Isabella. For details, see the trip note for the French Gulch, Boulder Gulch or Camp 9. The elevation is 2,650 feet. Open year-round.

42. ALDER CREEK

Reference: **In Sequoia National Forest; map G5, grid h1.**

Campsites, facilities: There are 12 sites for tents or motor homes up to 20 feet long. Fire grills and picnic tables are provided. Vault toilets are available. There is **no piped water**, so bring your own. Pets are permitted on leashes.

Reservations, fee: No reservations; no fee.

Who to contact: Phone the Sequoia National Forest Greenhorn Ranger District at (805) 871-2223.

Location: From Glennville, drive about eight miles east on Highway 155. Turn right (south) on Alder Creek Road and drive three miles to the campground.

Trip note: This primitive camp is just a quarter of a mile upstream from where Alder Creek meets Slick Rock Creek. There is a trail that runs north two miles along Slick Rock Creek. The elevation is 3,900 feet. Open from May to November.

43. GREENHORN MOUNTAIN PARK

Reference: **Near Shirley Meadows; map G5, grid h1.**

Campsites, facilities: There are 91 sites for tents or motor homes up to 24 feet long. Piped water, fire grills and picnic table are provided. Flush toilets and showers are available. Pets are permitted on leashes.

Reservations, fee: Reservations for groups only; $6 fee per night; $2 pet fee.

Who to contact: Phone the County Parks Department at (805) 861-2345 for group reservation or Sequoia National Forest Lake Isabella Office at (619) 379-5646 for information.

Location: From Wofford Heights (on the west shore of Lake Isabella), drive 10 miles west on Highway 155 to the park on the left side of the highway.

Trip note: This county campground is open all year and is near the Shirley Meadows ski area (open on weekends during the snow season). There are numerous back roads that can provide some sidetrips, all detailed on a Forest Service map. This camp is closed in the winter. The park covers 160 acres, the camp is set at 6,000 feet elevation.

44. CEDAR CREEK 🐟

Reference: **In Sequoia National Forest; map G5, grid h1.**

Campsites, facilities: There are 10 sites for tents only. Piped water (only from May to October), picnic tables, and fire grills are provided and restrooms are available. Pets are permitted on leashes.

Reservations, fee: No reservations; no fee.

Who to contact: Phone the Sequoia National Forest Greenhorn Ranger District at (805) 871-2223.

Location: From Glennville on Highway 155, drive nine miles east on Highway 155 to the campground. Or from Wofford Heights (on the west shore of Lake Isabella), drive 11 miles west on Highway 155 to the campground.

Trip note: This is a little-used Forest Service camp set along Cedar Creek, with easy access off "Highway" 155. Greenhorn Summit and Alder Creek provide alternatives. The elevation is 4,800 feet. Open year-round.

45. FRENCH GULCH GROUP CAMP   RV. **9**

🐟 ⚓ ♿ 🏊 🎣

Reference: **On Lake Isabella; map G5, grid h2.**

Campsites, facilities: There is one large group campsite for up to 100 people with tents or motor homes. Picnic tables, fire grills and piped water are provided. Flush toilets and solar-heated showers are available. A grocery store, a laundromat and propane gas are nearby. Pets are allowed on leashes.

Reservations, fee: For reservations, phone (800) 280-CAMP; $60 group fee per night.

Who to contact: Phone the Sequoia National Forest Lake Isabella Office at (619) 379-5646.

Location: From the town of Lake Isabella, drive three miles on Highway 155 to the campground entrance on the right.

Trip note: Take your pick from another in the series of camps along Lake Isabella. Rental boats are available at one of several marinas nearby. Sidetrips include the town of Keysville, the first of the gold rush towns on the Kern River. The elevation is 2,700 feet. Open year-round.

46. BOULDER GULCH 🐟 ⚓ ♿ 🏊 🎣   RV. **8**

Reference: **On Lake Isabella; map G5, grid h2.**

Campsites, facilities: There are 78 sites for tents, trailers or motor homes up to 30 feet long. Piped water, fire grills and picnic tables are provided. Flush toilets, showers, a playground and a fish cleaning station are available. Some facilities are **wheelchair accessible**. Pets are permitted on leashes. Supplies and a laundromat available in the town of Lake Isabella.

Reservations, fee: For reservations, phone (800) 280-CAMP; $14 fee per night.

Who to contact: Phone the Sequoia National Forest Lake Isabella Office at (619) 379-5646.

Location: From the town of Lake Isabella, drive four miles north on Highway 155.

Trip note: Boulder Gulch is set on the western shore of Lake Isabella, across the road from Hungry Gulch Camp. Take your pick. Isabella is the biggest lake for many miles and a prime destination point for Bakersfield area residents. Fishing for trout and bass is best in the spring. By the dog days of summer, when people are bowwowin' at the heat, waterskiers take over, along with folks just lookin' to cool off. Like a lot of lakes in the valley, Isabella is subject to drawdowns. The elevation is 2,650 feet. Open from April through September.

47. MAIN DAM 🐟 ⚓ 🏊 🎣   RV 8

Reference: On Lake Isabella; map G5, grid h2.

Campsites, facilities: There are 82 sites for tents, trailers or motor homes up to 30 feet long. Piped water, fire grills, and picnic tables are provided. Flush toilets and a dump station are available. Pets are permitted on leashes with proof of shots. Supplies and a laundromat are available in the town of Lake Isabella.

Reservations, fee: For reservations, phone (800) 280-CAMP; $14 fee per night.

Who to contact: Phone the Sequoia National Forest Lake Isabella Office at (619) 379-5646.

Location: From the town of Lake Isabella, drive 1.5 miles northwest on Highway 155 to the campground.

Trip note: This camp is located on the south shore of Lake Isabella. Open May to September.

48. CAMP 9 🐟 ⚓ 🏊 🎣 ✗   RV 8

Reference: On Lake Isabella; map G5, grid h2.

Campsites, facilities: There are 109 primitive sites for tents or motor homes. Piped water, flush toilets, a sanitary disposal station, a boat launch and a fish cleaning station are available. Supplies and a laundromat are available nearby in Kernville. Pets are permitted on leashes.

Reservations, fee: No reservations; $6 fee per night.

Who to contact: Phone the Sequoia National Forest Lake Isabella Office at (619) 379-5646.

Location: From Kernville, drive five miles south on Sierra Way to the north shore of Lake Isabella and the campground entrance.

Trip note: This campground is primitive and sparsely covered, but has several bonus features. It is set along the shore of Lake Isabella, known for good boating, waterskiing (in summer), and fishing (in the spring). Other options include great kayaking waters along the North Fork of the Kern River (located north of the lake), a good birdwatching area at the South Fork Wildlife Area (along the northeast corner of the lake), and an off-road-motorcycle park across the road from this campground. The elevation is 2,650 feet. Open year-round.

49. TILLIE CREEK 🐟 ⚓ ♿ 🏊 🎣   RV 9

Reference: On Lake Isabella; map G5, grid h2.

Campsites, facilities: There are 159 family sites and four group sites for tents or motor homes up to 30 feet long. Piped water, fire grills and picnic tables are provided. Flush toilets, showers, a sanitary disposal station, a playground, an amphitheater and a fish cleaning station are available. Four sites are **wheelchair accessible**. Pets are permitted on leashes. Supplies and a laundromat are nearby in Wofford Heights.

Reservations, fee: Reservations required for group sites; $14 fee per night for family sites; $60-$100 per night for group sites.

Who to contact: Phone the Sequoia National Forest Lake Isabella Office at (619) 379-5646.

Location: From Wofford Heights on the west side of Lake Isabella, drive one mile southwest on Highway 155.

Trip note: This is one of the two camps located along Tillie Creek, near Lake Isabella. See the trip note for the Camp 9. Open year-round.

50. LIVE OAK 🐟 ⚓ 🏊 🚶   RV 8

Reference: **On Lake Isabella; map G5, grid h2.**

Campsites, facilities: There are 150 family sites and one group site for tents or motor homes up to 30 feet long. Piped water, fire grills and picnic tables are provided. Flush toilets, and showers are available. Supplies and a laundromat are available nearby Wofford Heights. Pets are allowed on leashes.

Reservations, fee: Reservations required for group sites; phone (800) 280-CAMP; $14 fee per night for family site; $80 fee per night for group site.

Who to contact: Phone the Sequoia National Forest Lake Isabella Office at (619) 379-5646.

Location: From Wofford Heights on the west side of Lake Isabella, drive a half mile south on Highway 155 to the campground entrance road on your right.

Trip note: This is the second of the camps set along Tillie Creek, on Lake Isabella's northwest side. For details on the area, see the trip note for the Camp 9. The elevation is 2,600 feet. Open from May through September.

51. AUXILIARY DAM 🐟 ⚓ 🏊 🚶   RV 8

Reference: **On Lake Isabella; map G5, grid h2.**

Campsites, facilities: There are a number of primitive, undesignated sites for tents or motor homes. Piped water, flush toilets and a dump station are available. Pets are permitted on leashes. Supplies and a laundromat are available in the town of Lake Isabella.

Reservations, fee: No reservations; no fee.

Who to contact: Phone the Sequoia National Forest Lake Isabella Office at (619) 379-5646.

Location: From the town of Lake Isabella, drive a mile northeast on Highway 178.

Trip note: This is a primitive camp that is designed to be an overflow area if other camps at Lake Isabella are packed. It's the only camp directly on the shore of the lake—many people like it. Open year-round.

52. RIVERNOOK CAMPGROUND   RV 7

🐟 ⚓ 🏊 ✕

Reference: **On the North Fork of Kern River; map G5, grid h3.**

Campsites, facilities: There are 54 sites for tents or motor homes without hookups, 56 with partial hookups and 15 RV sites with full hookups. Picnic tables, piped water and full or partial hookups are provided. Restrooms, showers, a dump station and cable TV hookups are available. Pets are allowed on leashes.

Reservations, fee: Reservations accepted; $12-$18 fee per night.

Who to contact: Phone the park at (619) 376-2705.

Location: From Kernville, driven a half mile north to 14001 Sierra Way.

Trip note: This is a large, privately-operated park set near Lake Isabella. Boat rentals are available at one of the nearby marinas. Take a sidetrip to the town of Keysville, the first town to spring up on the Kern River during the gold rush days. The elevation is 2,665 feet. Open year-round.

53. HOBO 🐟 ✕   RV 7

Reference: **On Kern River in Sequoia National Forest; map G5, grid i1.**

Campsites, facilities: There are 25 sites for tents and 10 for motor homes up to 16 feet long. Fire grills and picnic tables are provided. Water is provided some of the time. Vault toilets and showers are available. Pets are allowed on leashes.

Reservations, fee: Reservations recommended; phone (800) 280-CAMP; $12 per night for first vehicle, $5 per night each additional vehicle; no fee when there is no water.

Who to contact: Phone the Sequoia National Forest Greenhorn Ranger District at (805) 871-2223.

Location: From the town of Lake Isabella, drive five miles south west on Highway 178. Turn left on Borel Road and drive south for about a third of a mile to the intersection of Old Kern Road. Turn right and drive about two miles to campground on your right.

Trip note: Because this camp is overshadowed by nearby Lake Isabella to the north, it is often overlooked. It is a small campground set along the Kern River, about two miles off Highway 178. The elevation is 2,300 feet. Open from May to October.

54. PARADISE COVE 🐟 ⚓ ♿ ≈ 🏃   RV 9

Reference: **On Lake Isabella; map G5, grid i2.**

Campsites, facilities: There are 58 sites for tents or motor homes, some with picnic tables and fire grills provided. Flush toilets, showers and a fish cleaning station are available. The restrooms are **wheelchair accessible**. Pets are permitted on leashes. Supplies, a trailer dump station, and a laundromat are available in the town of Lake Isabella.

Reservations, fee: Reservations required; $14 fee per night.

Who to contact: Phone the Sequoia National Forest Lake Isabella Office at (619) 379-5646. For reservations, phone (800) 280-2267.

Location: From the town of Lake Isabella, drive six miles northeast on Highway 178.

Trip note: Paradise Cove is on the south shore of Lake Isabella. The elevation is 2,600 feet. For details on the area, see the trip note for the Camp 9, Boulder Gulch and French Gulch campgrounds. Open all year.

55. MOUNTAIN MESA TRAILER COURT   RV 7

Reference: **On Lake Isabella; map G5, grid i2.**

Campsites, facilities: There are 45 motor home sites with full hookups. Restrooms, showers, a swimming pool, a recreation room, cable TV hookups and a laundromat are available. Pets are permitted on leashes.

Reservations, fee: Reservations accepted; $15.50-$17.50 fee per night.

Who to contact: Phone the park at (619) 379-2046.

Location: From the town of Lake Isabella, drive six miles northeast on Highway 178 to the signed entrance on the right.

Trip note: This quiet, privately-operated park is set up for motor homes across from Lake Isabella. It is one of many camps at the lake. Plan on plenty of company. For details on the area, see the trip note for the Eastside, Boulder Gulch and French Gulch camps. The elevation is 2,600 feet. Open all year.

56. KOA LAKE ISABELLA

Reference: Map G5, grid i3.

Campsites, facilities: There are 104 sites for tents or motor homes. Picnic tables, piped water and full or partial hookups are provided. Restrooms, showers, a playground, a swimming pool, a laundromat, a store, a dump station and propane gas are available. Pets are permitted on leashes.

Reservations, fee: Reservations accepted; $17-$25 per night.

Who to contact: Phone the park at (619) 378-2001.

Location: From the town of Lake Isabella, drive 10 miles east on Highway 178 and look for the KOA sign on the left.

Trip note: If the camps around Lake Isabella are jam-packed, the KOA camp provides an alternative. It is set in South Fork Valley (elevation is 2,600 feet).

---

57. WALKER PASS WALK-IN

Reference: On the Pacific Crest Trail southwest of Death Valley National Park; map G5, grid i7.

Campsites, facilities: There are two sites for tents and motor homes with limited parking, and nine walk-in sites for tents only. Water and pit toilets are available. No trash facilities are provided, so bring a garbage bag to pack out all refuse. A 14-day stay limit is enforced.

Reservations, fee: No reservations; no fee.

Who to contact: Phone the Caliente Resource Area at (805) 391-6000, or write Bureau of Land Management, Caliente Resource Area, 3801 Pegasus Drive, Bakersfield, CA 93308-6837.

Location: From Lake Isabella, drive east on Highway 178 and continue 14 miles past Onyx. At Walker Pass, look for the campground on the right side of the road, where a sign is posted for the Pacific Crest Trail. It is a quarter-mile walk from the parking area to the campground.

Trip note: Hikers on the Pacific Crest Trail treat this camp as if they were arriving at Valhalla. That's because it is set right on the trail, and better yet, piped water is available. Out here in the desert, there aren't many places where you can act like a camel and suck up all the liquids you can hold. The camp is set at 5,200 feet, southwest of Death Valley National Park. And if you guessed it was named for Joe Walker, the West's greatest trailblazer and one of my heroes, well, right you are. If you arrive by car instead of on the PCT, use this spot as a base camp, then head out from the trailhead on foot.

---

58. BRECKENRIDGE

Reference: In Sequoia National Forest; map G5, grid j0.

Campsites, facilities: There are eight tent sites. Picnic tables and fire grills are provided and portable restroom is available. There is **no piped water**, so bring your own. Pets are permitted on leashes.

Reservations, fee: No reservations; no fee.

Who to contact: Phone the Sequoia National Forest Greenhorn Ranger District at (805) 871-2223.

Location: From the town of Lake Isabella on Highway 178, turn south on Caliente Bodfish Road and drive about 12 miles to the town of Havilah. Continue south on Caliente Bodfish Road for two more miles. Turn right (west) on Forest

Service Road 28S06 and drive 10 miles to the campground.

Trip note: You join the One Percent Club by visiting this camp. In other words, *nobody* knows about it. It is a tiny, primitive camp set at 7,100 feet near Breckenridge Mountain (a good lookout here) in a little-traveled sector of the Sequoia National Forest. There are no other camps in the immediate area. Open from May to October.

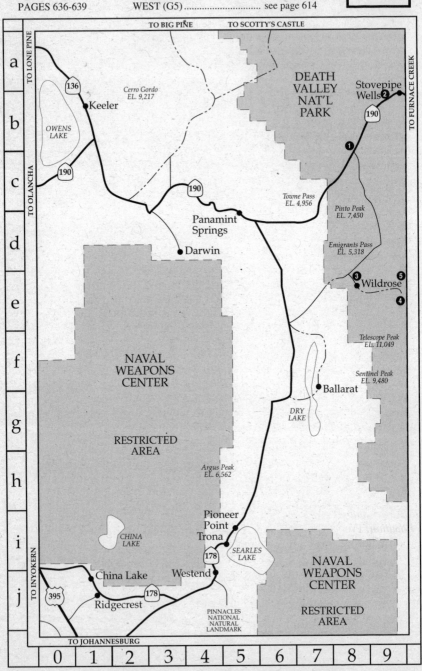

MAP G6

CEN-CAL MAP .... see page 512
adjoining maps
NORTH (F6) .... see page 590
EAST (G7) .... see page 640
SOUTH (H6) .... see page 678
WEST (G5) .... see page 614

5 LISTINGS
PAGES 636-639

TO BIG PINE — TO SCOTTY'S CASTLE

TO LONE PINE

136 Keeler

Cerro Gordo EL. 9,217

DEATH VALLEY NAT'L PARK

Stovepipe Wells ②

OWENS LAKE

190

TO FURNACE CREEK

190

TO OLANCHA

①

190

Panamint Springs

Towne Pass EL. 4,956

Pinto Peak EL. 7,450

Darwin

Emigrants Pass EL. 5,318

③ Wildrose ⑤
④

Telescope Peak EL. 11,049

NAVAL WEAPONS CENTER

Sentinel Peak EL. 9,480

Ballarat

RESTRICTED AREA

DRY LAKE

Argus Peak EL. 6,562

Pioneer Point

Trona

CHINA LAKE

SEARLES LAKE

178

NAVAL WEAPONS CENTER

TO INYOKERN

China Lake

Westend

395

178

Ridgecrest

PINNACLES NATIONAL NATURAL LANDMARK

RESTRICTED AREA

TO JOHANNESBURG

0 1 2 3 4 5 6 7 8 9

Map G6 featuring Death Valley National Park

1. EMIGRANT 👫 ⚓   RV 4

Reference: **In Death Valley National Park; map G6, grid b8.**

Campsites, facilities: There are 10 sites for tents or motor homes. Piped water and picnic tables are provided. Flush toilets are available. Pets are permitted on leashes.

Reservations, fee: No reservations; no fee.

Who to contact: Phone the Death Valley National Park at (619) 786-2331.

Location: In Stovepipe Wells Village, drive nine miles southwest on Highway 190. Turn left on Highway 178 and continue about 30 miles to the Wild Rose site. Take the signed turnoff to the campground on the left.

Trip note: The key here is the elevation, and Emigrant camp, at 2,000 feet, is out of the forbidding subzero elevations of Death Valley. That makes it one of the more habitable camps when others at Death Valley National Park are like furnaces. Open May through October.

2. STOVEPIPE WELLS 👫 ♿ 🏊 ⚓   RV 4

Reference: **In Death Valley National Park; map G6, grid b9.**

Campsites, facilities: There are 10 sites for tents only and 200 sites for tents or motor homes. Piped water is provided. Flush toilets, a dump station, a swimming pool, a camp store, gasoline and evening ranger programs are available. The restrooms are **wheelchair accessible**. Pets are allowed on leashes.

Reservations, fee: No reservations; $6 fee per night.

Who to contact: Phone the Death Valley National Park at (619) 786-2331.

Location: In Stovepipe Wells Village, drive to the north end of town on Highway 190 and make a right at the signed exit into the campground.

Trip note: This is a good base camp for four-wheel-drive cowboys because it is set near a rugged road that is routed into Cottonwood and Marble. (No cross-country vehicle travel is permitted in the park). The elevation is at sea level, on the edge of dropping off into never-never land. Open October through April.

3. WILDROSE 👫 ⚓   RV 4

Reference: **In Death Valley National Park; map G6, grid e8.**

Campsites, facilities: There are 30 sites for tents or motor homes. Picnic tables are provided. Piped water and pit toilets are available. Pets are permitted on leashes.

Reservations, fee: No reservations; no fee.

Who to contact: Phone the Death Valley National Park at (619) 786-2331.

Location: From Stovepipe Wells Village, drive 30 miles south on Highway 190 to Wildrose Canyon Road; turn left and follow the signs to the campground.

Trip note: The nearby Wildrose Ranger Station is the highlight at this camp, providing a chance to get the latest info on trail and road conditions. It is set on the road that heads out to the primitive country, eventually to Telescope Peak, the highest point in Death Valley National Park (11,049 feet). The elevation is 4,100 feet. Water is on April through November. Open year-round.

4. MAHOGANY FLAT 🚶🏕 🚰

Reference: **In Death Valley National Park; map G6, grid e9.**

Campsites, facilities: There are 10 sites for tents or motor homes. Picnic tables and
pit toilets are available. There is **no piped water**, so bring your own. The
campground is accessible by foot or four-wheel drive. Pets are allowed on
leashes.

Reservations, fee: No reservations; no fee.

Who to contact: Phone the Death Valley National Park at (619) 786-2331.

Location: From Stovepipe Wells Village, drive 38 miles south on Highway 190
to Wildrose Canyon Road; turn left and drive to the end of the road.

Trip note: This is one of two primitive, hard-to-reach camps set in Death Valley
National Park's high country. The trail that is routed to Bennett and Telescope
Peaks leads out from camp. Only the ambitious and well-conditioned should
attempt the climb. The elevation is 8,200 feet. This is one of the few shaded
camps, offering beautiful pinyon pines and junipers. Open from April through
October.

5. THORNDIKE 🚶🏕 🚰

Reference: **In Death Valley National Park; map G6, grid e9.**

Campsites, facilities: This backcountry campground is accessible by foot or four-
wheel drive and has eight campsites for tents or motor homes. Picnic tables and
pit toilets are available. There is **no piped water**, so bring your own. Pets are
permitted on leashes.

Reservations, fee: No reservations; no fee.

Who to contact: Phone the Death Valley National Park at (619) 786-2331.

Location: From Stovepipe Wells Village, drive 37 miles south on Highway 190
to Wildrose Canyon Road; turn left and drive to the end of the road. (The road
becomes extremely rough; four-wheel-drive is required.)

Trip note: This is one of Death Valley National Park's little-known camps. It is
set in the high country at 7,500 feet. It's free, of course. Otherwise they'd have
to actually send somebody out to tend to the place. Nearby are century-old
charcoal kilns that were built by Chinese laborers and tended by Shoshone
Indians. The trailhead that serves Telescope Peak (11,049 feet), the highest
point in Death Valley, can be found in nearby Mahogany Flat Campground. It
is a strenuous all-day hike. Open March to October.

NOTE: **For more camps in Death Valley National Park, see Chapter G7.**

MAP G7

CEN-CAL MAP .... see page 512
adjoining maps
NORTH .... no map
EAST .... no map
SOUTH (H7) .... see page 682
WEST (G6) .... see page 636

4 LISTINGS
PAGES 640-643

TO SCOTTY'S CASTLE

TO BEATTY, NV

TO STOVEPIPE WELLS

267

374

190

190

DEATH VALLEY NAT'L PARK

95

NEVADA

Amargosa Valley

TO INDIAN SPRINGS, NV

1

2

3

Furnace Creek Ranch

178

Aguersberry Point EL. 6,433

TO WILDROSE

Salt Pools

Ryan

190

127

Ash Meadows Ranch

Lowest Point in the U.S. EL. -282

BAD WATER

Dantes View

Death Valley Junction

178

Deadman Pass EL. 3,263

TO PAHRUMP, NV

Smith Mountain EL. 5,950

127

DEATH VALLEY NAT'L PARK

178

Salsberry Pass EL. 3,315

178

Shoshone

4

TO HWY. 160

Tecopa

SOUTH TO I-15

127

a b c d e f g h i j

0 1 2 3 4 5 6 7 8 9

Map G7 featuring Death Valley National Park

1. FURNACE CREEK 🚶 ♿ ⛺   RV 5

Reference: **In Death Valley National Park; map G7, grid c2.**

Campsites, facilities: There are 136 sites for tents or motor homes. Picnic tables and piped water are provided. Flush toilets, a dump station and evening ranger programs, are available. The restrooms are **wheelchair accessible**. Pets are allowed on leashes.

Reservations, fee: Reservations recommended; reserve through Destinet at (800) 365-CAMP; $14 fee per night.

Who to contact: Phone the Death Valley National Park at (619) 786-2331.

Location: From Furnace Creek Ranch, drive one mile north on Highway 190 to the signed campground exit on the left.

Trip note: This is a well developed national park site that provides a good base camp for exploring Death Valley, especially for newcomers. The nearby Visitor's Center and Death Valley Museum offer maps and suggestions for hikes and drives in this unique wildland. The elevation is 190 feet below sea level. This camp offers shady sites, a rarity in Death Valley. Open all year, but keep in mind that the summer temperatures commonly exceed 100 degrees.

2. SUNSET 🚶 ♿ ⛺   RV 4

Reference: **In Death Valley National Park; map G7, grid c2.**

Campsites, facilities: There are 1,000 sites for tents or motor homes. Piped water and picnic tables are provided. Flush toilets, a dump station and evening ranger programs are available. There are 16 **wheelchair accessible** sites near accessible restrooms. Pets are allowed on leashes.

Reservations, fee: No reservations; $10 fee per night.

Who to contact: Phone the Death Valley National Park at (619) 786-2331.

Location: From Furnace Creek Ranch, drive a quarter mile east on Highway 190 to the signed campground exit; turn left into the campground.

Trip note: This is one of several options for campers in the Furnace Creek area. Newcomers should check out the Visitor's Center for maps and suggested hikes and drives. Don't forget your canteen—and if you're backpacking, never set up a wilderness camp near water in Death Valley. A thirsty animal may think it has to fight you in order to get a drink. It'll probably win. The elevation is 190 feet below sea level. Open from October through April.

3. TEXAS SPRING 🚶 ⛺   RV 4

Reference: **In Death Valley National Park; map G7, grid c3.**

Campsites, facilities: There are 92 sites for tents or motor homes. There are also two group sites, each accommodating 70 people and 10 vehicles. Piped water and picnic tables are provided. Flush toilets, a dump station and evening ranger programs are available. Some **wheelchair accessible** sites. Pets are allowed on leashes.

Reservations, fee: No reservations; $6 fee per night.

Who to contact: Phone the Death Valley National Park at (619) 786-2331.

Location: From Furnace Creek Ranch, drive a half mile east on Highway 190 to the signed campground exit on the left.

Trip note: Death Valley is kind of like an ugly dog that you love. After awhile, you can't help it. This campground, like the others near Furnace Creek Ranch, offers a good headquarters to get a feel for Death Valley. The nearby Visitors Center and Death Valley Museum offer maps and suggestions for hikes and drives. This camp has one truly unique feature—bathrooms that are listed on the National Historic Register. Open from October to April.

4. TECOPA HOT SPRINGS COUNTY PARK

Reference: **Map G7, grid i8.**

Campsites, facilities: There are 300 sites for tents or motor homes. Piped water, fireplaces, picnic tables, and, in some cases electrical connections are provided. Flush toilets, showers, a dump station, a laundromat, groceries and propane gas are available nearby. Some facilities are **wheelchair accessible**. Pets are allowed on leashes.

Reservations, fee: No reservations; $6.50-$8 fee per night.

Who to contact: Phone the County Parks Department at (619) 852-4264.

Location: From Death Valley Junction, drive about 35 miles south on State Highway 127 to the park entrance on the left. (From Baker, drive north on Highway 127 for 57 miles to the signed exit to the park.)

Trip note: This one is out there in No Man's Land, and if it wasn't for the hot springs, all you'd see around here is a few skeletons. Regardless, it's quite an attraction in the winter, when the warm climate is a plus, and the nearby mineral baths are worth taking a dunk in. The elevation is 1,500 feet. Open all year.

MAP H2

CEN-CAL MAP .... see page 512
adjoining maps
NORTH (G2) .... see page 598
EAST (H3) .... see page 648
SOUTH .... no map
WEST .... no map

7 LISTINGS
PAGES 644-647

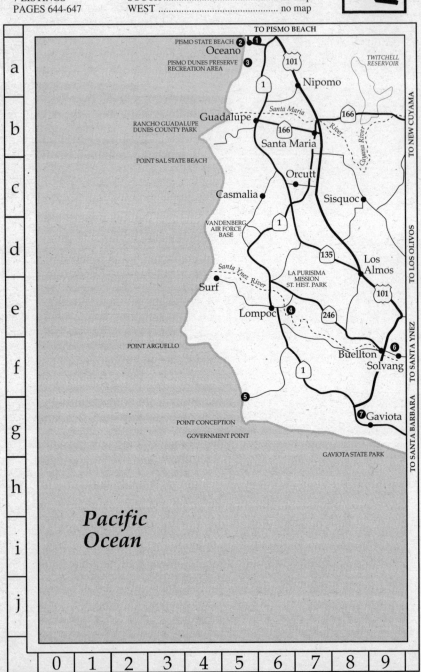

TO PISMO BEACH

PISMO STATE BEACH ❷ ❶

Oceano

PISMO DUNES PRESERVE
RECREATION AREA ❸

101

1

Nipomo

166

Santa Maria

Guadalupe

166

TWITCHELL
RESERVOIR

River

Guama River

TO NEW CUYAMA

RANCHO GUADALUPE
DUNES COUNTY PARK

Santa Maria

POINT SAL STATE BEACH

Orcutt

Casmalia

Sisquoc

VANDENBERG
AIR FORCE
BASE

1

135

Los
Almos

TO LOS OLIVOS

Santa Ynez River

LA PURISIMA
MISSION
ST. HIST. PARK

101

Surf

Lompoc ❹

246

Buellton ❻

Solvang

TO SANTA YNEZ

POINT ARGUELLO

1

❺

Gaviota ❼

TO SANTA BARBARA

POINT CONCEPTION

GOVERNMENT POINT

GAVIOTA STATE PARK

*Pacific
Ocean*

a b c d e f g h i j

0 1 2 3 4 5 6 7 8 9

1. OCEANO COUNTY CAMPGROUND ♿

Reference: **Near Arroyo; map H2, grid a5.**

Campsites, facilities: There are 24 sites for motor homes with full hookups. Fire grills and picnic tables are provided. Flush toilets and showers are available. A playground, a laundromat, a grocery store and propane gas are available nearby. Pets, with proof of vaccinations, are permitted on leashes.

Reservations, fee: No reservations; $20 fee per night; $2 pet fee.

Who to contact: Phone the park at (805) 781-5219.

Location: From Pismo Beach, drive south on US 101. Take the Arroyo-Grand Avenue exit west to Highway 1. Turn south for a short distance and turn right on Airpark. The campground is at 414 Airpark Drive.

Trip note: This county park often gets overlooked because it isn't on the state reservation system. That's other folks' loss, your gain. The location is a bonus, set near Pismo State Beach. Open year-round.

2. PISMO DUNES STATE RECREATION AREA

Reference: **Map H2, grid a5.**

Campsites, facilities: There are 1,000 primitive sites for off-road vehicles. Vault toilets are provided. There is **no piped water**, so bring your own. Horseback riding facilities, a grocery store, a laundromat and propane gas are available nearby. Pets are permitted on leashes.

Reservations, fee: Reserve by phoning Destinet at (800) 444-7275 ($6.75 Destinet fee); $8 fee per night.

Who to contact: Phone the park at (805) 549-3433 or (805) 473-7230.

Location: Northbound on US 101, take the Grand Avenue exit. Make a left at the signal. If you don't have reservations, continue westbound on Grand Avenue for about eight miles until the road ends at the beach. If you have reservations, continue westbound on Grand Avenue. Turn left at the last traffic light on Highway 1. Drive about 1.5 miles south to Pier Avenue. Turn right and follow the road to the dead end. Southbound on US 101, take the Pismo Beach Exit and continue straight to the fourth traffic light.

Trip note: This is "National Headquarters for All-Terrain Vehicles." You know, those three and four-wheeled motorcycles that turn otherwise normal people into lunatics. They roam wild on the dunes here, that's the law, so don't go planning a quiet stroll. If you don't like 'em, you are strongly advised to go elsewhere. Open year-round.

3. OCEANO

Reference: **In Pismo State Beach; map H2, grid a5.**

Campsites, facilities: There are 82 sites for tents, trailers or motor homes up to 36 feet long, some (42) with partial hookups. There are also some primitive hike-in and bike-in sites. Picnic tables and fire grills are provided. Piped water, restrooms and coin-operated showers are available. Horseback riding facilities, a grocery store, a laundromat and propane gas are nearby. Pets are allowed on leashes.

Reservations, fee: Reserve by phoning Destinet at (800) 444-7275 ($6.75 Destinet fee); $17-$19 fee per night; $6 per night for hiker/biker sites.

Who to contact: Phone the park at (805) 489-2684 or (805) 549-3312.

Location: From Pismo Beach, drive one mile south on Highway 1 to the campground entrance.

Trip note: This is the other campground at Pismo State Beach. With a world-famous beach, dunes, and all, plan on plenty of company. Open year-round.

---

4. RIVER PARK **RV 4**

Reference: In Lompoc; map H2, grid e6.

Campsites, facilities: There 34 motor home sites with full hookups and a large open area for tents. Piped water, flush toilets, showers, a dump station, a fishing pond and a playground are available. Supplies and a laundromat are nearby. Pets are permitted on leashes.

Reservations, fee: No reservations; $10-$15 fee per night; hikers and bikers $4 fee per night; $2 fee for dump station use; $1 pet fee.

Who to contact: Phone the park at (805) 736-6565.

Location: In Lompoc, drive to the junction of Highway 246 and Sweeney Road at the southwest edge of town.

Trip note: Before checking in here, you'd best get a lesson in how to pronounce Lompoc. It's "Lom-Poke." If you arrive and say, "Hey, it's great to be in Lom-Pock," they might just tell ya to get on back to Nebraska with the other cowpokes. It is set near the lower Santa Ynez River, which looks quite a bit different than it does up in Los Padres National Forest. There is a small fishing lake within the park which is stocked regularly with trout. Sidetrip possibilities include the nearby La Purisima Mission State Historical Park.

---

5. JALAMA BEACH COUNTY PARK **RV 8**

Reference: Near Lompoc on the Pacific Ocean; map H2, grid f5.

Campsites, facilities: There are 100 sites for tents or motor homes up to 35 feet long, including several group sites. Piped water, fire grills and picnic tables are provided. Flush toilets, showers, a dump station, a grocery store, a laundromat and propane gas are available. Pets are permitted on leashes.

Reservations, fee: No reservations except for groups; $13-$16 fee per night; $80 group fee per night; $1 pet fee.

Who to contact: Phone the park at (805) 736-6316.

Location: From Lompoc, drive south on Highway 1. Turn southwest on Jalama Road and drive 15 miles to the park.

Trip note: This is a pretty spot set where Jalama Creek empties into the ocean, about five miles north of Point Conception and just south of Vandenberg Air Force Base. The area is known for its beachcombing (occasional lost missiles) and sunsets.

---

6. FLYING FLAGS TRAVEL PARK **RV 3**

Reference: Near Solvang; map H2, grid f9.

Campsites, facilities: There are 100 sites for tents and 256 motor home sites with full or partial hookups. Picnic tables and fire grills are provided. Restrooms with **wheelchair access**, showers, a playground, a swimming pool, two hot therapy pools, a laundromat, a store, a dump station, ice, a recreation room, an arcade, five clubhouses and propane gas are available. Pets are permitted on leashes. A nine hole golf course is nearby.

Reservations, fee: Reservations recommended; $15-$21.50 fee per night; $0.50 pet fee.

Who to contact: Phone the park at (805) 688-3716.

Location: From Santa Barbara, drive 45 miles north on US 101 to its intersection with Highway 246. Turn left on Highway 246 and drive about one-half mile to the four-way stop. Turn left, drive about one block and look for the campground entrance on the left.

Trip note: This is one of the few privately-operated parks that welcomes tenters as well as motor homes. Nearby sidetrips include the Santa Ynez Mission, located just east of Solvang.

7. GAVIOTA STATE PARK

Reference: **Near Santa Barbara; map H2, grid g8.**

Campsites, facilities: There are 42 sites for tents and RVs up to 27 feet long. Fire grills and picnic tables are provided. Piped water, flush toilets, coin-operated showers and a boat hoist are available. A grocery store is nearby. Pets are permitted on leashes.

Reservations, fee: No reservations; $17-$19 fee per night; $1 pet fee.

Who to contact: Phone the park at (805) 968-1033 or (805) 899-1400.

Location: From Santa Barbara, drive 33 miles north on US 101 to park entrance.

Trip note: This is the granddaddy, the biggest of the three state beaches along Highway 1 northwest of Santa Barbara. The park covers 2,800 acres, providing both trails for hiking and horseback riding as well as a mile-long stretch of beautiful beach frontage. The ambitious can hike the beach to get more seclusion.

MAP H3

38 LISTINGS
PAGES 648-661

CEN-CAL MAP .... see page 512
adjoining maps
NORTH (G3) .... see page 606
EAST (H4) .... see page 662
SOUTH (I3) .... see page 694
WEST (H2) .... see page 644

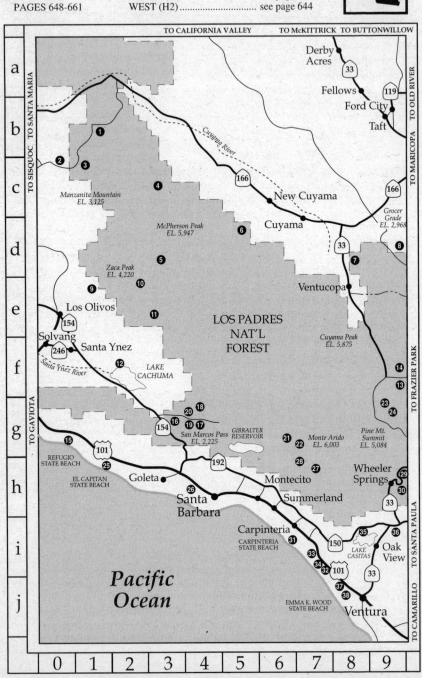

Map H3 featuring: Los Padres National Forest, Santa Ynez River, Lake Cachuma, Santa Barbara

1. WAGON FLAT

Reference: On the North Fork of La Brea Creek in Los Padres National Forest; map H3, grid b1.

Campsites, facilities: There are three sites for tents. Fire grills and picnic tables are provided. Vault toilets are available. There is **no piped water**, so bring your own. Pets are permitted on leashes.

Reservations, fee: No reservations; no fee.

Who to contact: Phone the Los Padres National Forest Santa Lucia District at (805) 925-9538.

Location: From Santa Maria, drive southeast on Foxen Canyon Road for eight miles to the town of Garey. Continue southeast on Santa Maria Mesa Road for four miles. Turn left on Tepusquet Road and drive 6.5 miles. Turn right on Colson Canyon Road (Forest Service Road 11N04) and drive 10 more miles.

Trip note: Not many folks know about this obscure spot, and if it's a hot, late summer day, they're probably better off for it. It is set at 1,400 feet, with a trail out of camp leading up Kerry Canyon. Open year-round.

2. COLSON

Reference: In Los Padres National Forest; map H3, grid c0.

Campsites, facilities: There are 10 tent sites. Fire grills and picnic tables are provided. Vault toilets are available. Pets are permitted on leashes.

Reservations, fee: No reservations; no fee.

Who to contact: Phone the Los Padres National Forest Santa Lucia District at (805) 925-9538.

Location: From Santa Maria on US 101, take the Betteravia Road exit. Drive eight miles southeast on Foxen Canyon Road. Bear left at the fork and continue southeast on Santa Maria Mesa Road. Turn left on Tepusquet Road and drive 6.5 miles. Turn right on Colson Canyon Road (Forest Service Road 11N04) and drive four miles to the campground.

Trip note: This area has two seasons to it, spring and fall. In the fall, it's hot and dry and with no water and is scarcely fit for habitation. The camp is deep in the Los Padres National Forest, with trails leading out of camp for ambitious hikers. The elevation is 2,100 feet. Open year-round.

3. BARREL SPRINGS

Reference: In Los Padres National Forest; map H3, grid c1.

Campsites, facilities: There are five tent sites. There is **no piped water**. Fire grills and picnic tables are provided. Vault toilets are available. Pets are permitted on leashes.

Reservations, fee: No reservations; no fee.

Who to contact: Phone the Los Padres National Forest Santa Lucia District at (805) 925-9538.

Location: From Santa Maria on US 101, take the Betteravia Road exit. Drive eight miles southeast on Foxen Canyon Road. Bear left at the fork and continue southeast on Santa Maria Mesa Road. Turn left on Tepusquet Road and drive 6.5 miles. Turn right on Colson Canyon Road (Forest Service Road 11N04) and drive eight miles to the campground. (The road is dirt and impassable when wet).

Trip note: This small, little-known camp is used primarily by backpackers starting wilderness expeditions. It is set at 1,000 feet along La Brea Creek and shaded by the oaks in La Brea Canyon. A trail near the camp is routed into the backcountry and into the San Rafael Wilderness, with more campgrounds spaced every 10 miles along the trail. Open year-round.

4. BATES CANYON

4

Reference: In Los Padres National Forest; map H3, grid c3.

Campsites, facilities: There are six tent sites. Fire grills and picnic tables are provided. Vault toilets are available. Pets are permitted on leashes. There is **no piped water**, so bring your own.

Reservations, fee: No reservations; no fee.

Who to contact: Phone the Los Padres National Forest Santa Lucia District at (805) 925-9538.

Location: From Santa Maria, drive 50 miles east on Highway 166. Turn right on Cottonwood Canyon Road and drive 7.5 miles southwest to the campground.

Trip note: This camp is located in the Sierra Madre Mountains, not far from the panoramic Bates Ridge Lookout. As with the other camps in this area, a Los Padres National Forest map will open up the area to you. The elevation is 2,900 feet. Open year-round.

5. NIRA

RV 7

Reference: On Manzana Creek in Los Padres National Forest; map H3, grid d3.

Campsites, facilities: There are 11 sites for tents and two sites for motor homes up to 16 feet long. Fire grills and picnic tables are provided. Vault toilets and horse hitching posts are available. There is piped water. Pets are permitted on leashes.

Reservations, fee: No reservations; no fee.

Who to contact: Phone the Los Padres National Forest Santa Lucia District at (805) 925-9538.

Location: From US 101 in Santa Barbara, drive 22 miles northeast on Highway 154. Turn right on Armour Ranch Road and drive 1.5 miles. Turn right on Happy Canyon Road and drive 11 miles to Cachuma Saddle. Continue straight (north) on Sunset Valley/Cachuma Road (Forest Service Road 8N09) for six miles to the campground.

Trip note: This premium jumpoff spot for backpackers is set at 2,100 feet along Manzana Creek on the border of the San Rafael Wilderness. A primary trailhead for the San Rafael Wilderness is located here and connects to numerous trails and backcountry camps. All are detailed on a Forest Service map. Today's history lesson? This camp was originally an NRA (National Recovery Act) camp during the Depression, hence the name Nira. Wow! Open year-round.

6. ALISO PARK

RV 5

Reference: In Los Padres National Forest; map H3, grid d5.

Campsites, facilities: There are 11 sites for tents or motor homes up to 22 feet long. Fire grills and picnic tables are provided. Vault toilets are available. There is

no piped water, so bring your own. Pets are permitted on leashes.

Reservations, fee: No reservations; no fee.

Who to contact: Phone the Los Padres National Forest Mt. Pinos District at (805) 245-3731.

Location: From Santa Maria, drive 59 miles east on Highway 166. Turn right on Aliso Canyon Road and drive six miles south to the campground.

Trip note: This primitive, quiet park is set at the foot of the Sierra Madre Mountains at 3,200 feet, directly below McPherson Peak (5,747 feet). Open year-round.

---

7. BALLINGER   RV 3

Reference: **In Los Padres National Forest; map H3 grid d8.**

Campsites, facilities: There are five sites for tents or motor homes up to 32 feet long. Fire grills and picnic tables are provided. Pit toilets are available. There is **no piped water**, so bring your own. Pets are permitted on leashes.

Reservations, fee: No reservations; no fee.

Who to contact: Phone the Los Padres National Forest Mount Pinos Ranger District at (805) 245-3731.

Location: From the junction of Highways 166 and 33 in Maricopa, drive 14 miles south on Highway 33. Where Highway 33 separates from Highway 166, turn left (south) on Highway 33 and drive 5.5 miles to Ballinger Canyon Road. Turn left (east) and drive three miles to the campground.

Trip note: Hope you like four-wheel-drive vehicles and dirt bikes. Why? Because that's the kind of company campers keep around this area. Off-road vehicles use the nearby Hungry Valley Recreation Area, which is near the boundary of Los Padres National Forest. Open year-round.

---

8. VALLE VISTA   RV 4

Reference: **In Los Padres National Forest; map H3, grid d9.**

Campsites, facilities: There are seven sites for tents or motor homes up to 32 feet long. Fire grills and picnic tables are provided. Vault toilets are available. There is **no piped water**, so bring your own. Pets are permitted on leashes.

Reservations, fee: No reservations; no fee.

Who to contact: Phone the Los Padres National Forest Mount Pinos Ranger District at (805) 245-3731.

Location: From the junction of Highways 166 and 33 in Maricopa, drive about nine miles south on Highway 166. Turn east (left) on Cerro Noroeste Road and drive 12 miles to the campground.

Trip note: The view of Bakersfield Valley is the highlight of this primitive camp. It is set at 4,800 feet, near the boundary of Los Padres National Forest. Visitors can usually spot a few buzzards circling around. If you don't bring your own water, they might just start circling you. Open year-round.

---

9. FIGUEROA 🚶 ♿   RV 6

Reference: **In Los Padres National Forest; map H3, grid e1.**

Campsites, facilities: There are 33 sites for tents and six sites for motor homes up to 22 feet long. Piped water, fire grills and picnic tables are provided. Vault toilets are available. Pets are permitted on leashes.

Reservations, fee: Groups may reserve by calling (800) 280-CAMP ($15 reservation fee); $6 fee per night; reservations available for groups of up to 56 people; $50 for groups.

Who to contact: Phone the Los Padres National Forest Santa Lucia District at (805) 925-9538.

Location: From Highway 154 in Los Olivos, turn northeast on Figueroa Mountain Road and drive 12.5 miles to the campground.

Trip note: This is one of the more attractive camps in Los Padres National Forest. Set at 4,000 feet beneath a unique stand of oak and huge manzanita trees, the camp offers a view of Santa Inez Valley. Several trailheads in the area provide access for hikers to the San Rafael Wilderness. The nearby Pino Alto Picnic Area offers a panoramic view of the adjacent wildlands and has a **wheelchair accessible** nature trail. Open year-round.

10. DAVY BROWN

Reference: **On Davy Brown Creek; map H3, grid e2.**

Campsites, facilities: There are 10 sites for tents and three sites for motor homes up to 18 feet long. Fire grills and picnic tables are provided. Vault toilets are available. There is **no piped water**, so bring your own. Pets are permitted on leashes.

Reservations, fee: No reservations in Los Padres National Forest; $5 fee per night.

Who to contact: Phone the Los Padres National Forest Santa Lucia District at (805) 925-9538.

Location: From US 101 in Santa Barbara, drive 22 miles northeast on Highway 154. Turn right on Armour Ranch Road and drive 1.5 miles. Turn right on Happy Canyon Road and drive 11 miles to Cachuma Saddle. Continue straight (north) on Sunset Valley/Cachuma Road (Forest Service Road 8N09) for four miles.

Trip note: This is a pretty spot, either to hunker down for awhile or to strap on a backpack and hoof it. Davy Brown Creek runs almost year-round, a big bonus. It is set at 4,000 feet, deep in Los Padres National Forest, near the border of the San Rafael Wilderness. A trail from the camp leads into the adjacent wildlands. Open year-round.

11. CACHUMA

Reference: **Near Cachuma Creek in Los Padres National Forest; map H3, grid e3.**

Campsites, facilities: There are five tent sites. Fire grills and picnic tables are provided. Vault toilets are available. There is **no piped water**, so bring your own. Pets are permitted on leashes.

Reservations, fee: No reservations; no fee.

Who to contact: Phone the Los Padres National Forest Santa Barbara District at (805) 967-3481.

Location: From US 101 in Santa Barbara, drive 22 miles northeast on Highway 154. Turn right on Armour Ranch Road and drive 1.5 miles. Turn right on Happy Canyon Road and drive 9.5 miles to the campground.

Trip note: Yes, Cachuma is the sound you make when sneezing. The stream here, which runs seven miles from camp downstream to Lake Cachuma, was named after an explorer known for his vociferous sneezing. A dirt road south of the camp follows the creek to the lake. The elevation is 2,200. Open year-round.

12. LAKE CACHUMA 🐟 ⚓ ♿ 🏊 RV 7

Reference: **Near Santa Barbara; map H3, grid f2.**

Campsites, facilities: There are 500 sites for tents or motor homes, some with full hookups. Fire grills and picnic tables are provided. Flush toilets, showers, a playground, a general store, propane gas, a swimming pool, a boat ramp, mooring, boat fuel, boat rentals, bicycle rentals, ice and a snack bar are available. Crafts under 10 feet are prohibited. Pets are allowed on leashes.

Reservations, fee: No reservations; $13-$18 fee per night; $1 pet fee.

Who to contact: Phone the park at (805) 688-4658.

Location: From Santa Barbara, drive 22 miles north on Highway 154 to the campground entrance.

Trip note: The climate is not only perfect for weekend vacationers, but for bass as well. Some monsters are known to swim in this lake along with plenty of little brothers. Premium weather and good fishing makes Lake Cachuma a popular destination for vacationers because of the fish. Note: No waterskiing or swimming is permitted. It is set at 600 feet in the foothill oaks-grassland country. Open year-round.

13. REYES CREEK 🚶 🏊 RV 7

Reference: **In Los Padres National Forest; map H3, grid f9.**

Campsites, facilities: There are 30 sites for tents only and six sites for tents or motor homes up to 22 feet long. Piped water, fire grills and picnic tables are provided. Vault toilets are available. Pets are permitted on leashes.

Reservations, fee: No reservations; $5 fee per night; $12 multi-family fee per night.

Who to contact: Phone the Los Padres National Forest Mount Pinos Ranger District at (805) 245-3731.

Location: From Ojai, drive 36 miles north on Highway 33. Turn right (east) on Lockwood Valley Road and drive about three miles to the campground entrance on your right.

Trip note: This developed camp is set at the end of an old spur, Forest Service Road 7N11. The trail leading out of camp goes south and connects to several backcountry camps set along small streams. The camp is set at 4,000 feet along Reyes Creek, which is stocked with trout in early summer. Open year-round. There is a good swimming hole nearby.

14. OZENA 🚶 🏊 RV 7

Reference: **In Los Padres National Forest; map H3, grid f9.**

Campsites, facilities: There are 12 sites for tents or motor homes up to 22 feet long. Fire grills and picnic tables are provided. Vault toilets are available. There is **no piped water**, so bring your own. Groceries and propane gas can be purchased nearby. Pets are permitted on leashes.

Reservations, fee: No reservations; no fee.

Who to contact: Phone the Los Padres National Forest Mount Pinos Ranger District at (805) 245-3731.

Location: From Ojai, drive 36 miles north on Highway 33. Turn right (east) on Lockwood Valley Road and drive 1.5 miles to the campground.

Trip note: This is a roadside campground near Boulder Canyon, Pine Mountain and Reyes Peak. The elevation is 3,600 feet. Open year-round.

15. REFUGIO STATE BEACH

Reference: Near Santa Barbara; map H3, grid g0.

Campsites, facilities: There are 85 sites for tents or motor homes up to 30 feet long. Fire grills and picnic tables are provided. Piped water, flush toilets, coin-operated showers, a grocery store and food service are available. The campground, food service area, and grocery store are **wheelchair accessible**. Pets are permitted on leashes.

Reservations, fee: Reserve through Destinet at (800) 444-PARK ($6.75 Destinet fee); $17-$19 fee per night; $1 pet fee.

Who to contact: Phone the park at (805) 968-1033 or (805) 899-1400.

Location: From Santa Barbara, drive 23 miles northwest on US 101.

Trip note: This is the smallest of the three beautiful state beaches located along Highway 1 north of Santa Barbara. The others are El Capitan to the east and Gaviota to the west. Open year-round.

16. FREMONT

Reference: On Santa Ynez River in Los Padres National Forest; map H3, grid g3.

Campsites, facilities: There are 15 sites for tents or motor homes up to 16 feet long. Piped water, fire grills, and picnic tables are provided. Flush toilets are available. Groceries and propane gas are nearby. Pets are permitted on leashes.

Reservations, fee: No reservations; $8 fee per night.

Who to contact: Phone the Los Padres National Forest Santa Barbara District at (805) 967-3481.

Location: From Santa Barbara, drive about ten miles northwest on Highway 154. Turn right on Paradise Road and drive 2.5 miles to the campground.

Trip note: It's a take-your-pick deal for campers who find their way to the Santa Ynez River. There are several camps set along the stream. This one is set at 900 feet. The eastern shore of Lake Cachuma is six miles away. Open from April to October.

17. LOS PRIETOS

Reference: On Santa Ynez River in Los Padres National Forest; map H3, grid g4.

Campsites, facilities: There are 38 sites for tents or motor homes up to 22 feet long. Piped water, fire grills and picnic tables are provided. Flush toilets are available. Pets are permitted on leashes.

Reservations, fee: No reservations; $8 fee per night.

Who to contact: Phone the Los Padres National Forest Santa Barbara District at (805) 967-3481.

Location: From Santa Barbara, drive 10 miles north on Highway 154. Turn right on Paradise Road and drive 3.8 miles to the campground.

Trip note: If you're coming here to hike, you are better off at the Sage Hill Camp, which is closer to the San Rafael Wilderness than Los Prietos. In fact, the trail out of this camp will lead hikers past other camps en route to the backcountry. It is set at 1,000 feet, and like the others in the area, is located next to the Santa Ynez River. Open April to October.

18. UPPER OSO 🚶🏇   RV 6

Reference: **Near Santa Ynez River in Los Padres National Forest; map H3, grid g4.**

Campsites, facilities: There are 28 sites for tents or motor homes up to 22 feet long. Piped water, fire grills, horse corrals and picnic tables are provided. Flush toilets are available. Pets are permitted on leashes.

Reservations, fee: No reservations; $8 fee per night.

Who to contact: Phone the Los Padres National Forest Santa Barbara District at (805) 967-3481.

Location: From Santa Barbara, drive about 10 miles north on Highway 154. Turn right on Paradise Road and drive 5.5 miles. Turn left on Camuesa Drive (Forest Service Road 5N15) and drive 1.5 miles to the campground.

Trip note: This is the most remote of the seven Forest Service campgrounds located in the immediate area. It is set in Oso Canyon at 1,100 feet, not far from the Santa Ynez River. A trailhead into the San Rafael Wilderness is nearby, and once on the trail, there are many primitive sites set in the backcountry. Open year-round.

19. PARADISE 🏇   RV 7

Reference: **On Santa Ynez River in Los Padres National Forest; map H3, grid g4.**

Campsites, facilities: There are 15 sites for tents or motor homes up to 22 feet long. Piped water, fire grills and picnic tables are provided. Flush toilets are available. Pets are permitted on leashes. Horseback riding facilities, groceries and propane gas can be found nearby.

Reservations, fee: Reservations requested; reserve by calling (800) 280-CAMP ($7.50 reservation fee); $8 fee per night.

Who to contact: For information phone Los Padres National Forest Santa Barbara District at (805) 967-3481.

Location: From Santa Barbara, drive about 10 miles north on Highway 154. Turn right on Paradise Road and drive three miles.

Trip note: This is a more developed option among the camps set along the Santa Ynez River. Sidetrips include west to Vista Point on Highway 154, which provides a nice lookout of Lake Cachuma. The lake itself is only six miles from the camp. Or drive east deep into the backcountry. Open year-round.

20. SAGE HILL GROUP CAMP   RV 7
🎣 🚶 🏊 🏇

Reference: **On Santa Ynez River in Los Padres National Forest; map H3, grid g4.**

Campsites, facilities: There are five loops with sites for tents or motor homes up to 32 feet long. Piped water, fire grills, picnic tables and flush toilets are available. Horse corrals are located nearby. Pets are permitted on leashes.

Reservations, fee: Reservations required; reserve by calling (800) 280-CAMP (2267); $15 reservation fee; $35-$45 fee per group per night.

Who to contact: For information phone Los Padres National Forest Santa Barbara District at (805) 967-3481.

Location: From Santa Barbara, drive 10 miles north on Highway 154. Turn right on Paradise Road and drive five miles to the ranger station. Turn left (north) and drive about one mile to the campground.

Trip note: This is another in the series of camps located along the Santa Ynez River in Los Padres National Forest. This one is set at 2,000 feet and designed for large groups. A trail from the camp is routed into the San Rafael Wilderness, where numerous primitive sites are available along the trails. Open year-round.

---

21. MONO HIKE-IN

Reference: **On Mono Creek in Los Padres National Forest; map H3, grid g6.**

Campsites, facilities: There are nine tent sites. Fire grills and picnic tables are provided. Vault toilets are available. There is **no piped water**, so bring your own. Pets are permitted on leashes.

Reservations, fee: No reservations; no fee.

Who to contact: Phone the Los Padres National Forest Santa Barbara District at (805) 967-3481.

Location: From US 101 in Santa Barbara, drive eight miles north on Highway 154. Turn east (right) on East Camino Cielo (paved most of the way) and drive 22 miles to Juncal Camuesa Road (a dirt road). Turn north (left) and drive 11.4 miles to the locked gate. Hike 1.7 miles to the campground, following the signs.

Trip note: Not many folks know about this spot. It is set beside Mono Creek, a feeder stream to Gibraltar Reservoir. The lake is small and narrow with no direct access. The camp is small and primitive. The elevation is 1,500 feet. Open year-round.

---

22. P-BAR FLAT

Reference: **On Santa Ynez River in Los Padres National Forest; map H3, grid g7.**

Campsites, facilities: There are three tent sites. Fire grills and picnic tables are provided. Vault toilets are available. There is **no piped water**, so bring your own. Pets are permitted on leashes.

Reservations, fee: No reservations; no fee.

Who to contact: Phone the Los Padres National Forest Santa Barbara District at (805) 967-3481.

Location: From US 101 in Santa Barbara, drive eight miles north on Highway 154. Turn east (right) on East Camino Cielo (paved most of the way) and drive 22 miles to Juncal Camuesa Road (a dirt road). Turn north (left) and drive 9.8 miles to the campground.

Trip note: This is one of the three smallish, primitive and little-known camps set along the Santa Ynez River between Gibraltar Reservoir to the west and little Jameson Lake to the east. The elevation is 1,800 feet. Open year-round.

---

23. PINE MOUNTAIN

Reference: **In Los Padres National Forest; map H3, grid g9.**

Campsites, facilities: There are eight tent sites. Fire grills and picnic tables are provided. Vault toilets are available. There is **no piped water**, so bring your own. Pets are permitted on leashes.

Reservations, fee: No reservations; no fee.

Who to contact: Phone the Los Padres National Forest Ojai Ranger District at (805) 646-4348.

Location: From Ojai, drive 33 miles north on Highway 33. Turn right (east) on

Reyes Peak Road and drive 2.5 miles to the campground.

Trip note: This is the kind of place a lot folks have no idea even exists. It's a tiny, primitive camp in a pretty area with a few trailheads in the area. The half-mile hike to Raspberry Spring (a backcountry camp is available there) is an easy trip, with the trailhead located immediately to the east of this camp. Immediately to the west is a trail that is routed along Boulder Canyon leading a mile down the mountain, where it meets another trail that is routed a quarter-mile to McGuire Spring Trail Camp (piped spring water is available there). It's advisable to obtain a Forest Service map. The elevation is 6,700 feet. Open from April to December.

24. REYES PEAK 🏃🏃

Reference: **In Los Padres National Forest; map H3, grid g9.**

Campsites, facilities: There are seven tent sites. Fire grills and picnic tables are provided. Vault toilets are available. There is **no piped water**, so bring your own. Pets are permitted on leashes.

Reservations, fee: No reservations; no fee.

Who to contact: Phone the Los Padres National Forest Ojai Ranger District at (805) 646-4348.

Location: From Ojai, drive 33 miles north on Highway 33. Turn right (east) on Reyes Peak Road and drive five miles to the campground.

Trip note: This camp is just down the road from Pine Mountain Camp. For hiking options, see the trip note for the Pine Mountain Camp. The elevation is 6,800 feet. Open from April to November.

25. EL CAPITAN STATE BEACH

Reference: **Near Santa Barbara; map H3, grid h1.**

Campsites, facilities: There are 140 sites for tents or motor homes up to 30 feet long. Fire grills and picnic tables are provided. Piped water, flush toilets, coin-operated showers, a dump station, food service and a grocery store are available. Pets are permitted on leashes. The campground, food service area, picnic grounds and grocery store are **wheelchair accessible**.

Reservations, fee: Reserve through Destinet at (800) 444-PARK ($6.75 Destinet fee); $17-$19 fee per night; pets $1.

Who to contact: Phone the park at (805) 968-1033 or (805) 899-1400.

Location: From Santa Barbara, drive 20 miles northwest on US 101.

Trip note: This is one in a series of beautiful state beaches along the Santa Barbara coast. The water is warm, the swimming good, and folks, the park ranger asks that you "Please keep your bathing suits on."

26. SANTA BARBARA SUNRISE RV PARK 🚻

Reference: **Near Santa Barbara; map H3, grid h4.**

Campsites, facilities: There are 33 sites for motor homes with full hookups and patios, and two tent sites. Restrooms, showers, cable TV, and a laundromat are available. A grocery store, golf course, tennis courts and propane gas are nearby. Pets are allowed on leashes.

Reservations, fee: Reservations accepted; $25 fee per night for two people.

Who to contact: Phone the park at (805) 966-9954, or (800) 345-5018.

Location: In Santa Barbara on US 101, take the Salinas Street exit going north or the Milpas Street exit going south and follow the blue camper signs to 516 South Salinas Street.

Trip note: Motor home cruisers get a little of two worlds here. For one thing, it's close to the beach, and for another, the downtown shopping area isn't too far distant either. Open year-round.

---

27. JUNCAL

Reference: On Santa Ynez River in Los Padres National Forest; map H3, grid h7.

Campsites, facilities: There are six tent sites. Fire grills and picnic tables are provided. Vault toilets are available. There is **no piped water**, so bring your own. Pets are permitted on leashes.

Reservations, fee: No reservations; no fee.

Who to contact: Phone the Los Padres National Forest Santa Barbara District at (805) 967-3481.

Location: From US 101 in Santa Barbara, drive eight miles north on Highway 154. Turn east (right) on East Camino Cielo (paved most of the way) and drive 22 miles to Juncal Camuesa Road (a dirt road). Turn north (left) and drive a quarter mile to the campground.

Trip note: We never did discover who Mr. Juncal was, but he got this campground, a road, and the dam at Jameson Lake named after him. As long as he wasn't a politician, that's okay with us. The camp is set on the Santa Ynez River at 1,800 feet. Open year-round.

---

28. MIDDLE SANTA YNEZ

Reference: On Santa Ynez River in Los Padres National Forest; map H3, grid h7.

Campsites, facilities: There are six tent sites. Fire grills and picnic tables are provided. Vault toilets are available. Pets are permitted on leashes. There's **no piped water.**

Reservations, fee: No reservations; no fee.

Who to contact: Phone the Los Padres National Forest Santa Barbara District at (805) 967-3481.

Location: From US 101 in Santa Barbara, drive eight miles north on Highway 154. Turn east (right) on East Camino Cielo (paved most of the way) and drive 22 miles to Juncal Camuesa Road (a dirt road). Turn north (left) and drive 8.8 miles to the campground.

Trip note: There are three camps set on the Santa Ynez River between Gibraltar Reservoir to the west and little Jameson Lake to the east. Look 'em over and pick the one you like. The elevation is 1,500 feet. Open year-round.

---

29. HOLIDAY GROUP CAMP

Reference: On Matilija Creek in Los Padres National Forest; map H3, grid h9.

Campsites, facilities: There are eight sites for tents or motor homes up to 22 feet long. Piped water, fire grills and picnic tables are provided. Vault toilets are available. Pets are permitted on leashes.

Reservations, fee: Reservations required; $40 group fee per night.

Who to contact: Phone the Los Padres National Forest Ojai Ranger District at (805) 646-4348.

Location: From Ojai, drive nine miles northwest on Highway 33 to the entrance.

Trip note: This group site, set at 2,000 feet, is very near the North Fork of the Matilija. Open from April to December.

30. WHEELER GORGE 🐟 👯 🏊 RV 7

Reference: **On Matilija Creek in Los Padres National Forest; map H3, grid h9.**

Campsites, facilities: There are 73 sites for tents or motor homes up to 16 feet long. Piped water, fire grills and picnic tables are provided. Pit toilets are available. Pets are permitted on leashes.

Reservations, fee: Reserve by calling (800) 280-CAMP (2267); $7.50 reservation fee; $12 fee per night.

Who to contact: Phone the Los Padres National Forest Ojai Ranger District at (805) 646-4348 or park concessionaire at (805) 646-3428.

Location: From Ojai, drive 8.5 miles northwest on Highway 33.

Trip note: This developed Forest Service camp is set at 2,000 feet and is one of the more popular spots in the area. The North Fork of the Matilija runs beside the camp and provides some fair trout fishing in the spring and good swimming holes in early summer. Nearby Matilija Reservoir provides a sidetrip option. Open year-round.

31. CARPINTERIA STATE BEACH ♿ 🏊 RV 8

Reference: **Near Santa Barbara; map H3, grid i6.**

Campsites, facilities: There are 100 sites for tents and 162 sites for motor homes up to 30 feet long. Piped water, fire grills, picnic tables and, in some cases, full hookups are provided. Flush toilets, coin-operated showers and a dump station are available. Pets are permitted on leashes. A grocery store, a laundromat and propane gas are nearby. Some areas are **wheelchair accessible**.

Reservations, fee: Reserve through Destinet at (800) 444-PARK ($6.75 Destinet fee); $17-$26 fee per night.

Who to contact: Phone the park at (805) 684-2811 or (805) 899-1400.

Location: From Santa Barbara, drive 10 miles south on US 101. Take the Casitas Pass exit and drive west to the campground (less than one mile).

Trip note: First, plan on reservations, then, plan on plenty of neighbors. This state beach is one pretty spot and a lot of folks cruising up the coast like the idea of taking off their cowboy boots here for awhile. Open year-round.

32. RINCON PARKWAY 🐟 🏊 RV 6

Reference: **On Pacific Ocean north of Ventura; map H3, grid i7.**

Campsites, facilities: There are 100 motor home sites for self-contained vehicles up to 34 feet long. A sanitary disposal station is available. Supplies are available nearby. Dogs are allowed on six foot leashes; two dog limit.

Reservations, fee: No reservations; $9-$12 fee per night.

Who to contact: Phone the County Parks Department at (805) 654-3951.

Location: From Ventura, drive six miles northwest on US 101 to the signed exit.

Trip note: This is basically a motor home park located near the ocean. Emma Wood State Beach, San Buenaventura State Beach and McGrath State Beach are all within 10 miles. Open year-round.

33. HOBSON COUNTY PARK

Reference: **On Pacific Ocean north of Ventura; map H3, grid i7.**

Campsites, facilities: There are 31 sites for tents or motor homes up to 34 feet long. Piped water, fire grills and picnic tables are provided. Flush toilets, showers and a snack bar are available. Pets are permitted on leashes.

Reservations, fee: Reservations accepted; $13-$16 fee per night; $1 pet fee.

Who to contact: Phone the County Parks Department at (805) 654-3951.

Location: From Ventura, drive nine miles northwest on US 101 to the signed exit.

Trip note: This county park is located at the end of Rincon Parkway with easy access to the beach and offers many sidetrip possibilities. Emma Wood State Beach, San Buenaventura State Beach and McGrath State Beach are all within 11 miles of the park. Open year-round.

34. FARIA COUNTY PARK

Reference: **On Pacific Ocean north of Ventura; map H3, grid i7.**

Campsites, facilities: There are 42 sites for tents or motor homes up to 34 feet long. Piped water, fire grills and picnic tables are provided. Flush toilets, a playground, showers and a snack bar are available. Pets are permitted.

Reservations, fee: Reservations accepted; $13-$16 fee per night; $1 pet fee.

Who to contact: Phone the County Parks Department at (805) 654-3951.

Location: From Ventura, drive seven miles north on US 101 to the signed exit.

Trip note: This county park provides a possible base of operations for beach trip adventures. It is set along the ocean, with Emma Wood State Beach, San Buenaventura State Beach and McGrath State Beach all within 10 miles of the park. Open year-round.

35. LAKE CASITAS RECREATION AREA

Reference: **North of Ventura; map H3, grid i8.**

Campsites, facilities: There are 480 sites for tents or motor homes up to 40 feet long, 150 of which offer partial hookups. Piped water, fire grills, and picnic tables are provided. Flush toilets, showers, two dump stations, seven playgrounds, a grocery store, propane gas, ice, a snack bar and a full-service marina (including boat ramps, boat rentals, slips, fuel, tackle and bait) are available. Pets are permitted on leashes.

Reservations, fee: Reservations should be made at least 14 days in advance and must be made 72 hours before arrival; phone (805) 649-1122; $12-$25 fee per night; $1.50 pet fee.

Who to contact: Phone the park at (805) 649-2233.

Location: From Ventura, drive 11 miles north on Highway 33. Turn left (west) on Highway 150 and drive about four miles to the campground entrance at 11311 Santa Ana Road.

Trip note: Known as southern California's world-class fish factory, Lake Casitas holds the state record for largemouth bass (21 pounds, 3 ounces) and also produces big catfish. The ideal climate in the foothill country (560 feet) gives the fish a nine-month growing season. The lake is managed primarily for anglers. Only boats between 11 and 24 feet are allowed on the lake. Swimming and waterskiing are prohibited. Open year-round.

36. CAMP COMFORT COUNTY PARK

Reference: **On San Antonio Creek; map H3, grid i9.**
Campsites, facilities: There are 43 sites for tents or motor homes up to 34 feet long. Fire grills, picnic tables, and in some cases electrical connections are provided. Piped water, flush toilets, showers and a playground are available. Supplies and a laundromat are nearby. Pets are permitted on leashes.
Reservations, fee: Reservations accepted; $12 fee per night; $1 pet fee.
Who to contact: Phone the County Parks Department at (805) 654-3951.
Location: From Ventura, take Highway 33 to Highway 150. Turn right (west) on Highway 150 and drive three miles to Creek Road. Turn right and drive one mile to the park.
Trip note: This county park gets missed by many tourists because it's not on the Destinet ticket system. It's set in a residential area in the foothill country at 1,000 feet along San Antonio Creek in the Ojai Valley. Lake Casitas Recreation Area is 10 miles away.

---

37. EMMA WOOD ST. BEACH-NORTH BEACH

Reference: **On Pacific Ocean near Ventura; map H3, grid j8.**
Campsites, facilities: There are 95 sites including group areas for tents or motor homes up to 40 feet long. Chemical toilets are available. There's **no piped water**, so bring your own. All conveniences are within one mile of the camp. Pets are permitted on leashes.
Reservations, fee: Reservations accepted for groups; $15 fee per night; $1 pet fee.
Who to contact: Phone the Channel Coast State Park District at (805) 654-4610 or (805) 899-1400.
Location: From Ventura, drive three miles northwest on US 101.
Trip note: This is one of the most popular county parks around, but you'd expect that with beachfront sites set within such close driving range of Highway 101. Open year-round.

---

38. EMMA WOOD ST. BEACH GROUP CAMP

Reference: **On Pacific Ocean north of Ventura; map H3, grid j8.**
Campsites, facilities: There are four group sites for tents that can accommodate groups of 30 to 50 people. There are some additional sites for hikers and bicyclists. Picnic tables and fire grills are provided. Piped water, pit toilets and cold showers are available. Supplies and a laundromat are nearby. Pets are allowed on leashes.
Reservations, fee: Reserve through Destinet at (800) 444-PARK ($6.75 Destinet fee); $48-$78 fee per night for group site; $6 for hiker/biker sites.
Who to contact: Phone the park at (805) 643-7532 or (805) 899-1400.
Location: From Ventura, drive two miles north on US 101.
Trip note: Plan on a reservation or don't plan on an overnight stay here. That's the way it is at popular state beaches, especially here. It is set along the ocean, a pretty spot with tidepools full of all kinds of little marine critters. It is also just a short drive to the town of Ventura and the Mission San Buenaventura. Open year-round.

MAP H4

CEN-CAL MAP .... see page 512
adjoining maps
NORTH (G4) .... see page 610
EAST (H5) .... see page 674
SOUTH (I4) .... see page 698
WEST (H3) .... see page 648

31 LISTINGS
PAGES 662-673

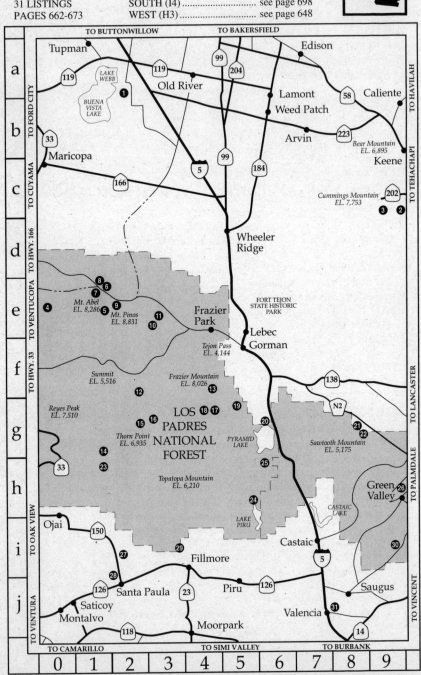

Map H4 featuring: Brite Lake, Los Padres National Forest, Mount Pinos, Alamo Mountain, Pyramid Lake, Angeles National Forest, Lake Piru, Elizabeth Lake

1. BUENA VISTA AQUATIC RECREATION AREA

Reference: **Near Bakersfield; map H4, grid a2.**

Campsites, facilities: There are 112 sites for tents or motor homes, many with full hookups. Picnic tables and fireplaces are provided. Restrooms, showers, a playground, three boat ramps, a store, a dump station and propane gas are available. Pets are permitted on leashes.

Reservations, fee: Reservations accepted; phone (800) 950-7275; $18-$26 fee per night; $3 pet fee.

Who to contact: Phone the park at (805) 763-1526.

Location: From Interstate 5 near Bakersfield, drive two miles west on Highway 119. Turn left (south) on Highway 43 and drive two miles to the campground.

Trip note: Lake Evans and Lake Webb are the highlights at this county park, providing separate lakes for fishing and boating. A public golf course is also nearby. The elevation is 330 feet. Open year-round.

2. INDIAN HILL RANCH CAMPGROUND

Reference: **Near Tehachapi; map H4, grid c9.**

Campsites, facilities: There are 225 sites for tents or motor homes, 46 with full hookups and some with water and electric. Picnic tables and fireplaces are provided. Restrooms, showers, a dump station and five stocked fishing ponds are available. Pets are allowed on leashes.

Reservations, fee: Reservations accepted; $12-$17 per night.

Who to contact: Phone the park at (805) 822-6613 or (800) 882-6613.

Location: From Highway 58 near Tehachapi, take the Highway 202 exit. Head west on Highway 202 for 3.5 miles to Banducci Road. Turn left and drive one mile to Indian Hill (Arosa) Road. Turn left and drive 1.5 miles to the campground.

Trip note: The five ponds here are stocked with trout and catfish which makes this a unique park. The campground is open year-round and offers spacious, private sites with oak trees and a view of Brite Valley. The elevation is 5,000 feet.

3. BRITE VALLEY AQUATIC RECREATION AREA

Reference: **At Brite Lake; map H4, grid c9.**

Campsites, facilities: There are 12 sites with water and electric, as well as several designated tent sites without hookups. Fireplaces and picnic tables are provided. Restrooms, showers, a dump station, a playground, three pavilions with electricity and tables and a fish cleaning station are available. Supplies are available nearby. Pets are permitted on leashes.

Reservations, fee: No reservations; $9-$12 fee per night.

Who to contact: Phone the park at (805) 822-3228.

Location: From Highway 58 near Tehachapi, take the Highway 202 exit. Head west on Highway 202 for 3.5 miles to Banducci Road. Turn left on Banducci Road and follow the signs for about a mile to the park.

Trip note: The highlight here is Brite Lake; it provides fishing for trout in the spring and catfish in the summer. No gas motors are permitted on the lake. The camp is near Tehachapi Mountain Park. Open from May to October.

4. NETTLE SPRING 🏃🏃

Reference: **In Los Padres National Forest; map H4, grid e0.**

Campsites, facilities: There are nine sites for tents only and four sites for tents or motor homes up to 22 feet long. Fireplaces and picnic tables are provided. Vault toilets are available. There is **no piped water**, so bring your own. Pets are permitted on leashes.

Reservations, fee: No reservations; no fee.

Who to contact: Phone the Los Padres National Forest Mount Pinos Ranger District at (805) 245-3731.

Location: From the junction of Highways 166 and 33 in Maricopa, drive 14 miles south on Highway 33. Where Highway 33 separates from Highway 166, turn left (south) on Highway 33 and drive about 13 miles to Apache Canyon Road. Turn left (east) and drive about 10 miles to the campground.

Trip note: This is a good headquarters for four-wheel-drive cowboys. A rough road (for four-wheel-drive vehicles only) leads northeast from camp and then forks after two miles. The fork that heads east is a winner, connecting two miles later with a primitive camp (Mesa Spring). From there, a trail leads into the backcountry. A Forest Service map is most advisable. In the fall, this campground is frequently used by hunters. The elevation is 4,400. Open year-round.

5. CAMPO ALTO 🏃🏃

Reference: **In Los Padres National Forest; map H4, grid e1.**

Campsites, facilities: There are 17 sites for tents or motor homes up to 22 feet long. Fireplaces and picnic tables are provided. Vault toilets are available, but there is **no piped water**. Pets are allowed on leashes.

Reservations, fee: No reservations; no fee.

Who to contact: Phone the Los Padres National Forest Mount Pinos Ranger District at (805) 245-3731.

Location: From Interstate 5, take the Frazier Park exit (just south of Lebec) and drive west on Lockwood Valley Road to Lake of the Woods. Turn right on Cuddy Valley Road and continue 15 miles west on Cuddy Valley Road (which becomes Mil Potrero Highway). Turn south on Cerro Noroeste Road and drive nine miles to the campground.

Trip note: It's primitive, little known, and little used, but a visit makes you an honorary member of the Five Percent Club. The camp is set high (8,200 feet) on Cerro Noroeste (Abel Mountain) in Los Padres National Forest. Don't show up thirsty. Open from May to November.

6. MARIAN

Reference: **In Los Padres National Forest; map H4, grid e1.**

Campsites, facilities: There are seven sites for tents or motor homes up to 16 feet long. Fireplaces and picnic tables are provided and vault toilets are available. There is **no piped water** at this site. Pets are permitted on leashes.

Reservations, fee: No reservations; no fee.

Who to contact: Phone the Los Padres National Forest Mount Pinos Ranger District at (805) 245-3731.

Location: From Interstate 5, take the Frazier Park exit (just south of Lebec) and drive west on Lockwood Valley Road to Lake of the Woods. Turn right on Cuddy Valley Road and continue 15.5 miles west on Cuddy Valley Road (which becomes Mil Potrero Highway) to the campground entrance. Proceed up the dirt entrance road one mile past the Caballo campground to this camp.

Trip note: This camp is a little higher (6,600 feet), a little farther up the road, and a little more primitive than the other nearby sites in Los Padres National Forest. Sidetrip options include heading to the top of several mountains in the area, including Abel Mountain (8,286 feet), Mt. Pinos (8,831 feet), and Frazier Mountain (8,026 feet). All are detailed on Forest Service maps. Open from May to November.

---

7. TOAD SPRING RV 4

Reference: **In Los Padres National Forest; map H4, grid e1.**

Campsites, facilities: There are four sites for tents only and three sites for tents or motor homes up to 16 feet long. Fireplaces and picnic tables are provided and vault toilets are available. There is **no piped water**, so bring your own. Pets are permitted on leashes.

Reservations, fee: No reservations; no fee.

Who to contact: Phone the Los Padres National Forest Mount Pinos Ranger District at (805) 245-3731.

Location: From Interstate 5, take the Frazier Park exit (just south of Lebec) and drive west on Lockwood Valley Road to Lake of the Woods. Turn right on Cuddy Valley Road and continue 15.5 miles west on Cuddy Valley Road (which becomes Mil Potrero Highway) to the campground entrance.

Trip note: This is one in a series of camps near Abel Mountain. Come prepared. The elevation is 5,700 feet. Open from May to November.

---

8. CABALLO RV 4

Reference: **In Los Padres National Forest; map H4, grid e1.**

Campsites, facilities: There are six sites for tents or motor homes up to 16 feet long. Fireplaces and picnic tables are provided. Vault toilets are available. There is **no water**, so bring your own. Pets are permitted on leashes.

Reservations, fee: No reservations; no fee.

Who to contact: Phone the Los Padres National Forest Mount Pinos Ranger District at (805) 245-3731.

Location: From Interstate 5, take the Frazier Park exit (just south of Lebec) and drive west on Lockwood Valley Road to Lake of the Woods. Turn right on Cuddy Valley Road and continue 15.5 miles west on Cuddy Valley Road (which becomes Mil Potrero Highway) to the campground entrance on the right.

Trip note: As one of several primitive camps in this immediate area, it is a take-your-pick offer. But it's an offer not many folks even know about. Caballo is set at 5,800 feet, not far from Abel Mountain (8,286 feet). Open from May to November.

9. MIL POTRERO PARK 🕊🐟♿🐎   RV. 5

Reference: **Near Mount Pinos; map H4, grid e2.**

Campsites, facilities: There are 43 sites for tents or motor homes. Fireplaces and picnic tables are provided. Piped water, flush toilets, showers and horse corrals are available. Pets are permitted on leashes.

Reservations, fee: Reservations required; $15 fee per night.

Who to contact: Phone the park at (805) 763-4246.

Location: From Interstate 5, take the Frazier Park exit (just south of Lebec) and drive 6.5 miles on Frazier Mountain Park Road. Bear right on Cuddy Valley Road and drive five miles to Mil Potrero Highway. Turn right and drive 5.5 miles to Pine Mountain Village Center. Continue 1.3 miles to the park entrance on the left.

Trip note: This quiet camp is set in the pines, but there are no lakes anywhere in the area. Instead, nearby Mt. Pinos is the highlight here with its dramatic 360-degree views. Also nearby are the Big Trees of Pleito Canyon. The elevation is 5,300 feet. Open year-round (except for occasional holidays—not exactly a brilliant business decision).

---

10. MOUNT PINOS 🐎   RV. 7

Reference: **In Los Padres National Forest; map H4, grid e3.**

Campsites, facilities: There are 19 sites for tents or motor homes up to 16 feet long. Piped water, fireplaces and picnic tables are provided. Vault toilets and horseback riding facilities are available. Pets are permitted on leashes. A note of caution: The water wells have been known to run dry in summer, so bring your own water at that time.

Reservations, fee: No reservations; $6 fee per night.

Who to contact: Phone the Los Padres National Forest Mount Pinos Ranger District at (805) 245-3731.

Location: From Interstate 5, take the Frazier Park exit (just south of Lebec) and drive west on Lockwood Valley Road to the town of Lake of the Woods. Turn right on Cuddy Valley Road and drive about seven miles. Turn left (south) on Mt. Pinos Road and drive about six miles to the campground.

Trip note: A lot of folks have no idea about the high country in southern California, but this camp provides a good clue to what is available. Set at 7,800 feet high on the slopes of Mt. Pinos (8,831 feet), it's a good place to watch for several varieties of raptors. Open from June to October.

---

11. McGILL 🚶🚶   RV. 5

Reference: **Near Mount Pinos in Los Padres National Forest; map H4, grid e3.**

Campsites, facilities: There are 73 family sites and two group sites for tents or motor homes up to 16 feet long. Piped water, fireplaces and picnic tables are provided. Vault toilets are available. Pets are permitted on leashes. A note of caution: The water wells have been known to run dry in summer, so bring your own water at that time.

Reservations, fee: Reservations required for group sites; phone (800) 280-CAMP (2267); $6 fee per night for family sites; $50 to $65 fee for a group site.

Who to contact: Phone the Los Padres National Forest Mount Pinos Ranger District at (805) 245-3731.

Location: From Interstate 5, take the Frazier Park exit (just south of Lebec) and drive west on Lockwood Valley Road to the town of Lake of the Woods. Turn right on Cuddy Valley Road and drive about seven miles. Turn left on Mt. Pinos Road and drive about six miles to the campground.

Trip note: If you wanted a great panoramic lookout, you came to the right place. The camp is set at 7,400 feet—it's an easy drive to the top of nearby Mt. Pinos—where you get a spectacular 360-degree view of the high Sierra, the San Joaquin Valley, the Channel Islands and Antelope Valley. Frazier Mountain Park, which is about seven miles from camp, provides a nearby sidetrip. Open from June to October.

12. PINE SPRING ≥   RV 3

Reference: **Near San Guillermo Mountain in Los Padres National Forest; map H4, grid f2.**

Campsites, facilities: There are eight sites for tents or motor homes up to 22 feet long. Fireplaces and picnic tables are provided. Vault toilets are available. There is **no piped water**, so bring your own. Pets are permitted on leashes.

Reservations, fee: No reservations; no fee.

Who to contact: Phone the Los Padres National Forest Mount Pinos Ranger District at (805) 245-3731.

Location: From Interstate 5, take the Frazier Park exit (just south of Lebec) and drive west on Lockwood Valley Road to the town of Lake of the Woods. Continue southwest (take the left fork) on Lockwood Valley Road and drive about 12 miles to the campground entrance road on your left.

Trip note: This primitive camp is set at 5,800 feet at the foot of San Guillermo Mountain (6,600 feet). It is one of the camps in the area that is easier to reach. Open from May to October.

13. KING'S CAMP ≥   RV 5

Reference: **Near Piru Creek in Los Padres National Forest; map H4, grid f4.**

Campsites, facilities: There are three sites for tents only and four sites for tents or motor homes up to 16 feet long. Fireplaces and picnic tables are provided. Vault toilets are available. There is **no piped water**, so bring your own. Pets are permitted on leashes.

Reservations, fee: No reservations; no fee. (Camp may be closed in 1996.)

Who to contact: Phone the Los Padres National Forest Mount Pinos Ranger District at (805) 245-3731.

Location: From Interstate 5, take the Gorman-Hungry Valley Road exit. Drive 13 miles south on Hungry Valley Road to the campground.

Trip note: This is a primitive but well-placed camp for four-wheel-drive vehicles. It is set near Piru Creek, five miles from the four-wheeler capital of Ventura County, the Hungry Valley State Vehicular Recreation Area. This camp may be closed in 1996; call before visiting.

14. LION CANYON ⌊ 🐟 👫 ≥ 🏇   RV 7

Reference: **On Sespe Creek in Los Padres National Forest; map H4, grid g1.**

Campsites, facilities: There are 22 sites for tents or motor homes up to 16 feet long. Piped water, fireplaces and picnic tables are provided. Vault toilets and horseback riding facilities are available. Pets are permitted on leashes.

Reservations, fee: No reservations; $7 fee per night.

Who to contact: Phone the Los Padres National Forest Ojai Ranger District at (805) 646-4348.

Location: From Ojai, drive about 15 miles north on Highway 33. Turn right (east) on Rose Valley Road and drive seven miles to the campground.

Trip note: Hikers might consider this spot, set on Sespe Creek at 3,000 feet. If you continue driving east on Forest Service Road 6N31, it will dead end at a trailhead for a hike that is routed east along Sespe Creek. It's about eight miles to Willett Hot Springs at Sycamore Flat. Open from April to December.

15. THORN MEADOWS 🚶🚶

Reference: **On Piru Creek in Los Padres National Forest; map H4, grid g2.**

Campsites, facilities: There are five sites for tents or motor homes up to 16 feet long. Fireplaces and picnic tables are provided. There is **no piped water**, so bring your own. Vault toilets are available. Pets are permitted on leashes.

Reservations, fee: No reservations; no fee.

Who to contact: Phone the Los Padres National Forest Mount Pinos Ranger District at (805) 245-3731.

Location: From Interstate 5, take the Frazier Park exit (just south of Lebec) and drive west on Lockwood Valley Road to the town of Lake of the Woods. Continue southwest (take the left fork) on Lockwood Valley Road and drive about 12 miles. Turn left on Mutau Flat Road (Forest Service Road 7N03) and drive seven miles to the campground entrance on your right.

Trip note: This is sure way out there in No Man's Land. It is tough to reach, but the reward is a small, quiet spot along Piru Creek at 5,000 feet, deep in Los Padres National Forest. A trail out of camp leads right up to Thorn Point, a magnificent 6,935-foot lookout. Worth the effort. Open from May to October.

16. HALF MOON 🚶🚶

Reference: **Near Piru Creek in Los Padres National Forest; map H4, grid g3.**

Campsites, facilities: There are 10 sites for tents or motor homes up to 22 feet long. Fireplaces and picnic tables are provided. Vault toilets are available. There is **no piped water**, so bring your own. Pets are permitted on leashes.

Reservations, fee: No reservations; no fee.

Who to contact: Phone the Los Padres National Forest Mount Pinos Ranger District at (805) 245-3731.

Location: From Interstate 5, take the Frazier Park exit (just south of Lebec) and drive west on Lockwood Valley Road to the town of Lake of the Woods. Continue southwest (take the left fork) on Lockwood Valley Road and drive about 12 miles. Turn left on Mutau Flat Road (Forest Service Road 7N03) and drive eight miles to the campground entrance on your left.

Trip note: This obscure camp, along with Thorn Meadows (about three miles southwest), is way out there in booger country. It is tough to reach, but in return, you get a quiet spot along little Piru Creek. The elevation is 4,700 feet. Open from May to November.

17. TWIN PINES 🚶🚶

Reference: **On Alamo Mountain in Los Padres National Forest; map H4, grid g4.**

Campsites, facilities: There are five tent sites. Fireplaces and picnic tables are provided. Vault toilets are available, but there is **no piped water**, so bring your own. Pets are permitted on leashes.

Reservations, fee: No reservations; no fee.

Who to contact: Phone the Los Padres National Forest Mount Pinos Ranger District at (805) 245-3731.

Location: From Interstate 5, take the Gorman-Hungry Valley Road exit (it's the northern exit for the Hungry Valley Recreation Area). Drive about 21 miles south on Hungry Valley Road and Alamo Mountain Road (a rough, dirt road).

Trip note: You'd best get a Forest Service map if you plan on exploring this area. Alamo Mountain is the jumpoff spot to a network of back roads, with many primitive camps sprinkled along the way. The elevation is 6,600 feet. Open from May to October.

---

18. DUTCHMAN

Reference: **At Alamo Mountain in Los Padres National Forest; map H4, grid g4.**

Campsites, facilities: There are 10 sites for primitive camping. Fire grills are available, but there is **no piped water**, so bring your own. Pets are permitted on leashes.

Reservations, fee: No reservations; no fee.

Who to contact: Phone the Los Padres National Forest Mount Pinos Ranger District at (805) 245-3731.

Location: From Interstate 5, take the Gorman-Hungry Valley Road exit (it's the northern exit for the Hungry Valley Recreation Area). Drive about 23 miles south on Hungry Valley Road and Alamo Mountain Road (a rough, dirt road) to the campground.

Trip note: This do-it-yourself camp is set near the top of Alamo Mountain at 6,800 feet. Nearby options are Twin Pines, Sunset and Cottonwood. A Forest Service map, which details the back roads in the area, is heartily advised. Open from May to October.

---

19. HARD LUCK

Reference: **On the Smith Fork of Piru Creek in Los Padres National Forest; map H4 grid g5.**

Campsites, facilities: There are eight sites for tents or motor homes up to 22 feet long. Fireplaces and picnic tables are provided. Vault toilets are available. There is **no piped water**, so bring your own. Pets are permitted on leashes.

Reservations, fee: No reservations; no fee.

Who to contact: Phone the Los Padres National Forest Mount Pinos Ranger District at (805) 245-3731.

Location: From Interstate 5, take the Gorman-Hungry Valley Road exit (it's the northern exit for the Hungry Valley Recreation Area). Drive about ten miles south on Hungry Valley Road. Turn left on Canada del los Alamos and drive three miles to the campground entrance on your right. Turn right and drive three miles to the campground.

Trip note: This is a developed Forest Service camp set on the Smith Fork of Piru Creek. It is just three miles upstream of popular Pyramid Lake, and there are no direct roads to the lake. Meanwhile the Hungry Valley State Vehicular Recreation Area, a popular four-wheel-drive area, is just a mile north of camp. This camp is popular with dirt bikers who don't or won't camp there. The elevation is 2,800 feet. Open from April to November.

20. LOS ALAMOS 🏃🏃

Reference: **Near Pyramid Lake in Angeles National Forest; map H4, grid g6.**

Campsites, facilities: There are 93 family sites for tents or motor homes and several group sites. Piped water, fire pits, flush toilets, and picnic tables are provided. A boat ramp is nearby at the Emigrant Landing Picnic Area. Pets are permitted on leashes.

Reservations, fee: No reservations; $7 fee per night.

Who to contact: Phone the Angeles National Forest Saugus Ranger District at (805) 296-9710.

Location: From Gorman, drive eight miles south on Interstate 5. Take the Smokey Bear Road exit. Drive west and follow the signs to the campground.

Trip note: Oak Flat is near the southwestern border of Angeles National Forest at 2,800 feet. It is a short drive north to Pyramid Lake, about 10 miles to the recreation area at Emigrant Landing. Open year-round.

21. SAWMILL 🏃🏃

Reference: **On Pacific Crest Trail in Angeles National Forest; map H4, grid g8.**

Campsites, facilities: There are eight tent sites. Picnic tables and fire pits, vault toilets are provided. There is **no piped water**, so bring your own. Pets are permitted on leashes.

Reservations, fee: No reservations; no fee.

Who to contact: Phone the Angeles National Forest Saugus District Office at (805) 296-9710.

Location: From Castaic, turn northeast on Lake Hughes Road and drive 27 miles to the town of Lake Hughes. Turn left on Pine Canyon Road and drive to Sawmill Mountain (northwest) on Sawmill Mountain-Liebre Ridge Road and drive about ten miles to the campground.

Trip note: This is one of the more appealing camps that hikers will find in the Angeles National Forest because it is set on the Pacific Crest Trail and is also one mile from the Burnt Peak Canyon trailhead into the backcountry. Take your pick. The elevation is 5,200 feet. Open from May to November, but the camp is inaccessible after the first snow.

22. UPPER SHAKE 🏃🏃

Reference: **Near Pacific Crest Trail in Angeles National Forest; map H4, grid g8.**

Campsites, facilities: There are 13 sites for tents or motor homes up to 22 feet long. Fire pits, vault toilets and picnic tables are provided. There is **no piped water**, so bring your own. Pets are allowed on leashes.

Reservations, fee: No reservations; no fee.

Who to contact: Phone the Angeles National Forest Saugus District Office at (805) 296-9710.

Location: From Castaic, turn northeast on Lake Hughes Road and drive 27 miles to the town of Lake Hughes. Turn left (northwest) on County Road N2 (Pine Canyon Road) and drive about 5.5 miles to the entrance road on the left.

Trip note: This camp is set a bit higher at 4,300 feet, with easy access and the Pacific Crest Trail, which passes nearby. Open from May to November, but the camp is inaccessible after the first snow.

23. ROSE VALLEY FALLS

Reference: **In Los Padres National Forest; map H4, grid h1.**
Campsites, facilities: There are nine sites for tents or motor homes up to 16 feet long. Piped water, fireplaces and picnic tables are provided. Vault toilets and horseback riding facilities are available. Pets are permitted on leashes.
Reservations, fee: No reservations; $7 fee per night.
Who to contact: Phone the Los Padres National Forest Ojai Ranger District at (805) 646-4348.
Location: From Ojai, drive about 15 miles north on Highway 33. Turn right (east) on Sespe River Road and drive 5.5 miles to the campground entrance.
Trip note: Rose Valley Falls is one of the scenic highlights in this section of Los Padres National Forest, especially in winter and spring, when the stream flow is highest. It is just a short hike from the camp to the falls. The camp is set at 3,400 feet next to Rose Valley Creek, about two miles from Sespe Creek.

24. LAKE PIRU RECREATION AREA

Reference: **Map H4, grid h5.**
Campsites, facilities: There are 238 sites for tents or motor homes. Fireplaces, picnic tables and, in some cases, electrical hookups are provided. Piped water, flush toilets, showers, a dump station, a snack bar, ice, bait, a boat ramp, temporary mooring, boat fuel, rentals for motorboats and tackle are available. Pets are permitted on leashes.
Reservations, fee: No reservations; $14-$22 fee per night; $1 pet fee.
Who to contact: Phone the park at (805) 521-1500.
Location: From Ventura, drive east on Highway 126 for about 30 miles to the Piru Canyon Road exit. Follow this road northeast for about 6 miles to the campground.
Trip note: Lake Piru is monopolized by power boats and waterskiers. In fact, the lake is designated for motorboats over 12 feet long; all others are prohibited. The lake is shaped kind of like a tear drop and was created by Santa Paula Dam on the Piru River. Bass fishing can be quite good in the spring, before the waterskiers take over. Open year-round.

25. OAK FLAT

Reference: **Near Pyramid Lake in Angeles National Forest; map H4, grid h6.**
Campsites, facilities: There are 27 sites for tents or motor homes up to 32 feet long. There is **no piped water**. Fire pits, vault toilets and picnic tables are provided. Pets are allowed on leashes.
Reservations, fee: No reservations; no fee.
Who to contact: Phone the Angeles National Forest Saugus Ranger District at (805) 296-9710.
Location: From Castaic, drive six miles north on Interstate 5. Turn left on Templin Highway and go under the freeway. Drive northwest for three more miles.
Trip note: Oak Flat is near the southwestern border of Angeles National Forest at 2,800 feet. It is a short drive north to Pyramid Lake, about 10 miles to the recreation area at Emigrant Landing. Open year-round.

26. COTTONWOOD 🐟   RV 5

Reference: **On Elizabeth Lake Canyon Creek in Angeles National Forest; map H4, grid h9.**

Campsites, facilities: There are 22 sites for tents or motor homes up to 22 feet long. There is **no piped water**. Fire pits, vault toilets and picnic tables are provided. Groceries are nearby. Pets are permitted on leashes.

Reservations, fee: No reservations; no fee.

Who to contact: Phone the Angeles National Forest Saugus District Office at (805) 296-9710.

Location: From Castaic, turn northeast on Lake Hughes Road and drive 21 miles.

Trip note: This is a quiet spot in Elizabeth Lake Canyon Creek with a small stream running by the camp. The elevation is 2,680 feet. Open year-round.

---

27. STECKEL COUNTY PARK 🐟 ♿   RV 7

Reference: **On Santa Paula Creek; map H4, grid i2.**

Campsites, facilities: There are 75 sites for tents or motor homes. Fireplaces, picnic tables and, in most cases, electrical connections are provided. Piped water, flush toilets and a playground are available. Some facilities are **wheelchair accessible**. Supplies and a laundromat are nearby. Pets are permitted on leashes.

Reservations, fee: No reservations; $12 fee per night; $1 pet fee.

Who to contact: Phone the County Parks Department at (805) 654-3951.

Location: From Ventura, drive south on US 101 to the Highway 126 turnoff. Travel 14 miles northeast on Highway 126. Turn northwest on Highway 150 and drive four miles to the park.

Trip note: You either know about this spot or you don't. You either have this book or you don't. Other than the locals, this park is not well known. It is a pretty spot set along little Santa Paula Creek in the foothill country. Open year-round.

---

28. MOUNTAIN VIEW RV PARK 🏊   RV 3

Reference: **In Santa Paula; map H4, grid i2.**

Campsites, facilities: There are 31 sites for self-contained vehicles. TV and a swim spa are available. A laundromat, a restaurant and a shopping center are nearby. Pets are allowed on leashes.

Reservations, fee: Call for available space; $19-$22 fee per night.

Who to contact: Phone the park at (805) 933-1942.

Location: From Ventura, drive south on US 101 to the Highway 126 turnoff. Travel 11 miles northeast on Highway 126. Take the Peck Drive exit and drive a short distance to Harvard Boulevard. Turn right and drive to 714 West Harvard Boulevard.

Trip note: The town of Santa Paula is known for its excellent weather and nearby recreation options. They include Steckel County Park, Los Padres National Forest and the beaches at Ventura. Open year-round.

---

29. KENNY GROVE COUNTY PARK   RV 4

Reference: **Near Fillmore; map H4, grid i3.**

Campsites, facilities: There are 40 sites for tents or motor homes, some with electrical hookups. Fireplaces and picnic tables are provided. Piped water, flush toilets and a playground are available. Supplies and a laundromat are nearby. Pets are permitted on leashes.

Reservations, fee: Reservations accepted; $12 fee per night; $1 pet fee.

Who to contact: Phone the County Parks Department at (805) 654-3951.

Location: From Ventura, drive south on US 101 to the Highway 126 turnoff. Travel 22 miles northeast on Highway 126. Take the Old Telegraph Road exit near the town of Fillmore and turn left. Drive to Seventh Street and turn right and drive two miles to the park.

Trip note: A lot of folks miss this spot. It is a county park set among the orchards and eucalyptus groves. It's just far enough off the highway to get some privacy. It is 12 miles from the Sespe Condor Sanctuary in Los Padres National Forest.

---

30. STREAMSIDE 🐟   7

Reference: **On Bouquet Canyon Creek in Angeles National Forest; map H4, grid i9.**

Campsites, facilities: There are nine tent sites. There is **no piped water**. Picnic tables, fire pits and vault toilets are provided. Pets are permitted on leashes.

Reservations, fee: No reservations; no fee.

Who to contact: Phone the Angeles National Forest Saugus District Office at (805) 296-9710.

Location: From Castaic, drive six miles south on Interstate 5 to the Magic Mountain Parkway exit. Take the exit and drive east to Valencia Boulevard. Turn left and drive about two miles to Bouquet Canyon Road. Turn north on Bouquet Canyon Road and drive about 14 miles to the campground.

Trip note: This is a nearby option to Bouquet Camp. For details, see the trip note for that camp. Do not drink the water from Bouquet Canyon Creek under any circumstances. The elevation is 2,300 feet. Open from April to October.

Special note: This campground is subject to closure at any time. A phone call prior to making your trip is mandatory.

---

31. VALENCIA TRAVEL VILLAGE 🐟 ⚓ ♿ 6

Reference: **In Valencia; map H4, grid j7.**

Campsites, facilities: There are 280 RV sites with full and partial hookups, plus 200 tent sites. A market and deli, three swimming pools, a spa, a lounge, billiards, a video and games arcade, a playground, shuffleboard, horseshoes, volleyball courts, a laundry, fire pits, propane and a dump station are provided. Some facilities are **wheelchair accessible.**

Reservations, fee: Reservations recommended; $18-$25 fee per night. Weekly and monthly rates are available.

Who to contact: 27946 Henry Mayo Road (Highway 126), Valencia, CA 91355; (805) 257-3333.

Location: From Los Angeles, take Highway 405 to Interstate 5, pass Magic Mountain Parkway and exit at Highway 126. Turn left (north), and the camp is about one mile up the road on the left hand side.

Trip note: This huge camp is located in the scenic San Fernando foothills, just five minutes from Six Flags Magic Mountain. Lake Piru and Lake Castaic are only 15 minutes away. The camp was built on a 65-acre horse ranch.

MAP H5

CEN-CAL MAP .... see page 512
adjoining maps
NORTH (G5) .... see page 614
EAST (H6) .... see page 678
SOUTH (I5) .... see page 704
WEST (H4) .... see page 662

4 LISTINGS
PAGES 674-677

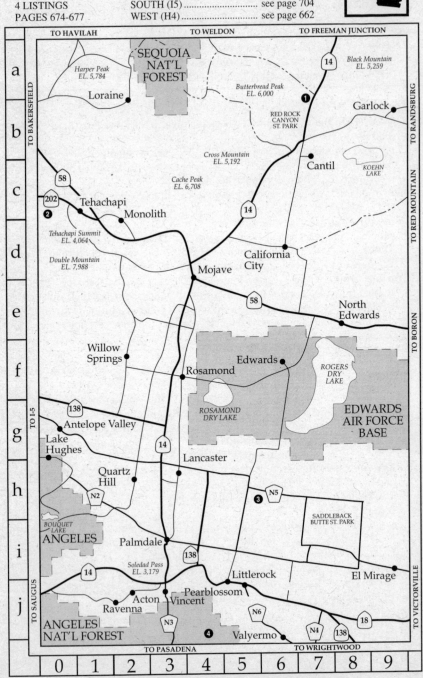

TO HAVILAH   TO WELDON   TO FREEMAN JUNCTION

a

b

c

d

e

f

g

h

i

j

TO BAKERSFIELD

TO RANDSBURG

TO RED MOUNTAIN

TO BORON

TO VICTORVILLE

TO I-5

TO SAUGUS

SEQUOIA NAT'L FOREST

Harper Peak EL. 5,784

Loraine

Butterbread Peak EL. 6,000

Black Mountain EL. 5,259

Garlock

Cross Mountain EL. 5,192

RED ROCK CANYON ST. PARK

Cantil

KOEHN LAKE

Cache Peak EL. 6,708

Tehachapi

Monolith

Tehachapi Summit EL. 4,064

Double Mountain EL. 7,988

Mojave

California City

North Edwards

Willow Springs

Rosamond

Edwards

ROGERS DRY LAKE

ROSAMOND DRY LAKE

EDWARDS AIR FORCE BASE

Antelope Valley

Lake Hughes

Quartz Hill

Lancaster

SADDLEBACK BUTTE ST. PARK

BOUQUET LAKE

ANGELES

Palmdale

Littlerock

El Mirage

Soledad Pass EL. 3,179

Acton

Ravenna

Vincent

Pearblossom

Valyermo

ANGELES NAT'L FOREST

TO PASADENA   TO WRIGHTWOOD

58   202   14   138   N2   N5   N6   N4   N3   18

0 1 2 3 4 5 6 7 8 9

Map H5 featuring: Angeles National Forest, Bouquet Reservoir, Little Rock Reservoir

1. REDROCK CANYON STATE PARK 🚶‍♂️ ♿ RV △5

Reference: Near Mojave; map H5, grid b7.

Campsites, facilities: There are 50 sites for tents or motor homes up to 30 feet long. Piped water, fire grills and picnic tables are provided. Pit toilets, a dump station, exhibits and a nature trail are available. Two campgrounds are **wheelchair accessible**. Pets are permitted on leashes.

Reservations, fee: No reservations; $10-$12 fee per night; $1 pet fee.

Who to contact: Phone the park at (805) 942-0662 or (818) 880-0350.

Location: From Highway 58 in the town of Mojave, turn northeast on Highway 14 and drive 25 miles to the park.

Trip note: Easy access makes this a prime attraction, along with the chance to see colorful rock formations. A side trip for geologically-oriented visitors or rock hounds is the drive up Jawbone Canyon Road in order to explore Jawbone and Last Chance Canyons. The elevation is 2,600 feet. Open year-round.

2. TEHACHAPI MOUNTAIN PARK RV △5 🚶‍♂️ ♿ 🐎

Reference: Map H5, grid c0.

Campsites, facilities: There are 61 sites for tents or motor homes. Piped water, showers, fire grills and picnic tables are provided. Pit and vault toilets, overnight corral facilities for equestrian groups are available. Pets are permitted on leashes.

Reservations, fee: No reservations; $8-$12 fee per night ($2 discount for seniors and the disabled); $2 pet fee.

Who to contact: Phone the County Parks Department at (805) 822-4632.

Location: From Tehachapi, drive eight miles southwest on Water Canyon Road to the park entrance at the end of the road.

Trip note: This is the kind of place that out-of-towners don't have a clue about, yet it is the most delightful spot to be found for many miles in the area. It is set on the slopes of the Tehachapi Mountains and covers 570 acres. The elevation in the park ranges from 5,500 to 7,000 feet. Winter sports are available during the snow season. Chains are often required in the winter. Open year-round.

3. SADDLEBACK BUTTE STATE PARK RV △6 🚶‍♂️ ♿

Reference: Near Lancaster; map H5, grid h6

Campsites, facilities: There are 50 sites for tents, trailers or self-contained motor homes up to 30 feet long. Piped water, picnic tables, stoves, flush toilets and a sanitary dump station are available. A group camp is also available for up to 40 people. Pets are permitted on leashes or otherwise restrained. The sites are **wheelchair accessible**.

Reservations, fee: No reservations for single sites; reserve group camp through Destinet at (800) 444-PARK (a reservation fee is charged). $13 camp fee per night.

Who to contact: Phone the park at (805) 942-0662 or (818) 880-0350.

Location: From Interstate 14 at Lancaster, turn east on Avenue J and drive 17 miles to the park entrance.

Trip note: This park was originally established to preserve the ancient Joshua Trees. In fact, it used to be called Joshua Tree State Park, but folks kept getting it confused with Joshua Tree National Park. The terrain is sparsely vegetated and desert-like, with excellent hiking trails up the nearby buttes. The elevation is 2,700 feet. Open year-round.

---

4. BASIN 🎣 🏊

Reference: **Near Little Rock Reservoir in Angeles National Forest; map H5, grid j4.**

Campsites, facilities: There are 15 sites for tents or motor homes up to 20 feet long. Piped water, fire pits, vault toilets and picnic tables are provided. A grocery store is nearby on the reservoir. Pets are permitted on leashes.

Reservations, fee: No reservations; $12 fee per night.

Who to contact: Phone the Angeles National Forest Valyermo District Office at (805) 944-2187.

Location: From Highway 14 near Palmdale, turn east onto Highway 138 and continue past the stoplight at the intersection. Turn right on Cheeseboro Road and continue six miles to the campground.

Trip note: If the camps at nearby Little Rock Reservoir (one mile to the north) are full, this camp provides an ideal alternative. It is set along Little Rock Creek at 3,400 feet, just south of a designated Off-Road-Vehicle Area. The entire area near Little Rock has been renovated. In addition to Basin Camp, there are two other new camps. Campsites are assigned at the entrance to Little Rock during the summer months. Open year-round.

MAP H6

CEN-CAL MAP .... see page 512
adjoining maps
NORTH (G6) .... see page 636
EAST (H7) .... see page 682
SOUTH (I6) .... see page 724
WEST (H5) .... see page 674

4 LISTINGS
PAGES 678-681

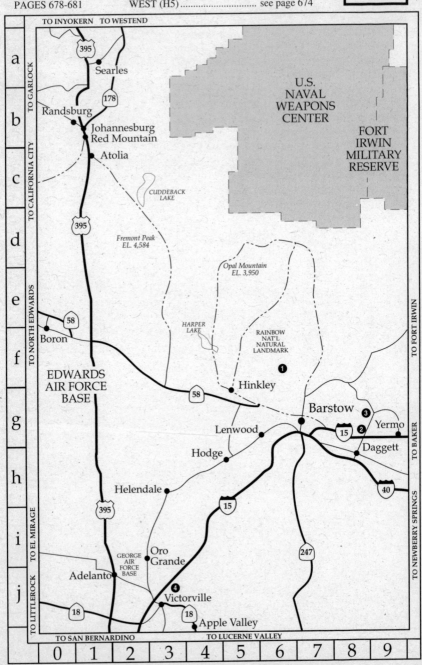

TO INYOKERN   TO WESTEND

TO GARLOCK

a

395

Searles

178

b

Randsburg

Johannesburg
Red Mountain

TO CALIFORNIA CITY

Atolia

c

CUDDEBACK
LAKE

U.S.
NAVAL
WEAPONS
CENTER

FORT
IRWIN
MILITARY
RESERVE

395

d

Fremont Peak
EL. 4,584

Opal Mountain
EL. 3,950

e

TO NORTH EDWARDS

58

Boron

HARPER
LAKE

RAINBOW
NAT'L
NATURAL
LANDMARK

TO FORT IRWIN

EDWARDS
AIR FORCE
BASE

f

58

Hinkley

①

g

Lenwood

Barstow

③

15

②

Yermo

TO BAKER

Hodge

Daggett

h

Helendale

40

395

15

i

TO EL MIRAGE

247

GEORGE
AIR
FORCE
BASE

Oro
Grande

TO NEWBERRY SPRINGS

TO LITTLEROCK

j

Adelanto

④

Victorville

18

18

Apple Valley

TO SAN BERNARDINO   TO LUCERNE VALLEY

| 0 | 1 | 2 | 3 | 4 | 5 | 6 | 7 | 8 | 9 |

Map H6 featuring: Calico Mountains, Calico Ghost Town Regional Park

1. OWL CANYON 🚶‍♂️ 🏇 ⚓ RV 3

Reference: **Near Barstow; map H6, grid f6.**

Campsites, facilities: There are 31 sites for tent or motor homes. Fire grills, picnic tables and vault toilets are provided. There is **limited piped water** so bring your own. Pets are permitted on leashes.

Reservations, fee: No reservations; $6 fee per night.

Who to contact: Phone the Bureau of Land Management at (909) 697-5200.

Location: From Barstow on Highway 58, drive eight miles north on Irwin Road. Turn on Fossil Beds Road and drive two miles west.

Trip note: The sparse BLM land out here is kind of like an ugly pet. After awhile, you love it anyway. It is best visited in the winter, of course, when hiking allows a new look at what appears, at first, to be a wasteland. The beauty is in the detail of it, tiny critters and tiny flowers seen against the unfenced vastness. Visitors can also see exposed fossils of ancient animals. The elevation is 2,600 feet.

2. BARSTOW CALICO KOA 🚶‍♂️ ♿ 🏊 RV 3

Reference: **Near Barstow; map H6, grid g8.**

Campsites, facilities: There are 78 sites for tents or motor homes, many with full or partial hookups. Picnic tables and fire grills are provided. Piped water, flush toilets, showers, a sanitary dump station, a playground, a swimming pool, a recreation room, a grocery store, propane gas, ice and a laundromat are available. Pets are permitted on leashes. Some facilities are **wheelchair accessible**.

Reservations, fee: Reservations accepted; $16-$23 fee per night.

Who to contact: Call (619) 254-2311.

Location: From Barstow, drive seven miles east on Interstate 15 North. Take the Ghost Town Road exit and drive west a short distance to the campground.

Trip note: Don't blame us if you end up way out here. But as long as you're here, you might as well take a side trip to the Calico Ghost Town, located about 10 miles to the northeast at the foot of the Calico Mountains. Rockhounding and hiking are other nearby options. The elevation is 1,900 feet. Open year-round.

3. CALICO GHOST TOWN REGIONAL PARK RV ♿ ⚓

Reference: **Near Barstow; map H6, grid g8.**

Campsites, facilities: There are 268 sites for tents or motor homes, 47 with full hookups. Piped water and fire grills are provided. Piped water, flush toilets, showers and a sanitary dump station are available. Groceries, propane gas and laundry facilities are available nearby. Pets are permitted on leashes.

Reservations, fee: Reservations requested; $15-$19 fee per night; $1 fee for off-road vehicles.

Who to contact: Phone the park at (619) 254-2122.

Location: From Barstow, drive seven miles northeast on Interstate 15. Take the Ghost Town Road exit and drive north for three miles to the park on the left.

Trip note: Let me tell you about this ghost town—there's probably more people here now than there's ever been. In the 1880s and 1890s, it was a booming silver mine town and there are still remnants of that. Alas, it now has lots of restaurants and shops. Recreation options include riding on a narrow gauge railroad, touring a silver mine, or watching an old-style play with villains and heroes. Open year-round.

4. SHADY OASIS VICTORVILLE KOA

Reference: **Near Victorville; map H6, grid j3.**

Campsites, facilities: There are 136 sites for tents or motor homes, many with full or partial hookups. Piped water, picnic tables and fire grills are provided. Restrooms, showers, a recreation room, a swimming pool, a playground, a grocery store, propane gas and a laundromat are available. Some facilities are **wheelchair accessible**. Pets are permitted on leashes.

Reservations, fee: Reservation accepted; $19-$23 fee per night.

Who to contact: Call (619) 245-6867.

Location: From Victorville, drive north on Interstate 15 to Stoddard Wells Drive. Turn south and drive a short distance to the campground at 16530 Stoddard Wells Drive.

Trip note: Keep your eyes open, Roy Rogers (the real one, not the rock star) might just ride by. He lives just minutes away from this park, where he sits happily in his living room with his horse, Trigger, which he stuffed. Open year-round.

MAP H7

CEN-CAL MAP .... see page 512
adjoining maps
NORTH (G7) .... see page 640
EAST (H8) .... see page 684
SOUTH (I7) .... see page 752
WEST (H6) .... see page 678

1 LISTING
PAGES 682-683

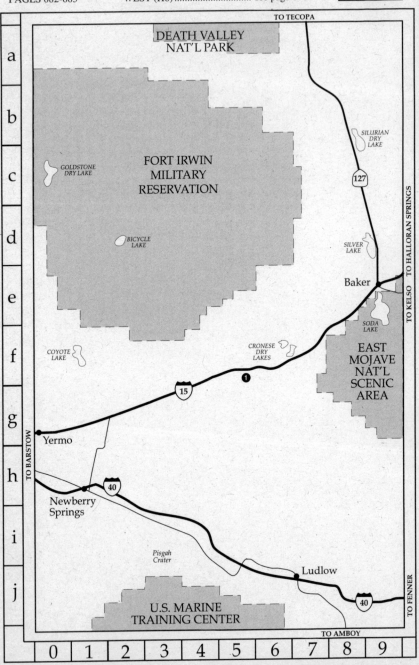

TO TECOPA

DEATH VALLEY NAT'L PARK

SILURIAN DRY LAKE

GOLDSTONE DRY LAKE

FORT IRWIN MILITARY RESERVATION

127

TO HALLORAN SPRINGS

BICYCLE LAKE

SILVER LAKE

Baker

TO KELSO

SODA LAKE

COYOTE LAKE

CRONESE DRY LAKES

EAST MOJAVE NAT'L SCENIC AREA

15

1

TO BARSTOW

Yermo

40

Newberry Springs

Pisgah Crater

Ludlow

40

TO FENNER

U.S. MARINE TRAINING CENTER

TO AMBOY

| 0 | 1 | 2 | 3 | 4 | 5 | 6 | 7 | 8 | 9 |

a b c d e f g h i j

1. AFTON CANYON 🏃🏿 🐎   RV 6

Reference: **Near Barstow in Mojave National Preserve; map H7, grid f5.**

Campsites, facilities: There are 22 sites for tents or motor homes. Fire rings, picnic tables, vault toilets are provided. There is **limited piped water** so bring your own. Pets are permitted on leashes.

Reservations, fee: No reservations; $6 fee per night.

Who to contact: Phone the California Desert Information Center at (619) 255-8760.

Location: From Barstow, drive 40 miles east on Interstate 15. Drive three miles south on Afton Canyon Road.

Trip note: This camp is set in a desert riparian habitat along the Mojave River. Remember, rivers in the desert are not like rivers in the cooler climates. There are lots of Tamarisk trees and no fish worth eating. Sidetrip options include Rainbow Basin Natural Area, Soda Springs and the Calico Early Man Site. This is one of several Bureau of Land Management areas in the East Mojave National Scenic Area.

MAP H8

CEN-CAL MAP .... see page 512
adjoining maps
NORTH .... no map
EAST (H9) .... see page 686
SOUTH (I8) .... see page 762
WEST (H7) .... see page 682

3 LISTINGS
PAGES 684-685

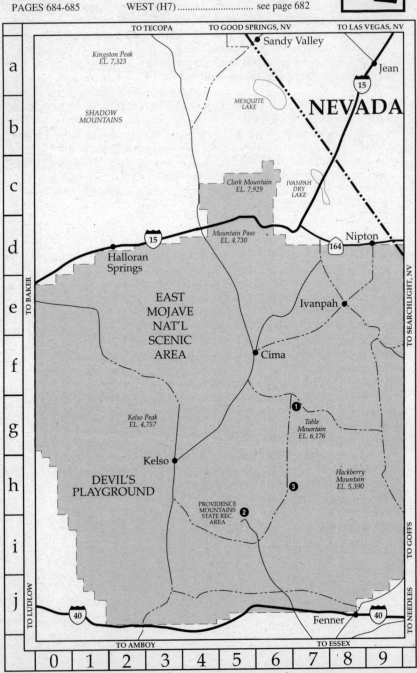

TO TECOPA   TO GOOD SPRINGS, NV   TO LAS VEGAS, NV

Sandy Valley

Jean

15

*Kingston Peak
EL. 7,323*

NEVADA

*MESQUITE
LAKE*

*SHADOW
MOUNTAINS*

*Clark Mountain
EL. 7,929*

*IVANPAH
DRY
LAKE*

15   *Mountain Pass
EL. 4,730*

164   Nipton

Halloran
Springs

TO BAKER

EAST
MOJAVE
NAT'L
SCENIC
AREA

Ivanpah

Cima

TO SEARCHLIGHT, NV

❶

*Table
Mountain
EL. 6,176*

*Kelso Peak
EL. 4,757*

Kelso

❸

*Hackberry
Mountain
EL. 5,390*

DEVIL'S
PLAYGROUND

PROVIDENCE
MOUNTAINS
STATE REC.
AREA

❷

TO LUDLOW

40

TO GOFFS

TO NEEDLES

Fenner   40

TO AMBOY   TO ESSEX

0   1   2   3   4   5   6   7   8   9

a b c d e f g h i j

Map H8 featuring Mojave National Preserve

1. MID HILLS 👥 RV 5

Reference: **In Mojave National Preserve; map H8, grid g7.**

Campsites, facilities: There are 26 sites for tents or motor homes. Fire grills, picnic tables and vault toilets are provided. There is **no piped water** so bring your own. Pets are permitted on leashes.

Reservations, fee: No reservations; $5 fee per night.

Who to contact: Phone the Mojave National Preserve at (619) 733-4040.

Location: From Interstate 40 near Essex, take the Essex Road exit and drive 16 miles north to Black Canyon Road. Turn north on Black Canyon Road and drive 19 miles, following the signs to the campground.

Trip note: This is a nice campground set among the junipers and pinyon trees in a mountainous area. It is one in a series of little-known camps that are sprinkled about the vast desert that is now managed by the National Park Service. The elevation is 5,500 feet. Open year-round.

2. PROVIDENCE MOUNTAINS STATE RECREATION AREA 👥 🏕 RV 5

Reference: **Near Mitchell Caverns; map H8, grid h5.**

Campsites, facilities: There are six sites for tents. Motor homes up to 32 feet long can park in the parking lot. Fire grills, flush toilets, piped water and picnic tables are provided. Pets are permitted on leashes.

Reservations, fee: No reservations; $14 fee per night; $1 pet fee.

Who to contact: Phone (805) 942-0662 or (818) 880-0350.

Location: From Interstate 40 near Essex, drive 17 miles northwest on Essex Road to the park.

Trip note: This desert park offers guided tours of Mitchell Caverns from mid-September through mid-June. It is a unique, remote park set at 4,300 feet.

3. HOLE-IN-THE-WALL 👥 RV 5

Reference: **In Mojave National Preserve; map H8, grid h6.**

Campsites, facilities: There are 35 sites for tents or motor homes. Fire grills, picnic tables, vault toilets and **piped water** are available. Pets are permitted on leashes.

Reservations, fee: No reservations; $4 fee per night.

Who to contact: Phone the Mojave National Preserve at (619) 733-4040.

Location: From Highway 40 near Essex, take the Essex Road exit and drive 16 miles north to Black Canyon Road. Turn north on Black Canyon Road and drive 12 miles, following the signs to the campground.

Trip note: An option to the previously-listed camp, Mid Hills is located about nine miles away. This is the tiniest and least known of the camps in the vast Mojave National Preserve. They even truck in water here, a big bonus. An interesting sidetrip is the Mitchell Caverns and Winding Stair Caverns in the nearby Providence Mountains State Recreation Area. To get there, go back to Essex Road, turn right and continue northeast for about six miles to the end of Essex Road. It's a good idea to reserve a place for the popular Mitchell Caverns tour. For reservations phone (805) 942-0662. The elevation is 5,000 feet. Open year-round.

MAP H9

3 LISTINGS
PAGES 686-688

CEN-CAL MAP .... see page 512
adjoining maps
NORTH .... no map
EAST .... no map
SOUTH (I9) .... see page 764
WEST (H8) .... see page 684

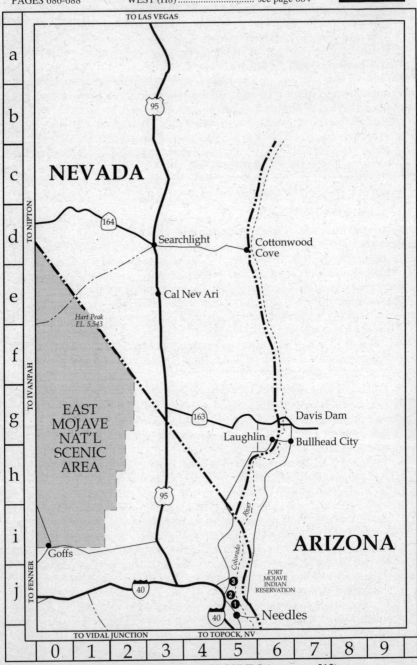

TO LAS VEGAS

a

b

95

c

NEVADA

TO NIPTON

164

d

Searchlight

Cottonwood
Cove

e

Cal Nev Ari

*Hart Peak
EL. 5,543*

TO IVANPAH

f

g

**EAST
MOJAVE
NAT'L
SCENIC
AREA**

163

Davis Dam

Laughlin

Bullhead City

h

95

i

ARIZONA

TO FENNER

Goffs

River

j

40

Colorado

3
2
1

FORT
MOJAVE
INDIAN
RESERVATION

40

Needles

TO VIDAL JUNCTION

TO TOPOCK, NV

| 0 | 1 | 2 | 3 | 4 | 5 | 6 | 7 | 8 | 9 |

Map H9 featuring Colorado River

1. NEEDLES KOA ≥   RV 2

Reference: **Near Colorado River; map H9, grid j5.**

Campsites, facilities: There are 90 sites for tents or motor homes, most with full or partial hookups. Flush toilets, showers, a recreation room, a swimming pool, a playground, a grocery store, a snack bar, propane gas and a laundromat are available. Pets are permitted on leashes.

Reservations, fee: Reservations accepted; $17 to $20 fee per night.

Who to contact: Call the Needles KOA at (619) 326-4207.

Location: In Needles on Interstate 40, take the River Road exit and drive 1.5 northwest on Old National Trails Highway.

Trip note: Now quit your yelpin'. So it's hot. So it's ugly. So you're on your way home from Las Vegas after getting cleaned out. At least you've got the Needles KOA, complete with swimming pool, where you can get a new start. Sidetrips include heading north to Lake Mead. Open year-round.

2. NEEDLES MARINA PARK   RV 6

Reference: **On Colorado River; map H9, grid j5.**

Campsites, facilities: There are 190 sites for motor homes with full hookups and picnic tables. Restrooms with showers, a heated pool, jacuzzi, a recreation room, a swimming pool, a playground, a boat ramp, boat slips, a grocery store, gas and a laundromat are available. Pets are allowed on leashes.

Reservations, fee: Reservations accepted; $22-$24 fee per night.

Who to contact: Call the Needles Marina Park at (619) 326-2197.

Location: From Highway 40 in Needles, take the "J" Street exit to Broadway. Turn left, then turn right on River Road and drive a half mile to the park.

Trip note: The campsites are on a stretch of the Colorado River that is smooth enough for waterskiing. An 18-hole golf course is adjacent to the camp. Compared to the surrounding desert, why it's almost a golden paradise.

3. RAINBO BEACH RESORT   RV 6

Reference: **On Colorado River; map H9, grid j5.**

Campsites, facilities: There are 70 motor home sites with full hookups and picnic tables. Restrooms with showers, a laundromat and a recreation room are available. In the summer, a restaurant, a swimming pool, a store, gas and a boat dock are also available. Pets are allowed on leashes.

Reservations, fee: Reservations accepted; $18-$20 per person fee per night.

Who to contact: Phone the Rainbo Beach Resort and Marina at (619) 326-3101.

Location: From Interstate 40 in Needles, drive 1.5 miles north on River Road.

Trip note: The big bonus at this resort beside the Colorado River is the full marina, making this a boat and waterskier's headquarters. Open year-round.

SOUTHERN AREA CAMPGROUNDS

SCENIC RATING

🔺1 🔺2 🔺3 🔺4 🔺5 🔺6 🔺7 🔺8 🔺9 🔺10

Poor... Fair ....Great

KEY TO THE SYMBOLS

 Boating

 Canoeing/ Rafting

 Fishing

Golf

 Hiking

Historical Site

 Horseback Riding

Hot Springs

Swimming

 Waterskiing

 Wheelchair Access

  Five Percent Club

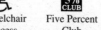   RV

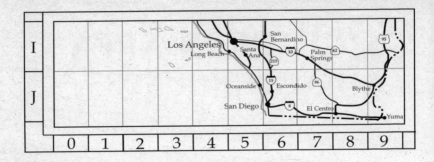

MAP I2

SO-CAL MAP .... see page 690
adjoining maps
NORTH (H2) .... see page 644
EAST (I3) .... see page 694
SOUTH .... no map
WEST .... no map

1 LISTING
PAGES 692-693

a

b

c

d

e

f

g

h

i

j

San
Miguel
Island ❶

Santa Rosa
Island

CHANNEL
ISLANDS
NAT'L PARK

*Pacific
Ocean*

0 1 2 3 4 5 6 7 8 9

Map I2 featuring San Miguel Island

1. SAN MIGUEL ISLAND

Reference: **Map I2, grid a7.**

Campsites, facilities: There are nine primitive tent sites. Pit toilets, picnic tables, wind breaks and food cabinets are provided. **No piped water** is available; you must bring your own. No open fires are allowed; bring a camp stove for cooking. No pets are permitted.

Reservations, fee: Reserve by calling Island Packers at (805) 642-1393. After arranging transportation, you must obtain a permit from the National Park Service. Phone (805) 658-5700 or write to Channel Islands National Park, 1901 Spinnaker Drive, Ventura, CA 93001. Camping is free; round-trip boat transportation is $90 for adults, $80 for children 12 and under. The boat ride takes four hours one-way.

Who to contact: For general information, phone Channel Islands National Park at (805) 658-5700. For camping and transportation information, phone Island Packers at (805) 642-7688. Ventura Visitors Bureau offers a free travel packet; phone (800) 333-2989.

Location: From US 101 in Ventura, take the Victoria exit and follow the signs to Ventura Harbor.

Trip note: This is the most unusual of the five islands, small, distant and extremely rugged. It is a home to some unusual birds and much wildlife, and only rarely do people take advantage of this island paradise. That is because it takes a four-hour boat ride to get here, a grueling trip for most. Spending a few days camping here is like renting your own personal island wilderness.

MAP I3

SO-CAL MAP .... see page 690
adjoining maps
NORTH (H3) .... see page 648
EAST (I4) .... see page 698
SOUTH .... no map
WEST (I2) .... see page 692

5 LISTINGS
PAGES 694-697

TO VENTURA

❶

Port Hueneme

TO OXNARD

a

b

Santa Cruz Island

❷

Santa Rosa Island

❸

❹

Anacapa Island

c

CHANNEL ISLANDS NAT'L PARK

d

e

Pacific Ocean

f

g

h

Santa Barbara Island ❺

CHANNEL ISLANDS NAT'L PARK

i

San Nicolas Island

j

0   1   2   3   4   5   6   7   8   9

Map I3 featuring: McGrath State Beach, Anacapa Island, Santa Cruz Island, Santa Rosa Island, Santa Barbara Island

1. McGRATH STATE BEACH

Reference: **On Pacific Ocean south of Ventura; map I3, grid a9.**

Campsites, facilities: There are 174 sites for tents or motor homes up to 34 feet long. Piped water, fire grills and picnic tables are provided. Flush toilets, coin-operated showers, a dump station, horseshoes and a visitor center are available. Supplies and a laundromat are nearby. Pets are permitted on leashes in the camping area only, not on the beach.

Reservations, fee: Reserve by phoning Destinet at (800) 444-7275 ($6.75 Destinet fee); $17-$19 fee per night; $1 pet fee.

Who to contact: Phone the park at (805) 899-1400.

Location: From Ventura, drive south on US 101. Take the Seaward Avenue/ Harbor Boulevard exit and drive four miles on Harbor Boulevard to the park.

Trip note: This is a pretty spot just south of Pierpoint Bay. The north tip of the park borders the Santa Clara River Estuary Natural Preserve and is close to Ventura Harbor and the Channel Islands National Park Visitor Center. Plan on a reservation or don't make a plan. Open year-round.

2. SANTA ROSA ISLAND

Reference: **Map I3, grid b1.**

Campsites, facilities: There are 10 primitive tent sites. Pit toilets, picnic tables, and wind breaks are provided. No piped water is available; you must bring your own. No open fires are allowed; bring a camp stove for cooking. No pets are permitted.

Reservations, fee: Reserve by calling Island Packers at (805) 642-1393. After arranging transportation, you must obtain a permit from the National Park Service. Phone (805) 658-5700 or write to Channel Islands National Park, 1901 Spinnaker Drive, Ventura, CA 93001. Camping is free; roundtrip boat transportation is $80 for adults, $70 for children 12 and under. The boat ride takes 3.5 hours one way.

Who to contact: For general information, phone Channel Islands National Park at (805) 658-5700. For camping and transportation information, phone Island Packers at (805) 642-7688. Ventura Visitors Bureau offers a free travel packet; phone (800) 333-2989.

Location: From US 101 in Ventura, take the Victoria exit and follow the signs to Ventura Harbor. Channel Islands Aviation offers a special flight to this island for campers who can't stomach the long boat ride. The flight takes 25 minutes and costs $150 roundtrip. Phone (805) 987-1301 for information.

Trip note: The "Painted Caves" of Santa Rosa make this a world-class trip for kayakers and an ideal camping trip, Fridays through Sundays. Because the boat ride to Santa Rosa is longer than the trip to Santa Cruz, this island is often overlooked by visitors on one-day trips. That makes it extra special.

3. SANTA CRUZ ISLAND

Reference: **Map I3, grid b6.**

Campsites, facilities: There are an undesignated number of primitive campsites. Pit toilets and picnic tables are provided. Fire rings are available, but fires are prohibited at certain times of the year; phone ahead to verify. **No piped water** is provided; you must bring your own. No pets are permitted.

Reservations, fee: Reserve through Island Packers at (805) 642-1393. Camping fee is $15 per person per night, except Friday and Saturday when the fee is $25; roundtrip boat transportation is $55 for adults, $45 for children 12 and under. The boat ride takes two hours one-way.

Who to contact: Phone Island Packers at (805) 642-7688.

Location: From US 101 in Ventura, take the Victoria exit and follow the signs to Ventura Harbor.

Trip note: This is the largest of the Channel Islands, perfect for camping and multi-day visits. This campground is the only one of the islands that is not managed by the National Park Service. The camp is set in a grove of eucalyptus in a valley, with a trailhead out of camp that hikers can take to reach the surrounding ridge line. A great hike is from Pelican Bay to Prisoner's Harbor, a three-miler that is routed through the interior of the island to a beautiful beach. Herds of wild sheep are abundant, and kayaking through sea caves is outstanding.

4. ANACAPA ISLAND

Reference: **Map I3, grid c7.**

Campsites, facilities: There are six primitive tent sites. Picnic tables and pit toilets are provided. **No piped water** is available; you must bring your own. No open fires are allowed; bring a camp stove for cooking. No pets are permitted.

Reservations, fee: Reserve by calling Island Packers at (805) 642-1393. After arranging transportation, you must obtain a permit from the National Park Service. Phone (805) 658-5700 or write to Channel Islands National Park, 1901 Spinnaker Drive, Ventura, CA 93001. Camping is free; roundtrip boat transportation is $48 for adults, $30 for children 12 and under. The boat ride takes 75 minutes one-way.

Who to contact: For general information, phone Channel Islands National Park at (805) 658-5700. For camping and transportation information, phone Island Packers at (805) 642-7688. Ventura Visitors Bureau offers a free travel packet; phone (800) 333-2989.

Location: From US 101 in Ventura, take the Victoria exit and follow the signs to Ventura Harbor.

Trip note: Little Anacapa, long and narrow, is known for its awesome caves, cliffs and sea lion rookeries that range near huge kelp beds. After landing on the island, you face a 154-step staircase trail that leaves you perched on an ocean bluff. The trails from there provide vast views of the channel. The inshore waters are an ecological preserve loaded with marine life, and with the remarkably clear water, makes a great destination for snorkeling and sea kayaking. Of the Channel Islands, the boat ride here is the shortest, only 75 minutes.

5. SANTA BARBARA ISLAND

Reference: **Map I3, grid h9.**

Campsites, facilities: There are eight primitive tent sites. Pit toilets and picnic tables are provided. **No piped water** is available; you must bring your own. No open fires are allowed; bring a camp stove for cooking. No pets are permitted.

Reservations, fee: Reserve by calling Island Packers at (805) 642-1393. After arranging transportation, you must obtain a permit from the National Park

Service. Phone (805) 658-5700 or write to Channel Islands National Park, 1901 Spinnaker Drive, Ventura, CA 93001. Camping is free; roundtrip boat transportation is $75 for adults, $65 for children 12 and under. The boat ride takes 3.5 hours one-way.

Who to contact: For general information, phone Channel Islands National Park at (805) 658-5700. For camping and transportation information, phone Island Packers at (805) 642-7688. Ventura Visitors Bureau offers a free travel packet; phone (800) 333-2989.

Location: From US 101 in Ventura, take the Victoria exit and follow the signs to Ventura Harbor.

Trip note: This is a veritable dot of an island, set well to the south of the four others, known for miles of hiking trails, solitude, snorkeling, swimming and excellent viewing of marine mammals. It is a breeding ground for elephant seals, with dolphins, sea lions and whales (in the winter) all common in the area. The snorkeling can be wonderful, as you dive amid playful seals. The only negative is the long boat ride, 3.5 hours from the mainland.

MAP I4

SO-CAL MAP .... see page 690
adjoining maps
NORTH (H4) .... see page 662
EAST (I5) .... see page 704
SOUTH .... no map
WEST (I3) .... see page 694

12 LISTINGS
PAGES 698-703

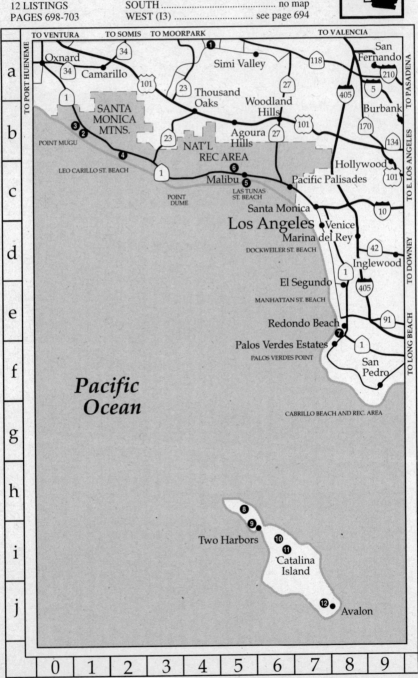

1. OAK COUNTY PARK 🚶‍♀️   RV 3

Reference: **Near Moorpark; map I4, grid a4.**

Campsites, facilities: There are 20 sites for tents only and 35 sites for motor homes. Fire grills, picnic tables and, in some cases, electrical hookups are provided. Piped water, flush toilets, a dump station and a playground are available. Supplies and a laundromat are nearby. Pets are allowed on leashes.

Reservations, fee: Reservations accepted; $12 fee per night; $1 pet fee.

Who to contact: Phone the County Parks Department at (805) 654-3951.

Location: From Ventura, drive south on US 101 to the Highway 126 turnoff. Travel six miles northeast on Highway 126 to Highway 118 (Los Angeles Avenue). Drive east for about 15 miles to the town of Moorpark. Continue east on Highway 118 for one mile to the park.

Trip note: This is an oft-overlooked county park set in the foothill country of Simi Valley. The park has many trails, offering good hiking possibilities. The camp is somewhat secluded, more so than you might expect.

2. SYCAMORE CANYON 🐟 🚶‍♀️ ♿ 🏊 🏇   RV 6

Reference: **In Point Mugu State Park; map I4, grid b1.**

Campsites, facilities: There are 54 sites for tents or motor homes up to 31 feet long. Picnic tables and fire grills are provided. Piped water, flush toilets and a sanitary disposal station are available. Supplies are available nearby. There is **wheelchair access** to trails, exhibits, picnic areas and Sycamore Canyon Campground. Pets are permitted on leashes.

Reservations, fee: Reserve by phoning Destinet at (800) 444-7275 ($6.75 Destinet fee); $17-$19 fee per night; $1 pet fee.

Who to contact: Phone the Point Mugu State Park at (818) 880-0350.

Location: From Oxnard, drive 16 miles south on Highway 1.

Trip note: This camp is set across the highway from the ocean, but is also part of Point Mugu State Park, which covers 14,980 acres in all. That gives you plenty of options. It is a popular surfing area. If that doesn't grab you, you can always just lay there in the sun and pretend you're a large, beached, marine mammal. Or you can head into the interior of the park by trail to explore the foothills of the Santa Monica Mountains. A recent fire has left its mark. Open year-round.

3. THORNHILL BROOME STATE BEACH   RV 7
🐟 🚶‍♀️ 🏊 🏇

Reference: **In Point Mugu State Park; map I4, grid b1.**

Campsites, facilities: There are 88 primitive sites for tents or motor homes up to 31 feet long. Picnic tables are provided. Piped water and pit toilets are available. Supplies are available nearby. Pets are permitted on leashes.

Reservations, fee: Reserve by phoning Destinet at (800) 444-7275 ($6.75 Destinet fee); $10-$12 fee per night; $1 pet fee.

Who to contact: Phone Point Mugu State Park at (818) 880-0350.

Location: From Oxnard, drive 15 miles south on Highway 1.

Trip note: This camp is set along the ocean, but it is also a chunk of Point Mugu State Park, covering 14,980 acres in all. That gives you plenty of options. It is a popular surfing area, or hey, you can always just lay there in the sun and pretend you're a beached whale. Or you can head into the interior of the park, exploring by trail the foothills of the Santa Monica Mountains. Open year-round.

4. LEO CARILLO STATE BEACH

Reference: **North of Malibu; map I4, grid b2.**

Campsites, facilities: There are 127 sites for tents or motor homes up to 31 feet long. Picnic tables and fire grills are provided. Piped water, flush toilets, showers and a dump station are available. Some facilities are **wheelchair accessible**. Supplies are available nearby. Pets are permitted on leashes.

Reservations, fee: Reserve by phoning Destinet at (800) 444-7275 ($6.75 Destinet fee); $17-$19 fee per night; $1 pet fee.

Who to contact: Phone the park at (818) 880-0350.

Location: From Santa Monica, drive 28 miles north on Highway 1 to the park. Or from Oxnard, drive 20 miles south on Highway 1 to the signed park exit on the right. Exit directly into the park.

Trip note: There are two camping areas, one along the beach, near the ocean, and another in an adjacent canyon. It's good either way. Reservations are essential.

5. MALIBU CREEK STATE PARK

Reference: **Near Malibu; map I4, grid b5.**

Campsites, facilities: There are 63 sites for tents or self-contained motor homes up to 24 feet long. Piped water, picnic tables, fire places (no wood fires allowed), hot showers and restrooms are provided. Pets are permitted on leashes or otherwise restrained. Some facilities are **wheelchair accessible.**

Reservations, fee: Reserve by phoning Destinet at (800) 444-7275 ($6.75 Destinet fee); $17 fee per night.

Who to contact: Phone the park at (800) 533-7275 or (818) 880-0350.

Location: From US 101 northeast of Malibu, take the Las Virgenes exit and drive six miles west on Las Virgenes Road to the park entrance. If you're coming from Highway 1 in Malibu, turn east on Malibu Canyon Road and drive about five miles to the park entrance.

Trip note: Be sure to get your reservation in early for this one. This 6,600-acre state park is set just a few miles out of Malibu between Highway 1 and US 101, two major tourist thoroughfares. Despite this, the park manages to retain a remote feel, with miles of trails for hiking, biking and horseback riding, and beautiful scenic views. It is a perfect spot for a two or three-day breather on a coastal road trip.

6. MALIBU BEACH RV PARK

Reference: **Map I4, grid c5.**

Campsites, facilities: There are 40 tent sites and 125 motor home sites with full or partial hookups. Picnic tables and barbecue grills are provided. Restrooms, showers, a playground, a laundromat, propane gas, ice, cable TV, a sanitary dump station and a grocery store are available. Some facilities are **wheelchair accessible**. Pets are permitted on leashes.

Reservations, fee: Reservations accepted; $15-$45 fee per night.

Who to contact: Phone the camp at (310) 456-6052.

Location: From Malibu, drive four miles north on Highway 1.

Trip note: This is one of the few privately-developed RV parks that provides some spots for tent campers as well. It's one of the nicer spots in the area, set on a bluff overlooking the Pacific Ocean, near both Malibu Pier (for fishing) and Paradise Cove. Each site has either an ocean or mountain view. And Hollywood is 10 miles to the east. Open year-round.

7. DOCKWEILER BEACH RV PARK

Reference: **On Pacific Ocean near Manhattan Beach; map I4, grid e8.**

Campsites, facilities: There are 118 sites for motor homes up to 35 feet long, 83 with full hookups. Picnic tables and barbecue grills are provided. Flush toilets, hot showers, a sanitary disposal station and a laundromat are available. Supplies are available nearby. Pets are permitted on leashes.

Reservations, fee: Reserve by phoning Destinet at (800) 444-7275 ($6.75 Destinet fee); $12-$22 fee per night.

Who to contact: Phone (800) 950-7275 or (310) 322-4951.

Location: From Santa Monica, drive 12 miles south on Interstate 405 to the Imperial West Highway exit. Drive about four miles west to Vista del Mar and the park.

Trip note: This layover spot for coast cruisers is just a hop from the beach and the Pacific Ocean. Open year-round.

8. PARSON'S LANDING

Reference: **On Catalina Island; map I4, grid h5.**

Campsites, facilities: There are six tent sites, each site accommodating a maximum of eight campers. Pit toilets, fire rings, barbecue pits and limited water are available. Pets are not permitted. Firewood, charcoal and lighter fluid must be obtained on the island, as U.S. Coast Guard regulations prohibit combustible materials in passenger vehicles when crossing the channel.

Reservations, fee: Reservations required; $15 fee per night for the first person per site, each additional camper is $5 per night to a maximum of eight campers ($50 maximum per night per site); check in at the visitor information booth to validate your camping permit. An adult round-trip ferry pass costs $35.

Who to contact: For ferry information or camp reservations, phone (310) 510-2800 or (310) 510-0303.

Location: From San Diego, San Pedro, or Long Beach a ferry is available that will take you to Two Harbors. From Two Harbors, travel by shoreboat (check schedule) to Emerald Bay. Hike one mile to the campground.

Trip note: This primitive campground, one of five on Catalina Island, is set on the island's northern end, seven miles from the island's isthmus and the village of Two Harbors. Primitive as it is, it can really fill up on a holiday weekend.

9. TWO HARBORS

Reference: **On Catalina Island; map I4, grid i5.**

Campsites, facilities: There are 52 sites, which can accommodate a total of 250 people. Chemical toilets, cold showers, fire rings, barbecues, picnic tables, sun shades and telephones are provided. A general store, a restaurant and saloon, a snack bar, tennis courts, volleyball, a laundromat and hot showers are available in the town of Two Harbors. Firewood, charcoal and lighter fluid must be obtained on the island, as U.S. Coast Guard regulations prohibit combustible materials in passenger vehicles when crossing the channel. Pets are not permitted.

Reservations, fee: Reservations requested; $6.50-$8.50 fee per person per night; check in at the visitor information booth to validate your camping permit. An adult round-trip pass on the ferry costs approximately $35.

Who to contact: For ferry information or camp reservations, phone (310) 510-2800 or (310) 510-0303.

Location: From San Pedro or Long Beach, a ferry is available that will take you directly to Two Harbors. If you are on the island at Avalon, take the bus to Two Harbors. Hike approximately a quarter-mile from the village of Two Harbors to the campground.

Trip note: This campground is only a quarter-mile away from the village of Two Harbors. Nearby attractions include the Two Harbors Dive Station with snorkeling equipment, paddleboard rentals, and scuba tank fills to 3000 psi. There are guided tours of the island and a scheduled bus service between Two Harbors and Avalon; the bus stops at all the interior campgrounds.

10. BLACK JACK

Reference: On Catalina Island; map I4, grid i6.

Campsites, facilities: There are accommodations for 75 campers. Water, chemical toilets, fire rings, barbecue pits and a public phone are available. Firewood, charcoal and lighter fluid must be obtained on the island, as U.S. Coast Guard regulations prohibit carrying any combustible materials in passenger vehicles when crossing the channel. Pets are not permitted.

Reservations, fee: Reservations recommended; $6.50-$8.50 fee per person per night. An adult round-trip pass on the ferry costs approximately $35.

Who to contact: Phone (310) 510-2800 or (310) 510-0303 for reservations.

Location: From San Pedro or Long Beach, a ferry is available that can take you to Avalon or Two Harbors. From either Avalon or Two Harbors take the shuttle bus to Black Jack Junction. Then hike one mile in from the junction to the campground.

Trip note: This camp, named after Mount Black Jack (2,008 feet), is a great place to hunker down for a spell. It's also the site of the old Black Jack Mine. The camp is set at 1,500 feet in elevation. If you stand in just the right spot, you can see the mainland.

11. LITTLE HARBOR

Reference: On Catalina Island; map I4, grid i6.

Campsites, facilities: There are accommodations for 150 campers. Chemical toilets, cold showers, barbecue pits, fire rings, picnic tables, phones and shuttle bus service are available. Firewood, charcoal and lighter fluid must be obtained on the island, as U.S. Coast Guard regulations prohibit carrying any combustible materials in passenger vehicles when crossing the channel. Pets are not permitted.

Reservations, fee: Reservations recommended; $6.50-$8.50 fee per person per night. An adult round-trip pass on the ferry costs approximately $35.

Who to contact: Phone (310) 510-2800 or (310) 510-0303.

Location: From San Diego, San Pedro or Long Beach, a ferry is available that can take you to Two Harbors. You then hike seven miles to the campground.

Trip note: Some folks consider this camp to be the pick of the campgrounds on the island. It is a gorgeous place; small wonder that some of the big Hollywood flicks have been shot here. There is plenty to do: You can swim, dive, fish or go for day hikes. It's also set plunk on top of an historic Indian site.

12. HERMIT GULCH

Reference: **On Catalina Island; map I4, grid j7.**

Campsites, facilities: There are 60 tent sites. Piped water, hot showers, flush toilets, picnic tables, fire rings, barbecue pits and a public phone are available. Firewood, charcoal and lighter fluid must be obtained on the island, as U.S. Coast Guard regulations prohibit carrying any combustible materials in passenger vehicles when crossing the channel. Some camping equipment is available for rent. Pets are not permitted.

Reservations, fee: Reservations requested; $6.50-$8.50 fee per person per night; children under six free. An adult round-trip pass on the ferry costs approximately $35.

Who to contact: Phone (310) 510-8368.

Location: From San Pedro or Long Beach a ferry is available that can take you to Avalon. From Sumner Avenue in Avalon, walk up Avalon Canyon. Follow the sign that says "Avalon Canyon Road" and walk one mile. The camp is across from the picnic grounds.

Trip note: This is the closest campground to the town of Avalon, the gateway to Catalina. Explore Avalon's underwater city park, play the nine-hole golf course, or visit the famous casino. Of course, there is fishing for a variety of fish, including sea bass, sheepshead, and the challenging marlin.

MAP I5

SO-CAL MAP .... see page 690
adjoining maps
NORTH (H5) .... see page 674
EAST (I6) .... see page 724
SOUTH (J5) .... see page 766
WEST (I4) .... see page 698

51 LISTINGS
PAGES 704-723

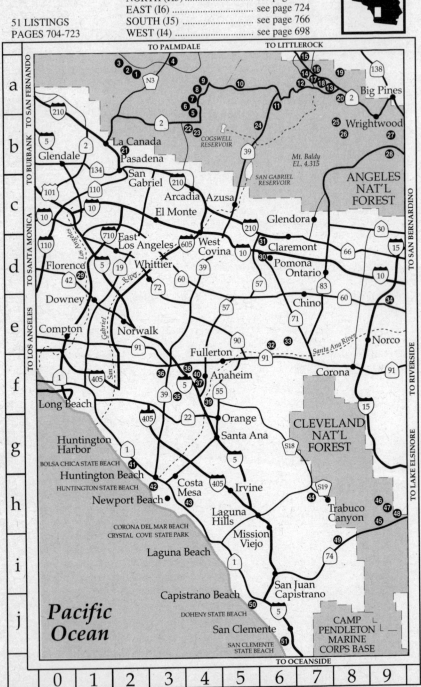

Map I5 featuring: Angeles National Forest, San Gabriel Wilderness, Crystal Lake, Jackson Lake, San Gabriel River, Mount Baldy, Puddingstone Lake, Santa Ana River, Cleveland National Forest, Santa Ana Mountains, Lake Elsinore, San Juan River, Dana Point Harbor

1. MOUNT PACIFICO

Reference: **On Pacific Crest Trail in Angeles National Forest; map I5, grid a2.**

Campsites, facilities: There are 10 tent sites. Picnic tables, fire pits and vault toilets are provided. There is **no piped water**, so bring your own. Pets are permitted on leashes.

Reservations, fee: No reservations; no fee.

Who to contact: Phone the Angeles National Forest Arroyo Seco District Office at (818) 790-1151.

Location: From Interstate 210 north of Pasadena, take the Angeles Crest Highway (Highway 2) exit and drive north for nine miles. Turn left onto Angeles Forest Highway (County Road N3) and drive about 12 miles to the intersection with Santa Clara Divide Road at Three Points (there is a sign). Turn left and drive about six miles to the signed gate. Turn left and then take the dirt road for four miles to the campground. The gate is locked in the winter when the road is impassable; walk in at that time.

Trip note: Backpackers can use Mount Pacifico as the launching pad for a multi-day trip. That is because the Pacific Crest Trail actually intersects with the camp. Being at 7,100 feet means hikers can start the hike by going down instead of up. Open from April to October.

2. LIGHTNING POINT GROUP CAMP

Reference: **Near Mount Gleason in Angeles National Forest; map I5, grid a2.**

Campsites, facilities: There are six group sites and 26 horse corrals. Piped water, picnic tables and fire pits are provided. Flush toilets are available. Pets are permitted on leashes.

Reservations, fee: Reservations required; $30 group fee per site per night.

Who to contact: Phone the Angeles National Forest Tujunga District Office at (818) 899-1900.

Location: From Interstate 210 north of Pasadena, take the Angeles Crest Highway (Highway 2) exit and drive north for nine miles. Turn left onto Angeles Forest Highway (County Road N3) and drive about 12 miles to the Santa Clara Divide Road intersection. Turn left and drive 10 miles to the entrance road on the left.

Trip note: This group camp is out in the middle of nowhere. If you want to climb Mount Gleason, trailheads are located at the Messenger Flats Camp and also three miles to the east on Forest Service Road 3N32 (left side of the road). Drive to the gate. There is also a one-mile interpretive trail within the camp boundaries. The elevation is 6,200 feet. Open from April to October.

3. MESSENGER FLAT

Reference: **Near Mt. Gleason in Angeles National Forest; map I5, grid a2.**

Campsites, facilities: There are 10 tent sites. Piped water (except in winter), picnic tables, fire pits and vault toilets are provided. There are two horse corrals available. Pets are permitted on leashes.

Reservations, fee: No reservations; $5 fee per night.

Who to contact: Phone the Angeles National Forest Tujunga District Office at (818) 899-1900.

Location: From Interstate 210 north of Pasadena, take the Angeles Crest Highway (Highway 2) exit and drive nine miles north. Turn left onto Angeles Forest Highway (County Road N3) and drive about 12 miles to the intersection with Santa Clara Divide Road. Turn left and continue 11 miles to the campground.

Trip note: The Pacific Crest Trail is routed right past this camp, which makes it a good jumpoff spot both for backpackers starting a multi-day trip or hikers looking to climb Mt. Gleason, about a half-mile trip to the east. The elevation is 5,900 feet. Open year-round but subject to snow closure from mid-November to March.

---

4. MONTE CRISTO ▮ 🐟 🏃 ♿   RV 7

Reference: **On Mill Creek in Angeles National Forest; map I5, grid a3.**

Campsites, facilities: There are 19 sites for tents or motor homes up to 32 feet long. Piped water, fire pits, vault toilets and picnic tables are provided. Pets are permitted on leashes. There are two **wheelchair accessible** sites with restrooms.

Reservations, fee: No reservations except for handicapped sites; $5 fee per night.

Who to contact: Phone the Angeles National Forest Tujunga District Office at (818) 899-1900.

Location: From Interstate 210 north of Pasadena, take the Angeles Crest Highway (Highway 2) exit and drive north for nine miles. Turn left onto Angeles Forest Highway (County Road N3) and drive about nine miles to the campground.

Trip note: This is a developed Forest Service camp set on Mill Creek at 3,600 feet, just west of Iron Mountain. Mill Creek flows eight months out of the year. The best fishing spot on the creek is located just two miles south of this camp. Open year-round.

---

5. BANDIDO GROUP CAMP 🏃 🏇   5

Reference: **Near Pacific Crest Trail in Angeles National Forest; map I5, grid a4.**

Campsites, facilities: There are 25 sites for tents or motor homes up to 16 feet long. The camp will accommodate up to 120 people. Piped water, fire pits, vault toilets and picnic tables are provided. Pets are permitted on leashes. Corrals and a water trough are available.

Reservations, fee: Reservations required; $50 fee per night per site. Groups can reserve half of the campground for $100 per night or the entire campground for $200 per night.

Who to contact: Phone the Angeles National Forest Concessionaire at (818) 578-1079 or (818) 449-1749.

Location: From Interstate 210 north of Pasadena, take the Angeles Crest Highway (Highway 2) exit and drive north for 29 miles to the intersection with Santa Clara Divide Road at Three Points (there is a sign). Turn left and drive two miles to the campground on the left.

Trip note: This is a base camp for groups preparing to hike off into the surrounding wilderness. A trail out of the camp heads north and intersects with the Pacific Crest Trail a little over one mile away at Three Points. Any questions? Rangers at the nearby Chilao Visitor Station (a mile to the west) can answer them. The elevation is 5,100 feet. Open from April to December.

6. HORSE FLATS 🚶🚶   ▲4

Reference: **Near San Gabriel Wilderness in Angeles National Forest; map I5, grid a4.**

Campsites, facilities: There are 25 sites for tents or motor homes up to 22 feet long. Piped water, fire pits, vault toilets and picnic tables are provided. A grocery store is nearby. Pets are permitted on leashes.

Reservations, fee: No reservations; $10 fee per night.

Who to contact: Phone the Angeles National Forest Arroyo Seco District Office at (818) 790-1151 or High Country Camping at (818) 578-1079.

Location: From Interstate 210 north of Pasadena, take the Angeles Crest Highway (Highway 2) exit and drive north for 29 miles to the intersection with Santa Clara Divide Road at Three Points (there is a sign). Turn left and drive three miles to the signed campground.

Trip note: This is one of the four options in the immediate area—Bandido, Chilao and Coulter are the other three. Horse Flats is set at 5,500 feet along a national recreation trail and is close to the Chilao Visitor Center. Several trails into the San Gabriel Wilderness are nearby. Open from May to November.

7. SULPHUR SPRINGS GROUP CAMP 🚶🚶 🐎   ▲4

Reference: **Near Pacific Crest Trail in Angeles National Forest; map I5, grid a4.**

Campsites, facilities: There are 10 sites for tents or motor homes up to 16 feet long. If reserved for a group, the campground will hold up to 50 people. Piped water, fire pits, vault toilets and picnic tables are provided. Pets are permitted on leashes.

Reservations, fee: No reservations for individual sites; reservations required for groups; $6 camp fee per night; $100 group fee per night.

Who to contact: Phone the Angeles National Forest Concessionaire at (818) 578-1079 or (818) 449-1749.

Location: From Interstate 210 north of Pasadena, take the Angeles Crest Highway (Highway 2) exit and drive north for 29 miles to the intersection with Santa Clara Divide Road at Three Points (there is a sign). Turn left and drive five miles to the campground entrance road on the right (it will seem like the continuation of the road you're on).

Trip note: Set in the pines along the Pacific Crest Trail, this makes a good base camp for groups preparing to hike off into the surrounding wilderness. Any questions? Rangers at the nearby Chilao Visitor Station can answer them. The elevation is 5,100 feet. Open from April to December.

8. CHILAO 🚶🚶   ▲4

Reference: **Near San Gabriel Wilderness in Angeles National Forest; map I5, grid a4.**

Campsites, facilities: There are 110 sites for tents or motor homes up to 22 feet long. Piped water, fire pits, vault toilets and picnic tables are provided. A dump station is available at Charlton Flat Picnic Area. Pets are permitted on leashes.

Reservations, fee: No reservations; $12 fee per night.

Who to contact: Phone the Angeles National Forest Arroyo Seco District Office at (818) 790-1151 or High Country Camping at (818) 578-1079.

Location: From Interstate 210 north of Pasadena, take the Angeles Crest Highway (Highway 2) exit and drive 26 miles northeast to the signed campground entrance road on the left.

Trip note: This popular trailhead camp gets a lot of use. And it's easy to see why, with the Chilao Visitor Center (any questions?) located nearby and a national recreation trail running right by the camp. Access to the Pacific Crest Trail is two miles north at Three Points, with parking available there. The elevation is 5,200 feet. Open from May to November.

---

9. COULTER GROUP CAMP 🚶🚶   4

Reference: **Near San Gabriel Wilderness in Angeles National Forest; map I5, grid a4.**

Campsites, facilities: There is one large campsite that will accommodate up to 50 people. No motor homes are permitted. Piped water, picnic tables, fire pits and vault toilets are provided. Pets are permitted on leashes.

Reservations, fee: Reservations requested; $100 group fee per night.

Who to contact: Phone the Angeles National Forest Concessionaire at (818) 449-1749 or (818) 578-1079.

Location: From Interstate 210 north of Pasadena, take the Angeles Crest Highway (Highway 2) exit and drive north for 26 miles to the signed campground.

Trip note: This specially designated group camp is actually set within the Chilao Camp. For details see the trip note for Chilao. The elevation is 5,300 feet. Open from May to November.

---

10. BUCKHORN 🚶🚶   6

Reference: **Near Kratka Ridge in Angeles National Forest; map I5, grid a5.**

Campsites, facilities: There are 40 sites for tents or motor homes up to 16 feet long. Piped water, fire pits, vault toilets and picnic tables are provided. Pets are permitted on leashes.

Reservations, fee: No reservations; $12 fee per night.

Who to contact: Phone the Angeles National Forest Arroyo Seco District Office at (818) 790-1151 or High Country Camping at (818) 578-1079.

Location: From Interstate 210 north of Pasadena, take the Angeles Crest Highway (Highway 2) and drive 35 miles northeast to the signed campground entrance.

Trip note: This is a prime jumpoff spot for backpackers in Angeles National Forest. The camp is set among huge pine and cedar trees, along a small creek near Mt. Waterman (8,038 feet). The High Desert National Recreational Trail leads northward from the camp into the backcountry, over Burkhart Saddle, west around Devil's Punchbowl County Park to the South Fork Campground. Then it heads south into the Islip Trailhead, east past Eagle's Roost and south again for the last mile back to Buckhorn Camp. It's a 20-mile hike, with the South Fork Camp situated perfectly 10 miles out to make it a weekend trip. A shorter trip to popular Cooper Canyon is 1.5 miles from Buckhorn and is accessible by trail. Open from May to October.

---

11. DEER FLAT GROUP CAMP 🚶🚶   4

Reference: **Near Crystal Lake in Angeles National Forest; map I5, grid a6.**

Campsites, facilities: There are nine group sites which will accommodate up to 300 people. Piped water, picnic tables, fire pits and vault toilets are provided. A grocery store and a visitor information center are nearby. Pets are permitted on leashes.

Reservations, fee: Reservations required with deposit; fee varies by site. Phone (800) 280-CAMP.

Who to contact: Phone L&L Concessionaire at (818) 910-2848.

Location: From Interstate 210, take the Azuza Canyon exit. Drive 25 miles north on San Gabriel Canyon Road (Highway 39) to the Crystal Lake Recreation Area.

Trip note: This is good spot to bring a Boy or Girl Scout troop. It is located about a mile from Crystal Lake at 6,300 feet. A nearby trail leads north from camp and in two miles, intersects with the Pacific Crest Trail. From there, you could go to Mexico or Canada, though it might take six months or so. Open year-round.

---

12. JACKSON FLAT GROUP CAMP 🏃‍♂️

Reference: **Near Pacific Crest Trail in Angeles National Forest; map I5, grid a7.**

Campsites, facilities: There are five group sites here which will accommodate 40 to 50 people each. Piped water, picnic tables, fire pits and flush toilets are provided. Pets are permitted on leashes.

Reservations, fee: Reservations requested; call for fee.

Who to contact: Phone the Angeles National Forest Concessionaire at (619) 249-3483.

Location: From Interstate 15 near Cajon, take Highway 138 west. Turn left (west) on Angeles Crest Highway and drive five miles to Wrightwood. Continue for three miles to Big Pines. Bear left and continue on Angeles Crest Highway for two miles. Turn right, opposite the sign for Grassy Hollow Campground, and drive one mile to the campground.

Trip note: This is a good spot for a group to overnight, assess themselves, and get information prior to heading out into the surrounding wildlands. The camp is set in the Angeles National Forest high country at 7,500 feet. The Pacific Crest Trail passes just north of camp and is reached by a short connecting link trail. Open June to October.

---

13. APPLE TREE

Reference: **Near Jackson Lake in Angeles National Forest; map I5, grid a7.**

Campsites, facilities: There are eight tent sites. Piped water, picnic tables, fire pits and vault toilets are provided. Pets are permitted on leashes.

Reservations, fee: No reservations; $8 fee per night.

Who to contact: Phone the Angeles National Forest Valyermo District Office at (805) 944-2187.

Location: From Interstate 15 near Cajon, take Highway 138 west. Turn left (west) on Angeles Crest Highway and drive five miles to Wrightwood. Continue for three miles to Big Pines. Bear right on Big Pines Highway (County Road N4) and drive two miles to the campground.

Trip note: This is one of the four camps set on Big Pines "Highway" near Jackson Lake, a small lake located about one-half mile up the road. Any questions? Rangers can answer them at the nearby Big Pines Visitor Information Center and Ski Complexes. The elevation is 6,200 feet. Open from April to November.

14. MOUNTAIN OAK

Reference: **Near Jackson Lake in Angeles National Forest; map I5, grid a7.**

Campsites, facilities: There are 17 sites for tents or motor homes up to 18 feet long. Piped water, fire pits and picnic tables are provided. Flush toilets are available. Groceries and propane gas are nearby. Pets are permitted on leashes.

Reservations, fee: No reservations; $10 fee per night.

Who to contact: Phone the Angeles National Forest Valyermo District Office at (805) 944-2187.

Location: From Interstate 15 near Cajon, take Highway 138 west. Turn left (west) on Angeles Crest Highway and drive five miles to Wrightwood. Continue for three miles to Big Pines. Bear right on Big Pines Highway (County Road N4) and drive three miles to the campground.

Trip note: This is one of four camps within a mile, set to the west of Jackson Lake on Big Pines Highway. The others are Lake, Peavine and Apple Tree. The elevation is 6,200 feet. Open from May to October.

---

15. BIG ROCK 🚶🚶

Reference: **On Big Rock Creek in Angeles National Forest; map I5, grid a7.**

Campsites, facilities: There are eight sites for tents. Fire pits, vault toilets and picnic tables are provided. There is **no piped water**, so bring your own. Pets are permitted on leashes.

Reservations, fee: No reservations; no fee.

Who to contact: Phone the Angeles National Forest Valyermo District Office at (805) 944-2187.

Location: From Highway 138 in Pearblossom, turn south on Longview Road. Turn left on Valyermo Road and drive past the ranger station. Turn right on Big Rock Road and continue up the canyon past the South Fork Camp turn and past Camp Fenner to the campground entrance road on the right.

Trip note: This is a good spot for four-wheel-drive cowboys. It is a primitive Forest Service camp set at the head of Fenner Canyon along Big Rock Creek. Forest Service Road 4N11 to the southeast is a four-wheel-drive road that connects to a network of backcountry roads and hiking trails. A Forest Service map is essential. The elevation is 5,550 feet. Open year-round.

---

16. SYCAMORE FLAT

Reference: **On Big Rock Creek in Angeles National Forest; map I5, grid a7.**

Campsites, facilities: There are 11 sites for tents or motor homes up to 22 feet long. Piped water, fire pits, vault toilets and picnic tables are provided. Pets are permitted on leashes.

Reservations, fee: No reservations; $8 fee per night.

Who to contact: Phone the Angeles National Forest Valyermo District Office at (805) 944-2187.

Location: From Highway 138 in Pearblossom, turn south on Longview Road. Drive to Valyermo Road and turn left. Drive past the ranger station. Turn right on Big Rock Road and drive about two miles up the canyon to the campground.

Trip note: This is a developed camp set just inside the northern boundary of Angeles National Forest. No trails lead out from the camp; the nearest trailhead is located at the South Fork Camp, which is a little over one mile to the north. The elevation is 4,300 feet. Open year-round.

17. LAKE

Reference: **On Jackson Lake in Angeles National Forest; map I5, grid a7.**

Campsites, facilities: There are eight sites for tents or motor homes up to 18 feet long. Piped water, fire pits, vault toilets and picnic tables are provided. Pets are permitted on leashes.

Reservations, fee: No reservations; $10 fee per night.

Who to contact: Phone the Angeles National Forest Valyermo District Office at (805) 944-2187.

Location: From Interstate 15 near Cajon, take Highway 138 west. Turn left (west) on Angeles Crest Highway and drive five miles to Wrightwood. Continue for three miles to Big Pines. Bear right on Big Pines Highway (County Road N4) and drive 2.5 miles to the campground.

Trip note: This is a pretty setting set on the southeast shore of little Jackson Lake. Of the four camps within a mile this is the only one set right along the lake. The elevation is 6,100 feet. Open from May to November.

18. PEAVINE

Reference: **Near Jackson Lake in Angeles National Forest; map I5, grid a7.**

Campsites, facilities: There are four tent sites. Piped water, picnic tables, fire pits and vault toilets are provided. A grocery store and propane gas are nearby. Pets are permitted on leashes.

Reservations, fee: No reservations; $8 fee per night.

Who to contact: Phone the Angeles National Forest Valyermo District Office at (805) 944-2187.

Location: From Interstate 15 near Cajon, take Highway 138 west. Turn left (west) on Angeles Crest Highway and drive five miles to Wrightwood. Continue for three miles to Big Pines. Bear right on Big Pines Highway (County Road N4) and drive 2.5 miles to the campground.

Trip note: This tiny camp, one of the four in the immediate area, is set at 6,100 feet. Little eight-acre Jackson Lake is located just a half mile to the west. Open from May to November.

19. TABLE MOUNTAIN

Reference: **In Angeles National Forest; map I5, grid a8.**

Campsites, facilities: There are 115 sites for tents or motor homes up to 32 feet long. Piped water, fire pits, vault toilets and picnic tables are provided. Pets are permitted on leashes.

Reservations, fee: No reservations; $12 fee per night.

Who to contact: Phone the Angeles National Forest Concessionaire at (619) 249-3483.

Location: From Interstate 15 near Cajon, take Highway 138 west. Turn left (west) on Angeles Crest Highway and drive five miles to Wrightwood. Continue for three miles to Big Pines. Turn right on Table Mountain Road and drive one mile to the campground.

Trip note: This is a family campground that accommodates both tenters and RVs. The road leading in is a paved two-lane county road, easily accessible by any vehicle. The nearby Big Pines Visitor Information Center, located one mile to the south, can provide maps and information on road conditions. The elevation is 7,200 feet. Open from May to October.

20. BLUE RIDGE

Reference: On Pacific Crest Trail in Angeles National Forest; map I5, grid a8.

Campsites, facilities: There are eight sites for tents or motor homes up to 16 feet long. Fire pits, vault toilets and picnic tables are provided. There is **no piped water**, so bring your own. Pets are permitted on leashes.

Reservations, fee: No reservations; no fee.

Who to contact: Phone the Angeles National Forest Valyermo District Office at (805) 944-2187.

Location: From Interstate 15 near Cajon, take Highway 138 west. Turn left (west) on Angeles Crest Highway and drive five miles to Wrightwood. Continue for three miles to Big Pines. Bear left and continue on Angeles Crest Highway for 1.5 miles. Turn left (opposite Inspiration Point) on Blue Ridge Road and drive three miles to the campground.

Trip note: Set high in Angeles National Forest at 8,000 feet, this makes an ideal jumpoff spot for a multi-day backpacking trip. The Pacific Crest Trail runs right alongside the camp. Guffy Camp, also located aside the PCT, provides an option two miles to the southeast, but it takes a four-wheel-drive vehicle to get there. Open from June to October.

21. MILLARD

Reference: Near Millard Falls in Angeles National Forest; map I5, grid b2.

Campsites, facilities: There are five tent sites. Piped water, picnic tables, fire pits and vault toilets are provided. Pets are permitted on leashes.

Reservations, fee: No reservations, no fee.

Who to contact: Phone the Angeles National Forest Arroyo Seco District Office at (818) 790-1151.

Location: From Interstate 210 north of Pasadena, take the Lake Avenue exit north to Loma Alta Drive. Turn west (left) on Loma Alta Drive and drive to the Chaney Trail (at the flashing yellow light). Follow the signs to the camp.

Trip note: This tiny camp can be used as a launching point for some excellent hikes. One trail out of camp leads to Inspiration Point and continues farther to San Gabriel Peak. Millard Falls, best viewed in late winter and early spring, is within a mile of the campground. The camp is set near a creek in oak and alder woodlands. The elevation is 1,200 feet. Open year-round.

22. WEST FORK WALK-IN

Reference: **On the West Fork of San Gabriel River in Angeles National Forest; map I5, grid b4.**

Campsites, facilities: There are seven tent sites. Picnic tables, fire pits and vault toilets are provided. There is **no piped water**, so bring your own. Pets are allowed on leashes.

Reservations, fee: No reservations; no fee.

Who to contact: Phone the Angeles National Forest Arroyo Seco District Office at (818) 790-1151.

Location: From Interstate 210 north of Pasadena, take the Angeles Crest Highway (Highway 2) and drive about 14 miles to the Red Box Ranger Station. Park in the lot there, walk in through the gate (on Red Box-Rincon Road) to the dirt road (not the paved one), and walk-in 4.5 miles to the campground.

Trip note: It takes a circuitous drive and a 4.5-mile hike to reach this camp, but for backpackers it is worth it. It is set along the West Fork of the San Gabriel River amid pine woodlands, with two national recreational trails intersecting just south of the camp. The elevation is 3,000 feet. Open from April to November, but subject to closure because of snow.

23. VALLEY FORGE WALK-IN

Reference: **On San Gabriel River in Angeles National Forest; map I5, grid b4.**
Campsites, facilities: There are 17 tent sites. Piped water, picnic tables, fire pits and vault toilets are provided. **No piped water.** Pets are allowed on leashes.
Reservations, fee: No reservations; no fee.
Who to contact: Phone the Angeles National Forest Arroyo Seco District Office at (818) 790-1151.
Location: From Interstate 210 north of Pasadena, take the Angeles Crest Highway (Highway 2) and drive about 14 miles to the Red Box Ranger Station. Park in the lot there, walk in through the gate (on Red Box-Rincon Road) to the dirt road (not the paved one), and walk-in three miles to the campground.
Trip note: This is a good camp for fishermen or hikers. For fishermen, the adjacent West Fork of the San Gabriel River is stocked with trout in the early summer. For hikers, a national recreation trail passes close to the camp. The elevation is 3,500 feet. Open from April to November, but subject to closure because of snow.

24. COLDBROOK

Reference: **On the North Fork of San Gabriel River in Angeles National Forest; map I5, grid b6.**
Campsites, facilities: There are 25 sites for tents or motor homes up to 22 feet long. Piped water, fire pits, vault toilets and picnic tables are provided. Campground host is on-site. Pets are permitted on leashes.
Reservations, fee: No reservations; $8 fee per night and $2 for each additional vehicle.
Who to contact: Phone the Angeles National Forest Mt. Baldy District Office at (818) 335-1251.
Location: From Interstate 210, take the Azuza Canyon exit. Drive 18 miles north on San Gabriel Canyon Road (Highway 39) to the campground entrance.
Trip note: This is one of the prime spots in the area because it is set along the North Fork of the San Gabriel River. The stream is often stocked with trout in the early summer. About a quarter mile from the camp is a trailhead for a backpacking trip into the San Gabriel Wilderness. The elevation is 3,300 feet. Open year-round.

25. LUPINE

Reference: **On Prairie Fork Creek in Angeles National Forest; map I5, grid b8.**
Campsites, facilities: There are 11 tent sites. Picnic tables and fire pits are provided. Vault toilets are available. There is **no piped water**, so bring your own. Pets are permitted on leashes.
Reservations, fee: No reservations; no fee.
Who to contact: Phone the Angeles National Forest Valyermo District Office at (805) 944-2187.
Location: From Interstate 15 near Cajon, take Highway 138 west. Turn left (west) on Angeles Crest Highway and drive five miles to Wrightwood. Continue for

three miles to Big Pines. Bear left and continue on Angeles Crest Highway for 1.5 miles. Turn left (opposite Inspiration Point) on Blue Ridge Road (it's a rough, dirt road after the first three miles) and drive 10 miles to the camp.

Trip note: This is a little-known, hard-to-reach camp, set at 6,500 feet along Prairie Fork Creek. There's a fantastic hike that starts here. The trail is routed from the camp over Pine Mountain Ridge and then eventually to the east up Dawson Peak. Open from June to October.

26. CABIN FLAT 🐟 🚶

Reference: **On Prairie Creek in Angeles National Forest; map I5, grid b8.**

Campsites, facilities: There are 12 tent sites. Picnic tables, fire pits and vault toilets are provided. There is **no piped water**, so bring your own. Pets are permitted on leashes.

Reservations, fee: No reservations; no fee.

Who to contact: Phone the Angeles National Forest Valyermo District Office at (805) 944-2187.

Location: From Interstate 15 near Cajon, take Highway 138 west. Turn left (west) on Angeles Crest Highway and drive five miles to Wrightwood. Continue for three miles to Big Pines. Bear left and continue on Angeles Crest Highway for 1.5 miles. Turn left (opposite Inspiration Point) on Blue Ridge Road and drive 12 miles to the campground (the road becomes a rough, dirt road after the first three miles).

Trip note: It takes a four-wheel drive to get here, but that done, you're guaranteed solitude along little Prairie Creek, deep in the Angeles National Forest. To get here, you will pass several other camps, including Guffy and Lupine. A short trail runs beside the stream for about a quarter mile. The elevation is 5,400 feet. Open from June to October.

27. GUFFY 🚶

Reference: **On Pacific Crest Trail in Angeles National Forest; map I5, grid b9.**

Campsites, facilities: There are six tent sites. Picnic tables and fire pits are provided. Vault toilets are available. There is **no piped water**, so bring your own. Pets are permitted on leashes.

Reservations, fee: No reservations; no fee.

Who to contact: Phone the Angeles National Forest Valyermo District Office at (805) 944-2187.

Location: From Interstate 15 near Cajon, take Highway 138 west. Turn left (west) on Angeles Crest Highway and drive five miles to Wrightwood. Continue for three miles to Big Pines. Bear left and continue on Angeles Crest Highway for 1.5 miles. Turn left (opposite Inspiration Point) on Blue Ridge Road and drive six miles to the campground (it's a rough, dirt road after the first three miles).

Trip note: A short trail right out of this camp connects with the Pacific Crest Trail, and from there you can hike to Canada if you want. The elevation is 8,300 feet. Open from June to October.

28. MANKER FLATS 🚶

Reference: **Near Mt. Baldy in Angeles National Forest; map I5, grid b9.**

Campsites, facilities: There are 22 sites for tents or motor homes up to 16 feet long. Piped water, flush toilets, picnic tables and fire grills are provided. Pets are permitted on leashes.

Reservations, fee: No reservations; $8 fee per night, $2 fee each additional vehicle.

Who to contact: Phone the Angeles National Forest Mount Baldy Ranger District at (818) 335-1251.

Location: From Ontario, drive six miles north on Highway 83 to Mt. Baldy Road. Drive nine miles north on Mt. Baldy Road to the campground.

Trip note: The camp is set between the Cucamonga Wilderness to the south and Sheep Mountain Wilderness to the west. There is a trail out of camp that leads to San Antonio Falls, a good side trip. Open May to October.

29. DEL RIO MOBILE HOME & RV PARK 🏊 RV 1

Reference: **In Los Angeles; map I5, grid d1.**

Campsites, facilities: There are 30 motor home sites. Piped water, electrical connections and sewer hookups are provided. A swimming pool, a jacuzzi and laundry facilities are available. Pets are allowed on leashes.

Reservations, fee: Reservations accepted; $20 fee for two people per night, $1 each additional camper (maximum of $24 for six or more people). Good Sam discounts.

Who to contact: Phone the park at (213) 560-2895.

Location: From Interstate 710 (Long Beach Freeway), take the Florence Avenue exit. Drive west on Florence Avenue to 5246 East Florence Avenue.

Trip note: This privately-operated, urban motor home park is located about 15 minutes from downtown Los Angeles and 20 minutes from Long Beach.

30. FAIRPLEX RV PARK 🐟 RV 4

Reference: **In Pomona; map I5, grid d5.**

Campsites, facilities: There are 185 pull-through sites, 158 with full hookups and 27 with water and electric hookups. Restrooms, showers, a heated pool and spa, a convenience store, dump station and laundry are provided.

Reservations, fee: Reservations accepted; $25 fee per night.

Who to contact: Fairplex, 2200 North White Avenue, Pomona, CA 91768; (909) 865-4318 or (909) 593-8915.

Location: From Interstate 10, take the Fairplex exit and go left. At the bottom of the hill, turn right on McKinley Avenue. Take McKinley all the way to White Avenue, then turn left. The RV park is at 2200 North White Avenue.

Trip note: This is what you might call an urban motor home park, but then again, the L.A. County Fairgrounds are right across the street, and there's always something interesting going on there, every weekend. Fishing at Bonelli Park is only 15 minutes away.

31. EAST SHORE RV PARK   RV 7
🐟 ⚓ 🚻 🏊 🚶

Reference: **At Puddingstone Lake; map I5, grid d6.**

Campsites, facilities: There are 25 walk-in tent sites and 426 motor home sites. Piped water, electrical connections, and sewer hookups are provided at most motor home sites. Restrooms, showers, a recreation room, a swimming pool, a grocery store, propane gas and a laundromat are available. Pets are permitted on leashes.

Reservations, fee: Reservations accepted; $23-$26 fee per night; $2 pet fee.

Who to contact: Phone the camp at (909) 599-8355.

Location: From Pomona, drive five miles west on Interstate 10. Take the Fairplex exit north to the first traffic light. Turn left on Via Verde and drive to the first stop sign. Turn right on Campers View and drive into the park.

Trip note: Puddingstone Lake is bigger than most folks expect any body of water in the Los Angeles basin to be and it provides all water sport activities, including boating, fishing, jet skiing and waterskiing. Side trip options include venturing north of Azusa on San Gabriel Canyon Road to Morris and San Gabriel Reservoirs or farther in Angeles National Forest. Open year-round.

---

32. CANYON RV

Reference: **Near Santa Ana River; map I5, grid e6.**

Campsites, facilities: There are 120 sites for tents or motor homes up to 40 feet long. Fire grills and picnic tables are provided. Piped water, flush toilets, showers, a dump station, a swimming pool and a playground are available. A grocery store, a laundromat and propane gas are nearby. Pets are permitted on leashes.

Reservations, fee: Reservations accepted; $22.50 fee per night; $1 pet fee.

Who to contact: Phone the park at (714) 637-0210.

Location: From Interstate 5 north of Anaheim, take the Gypsum Canyon Road exit. Drive 13 miles east on Highway 91 to the park entrance.

Trip note: In the mad rush to find a spot to park an RV in the area, this regional park is often overlooked. It is located near the Santa Ana River. Side trip possibilities include Chino Hills State Park to the north, Cleveland National Forest to the south, and Lake Mathews to the southeast. The park is also close to Disneyland and Knott's Berry Farm. Open year-round.

---

33. PRADO REGIONAL PARK

Reference: **On Prado Park Lake near Corona; map I5, grid e7.**

Campsites, facilities: There are 35 sites for RVs with full hookups and 15 tent sites. Twenty-five sites are available to groups. Picnic tables, fire pits, restrooms, laundry facilities and showers are provided. A snack bar, a picnic area, a boat ramp and boat rentals are available. Pets are permitted on leashes.

Reservations, fee: Reservations accepted; $15 per night; $1 pet fee. Weekly, monthly and senior rates available. Group rates are $11 per unit, with a maximum of two units per site. (There is also a $10 reservation fee for groups.) Proof of insurance for all vehicles is required.

Who to contact: Phone Prado Regional Park at (909) 597-4260.

Location: From Riverside, drive on Highway 91 west to Highway 71. Turn north on Highway 71 and proceed four miles to Highway 83/Euclid Avenue. Turn right on Euclid Avenue and drive one mile to the park entrance on the right.

Trip note: This little lake is a backyard fishing hole for folks in Corona and Norco. It doesn't look like much in the summer, and it doesn't produce much either. But in the early winter, it undergoes a complete transformation with a little rain, cool temperatures and trout plants making it a viable fishery.

---

34. RANCHO JURUPA COUNTY PARK

Reference: **Near Riverside; map I5, grid e9.**

Campsites, facilities: There are 80 sites for tents or motor homes. Electrical connections, piped water, fire grills and picnic tables are provided. Flush toilets, showers and a dump station are available. Pets are permitted on leashes.

Reservations, fee: Reservations accepted; $16 fee per night; $5 per pole fishing fee; $2 pet fee.

Who to contact: Phone the park at (909) 684-7032.

Location: From Interstate 15 in Riverside, turn west on Highway 60 for about three miles. Turn left on Rubidoux Boulevard and drive a half mile. Turn left on Mission Boulevard and drive about one mile to Crestmore Boulevard. Turn right and drive 1.5 miles to the park gate on the left.

Trip note: Lord, it gets hot here in the summertime. If you want a lake to jump into, you have your pick of Lake Mathews or Lake Perris, each about a 20-minute drive. In the cooler weather during spring, this county park stocks a fishing pond. That is also the best time to explore the park's hiking and equestrian trails. The elevation is 780 feet. Open year-round.

35. VACATIONLAND

Reference: **At Disneyland; map I5, grid f3.**

Campsites, facilities: There are 74 sites for tents and 298 sites for motor homes, with picnic tables and full hookups provided. Restrooms, showers, playground, swimming pool, laundromat, store, ice, dump station, recreation room, Disney movies nightly in the clubhouse and propane gas are available. Pets are allowed on leashes.

Reservations, fee: Reservations accepted; $20-$38 fee per night.

Who to contact: Phone the park at (714) 774-CAMP (2267).

Location: From Interstate 5 in Anaheim, take the Harbor Boulevard exit and drive one block north. Turn left on Ball Road and drive one quarter of a mile. Turn left on West Street to 1343 South West Street (on the right).

Trip note: When we advise calling for available space, we mean it. This camp is within walking distance of Disneyland and provides a Disneyland shuttle service plus packages that nobody else offers. Sometimes "Vacationland" looks like an RV sales lot, but the kids will have fun. Open year-round.

36. ANAHEIM VACATION PARK

Reference: **Near Knott's Berry Farm; map I5, grid f3.**

Campsites, facilities: There are 222 motor home sites with full hookups. Restrooms, showers, satellite TV, phone hookups, a playground, a swimming pool, a laundromat, a store, a recreation room and propane gas are available. A grocery store is nearby. Pets are permitted on leashes.

Reservations, fee: Reservations accepted; $25 fee per night; $1 pet fee.

Who to contact: Phone the park at (714) 821-4311.

Location: From Highway 91 in Anaheim, drive one mile south on Highway 39 to 311 North Beach Boulevard (Highway 39).

Trip note: Some of the most popular motor home parks in America are in this area, and it's easy to see why. Disneyland is nearby, and Knott's Berry Farm is within walking distance. Plus, where else are you going to park your rig?

37. TRAVELERS WORLD RV PARK

Reference: **Near Disneyland; map I5, grid f4.**

Campsites, facilities: There are 335 sites for tents or motor homes with full hookups, picnic tables and fire grills provided. Restrooms, showers, a playground, a swimming pool, a laundromat, a store, a dump station, ice, a recreation room and propane gas are available. Pets are permitted on leashes.

Reservations, fee: Call for available space; $20-$22 fee per night; $2 pet fee.

Who to contact: Phone the park at (714) 991-0100.

Location: Heading south into Anaheim on Interstate 5, take a left at the Ball Road exit and drive to East Vermont Street. Make a right and proceed to Lemon Street. Make another right on Lemon Street and a right again at Ball Road and continue half a block to the campground on the right at 333 West Ball Road.

Trip note: This is one of the premium and most popular motor home parks you can find anywhere. It is easy to see why, being located just a half of a mile from Disneyland, with a shuttle-tour bus option—the park bus will deliver you to Knott's Berry Farm, Wax Museum, Universal Studios, Marineland and the Queen Mary. Open year-round.

---

38. C C CAMPERLAND 🚶 🏊   RV ▲ 1

Reference: **Near Disneyland; map I5, grid f4.**

Campsites, facilities: There are 90 sites for tents or motor homes. Picnic tables and full hookups are provided. Restrooms, showers, a video arcade, a swimming pool, a laundromat, a store, a dump station, ice and a recreation room are available. Pets are allowed on leashes.

Reservations, fee: Call ahead for available space; $18-$24 fee per night.

Who to contact: Phone the park at (714) 750-6747.

Location: From Interstate 5 in Garden Grove, drive south on Harbor Boulevard to 12262 Harbor Boulevard.

Trip note: Camperland is located nine blocks south of Disneyland, and that right there is the number one appeal. Other side trip options include Knott's Berry Farm. Open year-round.

---

39. ANAHEIM KOA 🚶 🏊   RV ▲ 1

Reference: **Near Disneyland; map I5, grid f4.**

Campsites, facilities: There are 221 sites for motor homes with full hookups and picnic tables. Restrooms, showers, a playground, a swimming pool, a jacuzzi, a wading pool, a recreation room, a grocery store and propane gas are available. Pets are permitted on leashes.

Reservations, fee: Call for available space; $26-$38 fee per night; children camp for free.

Who to contact: Phone the park at (714) 533-7720.

Location: From Interstate 5 in Anaheim, take the Harbor Boulevard exit and drive one block north. Turn left on Ball Road and drive a half mile. Turn left on West Street to 1221 South West Street.

Trip note: This is another option for RV cruisers. Open year-round.

---

40. ORANGELAND RV PARK 🚶 🏊   RV ▲ 1

Reference: **Near Disneyland; map I5, grid f4.**

Campsites, facilities: There are 212 sites for motor homes with picnic tables, fire grills and full hookups provided. Restrooms, showers, a playground, a swimming pool, a therapy pool, a laundromat, a store, a carwash, a shuffleboard court, a dump station, ice and a recreation room are available. Pets are permitted on leashes.

Reservations, fee: Reservations accepted; $27 fee per night; $1 pet fee.

Who to contact: Phone the park at (714) 633-0414.

Location: From Interstate 5 in Orange, drive two miles north on Freeway 57. Turn east onto Katella Avenue and drive one-half mile to 1600 West Struck Avenue.

Trip note: This park is located about five miles east of Disneyland. If the RV parks on West Street near Disneyland are filled, this spot provides a viable alternative. Open year-round.

41. BOLSA CHICA STATE BEACH 🐟 ♿ 🏊 🚐 5

Reference: **Near Huntington Beach; map I5, grid g2.**

Campsites, facilities: This is a "destination" campsite (meaning that self-contained motor homes can park for one night stays, but they must leave by 12 p.m.). The beach park provides fire rings, dressing rooms, cold showers, picnic area, food service, a bicycle trail and a paved ramp for **wheelchair access** to the beach. Pets are allowed on leashes.

Reservations, fee: Reserve by phoning Destinet at (800) 444-CAMP ($6.75 Destinet fee); $17 fee per night.

Who to contact: Phone the park at (714) 846-3460 or (714) 492-0802.

Location: From Huntington Beach, drive three miles up the coast on Highway 1.

Trip note: This is basically a parking lot, but a popular one. Motor home drivers can park for the night, then say adios the next morning. Open year-round.

42. SUNSET VISTA 🐟 ♿ 🏊 🚐 7

Reference: **On Pacific Ocean; map I5, grid h2.**

Campsites, facilities: There are 160 sites for motor homes up to 30 feet long. Piped water and fire grills are provided. Flush toilets and a dump station are available. Supplies available nearby. No pets allowed.

Reservations, fee: Reservations accepted in winter months only; $15 fee per night.

Who to contact: Phone the park at (714) 536-5280.

Location: From Interstate 405 in Huntington Beach, take the Beach Boulevard exit and drive to Highway 1 (Pacific Coast Highway). Turn north and drive to the intersection with First Street and turn left into the campground parking area.

Trip note: This is the other of the two popular beachside camps in the immediate area, both prime layovers for Highway 1 cruisers. Bolsa Chica State Beach Camp provides an option. Open year-round.

43. NEWPORT DUNES 🐟 ⚓ ♿ 🏊 🚐 7

Reference: **Near Newport Beach; map I5, grid h3.**

Campsites, facilities: There are 406 sites for tents or motor homes, all with full hookups. Picnic tables and fire grills are provided. Restrooms, showers, a swimming pool area and spa, a saltwater lagoon , two playgrounds, planned kids' activities, a laundromat, store, restaurant, recreation room, boat ramp and boat rentals are available. Some facilities are **wheelchair accessible**. Pets are allowed on leashes.

Reservations, fee: Reservations accepted; phone (800) 288-0770; $23-$55 fee per night, except holidays when the fee is $75 per night.

Who to contact: Phone the park at (714) 729-3863.

Location: From Laguna Hills, take Interstate 405 north to the Highway 55 exit. Turn left (south) on Highway 55, proceed to Highway 73. Drive south on Highway 73 to for five miles to Back Bay Drive. Turn right (west) on Back Bay Drive and continue a short distance to the Newport Dunes exit and the campground entrance.

Trip note: This privately-operated park is set in a nice spot on the bay, with a beach, boat ramp, and storage area providing bonuses. Corona Del Mar State Beach to the west and Crystal Cove State Park to the south provide possible side trips. The park is five minutes' walking distance from charming Balboa Island, and is next to the largest estuary in California, the Upper Newport Bay Ecological Reserve. Open year-round.

44. O'NEILL REGIONAL PARK 🏃🚶 ♿   RV 3

Reference: Near Cleveland Forest; map I5, grid h7.

Campsites, facilities: There are 90 sites for tents or motor homes up to 35 feet long and several group camping areas. Piped water, fire grills and picnic tables are provided. Flush toilets, showers, a playground and a dump station are available. A grocery store is nearby. Pets are permitted on leashes.

Reservations, fee: No reservations are accepted, except for group sites; call for group-site fees; $12 fee per night for individuals; $2 pet fee.

Who to contact: Phone the park at (714) 858-9365.

Location: From Interstate 5 in Laguna Hills, take the County Road S18 (El Toro Road) exit and drive east (past El Toro) for seven miles. Turn right onto Live Oak Canyon Road (County Road S19) and drive about three miles to the park on the right.

Trip note: This park is just far enough off the main drag to get missed by the Highway 5 cruisers. It is set near Trabuco Canyon, adjacent to Cleveland National Forest to the east. Several roads near this park lead to trailheads into the Cleveland National Forest. The elevation is 1,000 feet. Open year-round.

45. UPPER SAN JUAN 🏃🚶   RV 4

Reference: In Cleveland National Forest; map I5, grid h9.

Campsites, facilities: There are 18 sites for tents or motor homes up to 18 feet long. Fire grills and picnic tables are provided. Piped water and vault toilets are available. Pets are permitted on leashes.

Reservations, fee: No reservations; $7 fee per night.

Who to contact: Phone the Cleveland National Forest, Trabuco District at (909) 736-1811.

Location: From Interstate 5 in San Juan Capistrano, drive 21 miles northeast on Highway 74 (Ortega Highway).

Trip note: This is the best camp for hikers in this region of Cleveland National Forest. It is set among the oaks, with trailheads for hikes south into San Mateo Canyon Wilderness and north into the Santa Ana Mountains. The elevation is 1,800 feet. Open from April to October.

46. FALCON GROUP CAMP 🏃🚶   4

Reference: In Santa Ana Mountains in Cleveland National Forest; map I5, grid h9.

Campsites, facilities: There are three sites for tents or motor homes up to 16 feet long. Piped water, fire grills and picnic tables are provided. Vault toilets are available. A grocery store is within five miles. Pets are permitted on leashes.

Reservations, fee: Reserve by calling (800) 280-CAMP ($15 reservation fee); $35-$70 fee per group per night.

Who to contact: Phone the Cleveland National Forest, Trabuco District at (909) 736-1811.

Location: From Interstate 15 in Lake Elsinore, take the Highway 74 exit and drive 12 miles east. Turn right (north) on Forest Service Road 6S05 and drive about seven miles to the campground entrance on your left.

Trip note: If you're planning a group outing, this camp provides an option to Blue Jay Camp. The campground is at the trailheads for the San Juan Trail and the Chiquito Trail, both of which lead into the backcountry wilderness and the Santa Ana Mountains. Open from May to September.

47. BLUE JAY

Reference: **In Santa Ana Mountains in Cleveland National Forest; map I5, grid h9.**

Campsites, facilities: There are eight sites for tents only and 43 sites for tents or motor homes up to 22 feet long. Piped water, fire grills, pedestal grills and picnic tables are provided. Chemical toilets are available and a grocery store is within five miles. Pets are permitted on leashes.

Reservations, fee: No reservations; $7 fee per night.

Who to contact: Phone the Cleveland National Forest, Trabuco District at (909) 736-1811.

Location: From Interstate 15 at Lake Elsinore, take the Highway 74 exit and drive 12 miles east. Turn right (north) on Forest Service Road 6S05 and drive about seven miles to the campground entrance on your left.

Trip note: The few hikers who know of this spot like it and keep coming back. It is one of three camps in the immediate area, located deep in the Santa Ana Mountains. The trailheads to the San Juan Trail and the Chiquito Trail, both of which lead into the backcountry wilderness and the Santa Ana Mountains, are adjacent to the camp. A Forest Service map is strongly advised. The elevation is 3,300 feet. Open year-round.

48. EL CARISO CAMPGROUNDS

Reference: **Near Lake Elsinore in Cleveland National Forest; map I5, grid h9.**

Campsites, facilities: There are 24 sites for tents or motor homes up to 22 feet long. Piped water, fire grills and picnic tables are provided. Vault toilets are available. Pets are permitted on leashes.

Reservations, fee: No reservations; $7 fee per night.

Who to contact: Phone the Cleveland National Forest, Trabuco District at (909) 736-1811.

Location: From Interstate 5 in San Juan Capistrano, drive 24 miles northeast on Highway 74 (Ortega Highway). Or from Interstate 15 in Lake Elsinore, drive 12 miles west on Highway 74 to the campground.

Trip note: This pretty, shaded spot at 3,000 feet is just inside the border of Cleveland National Forest with Lake Elsinore to the east. Hikers should head west to the Upper San Juan Campground. Open from April through November.

49. CASPERS REGIONAL PARK

Reference: **On San Juan River; map I5, grid i7.**

Campsites, facilities: There are about 40 sites for tents or motor homes and 30 additional sites for equestrian campers. Group sites are also available and

picic tables are provided. Barbecues, piped water, flush toilets, showers, a
dump station, corrals, stables, 30 miles of trails and a playground are available.
Must be accompanied by a ranger or group leader on the trails. Pets are not
allowed.

Reservations, fee: Reservations accepted; $12 fee per night; $2 fee per extra
vehicle; horses are $2 each per night.

Who to contact: Phone the park at (714) 831-2174.

Location: From San Juan Capistrano, drive 7.5 miles northeast on Highway 74 to
the signed park entrance on the left.

Trip note: Highway 74 provides easy access to this regional park, which is
bordered to the south by the San Juan River and to the east by the Cleveland
National Forest and the San Mateo Canyon Wilderness. Open year-round.

---

50. DOHENY STATE BEACH

Reference: **On Dana Point Harbor; map I5, grid j5.**

Campsites, facilities: There are 120 sites for tents or motor homes. No hookups
provided. Fire grills and picnic tables are provided. Flush toilets, showers, a
dump station, exhibits and food service (summer only) are available. Propane
gas is nearby. Camping, picnicking, food service and exhibit areas are
wheelchair accessible. Pets are permitted on leashes in campground only, not
on the beach.

Reservations, fee: Reserve by phoning Destinet at (800) 444-7275 ($6.75 Destinet
fee); $17-$24 fee per night; $1 pet fee.

Who to contact: Phone the park at (714) 496-6172 or (714) 492-0802.

Location: From San Juan Capistrano, drive three miles south on Interstate 5 to the
Coast Highway 1-Doheny State Beach exit. Turn left at 2nd light onto Dana
Point Harbor Drive. Drive one block and go left onto Park Lantern. The park
entrance is one block away.

Trip note: It's right in town but you should still plan on a reservation or don't make
a plan. It is set at the entrance to Dana Point Harbor, a pretty spot, with easy
access off the highway. San Juan Capistrano provides a nearby side trip. That's
too many good things not to expect a lot of folks to want to stay here for the
night. Open year-round.

---

51. SAN CLEMENTE STATE BEACH

Reference: **Near San Clemente; map I5, grid j6.**

Campsites, facilities: There are 157 sites for tents or motor homes, 72 with full
hookups. Fire grills and picnic tables are provided. Flush toilets and showers
are available. A grocery store, a laundromat and propane gas are nearby. The
camping area is **wheelchair accessible**. Pets are allowed on leashes.

Reservations, fee: Reserve by phoning Destinet at (800) 444-7275 ($6.75 Destinet
fee); $17-$23 fee per night.

Who to contact: Phone the park at (714) 492-3156 or (714) 492-0802.

Location: From Interstate 5 in San Clemente, take the Avenida Calafia exit. Drive
west for a short distance to the park entrance.

Trip note: In the series of three state beaches that provide easy access and
beachfront camping, this one offers full hookups. The others are Doheny State
Beach to the north, and San Onofre State Beach to the south. Open year-round.

MAP I6

SO-CAL MAP .... see page 690
adjoining maps
NORTH (H6) .... see page 678
EAST (I7) .... see page 752
SOUTH (J6) .... see page 770
WEST (I5) .... see page 704

67 LISTINGS
PAGES 724-751

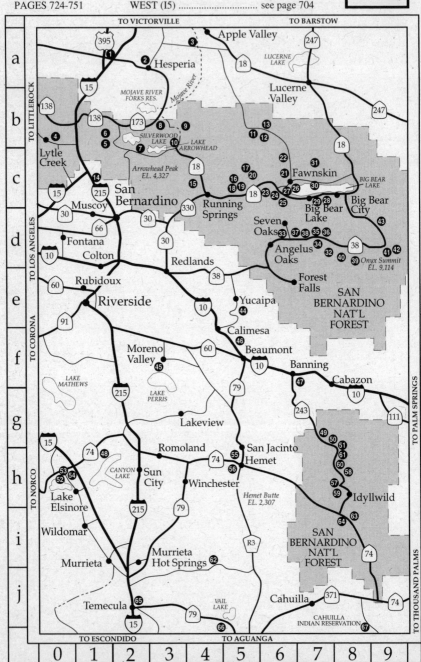

Map I6 featuring: **Mojave River, San Bernardino National Forest, Silverwood Lake, Lake Gregory, Lake Arrowhead, Big Bear Lake, Green Valley Lake, Children's Forest, San Gorgonio Wilderness, Santa Ana River, San Jacinto Wilderness, Lake Elsinore, Mount San Jacinto State Park, Lake Skinner, Cleveland National Forest, Agua Tibea Wilderness**

1. DESERT WILLOW RV PARK ♿ ≈   RV 2

Reference: **In Hesperia; map I6, grid a1.**

Campsites, facilities: There are 176 motor home sites with full hookups. Restrooms, hot showers, cable TV hookups, a convenience store, groceries, ice, laundry, propane gas, a swimming pool, an indoor spa, a recreation room, a library and cable TV are on the premises. Some facilities are **wheelchair accessible**. Pets are permitted on leashes.

Reservations, fee: Reservations accepted; $18-$20 fee per night; $2 pet fee.

Who to contact: Call (619) 949-0377.

Location: In Hesperia on Interstate 15, take the Main Street exit and drive west to 12624 Main Street West.

Trip note: This is a motor home park for Interstate 15 cruisers looking to make a stop. Silverwood Lake, 16 miles to the south, provides a side-trip option. The elevation is 3,200 feet. Open year-round, with limited winter facilities.

2. HESPERIA LAKE CAMPGROUND ↩ ♿   RV 5

Reference: **In Hesperia; map I6 grid a2.**

Campsites, facilities: There are 24 tent sites and 62 sites for tents, trailers or motor homes, some with electrical hookups. Picnic tables, barbecues, restrooms and showers are provided. A playground, horseshoe pits and a fishing pond are available. Pets are permitted on leashes in the camp, but not around the lake. The facilities are **wheelchair accessible**.

Reservations, fee: No reservations; $10-$13 fee per night; $2 pet fee.

Who to contact: Phone the park at (619) 244-5951.

Location: From Interstate 15 in Hesperia, take the Main Street exit and drive 12 miles east (the road curves around and becomes Arrowhead Lake Road). The park is on the left.

Trip note: This is a slightly more rustic option to Desert Willow RV Park in Hesperia. There is a fishing lake (a fee is charged but you don't need a license). No boating or swimming is allowed, but kids can feed the ducks and geese that live there.

3. MOJAVE NARROWS REGIONAL PARK   RV 6
   ↩ ⚓ 👥 ♿ 🐎

Reference: **On Mojave River; map I6, grid a4.**

Campsites, facilities: There are 110 sites for tents or motor homes, 38 of which have hookups. Picnic tables and barbecue grills are provided. Piped water, flush toilets, showers, a sanitary dump station, a snack bar, a bait house, boat rentals, horse rentals and horseback riding facilities are available. A grocery store, propane gas and a laundromat are available three miles from campground. Pets are permitted on leashes.

Reservations, fee: No reservations; $10-$15 fee per night; $1 pet fee.

Who to contact: This a county park; call (619) 245-2226 for information.

Location: From Interstate 15 south of Victorville, take the Bear Valley exit and drive east for six miles. Turn left on Ridgecrest and drive three more miles and make a left into the park.

Trip note: Just about nobody but the locals know about this little county park. It is set at 2,000 feet and provides a few recreation options, including fishing in a stocked pond, horseback riding facilities and trails. The "river level fluctuates," according to the ranger, which means that sometimes it just about disappears. Open year-round, but closed on Tuesdays.

---

4. APPLE WHITE

Reference: **Near Lytle Creek in San Bernardino National Forest; map I6, grid b0.**

Campsites, facilities: There are 42 sites for tents or motor homes up to 30 feet long. Piped water, flush toilets, picnic tables and fire grills are provided. The restrooms have sinks and electricity. A grocery store is nearby. Pets are allowed on leashes.

Reservations, fee: No reservations; $10 fee per night, $15 for multi-family sites.

Who to contact: Phone the Cajon Ranger District Office at (909) 887-2576.

Location: From Los Angeles, take Interstate 10 to Ontario. Continue past Ontario on Interstate 10 to the Interstate 15 North interchange. Drive 11 miles north on Interstate 15. Take the Sierra Avenue exit. Turn left, go under the freeway, and continue north for about nine miles to the campground.

Trip note: Nothing like a little inside know-how. You can reach the Middle Fork of Lytle Creek by driving north from Fontana via Serra Avenue to the Lytle Creek cabin area. To get to the stretch of water that is stocked with trout by the Department of Fish and Game, turn west on the first paved road past South Fork Road. The first mile upstream is stocked in early summer. The elevation is 3,300 feet. Open year-round.

---

5. WEST FORK GROUP CAMPS

Reference: On Silverwood Lake; map I6, grid b1.

Campsites, facilities: There are three group camps here with piped water, flush toilets, showers, a sanitary dump station, picnic tables and fire grills provided. Picnic areas, fishing, hiking, swimming, boating, food service and a grocery store are available. Pets are permitted on leashes.

Reservations, fee: Reserve by phoning Destinet at (800) 444-7275 ($6.75 Destinet fee); $150 group camp fee per night; $1 pet fee.

Who to contact: Phone the Silverwood Lake State Recreation Area at (619) 389-2303 or (909) 657-0676.

Location: From San Bernardino, drive north on Interstate 215. Continue north on Interstate 15 to the Highway 138 exit in Cajon. Drive 13 miles east on Highway 138 to the park.

Trip note: This is a group camping option at Silverwood Lake. Open from March through October.

6. MESA CAMPGROUND 🎣 ⚓ 🚶 ♿ 🏊 🏃 RV 6

Reference: **On Silverwood Lake; map I6, grid b1.**

Campsites, facilities: There are 128 sites for tents or motor homes up to 34 feet long. Piped water, flush toilets, showers, a sanitary dump station, picnic tables and fire grills are provided. There's **wheelchair access** to the campground facilities, picnic areas, fishing, hiking paths, exhibits, swimming areas, boating, food service and grocery store. Boat ramp and rentals available. Pets are allowed on leashes.

Reservations, fee: Reservations by phoning Destinet at (800) 444-7275 ($6.75 fee); $14-$18 fee per night; $1 pet fee.

Who to contact: Phone the Silverwood Lake State Recreation Area at (619) 389-2303 or (909) 657-0676.

Location: From San Bernardino, drive north on Interstate 215. Continue north on Interstate 15 to the Highway 138 exit in Cajon. Drive 13 miles east on Highway 138 to the park.

Trip note: This is a popular lake set at 3,355 feet and surrounded by National Forest land. Fishing is best for trout and bass in the spring, before the heat of summer and waterskiers take over. The park is located on the west side of the lake and offers both nature and bicycle trails. Open year-round.

7. CAMP SWITZERLAND 🎣 ⚓ 🚶 🏊 RV 7

Reference: **On Lake Gregory; map I6, grid b2.**

Campsites, facilities: There are 10 sites for tents, 30 sites for motor homes with full hookups and two cabins. Piped water, flush toilets, showers and picnic tables are provided. Propane gas is available nearby. Pets are permitted on leashes.

Reservations, fee: Reservations accepted; $17-$20 fee per night; cabins start at $50 per night; $2 pet fee.

Who to contact: Call Camp Switzerland at (909) 338-2731 or write POB 967, Crestline, CA 92325.

Location: From San Bernardino, drive eight miles north on Highway 18 to the Crestline/Highway 138 exit. Drive north two miles on Highway 138. Turn right (east) on Lake Drive and continue three miles to the signed entrance to the campground at Lake Gregory.

Trip note: Well, it really doesn't look anything like Switzerland, unless maybe you compare it to downtown Los Angeles. But it is pretty enough, set at 4,500 feet along little Lake Gregory. The lake is surrounded by San Bernardino National Forest. Open year-round, weather permitting.

8. MOJAVE RIVER FORKS REGIONAL PARK RV 5
🚶 ♿ 🏇

Reference: **Near Silverwood Lake; map I6, grid b3.**

Campsites, facilities: There are 30 sites for tents only, 25 motor home sites with full hookups, and 25 sites for tents or motor homes. Four group sites are also available. Picnic tables and fire grills are provided. Piped water, flush toilets, showers and a sanitary dump station are available. A convenience store and a recreation room are available in the summer. Pets are permitted on leashes with proof of shots and/or current license.

Reservations, fee: Reservations accepted for RV sites only; $13-$19 fee per night;

$2 pet fee.

Who to contact: Call the park at (619) 389-2322.

Location: From San Bernardino, drive north on Interstate 215/Interstate 15 the Highway 138 exit. Drive nine miles east to Highway 173. Stay to the left and drive seven miles to the park. From Hesperia on Interstate 15, take the Hesperia exit and drive four miles east to Hesperia. Continue southeast on Highway 173 for nine miles to the park entrance.

Trip note: The bonus here is the full hookups for motor homes and the park's close proximity to Silverwood Lake, which is 15 minutes away and does not have any sites with hookups available. The sites are well spaced. The nearby "river" is usually dry. The elevation is 3,000 feet. Open year-round.

9. DOGWOOD 🐟 ♿   RV 6

Reference: **Near Lake Arrowhead in San Bernardino National Forest; map I6, grid b3.**

Campsites, facilities: There are 93 sites for tents or motor homes up to 22 feet long. Piped water, flush toilets, a sanitary dump station, picnic tables and fire grills are provided. Some facilities are **wheelchair accessible**. A grocery store and a laundromat are nearby. Pets are allowed on leashes.

Reservations, fee: Reserve by calling (800) 280-CAMP ($7.50 reservation fee); $12-$16 fee per night; $16 for multi-family units.

Who to contact: Phone the Arrowhead Ranger District at (909) 337-2444.

Location: From San Bernardino, drive about 15 miles north on Highway 18 to Rimforest. Continue east on Highway 18 for two-tenths of a mile to Daley Canyon Road. Turn left on Daley Canyon Road and then an immediate right on the Daley Canyon access road. Turn left into the campground. Watch oncoming and turning traffic.

Trip note: This privately operated popular Forest Service camp is located near Lake Arrowhead, about a mile from the lake. Got a question? The rangers at the Arrowhead Ranger Station, located about 1.5 miles down the road to the east, can answer it. Lake Arrowhead is stocked regularly in the late spring and early summer and can provide good trout fishing. Lake Arrowhead is a private lake. One location is open to the public for fishing, but no swimming is allowed. The elevation is 5,600 feet. Open from May through October.

10. NORTH SHORE 🐟 🚶 ♿   RV 8

Reference: **On Lake Arrowhead in San Bernardino National Forest; map I6, grid b3.**

Campsites, facilities: There are 27 sites for tents or motor homes up to 22 feet long. Piped water, flush toilets, picnic tables and fire rings are provided. Some facilities are **wheelchair accessible**. A grocery store and a laundromat are nearby. Pets are permitted on leashes.

Reservations, fee: Reservations accepted; call (800) 280-CAMP (2267); $10 fee per night.

Who to contact: Call Arrowhead Ranger District at (909) 337-2444.

Location: From San Bernardino, drive about 17 miles north on Highway 18 to Highway 173. Turn left on Highway 173 and drive north for 1.6 miles to the traffic light. Turn right (still on Highway 173) and drive 2.9 miles to Hospital Road. Turn right and go a tenth of a mile to the top of the small hill. Turn left just past the hospital entrance and you will see the campground.

Trip note: This is the preferable camp of the two at Lake Arrowhead. It is set near the northeastern shore of the lake, which provides good trout fishing in the spring and early summer. A trail starts at the camp and is routed east in National Forest and connects to the Pacific Crest Trail. The elevation is 5,300 feet. Open from May through November.

11. BIG PINE HORSE CAMP 3

Reference: **In San Bernardino National Forest; map I6, grid b5.**

Campsites, facilities: This camp is expressly for equestrians. There is one group camp that can accommodate up to 60 people and 15 cars. Piped water, vault toilets, picnic tables and fire grills are provided. Pets are allowed on leashes.

Reservations, fee: Reservations are required; call (800) 280-CAMP (2267); $35 group fee per night.

Who to contact: Phone the Big Bear Ranger District Office at (909) 866-3437.

Location: From San Bernardino, take Highway 30 (the sign says "Mountain Resorts") to Highway 330. Drive about 35 miles on Highway 330 to the dam on Big Bear Lake. Take the left fork (Highway 38) and drive about four miles to the town of Fawnskin. Turn left on Rim of the World Road (it becomes Forest Service Road 3N14, a dirt road, after a half mile) and drive seven miles. Turn left on Forest Service Road 3N16 and drive one mile to the campground on the right.

Trip note: You might want to bring an apple or a carrot, or maybe some nose plugs. That's because this is a camp for the horse packers located adjacent to the Big Pine Fire Station. The elevation is 6,700 feet.

12. IRONWOOD GROUP CAMP 4

Reference: **In San Bernardino National Forest; map I6, grid b6.**

Campsites, facilities: There is one group camp that can accommodate up to 25 people and five cars (no trailers or motor homes). There is **no piped water**. Vault toilets, picnic tables and fire grills are provided. Pets are allowed on leashes.

Reservations, fee: Reservation required; $35 fee per night for groups.

Who to contact: Phone the San Bernardino National Forest Big Bear Ranger District at (909) 866-3437.

Location: From San Bernardino, take Highway 30 (the sign says "Mountain Resorts") to Highway 330. Drive about 35 miles on Highway 330 to the dam on Big Bear Lake. Take the left fork (Highway 38) and drive about four miles to the town of Fawnskin. Turn left on Rim of the World Road (it becomes Forest Service Road 3N14, a dirt road, after a half mile) and drive six miles. Turn left at the Forest Service Road 3N97 sign and go one mile to the campground.

Trip note: This nearby option to Hanna Flat Camp is a bit more isolated and in higher country. The camp is set in a wooded area near a meadow, and the rough road going in scares a lot of folks off. The elevation is 6,700 feet. Open from June through September.

13. BIG PINE FLATS 7

Reference: **In San Bernardino National Forest; map I6, grid b6.**

Campsites, facilities: There are 17 sites for tents or motor homes up to 30 feet long. Piped water, vault toilets, picnic tables and fire grills are provided. Pets are allowed on leashes.

Reservations, fee: No reservations; $10 fee per night.

Who to contact: Phone the Big Bear Ranger District Office at (909) 866-3437.

Location: From San Bernardino, take Highway 30 (the sign says "Mountain Resorts") to Highway 330. Drive about 35 miles on Highway 330 to the dam on Big Bear Lake. Take the left fork (Highway 38) and drive about four miles to the town of Fawnskin. Turn left on Rim of the World Road (it becomes Forest Service Road 3N14, a dirt road, after a half mile) and drive seven miles to Big Pine Flat Station and the campground on the right.

Trip note: This pretty spot, set at 6,800 feet in the National Forest, is popular with the folks who know about it. You get a little of both worlds; you are surrounded by wildlands near Redondo Ridge, yet you're not a long drive from Big Bear Lake to the south. Any questions? The firefighters at Big Flat Fire Station, just across the road, can answer them. Open from mid-May to mid-November.

14. SAN BERNARDINO-CABLE CANYON KOA 🚐 5

♿ 🏊

Reference: **Near Silverwood Lake; map I6, grid c1.**

Campsites, facilities: There are 155 tent and motor home sites with full or partial hookups and picnic tables. There are also two camping cabins. Piped water, flush toilets, showers, a laundromat, a playground, a swimming pool, a recreation room, a grocery store and propane gas are available. Some facilities are **wheelchair accessible**. Pets are permitted on leashes.

Reservations, fee: Reservations accepted; $18-$24 fee per night; cabins are $34 per night.

Who to contact: Call (909) 887-4098.

Location: From San Bernardino, drive 16 miles north on Interstate 215. Take the Devore exit and drive a short distance to Cable Canyon Road. Turn right and drive to 1707 Cable Canyon Road.

Trip note: This KOA camp provides space for tents as well as motor homes. It is set at 2,200 feet and virtually surrounded by National Forest. Silverwood Lake to the east provides a nearby side trip. Open year-round.

15. CANYON PARK 🚶🏇 🚐 5

Reference: **Near Running Lake; map I6, grid c4.**

Campsites, facilities: There are 30 sites for tents and five mobile home sites with full or partial hookups. Piped water, flush toilets, showers, picnic tables and fire grills are provided. Horses can be boarded here. Pets are allowed on leashes.

Reservations, fee: Call ahead for fee information.

Who to contact: Call (909) 867-2090.

Location: From San Bernardino, take Highway 30 to the Highway 330 turnoff. Turn left on Highway 330 and drive to Running Springs School Road, turn right and drive to the park at 2840 Running Springs Road.

Trip note: A quiet, privately-operated park with dirt roads, right smack in between Big Bear Lake to the east and Lake Arrowhead to the west; they are each about 15 miles away.

16. CRAB FLATS 🚐 4

Reference: **Near Crab Creek in San Bernardino National Forest; map I6, grid c5.**

Campsites, facilities: There are 29 sites for tents or motor homes up to 15 feet long.

Piped water, vault toilets, picnic tables and fire rings are provided. Pets are allowed on leashes.

Reservations, fee: No reservations; $8 fee per night.

Who to contact: Phone the San Bernardino National Forest Arrowhead Ranger District at (909) 337-2444.

Location: From San Bernardino, travel out Highway 30 and 330 to Running Springs. Continue east on Highway 18 (past the town of Running Springs). Turn north (left) on Green Valley Road and drive three miles to Forest Service Road 3N16 (a dirt road) on the left. Turn left and drive four miles. You will cross two creeks which vary in depth depending on season. High clearance is recommended, but it is not necessary if you are careful. After four miles you will come to an intersection. Bear left and you'll see the entrance on your right.

Trip note: This is a developed Forest Service camp set at a fork in the road, with Tent Peg Group Camp located just a half mile to the west on Forest Service Road 3N34 (a hiking trail is available there). The elevation is 6,200 feet. Open from mid-May through October.

---

17. GREEN VALLEY 🐟 🏊

Reference: **Near Green Valley Lake in San Bernardino National Forest; map I6, grid c5.**

Campsites, facilities: There are 36 sites for tents or motor homes up to 22 feet long. Piped water, flush toilets, picnic tables and fire rings are provided. A grocery store and a laundromat are nearby. Pets are allowed on leashes.

Reservations, fee: Reservations may be made by phoning (800) 280-CAMP (2267); $10 fee per night.

Who to contact: Phone the San Bernardino National Forest Arrowhead Ranger District at (909) 337-2444.

Location: From San Bernardino, travel out Highway 30 and 330 to Running Springs. Continue east on Highway 18 to Green Valley Road. Turn north (left) and go four miles up the road to the campground (one mile past town of Green Valley Lake).

Trip note: This spot is set along pretty Green Valley Creek. Little Green Valley Lake is located a mile to the west. The lake is stocked with trout by the Department of Fish and Game and is also a good spot to take a flying leap and belly flop. The elevation is 7,000 feet. Open from May through October.

---

18. TENT PEG GROUP CAMP 🐟 🥾

Reference: **Near the Pacific Crest Trail in San Bernardino National Forest; map I6, grid c5.**

Campsites, facilities: There is one group camp that will accommodate 10 to 30 people and five cars. There is **no piped water.** Vault toilets, picnic tables and fire rings are provided. A grocery store and a laundromat are five miles away. Pets are allowed on leashes.

Reservations, fee: Reservations required; $30 fee per night.

Who to contact: Call San Bernardino National Forest Arrowhead Ranger District at (909) 337-2444.

Location: From San Bernardino, travel out Highway 30 and 330 to Running Springs. Continue east on Highway 18 (past the town of Running Springs). Turn north (left) on Green Valley Road and drive three miles to Forest Service Road 3N16 (a dirt road) on the left. Turn left and drive four miles. You will cross two creeks which vary in depth depending on season. High clearance is recommended, but not necessary if you are careful. After four miles you will come to an intersection. Bear left on Forest Service Road 3N34, drive west for one mile, and the campground is on your left.

Trip note: This camp would be a lot easier to reach with a helicopter than a vehicle. But that's why it gets little use. It's a primitive camp for groups. The 2W08 trail from this camp links up with the Pacific Crest Trail. In early summer, nearby Holcomb Creek provides fishing for small trout. The elevation is 5,400 feet. Open May through October.

19. FISHERMAN'S HIKE-IN GROUP CAMP

Reference: **On Deep Creek in San Bernardino National Forest; map I6, grid c5.**

Campsites, facilities: There is one group camp that will accommodate 10 to 30 people. Vault toilets, picnic tables and fire rings are provided. There is **no piped water**, so bring in your own. Pack out your garbage. Pets are permitted on leashes.

Reservations, fee: Reservations required; $10 fee per night.

Who to contact: Call San Bernardino National Forest Arrowhead Ranger District at (909) 337-2444.

Location: From San Bernardino, travel out Highway 30 and 330 to Running Springs. Continue east on Highway 18 (past the town of Running Springs). Turn north (left) on Green Valley Road and drive three miles to Forest Service Road 3N16 (a dirt road) on the left. Turn left and drive four miles. You will cross two creeks which vary in depth depending on season. High clearance is recommended, but not necessary if you are careful. After four miles you will come to an intersection. Bear left on Forest Service Road 3N34, drive west for 1.3 miles to Forest Service Trail 2W07 on your left. Follow this hiking trail southwest for 2.5 miles and you will come to Deep Creek. The campground is on the other side of the creek.

Trip note: Get here and you join the Five Percent Club. It's a beautiful, secluded and wooded campground set deep in San Bernardino National Forest. Deep Creek runs alongside, providing stream trout fishing. It's worth the hike. The elevation is 5,400 feet.

20. SHADY COVE GROUP CAMP

Reference: **Near Children's Forest in San Bernardino National Forest; map I6, grid c5.**

Campsites, facilities: There is one camp that accommodates up to 100 people and 15 cars (no trailers or motor homes). Piped water, vault toilets, picnic tables and fire rings are provided. Pets are allowed on leashes.

Reservations, fee: Reservations required; special Forest Service arrangements are necessary for key access; phone (800) 280-CAMP (2267); $55-$100 fee per night.

Who to contact: Phone the San Bernardino National Forest Arrowhead Ranger District at (909) 337-2444.

Location: From San Bernardino, drive about 17 miles north on Highway 18 to the Arrowhead Ranger Station. Continue east on Highway 18 for seven miles (past the town of Running Springs). Turn south (right) on Keller Peak Road (just past Deer Lake Fire Station) and drive four miles to the Children's Forest. Bear left for the parking area (it requires a key to enter). The sites are 100 yards from parking area. Contact the district office for information.

Trip note: The highlight here is the adjacent short looped trail that is routed through the National Children's Forest. The camp is excellent for Boy Scout and Girl Scout troops. The elevation is 7,500 feet. Open from May through September.

21. HANNA FLAT 🏃🏃   RV 5

Reference: **Near Big Bear Lake in San Bernardino National Forest; map I6, grid c6.**

Campsites, facilities: There are 69 sites for tents and 19 sites for tents or motor homes up to 15 feet long. Piped water, vault toilets, picnic tables and fire grills are provided. Pets are allowed on leashes.

Reservations, fee: Make reservations by calling (800) 280-CAMP ($7.50 reservation fee); $12 fee per night; the second vehicle is $4.

Who to contact: Phone the San Bernardino National Forest Big Bear Ranger District at (909) 866-3437.

Location: From San Bernardino, take Highway 30 (the sign says "Mountain Resorts") to Highway 330. Drive about 35 miles on Highway 330 to the dam on Big Bear Lake. Take the left fork (Highway 38) and drive about four miles to the town of Fawnskin. Turn left on Rim of the World Road (it becomes Forest Service Road 3N14, a dirt road, after a half mile), and drive about three miles to the campground on the left.

Trip note: This is the largest, best maintained, and most popular of the Forest Service camps set in the Big Bear Lake district. All the trees and vegetation provide seclusion for individual sites. It is set at 7,000 feet, just under three miles from Big Bear Lake, which provides good trout fishing. The Pacific Crest National Scenic Trail passes by, one mile north of the camp. Open from May through September.

22. GRAY'S PEAK GROUP CAMP   RV 4

Reference: **Near Big Bear Lake in San Bernardino National Forest; map I6, grid c6.**

Campsites, facilities: There is one group camp that will accommodate up to 40 people and eight cars (limited use of trailers and motor homes). There is **no piped water.** Vault toilets, picnic tables and fire grills are provided. Pets are allowed on leashes.

Reservations, fee: Reservations may be made by phoning (800) 280-CAMP; there is a fee for group camping.

Who to contact: Phone the San Bernardino National Forest Big Bear Ranger District at (909) 866-3437.

Location: From San Bernardino, take Highway 30 (the sign says "Mountain Resorts") to Highway 330. Drive about 35 miles on Highway 330 to the dam on Big Bear Lake. Take the left fork (Highway 38) and drive about four miles to the town of Fawnskin. Turn left on Rim of the World Road (it becomes Forest Service Road 3N14, a dirt road, after a half mile) and drive about two miles to Forest Service Road 2N68. Turn left and drive about one mile to campground on the right.

Trip note: This primitive group camp is set at 7,200 feet, about two miles northwest of Big Bear Lake. The name "Gray's Peak Camp" is a bit of a misnomer, since Gray's Peak (7,952 feet) is located about a mile south of the camp. Open from June through September.

23. SIBERIA CREEK HIKE-IN GROUP CAMP

Reference: **In San Bernardino National Forest; map I6, grid c6.**

Campsites, facilities: There is one group camp that will accommodate up to 40 people. Fire rings are provided, but that's all. There is **no piped water**, so bring your own, and pack out your garbage. Pets are allowed on leashes.

Reservations, fee: Reservations requested; no fee.

Who to contact: Phone the San Bernardino National Forest Big Bear Ranger District at (909) 866-3437.

Location: From San Bernardino, take Highway 30 (the sign says "Mountain Resorts") to Highway 330. Drive about 20 miles on Highway 330 to just past Snow Valley Ski Area. Take the Camp Creek Trail turnoff and follow the signs to Trail Head.

Trip note: This is a primitive area that requires a fairly steep four-mile hike. Your reward is solitude at a camp that will hold up to 40 people. The camp is set near the confluence of Siberia Creek and larger Bear Creek. The latter is the major feeder stream into Big Bear Lake. The elevation is 4,800 feet.

24. BLUFF MESA GROUP CAMP

Reference: **Near Big Bear Lake in San Bernardino National Forest; map I6, grid c6.**

Campsites, facilities: There is one group camp that will accommodate up to 40 people and eight cars. There is **no piped water.** Pit toilets, picnic tables and fire grills are provided. Pets are allowed on leashes.

Reservations, fee: Reservations requested; $25 group fee per night.

Who to contact: Phone the San Bernardino National Forest Big Bear Ranger District at (909) 866-3437.

Location: From San Bernardino, take Highway 30 (the sign says "Mountain Resorts") to Highway 330. Drive about 35 miles on Highway 330 to the dam on Big Bear Lake. Bear right at the dam on Highway 18 and drive about four miles. Turn right on Mill Creek Road and drive about 1.5 miles to the sign at the top of the hill. Turn right on Forest Service Road 2N10 and drive three miles on the dirt road. Turn right on Road 2N86 and drive a quarter mile to the campground.

Trip note: This is one of the several camps located south of Big Bear Lake. Many Forest Service roads are available nearby for self-planned side trips. Maps are available at the ranger station in Fawnskin on the north side of the lake. The elevation is 7,600 feet. Open from June through September.

25. BOULDER GROUP CAMP

Reference: **Near Big Bear Lake in San Bernardino National Forest; map I6, grid c6.**

Campsites, facilities: There is one group camp that will accommodate up to 40 people and eight cars (limited use of trailers and motor homes). There is **no piped water.** Pit toilets, picnic tables and fire grills are provided. A grocery store and a laundromat are nearby. Pets are allowed on leashes.

Reservations, fee: Reservations required; $25 group fee per night.

Who to contact: Phone the San Bernardino National Forest Big Bear Ranger District at (909) 866-3437.

Location: From San Bernardino, take Highway 30 (the sign says "Mountain Resorts") to Highway 330. Drive about 35 miles on Highway 330 to the dam on Big Bear Lake. Bear right at the dam on Highway 18 and drive about four miles to Mill Creek Road. Turn right on Forest Service Road 2N10 and drive about two miles. Turn right on Road 2N10B and drive to the camp.

Trip note: This is a primitive camp, just far enough away from some prime attractions to make you wish the camp was in a slightly different spot. The headwaters of Metcalf Creek are hidden in the forest on the other side of the road, little Cedar Lake is about a half-mile drive north, and Big Bear Lake is about two miles north. You get the idea. The elevation is 7,500 feet. Open from June through September.

26. HOLLOWAY'S MARINA AND RV PARK RV 6

Reference: On Big Bear Lake; map I6, grid c6.

Campsites, facilities: There are 100 motor home sites with full or partial hookups. Picnic tables and fire grills are provided. Piped water, flush toilets, showers, a sanitary dump station, cable TV, a convenience store, ice, propane gas, a laundromat, a playground and a full marina with boat rentals are on the premises. Pets are allowed on leashes.

Reservations, fee: Reservations suggested; $20-$35 fee per night.

Who to contact: Call Holloway's Marina and RV Park at (909) 866-5706.

Location: From San Bernardino, take Highway 30 (the sign says "Mountain Resorts") to Highway 330. Drive about 17 miles to Highway 18 and bear right on Highway 18. Drive another 17 miles to the dam. Three miles past the dam, turn left on Edgemoor Road and drive to the park.

Trip note: Big Bear Lake is a large, popular lake set at 6,500 feet in the San Bernardino National Forest. There are tons of campgrounds to pick from here. Big Bear has good trout fishing in the spring and is well stocked. In the summer, a bonus is that a breeze off the lake keeps the temperature in the mid-80s.

27. HOLCOMB VALLEY RV 5

Reference: Near Pacific Crest Trail in San Bernardino National Forest; map I6, grid c7.

Campsites, facilities: There are 19 sites for tents or motor homes up to 25 feet long. There is **no piped water.** Pit toilets, picnic tables and fire grills are provided. Pack out your garbage. Pets are allowed on leashes.

Reservations, fee: No reservations; $7 fee per night.

Who to contact: Phone the Big Bear Ranger District Office at (909) 866-3437.

Location: From San Bernardino, take Highway 30 (the sign says "Mountain Resorts") to Highway 330. Drive about 35 miles on Highway 330 to the dam on Big Bear Lake. Take the left fork (Highway 38) and drive about 10 miles. Turn left on Van Dusen Canyon Road (3N09) and drive (dirt road) for three miles. Turn left 3N16 and the campground is on the right.

Trip note: The camp is set near the Holcomb Valley Historic Area and two miles north of the Pacific Crest Trail. The elevation is 7,400 feet. Open year-round, depending on the weather.

28. PINEKNOT ♿ 　　　　　　　RV. 6

Reference: Near Big Bear Lake in San Bernardino National Forest; map I6, grid c7.

Campsites, facilities: There are 52 sites for tents and RVs up to 45 feet long. Piped water, flush toilets, picnic tables and fire grills are provided. Facilities are **wheelchair accessible**. A grocery store and a laundromat are nearby. Pets are allowed on leashes.

Reservations, fee: Make reservations by calling (800) 280-CAMP ($7.50 reservation fee); $11 fee per night.

Who to contact: Phone the San Bernardino National Forest Big Bear Ranger District at (909) 866-3437.

Location: From San Bernardino, take Highway 30 (the sign says "Mountain Resorts") to Highway 330. Drive about 35 miles on Highway 330 to the dam on Big Bear Lake. Bear right at the dam on Highway 18 and drive about six miles to Summit Boulevard. Turn right and drive through the parking area and make a left into the campground just before the gate to the slopes.

Trip note: This popular, developed Forest Service camp is set just east of Big Bear Lake Village, about two miles from Big Bear Lake. The elevation is 7,000 feet. Open from mid-May through September.

29. BUTTERCUP GROUP CAMP 　　　　RV. 5

Reference: **Near town of Big Bear Lake in San Bernardino National Forest; map I6, grid c7.**

Campsites, facilities: There is one group camp that will accommodate up to 40 people and eight cars (limited use of trailers or motor homes). Piped water, portable toilets, picnic tables and fire grills are provided. A grocery store and a laundromat are nearby. Pets are allowed on leashes.

Reservations, fee: Reservation requested; $50 group fee per night.

Who to contact: Phone the San Bernardino National Forest Big Bear Ranger District at (909) 866-3437.

Location: From San Bernardino, take Highway 30 (the sign says "Mountain Resorts") to Highway 330. Drive about 35 miles on Highway 330 to the dam on Big Bear Lake. Bear right at the dam on Highway 18 and drive about six miles to Summit Boulevard. Turn right and drive through the parking area and make a left into the campground, just before the gate to the ski slopes.

Trip note: This is a forested camp, set up for large groups looking for a developed site near Big Bear Lake. The elevation is 7,000 feet. Open from June through September.

30. SERRANO 　🎣 🚶 ♿ 🏊 　　　　RV. 8

Reference: **On Big Bear Lake in San Bernardino National Forest; map I6, grid c7.**

Campsites, facilities: There are 132 sites for tents or motor homes up to 55 feet long. There are 30 sites that offer full hookups. Piped water, picnic tables, fire rings, restrooms, hot showers and a sanitary dump station are provided. Five sites are **wheelchair accessible**. There is a store nearby. Pets are allowed on leashes.

Reservations, fee: Reserve by calling (800) 280-CAMP ($7.50 reservation fee); $12-$20 fee per night; $24 for multi-families.

Who to contact: Phone the San Bernardino National Forest Big Bear Ranger District at (909) 866-3437.

Location: From San Bernardino, take Highway 30 (the sign says "Mountain Resorts") to Highway 330. Drive about 33 miles on Highway 330 to the dam on Big Bear Lake. Take the left fork (Highway 38) and drive about 2.5 miles east of Fawnskin and watch for the Serrano Campground signs. The campground entrance is off of North Shore Lane.

Trip note: This campground opened in 1991 and became the first National Forest campground to offer state-of-the-art restrooms and hot showers. That is why it costs so much to camp here. Recreational opportunities include fishing, birdwatching and hiking, and bonus is a **wheelchair accessible** walking/biking path that is paved. A trailhead for the Pacific Crest Trail is nearby. The shoreline is within walking distance. Elevation 7,000 feet. Open mid-April to mid-November.

---

31. TANGLEWOOD GROUP CAMP 👫 🚐 △ 4

Reference: **On Pacific Crest Trail in San Bernardino National Forest; map I6, grid c7.**

Campsites, facilities: There is one group camp that will accommodate up to 40 people and eight cars (limited use of trailers or motor homes). There is **no piped water.** Pit toilets, picnic tables and fire grills are provided. Pets are allowed on leashes.

Reservations, fee: Reservation required; $35 group fee per night.

Who to contact: Phone the San Bernardino National Forest Big Bear Ranger District at (909) 866-3437.

Location: From San Bernardino, take Highway 30 (the sign says "Mountain Resorts") to Highway 330. Drive about 35 miles on Highway 330 to the dam on Big Bear Lake. Take the left fork (Highway 38) and drive about 10 miles. Turn left on Van Dusen Canyon Road (Forest Service Road 3N09) and drive the dirt road for three miles. Turn right on Forest Service Road 3N16 and drive about two miles. Turn right on Forest Service Road 3N79 to the campground.

Trip note: This primitive group camp is set off an old spur road. The Pacific Crest Trail is accessible immediately to the south. It is set at 7,400 feet in a flat, but wooded area, with Big Bear Lake three miles to the southeast by road. Open from June through September.

---

32. SKYLINE GROUP CAMP 👫 △ 5

Reference: **In San Bernardino National Forest; map I6, grid d7.**

Campsites, facilities: There is one group site that will accommodate up to 25 people. Piped water, vault toilets and picnic tables are available. Pets are allowed on leashes.

Reservations, fee: Reserve by calling (800) 280-CAMP; $15 reservation fee; $25 fee per night.

Who to contact: Phone the San Bernardino National Forest, San Gorgonio Ranger District, at (909) 794-1123.

Location: From Redlands on Interstate 10, turn east on Highway 38 and drive 33.5 miles to Forest Service Road 1N02. Look for it on the right. Turn right and drive one mile to the campground, set just behind Heart Bar Campground.

Trip note: This camp is set just behind the Heart Bar Family Camp, at 6,900 feet, near Big Meadows. A trailhead is located about a half-mile to the north off the main road. It provides access to a great trail that runs along Wildhorse Creek and up to Sugarloaf Mountain, elevation 9,952 feet.

33. COUNCIL GROUP CAMP

Reference: **Near San Gorgonio Wilderness in San Bernardino National Forest; map I6, grid d7.**

Campsites, facilities: There is one group camp that will accommodate up to 50 people and 10 cars (no trailers or motor homes). Piped water, vault toilets, picnic tables and fire grills are provided. Pets are allowed on leashes.

Reservations, fee: Reserve by calling (800) 280-CAMP; $15 reservation fee; $25-$50 fee per night.

Who to contact: Phone the San Bernardino National Forest San Gorgonio Ranger District at (909) 794-1123.

Location: From Interstate 10 in Redlands, drive 26 miles east on Highway 38 to the campground on the left.

Trip note: This is a group camp that is about three miles away from South Fork Camp on Lost Creek. Campers who are not in large groups should consider South Fork Camp.

34. SOUTH FORK

Reference: **On the Santa Ana River in San Bernardino National Forest; map I6, grid d7.**

Campsites, facilities: There are 24 sites for tents or motor homes up to 30 feet long. Piped water, vault toilets, picnic tables and fire grills are provided. Pets are allowed on leashes.

Reservations, fee: No reservations; $7 fee per night; $3 for each additional car.

Who to contact: Phone the San Bernardino National Forest San Gorgonio Ranger District at (909) 794-1123.

Location: From Interstate 10 in Redlands, drive 29.5 miles east on Highway 38 to the campground on the right.

Trip note: This easy access Forest Service camp, just off Highway 38, is set at 6,400 feet on the Santa Ana River. It is part of the series of camps in the immediate area, just north of the San Gorgonio Wilderness. See the trip note for Barton Flats for more details. Open from mid-May through mid-October.

35. OSO GROUP CAMP

Reference: **Near San Gorgonio Wilderness in San Bernardino National Forest; map I6, grid d7.**

Campsites, facilities: This site will accommodate up to 100 people and 20 cars (limited use of trailers and motor homes). Piped water, flush toilets, picnic tables and fire grills are provided. Pets are allowed on leashes.

Reservations, fee: Reserve by calling (800) 280-CAMP (2267); $15 reservation fee; $75-$100 fee per night.

Who to contact: Phone the San Bernardino National Forest San Gorgonio Ranger District at (909) 794-1123.

Location: From Interstate 10 in Redlands, drive 29 miles east on Highway 38 to the campground entrance road on the left.

Trip note: This camp is set directly next to Lobo Camp. The elevation is 6,600 feet. Open from May through October.

36. LOBO GROUP CAMP 🚶🚶 　　　　　 RV 4

Reference: **Near Santa Ana River in San Bernardino National Forest; map I6, grid d7.**

Campsites, facilities: This site will accommodate up to 75 people and 15 cars (limited use of trailers and motor homes). Piped water, flush toilets, picnic tables and fire grills are provided. Pets are allowed on leashes.

Reservations, fee: Reserve by calling (800) 280-CAMP (2267); $15 reservation fee); $50-$75 fee per night.

Who to contact: Phone the San Bernardino National Forest San Gorgonio Ranger District at (909) 794-1123.

Location: From Interstate 10 in Redlands, drive 29 miles east on Highway 38 to the campground entrance road on the left.

Trip note: Lobo is right next to Oso Camp and is just north of the San Gorgonio Wilderness. The camp is about three-quarters of a mile from the Santa Ana River, which frequently has low flows in summer months. The elevation is 6,600 feet. Open spring through fall

---

37. BARTON FLATS 🚶🚶 ♿ 　　　　 RV 5

Reference: **Near San Gorgonio Wilderness in San Bernardino National Forest; map I6, grid d7.**

Campsites, facilities: There are 47 sites for motor homes up to 45 feet long. Piped water, flush toilets, showers, picnic tables and fire grills are provided. The facilities are **wheelchair accessible**. Pets are allowed on leashes.

Reservations, fee: Reserve by calling (800) 280-CAMP (2267); $7.50 reservation fee; $7 fee per night; $14 for multi-families; $3 for additional cars.

Who to contact: Phone the San Bernardino National Forest San Gorgonio Ranger District at (909) 794-1123.

Location: On Interstate 10 in Redlands, drive 27.5 miles east on Highway 38 to the campground on the left.

Trip note: This is one of the more developed Forest Service camps in southern California. The camp is set at 6,300 feet near Barton Creek—the "creek" part is a misnomer because there's rarely any water in it. The San Gorgonio Wilderness is located one mile to the south and is accessible via Forest Service roads to the trailhead. A wilderness permit is required and can be picked up on your way in from Redlands at the Mill Creek Ranger Station on Highway 38. Open from mid-May through October.

---

38. SAN GORGONIO 🚶🚶 　　　　　　 RV 4

Reference: **Near San Gorgonio Wilderness in San Bernardino National Forest; map I6, grid d7.**

Campsites, facilities: There are 55 sites for motor homes up to 43 feet long. Piped water, flush toilets, picnic tables, hot showers and fire grills are provided. Pets are allowed on leashes.

Reservations, fee: Reserve by calling (800) 280-CAMP (2267); $7.50 reservation fee; $7 camp fee per night; $14 for multi-family units; $3 for additional cars.

Who to contact: Phone the San Bernardino National Forest San Gorgonio Ranger District at (909) 794-1123.

Location: From Interstate 10 in Redlands, drive 28 miles east on Highway 38 to the campground on the left.

Trip note: This is another in the series of developed Forest Service camps in the immediate area. See the trip note for Barton Flats for details.

39. HEART BAR EQUESTRIAN GROUP CAMP

Reference: **In San Bernardino National Forest; map I6, grid d8.**

Campsites, facilities: There is one group camp with 46 corrals that will accommodate up to 65 people and 21 cars (limited use of trailers and motor homes). Piped water (equestrian use only), flush toilets, picnic tables, hot showers and fire grills are provided. Pets are allowed on leashes.

Reservations, fee: Reserve by calling (800) 280-CAMP (2267); $15 reservation fee; $65 fee per night.

Who to contact: Phone the San Bernardino National Forest San Gorgonio Ranger District at (909) 794-1123.

Location: From Interstate 10 in Redlands, drive 33.5 miles east on Highway 38 to Forest Service Road 1N02 on the right. Turn right and drive 1.5 miles to the campground.

Trip note: You might not meet Mr. Ed here, but bring an apple anyway. It's a horse camp, located less than a mile east of Heart Bar Group Camp. A good trail that leads east into the San Gorgonio Wilderness starts four miles down the road at Fish Creek. A wilderness permit is required. The elevation is 7,000 feet. Open from May through November.

40. HEART BAR FAMILY CAMP

Reference: **In San Bernardino National Forest; map I6, grid d8.**

Campsites, facilities: There are 94 sites for tents or motor homes up to 50 feet long. Piped water, vault toilets, picnic tables and fire grills are provided. Pets are allowed on leashes. All facilities are **wheelchair accessible.**

Reservations, fee: Reserve by calling (800) 280-CAMP (2267); $15 reservation fee; $7 fee per night for single family site; $14 for multi-family sites.

Who to contact: Phone the San Bernardino National Forest San Gorgonio Ranger District at (909) 794-1123.

Location: From Interstate 10 in Redlands, drive 33.5 miles east on Highway 38 to Forest Service Road 1N02 on the right. Turn right and drive one mile to the campground.

Trip note: It's a good thing there is piped water at this camp. Why? Because Heart Bar Creek often isn't much more than a trickle and can't be relied on for water. The camp is set at 6,900 feet near Big Meadows, the location of the Heart Bar Fire Station. A great trail that is routed along Wildhorse Creek to Sugarloaf Mountain (9,952 feet) starts just off the main road, about a half mile away to the north, midway between the camp and the fire station. Open from May through November.

41. GREEN CANYON GROUP CAMP

Reference: **Near Green Springs in San Bernardino National Forest; map I6, grid d8.**

Campsites, facilities: There is one group camp that will accommodate 40 people and eight cars (no trailers or motor homes). There is **no piped water.** Pit toilets, picnic tables and fire grills are provided. Pets are allowed on leashes.

Reservations, fee: Reservations required; $35 group fee per night.

Who to contact: Phone the San Bernardino National Forest Big Bear Ranger District at (909) 866-3437.

Location: From Interstate 10 in Redlands, drive about 45 miles east on Highway 38 (1.5 miles past the town of Lake Williams) to the campground entrance on the left (Forest Service Road 2N93). Turn left and then make another immediate left and follow the road for a half mile and you'll see the campground sign on your left.

Trip note: This primitive group camp provides an overflow area for Big Bear Lake campers that can't find a spot closer. It is set at 7,200 feet, with a trail located to the southwest just off the road (look for the gate) that is routed along Green Canyon to Wild Horse Creek. There it intersects with a great trail that goes west to Sugarloaf Mountain, 9,952 feet. Open from June through September.

42. COON CREEK CABIN GROUP CAMP 🏃🏃   **4**

Reference: **On Pacific Crest Trail in San Bernardino National Forest; map I6, grid d9.**

Campsites, facilities: There is one group camp that will accommodate up to 40 people and 14 cars (no trailers or motor homes). There is **no piped water.** Vault toilets, picnic tables and fire grills are provided. Pets are allowed on leashes.

Reservations, fee: Reserve by calling (800) 280-CAMP ($15 reservation fee); $30-$45 group fee per night.

Who to contact: Phone the San Bernardino National Forest San Gorgonio Ranger District at (909) 794-1123.

Location: From Interstate 10 in Redlands, drive 33.5 miles east on Highway 38 to Forest Service Road 1N02 on the right. Turn right and drive five miles to the campground (dirt road).

Trip note: This is a good jumpoff spot for ambitious backpackers. The camp is set beside the Pacific Crest Trail at 8,200 feet, near Coon Creek. Hikers should not count on getting water out of the creek; it often runs dry by early summer. The gate is closed on 1N02 during the winter months. So you need to hike or cross-country ski to the cabin. Open year-round.

43. JUNIPER SPRINGS GROUP CAMP   **RV** **3**

Reference: **In San Bernardino National Forest; map I6, grid d9.**

Campsites, facilities: There is one group camp that will accommodate up to 40 people and eight cars (limited use of trailers and motor homes). Piped water, pit toilets, picnic tables and fire grills are provided. Pets are allowed on leashes.

Reservations, fee: Reservation required; $50 fee per night.

Who to contact: Phone the San Bernardino National Forest Big Bear Ranger District at (909) 866-3437.

Location: From Interstate 10 in Redlands, drive about 40 miles east on Highway 38 (1.5 miles past Onyx Summit) to the campground entrance road (Forest Service Road 2N01) on the right. Turn in on the dirt road and drive three miles. Make a right (opposite the sign that says 2N04, on your left) and drive into the campground.

Trip note: This is a little-known group camp, set at 7,700 feet in a desert-like area, about 10 miles east of Big Bear Lake. The reason it is little known is because there are not a lot of reasons to camp here. You need to be creative. Watch the features of the land change colors as the day passes. Open from June through September.

---

44. YUCAIPA REGIONAL PARK

Reference: **Near Redlands; map I6, grid e5**

Campsites, facilities: There are nine tent sites and 26 sites for trailers or motor homes, 13 with full hookups. Piped water, rest rooms, picnic tables, showers and fire rings are provided. A swimming lagoon, fishing ponds, water slides and paddleboat rentals are available. Pets are permitted on leashed or otherwise restrained. The facilities are **wheelchair accessible**.

Reservations, fee: Reservations accepted; phone (909) 790-3127; $10-$17 fee per night. There are additional fees for fishing, swimming and the waterslide.

Who to contact: Phone the park at (909) 790-3127.

Location: From Redlands, drive east on Interstate 10. Take the Yucaipa exit and drive north on Yucaipa Boulevard to Oak Glen Road. Turn left and continue two miles to the park.

Trip note: This is a great family-oriented county park, complete with water slides and paddleboats for the kids and fishing access and hiking trails for adults. Three lakes are stocked weekly with catfish and bass in the summer and trout in the winter, almost always insuring a catch. Spectacular scenic views of the Yucaipa Valley, the San Bernardino mountains and Mount San Gorgonio can be seen from the park. Two museums are nearby for history buffs. Open Memorial Day through Labor Day.

---

45. LAKE PERRIS STATE RECREATION AREA

Reference: **Map I6, grid f3.**

Campsites, facilities: There are 261 sites for tents only, 265 sites for tents or motor homes up to 31 feet long, seven primitive horse camps with corrals and several group camps (by reservation only). There are no hookups in the group area. Picnic tables, fire grills, electrical connections and piped water are provided. Flush toilets, coin-operated showers, a dump station, a playground, a grocery store, boat launch, mooring and rentals are available. The exhibits, pathways, campgrounds and picnic areas are **wheelchair accessible**. Pets are permitted on leashes.

Reservations, fee: For family camping, reserve by phoning Destinet at (800) 444-7275 ($6.75 Destinet fee); $14-$18 fee per night; $1 pet fee. For group and horse camping, call the park contact number below.

Who to contact: Phone the park at (909) 940-5603 or (909) 657-0676.

Location: From Riverside, drive about 11 miles east on Highway 60. Exit on Moreno Beach Drive, turn right and drive four miles to Via Del Lago. Turn left on Via Del Lago into the park.

Trip note: This is a giant recreation area with many options, but the few elusive but giant spotted bass are the highlight. Some world-class level fish have been caught here. Spring months are best, when their cousins, the largemouth bass, provide the most consistent fishing of the year. By summer, the waterskiers take over, and if you can't beat 'em, join 'em. An Indian Museum features artifacts and handicrafts and is open Wednesdays and weekends. The park gates lock at 8 p.m. in the winter and 10 p.m. in the summer. The elevation is 1,575 feet. Open year-round.

46. BOGART COUNTY PARK 🚶‍♂️   RV 4

Reference: **In Cherry Valley; map I6, grid f5.**

Campsites, facilities: There are 40 sites for tents or motor homes as well as a group area. Fire grills and picnic tables are provided. Piped water, flush toilets and a playground are available. Supplies available in Beaumont. Pets are permitted on leashes.

Reservations, fee: Reservations for groups only; phone Destinet at (800) 234-7275. A reservation fee is charged; phone ahead for fee.

Who to contact: Phone the park at (909) 845-3818.

Location: From Interstate 10 in Beaumont, drive four miles north on Beaumont Avenue to 14th and Cherry Avenue; park is at 9600 Cherry Ave.

Trip note: A lot of Interstate 10 cruisers overlook this county park because they flat don't know it exists. But it does, and it is as pretty as it gets for this area. Some hiking trails provide a recreation option during the cooler months. The elevation is 2,800 feet. Open year-round.

47. BANNING TRAVEL PARK ♿ 🏊   RV 2

Reference: **In Banning; map I6, grid f6.**

Campsites, facilities: There are 106 sites for tents or motor homes, many with full hookups. Picnic tables and fire grills are provided. Cable TV, restrooms, showers, a playground, a swimming pool, a laundromat, a store, a dump station, ice, a recreation room, horseshoes, a video arcade and propane gas are available. Pets are permitted on leashes.

Reservations, fee: Reservations accepted; $12.50-$17.50 fee per night.

Who to contact: Phone the park at (909) 849-7513.

Location: From Interstate 10 in Banning, take the Highway 243 exit and drive one block south on 8th Avenue. Turn left on Lincoln and drive two blocks. Turn right on San Gorgonio and drive one mile to 1455 South San Gorgonio Avenue.

Trip note: Banning may not seem like a hotbed of civilization at first glance, but this clean, comfortable park is a good spot to make camp while exploring some of the area's hidden attractions, including Agua Caliente Indian Canyons and the Lincoln Shrine. It is set at 2,400 feet, 22 miles from Palm Springs. A good side trip is to head south on curving "Highway" 240 up to Vista Point in the San Bernardino National Forest. Open year-round.

48. PALM VIEW RV PARK 🐟 🏊   RV 4

Reference: **Near Lake Elsinore; map I6, grid g1.**

Campsites, facilities: There are 45 sites for tents or RVs, some with full hookups. Restrooms, fire rings, a sanitary dump station, a recreation area, a swimming pool and pond are provided. A laundromat, a store, ice and firewood are available. Pets are permitted on leashes.

Reservations, fee: Reservations accepted; $14-$16 fee per night. Group rates are available on request.

Who to contact: Phone the park at (909) 657-7791.

Location: From the Los Angeles area, travel south on Interstate 15 and exit at the Highway 74 (Central Avenue) turnoff. Drive east on Highway 74 for four miles to River Road. Drive south on River Road about one mile to 22200 River Road.

Trip note: This privately-operated RV park is located is a quiet valley between Lake Perris and Lake Elsinore, 700 feet. The park's recreation area offers basketball, volleyball, horseshoes, tetherball and a playground, which should tell you everything you need to know. For oddballs, bungy jumping and parachuting is available in the town of Perris. Open year-round.

49. BLACK MOUNTAIN GROUP CAMPS 🏃🏃   RV 6

Reference: Near Mt. San Jacinto in San Bernardino National Forest; map I6, grid g7.

Campsites, facilities: There are two group camps here for tents or motor homes up to 22 feet long. Each has a capacity of 50 people and 16 vehicles. Piped water, vault toilets, picnic tables and fire grills are provided. Pets are allowed on leashes.

Reservations, fee: Reserve by calling (800) 280-CAMP ($15 reservation fee); $50 fee per night.

Who to contact: Phone the San Bernardino National Forest San Jacinto Ranger District at (909) 659-2117.

Location: From Idyllwild, drive nine miles north on Highway 243. Turn right on Forest Service Road 4S01 (a narrow dirt road) and drive eight miles to the campground.

Trip note: This is a beautiful scenic area, particularly north on the edge of the San Jacinto Wilderness and east in Mt. San Jacinto State Park. The camp is set at 7,500 feet and has a trail routed out from the camp north into the National Forest and east into Mt. San Jacinto State Park. Open from May to October.

50. BOULDER BASIN 🏃🏃   RV 5

Reference: Near San Jacinto Wilderness in San Bernardino National Forest; map I6, grid g7.

Campsites, facilities: There are 34 sites for tents or motor homes up to 22 feet long (trailers are not recommended). Piped water, vault toilets, fire grills and picnic tables are provided. Pets are allowed on leashes.

Reservations, fee: Reservations accepted; phone (800) 280-CAMP; $9 fee per night.

Who to contact: Phone the San Bernardino National Forest San Jacinto Ranger District at (909) 659-2117.

Location: From Idyllwild, drive nine miles north on Highway 243. Turn right on Forest Service Road 4S01 and drive six miles to the campground. Note: This road is dirt and very narrow.

Trip note: Located near the San Jacinto Wilderness (to the northeast), this is an ideal trailhead camp for hikers. A trail heads west into a designated scenic area, starting at Black Mountain Lookout. The elevation is 7,300 feet. Open from May to mid-October.

51. DARK CANYON 🎣🏃🏃   RV 4

Reference: In San Jacinto Mountains in San Bernardino National Forest; map I6, grid g8.

Campsites, facilities: There are 22 sites for tents or motor homes up to 22 feet long. Piped water, vault toilets, fire grills and picnic tables are provided. Pets are permitted on leashes.

Reservations, fee: Reservations accepted; phone (800) 280-CAMP (2267); $7-$8 fee per night.

Who to contact: Phone the San Bernardino National Forest San Jacinto Ranger District at (909) 659-2117.

Location: From Idyllwild, drive seven miles north on Highway 243. Turn right on Forest Service Road 4S02 and drive three more miles on a narrowing road.

Trip note: This pretty setting is on the slopes of the San Jacinto Mountain. Hikers will find a trailhead at the end of Forest Service Road 4S02, less than a mile north of the camp. The trail leads east into Mt. San Jacinto State Park to Deer Springs, where it intersects with a major trail. A wilderness permit is required. The elevation is 5,800 feet. Open from May to mid-October.

52. ELSINORE WEST MARINA

Reference: On Lake Elsinore; map I6, grid h0.

Campsites, facilities: There are 195 sites for tents or RVs with full hookups. Picnic tables are provided. Restrooms, showers, a sanitary dump station, horseshoes, clubhouse, convenience store, telephone hookups, cable TV hookups, a boat ramp and boat rentals are available. Pets are allowed on leashes.

Reservations, fee: Reservations accepted for RV sites only; $14-$19 fee per night.

Who to contact: Phone the park at (909) 678-1300 or (800) 328-6844.

Location: From Interstate 15 in Lake Elsinore, take Highway 74 and drive four miles west to 32700 Riverside Drive.

Trip note: This privately operated motor home park is located just a half mile from Lake Elsinore. A nearby alternative RV park is Roadrunner, which used to be owned by the same folks.

53. ROADRUNNER

Reference: On Lake Elsinore; map I6, grid h0.

Campsites, facilities: There are 102 sites for motor homes with full hookups and 35 sites for tents only. Picnic tables are provided. Piped water, cable television, telephone hookups, a laundromat, sanitary dump station and boat ramp are available. Pets are permitted on leashes.

Reservations, fee: Reservations accepted; $12 to $16 fee per night.

Who to contact: Phone (909) 674-4900.

Location: From Elsinore on Interstate 15, turn west on Highway 74 and drive about four miles. Look for Roadrunner on the left side of the road, just a half mile past the city park.

Trip note: The Roadrunner, a privately operated park, features 600 feet of lakefront property along Lake Elsinore. It is best known as a quality lake for waterskiing, with hot weather to match, but only poor to fair fishing, with some bluegill, crappie and catfish. Boat ramps are located at both the north and south ends of the lake.

54. LAKE ELSINORE RECREATION AREA

Reference: Map I6, grid h0.

Campsites, facilities: There are 400 sites for tents or motor homes up to 40 feet long. Piped water, electrical connections, fire grills and picnic tables are provided. Flush toilets, showers, a dump station, playground, laundromat and a grocery store are available. Pets are permitted on leashes. The camping and picnicking areas are **wheelchair accessible**.

Reservations, fee: No reservations; $13.50-$17.50 fee per night.

Who to contact: Phone the park at (909) 674-3177.

Location: From Interstate 15 in Lake Elsinore, drive three miles west on Highway 74 to the park entrance.

Trip note: This is a pretty spot set along the northern shore of Lake Elsinore, a popular lake for waterskiing. The elevation is 1,250 feet. Open year-round.

55. CASA DEL SOL RV RESORTS   🛇 🏊 ⛳   RV 3

Reference: **In Hemet; map I6, grid h5.**

Campsites, facilities: There are 358 motor home sites. Piped water, electrical connections, cable TV, telephones and sewer hookups are provided. Restrooms, showers, a swimming pool, a recreation room, a billiard room, a jacuzzi and a laundromat are available. Pets are permitted on leashes.

Reservations, fee: Reservations accepted; $21 fee per night.

Who to contact: Phone the park at (909) 925-2515.

Location: From Interstate 215 south of Perris, turn east on Highway 74 and drive about 14 miles to Hemet (the highway becomes Florida Avenue in Hemet). Turn south on Kirby Avenue and continue to the campground on the corner of Kirby and Acacia at 2750 West Acacia Avenue.

Trip note: Hemet is a retirement town, so if you want excitement, the three lakes in the area are the best place to look for it: Lake Perris to the northwest, Lake Skinner to the south, and Lake Hemet to the east. Open year-round.

56. MOUNTAIN VALLEY RV PARK   🛇 🏊   RV 3

Reference: **In Hemet; map I6, grid h5.**

Campsites, facilities: There are 170 motor home sites. Piped water, cable TV, electrical connections and sewer hookups are provided. Restrooms, showers, a swimming pool, an enclosed jacuzzi, a laundromat, a recreation room, shuffleboard and telephone hookups are available. A grocery store and propane gas are available nearby. Pets are permitted on leashes.

Reservations, fee: Reservations accepted; $21 fee per night; $1 pet fee.

Who to contact: Phone the park at (909) 925-5812.

Location: From Interstate 215 south of Perris, turn east on Highway 74 and drive about 14 miles to Hemet (the highway becomes Florida Avenue in Hemet). Turn south (right) on Lyon Avenue and drive to 235 South Lyon Avenue.

Trip note: This is one of two motor home parks in the Hemet area. Three lakes in the area provide side trip possibilities: Lake Perris to the northwest, Lake Skinner to the south, and Lake Hemet to the east. Open year-round.

57. IDYLLWILD COUNTY PARK   🚶🚶   RV 6

Reference: **Near San Bernardino National Forest; map I6, grid h7.**

Campsites, facilities: There are 90 sites for tents or motor homes up to 34 feet long (30 for motor homes). Fire grills and picnic tables are provided. Flush toilets and showers are available. Pets are permitted on leashes. A grocery store, a laundromat and propane gas are available nearby.

Reservations, fee: Reservations accepted, phone Destinet at (800) 234-PARK (A reservation fee is charged); $10 fee per night.

Who to contact: Phone the park at (909) 659-2656.

Location: From Highway 243 in Idyllwild, drive a half mile west on Riverside County Playground Road (follow the signs) to the campground.

Trip note: Mt. San Jacinto State Park, San Jacinto Wilderness and the San Bernardino National Forest lands surround this park. That provides plenty of options for visitors. A trail from the State Park Headquarters nearby leads into the backcountry and connects with the Pacific Crest National Scenic Trail. The elevation is 5,300 feet. Open year-round.

---

58. STONE CREEK 🚶🏻🏇   RV 7

Reference: **In Mount San Jacinto State Park; map I6, grid h8.**

Campsites, facilities: There are 10 tent sites and 40 sites for tents or motor homes up to 24 feet long. Fire grills and picnic tables are provided. Piped water and pit toilets are available. Pets are permitted on leashes. Supplies and a laundromat are nearby.

Reservations, fee: Reserve by phoning Destinet at (800) 444-7275 ($6.75 Destinet fee); $12 fee per night; $1 pet fee.

Who to contact: Phone the Mt. San Jacinto State Park at (909) 659-2607 or (619) 767-5311.

Location: From Idyllwild, drive six miles north on Highway 243 to the entrance.

Trip note: This is a wooded camp located off the main road along Stone Creek, less than a mile from the Fern Basin Camp and less than three miles from Dark Canyon Camp. The elevation is 5,900 feet. Open year-round.

---

59. IDYLLWILD 🚶🏻🏇   RV 6

Reference: **In Mount San Jacinto State Park; map I6, grid h8.**

Campsites, facilities: There are 11 sites for tents only and 22 sites for tents or motor homes up to 24 feet long. Fire grills and picnic tables are provided. Piped water, flush toilets and showers are available. Pets are permitted on leashes. Supplies and a laundromat are nearby.

Reservations, fee: Reserve by phoning Destinet at (800) 444-7275 ($6.75 Destinet fee); $15-$17 fee per night; $1 pet fee.

Who to contact: Phone the Mt. San Jacinto State Park at (909) 659-2607 or (619) 767-5311.

Location: In Idyllwild, drive to the north end of town on Highway 243 to the entrance.

Trip note: This is a prime spot for hikers and one of the better jumpoff points in the area. A trail leading from the camp goes into the backcountry of Mt. San Jacinto State Park and San Jacinto Wilderness and connects with the Pacific Crest Trail. The elevation is 5,400 feet. Open year-round.

---

60. FERN BASIN 🚶🏻   RV 4

Reference: **Near Mt. San Jacinto State Park in San Bernardino National Forest; map I6, grid h8.**

Campsites, facilities: There are 22 sites for tents or motor homes up to 15 feet long. Piped water, vault toilets, fire grills and picnic tables are provided. Pets are allowed on leashes.

Reservations, fee: Reservations accepted; phone (800) 280-CAMP (2267); $9 fee per night.

Who to contact: Phone the San Bernardino National Forest San Jacinto Ranger District at (909) 659-2117.

Location: From Idyllwild, drive seven miles north on Highway 243. Turn right on Forest Service Road 4S02 and drive one mile to the campground.

Trip note: This is a nearby option to Black Mountain Camp. It is located a little over one mile south of Dark Canyon Camp. Backpackers should head north on Forest Service Road 4S02 for two miles until it dead ends at a Seven Pines trailhead. Wilderness permits are required. That trail is routed east into Mt. San Jacinto State Park, where it connects to a network of other trails. The elevation is 6,300 feet. Open from May to October.

61. MARION MOUNTAIN

Reference: **In San Bernardino National Forest; map I6, grid h8.**

Campsites, facilities: There are 24 sites for tents or motor homes up to 15 feet long. Piped water, vault toilets, fire grills and picnic tables are provided.

Reservations, fee: Reservations accepted; phone (800) 280-CAMP (2267); $9 fee per night.

Who to contact: Phone the San Bernardino National Forest San Jacinto Ranger District at (909) 659-2117.

Location: From Idyllwild, drive seven miles north on Highway 243. Turn right on Forest Service Road 4S02 and drive two miles to the campground.

Trip note: You get good nearby lookouts and a developed campground at this spot. The nearby trails head up the slopes to Marion Mountain and east into adjacent San Jacinto State Park. The elevation is 6,400 feet. Open from May to mid-October.

62. LAKE SKINNER RECREATION AREA

Reference: **Map I6, grid i4.**

Campsites, facilities: There are 257 sites for tents or motor homes, many with full hookups. Picnic tables and fire grills are provided. Restrooms, showers, a playground, a grocery store, ice, bait, a dump station, a swimming pool (in the summer), a boat ramp, mooring, boat rentals and propane gas are available. Pets are permitted on leashes.

Reservations, fee: Reservations requested; $15-$18 fee per night; $2 pet fee.

Who to contact: Phone Lake Skinner Recreation Area at (909) 926-1541.

Location: From Interstate 15 in Temecula, take the Rancho California exit and drive 9.5 miles northeast to the park entrance.

Trip note: Lake Skinner is a piece of water in the middle of some very dry, hot country. That's why it gets hit hard by boaters and sunbathers. However, note that no swimming or waterskiing is permitted here, and that non-motorized boats under 10 feet are prohibited. There is good fishing in the spring. The elevation is 1,500 feet. Open year-round.

63. HURKEY CREEK COUNTY PARK

Reference: **Near Lake Hemet; map I6, grid i8.**

Campsites, facilities: There are 105 family sites and 104 group sites for tents or motor homes up to 35 feet long. Fire grills and picnic tables are provided. Piped water, flush toilets and showers are available. A dump station is available for a fee at Lake Hemet campground nearby. Pets are permitted on leashes.

Reservations, fee: Reservations recommended; phone Destinet at (800) 234-7275 (A reservation fee is charged); $12 fee per night; phone ahead for fee.

Who to contact: Phone the park at (909) 659-2050.

Location: From Palm Desert, drive about 32 miles southwest on Highway 74 to the campground entrance on your right.

Trip note: This large county park is located just east (across the road) from Lake Hemet, beside Hurkey Creek (which runs in winter and spring). The highlight, of course, is the nearby lake, known for good fishing in the spring. No swimming is permitted. The elevation is 4,800 feet. Open year-round.

64. LAKE HEMET

Reference: Map I6, grid i8.

Campsites, facilities: There are 1,000 sites for tents or motor homes. Piped water, fire grills, picnic tables and, in some cases, electrical connections are provided. Flush toilets, showers, a dump station, a playground, a pond, a boat ramp, boat rentals, a grocery store, a laundromat and propane gas are available. Pets are allowed on leashes.

Reservations, fee: No reservations; $11.50-$14.75 fee per night.

Who to contact: Phone the camp at (909) 659-2680.

Location: From Palm Desert, drive 32 miles southwest on Highway 74 to the entrance.

Trip note: Hemet is a long, narrow lake, set on the South Fork of the San Jacinto River. It's a popular place for trout fishing, particularly in the spring. Boats under 10 feet or over 18 feet are prohibited and no swimming either. The elevation is 4,300 feet. Open year-round.

65. INDIAN OAKS TRAILER RANCH

Reference: In Temecula; Map I6, grid j2.

Campsites, facilities: There are 60 motor home sites with full hookups, 20 tent sites and several group camping sites. Showers, restrooms, a laundry, propane and a dump station are provided. Horseshoes, shuffleboard, a recreation room and volleyball are available. Pets are allowed on leashes.

Reservations, fee: Reservations are recommended; $13-$18 fee per night. Maximum two adults and two children per site; an additional person is $4 per night.

Who to contact: Indian Oaks Trailer Ranch, 38120 East Benton Road, P.O. Box 922, Temecula, CA 92593; (909) 676-5301.

Location: From Riverside, take Interstate 215 south into Temecula and take the Temecula/Rancho California Road exit east. Drive nine miles out of town, past the Lucky shopping center, then turn right on East Benton Road. Drive for 3.5 miles until you see the large sign for the camp.

Trip note: This camp is located in a 25-acre oak-studded valley, under giant oak trees they say are 600 years old. It was once a Native American campground. Scenic hiking trails and picnic areas are located in and nearby the camp, and Lake Skinner is only three miles away for fishing. Plus, you can always visit the many area wineries.

66. DRIPPING SPRINGS 🚶🚶

Reference: **Near Agua Tibia Wilderness in Cleveland National Forest; map I6, grid j5.**

Campsites, facilities: There are 24 sites for tents or motor homes up to 32 feet long. Piped water, fire rings, barbecue grills and picnic tables are provided. Vault toilets are available. Pets are permitted on leashes. A grocery store is nearby.

Reservations, fee: No reservations; $7 fee per night.

Who to contact: Phone the Cleveland National Forest, Palomar Ranger District at (619) 788-0250.

Location: From Interstate 15 in Temecula, drive 11 miles east on Highway 79 to the campground.

Trip note: This is one of the premium Forest Service camps, set just inside the northern border above Vail Lake and adjacent to the Agua Tibia Wilderness. The Dripping Springs Trail is routed south out of camp, starting at 1,500 feet and climbing near the peak of Agua Tibia Mountain, which is 4,779 feet. Open year-round.

67. KAMP ANZA RV RESORT 🐟 🏊

Reference: **Near Anza; map I6, grid j8.**

Campsites, facilities: There are 106 sites for tents or motor homes, many with full hookups. Horsecamping facilities are available. Picnic tables and fire grills are provided. Restrooms, showers, a playground, a fishing pond, a swimming spa, horseshoe pits, a laundromat, a store, a dump station, ice, a recreation room and propane gas are available.

Reservations, fee: Reservations accepted; $10-$15 fee per night; $5 fee per night per horse.

Who to contact: Phone the park at (909) 763-4819.

Location: From Palm Desert, drive west on Highway 74 for 24 miles. Turn left on Highway 371 and drive west to the town of Anza. Turn left on Kirby Road and drive one mile. Turn left on Wellman Road and drive one mile. Turn right on Terwilliger Road and drive to 41560 Terwilliger Road.

Trip note: This is a year-round motor home park set at 4,100 feet, with many nearby recreation options. Lake Hemet is 11 miles away, with hiking, motorbiking and jeep trails nearby in San Bernardino National Forest.

SO-CAL MAP .... see page 690
adjoining maps
NORTH (H7) .... see page 682
EAST (I8) .... see page 762
SOUTH (J7) .... see page 788
WEST (I6) .... see page 724

23 LISTINGS
PAGES 752-761

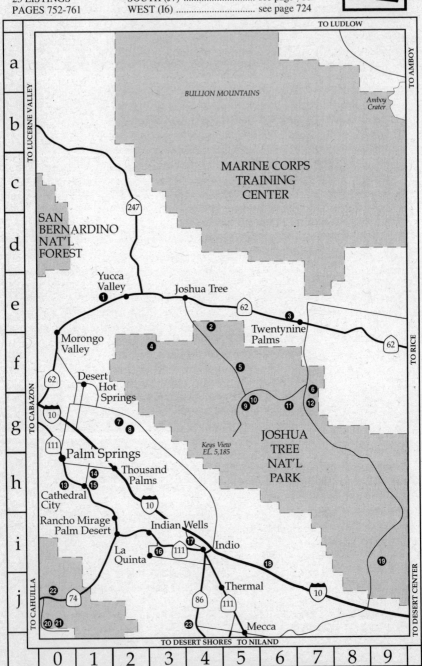

1. MORONGO PARK

Reference: Near Joshua Tree National Park; map I7, grid e1.

Campsites, facilities: There are six sites for tents or motor homes. There is **no potable piped water**, but pit toilets, picnic tables and fire grills are provided. Supplies can be purchased within one mile of the campground. Pets are permitted on leashes.

Reservations, fee: No reservations; no fee.

Who to contact: This is a city park. For information call (619) 363-6454.

Location: From Yucca Valley, drive five miles west on Highway 62 to signed campground entrance on the right.

Trip note: Not many folks use this camp. It's basically for desperate overnighters, stuck for a spot. So you really can't whine too much about the "no piped water." No nuthin', in fact. If it's summer, you'd best bring your own drinks or risk dying of dehydration. The elevation is 3,000 feet.

2. INDIAN COVE CAMPGROUND

Reference: In Joshua Tree National Park; map I7, grid e4.

Campsites, facilities: There are 107 sites for tents or motor homes to 32 feet long. Adjacent to this campground is a group camp with 13 sites for tents only that will accommodate 30 to 70 people each. Drinking water is available at the Indian Cove Ranger Station. Pit toilets, picnic tables and fire grills are provided. Gas, groceries, and laundry services are in town, which is about 10 miles from camp. Pets are permitted on leashes but not on backcountry trails.

Reservations, fee: Reserve by phoning Destinet at (800) 365-CAMP; Family sites are free; group sites are $15-$30 per night.

Who to contact: Phone the Joshua Tree National Park at (619) 367-7511.

Location: From Joshua Tree, drive about nine miles east on Highway 62 to Indian Cove Road. Turn right and drive three miles to the campground.

Trip note: This is one of the campgrounds that is near the northern border of Joshua Tree National Park. The vast desert park, covering 870 square miles, is best known for its unique granite formations and scraggly-looking trees. If you had to withstand the summer heat here, you'd look scraggly too. Drinking water is available at the Indian Cove Ranger Station.

3. KNOTT SKY PARK

Reference: Near Joshua Tree National Park; map I7, grid e6.

Campsites, facilities: There are 80 sites for tents or motor homes, some with water and electrical hookups. Picnic tables and fire grills are provided. Piped water, flush toilets, showers, a sanitary dump station and a playground are available. Supplies and a laundromat are available nearby. Pets are permitted

Reservations, fee: Reservations accepted; $7.50 to $17 fee per night.

Who to contact: Phone the County Parks at (619) 367-9669.

Location: From Twentynine Palms, drive one mile west on Highway 62 to the signed park entrance.

Trip note: What the heck, unlike the camps in the nearby national park to the south, this one has showers. And if you've spent any degree of time at Joshua Tree, you're probably in need in one. Whoo-eee! So turn that water on and dive in. The elevation is 2,000 feet. Open year-round.

4. BLACK ROCK CAMPGROUND

Reference: In Joshua Tree National Park; map I7, grid f3.

Campsites, facilities: There are 100 sites for tents or motor homes to 32 feet long. Picnic tables and fire grills are provided. Piped water, flush toilets and a sanitary disposal station are available. Pets are permitted on leashes, but not on backcountry trails. One site is **wheelchair accessible** (campsite #61).

Reservations, fee: Reserve by phoning Destinet at (800) 365-CAMP ($6.75 Destinet fee); $10 fee per night .

Who to contact: Phone the Joshua Tree National Park at (619) 367-7511.

Location: From the junction of Interstate 10 and Highway 62, drive about 22.5 miles north on Highway 62 to Yucca Valley. Turn south (right) on Joshua Lane and drive about five miles to the campground.

Trip note: This is the fanciest darn campground this side of the galaxy. Why they actually have piped water. Course, they charge you for it. It is set at the mouth of Black Rock Canyon, which provides good winter hiking possibilities amid unique (in other words, weird) rock formations. Show up in summer and you'll trade your gold for a sip of water. The elevation is 4,000 feet. Open October through May.

5. SHEEP PASS GROUP CAMP

Reference: **In Joshua Tree National Park; map I7, grid f5.**

Campsites, facilities: There are six sites for tents. Picnic tables and fire grills are provided. Pit toilets are available. There is **no piped water**, so bring plenty along. Pets are permitted on leashes.

Reservations, fee: Reserve by phoning Destinet at (800) 365-CAMP; $10 fee per night.

Who to contact: Phone the Joshua Tree National Park at (619) 367-7511.

Location: From Twentynine Palms, drive south on Utah Trail for about 16 miles to the campground on the south (left) side of the road.

Trip note: There are several camps located in this stretch of high desert. Ryan Camp is just one mile down the road and provides a nearby option. For details on the area, see the trip note for White Tank and Jumbo Rocks. Temperatures are routinely over 100 degrees in the summer months. Open year-round.

6. BELLE

Reference: **In Joshua Tree National Park; map I7, grid f7.**

Campsites, facilities: There are 17 sites for tents or motor homes up to 27 feet long. Picnic tables and fire grills are provided. Pit toilets are available. There is **no piped water**, so bring your own. Pets are permitted on leashes.

Reservations, fee: No reservations; no fee.

Who to contact: Phone the Joshua Tree National Park at (619) 367-7511.

Location: From Twentynine Palms, drive eight miles south on Utah Trail to the intersection with Cottonwood Springs Road. Turn south (bear left) on Cottonwood Road (goes to Interstate 10) and drive about 1.5 miles to the campground.

Trip note: This camp is at 3,800 feet in rocky high country. It is one of the six camps in the immediate area. For details, see the trip note for White Tank.

7. SAM'S FAMILY SPA ♿ 🏊 ♨

Reference: **Near Palm Springs; map I7, grid g2.**

Campsites, facilities: There are 180 RV sites, with full hookups and picnic tables. There is a separate area with fire grills. Restrooms, showers, a playground, swimming pool, a wading pool, four hot mineral pools, a sauna, a laundromat, a store and a restaurant are available. Pets are permitted on leashes.

Reservations, fee: No reservations; $30 fee per night.

Who to contact: Phone the park at (619) 329-6457.

Location: From Interstate 10, take the Palm Drive exit north and drive three miles north on Palm Drive. Turn east (right) on Dillon Road and drive 4.5 miles to 70-875 Dillon Road on the right.

Trip note: Hot mineral pools attract tons of winter vacationers to the Palm Springs area. This spot, being set 10 miles outside of Palm Springs, provides an alternative to the more crowded spots. The elevation is 1,000 feet. Open year-round.

---

8. SKY VALLEY EAST & WEST
🥾 ♿ 🏊 ♨

Reference: **Near Palm Springs; map I7, grid g2.**

Campsites, facilities: There are 614 RV sites. Piped water, cable TV hookups, electrical connections and sewer hookups are provided. Restrooms, showers, four swimming pools, nine natural hot mineral pools, two laundromats, two large recreation rooms, a social director, shuffleboard, tennis, horseshoes, a crafts room and walking trails are available. A grocery store and propane gas are nearby. Some facilities are **wheelchair accessible**. Pets are allowed on leashes.

Reservations, fee: Reservations accepted; $25-$29 fee per night.

Who to contact: Phone the park at (619) 329-2909.

Location: From Interstate 10, take the Palm Drive exit north and drive three miles north on Palm Drive. Turn east (right) on Dillon Road and drive 8.5 miles to 74-711 Dillon Road.

Trip note: A great spot for family fun and relaxation. Open year-round.

---

9. RYAN 🥾 🏇

Reference: **In Joshua Tree National Park; map I7, grid g5.**

Campsites, facilities: There are 29 sites for tents or motor homes up to 27 feet long. Picnic tables and fire grills are provided. Pit toilets are available. There is **no piped water**, so bring plenty along. Hitching posts are available at the campground (bring water for the horses). Pets are allowed on leashes.

Reservations, fee: No reservations; no fee.

Who to contact: Phone the Joshua Tree National Park at (619) 367-7511.

Location: From Twentynine Palms, drive south on Utah Trail about 20 miles to the signed campground entrance on the left.

Trip note: This is one of the high desert camps in the immediate area (see Jumbo Rocks Camp). Joshua Tree National Park is a forbidding paradise, huge, hot and waterless (most of the time). The unique rock formations look like some great artist made them with a chisel. The elevation is 4,300 feet.

10. HIDDEN VALLEY 🥾🥾   RV 🔺 4

Reference: **In Joshua Tree National Park; map I7, grid g5.**

Campsites, facilities: There are 39 sites for tents or motor homes up to 27 feet long. Picnic tables and fire grills are provided. Pit toilets are available. There is **no piped water**, so bring plenty along. Pets are permitted on leashes.

Reservations, fee: No reservations; no fee.

Who to contact: Phone the Joshua Tree National Park at (619) 367-7511.

Location: From Joshua Tree on Highway 62, turn south on Park Boulevard and drive 14 miles southwest to the campground.

Trip note: Set at 4,200 feet in the high desert country, this is one of several camping options in the area. Open year-round.

---

11. JUMBO ROCKS 🥾🥾   RV 🔺 4

Reference: **In Joshua Tree National Park; map I7, grid g6.**

Campsites, facilities: There are 125 sites for tents or motor homes up to 27 feet long. Picnic tables and fire grills are provided. Pit toilets are available. There is **no piped water**, so bring plenty along. Pets are permitted on leashes. Campsite #11 is **wheelchair accessible.**

Reservations, fee: No reservations; no fee.

Who to contact: Phone the Joshua Tree National Park at (619) 367-7511.

Location: From Twentynine Palms, drive south on Utah Trail for about 12 miles to the campground on the south (left) side of the road.

Trip note: Joshua Tree National Park covers more than 870 square miles. It is striking high desert with unique granite formations that seem to change color at different times of the day. This camp is one of the higher ones in the park at 4,400 feet. Open year-round.

---

12. WHITE TANK 🥾🥾   RV 🔺 4

Reference: **In Joshua Tree National Park; map I7, grid g7.**

Campsites, facilities: There are 15 sites for tents or motor homes up to 27 feet long. Picnic tables and fire grills are provided. Pit toilets are available, but there is **no piped water**, so bring plenty along. Pets are permitted on leashes.

Reservations, fee: No reservations; no fee.

Who to contact: Phone the Joshua Tree National Park at (619) 367-7511.

Location: From Twentynine Palms, drive eight miles south on Utah Trail to the intersection with Cottonwood Springs Road. Turn south (bear left) on Cottonwood Road (goes to Interstate 10) and drive three miles to the campground.

Trip note: Joshua Tree National Park is a unique area where the high and low desert meet. It looks kind of like high plains country. Winter is a good time to explore the beautiful boulder piles and rock formations amid scraggly Joshua trees. There are several trails in the area, but don't even think about hiking in summer. The elevation is 3,800 feet.

---

13. HAPPY TRAVELER RV PARK 🏊   RV 🔺 1

Reference: **In Palm Springs; map I7, grid h0.**

Campsites, facilities: There are 139 motor home sites with full hookups and picnic tables. Restrooms, showers, a recreation room, a swimming pool, a jacuzzi and a laundromat are available. Pets are permitted on leashes.

Reservations, fee: Reservations; $28 fee per night.

Who to contact: Phone the park at (619) 325-8518.

Location: In Palm Springs, drive one mile south on Palm Canyon Drive. Turn right on Mesquite Avenue to 211 West Mesquite Avenue.

Trip note: Are we having fun yet? They are at "Happy Traveler," which is within walking distance of Palm Springs shopping areas. Open year-round.

14. OUTDOOR RESORTS   RV 1

Reference: **Near Palm Springs; map I7, grid h1.**

Campsites, facilities: There are 1,213 motor home sites with full hookups. Restrooms, showers, eight swimming pools, 14 tennis courts, a health club with three saunas, ten jacuzzis, a 27-hole golf course, two club houses, a snack bar, a beauty salon, a laundromat, a store, shuffleboard and planned activities are available. Some facilities are **wheelchair accessible**. Pets are permitted on leashes.

Reservations, fee: Reservations accepted; $37.50-$47.50 fee per night.

Who to contact: Phone the park at (619) 324-4005 or (800) 843-3131 (California only).

Location: From Cathedral City, drive two miles north on Date Palm Drive to Ramon Road. Turn left and drive to 69-411 Ramon Road.

Trip note: This is the motor home park that was voted the "Most Likely To Succeed As a City." It's huge, it's flat, and it offers many activities. If you still can't think of anything to do, you can always compare tires. The park is located four miles from Palm Springs. Open year-round.

15. DE ANZA OASIS RV RESORT   RV 2

Reference: **Near Palm Springs; map I7, grid h1.**

Campsites, facilities: There are 140 motor home sites with full hookups. Restrooms, showers, cable TV hookups, a swimming pool, a jacuzzi, an 18- hole golf course, tennis courts, a laundromat, and propane gas are available. Pets are permitted on leashes.

Reservations, fee: Reservations accepted; $17-$25 fee per night.

Who to contact: Phone the park at (619) 328-4813.

Location: In Cathedral City, drive to 36-100 Date Palm Drive. The camp is on the corner of Gerald Ford Drive and Date Palm Drive.

Trip note: This popular wintering spot is for motor home cruisers looking to hole up in the Palm Springs area for awhile. Palm Springs is only six miles away. Open year-round.

16. INDIAN WELLS RV ROUNDUP   RV 1

Reference: **In Indio; map I7, grid i3.**

Campsites, facilities: There are 381 motor home sites, most with full hookups. Picnic tables and fire grills are provided. Restrooms, showers, cable TV hookups, three swimming pools, two therapy pools, a fitness room, horse-shoes, shuffleboard courts, a putting green, planned activities, ice, a dog run, a barbecue and a laundromat are available. Pets are allowed on leashes.

Reservations, fee: Reservations accepted; $16-$23 per night; adult-oriented.

Who to contact: Phone the park at (619) 347-0895.

Location: In Indio on Interstate 10, take the Jefferson exit. As you exit, stay in the right lane and turn right at the light. Follow Jefferson Street south for three miles. The park is on the left at 47-340 Jefferson Street.

Trip note: Indio is a good-sized town located midway between the Salton Sea to the south and Palm Springs to the north. In the summer, it is one of the hottest places in America.

17. OUTDOOR RESORTS MOTORCOACH ♿ RV 7

Reference: **In Indio; map I7, grid i3.**

Campsites, facilities: There are 165 sites for motor homes only. Full hookups and cable television are provided. Restrooms, showers, a swimming pool, tennis court, sauna, Jacuzzi, laundromat and nine-hole golf course are available. Some facilities are **wheelchair accessible**. Pets are permitted on leashes.

Reservations, fee: Reservations accepted; $38 fee per night.

Who to contact: Phone (619) 775-7255, (800) 371-9988 (California only), or (800) 982-2992 (outside California).

Location: From Palm Springs, take Interstate 10 east to the Jefferson exit. Stay in the right lane as you exit, then turn right at the light on Jefferson. Drive through the intersection at Highway 111 and continue one block south to 48th Avenue. Turn left and drive to the park on the left side of the road at 80394 48th Avenue.

Trip note: For owners of tour buses, motor coaches and lavish RVs, it doesn't get any better than this in Southern California. This is the only motor home-only park in California, and it is set close to golf, shopping and restaurants. Jeep tours of the surrounding desert canyons and organized recreation events are available.

18. CORN SPRINGS RV 4

Reference: **Near Indio; map I7, grid i6.**

Campsites, facilities: There are 10 sites for tents or motor homes, and there is also one group site. Picnic tables and fire rings are provided. Piped water and pit toilets are available. Pets are permitted on leashes.

Reservations, fee: No reservations; $6 fee per night.

Who to contact: Phone Palm Springs South Resource Area at (619) 251-4800, or write Bureau of Land Management, 63-500 Garnet Avenue, P.O. Box 2000, North Palm Springs, CA 92258.

Location: From Indio on Interstate 10, drive east 60 miles to Corn Springs Road. Exit right on Corn Springs Road and drive eight miles to the campground, which is adjacent to the road.

Trip note: Just think: If you spend a night here, you can say to darn near anybody, "I've camped some place you haven't." I don't know whether to offer my condolences or congratulations, but Corn Springs Camp offers a primitive spot in the middle of nowhere in desert country. What the heck, if you are stuck for a spot while cruising Interstate 10, this will seem like paradise. The sidetrip to Joshua Tree National Park to the north is also well worth the adventure. On the other hand, if it's a summer afternoon, tell me, just how do you spend the day here when it's 115 degrees?

19. COTTONWOOD 🚶🚶 RV 4

Reference: **In Joshua Tree National Park; map I7, grid i9.**

Campsites, facilities: There are 62 sites for tents or motor homes up to 27 feet long. There is a group campground adjacent to this one (Cottonwood Group Camp) that has three group sites for up to 30 people each. Group site #2 is **wheelchair accessible**. Piped water, picnic tables and fire grills are provided. Flush toilets are available. Pets are permitted on leashes.

Reservations, fee: No reservations for family sites; $8 fee per night; reserve group sites by phoning Destinet at (800) 365-CAMP; $15 group fee per night plus reservation fee.

Who to contact: Phone the Joshua Tree National Park at (619) 367-7511.

Location: From Indio, drive 26 miles east on Interstate 10. Take the Twentynine Palms exit (near Chiriaco Summit) and drive 10 miles north on the park entrance road to the campground.

Trip note: If you enter Joshua Tree National Park at its southern access point, this is the first camp you come to. The park visitor center, with maps available, is a mandatory stop. The Park is a vast, high desert, highlighted by unique rock formations, occasional scraggly trees, and vegetation that manages to survive the bleak, roasting summers. This camp is set at 3,000 feet. Open year-round.

---

20. TOOL BOX SPRING

Reference: In San Bernardino National Forest; map I7, grid j0.

Campsites, facilities: There are six tent sites. Vault toilets, fire grills and picnic tables are provided. **No piped water** is provided. Pets are permitted on leashes.

Reservations, fee: No reservations; no fee.

Who to contact: Phone the San Bernardino National Forest San Jacinto Ranger District at (909) 659-2117.

Location: Traveling southeast just past Lake Hemet on Highway 74, you'll see Forest Service Road 6S13 (paved, then dirt) on the right. Turn right (west) and drive about four miles. Turn left on Forest Service Road 5S13 and drive 4.5 miles to the camping area.

Trip note: This alternative to Thomas Mountain Camp is located two miles southwest, also on the flank of Thomas Mountain. The difference is this camp has a little creek that runs by a quarter mile away, though it turns into a trickle in summer, and a trail that runs right through the camp. If it is winter, call for road conditions to determine accessibility. The elevation is 6,500 feet.

---

21. THOMAS MOUNTAIN

Reference: In San Bernardino National Forest; map I7, grid j0.

Campsites, facilities: There are six tent sites. There is **no piped water**, but vault toilets, fire grills and picnic tables are provided. Pets are permitted on leashes.

Reservations, fee: No reservations; no fee.

Who to contact: Phone the San Bernardino National Forest San Jacinto Ranger District at (909) 659-2117.

Location: Traveling southeast just past Lake Hemet on Highway 74 you'll see Forest Service Road 6S13 (paved, then dirt) on the right. Turn right (west) and drive about four miles. Turn left on Forest Service Road 5S13 and drive three miles.

Trip note: If you don't want to be bugged by anything but a few bugs, this is the place. It's a small, primitive camp set just on the eastern flank of Thomas Mountain, 6,800 feet. There are no trails, no streams, no nuthin' in the immediate area. After you have purged your soul out here, you might consider a sidetrip to Lake Hemet, located four nautical miles (and a heck of a lot longer by car) to the north. Accessibility depends on weather conditions.

22. PINYON FLAT 🚶🦽   RV 4

Reference: **Near Cahuilla Tewanet Vista Point in San Bernardino National Forest; map I7, grid j0.**

Campsites, facilities: There are 18 sites for tents or motor homes up to 22 feet long. Piped water, vault toilets, fire grills and picnic tables are provided. The facilities are **wheelchair accessible.** Pets are permitted on leashes.

Reservations, fee: No reservations; $7 fee per night.

Who to contact: Phone the San Bernardino National Forest San Jacinto Ranger District at (909) 659-2117.

Location: From Palm Desert, drive 14 miles southwest on Highway 74 to the camp.

Trip note: The Cahuilla Tewanet Vista Point is just two miles east of the camp and provides a good, easy sidetrip. If you want to work harder at it, a trail that leads deep into the National Forest to the southeast starts less than one mile away. To get there, drive one mile south on Forest Service Road 7S01 and look for the trailhead on the left side of the road. The elevation is 4,000 feet. Open year-round. Have fun!

23. LAKE CAHUILLA COUNTY PARK   RV 7

🎣 ⚓ 🦽 🏊

Reference: **Near Indio; map I7, grid j4.**

Campsites, facilities: There are numerous undesignated, primitive sites and 60 RV sites (50 with electric and water hookups and 10 with no hookups). There is also a group area with collapsible horse corrals and equestrian trails. Fire grills and picnic tables are provided. Restrooms, showers, a dump station, a playground, a swimming pool and an unpaved boat ramp are available. Pets are permitted on leashes.

Reservations, fee: Reservations accepted; $12-$16 fee per night; $2 pet fee; monthly and midweek rates available.

Who to contact: Phone the park at (619) 564-4712.

Location: From Interstate 10 in Indio, take the Monroe Street exit, and follow Monroe Street south for seven or eight miles to Avenue 58. Turn right and continue three miles to the lake.

Trip note: Boaters beware. Even though Lake Cahuilla doesn't look big enough to cause much of a fuss, it can be quite dangerous when the Santa Ana winds are blowing. You can't swim in this lake, but they built a swimming pool a few years ago to make up for losing the swimming beach. A new equestrian camp is now available, complete with corrals.

SO-CAL MAP .... see page 690
adjoining maps
NORTH (H8) .... see page 684
EAST (I9) .... see page 764
SOUTH (J8) .... see page 798
WEST (I7) .... see page 752

0 LISTINGS
PAGES 762-763

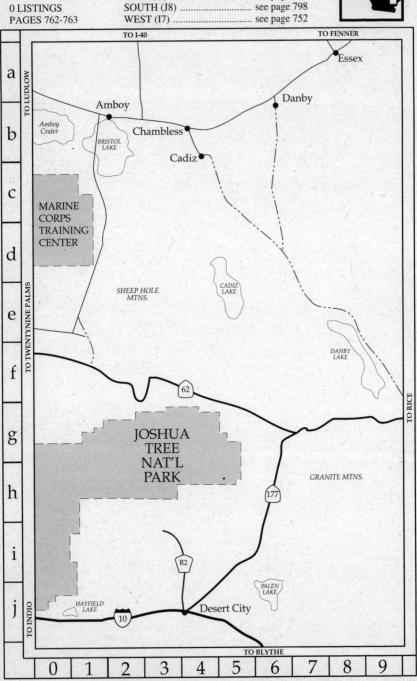

There are no campgrounds on this map. Turn to the chapters beginning on pages 684, 752, 764, and 798 to locate nearby camps.

MAP I9

1 LISTING
PAGES 764-765

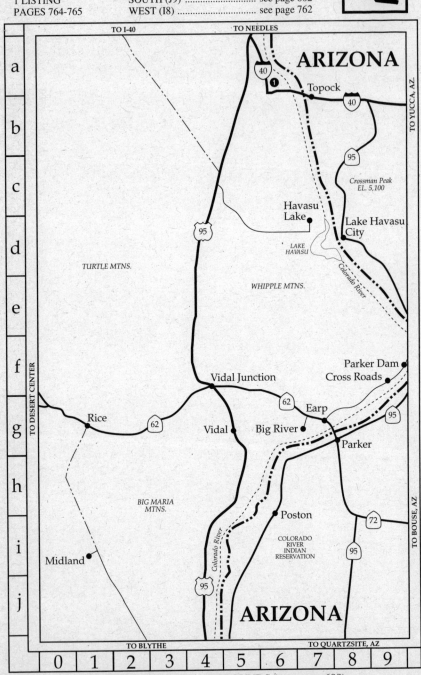

1. MOABI REGIONAL PARK

Reference: **On Colorado River; map I9, grid a6.**

Campsites, facilities: There are more than 600 sites for tents or motor homes, most with full hookups. Picnic tables and fire grills are provided at most sites. Flush toilets, showers, a laundromat, a store, ice, a playground, two sanitary dump stations and a boat ramp are available. Pets are permitted on leashes.

Reservations, fee: Reservations accepted (phone Monday through Thursday, 8 a.m. to 4 p.m.); $10-$20 fee per night; $1 pet fee.

Who to contact: Phone the Moabi Regional Park at (619) 326-3831.

Location: From Needles, drive 11 miles east on Interstate 40. Turn north on Park Moabi Road and drive a half mile to the park.

Trip note: The adjacent Colorado River provides the main attraction, with the beach and boat ramp a bonus. This is a popular boating area, with lots of wild and crazy types having the times of their lives on the water. Open year-round.

MAP J5

SO-CAL MAP .... see page 690
adjoining maps
NORTH (I5) .... see page 704
EAST (J6) .... see page 770
SOUTH .... no map
WEST .... no map

6 LISTINGS
PAGES 766-769

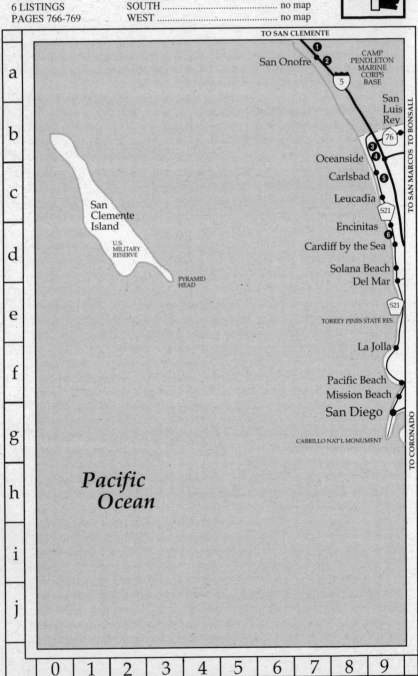

TO SAN CLEMENTE

San Onofre

❶
❷

CAMP
PENDLETON
MARINE
CORPS
BASE

5

San
Luis
Rey

76

❸
❹

Oceanside

Carlsbad ❺

Leucadia

S21

Encinitas ❻

Cardiff by the Sea

Solana Beach

Del Mar

S21

TORREY PINES STATE RES.

La Jolla

Pacific Beach

Mission Beach

San Diego

CABRILLO NAT'L MONUMENT

San
Clemente
Island

U.S.
MILITARY
RESERVE

PYRAMID
HEAD

TO BONSALL

TO SAN MARCOS

TO CORONADO

*Pacific
Ocean*

a b c d e f g h i j

0 1 2 3 4 5 6 7 8 9

1. SAN ONOFRE STATE BEACH - BLUFF AREA 🚐 7

Reference: **Near San Clemente; map J5, grid a7.**

Campsites, facilities: There are 230 sites for tents or motor homes. Piped water, fire grills and picnic tables are provided. Cold showers and flush toilets are available. A grocery store, a laundromat and propane gas are nearby. Pets are permitted on leashes.

Reservations, fee: Reserve by phoning Destinet at (800) 444-7275 ($6.75 Destinet fee); $17-$19 fee per night; $1 pet fee.

Who to contact: Phone the campground at (714) 492-4872 or (714) 492-0802.

Location: From San Clemente, drive three miles south on Interstate 5. Take the Basilone exit and drive to the park.

Trip note: Located just off the busy interstate highway, this park is one of three set along the beach near San Clemente. The others are San Clemente State Beach and Doheny State Beach, both located to the north. This area was one of the most popular areas in California for surfing and sits in the shadow of the San Onofre Nuclear Power Plant.

2. SAN ONOFRE ST. BEACH-SAN MATEO CAMP 🚐 7

Reference: **Near San Clemente; map J5, grid a7.**

Campsites, facilities: There are 162 sites for tents or motorhomes, 70 with electric and water hookups. A dump station, hot showers, fire grills and flush toilets are provided. A grocery store, propane gas and laundromat are nearby.

Reservations, fees: Reserve by phoning Destinet at (800) 444-7275 ($6.75 Destinet fee); $14-$20 fee per night; $1 pet fee.

Who to contact: Phone (714) 492-4872 or (714) 492-0802.

Location: From Interstate 5 at the southern end of San Clemente, take the Cristianitos exit and drive inland 1.5 miles to the park entrance.

Trip note: Folks cruising the coast highway yearn for spots just like this, but the only catch is that you'd better have a reservation during the vacation season or run the risk of finding yourself out of luck. State parks with oceanside camps and beach access like this one are beautiful and in demand.

3. PARADISE BY THE SEA RV PARK 🚐 7

Reference: **In Oceanside; map J5, grid b9.**

Campsites, facilities: There are 102 motor home sites with full hookups. Flush toilets, showers, cable TV hookups, a swimming pool, a jacuzzi, a clubhouse, a banquet room, laundry, RV supplies, a telephone and a mini-store are available. Boat rentals can be found nearby. Pets with proof of vaccination are permitted on leashes.

Reservations, fee: Reservations recommended; $28 fee per night; $1 pet fee.

Who to contact: Phone the park at (619) 439-1376.

Location: From Interstate 5 in Oceanside, take the Highway 78-Vista Way exit. Drive west for a half mile. Turn right on South Coast Highway to 1537 South Coast Highway.

Trip note: This is a classic oceanfront motor home park, but no tenters need apply. It's an easy walk to the beach. For boaters, Oceanside Marina to the immediate north is the place to go. Camp Pendleton, a huge marine corps training complex, is located to the north. Open year-round.

4. CASITAS POQUITOS

Reference: **In Oceanside; map J5, grid b9.**

Campsites, facilities: There are 140 motor home sites with full hookups, picnic tables and patios provided. Flush toilets, showers, cable TV hookups, a playground, a laundromat, a recreation room, a swimming pool, a jacuzzi, a billiard room, propane gas and a general store are available. Pets are allowed on leashes.

Reservations, fee: Reservations recommended; $22-$29 fee per night; $1 pet fee.

Who to contact: Phone the park at (619) 722-4404.

Location: From Interstate 5, in Oceanside, take the Oceanside Blvd. exit. Drive west for a half mile. Turn right on South Coast Highway to 1510 South Coast Highway.

Trip note: There are three options for motor home cruisers in the Oceanside area. This is one of them. For details on the area, see the trip note for Paradise By the Sea. Open year-round, a short distance to the beach.

5. SOUTH CARLSBAD STATE BEACH

Reference: **Near Carlsbad; map J5, grid c9.**

Campsites, facilities: There are 224 sites for tents or motor homes up to 35 feet long. Picnic tables and fire grills are provided. Piped water, flush toilets, showers and a dump station are available. Some facilities are **wheelchair accessible**. Supplies and a laundromat are available in Carlsbad. Pets are permitted on leashes.

Reservations, fee: Reserve by phoning Destinet at (800) 444-7275 ($6.75 Destinet fee); $17-$21 fee per night; $1 pet fee.

Who to contact: Phone the park at (619) 438-3143 or (619) 642-4200.

Location: From Carlsbad, drive four miles south on County Road S21 to the entrance.

Trip note: No reservation? Then likely you can forget about staying here. This is a beautiful state beach and as big as it is, the sites go fast to the coastal cruisers who used the Destinet reservation system. Open year-round.

Special note: This camp closed in September 1995 for renovation and is not expected to reopen until Memorial Day, 1996.

6. SAN ELIJO STATE BEACH

Reference: **In Cardiff by the Sea; map J5, grid d9.**

Campsites, facilities: There are 171 sites for tents or motor homes up to 35 feet long. Picnic tables and fire grills are provided. Piped water, flush toilets, showers, a dump station and a small store are available. Some of the campground and the store are **wheelchair accessible**. Pets are permitted on six foot leashes in the campground, but not on the beach.

Reservations, fee: Reserve by phoning Destinet at (800) 444-7275 ($6.75 Destinet fee); $17-$24 fee per night; $1 pet fee.

Who to contact: Phone the park at (619) 753-5091 or (619) 642-4200.

Location: From Cardiff by the Sea, drive a half mile northwest on County Road S21 to the park entrance.

Trip note: This is another in the series of popular state beaches along the San Diego County coast. This one is located along a beautiful beach just north of the small town of Cardiff by the Sea. Like at all state beaches, reservations are usually required to get a spot between Memorial Day weekend and Labor Day weekend. Open year-round.

MAP J6

SO-CAL MAP .... see page 690
adjoining maps
NORTH (I6) .... see page 724
EAST (J7) .... see page 788
SOUTH .... no map
WEST (J5) .... see page 766

43 LISTINGS
PAGES 770-787

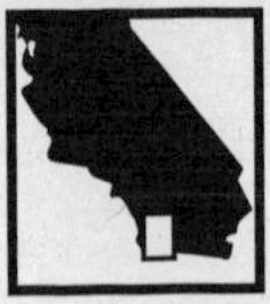

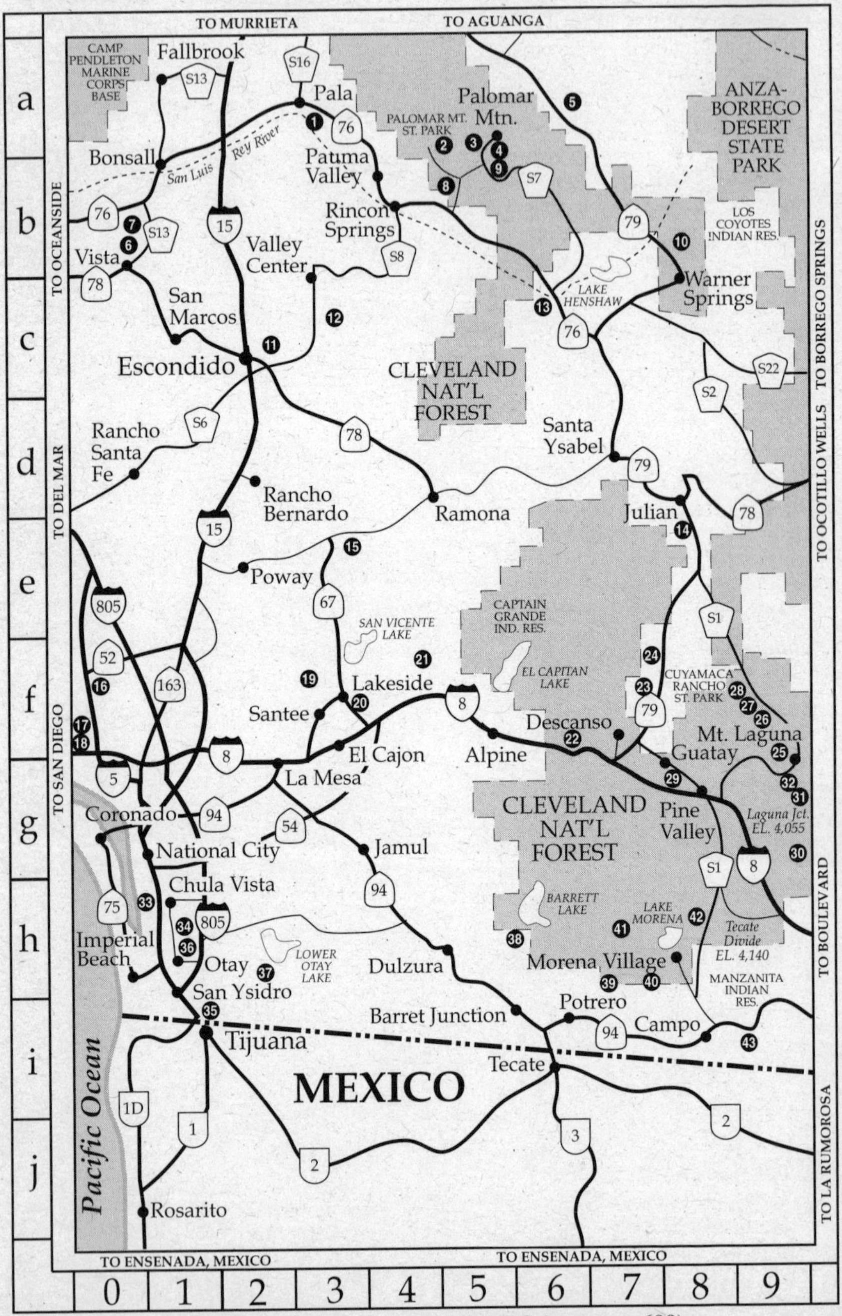
TO MURRIETA
TO AGUANGA
CAMP PENDLETON MARINE CORPS BASE
Fallbrook
S13
S16
Pala
Palomar Mtn.
PALOMAR MT. ST. PARK
ANZA-BORREGO DESERT STATE PARK
Bonsall
San Luis Rey River
76
Pauma Valley
S7
79
Rincon Springs
LOS COYOTES INDIAN RES.
15
Valley Center
S8
Vista
78
Warner Springs
LAKE HENSHAW
San Marcos
Escondido
CLEVELAND NAT'L FOREST
S22
S2
S6
Rancho Santa Fe
Santa Ysabel
Julian
Rancho Bernardo
Ramona
Poway
805
67
CAPTAIN GRANDE IND. RES.
SAN VICENTE LAKE
EL CAPITAN LAKE
S1
52
163
Lakeside
CUYAMACA RANCHO ST. PARK
Santee
8
Descanso
Mt. Laguna
El Cajon
Alpine
Guatay
5
La Mesa
Coronado
94
54
CLEVELAND NAT'L FOREST
Pine Valley
Laguna Jct. EL. 4,055
National City
Jamul
Chula Vista
BARRETT LAKE
LAKE MORENA
75
Imperial Beach
Otay
LOWER OTAY LAKE
Dulzura
Tecate Divide EL. 4,140
Morena Village
San Ysidro
MANZANITA INDIAN RES.
Potrero
Barret Junction
Campo
Tijuana
Tecate
MEXICO
Pacific Ocean
1D
1
2
3
Rosarito
TO ENSENADA, MEXICO
TO ENSENADA, MEXICO
TO OCEANSIDE
TO DEL MAR
TO SAN DIEGO
TO BORREGO SPRINGS
TO OCOTILLO WELLS
TO BOULEVARD
TO LA RUMOROSA
a
b
c
d
e
f
g
h
i
j
0
1
2
3
4
5
6
7
8
9

Map J6 featuring: Palomar Observatory, Cleveland National Forest, Lake Wohlford, Lake Henshaw, Mission Bay, Lake Jennings, Cuyamaca Rancho State Park, Little Laguna Lake, Imperial Beach, Lake Moreno

1. RANCHO CORRIDO

Reference: **Near Pala Mission; map J6, grid a3.**

Campsites, facilities: There are 120 sites for tents or motor homes. Picnic tables, fire pits, electrical connections, piped water and, in some cases, sewer connections are provided. Flush toilets, showers, a dump station, a playground, cable TV, a small store, a rifle range, propane gas, a fishing pond and a laundromat are available. Pets are permitted on leashes.

Reservations, fee: Reservations accepted; $14-$20 fee per night; $1 pet fee.

Who to contact: Phone the park at (619) 742-3755.

Location: From Interstate 15, take the Highway 76 exit and drive east past the town of Pala. Continue east on Highway 76 for four miles to the camp at 14715 Highway 76.

Trip note: This motor home layover spot is located ten miles east of the main drag, Interstate 15. It is a short drive to Pala Indian Reservation and the Pala Mission to the east. The Palomar Observatory is 20 miles to the east, another possible sidetrip. Their fishing pond is catch-and-release only. Open year-round.

2. PALOMAR MOUNTAIN STATE PARK

Reference: **Near Palomar Observatory; map J6, grid a4.**

Campsites, facilities: There are 21 sites for tents only and 10 sites for motor homes up to 21 feet long. Fire grills and picnic tables are provided. Piped water, flush toilets and showers are available. Some facilities are **wheelchair accessible**. Pets are permitted on leashes.

Reservations, fee: Reserve for group sites only by phoning Destinet at (800) 444-7275 ($6.75 Destinet fee); $15-$17 fee per night; $1 pet fee.

Who to contact: Phone the park at (619) 742-3462 or (619) 767-5311.

Location: From Interstate 15, turn east on Highway 76 and drive about 20 miles to County Road S6 (goes up to Palomar Mountain). Turn left (north) and drive 6.5 miles. Turn left on County Road S7 and drive 4.5 miles to the campground.

Trip note: This developed state park is a short drive from Palomar Observatory. It offers hiking trails and some fishing in Doane Pond. There are four other campgrounds in the immediate area that are a short distance from Palomar Observatory. The elevation is 4,700 feet. Open year-round.

3. FRY CREEK

Reference: **Near Palomar Observatory in Cleveland National Forest; map J6, grid a5.**

Campsites, facilities: There are 12 tent sites and eight sites for tents or motor homes up to 16 feet long. Piped water, fire pits and picnic tables are provided. Vault toilets are available. A grocery store is nearby. Pets are allowed on leashes.

Reservations, fee: No reservations; $7 fee per night.
Who to contact: Phone the Cleveland National Forest, Palomar Ranger District at (619) 788-0250.
Location: From Interstate 15, turn east on Highway 76 and drive about 20 miles to County Road S6 (goes up to Palomar Mountain). Turn left (north) and drive about nine miles to the campground entrance on the left. The road is not recommended for trailers.
Trip note: On a clear night, you can see forever from Palomar Mountain. Literally. That's because Palomar Observatory, just a short distance from this forested camp, houses America's largest telescope. A small stream runs nearby. The elevation is 5,200 feet. Open from May to November.

4. OBSERVATORY 🏃🏃   RV 4

Reference: **Near Palomar Observatory in Cleveland National Forest; map J6, grid a5.**
Campsites, facilities: There are 42 sites for tents or motor homes up to 22 feet long (a few sites will accommodate RVs up to 28 feet long). Fire grills, picnic tables and piped water are provided. Vault toilets are available. Pets are permitted on leashes.
Reservations, fee: No reservations; $7 fee per night.
Who to contact: Phone the Cleveland National Forest, Palomar Ranger District at (619) 788-0250.
Location: From Interstate 15, turn east on Highway 76 and drive about 20 miles to County Road S6 (goes up to Palomar Mountain). Turn left (north) and drive about 8.5 miles to the campground entrance on the right.
Trip note: This popular Forest Service camp is used primarily as a layover spot for campers visiting the nearby Palomar Observatory, housing the largest telescope in America. There are four other camps in the immediate area. The elevation is 4,800 feet. Open from May to November.

5. OAK GROVE   RV 4

Reference: **Near Temecula Creek in Cleveland National Forest; map J6, grid a6.**
Campsites, facilities: There are 81 sites for tents or motor homes. Piped water, fire grills and picnic tables are provided. Flush toilets are available. Propane gas and groceries are nearby. Pets are permitted on leashes.
Reservations, fee: No reservations; $7 fee per night.
Who to contact: Phone the Cleveland National Forest, Palomar Ranger District at (619) 788-0250.
Location: From Aguanga, drive 6.5 miles southeast on Highway 79.
Trip note: Easy access from Highway 79 makes this a popular camp. It is set at 2,800 feet. Vail Lake, located about 15 miles to the northwest, but is presently not open to the public. Lake Henshaw is 24 miles to the south. A boat ramp and boat rentals are available there. Open year-round.

6. SUNRISE TERRACE RV PARK   RV 2

Reference: **Near Vista; map J6, grid b0.**
Campsites, facilities: There are 32 motor home sites with full hookups. Flush toilets, showers, laundry, telephones, cable and propane gas are available. There is a grocery store nearby. Pets are allowed on leashes.
Reservations, fee: Reservations accepted; $20 fee per night.

Who to contact: Phone the park at (619) 724-6654.

Location: From Interstate 15 northbound, take the Gopher Canyon Road exit. Turn left on East Vista Way. Turn right on East Taylor and drive to 817 East Taylor Street. From Interstate 15 southbound, turn right on Gopher Canyon Road, then make a left on East Vista Way then right again on East Taylor Street and drive to 817 East Taylor Street.

Trip note: This rural country park provides an overnight spot for highway cruisers. The San Diego Wild Animal Park is located about 20 miles southeast via Highway 15 and 78. Seasonal rentals are accepted. Open year-round.

7. GUAJOME COUNTY PARK 👁‍🗨 ♿ 🚐 3️⃣

Reference: In Oceanside; map J6, grid b0.

Campsites, facilities: There are 17 motor home sites with water and electrical hookups. Picnic tables and fire grills are provided. Flush toilets, showers, a dump station and a playground are available. A grocery store and propane gas are nearby. Pets are permitted on leashes.

Reservations, fee: Reservations accepted; $3 reservation fee; $14 per night; $1 pet fee.

Who to contact: Phone the County Parks Department at (619) 565-3600 or (619) 694-3049.

Location: From Oceanside, drive seven miles east on Highway 76/Mission Avenue. Turn right on Guajome Lakes Road (Santa Fe Road) and drive to the entrance.

Trip note: This is one of the several options for motor home drivers cruising Highway 5 along the coast. It's not far from Mission San Luis Rey. Open year-round.

Special note: This park will be re-opened after renovation in summer 1996.

8. CRESTLINE GROUP CAMP 4️⃣

Reference: Near Palomar Observatory in Cleveland National Forest; map J6, grid b5.

Campsites, facilities: There is one group campsite for tents. Piped water, fire grills and picnic tables are provided, and vault toilets are available. A grocery store is nearby. Pets are allowed on leashes.

Reservations, fee: Reservations required; phone (800) 280-CAMP (2267); $50 group fee per night.

Who to contact: Phone the Cleveland National Forest, Palomar Ranger District at (619) 788-0250.

Location: From Interstate 15, turn east on Highway 76 and drive about 20 miles to County Road S6 (goes up to Palomar Mountain). Turn left (north) and drive 6.5 miles. The campground is at the junction of County Roads S6 and S7.

Trip note: This Forest Service camp is designed expressly for large groups planning to visit Palomar Observatory. The elevation is 4,800 feet. Open from May to November.

9. OAK KNOLL CAMPGROUND 🏊 🚐 5️⃣

Reference: Near Palomar Observatory; map J6, grid b5.

Campsites, facilities: There are 46 sites for tents or motor homes, many with full or partial hookups. Flush toilets, showers, a playground, a swimming pool, a clubhouse, a baseball diamond, a dump station, laundry, propane gas and groceries are available. Pets are allowed on leashes.

Reservations, fee: Call ahead for available space; $15 fee per night; $1 pet fee.

Who to contact: Phone the park at (619) 742-3437.

Location: From Interstate 15, turn east on Highway 76 and drive about 20 miles to County Road S6 (goes up to Palomar Mountain). Turn left (north) and drive one block to the campground.

Trip note: This is one in a series of camps where visitors can set up shop while visiting nearby Palomar Observatory, which houses the largest telescope in the world. The camp is set at 3,000 feet in the San Diego County foothill country, among giant old California Oaks. Open year-round.

---

10. INDIAN FLATS CAMP 🏃🏃   RV. 4

Reference: **Near Pacific Crest Trail in Cleveland National Forest; map J6, grid b8.**

Campsites, facilities: There are 17 sites for tents or motor homes. Piped water, fire grills and picnic tables are provided. Vault toilets are available. Pets are permitted on leashes.

Reservations, fee: No reservations; $6 fee per night.

Who to contact: Phone the Cleveland National Forest, Palomar Ranger District at (619) 788-0250.

Location: From Warner Springs on Highway 79, drive two miles northwest on Highway 79. Turn right (north) on Forest Service Road 9S05 and drive six miles to the campground.

Trip note: The Pacific Crest Trail passes only two miles away, providing the opportunity for a day hike or a multi-day adventure for backpackers. A possible sidetrip is Lake Henshaw, about 15 miles away, where fishing for bass and catfish can be good and no waterskiers are allowed. The elevation is 3,600 feet. Open year-round.

---

11. DIXON LAKE RECREATION AREA   RV. 7

🐟 ⚓ ♿

Reference: **Near Escondido; map J6, grid c2.**

Campsites, facilities: There are 45 sites for tents or motor homes, some with full hookups. Picnic tables, fire grills and piped water are provided. Flush toilets, showers, boat rentals, bait, ice, a snack bar and a playground are available. Pets are not permitted.

Reservations, fee: Reservations available; $10-$14 fee per night.

Who to contact: Phone the park at (619) 741-3328 or (619) 741-4680.

Location: In Escondido, drive four miles northeast on El Norte Parkway to La Honda Drive. Turn left and drive to 1700 North La Honda Drive at Dixon Lake.

Trip note: On this small lake, set near Escondido, boating is restricted to rental boats only. The lake is primarily used by anglers. Nearby Lake Hodges to the south is much bigger, has big bass, and no restrictions on boating. The elevation is 1,000 feet. Open year-round.

---

12. WOODS VALLEY KAMPGROUND   RV. 5

🐟 🏊

Reference: **Near Lake Wohlford; map J6, grid c3.**

Campsites, facilities: There are 59 motor home sites and 30 sites for tents or motor homes. Picnic tables, fire grills, electrical connections, piped water and, in some cases, sewer hookups are provided. Flush toilets, showers, a dump station, a swimming pool, a kid's fishing pond, hay rides, a mini farm and a playground are available. Supplies and a laundromat are nearby. Pets are permitted on leashes.

Reservations, fee: Reservations accepted; $19-$26 fee per night; $3 pet fee.

Who to contact: Phone the park at (619) 749-2905.

Location: From Escondido on Interstate 15, turn east on County Road S6 and drive northeast to Valley Center. Turn right on Woods Valley Road and drive two miles east to 15236 Woods Valley Road.

Trip note: This privately-operated park is set up primarily for motor homes. It is a short drive from Lake Wohlford to the south. Other possible sidetrips include the San Pasqual Battlefield State Historic Park on Highway 78 to the south and big Lake Hodges, located south of Escondido. Open year-round.

13. LAKE HENSHAW RESORT RV

Reference: Near San Ysabel; map J6, grid c6.

Campsites, facilities: There are 164 sites for tents or motor homes, many with full hookups. There are also 18 cabins with linens and kitchenettes. Flush toilets, showers, a swimming pool, a jacuzzi, a clubhouse, a playground, a dump station, laundry, propane gas, boat and motor rentals, a boat launch, a bait and tackle shop, a restaurant and groceries are available. A golf course is nearby. Pets are permitted on leashes.

Reservations, fee: No reservations accepted; $14-$16 fee per night; cabin fees are $45-$80 per night.

Who to contact: Phone (619) 782-3487 or (619) 782-3501.

Location: From San Ysabel, drive seven miles north on Highway 79. Turn left on Highway 76 and drive four miles to the campground on the left.

Trip note: Lake Henshaw is the biggest lake in San Diego County, yet it only has one camp. This one is located on the southern corner of the lake. The lake is fed by several streams and provides good trout fishing in the winter and spring and good catfishing in the summer. It is stocked annually with 10,000 pounds—and sometimes more—of channel catfish and rainbow trout. The elevation is 2,700 feet. Open year-round.

14. WILLIAM HEISE COUNTY PARK

Reference: Near Julian; map J6, grid d8.

Campsites, facilities: There are 43 sites for tents only, 40 sites for tents or motor homes and several group sites. Fire grills and picnic tables are provided. Piped water, flush toilets, showers, a laundromat, a dump station and a playground are available. Supplies are available nearby in Julian. Pets are permitted on leashes.

Reservations, fee: Reservations accepted; $11 per night; $1 pet fee.

Who to contact: Phone the County Parks Department at (619) 565-3600 or (619) 694-3049.

Location: From Highway 78 west of Julian, turn south on Pine Hills Road and drive two miles. Turn left on Frisius Drive and drive two miles to the park.

Trip note: This little-known spot, set at 4,200 feet, offers hiking trails and a playground, and is surrounded by recreation options. They include Cleveland

National Forest to the immediate south, Lake Cuyamaca and Cuyamaca State Park to the southeast, and the vast Anza-Borrego Desert State Park to the east. Open year-round.

15. DOS PICOS COUNTY PARK

Reference: **Near Ramona; map J6, grid e3.**

Campsites, facilities: There are 14 tent sites and 50 motor home sites with water and electrical hookups. Picnic tables and fire grills are provided. Flush toilets, showers and a playground are available. Supplies and a laundromat are nearby in Ramona. Pets are permitted on leashes.

Reservations, fee: Reservations accepted; $10-$14 per night; $1 pet fee.

Who to contact: Phone the county parks department at (619) 565-3600 or (619) 694-3049.

Location: From Interstate 8 in El Cajon, drive 22 miles north on Highway 67. Make a sharp right on Mussey Grade Road and drive two miles to the park.

Trip note: As a county park, this camp is often missed by folks relying on less complete guides. The park is quite picturesque, with plenty of shade trees and a small pond. Several nearby recreation options are in the area. San Vicente Lake is about 15 miles away, a prime bass lake open Thursday through Sunday from September through June. The Barona Ranch Indian Reservation and Barona Mission, also 15 miles from the park, are located to the southeast. The elevation is 1,500 feet. Open year-round.

16. DE ANZA HARBOR RESORT

Reference: **On Mission Bay; map J6, grid f0.**

Campsites, facilities: There are 250 motor home sites with full hookups and patios. Flush toilets, showers, a playground, a dump station, a laundromat, a recreation room, bike rentals, a boat ramp, propane gas and a grocery store are available. Pets are allowed on leashes.

Reservations, fee: Reservations recommended; $25-$44 fee per night.

Who to contact: Phone the park at (619) 273-3211.

Location: From southbound Interstate 5, take the Clairemont exit to Mission Bay Drive. Turn left and drive to North Mission Bay Drive. Turn right on De Anza Road and drive to 2727 De Anza Road.

Trip note: Location means everything in real estate and campgrounds, and this private park passes the test. It is set on a small peninsula that is surrounded on three sides by Mission Bay, Sea World and the San Diego Zoo. A beach and golf course are adjacent. Open year-round.

17. CAMPLAND ON THE BAY

Reference: **On Mission Bay; map J6, grid f0.**

Campsites, facilities: There are 750 tent and motor home sites, most with full or partial hookups. Picnic tables and fire grills are provided. Flush toilets, showers, phone hookups, swimming pools, a jacuzzi, a recreation hall, a playground, a dump station, a laundromat, a grocery store, RV supplies, propane gas, a boat ramp, boat docks, boat and bike rentals, and groceries are available. Pets are permitted on leashes.

Reservations, fee: Reservations accepted; $19-$52 per night; $3 pet fee.

Who to contact: Phone the park at (800) 422-9386.

Location: From southbound Interstate 5 in San Diego, take the Balboa-Garnet exit. Drive straight on Mission Bay Drive to Grand Avenue. Turn right and drive one mile. Turn left on Olney Avenue and drive a short distance to the campground entrance. From northbound Interstate 5 in San Diego, take the Grand-Garnet exit. Stay in the left lane and turn left on Grand Avenue. Turn left on Olney Avenue as above.

Trip note: No kidding, this is one of the biggest campgrounds on this side of the galaxy. With space for both tenters and motor homes, you can usually find a spot to shoehorn your way into. It is set on Mission Bay, a beautiful spot. Sea World, located just north of San Diego, offers a premium sidetrip. Open year-round.

---

18. SANTA FE TRAVEL TRAILER PARK

Reference: **In San Diego; map J6, grid f0.**

Campsites, facilities: There are 129 motor home sites with full hookups. Flush toilets, showers, a playground, a swimming pool, a dump station and laundry facilities are available. Pets are permitted on leashes.

Reservations, fee: Reservations recommended; $25 fee per night; $2 pet fee.

Who to contact: Phone the park at (619) 272-4051.

Location: In San Diego from Interstate 5, take the Balboa-Garnet exit (southbound). Drive straight (south) on West Mission Bay Drive for a short distance to Damon Street (second light). Go left and follow to Santa Fe Street. Turn left and drive to 5707 Santa Fe Street.

Trip note: This camp is a short drive from a variety of sidetrips, including the San Diego Zoo, Sea World, golf courses, beaches, sport fishing and Tijuana. No tent camping is allowed. Open year-round.

---

19. SANTEE LAKES REGIONAL PARK

Reference: **Near Santee; map J6, grid f3.**

Campsites, facilities: There are 152 sites for motor homes with full hookups. There are 50 sites (out of the total 152) which can be used for tents. Some barbecue grills are provided. Flush toilets, showers, a dump station, boat rentals, a playground, a swimming pool, a grocery store, a recreation center and a laundromat are available. A snack bar is nearby. Pets are permitted on leashes in campground, but not in park.

Reservations, fee: Reservations accepted; $13-$18 fee per night; $1 pet fee.

Who to contact: Phone the park at (619) 448-2482.

Location: From Interstate 8 in El Cajon, drive two miles north on Highway 67 to the town of Santee. Turn left on Mission Gorge Road and drive 2.5 miles to Carlton Hills Boulevard. Turn right and drive one mile to the park on the right.

Trip note: This small regional park is located 20 miles east of San Diego. Quiet, low-key boating is the name of the game here. Rowboats, pedal boats and canoes are available for rent. The camp is set at 400 feet. Open year-round.

---

20. RANCHO LOS COCHES RV PARK

Reference: **Near Lake Jennings; map J6, grid f4.**

Campsites, facilities: There are four tent areas and 142 motor home sites with full hookups. Flush toilets, showers, a dump station and laundry facilities are available. A grocery store is nearby. Pets up to 30 pounds are allowed on leashes.

Reservations, fee: Reservations recommended; $20 fee per night.

Who to contact: Phone the park at (619) 443-2025.

Location: From El Cajon, drive east on Interstate 8 to the Los Coches Road exit. Go under the freeway. Turn right on Highway 8 Business and drive to park entrance on the left at 13468 Highway 8 Business

Trip note: Nearby Lake Jennings provides an option for boaters and anglers and also has a less developed camp located on its northeast shore. Vista Point on the southeastern side of the lake provides a sidetrip.

21. LAKE JENNINGS COUNTY PARK

Reference: Map J6, grid f4.

Campsites, facilities: There are 35 sites for tents only, 13 sites for tents or motor homes and 63 motor home sites, most with full hookups. Picnic tables and fire grills are provided. Flush toilets, showers, a playground and a dump station are available. A grocery store is nearby. Pets are permitted on leashes.

Reservations, fee: Reservations accepted; $10-$16 per night; $1 pet fee.

Who to contact: Phone the County Parks Department at (619) 565-3600 or (619) 694-3049.

Location: From San Diego, drive 16 miles east on Interstate 8. Take Lake Jennings Park Road north to the park.

Trip note: Only one camp is available at little Lake Jennings and this is it. It is set on the northeastern shore at 800 feet. Easy access from Highway 8 is a bonus. The lake is known for bass and catfish, and has a boat ramp and rentals available nearby on the east shore of the lake. Open year-round.

22. ALPINE RV RESORT

Reference: Near Lake Jennings; map J6, grid f6.

Campsites, facilities: There are 340 sites for tents or motor homes, some with full or partial hookups. Picnic tables are provided. Flush toilets, showers, a dump station, a laundromat, a recreation room and a swimming pool are available. No pets over 15 pounds are permitted.

Reservations, fee: Reservations accepted; $12-$20 fee per night.

Who to contact: Phone the park at (619) 445-3162.

Location: From Interstate 8 just east of Alpine, take the East Willows exit. Cross over the freeway and drive a third mile to 5635 Willows Drive.

Trip note: This is one of the few motor home parks in the area that welcomes tent campers. It is set in the foothill country in Alpine, eight miles from Lake Jennings to the west. The small lake has good fishing in the spring, (a boat ramp, boat rentals, and supplies are available). Other nearby lakes include larger El Capitan to the north and Loveland Reservoir to the south. Open year-round.

23. PASO PICACHO

Reference: In Cuyamaca Rancho State Park; map J6, grid f7.

Campsites, facilities: There are 85 sites for tents or motor homes. Fire grills and picnic tables are provided. Piped water, flush toilets, coin-operated showers and a dump station are available. Pets are permitted. Supplies are nearby in Cuyamaca.

Reservations, fee: Reserve by phoning Destinet at (800) 444-7275 ($6.75 Destinet fee); $15-$17 fee per night; $1 pet fee.

Who to contact: Phone the Cuyamaca Rancho State Park at (619) 765-0755 or (619) 767-5311.

Location: From Julian, drive 11 miles south on Highway 79 to the park entrance.

Trip note: This camp, in Cuyamaca State Park, is located just south of Lake Cuyamaca. It is set at 4,900 feet, not far from the park headquarters, where exhibits about the area's Native Americans, gold mining and natural history are available for your perusal. Perusal? That means for you to look at, podnah. Open year-round.

24. GREEN VALLEY FALLS

Reference: **In Cuyamaca Rancho State Park; map J6, grid f7.**

Campsites, facilities: There are 81 sites for tents or motor homes. Piped water, fire grills and picnic tables are provided. Flush toilets and coin-operated showers are available. Some of the campgrounds, picnic areas, and exhibits are **wheelchair accessible**. A grocery store and propane gas are nearby. Pets are allowed on leashes.

Reservations, fee: Reserve by phoning Destinet at (800) 444-7275 ($6.75 Destinet fee); $15-$17 fee per night; $1 pet fee.

Who to contact: Phone the Cuyamaca Rancho State Park at (619) 765-0755 or (619) 767-5311.

Location: From San Diego, drive approximately 40 miles east on Interstate 8 to Highway 79. Turn north and drive seven miles. Turn left (west) on Green Valley road, the entrance road into the park.

Trip note: This is the southernmost camp in Cuyamaca Rancho State Park. It is set at 3,900 feet, with Cuyamaca Mountain (6,512 feet) looming overhead to the northwest. Newcomers should visit the park headquarters, where there are exhibits detailing the natural history of the area. Open year-round.

25. HORSE HEAVEN GROUP CAMP

Reference: **Near Pacific Crest Trail in Cleveland National Forest; map J6, grid f9.**

Campsites, facilities: There are three group sites for tents or motor homes. Piped water, fire grills and picnic tables are provided. Vault toilets are available. Supplies can be purchased in Mount Laguna. Pets are allowed on leashes.

Reservations, fee: Reserve by calling (800) 280-CAMP ($15 reservation fee); $35-$75 fee per group per night.

Who to contact: Phone the Cleveland National Forest, Descanso District at (619) 445-6235.

Location: From San Diego, drive about 50 miles east on Interstate 8 to the Laguna Junction exit. Drive about 11 miles north on Sunrise Highway to the town of Mt. Laguna. Continue north for two miles on Sunrise Highway-Laguna Mountain Road to the campground entrance road on the left.

Trip note: Horse Heaven is set on the northeastern border of Cleveland National Forest at 5,500 feet, near Mt. Laguna in the Laguna Recreation Area. The Pacific Crest Trail passes near the camp. Laguna and El Prado camps provide nearby options. Sidetrip possibilities include visiting Little Laguna Lake, to the immediate west, and Desert View Picnic Area, to the south at Mt. Laguna.

26. LAGUNA 🚶 RV 4

Reference: **Near Little Laguna Lake in Cleveland National Forest; map J6, grid f9.**

Campsites, facilities: There are 75 sites for tents only, 25 motor home sites, and 20 sites for tents or motor homes. Piped water, fire grills and picnic tables are provided. Vault toilets are available. A grocery store and propane gas are nearby. Pets are allowed on leashes.

Reservations, fee: Some sites by reservation only; phone (800) 280-CAMP ($7.50 reservation fee); $9 fee per night.

Who to contact: Phone the Cleveland National Forest, Descanso District at (619) 445-6235.

Location: From San Diego, drive about 50 miles east on Interstate 8 to the Laguna Junction exit. Drive about 11 miles north on Sunrise Highway to the town of Mt. Laguna. Continue north for 2.5 miles on Sunrise Highway-Laguna Mountain Road to the campground entrance road on the left.

Trip note: Little Laguna Lake is located to the southwest, and the Pacific Crest Trail passes near the camp. The elevation is 5,550 feet. Open year-round.

27. EL PRADO GROUP CAMP 🚶 🐎 RV 3

Reference: **In Cleveland National Forest; map J6, grid f9.**

Campsites, facilities: There are five group sites for tents or motor homes. Piped water, fire grills and picnic tables are provided. Vault toilets are available. Supplies can be purchased in Mt. Laguna. Pets are allowed on leashes.

Reservations, fee: Reserve by calling (800) 280-CAMP ($15 reservation fee); $30-$80 fee per group per night.

Who to contact: Phone the Cleveland National Forest, Descanso District at (619) 445-6235.

Location: From San Diego, drive about 50 miles east on Interstate 8 to the Laguna Junction exit. Drive about 11 miles north on Sunrise Highway to the town of Mt. Laguna. Continue north for 2.5 miles on Sunrise Highway-Laguna Mountain Road to the campground entrance road on the left.

Trip note: This is a nearby option to Horse Heaven Group Camp. See that trip note for recreation details. The elevation is 5,500 feet. Open from May to October.

28. AGUA DULCE GROUP CAMP 🚶 6

Reference: **Near Pacific Crest Trail in Cleveland National Forest; map J6, grid f9.**

Campsites, facilities: There are seven group sites for tents. Piped water, fire grills, and picnic tables are provided. Vault toilets are available. A grocery store is nearby. Pets are allowed on leashes.

Reservations, fee: Reserve by calling (800) 280-CAMP ($15 reservation fee); $25-$40 fee per group per night.

Who to contact: Phone the Cleveland National Forest, Descanso District at (619) 445-6235.

Location: From San Diego, drive approximately 50 miles east on Interstate 8 to the Laguna Junction exit. Drive about eight miles north on Sunrise Highway-Laguna Mountain Road to the campground entrance road on the left.

Trip note: This is one of the three camps that are set on the southern flanks of Mt. Laguna. Little Agua Dulce Creek runs nearby, and the Desert View Picnic

Area, located two miles to the northwest, provides a sidetrip option. The Pacific Crest Trail passes nearby, running past the Burnt Rancheria Camp. The elevation is 5,000 feet. Open from May to October.

29. PINE VALLEY TRAILER PARK 🏇   RV 3

Reference: **Near Cuyamaca Rancho State Park; map J6, grid g8.**
Campsites, facilities: There are 85 motor home sites with full hookups, including telephone. Laundromat facilities are available. Riding stables and a grocery store are nearby. Pets are allowed on leashes.
Reservations, fee: Call ahead for available space; $15-$18 fee per night.
Who to contact: Phone the park at (619) 473-9040.
Location: From San Diego, drive 45 miles east on Interstate 8 to the Pine Valley exit. Go left and at the first stop sign go left again onto Olde Highway 80. Drive for about 3 miles to the park at 27521 Olde Highway 80.
Trip note: This privately-operated park provides a refined option to the more primitive camps located north in Cuyamaca Rancho State Park. It is set in a rustic area that is surrounded by National Forest land. Open year-round.

30. CIBBETS FLAT 🚶🚶   RV 4

Reference: **On Troy Canyon Creek in Cleveland National Forest; map J6, grid g9.**
Campsites, facilities: There are 23 sites for tents or small motor homes. Piped water, fire grills and picnic tables are provided. Vault toilets are available. Pets are permitted on leashes.
Reservations, fee: No reservations; $7 fee per night.
Who to contact: Phone the Cleveland National Forest, Descanso District at (619) 445-6235.
Location: From San Diego, drive about 53 miles east on Interstate 8 to the Kitchen Creek-Cameron Station exit. Turn north on Kitchen Creek Road and drive 4.5 miles to the campground entrance on the right.
Trip note: This small camp is set along Troy Canyon Creek, less than a mile from the Pacific Crest Trail. The elevation is 4,000 feet. Open from May to October.

31. BURNT RANCHERIA 🚶🚶 🏇   RV 6

Reference: **Near Pacific Crest Trail in Cleveland National Forest; map J6, grid g9.**
Campsites, facilities: There are 64 sites for tents only and 45 sites for tents or motor homes. Piped water, fire grills and picnic tables are provided. Vault toilets are available. Supplies are nearby in Mount Laguna. Pets are allowed on leashes.
Reservations, fee: Some sites by reservation only; reserve by calling (800) 280-CAMP ($7.50 reservation fee); $9 fee per night.
Who to contact: Phone the Cleveland National Forest, Descanso District at (619) 445-6235.
Location: From San Diego, drive approximately 50 miles east on Interstate 8 to the Laguna Junction exit. Drive about nine miles north on Sunrise Highway-Laguna Mountain Road to the campground entrance on the right.
Trip note: Set high (6,000 feet) on the slopes of Mt. Laguna in Cleveland National Forest, the Pacific Crest Trail runs right alongside this camp. It is quiet and

private with large, roomy sites. Desert View Picnic Area, a mile to the north, provides a good sidetrip. Open from May to October.

32. WOODED HILL GROUP CAMP 👫   RV 4

Reference: **Near Pacific Crest Trail in Cleveland National Forest; map J6, grid g9.**

Campsites, facilities: There are 22 sites for tents or motor homes. Piped water, fire grills and picnic tables are provided. Vault toilets are available. A grocery store is nearby. Pets are allowed on leashes.

Reservations, fee: Reserve by calling (800) 280-CAMP ($15 reservation fee); $85 group fee per night.

Who to contact: Phone the Cleveland National Forest, Descanso District at (619) 445-6235.

Location: From San Diego, drive approximately 50 miles east on Interstate 8 to the Laguna Junction exit. Drive about eight miles north on Sunrise Highway-Laguna Mountain Road to the campground entrance road on the left.

Trip note: This camp is set right along side Agua Dulce Camp, on the southern flank of Mt. Laguna. The Pacific Crest Trail passes right by the Burnt Rancheria Campground, located a mile up the road to the northwest. The elevation is 6,000 feet. Open from May to October.

33. INTERNATIONAL MOTOR INN RV PARK   RV 3
♿ 🏊

Reference: **Near Imperial Beach; map J6, grid h0.**

Campsites, facilities: There are 42 motor home sites with full hookups. Picnic tables and patios are provided. Flush toilets, showers, a swimming pool, a jacuzzi and a laundromat are available. Pets are permitted on leashes.

Reservations, fee: Reservations accepted; $22 fee per night.

Who to contact: Phone the park at (619) 428-4486.

Location: From Interstate 5, take the Via de San Ysidro exit and drive south on Calle Primera to 190 East Calle Primera, next to Motel 6.

Trip note: Easy access from Highway 5 is a big plus here, but be advised to call ahead for available space. Nearby sidetrips include west to Imperial Beach, south to Tijuana, and east to Otay Lake. Open year-round.

34. CHULA VISTA MARINA AND RV PARK   RV 6
🐟 ⚓ ♿ 🏊

Reference: **In Chula Vista; map J6, grid h1.**

Campsites, facilities: There are 237 motor home sites with full hookups. Flush toilets, showers, TV hookups, a playground, a heated swimming pool and spa, a game room, a marina, a fishing pier, a free boat launch, free transportation to the San Diego Trolley, a laundromat, propane gas and groceries are available. Some facilities are **wheelchair accessible**. Pets are permitted on leashes.

Reservations, fee: Reservations recommended; $24.50-$40.50 fee per night; $1 pet fee.

Who to contact: Phone the park at (619) 422-0111.

Location: From Interstate 5 in Chula Vista, take the J Street exit and drive west a short distance to Sandpiper. Go left and drive to 460 Sandpiper Way.

Trip note: This is one of two parks in Chula Vista. See the trip note for San Diego Metropolitan KOA for detailed trip options. Open year-round.

35. BORDER GATE RV PARK   ♿ ≋

Reference: In San Ysidro; map J6, grid h1.

Campsites, facilities: There are 179 motor home sites with full hookups and individual lawns and patios. Flush toilets, showers, a playground, a heated swimming pool, a dump station, laundry, propane gas and groceries are available. Some facilities are **wheelchair accessible**. Pets are permitted on leashes.

Reservations, fee: Reservations recommended; $20 fee per night; $1 pet fee.

Who to contact: Phone the park at (619) 428-4411.

Location: From Interstate 5 in San Ysidro, drive east on Dairymart Road to San Ysidro Boulevard. Turn left and drive to 1010 San Ysidro Boulevard.

Trip note: Border Gate is literally that. It is less than two miles from the Mexican border, with a regular Mexicoach bus service from the park to downtown Tijuana and back. Open year-round.

36. SAN DIEGO METROPOLITAN KOA ♿ ≋

Reference: In Chula Vista; map J6, grid h1.

Campsites, facilities: There are 64 tent sites and 206 motor home sites with full hookups. Picnic tables and barbecue grills are provided. Flush toilets, showers, a playground, a dump station, a laundromat, a swimming pool, a jacuzzi, bike rentals, propane gas and groceries are available. Some facilities are **wheelchair accessible**. Pets are permitted on leashes.

Reservations, fee: Reservations accepted; $25-$32 fee per night.

Who to contact: Phone the park at (619) 427-3601.

Location: From Interstate 5 in Chula Vista, take the E Street exit and drive three miles east. Turn north on Second Street and drive to 111 North Second Street.

Trip note: This is one in a series of parks set up primarily for motor homes cruising Highway 5. Chula Vista is located between Mexico and San Diego, allowing visitors to make sidetrips east to Lower Otay Lake, north to the San Diego attractions, south to Tijuana, or "around the corner" on Highway 75 to Silver Strand State Beach. Open year-round.

37. SWEETWATER SUMMIT REGIONAL PARK ⌐● ⚓ 🏇

Reference: At Lower Otay Lake; map J6, grid h2.

Campsites, facilities: There are 60 sites for tents or motor homes with partial hookups. Twenty-two of the sites have horse corrals. Picnic tables and fire grills are provided. Piped water, flush toilets, showers and a dump station are available. Pets are permitted on leashes.

Reservations, fee: Reservations accepted; $12-$16 fee per night; $1 pet fee.

Who to contact: Phone the County Parks Department at (619) 565-3600 or (619) 694-3049.

Location: From San Diego, drive southeast about 10 miles on Highway 805 to Bonita Road. Go east on Bonita Road to San Miguel Road. Proceed on San Miguel Road another two miles to the park entrance on the left.

Trip note: This is an ideal base camp for campers and anglers in pursuit of Otay Lakes giant Florida strain of largemouth bass. I was fishing with Jack Neu the day he caught the California record for the largest five-fish limit of bass, 53 pounds, 14 ounces (using crawdads for bait). The camp is located at the southern tip of Lower Otay Lake. A paved boat ramp, boat rentals, tackle, a snack bar and groceries are available on the west shore of the lake. The lake and its facilities are open Wednesdays, Saturdays, and Sundays, February through mid-October. Open year-round.

38. BARRETT LAKE MOBILE HOME & RV PARK

Reference: **North of Tecate; map J6, grid h5.**
Campsites, facilities: There are 40 RV sites with full or partial hookups. Flush toilets, showers, picnic tables, a dump station, laundry, a clubhouse, cable TV and two swimming pools are available. Pets are allowed on leashes.
Reservations, fee: Call ahead for available space; $14 fee per night; group rate of $12 per night per RV applies to groups of six or more RVs.
Who to contact: Phone the park at (619) 468-3332.
Location: From San Diego, drive 40 miles on Highway 94 to Barrett Lake Road on the left. Drive north on Barrett Lake road to the campground at 1250 Barrett Lake Road.
Trip note: This is just enough off the beaten path to get missed by a lot of folks. It is set near Barrett Lake amid the surrounding Cleveland National Forest (but you can't see Barrett Lake from the camp). The lake is only about 10 miles north of the Mexican border, and here's a tip: It provides the best fishing of any lake in the western US, but access is restricted on a lottery basis only. Call the San Diego City Lakes program for information. Open year-round.

39. POTRERO COUNTY PARK

Reference: **Near Mexican border; map J6, grid h7.**
Campsites, facilities: There are 32 sites for tents or motor homes. Picnic tables, fire grills, electrical hookups and piped water are provided. Flush toilets, showers, a playground and a dump station are available. Supplies can be purchased in Potrero. Pets are permitted on leashes.
Reservations, fee: Reservations accepted; $10-$12 per night; $1 pet fee.
Who to contact: Phone the County Parks Department at (619) 565-3600 or (619) 694-3049.
Location: From San Diego, drive 42 miles east on Highway 94 to Potrero Valley Road. Drive north one mile on Potrero Valley Road to Potrero Park Road. Continue east on Potrero Park Road one mile to the park entrance.
Trip note: If you want to hole up for the night before getting through customs, this is the place. It is set just a heartbeat away from the customs inspection station in Tecate. A good sidetrip is to the nearby Tecate Mission Chapel, where you can pray the guards do not rip your car up in the search for contraband. It's a lot easier just to be clean, live clean. Open year-round.

40. LAKE MORENA RV PARK

Reference: **Near Campo; map J6, grid h7.**

Campsites, facilities: There are 27 motor home sites with full hookups and 17 with partial hookups. Picnic tables are provided. Flush toilets, showers, propane gas and a laundromat are available. Pets are allowed on leashes.

Reservations, fee: Reservations recommended; $18 fee per night; deposit required on three-day weekends.

Who to contact: Phone the park at (619) 478-5677.

Location: From San Diego, drive approximately 53 miles east on Interstate 8. Take the Buckman Springs Road exit (County Road S1) and drive 5.5 miles south. Turn right (west) on Oak Drive and drive 2.5 miles. Turn left on Lake Morena Drive and drive to 2330 Lake Morena Drive. From Campo on Highway 94, turn north on County Road S1 and drive five miles to Oak Drive. Turn left on Oak Drive. Turn left on Lake Morena Drive and drive to 2330 Lake Morena Drive.

Trip note: The camp is set near the southern side of Lake Morena. It is one of the three camps near the lake and the best for motor homes. Lake Morena, at 3,200 feet, is a large reservoir set in the San Diego County foothills and is known for the big bass. The lake record weighed 19 pounds, 2 ounces. The lake has a paved ramp and rowboat rentals. Open year-round.

41. LAKE MORENA COUNTY PARK

Reference: Near Campo; map J6, grid h7.

Campsites, facilities: There are 90 sites for tents or motor homes, some with partial hookups. Picnic tables and fire grills are provided. Piped water, flush toilets and showers are available. A grocery store, a boat ramp and rowboat rentals are nearby. Pets are permitted on leashes.

Reservations, fee: Reservations accepted; $10-$12 per night; $1 pet fee.

Who to contact: Phone the park at (619) 565-3600 or (619) 478-5473.

Location: From San Diego, drive approximately 53 miles east on Interstate 8. Take the Buckman Springs Road exit (County Road S1) and drive 5.5 miles south. Turn right (west) on Oak Drive and follow signs to the park. Turn left on Lake Morena Drive and drive to 2330 Lake Morena Drive.

Trip note: This camp is set along the southern shore of Lake Morena at 3,150 feet. Morena is a large reservoir, not far from the California-Mexico border, that is known for occasionally producing giant bass. The lake record weighed 19 pounds, 2 ounces. Rowboat rentals are available nearby. Open year-round.

42. BOULDER OAKS

Reference: Near Lake Morena in Cleveland National Forest; map J6, grid h8.

Campsites, facilities: There are six sites for tents only, 12 sites for tents or motor homes, and 14 equestrian sites. Picnic tables, fire grills and piped water are provided. Vault toilets are available. A grocery store is nearby. Pets are allowed on leashes.

Reservations, fee: Equestrian sites by reservation only; phone (800) 280-CAMP (2267); $7.50 reservation fee; $7-$8 fee per night.

Who to contact: Phone the Cleveland National Forest, Descanso District at (619) 445-6235.

Location: From San Diego, drive approximately 55 miles east on Interstate 8 to the Kitchen Creek-Cameron Station exit. Turn right on the southern frontage road and drive about one mile to the campground.

Trip note: This campground is about 10 miles (by car) from Lake Morena, a large reservoir that is the home of some big bass in the 15-pound class, as elusive as they can often prove to be. Rowboat rentals are available. The Pacific Crest Trail passes nearby, the same trail that extends north for 2,700 miles to the Washington-Canada border. The elevation is 3,500 feet. Open year-round.

43. OUTDOOR WORLD RV PARK 🚶 🐟 ♨ RV 4

Reference: **In Campo; map J6, grid i8.**

Campsites, facilities: There are 138 sites for RVs, 122 have full hookups and 16 have partial hookups. There are also some primitive tent camping sites. A clubhouse, pool table, restrooms, showers, horseshoes, fire rings and a group camping area are provided.

Reservations, fee: Reservations are recommended; $10-$15 fee per night.

Who to contact: Outdoor World, 37133 Highway 94, Campo, CA 92006; (619) 766-4480.

Location: From San Diego, take Interstate 8 to the Boulevard/Campo exit. Turn right and drive three-quarters of a mile to the Olde Highway 80/Highway 94 exit. Turn right and drive to the fork where Olde Highway 80 and Highway 94 split. Make a left turn and drive 3.5 miles to the signed campground turnoff at Shasta Way.

Trip note: Hiking and nature trails on Mount Laguna are the big highlight here, as well as the camp's proximity to Mexico. The nearest point of entry, Tecate, is only 30 minutes away. Fishing at Lake Morena or Lake Cuyamaca is also a possibility, or soaking in nearby hot springs. Weekly and monthly rates are also available.

MAP J7

SO-CAL MAP .... see page 690
adjoining maps
NORTH (I7) .... see page 752
EAST (J8) .... see page 798
SOUTH .... no map
WEST (J6) .... see page 770

22 LISTINGS
PAGES 788-797

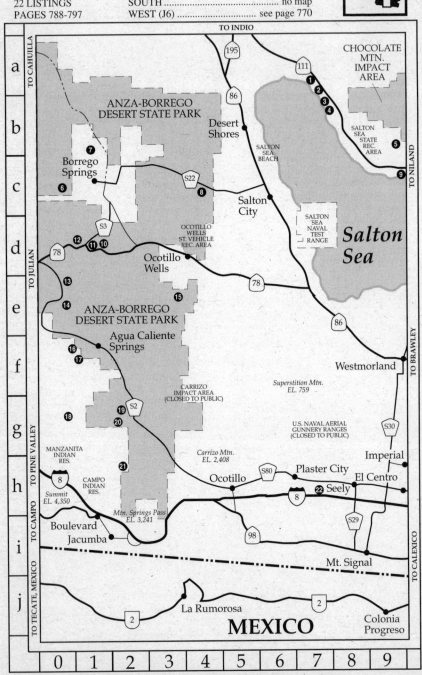

1. HEADQUARTERS 🐟 ⚓ 👫 ♿ 🏊 RV 5

Reference: **In Salton Sea State Recreation Area; map J7, grid a7.**

Campsites, facilities: There are 25 sites for tents or motor homes up to 32 feet long. Piped water, fire grills and picnic tables are provided. Sixteen sites have electrical connections and sewer hookups. Restrooms, showers, a dump station, a grocery store and propane gas are available nearby. There is **wheelchair access** to camping, picnicking, boating, fishing and exhibit areas. Pets are permitted on leashes.

Reservations, fee: Reserve by phoning Destinet at (800) 444-7275 ($6.75 Destinet fee); $10-$16 fee per night; $1 pet fee.

Who to contact: Phone Salton Sea State Recreation Area at (619) 393-3052 or (619) 767-5311.

Location: From Mecca, drive 10 miles southeast on Highway 111 to the entrance.

Trip note: This is the northernmost of the camps on the shore of the giant Salton Sea, that vast, shallow, and unique lake. It is set at the recreation area headquarters, just south of the town of Desert Beach at an elevation of 220 feet below sea level. Corvina fishing can be quite good at this lake. The best time to visit is from October through May. Summer is like visiting the devil, and spring and fall can be quite windy. If winds are hazardous, a red beacon on the northeast shore of the lake will flash. If you see it, it's time to flat git to the nearest shore. Open year-round.

2. MECCA BEACH 🐟 ⚓ 👫 ♿ 🏊 RV 5

Reference: **In Salton Sea State Recreation Area; map J7, grid a7.**

Campsites, facilities: There are 110 sites for tents or motor homes up to 30 feet long. Piped water, fire grills and picnic tables are provided. Flush toilets, showers, groceries and propane gas are available. Pets are permitted on leashes.

Reservations, fee: No reservations; $10-$16 fee per night; $1 pet fee.

Who to contact: Phone the Salton Sea State Recreation Area at (619) 393-3052 or (619) 767-5311.

Location: From Mecca, drive 12 miles southeast on Highway 111 to the entrance.

Trip note: This is one of the camps set in the Salton Sea State Recreation Area on the northeastern shore of the lake. For details, see the trip note for Headquarters Camp.

3. CORVINA BEACH 🐟 ⚓ 👫 ♿ 🏊 RV 5

Reference: **In Salton Sea State Recreation Area; map J7, grid b7.**

Campsites, facilities: There are 500 primitive sites for tents or motor homes. Piped water is provided. Chemical toilets and a boat ramp are available. Groceries and propane gas are available nearby. Pets are permitted on leashes.

Reservations, fee: No reservations; $10-$16 fee per night; $1 pet fee.

Who to contact: Phone the Salton Sea State Recreation Area at (619) 393-3052 or (619) 767-5311.

Location: From Mecca, drive 14 miles southeast on Highway 111 to the entrance.

Trip note: This is by far the biggest of the campgrounds on the Salton Sea. For details, see the trip note for Headquarters Camp. Open year-round.

---

4. SALT CREEK PRIMITIVE AREA

Reference: **In Salton Sea State Recreation Area; map J7, grid b7.**

Campsites, facilities: There are 150 primitive sites for tents or motor homes. Chemical toilets are available, but **no piped water** is available, so bring your own. Pets are permitted on leashes.

Reservations, fee: No reservations; $10-$16 fee per night; $1 pet fee.

Who to contact: Phone the Salton Sea State Recreation Area at (619) 393-3052 or (619) 767-5311.

Location: From Mecca, drive 17 miles southeast on Highway 111 to the entrance.

Trip note: Every camp has some claim to fame, however obscure. This one gets the award for the least likely place you want to visit on the Salton Sea. Why? No water. Even a water purifier won't work with the lake water, unless you're a corvina. For details on the area, see the trip note for Headquarters Camp.

5. FOUNTAIN OF YOUTH SPA

Reference: **Near Salton Sea; map J7, grid b9.**

Campsites, facilities: There are 400 primitive sites and 546 motor home sites with full hookups. Flush toilets, showers, natural artesian steam rooms, hydrojet pools, swimming pools, recreation centers, dump stations, laundry, a barber shop, a beauty parlor, a masseur, church services, propane gas and groceries are available. Pets are allowed on leashes.

Reservations, fee: No reservations; $11.75-$18 fee per night.

Who to contact: Phone the park at (619) 354-1340.

Location: From Indio, drive 44 miles south on Highway 111 to Hot Mineral Spa Road. Or from Niland, drive 15 miles north on Highway 111 to Hot Mineral Spa Road. Turn north on Hot Mineral Spa Road and drive about four miles to the park.

Trip note: Natural artesian steam rooms are the highlight here, but I didn't seem to get any younger. It is a vast private park, set near the Salton Sea. See the trip note for Red Hill County Park, located nearby, for side trip options.

---

6. CULP VALLEY PRIMITIVE CAMP AREA

Reference: **Near Pena Springs in Anza-Borrego Desert State Park; map J7, grid c0.**

Campsites, facilities: This is an open camping area in Anza-Borrego Desert State Park. It can be used for tents or motor homes. Open fires are not allowed and there is **no piped water**, so bring your own. Pets are allowed on leashes.

Reservations, fee: No reservations; no fee.

Who to contact: Phone the Anza-Borrego Desert State Park at (619) 767-5311.

Location: From Borrego Springs, drive 10 miles southwest on County Road S22.

Trip note: Culp Valley is set near Pena Springs and offers a trailhead for a hike that is routed to the northeast to the high desert. An advisable side trip is to the Panorama Outlook, located at the Visitor Center about a 15-minute drive north on County Road S22. The elevation is 3,400 feet. Open year-round.

7. BORREGO PALM CANYON 🏃 ♿ 🐎 ⛪ 🚐 △ 4

Reference: **In Anza-Borrego Desert State Park; map J7, grid c1.**

Campsites, facilities: There are 52 motor home sites with full hookups and 65 sites for tents or motor homes. Piped water, fire grills and picnic tables are provided. Flush toilets and showers are available. A grocery store, laundromat and propane gas are nearby. There are also five group tent camps that can accommodate 10 to 24 people. Pets are allowed on leashes.

Reservations, fee: Phone Destinet at (800) 444-7275 ($6.75 Destinet fee); $13-$21 fee per night; $36 group fee.

Who to contact: Phone the Anza-Borrego Desert State Park at (619) 767-5311.

Location: From Borrego Springs, drive 2.5 miles west on County Road S22 and Palm Canyon Drive.

Trip note: This is the place to go for motor home cruisers. The Panorama Outlook Trail starts here, and a Visitors Center is also available. The latter offers exhibits and a slide show. The elevation is 760 feet. Open year-round.

8. ARROYO SALADO PRIMITIVE CAMP AREA 🚐 △ 5
🏃 🐎 ⛪ 🧍

Reference: **In Anza-Borrego Desert State Park; map J7, grid c4.**

Campsites, facilities: This is an open camping area in the Anza-Borrego Desert State Park. It can be used for tents or motor homes. Open fires are not allowed and there is **no piped water**, so bring your own. Pets are allowed on leashes.

Reservations, fee: No reservations; no fee.

Who to contact: Phone the Anza-Borrego Desert State Park at (619) 767-5311.

Location: From Borrego Springs, drive 16 miles east on County Road S22.

Trip note: The camp is a primitive spot set along (and named after) an ephemeral stream, the Arroyo Salado. A few miles to the west is the trailhead for the Thimble Trail, which is routed south into a wash in the Borrego Badlands. The elevation is 800 feet. Open year-round.

9. BOMBAY BEACH 🛶 🐟 ⚓ 🏃 ♿ 🏊 🚐 △ 5

Reference: **In Salton Sea State Recreation Area; map J7, grid c9.**

Campsites, facilities: There are 200 sites for tents or motor homes. Piped water and chemical toilets are available. Pets are permitted on leashes.

Reservations, fee: No reservations; $10-$16 fee per night; $1 pet fee.

Who to contact: Phone the Salton Sea State Recreation Area at (619) 393-3052 or (619) 767-5311.

Location: From Niland, drive 18 miles northwest on Highway 111 to the entrance.

Trip note: All in all, this is a strange looking place, the vast body of water surrounded by stark countryside. Salton Sea is the unique saltwater lake set below sea level, where corvina provide a lively sports fishery. This camp is set in a bay along the southeastern shoreline, where a beach and nature trails are available. Nearby, to the south, is the Wister Waterfowl Management Area. Open year-round.

10. YAQUI WELL PRIMITIVE CAMP AREA

Reference: **In Anza-Borrego Desert State Park; map J7, grid d1.**

Campsites, facilities: This is an open camping area in Anza-Borrego Desert State Park. It can be used for tents or motor homes. Pit toilets are available. Open fires are not allowed and there is **no piped water**, so bring your own. Pets are allowed on leashes.

Reservations, fee: No reservations; no fee.

Who to contact: Phone the Anza-Borrego Desert State Park at (619) 767-5311.

Location: From Borrego Springs, drive about five miles south on County Road S3. Turn right on Yaqui Pass Road (County Road S3) and drive about six miles to the camping area on the right.

Trip note: This camp is used primarily as an overflow area if the more developed Tamarisk Grove Camp is full. A hiking trail, the Cactus Loop Trail, starts at Tamarisk Grove. The elevation is 1,400 feet. Open year-round.

11. YAQUI PASS PRIMITIVE CAMP AREA RV 3

Reference: **In Anza-Borrego Desert State Park; map J7, grid d1.**

Campsites, facilities: This is an open camping area in Anza-Borrego Desert State Park. It can be used for tents or motor homes. There are no toilets. Open fires are not allowed and there is **no piped water**, so bring your own. Pets are allowed on leashes.

Reservations, fee: No reservations; no fee.

Who to contact: Phone the Anza-Borrego Desert State Park at (619) 767-5311.

Location: From Borrego Springs, drive about five miles south on County Road S3. Turn right on Yaqui Pass Road (County Road S3) and drive about four miles to the camping area on the left.

Trip note: Set beside primitive Yaqui Pass Road, at 1730 feet elevation. The trailhead for the Kenyan Loop Trail, a side trip possibility, is located to the immediate south. This spot is often overlooked because the Tamarisk Grove Camp nearby provides piped water. Open year-round.

12. TAMARISK GROVE RV 5
Reference: **In Anza-Borrego Desert State Park; map J7, grid d1.**

Campsites, facilities: There are 27 sites for tents or motor homes. Piped water, fire grills and picnic tables are provided. Flush toilets and showers are available. Pets are permitted on leashes.

Reservations, fee: Reserve through Destinet at (800) 444-7275 ($6.75 Destinet fee); $13-$17 fee per night; $1 pet fee.

Who to contact: Phone the Anza-Borrego Desert State Park at (619) 767-5311.

Location: From Borrego Springs, drive 12 miles south on County Road S3 (which becomes Yaqui Pass Road) to the intersection with Highway 78.

Trip note: They've got piped water here, and right there is the number one reason that this is one of the most popular camps in this desert park. It is one of the three camps in the immediate area, so if this camp is full, primitive Yaqui Well to the immediate west and Yaqui Pass to the north on Yaqui Pass Road, provide options. The Cactus Loop Trail, with the trailhead just north of camp, provides a hiking option. The elevation is 1,400 feet. Open year-round.

13. BUTTERFIELD RANCH 🐟 ♿ 🏊 RV 3

Reference: **Near Anza-Borrego Desert State Park; map J7, grid e0.**

Campsites, facilities: There are 500 sites in all, with 300 full hookup RV sites and 200 tent sites. Restrooms, hot showers, a sanitary dump station, a playground, a swimming pool, a jacuzzi, a laundromat, a cafe, a recreation room, a store, a fish pond and a petting farm are available. Pets are allowed on leashes.

Reservations, fee: Reservations accepted; $12-$20 fee per night.

Who to contact: Phone the park at (619) 765-1463.

Location: From San Diego, turn east on Interstate 8 and drive 35 miles east to Highway 79. Turn north and 24 miles to the town of Julian, then turn east on Highway 78 and drive about 12 miles to County Road S2. Turn south and continue to the campground entrance.

Trip note: This is an ideal layover spot for motor home cruisers visiting nearby Anza-Borrego Desert State Park who want a developed park in which to stay overnight. Note that there is no gas available in Julian after 6 p.m. and that the nearest gas station is 36 miles east.

---

14. BLAIR VALLEY ENVIRONMENTAL CAMP 5% CLUB 4
🚶🚶 🐎 ⛪

Reference: **In Anza-Borrego Desert State Park; map J7, grid e0.**

Campsites, facilities: There are several primitive, walk-in sites. **No piped water** is available, so bring your own. Fires are not permitted. Pets are allowed on leashes.

Reservations, fee: No reservations; no fee.

Who to contact: Phone the Anza-Borrego Desert State Park at (619) 767-5311.

Location: From Julian on Highway 78, drive 12 miles east. Turn right (south) on County Road S2 and drive about five miles to the campground entrance road.

Trip note: These sites have been developed to offer maximum seclusion for the camper. The sites are walk-in and are about 100 yards from their parking areas. An attraction of this camp is the nearby hiking, with the Morteros Trail (drive three miles) and Pictograph Trail (drive six miles) located down the road—look for the trailheads on the right side. The elevation is 2,500 feet. Open year-round.

---

15. FISH CREEK 🚶🚶 🐎 ⛪ RV 3

Reference: **In Anza-Borrego Desert State Park; map J7, grid e3.**

Campsites, facilities: There are eight sites for tents or motor homes. Pit toilets are available, but there is **no piped water**, so bring your own. Pets are allowed on leashes.

Reservations, fee: No reservations; no fee.

Who to contact: Phone the Anza-Borrego State Park at (619) 767-5311.

Location: From Highway 78 in Ocotillo Wells, drive 12 miles south on Split Mountain Road to the campground.

Trip note: This primitive camp is set just inside the eastern border of Anza-Borrego State Park, at the foot of the Vallecito Mountains to the west. A possible side trip is to hike the Elephant Trees Discovery Trail, located a few miles to the north. This is the closest camp to the Ocotillo Wells State Vehicular Recreation Area, which is located 12 miles to the north.

16. VALLECITO COUNTY PARK

RV. 3

Reference: **Near Anza-Borrego Desert State Park; map J7, grid f0.**

Campsites, facilities: There are 44 sites for tents or motor homes. Fire grills and picnic tables are provided. Piped water, flush toilets and a playground are available. Pets are permitted on leashes.

Reservations, fee: No reservations; $10-$14 fee per night; $1 pet fee.

Who to contact: Phone the County Parks Department at (619) 565-3600 or (619) 694-3049.

Location: From Julian, drive 12 miles east on Highway 78. Turn right (south) on County Road S2 and drive 18 miles to the park entrance on the right.

Trip note: This nice county park in the desert gets little attention in the face of the other nearby attractions. Nearby are the Agua Caliente Hot Springs, Anza-Borrego Desert State Park to the east, and Cuyamaca Reservoir and Cuyamaca Rancho State Park are about 35 miles away. The elevation is 1,500 feet. Open from October to June.

17. AGUA CALIENTE COUNTY PARK

RV. 3

Reference: **Near Anza-Borrego Desert State Park; map J7, grid f1.**

Campsites, facilities: There are 104 motor home sites with full or partial hookups and 36 sites for tents or motor homes. Piped water, fire grills and picnic tables are provided. Flush toilets, showers, a swimming pool, a therapy pool and a playground are available. Groceries and propane gas are nearby. No pets are allowed.

Reservations, fee: Reservations accepted; $10-$14 fee per night.

Who to contact: Phone the County Parks Department at (619) 565-3600 or (619) 694-3049.

Location: From San Diego, take Interstate 8 east to Ocotillo. In the town of Ocotillo, take County Road S2 north 25 miles to the park entrance on the right. Alternate directions: From Julian, drive 12 miles east on Highway 78. Turn right (south) on County Road S2 and drive 21 miles south to the park entrance road on the right.

Trip note: Everything is hot here. The weather is hot, the coffee is hot, and the water is hot, and hey, that's what "Agua Caliente" means. Hot water, named after the nearby hot springs. Anza-Borrego Desert State Park is also nearby. If you like to see some cold water, Lake Cuyamaca and Cuyamaca Rancho State Park are about 35 miles away. The elevation is 1,350 feet. Open Labor Day through Memorial Day weekend.

18. COTTONWOOD

RV. 4

Reference: **In McCain Valley Wildlife Management Area; map J7, grid g0.**

Campsites, facilities: There are 29 sites for tents or motor homes. Piped water, fire grills and picnic tables are provided. Vault toilets are available. Pets are permitted on leashes.

Reservations, fee: No reservations; $4 fee per night.

Who to contact: Phone the Bureau of Land Management at (909) 697-5200.

Location: From San Diego, drive approximately 70 miles east on Interstate 8 to the McCain Valley-Boulevard exit. Turn right, then left on the southern frontage (county) road and continue east for two miles to the intersection with McCain Valley Road. Turn left (north) on McCain Valley Road and drive about 14 miles to the campground.

Trip note: This camp is set on the western edge of the McCain Valley National Cooperative Land and Wildlife Management Area. The area is not well known by out of towners. The elevation is 4,000 feet. Open year-round.

19. BOW WILLOW 🚶🏻 ♿ 🏇 ⛪   RV 🔺4

Reference: **Near Bow Willow Canyon in Anza-Borrego Desert State Park; map J7, grid g2.**

Campsites, facilities: There are 14 sites for tents or motor homes. Picnic tables and ramadas are provided. **Piped water is limited** and vault toilets are available. Pets are permitted on leashes.

Reservations, fee: No reservations; $7-$9 fee per night; $1 pet fee.

Who to contact: Phone the Anza-Borrego Desert State Park at (619) 767-5311.

Location: From Interstate 8 in Ocotillo, turn north on County Road S2 and drive 14 miles to the campground gravel entrance road on the left.

Trip note: Bow Willow Canyon is a rugged setting that can be explored by hiking the trail that starts at this camp. A short distance east of the camp, the trail forks to the south to Rockhouse Canyon. A good side trip is to drive back to County Road S2 and head south over Sweeney Pass for the view at the Carrizo Badlands Overlook. Open year-round.

20. MOUNTAIN PALM SPRINGS   RV 🔺4
   ### PRIMITIVE CAMP AREA 🚶🏻 🏇 ⛪

Reference: **In Anza-Borrego Desert State Park; map J7, grid g2.**

Campsites, facilities: This is an open camping area in Anza-Borrego Desert State Park. It can be used for tents or motor homes. Pit toilets are available. Open fires are not allowed and there is **no piped water**, so bring your own. Pets are allowed on leashes.

Reservations, fee: No reservations, no fee.

Who to contact: Phone the Anza-Borrego Desert State Park at (619) 767-5311.

Location: From Interstate 8 in Ocotillo, turn north on County Road S2 and drive 15 miles to the camping entrance road on the left.

Trip note: Easy access from County Road S2 is a plus, but no water is a minus at this camp. Regardless of either, to get the full benefit of this camp, you need to get out and hoof it. A trail leads south to Bow Willow Creek (and Bow Willow Camp) and onward into Bow Willow Canyon. The Carrizo Badlands Overlook is located on the southeast side of Sweeney Pass, about a 10-minute drive south on County Road S2. The elevation is 950 feet. Open year-round.

21. LARK CANYON 🚶🏻 🏇   RV 🔺5

Reference: **In McCain Valley Wildlife Management Area; map J7, grid h2.**

Campsites, facilities: There are 15 sites for tents or motor homes. Fire grills and picnic tables are provided. Piped water and pit toilets are available. Pets are permitted on leashes.

Reservations, fee: No reservations; $4 fee per night.

Who to contact: Phone the Bureau of Land Management at (909) 697-5200.

Location: From San Diego, drive approximately 70 miles east on Interstate 8 to the McCain Valley-Boulevard exit. Turn right, then left on the frontage (county) road and continue east for two miles to the intersection with McCain

Valley Road. Turn left (north) on McCain Valley Road and drive seven miles to the campground.

Trip note: This is a small camp that few know of, set at 4,000 feet in the McCain Valley National Cooperative and Wildlife Management Area. It is near a popular off-highway-vehicle area. Many bikers use it as their base camp. Open year-round.

22. RIO BEND RV PARK

Reference: **Near El Centro; map J7, grid h7.**

Campsites, facilities: There are 228 sites with full hookups for motor homes, and a group area with 42 sites with partial hookups. Picnic tables are provided. There is also a heated pool, spa, shuffleboard, volleyball, two small stocked lakes, a golf course and laundromat. Telephone and cable television hookups are available. A small store is located nearby. Pets are permitted on leashes. The park is **wheelchair accessible**.

Reservations, fee: Reservations accepted; $13 to $21 fee per night.

Who to contact: Phone (619) 352-7061.

Location: From El Centro, drive west on Interstate 8 for seven miles. Take the Drew Road exit, then drive south on Drew Road for one-quarter mile to the park, located at 1589 Drew Road.

Trip note: To some travelers, this part of America is a god-forsaken wasteland, but hey, that makes arriving at this park all the more like coming to a mirage in the desert. The park is usually well maintained, and management does what it can to offer visitors recreational options. It's hot out here—sizzlin' most of the year—but dry and cool in the winter, which is the best time to visit. The park is set at 50 feet below sea level near Mt. Signal, and it's about a 20-minute drive north to the Salton Sea.

MAP J8

SO-CAL MAP .... see page 690
adjoining maps
NORTH (I8) .... see page 762
EAST (J9) .... see page 802
SOUTH .... no map
WEST (J7) .... see page 788

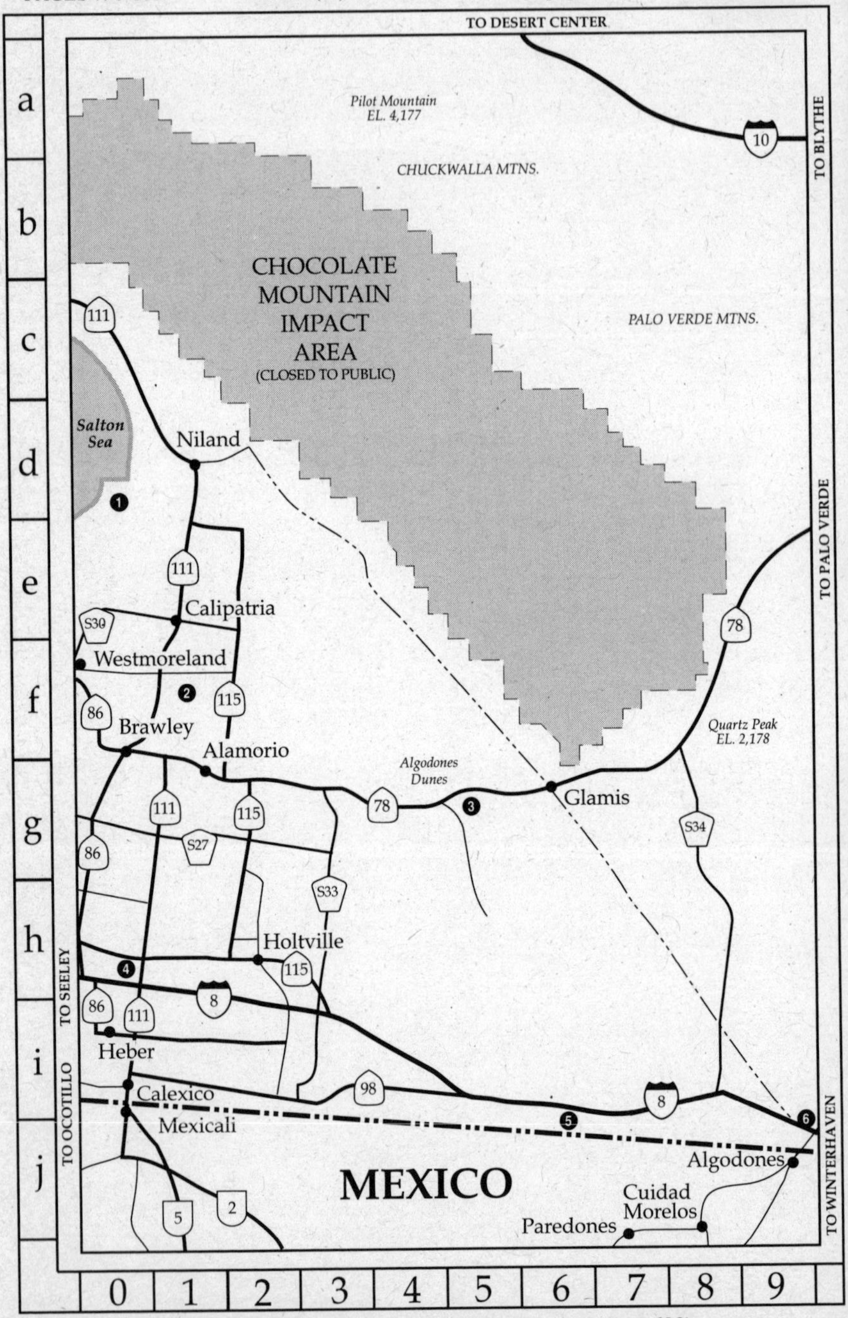

6 LISTINGS
PAGES 798-801

TO DESERT CENTER

TO BLYTHE

Pilot Mountain
EL. 4,177

CHUCKWALLA MTNS.

111

CHOCOLATE
MOUNTAIN
IMPACT
AREA
(CLOSED TO PUBLIC)

PALO VERDE MTNS.

Salton Sea

Niland

1

10

TO PALO VERDE

111

Calipatria

S30

78

Westmoreland

86

2

115

Brawley

Alamorio

Algodones Dunes

78

3

Glamis

Quartz Peak
EL. 2,178

S34

111

115

86

S27

S33

Holtville

115

TO SEELEY

4

8

86

111

TO OCOTILLO

Heber

Calexico

98

8

Mexicali

5

6

TO WINTERHAVEN

MEXICO

Algodones

Cuidad
Morelos

Paredones

5

2

0 1 2 3 4 5 6 7 8 9

a b c d e f g h i j

1. RED HILL MARINA COUNTY PARK   RV 3

Reference: **Near Salton Sea; map J8, grid d0.**

Campsites, facilities: There are 400 sites for tents or motor homes, some with hookups. Picnic tables and piped water are provided. Flush toilets and showers are available. Pets are allowed on leashes.

Reservations, fee: No reservations; call for fees.

Who to contact: Phone the park at (619) 348-2310.

Location: From Niland, drive five miles south on Highway 111 to Sinclair Road. Turn right and drive to Garst Road. Go right and follow to end (about 1.5 miles). Go left on Red Hill Road and follow it to the marina and campground.

Trip note: This county park is set near the south end of the Salton Sea. Several wildlife refuges are in the immediate area, including two separate chunks of the Imperial Wildfowl Management Area, to the west and south, and the huge Wister Waterfowl Management Area, northwest of Niland. For sidetrip options, see the trip note for Bombay Beach.

2. WIEST LAKE COUNTY PARK   RV 4

Reference: **On Wiest Lake; map J8, grid f1.**

Campsites, facilities: There are 20 tent sites and 24 motor home sites with full hookups. Picnic tables, fire grills, piped water, a boat ramp and a dump station are provided. Flush toilets and showers are available. A grocery store, a laundromat and propane gas are nearby. Pets are allowed on leashes.

Reservations, fee: No reservations; $7-$12 fee per night.

Who to contact: Phone the park at (619) 344-3712 or (619) 339-4384.

Location: From Brawley, drive approximately five miles north on Highway 111. Turn right (east) on Rutherford Road and drive two miles to the park entrance on the right.

Trip note: This is a developed county park set along the southern shore of Wiest Lake, which adjoins the Imperial Wildfowl Management Area to the north. The park is actually below sea level. The Salton Sea, about a 20-minute drive to the northwest, provides a nearby side trip.

3. GECKO   RV 1

Reference: **Near Brawley; map J8, grid g5.**

Campsites, facilities: There are numerous dispersed sites for tents or motor homes. Vault toilets and a dumpster are provided, but there is **no piped water**, so bring your own. Pets are permitted on leashes.

Reservations, fee: No reservations; no fee.

Who to contact: Phone the Bureau of Land Management at (619) 337-4400.

Location: From Brawley, drive 27 miles east on Highway 78 to Gecko Road. Turn south on Gecko Road and drive three miles to the campground entrance on the right.

Trip note: There isn't a tree within a million miles of this camp. People who wind up here all have the same thing in common—they're ready to ride across the dunes in their dune buggies. Other recreation options include watching the sky and waiting for a cloud to show up. Open year-round.

4. COUNTRY LIFE RV ♿ 🏊   RV 2

Reference: **Near El Centro; map J8, grid h0.**

Campsites, facilities: There are 30 tent sites and 175 motor home sites with full hookups. Flush toilets, showers, swimming pool, clubhouse, laundry, propane gas and groceries are available. Some facilities are **wheelchair accessible**. Pets are permitted on leashes.

Reservations, fee: Reservations recommended; $15-$18.50 fee per night.

Who to contact: Phone the park at (619) 353-1040.

Location: From Interstate 8 in El Centro, take the Highway 111 exit and drive a quarter mile north. Turn left on Ross Road and drive a short distance to the campground entrance.

Trip note: You'd best have air conditioning. This is a motor home parking lot on the desert flats about a 10-minute drive north of the Mexican border. Nearby sidetrips include the Salton Sea to the north, little Sunbeam Lake County Park to the west, and, if you need to sober up, the border customs to the south. Open year-round.

5. MIDWAY   RV 6

Reference: **In Imperial Sand Dunes Recreation Area; map J8, grid i6.**

Campsites, facilities: There are several primitive sites for tents or motor homes. Pit toilets are available. **No piped water** is provided.

Reservations, fee: No reservations; no fee.

Who to contact: Phone El Centro Resource Area at (619) 337-4400, or write Bureau of Land Management, 1661 South Fourth Street, El Centro, CA 92243.

Location: From El Centro, drive east on Interstate 8 for about 40 miles to Sand Hills. Turn south on Gray's Wells Road and drive three miles. The road turns from pavement to dirt and then deadends; camping is permitted anywhere in this region.

Trip note: This is off-road headquarters, a place where people bring their three-wheelers, four-wheelers and motorcycles and act like lunatics without anybody even raising an eyebrow. That's because a large area has been set aside for this type of recreation. As you drive in, you will enter the Buttercup Recreation Area, which is part of the Imperial Sand Dunes Recreation Area. You do what you please, camp wherever you like, and nobody beefs.

6. PILOT KNOB CAMPGROUND 🏊   RV 3

Reference: **Near Colorado River; map J8, grid j9.**

Campsites, facilities: There are 105 motor home sites with full hookups and picnic tables. Flush toilets, showers, a recreation room, a swimming pool, a spa and a laundromat are available. Pets are permitted on leashes.

Reservations, fee: Reservations recommended; $18 fee per night.

Who to contact: Phone the park at (619) 572-5232.

Location: From Interstate 8 in Winterhaven, take the Sidewinder Road exit and drive to the southern frontage road. Drive a half-mile west on the frontage road to the campground on the left.

Trip note: They don't call the town Winterhaven for nothing. Just try visiting in the summer and you'll find out why winter is preferred. This is a privately-operated motor home park that is a winter attraction for folks in the Pacific Northwest who are starting to rust from all the rain up there. The Colorado River and the Mexican border are to the south. Open year-round.

SO-CAL MAP .... see page 690
adjoining maps
NORTH (I9) .... see page 764
EAST .... no map
SOUTH .... no map
WEST (J8) .... see page 798

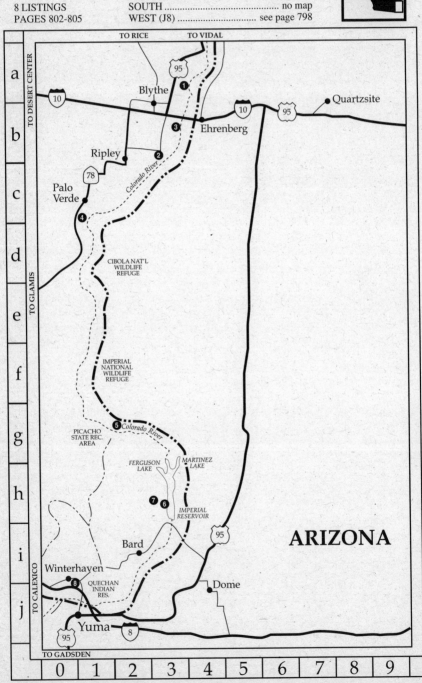

Map J9 featuring: Colorado River, Taylor Lake, Senator Wash Reservoir

1. MAYFLOWER COUNTY PARK

Reference: On Colorado River; map J9, grid a4.

Campsites, facilities: There are 28 tent sites and 152 motor home sites with piped water and electrical hookups provided. Picnic tables and barbecues are provided. Flush toilets, showers, a dump station and a boat ramp are available. Pets are permitted on leashes.

Reservations, fee: No reservations; $15-$16 fee per night; $2 pet fee.

Who to contact: Phone the park at (619) 922-4665.

Location: From Blythe, drive seven miles northeast on Intake Boulevard (US 95) to Sixth Avenue. Turn right on Sixth Avenue and drive three miles to the park entrance directly ahead.

Trip note: The Colorado River is the fountain of life around these parts, and for campers, it provides the main element that makes it an attraction. It is a popular spot for waterskiing. Open year-round.

2. McINTYRE PARK

Reference: Near Colorado River; map J9, grid b3.

Campsites, facilities: There are 140 tent sites and 160 motor home sites, with picnic tables, piped water and electrical connections provided. Restrooms, showers, a dump station, propane gas, a snack bar, a grocery store, bait, ice and a boat ramp are available. Some facilities are **wheelchair accessible**. Pets are not permitted.

Reservations, fee: No reservations; $16-$20 fee per night.

Who to contact: Phone the park at (619) 922-8205.

Location: From Blythe on Interstate 10, drive seven miles south on Intake Boulevard to the foot of 26th Avenue and the park entrance.

Trip note: How you rate this place depends on whether you are coming or going to Las Vegas. If you are arriving, you'll probably just keep on cruising to the bright lights. If you're returning with darn near empty pockets, well, even a motor home park on the outskirts of Blythe starts to look good. The park is two miles from the Colorado River. Open year-round.

3. RIVIERA BLYTHE MARINA

Reference: Near Colorado River; map J9, grid b3.

Campsites, facilities: There are 285 motor home sites, many with full or partial hookups. Picnic tables are provided. Restrooms, showers, a swimming pool, spa, cable TV, a laundromat, a store, a card room, a boat ramp and propane gas are available. A golf course is nearby. Pets are allowed on leashes.

Reservations, fee: Reservations accepted; $16-$23 fee per night.

Who to contact: Phone the park at (619) 922-5350.

Location: From Blythe, drive two miles east on Interstate 10 to Riviera Drive exit. Follow to 14100 Riviera Drive.

Trip note: This motor home park is set up for camper-boaters who want to hunker down for awhile along the Colorado River and cool off. Open year-round.

---

4. PALO VERDE COUNTY PARK   RV. 5

Reference: **Near Colorado River; map J9, grid c1.**
Campsites, facilities: There are an undesignated number of sites for tents or motor homes. Piped water, flush toilets and a playground are available. A boat ramp is available at the Palo Verde Oxbow BLM site five miles west on the Colorado River (see trip note for instructions). A grocery store, laundromat and propane gas are available in Palo Verde. Pets are allowed on leashes.
Reservations, fee: No reservations; no fee.
Who to contact: Phone the park at (619) 339-4384.
Location: From Palo Verde, drive three miles south on Highway 78 to the signed campground exit on the left.
Trip note: Now that you're out here, don't start getting picky. This is the only game in town, with no other camps for many miles. It is set near a bend in the Colorado River, not far from the Cibola National Wildlife Refuge. To get to the boat ramp, available at the Palo Verde Oxbow BLM site on the Colorado River, take the gravel road between mileposts 77 and 78 off Highway 78. Drive west for five miles to the river. Open year-round.

---

5. PICACHO STATE RECREATION AREA   RV. 6

Reference: **By Taylor Lake on Colorado River; map J9, grid g2.**
Campsites, facilities: There are 58 sites for tents or small motor homes. Picnic tables and fire grills are provided. There are also several boat-in campsites available. Piped water, pit toilets, a sanitary disposal station, solar showers and a boat launch are available. Pets are permitted on leashes.
Reservations, fee: No reservations except for group sites; $9-$12 fee per night.
Who to contact: Phone (619) 393-3059 or (619) 996-2963 or (619) 767-5311.
Location: From Highway 8 in Winterhaven, take the Winterhaven-Fourth Avenue exit. Turn left on Fourth Avenue. Turn right on County Road S24. Turn left on Picacho Road and drive under the railroad tracks. Continue on Picacho Road. When you cross the American Canal the road becomes dirt. Continue north for 18 miles on the winding dirt road (not suitable for large motor homes) to the campground. This takes about one hour.
Trip note: To get here, you really have to want it. It's way out there, requiring a long drive north out of Winterhaven on a spindly little road. The camp is on the southern side of Taylor Lake on the Colorado River. The park is the best deal around for many miles, though, with a boat ramp, waterskiing, good bass fishing, and occasionally, crazy folks having the time of their life. The sun and water make a good combination. Open year-round.

---

6. SENATOR WASH RECREATION AREA   RV. 6

Reference: **Near Senator Wash Reservoir; map J9, grid h3.**
Campsites, facilities: There are an undesignated number of sites for tents or self-contained motor homes. There is **no piped water**, so bring your own. A boat

ramp is available. Camping at the boat ramp is not allowed. Pets are allowed on leashes.

Reservations, fee: No reservations; no fee; maximum 14-day stay.

Who to contact: Phone the Bureau of Land Management at (602) 726-6300.

Location: From Yuma, Arizona, drive approximately 23 miles northeast on Imperial Highway (County Road S24) to Senator Wash Road. Turn left and drive about three miles to the campground.

Trip note: This campground is set in a large recreation area that borders the Colorado River. More specifically, it is nestled between Senator Wash Reservoir to the west and Squaw Lake (created by Imperial Dam on the Colorado River) to the southeast. It is a vast, virtually unmonitored area. Within this area is the Imperial Dam Long-Term Visitor Area. For $50, campers can stay from September 15th through April 14th. The rest of the year, camping is free, but there is a limit of 14 days.

---

7. SQUAW LAKE

Reference: **Near Colorado River; map J9, grid h3.**

Campsites, facilities: There are 80 sites for tents or motor homes. Picnic tables and fire grills are provided. Piped water, flush toilets, cold showers and a boat ramp are available. Some facilities are **wheelchair accessible**. Pets are permitted on leashes.

Reservations, fee: No reservations; call for fees.

Who to contact: Phone the Bureau of Land Management at (602) 726-6300.

Location: From Yuma, Arizona, drive approximately 23 miles northeast on Imperial Highway (County Road S24) to Senator Wash Road. Turn left and drive about three miles to the campground.

Trip note: Take your pick. There are two camps near the Colorado River in this area. This one is near Squaw Lake, created by the nearby Imperial Dam on the Colorado River. Open year-round.

---

8. SANS END RV PARK

Reference: **In Winterhaven; map J9, grid i0.**

Campsites, facilities: There are 167 sites for motor homes and a few sites for tents. Restrooms, showers, a recreation hall, a pool table, a laundry and shuffleboard are available. Pets are allowed on leashes.

Reservations, fee: No reservations; $17 fee per night.

Who to contact: Phone or write to 2209 West Winterhaven Drive, Winterhaven, CA 92283; (619) 572-0797.

Location: From Yuma, take Interstate 8 west and exit on Winterhaven Drive. Follow Winterhaven Drive to the RV park at 2209.

Trip note: The high season at this RV park is January to March, and no wonder, because it is blazing hot here in summer. Sans End is only seven miles from Mexico, and lots of people who stay here like to cross the border for shopping and fun.

INDEX

ALL CAMPGROUND LISTINGS ARE IN CAPITAL LETTERS

ALL CAMPGROUND LISTINGS ARE IN CAPITAL LETTERS

ALL CAMPGROUND LISTINGS ARE IN CAPITAL LETTERS

ALL CAMPGROUND LISTINGS ARE IN CAPITAL LETTERS

ALL CAMPGROUND LISTINGS ARE IN CAPITAL LETTERS

ALL CAMPGROUND LISTINGS ARE IN CAPITAL LETTERS

ALL CAMPGROUND LISTINGS ARE IN CAPITAL LETTERS

ALL CAMPGROUND LISTINGS ARE IN CAPITAL LETTERS

ALL CAMPGROUND LISTINGS ARE IN CAPITAL LETTERS

ALL CAMPGROUND LISTINGS ARE IN CAPITAL LETTERS

HAWKINS LANDING 191
HAYDEN FLAT 160
Hayfork 170, 175
Haypress Creek 304, 305
Haypress Trail 305
Haystack Mountain 353
HAYWARD FLAT 165
Hazel Creek 383
HEADQUARTERS 135, 627, 789
Headquarters Camp 789, 790
Headwaters Trail 211
Healdsburg 319
Hearst Castle 600, 601
Heart Bar Campground 737
Heart Bar Creek 740
HEART BAR EQUESTRIAN GROUP CAMP 740
HEART BAR FAMILY CAMP 740
Heart Bar Fire Station 740
Heart's Desire Beach 325
Hebron Summit 129
HEDRICK POND 619
HEISE COUNTY PARK, WILLIAM 775
Helena 159, 161, 162
HELL GATE 176
HELL HOLE 374
Hell Hole Reservoir 370, 373, 374, 375
HELL HOLE WALK-IN, UPPER 375
Hemet 746
HEMET, LAKE 749
Hemet, Lake 746, 748, 749, 750, 759
HEMLOCK 135
Henderson Point 333
HENDY WOODS STATE PARK 246
HENRY COWELL REDWOODS STATE PARK 515
HENRY W. COE STATE PARK 441
Henshaw, Lake 774, 775
HENSHAW RESORT RV, LAKE 775
HENSLEY GROUP SITE 536
Hensley Lake 536
HERMIT GULCH 703
Hermit Hut 246
HERMIT VALLEY 414

Hermon, Mount 429
Hesperia 725, 728
HESPERIA LAKE CAMPGROUND 725
Hetch Hetchy Reservoir 479, 482
HI MOUNTAIN 604
Hi Mountain Campground 608
HICKEY 237
HIDDEN CREEK 140
HIDDEN FALLS 616
Hidden Falls 617
Hidden Lake 411
HIDDEN SPRINGS 148
HIDDEN VALLEY 756
HIDDEN VALLEY CAMPGROUND 241
HIDDEN VIEW CAMPGROUND 536
HIGH BRIDGE 276
High Country Camping 708
High Desert National Recreational Trail 708
High Rock 149, 150
Highland Lakes 416
HIGHLAND LAKES, LOWER 464
HIGHLAND LAKES, UPPER 464
Highlands Lakes 465
HIGHLANDS RV PARK 572
Highway 299 Bridge 213
hike-in camping 102-103, 105, 154, 237, 244, 321, 332, 367, 369, 402-403, 419-421, 494, 576, 587, 645, 732, 734
hiking (see also backpacking)
Northern California: 98-100, 102-108, 110-111, 115-120, 123-125, 127-128, 130, 133, 137, 139-143, 146-150, 153-159, 162-163, 170-171, 173, 175, 177-178, 181-189, 191, 194, 198, 200-204, 206, 211-215, 217-219, 225-230, 233-239, 242-244, 246, 249-250, 252, 254, 257-263, 266-271, 273-276, 278-280, 282, 287, 292-299, 302-303, 305, 308, 310, 314, 317, 319-321, 323-325, 327, 329-333, 336-340, 342,

349, 353-356, 358-366, 369, 372-373, 375-376, 383-387, 396-397, 399-408, 410-416, 419-429, 438-440, 442, 447-449, 451, 454, 463-471, 473-474, 476-480, 482, 486-488, 490-498, 501-502, 504-510
Central California: 515-516, 519, 521-526, 532, 540-543, 545, 547-553, 555-556, 558-561, 566, 569-570, 572-577, 581-588, 592, 595-596, 601, 603-605, 607-608, 612, 615-626, 628-631, 633-634, 637-638, 645-647, 649-650, 652-657, 659, 661, 664, 668, 670, 675-676, 679, 687
Southern California: 699-700, 705-710, 712-715, 717, 719-722, 725-727, 729, 731-745, 747-750, 753-756, 759-760, 771-772, 774-775, 777, 779-782, 786, 790-793, 795
HILTON PARK 338
Hiouchi 102, 103
HIOUCHI HAMLET RV RESORT 102
Hiram Peak 414, 465
HIRZ BAY 199
HIRZ BAY GROUP CAMP 199
HOBO 633
HOBO GULCH 159
Hobo Gulch Trailhead 162
HOBSON COUNTY PARK 660
Hocket Lakes 615
HODGDON MEADOW 493
Hodges, Lake 774, 775
Hoffman, Mount 494
Holcomb Creek 732
HOLCOMB VALLEY 735
Holcomb Valley Historic Area 735
HOLE-IN-THE-GROUND 274
HOLE-IN-THE-WALL 685
HOLEY MEADOW 624
HOLIDAY GROUP CAMP 658
HOLIDAY HARBOR 198

ALL CAMPGROUND LISTINGS ARE IN CAPITAL LETTERS

ALL CAMPGROUND LISTINGS ARE IN CAPITAL LETTERS

ALL CAMPGROUND LISTINGS ARE IN CAPITAL LETTERS

ALL CAMPGROUND LISTINGS ARE IN CAPITAL LETTERS

ALL CAMPGROUND LISTINGS ARE IN CAPITAL LETTERS

O

OAK BOTTOM 200
Oak Bottom Amphitheater 201
OAK BOTTOM ON THE SALMON RIVER 121
OAK COUNTY PARK 699
OAK CREEK 583
OAK DELL 516
OAK FLAT (Richardson Grove State Park) 236
OAK FLAT (Lake Pillsbury) 254
OAK FLAT (Pyramid Lake) 671
Oak Flat 164, 255, 670, 671
OAK GROVE 772
OAK HOLLOW 449
OAK KNOLL 448
Oak Knoll 447
OAK KNOLL CAMP-GROUND 773
Oakdale 452, 453
Oakhurst 489, 498, 539, 540, 541
Oakland 424
Oakley 436
OAKS RV PARK, THE 128
OAKWOOD LAKE RESORT 438
OBSERVATORY 772
OBSIDIAN 474
Obsidian Dome 503, 505
Ocean Cove 321
OCEAN COVE CAMP-GROUND 320
OCEANO 645
OCEANO COUNTY CAMPGROUND 645
Oceanside 767, 768, 773
Ocotillo 793, 794, 795
Ocotillo Wells State Vehicular Recreation Area 793
off-road vehicles 205, 532, 676, 793
OH! RIDGE 503
Ohlone Wilderness Trail 438
Ojai 653, 656, 657, 658, 659, 661, 668, 671
Old Battle Creek 206
Old Cow Creek 205
OLD COW MEADOWS 205
OLD LEWISTON BRIDGE RV RESORT 171
OLD MILL 259

OLD ORCHARD RV PARK 268
Old Oregon Trail 202
Old River 435, 436
OLD SHADY REST 509
Old Station 213, 214, 216
Olema 325, 419, 420, 421
OLEMA RANCH CAMP-GROUND 419
Omega Overlook 361
O'NEIL CREEK 117
O'Neill Forebay 530
O'NEILL REGIONAL PARK 720
ONION VALLEY 585
O'NITE PARK 265
Ontario 715, 726
Onyx 634
Orange 719
ORANGELAND RV PARK 718
Orchard Camp 234
Orchard Creek 234
ORCHARD RV PARK 438
Oregon 97, 137
Orem, UT 364, 365, 366, 369, 370, 371, 372
Orick 110, 112
Orland 268, 269, 282, 283
ORLAND BUTTES 267
Orleans 118, 121, 123, 124, 153
Orleans, Mount 124
Oroville 270, 271, 283, 285, 286, 287, 288, 289, 290, 291, 292, 293, 294, 296
Oroville dam 270
Oroville, Lake 269, 270, 271, 291, 341, 343
Orr Lake, Little 133
Orr Mountain 133
Oso Camp 739
Oso Canyon 655
OSO GROUP CAMP 738
Osprey Management Area 221
Ostrander Lake 488
Otay Lake 782, 783, 784
OUTDOOR RESORTS 757
OUTDOOR RESORTS MOTORCOACH 758
OUTDOOR WORLD RV PARK 786
Owens River 572
Owens Valley 568
OWL CANYON 679
Oxnard 699, 700

OZENA 653
Ozena Camp 657

P

P-BAR FLAT 656
Pacheco Pass 529
Pacific Coastal Trail 104, 105
Pacific Creek 414
Pacific Crest Trail 118, 181, 182, 183, 184, 185, 189, 211, 276, 287, 293, 356, 358, 372, 401, 408, 412, 465, 469, 470, 490, 491, 492, 494, 495, 506, 569, 576, 585, 588, 628, 634, 670, 705, 706, 707, 708, 709, 712, 714, 729, 731, 732, 733, 735, 737, 741, 747, 774, 779, 780, 781, 782, 786
Pacific Ocean 112, 146, 149, 238, 239, 242, 251, 426, 516, 517, 518, 595, 596, 646, 659, 660, 661, 695, 701, 719
PACIFIC PARK 425
Pacific Ranger District 376, 379, 380, 381, 382
PACIFIC VALLEY 414
Pacifica 425
PACIFICO, MOUNT 705
Packer Creek 296, 297
Packer Lake 296, 297, 298
PACKSADDLE 297
PAHA 475
Painted Caves 695
Pala Indian Reservation 771
Pala Mission 771
Palace Hotel Tree 449
PALISADE 566
PALISADE GROUP CAMP 576
Palisades 577
Palm Desert 749, 750, 760
Palm Springs 743, 755, 756, 757, 758
Palm Springs South Resource Area 758
PALM VIEW RV PARK 743
Palmdale 676
Palo Alto 428
Palo Colorado (redwood) Canyon 522
Palo Verde 804
PALO VERDE COUNTY PARK 804

ALL CAMPGROUND LISTINGS ARE IN CAPITAL LETTERS

ALL CAMPGROUND LISTINGS ARE IN CAPITAL LETTERS

Acknowledgments

The following camping specialists reviewed this book to help make it as accurate as possible:

Kris Fister, Yosemite National Park
James Dahlgren, Yosemite National Park
Janelle Miller, California State Parks Department
Matt Mathes, U.S. Forest Service, Pacific Southwest
    Regional Headquarters
Susie Wood, Angeles National Forest
Gail van der Bie, Cleveland National Forest
Karen Finlayson, Eldorado National Forest
Heide Anderson, Inyo National Forest
Ray Orlanskis, Klamath National Forest
Ken Karkula, Lake Tahoe Basin
Elizabeth Norton, Lassen National Forest
Jim Barnhart, Lassen National Forest
Rich Tobin, Los Padres National Forest
Charles Smay, Mendocino National Forest
Jeni Bradley, Modoc National Forest
Judy Schaber, Plumas National Forest
Rodney Bennett, San Bernardino National Forest
Marilee Reese, Sequoia National Forest
Marla Schardin, Shasta-Trinity National Forest
Delora Kurth, Sierra National Forest
Peggy Lawrence, Six Rivers National Forest
Art Smith, Stanislaus National Forest
Phil Horn, Tahoe National Forest
Scott Lamoreux, Toiyabe National Forest
Ned MacKay, East Bay Regional Parks
Larry Mercu, Bureau of Land Management
Bob Wick, Bureau of Land Management
Johna Cochran, Bureau of Land Management

Books Building Community

Foghorn Press is pleased to support environmental and social causes nationwide. In an effort to create an awareness of and support for these worthy causes, the Books Building Community program unites Foghorn's media, bookstore, and outdoor retail partners with nonprofit organizations such as:

THE CALIFORNIA STATE PARKS FOUNDATION

Walk among the towering and ancient redwood trees, gaze up a 1,200-mile coastline that stretches from Mexico to Oregon, wade through beautiful inland lakes, push onward through the Sierras, and revel in the vastness of California's deserts. For more than 25 years, the California State Parks Foundation has protected these natural and historic state treasures.

Now numbering more than 265 state parks, our California system is truly unique and offers many recreational and educational opportunities for the benefit of all Californians and visitors to this great state. The mission of the California State Parks Foundation is very straightforward: acquire land and artifacts for our state parks, protect endangered land, and provide funding to the California Department of Parks and Recreation to complete urgently needed projects and programs in our state park system. The Foundation joins private citizens, corporations, and foundations that wish to contribute to the state park system. This private support makes possible vital projects that benefit all Californians.

We are a public non-profit organization that does not receive government funding and is solely dependent upon grants and gifts from private individuals, corporations, and foundations, as well as annual contributions from our members.

The state park system is not frozen in time. New ideas, new lands to incorporate into parks, and new buildings and services that serve tens of millions of visitors all contribute to a system that grows each year.

You are an owner of the state park system considered by many to be the finest in the world. The most beautiful areas of California are found in these parks. They should and will last forever. As a guardian of our parks, we can help insure that future with your tax-deductible contribution to the California State Parks Foundation. Many opportunities exist for interested people and companies to contribute to our state parks and improve the quality of life in our California home. Your support is needed. To learn more about how you can help California state parks and enjoy membership benefits, please call or write to:

California State Parks Foundation
800 College Avenue, P.O. Box 548
Kentfield, CA 94914
(415) 258-9975

The California State Parks Foundation is an independent membership organization dedicated to protecting and preserving California's state parks.

Leave No Trace

Leave No Trace, Inc., is a program dedicated to maintaining the integrity of outdoor recreation areas through education and public awareness. Foghorn Press is a proud supporter of this program and its ethics.

Here's how you can Leave No Trace:

Plan Ahead and Prepare
- Learn about the regulations and special concerns of the area you are visiting.
- Visit the backcountry in small groups.
- Avoid popular areas during peak-use periods.
- Choose equipment and clothing in subdued colors.
- Pack food in reusable containers.

Travel and Camp with Care
On the trail:
- Stay on designated trails. Walk single file in the middle of the path.
- Do not take shortcuts on switchbacks.
- When traveling cross-country where there are no trails, follow animal trails or spread out your group so no new routes are created. Walk along the most durable surfaces available, such as rock, gravel, dry grasses, or snow.
- Use a map and compass to eliminate the need for rock cairns, tree scars, or ribbons.
- If you encounter pack animals, step to the downhill side of the trail and speak softly to avoid startling them.

At camp:
- Choose an established, legal site that will not be damaged by your stay.
- Restrict activities to areas where vegetation is compacted or absent.
- Keep pollutants out of the water by camping at least 200 feet (about 70 adult steps) from lakes and streams.
- Control pets at all times, or leave them at home with a sitter. Remove dog feces.

Pack It In and Pack It Out
- Take everything you bring into the wild back out with you.
- Protect wildlife and your food by storing rations securely. Pick up all spilled foods.

- Use toilet paper or wipes sparingly; pack them out.
- Inspect your campsite for trash and any evidence of your stay. Pack out all trash—even if it's not yours!

Properly Dispose of What You Can't Pack Out
- If no refuse facility is available, deposit human waste in catholes dug six to eight inches deep at least 200 feet from water, camps, or trails. Cover and disguise the catholes when you're finished.
- To wash yourself or your dishes, carry the water 200 feet from streams or lakes and use small amounts of biodegradable soap. Scatter the strained dishwater.

Keep the Wilderness Wild
- Treat our natural heritage with respect. Leave plants, rocks, and historical artifacts as you found them.
- Good campsites are found, not made. Do not alter a campsite.
- Let nature's sounds prevail; keep loud voices and noises to a minimum.
- Do not build structures or furniture or dig trenches.

Minimize Use and Impact of Fires
- Campfires can have a lasting impact on the backcountry. Always carry a light-weight stove for cooking, and use a candle lantern instead of building a fire whenever possible.
- Where fires are permitted, use established fire rings only.
- Do not scar the natural setting by snapping the branches off live, dead, or downed trees.
- Completely extinguish your campfire and make sure it is cold before departing. Remove all unburned trash from the fire ring and scatter the cold ashes over a large area well away from any camp.

For more information, call 1-800-332-4100.